Lecture Notes in Computer Science 11962

More information about this series at http://www.springer.com/series/7409

Yong Man Ro · Wen-Huang Cheng ·
Junmo Kim · Wei-Ta Chu ·
Peng Cui · Jung-Woo Choi ·
Min-Chun Hu · Wesley De Neve (Eds.)

MultiMedia Modeling

26th International Conference, MMM 2020
Daejeon, South Korea, January 5–8, 2020
Proceedings, Part II

Editors
Yong Man Ro
Korea Advanced Institute of Science and Technology
Daejeon, Korea (Republic of)

Junmo Kim
Korea Advanced Institute of Science and Technology
Daejeon, Korea (Republic of)

Peng Cui
Tsinghua University
Beijing, China

Min-Chun Hu
National Tsing Hua University
Hsinchu, Taiwan

Wen-Huang Cheng
National Chiao Tung University
Hsinchu, Taiwan

Wei-Ta Chu
National Cheng Kung University
Tainan City, Taiwan

Jung-Woo Choi
Korea Advanced Institute of Science and Technology
Daejeon, Korea (Republic of)

Wesley De Neve
Ghent University
Ghent, Belgium

ISSN 0302-9743 ISSN 1611-3349 (electronic)
Lecture Notes in Computer Science
ISBN 978-3-030-37733-5 ISBN 978-3-030-37734-2 (eBook)
https://doi.org/10.1007/978-3-030-37734-2

LNCS Sublibrary: SL3 – Information Systems and Applications, incl. Internet/Web, and HCI

This Springer imprint is published by the registered company Springer Nature Switzerland AG
The registered company address is: Gewerbestrasse 11, 6330 Cham, Switzerland

Preface

These proceedings contain the papers presented at MMM 2020, the 26th International Conference on MultiMedia Modeling, held in Daejeon, South Korea, during January 5–8, 2020. MMM is a leading international conference for researchers and industry practitioners to share new ideas, original research results, and practical development experiences from all MMM-related areas, broadly falling into three categories: multimedia content analysis; multimedia signal processing and communications; and multimedia applications and services. MMM 2020 received 241 paper submissions across 4 categories: 171 full research paper submissions, 49 special session paper submissions, 11 demonstration submissions, and 10 submissions to the Video Browser Showdown (VBS 2020). Of the 171 full papers submitted, 40 were selected for oral presentation and 46 for poster presentation. Of the 49 special session papers submitted, 28 were selected for oral presentation and 8 for poster presentation. In addition, 9 demonstrations and 10 VBS submissions were accepted. The overall acceptance percentage across the conference was thus 58.51%, but 50.29% for full papers and 23.39% of full papers for oral presentation. The submission and review process was coordinated using the EasyChair conference management system. All full-paper submissions were assigned for review to at least three members of the Program Committee. We owe a debt of gratitude to all these reviewers for providing their valuable time to MMM 2020. We would like to thank our invited keynote speakers for their stimulating contributions to the conference. We also wish to thank our organizational team: Special Session chairs Changick Kim and Benoit Huet; Demonstration Chairs Munchurl Kim and Kai-Lung Hua; Video Browser Showdown Chairs Klaus Schoeffmann, Werner Bailer, and Jakub Lokoč; Publicity Chairs Phoebe Chen, Kiyoharu Aizawa, Yo-Sung Ho, Björn ór Jónsson, Yan-Ying Chen, and Bing-Kun Bao; Finance Chair Hoirin Kim; Tutorial Chairs Jitao Sang and Jinah Park; Industrial Chair Young Bok Lee; Panel Chairs Shin'ichi Satoh and Guo-Jun Qi; Web Chair Seung Ho Lee; Conference Secretariat Seul Lee, Minjeong Lee, and A-Young Kim. We would like to thank KAIST for hosting MMM 2020. Special thanks go to the Steering Committee for timely support and advice. In addition, we wish to thank all authors who spent time and effort submitting their work to MMM 2020, and all of the participants and student volunteers for their contributions and valuable support.

October 2019

Yong Man Ro
Wen-Huang Cheng
Junmo Kim
Wei-Ta Chu
Peng Cui
Jung-Woo Choi
Min-Chun Hu
Wesley De Neve

The original version of the book was revised: the first volume editor and a missing funding number in the acknowledgement section of chapter 46 were added. The correction to the book is available at https://doi.org/10.1007/978-3-030-37734-2_75

Organization

Organizing Committee

General Chairs

Yong Man Ro	Korea Advanced Institute of Science and Technology, South Korea
Wen-Huang Cheng	National Chiao Tung University, Taiwan

Program Chairs

Junmo Kim	Korea Advanced Institute of Science and Technology, South Korea
Wei-Ta Chu	National Cheng Kung University, Taiwan
Peng Cui	Tsinghua University, China

Organizing Chair

Jung-Woo Choi	Korea Advanced Institute of Science and Technology, South Korea

Special Session Chairs

Changick Kim	Korea Advanced Institute of Science and Technology, South Korea
Benoit Huet	Eurecom, France

Panel Chairs

Shin'ichi Satoh	National Institute of Informatics, Japan
Guo-Jun Qi	University of Central Florida, USA

Tutorial Chairs

Jitao Sang	Beijing Jiaotong University, China
Jinah Park	Korea Advanced Institute of Science and Technology, South Korea

Demo Chairs

Munchurl Kim	Korea Advanced Institute of Science and Technology, South Korea
Kai-Lung Hua	National Taiwan University of Science and Technology, Taiwan

Video Browser Showdown Chairs

Klaus Schoeffmann	University of Klagenfurt, Austria
Werner Bailer	Joanneum Research, Austria
Jakub Lokoč	Charles University in Prague, Czech Republic

Publicity Chairs

Phoebe Chen	La Trobe University, Australia
Kiyoharu Aizawa	University of Tokyo, Japan
Yo-Sung Ho	Gwangju Institute of Science and Technology, South Korea
Björn Þór Jónsson	IT University of Copenhagen, Denmark
Yan-Ying Chen	FXPAL, Taiwan
Bing-Kun Bao	Nanjing University of Posts and Telecommunications, China

Publication Chairs

Min-Chun Hu	National Tsing Hua University, Taiwan
Wesley De Neve	Ghent University, Belgium

Industrial Chair

Young Bok Lee	Genesis Lab, South Korea

Financial Chair

Hoirin Kim	Korea Advanced Institute of Science and Technology, South Korea

Web Chair

Seung Ho Lee	Korea University of Technology and Education, South Korea

Steering Committee

Phoebe Chen	La Trobe University, Australia
Tat-Seng Chua	National University of Singapore, Singapore
Kiyoharu Aizawa	University of Tokyo, Japan
Cathal Gurrin	Dublin City University, Ireland
Benoit Huet	Eurecom, France
Klaus Schoeffmann	University of Klagenfurt, Austria
Richang Hong	Hefei University of Technology, China
Björn Þór Jónsson	IT University of Copenhagen, Denmark
Guo-Jun Qi	University of Central Florida, USA
Wen-Huang Cheng	National Chiao Tung University, Taiwan
Peng Cui	Tsinghua University, China

Special Sessions Organizers

SS1: AI-Powered 3D Vision

You Yang	Huazhong University of Science and Technology, China
Qifei Wang	Google Inc., USA

SS2: Multimedia Analytics: Perspectives, Tools and Applications

Björn Þór Jónsson	IT University of Copenhagen, Denmark
Laurent Amsaleg	CNRS-IRISA, France
Cathal Gurrin	Dublin City University, Ireland
Stevan Rudinac	University of Amsterdam, The Netherlands
Xirong Li	Renmin University of China, China

SS3: MDRE: Multimedia Datasets for Repeatable Experimentation

Cathal Gurrin	Dublin City University, Ireland
Duc-Tien Dang-Nguyen	Dublin City University, Ireland
Klaus Schoeffmann	University of Klagenfurt, Austria
Björn Þór Jónsson	IT University of Copenhagen, Denmark

SS4: MMAC: Multi-modal Affective Computing of Large-Scale Multimedia Data

Sicheng Zhao	University of California, USA
Jufeng Yang	Nankai University, China
Hatice Gunes	University of Cambridge, UK

SS5: MULTIMED: Multimedia and Multimodal Analytics in the Medical Domain and Pervasive Environments

Georgios Meditskos	Centre for Research and Technology Hellas, Greece
Klaus Schoeffmann	University of Klagenfurt, Austria
Leo Wanner	ICREA, Universitat Pompeu Fabra, Spain
Kunwadee Sripanidkulchai	Chulalongkorn University, Thailand
Stefanos Vrochidis	Centre for Research and Technology Hellas, Greece

SS6: Intelligent Multimedia Security

Youliang Tian	Guizhou University, China
Hongtao Xie	University of Science and Technology of China, China
Bing-Kun Bao	Nanjing University of Posts and Telecommunications, China
Zhineng Chen	Institute of Automation, Chinese Academy of Sciences, China
Changgen Peng	Guizhou University, China

Tutorial Organizers

Tutorial 1: Introduction to Biometrics and Anti-Spoofing

Wonjun Kim — Konkuk University, South Korea

Tutorial 2: Recent Advances in Deep Novelty Detection for Medical Imaging

Jaeil Kim — Kyungpook National University, South Korea

Tutorial 3: Haptic Interaction with Multimedia Data

Sang-Youn Kim — Korea University of Technology and Education, South Korea

Program Committee

Aaron Duane	Insight, Ireland
Adam Jatowt	Kyoto University, Japan
Adrian Muscat	University of Malta, Malta
Alan Smeaton	Dublin City University, Ireland
Amon Rapp	University of Turin, Italy
Anastasios Karakostas	Aristotle University of Thessaloniki, Greece
Andreas Leibetseder	University of Klagenfurt, Austria
Antonino Furnari	Università degli Studi di Catania, Italy
Athina Tsanousa	Centre for Research and Technology Hellas, Greece
Benjamin Bustos	University of Chile, Chile
Benoit Huet	Eurecom, France
Bing-Kun Bao	Nanjing University of Posts and Telecommunications, China
Björn Jónsson	IT University of Copenhagen, Denmark
Björn Thor Jonsson	IT University of Copenhagen, Denmark
Bogdan Ionescu	Politehnica University of Bucharest, Romania
Borja Sanz	University of Deusto, Spain
Byoung Tae Oh	Korea Aerospace University, South Korea
Cathal Gurrin	Dublin City University, Ireland
Cem Direkoglu	Middle East Technical University, Turkey
Changick Kim	Korea Advanced Institute of Science and Technology, South Korea
Chong-Wah Ngo	City University of Hong Kong, Hong Kong, China
Christian Timmerer	University of Klagenfurt, Austria
Claudiu Cobarzan	University of Klagenfurt, Austria
Cong-Thang Truong	University of Aizu, Japan
Daniel Stanley Tan	De La Salle University, Philippines
Debesh Jha	Simula Research Laboratory, Norway
Dongyu She	Nankai University, China
Duc Tien Dang Nguyen	University of Bergen, Norway
Edgar Chavez	Ensenada Center for Scientific Research and Higher Education, Mexico

Esra Açar	Middle East Technical University, Turkey
Estefania Talavera	University of Groningen, The Netherlands
François Destelle	Dublin City University, Ireland
Frank Hopfgartner	The University of Sheffield, UK
Fuli Feng	National University of Singapore, Singapore
Georges Quénot	Laboratoire d'Informatique de Grenoble, CNRS, France
Georgios Meditskos	Centre for Research and Technology Hellas, Greece
Gylfi Gudmundsson	Reykjavik University, Iceland
Henning Müller	HES-SO, Switzerland
Hong Wu	University of Science and Technology of China, China
Hong-Han Shuai	National Chiao Tung University, Taiwan
Hongtao Xie	University of Science and Technology of China, China
Hyowon Lee	Singapore University of Technology and Design, Singapore
Ichiro Ide	Nagoya University, Japan
Ioannis Kompatsiaris	Centre for Research and Technology Hellas, Greece
Jakub Lokoč	Charles University in Prague, Czech Republic
Jan Zahálka	Czech Technical University in Prague, Czech Republic
Jean-Marc Ogier	University of La Rochelle, France
Jenny Benois-Pineau	University of Bordeaux, France
Jen-Wei Huang	National Cheng Kung University, Taiwan
Jianjun Qian	Nanjing University of Science and Technology, China
Jie Shao	University of Science and Technology of China, China
Jiro Katto	Waseda University, Japan
Jochen Laubrock	University of Potsdam, Germany
Jochen Meyer	OFFIS Institute for Information Technology, Germany
John See	Multimedia University, Malaysia
John Virtusio	National Taiwan University of Science and Technology, Taiwan
Josep Blat	Universitat Pompeu Fabra, Spain
Jun Shi	Harbin Institute of Technology, China
Jung-Woo Choi	Korea Advanced Institute of Science and Technology, South Korea
Junmo Kim	Korea Advanced Institute of Science and Technology, South Korea
Jun-Wei Hsieh	National Taiwan Ocean University, Taiwan
K. Selcuk Candan	Arizona State University, USA
Kai-Lung Hua	National Taiwan University of Science and Technology, Taiwan
Kathy Clawson	University of Sunderland, UK
Keiji Yanai	The University of Electro-Communications, Japan
Kevin Mcguinness	Dublin City University, Ireland
Klaus Schöffmann	University of Klagenfurt, Austria
Koichi Shinoda	Tokyo Institute of Technology, Japan
Konstantin Pogorelov	Simula Research Laboratory, Norway

Konstantinos Avgerinakis	Centre for Research and Technology Hellas, Greece
Ladislav Peska	Charles University in Prague, Czech Republic
Lai-Kuan Wong	Multimedia University, Malaysia
Laurent Amsaleg	CNRS-IRISA, France
Lei Huang	Ocean University of China, China
Li Su	Chinese Academy of Sciences, China
Lianli Gao	University of Science and Technology of China, China
Lifeng Sun	Tsinghua University, China
Linjun Zhou	Tsinghua University, China
Marcel Worring	University of Amsterdam, The Netherlands
Marco A. Hudelist	University of Klagenfurt, Austria
Mariana Damova	Mozaika, Bulgaria
Mario Taschwer	University of Klagenfurt, Austria
Markus Koskela	CSC - IT Center for Science Ltd., Finland
Martin Winter	Joanneum Research, Austria
Mathias Lux	University of Klagenfurt, Austria
Mathieu Delalandre	Laboratoire d'Informatique, France
Matthias Zeppelzauer	University of Applied Sciences St. Pölten, Austria
Mei-Ling Shyu	University of Miami, USA
Michael E. Houle	National Institute of Informatics, Japan
Michael Lew	Leiden University, The Netherlands
Miloš Radovanović	University of Novi Sad, Serbia
Min H. Kim	Korea Advanced Institute of Science and Technology, South Korea
Min-Chun Hu	National Tsing Hua University, Taiwan
Ming Sun	SenseTime, Hong Kong, China
Minh-Son Dao	National Institute of Information and Communications Technology, Japan
Mitsunori Matsushita	Kansai University, Japan
Mohan Kankanhalli	National University of Singapore, Singapore
Monica Dominguez	Universitat Pompeu Fabra, Spain
Munchrl Kim	Korea Advanced Institute of Science and Technology, South Korea
Mylene Farias	University of Brasília, Brazil
Naoko Nitta	Osaka University, Japan
Neil O'Hare	Yahoo Research, Spain
Ognjen Arandjelovic	University of St Andrews, UK
Olfa Ben Ahmed	Eurecom, France
Panagiotis Sidiropoulos	Cortexica, UK
Peiguang Jing	Tianjin University, China
Peng Cui	Tsinghua University, China
Pengming Feng	China Aerospace Science and Technology Corporation, China
Petros Alvanitopoulos	Centre for Research and Technology Hellas, Greece
Phivos Mylonas	National Technical University of Athens, Greece

Pyunghwan Ahn	Korea Advanced Institute of Science and Technology, South Korea
Qi Dai	Microsoft, China
Qiao Wang	Southeast University, China
Qifei Wang	Google, USA
Qiong Liu	Huazhong University of Science and Technology, China
Richang Hong	Hefei University of Technology, China
Robert Mertens	HSW University of Applied Sciences, Germany
Roger Zimmermann	National University of Singapore, Singapore
Sabrina Kletz	University of Klagenfurt, Austria
Sanghoon Lee	Yonsei University, South Korea
Savvas Chatzichristofis	Neapolis University, Cyprus
Seiji Hotta	Tokyo University of Agricultural and Technology, Japan
Sen Xiang	Wuhan University of Science and Technology, China
Seong Tae Kim	Technical University of Munich, Germany
Shaoyi Du	Xi'an Jiaotong University, China
Shijie Hao	Hefei University of Technology, China
Shingo Uchihashi	Fuji Xerox Co., Ltd., Japan
Shin'Ichi Satoh	National Institute of Informatics, Japan
Shintami Hidayati	Institute of Technology Sepuluh Nopember, Indonesia
Sicheng Zhao	University of California, Berkeley, USA
Silvio Guimaraes	Pontificia Universidade Católica de Minas Gerais, Brazil
Simon Mille	Universitat Pompeu Fabra, Spain
Stefan Petscharnig	AIT Austrian Institute of Technology, Austria
Stefanos Vrochidis	Center for Research and Technology Hellas, Greece
Stevan Rudinac	University of Amsterdam, The Netherlands
Thanos Stavropoulos	Aristotle University of Thessaloniki, Greece
Thomas Koehler	TU Dresden, Germany
Tianzhu Zhang	University of Science and Technology of China, China
Tien-Tsin Wong	The Chinese University of Hong Kong, Hong Kong, China
Tomas Grosup	Charles University in Prague, Czech Republic
Tongwqei Ren	Nanjing University, China
Tong-Yee Lee	National Cheng Kung University, Taiwan
Toshihiko Yamasaki	The University of Tokyo, Japan
Tse-Yu Pan	National Tsing Hua University, Taiwan
Vasileios Mezaris	Centre for Research and Technology Hellas, Greece
Vincent Oria	New Jersey Institute of Technology, USA
Weiming Dong	Chinese Academy of Sciences, China
Weiqing Min	Chinese Academy of Sciences, China
Wei-Ta Chu	National Cheng Kung University, Taiwan
Wen-Huang Cheng	National Chiao Tung University, Taiwan

Wen-Ze Shao	Nanjing University of Posts and Telecommunications, China
Werner Bailer	Joanneum Research, Austria
Wolfgang Minker	University of Ulm, Germany
Wolfgang Weiss	Joanneum Research, Austria
Wu Liu	JD AI Research of JD.com, China
Xi Shao	Nanjing University of Posts and Telecommunications, China
Xiang Wang	National University of Singapore, Singapore
Xiangjun Shen	Jiangsu University, China
Xiao Wu	Southwest Jiaotong University, China
Xiaofeng Zhu	Guangxi Normal University, China
Xiaoqing Luo	Jiangnan University, China
Xiaoxiao Sun	Nankai University, China
Xirong Li	Renmin University of China, China
Xu Wang	Shenzhen University, China
Xueting Liu	The Chinese University of Hong Kong, Hong Kong, China
Yang Yang	University of Science and Technology of China, China
Yannick Prié	University of Nantes, France
Yanwei Fu	Fudan University, China
Ying Cao	City University of Hong Kong, Hong Kong, China
Yingbo Li	Eurecom, France
Ying-Qing Xu	Tsinghua University, China
Yong Man Ro	Korea Advanced Institute of Science and Technology, South Korea
Yongju Jung	Gachon University, South Korea
Yo-Sung Ho	Gwangju Institute of Science and Technology, South Korea
You Yang	Huazhong University of Science and Technology, China
Yue Gao	Tsinghua University, China
Yue He	Tsinghua University, China
Yu-Kun Lai	Cardiff University, UK
Zan Gao	Tianjin University of Technology, China
Zhaoquan Yuan	Southwest Jiaotong University, China
Zhe-Cheng Fan	Academia Sinica, Taiwan
Zhenzhen Hu	Nanyang Technological University, Singapore
Zhineng Chen	Chinese Academy of Sciences, China
Zhiyong Cheng	Shandong Artificial Intelligence Institute, China
Zhongyuan Wang	Wuhan University, China
Zhu Li	University of Missouri, USA
Zhuangzhi Yan	Shanghai University, China
Ziyu Guan	Northwest University of China, China

Additional Reviewers

Ahn, Jaesung
Alvanitopoulos, Petros
Avgerinakis, Konstantinos
Chatzilari, Elisavet
Ding, Yujuan
Giannakeris, Panagiotis
Gkountakos, Konstantinos
Guo, Yangyang
Healy, Graham
Hu, Wenbo
Hu, Xinghong
Huang, Tianchi
Huyen, Tran Thi Thanh
Kim, Hyungmin
Krestenitis, Marios
Le Capitaine, Hoel
Liu, Fan
Lu, Jian
Lu, Steve
Lu, Yu
MacFarlane, Kate
Michail, Manos
Mouchère, Harold
Orfanidis, Georgios
Ortego, Diego
Park, Byeongseon
Patrocínio Jr., Zenilton K. G.
Rudinac, Stevan
Ruiz, Ubaldo
Sadallah, Madjid
Shimoda, Wataru
Vystrcilova, Michaela
Wang, Wenxuan
Xia, Menghan
Xiao, Junbin
Xu, Pengfei
Yang, Juyoung
Yao, Xin
Yu, Jaemyung
Yu, Sha
Zhang, Haoran
Zhang, Ruixiao
Zhang, Zhuming
Zhao, Wanqing
Zhou, Liting
Zhou, Yuan
Zhu, Haichao
Ètefan, Liviu-Daniel

Contents – Part II

Poster Papers

Special Session Papers SS1: AI-Powered 3D Vision

SS2: Multimedia Analytics: Perspectives, Tools and Applications

SS3: MDRE: Multimedia Datasets for Repeatable Experimentation

SS4: MMAC: Multi-modal Affective Computing of Large-Scale Multimedia Data

SS5: MULTIMED: Multimedia and Multimodal Analytics in the Medical Domain and Pervasive Environments

SS6: Intelligent Multimedia Security

Demo Papers

VBS Papers

Contents – Part I

Oral Session 3A: Color Processing and Art

Oral Session 4A: Detection and Classification

Oral Session 5A: Face

Oral Session 7B: Video Processing

Poster Papers

Poster Papers

Multi-scale Comparison Network for Few-Shot Learning

Pengfei Chen, Minglei Yuan, and Tong Lu(✉)

National Key Lab for Novel Software Technology, Nanjing University, Nanjing, China
{mf1833006,mlyuan}@smail.nju.edu.cn, lutong@nju.edu.cn

Abstract. Few-shot learning, which learns from a small number of samples, is an emerging field in multimedia. Through systematically exploring influences of scale information, including multi-scale feature extraction, multi-scale comparison and increased parameters brought by multiple scales, in this paper, we present a novel end-to-end model called Multi-scale Comparison Network (MSCN) for few-shot learning. The proposed MSCN uses different scale convolutions for comparison to solve the problem of excessive gaps between target sizes in the images during few-shot learning. It first uses a 4-layer encoder to encode support and testing samples to obtain their feature maps. After deep splicing these feature maps, the proposed MSCN further uses a comparator comprising two layers of multi-scale comparative modules and two fully connected layers to derive the similarity between support and testing samples. Experimental results on two benchmark datasets including Omniglot and *mini*Imagenet shows the effectiveness of the proposed MSCN, which has averagely 2% improvement on *mini*Imagenet in all experimental results compared with the recent Relation Network.

Keywords: Few-shot learning · MSCN · Metric learning · Multi-scale comparison

1 Introduction

In the past years, deep learning methods based on big data have achieved great success in computer vision and natural language processing tasks. For example, on ImgaeNet dataset, GoogLeNet [5] and ResNet [1] have achieved very high accuracies, some of which are even more accurate than humans. However, there are still many problems in real life tasks, especially when people do not have enough labeled data, and the cost of labeling all the data is too large. For these cases, it is very easy to cause over-fitting due to the small number of training samples. As a result, traditional deep learning methods often do not perform well.

How to learn from a small number of samples, which is called few-shot learning, is a new field in multimedia research. Metric learning is one of the methods for few-shot learning. Metric learning models attempt to learn feature representation and use distance metric to determine object categories in new tasks.

Y. M. Ro et al. (Eds.): MMM 2020, LNCS 11962, pp. 3–13, 2020.
https://doi.org/10.1007/978-3-030-37734-2_1

Although metric learning models have achieved successes in few-shot learning, the recent methods [3,7,12] only use simple metrics such as cosine similarity or 3×3 convolution to calculate similarity between samples, which may result in a lower classification accuracy when the targets are in different sizes.

To solve the above problem, in this paper, we propose a novel Multi-Scale Comparison Network (MSCN) for few-shot learning. We believe that synthesizing different scales information of the images has a positive effect for few-shot learning. We thus explore the effects of multi-scale feature extraction and multi-scale comparison. We find out that only multi-scale comparison plays role in few-show learning, while multi-scale feature extraction has a negative effect. Therefore, the proposed MSCN considers only multi-scale comparison and uses different convolutional kernels in the comparison phase to extract comparison information of different scales. In addition, the proposed MSCN also explores influences of increased parameters brought by multi-scale and different scales on few-shot learning.

Specially, the proposed MSCN first uses a 4-layer encoder to encode support samples and testing samples to obtain their feature maps, then deep splices the feature maps, and finally uses a comparator comprising two layers of multi-scale comparative modules and two fully connected layers to derive the similarity between support samples and testing samples, and according to the similarity the categories of testing samples are obtained.

To the best of our knowledge, this is the first work to propose multi-scale comparison for few-shot learning. We systematically explore the effects of multi-scale comparison and multi-scale feature extraction, and the influences of increased parameters brought by multi-scale and different scales. We do experiments on two benchmark datasets for few-shot learning, including Omniglot [2] and *mini*Imagenet [7]. Experimental results show that comparing with the state-of-the-art method [3], the proposed MSCN performs better on Omniglot and has about 2% improvement on the *mini*Imagenet in all experimental results.

2 Related Work

There are already a number of relatively mature methods for few-shot learning and the most common methods are transfer learning, meta learning and metric learning.

2.1 Transfer Learning

Transfer learning's basic idea is to train a model with a large amount of labeled data at first, then fine tune it to generalize to a specific task. Fine-tuning generally involves fixing partial network parameters and adjusting learning rate. This method is easy to implement and improves the experiment result for it gives a good initilazation, but fine-tuning model with few number of samples often results in violent overfitting. Meta-learning methods were proposed to handle this suituation.

2.2 Meta Learning

The main goal of meta-learning is to use metadata to change the learning algorithm's fit in solving different problems, so that the learning algorithm becomes more flexible and better in the face of different problems. Both meta-learning LSTM [9] and Memory-Augmented Neural Networks (MANN) [11] are good meta-learning methods for few-shot learning.

2.3 Metric Learning

Another solution to few-shot learning is to model the distance distribution between samples, similar to K-NearestNeighbor (KNN) [6], and the ultimate goal is to make similar samples close to each other, and heterogeneous samples are far away from each other. This method is also called metric learning. At present, Prototypical Networks [12], Matching Network [7] and Relation Network [3] are all excellent metric learning methods.

The basic idea of the Prototypical Networks [12] is very similar to KNN. It proposed to learn a embedding model which can map samples to a metric space. It assumed that each category should be a cluster, and samples in the same category should be clustered around the center of this category. The center of each category is obtained by calculating the mean of each samples in the same category. When facing the new test sample, its category is obtained by calculating the distance between it and each category center.

Matching network [7] is based on the principle that training and testing are performed under the same conditions to solve few-shot learning problems. The core idea of the Matching Network is to learn a mapping from a small labelled support set (for more details see Sect. 3.1) and an unlabelled example to its label. Its main function is realized by attention and LSTM.

Relational Network [3] draws on the idea of the above methods and directly uses Convolutional Neural Networks [4] to encode and compare samples. The training and testing methods are similar to Matching Network. Relational Network learns the similarity of two samples at a time. It is an end-to-end classifier, the effect is good, and the training cost and speed are also satisfactory. However, Relational Network does not make full use of the multi-scale information of the samples. For this reason, we propose MSCN to further improve the performance of the network, and there are some improvements in most indicators compared to Relational Network.

3 Methodology

This section will detail the definition of few-shot learning, the model and the network structure of the MSCN for few-shot learning.

3.1 Problem Definition

The task of few-shot learning in this paper refers to the image classification problem with few samples. For example, there are K categories, each with Z samples, which is the few-shot learning task called K-way Z-shot. One of the most intuitive solutions to this type of task is to train a classifier with few samples, but the effect of this method is often unsatisfactory due to overfitting and the like. Therefore, we propose a new multi-scale comparison network, which can compare feature maps of different kernel size, and more accurately compare and analyze, further improving our accuracy.

The few-shot data set generally consists of three parts: a training set, a support set, and a testing set. The support set and the testing set have the same label space, but their label space and the training set's label space intersection are empty sets. When training, we divide the training set into two parts to simulate the support set and the testing set, called the sample set and the query set. The images of the sample set and the query set and the labels of the sample set are used to predict the labels of the query set, and we train our model using the labels of the query set; when testing, we use the images of the support set and test set and the labels of the support set to predict the labels of the test set (For more specific training and testing process, see Sect. 3.2).

3.2 Model

MSCN consists of two modules: an encoder and a comparator. First, the images in the sample set and the query set are input into the encoder to obtain two sets of feature maps, and then they are input into the comparator by filter concatenation to obtain their similarities. The specific model structure is shown in Fig. 1. For example, x from the sample set and x_i from the query set respectively obtain the feature maps $f(x)$ and $f(x_i)$ of the two samples through the encoder, and then obtain $C(f(x), f(x_i))$ by deep splicing, which is finally input into the comparator to obtain the similarity $s(x, x_i)$ of the two samples, and the specific workflow of the model is as Eq. (1):

$$s(x, x_i) = g(C(f(x), f(x_i))) \quad (1)$$

Because the target sizes in samples sometimes vary greatly, the traditional metric learning method can not accurately measure the differences between objects of different sizes. Therefore, we use different scales convolutions to compare features at different scales, further improving the accuracy of prediction.

In training, for 1 shot, we use one sample in each category to represent the category by the feature map obtained by the encoder; for Z shot ($Z > 1$), we take Z samples through the encoder to derive Z feature maps, and then represent the categories by calculating the arithmetic mean of these features. For K way, we obtain K feature combinations by deep splicing the feature maps of the image to be tested and the features of each category, and these combinations are input into the comparator to derive the similarity between the sample to be tested and

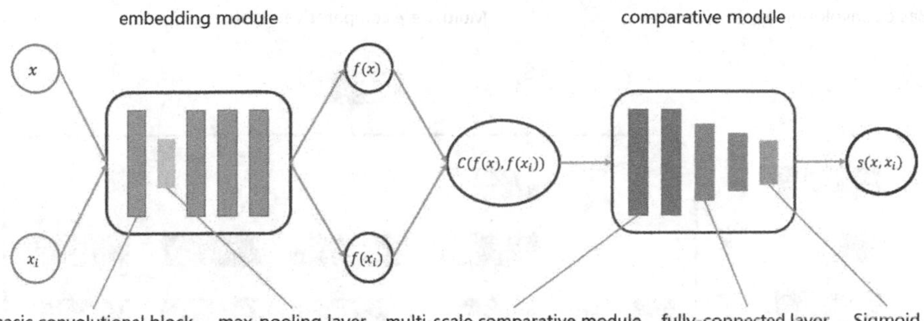

Fig. 1. The architecture of multi-scale comparison network is shown. The network obtains the similarity of the two images by first encoding, then deep splicing and finally comparing.

each category sample. Finally, the back propagation training network is realized by using the prediction result and the label of the sample to be tested to calculate the loss function.

The final output of the network is the similarity of the two features, ranging from 0 to 1. We use mean-square error (MSE) as loss funtion, as shown in Eq. (2). For K way, the variance of the K prediction results and the labels of the samples to be tested is calculated to evaluate the network performance.

$$Loss = \sum_{i=1}^{K} (s(x, x_i) - 1(y(x) == y(x_i)))^2 \tag{2}$$

Where $y(x)$ is the label of x and $y(x_i)$ is the label of x_i.

3.3 Network Architecture

In order to compare fairly with other networks, we use a 4-layer 3×3 convolution structure similar to [3,7,12] in terms of encoders. Since the multi-scale comparison has certain requirements on the size of the feature map, the first layer of the encoder is fine-tuned for data sets with different image sizes. For Omniglot, each convolution block contains a 64-filter 3×3 convolution whose stride and padding are both 1, a batch normalisation and a ReLU nonlinearity layer respectively, and a 2×2 maxpool pooling layer is added after the first convolution block; for the *mini*Imagenet, except for the padding of the convolution in the first convolution block is changed to 0, the last three convolution blocks and the maxpool pooling layer are the same as these of Omniglot.

The first two convolutional blocks of the comparator are similar in structure, which we call the multi-scale comparison module. The multi-scale comparison module consists of five convolutional parts of different scales, and a relu nonlinearity layer is added to the end of each convolutional layer: the first part has a 1×1 convolutional layer; the second part has a 3×3 average pooling layer and

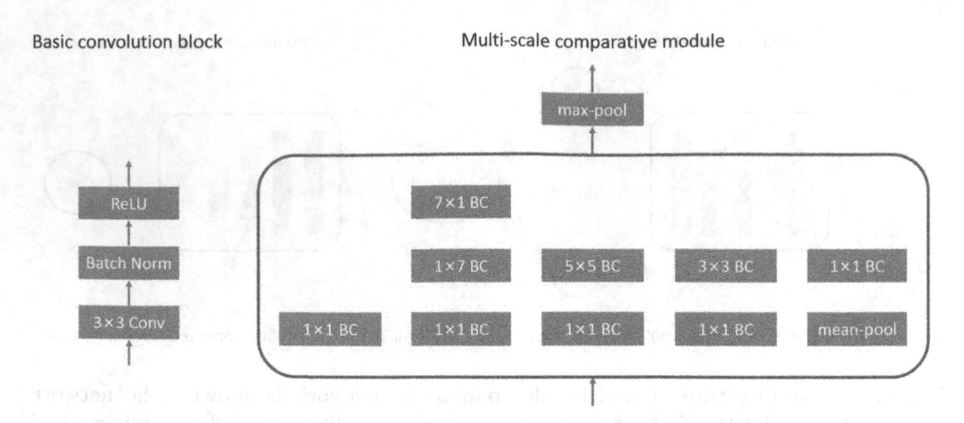

Fig. 2. The architecture of the basic convolutional block (BC) and the multi-scale comparative module are shown.

a 1×1 convolutional layer; the third part has a 1×1 convolutional layer and a 3×3 convolutional layer; the fourth part has the 1×1 convolutional layer and a 5×5 convolutional layer; the fifth part has a 1×1 convolution layer and a 1×7 convolution layer and a 7×1 convolution layer. At the end of the module, the output of each part is spliced in depth, and then the 2×2 max-pooling layer is used to compress the size (see Fig. 2 for the specific architecture). The input dimension of the first convolutional blocks is $64 \times 2 = 128$, the output dimension of each part is 32; the input dimension of the second convolutional blocks is $32 \times 5 = 160$, and the output dimension of each part is 16, and final output dimension is $16 \times 5 = 80$.

Then, different average pooling operations are performed for different sizes of data in different datasets: 4×4 average pooling with a step size of 3 and a zero padding number of 0 for Omniglot; 5×5 average pooling with a step size of 5 and a zero padding number of 0 for the *mini*Imagenet. The output is obtained by using two fully connected layers: the output dimension of the first fully connected layer is 16, and the output dimension of the second fully connected layer is 1. Finally, the sigmoid function is used to normalize the prediction result between 0 and 1.

4 Experiments

We used two data sets to evaluate the performance of the multiscale comparison network: Omniglot [2] and the *mini*Imagenet [7]. The model is all implemented using PyTorch [10]. The optimizer uses Adam [8], the initial learning rate is 10^{-3}, and the learning rate is reduced by half at every 100,000 episodes. Due to the small number of model parameters, the end-to-end training mode model can achieve convergence around 107,000. In order to make a fair comparison, the data processing, training and testing strategies of the experiments in this paper are the same as [3].

4.1 Omniglot

Omniglot [2] contains 1,623 different handwritten characters from 50 different letters. Each character is drawn online by 20 different people through Amazon's Mechanical Turk. We first adjust the picture to 28 × 28, 1200 characters for training, 423 characters for testing, and in the process of training and testing, the data set is expanded by rotating the characters clockwise by 90, 180, 270 degrees to obtain new categories. For each case, the number of training sample sets and query sets is shown in Table 1.

Table 1. The number of images in each training episode for Omniglot.

	Query images	Sample images	Total
5-way 1-shot	$19 \times 5 = 95$	$1 \times 5 = 5$	100
5-way 5-shot	$15 \times 5 = 75$	$5 \times 5 = 25$	100
20-way 1-shot	$10 \times 20 = 200$	$1 \times 20 = 20$	220
20-way 5-shot	$5 \times 20 = 100$	$5 \times 20 = 100$	200

The experimental results on Omniglot [2] are shown in Table 2. Although our method has no improvement on **5-way 1-shot** and **5-way 5-shot** compared to the previous methods, the difference between the accuracy rates is not large. We think this is because the method for solving these two tasks has been done to the extreme. When facing the more difficult tasks: **20-way 1-shot** and **20-way 5-shot**, we achieved state-of-the-art performance compared to other methods. Since the size gap between the samples on Omniglot is not large, the improvement of MSCN is not very obvious, but it has almost the highest accuracy.

Table 2. The results of few-shot classifications on Omniglot. '-' means no report. The highest rates of accuracy are bolded.

Model	5-way acc.		20-way acc.	
	1-shot	5-shot	1-shot	5-shot
MANN [11]	82.8%	94.9%	-	-
Convolutional siamese nets [13]	97.3%	98.4%	88.1%	97.0%
Matching nets [7]	98.1%	98.9%	93.8%	98.7%
Siamese nets with memory [14]	98.4%	99.6%	95.0%	98.6%
Neural statistician [15]	98.1%	99.5%	93.2%	98.1%
Meta nets [16]	99.0%	-	97.0%	-
Prototypical nets [12]	98.8%	99.7%	96.0%	98.9%
MAML [17]	98.7%	**99.9%**	95.8%	98.9%
Relation net [3]	**99.6%**	99.8%	97.6%	99.1%
Multi-scale comparison net	**99.6%**	99.8%	**98.0%**	**99.2%**

4.2 *mini*Imagenet

The *mini*Imagenet [7] was selected from the Imagenet dataset for few-shot learning. This dataset has 100 categories, 600 images per category. We adjusted the picture to 84 × 84, 64 categories for training, 16 categories for validation, and 20 categories for testing. For each case, the number of training sample sets and query sets is shown in Table 3.

Table 3. The number of images in each training episode for the *mini*Imagenet.

	Query images	Sample images	Total
5-way 1-shot	$15 \times 5 = 75$	$1 \times 5 = 5$	80
5-way 5-shot	$10 \times 5 = 50$	$5 \times 5 = 25$	75

From Table 4 we can see that MSCN has greatly improved both accuracy rates compared to the similar model [3] and achieves the highest accuracy on **5-way 1-shot** compared to other methods. Although MSCN does not perform additional optimizations on **5-way 5-shot**, it achieves a competitive result. Compared to the latest methods, since MSCN uses the simple arithmetic mean to calculate the feature of each category, MSCN doesn't perform very well on **5-way 5-shot**.

Table 4. The results of few-shot classifications on the *mini*Imagenet. '-' means no report. The highest rates of accuracy are bolded. 5 and 7 represent the number of parts in the multi-scale comparative module, and for more details see Sect. 5.2.

Model	5-way acc.	
	1-shot	5-shot
Matching nets [7]	43.56%	55.31%
Meta-learning LSTM [9]	43.44%	60.60%
MAML [17]	48.70%	63.11%
Meta nets [16]	49.21%	-
Prototypical nets [12]	49.42%	68.20%
Prototypical nets + fsL + CP [18]	49.64%	69.45%
Deep nearest neighbor neural network [19]	51.24%	**71.02%**
Relation net [3]	50.44%	65.32%
Multi-scale comparison net: 5 parts	52.23%	67.41%
Multi-scale comparison net: 7 parts	**52.32%**	67.44%

5 Analysis

In order to further explore the effectiveness of multi-scale comparison networks, we conducted comparative experiments on two aspects. The experimental data set is still the *mini*Imagenet [7], and the other settings of the experiment are the same as Sect. 4.

5.1 Comparison of Multi-scale Extraction Features and Increasing Parameters with MSCN

One possible reason for the multi-scale comparison network to be effective is that the effect of feature extraction or the increased number of parameters. So we did the following two comparison experiments: the first one, replacing the multi-scale comparative modules of the comparator with the basic convolution blocks similar to the encoder, and replacing the last two basic convolution blocks of the encoder with the proportional multi-scale comparative modules; the second one, replacing the convolutions in the multi-scale comparative modules with the 3×3 convolutions to ensure roughly the same quantity of parameters. The experimental results are shown in Table 5. It can be seen that only multi-scale convolution in the comparison phase can really improve the effect, which means that our work is a universal improvement method for few-shot learning and it is not using the previous method to optimize the feature extraction.

Table 5. The results of multi-scale extraction features, increasing parameters and MSCN. The highest rates of accuracy are bolded.

Model	5-way acc.	
	1-shot	5-shot
Multi-scale extraction features	49.68%	64.22%
Increasing parameters	51.82%	66.87%
Multi-scale comparison net: 5 parts	**52.23%**	**67.41%**

5.2 Self-contrast of Multi-scale Comparison Network

In order to explore the effects of different scale convolutions on the experimental results, we performed different deletions and additions to the components of the multiscale comparison module, as shown in Table 6: the first experiment (3 parts) removed the fourth and fifth parts; the second experiment (4 parts) removed the fifth part; the third experiment (6 parts) added the sixth part: 1×1 convolution layer and 1×9 convolution layer and 9×1 convolution layer; the fourth experiment (7 parts) added the sixth part and the seventh part: 1×1 convolution layer and 1×11 convolution layer and 11×1 convolution layer. The experimental results are shown in Table 6. It can be seen that the effect of the model gradually becomes better with the addition of convolutional layers of different scales at the beginning, but since the multi-scale comparison information has been completed, the effect of the model is not significantly improved.

Table 6. The results of MSCN with different scale convolutions. The highest rates of accuracy are bolded.

Model	5-way acc.	
	1-shot	5-shot
Multi-scale comparison net: 3 parts	51.17%	66.34%
Multi-scale comparison net: 4 parts	51.79%	66.79%
Multi-scale comparison net: 5 parts	52.23%	67.41%
Multi-scale comparison net: 6 parts	52.31%	**67.48%**
Multi-scale comparison net: 7 parts	**52.32%**	67.44%

6 Conclusion and Future Work

We propose a model for few-shot learning using multi-scale information for comparison which has achieved good results on Omniglot and the *mini*Imagenet. And we delved into the effects of a variety of different methods on the effects of the model. Since our work is mainly for one-shot, the effect improvement on the few-shot is not obvious like one-shot, so the next step is to make the model optimize the case of the few-shot. Further work is to extend the scope of comparison and let the model learn more distance relationships when facing new support set and test set.

Acknowledgement. This work is supported by the Natural Science Foundation of China under Grant 61672273 and Grant 61832008, and Scientific Foundation of State Grid Corporation of China (Research on Ice-wind Disaster Feature Recognition and Prediction by Few-shot Machine Learning in Transmission Lines).

References

1. He, K., Zhang, X., Ren, S., Sun, J.: Deep residual learning for image recognition. In: Proceedings of the IEEE Conference on Computer Vision and Pattern Recognition, pp. 770–778 (2016)
2. Lake, B., Salakhutdinov, R., Gross, J., Tenenbaum, J.: One shot learning of simple visual concepts. In: Proceedings of the Annual Meeting of the Cognitive Science Society, vol. 33 (2011)
3. Sung, F., Yang, Y., Zhang, L., Xiang, T., Torr, P.H., Hospedales, T.M.: Learning to compare: relation network for few-shot learning. In: Proceedings of the IEEE Conference on Computer Vision and Pattern Recognition, pp. 1199–1208 (2018)

4. Krizhevsky, A., Sutskever, I., Hinton, G.E.: Imagenet classification with deep convolutional neural networks. In: Advances in Neural Information Processing Systems, pp. 1097–1105 (2012)
5. Szegedy, C., et al.: Going deeper with convolutions. In: Proceedings of the IEEE Conference on Computer Vision and Pattern Recognition, pp. 1–9 (2015)
6. Hastie, T., Tibshirani, R.: Discriminant adaptive nearest neighbor classification and regression. In: Advances in Neural Information Processing Systems, pp. 409–415 (1996)
7. Vinyals, O., Blundell, C., Lillicrap, T., Wierstra, D., et al.: Matching networks for one shot learning. In: Advances in Neural Information Processing Systems, pp. 3630–3638 (2016)
8. Kingma, D.P., Ba, J.: Adam: a method for stochastic optimization. arXiv preprint arXiv:1412.6980 (2014)
9. Ravi, S., Larochelle, H.: Optimization as a model for few-shot learning (2016)
10. Paszke, A., et al.: Automatic differentiation in pytorch (2017)
11. Santoro, A., Bartunov, S., Botvinick, M., Wierstra, D., Lillicrap, T.: Meta-learning with memory-augmented neural networks. In: International Conference on Machine Learning, pp. 1842–1850 (2016)
12. Snell, J., Swersky, K., Zemel, R.: Prototypical networks for few-shot learning. In: Advances in Neural Information Processing Systems, pp. 4077–4087 (2017)
13. Koch, G., Zemel, R., Salakhutdinov, R.: Siamese neural networks for one-shot image recognition. In: ICML Deep Learning Workshop, vol. 2 (2015)
14. Kaiser, Ł., Nachum, O., Roy, A., Bengio, S.: Learning to remember rare events. arXiv preprint arXiv:1703.03129 (2017)
15. Edwards, H., Storkey, A.: Towards a neural statistician. arXiv preprint arXiv:1606.02185 (2016)
16. Munkhdalai, T., Yu, H.: Meta networks. In: Proceedings of the 34th International Conference on Machine Learning, vol. 70, pp. 2554–2563. JMLR.org (2017)
17. Finn, C., Abbeel, P., Levine, S.: Model-agnostic meta-learning for fast adaptation of deep networks. In: Proceedings of the 34th International Conference on Machine Learning, vol. 70, pp. 1126–1135. JMLR.org (2017)
18. Wertheimer, D., Hariharan, B.: Few-shot learning with localization in realistic settings. In: Proceedings of the IEEE Conference on Computer Vision and Pattern Recognition, pp. 6558–6567 (2019)
19. Li, W., Wang, L., Xu, J., Huo, J., Gao, Y., Luo, J.: Revisiting local descriptor based image-to-class measure for few-shot learning. In: Proceedings of the IEEE Conference on Computer Vision and Pattern Recognition, pp. 7260–7268 (2019)

Semantic and Morphological Information Guided Chinese Text Classification

Jiayu Song(✉), Qinghua Xu(✉), Wei Liu(✉), Yueran Zu(✉), and Mengdong Chen(✉)

School of Computer Science and Engineering, Beihang University, Beijing, China
jiayu_buaa@163.com,
{xuqh_buaa,liuwei1206,yueranzu,cmd}@buaa.edu.cn

Abstract. Recently proposed models such as BERT, perform well in many text processing tasks. They get context-sensitive features, which is a good semantic for word sense disambiguation, through deeper layer and a large number of texts. But, for Chinese text classification, majority of datasets are crawled from social networking sites, these datasets are semantically complex and variable. How much data is needed to pre-train these models in order for them to grasp semantic features and understand context is a question. In this paper, we propose a novel shallow layer language model, which uses sememe information to guide model to grasp semantic information without a large number of pre-trained data. Then, we use the Chinese character representations generated from this model to do text classification. Furthermore, in order to make Chinese as easy to initialize as English, we employ convolution neural networks over Chinese strokes to get Chinese character structure initialization for our model.

This model pre-trains on a part of the Chinese Wikipedia dataset, and we use the representations generated by this pre-trained model to do text classification. Experiments on text classification datasets show our model outperforms other state-of-arts models by a large margin. Also, our model is superior in terms of interpretability due to the introduction of semantic and morphological information.

Keywords: Text classification · Sememe · Stroke n-grams · Chinese character representation

1 Introduction

Text categorization is a fundamental and traditional task in natural language processing (NLP), which can be applied in various applications such as sentiment analysis [14], question classification [20] and topic classification [15]. Since Mikolov et al. proposed pre-trained word embeddings [10], many tasks have been greatly improved including text classification. After that, some methods start to improve the text classification task by improving the word embeddings, where they learn word semantic information from context or subword information [1,9].

Y. M. Ro et al. (Eds.): MMM 2020, LNCS 11962, pp. 14–26, 2020.
https://doi.org/10.1007/978-3-030-37734-2_2

Pre-trained word representations become a compulsory component in many neural language understanding models.

Although the above pre-training methods bring many benefits, this kind of word representation can not be used variably across linguistic contexts. To address this problem, Peter et al. provided another idea [12]. They take advantage of language model to produce word representations according to the entire input sentence, which makes a word get different representation in various contexts. BERT [3] also adopts this idea, which uses deeper bidirectional model as well as fine-tunes the parameters for different downstream tasks. This method believes that deep bidirectional model is strictly more powerful, which can extract context-sensitive features, and this kind of feature is a good semantic for word sense disambiguation. That's need large amounts of texts and deep networks can help models understand text more profoundly. However, BERT is notorious for the complexity of its network structure which contains billions of trainable parameters. That is, the model needs a deeper layer to help understand contextual semantic, at the same time, deep network requires large number texts to fit. Unfortunately, the majority of text classification datasets are crawled from social networking sites and the information of these datasets are more diverse and complicated. How much text is needed to get enough semantic knowledge for the model, and how deep the network should be to meet the demand? In this case, we believe that buying a little higher accuracy with a lot more data is meaningless. What we should do is turn to external knowledge for help, just like when humans turn to dictionaries for help when they come across an unfamiliar sentence or article. With the assistance of external knowledge, state-of-art predictions can still be made with shallow layer networks and much less data.

In this paper, we propose a shallow layer language model named glyph-sememe Language Model (gs-LM). In this model, we use sememe information, which likes a dictionary, to make the model learn to look up the dictionary itself by pre-training it on a part of Chinese Wikipedia datasets. Sememes are minimum semantic units [17,18] and it can be used as explanatory information to understand different words. We will elaborate on this later. Besides that, Chinese character structure is also rich in semantic information. In order to avoid incomplete and noisy subword information such as radicals [13] and components [19], Cao et al. [2] use Chinese character strokes and slide window to get subword information, then they add this information together. In our model, we do convolution on strokes to concatenate these subword features instead of summation and get semantic information behind Chinese character structures. Finally, we perform text classification with this character representation generated by the pre-trained gs-LM.

We demonstrate the effectiveness of our architecture on five widely-used datasets. Experimental results show that our proposed model outperforms other state-of-art models on the five datasets. Our contributions of this paper can be concluded as follows:

1. We propose a novel model glyph-sememe Language Model (gs-LM) to incorporate sememe information into Chinese character representation. This

method demonstrates that even without deep-layer networks and large amounts of data, good results can also be achieved.
2. We adopt a different method for Chinese to capture character structure and get semantic information behind this structure to optimize our model.
3. Our proposed model outperforms the other models and achieves the best performance on five text classification datasets.

2 Related Work

Learning excellent text semantic representation has always been an effective way to improve text classification, no matter through models [6,8] or improving the word embeddings [1,9].

Subword Information. Due to their ability to capture syntactic and semantic information from large scale unlabeled text, pre-trained word embeddings become a component of various NLP tasks, and many strategies have been proposed to learn widely applicable representations of words. Except for the use of contextual information, subword information is also added to the word representation. Bojanowski [1] proposes a different score function to take into account the internal structure of word. Internal structure is an important factor for morphologically rich languages, especially for Chinese. Li [9] considers different meaningful components of Chinese character such as Chinese radicals and radical-like components. Considering of such information might be incomplete and noisy, Cao [2] explores the smallest unit of Chinese character, strokes, to extract internal structures of Chinese words and characters. This method, which is similar to FastText [1], uses slide window to get stroke n-gram information of a character or a word, and adds these features together to ensure the final vector dimensions are consistent. But the summation of the feature embeddings does not show these features well. Although our approach also benefits from stroke n-gram information, we use Convolutional Neural Network (CNN) to get this information and concatenate these feature embeddings. Then we can also obtain the final representation with consistent dimensions and richer features.

Pre-trained Word Representation. In addition the use of subword information, Peter et al. [12] provide another way of thinking to improve word embeddings. The representation for each word depends on the entire context in which it is used, and the semantic information obtained by different network layers is also different. BERT [3] builds upon recent work in pre-training contextual representations, including ELMo [12] and ULMFit [4]. This method uses Multi-Task Learning (MTL) to do pre-training task with Masked LM and Next Sentence Prediction (NSP). After pre-training, they simply plug in the task specific inputs and outputs into BERT and fine-tune all the parameters end-to-end for each task. The above models believe that deep layer and large texts help them to get more various semantic information (BERT even uses 12 layers as base model, 24 layers for large model). They rely on this to achieve good performance on different downstream tasks. We take advantage of this kind of models with shallow layers, but gain semantic information with the help of external knowledge.

Character-Based Model for Chinese Text Classification. Unlike English, there is no interval between words in Chinese text, which makes Chinese word segmentation become a peculiar step in Chinese text preprocessing. Although the development of this algorithm is much more mature, it still makes mistakes when it comes to new words. Therefore many Chinese text classification do two groups of controlled experiments, one based on Chinese word and the other based on Chinese character [9,21]. Chinese character shows a better performance on text classification. Our model adopts character-based model to pre-train and do text classification.

3 Methodology

In this section, we introduce our model, glphy-sememe Language Model (gs-LM), and its detailed implementation. In our process, we first pre-train our model, then use the Chinese character representation generated from the pre-trained model to do text classification.

3.1 Model Architecture

The gs-LM is a language model based on the original implementation described in [7]. Because the use of language model has become common, and we also want to implement the structure initialization of Chinese characters in a more convenient way. Our proposed model consists of two parts. The first part is a CNN, which is for Chinese character structure initialization, and the second part is a bidirectional LSTM and a LSTM. In the second part, we take two strategies to add sememe information into the bi-LSTM, in order the model to better understand the text and get well character representation from LSTM.

3.2 Encode Strokes for Character Embedding

Chinese character stroke information can be got from the Xinhua Dictionary[1], where the strokes of each character are encoded into numbers and arranged in the order in which they are written. According to the rules in the dictionary, the strokes are divided into five different types. They are horizontal, vertical, left-falling, right-falling and Turning and numbered as 1, 2, 3, 4 and 5. These stroke numbers are concatenated on the basis of the guideline provided by the Chinese writing system. The example is shown in Fig. 1.

Convolutional neural network (CNN) is a type of neural network architecture, particularly suited for getting n-gram information, whether it is a word or a text, and has also shown to be effective for various NLP applications. Therefore,

[1] http://xh.5156edu.com/.

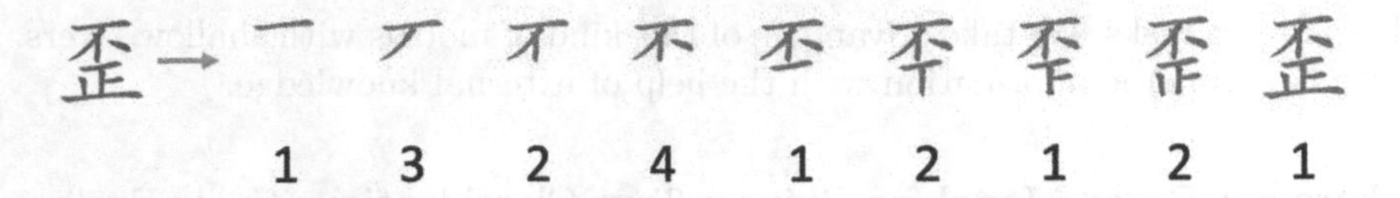

Fig. 1. Taking "歪" as an example to show the rules of Chinese character stroke coding. In the figure, from left to right is the writing order of Chinese character strokes, the newly marked red stroke in each position are the stroke to be written at present, the number denotes the current stroke. Chinese character "歪" can be expressed as "132412121"

we plan to use CNN to get stroke n-gram information. Let us give an example to illustrate. For Chinese character "歪(aslant)", we want to get two components "不(not)" and "正(upright)" from "歪", which can give the basic semantics of "歪". That is, the n-gram information extracted by CNN can be used to initialize Chinese characters and get semantic information [2] behind the Chinese character structure.

Before introduce this method, we first declare some variables. Assume that we have a Chinese character k, the corresponding stroke sequence of the character k is $\{s_1, s_2, \ldots, s_l\}$, where l is the length of the stroke sequence of character k. We can also get the matrix stroke embeddings of character k denoted by $\mathbf{S}^k \in \mathbb{R}^{d \times l}$, and d is the dimensionality of stroke embeddings.

A convolution operation involves a filter $\mathbf{H} \in \mathbb{R}^{w \times d}$, which is applied to a window of w strokes to produce a new feature. A feature f_i^k of character k is generated from a window of character stroke sequence $S_{i:i+w-1}$ by

$$\mathbf{f}_i^k = \tanh\left(\mathbf{H}_k^{\mathrm{T}} \cdot \mathbf{S}_{i:i+w-1} + b\right) \tag{1}$$

Here $b \in \mathbb{R}$ is a bias term. We then apply a max-overtime pooling operation over the feature map to capture the most important feature, also the highest value for each feature map.

$$y^k = \max_i f_i^k \tag{2}$$

Finally, we concatenate these selected features. In other words, when we have h filters, $\left\{y_1^{(k)}, y_2^{(k)}, \ldots, y_h^{(k)}\right\}$ is the final representation of character k. A fixed-length and context-independent vector is available.

3.3 Sememes, Senses and Characters in HowNet

In this paper, we compare the sememe collection to a dictionary, our explanation as follows. HowNet lexicon[2] is a general knowledge base of Chinese and English words. There are two basic terminologies in HowNet, which are "concept" and "sememe". In Chinese, concept is a description of the semantic of word/character. Every word/character can be expressed as one concept or a

[2] http://www.keenage.com/.

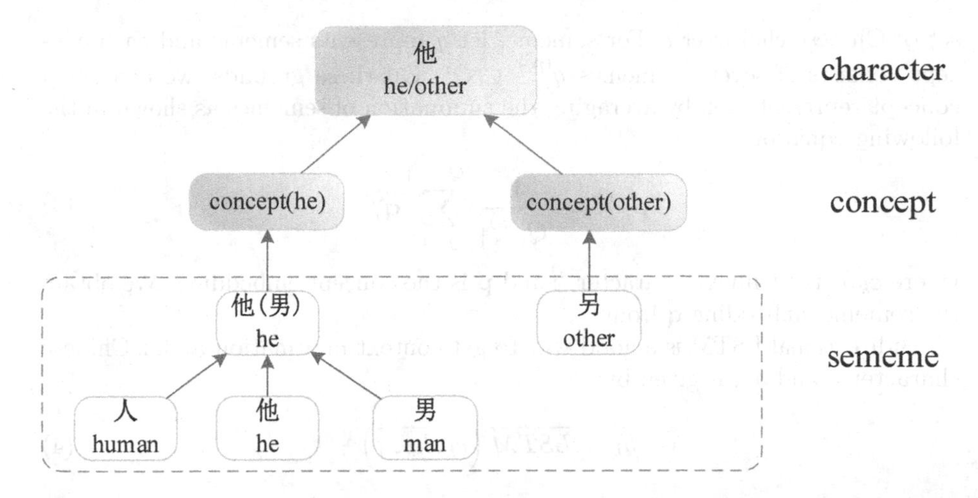

Fig. 2. The first layer is Chinese character '他' the character has two concepts shown in the second layer: the first concept is a pronoun, especially a male, the second one means other. The following layers are sememes used to explain these concepts.

few concepts. Sememe denotes the minimum semantic unit to describe the concept. Each concept in HowNet lexicon is described by several sememes, and the sememes are organized to form a tree structure according to the relation of hyponyms and hypernym. The fundamental function of HowNet lexicon is to uncover the associative relationship among the concepts and relations between the attributes of concepts [17]. In other words, this information can provide Chinese characters or words with the fundamental explanations, that's why we compare it as a dictionary. Figure 2 shows the example of character, concepts and sememes in HowNet.

In this model, we hope to be able to choose the most suitable interpretation of the Chinese characters through contextual information, which is like looking up a dictionary. After pre-training, even if the model encounters text that has not been seen before, it can use the "dictionary" to understand the text information reasonably and accurately.

The similarity between two words in HowNet lexicon is calculated by the similarity between their concepts. Furthermore, the similarity of two concepts is calculated by the similarity of their sememes. Inspired by this, we try to use this semantic similarity to obtain the concept, which Chinese characters are expressing in different contexts. Therefore, we use the attention mechanism to "look up the dictionary", that is, select the most appropriate explanation of Chinese characters according to the context. After that, we add it to the hidden states to get a more accurate character representation.

Attention. We obtain contextual information with bi-LSTM and use it to extract an appropriate concept by attention mechanism. Suppose that a Chinese character contains several different concepts $p_i^c \in P^c$, where P^c is the concept set of Chinese character c. For sememe, let q represents sememe and each concept consists of several sememes $q_j^{(p_i)} \in Q_i^c$. On these grounds, we can get a concept representation by averaging the summation of sememes as shown in the following equation:

$$\mathbf{p}_i^{(c_k)} = \frac{1}{|Q_i^{(c_k)}|} \sum_{j=1}^{|Q_i^{(c_k)}|} \mathbf{q}_j^{(p_i)} \tag{3}$$

where c_k is the Chinese character k and $\mathbf{p}$ is the concept embedding. We obtain the sememe embedding $\mathbf{q}$ from[3]

Bidirectional LSTM is a good way to get context information h_k for Chinese character k and h_k, is given by:

$$\overrightarrow{h_k} = \overrightarrow{LSTM}\left(c_k, \overrightarrow{h_{k-1}}\right) \tag{4}$$

$$\overleftarrow{h_k} = \overleftarrow{LSTM}\left(c_k, \overleftarrow{h_{k+1}}\right) \tag{5}$$

$$h_k = \left[\overrightarrow{h_k}; \overleftarrow{h_k}\right] \tag{6}$$

Then, we use an attention scheme to automatically filter out the most appropriate concept of character k, which is according the context information.

$$att\left(p_i^{(C_k)}\right) = \frac{\exp\left(h_k' \cdot p_i^{(C_k)}\right)}{\sum_{r=1}^{|p^{(C_k)}|} \exp\left(h_k' \cdot p_r^{(C_k)}\right)} \tag{7}$$

The weight of each concept $att\left(p_i^{(C_k)}\right)$ depends on the similarity between them and the context information. Finally, we can a get context dependent semantic representation $\mathbf{z}_1^k$ of character k as following:

$$\mathbf{z}_1^k = \sum_{i=1}^{|p^{(C_k)}|} att(p_i^{(C_k)}).p_i^{(C_k)} \tag{8}$$

Average. In addition to the above strategy, we also propose another rough strategy as a comparison. This strategy averages all concepts of a character and allows us to get a context independent semantic representation $\mathbf{z}_2^k$ of character k, which is a rough semantic information. Similarly, we also add it to the hidden states.

$$\mathbf{z}_2^k = \frac{1}{|P^{(C_k)}|} \sum_{i=1}^{|P^{(C_k)}|} p_i^{(C_k)} \tag{9}$$

[3] https://github.com/thunlp/SE-WRL.

Chinese Text Classification. As the final step, text classification, we adopt CNN to finish this task. We only define a convolution kernel $\mathbf{G} \in \mathbb{R}^{h \times k}$, where h denotes the size of the kernel, and k is the dimensionality of Chinese character representation from pre-trained model. convolution operation apply over the text sequence X, and the resulting $\mathbf{context}_i$ constitutes a feature map.

$$\mathbf{context}_i = f\left(\mathbf{G} \cdot \mathbf{X}_{i:i+h-1} + b\right) \tag{10}$$

Here $b \in \mathbb{R}$ is a bias term and f is a non-linear function. After convolution, we select the maximum value from a feature map, and concatenate all these maximum values together as the final representation of text to classify.

4 Experiments

4.1 Datasets and Experimental Setup

Pre-training Task. We experiment with several variants of the model. The first one is gs-LM without any sememe information (gs-LM without sememe), the second one combines sememes with attention mechanism (gs-LM + attention) and the last one uses average to add sememe information (gs-LM + average). We pre-train these three models separately on only 500M Chinese (simplified) Wikipedia dataset. As is standard in language modeling, we use perplexity (PPL) to evaluate the performance of these models following the standard described in [7].

Implementation Details. The Chinese character stroke order information is from Xinhua Dictionary and the sememe embeddings with 200 dimensions are pre-trained in [11]. For hyper-parameter configurations, we mostly refer to the settings in [7]. In addition, for CNN, it has filters of width [1, 2, 3, 4, 5, 6] of size [25, 50, 75, 100, 100, 100]. The model has one layer biLM with 150 hidden states and one layer LSTM with 300 hidden states. For gs-LM without sememe, we backpropagate for 35 time steps using stochastic gradient descent where the learning rate is initially set to 1.0 and halved if the perplexity does not decrease by more than 1.0 on the validation set after an epoch. But, for gs-LM with sememe, we find this learning rate is too large for it, so we set 0.1 for it and also use stochastic gradient descent. To avoid overfitting, we apply dropout to LSTM with a rate of 0.5. Furthermore, we use a batch size of 40, parameters of the model are randomly initialized over a uniform distribution with support [−0.05, 0.05].

As for text classification, we conduct a simple Convolutional Neural Network (CNN). For all datasets we use: filter windows of 5 with 256 feature maps, dropout rate of 0.5 and batch size of 256.

We evaluate our method on five widely-studied datasets with varying numbers of documents, and experiment on two common text classification tasks: sentiment analysis and topic classification. We show the statistics for each dataset and task in Table 1.

Table 1. Text classification datasets and tasks with number of classes and training examples and testing examples.

Dataset	Type	Classes	Training	Testing
Dianping	Sentiment	2	450k	45k
JD full	Sentiment	5	200k	20k
JD binary	Sentiment	2	300k	30k
ChnSentiCorp	Sentiment	2	9.6k	1.2k
Ifeng	Topic	5	45k	4.5k

Dianping. The Dianping dataset consists of user reviews crawled from Chinese online restaurant review website dianping.com. This dataset was developed and used by Zhang et al. [21] and it's a binary classification. We randomly selected 450,000 samples for training and 45,000 samples for testing.

JD. The JD dataset consists of user reviews crawled from the Chinese online shopping website jd.com. it was divided into 2 sentiment classification datasets, in which one is to predict the full 5 stars (JD-full) and the other is binary (JD-binary), and also provided by Zhang et al. [21].

Ifeng. The Ifeng dataset consists of first paragraphs of news articles from the Chinese news website ifeng.com. Zhang et al. [21] crawled all news from the year 2006 to the year 2016, and selected 5 different news channels as 5 topic classes.

ChnSentiCorp. This dataset is a larger hotel review corpus [16] and it's a binary classification.

4.2 Experimental Result

Pre-trained Tasks. We pre-train our three models on the Chinese (simplified) Wikipedia and the performance can be seen from Table 2.

Table 2. Performance of our three models on the Chinese (simplified) Wikipedia. PPL refers to perplexity (lower is better).

	PPL
gs-LM without sememe	61.23
gs-LM + attention	1.23
gs-LM + average	1.31

The model with sememe information significantly outperforms than the one without sememes, and the gs-LM with an attention mechanism performs a little better than the average strategy. This results show that the addition of sememe information is beneficial to increase the prediction probability of the model.

Text Classification. For consistency, we report all results as correct rates (higher is better). Table 3 shows the experimental results on five various datasets, among them, JD, Dianping and ChnSentiCorp are datasets for sentiment analysis and Ifeng for topic classification. The result of fastText method [21] shows that the character-level 5-gram fastText [5] model performs better than word-level fastText model on almost all datasets. Some experimental results on ChnSentiCorp and Ifeng are from [16], they use character-level BERT and their own model, Glyce+BERT, to do text classification on these datatsets. This experiment demonstrates the importance of Chinese character structure. Although these methods have achieved good performance, our model shows the best results on these datasets. We note that our model achieves great performance on JD and Dianping, especially for JD. JD are user reviews crawled from the Chinese online shopping website, there are many irregular expressions in this dataset, moreover, sememe information can really help the model understand text semantics. The strategy of attention is indeed better than the second strategy.

Table 3. Test correct rates (%) on five text classification datasets used by Zhang et al. [21] and Meng et al. [16]. The results about fastText are from [21] and the results of BERT and Glyce+BERT on ChnSentiCorp and Ifeng are from [16]

Model	Dianping	JD Full	JD Binary	ChnSentiCorp	Ifeng
char-fastText	77.66	52.01	91.28	-	83.69
word-fastText	77.38	51.89	90.89	-	83.35
BERT	79.13	55.26	92.73	95.4	87.1
Glyce+BERT	-	-	-	95.9	87.5
gs-LM + attention	**88.56**	**86.68**	**96.37**	**96.17**	**90.34**
gs-LM + average	87.84	85.43	95.65	95.25	86.17

4.3 Analysis

The above experiments verify the effectiveness of our pre-trained modle for text classification. Here we show some examples of attention strategy.

Effect of Attention Mechanism. The strategy of attention performs better than the strategy of average, and we also want to know, whether the attention mechanism can choose the most appropriate sememe information. Therefore, we use a portion of Chinese Wikipedia data as test data, as well as we look at the weight values of concepts of each character, which is computed by the attention mechanism. The larger the weight value of the concept is, the closer the concept and context semantics are. There are some examples shown in Table 4.

Table 4. Examples of concept selected by attention mechanism. The bold number indicates the maximum weight value

sentence1: 两个算法采用的旋转因子都是纯虚数
(The twiddle factors used by both algorithms **are** pure imaginary numbers)
sentence2: 重要城市多位于维多利亚湖畔，包括首都坎帕拉
(Important cities are located on the shores of Lake Victoria, including the **capital** Kampala.)

Character: 都	concept1: function word	concept2: capital	concept3: family name
attention value(sentence1):	**0.00984303**	0.00319137	0.00135343
attention value(sentence2):	0.00033568	**0.0065304**	-0.00150997

sentence1: 软体模拟器来提供更好的效能
(Software simulator to provide **better** performance)
sentence2: 后来中央电影公司要求更改为其他人
(Later, the Central Film Company requested to **change** to other people.)
sentence3: 政府没有更换改革部长
(The government has not **chang** the reform minister)

Character: 更	concept1: change	concept2: more	concept3: replace
attention value(sentence1):	0.00218466	**0.01004492**	0.00036887
attention value(sentence2):	**0.00726613**	0.00096601	0.00555996
attention value(sentence3):	**0.00489333**	0.00238795	0.00396619

We choose two Chinese characters as an example to analyze. The first Chinese character is "都", which has three concepts. The table lists the calculated weight of each concept of "都" in each sentence, the concept with the greatest weight value is obviously the same as the semantics of the character in a sentence. As for the Chinese character "更", what we would like to mention more is sentence 3. In the sentence 3, The meaning of the character "更" tends not only to the first concept (change) but also to the second concept (replace), attention mechanism also gives them two higher weights. This is the reason, why we do not select the concept which has the highest weight value, instead to add them together. We want to use weights to influence semantic expression, rather than picking the only one. Unfortunately, If it fails to calculate the most correct semantics, it will not greatly affect the final semantic expression.

4.4 Conclusion and Future Work

In this paper, we propose a novel model to generate character representations, which for character-based Chinese text classification. In this method, we use Convolutional Neural Network (CNN) to achieve structural initialization of Chinese characters, as well as take advantage of sememe information to guide model to learn semantic information. In this way, we do not need deep layer or a large number of datasets, this model can also be adequate for coping with diverse texts. Experiments on datasets in different domains show that our model is more efficient and outperforms other state-of-art models.

In the future, we plan to improve the robustness and adaptability of our model by exploring more complicated language phenomenon. For example, "神马" derives from the word "什么" because they resemble each other in terms of pronunciation and they share the exact same meaning of "what". And, since "神马" is a newly-emerged word from the Internet, most existing models can not understand its meaning. In this case, we hope to teach our model of its meaning with the help of the word "什么". Also, we want to try our proposed character representations on other Chinese NLP tasks, such as CWS and Named Entity Recognition (NER).

References

1. Bojanowski, P., Grave, E., Joulin, A., Mikolov, T.: Enriching word vectors with subword information. Trans. Assoc. Comput. Linguist. **5**, 135–146 (2017)
2. Cao, S., Lu, W., Zhou, J., Li, X.: cw2vec: learning Chinese word embeddings with stroke n-gram information. In: Thirty-Second AAAI Conference on Artificial Intelligence (2018)
3. Devlin, J., Chang, M.W., Lee, K., Toutanova, K.: Bert: pre-training of deep bidirectional transformers for language understandingßß. arXiv preprint arXiv:1810.04805 (2018)
4. Howard, J., Ruder, S.: Universal language model fine-tuning for text classification. arXiv preprint arXiv:1801.06146 (2018)
5. Joulin, A., Grave, E., Bojanowski, P., Mikolov, T.: Bag of tricks for efficient text classification. arXiv preprint arXiv:1607.01759 (2016)
6. Kim, Y.: Convolutional neural networks for sentence classification. arXiv preprint arXiv:1408.5882 (2014)
7. Kim, Y., Jernite, Y., Sontag, D., Rush, A.M.: Character-aware neural language models. In: Thirtieth AAAI Conference on Artificial Intelligence (2016)
8. Lai, S., Xu, L., Liu, K., Zhao, J.: Recurrent convolutional neural networks for text classification. In: Twenty-Ninth AAAI Conference on Artificial Intelligence (2015)
9. Li, Y., Li, W., Sun, F., Li, S.: Component-enhanced Chinese character embeddings. arXiv preprint arXiv:1508.06669 (2015)
10. Mikolov, T., Sutskever, I., Chen, K., Corrado, G.S., Dean, J.: Distributed representations of words and phrases and their compositionality. In: Advances in Neural Information Processing Systems, pp. 3111–3119 (2013)
11. Niu, Y., Xie, R., Liu, Z., Sun, M.: Improved word representation learning with sememes. In: Proceedings of the 55th Annual Meeting of the Association for Computational Linguistics (vol. 1: Long Papers), vol. 1, pp. 2049–2058 (2017)
12. Peters, M.E., et al.: Deep contextualized word representations. arXiv preprint arXiv:1802.05365 (2018)
13. Sun, Y., Lin, L., Yang, N., Ji, Z., Wang, X.: Radical-enhanced Chinese character embedding. In: Loo, C.K., Yap, K.S., Wong, K.W., Teoh, A., Huang, K. (eds.) ICONIP 2014. LNCS, vol. 8835, pp. 279–286. Springer, Cham (2014). https://doi.org/10.1007/978-3-319-12640-1_34
14. Tang, D., Qin, B., Liu, T.: Document modeling with gated recurrent neural network for sentiment classification. In: Proceedings of the 2015 Conference on Empirical Methods in Natural Language Processing, pp. 1422–1432 (2015)
15. Tong, S., Koller, D.: Support vector machine active learning with applications to text classification. J. Mach. Learn. Res. **2**(Nov), 45–66 (2001)

16. Wu, W., et al.: Glyce: Glyph-vectors for Chinese character representations. arXiv preprint arXiv:1901.10125 (2019)
17. Xianghua, F., Guo, L., Yanyan, G., Zhiqiang, W.: Multi-aspect sentiment analysis for chinese online social reviews based on topic modeling and hownet lexicon. Knowl.-Based Syst. **37**, 186–195 (2013)
18. Xie, R., Yuan, X., Liu, Z., Sun, M.: Lexical sememe prediction via word embeddings and matrix factorization. In: IJCAI, pp. 4200–4206 (2017)
19. Yu, J., Jian, X., Xin, H., Song, Y.: Joint embeddings of Chinese words, characters, and fine-grained subcharacter components. In: Proceedings of the 2017 Conference on Empirical Methods in Natural Language Processing, pp. 286–291 (2017)
20. Zhang, D., Lee, W.S.: Question classification using support vector machines. In: Proceedings of the 26th Annual International ACM SIGIR Conference on Research and Development in Information Retrieval, pp. 26–32. ACM (2003)
21. Zhang, X., LeCun, Y.: Which encoding is the best for text classification in Chinese, English, Japanese and Korean? arXiv preprint arXiv:1708.02657 (2017)

A Delay-Aware Adaptation Framework for Cloud Gaming Under the Computation Constraint of User Devices

Duc V. Nguyen(✉), Huyen T. T. Tran, and Truong Cong Thang

The University of Aizu, Aizuwakamatsu, Japan
nvduc712@gmail.com, tranhuyen1191@gmail.com, thang@u-aizu.ac.jp

Abstract. Cloud gaming has emerged as a new trend in the gaming industry, bringing a lot of benefits to both players and service providers. In cloud gaming, it is essential to ensure low end-to-end delay for good use experience. Hence, sufficient computational resources must be available at the client in order to process video in a timely manner. However, thin clients such as mobile devices generally have limited computation capabilities. Thus, the available computational resources may be insufficient to support the client, such as in case of low battery. In this paper, we propose a new adaptation framework for resource-constrained cloud gaming clients. The proposed framework combines frame skipping at the server and frame discarding at the client according to available computational resources of the client. Experiment results show that the proposed framework can significantly improve video quality given a delay constraint compared to conventional methods.

Keywords: Cloud gaming · Adaptation · Computation constraint

1 Introduction

Thanks to the popularity of cloud infrastructure and broadband internet connections, cloud gaming has emerged as a new trend in the gaming industry [1,2]. According to [4], the global cloud gaming market is expected to grow at a rate of 33.7% in the period 2015–2020. The same report also suggests that more core gamers will soon switch to cloud gaming.

The principle of cloud gaming is that games are executed on a powerful cloud server. Then, the rendered game scenes are encoded into video and streamed to a client running on a user device. The client decodes the video and displays game scenes to gamers while sending the commands from input devices such as keyboard and mouse to the cloud server [7]. The client and cloud server communicate over the best-effort Internet.

Cloud gaming can help gamers avoid regular, costly hardware and software upgrade. Also, they can play their favorite games anywhere on any devices at anytime. For game developers, cloud gaming eliminates the need of multiple

Y. M. Ro et al. (Eds.): MMM 2020, LNCS 11962, pp. 27–38, 2020.
https://doi.org/10.1007/978-3-030-37734-2_3

game versions for different platforms, thus eases the developing process. Besides, piracy can be completely avoided as game softwares are not downloaded to the client devices.

So far, a number of adaptation methods for cloud gaming have been proposed. However, all previous methods focus on quality improvement under the constraints of network [6,7,17–19] or server [6]. The client-related constraints have not been considered. According to a recent survey [3], 76% of players prefer playing games on mobile devices. However, mobile devices generally have limited computation capabilities. Despite the fact that modern mobile devices are equipped with more powerful CPU, a game client has to share computation resources with other applications (i.e., multitasking). Also, increases in the processor temperature can lead to a significant throttling of CPU frequency [12]. The CPU frequency can also be throttled under low battery mode to save energy [11]. In these circumstances, the client may not always have enough resources to support the game video sent by the cloud server, resulting in increased delay and degraded video quality. Hence adaptation approaches to provide satisfactory gaming experience in resource-constrained clients are especially necessary. To the best of our knowledge, this is the first work that addresses the resource constraints at clients in cloud gaming.

In this paper, we propose a new adaptation framework for cloud gaming that can dynamically adapt to varying computational resources of the client. Because, among encoding parameters, frame rate is found to have the highest impact on CPU utilization and power consumption of user devices [8], we will employ frame rate modification as the key adaptation operation. Also, we propose and evaluate different potential adaptation approaches at both the client and the server sides. Our framework is implemented and evaluated using a real test-bed. Experimental results demonstrate that the proposed framework is effective in adapting cloud gaming systems to meet the computation constraint at the client. In addition, the tradeoff between buffering delay and playback smoothness can be controlled using our method.

The remainder of this paper is as follows. Related work is discussed in Sect. 2. The proposed framework is given in Sect. 3. The evaluation is described in Sect. 4. Finally, conclusions and future work are presented in Sect. 5.

2 Related Work

Previous studies have proposed a number of adaptation methods for cloud gaming systems. However, all the existing methods deal with either server-related constraints (e.g., power [17] and GPU utilization [6]) or network-related constraints (e.g., bandwidth [7,18], delay [10] and packet loss [19]).

In [17], the authors propose a rendering adaptation technique to address server computation capacity. Specifically, four rendering parameters of realistic effect, texture detail, view distance, and enabling grass are considered. In [6], a selective object encoding method is proposed to save the processing power of the server.

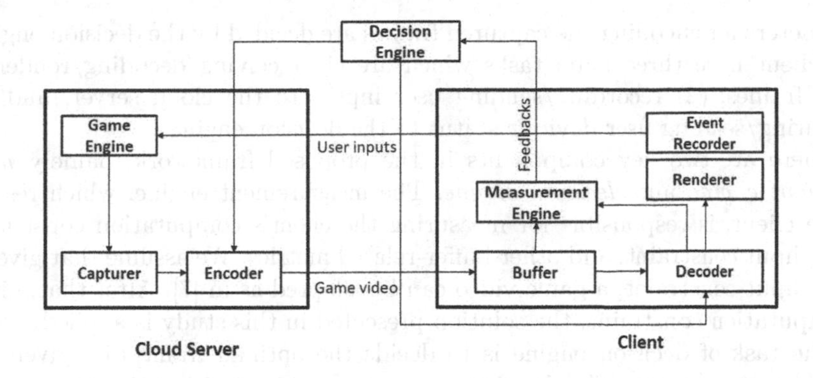

Fig. 1. System architecture. Decision engine for adaptation can reside at either the server or the client.

In [7,18], the authors propose to adapt the bitrate and frame rate of game video according to available network throughput. It is also found that the frame rate can be reduced to as low as 10 fps without significantly affecting user experience. In [16], the authors study the adaptation mechanism used by GerForce NOW and find that it adapts both video resolution and frame rate to cope with bandwidth variations. The study in [10] presents a method that can render speculative frames of future possible outcomes, deliver them to the client one entire RTT ahead of time, and recover quickly from mis-speculations when they occur. The results show that the method is able to mask up to 120 ms of network latency. In [19], the authors propose an adaptation framework called APHIS that dynamically adjusts the video traffic load and forward error correction (FEC) coding in mobile cloud gaming. In [20], a client-based frame discarding algorithm for low-latency video streaming is proposed using HTTP/2's stream termination feature.

As for response latency, games that require intensive interactions like action and racing games are more sensitive to delay than puzzle and strategy games [13]. In [9], it is found that players start to notice the lag when the response delay exceeds 160 ms and 600 ms for a fast-paced game and a slow-paced game, respectively. The mobile device-imposed delays are found to be the biggest components in the end to end latency [5]. In [8], it is found that among encoding parameters, frame rate has the highest impact on the CPU utilization and power consumption of user devices.

3 Proposed Adaptation Framework

3.1 System Architecture

The architecture of the proposed adaptation framework is shown in Fig. 1. The cloud server is responsible for receiving the user inputs (e.g., keyboard strokes), executing the game, and capturing/encoding/sending video frames to the client.

Parameters for encoding the captured frames are decided by the decision engine. The client have three main tasks which are (1) receiving/decoding/rendering video frames, (2) recording/sending user inputs to the cloud server, and (3) measuring/sending user device's status to the decision engine.

There are two key components in the proposed framework, namely *measurement engine* and *decision engine*. The measurement engine, which resides at the client, is responsible for measuring the client's computation constraint, throughput constraint, and other buffer-related metrics. We assume that given a throughput constraint, a game video can be adapted as in [7]. After that, given a computation constraint, the solution presented in this study is applied.

The task of decision engine is to decide the optimal frame rate given the current system status. The decision engine can reside at either the client or the sever. The system performs adaptation periodically with an interval of T s. The optimal adaptation interval depends on client devices, game genres, and also network characteristics. Short adaptation intervals are good to adapt quickly to changes in the system, but longer intervals help reduce system complexity. In [7], an adaptation interval of 60 s is used. In cloud gaming, possible adaptation operators include modifying frame rate, modifying resolution, and modifying bitrate. In this paper, we will consider the first adaptation operator, i.e. modifying video frame rate. The other operators will be reserved for our future work.

3.2 Measurement Engine

The measurement engine resides at the client and is responsible for measuring the computation constraint F^c, estimating the maximum buffering delay d^{buf}_{max}, and measuring the number of video frames in the client buffer. Here, the maximum buffering delay d^{buf}_{max} is the buffering delay to be experienced by the last received frame in the buffer.

The computation constraint F^c is computed as follows. The client calculates the time required to process each frame as the duration from when a frame is retrieved from the buffer until when that frame is rendered. The average processing time t^{proc}_{avg} over the last N frames is then computed. The computation constraint F^c is given by

$$F^c = \frac{1}{t^{proc}_{avg}}. \tag{1}$$

Let d^{proc}_n, d^{buf}_n, and m denote the processing delay (i.e., the time required to decode and render) and the buffering delay of the last playout frame n and the index of the last received frame in the buffer. The server generates and transmits video frames periodically as determined by a frame rate. If the frame rate is F fps, then a video frame is sent out every $\tau = 1/F(s)$. If the computation constraint is less than or equal to the current frame rate, i.e., $F^c \geq F$, the buffering delay and the number of frames in the client buffer is zero. If $F^c < F$, the number of frames in the client buffer is $(m-n)$. The maximum buffering delay d^{buf}_{max}, which is the buffering delay of frame m, can be estimated from d^{buf}_n and F^c as follows.

$$d^{buf}_{max} = d^{buf}_m = d^{buf}_n + (m-n) \times (d^{proc}_n - \tau). \tag{2}$$

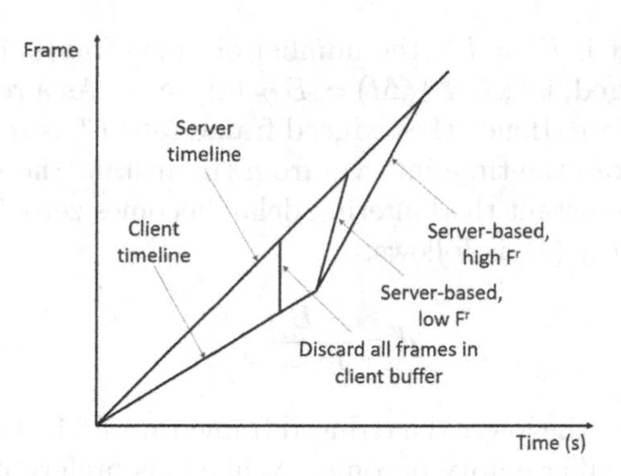

Fig. 2. Tradeoff between the delay and smoothness.

The computation constraint, the maximum buffering delay, and the number of video frames in the buffer are calculated at every frame.

3.3 Decision Engine

In our proposed system, the decision engine receives necessary information from the measurement engine and decides the optimal frame rate of the game video. At the beginning of each adaptation interval, the decision engine will decide the optimal frame rate of the encoder in that interval.

The system has two stages depending on the maximum buffering delay. Initially, the system is in Stage 1 and the optimal frame rate is set to the computation constraint F^c. The system will enter Stage 2 if it detects that the maximum buffering delay has exceeded a predefined delay threshold d^{buf}_{thres}. In Stage 2, the objective is to remove the buffering delay. The system will leave Stage 2 and enter Stage 1 when the buffering delay becomes zero.

Assume that at time t when the decision engine is going to decide the optimal frame rate of the next adaptation interval, the maximum buffering delay d^{buf}_{max} reported in the last feedback has exceeded the delay threshold d^{buf}_{thres}. The decision engine decides to reduce the server's frame rate from the current frame rate F fps to a reduced frame rate F^r fps to eliminate the buffering delay. So, the number of video frames in the client buffer at time $(t + \Delta t)$ can be estimated by

$$B(t + \Delta t) = B(t) - (F^c - F^r) \times \Delta t, \tag{3}$$

where $B(t)$ denotes the number of frames in the client buffer at time t. Let B_{fb} denote the number of video frames in the client buffer reported in the last feedback. Because of the network delay, $B(t)$ may not necessarily equal to B_{fb}. However, since the client sends a feedback every frame, and the network delay is considered small, the value of $B(t)$ is approximated by B_{fb} in this paper. As a result, the value of $B(t + \Delta t)$ is estimated at the server by

$$B(t + \Delta t) = B_{fb} - (F^c - F^r) \times \Delta t \tag{4}$$

It can be noted that if $F^r = F^c$, the number of video frames in the client buffer will remain unchanged, i.e., $B(t+\Delta t) = B_{fb}$ ($\Delta t \geq 0$). As a result, the buffering delay will not decrease. Hence the reduced frame rate F^r is required to be lower than F^c. Let d denote the time interval from the instant the server changes the frame rate until the instant the buffering delay becomes zero. The value of d can be computed from Eq. (4) as follows.

$$d = \frac{B_{fb}}{F^c - F^r} \tag{5}$$

According to Eq. (5), the lower the reduced frame rate F^r is, the shorter the time to make the client buffer empty becomes. While it is preferable to eliminate the buffering delay as fast as possible, a very low frame rate can greatly decrease the smoothness of the rendered game video, and therefore the user experience may be negatively affected. The tradeoff between the delay and smoothness will be considered when deciding the reduced frame rate F^r. Figure 2 illustrates the tradeoff between the delay and smoothness.

Our framework supports two adaptation approaches, namely *server-based approach* and *hybrid approach.*

Server-Based Approach. Firstly, we formulate the problem of selecting the reduced frame rate F^r in the server-based approach as follows. For a given computation constraint F^c, there are more than one feasible frame rate F^r that satisfy the condition $F^r < F^c$. To reflect the tradeoff between the smoothness and delay, we use a cost function, $C(F^r)$, to quantify the cost associated with a frame rate F^r. The optimal frame rate selection can be formulated as follows.

Find a frame rate F^r that minimizes the associated cost $C(F^r)$ and satisfies

$$F^r < F^c. \tag{6}$$

As mentioned, if a low frame rate is selected, the buffering delay could be eliminated very quickly. Yet, the smoothness of the video is greatly reduced, and the user experience may be adversely affected. On the other hand, the smoothness of the video could be maintained with a high value of frame rate. However, it will take a longer time to eliminate the buffering delay. To solve the above problem, we propose to compute the cost C as a weighted sum of two element costs which are the cost of delay C_d and the cost of smoothness C_s. The cost C is given by

$$C = \alpha \times C_d + (1 - \alpha) \times C_s, \tag{7}$$

where the weight α is in range $[0, 1]$. Good values of α are dependent on the game types. Specifically, the value of α should be high if the considered games are very sensitive to delay such as First-Person Shooter. On the other hand, for games that can tolerate longer delay, lower values of α could be chosen.

It can be noted that the higher the delay is, the longer the duration of the problems caused by the buffering delay would become. Hence the delay cost C_d should be an increasing function of the delay d. On the other hand, the smoothness can be improved when the frame rate is increased. Thus, the smoothness cost C_s should be a decreasing function of the reduced frame rate F^r. In this paper, the delay and smoothness costs are defined as follows.

$$C_d = \frac{d}{d_{max}}. \tag{8}$$

$$C_s = \frac{F_{min}}{F^r}. \tag{9}$$

Here, d_{max} and F_{min} respectively denote the maximum delay and the minimum allowable frame rate.

Given the processing constraint F^c, the current frame rate F, and the number of frames in the client buffer B_{fb}, the general procedure to determine the optimal reduced frame rate F^r is summarized in Algorithm 1.

Algorithm 1. Optimal frame rate selection algorithm

```
C_min = ∞;
F^r = 1;
for F = 1 to F^c do
    Calculate the delay d using (5);
    Calculate the cost C using (7)(8)(9);
    if C < C_min then
        F^r = F;
        C_min = C;
    end
end
```

In Algorithm 1, we only consider the frame rates which are integer numbers between 1 and F^c. As the number of possible frame rates is limited, the complexity of this procedure is negligible. Finally, the operations of the decision engine is summarized in Algorithm 2.

Hybrid Approach. In the hybrid approach, the adaptation will be performed by both the client and the server. This approach combines discarding video frames at the client and adjusting frame rate at the server. The decision engine actually may be located or distributed at the server and/or the client. In our current implementation, the decision engine resides at the server.

In this study, we focus on evaluating the server-based approach. Thus, for our evaluation, a special case of the hybrid approach where the client discards all video frames in the buffer while the server reduces its frame rate to F^c is considered. In this way, the removal of buffering delay can be done immediately while, at the same time, achieving optimal frame rate. The general solution for the hybrid-based approach will be reserved for our future work.

Algorithm 2. General adaptation algorithm

Input: F^c, T, d_{thres}^{buf}, d_{max}^{buf}, d_{max}, F_{min}
Output: Optimal frame rate F
Stage = 1;
while *not end of the session* **do**
  retrieve F^c, d_{max}^{buf} from the last feedback;
  if $d_{max}^{buf} > d_{thres}^{buf}$ **or** *(Stage == 2* **and** $d_{max}^{buf} > 0$*)* **then**
    Stage = 2;
  else
    Stage = 1;
  end
  if *Stage == 1* **then**
    $F = F^c$;
  else
    Calculate the optimal reduced frame F^r using Algorithm 1; $F = F^r$;
  end
  sleep for T seconds;
end

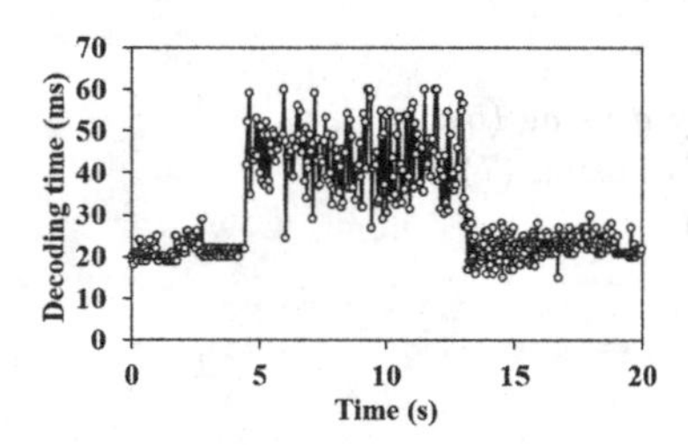

Fig. 3. Decoding times of video frames increases significantly when the CPU clock is throttled from t = 5 s to t = 13 s.

4 Evaluation

4.1 Experiment Settings

In the experiments, we use a 20-second long video of Final Fantasy[1], a Massively multiplayer online role-playing game (MMORPG). The video has a resolution of 1280 × 720 and a frame rate of 30 fps. The video is encoded using x264 with a GoP size of 48, zero latency, and intra-refresh. In the intra-refresh mode, key frames are replaced by using a column of intra blocks that move across the video frame from left to right, refreshing video every GoP [15]. The network bandwidth is set to 5 Mbps, the round-trip time delay is set to 20 ms using DummyNet [14]. The adaptation interval T is set to 1 s. The values of d_{max}, N, and F_{min} are set to 10 s, 30, and 1 fps, respectively. The proposed approach is implemented based on Gaming Anywhere [7], an open-source cloud gaming platform. The

[1] https://www.youtube.com/watch?v=gje2nTPERAs, 00:11:40-00:12:00.

client is running on a Ubuntu 14.04 LTS 64 bit machine with 4 GB RAM and Intel Core i5-3210M CPU 2.5 GHz (4 cores). The server is running on another Ubuntu 14.04 LTS 64 bit machine with 8 GB RAM and Intel Core i5-2500 CPU 3.3 GHz (4 cores). Client feedbacks and server control messages are delivered over an UDP connection.

To emulate the computation constraint at the client, the case of low battery is considered. When the battery is low, the CPU frequency will be throttled to save energy until the device is charged again. The time required to decode each video frame under such a case is shown in Fig. 3. Here, the mobile device is in low-battery mode from time t = 5 s to time t = 13 s. We can see that video decoding time almost doubles during the period CPU frequency is throttled.

For the server-based approach, we consider three values of α which are 0.05, 0.5, and 0.9. As mentioned above, a special case of the hybrid approach in which the client discards all frames in the client buffer called *discard* is considered. These approaches are compared with a reference approach, called *no-adapt*, that does not employ any adaption mechanisms. A delay thresholds of 400 ms is considered. In practice, the value of the delay threshold should depend on the game genre. The problem of deciding good threshold values is reserved for our future work.

4.2 Experiment Results

Figure 4 shows the playout curves, frame rates, buffering delays and frame PSNRs of the proposed method and *no-adapt* when the delay threshold is 400 ms. Each playout curve in Fig. 4a shows the frame being played at each time instant. The curve when all video frames are played on time is denoted by **normal**. Separations from the **normal** curve indicate that the client is behind the original playout schedule. In other words, a buffering delay is occurring at the client. For clear observations, only the parts from time t = 5 s to time t = 9 s are shown.

During the first 5 s, it can be seen that all methods select the same frame rate of 30 fps and do not experience any buffering delay. This is because the computation constraint is sufficient to support the highest frame rate. From time t = 5 s, the decoding time required for each frame is increased significantly as the client has to spend a part of its computation for broadcasting the gameplay. As a result, the buffering delay starts to increase as shown in Fig. 4c. For *no-adapt*, the buffering delay continues to increase and reaches 2 s at time t = 13 s. Such a high delay is considered as unacceptable in cloud gaming [9]. Meanwhile, the proposed method (both server-based and *discard*) can effectively eliminate the buffering delay and achieve the optimal frame rate thereafter by adapting the video frame rate. Once the buffering delay is eliminated, the frame rate is increased to 18 fps which is the optimal value under the computation constraint. After the broadcast finishes at time t = 13 s, the video frame rate is increased to 30 fps.

The tradeoff between delay and smoothness in case of the server-based approach can be controlled via the value of α. Specifically, if a high value of α is selected, e.g., $\alpha = 0.9$, it takes only 1s to remove the buffering delay by reducing

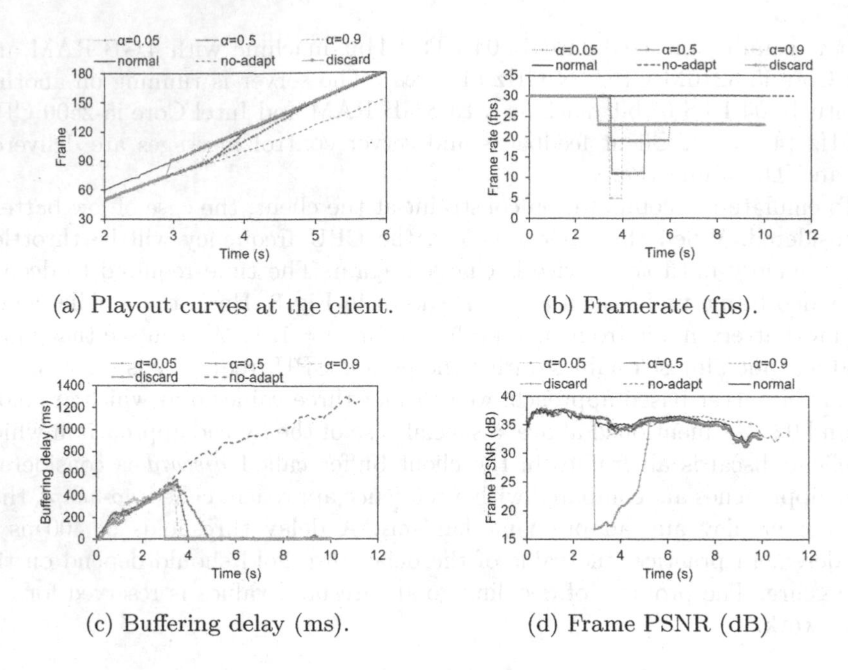

(a) Playout curves at the client.

(b) Framerate (fps).

(c) Buffering delay (ms).

(d) Frame PSNR (dB).

Fig. 4. Playout curves, frame rate, buffering delay, and frame PSNR when the delay threshold is 400 ms.

the frame rate to 5 fps as shown in Fig. 4b. On the other hand, the smoothness of video frame rate could be improved by selecting a low value of α. When $\alpha = 0.5$, the reduced frame rate F^r is much higher at 9 fps. However, in this case, the time required to eliminate the buffering delay is 2 s which is two times higher compared to that of $\alpha = 0.9$. By further reducing the value of α to 0.05, a high frame rate of 17 fps can be achieved. Yet, it takes approximately 3 s to eliminate the buffering delay as can be seen in Fig. 4c. In practice, good values of α should depend on game genres. For example, high value of α should be used in case of fast-spaced games that require extremely low response delay. It can also be noted that reducing the frame rate does not visible impact to the video quality as can be seen in Fig. 4d.

By discarding all video frames in the client buffer (i.e., 14 frames from the 166th to 178th frame), the *discard* approach can remove the buffering delay immediately at time t = 6 s as can be seen in Fig. 4c. The frame rate is also reduced to the optimal value of 18 fps at the same time as can be seen in Fig. 4b. However, the *discard* approach results in severe quality degradations in which the frame PSNR drops below 25 dB for approximately 1.5 s as shown in Fig. 4d. This is because of (1) a number of video frames are lost and (2) the intra-refresh coding mode that disables I frames. Thus, a frame loss causes decoding errors of one or more following frames.

Considering the case of $\alpha = 0.9$, it can be seen that the buffering delay exceeds the delay threshold at time t = 5.8 s. However, since the server can only adapt the frame rate every $T = 1$ s, the frame rate is actually unchanged until time t = 6 s. As a result, the buffering delay is increased to about 420 ms when the server changes the frame rate from 30 fps to 5 fps at time t = 6 s. For the server-based approach, the buffering delay continues to increase even though the server has already reduced the frame rate. This is caused by the ealier-arriving frames in the client buffer. Once all those frames have been processed, the buffering delay starts to decrease as the frames associated with the new frame rate are processed. When $\alpha = 0.9$, it takes additionally 500 ms until the buffering delay starts decreasing at time t = 6.5 s. Meanwhile, since all ealier-arrived frames are discarded, the *discard* approach is able to eliminate the buffering delay instantly.

5 Conclusion

In this paper, we have proposed a new adaptation framework for cloud gaming that can adapt to the constraint of computation resource at clients. Different potential approaches, namely server-based, and hybrid approaches were investigated. For the server-based approach, it was found that the proposed solution could enable a trade-off between buffering delay and quality smoothness by adapting the frame rate. Meanwhile, the hybrid approach is the fastest way to eliminate the buffering delay; however, it experiences significant quality degradations due to frame discarding. In the future work, we will extend the current framework with advanced encoding features.

References

1. Geforcenow. http://www.geforce.com/geforcenow. Accessed 01 Mar 2019
2. PS NOW. https://www.playstation.com/en-gb/explore/playstation-now/ps-now-on-pc/. Accessed 25 Mar 2019
3. Customer preferred gaming platforms according to gaming companies worldwide. Technical report (2016). https://www.statista.com/statistics/608933/gaming-companies-customer-preferred-gaming-platforms-worldwide/
4. Global cloud gaming market by technology. Technical report (2017). https://www.marketresearchengine.com/reportdetails/global-cloud-gaming-market
5. Echeverria, V., Falcones, G., Castells, J., Granda, R., Chiluiza, K.: Multimodal collaborative workgroup dataset and challenges. In: CEUR Workshop Proceedings, vol. 1828, pp. 94–98 (2017)
6. Hemmati, M., Javadtalab, A., Nazari Shirehjini, A.A., Shirmohammadi, S., Arici, T.: Game as video: bit rate reduction through adaptive object encoding. In: ACM NOSSDAV, Oslo, Norway, pp. 7–12 (2013)
7. Hong, H.J., Hsu, C.F., Tsai, T.H., Huang, C.Y., Chen, K.T., Hsu, C.H.: Enabling adaptive cloud gaming in an open-source cloud gaming platform. IEEE Trans. Circuits Syst. Video Technol. **25**(12), 2078–2091 (2015)
8. Huang, C.Y., Chen, P.H., Huang, Y.L., Chen, K.T., Hsu, C.H.: Measuring the client performance and energy consumption in mobile cloud gaming. In: Annual Workshop on Network and Systems Support for Games, Nagoya, Japan, pp. 4–6 (2014)

9. Jarschel, M., Schlosser, D., Scheuring, S., Hoßfeld, T.: An evaluation of QoE in cloud gaming based on subjective tests. In: The Fifth International Conference on Innovative Mobile and Internet Services in Ubiquitous Computing, Washington DC, USA, pp. 330–335 (2011)
10. Lee, K., Chu, D., Cuervo, E., Wolman, A., Flinn, J.: Outatime: using speculation to enable low-latency continuous interaction for mobile cloud gaming. In: Proceedings of the MobiSys 2014, Florence, Italy, pp. 347–347 (2014)
11. Natvig, L., Iordan, A.C.: Green computing: saving energy by throttling, simplicity and parallelization. Green ICT: Trends and Challenges, p. 49 (2011)
12. Prakash, A., Amrouch, H., Shafique, M., Mitra, T., Henkel, J.: Improving mobile gaming performance through cooperative CPU-GPU thermal management. In: The 53rd Annual Design Automation Conference, Austin, Texas, pp. 47:1–47:6 (2016)
13. Quax, P., Beznosyk, A., Vanmontfort, W., Marx, R., Lamotte, W.: An evaluation of the impact of game genre on user experience in cloud gaming. In: IEEE Consumer Electronics Society International Games Innovation Conference, IGIC, Vancouver, Canada, pp. 216–221 (2013)
14. Rizzo, L.: Dummynet: a simple approach to the evaluation of network protocols. ACM SIGCOMM Comput. Commun. Rev. **27**(1), 31–41 (1997)
15. Schreier, R.M., Rothermel, A.: Motion adaptive intra refresh for the H.264 video coding standard. IEEE Trans. Consum. Electron. **52**(1), 249–253 (2006)
16. Suznjevic, M., Slivar, I., Skorin-Kapov, L.: Analysis and QoE evaluation of cloud gaming service adaptation under different network conditions: the case of NVIDIA GeForce NOW. In: QoMEX 2016, Lisbon, Portugal, pp. 1–6 (2016)
17. Wang, S., Dey, S.: Rendering adaptation to address communication and computation constraints in cloud mobile gaming. In: 2010 IEEE Global Telecommunications Conference GLOBECOM 2010, Miami, USA, pp. 1–6, December 2010
18. Wang, S., Dey, S.: Addressing response time and video quality in remote server based internet mobile gaming. In: IEEE WCNC, Sydney, Australia, pp. 1–6 (2010)
19. Wu, J., Yuen, C., Cheung, N.M., Chen, J., Chen, C.W.: Enabling adaptive high-frame-rate video streaming in mobile cloud gaming applications. IEEE Trans. Circuits Syst. Video Technol. **25**(12), 1988–2001 (2015)
20. Yahia, M.B., Louedec, Y.L., Simon, G., Nuaymi, L., Corbillon, X.: HTTP/2-based frame discarding for low-latency adaptive video streaming. ACM Trans. Multimed. Comput. Commun. Appl. **15**(1), 181–1823 (2019)

Efficient Edge Caching for High-Quality 360-Degree Video Delivery

Dongbiao He[1], Jinlei Jiang[1(✉)], Cédric Westphal[2], and Guangwen Yang[1]

[1] Department of Computer Science and Technology, Tsinghua University, Beijing 100084, China
hdb13@mails.tsinghua.edu.cn, {jjlei,ygw}@tsinghua.edu.cn

[2] Department of Computer Science and Engineering, University of California, Santa Cruz, CA 95064, USA
cedric@soe.ucsc.edu

Abstract. 360-degree video streaming, which offers an immersive viewing experience, is getting more and more popular. However, delivering 360-degree video streams at scale is challenging due to the extremely large video size and the frequent viewport variations. In order to ease the burden on the network and improve the delivered video quality, we present a caching scheme that places the frequently requested contents at the edge. Our scheme achieves this purpose by presenting: (i) an online learning approach to predict video popularity, and (ii) some strategies for allocating cache for videos and tiles. A thorough evaluation shows that the proposed scheme yields significant traffic reduction over other strategies and does improve the quality of the delivered videos.

Keywords: Edge computing · Caching policy · 360-degree video · QoE

1 Introduction

360-degree (or 360°) video, also known as panoramic videos or immersive video, is predicted to become a global market that will reach $47.7 billion by 2024[1]. Such a prediction assumes that the network infrastructure can support this type of video efficiently. Unfortunately, even with the roll-out of 5G, the delivery infrastructure needs some updates [15]. One solution is to provide an adaptive streaming strategy based on users' field of view (FoV), which is only a small slice of the whole 360° video stream. For instance, the network could only transmit the content within the FoV, or lower the resolution of content out of FoV in order to save bandwidth.

To do FoV-adaptive streaming, 360° videos are spatially segmented into small *tiles* based on their relative position on the viewing sphere. Each tile is encoded and transmitted independently. Even so, a caching infrastructure [1] can still

[1] https://www.mordorintelligence.com/industry-reports/virtual-reality-market/.

This work is sponsored by Natural Science Foundation of China (61572280).

Y. M. Ro et al. (Eds.): MMM 2020, LNCS 11962, pp. 39–51, 2020.
https://doi.org/10.1007/978-3-030-37734-2_4

help improve content delivery. To get the most benefit, caching must take into account the characteristics of 360° video streaming. Indeed, previous studies (e.g., [5,16]) have shown that the behaviors of users are relatively similar for the same video: most users keep their focus on the same small subset of tiles. Thus, placing the most requested video tiles at the edge would ease the burden on the network, reduce access latency and give users a better immersive experience. This is the basic idea behind edge caching and our work as well.

For 360° video delivery, the task of selecting the content to be cached is particularly challenging due to a number of factors involved, including request patterns in tiles and FoV, resolution, cache size, source server locations, and content size. Here we present a new edge caching scheme that distinguishes itself from the existing ones by considering the request characteristics of both the video and the tiles of the video. This scheme can reduce computation overhead and adapt to heterogeneous request patterns.

Our scheme is distributed at the edge and works reactively. It can be viewed as a complement to a, say, daily content placement problem backed by some centralized algorithm such as the ones currently used in content delivery networks (CDNs). Each edge cache compiles information based upon the locally-observed requests and feeds it into a cache optimization algorithm. The collected information includes video request history (frequency and access time), as well as tiles distribution. We find that not only popularity but also the FoV distribution can impact the caching strategy. For example, if many users watch the same few tiles of a popular video, only these tiles should be cached. However, if the FoVs viewed by different users are far apart, the whole 360° video needs to be cached.

We devise an online learning strategy to predict video access so that caching decisions can be made. The decision aims at maximizing the reward associated with network traffic reduction. To do so, we allocate the caching space according to a comprehensive metric covering not only popularity (as in a typical caching system) but also the required cache space of each video. To the best of our knowledge, it is the first 360° video caching solution which considers caching at both the video and more fine-grained tile levels.

Our main contributions are as follows:

- We formulate the 360° videos caching problem and devise an effective and efficient caching scheme that makes use of the history of video access via an online learning algorithm. The scheme predicts the video popularity without any assumption of the underlying request distributions and offers a comprehensive cache allocation strategy.
- We devise a cache allocation solution for tiles which takes the user's quality of experience (QoE) as the primary goal. The requested tiles are divided into multiple groups and the most frequently-accessed tiles are cached with high resolution. The solution can also reduce computation overhead when compared with existing tile-based video caching solutions.
- Thorough evaluation is conducted to evaluate the newly designed caching scheme under various settings. The experimental results show our solution yields significant traffic reduction over the caching schemes considering only

a single factor. Moreover, the results also indicate that partitioning tiles into two fixed groups is enough from the perspective of QoE.

2 Background and Related Work

2.1 Edge Caching for 360° Video Delivery

360° videos are usually shot with a set of cameras, whose FoVs jointly cover an entire sphere. The video frames captured from each camera are stitched and projected onto the sphere, which is further mapped to a plane as a 360° video frame. Afterward, the video data is compressed for delivery. As there are many types of terminal devices (e.g., VR glasses, smart phones, or laptops), multiple formats with different projection methods should be stored. Furthermore, the bandwidth required to stream a 360° video is significantly larger than that required by a regular video. For example, the data rate for delivering a 4K 360° video to each eye with full viewing range is 400 Mbps while only about 25 Mbps is required for delivering a traditional 4K video [4,17].

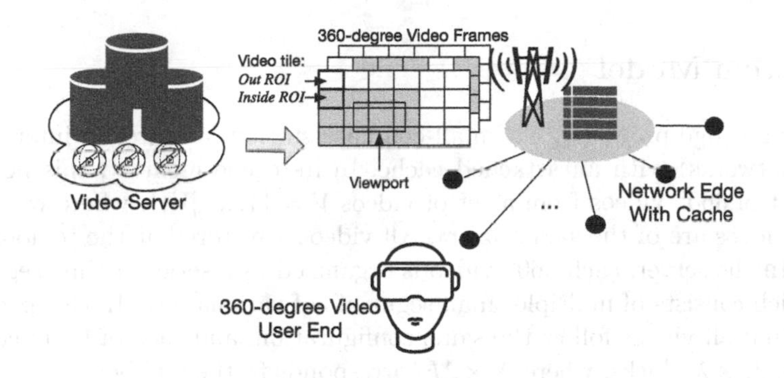

Fig. 1. The architecture of 360° video cache

To alleviate the bandwidth crunch, region-of-interest (ROI) has been proposed for streaming. Human eyes have a limited viewport, and only the view that is actively watched should be transmitted in high resolution, while the other views are transmitted in low resolution. Obviously, this idea could also be used in edge caching to cache the popular ROIs obtained from users.

An overview of our edge caching enabled 360° video delivery architecture is shown in Fig. 1. The architecture is comprised of three major components: video server, transport network, and edge cache. The video server is responsible for the generation, storage, and preparation of 360° videos. The transport network fulfills the delivery of videos. Finally, the edge cache establishes a tight interaction between the clients and the server to meet the stringent delay requirements of 360° video streaming.

2.2 Related Work

360° video caching can be done at the *tiles* or *videos* levels. At the tiles level, each tile is considered independent and more popular tiles can be cached with limited cache capacity. In contrast, caching at the video level caches the whole video and may lead to some waste, for some tiles may not be requested.

Recently, tile-based caching solutions [8,9,11] have been suggested to save the cache capacity and improve caching efficiency. Since tiles are small in size, operating on tiles introduces a lot of overhead. For example, a 20-minute 360° video has 1.4×10^5 tiles when the video segments last 2 s with a 6×4 tiling scheme. As mentioned before, the ROI has been used for streaming 360° videos selectively, and users only focus on specific parts of a video. A previous study [16] showed that: (1) most users are drawn to a common ROI on the same 360° video; (2) the spread of ROIs across users varies across videos. Besides this, we also find that the tile popularity of each video could be estimated via certain sample statistics methods.

Different from existing solutions, our work delves into the use of caching for improving 360° video delivery at both the tiles and video levels. It reduces the model complexity and is more efficient.

3 System Model

Consider an edge proxy (e.g., a small-cell base station, a router in information-centric networks) with an attached cache. In its cache memory, this node can store part of 360° videos from a set of videos $\mathcal{V} = \{1, ..., |V|\}$, where we assume that all videos are of the same size $\mathfrak{m}$. All videos are stored at the remote video servers. In the server, each 360° video is organized as a series of time segmentation, which consists of multiple small segments of various tiles. In this paper, we assume that all videos follow the same configuration, and each of them contains $H = N \times M \times \lambda$ blocks, where $N \times M$ corresponds to the number of tiles, and λ to the number of time segments. Therefore, the segments of each video v could be represented as $\{v(1), v(2), ..., v(H)\}$.

In order to solve the caching problem, consider a system that works in a discrete-time setting $\mathcal{T} = 1, 2, ..., T$, where T is finite and at each time t the following events happen sequentially: (i) the node observes the video content request vector which characterizes the user demand for the system in this period; (ii) based on the features of the observed vector, the caching node refreshes the cached video files, and sends a broadcast message to all users connecting to it to updated their content lists.

To inform the attached users of the available videos, the node sends the information periodically to the forwarding gateway. When a user requests a video that the caching node has cached, the video is retrieved from the node via local communications. Otherwise, the user has to download the video from the video server, which is of high latency and lowers the quality of the required video. In order to make full use of the caching node, we aim at optimizing the cached videos such that the traffic served directly by the caching node is maximized.

(1) User Request: In 360° video delivery, the request from a user to a single video is serialized into chunks with different tile identities embedding the position and time. We use $x^t = (x_v^t, v \in \mathcal{V})$ to represent the request for video v at slot t, with all requests denoted by $\mathcal{X} = \{x \in \{0,1\}^V | \sum_{n=1}^{H} x_v = 1\}$. Hence, $x_v^t = 1$ indicates video v is requested at time slot t. We use $\{x_{v(1)}^t, x_{v(2)}^t, ..., x_{v(H)}^t\}$ to denote the list of requests for each tile of video v, where $x_{v(k)}^t$ indicates the request at time period t for segment k of video v.

(2) Caching Policy: The cache is managed with the caching policy represented by the vector $m_t^v \in [0, \mathfrak{m}]$, which denotes the fraction of cache capacity allocated to video v in slot t. Taking into account the cache size C, the set $\mathcal{M}$ of admissible caching configurations is:

$$\mathcal{M} = \{m \in [0, \mathfrak{m}]_V | \sum_{v=1}^{V} m_v \leq C\} \tag{1}$$

A caching policy σ is a rule that maps the past observations $x^1, ..., x^{t-1}$ and configurations $m^1, ..., m^{t-1}$ to the cache allocation $m^t(\sigma) \in \mathcal{M}$ at each slot $t = 1, 2, ..., T$.

(3) Reward: As the size of the cached video v is m_v, we use $m_v^{\beta_v}$ to denote the reward of accessing a cached version, where $\beta_v \in (0,1)$ is the traffic cost saved by replacing access to the source server with access to the cache node. Combine this reward with the hit ratio γ_v and we then have the reward for caching video v as $R_v = \gamma_v m_v^{\beta_v}$. Therefore, the caching problem can be expressed as follows:

$$\textbf{P1:} \quad \max_\sigma \sum_{t=1}^{T} \sum_{v=1}^{V} R_v(t)$$
$$\text{s.t.} \quad \sum_{i=1}^{V} m_v \leq C$$

where T is the time horizon and the maximization is over the admissible adversary distributions according to the possibly randomized x_t and m_t. By solving the above formula we can then get the desired caching policy σ.

Theorem 1. *Assuming $\beta_v = \beta$ (that is, all videos are retrieved from the same video server upon cache miss), $\forall v$, the optimal allocation which maximizes the performance gain $m^* = argmax_m R(\gamma, m)$ is given by*

$$m_v^* \propto \gamma_v^{\frac{1}{1-\beta}} \tag{2}$$

Proof. The result is an immediate consequence of Hölder's inequality [2]. Note that the reward function could be written as $\sum_{v=1}^{V} (\gamma_v^{\frac{1}{1-\beta}})^{1-\beta} m_v^{\beta_v}$ for a given time slot t. Therefore, we have

$$\sum_{v=1}^{V} (\gamma_v^{\frac{1}{1-\beta}})^{1-\beta} m_v^{\beta} \leq (\sum_{i=1}^{V} (\gamma_v^{\frac{1}{1-\beta}}))^{1-\beta} (\sum_{i=1}^{V} m_v)^{\beta}$$

Then equality occurs if and only if

$$\frac{m_1}{\gamma_1^{\frac{1}{1-\beta}}} = \frac{m_2}{\gamma_2^{\frac{1}{1-\beta}}} = ... = \frac{m_V}{\gamma_V^{\frac{1}{1-\beta}}}.$$

So it yields $m_v^* \propto \gamma_v^{\frac{1}{1-\beta}}$.

4 Cache Allocation Solution

Our scheme is composed of three phases. First, it makes a prediction on the likelihood of a video being requested over the next time horizon (Sect. 4.1). Next, it uses the result to make a cache allocation for the videos (Sect. 4.2). Finally, the allocation is refined at the tile level (Sect. 4.3).

4.1 Video Popularity Prediction

In this paper, we focus on caching 360° videos to provide low latency with low data redundancy in the network. The mechanism we develop here does not require changes in packet headers or modifications to any existing protocol in the network. The content placement approach we develop operates in each caching node to integrate different features observed from the past video requests. In other words, the video popularity estimation is dependent on the request features within different dimensions. Hence, our approach can be enriched with other new features when applied in practice.

The challenge arising is how to define the features with the changing access vectors (denoted by $\mathcal{X}$). In this paper, three features are identified for the prediction. Besides past accesses that can provide some positive influence on future popularity, the gap between two successive accesses for a video is also an indicator for future requests. Indeed, the past access features, namely "Frequency" and "Age", have been widely adopted by existing caching systems. Based on the principles mentioned, we adopt the self-exciting point process [10] to combine all the features:

$$\gamma_v(t) = \sum_{\tau=1}^{t} \sum_{t'=t+1}^{T} x_v^t \phi(t' - \tau) \tag{3}$$

where $\phi(t' - \tau)$ is a kernel function describing the influence of "Recency". It is a non-increasing function with regard to the variable $t' - \tau$, indicating the video demand would be decreased when it is getting "old" (large age). $\sum_{\tau=1}^{t} x^\tau$ represents the access frequency, which is easy to understand.

4.2 Cache Allocation for Videos

A simple approach for solving our problem is treating each video as an arm so that the existing Multi-arm Bandit algorithms [14] could be applied directly. To

Algorithm 1. Cache Allocation for Videos

1 Initialize the value $R_v = 0$ for all the videos;
2 Allocate $m_v^0 = C/V$ for all the videos;
3 **for** $t = 1$ *in* T **do**
4 Record the previous allocation m^{t-1};
5 Allocate the cache capacity by:

$$m_v^t = \begin{cases} \text{argmax}_v R(x_v^t, m_v^t) \text{ w.r.t. } 1 - \epsilon_t \\ \text{random}\{m_v^t | v \in \mathcal{V}\} \text{ w.r.t. } \epsilon_t \end{cases}$$

6 Observe the user request x_v^t;
7 Calculate the reward based on Eq. 3;
8 Get the instantaneous error based on Eq. 4;
9 **end**

allocate the cache efficiently, we provide an approach that could leverage the structure of the 360° video.

The procedure of our scheme is displayed in Algorithm 1. Initially, the algorithm allocates an equal amount C/V of caching space to each video. At each time slot, the algorithm computes the parameter γ_v according to Eq. 3. Based on Theorem 1, the algorithm allocates $m_i(\gamma_1, ..., \gamma_V)$ according to the results obtained. In other words, each video gets the cache resource with its estimated future reward and popularity. Note that the cache node only has limited information about the past access, and the request distribution $\mathcal{X}$ of each video is arbitrary. It is challenging to find an optimal policy by applying a pure-exploitation phase at the beginning.

In order to guarantee convergence, a probabilistic exploration-exploitation approach is utilized to determine cache allocation. The trade-off between exploration and exploitation is balanced by the instantaneous error $\epsilon \in (0, 1)$ at time slot t. The variation of ϵ follows such a principle: an increase of the reward means that the current learning sample is efficient for making caching decisions and less exploration is needed, so we decrease ϵ; otherwise, we increase ϵ so as to cache more undetected (say, new) videos. The equation is shown below:

$$\epsilon_t = \max(\epsilon_{min}, \epsilon_{t-1} - \kappa dR/dt) \tag{4}$$

where dR/dt indicates the changing rate of the reward, $\kappa > 0$ is a constant, and $\epsilon_{min} \geq 0$ is the lower bound of the exploration variable.

4.3 Cache Allocation for Tiles

Since the user's viewport is in the spatial domain when watching a 360° video, ideally, the cache node should only store the required tiles rather than the whole video to save storage resources. In practice, we could use the saliency of 360° videos [13] and user behavior information [16] to *detect ROIs* and the tiles to be cached. Here, we aim at optimizing the user QoE by selecting the specific tiles to be cached, represented by $H'(H' < H)$. To assess the QoE of 360° video streaming, not only the video quality should be considered, but other factors related to quality transition are also important. According to the incoming requests for video v, we could easily compute the accumulated video quality: $\sum_{i=1}^{H'} x_{v(i)} m_v(i)$. The excepted transition of the video quality is calculated by $\sum_{i,k=1}^{H'} |m_v(i) - m_v(k)|$, where i and k are two successively viewed tiles. With the goal of maximizing video quality and minimizing video quality transition, user QoE optimization can be formulated as:

$$\textbf{P2:} \quad \max \sum_{t=1}^{T} \mathbb{E}[\sum_{i=1}^{H'} x_{v(i)}^t m_v^t(i)] \quad \& \quad \min \sum_{t=1}^{T} \mathbb{E}[\sum_{i,k=1}^{H'} |m_v^t(i) - m_v^t(k)|]$$

$$\text{s.t.} \sum_{i=1} m_v^t(i) \leq m_i^t$$

According to the previous analysis, we need to make a balance between video quality and quality transition. To solve this problem, the following three strategies are offered:

(1) Uniform allocation (UA): The cache node saves every tile with the same quality. Obviously, this strategy has minimum quality transitions if the cache node could serve all the requests from the client.

(2) Frequency-based allocation (FA): The cache node adapts the size allocated to each tile according to the access frequency. By doing so, each tile is treated independently and saved with a certain resolution. This could lead to frequent quality changes but offer the best overall video quality.

(3) Static partition allocation (SP): This strategy makes a trade-off between video quality and quality transition of tiles. The key idea is to use a constant parameter to determine the number of video quality partitions. The frequencies of the tiles selected would also be divided into several parts to match the tile cache size with the tile frequency.

5 Performance Evaluation

We implement an HTTP server for 360° video streaming based on the DASH-enabled platform [7] and use NS-3 to evaluate the effectiveness and performance of our proposed edge caching scheme.

5.1 Experimental Settings

The simulation uses 700 videos in total. The tile distribution of each video is generated by a Markov-based tool [5] that creates accurate synthetic traces. Based upon the results in [3], each video is partitioned into 6×4 tiles for efficient encoding and bandwidth saving. In all, each video has 3,600 tiles with a fixed segmentation of 4 s. Additionally, the bitrate of each video segment on the video server is adaptable according to the network bandwidth. The workloads for the videos are generated by GlobeTraff [6].

For performance measures, three parameters of interest are: (i) cache capacity $\mathcal{C}$; (ii) content population $\mathcal{V}$; (iii) Zipf distribution parameter α. The default settings of these parameters are 20%, 400, and 0.8. The traffic cost reduction is recorded as the evaluation metric.

We evaluate our caching allocation scheme (referred to as $PLCS$) against well-known benchmarks by comprehensive experiments with *(1) random caching strategy (Random)*, which updates the cached videos randomly at each time slot, *(2) offline greedy caching strategy (OGCS)*, which uses an offline greedy algorithm for cache allocation, with the parameter ϵ set to 0.01 and remaining unchanged during the evaluation, *(3) frequency caching strategy (FCS)*, which predicts the future request popularity only with the frequency, *(4) age caching strategy (ACS)*, which predicts the future request popularity only with the video access age.

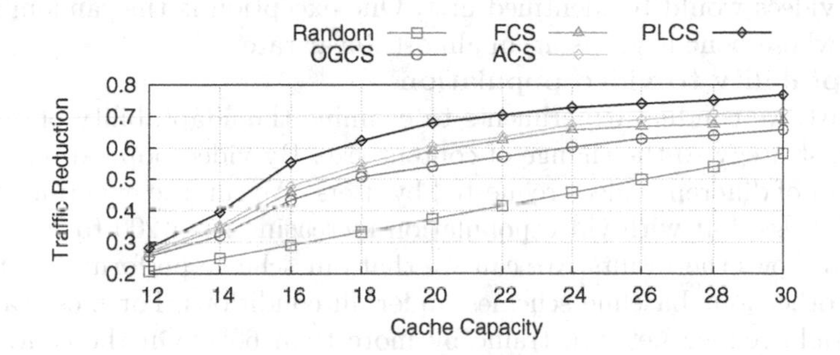

Fig. 2. Performance with various cache capacities

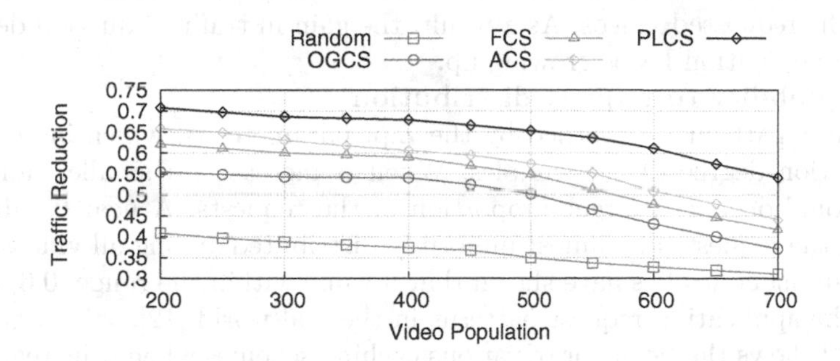

Fig. 3. Performance with various video population

Since the caching node could only obtain the requests of the cached videos, the strategies (3) and (4) are equivalent to least frequently used (LFU) and least recently used (LRU) strategy respectively. The kernel function of Eq. (3)

in the simulation is defined as $\phi(t-\tau) = e^{-(t-\tau)}$. As the distribution of the tile requests for a video is similar across users and tile-based cache schemes are computation-intensive, no comparison with them is done here.

5.2 Caching Performance

(1) Adaptability to cache capacity
The cache capacity of a node is denoted by the ratio of available cache space to the total size of videos in the network. A node with a larger cache capacity can cache more required contents. We evaluate the performance of our caching scheme using default settings, but with cache capacity increasing from 12% to 30% and display the results in Fig. 2.

With no doubt, the benefit of all five caching schemes improves monotonically because more content can be cached as the cache capacity increases. Our proposal reduces the traffic by 76.8% while the random caching strategy only contributes 58.2%. We can see that the marginal benefit increase is higher for most policies when the cache capacity is small. This is because the most popular tiles and videos would be identified first. One exception is the random caching strategy, whose benefit grows at an almost linear rate.

(2) Adaptability to video population
In this part, we conduct experiments to examine the adaptability of our cache allocation strategy to the change of content size. By video population we mean the number of different videos requested by users. We run the experiments using default settings, but with video population increasing from 200 to 700.

Figure 3 shows the results. We can see that our scheme performs much better than the other four baseline schemes under all conditions. For most cases, our scheme could reduce network traffic by more than 60%. On the contrast, the other approaches can at most reduce the traffic by 65%. It can also be seen from the figure that the benefit of caching drops faster when the number of videos grows beyond 400. This is because the available cache space is fixed and cannot hold all the requested videos. As a result, the gain in traffic reduction decreases when the population keeps growing up.

(3) Adaptability to request distribution
The request pattern is governed by the Zipf parameter α, which indicates the concentration degree of the samples. When α increases, a smaller number of videos would occupy a larger proportion of the requests. A near 0 value of α indicates the requests are almost uniformly distributed among all videos. Existing measurement studies have shown that a value within the range $[0.6, 1.1]$ can best fit the application request patterns in the real world [12].

Figure 4 shows the behavior of various caching schemes when α increases from 0.6 to 1.0, which implies that the requests are getting more and more concentrated. It is quite normal that the traffic reduction is increasing as α grows, for a small amount of content receives a relatively higher proportion of the requests. For this reason, the Zipf parameter has a greater impact on the caching performance when compared with the cases of Figs. 2 and 3. As for comparison with other caching strategies, our solution always achieves the best performance

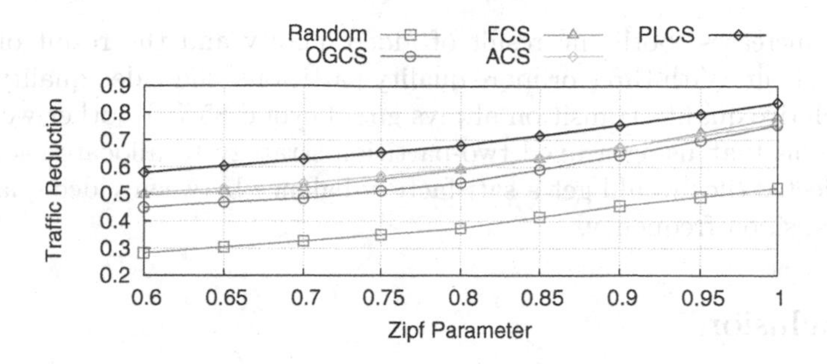

Fig. 4. Performances under different workloads

against all ranges of the Zipf parameter α. Specifically, our scheme achieves traffic reduction by 70% on average. As we can see from Fig. 4, *ACS* outperforms *OGCS* when α is larger than 0.95. Moreover, the gap between our scheme and *ACS* or *FCS* becomes narrower when α keeps growing, which implies that the feature of frequency becomes more and more critical so that it alone dominates the prediction of future access. Please note that the typical α value for web traffic is about 0.75.

5.3 QoE Results

In this part, we run the three tile allocation strategies (namely UA, FA and SP) mentioned in Sect. 4.3 to examine how the number of quality partitions affects the overall QoE. The high video resolution and low rate in quality transition indicate a good QoE. The frequency-based allocation strategy is set as the baseline. Since tiles of very low frequency have been filtered out by ROI detection, for static partition we only provide results covering two to four partitions (SP2 SP4). The performance of relative QoE is displayed in Fig. 5. As the number of quality

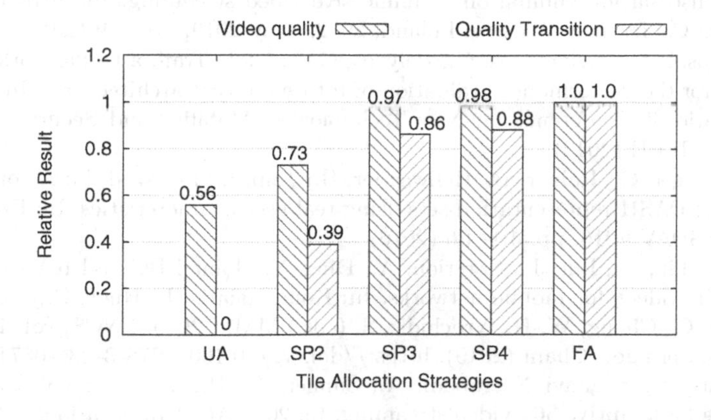

Fig. 5. The QoE with different tile allocation strategies

partitions increases, both the result of video quality and the result of quality transition climb. With three or more quality partitions, the video quality is high, but the relative quality transition always goes beyond 85%. In other words, this figure tells us that using a fixed two-partition strategy to allocate cache space for the selected tiles would get a satisfactory balance between video quality and quality transition frequency.

6 Conclusion

In this paper, we presented an edge caching scheme for 360° video streaming. It fulfills the work at two levels: at the video level, an online learning algorithm is devised to predict the most wanted videos, forming the basis for effective cache allocation at the tiles level. Simulations with real-world traces show that our proposed scheme outperforms other strategies for a wide range of cache capacity, content population, and popularity distribution.

References

1. Coileáin, D.Ó., Omahony, D.: Accounting and accountability in content distribution architectures: a survey. ACM Comput. Surv. (CSUR) **47**(4), 59 (2015)
2. Cvetkovski, Z.: Hölder's inequality, Minkowski's inequality and their variants. In: Cvetkovski, Z. (ed.) Inequalities, pp. 95–105. Springer, Heidelberg (2012). https://doi.org/10.1007/978-3-642-23792-8_9
3. Graf, M., Timmerer, C., Mueller, C.: Towards bandwidth efficient adaptive streaming of omnidirectional video over HTTP: design, implementation, and evaluation. In: ACM MMSys 2017, pp. 261–271. ACM (2017)
4. He, D., Westphal, C., Garcia-Luna-Aceves, J.: Network support for AR/VR and immersive video application: a survey. In: Proceedings of the 15th International Joint Conference on e-Business and Telecommunications, ICETE 2018, SIGMAP and WINSYS, Porto, Portugal, 26–28 July 2018, pp. 525–535 (2018)
5. He, D., Westphal, C., Jiang, J., Yang, G., Garcia-Luna-Aceves, J.: Towards tile based distribution simulation in immersive video streaming. In: 2019 IFIP Networking Conference, Warsaw, Poland, 20–22 May 2019, pp. 1–9 (2019)
6. Katsaros, K.V., Xylomenos, G., Polyzos, G.C.: GlobeTraff: a traffic workload generator for the performance evaluation of future internet architectures. In: 2012 5th International Conference on New Technologies, Mobility and Security (NTMS), pp. 1–5. IEEE (2012)
7. Kreuzberger, C., Rainer, B., Hellwagner, H., Toni, L., Frossard, P.: A comparative study of DASH representation sets using real user characteristics. In: Proceedings of NOSSDAV 2016, pp. 4:1–4:6 (2016)
8. Liu, K., Liu, Y., Liu, J., Argyriou, A., Ding, Y.: Joint EPC and RAN caching of tiled VR videos for mobile networks. In: Kompatsiaris, I., Huet, B., Mezaris, V., Gurrin, C., Cheng, W.-H., Vrochidis, S. (eds.) MMM 2019. LNCS, vol. 11295, pp. 92–105. Springer, Cham (2019). https://doi.org/10.1007/978-3-030-05710-7_8
9. Mahzari, A., Taghavi Nasrabadi, A., Samiei, A., Prakash, R.: FoV-aware edge caching for adaptive 360 video streaming. In: 2018 ACM International Conference on Multimedia, pp. 173–181. ACM (2018)

10. Mishra, S., Rizoiu, M.A., Xie, L.: Feature driven and point process approaches for popularity prediction. In: Proceedings of the 25th ACM International on Conference on Information and Knowledge Management, pp. 1069–1078. ACM (2016)
11. Papaioannou, G., Koutsopoulos, I.: Tile-based caching optimization for 360 videos. In: ACM MobiHoc 2019, pp. 171–180. ACM (2019)
12. Saino, L., Psaras, I., Pavlou, G.: Understanding sharded caching systems. In: IEEE INFOCOM 2016, pp. 1–9. IEEE (2016)
13. Sitzmann, V., et al.: Saliency in VR: how do people explore virtual environments? IEEE Trans. Visual Comput. Graph. **24**(4), 1633–1642 (2018)
14. Vermorel, J., Mohri, M.: Multi-armed bandit algorithms and empirical evaluation. In: Gama, J., Camacho, R., Brazdil, P.B., Jorge, A.M., Torgo, L. (eds.) ECML 2005. LNCS (LNAI), vol. 3720, pp. 437–448. Springer, Heidelberg (2005). https://doi.org/10.1007/11564096_42
15. Westphal, C.: Challenges in networking to support augmented reality and virtual reality. In: ICNC 2017, Silicon Valley, CA, USA, 26–29 January 2017 (2017)
16. Xie, L., Zhang, X., Guo, Z.: CLS: a cross-user learning based system for improving QoE in 360-degree video adaptive streaming. In: 2018 ACM International Conference on Multimedia, pp. 564–572. ACM (2018)
17. Zink, M., Sitaraman, R., Nahrstedt, K.: Scalable 360° video stream delivery: challenges, solutions, and opportunities. Proc. IEEE **107**(4), 639–650 (2019)

Inferring Emphasis for Real Voice Data: An Attentive Multimodal Neural Network Approach

Suping Zhou[1], Jia Jia[1(✉)], Long Zhang[2], Yanfeng Wang[3], Wei Chen[3], Fanbo Meng[3], Fei Yu[2], and Jialie Shen[4]

[1] Department of Computer Science and Technology, Tsinghua University, Beijing, China
1874504489@qq.com, jjia@mail.tsinghua.edu.cn

[2] The Spectrum Division of China Electronic Equipment System Engineering Company, Beijing, China
976890413@qq.com, yfei0210@163.com

[3] Sogou Corporation, Beijing, China
{wangyanfeng,chenweibj8871,mengfanbosi0935}@sogou-inc.com

[4] Queen's University Belfast, Belfast, UK
j.shen@qub.ac.uk

Abstract. To understand speakers' attitudes and intentions in real Voice Dialogue Applications (VDAs), effective emphasis inference from users' queries may play an important role. However, in VDAs, there are tremendous amount of uncertain speakers with a great diversity of users' dialects, expression preferences, which challenge the traditional emphasis detection methods. In this paper, to better infer emphasis for real voice data, we propose an attentive multimodal neural network. Specifically, first, beside the acoustic features, extensive textual features are applied in modelling. Then, considering the feature in-dependency, we model the multi-modal features utilizing a Multi-path convolutional neural network (MCNN). Furthermore, combining high-level multi-modal features, we train an emphasis classifier by attending on the textual features with an attention-based bidirectional long short-term memory network (ABLSTM), to comprehensively learn discriminative features from diverse users. Our experimental study based on a real-world dataset collected from Sogou Voice Assistant (https://yy.sogou.com/) show that our method outperforms (over 1.0–15.5% in terms of F1 measure) alternative baselines.

Keywords: Emphasis detection · Voice dialogue applications · Attention

Y. M. Ro et al. (Eds.): MMM 2020, LNCS 11962, pp. 52–62, 2020.
https://doi.org/10.1007/978-3-030-37734-2_5

1 Introduction

With the rapid development of technology, the Voice Dialogue Applications (Siri[1], Nina[2], Alexa[3], etc.) have gained popularity in recent years. Emphasis plays an important role in conveying speaker's attitudes and intentions in VDAs. Meanwhile, emphasis detection also attracts considerable attention in the field of speech-to-speech translation, emphatic speech synthesis, automatic prosodic event detection, human-computer interaction [2,18].

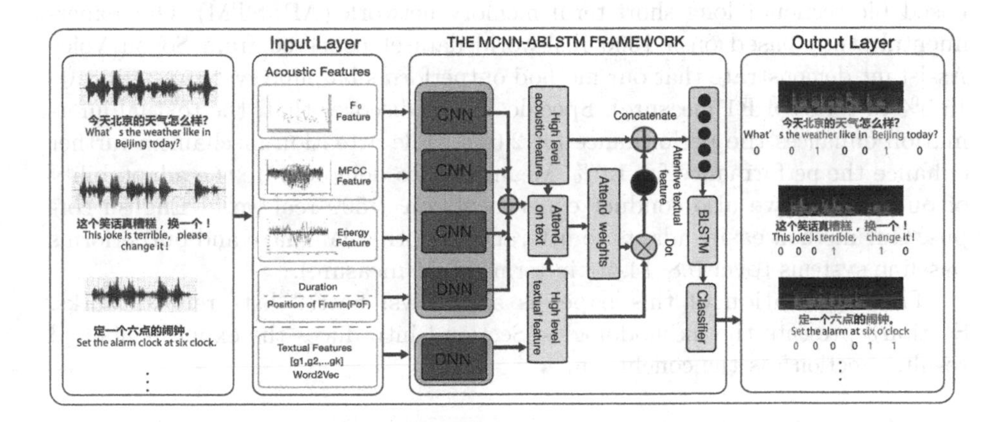

Fig. 1. The workflow of our framework.

Although there have amounts of attempts on emphasis detection, fulfilling the task is still a non-trivial issue. Traditionally, emphasis mainly detected utilizing acoustics information. Kennedy *et al.* [12] propose the use of pitch features as its only acoustic predictor. Ferrer *et al.* [9] uses filtered spectral and segmental features to detect emphasis for each syllable in a word. Although some work also try to utilize both acoustic and textual features [2] for emphatic words detection, they are mainly done on acted corpora data.

Therefore, there remains two challenges unsolved for emphasis detection in the specific situation of real-world VDAs: (1) Except speech information, the speech-to-text information is also provided by VDAs. Can we integrate multiple modalities (speech and text) to help enhance the performance on inferring emphasis? (2) Distinguished from the traditional speech emphasis recognition methods based on acted labeled data, the tremendous amount of uncertain speakers bring in a great diversity of users' dialects and expression preferences. Therefore, how to comprehensively learn user-invariant features by strengthening single modal features to increase the emphasis inferring effectiveness?

---

[1] https://www.apple.com/cn/ios/siri/.
[2] https://www.nuance.com/index.html.
[3] https://developer.amazon.com/alexa/.

To solve this problem, we introduce a novel approach to detect emphasis in VDAs with extra attention on textual information. Figure 1 illustrates detail architecture. In particular, first we employ a Multi-path convolutional neural network (MCNN) component which considers the independency nature of features [21,22], to extract high-level representation of acoustic features (fundamental frequency (F0), Mel Frequency Cepstral Coefficients (MFCCs), energy, duration and position of frame (POF) [21]) and high-level textual features individually. Then, combining both high-level acoustic features and textual features, we train an emphasis classifier by attending on the textual features with an attention-based bidirectional long short-term memory network (ABLSTM). Our experimental study based on a 1500 real-world dataset collected from Sogou Voice Assistant demonstrate that our method outperforms baseline systems (over 1.0–15.5% in terms of F1 measure). Specifically, we discover that, the textual information enhances the performance for 2.6%, while attention mechanism further enhance the performance for 1.0%. Meanwhile, to demonstrate the adaptability of our method, we also conduct experiments on a 500 real-world English corpus. Our method easily adapts to utterances of other language and outperforms baseline systems (over 0.8–14.4% in terms of F1 measure).

The organization of this paper is as follows: Sect. 2 lists related works. Section 3 presents the methodologies. Section 4 introduces the experiments and results. Section 5 is the conclusion.

2 Related Work

Emphasis Detection Methods. Previous researches on emphasis detection have focused on the features and models perspectives: Ladd *et al.* [15] utilize fundamental frequency to analysis 'normal' and 'emphatic' accent peaks. Heldner *et al.* [11] and Ferrer *et al.* [9] uses spectral features to detect emphasis. In [2], fundamental frequencies, duration, spectral features, lexical features, and identity features are combined together to get a better performance in emphatic words detection. Meanwhile, some previous works have been done on modelling methods. Cernak *et al.* [3] used a probabilistic amplitude demodulation (PAD) method to predict word prominence in speech. Do *et al.* [6] used linear regression HSMMs method (LR-HSMMs) for preserving word-level emphasis. Ning *et al.* [18] propose a multilingual BLSTM model for prosodic event detection. However, these researches mainly focus on inferring emphasis from acted corpora, few have been done to address the problem in real-world VDAs.

Multi-media Modeling. Recently, methods in Multi-media Modeling have shown significant performance improvements. Zhou *et al.* [22] propose a Multi-path Generative Neural Network which consider both acoustic and textual features. Zhang *et al.* [21] propose a MCNN model for emphasis detection. Meanwhile, attention mechanism [1] is gaining its popularity. It have been proved to be effective in learning more attentive features for many areas like sentiment analysis [5]. Therefore, we suppose that these methods may also be helpful for multi-modal emphasis detection in VDAs.

3 Methodology

In this paper, to infer users' emphasis in VDAs. We propose a novel scheme for emphasis detection with extra attention on textual information. Specifically, (1) considering the in-dependency nature in features, we first model the acoustic and textual features utilizing a Multi-path convolutional neural network (MCNN) individually. (2) to comprehensively learn discriminative features from diverse users in VDAs, combining high-level multi-modal features, we train an emphasis classifier by attending on the textual features with an attention-based bidirectional long short-term memory network (ABLSTM).

3.1 Multi-path Convolutional Neural Network Component

As discussed above, traditionally, to model high-level features for emphasis analysis, SVM, CRF [19], HSMMs [7], DNNs, CNNs [14] have been adopted. However, since the different feature has its own characteristics, the traditional methods which utilize the low-level features like F0, MFCCs, energy, et al. as input together may not fully consider the independency nature of different features. These may limit the performance in emphasis detection while combining multi-features [21]. In our solution, considering both textual feature and six kinds of acoustic feature, we employ a multi-path convolutional neural network (MCNN) component to extract high-level representation from multi-modal features respectively to enhance the performance of our proposed approach.

Specifically, for F0, MFCCs and energy, we perform convolution on modelling. We define $\mathbb{F}$, $\mathbb{E}$, $\mathbb{M}$ as the high-level features representation for F0, energy, MFCCs. Let $\boldsymbol{s} \in \mathbb{R}^{L\times d}$ represents a L-frame sentence. For each frame, it has d-dimensional features. The convolution involves a filter $\boldsymbol{m} \in \mathbb{R}^{k\times k}$, which is applied to a window $\boldsymbol{w} \in \mathbb{R}^{k\times k}$ to produce a new feature $\boldsymbol{y} \in \mathbb{R}^{L\times d}$. Each feature $\boldsymbol{y}_i$ is produced as [13]:

$$\boldsymbol{y}_i = f(\boldsymbol{w} \cdot \boldsymbol{m} + b) \tag{1}$$

b respectively denotes bias term and f is nonlinear transformation function. This filter is applied to each possible window in the sentence $\boldsymbol{s}$ to produce a feature map:

$$\boldsymbol{y} = [\boldsymbol{y}_1; \boldsymbol{y}_2; ...; \boldsymbol{y}_n] \tag{2}$$

For duration, POE feature and textual features, we choose the DNNs to model their high-level representation which preforms well for these three features and can make our model more efficient. We define them as $\mathbb{D}$, $\mathbb{P}$ and $\mathbb{W}$. We train all these feature extractors together. Then, all the acoustic features are merged together to generate $\mathbb{A}$ as follows:

$$\mathbb{A} = concat[\mathbb{F}, \mathbb{E}, \mathbb{M}, \mathbb{D}, \mathbb{P}] \tag{3}$$

The output hiddens $\mathbb{A}$ and $\mathbb{W}$ for high-level acoustic and textual features are then fed to the ABLSTM component for further computation directly.

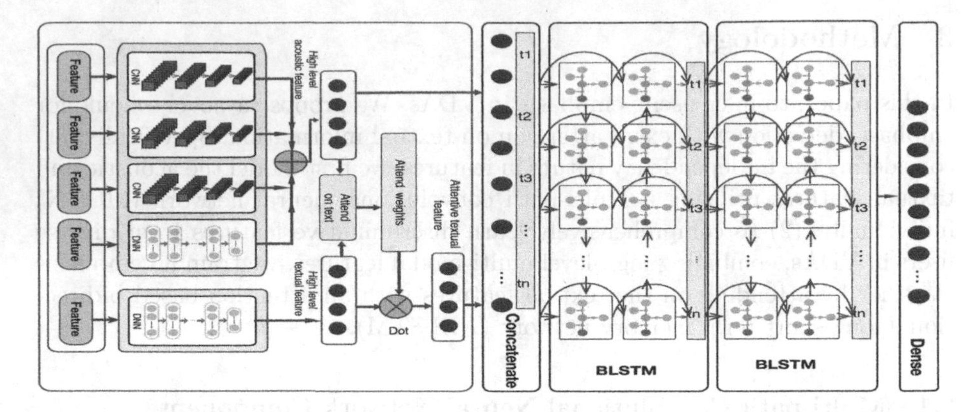

Fig. 2. The multi-path convolutional and attention-based bidirectional long short-term memory neural network (MCNN-ABLSTM)

3.2 Attention-Based BLSTM

Long short-term memory (LSTM) units have been extensively used to learn long span temporal information. In our proposed framework, we apply recurrent neural network architecture with bi-directional long short-term memory (BLSTM) to achieve effective modeling.

Sepecifically, we apply Bidirectional RNN [20] to make full use of speech sequences in the forward and backward directions. Given an input sequence $\boldsymbol{x} = (\boldsymbol{x}_1, \ldots, \boldsymbol{x}_T)$, T is the length. $\overrightarrow{h}$ is forward hidden layer, and $\overleftarrow{h}$ is backward hidden layer. The iterative process is as follows [8]:

$$\overrightarrow{h}_t = \mathcal{H}(\boldsymbol{W}_{x\overrightarrow{h}} x_t + \boldsymbol{W}_{\overrightarrow{h}\overrightarrow{h}} \overrightarrow{h}_{t+1} + b_{\overrightarrow{h}}) \tag{4}$$

$$\overleftarrow{h}_t = \mathcal{H}(\boldsymbol{W}_{x\overleftarrow{h}} x_t + \boldsymbol{W}_{\overleftarrow{h}\overleftarrow{h}} \overleftarrow{h}_{t-1} + b_{\overleftarrow{h}}) \tag{5}$$

$$y_t = \boldsymbol{W}_{\overrightarrow{h}y} \overrightarrow{h}_t + \boldsymbol{W}_{\overleftarrow{h}y} \overleftarrow{h}_t + b_y \tag{6}$$

$\boldsymbol{y}$ is the outputs sequence and $\boldsymbol{W}$ is the weight matrix for different layers. b_h is the bias vector for hidden state vector and b_y is the bias vector for output vector. $\mathcal{H}$ is an activation function. For $\mathcal{H}$ in conventional RNN models, it has the limitations of storing past and future information in speech. The Bidirectional long short-term memory (BLSTM) with a memory cell built inside can overcome it. The $\mathcal{H}$ of BLSTM is as follows [10]:

$$i_t = \sigma(\boldsymbol{W}_{xi} x_t + \boldsymbol{W}_{hi} h_{t-1_+} \boldsymbol{W}_{ci} c_{t-1} + b_i) \tag{7}$$

$$f_t = \sigma(\boldsymbol{W}_{xf} x_t + \boldsymbol{W}_{hf} x_{t-1_+} \boldsymbol{W}_{cf} c_{t-1} + b_f) \tag{8}$$

$$c_t = f_t c_{t-1} + i_t tanh(\boldsymbol{W}_{xc} x_t + \boldsymbol{W}_{hc} h_{t-1} + b_c) \tag{9}$$

$$o_t = \sigma(\boldsymbol{W}_{x0} x_t + \boldsymbol{W}_{ho} h_{t-1_+} \boldsymbol{W}_{co} c_t + b_o) \tag{10}$$

$$h_t = o_t tanh(c_t) \tag{11}$$

In order to take advantage of the textual information, we adopt the attention mechanism mentioned in [5] and modify the input layer into the BLSTM units. Let $\boldsymbol{a}_t$ represents the current high-level acoustic feature input and $\boldsymbol{w}_t$ be the current high-level textual feature input learned from MCNN. We first obtain the attentive textual feature $\boldsymbol{v}_t$ as an weighted average of the high-level textual feature $\boldsymbol{w}_t$ based on the self-selected attention mechanism. Let $\boldsymbol{w}_t$, $t \in (1, T)$ represent the t-th frame feature of textual feature $\boldsymbol{w}$ and $f_{att}(\cdot, \boldsymbol{a}_t)$ denote the attention function conditioned on the current high-level acoustic feature $\boldsymbol{a}_t$. The attention weight $\boldsymbol{\alpha}_i$ and attentive textual feature $\boldsymbol{v}_t$ is formulated as follows:

$$u_t = f_{att}(\boldsymbol{w}_t, \boldsymbol{a}_t) \tag{12}$$

$$\alpha_t = \frac{exp(u_t)}{\sum_{t=1}^{T} exp(u_t)} \tag{13}$$

$$\boldsymbol{v}_t = \alpha_t \cdot \boldsymbol{w}_t \tag{14}$$

We choose a fully-connected layer with ELU activation as the attention function, and the attention vector $\boldsymbol{v}_t$ is concatenated with the high-level acoustic feature $\boldsymbol{a}_t$ as the new input of the BLSTM. Thus the input vector $\boldsymbol{x}_t$ becomes $[\boldsymbol{a}_t, \boldsymbol{v}_t]$. The output of the final BLSTM unit is then fed into a fully-connected layer with softmax activation to predict emphasis results. Categorical cross-entropy loss is used as the objection function.

The motivation of this acoustic-guide Attention-based BLSTM (ABLSTM) as shown in Fig. 2 with the textual feature is that we use the acoustic feature to guide the attention weights of the textual feature in order to enforce the model to self-select which frame feature it should attend on. With this mechanism, it can help comprehensively learn discriminative features from diverse users in order to improve the emphasis detection accuracy in VDAs.

4 Experiments

4.1 Corpus and Annotation

Mandarin Corpus. We establish a real-world corpus of voice data from Sogou Voice Assistant containing 1500 Mandarin utterances recorded by 176 users. Every utterance is assigned with its corresponding speech-to-text information provided by Sogou Corporation.

English Corpus. We establish a corpus of voice data containing 500 English utterances. Every utterance is assigned with its corresponding speech-to-text information provided by Sogou Corporation.

Data Annotation. The corpus is labeled by three well-trained annotators. The annotators are asked to label the emphasis by listening to the utterances and reading corresponding words simultaneously. The words are then classified into labels of 0 and 1 indicating normal and emphasized words. Labels are regarded as emphasis only when three inter-annotator reach an agreement. If they are controversial or ambiguous about labels, utterance will be labeled as ambiguous or discarded. Finally, 1500 Mandarin utterances and 500 English utterances are labeled emphasis. Each of the utterances contains one or more emphatic words. These emphatic words are located at different positions in sentences. The emphasis distributions of these utterances are: emphasis: 27.03%, normal: 72.97%. An example of the label sentences is shown in Fig. 3.

Mandarin : 今天北京的天气怎么样？
Mandarin Labels : 0 0 1 1 0 1 1 0 0 0
English : What's the weather like in Beijing today?
English Labels : 0 0 1 0 0 1 0

Fig. 3. An example of emphasis labels in Mandarin and English from the VDAs.

4.2 Features

Acoustic Feature. Previous works indicate that emphasis usually has higher F0, longer duration and higher energy [4]. Therefore, we use 19-dimensional acoustic features, including Log F0 (lf0) (1), energy (1), duration (1), Position of Frame (PoF) (4) and Mel Frequency Cepstral Coefficients (MFCCs) (12) prosodic features. The used PoF features include the position of the syllables in the sentence, the position of the frame in syllable and the position of the frame in sentence [21]. The frame length of voice segments is 25 ms and frame shift is 5 ms. Features are normalized to the mean 0 and the variance 1.

Textual Feature. For textual information in Mandarin Corpus, we first use Thulac Tool [17] which is an efficient Chinese word segmentation to get words of an utterance. Then we utilize word2vec to learn word embeddings. Specifically, we use the whole 31.2 million chinese word corpora collected from the 7.5 million utterance from SVAD13 [22] as the training corpora for word2vec. As for the textual information for English databases, we adopt the publicly available 300-dimensional word2vec vectors, which are trained on 100 billion words from Google News to represent word vector.

4.3 Experimental Setup

Comparison Methods. We compared the performance of emphasis detection with some well-known LSTM baseline models for comparison, bi-directional long short-term memory (BLSTM) [18], convolutional bidirectional long short-term memory (CNN-BLSTM) [16], Multi-path convolutional bi-directional long short-term memory neural networks (MCNN-BLSTM) [21]. Our proposed model is

Table 1. The performance on Mandarin corpus and English corpus with different comparison methods.

Method	Mandarin corpus			English corpus		
	Precision	Recall	F1-measure	Precision	Recall	F1-measure
BLSTM	0.396	0.453	0.422	0.387	0.639	0.477
CNN-BLSTM	0.493	0.541	0.516	0.524	0.560	0.538
MCNN-BLSTM	**0.542**	0.595	0.567	**0.632**	0.595	0.613
MCNN-ABLSTM	0.523	**0.643**	**0.577**	0.627	**0.616**	**0.621**

Attention-base Multi-path convolutional bi-directional long short-term memory neural networks (MCNN-ABLSTM).

Metrics. In all the experiments, we evaluate the performance in terms of F1-measure, Precision, Recall. The datasets are split by train:val:test = 8:1:1.

4.4 Experimental Results

4.4.1 Performance Comparision

To evaluate the effectiveness of our proposed MCNN-ABLSTM, we compare the performance of emphasis detection with some baseline methods: BLSTM, CNN-BLSTM, MCNN-BLSTM for both Mandarin corpus and English corpus. Table 1 shows the results of emphasis detection with acoustic information and textual information.

For the Mandarin corpus from Sogou Voice Assistant, in terms of F1-measure, the proposed MCNN-ABLSTM outperforms all the baseline methods: +15.5% compared with BLSTM, +6.1% compared with CNN-LSTM, and +1.0% compared with MCNN-BLSTM. Specifically, (1) to demonstrate the Multi-path solution of our proposed method, the MCNN-BLSTM also outperforms the BLSTM (+14.5%) and CNN-BLSTM (+5.1%). This proves the effectiveness of the proposed MCNN component which considers the in-dependency nature of different features, in modeling the multi-modal high-level features. (2) To demonstrate the ABLSTM part of our proposed method, comparing MCNN-BLSTM and MCNN-ABLSTM, although MCNN-BLSTM has a better performance in terms of precision, MCNN-ABLSTM has a more balanced overall performance, +4.8% in terms of recall, +1.0% in terms of F1-measure. Therefore, our proposed MCNN-ABLSTM with acoustic-guide attention on textual feature is a more effective way for emphasis detection in VDAs.

To demonstrate the comparability and the adaptability of our method, we also report experimental results on a real-world English corpus from Sogou Corporation. As shown in Table 1, the F1-measure reaches 0.621, showing +14.4% improvement compared with BLSTM, +8.3% improvement compared with CNN-BLSTM, +0.9% improvement compared with MCNN-BLSTM, indicating that our method still shows advantages on utterances of other language.

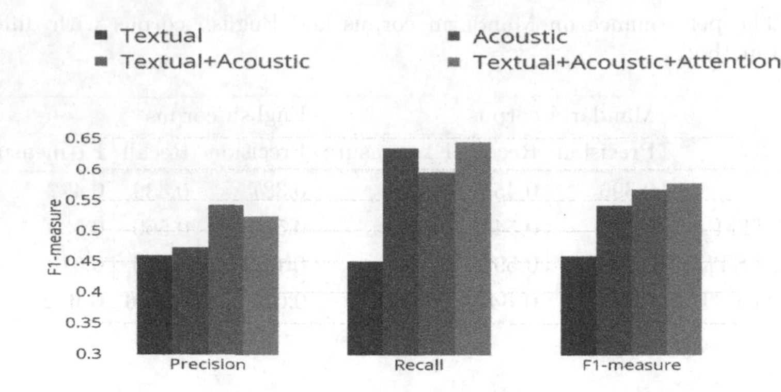

Fig. 4. Feature contribution analysis.

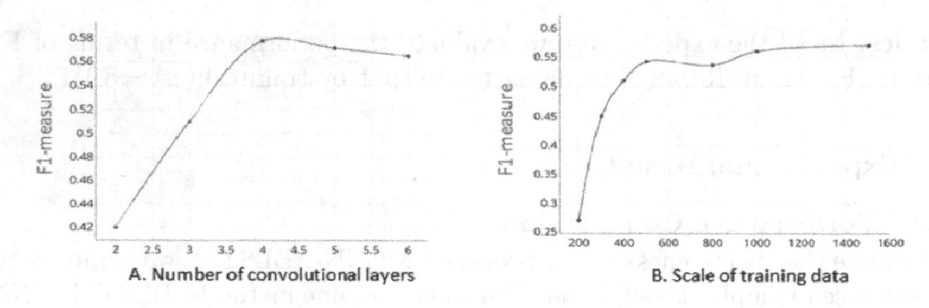

Fig. 5. Parameters analysis.

4.4.2 Feature Contribution Analysis

Then we discuss the contributions of acoustic and textual features. The F1-measure, precision, recall for emphasis detection results for Mandarin Corpus are shown in Fig. 4. Specifically, for 'Textual Only', 'Acoustic Only', 'Textual+Acoustic', we utilize MCNN-BLSTM model, and for 'Textual+Acoustic+Attention', we utilize MCNN-ABLSTM model. As in Fig. 4, the performance of 'Acoustic Only' is better than 'Textual Only', which indicates that the acoustic information can contribute more to the emphasis detection in the real world VDAs. Moreover, 'Textual+Acoustic' which contains both textual information and acoustic information performs better than 'Acoustic Only' +2.6% in terms of F1-measure. The results validate the necessity of taking the textual information into consideration. Moreover, 'Textual+Acoustic+Attention' which consider both acoustic feature and textual feature with our proposed MCNN-ABLSTM has the best performance. Compared with 'T+A', 'T+A+attention' +1.0% in terms of F1-measure and +4.8% in terms of recall. These convince that our proposed attention mechanism can be more effective in modeling multi-modal features.

4.4.3 Parameter Sensitivity Analysis

We show how changes of parameters in MCNN-ABLSTM affect the performance of emphasis detection in Mandarin Corpus.

Multi-path Convolutional Layers Analysis. We first test the parameter sensitivity about Multi-path Convolutional Layers. As shown in Fig. 5(a), the performance reached the highest performance when the layer of Multi-path Convolutional is 4. With the increase of the number of the layers, the performance decreased for over-fitting. So we choose the four convolutional layers as the experimental setup.

Training Data Scalability Analysis. We further test the parameter sensitivity about training data size of Mandarin Corpus. As shown in Fig. 5(b), with the increase of the amount of training data, F1-score performance with rapid ascension, but when the size of training data over 1500, the performance reaches convergence. Considering time efficiency, we choose 1500 as our experiment dataset.

5 Conclusions

In this paper, we propose a novel scheme for emphasis detection with extra attention on textual information. Specifically, we first model the acoustic features and textual features utilizing a MCNN component individually. Then combining high-level multi-modal features, we train an attention-based emphasis classifier ABLSTM, to comprehensively learn discriminative features from diverse users. Experiments based on real-world Mandarin and English corpus show the effectiveness of our methods. Based on our work, VDAs can better understand speakers' attitudes and intentions which contributes to more humanized intelligent service.

Acknowledgements. This work is supported by Tiangong Institute for Intelligent Computing, Tsinghua University and the state key program of the National Natural Science Foundation of China (NSFC) (No. 61831022).

References

1. Bahdanau, D., Cho, K., Bengio, Y.: Neural machine translation by jointly learning to align and translate. arXiv preprint arXiv:1409.0473 (2014)
2. Brenier, J.M., Cer, D.M., Jurafsky, D.: The detection of emphatic words using acoustic and lexical features. In: Ninth European Conference on Speech Communication and Technology (2005)
3. Cernak, M., Honnet, P.E.: An empirical model of emphatic word detection. In: Interspeech, pp. 573–577 (2015)
4. Chen, J.Y., Lan, W.: Automatic lexical stress detection for Chinese learners' of English. In: International Symposium on Chinese Spoken Language Processing (2011)
5. Chen, Y., Yuan, J., You, Q., Luo, J.: Twitter sentiment analysis via bi-sense emoji embedding and attention-based LSTM. arXiv preprint arXiv:1807.07961 (2018)

6. Do, Q.T., Takamichi, S., Sakti, S., Neubig, G., Toda, T., Nakamura, S.: Preserving word-level emphasis in speech-to-speech translation using linear regression HSMMs. In: Sixteenth Annual Conference of the International Speech Communication Association (2015)
7. Do, Q.T., Toda, T., Neubig, G., Sakti, S., Nakamura, S.: Preserving word-level emphasis in speech-to-speech translation. IEEE/ACM Trans. Audio Speech Lang. Process. **25**(3), 544–556 (2017)
8. Fan, Y., Qian, Y., Xie, F.L., Soong, F.K.: TTS synthesis with bidirectional LSTM based recurrent neural networks. In: Fifteenth Annual Conference of the International Speech Communication Association (2014)
9. Ferrer, L., Bratt, H., Richey, C., Franco, H., Abrash, V., Precoda, K.: Lexical stress classification for language learning using spectral and segmental features. In: IEEE International Conference on Acoustics, Speech and Signal Processing, pp. 7704–7708 (2014)
10. Gers, F.A., Schraudolph, N.N., Schmidhuber, J.: Learning precise timing with LSTM recurrent networks. J. Mach. Learn. Res. **3**(Aug), 115–143 (2002)
11. Heldner, M.: Spectral emphasis as an additional source of information in accent detection. In: ISCA Tutorial and Research Workshop (ITRW) on Prosody in Speech Recognition and Understanding (2001)
12. Kennedy, L.S., Ellis, D.P.W.: Pitch-based emphasis detection for characterization of meeting recordings. In: 2003 IEEE Workshop on Automatic Speech Recognition and Understanding, ASRU 2003, pp. 243–248 (2003)
13. Kim, Y.: Convolutional neural networks for sentence classification. arXiv preprint arXiv:1408.5882 (2014)
14. Krizhevsky, A., Sutskever, I., Hinton, G.E.: Imagenet classification with deep convolutional neural networks. In: Advances in Neural Information Processing Systems, pp. 1097–1105 (2012)
15. Ladd, D.R., Morton, R.: The perception of intonational emphasis: continuous or categorical? J. Phon. **25**(3), 313–342 (1997)
16. Li, L., Wu, Z., Xu, M., Meng, H.M., Cai, L.: Combining CNN and BLSTM to extract textual and acoustic features for recognizing stances in mandarin ideological debate competition. In: Interspeech, pp. 1392–1396 (2016)
17. Li, Z., Sun, M.: Punctuation as implicit annotations for Chinese word segmentation. Comput. Linguist. **35**(4), 505–512 (2009)
18. Ning, Y., et al.: Learning cross-lingual knowledge with multilingual BLSTM for emphasis detection with limited training data. In: ICASSP 2017–2017 IEEE International Conference on Acoustics, Speech and Signal Processing, pp. 5615–5619 (2017)
19. Schnall, A., Heckmann, M.: Integrating sequence information in the audio-visual detection of word prominence in a human-machine interaction scenario. In: Fifteenth Annual Conference of the International Speech Communication Association (2014)
20. Schuster, M., Paliwal, K.K.: Bidirectional recurrent neural networks. IEEE Trans. Sig. Process. **45**(11), 2673–2681 (1997)
21. Zhang, L., et al.: Emphasis detection for voice dialogue applications using multi-channel convolutional bidirectional long short-term memory network. In: 2018 11th International Symposium on Chinese Spoken Language Processing (ISCSLP), pp. 210–214. IEEE (2018)
22. Zhou, S., Jia, J., Wang, Q., Dong, Y., Yin, Y., Lei, K.: Inferring emotion from conversational voice data: a semi-supervised multi-path generative neural network approach. In: Thirty-Second AAAI Conference on Artificial Intelligence (2018)

PRIME: Block-Wise Missingness Handling for Multi-modalities in Intelligent Tutoring Systems

Xi Yang[1(✉)], Yeo-Jin Kim[1], Michelle Taub[2], Roger Azevedo[2], and Min Chi[1(✉)]

[1] North Carolina State University, Raleigh, NC 27606, USA
{yxi2,ykim32,mchi}@ncsu.edu
[2] University of Central Florida, Orlando, FL 32816, USA
{michelle.taub,roger.azevedo}@ucf.edu

Abstract. Block-wise missingness in multimodal data poses a challenging barrier for the analysis over it, which is quite common in practical scenarios such as the multimedia intelligent tutoring systems (ITSs). In this work, we collected data from 194 undergraduates via a biology ITS which involves three modalities: student-system logfiles, facial expressions, and eye tracking. However, only 32 out of the 194 students had all three modalities and 83% of them were missing the facial expression data, eye tracking data, or both. To handle such a block-wise missing problem, we propose a *Progressively Refined Imputation for Multi-modalities by auto Encoder (PRIME)*, which trains the model based on single, pairwise, and entire modalities for imputation in a progressive manner, and therefore enables us to maximally utilize all the available data. We have evaluated PRIME against single-modality log-only (without missingness handling) and five state-of-the-art missing data handling methods on one important yet challenging student modeling task: to predict students' learning gains. Our results show that using multimodal data as a result of missing data handling yields better prediction performance than using logfiles only, and PRIME outperforms other baseline methods for both learning gain prediction and data reconstruction tasks.

Keywords: Multimodal · Block-wise missing · Learning gain prediction

1 Introduction

Intelligent tutoring systems (ITSs) play an important role in aiding students to achieve better learning outcomes. Recent studies show that learning with an ITS produces measurable larger learning gains compared to learning without it [19]. One crucial component of an effective ITS is the student modeling, which infers students' competencies and learning outcomes based on the data collected during the interaction [20]. The student modeling is of great importance and enables the tutor to adapt its pedagogical interventions by addressing

Y. M. Ro et al. (Eds.): MMM 2020, LNCS 11962, pp. 63–75, 2020.
https://doi.org/10.1007/978-3-030-37734-2_6

students' learning needs and providing tailored scaffolding and feedback accordingly. However, the student modeling is known to be challenging [6], because there is often a large gap between students' behaviors observed by an ITS and the students' underlying learning status that ITS needs to model. In classrooms, teachers can leverage multiple sources of information to understand students' learning, e.g., facial expressions, eye contact, etc. [20]. Most student modeling in ITSs are primarily based on the student-system interactions recorded in logfiles (*Log-only*). Given the recent development of multimedia ITSs, different sources of information are increasingly collected and incorporated during the student modeling [7,8,11,23].

In this work, we collected multimodal data from 194 undergraduates via a hypermedia biology ITS. In addition to the logfile, we had two additional modalities: facial expression (*Face*) and eye tracking (*Eye*). Unlike most previous works that took post-test scores as students' learning outcomes for modeling [12], we aimed to utilize the multimodal data to predict the students' learning gain. Both post-test scores and learning gain are important learning outcomes. Post-test scores are directly obtained at the end of the learning session; Learning gain, on the other hand, measures how much a student has learned from pre-test to post-test: the higher a student's learning gain, the more the student benefits from the ITS. To find whether a tutor is indeed effective, the latter can be more important and also more challenging because students who perform well on the pre-test often perform well on the post-test, but may or may not benefit from the tutor. For example, in our data we found a significant positive correlation between students' pre- and post-test scores ($r = 0.65$, $p \approx 0 \ll 0.0001$).

When applying the *Log-only* data to predict students' learning gain for measuring if they benefitted from the ITS, we got the accuracy of 61.9%, just above 58.2% by the simple majority voting classifier. One possible reason for this result is that the *Log-only* conveys limited observations on students' performance [14]. Therefore, we expect to take advantage of multimodal data to fully capture the students' states [3]. Despite the great promise of multi-modalities, student modeling using multimodal data often faces one practical challenge: *the block-wise missingness*, as some modalities are inaccessible probably because the equipment is not configured or offline. In our data, only 32 out of 194 students had all three modalities: Log, Face, and Eye; and for the remaining 162 students, either one of Face or Eye, or both of them were missing. That is, more than 83% of our data was block-wise missing. When using the 32 students with all three modalities for learning gain prediction, the multimodal data shows better accuracy compared to any single modality. Therefore, it is highly desired to impute the data of the missing modalities for the rest of the 162 students, not only to *maximally* utilize all the available data, but also to improve the prediction performance.

In this work, we proposed a general neural network-based imputation framework: ***P**rogressively **R**efined **I**mputation for **M**ulti-modalities by auto-**E**ncoder (PRIME)* to impute the block-wise missing data. Specifically, we first used autoencoder to capture the latent pattern for each *single* modality. Then we trained the mappings between the captured latent patterns of any *pairwise* modalities, which aims at inferring the latent pattern of the missing modality based on available modalities. Meanwhile, we refined the decoder from the latent patterns to the original data, because the inferred latent patterns from other modalities may have slightly different distributions. After that, we used the data available from *entire* modalities to further refine the pairwise mappings across different modalities and also the decoders from the latent patterns to the original data. Finally, the refined pairwise mappings and decoders could be utilized to impute the block-wise missing data. The imputed multimodal data was then concatenated for feature selection and fed into a classifier for learning gain prediction.

2 Related Work

Multimodal Student Modeling: With multi-channel sensors, an increasing number of ITSs collect multimodal data, e.g., facial expressions, eye tracking, etc., along with the traditional student-system interaction logfiles [8,11,15,23]. The benefit of such multimodal data is twofold: *on one hand*, multi-modalities contain overlapping information, such as the emotional information captured from logfiles based on student's self-reported questionnaires and that extracted from facial expression. Such overlapping is desired because it can filter the noise and uncertainty among different modalities. *On the other hand*, each modality can convey distinct information. For example, eye tracking can capture informative attention patterns via eye gaze, fixations, and saccade movements; and logfiles contain specific information such as a tutor's actions, students' self-regulated learning strategies, etc. Therefore, a growing number of multimodal data have been collected for better understanding and evaluating the student learning process. Some previous work has emphasized the effectiveness of multimodal data in student modeling. Bosch employed logfiles and facial data for students' affect detection [7]. They demonstrated that complemented by logfile, facial data could achieve better prediction, with the AUC improved from 57.4% to 67.1%. Kapoor *et al.* employed facial and postural data to detect learning interest [11]. In their work, the multimodal Gaussian Process approach had an accuracy of 86.6% and significantly outperformed the strongest individual modality with an accuracy of 81.9%. Grafsgaard *et al.* employed multi-modalities including facial expression, posture, and gesture to predict engagement and frustration during the learning session [8]. They showed the combined set of trimodal features was the most predictive of learning comparing to unimodal and bimodal data. Zhong *et al.* proposed a temporal framework to model the relationship between emotional and physiological states [23]. Their experiments showed that the fusion of facial expressions and physiological responses can capture complementary information to improve recognition performance. Note that previous work using multimodalities were generally based on data without missingness [8,11,23], while in this work, more than 83% of data were block-wise missing.

Handling Missing Data: One way to handle missingness is data imputation. The commonly applied imputation approaches include MEAN/median-filling, k-nearest neighbor (KNN) [9], etc. Some *latent pattern*-based approaches explored the mapping from features to interpretative latent patterns for handling the missingness, e.g., the SVD matrix decomposition based imputation [9]. However, the aforementioned methods generally assumed the data to be missing completely at random, i.e., the missing entries were randomly scattered among the data. To adapt for the missing not at random case, Beaulieu-Jones *et al.* applied a denoising autoencoder [5] for imputation. Specifically to solve the block-wise missing problem in multimodal data, Tran *et al.* proposed a cascaded residual autoencoder [17], which modeled the residual between current prediction and original multimodal input. Shang *et al.* proposed a modality imputation via generative adversarial network [13] that worked for imputing the block-wise missing data when there are *two* modalities. Jaques *et al.* proposed a multimodal autoencoder (MMAE) [10] to extract latent patterns from all modalities simultaneously with a single autoencoder and trained together with a classifier in order to fully leverage either unlabeled data or the data with block-wise missingness. Another way to handle missing data is to circumvent the missingness. In [7], the available data in each individual modality was modeled separately and then late fusion was applied to merge the outputs by training an additional classifier. Yuan *et al.* proposed an incomplete multi-source feature learning algorithm with a *grouping mechanism* to partition modalities into different groups to get rid of missingness [22]. The grouping mechanism made full use of multimodal data and could unify simple feature selection models among different groups. Considering varying importance among different modalities, Xiang *et al.* followed the idea of grouping mechanism proposed in [22] based on data availability and further proposed an incomplete source-feature selection (iSFS) algorithm [21]. Their experiments demonstrated that iSFS achieved better performance than [22].

Motivated by the *latent pattern*-based imputation and the *grouping mechanism*-based circumvention of missingness, we proposed a PRIME imputation in this paper to take advantage of their respective strengths to achieve better performance in multimodal student modeling.

3 Methodology

3.1 Data Imputation Phase

To impute the block-wise missing entries, PRIME first extracts latent patterns from all available data for every single modality. Based on these extracted latent patterns, the missing data for each target modality is imputed by two steps. In *Step 1*, pairwise mappings from every other modality are trained by the available pairwise data. In *Step 2*, we aggregated the imputation models from different modalities by constraining the latent patterns for the same target modality that learned from different input modalities to be similar. PRIME is motivated to maximally take advantage of all available data from every *single* modality, each *pairwise* of modalities, and the *entire* modalities respectively to conduct data imputation. Figure 1 shows the entire process using three modalities $\Psi = \{\mathrm{A}, \mathrm{B}, \mathrm{C}\}$ as an illustration.

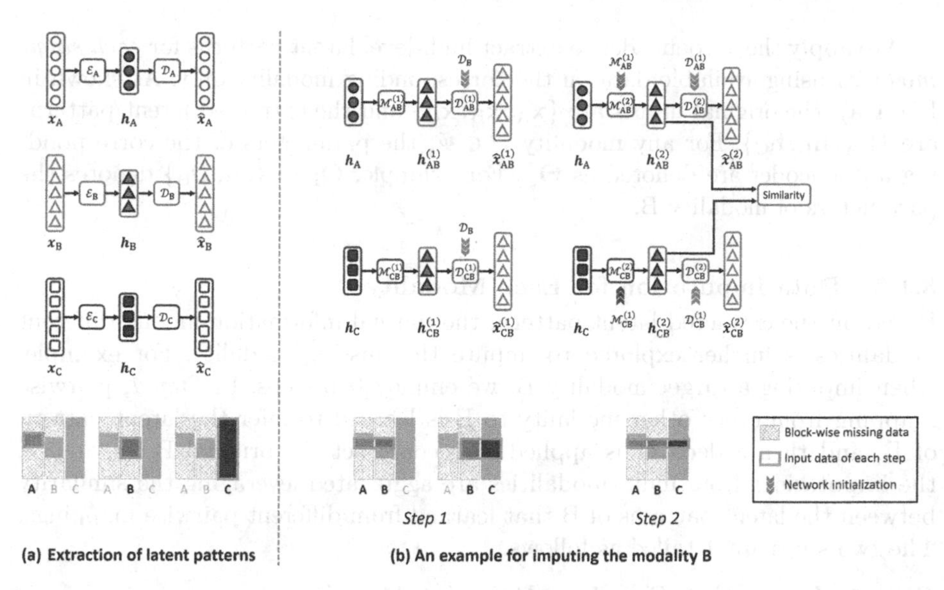

Fig. 1. The framework of PRIME using three modalities {A, B, C} as an illustration: (a) Extraction of latent patterns from each modality with autoencoder; (b) An example of data imputation for modality B with two steps: *Step 1*: Pairwise mapping for imputation from every other modality; *Step 2*: Aggregation of multimodal imputations leveraging the similarity of latent patterns learned from different pairwise mappings.

3.1.1 Extraction of Latent Patterns from Each Modality

To reduce the redundancy and noise of each original single modality data and to facilitate the subsequent cross-modality imputation, PRIME first uses an autoencoder to extract high-level latent pattern from the original data in a non-linear way. It consists of an encoder and a decoder [4]. The encoder compresses the high-dimensional input into a low-dimension representation and the decoder decompresses the low-dimension representation to reconstruct the high-dimension original input. By minimizing the distance between the original and the reconstructed data in such a "bottle-neck" structure, the hidden layer can capture the high-level and low-dimensional patterns from the input data, i.e., latent pattern.

We denote the input and reconstructed data of an autoencoder as $\mathbf{x}$ and $\hat{\mathbf{x}}$, and the hidden layer to be extracted as $\mathbf{h}$. The *Encoder* compresses the original data $\mathbf{x}$ as: $\mathbf{h} = \mathcal{F}_e(\mathbf{x}; \mathbf{W}, \mathbf{b})$, using non-linear encoding function $\mathcal{F}_e$ with parameters $\mathbf{W}, \mathbf{b}$; Then the *Decoder* reconstructs the data as: $\hat{\mathbf{x}} = \mathcal{F}_d(\mathbf{h}; \mathbf{W}', \mathbf{b}')$, using non-linear decoding function $\mathcal{F}_d$ with parameters $\mathbf{W}', \mathbf{b}'$. Therefore, the autoencoder can be denoted as: $\hat{\mathbf{x}} = \mathcal{F}(\mathbf{x}; \boldsymbol{\Theta})$, where $\boldsymbol{\Theta} = \{\mathcal{E}, \mathcal{D}\}$, with $\mathcal{E} = \{\mathbf{W}, \mathbf{b}\}$ and $\mathcal{D} = \{\mathbf{W}', \mathbf{b}'\}$ being parameters of the *Encoder* and *Decoder*, respectively. The mean squared error loss function $\mathcal{L}(.)$ between $\mathbf{x}$ and $\hat{\mathbf{x}}$ is used to train representation parameters $\boldsymbol{\Theta}$, i.e., $\text{argmin}_{\boldsymbol{\Theta}}\, \mathcal{L}(\hat{\mathbf{x}}, \mathbf{x}; \boldsymbol{\Theta})$. To avoid potential overfitting, the dropout strategy was applied over the input and hidden layers.

We apply the autoencoder to extract high-level latent patterns for *each single modality* using available data on the corresponding modality only. As shown in Fig. 1(a), the original inputs are $\{\mathbf{x}_A, \mathbf{x}_B, \mathbf{x}_C\}$ and the extracted latent patterns are $\{\mathbf{h}_A, \mathbf{h}_B, \mathbf{h}_C\}$. For any modality $\psi \in \Psi$, the parameters of the corresponding autoencoder are denoted as $\boldsymbol{\Theta}_\psi$. For example, $\boldsymbol{\Theta}_B = \{\mathcal{E}_B, \mathcal{D}_B\}$ denotes the parameters of modality B.

3.1.2 Data Imputation for Each Modality

Based on the extracted latent pattern, the mutual information among different modalities is further explored to impute the missing modality. For example, when imputing a target modality B, we employ two steps. In *Step 1*, pairwise mapping from every other modality to B is learned to infer the latent pattern of B, and then a decoder is applied to reconstruct the original B. In *Step 2*, the imputations from multi-modalities are aggregated leveraging the similarity between the latent patterns of B that learned from different pairwise mappings. The two steps are detailed as follows.

Step 1: Imputation Based on Pairwise Mapping

The pairwise mappings between any two modalities are learned using neural networks. Herein, the mappings across modalities are built upon latent patterns instead of the original data, because: (1) the extracted latent pattern can filter out heterogeneous noise among different modalities, thus more accurate mappings can be learned; (2) the extracted latent pattern can decrease the dimension of units to be inferred therefore facilitating the imputation task. In addition, considering that the inferred latent patterns from other modalities may have slightly different distributions with the latent pattern extracted in autoencoder, the decoder from the inferred latent pattern to the original data needs to be adjusted accordingly. Therefore, we further refine the decoder to restore the missing data from the inferred latent pattern. Note that this decoder is initialized by the decoder parameters from the autoencoder, rather than training from scratch. Because the decoder parameters from the autoencoder has already achieved a good initialization to restore data from the latent pattern, what we need is to adapt it for the inferred latent pattern.

Figure 1(b) at *Step 1* shows an example for imputing the target modality B: applying each of the remaining modalities $\psi \in \{A, C\}$ with available data as the input. The *pairwise Mapping* $\mathcal{M}_{\psi B}^{(1)}$ and the *Decoder* $\mathcal{D}_{\psi B}^{(1)}$ are learned, with superscript $^{(1)}$ indicating *Step 1*. Note that the decoders in this step are initialized by the $\mathcal{D}_B$ from the autoencoder. The loss function for the pairwise mapping is specifically designed to support the refinement. Without losing generality, taking the example of representing latent patterns of modality B using latent pattern of modality A, the loss function is formulated as:

$$\underset{\boldsymbol{\Theta}_{AB}^{(1)}}{\operatorname{argmin}}\ \mathcal{L}(\mathbf{h}_{AB}^{(1)}, \mathbf{h}_B; \boldsymbol{\Theta}_{AB}^{(1)}) + \lambda^{(1)} \mathcal{L}(\hat{\mathbf{x}}_{AB}^{(1)}, \mathbf{x}_B; \boldsymbol{\Theta}_{AB}^{(1)}), \tag{1}$$

which consists of two terms. The first term encourages the inferred latent pattern from A to B, i.e., $\mathbf{h}_{\mathrm{AB}}^{(1)}$, to be close to the latent pattern $\mathbf{h}_{\mathrm{B}}$ obtained from autoencoder of B; while the second term encourages the restored data from the inferred latent pattern $\hat{\mathbf{x}}_{\mathrm{AB}}^{(1)}$ to be close to the original data $\mathbf{x}_{\mathrm{B}}$. These two terms are balanced via a coefficient $\lambda^{(1)}$, and $\boldsymbol{\Theta}_{\mathrm{AB}}^{(1)}$ denotes the parameters of the pairwise mapping network that needs to be optimized. For any other two modalities, We can naturally get similar loss functions as Eq. (1) quite straightforwardly.

Step 2: Aggregation of Multimodal Imputations

For a target modality, if there is only one pairwise mapping model generated in *Step 1*, the imputation is done; otherwise we proceed to *Step 2* to aggregate the multimodal imputations leveraging the similarity of latent patterns learned from pairwise mappings of different input modalities. Specifically, we applied the data available at all modalities to further refine the pairwise mapping modeled in *Step 1*. The motivation is that when representing the latent pattern of the same modality from two different modalities, the consistency of the inferred latent pattern from different modalities could be used as a regularizer. As illustrated in Fig. 1(b) at *Step 2*, we are representing the modality B using modality A and C, where the superscript $^{(2)}$ indicates *Step 2*. The latent patterns $\mathbf{h}_{\mathrm{AB}}^{(2)}$ and $\mathbf{h}_{\mathrm{CB}}^{(2)}$ from A and C to B should be consistent, because both of them will be used to decode the same $\mathbf{x}_B$. This consistency can be leveraged to further refine the pairwise mapping between two modalities. Therefore, we further use the similarity of $\mathbf{h}_{\mathrm{AB}}^{(2)}$ and $\mathbf{h}_{\mathrm{CB}}^{(2)}$ as the additional loss to penalize their inconsistency. Of note, we use the $\boldsymbol{\Theta}_{\psi\mathrm{B}}^{(1)}, \psi \in \{A, C\}$ obtained in *Step 1* to initialize the pairwise mapping model. The loss function can be formulated as:

$$\begin{aligned} \underset{\boldsymbol{\Theta}_{\mathrm{AB}}^{(2)},\boldsymbol{\Theta}_{\mathrm{CB}}^{(2)}}{\operatorname{argmin}} \ & \lambda_1^{(2)}\mathcal{L}(\hat{\mathbf{x}}_{\mathrm{AB}}^{(2)}, \mathbf{x}_{\mathrm{B}}; \boldsymbol{\Theta}_{\mathrm{AB}}^{(2)}) + \lambda_2^{(2)}\mathcal{L}(\mathbf{h}_{\mathrm{AB}}^{(2)}, \mathbf{h}_{\mathrm{CB}}^{(2)}; \boldsymbol{\Theta}_{\mathrm{AB}}^{(2)}, \boldsymbol{\Theta}_{\mathrm{CB}}^{(2)}) \\ & + \lambda_3^{(2)}\mathcal{L}(\hat{\mathbf{x}}_{\mathrm{CB}}^{(2)}, \mathbf{x}_{\mathrm{B}}; \boldsymbol{\Theta}_{\mathrm{CB}}^{(2)}), \end{aligned} \tag{2}$$

with $\boldsymbol{\Theta}_{\mathrm{AB}}^{(2)}$ and $\boldsymbol{\Theta}_{\mathrm{CB}}^{(2)}$ being the parameters to be refined. For $\psi \in \{\mathrm{A}, \mathrm{C}\}$, $\boldsymbol{\Theta}_{\psi\mathrm{B}}^{(2)} = \{\mathcal{M}_{\psi\mathrm{B}}^{(2)}, \mathcal{D}_{\psi\mathrm{B}}^{(2)}\}$. $\mathbf{h}_{\psi\mathrm{B}}^{(2)}$ and $\hat{\mathbf{x}}_{\psi\mathrm{B}}^{(2)}$ denote the inferred latent pattern from ψ to B and the decoded data B.

Given that the representations from A to B and from C to B are heterogeneous, this means the initialization parameters $\boldsymbol{\Theta}_{\mathrm{AB}}^{(1)}$ and $\boldsymbol{\Theta}_{\mathrm{CB}}^{(1)}$ would achieve heterogeneous performance for representing the same modality data $\mathbf{x}_B$. To address this issue, we obtain the refined $\boldsymbol{\Theta}_{\mathrm{AB}}^{(2)}$ and $\boldsymbol{\Theta}_{\mathrm{CB}}^{(2)}$ in two different refinements using the same network structure and same initialization in Fig. 1(b) at *Step 2*, but with different loss configurations. *In one refinement*, we obtain $\boldsymbol{\Theta}_{\mathrm{AB}}^{(2)}$ with $\lambda_1^{(2)} \gg \lambda_2^{(2)}, \lambda_3^{(2)}$. Under this loss configuration, the joint representation network will focus more on representing modality B from modality A; *in another refinement*, we obtain $\boldsymbol{\Theta}_{\mathrm{CB}}^{(2)}$ with $\lambda_3^{(2)} \gg \lambda_2^{(2)}, \lambda_1^{(2)}$. Similarly, this time the joint representation network will focus more on representing modality B from modality C. By alternating weights of the loss function components, we are able to adaptively use the structural information embedded in multimodal data to specifically refine each pairwise mapping. Note that the three terms in Eq. (2) are normalized to have the same scale.

After all models have been finalized with the refinement procedure, they are employed for imputing the block-wise missing data. For example, to impute the missing block in modality B, we employ the *complimentary* data in modalities A and C. Specifically, the data will go through $\mathcal{E}_{\text{A}}$ and $\mathcal{E}_{\text{C}}$ to extract latent patterns, then be mapped to modality B via $\mathcal{M}^{(2)}_{\text{AB}}$ and $\mathcal{M}^{(2)}_{\text{CB}}$, and finally be reconstructed by $\mathcal{D}^{(2)}_{\text{AB}}$ and $\mathcal{D}^{(2)}_{\text{CB}}$. The imputed modality B is:

$$\tilde{\mathbf{x}}_{\text{B}} = \begin{cases} \frac{1}{2}(\hat{\mathbf{x}}^{(2)}_{\text{AB}} + \hat{\mathbf{x}}^{(2)}_{\text{CB}}) & \text{If } \mathbf{x}_{\text{B}} \text{ was missing;} \\ \mathbf{x}_{\text{B}} & \text{Otherwise.} \end{cases} \tag{3}$$

For each target modality we follow the above two steps for data imputation. After we fill in the block-wise missing data in each modality, the multimodal data will be further concatenated together as $\mathbf{v} = [\tilde{\mathbf{x}}_{\text{A}}\ \tilde{\mathbf{x}}_{\text{B}}\ \tilde{\mathbf{x}}_{\text{C}}]$ and then fed into the subsequent *prediction phase*. It is worth noting that although we describe PRIME using three modalities only, it can be easily extended to $N > 3$ modalities.

3.2 Prediction Phase

In the prediction phase, given the concatenated multimodal feature $\mathbf{v}$, we employed the LASSO [16] feature selection scheme to choose the most relevant features for classification. Denote the feature of n-th student as $\mathbf{v}_n, n = 1, ..., N$, with N being total number of students, and the corresponding class label as $y_n \in \{0, 1\}$. Then, the objective function of LASSO is:

$$\underset{\alpha,\beta}{\text{argmin}} \sum_{n=1}^{N} \log[1 + \exp(-y_n(\alpha^T \mathbf{v}_n + \beta))] + \gamma \|\alpha\|_1 \tag{4}$$

where α is the weight coefficient vector. β is the intercept and γ is the regularization parameter. The features with non-zero elements of α were selected and fed into the classifier. With LASSO, the redundant features among multimodal data can be removed and the potential complementary features can be captured. Once the features are selected, we further use the SVM for the prediction.

4 Data Description

194 undergraduates from four cities across the US and Canada were involved in this work. All students followed the same procedure when interacting with a hypermedia based biology ITS to learn about the human circulatory system [1,2]. Before the learning session, a *pre-test*, which contained 30 multiple-choice questions was administered for assessing students' prior knowledge. When the learning session ended, a *post-test*, which was isomorphic to the pre-test and contained 30 multiple-choice questions was given to evaluate the learning outcomes.

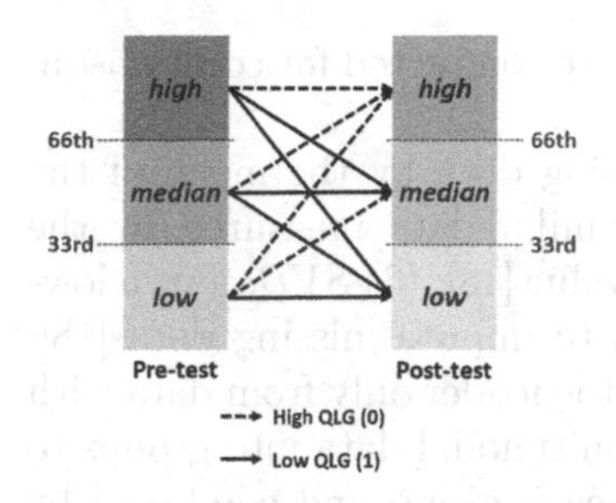

Fig. 2. Determine QLG based on pre- and post-test scores.

Table 1. Numbers of available High/Low QLG students in each single modality and in three modalities, and the corresponding χ^2 test against all remaining individuals among the total 194 students.

Modality	Stu#	High	Low	$\chi^2(1, 194)$	p
Log	194	81	113	–	–
Face	58	21	37	0.7463	0.3877
Eye	34	12	22	0.4217	0.5161
Log+Face+Eye	32	11	21	0.5328	0.4654

We measured students' learning performance using a quantized learning gain (QLG) [12], which is a binary indicator reflecting whether the student benefits from the ITS with High (0) or Low (1) level. It is determined by pre- and post-test scores as shown in Fig. 2. Specifically, both pre- and post-test scores are divided by 33rd and 66th percentiles into *high*, *median* and *low*. The transitions from pre- to post-tests in dashed lines indicate the High group and that in solid lines represent the Low group. When moving from a lower performance group on the pre-test to a higher group on the post-test or remaining in the *high* group, the QLG is labeled as High, because the student needs to perform well for increasing to or maintaining *high* scores; otherwise, the QLG is labeled as Low. We got 81 students in the High group and 113 students in the Low group accordingly.

Table 1 shows student numbers for the three modalities, i.e., logfiles (*Log*), facial expressions (*Face*), and eye tracking (*Eye*). Among the 194 participants who all had Log, 58 had Face and 34 had Eye, with the missing rate being 70.1% and 82.5%, respectively. When considering all three modalities, i.e., Log+Face+Eye, there were 32 students available. The χ^2 test in Table 1 shows the incorporation of additional modalities does not significantly affect the QLG distribution.

We extracted 125 features and normalized them to the range of 0 to 1. Specifically, *Log* has 59 features, including quiz accuracy, interaction duration, self-reported emotions in the questionnaires, etc.; *Face* has 40 features extracted from the data captured by a facial analysis tool in iMotions[1], including evidence scores calculated as the likelihood on a log scale, for 28 pre-defined action units and 12 emotions; and *Eye* has 26 features extracted from the data collected by a SMI EYERED 250 eye-tracker, including the frequency and duration fixating on 9 areas of interest (AOIs) and the transition frequencies between AOIs [14].

5 Experiments and Results

We compared a single modality of *Log-only* without missingness handling to multi-modalities, i.e., Log+Face+Eye, in which the missing data was handled by

[1] iMotions: www.imotions.com.

either *five baselines* or *three PRIMEs*. Two tasks were conducted for comparison, i.e., *learning gain prediction* and *data reconstruction*.

Five baselines include: (1) *MEAN:* fills missing data by the mean of the corresponding feature; (2) *KNN:* finds K most similar data measured by the present modalities and takes the mean as imputed value [18]; (3) *SVD:* uses a low-rank singular value decomposition approximation to impute missing data [18]; (4) *MMAE:* extracts latent patterns via a single autoencoder only from data with all modalities available [10]; (5) *iSFS:* partitions multimodal data into groups to circumvent missingness with a classifier built for each group and combined by late fusion.

Three PRIMEs were compared to measure the effectiveness of the two progressive refinement steps in the framework. Specifically, we looked into *Step 1* in which the decoder was refined and *Step 2* in which both pairwise mapping and the decoder were further refined. Three combinations of pairwise mappings ($\mathcal{M}$) and decoders ($\mathcal{D}$) were compared accordingly (the superscript indicates which step the $\mathcal{M}/\mathcal{D}$ came from), including: (1) *PRIME-0*: $\mathcal{M}^{(1)} + \mathcal{D}$, i.e., pairwise mapping was from *Step 1* and decoder was from autoencoder, both without any refinement; (2) *PRIME-1*: $\mathcal{M}^{(1)} + \mathcal{D}^{(1)}$, i.e., pairwise mapping was from *Step 1* without refinement, while decoder was refined by *Step 1*; (3) *PRIME*: $\mathcal{M}^{(2)} + \mathcal{D}^{(2)}$, i.e., both pairwise mapping and decoder were refined by *Step 2*.

We implemented the PRIME framework using Tensorflow. The involved parameters were determined by grid search: when extracting latent pattern, hidden neurons were $\{20, 14, 8, 14, 20\}$, $\{15, 5, 15\}$, and $\{10, 5, 10\}$ for Log, Face, and Eye. In *Step 1*, hidden neurons in pairwise mappings was 3. The centralized term in Eq. (2) was assigned a coefficient of 0.8 in turn with the other coefficients being 0.1. Adam was applied as the optimizer. The γ in LASSO Eq. (4) was 0.03, and SVM utilized RBF kernel. The leave-one-out cross validation was employed.

5.1 Task I: Learning Gain Prediction

The Task I section in Table 2 shows the QLG prediction results measured by: accuracy (Acc), recall (Rec), precision (Prec), F-score (F1), and AUC. The higher the metrics, the better. The best results among baselines and PRIMEs are in bold, and the overall best results are marked with *.

First, note that the simple majority voting classifier has an accuracy of 0.582 (113 out of 194 students). Using Log-only and eight missing data handling methods all beat the majority voting. Second, all eight block-wise missingness handling methods outperformed the Log-only. This suggests that using multimodal Log+Face+Eye can provide complementary information to enhance prediction power than the traditional Log-only. Third, among the five baselines, iSFS got the best results, except for recall, where SVD was the best. PRIME was better than both MMAE and iSFS, which demonstrated that it could take advantage of the respective strengths of latent pattern-based imputation and grouping mechanism-based circumvention of missingness. PRIME performed the best, which suggested that it was effective in maximally utilizing all available data

Table 2. Log-only vs. Log+Face+Eye (five baselines vs. three PRIMEs) over Task I: Learning gain prediction and Task II: Data reconstruction (RMSE).

Modality	Method	Task I					Task II	
		Acc	Rec	Prec	F1	AUC	Face	Eye
Log	–	.618	.664	.676	.670	.659	–	–
Log+Face+Eye	MEAN	.613	.717	.653	.683	.662	**.179**	**.182**
	KNN	.634	.690	.684	.687	.683	.198	.223
	SVD	.629	**.743**	.661	.700	.671	.211	.257
	MMAE	.649	.690	.678	.684	.672	.194	.264
	iSFS	**.670**	.708	**.721**	**.714**	**.705**	–	–
	PRIME-0	.644	.690	.696	.693	.686	.192	.271
	PRIME-1	.665	.735	.703	.719	.726	.176	.214
	PRIME	**.691***	**.743***	**.730***	**.737***	**.742***	**.163***	**.158***

for imputation to handle the block-wise missingness problem. In addition, both *Step 1* and *Step 2* in PRIME triggered an improvement via refinement.

5.2 Task II: Data Reconstruction

To further look into the performance of data imputation methods, we conducted a data reconstruction task. The Task II section in Table 2 shows the results: the reconstruction error when artificially erasing the Face or Eye block from testing data, respectively. Specifically, an existing modality of Face or Eye was removed from testing data and was imputed by different methods. The reconstruction performance was measured by root-mean-square error (RMSE). Note that the Log-only and iSFS does not involve imputation, so the RMSE is not applicable. The lower the RMSE, the better, and the best results are in bold with *.

First, compared to baseline methods, PRIME led to less RMSE, suggesting that PRIME can better capture latent patterns to reconstruct missing blocks more accurately. Second, compared to PRIME-0, PRIME-1 reached lower RMSE for both modalities, which indicates the effectiveness of decoder refinement in *Step 1* to filter the induced noise in latent pattern when mapping from other modalities. Additionally, PRIME got the best reconstruction performance among the three PRIMEs, which demonstrates that the interaction across multi-modalities was beneficial for refining both pairwise mapping and decoder in *Step 2*.

6 Conclusions

In this work, we proposed a data imputation method called PRIME for block-wise missingness handling in multimodal data and measured its effectiveness in a student modeling task to predict students' learning gain in an ITS. Through experiments, we demonstrated that: (1) the multimodal data is more effective than the single-modal data; (2) compared to competitive baseline missing data handling methods, the PRIME can not only improve the prediction performance, but also achieve more accurate reconstruction results. In future work, we will take temporal properties of ITS data into consideration and will also explore other multimodal datasets to further validate the PRIME framework.

Acknowledgements. This research was supported by the NSF Grants: #1660878, #1726550, and #1651909.

References

1. Azevedo, R., Taub, M., Mudrick, et al.: Using multi-channel trace data to infer and foster self-regulated learning between humans and advanced learning technologies. In: Handbook of Self-Regulation of Learning and Performance, vol. 2 (2018)
2. Azevedo, R., Mudrick, N.V., Taub, M., Bradbury, A.E.: 23 self-regulation in computer-assisted learning systems (2019)
3. Azevedo, R., et al.: Analyzing multimodal multichannel data about self-regulated learning with advanced learning technologies: issues and challenges (2019)
4. Beaulieu-Jones, B.K., Greene, C.S., et al.: Semi-supervised learning of the electronic health record for phenotype stratification. JBI **64**, 168–178 (2016)
5. Beaulieu-Jones, B.K., Moore, J.H.: Missing data imputation in the electronic health record using deeply learned autoencoders. In: Pacific Symposium on Biocomputing 2017, pp. 207–218 (2017)
6. Bondareva, D., Conati, C., Feyzi-Behnagh, R., Harley, J.M., Azevedo, R., Bouchet, F.: Inferring learning from gaze data during interaction with an environment to support self-regulated learning. In: Lane, H.C., Yacef, K., Mostow, J., Pavlik, P. (eds.) AIED 2013. LNCS (LNAI), vol. 7926, pp. 229–238. Springer, Heidelberg (2013). https://doi.org/10.1007/978-3-642-39112-5_24
7. Bosch, N.: Multimodal affect detection in the wild: accuracy, availability, and generalizability. In: Proceedings of the 2015 ICMI, pp. 645–649. ACM (2015)
8. Grafsgaard, J.F., et al.: The additive value of multimodal features for predicting engagement, frustration, and learning during tutoring. In: Proceedings of the 16th International Conference on Multimodal Interaction, pp. 42–49. ACM (2014)
9. Hastie, T., Tibshirani, R., Sherlock, G., Eisen, M., Brown, P., Botstein, D.: Imputing missing data for gene expression arrays (1999)
10. Jaques, N., Taylor, S., Sano, A., Picard, R.: Multimodal autoencoder: a deep learning approach to filling in missing sensor data and enabling better mood prediction. In: 2017 7th ACII, pp. 202–208. IEEE (2017)
11. Kapoor, A., Picard, R.W.: Multimodal affect recognition in learning environments. In: 13th ACM Multimedia, pp. 677–682. ACM (2005)
12. Mao, Y., Lin, C., Chi, M.: Deep learning vs. Bayesian knowledge tracing: student models for interventions. J. EDM **10**(2), 28–54 (2018)
13. Shang, C., et al.: VIGAN: missing view imputation with generative adversarial networks. In: 2017 IEEE Big Data, pp. 766–775. IEEE (2017)
14. Taub, M., Azevedo, R.: How does prior knowledge influence eye fixations and sequences of cognitive and metacognitive SRL processes during learning with an intelligent tutoring system? Int. J. AIED **29**(1), 1–28 (2019)

15. Taub, M., Mudrick, N.V., Azevedo, R., Millar, G.C., Rowe, J., Lester, J.: Using multi-channel data with multi-level modeling to assess in-game performance during gameplay with CRYSTAL ISLAND. Comput. Hum. Behav. **76**, 641–655 (2017)
16. Tibshirani, R.: Regression shrinkage and selection via the lasso. J. Roy. Stat. Soc.: Ser. B (Methodol.) **58**(1), 267–288 (1996)
17. Tran, L., et al.: Missing modalities imputation via cascaded residual autoencoder. In: Proceedings of the IEEE Conference on CVPR, pp. 1405–1414 (2017)
18. Troyanskaya, O., et al.: Missing value estimation methods for DNA microarrays. Bioinformatics **17**(6), 520–525 (2001)
19. VanLehn, K., Lynch, C., et al.: The Andes physics tutoring system: lessons learned. Int. J. Artif. Intell. Educ. **15**(3), 147–204 (2005)
20. Woolf, B.P.: Student modeling. In: Nkambou, R., Bourdeau, J., Mizoguchi, R. (eds.) Advances in Intelligent Tutoring Systems. Studies in Computational Intelligence, vol. 308, pp. 267–279. Springer, Heidelberg (2010). https://doi.org/10.1007/978-3-642-14363-2_13
21. Xiang, S., Yuan, L., et al.: Multi-source learning with block-wise missing data for Alzheimer's disease prediction. In: 19th ACM SIGKDD, pp. 185–193. ACM (2013)
22. Yuan, L., et al.: Multi-source learning for joint analysis of incomplete multi-modality neuroimaging data. In: 18th ACM SIGKDD, pp. 1149–1157. ACM (2012)
23. Zhong, B., et al.: Emotion recognition with facial expressions and physiological signals. In: 2017 IEEE SSCI, pp. 1–8. IEEE (2017)

A New Local Transformation Module for Few-Shot Segmentation

Yuwei Yang, Fanman Meng(✉), Hongliang Li, Qingbo Wu, Xiaolong Xu, and Shuai Chen

School of Information and Communication Engineering, University of Electronic Science and Technology of China, Chengdu, China
fmmeng@uestc.edu.cn

Abstract. Few-shot segmentation segments object regions of new classes with a few of manual annotations. Its key step is to establish the transformation module between support images (annotated images) and query images (unlabeled images), so that the segmentation cues of support images can guide the segmentation of query images. The existing methods form transformation model based on global cues, which however ignores the local cues that are verified in this paper to be very important for the transformation. This paper proposes a new transformation module based on local cues, where the relationship of the local features is used for transformation. To enhance the generalization performance of the network, the relationship matrix is calculated in a high-dimensional metric embedding space based on cosine distance. In addition, to handle the challenging mapping problem from the low-level local relationships to high-level semantic cues, we propose to apply generalized inverse matrix of the annotation matrix of support images to transform the relationship matrix linearly, which is non-parametric and class-agnostic. The result by the matrix transformation can be regarded as an attention map with high-level semantic cues, based on which a transformation module can be built simply. The proposed transformation module is a general module that can be used to replace the transformation module in the existing few-shot segmentation frameworks. We verify the effectiveness of the proposed method on Pascal VOC 2012 dataset. The value of mIoU achieves at 57.0% in 1-shot and 60.6% in 5-shot, which outperforms the state-of-the-art method by 1.6% and 3.5%, respectively.

Keywords: Few-shot segmentation · Transformation module · Attention · Matrix transformation

1 Introduction

Image segmentation is a basic computer vision task [1]. In recent years, with the rapid development of deep learning method, several convolution neural network based segmentation methods have improved the performance of image segmentation greatly, such as FCN [1] and DeepLab v3 [2]. However, these methods rely

Y. M. Ro et al. (Eds.): MMM 2020, LNCS 11962, pp. 76–87, 2020.
https://doi.org/10.1007/978-3-030-37734-2_7

heavily on a large amount of annotations. In order to overcome this shortcoming, few-shot segmentation task [3] is proposed to achieve segmentation of new class with a few of manual annotations, such as one annotation (1-shot segmentation) and five annotations (5-shot segmentation). Few-shot segmentation is a challenging task due to the asymmetry of training data and testing data.

In few-shot segmentation task, the annotated and unlabeled images are called support images and query images respectively [3]. The existing models [3–7] usually consist of three terms. (1) The support branch that extracts feature from support images. (2) The query branch that extracts feature from query images. (3) The transformation module that transfers the features between support branch and query branch to facilitate the segmentation of query branch. The essential term is the transformation module and the most challenging obstacle is how to design a transformation module that is class-agnostic, so that the transformation module can be generalized to new classes efficiently. The existing methods [5,7] use the global cues of the support image to model the transformation process, which however ignores the geometry relationships of the local features. This paper demonstrates that the geometry relationships of the local features are very useful to the transformation module.

This paper proposes a new transformation module based on local cues, where the relationship of the local features is used to accomplish the transformation. Our idea is to use linear transformation of the relationship matrix in a high-dimensional metric embedding space to accomplish the transformation. To this end, we firstly map the local features into an embedding space, where cosine distance is used to obtain the relationship matrix of local features. Then, the relationship matrix is transformed linearly by the generalized inverse matrix of the annotated matrix of support image. After linear transformation, the result is regarded as an attention map containing high-level semantic information, by which we establish a new attention transformation module. We verify the effectiveness of our transformation module on Pascal VOC 2012 dataset [9]. The value of mIoU achieves at 57.0% in 1-shot and 60.6% in 5-shot, which outperform the state-of-the-art method by 1.6% and 3.5%, respectively.

2 Proposed Method

2.1 Problem Definition

Few-shot segmentation is a task that uses a few of annotations to segment unknown images for new classes. Let $S = \{(I_s^i, Y_s^i)\}_{i=1}^k$ be a set of support images and the corresponding manual annotations. Let $Q = \{I_q\}$ be query images set that needs to be segmented. The images in S and Q belong to the same new class $l \in \{L_{test}\}$. Let $\{L_{train}\}$ be the training dataset of known classes that already exist, and $\{L_{train}\} \cap \{L_{test}\} = \emptyset$. The goal of few-shot segmentation is to build a model $f(I_q, S)$ by $\{L_{train}\}$ that outputs binary mask Y_q for query image I_q based on S.

2.2 Overview

Similar to the existing few-shot segmentation network, the proposed framework includes a support branch, a query branch and a transformation module, as shown in Fig. 1. In order to make the network more generalized to unseen classes, our feature extraction backbone adopts relatively shallow layers, such as the first three layers of *Resnet*50 [18]. In addition, the support branch and the query branch share the feature extraction backbone.

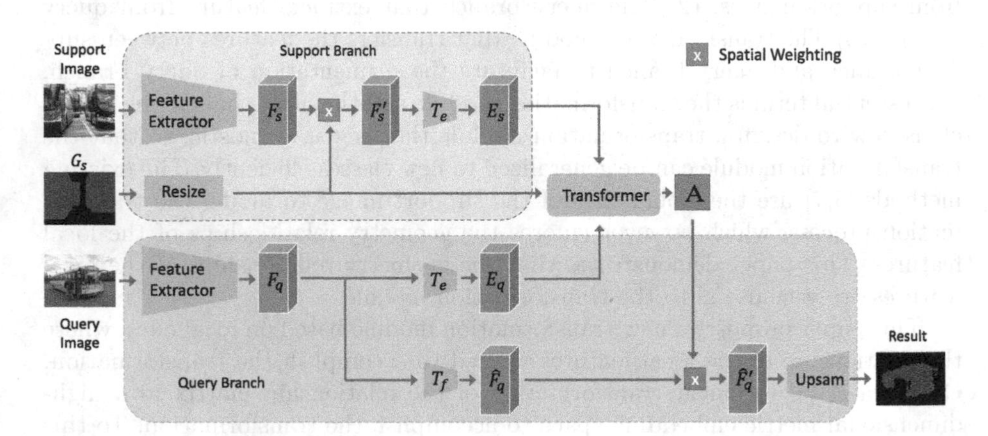

Fig. 1. The pipeline of the proposed method. The *Feature Extractor* extracts the features F_s and F_q. The feature F_s is weighted spatially by the groundtruth mask G_s to obtain the feature $F_s^{'}$. The deep features F_q and $F_s^{'}$ are mapped into an embedding space by T_e to get E_q and E_s respectively. Simultaneously, the feature F_q is learned by T_f to get $\hat{F}_q$. Based on E_s, E_q and G_s, the proposed $Transformer$ outputs attention map A, which weights $\hat{F}_q$ spatially. The segmentation result is obtained through $Upsam$ module finally.

After obtaining deep features F_s and F_q from support image and query image, F_s is weighted spatially by the annotated mask G_s to get the features $F_s^{'}$, which guarantees the features $F_s^{'}$ only containing corresponding foreground regions. Such process can be represented as

$$F_s^{'}(i,j) = F_s(i,j) \times G_s(i,j) \tag{1}$$

where i, j is spatial location of feature map F_s or annotated mask G_s.

Then, the learned features F_q and $F_s^{'}$ are mapped into a high-dimensional embedding space by further convolution operations T_e to get corresponding embedding features E_q and E_s respectively, so that cosine distance can be used to calculate the relationship between the feature pixels in this space. Simultaneously, the feature F_q is learned by convolution operation T_f to get $\hat{F}_q$.

Based on the embedding E_s, E_q and the groundtruth mask of support images G_s, the proposed $Transformer$ applies linear transformation of matrix to obtain the attention map A with high-level semantic cues. The detailed description refers to Sect. 2.3. The attention map A finally filters the deep features $\hat{F}_q$ to $\hat{F}'_q$ by

$$\hat{F}'_q(i,j) = \hat{F}_q(i,j) \times A(i,j) \tag{2}$$

where i, j is spatial location of feature maps $\hat{F}_q$ or attention map A. It is seen that the attention map A indicates a rough object area to be segmented. This coarse object area provides high-level semantic information for the subsequent *Upsam* sub-network.

We next use *Upsam* sub-network to generate segmentation mask from $\hat{F}_q$. The *Upsam* sub-network is shown in Fig. 2. Specifically, in order to handle the scale changes of the object better, we introduce multi-scale feature fusion module ASPP [15] and residual connection [18] in *Upsam*. The output of *Upsam* is the probability map M with the same size to the query image, and the cross entropy loss in Eq. (3) is used to supervise the training of the model, i.e.,

$$L_m = \sum_i \sum_j -(Y(i,j)log(M(i,j)) + (1 - Y(i,j))log(1 - M(i,j))) \tag{3}$$

where Y is the groundtruth mask of the query image, M is the predicted probability map of our few-shot segmentation model, and i, j is the spatial location of Y or M.

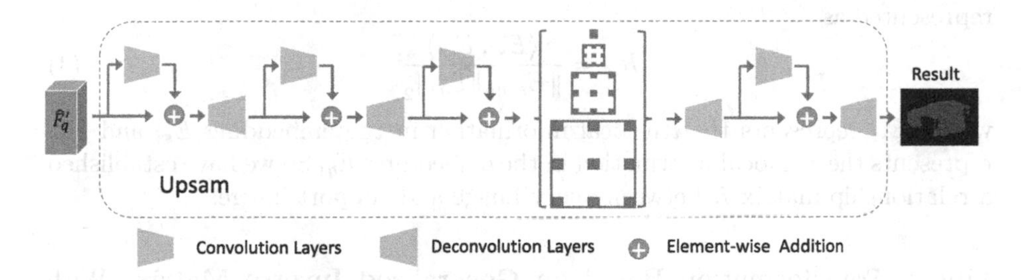

Fig. 2. The structure of *Upsam* module. The residual connection [18] and multi-scale strategy ASPP [15] are implemented to handle the scale variations of object.

2.3 Transformation Module

Existing methods often establish the transformation between support image and query image by the global features of the support image, thus lose local geometric information, which however is also important to the transformation. The proposed transformation module is designed based on the relationship between local pixels (represented by the relationship matrix in NON-Local model [8]), and more accurate segmentation can be realized by propagating local relationships.

The detailed steps are illustrated in Fig. 3. The transformation is achieved by the linear transformation of the relationship matrix. Specifically, the relationship matrix between E_s (for support image) and E_q (for query image) is linearly transformed by the generalized inverse matrix of G_s (groundtruth mask matrix of the support image), which overcomes the difficulty of transforming local relationship matrix to high-level semantic information. The result of linear transformation is the attention map A of the query image.

Relationship Matrix. For few-shot segmentation task, it is very important to model the relationship between each pair of deep local features of support image and query image. Due to the local computational nature of the convolution operation, the relationships between long-distance pixels cannot be established directly. Therefore, NON-Local [8] structure was proposed to conquer it, where the feature tensor is reshaped into a matrix, and a relationship matrix is established by matrix product. This relationship matrix contains the relationships between each pair of local deep features. We imitate the relationship matrix in NON-Local [8] to establish the relationship in few-shot segmentation.

In NON-Local [8], it is only desirable to establish long-distance constraints, and the matrix product is just used to describe the relationship between two local features. For few-shot segmentation task, this is a rough description of feature similarity. Therefore, in our proposed transformation module, the feature is firstly mapped into an embedding space, in which the cosine distance can be used to calculate the relationship between local features. Such process is represented as

$$R_{ij} = \frac{\langle E_{si}, E_{qj} \rangle}{\|E_{si}\|_2 \|E_{qj}\|_2} \tag{4}$$

where E_{si} represents the ith local information in the embedding E_s, and E_{qj} represents the jth local information in the embedding E_q. So we have established a relationship matrix R between query image and support image.

Linear Transformation Based on Generalized Inverse Matrix. With the above relationship matrix R, how to convert this relationship matrix R to high-level semantic information of query image becomes another key point. Let G_s and G_q be the binary groundtruth mask of support image and query image respectively. Based on Eq. (4), the true relationship matrix R_{truth} between query image and support image can be simplified by matrix product between G_s and G_q, i.e.,

$$R_{truth} = G_q \cdot G_s \tag{5}$$

where $\cdot$ demonstrates matrix product. The original size of G_s and G_q are $H \times W$. The reshaped size of G_s and G_q are $1 \times HW$ and $HW \times 1$ respectively. The size of R_{truth} is $HW \times HW$, which contains the relationship information of each pair of local feature pixels of E_q and E_s. Our target is to obtain G_q based on Eq. (5).

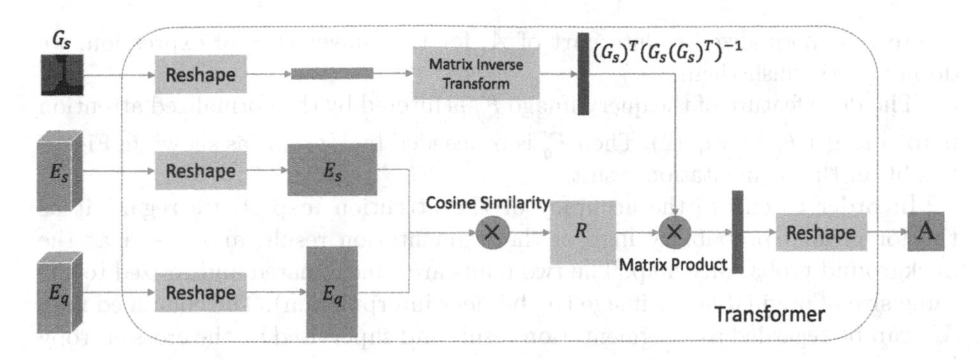

Fig. 3. The detailed information of the proposed transformation module. The embedding E_s and E_q are reshaped to matrix. Then, the relationship matrix R is obtained based on E_q and E_s by cosine similarity. Finally, the relationship matrix R is transformed linearly by the matrix of generalized inverse matrix of G_s. After reshape operator, the attention map A is obtained.

We suppose the matrix R is approximately equal to the true relationship matrix R_{truth} between query image and support image. Furthermore, we relax the binary groundtruth mask G_q to the soft attention map A, which provides high-level semantic information. Since G_s is known for few-shot segmentation task, the problem is transformed to get the attention map A based on,

$$R = A \cdot G_s \tag{6}$$

Moreover, since the G_s is not square matrix, its inverse matrix does not exist. But it can be regarded as matrix with row full rank. According to the generalized inverse matrix theory [19], the transformation problem can be represented by:

$$A = R \cdot [(G_s)^T (G_s (G_s)^T)^{-1}] \tag{7}$$

where $\cdot$ demonstrates matrix product. $(G_s)^T (G_s (G_s)^T)^{-1}$ is the right inverse matrix (one type of generalized inverse matrix) of G_s. This is just a process that applies the generalized inverse matrix of G_s to linearly transform the relationship matrix R. Finally, the attention map can be obtained by Eq. (7) directly.

In order to ensure that the learned relation matrix R is consistent with R_{truth} during training, the mean square error loss is used to supervise it, i.e.,

$$L_r = \|R - R_{truth}\|_2^2 \tag{8}$$

Attention Map. By linearly transforming the relationship matrix R by Eq. (7), the attention map of the query image A is obtained, with reshaped size to $H \times W$. Moreover, we normalize it to $0 \sim 1$ by

$$\hat{A} = \frac{A - min(A)}{max(A) - min(A)} \tag{9}$$

where $\hat{A}$ is normalized counterpart of A, for the convenience of expression, we do not distinguish them.

The deep feature of the query image $\hat{F_q}$ is filtered by the normalized attention map $\hat{A}$ to get $\hat{F_q'}$ by Eq. (2). Then $\hat{F_q'}$ is proceeded by $Upsam$ (as shown in Fig. 2) to obtain the segmentation result.

In order to ensure the accuracy of the attention map A, we regard it as the foreground probability map of the segmentation result, and $1 - A$ as the background probability map. The two maps are concatenated and resized to the same size of original query image (by bilinear interpolation). The combined map M_a can be regarded as a segmentation result and supervised by the cross entropy loss.

$$L_a = \sum_i \sum_j -(Y(i,j)log(M_a(i,j)) + (1 - Y(i,j))log(1 - M_a(i,j))) \tag{10}$$

where Y is the groundtruth mask of the query image, M_a is the probability map derived from attention map A. i and j are the spatial location of Y and M_a.

For 5-shot, there are five support images. In order to combine the attention maps provided by the five different images, we simply average the attention maps by

$$A_{5-shot} = \frac{1}{5} \sum_i A_i \tag{11}$$

In the training stage, we combine the three losses in Eqs. (3), (10) and (8) to supervise the learning of our model, i.e.,

$$L = \lambda_m L_m + \lambda_a L_a + \lambda_r L_r \tag{12}$$

where λ_m, λ_a, λ_r are the weights of corresponding loss function.

3 Experiment

The project of our method is built based on the Pytorch library, Adam [16] optimizer is adopted to update the parameters, and all experimental code is executed on a machine equipped with a Titan XP GPU. We set the initial learning rate to 1e-4. The backbone network of our feature extraction is pre-trained on ImageNet [17] dataset, and the parameters of the previous layers of backbone are frozen, and we apply the first three layers of $Resnet50$ [18] as our backbone.

3.1 Detail of Implementation

We validate the proposed method on the Pascal VOC 2012 [9] dataset and its enhanced dataset SDS [12]. Similar to the existing methods [3–7], we split images of 20 classes into four subsets, each of which contains images of five classes, the detailed description can be found in Table 1. For these four subsets, three of

Table 1. The detailed setting for splitting the sub-dataset to evaluate the few-shot segmentation. There are 4 sub-datasets, and $PASCAL-5^i$ represents the ith subset, where $i = \{0,1,2,3\}$. When the i-th sub-dataset is selected for evaluation, the rest three datasets are used for training.

Sub-dataset	Corresponding classes
$PASCAL-5^0$	Aeroplane, bicycle, bird, boat, bottle
$PASCAL-5^1$	Bus, car, cat, chair, cow
$PASCAL-5^2$	Diningtable, dog, horse, motorbike, person
$PASCAL-5^3$	Potted plant, sheep, sofa, train, tv/monitor

them are selected as the training set, and the rest one is used as the test set to validate the effectiveness of the proposed method. In the training stage, we randomly select two images for each class, one as a support image and another as a query image until all images of training classes were selected. In the testing stage, in order to make a fair comparison with the existing methods, we use the same random seed in the existing method to sample the same 1000 pairs of images as the test data for each evaluation sub-dataset.

Table 2. The comparison results (mIoU value) on four evaluation sub-datasets in 1-shot. The best results are in bold.

Methods	$PASCAL-5^0$	$PASCAL-5^1$	$PASCAL-5^2$	$PASCAL-5^3$	Mean
1-NN	25.3	44.9	41.7	18.4	32.6
LogReg	26.9	42.9	37.1	18.4	31.4
Siamese	28.1	39.9	31.8	25.8	31.4
OSVOS [10]	24.9	38.8	36.5	30.1	32.6
OSLSM [3]	33.6	55.3	40.9	33.5	40.8
co-FCN [4]	36.7	50.6	44.9	32.4	41.1
SG-One [5]	40.2	58.4	48.4	38.4	46.3
CA-Net [7]	52.5	65.9	51.3	51.9	55.4
Ours	**52.8**	**69.6**	**53.2**	**52.3**	**57.0**

We use the mean intersection over union of foreground (mIoU) to measure the performance of our proposed method, which is widely used in few-shot segmentation. In addition, the FB-IoU proposed in co-FCN [4] is also considered, which includes mean intersection over union of foreground and background.

3.2 Comparison with Benchmarks

In order to verify the effectiveness of our method, we compare with existing method in 1-shot and 5-shot. We follow CA-Net [7] to adopt DenseCRF [14] and multi-scale evaluation strategy to improve the performance, which are always

Table 3. The comparison results (mIoU value) on four evaluation sub-datasets in 5-shot. The best results are in bold.

Methods	$PASCAL-5^0$	$PASCAL-5^1$	$PASCAL-5^2$	$PASCAL-5^3$	Mean
1-NN	34.5	53.0	46.9	25.6	40.0
LogReg	25.9	51.6	44.5	25.6	39.3
Co-segmentation [13]	25.1	28.9	27.7	26.3	27.1
OSLSM [3]	35.9	58.1	42.7	39.1	43.9
co-FCN [4]	37.5	50.0	44.1	33.9	41.4
SG-One [5]	41.9	58.6	48.6	39.4	47.1
CA-Net [7]	55.5	67.8	51.9	53.2	57.1
Ours	**57.9**	**69.9**	**56.9**	**57.5**	**60.6**

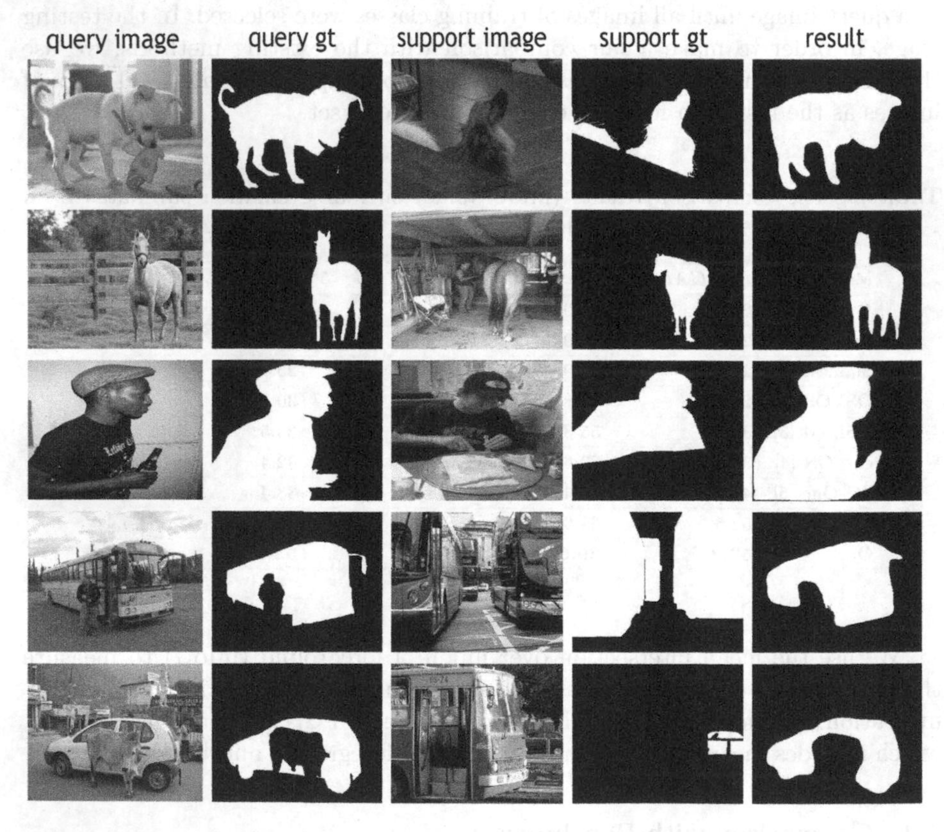

Fig. 4. The subjective results of the proposed method. From left to right: query image, ground-truth mask of the query image, the support image, ground-truth mask of the support image and the segmentation result, respectively.

Table 4. The comparison results (FB-IoU value) on four evaluation sub-datasets in 1-shot and 5-shot. The best results are in bold.

Methods	OSLSM [3]	co-FCN [4]	PL [11]	SG-One [5]	A-MCG [6]	CA-Net [7]	Ours
1-shot	61.3	60.1	61.2	63.1	61.2	66.2	**71.8**
5-shot	61.5	60.2	62.3	65.9	62.2	69.6	**74.6**

Table 5. The ablation results of three loss functions. The ticking indicates that the loss function is used.

k-shot	L_m	L_r	L_a	mIoU	FB-IoU
1-shot	✓			55.3	70.2
1-shot	✓	✓		55.9	70.9
1-shot	✓		✓	56.0	71.1
1-shot	✓	✓	✓	57.0	71.8

employed in existing [15] semantic segmentation method. The detailed results can be found in Tables 2, 3 and 4. We can see the values of mIoU by our method achieve at 57.0% in 1-shot and 60.6% in 5-shot, which outperform the state-of-the-art few-shot segmentation method CA-Net [7] by 1.6% and 3.5% respectively. The improvement in 5-shot indicates the superiority of our method when it comes to more annotations. In addition, the values of FB-IoU in 1-shot and 5-shot achieve at 71.8%, 74.6% respectively, which also outperforms the comparison methods obviously.

Table 6. The effectiveness of Dense-CRF post-processing and Multi-scale strategy are demonstrated. The ticking indicates that the strategy is used.

k-shot	Dense-CRF	Multi-scale	mIoU	FB-IoU
1-shot			56.1	71.0
1-shot	✓		56.7	71.5
1-shot		✓	56.6	71.3
1-shot	✓	✓	57.0	71.8

3.3 Ablation

In the training stage, the weight λ_m, λ_a and λ_r are set to 1. In order to validate the effectiveness of our three loss functions, ablation experiment is implemented. The detailed results can be found in Table 5. We can see L_a and L_r improve the performance by 1.1% and 1.0% respectively. In addition, we follow CA-Net [7] to employ DenseCRF [14] and multi-scale evaluation in our test stage. The ablation of these two strategies is also conducted, and the detailed results can be found in Table 6. We can see that DenseCRF [14] and the multi-scale evaluation strategy can improve the mIoU value by 0.4% and 0.3% respectively.

3.4 Subjective Result

The subjective results of the proposed method are shown in Fig. 4. The support image, the ground-truth mask of the support image, the query image, the ground-truth mask of the query image and the segmentation result are displayed from left column to right column, respectively. It is seen that the proposed method segments objects from these images successfully.

4 Conclusion

This paper proposes a new transformation module for few-shot segmentation. Rather than focusing on global cues, the relationships of local features are used to form the transformation. Local feature relationship matrix calculated by the cosine similarity is used to represent the relationships of local features. Linear transformation of relationship matrix based on generalized inverse of the groundtruth matrix is implemented to transform the relationship matrix. We also map the features into a high-dimensional metric embedding space to enhance the generalization of the proposed module. We propose a new few-shot segmentation network based on transformation module, and better results are obtained in terms of both mIoU value and FB-IoU value.

Acknowledgment. This work was supported in part by the National Natural Science Foundation of China under Grant 61871087, Grant 61502084, Grant 61831005, and Grant 61601102, and supported in part by Sichuan Science and Technology Program under Grant 2018JY0141.

References

1. Long, J., Shelhamer, E., Darrell, T.: Fully convolutional networks for semantic segmentation. In: Proceedings of the IEEE Conference on Computer Vision and Pattern Recognition, pp. 3431–3440 (2015)
2. Chen, L.C., Papandreou, G., Schroff, F., Adam, H.: Rethinking atrous convolution for semantic image segmentation (2017). arXiv preprint arXiv:1706.05587
3. Shaban, A., Bansal, S., Liu, Z., Essa, I., Boots, B.: One-shot learning for semantic segmentation. In: BMVC (2017)
4. Rakelly, K., Shelhamer, E., Darrell, T., Efros, A., Levine, S.: Conditional networks for few-shot semantic segmentation. In: ICLR workshop (2018)
5. Zhang, X., Wei, Y., Yang, Y., Huang, T.: Sg-one: similarity guidance network for one-shot semantic segmentation (2018). arXiv preprint arXiv:1810.09091
6. Hu, T., Yang, P., Zhang, C., Yu, G., Mu, Y., Snoek, C.G.: Attention-based multi-context guiding for few-shot semantic segmentation. In: Proceedings of the Association for the Advance of Artificial Intelligence (2019)

7. Zhang, C., Lin, G., Liu, F., Yao, R., Shen, C.: CANet: class-agnostic segmentation networks with iterative refinement and attentive few-shot learning. In: Proceedings of the IEEE Conference on Computer Vision and Pattern Recognition, pp. 5217–5226 (2019)
8. Wang, X., Girshick, R., Gupta, A., He, K.: Non-local neural networks. In: Proceedings of the IEEE Conference on Computer Vision and Pattern Recognition, pp. 7794–7803 (2018)
9. Everingham, M., Eslami, S.A., Van Gool, L., Williams, C.K., Winn, J., Zisserman, A.: The pascal visual object classes challenge: a retrospective. Int. J. Comput. Vis. **111**(1), 98–136 (2015)
10. Caelles, S., Maninis, K.K., Pont-Tuset, J., Leal-Taixé, L., Cremers, D., Van Gool, L.: One-shot video object segmentation. In: Proceedings of the IEEE Conference on Computer Vision and Pattern Recognition, pp. 221–230 (2017)
11. Dong, N., Xing, E.: Few-shot semantic segmentation with prototype learning. In: BMVC, vol. 1, p. 6 (2018)
12. Hariharan, B., Arbelaez, P., Bourdev, L.D., Maji, S., Malik, J.: Semantic contours from inverse detectors. In: IEEE International Conference on Computer Vision, ICCV 2011, Barcelona, Spain, 6–13 November 2011. IEEE (2011)
13. Faktor, A., Irani, M.: Co-segmentation by composition. In: Proceedings of the IEEE International Conference on Computer Vision, pp. 1297–1304 (2013)
14. Krähenbühl, P., Koltun, V.: Efficient inference in fully connected crfs with gaussian edge potentials. In: Advances in Neural Information Processing Systems, pp. 109–117 (2011)
15. Chen, L.C., Papandreou, G., Kokkinos, I., Murphy, K., Yuille, A.L.: Deeplab: semantic image segmentation with deep convolutional nets, atrous convolution, and fully connected crfs. IEEE Trans. Pattern Anal. Mach. Intell. **40**(4), 834–848 (2017)
16. Kingma, D. P., Ba, J.: Adam: a method for stochastic optimization (2014). arXiv preprint arXiv:1412.6980
17. Deng, J., Dong, W., Socher, R., Li, L.J., Li, K., Fei-Fei, L.: imagenet: a large-scale hierarchical image database. In: 2009 IEEE Conference on Computer Vision and Pattern Recognition, pp. 248–255. IEEE, June 2009
18. He, K., Zhang, X., Ren, S., Sun, J.: Deep residual learning for image recognition. In: Proceedings of the IEEE Conference on Computer Vision and Pattern Recognition, pp. 770–778 (2016)
19. Rao, C.R., Mitra, S.K.: Generalized inverse of a matrix and its applications. In: Icams Conference, vol. 1 (1972)

Background Segmentation for Vehicle Re-identification

Mingjie Wu[1], Yongfei Zhang[1,2(✉)], Tianyu Zhang[1], and Wenqi Zhang[1]

[1] Beijing Key Laboratory of Digital Media, School of Computer Science and Engineering, Beihang University, Beijing 100191, China
yfzhang@buaa.edu.cn
[2] State Key Laboratory of Virtual Reality Technology and Systems, Beihang University, Beijing 100191, China

Abstract. Vehicle re-identification (Re-ID) is very important in intelligent transportation and video surveillance. Prior works focus on extracting discriminative features from visual appearance of vehicles or using visual-spatio-temporal information. However, background interference in vehicle re-identification have not been explored. In the actual large-scale spatio-temporal scenes, the same vehicle usually appears in different backgrounds while different vehicles might appear in the same background, which will seriously affect the re-identification performance. To the best of our knowledge, this paper is the first to consider the background interference problem in vehicle re-identification. We construct a vehicle segmentation dataset and develop a vehicle Re-ID framework with a background interference removal (BIR) mechanism to improve the vehicle Re-ID performance as well as robustness against complex background in large-scale spatio-temporal scenes. Extensive experiments demonstrate the effectiveness of our proposed framework, with an average 9% gain on mAP over state-of-the-art vehicle Re-ID algorithms.

Keywords: Vehicle re-identification · Background segmentation · Triplet loss

1 Introduction

Vehicle re-identification (Re-ID) targets to retrieve images of a query vehicle in different scenes [10]. In recent years, the number of cars has increased rapidly, and the application scenarios of intelligent transportation and video surveillance have pervasively expanded [13]. As one of the most important techniques therein, vehicle Re-ID has become a popular field, attracting widespread attention from both academia and industry.

Prior works focus on visual appearance of vehicles [11,21,28] only or introduce spatial-temporal clues for more accurate vehicle Re-ID [20,23]. With the

Y. M. Ro et al. (Eds.): MMM 2020, LNCS 11962, pp. 88–99, 2020.
https://doi.org/10.1007/978-3-030-37734-2_8

nice exploration of visual appearance of vehicles and/or spatial-temporal constraints, as well as the carefully designed deep learning architectures, the performance of vehicle Re-ID has been largely improved, yet there are still unexplored issues. One of them is the background interference problem. In the actual large-scale scenes, the same vehicle often appears in different backgrounds and different vehicles may appear in the same background, which will seriously affect the Re-ID performance, due to background interference. As shown in the first row of Fig. 1, different vehicles share the same background, making it harder to distinguish. The second row shows the same car in different cameras. The various background may lead Re-ID systems to extract background-related features and result in unsatisfying Re-ID performance.

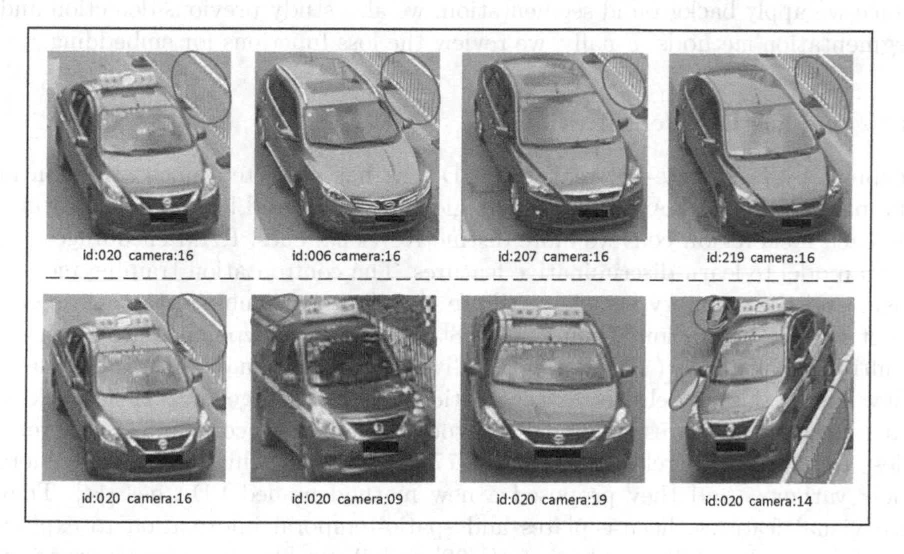

Fig. 1. The background interference information in datasets [12]. The first row of pictures shows the different vehicles shot under the same camera. The second row shows the pictures taken for the same car under different cameras.

In this paper, we propose to use vehicle background segmentation to reduce the harmful impact of interference information and improve the vehicle Re-ID performance as well as robustness against complex background in large-scale spatio-temporal scenes. The extensive experiments demonstrate that the proposed framework can accurately extract the vehicle characteristics and outperform several state-of-the-art methods. Our contributions are summarized as follows:

- We construct a vehicle background segmentation dataset based on the Cityscapes [2] dataset, and then use the new dataset to train the vehicle background segmentation model.
- We propose a novel post processing method for more accurate background segmentation. The post processing procedure ensures the segmented images

reserve the vehicle area as much as possible, thus the segmentation suffers less information loss.
- We develop a new background interference removal (BIR) pipeline and evaluate our methods on two large-scale vehicle Re-ID datasets [12,13]. Experiment results demonstrate that by reducing background interference, the Re-ID performance can be boosted significantly.

2 Related Works

Vehicle Re-ID is an essential task in the field of intelligent transportation and video surveillance. In this section, we first review prior works on vehicle Re-ID. Since we apply background segmentation, we also study previous detection and segmentation methods. Finally, we review the loss functions for embedding.

2.1 Vehicle Re-Identification

Inspired by person Re-ID, vehicle Re-ID task has attracted much attention in the past few years. RAM [11] extracts global features and local regions feature. As each local region conveys more distinctive visual cues, RAM encourages the deep model to learn discriminative features. The confrontation training mechanism and the auxiliary vehicle attribute classifier are combined to achieve efficient feature generation. Zhou *et al.* [28] proposed a viewpoint-aware attentive multi-view inference (VAMI) model. Given the attentional features of single-view input, this model designs a conditional multi-view generation network to infer the global features of different viewpoint information containing input vehicles. Liu *et al.* [12] released the VeRi-776 dataset, in which there exist more view variants. And they proposed a new mathod named FDA-net [14]. They use visual features, license plates and spatio-temporal information to explore Re-ID tasks. In addition, Shen *et al.* [20] and Wang [21] respectively proposed visual-space-time path suggestion and spatio-temporal regularization, focusing on the development of vehicle spatio-temporal information to solve vehicle Re-ID problem.

2.2 Target Detection and Background Segmentation

Conventional target detection systems utilize classifiers to perform detection. For example, Dean *et al.* [3] adopts the method of deformable parts models (DPM), and the recent R-CNN [5] method uses region proposal methods. The flow of such methods is complicated, and there are problems of slow speed and difficult training. The YOLOv3 [16] detection system runs a single convolutional network on the image, and the threshold of the obtained detection is dealt by the confidence of the model. The detection is quite quick and the process is simple. YOLOv3 can utilize the full map information in the training and prediction process. Compared to Fast R-CNN [4], the YOLOv3 background prediction error rate is half lower.

With the application of convolutional neural networks (CNN) [18] to image segmentation, there has been increasing interest in background pixel annotation using CNN with dense output, such as F-CNN [26], deconvolution neural network [15], encoder decoder SegNet [1], and so on. DilatedResNet [24] and PPM [25] have made great progress in the field of background segmentation. Compared with other CNN-based methods, this method has higher applicability and stable performance.

2.3 Loss Functions for Embedding

Hermans *et al.* [7] demonstrated that the use of triplet-based losses to perform end-to-end depth metric learning is effective for person Re-ID tasks. Kanac [8] proposed a similar method for vehicle embedding based on the training model of vehicle model classification. Cross entropy loss ensures separability of features, but these features may not be distinguishable enough to separate identities that are unseen in the training data. Some recent works [17,19,22] combined the classification loss through metric learning. Kumar *et al.* [9] conducted an in-depth analysis of the vehicle triplet embeddings, extensively evaluated the loss function, and proved that the use of triplet embeddings is effective.

3 Approach

Since there is no background segmentation dataset specially designed for vehicle segmentation, we first explain how we use the target detection algorithm to construct the dataset and then we introduce the BIR module and the overall framework.

3.1 Constructing Vehicle Background Segmentation Dataset

Given the powerful performance and good stability of Yolov3, we use Yolov3 as a target detection tool. The Cityscapes dataset is powered by Mercedes-Benz and provides image segmentation annotations. Cityscapes contains 50 scenes of different views, different backgrounds and different seasons. Because they are high definition images and most of them are street view pictures, this dataset image is suitable for further cropping as a vehicle background segmentation dataset.

When adopting Yolov3 for vehicle detection, we ignore the detected vehicle images smaller than 256×256 because the small images are unclear and affect the segmentation effect. And we generated the small dataset named Cityscapes-vehicle (CS-vehicle for short) which contains cropped 2,686 vehicle images and only vehicle segmentation annotations as well as two labels (the vehicle and the background), as shown in Fig. 2

However, CS-vehicle has rather less images, so we construct a large vehicle background segmentation dataset named Vehicle-Segmentation to train the vehicle background segmentation model. The Vehicle-Segmentation contains a total

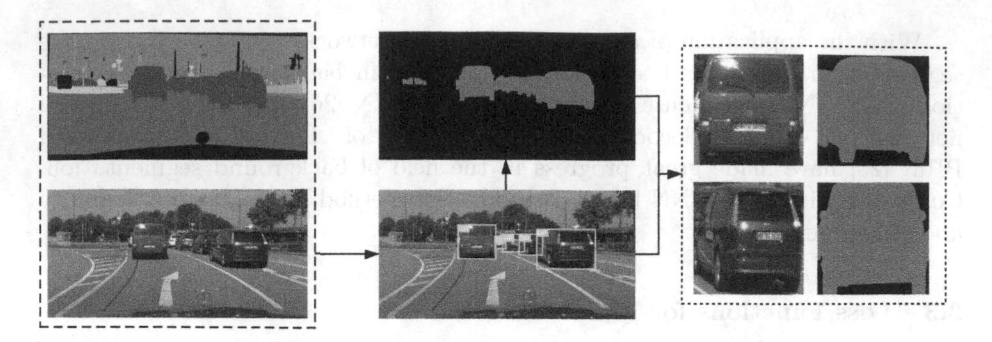

Fig. 2. Generating CS-vehicle. On the left is the Cityscapes dataset. We use yolov3 on this dataset to detect the vehicles (middle), remove the detected vehicles with less than 256×256, and then generate the images we need (right).

of 27,896 images: 2,686 vehicle images from CS-Vehicle, 5,000 street view images from Cityscapes and 20,210 all kinds of scenes images from ADE20K [27]. Using Cityscapes and ADE20K are aimed to extract more semantic features, while using CS-Vehicle can make our model pay more attention on vehicle segmentation. All of the annotated images in Vehicle-Segmentation have a resolution greater than 256*256, which is very suitable for background segmentation tasks in vehicle Re-ID.

3.2 Vehicle Re-ID with Background Inteference Removal

In this section, we introduce a vehicle Re-ID framework with background interference removal (BIR) as illustrated in Fig. 3. Our framework consists of three components, a background segmentation module to remove background interference, a random selection module to enhance robustness and a CNN-Loss module to achieve Re-Id tasks. We will explain the details of the three main components in this section.

Background Segmentation. Based on the original semantic segmentation method, we find that the background segmentation results are unsatisfying, which affects the vehicle Re-ID accuracy seriously when directly used to train the Re-ID network. This is due to the presence of uncomplete segmented vehicle bodies with holes and interference factors such as labels, license plates, and faces. Therefore, we propose a post processing method for more accurate background segmentation. We use the DilatedResNet-50 network as the encoder and the PPM network as the decoder for the initial scene segmentation to generate the intermediate segmentation results. Then we combine the edge detection results with intermediate segmentation results, and we further process them with our post processing method. First, the flood water filling algorithm are used to fill the holes; second, we detect the number of connected regions in the binary image and mark each connected domain, leaving only the largest connected domain;

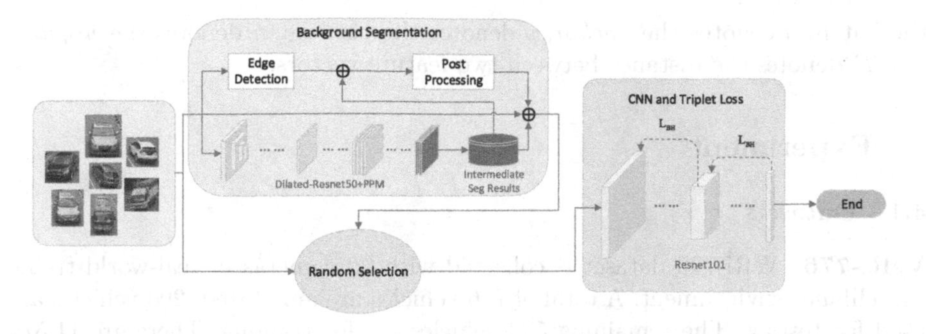

Fig. 3. Structure of the Vehicle Re-ID with background interference removal (BIR), which is composed of three components. Background segmentation, random selection, CNN and loss function.

finally, we discard those segmented images in which the car contains a pixel area smaller than 0.60 of the overall picture area.

Random Selection. Considering the fact that vehicle background segmentation effect is not perfect, we design a random selection module in our framework. All images has a probability of k ($k \in [1]$) to be selected to use their images with background segmentation. These segmentation images, together with other $1-k$ ratio original images, are put into CNN to train the Re-ID module.

By using this random selection module, we reduce the risk of imperfect segmentation results and increase the diversity of vehicle images. This further encourages the model to extract more discriminative features from vehicle body areas and improve the generalization ability.

Loss Function. The training images are first fed into a CNN backbone to produce feature vectors. In view of the excellent characteristics of batch hard triplet loss in the field of person Re-ID, we use it for vehicle re-identification.

To reduce the number of triples, the authors [7] construct a data batch by randomly sampling P identities and then randomly sampling K images for each identity, thus resulting in a batch size of PK images. For each sample in the batch, the most difficult positive sample and the most difficult negative sample in this batch are selected when forming the triplet for calculating the loss, as shown in Eq. 1.

$$\begin{aligned}\mathcal{L}_{BH}(\theta) = \sum_{i=1}^{P}\sum_{a=1}^{K}[&\max_{p=1\ldots K} D(f_\theta(x_i^a), f_\theta(x_i^p)) - \\ &\min_{\substack{n=1\ldots K\\ j=1\ldots P\\ j\neq i}} D(f_\theta(x_i^a), f_\theta(x_j^n)) + m]_+\end{aligned} \tag{1}$$

where θ is the parameter that model learns in deep neural network, f_θ is the feature vector of image, x_i^j corresponds to the j-th image of the i-th vehicle in the batch. a denotes the *anchor*, p denotes the *positive*, n denotes the *negative* and D denotes the distance between two feature vectors.

4 Experiment

4.1 Datasets

VeRi-776. VeRi-776 dataset is collected with 20 cameras in real-world traffic surveillance environment. A total of 776 vehicles are annotated. 200 vehicles are used for testing. The remaining 576 vehicles are for training. There are 11,579 images in the test set, and 37,778 images in the training set.

VehicleID. VehicleID dataset is captured by multiple surveillance cameras and there are 221,763 images of 26,267 vehicles in total (8.44 images/vehicle in average). This dataset is split into two parts for model training and testing. The first part contains 110,178 images of 13,134 vehicles and 47,558 images have been labeled with vehicle model information. The second part contains 111,585 images of 13,133 vehicles and 42,638 images have been labeled with vehicle model information. This dataset extracts three subsets, *i.e.* small, medium and large, ordered by their size from the original testing data for vehicle retrieval and vehicle Re-ID tasks.

4.2 Implementation Details

We use the ResNet-101 architecture and the pre-trained weights provided by He *et al.* [6]. In a mini-batch, we randomly select 18 vehicles and for each vehicle, we randomly select 4 images, thus the batch size is 72. We run 300 epochs with a base learning rate 2×10^{-4}. The input image size is set to 256×256. We use two GTX 2080ti GPUs for training.

4.3 Performance Evaluation

In this section, we show the effect of background segmentation, experiment results of BIR and comparisons with state-of-the-art methods. The baseline model involves no segmentation. The evaluation is conducted in four steps:

- *Seg* first trains the model only using the dataset processed by the Dilated-Resnet50+PPM module.
- *Seg+Post* further adds the post processing to the background removal module then uses the new dataset to train vehicle Re-ID model.
- *TrainS+TestN* uses the training dataset that processed by *Seg+Post* as new training dataset and uses original image without any processing as test dataset.
- *Random-k* randomly uses k percent images processed by *Seg+Post* and others original images for both training and test to evaluate the vehicle Re-ID model.

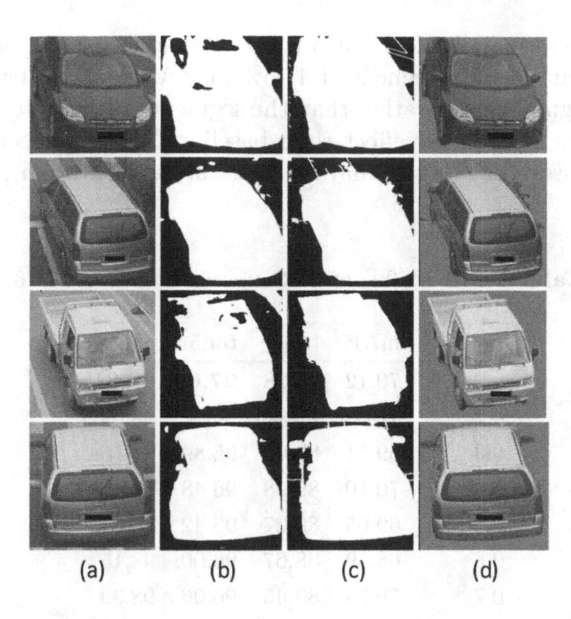

Fig. 4. The vehicle segmentation results. (a) original image, (b) intermediate segmentation results, (c) our background removal results, (d) final results.

Effect of Background Segmentation. The vehicle background removal results are shown in Fig. 4. It is obvious that our background removal results are better than preliminary results. We show the improvements gained by improving background removal methods and the experimental results on VeRi-776 are summarized in Table 1. We found that the results of *Seg* have not been improved, but have been reduced. We believe that the segmentation effect is not good. It can be seen that the effect of *Seg+Post* is significantly improved. Therefore, background removal is effective for the vehicle to identify. *TrainS+TestN* shows the effectiveness of background interference removal.

Table 1. Results(%) of ablation experiment on VeRi-776

Method	mAP	top1	top5	top10
Seg	57.53	81.70	82.01	94.76
Seg+Post	64.79	86.89	95.47	97.85
TrainS+TestN	66.08	86.89	94.87	97.14
Baseline	65.78	86.29	94.76	96.96

Experiment Result of BIR. In this section, we experimentally verify the impact of the parameter k on the performance and determine the best one accordingly. As shown in Table 2, when the k is equal to 0.2, the effect is best. It exhibits a substantial improvement of 4.96% in mAP over the baseline method that uses the original images rather than the segmented images to train and test. All of our results have better effect than baseline. But the effect is not significant as k increases. The reason may be that the segmentation performance is not perfect.

Table 2. Results(%) of BIR experiment on VeRi-776

k	mAP	top1	top5	top10
0.1	70.12	90.28	**97.08**	**98.81**
0.2	**70.74**	**90.46**	96.96	98.69
0.3	69.61	89.03	95.89	98.15
0.4	70.10	89.98	96.48	98.15
0.5	69.65	89.27	96.42	98.51
0.6	68.59	88.67	96.00	98.15
0.7	70.34	89.45	96.06	98.39
0.8	67.69	88.73	95.59	97.79
0.9	67.22	87.72	95.89	97.79
Baseline	65.78	86.29	94.76	96.96

Comparisons with State-of-the-art Methods. As shown in Table 3, our vehicle Re-ID framework with BIR outperforms state-of-the-art methods and compared baselines, which demonstrates the effectiveness of our overall framework and individual components. Compared with *FDA-net* [14], BIR has a gain of 15% in terms of mAP and 6% in terms of top-1 accuracy. Such a performance increase shows that the batch hard triplet loss does provide vital priors for robustly estimating the vehicle similarities. Compared with *MOV1+BH* [9] only, BIR also has a 5.6% increase in terms of mAP. This is because that the our method eliminates background interference information. It strongly proves that background segmentation is of great significance in vehicle Re-ID.

Although BIR only uses visual information, our final approach also has a 17% and 12% increase in terms of mAP, as compared with Siamese-CNN+path-LSTM [20] and AFL+CNN [23], which also use spatio-temporal information. It proves that making full use of image information can improve accuracy. Compared with the *VAMI* [28] and *RAM* [11], BIR is not complicated and we don't have to pick a dataset image and our method has a 9% mAP gain

It should be noted that, BIR does not use local information features, nor does it add spatio-temporal information, and only considers the global feature, and the performance is greatly improved. This shows that the background of the picture has a great interference to vehicle Re-ID and removing the background is of great significance for vehicle Re-ID.

Table 3. Comparisons (%) with State-of-the-art Re-ID methods on VeRi-776 and VehicleID

Dataset	VeRi		VehicleID					
Method	All		Small		Medium		Large	
	mAP	top1	mAP	top1	mAP	top1	mAP	top1
MOV1+BH [9]	65.10	87.30	83.34	**77.90**	78.72	72.14	**75.02**	67.56
RAM [11]	61.50	88.60	-	75.20	-	72.30	-	**67.70**
FDA-Net [14]	55.49	84.27	-	-	65.33	59.84	61.84	55.53
Siamese-CNN+path-LSTM [19]	58.27	83.94	-	-	-	-	-	-
AFL+CNN [23]	53.35	82.06	-	-	-	-	-	-
VAMI [28]	61.32	85.92	-	63.12	-	52.87	-	47.34
Our Method	**70.74**	**90.46**	**85.46**	77.17	**84.41**	**75.81**	74.13	63.71

4.4 Discussion

Our proposed BIR is suitable for pictures taken under different cameras across large spatial-temporal span. During the experiment, we find that background removal results for white vehicles are better than that for black vehicles, because the road is mostly dark gray, thus black vehicles are more difficult to segment. We will consider this effect in the background removal, and optimize to generate a more widely used algorithm in the future work.

5 Conclusion

In this paper, we proposed a new vehicle Re-ID framework with background interference removal to improve the generalization ability over large spatio-temporal span. Due to the absence of vehicle background segmentation datasets, we construct a vehicle background segmentation dataset based on Cityscapes, and then use this dataset for the training of vehicle background segmentation models. In the later stage of segmentation, we use the traditional image operation to post-process the segmentation results, and generate a vehicle image with better background removal. We use proposed BIR for the Re-ID task, and the vehicle Re-ID accuracy is significantly improved, outperforming state-of-the-art vehicle Re-ID algorithms. It should also be noted that different from existing methods, which either introduced local visual information or spatio-temporal information, the proposed scheme uses only the global visual information of vehicles, which can be easily integrated with these algorithms to further enhance the vehicle Re-ID accuracy.

Acknowledgments. This work was partially supported by the National Natural Science Foundation of China (No. 61772054), and the NSFC Key Project (No. 61632001) and the Fundamental Research Funds for the Central Universities.

References

1. Badrinarayanan, V., Kendall, A., Cipolla, R.: Segnet: a deep convolutional encoder-decoder architecture for image segmentation. IEEE Trans. Pattern Anal. Mach. Intell. **39**(12), 2481–2495 (2017)
2. Cordts, M., et al.: The cityscapes dataset for semantic urban scene understanding. In: Proceedings of the IEEE Conference on Computer Vision and Pattern Recognition, pp. 3213–3223 (2016)
3. Dean, T., Ruzon, M.A., Segal, M., Shlens, J., Vijayanarasimhan, S., Yagnik, J.: Fast, accurate detection of 100,000 object classes on a single machine. In: Proceedings of the IEEE Conference on Computer Vision and Pattern Recognition, pp. 1814–1821 (2013)
4. Girshick, R.: Fast r-cnn. In: Proceedings of the IEEE International Conference on Computer Vision, pp. 1440–1448 (2015)
5. Girshick, R., Donahue, J., Darrell, T., Malik, J.: Rich feature hierarchies for accurate object detection and semantic segmentation. In: Proceedings of the IEEE Conference on Computer Vision and Pattern Recognition, pp. 580–587 (2014)
6. He, K., Zhang, X., Ren, S., Sun, J.: Deep residual learning for image recognition. In: Proceedings of the IEEE International Conference on Computer Vision, pp. 770–778 (2016)
7. Hermans, A., Beyer, L., Leibe, B.: In defense of the triplet loss for person re-identification. arXiv preprint arXiv:1703.07737 (2017)
8. Kanacı, A., Zhu, X., Gong, S.: Vehicle reidentification by fine-grained cross-level deep learning. In: BMVC AMMDS Workshop, vol. 2, pp. 772–788 (2017)
9. Kumar, R., Weill, E., Aghdasi, F., Sriram, P.: Vehicle re-identification: an efficient baseline using triplet embedding. arXiv preprint arXiv:1901.01015 (2019)
10. Liu, H., Tian, Y., Yang, Y., Pang, L., Huang, T.: Deep relative distance learning: tell the difference between similar vehicles. In: Proceedings of the IEEE Conference on Computer Vision and Pattern Recognition, pp. 2167–2175 (2016)
11. Liu, X., Zhang, S., Huang, Q., Gao, W.: Ram: a region-aware deep model for vehicle re-identification. In: 2018 IEEE International Conference on Multimedia and Expo, pp. 1–6. IEEE (2018)
12. Liu, X., Liu, W., Ma, H., Fu, H.: Large-scale vehicle re-identification in urban surveillance videos. In: 2016 IEEE International Conference on Multimedia and Expo (ICME)', pp. 1–6. IEEE (2016)
13. Liu, X., Liu, W., Mei, T., Ma, H.: A deep learning-based approach to progressive vehicle re-identification for urban surveillance. In: Leibe, B., Matas, J., Sebe, N., Welling, M. (eds.) ECCV 2016. LNCS, vol. 9906, pp. 869–884. Springer, Cham (2016). https://doi.org/10.1007/978-3-319-46475-6_53
14. Lou, Y., Bai, Y., Liu, J., Wang, S., Duan, L.: Veri-wild: a large dataset and a new method for vehicle re-identification in the wild. In: Proceedings of the IEEE Conference on Computer Vision and Pattern Recognition, pp. 3235–3243 (2019)
15. Noh, H., Hong, S., Han, B.: Learning deconvolution network for semantic segmentation. In: Proceedings of the IEEE International Conference on Computer Vision, pp. 1520–1528 (2015)
16. Redmon, J., Farhadi, A.: Yolov3: An incremental improvement. arXiv preprint arXiv:1804.02767 (2018)
17. Rippel, O., Paluri, M., Dollar, P., Bourdev, L.: Metric learning with adaptive density discrimination. arXiv preprint arXiv:1511.05939 (2015)

18. Sharif Razavian, A., Azizpour, H., Sullivan, J., Carlsson, S.: Cnn features off-the-shelf: an astounding baseline for recognition. In: Proceedings of the IEEE Conference on Computer Vision and Pattern Recognition Workshops, pp. 806–813 (2014)
19. Shen, L., Lin, Z., Huang, Q.: Relay backpropagation for effective learning of deep convolutional neural networks. In: Leibe, B., Matas, J., Sebe, N., Welling, M. (eds.) ECCV 2016. LNCS, vol. 9911, pp. 467–482. Springer, Cham (2016). https://doi.org/10.1007/978-3-319-46478-7_29
20. Shen, Y., Xiao, T., Li, H., Yi, S., Wang, X.: Learning deep neural networks for vehicle re-id with visual-spatio-temporal path proposals. In: Proceedings of the IEEE International Conference on Computer Vision, pp. 1900–1909 (2017)
21. Wang, Z., et al.: Orientation invariant feature embedding and spatial temporal regularization for vehicle re-identification. In: Proceedings of the IEEE International Conference on Computer Vision, pp. 379–387 (2017)
22. Wojke, N., Bewley, A.: Deep cosine metric learning for person re-identification. In: 2018 IEEE Winter Conference on Applications of Computer Vision, pp. 748–756. IEEE (2018)
23. Wu, C.W., Liu, C.T., Chiang, C.E., Tu, W.C., Chien, S.Y.: Vehicle re-identification with the space-time prior. In: Proceedings of the IEEE Conference on Computer Vision and Pattern Recognition Workshops, pp. 121–128 (2018)
24. Yu, F., Koltun, V.: Multi-scale context aggregation by dilated convolutions. arXiv preprint arXiv:1511.07122 (2015)
25. Zhao, H., Shi, J., Qi, X., Wang, X., Jia, J.: Pyramid scene parsing network. In: Proceedings of the IEEE Conference on Computer Vision and Pattern Recognition, pp. 2881–2890 (2017)
26. Zhao, W., et al.: F-cnn: an fpga-based framework for training convolutional neural networks. In: 2016 IEEE 27th International Conference on Application-specific Systems, Architectures and Processors, pp. 107–114. IEEE (2016)
27. Zhou, B., Zhao, H., Puig, X., Fidler, S., Barriuso, A., Torralba, A.: Scene parsing through ade20k dataset. In: Proceedings of the IEEE Conference on Computer Vision and Pattern Recognition, pp. 633–641 (2017)
28. Zhou, Y., Shao, L.: Aware attentive multi-view inference for vehicle re-identification. In: Proceedings of the IEEE Conference on Computer Vision and Pattern Recognition, pp. 6489–6498 (2018)

Face Tells Detailed Expression: Generating Comprehensive Facial Expression Sentence Through Facial Action Units

Joanna Hong[1], Hong Joo Lee[1], Yelin Kim[2], and Yong Man Ro[1(✉)]

[1] Image and Video Systems Laboratory, School of Electrical Engineering, KAIST, Daejeon, South Korea
{joanna2587,dlghdwn008,ymro}@kaist.ac.kr
[2] Amazon Lab126, Sunnyvale, CA, USA
kimyelin@amazon.com

Abstract. Human facial expression plays the key role in the understanding of the social behavior. Many deep learning approaches present facial emotion recognition and automatic image captioning considering human sentiments. However, most current deep learning models for facial expression analysis do not contain comprehensive, detailed information of a single face. In this paper, we newly introduce a text-based facial expression description using several essential components describing comprehensive facial expression: gender, facial action units, and corresponding intensities. Then, we propose comprehensive facial expression sentence generating model along with facial expression recognition model for a single facial image to verify the effectiveness of our text-based dataset. Experimental results show that the proposed two models are supporting each other improving their performances: the text-based facial expression description provides comprehensive semantic information to the facial emotion recognition model. Also, the visual information from the emotion recognition model guides the facial expression sentence generation to produce a proper sentence describing comprehensive description. The text-based dataset is available at https://github.com/joannahong/Text-based-dataset-with-comprehensive-facial-expression-sentence.

Keywords: Facial action unit based · Facial expression sentence generation · Explaining expression from a single face image · Deep learning

1 Introduction

Facial expression recognition, as one of the most important factors for human beings to interpret their emotions and intensions in communication, plays the key role in the understanding of the social behavior. Containing a vast range of information and carrying emotional meaning, facial expressions become one

Y. M. Ro et al. (Eds.): MMM 2020, LNCS 11962, pp. 100–111, 2020.
https://doi.org/10.1007/978-3-030-37734-2_9

of the main information channels in interpersonal communication [8]. Because of their importance, facial expressions recognition has been widely studied in the field of computer vision [7,14,19,20]. These studies make a computer better understand human emotions and interact more naturally with human.

Recently, many deep learning based facial emotion recognition models have been proposed [7,14,19]. Among deep models, deep convolution neural networks (CNNs) have achieved the state-of-the-art performances. Tang [14] introduced the emotion recognition model using CNNs and linear support vector machines. Kau et al. [7] used CNNs extracting visual features with audio features to detect faces areas and remove irrelevant noises. While these approaches achieve great performances in recognizing facial emotions, they only predict certain emotion class with a discrete sense. The facial expressions reflect not only emotions, but also cognitive processes, social interaction, and physiological signals, so directly mapping facial expressions towards discrete class of emotions possibly becomes ill-posed problem [5]. Therefore, it is necessary to describe comprehensive facial expression as a further analysis of the emotion classification.

One way of describing visual information in a comprehensive aspect is to use a descriptive language. Explaining the content of an image using properly formed sentences helps people better understand the content of images. Regarding as the core of image understanding, automatic image caption generation has been widely studied [16,18]. However, the generated captions are mostly reflected only in the factual aspects of an image. A few deep learning-based models have incorporated non-factual information such as sentiment into image captions to describe facial expressions. Nezami et al. [11] introduced automatic image captioning incorporating with emotional contents. This model only considered sentiments in terms of neutral, positive, and negative aspects. More comprehensive descriptions showing face expression (e.g. facial AUs) changes are yet to be provided in the facial expression sentence generation.

To solve the aforementioned problems, this paper introduces a novel dataset, namely text-based facial expression description, that includes additional comprehensive text-based descriptions on the existing facial expression datasets. The dataset is built based on the peak facial expression frames from the public video facial datasets [9,10,12]. To generate description sentences, we use facial action units (AUs), which describe the basic emotions [3] in a comprehensive manner, from the facial action coding system (FACS) [4] with their intensities. These description sentences include three types of information: gender, facial AUs, and the following intensities. To effectively describe a facial expression on each image, we make the sentence with random grammatical order and random word choice in a given condition.

Based on our proposed dataset, we develop a comprehensive facial expression sentence generating model along with facial expression recognition model for a single facial image. This architecture is composed of two deep learning models: facial expression sentence generation (FES) model and facial emotion recognition (FER) model. The FES model consists of visual feature encoder and sentence generator. This model automatically produces a sentence that describes the given input facial expression image. The FER model receives the semantic information (i.e. output features from the sentence generator) and the visual information (i.e. visual features from the visual feature encoder) from the sentence generation model. With those information, the FER model predicts a facial emotion. As a result, it employs the comprehensive information in recognizing the emotion. Two models have in common that they contain the visual and semantic features; thus, they are mutually beneficial by helping each other to improve their performances. The main contributions of this paper are the following:

1. We introduce a new dataset that describes comprehensive human facial expressions of facial images using natural language description. The text-based facial expression description dataset is generated based on the three categories: gender, facial AUs, and the following intensities.
2. We propose the FES model with the FER model, describing human face expression with facial AUs and the corresponding intensities. We also show that both models have high correlation and are mutually advantageous. To the best of our knowledge, this is the first study to use facial AUs and intensities for describing facial expressions.

2 Facial Expression Description Modeling

2.1 Comprehensive Facial Expression

To deliver the comprehensive information on facial expression of image, we utilize three useful categories: a gender, facial AUs, and their intensities of a single facial image. A gender demonstrates the fundamental information of a single face. Facial AUs are essential to decode human facial expressions. They show the significance of different facial regions for each expression. Using facial AUs, we are able to consider the face parts with the highest diagnostic value for expression identification [17]. Also, with corresponding intensities, deeper analysis on each facial AU could be adapted.

2.2 Building Text-Based Dataset with Comprehensive Facial Expression Sentence

We introduce a text-based facial expression description dataset for analysis of facial expression. The dataset is built to express a facial image with comprehensive aspects: gender, facial AUs, and following intensities. Firstly, we select the video frames with relatively high facial AU intensities and use it as a peak facial expression frame of videos and crop the image frames where the faces are centered. Then we utilize the facial AUs with their intensities, and generate the corresponding sentences. Thus, the generated sentences are basically a combination of three categories: gender (0: male, 1: female), facial AUs, and intensity (1 to 5) of each AU so that each peak image frame well describes a facial expression. Figure 1(a) shows an example of the combination set of categories. The direct emotion information is not given so that the facial expression sentence generator focuses on the comprehensive facial expression description.

Peak frame	Gender	Action Unit	Intensity
	0	6	3
		12	5
		25	5
		26	2

(a) Example of three categories for text-based dataset generation with peak image frame.

Text-based dataset modeling	A [Gender]'s [AU subject] is/are [AU intensity] [AU description], [Gender(pronoun)] ... interchangeable
Example	Ex) A man's cheek is quite lifted, his lip corner is highly stretched, his lip is separated strongly, and his jaw is lightly dropped.

(b) Text-based dataset generation rule and example sentence.

Action Unit	Description	AU subject	AU description 1	AU description 2
6	Cheek Raiser	cheek	raised	lifted
12	Lip Corner Puller	lip corner	pulled	stretched
25	Lips Part	lips	parted	separated
26	Jaw Drop	jaw	dropped	fallen

(c) Facial action units description for example facial image.

1	2	3	4	5
marginally	slightly	kind of	positively	strongly
insignificantly	lightly	fairly	reasonably	highly
very slightly	somewhat	quite	sensibly	significantly

(d) Facial action unit intensities description. Each intensity is described as three different words with equivalent meaning.

Fig. 1. Example of text-based dataset with comprehensive facial expression sentence. (a) A sample peak image frame with gender, facial AUs, and intensities for text-based dataset generation, (b) text-based dataset generation rule and example sentence, (c) the facial action units (AUs) description for example facial image, and (d) description for facial action unit intensities with three different words of equivalent meanings.

In order to generalize the text-based dataset, we design a number of candidates in terms of word choice and grammatical sense. Firstly, we collect all facial AUs descriptions from FACS [4] and divide each description into a subject and a describing word which we refer to as AU subject and AU description, respectively. To avoid bias during training, we add multiple AU descriptions that have equivalent meanings besides the word used in the description in FACS. Figure 1(c) shows the facial AUs description for an example facial image. Next, AU intensities corresponding to the facial AUs are set to be the range of 1 to 5, where 1 means that the facial AU is very slightly activated and 5 is that the facial AU is very largely appeared. We also bring three words of equivalent meanings that describe the intensity range for maintaining diversity (Fig. 1(d)). With all categories set, the text-based dataset is automatically built based on the rule shown in Fig. 3(b). In order to maintain diversity of the dataset, we build multiple sentences per each facial image with random choice among words of equivalent meanings. Also, the order of AU combination can change while obeying grammatical rule. This facial expression description modeling is applicable for existing facial datasets containing facial AUs and following intensities. We utilize CK+ [9], DISFA+ [10], and MMI [12] datasets to build the text-based facial expression dataset. Detailed explanation will be shown in Sect. 4.

3 Automatic Generation of Comprehensive Facial Expression Description

3.1 Overview of Facial Expression Description Framework

With the text-based facial expression dataset, we propose a method for automatically describing comprehensive facial expression, shown in Fig. 2. The proposed framework consists of two models: FES model and FER model.

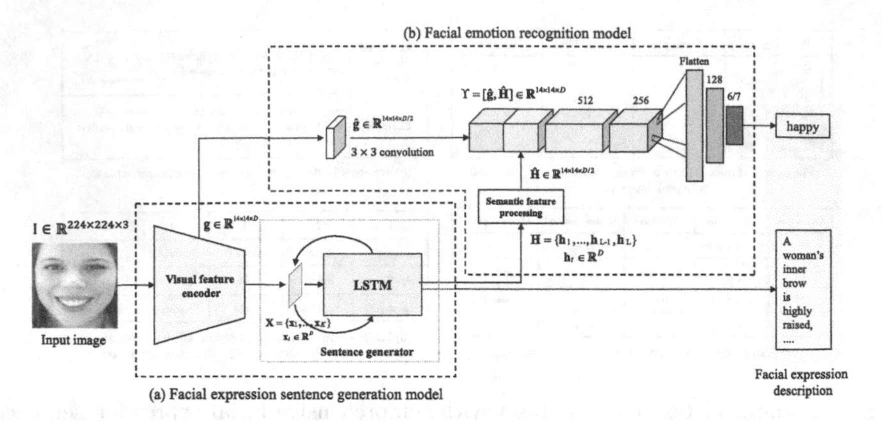

Fig. 2. The overall proposed deep network for comprehensive facial expression description, composed of two models: (a) facial expression sentence generation (FES) model through facial action units and (b) facial emotion recognition (FER) model.

Figure 2(a) shows the proposed FES model. It consists of visual feature encoder and sentence generator. The model is trained to generate a facial expression sentence describing an input facial expression image using the text-based dataset based on facial AUs. During evaluation, the model automatically generates a sentence containing comprehensive expression information, e.g. the facial AUs, without any guided facial expression information. The input of the FES is $\mathrm{I} \in \mathbb{R}^{224\times224\times3}$, and it is encoded through visual feature encoder and sentence generator. The model produces visual features $\mathbf{g}$ and semantic features $\mathbf{H}$. Figure 2(b) shows the FER model. This model receives both visual and semantic features from the facial expression sentence generator. Using both the visual and the semantic information, the model predicts a facial emotion. Detailed explanation for the overall architecture is described in the following sections.

3.2 Facial Expression Sentence Generation

In this section, we describe our proposed FES model (Fig. 2(a)). The input facial image I is encoded through the visual feature encoder. The visual feature encoder extracts D-dimensional facial features, $\mathbf{X} = \{\mathbf{x}_1, ..., \mathbf{x}_{K-1}, \mathbf{x}_K\}$, $\mathbf{x}_i \in \mathbb{R}^D$, where K denotes the length of the output vector. The facial feature is obtained from the lower convolutional layer (i.e. fifth convolution layer before max-pooling) to match with the portions of the input facial image.

The sentence generator receives the facial feature X and generates facial expression sentence containing L words, $\mathbf{Y} = \{\mathbf{y}_1, ..., \mathbf{y}_{L-1}, \mathbf{y}_L\}$, $\mathbf{y}_i \in \mathbb{R}^N$, where N is number of vocabulary. As shown in Fig. 3(a), we utilize soft LSTM [11], and the soft LSTM produces a facial expression sentence by generating facial expression word at each time step (t), conditioned on previously embedded word $(\mathbf{s}_{t-1})$, previous hidden state vector $(\mathbf{h}_{t-1})$ and facial information vector $(\mathbf{q}_t)$.

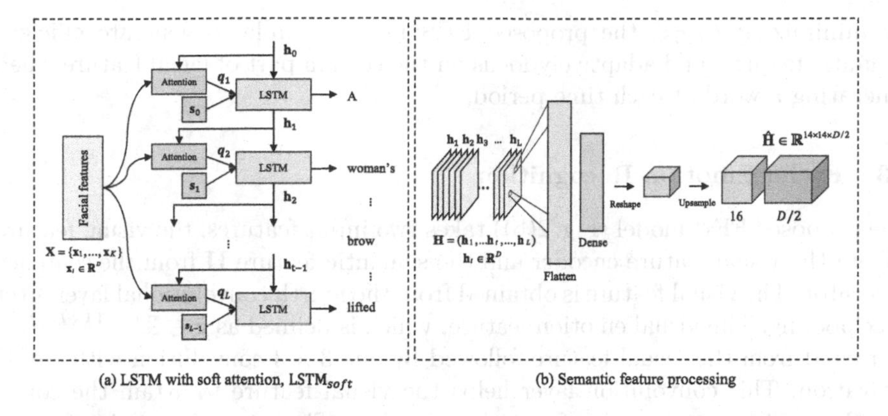

Fig. 3. The detailed explanation of the architecture: (a) the recurrent neural network, LSTM with soft attention and (b) the semantic feature processing module.

Each cell of LSTM_{soft} can be written as

$$\mathbf{h}_t = \mathrm{LSTM}_{soft}(\mathbf{h}_{t-1}, \mathbf{s}_{t-1}, \mathbf{q}_t). \tag{1}$$

Also, the embedded facial expression word $\mathbf{s}_t$ is computed as,

$$\mathbf{s}_t = \mathbf{W}_{embed}\mathbf{y}_t^*,\ t \in (0, ..., L-1). \tag{2}$$

$\mathbf{W}_{embed}$ is the learnable embedding matrix, $\mathbf{W}_{embed} \in \mathbb{R}^{N \times M}$, where M is the embedding dimensionality. Here, $\mathbf{y}_t^*$ is a ground truth of facial expression word during training, where $\mathbf{y}_t^* \in \mathbb{R}^N$, and it becomes $\mathbf{y}_t$ during evaluation. The facial information vector $\mathbf{q}_t$ is generated through the soft attention module, $f_{attention}$. This module helps the network selectively activate a specific facial part (e.g. facial AUs) corresponding to a facial expression word. Each layer of LSTM_{soft} focuses on the certain part of the input facial image when generating the output word at each time.

$$att_{t.i} = \mathrm{softmax}(f_{attention}(\mathbf{x}_i, \mathbf{h}_{t-1})), \tag{3}$$

$$\mathbf{q}_t = \sum_{i-1}^{K} att_{t,i}\mathbf{x}_i. \tag{4}$$

Thus, the facial information vector is basically the facial feature weighted on attention module after taking softmax at each time period t.

The initial input states of the LSTM, i.e. the memory state and the hidden state, are initialized as the reduced mean of the input image feature vector $\mathbf{x}_i$. Then, they are fed through multilayer perceptrons. The model is then trained to minimize the sum of the negative log likelihood of the correct facial expression word at each step:

$$L_{FES} = -\sum_{t=1}^{L} \log p(\mathbf{y}_t|\mathbf{X}) + \beta \sum_{i=1}^{K}(1 - \sum_{t=1}^{L} att_{ti})^2. \tag{5}$$

By minimizing L_{FES}, the proposed FES model is able to generate efficient semantic features and adaptively focus on the certain part of facial feature when generating a word at each time period.

3.3 Facial Emotion Recognition

The proposed FER model (Fig. 2(b)) takes two input features: the visual feature $\mathbf{g}$ from the visual feature encoder and the semantic feature $\mathbf{H}$ from the sentence generator. The visual feature is obtained from the fourth convolutional layer after max-pooling. The visual emotion feature, which is defined as $\hat{\mathbf{g}} \in \mathbb{R}^{14\times 14\times D/2}$, is extracted from the visual feature followed by one 3×3 convolution with ReLU activation. This convolution layer helps the visual feature to attain the correspondence of feature domain of two input features. The semantic emotion feature matrix is obtained through semantic feature processing, shown in Fig. 3(b). This process is implemented so that the semantic features are efficiently encoded in keeping with their facial information (e.g. facial AUs) thoroughly. In the semantic feature processing, the semantic feature vector is extracted from the output hidden state vector of each LSTM cell at every time step t. The semantic feature vector can be written as

$$\mathbf{H} = \{\mathbf{h}_1, ...\mathbf{h}_t, ..., \mathbf{h}_L\},\ \mathbf{h}_t \in \mathbb{R}^D.$$

Then, the stacked output hidden state vectors, $\mathbf{H} \in \mathbb{R}^{L\times D}$, is flattened and sent to one fully connected layer. The output vector from the dense layer is mapped into 2-dimensionality in order to obtain the correspondence of the visual feature $\hat{\mathbf{g}}$. It is encoded through one 2-dimensional upsampling layer with size 2×2 and two 3×3 convolutions with ReLU activation function. This results the final output sementic emotion feature, $\hat{\mathbf{H}} \in \mathbb{R}^{14\times 14\times D/2}$. As a result, the visual feature and the semantic feature are encoded to adapt both feature domain while maintaining their information. After obtaining both features from two different domains, these features are combined into visual-semantic feature, $\Upsilon = [\hat{\mathbf{g}}, \hat{\mathbf{H}}] \in \mathbb{R}^{14\times 14\times D}$, which is concatenated along with the channel dimension. The combined visual-semantic feature is encoded through the convolution layers and the fully-connected layers. Then it predicts a facial emotion. The proposed FER model is trained by minimizing the following loss,

$$L_{FER} = -\log P(c|\Upsilon), \tag{6}$$

where c is an emotion label of an input facial image.

Thus, the total loss, L_{total}, is to be minimized in order to generate a reasonable facial expression sentence and classify a correct facial emotion. The objective function can be written as

$$\begin{aligned} L_{total} &= -\lambda_1[\sum_{t=1}^{L} \log p(\mathbf{y}_t|\mathbf{X}) + \beta \sum_{i=1}^{K} (1 - \sum_{t=1}^{L} att_{ti})^2] - \lambda_2 \log P(c|\Upsilon) \\ &= \lambda_1 L_{FES} + \lambda_2 L_{FER}, \end{aligned} \tag{7}$$

where λ_1 and λ_2 are hyper-parameters controlling the relative importance of the FES loss and the FER loss. The overall loss is trained to minimize L_{total}. As the total loss gets minimized, it is expected that both updated visual features and semantic features help our proposed multi-modal architecture to obtain comprehensive information, thus mutually improving performances of both models.

4 Experiment

4.1 Dataset

Our proposed text-based facial expression description dataset includes image frames and facial AU with intensities. We used three public datasets to generate our proposed dataset and modified them fit to train our proposed model.

CK+. This dataset contains 123 subjects with seven emotions: anger, contempt, disgust, fear, happy, sad, and surprise. There were only 327 peak frames containing highest intensities with both emotions and facial action units, so 10-fold cross-validation was adopted to generalize the performance. If intensities of the facial AUs were not listed, we compared all images and assigned the relative intensity corresponding to each facial AU. Five randomly augmented sentences for each image were built.

DISFA+. This dataset consists of six emotions, the same as those of the CK+ except for contempt, and 9 subjects. The total of 1,940 images contains both facial AUs and intensities, but only 858 images have emotion data. For images without emotion, we trained them through the well-known emotion recognition network using CNN [19] with those with emotions and tested with those without emotion. Then, we checked the emotion evaluated dataset through human subjective evaluation to maintain authenticity. Three text-based datasets per each image were built. The dataset was trained with 9-fold cross-validation.

MMI. Since there were only 9 videos containing all emotions, facial AUs, and intensities, we chose video frames with only facial AUs and intensities, total of 1,015. The intensities were ranged from 0 to 3, so we selected frames with top 2 highest intensities and rescale them to the range from 1 to 5. To obtain emotion data, we used pre-trained emotion recognition network same as we used in DISFA+ and checked them with 5-human subjective evaluations. Five random augmented sentences were built per image. 10-fold cross-validation was adopted.

4.2 Experimental Setup

Implementation Details. We used pre-trained VGGFace [10] as visual feature encoder. The weights of the CNN component of the visual feature encoder are fixed. The dimensionality of output feature vectors D and the embedding

Table 1. Comparisons of facial expression sentence generation and emotion recognition task. FES-only considers facial expression sentence model only; also, FER-only considers facial emotion recognition only. BLEU-1,2,3,4, Meteor, CIDEr-D, and SPICE evaluation metrics are used. Emotion classification score is also considered. *Note that CIDEr-D score is 10 multiplied by the original CIDEr score.*

		BLEU							
Dataset	Model	BLEU-1	BLEU-2	BLEU-3	BLEU-4	METEOR	CIDEr	SPICE	Emotion
CK+	FES-only	61.85	47.70	35.22	23.70	30.00	108.68	51.12	
	FER-only								97.33
	Ours	**65.39**	**50.72**	**37.59**	**25.36**	**31.12**	**119.43**	**52.42**	**97.78**
DISFA	FES-only	57.24	42.57	30.75	20.18	28.41	63.53	45.87	
	FER-only								54.98
	Ours	**59.64**	**45.98**	**34.05**	**22.96**	**30.22**	**75.37**	**50.33**	**64.11**
MMI	FES-only	45.25	31.51	21.61	13.57	21.64	45.97	27.66	
	FER-only								42.08
	Ours	**50.05**	**35.69**	**25.14**	**16.27**	**22.76**	**61.05**	**33.81**	**45.72**

dimensionality M are both set to 512. During training, Adam optimizer with $\beta_1 = 0.9$ and $\beta_2 = 0.999$ was used with the initial learning rate 0.0001. The hyper-parameters controlling the relative importance two models were set to be $\lambda_1 = 1$ and $\lambda_2 = 0.00001$.

Evaluation. In testing, we utilized beam search, a widely-used approximate search algorithm, to decode the output sentence generated from the output vectors of our model. Beam search is an iterative method that considers all possible next steps output word and keeps k most likely ones to output best sentences up to time t. We set k as 3.

Since we newly adopted the dataset, we provided a direct comparison. For each dataset, we tested on different subjects from what we have trained. We separated our architecture into two separate individual architectures, the FES model and the FER model, respectively, and observed our proposed method is actually efficient. To evaluate the performance of the proposed method, we used standard evaluation metrics in natural language processing. We used BLEU-1,2,3,4 [13], METEOR [2], CIDEr [15], and SPICE [1]. Especially, CIDEr and SPICE are proposed specifically on evaluation image description generation.

4.3 Quantitative Analysis

Table 1 shows the comparison of our proposed method and the separated individual model: the FES-only model and the FER-only model, using several metrics. Overall, our method outperformed each separated model for all three datasets. Compared to single FES-only model, the proposed method notably improved 10.75%, 11.84%, and 15.08% in CIDEr for CK+, DISFA+, and MMI dataset, respectively. For recognizing a facial emotion, our proposed architecture achieved the highest performance gain for DISFA+, from 54.98% to 64.11%, with 9.13% performance improvement. Our model also improved the emotion recognition performance in CK+ and MMI, improving 0.45% and 3.64%, respectively.

Input image	Generated sentence	Ground truth
	A woman's lip corner is depressed slightly, her chin is lifted sensibly, her brow is kind of down, and her cheek is lifted slightly.	A woman's brow is reasonably lowered, her lip corner is somewhat pushed down, her chin is reasonably lifted, and her jaw is fallen slightly.
	A man's lips are separated significantly, his brow is quite lowered, his nose is creased strongly, his jaw is dropped very slightly, and his cheek is raised fairly.	A man's cheek is slightly lifted, his brow is down marginally, his jaw is dropped lightly, his nose is positively wrinkled, his lips are significantly parted, and his upper lid is kind of lifted.
	A woman's lip corner is pulled lightly, her brow is down sensibly, her lip is stretched lightly, and her chin is lifted lightly.	A woman's lip is slightly stretched, her brow is highly lowered, her jaw is very slightly fallen, and her upper lid is lifted reasonably.
	A woman's lip corner is pulled significantly, her lips are reasonably parted, her jaw is fallen slightly, her upper lid is lifted lightly, and her cheek is raised quite.	A woman's lip corner is stretched strongly, her lips are separated sensibly, her cheek is raised quite, and her jaw is fallen marginally.
	A woman's lip corner is somewhat pushed down, her brow is down quite, her lip is somewhat spread, and her chin is raised insignificantly.	A woman's chin is raised lightly, her lip corner is reasonably depressed, her brow is lightly lowered, her lip is stretched lightly, and her inner brow is raised lightly.
	A man's upper lid is raised lightly, his outer brow is lifted highly, his jaw is kind of dropped, his inner brow is raised sensibly, and his lips are highly parted.	A man's jaw is fallen positively, his upper lid is lifted sensibly, his outer brow is highly lifted, his lips are parted strongly, and his inner brow is strongly raised.

Fig. 4. Facial expression sentence generation result on DISFA+. Each facial AU with intensity of generated sentence is highlighted to same color with that of ground truth. The underlined action units and intensities in generated sentence indicate that they do not match with the ground truth sentence. *The facial emotion from top to bottom: anger, disgust, fear, happiness, sadness, and surprise.*

While the sentence datasets do not contain emotion information, the combination of facial action units and intensities well implies emotion of each image, thus improving the recognition accuracy. This shows that both visual emotion feature and semantic emotion feature summarize useful information in generating a sentence and recognizing an emotion. Also, they are effective in generating a facial expression sentence and recognizing a facial emotion.

4.4 Qualitative Analysis

We verified the effectiveness of our dataset and the proposed model in Fig. 4. The figure shows the qualitative results on the facial expression sentence generation. We show results from DISFA+ dataset since it contains spontaneous but clear expression in the facial images. The FES model clearly outputs the facial expression sentence without any grammatical error. Shown in the figure, the order of the facial action units and their intensities are all varied, meaning that the model actually learned the location of the facial action units and their corresponding words.

As shown in Fig. 4, the word combinations of each facial action unit with intensity from the generated sentence and the ground truth are highlighted with same color. Mostly, the generated sentences match with the ground truth sentences. Few descriptions of following intensities are different. For example, a *disgusted* man in the figure is described that his nose is creased *strongly*, where a word *strongly* belongs to intensity 4, but the ground truth says that his nose is *positively* wrinkled, where *positively* belongs to intensity 5 (see Fig. 1(d)). Moreover, a *happy* woman has *marginally* (intensity 1) fallen jaw, but the generated sentence says her jaw is *slightly* (intensity 2) fallen. Those AU intensities have differences of 1, which is generally tolerable because there might be some differences depending on subject's facial movement. Moreover, the underlined AUs and intensities in generated sentence of the figure do not match with the ground truth sentence; however, they stand to reason that those AUs and intensities also well describe the input facial image. This shows that the model actually learned where the action units were activated and how they were to be described. Thus, the overall result verifies that the generated sentences clearly describe the facial image with activated facial AUs.

5 Conclusion

In this paper, we introduced a novel text-based dataset using gender, facial AUs, and the corresponding intensities for comprehensive facial expression analysis. We also proposed a facial expression description framework which contains the FES and FER model. The proposed framework verified the effectiveness of the comprehensive facial expression description. Both models were supporting each other improving their performances: our text-based facial expression description provided comprehensive semantic information to the proposed FER model so that the model improved the performances. Also, the visual information from the FER model guided the FES model to produce a proper sentence describing comprehensive, detailed description. Thus, our FES model also could be used in human interaction technologies such as a dialogue generation [6] that explicitly describes human expressions.

Acknowledgement. The authors would like to express their gratitude to Wissam J. Baddar for his discussion and efforts in building the text-based facial expression dataset.

References

1. Anderson, P., Fernando, B., Johnson, M., Gould, S.: SPICE: semantic propositional image caption evaluation. In: Leibe, B., Matas, J., Sebe, N., Welling, M. (eds.) ECCV 2016. LNCS, vol. 9909, pp. 382–398. Springer, Cham (2016). https://doi.org/10.1007/978-3-319-46454-1_24
2. Banerjee, S., Lavie, A.: METEOR: an automatic metric for MT evaluation with improved correlation with human judgments. In: Proceedings of the ACL Workshop on Intrinsic and Extrinsic Evaluation Measures for Machine Translation and/or Summarization, pp. 65–72 (2005)

3. Ekman, P.: Basic emotions. Handb. Cogn. Emot. **98**(45–60), 16 (1999)
4. Ekman, R.: What the Face Reveals: Basic and Applied Studies of Spontaneous Expression Using the Facial Action Coding System (FACS). Oxford University Press, USA (1997)
5. Fasel, B., Luettin, J.: Automatic facial expression analysis: a survey. Pattern Recogn. **36**(1), 259–275 (2003)
6. Huber, B., McDuff, D., Brockett, C., Galley, M., Dolan, B.: Emotional dialogue generation using image-grounded language models. In: Proceedings of the 2018 CHI Conference on Human Factors in Computing Systems, p. 277. ACM (2018)
7. Kahou, S.E., et al.: EmoNets: multimodal deep learning approaches for emotion recognition in video. J. Multimodal User Interfaces **10**(2), 99–111 (2016)
8. Ko, B.: A brief review of facial emotion recognition based on visual information. Sensors **18**(2), 401 (2018)
9. Lucey, P., Cohn, J.F., Kanade, T., Saragih, J., Ambadar, Z., Matthews, I.: The extended Cohn-Kanade dataset (ck+): a complete dataset for action unit and emotion-specified expression. In: 2010 IEEE Computer Society Conference on Computer Vision and Pattern Recognition-Workshops, pp. 94–101. IEEE (2010)
10. Mavadati, M., Sanger, P., Mahoor, M.H.: Extended DISFA dataset: investigating posed and spontaneous facial expressions. In: Proceedings of the IEEE Conference on Computer Vision and Pattern Recognition Workshops, pp. 1–8 (2016)
11. Mohamad Nezami, O., Dras, M., Anderson, P., Hamey, L.: Face-cap: image captioning using facial expression analysis. In: Berlingerio, M., Bonchi, F., Gärtner, T., Hurley, N., Ifrim, G. (eds.) ECML PKDD 2018. LNCS (LNAI), vol. 11051, pp. 226–240. Springer, Cham (2019). https://doi.org/10.1007/978-3-030-10925-7_14
12. Pantic, M., Valstar, M., Rademaker, R., Maat, L.: Web-based database for facial expression analysis. In: 2005 IEEE International Conference on Multimedia and Expo, pp. 5-pp. IEEE (2005)
13. Papineni, K., Roukos, S., Ward, T., Zhu, W.J.: BLEU: a method for automatic evaluation of machine translation. In: Proceedings of the 40th Annual Meeting on Association for Computational Linguistics, pp. 311–318. Association for Computational Linguistics (2002)
14. Tang, Y.: Deep learning using linear support vector machines. arXiv preprint. arXiv:1306.0239 (2013)
15. Vedantam, R., Lawrence Zitnick, C., Parikh, D.: CIDEr: consensus-based image description evaluation. In: Proceedings of the IEEE Conference on Computer Vision and Pattern Recognition, pp. 4566–4575 (2015)
16. Vinyals, O., Toshev, A., Bengio, S., Erhan, D.: Show and tell: a neural image caption generator. In: Proceedings of the IEEE Conference on Computer Vision and Pattern Recognition, pp. 3156–3164 (2015)
17. Wegrzyn, M., Vogt, M., Kireclioglu, B., Schneider, J., Kissler, J.: Mapping the emotional face. How individual face parts contribute to successful emotion recognition. PloS One **12**(5), e0177239 (2017)
18. Xu, K., et al.: Show, attend and tell: neural image caption generation with visual attention. In: International Conference on Machine Learning, pp. 2048–2057 (2015)
19. Yu, Z., Zhang, C.: Image based static facial expression recognition with multiple deep network learning. In: Proceedings of the 2015 ACM on International Conference on Multimodal Interaction, pp. 435–442. ACM (2015)
20. Zeng, N., Zhang, H., Song, B., Liu, W., Li, Y., Dobaie, A.M.: Facial expression recognition via learning deep sparse autoencoders. Neurocomputing **273**, 643–649 (2018)

A Deep Convolutional Deblurring and Detection Neural Network for Localizing Text in Videos

Yang Wang, Ye Qian, Jiahao Shi, and Feng Su(✉)

State Key Laboratory for Novel Software Technology, Nanjing University, Nanjing 210023, China
suf@nju.edu.cn

Abstract. Scene text in the video is usually vulnerable to various blurs like those caused by camera or text motions, which brings additional difficulty to reliably extract them from the video for content-based video applications. In this paper, we propose a novel fully convolutional deep neural network for deblurring and detecting text in the video. Specifically, to cope with blur of video text, we propose an effective deblurring subnetwork that is composed of multi-level convolutional blocks with both cross-block (long) and within-block (short) skip connections for progressively learning residual deblurred image details as well as a spatial attention mechanism to pay more attention on blurred regions, which generates the sharper image for current frame by fusing multiple surrounding adjacent frames. To further localize text in the frames, we enhance the EAST text detection model by introducing deformable convolution layers and deconvolution layers, which better capture widely varied appearances of video text. Experiments on the public scene text video dataset demonstrate the state-of-the-art performance of the proposed video text deblurring and detection model.

Keywords: Scene text · Detection · Deblurring · Video · Fully convolutional network

1 Introduction

Rapid development of Internet and multimedia technologies nowadays leads to a massive and ever increasing amount of video data, in which scene text usually conveys important semantic information about the video content. Similar to text appearing in static scene images, scene text in the video has widely varied appearances (e.g. size, orientation, color, style) and is usually subjected to complex contextual interferences (e.g. background, lighting condition, occlusion). On the other hand, video text also exhibits some distinct characteristics specific to the video context such as various degradations caused by motions, which may bring extra difficulties to reliable detection of text in the video.

Y. M. Ro et al. (Eds.): MMM 2020, LNCS 11962, pp. 112–124, 2020.
https://doi.org/10.1007/978-3-030-37734-2_10

To detect scene text in one video sequence, one can exploit the existing large numbers of text detection methods originally designed for static images, which traditionally can be categorized into two groups. The connected component based methods exploit connected component analysis such as Maximally Stable Extremal Regions (MSERs) [11] and Stroke Width Transform (SWT) [4] to extract text candidates. The region based methods [17] detect text by shifting a multi-scale window on the image to extract various features and then employ certain machine learning methods (e.g. SVM and AdaBoost) to classify a window region as text candidate or not.

More recently, as deep neural networks such as convolutional neural network (CNN) and recurrent neural network (RNN) are extensively applied in computer vision field, there have appeared some scene text detection methods based on various deep neural networks [6,13,18,23], which can be classified roughly into two categories: proposals based methods [13,18] and direct regression methods [6,23]. The proposals based methods employ certain object detection networks like Faster R-CNN [12] to generate a set of text proposals, which are then filtered to obtain final detection results. For example, Tian *et al.* [18] proposed Connectionist Text Proposal Network (CTPN) that extracts sequences of fixed-width text proposals from convolutional feature maps of the input image, whose correlations are then depicted by a RNN model and utilized for obtaining text candidates. The direct regression methods predict classification scores and coordinates of potential text boxes directly using certain Fully Convolutional Network (FCN) variant. For example, Zhou *et al.* [23] proposed a FCN-based model for scene text detection, which predicts parameters of text candidates at every location in output feature maps based on extracted convolutional features.

To further exploit correlations of text cues across video frames to help robustly localize text in the video, especially for those frames that a text detection method for static images fails due to unfavorable detection conditions (e.g. highlight, low contrast, blur), some multi-frame based video text detection methods [19,20,22] have been proposed on the basis of image oriented text detection techniques, in which, variant techniques such as spatial-temporal analysis, multi-frame integration and tracking are exploited to improve overall detection performance. For example, Yang *et al.* [20] proposed a tracking based video text detection framework, which exploits multi-aspect information to detect text candidates in every frame, and then utilizes tracking and dynamic programming algorithms to refine detection results.

Despite the promising results having been achieved by existing video text detection methods, the difficulty brought by blurs to video text detection is relatively seldom addressed so far [10], which can significantly affect the performance of a video text detection method, especially those trained with non-blurry text samples. Figure 1 presents an example that illustrates the influence of blurs on video text detection, in which, blurs caused by camera motions significantly degrade the edge features of text and therefore lead to lowered detection performance.

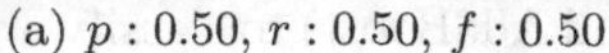

(a) $p: 0.50$, $r: 0.50$, $f: 0.50$

(b) $p: 0.67$, $r: 0.67$, $f: 0.67$

Fig. 1. An illustration of the influence of blurs on video text detection. (a) shows the detection results on a blurry image with no deblurring processing performed, while (b) shows the detection results on the deblurred image. The green boxes indicate the bounding boxes of ground truth text, while the red boxes indicate those of detected text. p, r, and f denote precision, recall, and f-measure of the detection results respectively. It can be seen that introducing the deblurring processing helps improve text detection results on blurry video frames. (Color figure online)

In this paper, we propose a novel deep neural network for deblurring and detecting scene text in videos. The key contributions of our work are summarized as follows:

- We propose a fully convolutional network for detecting text in the video, which seamlessly combines an effective deblurring subnetwork for video frames and a robust hierarchical text detection subnetwork to attain enhanced text detection performance.
- We propose a deblurring network that generates sharper representation of a video frame to be used as the input to the text detection network. The deblurring network fuses information from multiple adjacent frames by multi-level convolutional blocks with both cross-block (long) and within-block (short) skip connections to progressively learn residual deblurred image details, and attentively focuses on blurred regions with a spatial attention mechanism.
- We enhance the EAST text detection network [23] by introducing deformable convolution layers and deconvolution layers to better capture widely varied appearances of video text.
- The proposed model achieves higher text detection performance than the baseline models and state-of-the-art methods on the public ICDAR 2013 video text dataset [7] in the experiment.

2 Approach

In this work, we propose a novel deep neural network for video text deblurring and detection, which effectively improves the text detection result on a video frame by alleviating blurs of text via fusing information of multiple adjacent frames as well as a robust hierarchical text detection network. The proposed network is composed of two main components - the deblurring subnetwork and the detection subnetwork, as shown by Fig. 2.

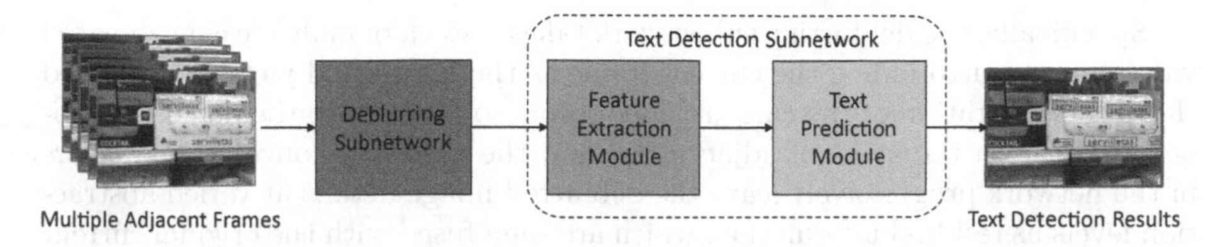

Fig. 2. The architecture of the proposed video text deblurring and detection model.

2.1 Deblurring Subnetwork

Most existing video deblurring methods [1,3] exploit complementary information from adjacent video frames to sharpen the current blurry frame. However, in many of these methods, the adjacent frames must be aligned before aggregation of multiple video frames can be performed. To avoid expensive computation cost and the warping artifacts caused by alignment of video frames, we propose an effective fully convolutional encoder-decoder network for deblurring a video frame on the basis of its (unaligned) surrounding frames, which enhances the original DeBlurNet proposed in the work [16] and acts as an early fusion mechanism of information from multiple related video frames.

The proposed deblurring subnetwork, as illustrated in Fig. 3, is composed of multiple cascaded convolutional blocks with long symmetric skip connections between the encoder and the decoder sides of the network. Specifically, compared to [16], we introduce ***short skip connections*** within each convolutional block to better integrate local information, and the *spatial attention* mechanism to focus on blurry regions, which are proved by the experiments to be capable of effectively improving the deblurring performance and yielding sharper representation of video frames.

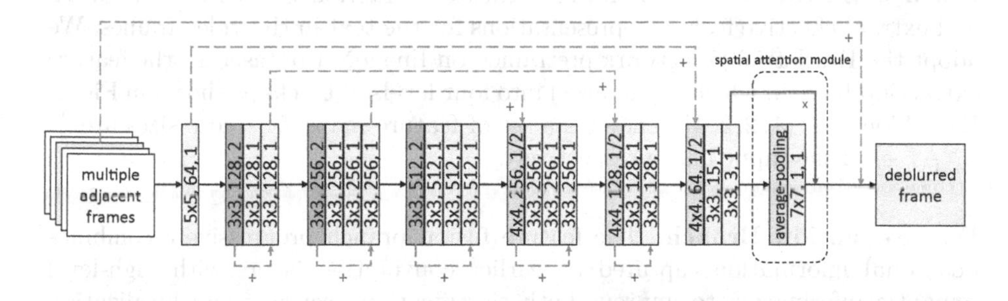

Fig. 3. The architecture of the proposed deblurring subnetwork. The orange dotted lines denote the long skip connections between different convolutional blocks. The green dotted lines denote the short skip connections within a convolutional block. The purple line denotes the element-wise multiplication of the two ends of the connection in the spatial attention module. The blue component in a convolutional block denotes the convolutional downsampling layer, while the yellow component denotes the deconvolutional upsampling layer. (Color figure online)

Specifically, the deblurring subnetwork takes a stack of multiple concatenated video frames surrounding the current frame as the input, and yields a deblurred sharp representation of the current video frame to be fed into the detection subnetwork. Given the stack of adjacent frames, the cascaded convolutional layers in the network progressively learn the deblurred image details at varied abstraction levels as residual information, which are then fused with the original current frame by skip connection. For each skip connection (either long or short), the feature maps at both ends of the connection are added element-wise, which facilitates the propagation of gradients so as to significantly accelerate the training of the network.

For the spatial attention mechanism, we first apply average pooling operation on the input feature maps along the channel axis, followed by a 7×7 convolution layer to generate the spatial attention map that adaptively emphasizes blurred regions while suppressing non-blurry regions, and then multiply it element-wise with the input feature maps. To train the deblurring subnetwork, we adopt the mean squared error (MSE) between the deblurred image and the ground truth sharp image as the loss function of the network.

2.2 Text Detection Subnetwork

To localize text candidates in the deblurred representation of one video frame, we extend the EAST text detection model [23] by introducing deconvolution layers and deformable convolution layers into the multi-level fully convolutional network to better capture widely varied text appearances for enhanced detection performance. As shown in Fig. 4, the text detection subnetwork has an U-shape architecture composed of *feature extraction branch*, *feature fusion branch* and *text prediction module*.

Feature Extraction Branch. The feature extraction branch aims to learn and extract effective feature representations for the text in the video frames. We adopt the ResNet-50 [5] network pretrained on ImageNet dataset for the feature extraction branch, which is organized into four levels of blocks as shown in Fig. 4. Each block $i \in \{1, 2, 3, 4\}$ generates a set of feature maps f_i, whose sizes are $\frac{1}{4}$, $\frac{1}{8}$, $\frac{1}{16}$, $\frac{1}{32}$ of the input image respectively.

Feature Fusion Branch. The feature fusion branch progressively combines positional information captured by earlier convolution layers with high-level semantic information to improve both classification accuracy and localization precision of text candidates.

Specifically, in each feature fusion stage $i \in \{3, 2, 1\}$, we substitute the unpooling operation adopted in the EAST model by a deconvolution layer for increased flexibility, which doubles the sizes of the feature maps h_{i+1} from the previous fusion stage. Next, the resulting feature maps are concatenated with the feature maps f_i from the corresponding feature extraction block, and then a 1×1 and a 3×3 convolution layers are successively applied to

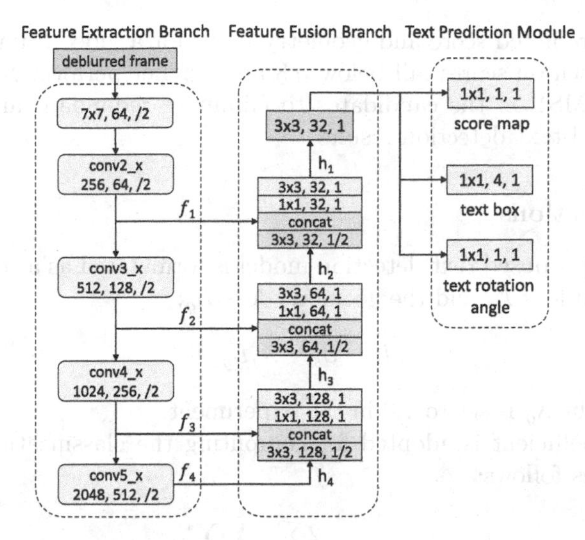

Fig. 4. The architecture of the proposed text detection subnetwork. The yellow component in each feature fusion stage denotes the deconvolution layer. The purple block at the end of the feature fusion branch denotes the deformable convolution layer. (Color figure online)

reduce the number of channels and produce the output of current feature fusion stage, respectively.

Finally, as shown in Fig. 4, we propose to cascade a *deformable convolution* [2] layer after the last feature fusion stage, which enhances the standard 2-D convolution with learnable sampling positions to adapt to spatial relocation of features involved in computing the convolution. Introducing this additional deformable convolution layer in the network increases the proposed detection subnetwork's capability of modelling various local spatial deformations of text in the video.

Text Prediction Module. On the basis of the feature maps outputted by the feature fusion branch, the prediction module yields potential text candidates for every position in the output feature maps, which are composed of a 1-channel score map F_s and a 5-channels geometry map F_g, with 4 channels giving the axis-aligned bounding box of the text candidate and 1 channel encoding its rotation angle.

We generate appropriate labels for corresponding prediction channels as adopted in [23]. Given the rectangular bounding box of one ground truth text, every endpoint of its edge is moved inward by 15% of the edge length, and the shrunk rectangle is taken as the positive area of text on the score map. For the geometry map, the distances of one pixel to every edge of the rectangular bounding box are taken as the values in the first 4 channels, while the angle between the rectangle and the horizontal axis is used for the last channel.

Given the predicted score and geometry maps for a video frame, we discard the candidates whose scores fall below 0.8 and further perform Non-Maximum Suppression (NMS) on the candidates to eliminate redundant and false ones, yielding the final text detection results.

2.3 Loss Functions

The loss of the proposed text detection model is formulated as a combination of the classification loss L_s and the geometry loss L_g:

$$L = L_s + \lambda_g L_g \tag{1}$$

where, the weight λ_g is set to 1.0 in the experiment.

The Dice coefficient is adopted for computing the classification loss L_s on the score map as follows:

$$L_s = 1 - \frac{2\sum_i^N \hat{\mathbf{Y}}_i \mathbf{Y}_i^*}{\sum_i^N \hat{\mathbf{Y}}_i + \sum_i^N \mathbf{Y}_i^*} \tag{2}$$

where, $\hat{\mathbf{Y}}$ is the predicted value for the score map while $\mathbf{Y}^*$ being the ground truth, and N denotes the number of elements in the score map.

The geometry loss L_g on the geometry map combines the boundary loss L_b and the rotation angle loss L_θ:

$$L_g = L_b + \lambda_\theta L_\theta \tag{3}$$

where, $\lambda_\theta = 20$ is used in the experiment, and the boundary loss L_b and the rotation angle loss L_θ are computed respectively as follows:

$$L_b = -log\frac{|\hat{\mathbf{R}} \cap \mathbf{R}^*|}{|\hat{\mathbf{R}} \cup \mathbf{R}^*|} \qquad L_\theta(\hat{\theta}, \theta^*) = 1 - cos(\hat{\theta} - \theta^*) \tag{4}$$

where, $\hat{\mathbf{R}}$ and $\hat{\theta}$ denote the predicted boundary parameters and the rotation angle respectively, with $\mathbf{R}^*$ and θ^* being the ground truth.

2.4 Implementation Details

The kernel size, number of filters and stride of every convolution and deconvolution layer in the deblurring subnetwork and text detection subnetwork are labeled in Figs. 3 and 4.

We first train the deblurring subnetwork with the ADAM optimizer on the training dataset in [16] for 80000 iterations. In each iteration, we randomly crop 128 × 128 patches from the training video frames, and use a stack of 5 corresponding patches from consecutive 5 frames as one training sample, while one batch is composed of 64 samples. The learning rate is fixed to 0.005 in the first 24000 iterations, and then halves for every 8000 iterations in the remaining training process.

To train the text detection subnetwork, we fix the parameters of the pre-trained deblurring subnetwork and exploit the ADAM optimizer with the learning rate starting from 10^{-4} and stopping at 10^{-5} with a decay of 0.9 every 10000 iterations, in which we randomly crop 512×512 patches from training frames to augment the training data and generate mini-batches of size 6. The training is terminated when the network performance no longer improves.

3 Experiments

3.1 Dataset

We adopt the deblurring video dataset presented in [16] to evaluate the effectiveness of our enhancement to the original DeBlurNet [16]. The dataset consists of 71 video sequences containing 6708 synthetic blurry frames with corresponding ground truth, which are split into 61 training videos and 10 testing videos, with an average duration of 3–5 s for one video sample. The blurry video samples in the dataset are synthetically created by accumulating a number of consecutive frames from some real-world sharp videos captured at very high frame rate, which approximates a long exposure resulting in certain degree of blur.

To evaluate video text detection performance, we adopt the public scene text video dataset of ICDAR 2013 Robust Reading Competition Challenge 3: Text in Videos [7], which consists of 28 video sequences with 13 videos for training and 15 videos for testing. The duration of a video sequence ranges from 10 s to 1 min.

We adopt the standard evaluation metrics of ICDAR 2013 dataset [7], i.e. precision p, recall r, and f-measure (the harmonic mean value $\frac{2*p*r}{p+r}$ of p and r), for measuring text detection performance.

3.2 Evaluation of Deblurring Subnetwork

To verify the effectiveness of the proposed enhancements to the original DeBlurNet [16] on general image deblurring, in Table 1, we compare the peak signal-to-noise ratio (PSNR) of the deblurring results by the proposed deblurring subnetwork and DeBlurNet on the deblurring video dataset [16], along with the PSNRs of the original input videos. It can be seen that, the proposed enhancements to DeBlurNet, i.e. the short skip connections and the spatial attention mechanism, progressively improve the deblurring performance, and altogether increase the average PSNR by 0.68 over all 10 videos in the dataset, demonstrating the effectiveness of the proposed deblurring model.

3.3 Evaluation of Text Detection Subnetwork and Combination with Deblurring Module

We first investigate the effectiveness of the proposed text detection subnetwork on video frames by comparing its performance with that of the popular EAST

Table 1. Comparison of delurring performances of the proposed deblurring subnetwork and the original DeBlurNet (NOALIGN) [16] on PSNR, which are averaged over all frames in each of 10 test videos (#1 to #10) in the deblurring video dataset. (a) denotes DeBlurNet; (b) denotes combining DeBlurNet with the proposed short skip connections (SSC); (c) denotes the proposed deblurring subnetwork that enhances DeBlurNet with SSC and the spatial attention mechanism (SA).

Method	Video sample										Avg.
	#1	#2	#3	#4	#5	#6	#7	#8	#9	#10	
Input	24.14	30.52	28.38	27.31	22.60	29.31	27.74	23.86	30.59	26.98	27.14
(a)	27.83	33.11	31.29	29.73	25.12	31.52	30.80	27.28	33.31	29.51	30.05
(b)	28.63	33.28	31.60	30.51	25.55	33.00	30.90	27.12	34.71	30.16	30.54
(c)	**28.79**	**33.58**	**31.70**	**30.70**	**25.76**	**33.15**	**31.01**	**27.29**	**34.98**	**30.36**	**30.73**

network [23], which exploits a FCN framework with fundamental U-shape structure. Note that, as only the detection results of the EAST network on the static scene image dataset of ICDAR 2013 (different from the video dataset used in our experiments) were presented in [23], we reimplemented the EAST network, which is denoted as EAST* in Table 2. The detection results on ICDAR 2013 video text dataset show that, compared to EAST*, the proposed text detection subnetwork achieves improved text detection performance on all precision, recall and f-measure metrics, i.e. 0.67% on precision, 0.83% on recall, 0.57% on f-measure.

We further evaluate the video text detection performance of combining the proposed detection subnetwork with the proposed deblurring subnetwork as well as the original DeBlurNet [16] in Table 2. It can be seen that, introducing deblurring modules (either the proposed one or DeBlurNet) generally helps enhance the detection performance, revealing the positive effect of the deblurring processing on video text detection. The results also show that the proposed deblurring network is more effective than DeBlurNet as a preceding image enhancement module for subsequent text detection. Specifically, compared to no deblurring mechanism adopted, the text detection model incorporating the proposed deblurring subnetwork effectively increases the f-measure on 12 videos among the total 15 test videos of the ICDAR 2013 video text dataset, i.e., 8.43% increase on 1 video, 5–6% increases on 2 videos and 1–3% increases on the other 9 videos, which leads to significant increases on average precision (1.14%), recall (2.32%), and f-measure (2.17%) due to the improved text quality, demonstrating the effectiveness of the proposed video text detection model.

Figure 5 illustrates two examples of the deblurring results by DeblurNet [16] and the proposed network along with the detection results. It can be observed that, despite the visually notable improvement of image quality attained by DeblurNet relative to the input image, the detection results may not be improved as much. Compared to DeblurNet, the proposed deblurring network demonstrates its capability of enhancing the blurry image in a way more favorable to the text detection task.

Table 2. Comparison of text detection performances (%) of the proposed network and the original EAST network [23] on ICDAR 2013 video text dataset.

Method	p	r	f
EAST*	65.22	54.63	57.71
Proposed Detection Subnetwork	65.89	55.46	58.28
DeBlurNet & **Proposed Detection Subnetwork**	66.48	56.97	59.67
Proposed Deblurring & Detection Network	**67.03**	**57.78**	**60.45**

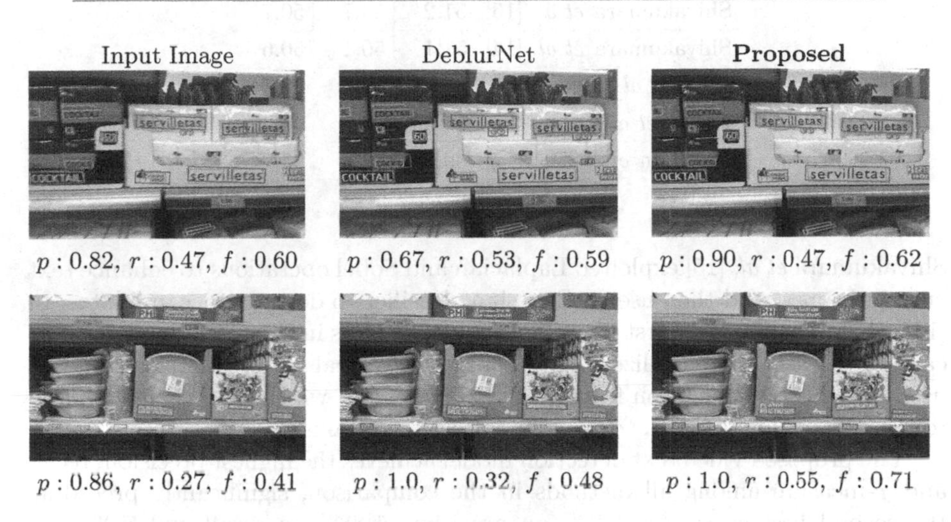

Fig. 5. Examples of video text detection results on the blurry input images and the deblurred images by DeblurNet and the proposed deblurring network respectively. The green boxes indicate the bounding boxes of ground truth text, while the red boxes indicate those of detected text. (Color figure online)

3.4 Comparison with State-of-the-Art Video Text Detection Methods

We compare video text detection performances of the proposed model and some state-of-the-art methods in Table 3. Specifically, Wang *et al.* [19] first employed a deep neural network to detect text candidates in a video frame, and on the other hand, the method extracted potential background regions of text, which were used to filter out some false text candidates based on correspondence between text and its background. The method then tracked text candidates across frames as the supplement to individual-frame detection. Khare *et al.* [8] classified a video frame's pixels to ones exclusively belonging to caption text, scene text or background with the proposed Higher Order Moments descriptor, and then localized text candidates in the video frame based on gradient directions of pixel clusters. Yin *et al.* [21] localized potential text candidates in video frames based on MSERs and corresponding pruning and clustering algorithms, and then employed a classifier to identify the text based on its posterior probability.

Table 3. Comparison of text detection performance (%) on ICDAR 2013 video text dataset.

Method	p	r	f
Proposed	**67.03**	**57.78**	**60.45**
Wang *et al.* [19]	58.3	51.7	54.5
Khare *et al.* [8]	57.9	55.9	51.7
Yin *et al.* [21]	48.6	54.7	51.6
Shivakumara *et al.* [15]	51.2	53.7	50.7
Shivakumara *et al.* [14]	51.1	50.1	50.6
Zhao *et al.* [22]	47.0	46.3	46.7
Khare *et al.* [9]	41.4	47.6	44.3
Epshtein *et al.* [4]	39.8	32.5	35.9

Shivakumara *et al.* [15] exploited Laplacian and Sobel operations to enhance text cues in frames, and then used a Bayesian classifier to detect text candidates. In [14], Shivakumara *et al.* first identified the text frames in the video, in which text candidates were then localized using Fourier-statistical features. Zhao *et al.* [22] used optical flow as motion features for frame pixels, which were then exploited to localize moving caption text regions in a video frame.

The proposed video text detection model achieves the highest precision, recall and f-measure among all methods in the comparison, significantly preceding the second best scores by 8.73% on precision, 1.88% on recall and 5.95% on f-measure, which demonstrate the effectiveness of the proposed model. Specifically, compared to the method [19] that achieved the second best f-measure and employed the tracking algorithm as a late multi-frame fusion mechanism for detection results, our method introduces deblurring as a specific early fusion measure to integrate relevant information from multiple video frames and achieves overall better detection performance. On the other hand, the proposed model can also be combined with tracking-based fusion measures to further enhance video text detection performance. Moreover, possible extensions to the proposed multi-frame fusion model will be explored in the future work to deal with other challenging factors in videos that affect robust detection of video text.

4 Conclusions

In this paper, we present a novel fully convolutional deblurring and detection network for text in the videos. The network combines an effective deblurring subnetwork, which generates sharper representation of a video frame by fusing information of its multiple adjacent frames, and a robust hierarchical text detection subnetwork to localize text in the deblurred frames. The experiments demonstrate the effectiveness of the proposed video text deblurring and detection network.

Acknowledgments. Research supported by the Natural Science Foundation of Jiangsu Province of China under Grant No. BK20171345 and the National Natural Science Foundation of China under Grant Nos. 61003113, 61321491, 61672273.

References

1. Cho, S., Wang, J., Lee, S.: Video deblurring for hand-held cameras using patch-based synthesis. ACM Trans. Graph. (TOG) **31**(4), 64 (2012)
2. Dai, J., et al.: Deformable convolutional networks. In: ICCV, October 2017
3. Delbracio, M., Sapiro, G.: Burst deblurring: removing camera shake through fourier burst accumulation. In: CVPR, pp. 2385–2393 (2015)
4. Epshtein, B., Ofek, E., Wexler, Y.: Detecting text in natural scenes with stroke width transform. In: CVPR, pp. 2963–2970 (2010)
5. He, K., Zhang, X., Ren, S., Sun, J.: Deep residual learning for image recognition. In: CVPR, pp. 770–778 (2016)
6. He, P., Huang, W., He, T., Zhu, Q., Qiao, Y., Li, X.: Single shot text detector with regional attention. In: ICCV, pp. 3047–3055 (2017)
7. Karatzas, D., et al.: ICDAR 2013 robust reading competition. In: ICDAR, pp. 1484–1493 (2013)
8. Khare, V., Shivakumara, P., Paramesran, R., Blumenstein, M.: Arbitrarily-oriented multi-lingual text detection in video. Multimedia Tools Appl. **76**(15), 16625–16655 (2017)
9. Khare, V., Shivakumara, P., Raveendran, P.: A new histogram oriented moments descriptor for multi-oriented moving text detection in video. Expert Syst. Appl. **42**(21), 7627–7640 (2015)
10. Khare, V., Shivakumara, P., Raveendran, P., Blumenstein, M.: A blind deconvolution model for scene text detection and recognition in video. Pattern Recogn. **54**(C), 128–148 (2016)
11. Matas, J., Chum, O., Urban, M., Pajdla, T.: Robust wide-baseline stereo from maximally stable extremal regions. IVC **22**(10), 761–767 (2004)
12. Ren, S., He, K., Girshick, R., Sun, J.: Faster R-CNN: towards real-time object detection with region proposal networks. In: NIPS, pp. 91–99 (2015)
13. Shi, B., Bai, X., Belongie, S.: Detecting oriented text in natural images by linking segments. In: CVPR, pp. 3482–3490 (2017)
14. Shivakumara, P., Phan, T.Q., Tan, C.L.: New fourier-statistical features in RGB space for video text detection. IEEE TCSVT **20**(11), 1520–1532 (2010)
15. Shivakumara, P., Sreedhar, R.P., Phan, T.Q., Lu, S., Tan, C.L.: Multioriented video scene text detection through Bayesian classification and boundary growing. IEEE TCSVT **22**(8), 1227–1235 (2012)
16. Su, S., Delbracio, M., Wang, J., Sapiro, G., Heidrich, W., Wang, O.: Deep video deblurring for hand-held cameras. In: CVPR, pp. 1279–1288, July 2017
17. Tian, S., Pan, Y., Huang, C., Lu, S., Yu, K., Tan, C.L.: Text flow: a unified text detection system in natural scene images. In: ICCV, pp. 4651–4659 (2015)
18. Tian, Z., Huang, W., He, T., He, P., Qiao, Y.: Detecting text in natural image with connectionist text proposal network. In: Leibe, B., Matas, J., Sebe, N., Welling, M. (eds.) ECCV 2016. LNCS, vol. 9912, pp. 56–72. Springer, Cham (2016). https://doi.org/10.1007/978-3-319-46484-8_4
19. Wang, L., Wang, Y., Shan, S., Su, F.: Scene text detection and tracking in video with background cues. In: ICMR, pp. 160–168 (2018)

20. Yang, C., et al.: Tracking based multi-orientation scene text detection: a unified framework with dynamic programming. IEEE TIP **26**(7), 3235–3248 (2017)
21. Yin, X.C., Yin, X., Huang, K., Hao, H.W.: Robust text detection in natural scene images. IEEE TPAMI **36**(5), 970–983 (2014)
22. Zhao, X., Lin, K.H., Fu, Y., Hu, Y., Liu, Y., Huang, T.S.: Text from corners: a novel approach to detect text and caption in videos. IEEE TIP **20**(3), 790–799 (2011)
23. Zhou, X., et al.: EAST: an efficient and accurate scene text detector. In: CVPR, pp. 2642–2651 (2017)

Generate Images with Obfuscated Attributes for Private Image Classification

Wei Hou[1,2], Dakui Wang[2(✉)], and Xiaojun Chen[2]

[1] School of Cyber Security, University of Chinese Academy of Sciences, Beijing 100049, China
[2] Institute of Information Engineering, Chinese Academy of Sciences, Beijing 100093, China
{houwei,wangdakui,chenxiaojun}@iie.ac.cn

Abstract. Image classification is widely used in various applications and some companies collect a large amount of data from users to train classification models for commercial profitability. To prevent disclosure of private information caused by direct data collecting, Google proposed federated learning to share model parameters rather than data. However, this framework could address the problem of direct data leakage but cannot defend against inference attack, malicious participants can still exploit attribute information from the model parameters.

In this paper, we propose a novel method based on StarGAN to generate images with obfuscated attributes. The images generated by our methods can retain the non-private attributes of the original image but protect the specific private attributes of the original image by mixing the original image and the artificial image with obfuscated attributes. Experimental results have shown that the model trained on the artificial image dataset can effectively defend against property inference attack with neglected accuracy loss of classification task in a federated learning environment.

Keywords: Private image classification · Federated learning · Generated adversarial network

1 Introduction

With the development of mobile networks and data storage technology, smartphone users have created more and more multimedia data such as photos and videos. Many Internet business companies, like Facebook and Google, collect these data and train deep models to analysis users' behavior and preferences. Deep models on users' data bring real economic benefits for these companies but

Supported by the Strategic Priority Research Program of Chinese Academy of Sciences, Grant No. XDC02040400.

Y. M. Ro et al. (Eds.): MMM 2020, LNCS 11962, pp. 125–135, 2020.
https://doi.org/10.1007/978-3-030-37734-2_11

such data collection is restrained by regulatory frameworks such as the European Union's General Data Protection Regulations (GDPR) [1], as it may lead to privacy leakage of users. To solve this problem, Google proposed federated learning [2] to build machine learning models based on distributed data. This framework allows data holders to share model parameters rather than data with service providers.

However, there still exist risks of privacy leakage in the federated learning environment. For example, property inference attack [3] can infer attribute information of other participants through training in federated learning. One can infer any property information other than main task through property inference attack, for instance, infer the race in gender classification training.

In order to protect image data from being inferred by an attacker, we propose a new method by generating images with obfuscated attributes. We invert the private attributes to produce new image data and add such data to the training process, misleading attackers to make wrong inferences on private attributes. This article has two main contributions:

1. We proposed two metrics to measure the inherent characteristics of images, include anti-classification ability and confusion ability. One is the ability to mislead classifiers, and the other is the ability to make the classifier unable to give valid confidence.
2. We proposed an obfuscation method to generate images to defend against the property inference attack. Our approach can significantly reduce the accuracy of the attack model and can confuse attackers in a controlled way.

The rest of the paper is structured as follows: Sect. 2 introduces some related methods and analyze the defects. In Sect. 3, a new method of protecting private attributes and the corresponding evaluation methods are proposed. The experimental results are shown in Sect. 4. Section 5 summarizes this paper and promotes prospects for future work.

2 Related Work

Federated learning [2] was proposed to deal with data privacy issues because it allows participants to train a joint model without sharing data. However, several attacks [3–5] proposed in recent research can steal private information of participants in a federated learning environment. There are roughly two types of methods to defend against these attacks, one improves the data security through security protocols and the other is concerning on confusing data to conceal the private attributes.

Secure Aggregation [6] is the earliest method of security protocol used in federated learning. Similar to homomorphic encryption [7], secure aggregation protocol provides protection against malicious central server through encrypting parameter updates. The shortcoming is that it cannot defend against inference attacks from malicious participants because the training process must be visible to all participants. Differential privacy [8,9] is another method of security protocol by adding noise to uploaded parameters. It can effectively defend against attacks from malicious participants like model inverse attack [4], GAN attack [5]. But at the same time, the accuracy of the model will be reduced.

Data obfuscation is another type of method to protect privacy. Adding noise to images to avoid identificating [10] is an intuitive method that can defend against attacks from participants. However, blurring images leads to the accuracy loss of the target model. Another method is disguising images [11], which permutates and transforms images to avoid identification. However, this method cannot be used to train the joint model or share model to others who don't know transforming rules. One more method is generating artificial data [12], which is similar to our method. But such generated fake data from datasets is not suitable in face identification tasks and cannot defend against property inference attack [3] because it keeps the same statistical information.

Based on the analysis above, none of these methods could effectively defend against the property inference attack. So our work focuses on protecting private attributes in images and we use StarGAN [13] to achieve this goal. StarGAN is a novel and scalable approach that can perform image-to-image [14] translations for multiple domains using only a single model. Inspired by StarGAN, we convert the attributes of one image to opposing attributes, which we call property inversion. We apply translation for multiple attributes on images to generate results that we call inverse property images. We add inverse property images to original datasets to protect private attributes and maintain the original features. One similar method in [15] is to protect face privacy controllably by synthesis. However, our method can protect various types of images with privacy attributes, which is more general.

3 Methodology

3.1 Threat Model

Our method is proposed under a federated learning environment [8]. We assume that $K (K \geq 2)$participants, each represents a user or a data holder, jointly train a classification model on their own dataset, represents as D^j, and exchange parameters via a parameter server per each turn.

We define the attribute set of an image data set D by

$$Attr_D = [p_1, p_2, ..., p_n],$$

where p_i represents the proportion of property i which may be valued from 0 to 1. When D has only one image, we think the image has property i when $p_i = 1$. For example, we index attribute *male* as 1, then one face image has *male* property when $p_1 = 1$.

An attribute classifier is a model $f_\theta^{p_i}(\cdot)$ trained on D that can give confidence of property i of input data. Then we define participants' main task is to train a classifier $f_\theta^{p_i}(\cdot)$ of object property o.

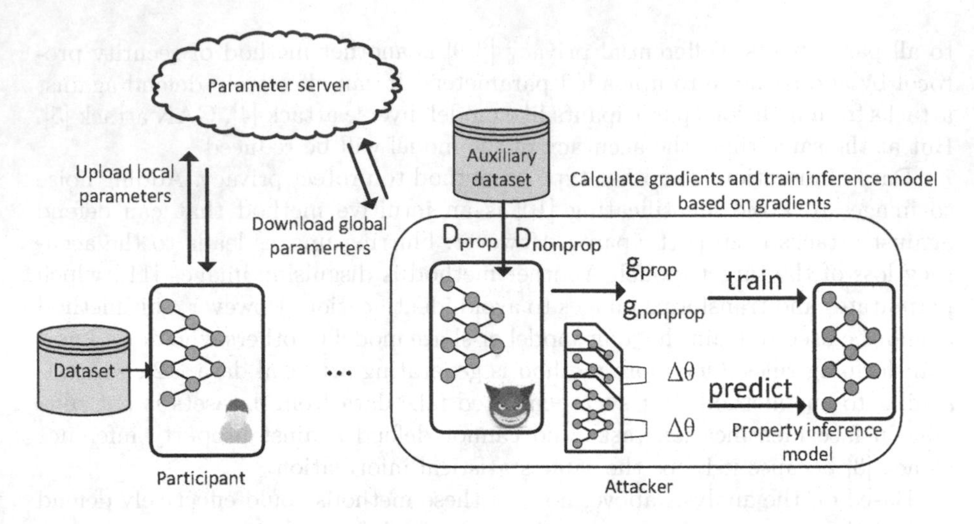

Fig. 1. Federated learning and property inference attack.

We then consider a property inference attacker among participants who aims to infer the target property p_t of other participants' training data. For example, if an adversary is interested in the gender distribution of other participants' data D^j, the attacker can use property inference attack [3] to estimate p_t on D^j.

The process of property inference attack is shown in Fig. 1, the attacker collects global model parameters from parameter server every turn and calculate gradients $\Delta\theta = \theta_t - \theta_{t-1}$ as predicting set. Given global model parameter θ, the attacker calculates gradient g_{prop} and $g_{nonprop}$ based on auxiliary data. Finally, the attacker trains a binary classifier f_{prop} based on g_{prop} and $g_{nonprop}$ and test on $\Delta\theta$ to indicate the probability that a batch has the property [3]. We use M_A to represent classifier f_{prop} as property inference attack model.

The adversary is honest but curious in cryptographic parlance and needs auxiliary data with label of target property(e.g. face image with label of gender if goal is infer gender) to build attack model. The auxiliary data set is not intersect with data set held by other participants.

3.2 Images with Obfuscated Private Attributes

We propose a method to protect private attributes under the threat model described in Sect. 3.1. We train StarGAN model of selected private attributes and use the model to translate original images to generated images which we call inverse property images. For example, we select skin color as private attribute and we use StarGAN to translate an image with black color to an image with white color. We mix inverse property images and original images as training data set.

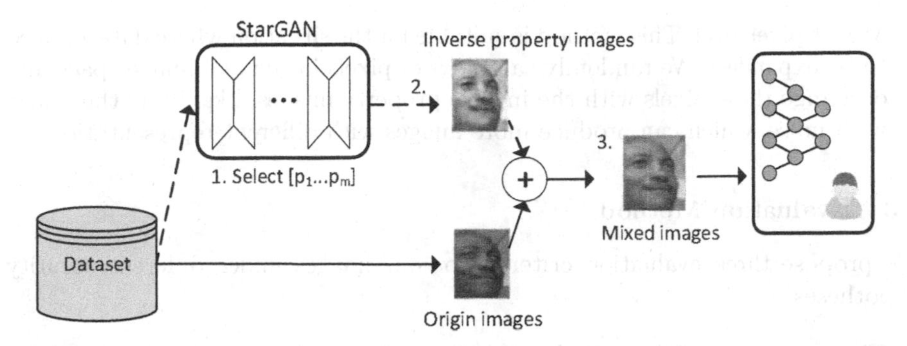

Fig. 2. Overview of obfuscating attributes method. We first select private attributes. Then use StarGAN to generate inverse property images. Finally, mix them to original images as training set.

Detaily, the process is described as follows:

1. The participant secretly decides m attributes $Attr_D^s = [p_1, p_2 ... p_m]$ that need to be protected with $Attr_D^s \in Attr_D$. The goal is to make the images cannot be classified by the classifiers of these attributes. At the same time, we need to guarantee the accuracy of the object attribute, that means $p_o \notin Attr_D^s$. For example, in the task of face recognition, the protection of gender property will confuse the gender classifiers but no influence to face recognition (Fig. 2).
2. Use generative adversary network to generate images with inverse properties. For the selected attribute set $Attr_D^s$ of the original dataset D_{org}, we use StarGAN [13] to translate images with inverse properties. We use M^s to represent StarGAN model. For each $p_i \in Attr_D^s$, we build a StarGAN model M_i^s that can inverse image's property which means $p_i \leftarrow 1 - p_i$. For example, in terms of gender attributes in face images, images labeled as male are translated to images that will be classfied as female by classifiers. This can increase the confusion of private attributes. We use D_{inv} to represent inverse property images.
3. Mix inverse property images and original images to generate training set.

We mix two type of images to obfuscate private attributes. We propose three different mixing methods, using hyperparameter α to control the proportion of inverse property images.

1. Mix at dataset level. This method is suitable for defending property inference attack because attackers observe gradients for each batch rather than specific record. The inverse property images and the original images are put into a dataset and the proportion of the inverse property images is α.
2. Mix at image level. This method is suitable for the situation where a single image needs to be protected. The inverse property images is superimposed with a certain ratio, $D_{mix} = (1 - \alpha) * D_{org} + \alpha * D_{inv}$. The smaller the α, the closer to the real image.

3. Mix at pixel level. This method is suitable for the situation where dataset need to be expanded. We randomly sample α of pixels in the real image space and exchange these pixels with the inverse property images, like filling the image with noise, which can produce more images with different representations.

3.3 Evaluation Method

We propose three evaluation criterias for our images under different security hypotheses.

1. The assessment of the anti-classification ability on images. An honest participant needs to protect specific attributes of his own data from being inferred. The method of evaluating anti-inference ability of image is as follows: training an attribute classifier based on public data, and sequentially determining the attributes in $Attr^s_D$. The image data's anti-classification score is defined as:

$$P^c(D) = \frac{1}{m}\sum_{i=1}^{m}(1 - f_\theta^{p_i}(D))$$

where $f_\theta^{p_i}(D)$ is the output of the classifier for property i trained on public data. The greater the $P^c(D)$, the stronger the ability of D to mislead classifiers of private attribute.
2. Confusion ability assessment in the open environment. When an attacker knows that the participants will take this defense method, the ability of anti-classification is no longer appropriate for evaluation, because an attacker can train attack model with opposite label and steal information as well. Confusion score is defined as:

$$P^f(D) = \frac{1}{m}\sum_{i=1}^{m}\sqrt{1 - (f_\theta^{p_i}(D) - E_i)^2}$$

where E_i is expectation which can be easily obtained from public data statistics. The greater the $P^f(D)$, the less useful information the attribute classifier f^{p_i} can get from D.
3. Accuracy loss measure the negative influence to main task. Accuracy loss is defined as:

$$L_{acc}(D) = accuracy(f_{\theta_{org}}^{p_o}) - accuracy(f_{\theta_{mix}}^{p_o})$$

where D_{org} represents original data set and D_{mix} represents the obfuscated data set. $f_{\theta org}^{p_o}$ represents classifier trained on D_{org} and $f_{\theta mix}^{p_o}$ represents classifier trained on D_{mix}. The smaller $L_c(D)$, the smaller the accuracy cost of the images with obfuscated attributes on main task.

4 Experiment

We evaluate our work on tow datasets namely LFW [16] and CelebA [17]. All experiments were performed on a workstation running CentOS 7 equipped with a 3.3 GHz CPU i9-7900X, 32 GB RAM, and an NVIDIA TitanXp GPU card. We use Pytorch as the deep learning framework, AlexNet [18] to implement neural network classifiers and StarGAN [13] to generate inverse property images. We evaluate the performance of both the main task model and attack model based on the criteria described in Sect. 3.3.

4.1 Generate Inverse Property Images

We first verify whether inverse property images can cause misclassification of the private attributes classifiers.

We set gender, age, glasses wearing as private attributes, and train StarGAN model to generate inverse property images of corresponding attributes. The generated results are shown in the fourth line in Fig. 3.

We set the original task as classification of face emotions (is smilling or not). We train models after inverting properties and compare them with the results of the original images. We use AlexNet with learning rate 0.001 to train on CelebA dataset. The test results are shown in Table 1.

Table 1. Accuracy of inverse property images on three private attributes(Male, Young and Glasses) compare to original images. The results have shown that the classification model trained on inverse property images has a high misclassification rate of private attributes with neglected accuracy loss on inversed attribute.

Attributes	Origin images(%)	Inverse private attributes images(%)	L_{acc}
Male	90.4	9.2	81.2
Young	92.1	5.1	87.0
Glasses	89.7	6.8	82.9
Smilling	91.2	90.7	0.5

The results show that the images still retains the features of the non-private part after inverting private properties, resulting in misclassification of classifiers, thereby preventing the real attribute information from being leaked.

However, in this way of inverting attributes, the protection ability is reduced in the training steps of the public protocol. Because if the attacker who takes the property inference attack knows about the protection method, it also adopts the opposite label attack method, which will make this method invalid. This is more like a game problem, but we mainly focus on the confusing ability of private properties in images.

4.2 Evaluation on Obfuscated Images

After generating inverse property images, we mix the original image and the inverted attribute image in three ways described in Sect. 3.2. The implementations are as follows:

Fig. 3. Obfuscated attributes images using superposition and pixel-swap on three attributes: Male, Glasses and Young. When α values 0 or 1, they becomes original images or inverse property images.

Record swap for dataset level mixing. For the original data and the records in D_{org}, the records of the random ratio α are exchanged with the inverted attribute dataset D_{inv} and finally get D_{mix} as training data.

Linear superposition for image level mixing. Add each pair of images in D_{org} and D_{inv}, $D_{mix} = D_{inv} * \alpha + D_{org} * (1 - \alpha)$.

Pixel swap for pixel level mixing. For each pair of images in D_{org} and D_{inv}, α of the pixels in the original image were randomly selected to be replaced with the inverse property image of the same position.

We set $\alpha = 0, 0.5, 1.0$ to generate images. The result of linear superposition and pixel swap is compared as shown in Fig. 3.

We verified the anti-classification ability of the image from α from 0 to 1 as shown in Fig. 4. It can be found that the score positively correlated with α. The accuracy of the model for mixed image training is tested in Fig. 4.

Through the above observation, we assume $E_i = 1 - \alpha$ to get confusion score of three mix methods. Figure 5 has shown confusion ability of three methods. We found that record-swap method has stable results to various α.

4.3 Defend Against Property Inference Attack

In this section, we want to test the performance of our approach under attacks in a real environment.

We use same CNN network and federated learning setting as in [3]. We set $K = 2$ for the best condition of attack. Our private attribute is black skin and main task is gender classification. Attacker's target is to infer race information.

We apply images with obfuscated attributes to training process. We set $\alpha = 0, 2, 0.5, 0.8$, and choose $record - swap$ method because of its stability.

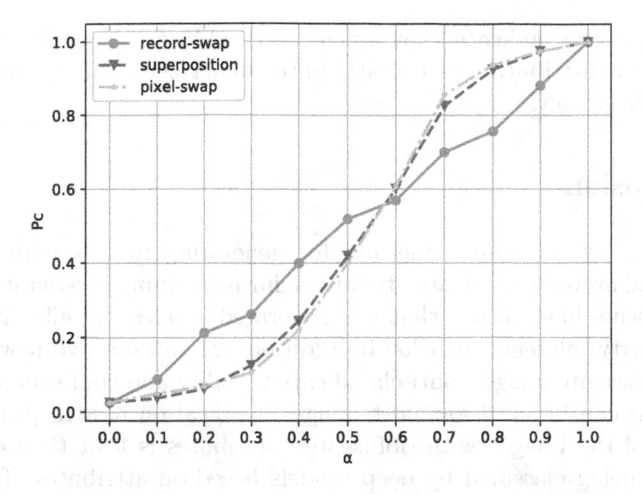

Fig. 4. Anti-classification score P^c of three mix methods controlled under α from 0 to 1.

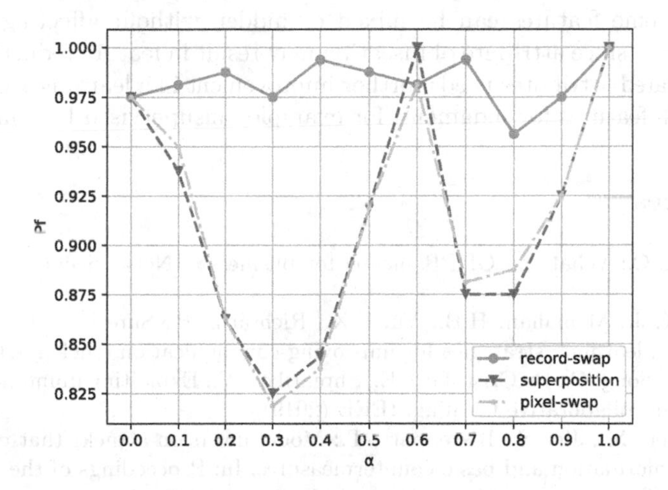

Fig. 5. Confusion score P^f of three mix methods controlled under α from 0 to 1.

Table 2. Accuracy score of property inference attack on images with obfuscated attribute on black.

Attributes	without defend(%)	$\alpha = 0.2$(%)	$\alpha = 0.5$(%)	$\alpha = 0.8$(%)
Black(attack target)	90.4	74.1	46.8	21.2
Male(main task)	92.4	92.4	92.2	92.1

Table 2 shows that the images with obfuscated attributes can effectively reduce the impact of property inference attack with neglected impact on gender classification tasks. We find that the accuracy rate will decrease when α

increases. This may indicate that images with obfuscated attributes can hide the probability distribution of the attributes under the security assumption of protocol transparency.

5 Conclusion

In this paper, we propose a method for generating images with obfuscated attributes and protecting private attributes during training in federated learning. Our experiments have shown that our generated images can effectively defend against property inference attacks. In addition, we propose two new evaluation methods to measure images' anti-classification ability and confusion ability. The two criterions can be used for most image classification hidden problems. One more merit of the images with obfuscated attributes is that they can be prevented from being classified by deep models based on attributes. The mixture parameter can effectively control the leakage of attribute information.

The success of obfuscation indicates that the image data has some rich features, and some features can be mixed or hidden without affecting the main task. However, since attribute obfuscating may result in feature reduction, image with obfuscated attributes needs further improvement in a learning scenario that requires rich features for judgment, for example, unsupervised learning.

References

1. Tankard, C.: What the GDPR means for businesses. Netw. Secur. **2016**(6), 5–8 (2016)
2. Konečný, J., Mcmahan, H.B., Yu, F.X., Richtárik, P., Suresh, A.T., Bacon, D.: Federated learning: strategies for improving communication efficiency (2016)
3. Melis, L., Song, C., De Cristofaro, E., Shmatikov, V.: Exploiting unintended feature leakage in collaborative learning. IEEE (2019)
4. Fredrikson, M., Jha, S., Ristenpart, T.: Model inversion attacks that exploit confidence information and basic countermeasures. In: Proceedings of the 22nd ACM SIGSAC Conference on Computer and Communications Security, pp. 1322–1333. ACM (2015)
5. Hitaj, B., Ateniese, G., Pérez-Cruz, F.: Deep models under the GAN: information leakage from collaborative deep learning. In: Proceedings of the 2017 ACM SIGSAC Conference on Computer and Communications Security, pp. 603–618. ACM (2017)
6. Bonawitz, K., Ivanov, V., Kreuter, B., Marcedone, A., Seth, K.: Practical secure aggregation for privacy-preserving machine learning. In: ACM SIGSAC Conference on Computer & Communications Security (2017)
7. Le, T.P., Aono, Y., Hayashi, T., Wang, L., Moriai, S.: Privacy-preserving deep learning via additively homomorphic encryption. IEEE Trans. Inf. Forensics Secur. **PP**(99), 1 (2017)
8. Shokri, R., Shmatikov, V.: Privacy-preserving deep learning. In: Proceedings of the 22nd ACM SIGSAC Conference on Computer and Communications Security, pp. 1310–1321. ACM (2015)

9. Abadi, M., et al.: Deep learning with differential privacy. In: Proceedings of the 2016 ACM SIGSAC Conference on Computer and Communications Security, pp. 308–318. ACM (2016)
10. Zhang, T., He, Z., Lee, R.B.: Privacy-preserving machine learning through data obfuscation (2018)
11. Sharma, S., Chen, K.: Poster: image disguising for privacy-preserving deep learning (2019)
12. Triastcyn, A., Faltings, B.: Generating artificial data for private deep learning (2018)
13. Choi, Y., Choi, M., Kim, M., Ha, J.W., Kim, S., Choo, J.: StarGAN: unified generative adversarial networks for multi-domain image-to-image translation (2017)
14. Zhu, J.Y., Park, T., Isola, P., Efros, A.A.: Unpaired image-to-image translation using cycle-consistent adversarial networks. In: IEEE International Conference on Computer Vision (2017)
15. Sim, T., Zhang, L.: Controllable face privacy. In: 2015 11th IEEE International Conference and Workshops on Automatic Face and Gesture Recognition (FG), vol. 4, pp. 1–8. IEEE (2015)
16. Huang, G.B., Mattar, M., Berg, T., Learned-Miller, E.: Labeled faces in the wild: a database for studying face recognition in unconstrained environments. In: Workshop on Faces in 'Real-Life' Images: Detection, Alignment, and Recognition (2008)
17. Liu, Z., Luo, P., Wang, X., Tang, X.: Large-scale celebfaces attributes (celeba) dataset (2018). Accessed 15 Aug 2018
18. Krizhevsky, A., Sutskever, I., Hinton, G.E.: Imagenet classification with deep convolutional neural networks. In: Advances in Neural Information Processing Systems, pp. 1097–1105 (2012)

Context-Aware Residual Network with Promotion Gates for Single Image Super-Resolution

Xiaozhong Ji[1], Yirui Wu[2], and Tong Lu[1](✉)

[1] National Key Lab for Novel Software Technology, Nanjing University, Nanjing, China
shawn_ji@163.com, lutong@nju.edu.cn
[2] College of Computer and Information, Hohai University, Nanjing, China
wuyirui@hhu.edu.cn

Abstract. Deep learning models have achieved significant success in quantities of vision-based applications. However, directly applying deep structures to perform single image super-resolution (SISR) results in poor visual effects such as blurry patches and loss in details, which are caused by the fact that low-frequency information is treated equally and ambiguously across different patches and channels. To ease this problem, we propose a novel context-aware deep residual network with promotion gates, named as G-CASR network, for SISR. In the proposed G-CASR network, a sequence of G-CASR modules is cascaded to transform low-resolution features to high informative features. In each G-CASR module, we also design a dual-attention residual block (DRB) to capture abundant and variant context information by dually connecting spatial and channel attention scheme. To improve the informative ability of extracted context information, a promotion gate (PG) is further applied to analyze inherent characteristics of input data at each module, thus offering insight for how to enhance contributive information and suppress useless information. Experiments on five public datasets consisting of Set5, Set14, B100, Urban100 and Manga109 show that the proposed G-CASR has achieved averagely 1.112/0.0255 improvement for PSNR/SSIM measurements comparing with the recent methods including SRCNN, VDSR, lapSRN and EDSR. Simultaneously, the proposed G-CASR requires only about 25% memory cost comparing with EDSR.

Keywords: Context-aware residual network · Channel and spatial attention scheme · Promotion gate · Single image super-resolution

1 Introduction

Recently, numerous deep learning methods have been proposed to reconstruct high-resolution images based on single low-resolution images in multimedia. However, these methods still suffer from drawbacks in visual effects. We show

Y. M. Ro et al. (Eds.): MMM 2020, LNCS 11962, pp. 136–147, 2020.
https://doi.org/10.1007/978-3-030-37734-2_12

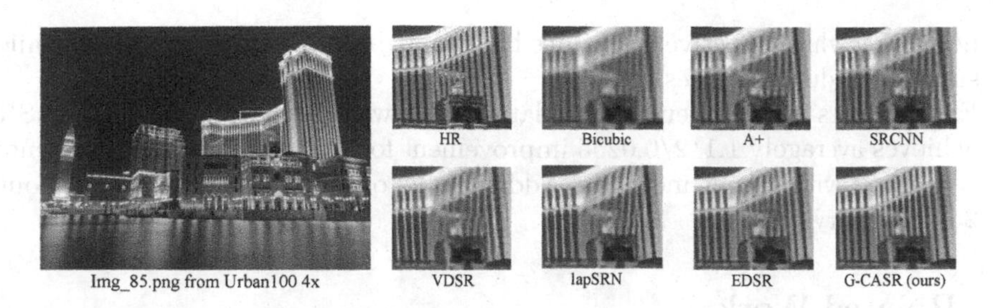

Fig. 1. Comparisons on SISR results achieved by G-CASR and comparative methods, where HR refers to the high-resolution image of the yellow rectangle region. (Color figure online)

examples of reconstructing a high-resolution image as in Fig. 1 (Left) to show these unpleasant effects. Based on the comparisons between the ground truth (HR in Fig. 1) and the generated high-resolution images of different methods in Fig. 1, we can observe blurry patches, failures in reconstructing high-frequency image details, and loss of low-frequency features like straight lines for the existing methods consisting of Bicubic, A+, SRCNN, VDSR, lapSRN and EDSR. The reason for unpleasant visual effects lies in the fact that the existing methods lack context information to capture the unique characteristics of low-resolution images. Essentially, the lack of context descriptor is one of the main drawbacks in most deep residual networks.

Based on these limitations of existing methods for single image super-resolution (SISR), we propose a novel Gated Context-Aware Super-Resolution network, which is named as G-CASR. The proposed G-CASR network consists of two main parts, namely, a dual-attention residual block (DRB) and a promotion gate (PG). By modeling channel-wise and spatial attention information to describe the inherent property of context information, the proposed DRB can restore high-frequency features and maintain low-frequency features simultaneously. On the other side, the proposed PG is used to enhance informativeness of context information with an adaptive gating signal.

By involving these two parts, we conduct a light-scale deep residual network to capture the unique and informative context characteristics. The proposed G-CASR network learns an end-to-end mapping between low-resolution image and reconstructed high-resolution image. As shown in G-CASR in Fig. 1, we can see the result of the same input is greatly improved by G-CASR.

The contributions of this paper are three-fold:

- We propose a novel and context-aware residual network G-CASR for SISR, in which dual-attention residual structure and promotion gate mechanism are proposed to enhance feature representative ability based on multi-level features and context information.
- We design a new dual-attention residual block (DRB) by involving channel and spatial attention scheme to modeling context information. Furthermore, we are the first to propose promotion gate (PG) for attention-based residual

networks, which effectively enhance high contribution features and meanwhile suppress redundant ones.
- Experiments on five benchmark datasets show that the proposed G-CASR achieves averagely 1.112/0.0255 improvement for PSNR/SSIM measurements compared with recent methods. Additionally, our model requires only about 25% memory cost.

2 Related Work

We category the existing deep learning methods for SISR into two types, i.e., convolutional neural networks (CNN) and generative adversarial networks. CNN-based SISR methods are quite larger in the amount due to more years of development and their impressive high-resolution reconstruction results. The first work to solve SISR problem, i.e., SRCNN, is introduced by Dong et al. [3]. Their proposed three-layer CNN network directly learns an end-to-end mapping between interpolated low-resolution image and the corresponding high-resolution output image. Inspired by the success of very deep networks like Res-Net, Kim et al. [8] propose very deep convolutional networks (VDSR), in which global residual learning is utilized to recover high-frequency details. Moreover, VDSR stacks 20 convolutional layers to construct a very deep network for accurate SISR and thus has an impressive property of fast convergence.

To pursue a deeper network for SISR task, Tong et al. [15] present a novel SISR method by introducing dense skip connections in a very deep network. By propagating feature maps of each layer into all the subsequent layers and allowing dense skip connection, their model combines low-level and high-level features in a reasonable way to boost reconstruction performance. Lim et al. [11] develop an enhanced deep super-resolution network (EDSR) with its performance exceeding the current state-of-the-art SISR methods. Their method performs optimization by removing unnecessary modules in convolutional residual networks and expanding model depth with a stable training procedure.

Most recently, Kim et al. [9] propose a novel channel-wise and spatial attention mechanism specially optimized for super-resolution, which prefers to fuse spatial and channel attention for a unity representation before assigning weights, rather than two separate weight schemes. However, their work is only tested on two simplified attention schemes. Woo et al. [16] construct convolutional block attention module (CBAM) as a lightweight and general attention module, which sequentially infers attention maps along spatial and channel dimensions at first and then multiply attention maps to the input feature map for adaptive feature refinement. Their proposed light-scale attention module has achieved excellent performance in lots of recognition and classification tasks.

3 The Proposed Method

In this section, we describe the network architecture of G-CASR, and the structures of the proposed DRB and PG.

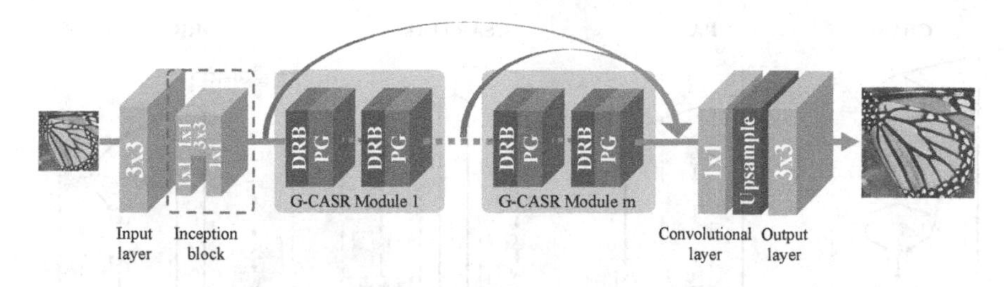

Fig. 2. The framework of proposed G-CASR method, which consists of an input layer, an inception block, G-CASR modules, a convolutional layer, an upsampling layer, and an output layer.

3.1 Network Architecture Design

As shown in Fig. 2, the proposed G-CASR network mainly consists of six parts, that is, an input layer, an inception block, G-CASR modules, a convolutional layer, an upsampling layer, and an output layer. The input low-resolution image I_L is firstly processed by a convolutional kernel of the input layer to generate shallow feature and then enhanced by an inception block, which can be formulated as

$$F_I = H_I(H_S(I_L)) \tag{1}$$

where function $H_S()$ denotes convolutional operation in the input layer, and $H_I()$ refers to multi-branch operations of inception block.

After that, the first G-CASR module is adopted to generate deep feature F_{G_1} based on enhanced feature F_I:

$$F_{G_1} = H_{G_1}(F_I) \tag{2}$$

where function $H_{G_1}()$ denotes the operation of the first G-CASR module. Take G-CASR as the basic module of the whole network, we thus construct deeper network by cascading a quantity of DRBs and PGs. The generated feature after processing of the mth G-CASR can be represented as

$$F_{G_m} = H_{G_m}(F_{G_{m-1}}) \tag{3}$$

To increase the width of the network and generate global features, the convolutional layer accepts input from different modules. G-CASR network obtains a high-resolution image I_H by firstly performing the upsampling layer and then generating the image after operation of the output layer:

$$I_H = H_O(H_U(H_C([F_I, H_{G_1}(F_I), \cdots, H_{G_m}(H_{G_{m-1}}(\cdots H_{G_1}(F_I)\cdots))]))) \tag{4}$$

where function $H_C()$, $H_U()$ and $H_O()$ represent the convolutional layer, upsampling, and the output layer, respectively, while [,] denotes concatenation along channel dimension.

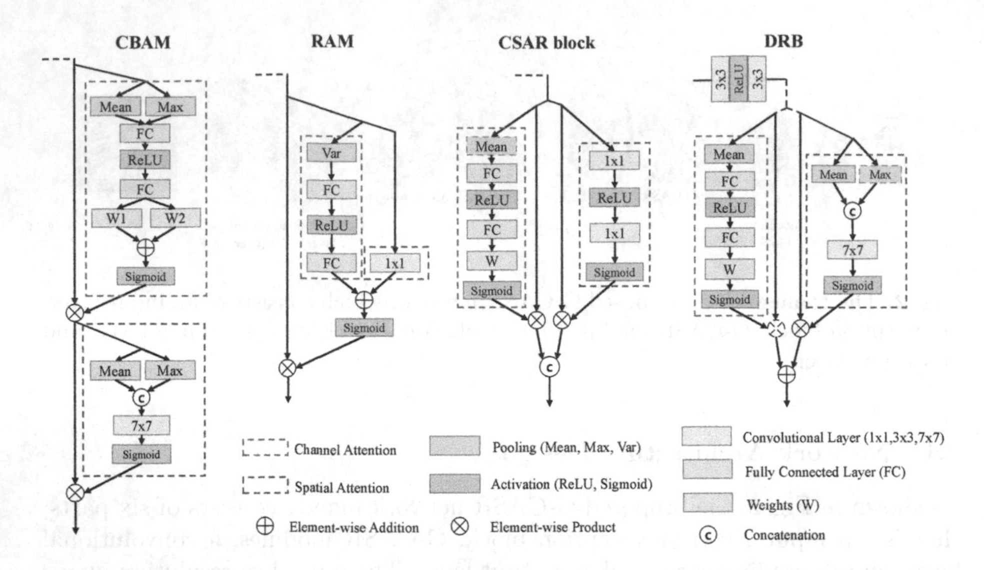

Fig. 3. Structure of the proposed DRB and three other different attention schemes, where the rightmost structure is the proposed DRB.

3.2 Structure of Dual-Attention Residual Block

Inspired by attention schemes applied in other domains and related SISR work based on attention scheme, we propose a lightweight DRB structure, which combines channel-wise and spatial attention in a dual form to adaptively modulate feature representations with context information among feature channels and different regions.

We show structures of various attention schemes including CBAM [16], RAM [9], CSAR block [6] and the proposed DRB in Fig. 3. We can observe DRB is different from other schemes in structure design and combination form. Applying an additional max-pooling to construct spatial attention scheme is adopted by CBAM and DRB, which exploits maximal context characteristics of the feature map to enhance its representative ability. Essentially, regions with the maximal values can be edges, corners or places with high gradient values, which are more salient than other regions and require more attention to their high-frequency details reconstruction. Meanwhile, we use mean-pooling operation in the construction of channel-wise attention scheme, due to the fact that maximal information is weak to exploit the inter-channel relationship.

We prefer dual form to combine the channel and spatial attention scheme rather than a cascade form. This is because usually for recognition and classification tasks, feature information needs to be highly compressed to resolve high-level and semantic information; however, a SISR task requires to restore high-frequency details based on generated feature maps. Cascade combination form often leads passed-by information to be compressed, while dual form can increase bandwidth for information transmission to obtain abundant information for high-frequency detail reconstruction.

Take the first G-CASR module H_{G_1} as an example and assume only one DRB and PG inside, we firstly adopt two convolutional layers and an activation layer to extract feature $\tilde{F_I} = H_E(F_I)$. Then, we construct the dual form of attention scheme to extract informative part of the generated feature, which can be represented as

$$F_D = C(\tilde{F_I}) \odot \tilde{F_I} + S(\tilde{F_I}) \odot \tilde{F_I} \tag{5}$$

where $\odot$ denotes element-wise multiplication, $C()$ and $S()$ represent channel and spatial attention scheme, respectively.

Channel Attention Scheme. Considering that a convolutional layer consists of different channel filters, each 2D slice of the output 3D feature map essentially encodes spatial-visual responses raised by a channel filter. By stacking different layers, CNN extracts image features through a hierarchical representation of visual abstractions [17]. Therefore, features extracted from CNN structure are essentially channel-wise and multi-layer. However, not all the channel-wise features are equally important and informative for recovering high-frequency details. We thus utilize channel attention scheme to compute task-specified feature map for SISR by exploiting the cross-channel relationship.

As shown in Fig. 3, a global mean-pooling is firstly performed on input feature map $\tilde{F_I}$ to output global mean-pooled feature map F_c with size $C \times 1 \times 1$. Then, F_c will be fed into a multi-layer perception with two hidden layers. It is noted that the first hidden layer is used to perform dimension reduction for compact feature representation. Finally, a sigmoid activation function is applied to squeeze the output, thus generating channel attention weight as follows:

$$C(\tilde{F_I}) = sig(W_1 * (relu(W_0 * P_a(\tilde{F_I})))) \tag{6}$$

where function $P_a()$, $sig()$ and $relu()$ refer to the global mean-pooling operation, Sigmoid and ReLU activation function respectively, W_0 and W_1 are learnable parameter matrices and defined with size $\frac{C}{r} \times C$ and $C \times \frac{C}{r}$ respectively, and r is a pre-defined dimension reduction parameter and we set it as 16 by experiments.

Spatial Attention Scheme. We observe the information contained in feature maps and low-resolution images is diverse over spatial positions. For example, edge or texture regions usually contain high-frequency information, while smooth areas have low-frequency information. To better recover high-frequency details and maintain low-frequency parts for a SISR task, we thus propose a spatial attention scheme to adaptively optimize feature map in different regions with suitable operations. Spatial attention scheme is constructed based on the difference of feature map of different positions, which essentially explores the spatial relationship to construct context descriptor.

As shown in Fig. 3, a global max-pooling operation is first performed on input feature map $\tilde{F_I}$ to output max-pooled feature map F_m with size $1 \times m \times n$. Then, we perform mean-pooling operation along channel dimension to generate

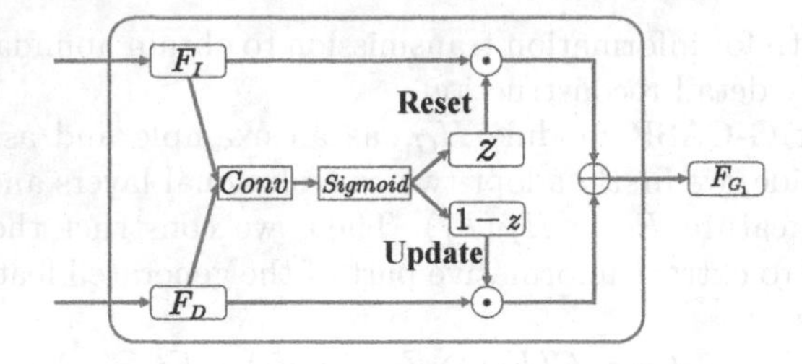

Fig. 4. Architecture of the proposed PG for residual network.

mean-pooled feature map F_a. Finally, a convolutional layer and a sigmoid activation function are performed on the concatenated feature map of F_a and F_m to generate spatial attention weight:

$$S(\tilde{F_I}) = sig(Conv([P_m(\tilde{F_I}), P_{ac}(\tilde{F_I})])) \tag{7}$$

where function $P_m()$, $P_{ac}()$ and $Conv()$ refer to the global max-pooling operation, mean-pooling operation along channel dimension and convolutional layer with 7×7 kernel, respectively.

3.3 Promotion Gate for Residual Network

During modeling a SISR task, missing pixels of high-resolution images can be generated from clues by analyzing low-frequency information from the input low-resolution images. Such highly non-linear processing can be properly achieved by constructing deep neural network to learn from a large training set. However, gradient disappearance from layer to layer leads to shallow structure, thus preventing to obtain deep CNN-based structure.

Inspired by GRU [2] and LSTM [5] for time-varying signal processing, we design PG to work on residual network for deeper layers, where we show its architecture in Fig. 4. Essentially, a GRU or LSTM-based network can build long-term dependencies based on complicated and time-varying information due to their unique gate design, which allows to efficiently update memory with the useful part of a signal. This inspires us to borrow the most important concept of GRU, i.e., gating mechanism, to help build a deeper residual network by enhancing informative part of features, thus relieving the burden of gradient disappearance.

As shown in Fig. 4, the feature F_D is computed by the proposed DRB block for reconstruction, and also the input of the proposed PG. By comparing between the original signal F_I and F_D, the proposed PG decides the proportion of enhancing and forgetting information with a simple but effective gating signal z, which is constructed as a lightweight structure of a convolutional layer with 1×1 kernel and a sigmoid activation function:

$$z = sig(Conv([F_I, F_D])) \tag{8}$$

Table 1. Comparisons on PSNR/SSIM measurement with or without DRB and PG. It is noted that the scale factor is 2×, √ and × represent network design with or without structure, respectively.

DRB	PG	Set5	Set14	B100	Urban100	Manga109
×	×	37.97/0.9604	33.54/0.9169	32.17/0.8996	31.99/0.9270	38.40/0.9767
√	×	37.98/0.9605	33.49/0.9163	32.15/0.8994	32.06/0.9275	38.61/0.9769
×	√	38.03/0.9606	33.62/0.9179	32.20/0.8999	32.10/0.9283	38.52/0.9769
√	√	38.01/0.9606	33.68/0.9186	32.19/0.9000	32.19/0.9288	38.70/0.9772

Since z is of the same size as F_I and F_D, it can be directly applied as weight to process both features:

$$F_{G_1} = z \odot F_I + (1 - z) \odot F_D \tag{9}$$

Essentially, z resets F_I by assisting to forget useless information, meanwhile $1 - z$ updates F_D by selectively enhancing valuable information. Since z and $1-z$ change synchronously, the PG allows the residual network to keep balance in remembering and forgetting, thus relieving the burden of gradient disappearance.

4 Experimental Results

In this section, we firstly introduce datasets. Then, we conduct four groups of ablation studies to demonstrate the proposed DRB and PG are effective for SISR task. After that, we show performance of our final model on five benchmark datasets. Finally, we describe implementation details for readers' convenience.

4.1 Datasets and Metrics

We conduct experiments on five datasets, i.e., Set5 [1], Set14 [18], B100 [12], Urban100 [7] and Manga109 [4]. Note that Set5, Set14 and B100 consist of natural scenes, Urban100 contains challenging urban scenes images with details, and Manga109 is a dataset of Japanese cartoon drawing. Besides these benchmark datasets, DIV2K [13], which served as the benchmark for NTIRE 2017 challenge, is adopted as a part of the training set. We achieve pairs of low-resolution and high-resolution images by a bicubic operator on high-resolution images. Above all, we obtain 800 images for training and 100 images to perform cross-validation for evaluating SISR methods. Peak signal to noise ratio (PSNR) and structural similarity index (SSIM) are used to measure reconstruction performances for SISR.

4.2 Ablation Study

To verify the effect of the proposed DRB and PG, we conduct four ablation experiments with different network design. To be clear, we define the number of

Table 2. Quantitative evaluation of state-of-the-art SISR algorithms, where average PSNR/SSIM for scale factors 2×, 3×, 4× are listed. Best results are **highlighted**.

Methods	Scale	Set5	Set14	B100	Urban100	Manga109
Bicubic	2×	33.66/0.9299	30.24/0.87688	29.56/0.8431	26.88/0.8403	30.80/0.9339
A+ [14]	2×	36.54/0.9544	32.28/0.9056	31.21/0.8863	29.20/0.8938	35.57/0.9663
SRCNN [3]	2×	36.66/0.9542	32.45/0.9067	31.36/0.8879	29.50/0.8946	35.60/0.9663
VDSR [8]	2×	37.53/0.9590	33.05/0.9130	31.90/0.8960	30.77/0.9140	37.22/0.9750
LapSRN [10]	2×	37.52/0.9591	33.08/0.9130	31.80/0.8950	30.41/0.9101	37.27/0.9740
EDSR [11]	2×	38.11/0.9601	33.92/0.9195	32.32/0.9013	**32.93/0.9351**	39.10/0.9773
G-CASR	2×	**38.22/0.9614**	**33.94/0.9214**	**32.33/0.9015**	32.79/0.9344	**39.24/0.9782**
Bicubic	3×	30.39/0.8682	27.55/0.7742	27.21/0.7385	24.46/0.7349	26.95/0.8556
A+ [14]	3×	32.58/0.9088	29.13/0.8188	28.29/0.7835	26.03/0.7973	29.93/0.9089
SRCNN [3]	3×	32.75/0.9090	29.30/0.8215	28.41/0.7863	26.24/0.7989	30.48/0.9117
VDSR [8]	3×	33.67/0.9210	29.78/0.8320	28.83/0.7990	27.14/0.8290	32.01/0.9340
LapSRN [10]	3×	33.82/0.9227	29.87/0.8320	28.82/0.7980	27.07/0.8280	32.21/0.9350
EDSR [11]	3×	34.65/0.9282	30.52/0.8462	29.25/0.8093	**28.80/0.8653**	34.17/0.9476
G-CASR	3×	**34.66/0.9294**	**30.55/0.8464**	**29.26/0.8094**	28.76/0.8637	**34.18/0.9480**
Bicubic	4×	28.42/0.8104	26.00/0.7027	25.96/0.6675	23.14/0.6577	24.89/0.7866
A+ [14]	4×	30.28/0.8603	27.32/0.7491	26.82/0.7087	24.32/0.7183	27.03/0.8439
SRCNN [3]	4×	30.48/0.8628	27.50/0.7513	26.90/0.7101	24.52/0.7221	27.58/0.8555
VDSR [8]	4×	31.35/0.8838	28.01/0.7674	27.29/0.7251	25.18/0.7524	28.83/0.8870
LapSRN [10]	4×	31.54/0.8850	28.19/0.7720	27.32/0.7270	25.21/0.7560	29.09/0.8900
EDSR [11]	4×	32.46/0.8968	28.80/0.7876	27.71/0.7420	26.64/0.8033	31.02/0.9148
G-CASR	4×	**32.54/0.8996**	**28.88/0.7882**	**27.72/0.7424**	**26.69/0.8038**	**31.14/0.9163**

G-CASR modules as m, the number of DRB with PG in each G-CASR module as n and filter number of each convolutional layer as k. The setting for ablation experiments is $m = 4$, $n = 4$ and $k = 64$. For parameter balancing, two convolutional layers with an activation function replace the proposed structure to construct original network.

By comparing the first and second rows of Table 1, we can observe the effectiveness of DRB structure since PSNR/SSIM values achieved by G-CASR with DRB structure are higher than those of the original network on most datasets. It is noted that G-CASR with DRB fails to improve reconstruction effect on Set14 and B100 datasets. This is caused by unsuccessful modeling of complicated and multi-type context information embedded in natural scene scenario. This conclusion can be further proved by tests on Manga109 dataset, where G-CASR with and without DRB achieve results of 38.61/0.9769 and 38.40/0.9767, respectively. Manga109 dataset contains only cartoon drawings, which makes it easy to model context information. By comparing the first and third rows of Table 1, we can observe the effectiveness of PG since PSNR/SSIM values achieved by G-CASR are higher than those of the original network on all the datasets including B100 and Urban100.

Between the results of the first and last rows, we can notice the network with DRB and PG achieves improvements on all listed datasets, which proves the effectiveness of the proposed DRB and PG for feature map enhancement. Moreover, PG enhances reconstruction performance based on the network only with DRB, which can be proved by the fact that DRB with PG achieves 0.13/0.0013 and 0.09/0.0003 improvement on Urban100 and Manga109.

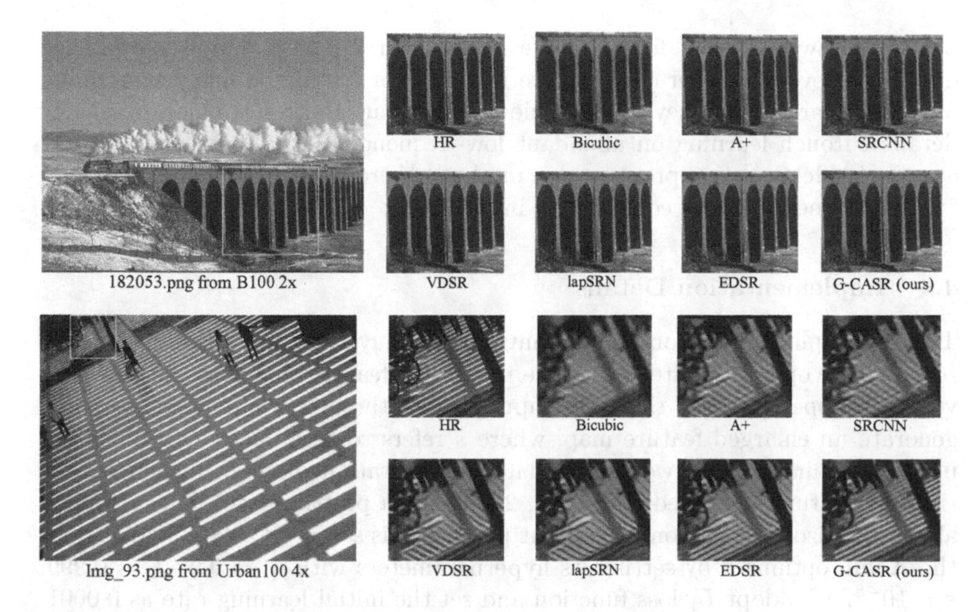

Fig. 5. Visual comparisons for SISR on B100 and Urban100 dataset, where the yellow rectangle represents enlarged regions for comparisons. (Color figure online)

4.3 SISR Performance and Analysis

Table 2 shows quantitative comparative results with 6 SISR algorithms for 2×, 3× and 4× SISR, respectively. It is noted that we obtain results of all comparative methods on five public datasets directly from their published papers. Among these methods, we pay special attention to EDSR since it is the current state-of-the-art algorithm for SISR. We test G-CASR by setting $m = 4$, $n = 8$ and $k = 128$.

From Table 2, we can notice G-CASR achieves better performance on Set5, Set14, B100 and Manga109 datasets compared with EDSR at 2×, 3× and 4×. This is due to their context information is easy to be captured and described by the proposed structure, thus enhancing feature map by context information. In fact, less performance improvement on Urban100 can be viewed by comparing G-CASR with EDSR because the former suffers from fewer model parameters. With only 25% model size of EDSR, G-CASR still produces superior SISR results. For example, the PSNR/SSIM value of G-CASR and EDSR on Manga109 are 31.14/0.9163 and 31.02/0.9148, respectively. The proposed structure acts well in most cases to partly describe context information embedded in complex urban and natural scenes, which are difficult to completely modeling. This can be proved by the fact that G-CASR obtains all the best performance during testing on B100 and Urban100 at 4×.

Figure 5 shows comparisons of visual effects achieved by G-CASR and comparative methods on B100 and Urban100. We can notice that G-CASR accurately reconstructs straight lines and parallel grid patterns on building surface and ground texture. This is because the proposed G-CASR network well preserves low-frequency features. We notice blurry effects and loss of image details achieved by other comparative methods for testing on image containing hair and beards since they fail to achieve clear focus and restore high-frequency details through learning on abundant low-frequency features. In contrast, our approach effectively suppresses these methods by removing redundant information but remember high contributive information.

4.4 Implementation Details

The upsampling layer contains a convolutional layer with 3×3 kernel and a pixel-shuffle operation afterward. The number of feature channels after the convolutional operation is s times the input so that the pixel-shuffle operation can generate an enlarged feature map, where s refers to scale factor. To make full usage of training data, we used a data augmentation method, in which each training picture is rotated 90°, 180°, 270° with a probability of 0.5, or flipped along a horizontal position. The input patch size is set as $48 \times 48 \times 3$. We adopt the Adam optimizer by setting its hyperparameters with $\beta_1 = 0.9$, $\beta_2 = 0.999$, $\epsilon = 10^{-8}$. We adopt L_1 loss function and set the initial learning rate as 0.0001. It is noted the learning rate decays by 0.5 for every 100 epochs and the total number of training epoch is 300. All of these experiments are performed on a single GTX 1080Ti GPU with 12 GB memory.

5 Conclusion

In this work, we propose a deep and lightweight context-aware residual network named as G-CASR, which appropriately encodes channel and spatial attention information to construct a context-aware feature map for SISR. Comparative results show that G-CASR not only achieves superior SISR performances than the current state-of-the-art method, i.e., EDSR, but also has the advantages of fewer parameters and less memory requirement. Our future work includes explorations to achieve real-time performance and better visual effects with extreme imaging situations.

Acknowledgment. This work is supported by the Natural Science Foundation of China under Grant 61672273, Grant 61832008, and Grant 61702160, Scientific Foundation of State Grid Corporation of China (Research on Ice-wind Disaster Feature Recognition and Prediction by Few-shot Machine Learning in Transmission Lines), National Key R&D Program of China under Grant 2018YFC0407901, and the Science Foundation of Jiangsu under Grant BK20170892.

References

1. Bevilacqua, M., Roumy, A., Guillemot, C., Alberi-Morel, M.L.: Low-complexity single-image super-resolution based on nonnegative neighbor embedding. In: Proceedings of BMVC (2012)

2. Cho, K., et al.: Learning phrase representations using RNN encoder-decoder for statistical machine translation. arXiv preprint arXiv:1406.1078 (2014)
3. Dong, C., Loy, C.C., He, K., Tang, X.: Learning a deep convolutional network for image super-resolution. In: Fleet, D., Pajdla, T., Schiele, B., Tuytelaars, T. (eds.) ECCV 2014. LNCS, vol. 8692, pp. 184–199. Springer, Cham (2014). https://doi.org/10.1007/978-3-319-10593-2_13
4. Fujimoto, A., Ogawa, T., Yamamoto, K., Matsui, Y., Yamasaki, T., Aizawa, K.: Manga109 dataset and creation of metadata. In: Proceedings of the 1st International Workshop on coMics ANalysis, Processing and Understanding, p. 2 (2016)
5. Hochreiter, S., Schmidhuber, J.: Long short-term memory. Neural Comput. **9**(8), 1735–1780 (1997)
6. Hu, Y., Li, J., Huang, Y., Gao, X.: Channel-wise and spatial feature modulation network for single image super-resolution. arXiv preprint arXiv:1809.11130 (2018)
7. Huang, J.B., Singh, A., Ahuja, N.: Single image super-resolution from transformed self-exemplars. In: Proceedings of CVPR, pp. 5197–5206 (2015)
8. Kim, J., Kwon Lee, J., Mu Lee, K.: Accurate image super-resolution using very deep convolutional networks. In: Proceedings of CVPR, pp. 1646–1654 (2016)
9. Kim, J.H., Choi, J.H., Cheon, M., Lee, J.S.: Ram: residual attention module for single image super-resolution. arXiv preprint arXiv:1811.12043 (2018)
10. Lai, W.S., Huang, J.B., Ahuja, N., Yang, M.H.: Deep Laplacian pyramid networks for fast and accurate super-resolution. In: Proceedings of CVPR (2017)
11. Lim, B., Son, S., Kim, H., Nah, S., Lee, K.M.: Enhanced deep residual networks for single image super-resolution. In: Proceedings of CVPR, vol. 1, p. 4 (2017)
12. Martin, D., Fowlkes, C., Tal, D., Malik, J.: A database of human segmented natural images and its application to evaluating segmentation algorithms and measuring ecological statistics. In: Proceedings of ICCV, vol. 2, pp. 416–423 (2001)
13. Timofte, R., Agustsson, E., Van Gool, L., Yang, M.H., Zhang, L.: NTIRE 2017 challenge on single image super-resolution: methods and results. In: Proceedings of Computer Vision and Pattern Recognition Workshops, pp. 114–125 (2017)
14. Timofte, R., De Smet, V., Van Gool, L.: A+: adjusted anchored neighborhood regression for fast super-resolution. In: Cremers, D., Reid, I., Saito, H., Yang, M.-H. (eds.) ACCV 2014. LNCS, vol. 9006, pp. 111–126. Springer, Cham (2015). https://doi.org/10.1007/978-3-319-16817-3_8
15. Tong, T., Li, G., Liu, X., Gao, Q.: Image super-resolution using dense skip connections. In: Proceedings of ICCV, pp. 4809–4817 (2017)
16. Woo, S., Park, J., Lee, J.-Y., Kweon, I.S.: CBAM: convolutional block attention module. In: Ferrari, V., Hebert, M., Sminchisescu, C., Weiss, Y. (eds.) ECCV 2018. LNCS, vol. 11211, pp. 3–19. Springer, Cham (2018). https://doi.org/10.1007/978-3-030-01234-2_1
17. Zeiler, M.D., Fergus, R.: Visualizing and understanding convolutional networks. In: Fleet, D., Pajdla, T., Schiele, B., Tuytelaars, T. (eds.) ECCV 2014. LNCS, vol. 8689, pp. 818–833. Springer, Cham (2014). https://doi.org/10.1007/978-3-319-10590-1_53
18. Zeyde, R., Elad, M., Protter, M.: On single image scale-up using sparse-representations. In: Boissonnat, J.-D., et al. (eds.) Curves and Surfaces 2010. LNCS, vol. 6920, pp. 711–730. Springer, Heidelberg (2012). https://doi.org/10.1007/978-3-642-27413-8_47

A Compact Deep Neural Network for Single Image Super-Resolution

Xiaoyu Xu, Jian Qian, Li Yu(✉), Shengju Yu, HaoTao, and Ran Zhu

Huazhong University of Science and Technology, Wuhan, China
{hustxyxu,qianjian,shengju_yu,husthtao,ran_zhu}@hust.edu.cn,
hustlyu@mail.hust.edu.cn

Abstract. Convolutional neural network (CNN) has recently been applied into single image super-resolution (SISR) task. But the applied CNN models are increasingly cumbersome which will cause heavy memory and computational burden when deploying in realistic applications. Besides, existing CNNs for SISR have trouble in handling different scales information with same kernel size. In this paper, we propose a compact deep neural network (CDNN) to (1) reduce the amount of model parameters (2) decrease computational operations and (3) process different scales information. We devise two kinds of channel-wise scoring units (CSU), including adaptive channel-wise scoring unit (ACSU) and constant channel-wise scoring unit (CCSU), which act as judges to score for different channels. With further sparsity regularization imposed on CSUs and ensuing pruning of low-score channels, we can achieve considerable storage saving and computation simplification. In addition, the CDNN contains a dense inception structure, the convolutional kernels of which are in different sizes. This enables the CDNN to cope with different scales information in one natural image. We demonstrate the effectiveness of CSUs, dense inception on benchmarks and the proposed CDNN has superior performance over other methods.

Keywords: Single image super resolution · Channel-wise scoring · Dense inception structure

1 Introduction

Image super-resolution (SR) technology aiming at reconstructing high resolution images from low resolution images has recently gained increasing interests

This work was supported in part by the National Natural Science Foundation of China under Grant 61871437 and in part by the Natural Science Foundation of Hubei Province of China under Grant 2019CFA022.
J. Qian—Equal contribution.

Electronic supplementary material The online version of this chapter (https://doi.org/10.1007/978-3-030-37734-2_13) contains supplementary material, which is available to authorized users.

Y. M. Ro et al. (Eds.): MMM 2020, LNCS 11962, pp. 148–160, 2020.
https://doi.org/10.1007/978-3-030-37734-2_13

in applications like surveillance [41], medical imaging [18]. Among SR problems, the single image super-resolution (SISR) focusing on mapping of single low resolution image to single high resolution image is considered complicated for its ill-posedness. The ill-posedness of SISR refers to a one-to-many mapping from domains of input to ranges of output which deteriorates with the increment of down-sampling factor.

In realistic scene, people always require SR methods to consume less memory and run at a high speed. Therefore, a light weight and fast SR method is urged. Generally speaking, in an inference stage of CNN, the memory consumption mainly comes from model parameters plus intermediate activation. For example, the state-of-the-art methods like [25,39] have more than 40 million parameters. They will even consume 10 times more memory in inference stage. Therefore we can conclude that three problems need to be solved simultaneously to obtain a compact model. (1) Reducing model size, it means model parameters should not be excessive. That is to say, we need to use less parameters to achieve favorable performance. (2) Decreasing computation complexity. It means less multiplication and addition operations are needed to complete a forward process. (3) Introducing as few overheads as possible. Since the scoring unit will also increase computation complexity, we should control the increment to a low level. Many works for getting a compact model have been carried out. A group is proposed [14] in convolution to efficiently simplify convolution operation. But this method takes no effect on memory reduction. Liu, Ye, etc. [26,35] tried to impose sparsity regularization on batch normalization layer and prune unimportant layers according to their scores. However, these methods require specific batch normalization layer which has been demonstrated ineffective in SR task. In addition, the scoring units become constant once model is trained over. These drawbacks limit model performance when processing different images. Furthermore, Yu, etc. [37] attempted to score all neurons in CNN but they introduced much overhead to the model.

In another aspect, solving SISR problem requires prolific prior information. Unlike video SR [22] which can utilize spatial and temporal information to

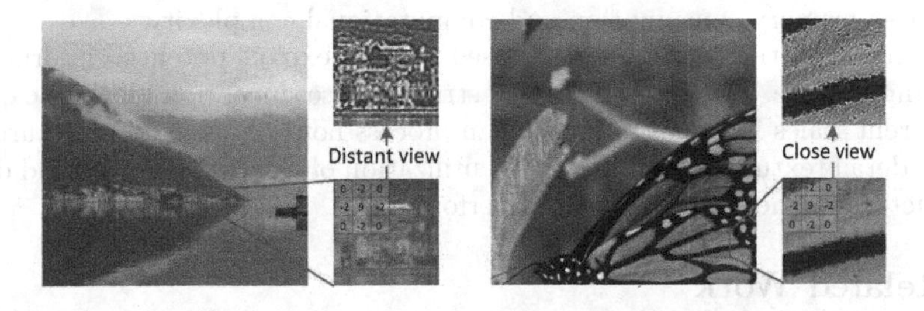

Fig. 1. An instance of different scale images in natural scenery. The left image is obtained from a distant view. With 3×3 convolution, the kernel has a broader receptive field which will process a holistic region thus being unable to focus on details. The right image has a close view. With 3 × 3 convolution, the kernel concentrates on details like textures in butterfly wings.

enhance performance, SISR has to delve into single image information to achieve superior performance. In a CNN model, kernel size determines how detail the model can process the input image. As for natural scenery SISR, the input image are always in different scales. As shown in Fig. 1, if the same size kernel is employed to different scale images, the kernel will cover a broader region in a larger scale image, which will cause information loss. That is to say, a fixed size of convolution kernel is not able to process both holistic structure and detail texture.

To address these problems, we design a compact deep neural network (CDNN). The CDNN mainly contains CSUs to realize model slimming and dense inception structure to exploit different scales information. Specifically, the CSU is divided into two types. The first type is ASCU which extracts information from channel-wise features, then crystalize the information into adaptive scoring weights. Afterwards, we impose smooth L1 regularization to these scoring weights to force their values to zero. With it, we can obtain a sparse scoring weight vector. The channels with low weights will eventually be clipped off from the model. In addition, we propose another type CSCU which introduces less overhead. The difference from ASCU is the scoring weights of ASCU are constant once the model is trained over. The compact network reduces parameters redundancy and subsequently improve performance to some extents. Besides, we also devise a dense inception structure to exploit different scales information. The dense inception structure adopts inception [30] block as basis. The inception block has different size kernels. In addition, the residual [11] learning has been indispensable in increasing CNN depth. Besides, the dense [23] structure is beneficial for memorizing all shallow layer features. The combination of these two techniques improve model performance to another level. So we devise a dense residual structure and integrate the basis inception block into it.

In this work, our contributions can be summarized as two aspects:

- We propose two types of channel-wise scoring units to make the model compact. The CSUs adopt smooth L1 regularization to make the weight vectors more sparse. Then we proceed a pruning to the sparse model to clip off channels with low scores. This strategy makes full use of channels, which further reduces memory consumption and computational complexity.
- A dense inception structure is devised to fully exploit potential information in single image. The dense inception structure uses inception block to capture different scales information which can process not only holistic structure but also detail textures. In addition, the utilization of residual learning and dense structure further improves model performance.

2 Related Work

In this section, we will describe the background knowledge, previous work on model slimming and methods on SISR.

Model Slimming. Current methods on model slimming mainly center on image classification task. It can be divided into three aspects: weight quantization, model distilling and model pruning. Han [10] proposed an improved model compression pipeline which can compress model 35× smaller than the primary. But it can not reduce inference computation complexity. XNOR-net is used in [28] to quantize model weights to binary values which only contains $\{-1, 0, 1\}$. Although this method achieves high compression rate, it also suffers high performance deterioration. A new concept of distilling a smaller model based on a trained complicated model is proposed in [12]. The distilling is realized with a cumbersome model as teacher to guide the training of the simple model. But this method introduces a 'temperature' concept to softmax activation. It is not suitable for SR task because SR task adopts L2 or L1 loss to evaluate the training. A neuron scoring method is used by [37] for each neuron in th model, but it introduced many overheads into the processing. [26,35] also came up with the channel-wise scoring methods, but they scored the channel on batch normalization layer. The batch normalization layer has been proved ineffective [25] in SR task.

Single Image Super Resolution (SISR). SISR is formulated as ill-posed problem and many researches have been conducted to solve it. Some previous solutions [6,7,20,24,34] tried to get accurate interpolation kernel or improve sampling skills. However these methods are not effective in capturing image details and always result in artifacts. Other works focused on learning-based methods. The random field methods [8,9,32] has also been studied in SR problem. Meanwhile, sparse-coding based methods [17,33,38] were proposed to better reconstruct high resolution images. These methods are limited by sampling skills, representation capability of models and high computational complexity. Recently, deep convolutional neural network achieves outstanding performance in SR. Dong et al. [3] proposed SRCNN for image SR and get superior performance over the conventional methods. Following methods such as FSRCNN [4], VDSR [19] reformed the SRCNN in training speed and model structure. These methods interpolate low resolution images before putting them into networks. It implicitly transfers input domain of mapping function. [21] proposed SRResnet to directly map low resolution images to high resolution images, and employed perceptual loss and adversarial loss to make outputs more visually realistic. While the SRResnet can result in PSNR loss, [25] removed batch normalization layer and aggregated residual blocks together with dense blocks to improve PSNR. [31] introduced densenet to SISR and MemNet [36] stepped further with densenet. In addition, [5,40] modeled the SR problem as recursive model. Unfortunately, most of these methods didn't consider the impact of kernel size.

In the following sections, we will firstly introduce two types of CSUs, and the framework of the proposed method in Sect. 3. After, extensive experimental results will be exhibited in Sect. 4. Finally, we will make a concise summary of the work in Sect. 5.

3 Proposed Method

We aim to achieve a compact deep neural network for SISR. In this section, we first introduce details about CSUs which help slim the nrural network. Then the framework of the proposed model will be illuminated.

3.1 Channel-Wise Scoring Unit

We propose a simple and applicable method to make the model sparse. Generally speaking, a CNN contains several convolution layers. The convolution layer has I input channels and J output channels. Each input channel is connected to every output channel. So there have to be $I \times J$ connections for a layer. But in fact, not all of these connections take effect for final output. Some connections may have lower values and will not change output even it is omitted. Therefore, we can devise a scoring unit to judge whether the connections, namely channels, need to be preserved or clipped off. Motivated by this, we design two types channel-wise scoring units (CSU): adaptive channel-wise scoring unit (ACSU), constant channel-wise scoring unit (CCSU). We allocate a unique weight for each channel which represents the importance of the channel. The J weights from one layer form into a weight vector. This weight vector is called CSU and values of which range from 0.0 to 1.0. Then we impose a smooth L1 [29] regularization to the weight vector in training phase to make it more sparse. So once we got the weight vector, the channel-wise multiplication is performed between the weight vector and J output features. What's worth mentioning is although generally used L1 regularization can achieve higher sparsity but it has drawbacks of being not stable to train. In contrast, smooth L1 regularization is more robust. So we adopt smooth L1 rather than L1. Eventually, we can prune the network according to the values of CSU. Specifically, the optimizing objective of the model is formulated as following:

$$\hat{\theta}, \hat{\omega} = \underset{\theta,\omega}{\arg\min} \left[\frac{1}{N} \sum_{n=1}^{N} ||I^{HR}, M_\theta(I^{LR})||_1 + \lambda * \frac{1}{K} \sum_{k=1}^{K} \Re(\omega_k) \right] \tag{1}$$

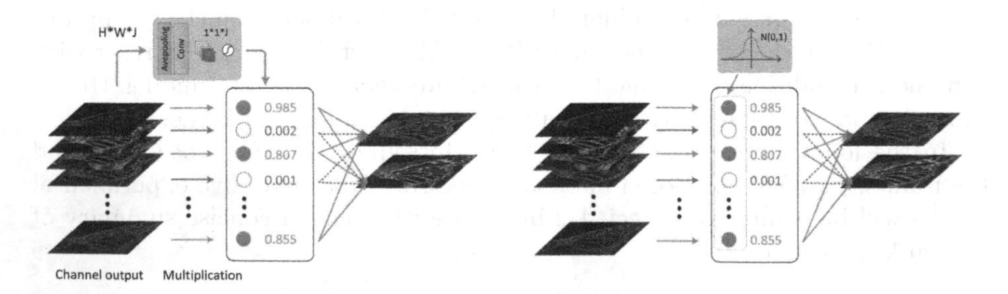

Fig. 2. Framework of ACSU and CCSU. The left is ACSU, the weight vector of which is derived from $H \times W \times J$ channel outputs. The right is CCSU, the weight vector of which is initialized with normal distribution.

where (I^{LR}, I^{HR}) denotes input and output of the model. L1 loss function is used here to avoid the impact from outlier samples. $\Re(\omega_k)$ regularizes the weight vector to achieve weight sparsity. λ balances the performance and sparsity.

ACSU. The reason we call it ACSU ascribes to the origination of the scoring weight vector. In ACSU, the weight vector is derived from each channel output. As shown in Fig. 2, the output first gets through an adaptive pooling layer. This operation makes features with size $H \times W \times J$ into a weight vector with size $1 \times 1 \times J$. Then this weight vector is sent to a sigmoid layer thus values of which are squashed in [0,1]. Finally features from all channel are multiplied with the vector. In the process of getting the weight vector, if different images are fed to the model, the weight vector for same layer will also changes according to channel output. Taking a middle layer CSU as example, as an image of mountains is sent to the model, the first quarter of the CSU have high values while other values are 0, so just high values corresponded features contribute to the result. However when an image of butterfly is sent to the model, only last quarter of CSU values are high, namely last quarter values are available for output. That indicates the model will judge the importance of channels in an adaptive way. That is why we call it 'adaptive channel-wise scoring unit'. This is also where we outperform the method in [10].

Run-Time Pruning. Since the ASCU has adaptive weight vectors, the pruning process should also change accordingly. As we know, general pruning [10] operation is executed before inference. It cut off unimportant channels after model is trained. Once these channels are pruned, they will never be used again, we call this static pruning. However, in our work, the static pruning is not suitable anymore. As mentioned above, the weight vectors for ASCU changes every time the input is altered. That manifests the weight vectors are able to learn which channels are useful for the input. So we need to employ a run-time pruning for it. We exhibit the whole process of run-time pruning in Algorithm 1. The key step in run-time pruning is 2. In this step, we first sort values of the weight vector and then prune the channels according to their scores. Those channels with low scores close to 0 will be pruned. Then only preserved channels are connected to next layer. With the loop of this process, we can prune the model layer by layer. Finally we get the output I^{SR}.

CCSU. In some situations, memory consumption is extremely restricted. So we devise another CCSU based on the ACSU. The CCSU introduces less overhead than ACSU but not as efficient as CCSU. So we provide these two solutions for different demands. As for the CCSU, its weight vectors are preassigned before the training. Here we initialize them to normalization distribution which has means 0, variance 1. In the training phase, the smooth L1 regularization is imposed to them. So the optimal weight vectors will be acquired after the training finishes. That means once the training is over, weight vectors of CCSU will be constant. The difference between CCSU and [10] is weight vectors of CCSU is preassigned and are directly applied to each channel but [10] uses γ in batch normalization layers as weight vectors.

Algorithm 1. Framework of run-time pruning.

Require:
The trained model M;
The set of input images I^{LR}, ground-truth images I^{HR};
Ensure:
The pruned model $\hat{M}$;
The set of output images I^{SR};
1: Feed I^{LR} to the M and get the weight vector w_0 form CSU_0, features f_0;
2: Sort values of the w_0 and prune the elements whose values are close to 0, the pruned weight vector is $\hat{w_0}$;
3: $\hat{f_0} = \hat{w_0} \cdot f_0$;
4: Feed $\hat{f_0}$ to next layer and loop from 1;
5: **return** I^{HR};

Static Pruning and Fine-Tuning. Unlike ACSU, the weight vectors of CCSU are constant once the training is over. So we prune unimportant channels before inference phase. We compare values of weight vectors with a threshold. The channels with lower values than the threshold will be pruned. Therefore, after the pruning process is over, the model will also be fixed. Compared with CCSU, it is needless for ACSU to derive weight vectors from channel outputs, for that no computational overhead will be brought in. But the ACSU can not allocate adaptive weights to channels, which indicates CCSU can't distinguish which channels are important for different input images. So we proceed a fine-tuning operation for the pruned model. The fine-tuning refers to extra training of the pruned model, which will improve performance in some cases. So we can conclude that the ACSU is more intelligent and CCSU is thiner.

3.2 Dense Inception Structure

This section mainly focuses on explanation of the proposed dense inception structure. Contemporary methods are unable to capture multiple scale information of input. It is mainly caused by the kernel size of their models is fixed to 3×3. Motivated by it, we adopt four kinds of kernel sizes in our dense inception structure. Besides, dense network and residual learning are also employed to improve model performance.

Inception Structure. Existing SISR methods like [5,31,36,40] just adopt convolution kernels with same size 3×3. However, [30] illustrates that different size kernels capture different scales information, small size kernel focuses more on details while big size kernel benefits for processing coarse outlines. Therefore, we set kernel sizes for each convolution operation in residual blocks 1×1, 3×3, 5×5, 7×7. As shown in Fig. 3 all outputs from the convolution layers are concatenated together and sent to local fusion layer. Finally a short skip connection is applied. The process of dense inception is formulated as following:

$$f_m = f_{m-1} + LF(ReLU(cat[Conv_1(f_{m-1}), ..., Conv_k(f_{m-1})])) \tag{2}$$

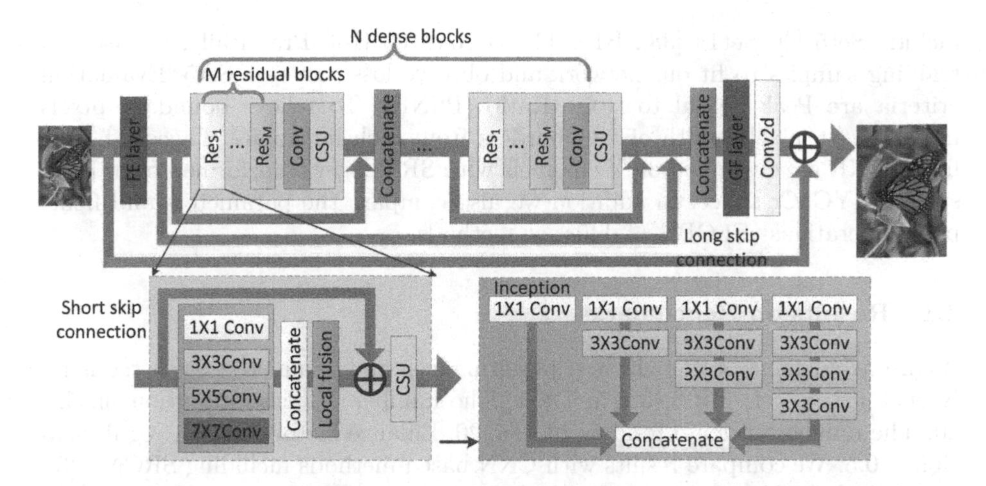

Fig. 3. Framework of CDNN.

Where f_{m-1} denotes input of dense inception block, f_m is output of dense inception block. k is the kernel size, and activation function here is Rectifier Linear Unit (ReLU). The processed features are then added with input f_{m-1} which means the residual block just needs to learn the representation of differential information between f_{m-1} and f_m. Eventually, the channel outputs are sent to CSU. By the way, in order to reduce parameters and computations, we use cascaded 3×3 kernels to represent 5×5 and 7×7 kernels.

Dense Residual Structure. Existing methods neglect utilizing hierarchical features in neural network. For example, shallow features contain texture information. As [15] illuminates, dense network can improve model's depth and utilize hierarchical information. But the dense network increases memory consumption as it concatenates all shallow features. So we design a dense residual structure as Fig. 3 shows. Unlike the fully connected dense network which consumes much memory, we just concatenate the output of each dense residual block. The concatenated features are then fed to next dense residual block. Besides, each dense residual block contains multiple inception blocks. In summary, the CDNN contains multiple dense residual blocks and each dense residual block contains several inception blocks.

$$f_m^n = cat[f_m^{n-1}, DR(f_m^{n-1})] \quad (3)$$

As denoted in equation above, f_m^{n-1} is input and f_m^n is output. $DR(*)$ denotes dense residual block. The f_m^{n-1} is fed to $DR(*)$ and processed by cascaded dense inception blocks.

4 Experimental Results

DIV2K is proposed by [1] for high quality image restoration tasks, it contains 800 training samples, 100 evaluation samples and 100 test samples. Benchmarks include Set5 [2], Set14 [38], B100 [27], Urban100 [16]. Practically, we use 800 training samples to fit our network and observe loss curve on Set5. Evaluation criteria are Peak Signal to Noise Ratio (PSNR). To relieve boundary pixels influence, 10 pixels width of four borders from each image are shaved off. The final PSNR are evaluated on Y channels with SR images transformed from RGB space to YCbCr space. In addition we also compare the parameters and float-point-operations (FLOPs) of different methods.

4.1 Results on Benchmarks

As discussed above, to get the best performance, final parameters are listed here. Kernel size: 1×1, 3×3, 5×5, 7×7. The number of dense inception blocks: 20. The number of dense residual blocks: 20. Balance factor λ for L1 regularization is 0.5. We compare results with CNN based methods including SRCNN [3], EDSR [25], RDN [40], Meta-RDN [13]. In the test, all images are transferred to YCbCr color space and we calculate PSNR in Y channel. To avoid edge pixels reconstruction errors, 10 boundary pixels from each side are shaved off. Further, we execute additional self-ensemble [25] testing for our model. Quantitative results are shown in Table 1. It is explicit that the proposed CDNN (last column) achieves the best performance in PSNR. It also shows that ASCU can decrease the amount of FLOPs by 25.4%, parameters by 40.1% but the PSNR loses a little. As for CCSU, it can lead to 29.2% and 16.8% decrement of Parameters and FLOPs. Compared with ACSUs it causes less performance loss. Subjective results are shown in Fig. 4. It is shown that our CDNN can reconstruct low resolution image more precisely. Detailed analyses are presented in supplementary material.

Table 1. Benchmark results with compared methods. Averaging PSNR(dB) with scaling factor ×2,×3,×4, the amount of parameters and FLOPs(input size is $3 \times 96 \times 96$). The best two results are highlighted in red and blue.

Methods		Bicubic	SRCNN	EDSR	RDN	Meta-RDN	CDNN-A (ACSU)	CDNN-C (CCSU)	CDNN+
Params		-	-	40.7M	22.1M	22.1M	15.5M	13.1M	21.9M
Flops		-	-	417.1G	231.9G	231.9G	142.2G	127.4G	170.8G
Set5	×2	33.66	36.66	38.11	38.24	-	38.28	38.23	38.32
	×3	30.39	32.75	34.66	34.71	-	34.77	34.70	34.82
	×4	28.42	30.48	32.50	32.47	-	32.55	32.50	32.65
Set14	×2	30.24	32.45	33.85	34.01	34.04	34.05	34.00	34.16
	×3	27.55	29.30	30.44	30.57	30.55	30.58	30.55	30.69
	×4	26.00	27.50	28.72	28.81	28.84	28.81	28.79	28.90
B100	×2	29.56	31.36	32.29	32.34	32.35	32.37	32.34	32.42
	×3	27.21	28.41	29.25	29.26	29.30	29.31	29.27	29.33
	×4	25.96	26.90	27.72	27.72	27.75	27.78	27.70	27.80
Urban100	×2	26.88	29.50	32.84	32.89	-	32.98	32.90	33.05
	×3	24.46	26.24	28.79	28.80	-	28.90	28.85	28.93
	×4	23.14	24.52	26.67	26.61	-	26.69	26.65	26.86

Fig. 4. Subjective results on benchmarks. The SR results are for image "3002008" from B100, "barbara" from Set14 and "img096" from Urban100 respectively.

5 Discussion and Conclusion

We proposed two types of channel-wise scoring methods to slim the model and devised a new structure for SISR. The smooth L1 regularization is imposed to get a compact neural network. On benchmarks, we demonstrate the proposed method not only achieves PSNR improvement compared with state-of-the-art methods but also have less parameters and FLOPs. The result also shows that the adaptive scoring have better PSNR while constant scoring have less parameters and FLOPs. So these two kinds of scoring strategies are suitable for different applications. Finally, the quantitative result also indicates the dense inception structure makes superior contributions compared with other methods.

References

1. Agustsson, E., Timofte, R.: NTIRE 2017 challenge on single image super-resolution: dataset and study. In: IEEE Conference on Computer Vision and Pattern Recognition Workshops (CVPRW) (2017)
2. Bevilacqua, M., Roumy, A., Guillemot, C., Alberi-Morel, M.L.: Low-complexity single-image super-resolution based on nonnegative neighbor embedding. In: BMVC (2012)
3. Dong, C., Loy, C.C., He, K., Tang, X.: Learning a deep convolutional network for image super-resolution. In: Fleet, D., Pajdla, T., Schiele, B., Tuytelaars, T. (eds.) ECCV 2014. LNCS, vol. 8692, pp. 184–199. Springer, Cham (2014). https://doi.org/10.1007/978-3-319-10593-2_13
4. Chao, D., Chen, C.L., Tang, X.: Accelerating the super-resolution convolutional neural network. In: CVPR (2016)
5. Dahl, R., Norouzi, M., Shlens, J.: Pixel recursive super resolution. In: ICCV (2017)
6. Duchon, C.E.: Lanczos filtering in one and two dimensions. J. Appl. Meteorol. **18**(8), 1016–1022 (1979)
7. Fattal, R.: Image upsampling via imposed edge statistics. ACM Trans. Graph. **26**(3), 95 (2007)
8. Freeman, W.T., Jones, T.R., Pasztor, E.C.: Example-based super-resolution. Comput. Graph. Appl. IEEE **22**(2), 56–65 (2002)
9. Haichao, Z., Yanning, Z., Haisen, L., Huang, T.S.: Generative Bayesian image super resolution with natural image prior. IEEE Trans. Image Process. **21**(9), 4054–4067 (2012)
10. Han, S., Pool, J., Tran, J., Dally, W.: Learning both weights and connections for efficient neural network. In: Advances in Neural Information Processing Systems, pp. 1135–1143 (2015)
11. He, K., Zhang, X., Ren, S., Sun, J.: Deep residual learning for image recognition. In: CVPR (2016)
12. Hinton, G., Vinyals, O., Dean, J.: Distilling the knowledge in a neural network. arXiv preprint arXiv:1503.02531 (2015)
13. Hu, X., Mu, H., Zhang, X., Wang, Z., Tan, T., Sun, J.: Meta-SR: a magnification-arbitrary network for super-resolution. In: Proceedings of the IEEE Conference on Computer Vision and Pattern Recognition, pp. 1575–1584 (2019)
14. Huang, G., Liu, S., Laurens, V.D.M., Weinberger, K.Q.: CondenseNet: an efficient DenseNet using learned group convolutions (2017)
15. Huang, G., Liu, Z., Weinberger, K.Q.: Densely connected convolutional networks. CoRR abs/1608.06993 (2016). http://arxiv.org/abs/1608.06993
16. Huang, J.B., Singh, A., Ahuja, N.: Single image super-resolution from transformed self-exemplars. In: CVPR (2015)
17. Jianchao, Y., John, W., Thomas, H., Yi, M.: Image super-resolution via sparse representation. IEEE Trans. Image Process. **19**(11), 2861–2873 (2010)
18. Jun, X.U., Liu, H., Yin, Y.: Medical image super-resolution reconstruction method based on non-local autoregressive learning. Pattern Recog. Artif. Intell. **30**(8), 747–753 (2017)
19. Kim, J., Lee, J.K., Lee, K.M.: Accurate image super-resolution using very deep convolutional networks. In: CVPR (2016)
20. Kwang In, K., Younghee, K.: Single-image super-resolution using sparse regression and natural image prior. IEEE Trans. Pattern Anal. Mach. Intell. **32**(6), 1127 (2010)

21. Ledig, C., et al.: Photo-realistic single image super-resolution using a generative adversarial network. In: ICCV (2017)
22. Li, S., He, F., Du, B., Zhang, L., Xu, Y., Tao, D.: Fast spatio-temporal residual network for video super-resolution. In: The IEEE Conference on Computer Vision and Pattern Recognition (CVPR), June 2019
23. Li, T., Xu, M., Yang, R., Tao, X.: A DenseNet based approach for multi-frame in-loop filter in HEVC. In: 2019 Data Compression Conference (DCC), pp. 270–279. IEEE (2019)
24. Li, X., Orchard, M.T.: New edge-directed interpolation. IEEE Trans. Image Process. **10**(10), 1521–1527 (2001)
25. Lim, B., Son, S., Kim, H., Nah, S., Lee, K.M.: Enhanced deep residual networks for single image super-resolution. In: Computer Vision and Pattern Recognition Workshops (CVPRW) (2017)
26. Liu, Z., Li, J., Shen, Z., Huang, G., Yan, S., Zhang, C.: Learning efficient convolutional networks through network slimming (2017)
27. Martin, D., Fowlkes, C., Tal, D., Malik, J.: A database of human segmented natural images and its application to evaluating segmentation algorithms and measuring ecological statistics. In: ICCV 2001 (2001)
28. Rastegari, M., Ordonez, V., Redmon, J., Farhadi, A.: XNOR-Net: ImageNet classification using binary convolutional neural networks. In: Leibe, B., Matas, J., Sebe, N., Welling, M. (eds.) ECCV 2016. LNCS, vol. 9908, pp. 525–542. Springer, Cham (2016). https://doi.org/10.1007/978-3-319-46493-0_32
29. Schmidt, M., Fung, G., Rosales, R.: Fast optimization methods for L1 regularization: a comparative study and two new approaches. In: Kok, J.N., Koronacki, J., Mantaras, R.L., Matwin, S., Mladenič, D., Skowron, A. (eds.) ECML 2007. LNCS (LNAI), vol. 4701, pp. 286–297. Springer, Heidelberg (2007). https://doi.org/10.1007/978-3-540-74958-5_28
30. Szegedy, C., et al.: Going deeper with convolutions. CoRR abs/1409.4842 (2014). http://arxiv.org/abs/1409.4842
31. Tong, T., Li, G., Liu, X., Gao, Q.: Image super-resolution using dense skip connections. In: ICCV (2017)
32. Wang, X., Hou, C., Pu, L., Hou, Y.: A depth estimating method from a single image using FoE CRF. Multimedia Tools Appl. **74**(21), 9491–9506 (2015)
33. Yang, J., Wright, J., Huang, T.S., Yi, M.: Image super-resolution as sparse representation of raw image patches. In: CVPR (2008)
34. Yang, P., Zhang, N., Zhang, S., Yu, L., Zhang, J., Shen, X.: Content popularity prediction towards location-aware mobile edge caching. IEEE Trans. Multimed. **21**(4), 915–929 (2019). https://doi.org/10.1109/TMM.2018.2870521
35. Ye, J., Lu, X., Lin, Z., Wang, J.Z.: Rethinking the smaller-norm less-informative assumption in channel pruning of convolution layers. arXiv preprint arXiv:1802.00124 (2018)
36. Ying, T., Jian, Y., Liu, X., Xu, C.: MemNet: a persistent memory network for image restoration. In: ICCV (2017)
37. Yu, R., et al.: NISP: pruning networks using neuron importance score propagation (2017)
38. Zeyde, R., Elad, M., Protter, M.: On single image scale-up using sparse-representations. In: Boissonnat, J.-D., et al. (eds.) Curves and Surfaces 2010. LNCS, vol. 6920, pp. 711–730. Springer, Heidelberg (2012). https://doi.org/10.1007/978-3-642-27413-8_47
39. Zhang, Y., Tian, Y., Kong, Y., Zhong, B., Fu, Y.: Residual dense network for image super-resolution. In: CVPR, June 2018

40. Zhang, Y., Tian, Y., Kong, Y., Zhong, B., Fu, Y.: Residual dense network for image super-resolution. In: Proceedings of the IEEE Conference on Computer Vision and Pattern Recognition, pp. 2472–2481 (2018)
41. Zou, W.W.W., Yuen, P.C.: Very low resolution face recognition problem. IEEE Trans. Image Process. Publ. IEEE Sig. Process. Soc. **21**(1), 327–40 (2012)

An Efficient Algorithm of Facial Expression Recognition by TSG-RNN Network

Kai Huang[1], Jianjun Li[1(✉)], Shichao Cheng[1(✉)], Jie Yu[1], Wanyong Tian[2], Lulu Zhao[2], Junfeng Hu[2], and Chin-Chen Chang[1,3]

[1] Institute of Graphics and Image, Hangzhou Dianzi University, Hangzhou 310018, China
{jianjun.li,sccheng}@hdu.edu.cn, alan3c@gmail.com
[2] CETC Key Laboratory of Data Link, XiAn 710071, China
[3] Department of Information Engineering and Computer Science, Feng Chia University, Taichung, Taiwan

Abstract. Facial expression recognition remains a challenging problem and the small datasets further exacerbate the task. Most previous works realize facial expression by fine-tuning the network pre-trained on a related domain. They have limitations inevitably. In this paper, we propose an optimal CNN model by transfer learning and fusing three characteristics: spatial, temporal and geometric information. Also, the proposed CNN module is composed of two-fold structures and it can implement a fast training. Evaluation experiments show that the proposed method is comparable to or better than most of the state-of-the-art approaches in both recognition accuracy and training speed.

Keywords: Facial expression recognition · Facial landmark · Feature fusion

1 Introduction

Facial expression is one of the most important ways for human expression of emotions, and it also plays an extremely important role in the process of social communication. The understanding of human emotion from images has become increasingly important with the recent advances in deep learning and human computer interaction [17], this technology is increasingly used in human-computer interaction [27], health care [23] and photography [28]. Early recognition of facial expressions is usually based on static images. These methods recognize and classify expressions by extracting the texture information of a single image, such as LBP [8], BoW [10], HoG [1], and SIFT [6]. However, with the deep learning method is different with the traditional machine learning method.

Supported by National Science Fund of China No. 61871170 and The National Defense Basic Research Program of JCKY2017210A001.

Y. M. Ro et al. (Eds.): MMM 2020, LNCS 11962, pp. 161–174, 2020.
https://doi.org/10.1007/978-3-030-37734-2_14

It can independently extract and classify the features of the image by training, without designing these features manually. Nowadays, the dataset for facial expression is not as many as target detection and recognition and the mainstream dataset includes: CK+[13], MMI [14], Oulu-CASIA [29] and so on. Besides, the facial expression data set is relatively small and not enough for training.

Facial expression recognition is a special existence in image classification tasks. On the one hand, the expression can be regarded as the dynamic change of the face over a period of time. Therefore, based on this, the sequence-based approach is proposed to capture temporal information of facial expressions in a video frame. On the other hand, the recognition result of the static expression picture is greatly affected by the posture, the background, the obstacle, etc., and the classification result cannot be obtained in the case of a lot of interference. Therefore, the various information fusion in the expression recognition is the key point. Among them, the spatial texture information carried by the expression picture, the geometric information represented by the key points of the face, and the temporal dynamic change information contained in the sequence are utilized by more and more researchers. By observation, there are a lot of neutral expressions in sequences that are difficult to be distinguished and its spatial, temporal and geometry features of the expression are not obvious and hard to be recognized.

In this paper, we propose a recurrent neural network based on migration learning and feature fusion, named temporal spatial-geometry recurrent neural network (TSG-RNN). In order to enable the model to fully learn the three characteristics, the network is divided into two parts. In the first part, the transfer learning can adapt the source domain into the target domain since the data for face recognition and the data for facial expression are intrinsically related. Therefore, we focus on training the ability of spatial feature extraction of the network by applying transfer learning into static face images. In the second part, the expression sequence and the corresponding key points are used as training data. The purpose is to fuse the spatial features represented by the images with the geometric features provided by face landmarks, and further obtain their common temporal features using RNN. The features obtained will have better classification capabilities. The main contributions in this paper can be summarized as follows:

1. We propose a recursive neural network with spatial-geometric feature fusion for the recognition of expression sequences, which can fully extract the spatial, geometric and temporal features of the expression sequence.
2. We propose a distributed training method using transfer learning to transfer the knowledge of face recognition to expression recognition, and further integrate geometric features and extract temporal features while ensuring that the model has good spatial coding ability for expressions. Meanwhile, the problem of weak generalization of the model brought by the small data set is solved to some extent.
3. The proposed method achieves a higher recognition result on the MMI data set with fewer iterations.

2 Related Work

2.1 Facial Expression Recognition

Facial expression recognition methods can be classified in two categories: frame-based and sequence-based methods. Early research on Facial expressions is usually based on static images, which is similar to general image classification methods as shown in [8,10]. However, it is considered that the facial expression recognition based on the still image is influenced by factors such as posture, background, obstacles, etc., and the facial expression can be regarded as the continuous dynamic change of the face over a period of time. In recent years, recognizing the facial expressions by the continuous frames of a video have been proven to be a more efficient treatment and can achieve better results. Since an expression sequence can be considered as multiple static emoticons stacked in temporal dimension, some of the earlier proposed sequence-based methods are upgraded to the 3D version on the original basis (i.e, the time is the third dimension), such as 3D-HOG [3], LBP-TOP [21] and 3D-SIFT [9]. Meanwhile, STM-ExpLet [5] used expressionlet-based spatial-temporal manifold to model the expression sequence and achieved better performance on CK+ and MMI databases. Guo et al. [20] proposes a new scheme to formulate the dynamic facial expression recognition problem as a longitudinal atlases construction and deformable groupwise image registration problem. LOMO [25] combines multiple information as features to make use of information in images, such as facial landmarks, LBP, SIFT and so on.

2.2 Deep Neural Networks

With the emergence of deep learning methods in recent years, CNN [22] and RNN [19] have shown the outstanding potential in extracting spatial and temporal features, and they are increasingly used in the field of computer vision. At the same time, the transfer learning method also shows an excellent potential in dealing with small data sets [26]. In the field of sequence expression recognition, Kuo et al. [17] proposed a streamlined sequence-based expression recognition model and a data enhancement method to deal with the image illumination unevenness problem. Papers [2,4,7,11,12,16] recognize facial expression by combining facial expression images and face landmarks. DTAGN [2] proposed two deep learning models, DTAN and DTGN, to encode sequence emoticons and face landmarks into feature vectors using 3D convolution and fully connected layers, respectively, but they are more sensitive to temporal information compared to RNNs since DTAGN cannot fully utilize the dynamic changes of the expression sequence to promote the classification result. In DFSN [16], the face landmarks were physiologically analyzed, modeled and merged with the spatial features. Zhang et al. [11] proposed PHRNN-MSCNN and divided the landmarks into four parts: eyebrow, nose, mouth and glasses as the geometric features of the expression and extracted the temporal features with BRNN respectively, and then fused the temporal features of the face landmarks. Therefore,

PHRNN-MSCNN pays more attention to the geometric temporal information of the expression sequence while ignoring the spatial information. These above methods have different emphases on the expression information, but their weakness is that they do not adequately deal with the relationship between the three features of temporal, space and geometry, ignoring the strong representation ability of the space-geometry feature in time.

2.3 Facial Expression Data Set

At present, the more mainstream expression data sets are CK+ [13], MMI [14], and Oulu-CASIA [29], which are widely used in static and sequential expression recognition research. Each of them has a sequence length of more than 10 frames and a wide distribution of character types is why they are more widely adopted than other data sets. In addition, there are other expression data sets such as FER2013, SFEW [18]. Our experiments were mainly carried out on the MMI dataset, which is biggest and the most complex dataset for facial expression recognition.

3 Our Approach

The proposed network for expression sequence recognition is a recursive neural network model based on transfer learning and feature fusion. It combines spatial features with geometric features and extracts their common temporal features. The research object is continuous frames of expression sequences. First, for each frame of the facial expression image in the sequence, the face landmarks are extracted as geometric features. Then the image and face landmarks are re-encoded into feature vectors by VGG-Expression and Deep Geometry Network (DGN) respectively. Finally, the two features from the same sequence are fused in time dimension to enrich the expression motion in time dimension. The above features are passed by the long-term short-term memory module (LSTM)[19] to capture the dynamic information of the superimposed features in the expression changes in order to promote subsequent classification tasks. Therefore, TSG-RNN contains three kinds of structures: encoding structure, recurrent neural network structure and expression classification structure. The overall structure of the network is shown in Fig. 1.

3.1 Encoding Structure

The encoding structure is composed of a model of VGG-Expression that processes the expression space features and a model of DGN that processes the geometric features.

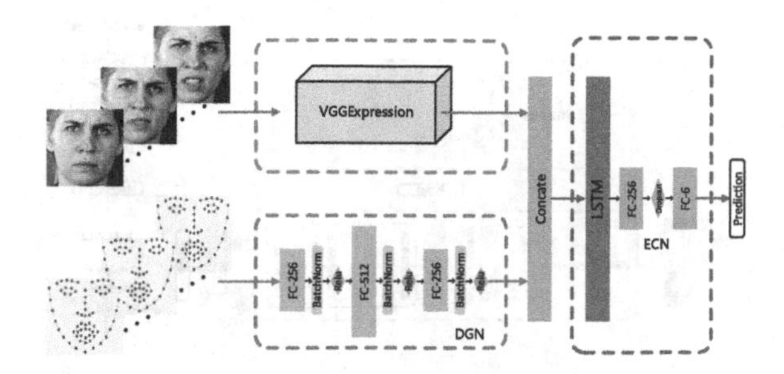

Fig. 1. Our proposed TSG-RNN network for facial expression recognition. The blue dotted frame is the pre-trained VGGExpression network for extracting the spatial features of the expression sequence; The green dotted frame is used for the DGN network to extract the geometric features of the key sequence; After cascading spatial features and geometric features, the LSTM + ECN of the purple dotted frame is used to extract timing features and perform expression prediction. The network takes the expression sequence and key sequence as input. (Color figure online)

VGG-Expression for Extracting Spatial Features. In this section, we describe VGG-Expression model. It is learned by VGGFace [15] with facial expression data sets. VGGFace is a robust face recognition model trained by VGG16 on a mixture of 2.6M wild face samples. According to the knowledge of the transfer learning and compared with the weight of the random initialization network, it is better to use the parameters of VGGFace to initialize the network because of the commonality between the face dataset and the expression dataset. However, since the dimension of the full connection layer is relatively high by the original data and is not suitable for expression classification, the parameters of the full connection layer are randomly initialized. At the same time, in order to better promote the transfer learning of features, we have made some modifications to the network structure of VGG16: (1) Reduce the fully connected layers from three layers into two layers and decrease the output dimensions to 512 respectively. (2) Adding batch normalization after both the last layer of the convolutional layer and the first layer of the fully-connected layer to change the output distribution of the features of the previous layer, and accelerate the convergence of the model. The transfer learning method is shown in Fig. 2. In the end, we obtained the VGG-Expression model with high recognition accuracy on the facial expression dataset. It also means that we can perform high-quality spatial coding on the expression image, which lays a foundation for the later feature fusion and timing coding. The data set of the training network I_e can be expressed as:

$$f_i^1, f_i^2, \ldots, f_i^n \in Seq_i \tag{1}$$

$$I_e = \{f_1^1, \ldots, f_1^n, f_2^1, \ldots, f_2^n, f_i^1 \cdots, f_i^n\}_{shuffle} \tag{2}$$

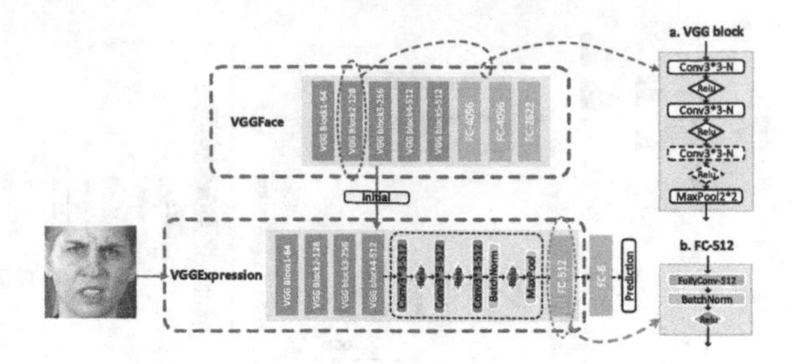

Fig. 2. Our proposed VGGExpression network for extracting spatial features. VGGFace uses its own convolutional layer parameters to initialize the parameters of the VGGExpression corresponding layer (corresponding to the blue background area in the figure) to achieve facial recognition knowledge transfer expression recognition. (Color figure online)

Seq_i represents the $i-th$ sequence in the sequence of expression data, and each sequence takes n peak expression frames to form a static expression data set I_e, and randomly shuffles the order when inputting. The entire migration learning process is summarized as:

$$T_f = p_{\theta_f}\left(g_{\theta_{f,c}}\left(I_f\right)\right) \tag{3}$$

$$T_e = q_{\theta_e}\left(g_{\theta_{e,c}}\left(I_e\right)\right) \tag{4}$$

For the face recognition task of T_f and the expression recognition task of T_e with their own datasets, I_f and I_e. $g(\theta)$ represents their common feature extraction function. $p(\theta)$ and $q(\theta)$ represent the respective classification functions, and θ represents the corresponding parameters of the function. The goal of the network is to use the transfer learning to enable VGG-Expression to inherit the common parameters of the two tasks, θ_c, and transfer the face recognition parameter θ_f into the expression recognition parameter θ_e by learning so that the spatial coding ability of the network can be excellently demonstrated.

DGN for Extracting Geometry Features. Facial expression changes can be characterized by changes of the facial landmarks. Changes in these key parts can be described by the movement of the geometric features of the face landmarks. The parts of face that have a greater influence on the expression mainly include eyebrows, glasses, nose and mouth. So we need to extract the key landmarks used to characterize these parts. We use the Dlib library for face detection and extraction of face landmarks, a total of 51 face key points, including two eyebrows (10), one nose (9), two eyes (12) and one mouth (20). The coordinates of obtained feature points are a two-dimensional array of 51×2 and defined as follows:

$$X^{(t)} = \left[\left[x_1^{(t)}, y_1^{(t)}\right], \left[x_2^{(t)}, y_2^{(t)}\right], \ldots, \left[x_{51}^{(t)}, y_{51}^{(t)}\right]\right]^T. \tag{5}$$

Where $x_k^{(t)}$ and $y_k^{(t)}$ represent the x and y coordinates of the $i-th$ facial expression key point of the $t-th$ frame image in the sequence, respectively. However, these landmarks are inappropriate for direct use as an input to the deep network, because they are not normalized, and the coordinates need to be normalized as follows:

$$\overline{x}_i^{(t)} = \frac{x_i^{(t)} - x_o^{(t)}}{\delta_x^{(t)}} \tag{6}$$

Where $x_i^{(t)}$ represents the x-axis coordinate of the $i-th$ personal facial expression landmarks of the $t-th$ frame image in the sequence, and $\delta_x^{(t)}$ is the standard deviation of the x-coordinates of all key points of the $t-th$ frame. We also use the same processing method for the y coordinate. Finally, the normalized 2D coordinate array is expanded into a 1D vector as follows:

$$\overline{X}^{(t)} = \left[\overline{x}_1^{(t)}, \overline{y}_1^{(t)}, \overline{x}_2^{(t)}, \overline{y}_2^{(t)}, \ldots, \overline{x}_{51}^{(t)}, \overline{y}_{51}^{(t)}\right]^T \tag{7}$$

We will get the landmark vector as the input of DGN. The network structure is a three-layer fully connected layer. Since it is a similar sequence of face images instead of the disordered sequence of samples entering the network, this is not conducive to parameter learning. We add a BN layer after each fully connected layer to adjust the output distribution, and finally encode the 1×102-dimensional of face landmark coordinates into 1×256-dimensional geometric feature vectors.

3.2 Recurrent Neural Network and Expression Classification Network

The above two models respectively encode and model the facial expression spatial features and geometric texture features. The recurrent neural network proposed in this section adopts the LSTM structure, which mainly combines these two features in the time dimension and extracts the merged sequence-based dynamic expression information through LSTM. The structure complements each other in the time dimension by combining the two features, which enhances the ability of the feature expression, resulting in a better classification result for the expression sequence. Given a sequence of T consecutive frames with $F^t, t = 1, 2, ..., T$, the encoded spatial feature vector and geometric feature vector are represented as $V_S^{(t)} \in R^{1\times n}$ and $V_G^{(t)} \in R^{1\times m}$, n, m represent the number of channels, and the two features are fused in a splicing manner. Then the mixed features at time t after fusion are expressed as:

$$V_{SG}^{(t)} = \left\{V_S^{(t)}, V_G^{(t)}\right\} \in R^{1\times(n+m)} \tag{8}$$

The hybrid feature vector $V_{SG}^{(t)}$ is then used as the input of t moments in the LSTM for extracting richer dynamic expression features in the time dimension. Figure 3 shows the time-based recursive learning expansion of the mixed feature vector V_{SG} for each frame.

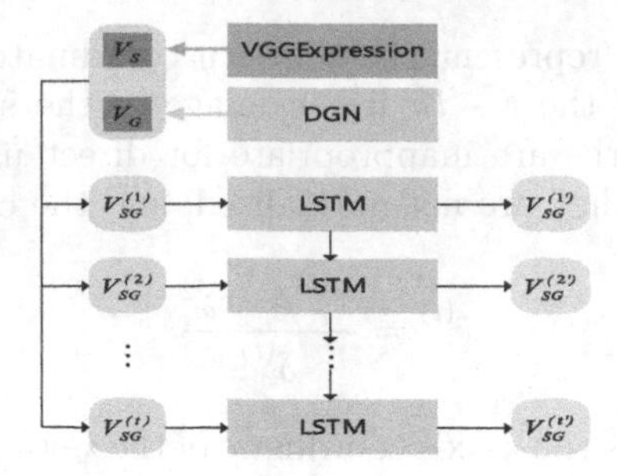

Fig. 3. LSTM structure for extracting temporal information of spatial-geometry features.

The goal is to obtain the nonlinear mapping function f_{tem}, generate the hidden state of $h_t, t = 1, 2..., T$ at each moment and pass it backward. The formula is defined as follows:

$$h_t = p\left(V_{SG}^{(t)}, h_{t-1}; \theta_{tem}\right) \tag{9}$$

$$V_{SG}^{t'} = q\left(h_t, \theta_{tem}\right), t = 1, \ldots, T \tag{10}$$

Where $p(\Delta)$ and $q(\Delta)$ are functions of f_{tem}, $V_{SG}^{(t')}$ is the output of the network at t time, and θ_{tem} represents a parameter corresponding to the LSTM layer. We set the number of the hidden layer node to 768. This experiment takes the output $V_{SG}^{(T')}$ at the final moment of each sequence as the captured time-space-geometric information. The output vector is then sent to the expression classification structure of ECN. The expression classification function is represented by f_{ECN}, and its output is the predicted facial expression category. In this experiment, we predict the six types of facial expressions, namely, anger, sadness, fear, fear, happiness, and surprise. The actual predicted output of the expression classification model is expressed as:

$$y = f_{ECN}\left(V_{SG}^{(T')}, \theta_{ECN}\right) \tag{11}$$

θ_{ECN} is the parameter corresponding to the ECN part of the expression classification structure. The entire TSG-RNN model uses softmax cross entropy to calculate the loss. The final loss function of L_{EC} can be further expressed as:

$$\arg\min\left(\theta_{DGN}, \theta_{tem}, \theta_{ECN} | \theta_{VGGErpression}\right) L_{EC}(\hat{y}, y) \tag{12}$$

$\hat{y}$ is the expression of the sequence. The parameters of $\theta_{VGGErpression}$ have been fixed by training in Sect. 3.1, and are not involved in the optimization of the subsequent training process. The other three model parameters, $\theta_{DGN}, \theta_{tem}, \theta_{ECN}$ will be optimized based on the condition.

3.3 Distributed Training Method

We have designed the following four models to train:

(1) Pre-training VGG-Expression and DGN. The parameters of the two models are fixed when training TSG-RNN, and only the training of recurrent neural network and classification network is performed.
(2) Train TSG-RNN as a whole, and carry out VGG-Expression transfer learning and tran DGN, recurrent neural network, and classification network in one training.
(3) Only pre-train VGG-Expression, fix VGG-Expression model parameters when training TSG-RNN, and train the remaining networks.
(4) Only VGG-Expression is pre-trained, but TSG-RNN is not fixed with its parameters so that it can continue to be optimized.

Through experiments, we know that only (3) of these four methods can get higher classification results. (1) Tell us that the spatial features and geometric features obtained by separate pre-training conflict when extracting common time series features. However, (2) and (4) conclude that the network structure cannot be effectively learned at the same time. Even though the encoding ability of the spatial feature network is prioritized, it will be destroyed in the overall training. Therefore, we define that training the spatial encoding ability at first, and then adapt the extracted geometric features and time series features to the distributed training method of the established spatial features.

4 Experiments

The above mentioned sequence-based expression recognition has three widely used data sets, named CK+ [13], MMI [14], and Oulu-CASIA [29]. MMI is the most difficult of the three, so we prefer to experiment on the MMI dataset to verify the performance of our network.

4.1 MMI Database

The MMI contains 30 subjects from different ethnicities and ages ranging from 19–62 years [14]. A total of 213 expression sequences were marked as 6-minute basic expressions, of which 205 were frontal views. Compared with CK+ and Oulu-CASIA, MMI has two different points: (1) each expression sequence starts with a central expression and gradually develops into a peak expression, eventually ending in a neutral expression; (2) The expressions of the same type of expression of different characters are quite different, and are accompanied by gesture differences, beards, glasses, headscarves and the like. In this paper, we intercepted two random peak expression frames from all 205 frontal face sequences as a static expression image library for training VGG-Expression. For TSG-RNN, we conduct our experiments on all of the 205 frontal facial sequences. In the experiment, we randomly divided all sequences into 10 groups for cross-validation.

4.2 Processing

Since the source frame of the video sequence contains many background regions, we first crop and scale the video frame to obtain a color face image of 256×256 size. Considering that the facial expression dataset is generally small, we use the method in DTAGN [2] to augment the image. First flip the image horizontally, then the original image and the flipped image. The rotation includes: $\{-15°, -10°, -5°, 5°, 10°, 15°\}$. We can finally get a new data set $2 \times (6+1) = 14$ times larger than the original data set. At the same time, the random cropping of the input image during training also greatly increases the number of samples.

4.3 Model Training and Parameter Setting

The network is divided into three parts: spatial feature coding structure VGG-Expression, the geometric feature coding structure DGN, and the recurrent neural network structure and the expression classification network structure ECN. VGG-Expression is a convolutional neural network structure. In the first stage of training, its structure is expressed as $I(256,3) - C1_1(64) - C1_2(64) - C2_1(128) - C2_2(128) - C3_1(256) - C3_2(256) - C3_3(256) - C4_1(512) - C4_2(512) - C4_3(512) - C5_1(512) - C5_2(512) - C5_3(512) - FC(512) - FC(6)$. $I(256,3)$ indicates that the input of the network is $256 \times 256 \times 3$ images, $C1_1(64)$ indicates that the number of convolution kernels is 64, and $FC(512)$ indicates that the output is a spatial feature vector of 1×512 dimensions, the size of the convolution kernel is 3×3. The batch size is 32, the loss function is calculated by softmax cross entropy, the initial learning rate is set to 0.0001, and the learning rate reduction strategy and the ADAM optimization method of gamma $= 0.001$ and power $= 0.75$ are used to iterate 500 times, and the momentum is set to 0.9. The weight is attenuated to 0.0005. In the TSG-RNN training phase we remove the last layer of the VGG-Expression fully connected layer and freeze all its parameters. GCN is a fully connected network, and its structure is represented as $I(102) - FC(256) - FC(512) - FC(256)$. The network input is 1×102 face landmark coordinates, and the output is a geometric feature vector of 1×256 dimensions. In the two-stage training, we set the sequence size of the sequence to 8, which means that the input of VGG-Expression and GCN is 8 emoticons and face landmark vectors for each iteration. The recursive neural network structure utilizes a one-way LSTM, and we set the number of hidden layer nodes to 768. The ECN is used to predict the temporal category of the temporal spatial-geometry features at time T. The structure is expressed as $FC(256) - FC(6)$, and dropout is added after the first fully connected layer, and ratio is set to 0.5 to prevent the network with overfitting. The network parameters of the training of the two-stage model are all based on the random initialization method. The optimizer and the training parameters are the same as the first stage, and the iteration is set to 1000.

4.4 Time-Based Spatial-Geometric Fusion Experiment

In order to complement the three characteristics of the proposed network, we performed experiments using different combination of features. The first set of experiments did not include feature fusion, just using VGG-Expression with spatial features and DGN for facial expression recognition with only geometric features; the second set of experiments used VGG-Expression+LSTM to extract temporal features only for spatial features. The third group adds geometric features based on the second group, that is, using our proposed TSG-RNN network for facial expression recognition. Table 1 shows the results of our three sets of experiments on the MMI dataset. It can be observed that spatial features can obtain better results for expression recognition than geometric features from this table. This DTAGN [2] and PHRNN [11] also show similar results. At the same time, the accuracy is significantly improved when fusing the time series features in our network, which proves that our network can effectively capture the dynamic change information in the expression sequence and promote the recognition of expressions. The TSG-RNN network achieved the highest precision in these sets of experiments, and it also proved that the spatial-geometric features after fusion can represent more powerful information of expression images.

Table 1. Ablation experiments in our network

Model	Explanation	Input	Accuracy
VGGExpression	Spatial features	Frame	76.7%
DGN	Geometry features	Frame	75%
VGGExpression-LSTM	Temporal spatial features	Sequence	79.8%
TSG-RNN	**Temporal spatial-geometry features**	**Sequence**	**81.7%**

4.5 Comparison and Analysis of Experimental Results

Table 2 compares the performance of our models with current state-of-the-art methods on MMI dataset. Among the better performing methods, STM-ExpLet [5] is based on the traditional method, Jung et al. [2] proposed the DTAGN model for joint training appearance feature network and geometric network, Hasani et al. [7] used 3DCNN-LSTM to achieve an accuracy of 77.50% by adding landmarks to the convolution,

A recursive neural network model (PHRNN) by gradually fusion of facial landmarks is also proposed by Zhang et al. [11] and it used recognition and verification signals as the supervised convolutional neural network (MSCNN) and combined the two CNN networks, PHRNN-MSCNN, to achieve an accuracy of 81.18%, and all the experiments used the same 10-fold cross-validation method to process the data set. Table 2 shows that our designed temporal spatial-geometry recurrent neural network achieved satisfactory performance.

Table 2. Comparison of different methods on the MMI database.

Methods	Accuracy
HOG 3D [3]	60.89%
3DCNN-DAP [4]	63.40%
3D SIFT [9]	64.39%
DTAGN [2]	70.24%
CNN-DBN [12]	71.43%
STM-ExpLet [5]	75.12%
3DCNN-LSTM + landmark [7]	77.50%
PHRNN [11]	76.17%
PHRNN-MSCNN [11]	81.18%
VGGExpression-LSTM	79.81%
TSG-RNN	**81.71%**

4.6 Model Convergence Speed

Take advantage of transfer learning, our model can achieve convergence and obtain high precision in a short time. Figure 4 shows that VGGExpression and TSG-RNN can converge quickly in no more than 1000 iterations because the model is initialized with excellent pre-trained parameters. We only need less than an hour to complete all the training with just one TITAN X card.

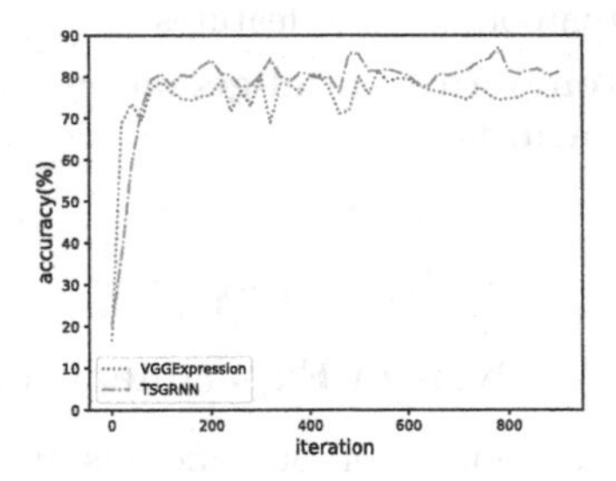

Fig. 4. Comparison of VGGExpression and TSG-RNN during training.

5 Conclusion

In this paper, we propose a neural network based on transfer learning. We propose VGGExpression to capture facial texture information of faces in video frames by using the correlation between face recognition and expression recognition. At the same time, in order to make use of the expression of information in the network of expression sequences, we propose the TSG-RNN to fuse the spatial-geometric features of the expression sequences and captures the dynamic evolution information. The network can eventually converge with very few iterations while greatly reducing the time required for training. The experimental results on the MMI database prove that the proposed method has achieved satisfactory performance. Our current experiments only are conducted on the MMI dataset, but we have not tested the performance of our network on other mainstream datasets such as CK+, Oulu-CASIA, etc. This will be our next major work. Secondly, the method of our extracting facial expression information by landmarks is relatively simple, and some information may be lost, and face alignment in frames from sequences can be implemented to further reduce the error in our future work.

References

1. Dalal, N., Triggs, B.: Histograms of oriented gradients for human detection (2005)
2. Jung, H., Lee, S., Yim, J., Park, S., Kim, J.: Joint fine-tuning in deep neural networks for facial expression recognition. In Proceedings of the IEEE International Conference on Computer Vision, pp. 2983–2991 (2015)
3. Klaser, A., Marszałek, M., Schmid, C.: A spatio-temporal descriptor based on 3D-gradients (2008)
4. Liu, M., Li, S., Shan, S., Wang, R., Chen, X.: Deeply learning deformable facial action parts model for dynamic expression analysis. In: Cremers, D., Reid, I., Saito, H., Yang, M.-H. (eds.) ACCV 2014. LNCS, vol. 9006, pp. 143–157. Springer, Cham (2015). https://doi.org/10.1007/978-3-319-16817-3_10
5. Liu, M., Shan, S., Wang, R., Chen, X.: Learning expressionlets on spatio-temporal manifold for dynamic facial expression recognition. In: Proceedings of the IEEE Conference on Computer Vision and Pattern Recognition, pp. 1749–1756 (2014)
6. Lowe, D.G., et al.: Object recognition from local scale-invariant features. In: ICCV, vol. 99, pp. 1150–1157 (1999)
7. Hasani, B., Mahoor, M.H., et al.: Facial expression recognition using enhanced deep 3D convolutional neural networks. In: Proceedings of the IEEE Conference on Computer Vision and Pattern Recognition Workshops, pp. 30–40 (2017)
8. Ojala, T., Pietikäinen, M., Mäenpää, T.: Multiresolution gray-scale and rotation invariant texture classification with local binary patterns. IEEE Trans. Pattern Anal. Mach. Intell. **7**, 971–987 (2002)
9. Scovanner, P., Ali, S., Shah, M.: A 3-dimensional sift descriptor and its application to action recognition. In: Proceedings of the 15th ACM International Conference on Multimedia, pp. 357–360. ACM (2007)
10. Sikka, K., Wu, T., Susskind, J., Bartlett, M.: Exploring bag of words architectures in the facial expression domain. In: Fusiello, A., Murino, V., Cucchiara, R. (eds.) ECCV 2012. LNCS, vol. 7584, pp. 250–259. Springer, Heidelberg (2012). https://doi.org/10.1007/978-3-642-33868-7_25
11. Zhang, K., Huang, Y., Yong, D., Wang, L.: Facial expression recognition based on deep evolutional spatial-temporal networks. IEEE Trans. Image Process. **26**(9), 4193–4203 (2017)
12. Zhang, S., Pan, X., Cui, Y., Zhao, X., Liu, L.: Learning affective video features for facial expression recognition via hybrid deep learning. IEEE Access **7**, 32297–32304 (2019)

13. Lucey, P., Cohn, J.F., Kanade, T., Saragih, J., Ambadar, Z., Matthews, I.: The extended Cohn-Kanade dataset (ck+): a complete dataset for action unit and emotion-specified expression. In: 2010 IEEE Computer Society Conference on Computer Vision and Pattern Recognition-Workshops, pp. 94–101. IEEE (2010)
14. Pantic, M., Valstar, M., Rademaker, R., Maat, L.: Web-based database for facial expression analysis. In: 2005 IEEE International Conference on Multimedia and Expo, pp. 5–pp. IEEE (2005)
15. Parkhi, O.M., Vedaldi, A., Zisserman, A., et al.: Deep face recognition. In: BMVC, vol. 1, p. 6 (2015)
16. Tang, Y., Zhang, X.M., Wang, H.: Geometric-convolutional feature fusion based on learning propagation for facial expression recognition. IEEE Access **6**, 42532–42540 (2018)
17. Kuo, C.-M., Lai, S.-H., Sarkis, M.: A compact deep learning model for robust facial expression recognition. In: Proceedings of the IEEE Conference on Computer Vision and Pattern Recognition Workshops, pp. 2121–2129 (2018)
18. Dhall, A., Goecke, R., Lucey, S., Gedeon, T.: Static facial expression analysis in tough conditions: data, evaluation protocol and benchmark. In: 2011 IEEE International Conference on Computer Vision Workshops (ICCV Workshops), pp. 2106–2112. IEEE (2011)
19. Graves, A.: Long short-term memory (2012)
20. Guo, Y., Zhao, G., Pietikäinen, M.: Dynamic facial expression recognition using longitudinal facial expression atlases. In: Fitzgibbon, A., Lazebnik, S., Perona, P., Sato, Y., Schmid, C. (eds.) ECCV 2012. LNCS, pp. 631–644. Springer, Heidelberg (2012). https://doi.org/10.1007/978-3-642-33709-3_45
21. Zhao, G., Pietikainen, M.: Dynamic texture recognition using local binary patterns with an application to facial expressions. IEEE Trans. Pattern Anal. Mach. Intell. **29**(6), 915–928 (2007)
22. Krizhevsky, A., Sutskever, I., Hinton, G.E.: ImageNet classification with deep convolutional neural networks. In: International Conference on Neural Information Processing Systems (2012)
23. Lucey, P., Cohn, J., Lucey, S., Matthews, I., Sridharan, S., Prkachin, K.M.: Automatically detecting pain using facial actions. In: 2009 3rd International Conference on Affective Computing and Intelligent Interaction and Workshops, pp. 1–8. IEEE (2009)
24. Shin, H.C., et al.: Deep convolutional neural networks for computer-aided detection: CNN architectures, dataset characteristics and transfer learning. IEEE Trans. Med. Imaging **35**(5), 1285–1298 (2016)
25. Sikka, K., Sharma, G., Bartlett, M.: LOMo: latent ordinal model for facial analysis in videos. In: Proceedings of the IEEE Conference on Computer Vision and Pattern Recognition, pp. 5580–5589 (2016)
26. Tzeng, E., Hoffman, J., Zhang, N., Saenko, K., Darrell, T.: Deep domain confusion: maximizing for domain invariance. Computer Science (2014)
27. Vinciarelli, A., Pantic, M., Bourlard, H.: Social signal processing: survey of an emerging domain. Image Vis. Comput. **27**(12), 1743–1759 (2009)
28. Wilson, M.: Photography, emotions, & OT (2018)
29. Zhao, G., Huang, X., Taini, M., Li, S.Z., PietikäInen, M.: Facial expression recognition from near-infrared videos. Image Vis. Comput. **29**(9), 607–619 (2011)

Structured Neural Motifs: Scene Graph Parsing via Enhanced Context

Yiming Li[1,4], Xiaoshan Yang[2,3,4], and Changsheng Xu[1,2,3,4](✉)

[1] HeFei University of Technology, Hefei, China
liym@mail.hfut.edu.cn
[2] National Lab of Pattern Recognition, Institute of Automation, Chinese Academy of Sciences, Beijing, China
{xiaoshan.yang,csxu}@nlpr.ia.ac.cn
[3] University of Chinese Academy of Sciences, Beijing, China
[4] Peng Cheng Laboratory, Shenzhen, China

Abstract. Scene graph is one kind of structured representation of the visual content in an image. It is helpful for complex visual understanding tasks such as image captioning, visual question answering and semantic image retrieval. Since the real-world images always have multiple object instances and complex relationships, the context information is extremely important for scene graph generation. It has been noted that the context dependencies among different nodes in the scene graph are asymmetric, which meas it is highly possible to directly predict relationship labels based on object labels but not vice versa. Based on this finding, the existing motifs network has successfully exploited the context patterns among object nodes and the dependencies between the object nodes and the relation nodes. However, the spatial information and the context dependencies among relation nodes are neglected. In this work, we propose Structured Motif Network (StrcMN) which predicts object labels and pairwise relationships by mining more complete global context features. The experiments show that our model significantly outperforms previous methods on the VRD and Visual Genome datasets.

Keywords: Scene graph · Deep learning · LSTMs

1 Introduction

Scene graph is a structured representation of the visual content in an image. It is firstly proposed in [4] to represent object instances as well as the relationships between them using a scene graph structure. A pair of objects and the relationship of them are represented as a triplet <*subject* − *relationship* − *object*>, where *subject* and *object* denotes the roles of object instances in the relationship. Specifically, both object instances and relationships are represented as nodes in a scene graph as shown in Fig. 1. The neighbors of each object node are relationship nodes, vice versa. Since the subject-predicate structure in the natural

Y. M. Ro et al. (Eds.): MMM 2020, LNCS 11962, pp. 175–188, 2020.
https://doi.org/10.1007/978-3-030-37734-2_15

language is necessary in the relationship description, the edge direction in the scene graph is specified either from the subject node to the relationship node or from the relationship node to the object node. Note that a subject instance in one relationship pair might be an object in another. With the successful application in image captioning [9,21], visual question answering [2,18], the problem of generating scene graphs from images becomes an active research topic in computer vision.

A major challenge in scene graph generation task is relational reasoning, as the relationship depends on both the subject and object instances instead of direct visual features of a single object. Several previous works [11,12,17] adopt the deep neural networks to capture the better visual features and make independent relationship prediction for each pair of objects. These kinds of local prediction methods ignore the impact of contextual information. To resolve this problem, [20] explicitly model the graphical structure of the objects and their relationships. Based on the topological structure, the joint inference is implemented by iteratively passing contextual messages.

Zellers *et al.* [22] show a key finding that it is highly possible to directly predict relationship labels based on object labels but not vice-versa. They proposed a global context embedding model to jointly capture the asymmetric dependence and larger contextual patterns in the scene graph. Firstly, the global context patterns were captured through accumulating the information of all objects in the image with bidirectional LSTMs. Then, the relationships of object pairs were predicted based on both the visual features and the class labels of the object instances. Though this method achieves much better performance than previous methods, it has two limitations at least. (1) The image regions are sequentially imported in the LSTMs without considering their spatial relationships. This will damage the accuracy of predicting the geometric relationships, such as "above", "behind" and "in front of". This issue is even worse on the most widely used scene graph dataset Visual Genome [6], where 50% instances have the geometric relation type according the data analysis in [22]. (2) The context patterns among object nodes and the dependencies between the object nodes and the relation nodes are considered while the context dependencies among relation nodes are ignored. Thus, this method [22] practically does not capture the complete global dependencies among the different nodes in the scene graph.

In order to resolve the above problems, we propose Structured Motif Network, a model for scene graph parsing using enhanced global context. To completely capture the global context, we exploit two kinds of extra dependencies in the scene graph. (1) Location-aware dependencies among object nodes. (2) Context dependencies among relation nodes. The first one is implemented by accumulating the object information through LSTMs and encoding the location coordinates of local regions through position encoding. The second one is implemented by formulating the relationship prediction as a conditional random field. The context patterns were iteratively passed between object nodes and relation nodes in the scene graph. The proposed method takes advantage of both the structured prediction methods [20] with independency assumptions and the methods [22] which rely on global context of object instances.

Figure 2 shows the framework of the proposed model. It firstly detects object regions with Faster-RCNN pretrained on the dataset we used. Object context is obtained by bidirectional LSTMs with both visual feature and object label as input. Then another specialized layer of bidirectional LSTMs is used to propagate relation context by the object labels and object context embedding computed in the previously bidirectional LSTMs. Finally, we adopt CRFs for modeling the dependencies between the object nodes and the relationship nodes of scene graph and generating the final predictions. The main contributions of this paper are concluded as follows. (1) We proposed a scene graph parsing framework with enhanced context modeling which, as far as we know, captures most complete global context information. (2) We proposed a flexible 4-dimensional position encoding scheme to model the spatial relationships of object regions. (3) We proposed a structured relationship prediction model based on the global context features of the object nodes. (4) We demonstrated the effectiveness of the proposed method with extensive experimental results on two widely used scene graph datasets.

Fig. 1. An example of the scene graph. The blue nodes represent object instances while the red ones denote relationships. (Color figure online)

2 Related Work

In this section, we briefly review the scene graph parsing and discuss the work that is most related to the proposed method.

Recent years, with the success of deep learning based recognition models [7], the interest of researchers has turned to the study on detail structures of the visual scene. Johnson *et al.* [4] proposed the first graph structure to describe the visual content–Scene Graph, which can explicit model objects and relationships. In short, scene graph represents the objects contained in the image and the relationship between them as a graph structure composed of nodes and edges.

One of the major challenges in scene graph generation is reasoning about relationships between subjects and objects. Lu *et al.* [12] attempted to use a visual model to predict objects and relationships independently, and they also fine-tuned the model with the help of language prior provided by a pretrained word2vec [14] model. But this method ignores the context information, which has been proved to be extremely valuable in the scene graph generation task [22].

In order to utilize context information, Xu *et al.* [20] investigated the relationship reasoning problem with considering surrounding context according to the topological structure of scene graph. The visual characteristics of each node in the scene graph was fine-tuned by using the information in the surrounding environment. Although the performance of scene graph generation has been improved, Cong *et al.* [1] point out that it is likely to confuse subjects and objects. The real world images always have complex relationships and large number of fuzzy entities, the performance will significantly degraded.

Recently, a lot of improved methods based on [20] have been proposed. Li *et al.* [11] trained the scene graph generation model and the image caption model simultaneously to capture the semantic-level relevance between these two tasks. In order to capture low-level visual features for relationship prediction, Li *et al.* [10] further proposed to implement message passing in the convolutional layer [20]. More recently, Zellers *et al.* [22] analyzed the co-occurrence frequency of relationship and object pairs on the Visual Genome [6] dataset. They concluded that the frequency has important help for relationship prediction and designed a Stacked Motif Network to capture global context information by stacked bidirectional LSTMs [3]. Our work is closely related to [22]. The major difference is that [22] directly decodes relationships from embedded object feature pairs while the proposed method extensively captures dependencies between object nodes and relationship nodes in the scene graph. Another difference is that [22] ignores the locations of the object regions while the proposed method models them with a 4-dimensional position encoding scheme.

As a classical complex structural modeling tool, Conditional Random Fields (CRFs) have been widely used in graph inference task. CRFs jointly compute the relationship between nodes in the graph. It has been successfully applied in many classical tasks, such as image segmentation [5,23], image retrieval [4] and named-entity recognition [8,13]. Johnson *et al.* [4] proposed a CRFs model that calculates the similarity between an image and ground-truth scene graph. As an extra application, the scene graph was used to guide the image retrieval task. Inspired by this work, Xu *et al.* [20] proposed a scene graph generation method by using CRFs meanfield approximate inference algorithm. As an improvement, Cong *et al.* [1] used a message passing [20] to capture the compatibility of objects in the word semantic level and significantly improved the performance. Our work is closely related to [20]. The major difference is that the structured prediction is implemented directly on object features in [20] while the proposed method structurally predicts the relationships based on both the object features and the object labels which have been proved to be extremely important for scene graph parsing [22].

3 Methods

3.1 Problem Formulation

Our work aims to generate a *scene graph*, G, which is a structured semantic representation for a given image I. It consists of:

- A *bounding box* set $B = \{b_1, b_2, \ldots, b_N\}$, where $b_i \in \mathbb{R}^4$ represents the coordinate.
- An *object* set $O = \{o_1, o_2, \ldots, o_N\}$, where $o_i \in \mathcal{C}$ represents the class label of b_i.
- A *relationship* set $R = \{r_1, r_2, \ldots, r_M\}$ which represents the binary relationships between objects.

Each $r_k \in R$ is a triplet which consists of a subject node $(b_i, o_i) \in B \times O$, the corresponding object node $(b_j, o_j) \in B \times O$, and a relationship label $rel_{i \to j} \in \mathcal{R}$. The $\mathcal{R}$ contains all relationship categories including the "background" predicate, BG, which represents that there is no relation between the subject and the object. Figure 1 shows an example of the scene graph.

Zellers *et al.* [22] demonstrated that the dependence between objects and their relations is asymmetric, which means the relation prediction closely depends on object labels, but not vice versa. Based on this, we denote the probability of a graph G for a given image I as a product of three items:

$$P(G|I) = P(B|I)P(O|B, I)P(R|O, B, I) \tag{1}$$

The probability of the bounding box coordinates $P\ (B|I)$ and object class labels $P\ (O|B, I)$ can be computed by a standard object detection model which will be illustrated in Sect. 3.2. The difference is that we capture the contextual information of objects. We adopt a LSTM to sequentially process each box in B to obtain a contextualized representation and then decode it into the object label. We encode the coordinates of the boxes using positional encoding which will be illustrated in Sect. 3.2. We fuse the position embedding features and visual features, which will be illustrated in Sect. 3.2.

In order to exploit the contextual dependencies between relations and object class labels, we formulate $P\ (R|O, B, I)$ as a structured prediction problem. Specifically, we adopt CRFs to predict the relationships of the graph G. Each relation $r_{i \to j}$ is predicted based on the coordinates, labels and visual features of the objects. Different from conventional CRFs, where individual input features are used, we adopt the contextualized representation of spatial features, class labels and visual features as input. The details will be illustrated in Sect. 3.3. In the experiment, we will show that this kind of feature-level structure is useful to improve the performance.

3.2 Object Prediction

Now, we will introduce how to compute the $P\ (B|I)$ and $P\ (O|B, I)$ based on the conventional object detection framework.

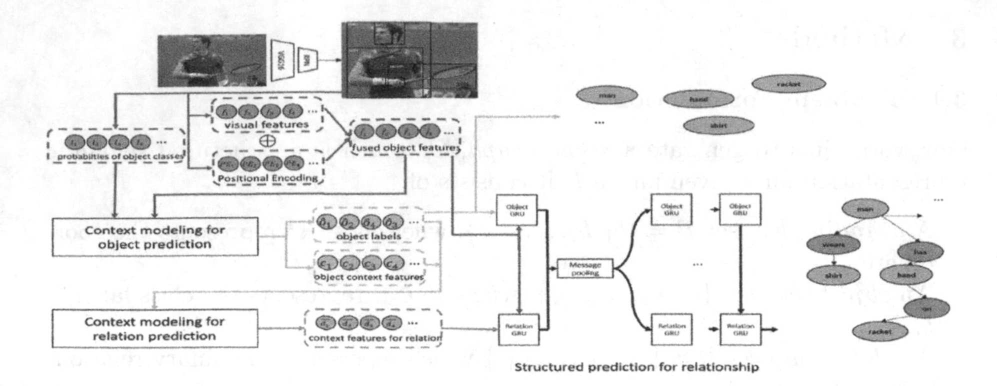

Fig. 2. The pipeline of the proposed structured motifs networks.

Bounding Boxes. We use Faster R-CNN [16] as the object detector of a given image I. The detector predicts a region proposal set $B = \{b_1, b_2, \ldots, b_N\}$. For each box $b_i \in B$, the detector outputs a visual feature vector $f_i \in \mathbb{R}^{d_{model}}$ by ROI-pooling and a probability vector $l_i \in \mathbb{R}^C$ by object classifier. Note that the classification output of each bounding box is not the final prediction, we will use LSTMs for contextualized prediction in next steps.

Position Encoding. Most of existing scene graph generating methods adopt ROI-pooling to sample visual features of objects from the convolutional maps of the image. The problem of these methods is that the spatial structure information of objects lost in ROI-pooling. To resolve this problem, we adopt a 4-dimensional positional encoding scheme to obtain the spatial features of the objects. The encoded position features have the same dimension d_{model} as the visual features, so that they can be fused together with simple sum-pooling. Considering the successful application of position encoding in NLP tasks [19], we use sine and cosine functions to encode spatial information:

$$
\begin{aligned}
pos &= \left(\frac{x_l}{h_{img}}, \frac{y_l}{w_{img}}, \frac{x_r}{h_{img}}, \frac{y_r}{w_{img}}\right)^T \\
PE_{(j\frac{1}{4}d_{model}+2i)} &= sin(pos_{[j]}/10000^{2i/d_{model}}) \\
PE_{(j\frac{1}{4}d_{model}+2i+1)} &= cos(pos_{[j]}/10000^{2i/d_{model}})
\end{aligned} \tag{2}
$$

where $i = \{0, 1, \ldots, \frac{1}{8}d_{model} - 1\}$ and $j = \{0, 1, 2, 3\}$. The (x_l, y_l) and (x_r, y_r) are upper left and lower right coordinates of the bounding box. The h_{img} and w_{img} are the height and width of the box. Thus, the pos represents the relative position of the bounding box in the image. The i and j are used to assign the index of the final spatial feature vector $PE \in \mathbb{R}^{d_{model}}$. Each dimension of the positional encoded feature corresponds to a sinusoid. The wavelengths form a geometric progression from 2π to $10000 \cdot \pi$.

Global Context Based Prediction. In order to get the contextual visual features of objects, we fuse the visual feature and the spatial feature as $\hat{f}_i$ by sum-pooling. Now the bounding box set B can be represented by a sequence $\left[(\hat{f}_1, l_1), (\hat{f}_2, l_2), \ldots, (\hat{f}_N, l_N)\right]$. Then, the contextualized visual features C are computed using a bidirectional LSTM:

$$C = BiLSTM_1([\hat{f}_i; W_1 l_i]_{i=1,2,\ldots,N}) \tag{3}$$

where each $c_i \in C$ is the hidden state vector of the $BiLSTM_1$ for the corresponding i^{th} box in B. The W_1 is a parameter matrix which maps l_i to $\mathbb{R}^{100}$. The recursive structure of BiLSTM guarantees that every box in B contributes to the final classification of other objects.

To decode the final category label based on the object context feature C, we use another LSTM to iteratively process each contextualized representation in C:

$$\begin{aligned} h_i &= LSTM_i\left([c_i; \hat{o}_{i-1}]\right) \\ \hat{o}_i &= \arg\max\left(W_o h_i\right) \end{aligned} \tag{4}$$

where the h_i is the hidden state of the LSTM layer. The weight matrix W_o maps h_i to the probability vector of object categories. The object label $\hat{o}_i$ will be further used as an input for the relation prediction.

3.3 Relation Prediction

Object-Aware Context Modeling. In the previous steps, we have computed the contextualized representations of all bounding boxes. These context features have been used to predict the object labels. Here, we feed them into another bidirectional LSTM to generate context features for relation prediction:

$$D = BiLSTM_2([c_i; W_2 \hat{o}_i]_{i=1,2,\ldots,N}) \tag{5}$$

where W_2 is a weight matrix which maps $\hat{o}_i$ to $\mathbb{R}^{100}$. Each $d_i \in D$ is the hidden state vector for the corresponding bounding box at the final layer of the $BiLSTM_2$. The d_i will be further used as an input for the structured relation prediction.

Structured Prediction. To comprehensively consider two kinds of dependencies of object-to-relation and relation-to-relation, we predict the probability of relationships $P\ (R|O, B, I)$ using CRFs. Specifically, we find optimal relationship labels $\mathbf{r}^* = \arg\max_{\mathbf{r}} P\ (R|O, B, I)$ that maximizes the following probability function given the image I, region proposals B and predicted object labels O:

$$P(R|O, B, I) = \prod_{i \in N} \prod_{j \neq i} P(r_{i \to j}|O, B, I). \tag{6}$$

In this work we adopt mean field to approximate CRFs. The probability of each relation node r is expressed as $Q(r|\cdot)$, and suppose that the probability only related to the states of neighbor nodes at each iteration. Zheng *et al.* [23] demonstrated that the message passing can be approximately computed by the RNN module. The difference is that we choose Gated Recurrent Units (GRU) due to its simplicity and efficiency. For each node, we use the hidden state of the GRU to represent the current state. Specifically, the state of the ith object node is denoted as h_i while the state of the relation from the ith object to the jth object is represented as $h_{i\to j}$. Then the structured relation prediction can be formulated as:

$$Q(\mathbf{r}|O,B,I) = \prod_{j\neq i} Q(r_{i\to j}|h_{i\to j})Q(h_{i\to j}|d_{i\to j}) \tag{7}$$

where $d_{i\to j}$ is the contextual feature of the relation $i \to j$. It is initialized by combining d_i and d_j which have been computed in Sect. 3.3.

In the topology of the scene graph, all neighbors of the relation nodes are object nodes, and vice versa. Thus, if we want to consider the contextual dependencies among relation nodes, we can only pass the messages with the object nodes as intermediaries. To conveniently implement the message passing through the object nodes and the relation nodes in the scene graph, we build two sub-graphs of objects and relations respectively with the same scheme as in [22]. In the object-centric sub-graph, an object GRU gets messages from its inbound and outbound relation GRUs. The hidden state h_i of the ith object is computed with the input of the concatenation of the category probability $\hat{o}_i$ and the feature vector $\hat{f}_i$. In the relation-centric sub-graph, a relation GRU gets messages from its subject node GRUs and object node GRUs. The hidden state $h_{i\to j}$ of the relation $i \to j$ is computed with the input of the context feature $d_{i\to j}$. We adopt message pooling to process the multiple inputs of each GRU. The update messages of the ith object node are denoted as m_i. It can be computed based on its own hidden state h_i and the hidden state $h_{i\to j}$ and $h_{j\to i}$ of it's neighbor relation nodes. Similarly, we use $m_{i\to j}$ to denote the messages of the relation node which connects the ith object node and the jth object node. Then, the message updating rules can be defined as follows:

$$m_i = \sum_{j:i\to j} \sigma\left(W_3^T\left[h_i, h_{i\to j}\right]\right) h_{i\to j} + \sum_{j:j\to i} \sigma\left(W_4^T\left[h_i, h_{j\to i}\right]\right) h_{j\to i} \tag{8}$$

$$m_{i\to j} = \sigma\left(W_5^T\left[h_i, h_{i\to j}\right]\right) h_i + \sigma\left(W_6^T\left[h_j, h_{i\to j}\right]\right) h_j \tag{9}$$

where the σ denotes a sigmoid function. The W_3, W_4, W_5, W_6 are learnable parameters. More details of the message passing for scene graph generation are referred to [20]. The difference is that we predict the relation labels using pre-processed context information instead of individual visual features. Besides, the object GRUs are only used as intermediaries for message passing of relation prediction in our work.

4 Experiment

4.1 Datasets

VRD dataset was firstly proposed in [12]. It has 100 object categories, 70 relationship categories, and 37,993 relationship instances. There are totally 5,000 images where 4,000 ones are used for training and the remaining for test. VRD has been widely used in real-world relationship detection task due to its diversity. *Visual Genome* [6] is the largest and most complex scene graph dataset. It contains 108,077 images with an average of 38 objects and 22 relationships per image. We use the same training and testing split as in [20].

4.2 Implementation Details

Similar to previous works in scene graph parsing, we use Faster RCNN [16] with a VGG backbone as the object detector. All input images are firstly reshaped to 592×592 before detection. Similar to YOLO-9000 [15], we adjust the bounding box proposal scales and dimension ratios to adapt different box shapes in Visual Genome and VRD dataset. To train the proposed structured motifs networks, the batch size is set to 3 on both the Visual Genome dataset and the VRD dataset. For each batch we sample 256 RoIs per image based on the detected region boxes, then we use non-maximal suppression (NMS) with 0.3 IoU to choose the 64 proposals with the highest confidence and pass them to the object prediction and relation prediction modules. In order to avoid gradient vanishing problem, we adopt the similar highway connection for all LSTMs as in [22]. The input and output dimensions of each node in CRFs are set to 612. We use cross entropy loss to constrain the learning of overall parameters with the SGD as optimizer. The learning rate is set to 0.018. It will be rescaled by 1/10 after the validation mAP plateaus. To keep a balance between the performance and time consumption, the GRU networks of the message passing are iterated for 2 times.

4.3 Metrics and Baselines

We evaluate the performance of our model with the metric of Recall@K (R@K), which measures the correct number of instances in the top K predicted relationships with the highest confidences. We adopt three popularly used metrics of R@20, R@50 and R@100. We follow previous works in scene graph parsing to evaluate our model under the following three kinds of tasks:

Predicate Classification (PredCls): Predict the predicates of all pairwise relationships of the objects with given ground-truth bounding boxes and category labels. This task test the performance on relational prediction.

Scene Graph Classification (SGCls): Predict both the pairwise relations and the class labels of objects with given ground-truth bounding boxes.

Scene Graph Detection (SGDet): Detect the objects and predict the relationships of object pairs. It means models need to simultaneously predict object boxes, object labels and pairwise relations. An object box is considered to be correctly detected only if the predicted box has at least 0.5 IoU overlap with the ground-truth box.

On the VRD dataset, most of the early methods used different metrics. Here, we compare our model with three competitive works which used the same evaluation settings. The Message Passing [20] which predicts both the object labels and the relationships under conditional random fields. The Motifs Network [22] which exploits the global context features with BiLSTMs. The recent method SG-CRF [1] which learns the sequential order of the subject and the object in a relationship triplet. On the more widely used dataset Visual Genome, we add two extra baselines. The early method VRD [12] which does not consider the context information. The improved version of the Message Passing (Message Passing$^+$) [22] which adopts a better detector.

Table 1. Results on the VRD dataset. All numbers are in %. For the methods which do not have R@20 results, we only average the results of the R@50 and R@100.

Model	SGDet			SGCls			PredCls			Mean
	R@20	R@50	R@100	R@20	R@50	R@100	R@20	R@50	R@100	
MESSAGE PASSING [20]		21.2	21.9		26.3	27.3		40.0	41.9	29.7
SG-CRF [1]		24.9	25.4		31.4	32.1		49.1	50.4	35.5
MOTIFNET [22]	22.9	**28.4**	29.7	33.2	37.3	38.1	52.8	57.6	60.4	41.9
Ours	**23.1**	28.3	**30.2**	**37.5**	**40.2**	**41.1**	**55.3**	**61.9**	**63.7**	**44.2**

Table 2. Results on the Visual Genome dataset. All numbers are in %. For the methods which do not have R@20 results, we only average the results of the R@50 and R@100.

Model	SGDet			SGCls			PredCls			Mean
	R@20	R@50	R@100	R@20	R@50	R@100	R@20	R@50	R@100	
VRD [12]		0.3	0.5		11.8	14.1		27.9	35.0	14.9
MESSAGE PASSING [20]		3.4	4.2		21.7	24.4		44.8	53.0	25.3
MESSAGE PASSING$^+$ [22]	14.6	20.7	24.5	31.7	34.6	35.4	52.7	59.3	61.3	39.3
SG-CRF [1]		22.9	23.5		29.2	30.1		53.1	54.7	35.6
MOTIFNET [22]	**21.4**	27.2	30.3	32.9	35.8	36.5	58.5	65.2	67.1	43.6
Ours	21.3	**27.6**	**30.5**	**37.1**	**39.5**	**40.2**	**60.8**	**65.7**	**67.9**	**45.2**

4.4 Result

Results of the baselines and the proposed method are shown in Table 1 and Table 2. As shown in Table 1, we improve the mean recall by 2.3% over the second best method MOTIFNET on the VRD dataset. On the larger dataset Visual

Genome as shown in Table 2, our model also achieves the best performance compared to all the other methods. It improves the mean recall by 1.6% over second best method MOTIFNET. This is primarily due to improvements on the scene graph classification task, where our method outperforms MOTIFNET by 3.7% on the R@100 metric. This demonstrates that the effectiveness of the proposed method in predicting object labels and relationships through the enhanced global context. On the scene graph detection task, our method does not completely outperform the MOTIFNET. But the results are extremely close. Because the performance of the object detector plays a key role on this task.

Table 3. Ablation studies on the Visual Genome dataset. All numbers are in %.

Position encoding	CRFs	SGDet			SGCls			PredCls			Mean
		R@20	R@50	R@100	R@20	R@50	R@100	R@20	R@50	R@100	
✓		19.3	23.2	27.1	34.9	37.5	38.9	52.2	58.3	63.1	41.3
	✓	21	25.7	29.8	36.6	39.1	39.7	57.1	64.7	66.3	44.2
✓	✓	21.3	27.6	30.5	37.1	39.5	40.2	60.8	65.7	67.9	45.1

4.5 Qualitative Analysis

Figure 3 shows two scene graph examples generated by the proposed method. These results demonstrate that our model is able to capture the complex structure of the object relationships. The blue relation node in Fig. 3(a) shows that our model even can detect positive result that is not included in manually labeled ground-truth.

4.6 Discussions

To evaluate the effectiveness of the two key modules of the proposed method: the positional encoding and the CRF-based structured relation prediction, we show the ablation experiment results in Table 3. As shown, the structured relation prediction has the most contribution to the performance improvement. And the mean recall decreases by about 1% without positional encoding.

As introduced in Sect. 3, the CRF-based structured prediction module is approximately implemented by the message passing scheme. Here, we study the impact of the iteration times of the message passing. The results are shown in Table 4. With only 2 iterations, the model has achieved relatively good performance and more iterations have no more help for the relation prediction. This demonstrates that the message passing is efficient to capture the contextual dependency among the relations.

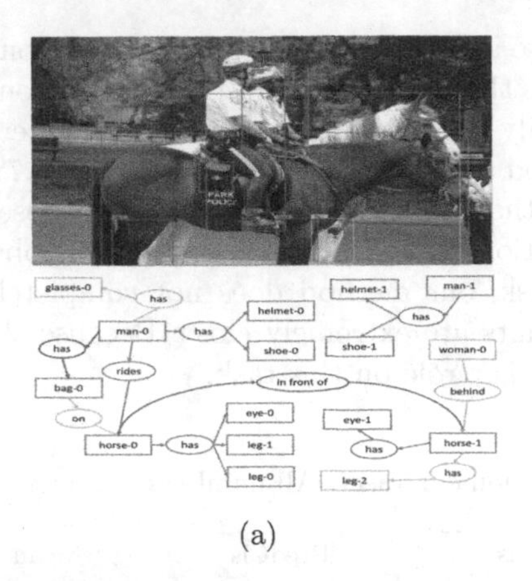

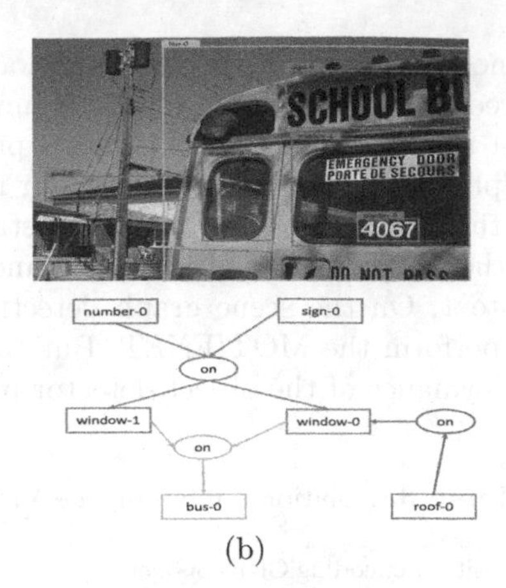

Fig. 3. Scene graph examples generated by the proposed method. Green boxes are correctly predicted objects while yellow ones are groundtruth with no prediction. For the relation nodes, green ones represent the correctly predicted relations under the R@20 metric. Yellow ones are groundtruth with no prediction. Red and blue ones are relations that do not exist in groundtruth. The difference is that blue ones are positive. (Color figure online)

Table 4. Results on the Visual Genome dataset with different iterations of the message passing in the structured relation prediction.

Iterations	PredCls		
	R@20	R@50	R@100
0	36.2	41.4	48.5
1	53.0	59.2	64.6
2	60.8	65.7	67.9
3	61.0	65.8	68.3

5 Conclusion

In this work, we exploited two kinds of dependencies which were neglected by the conventional motifs network in the scene graph generation task: the location-aware dependencies among object nodes and the context dependencies among relation nodes. The former were captured by accumulating the object information through LSTMs and encoding the location coordinates of local regions through position encoding. The later were captured by formulating the relationship prediction as a conditional random field. We demonstrated the effectiveness of the proposed method with extensive experimental results on two widely used scene graph datasets.

Acknowledgments. This work was supported by National Key Research and Development Program of China (No. 2018AAA0100604, 2017YFB1002804), National Natural Science Foundation of China (No. 61872424, 61702511, 61720106006, 61728210, 61751211, 61620106003, 61532009, 61572498, 61572296, 61432019, U1836220, U1705262) and Key Research Program of Frontier Sciences, CAS, Grant NO. QYZD-JSSWJSC039. This work was also supported by Research Program of National Laboratory of Pattern Recognition (No. Z-2018007) and CCF-Tencent Open Fund.

References

1. Cong, W., Wang, W., Lee, W.C.: Scene graph generation via conditional random fields. arXiv preprint arXiv:1811.08075 (2018)
2. Ghosh, S., Burachas, G., Ray, A., Ziskind, A.: Generating natural language explanations for visual question answering using scene graphs and visual attention. arXiv preprint arXiv:1902.05715 (2019)
3. Hochreiter, S., Schmidhuber, J.: Long short-term memory. Neural Comput. **9**(8), 1735–1780 (1997)
4. Johnson, J., et al.: Image retrieval using scene graphs. In: CVPR, pp. 3668–3678 (2015)
5. Krähenbühl, P., Koltun, V.: Efficient inference in fully connected CRFs with Gaussian edge potentials. In: NIPS, pp. 109–117 (2011)
6. Krishna, R., et al.: Visual genome: Connecting language and vision using crowdsourced dense image annotations. IJCV **123**(1), 32–73 (2017)
7. Krizhevsky, A., Sutskever, I., Hinton, G.E.: Imagenet classification with deep convolutional neural networks. In: NIPS, pp. 1097–1105 (2012)
8. Lample, G., Ballesteros, M., Subramanian, S., Kawakami, K., Dyer, C.: Neural architectures for named entity recognition. arXiv preprint arXiv:1603.01360 (2016)
9. Li, X., Jiang, S.: Know more say less: image captioning based on scene graphs. TMM **21**(8), 2117–2130 (2019)
10. Li, Y., Ouyang, W., Wang, X., Tang, X.: ViP-CNN: visual phrase guided convolutional neural network. In: CVPR, pp. 1347–1356 (2017)
11. Li, Y., Ouyang, W., Zhou, B., Wang, K., Wang, X.: Scene graph generation from objects, phrases and region captions. In: ICCV, pp. 1261–1270 (2017)
12. Lu, C., Krishna, R., Bernstein, M., Fei-Fei, L.: Visual relationship detection with language priors. In: Leibe, B., Matas, J., Sebe, N., Welling, M. (eds.) ECCV 2016. LNCS, vol. 9905, pp. 852–869. Springer, Cham (2016). https://doi.org/10.1007/978-3-319-46448-0_51
13. McCallum, A., Li, W.: Early results for named entity recognition with conditional random fields, feature induction and web-enhanced lexicons. In: NAACL (2003)
14. Mikolov, T., Sutskever, I., Chen, K., Corrado, G.S., Dean, J.: Distributed representations of words and phrases and their compositionality. In: NIPS (2013)
15. Redmon, J., Farhadi, A.: YOLO9000: better, faster, stronger. In: CVPR (2017)
16. Ren, S., He, K., Girshick, R., Sun, J.: Faster R-CNN: towards real-time object detection with region proposal networks. In: NIPS, pp. 91–99 (2015)
17. Sadeghi, M.A., Farhadi, A.: Recognition using visual phrases. In: CVPR (2011)
18. Teney, D., Liu, L., van den Hengel, A.: Graph-structured representations for visual question answering. In: CVPR, pp. 1–9 (2017)
19. Vaswani, A., et al.: Attention is all you need. In: NIPS, pp. 5998–6008 (2017)
20. Xu, D., Zhu, Y., Choy, C.B., Fei-Fei, L.: Scene graph generation by iterative message passing. In: CVPR, pp. 5410–5419 (2017)

21. Yang, X., Tang, K., Zhang, H., Cai, J.: Auto-encoding scene graphs for image captioning. In: CVPR, pp. 10685–10694 (2019)
22. Zellers, R., Yatskar, M., Thomson, S., Choi, Y.: Neural motifs: scene graph parsing with global context. In: CVPR, pp. 5831–5840 (2018)
23. Zheng, S., et al.: Conditional random fields as recurrent neural networks. In: ICCV, pp. 1529–1537 (2015)

Perceptual Localization of Virtual Sound Source Based on Loudspeaker Triplet

Duanzheng Guan[1], Dengshi Li[1(✉)], Xuebei Cai[2], Xiaochen Wang[2], and Ruimin Hu[2]

[1] School of Mathematics and Computer Science, Jianghan University, Wuhan 430056, China
1747899323@qq.com, realldS@126.com

[2] National Engineering Research Center for Multimedia Software, School of Computer, Wuhan University, Wuhan 430072, China
928886418@qq.com, clowang@163.com, hrm1964@163.com

Abstract. When using a loudspeaker triplet for virtual sound localization, the traditional conversion method will result in inaccurate localization. In this paper, we constructed a perceptual localization distortion model based on the basic principle of binaural perception sound source localization and relying on the known PKU HRTFs database. On this basic, the perceptual localization errors of virtual sources were calculated by using PKU HRTFs. After analyzing the perceptual localization errors of virtual sources reproduced by loudspeaker triplets, it was found that the main influence factor, i.e., the convergence angle of the loudspeaker triplet, could constrain the perceptual localization distortion. Simulation and subjective evaluation experiments indicate that the proposed selection method outperforms the traditional method, and that the proposed method can be successfully applied to perceptual localization of the moving virtual source.

Keywords: Virtual sound source · Loudspeaker triplet · Head related transfer function · Perceptual localization

1 Introduction

With the development of 3D movies, it needs more effective means to improve the 3D audio-visual experience. In recent years, many 3D multichannel sound systems [1,2] have been played by loudspeaker arrays, such as Dolby Atoms, Barco Auro-3D and NHK 22.2, which can provide a better 3D sound immersive experience than traditional stereophony [3] or 5.1 multi-channel sound systems [4].

Since the position of a virtual or phantom sound source can be rendered by a given loudspeaker array, it can provide the 3D sound experience of the original sound source while the position of a virtual sound source corresponds to

Supported by National Nature Science Foundation of China (No. 61701194, U1736206, 61762005) and Nature Science Foundation of Hubei Province (No. 2017CFB756).

Y. M. Ro et al. (Eds.): MMM 2020, LNCS 11962, pp. 189–200, 2020.
https://doi.org/10.1007/978-3-030-37734-2_16

the position of the original source [5]. There are two main approaches, physical sound field reproduction and auditory event reproduction, to generate 3D virtual sound source. Wave field synthesis (WFS) [6] and Ambisonics [7] belong to physical sound field reproduction. However, WFS needs at least 735 loudspeakers to reproduce an original sound field generated by a 20 KHz sound source with 1 m radius and ring shaped region. Ambisonics requires at least 1936 loudspeakers to reproduce an original sound field generated by a 20 KHz sound source within a sphere with a radius of 8.5 cm [8]. That is, physical sound field reproduction uses a loudspeaker array with very large number of loudspeakers to reproduce the original sound field within the given region, which provides the audience with a perfect 3D sound immersion.

Therefore, in recent years, auditory event reproduction is mainly used in mainstream 3D multichannel sound systems. The key point of this method is to let the perceived location of the virtual source correspond to the location of the original or given source. Because humans perceive the direction of the sound source through both ears, the researchers introduced two binaural clues [9], the interaural level difference (ILD) and the interaural time difference (ITD), to adjust the spatial orientation of the virtual sound source. Subsequently, using binaural clues, many practical techniques were produced, the most famous of which included Head Related Transfer Function(HRTF) [10] technology using headphone playback and Panning technology using two or three loudspeaker playbacks. Since the playback device for the auditory event reproduction is easier than the playback device for the sound field reproduction, the auditory event reproduction is more popular nowadays. The auditory event reproduction based on loudspeaker triplet (i.e., three loudspeakers) will be discussed in this paper.

1.1 Related Work

Panning is a well-known practical technique for auditory event reproduction. Based on the sine panning law [11], the ILD (or amplitude difference) generated by two loudspeakers must be equal to that generated by the phantom source provided by an alternative sound source (or a loudspeaker). From the listening point, the direction vector (i.e., unit vector) can be set to the sound source (or loudspeaker array). According to the vector-base amplitude panning (VBAP) [12] technique, the direction vector of the phantom source must be equal to the sum of the direction vectors of two or three loudspeakers. The phantom source may be placed in a full azimuthal circle(or spherical triangular region, as 3D-VBAP) around the listener by controlling the direction vectors of two or three loudspeakers. That is, three loudspeakers can be used to generate a phantom or virtual source in 3D-VBAP. Moreover, Professor Ando introduced an multichannel conversion [13], which the signal of a sound source (or a loudspeaker in the original multimedia system) can be allocated to three loudspeakers of a loudspeaker triplet in the reproduced multichannel system while maintaining the sound pressure properties at the listening point(shown in Fig. 1(a)).

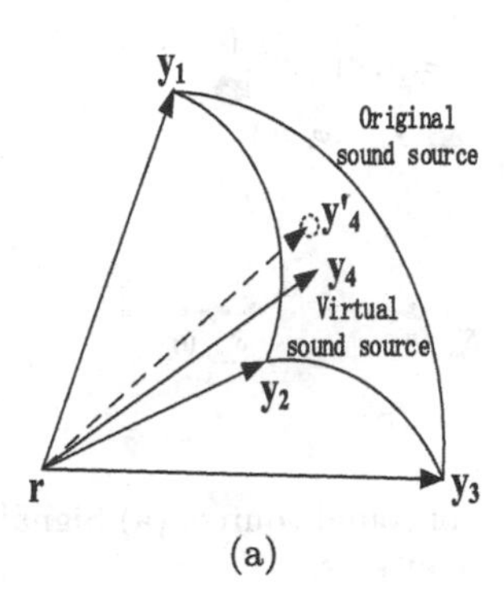

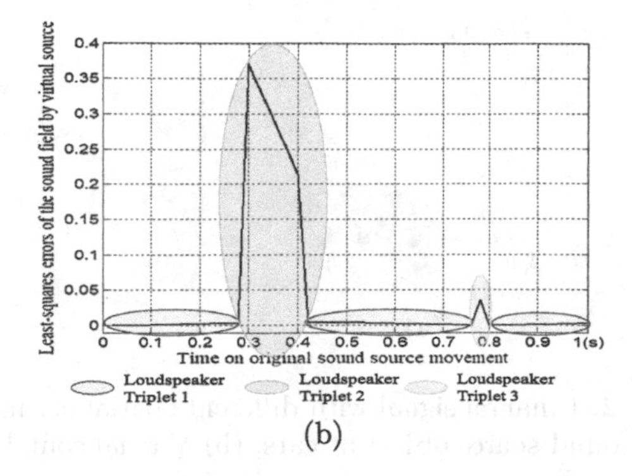

Fig. 1. (a) Ando's conversion for synthesizing the spatial orientation of the original sound source; (b) Errors of sound field reproduction distortion by different loudspeaker triplets.

The key point of 3D-VBAP and Ando's conversion is to allocate a sound source (or a loudspeaker) signal to a given loudspeaker triplet, while the observation point (or the listening point) is simply the center of the listener's head. However, only limiting the sound properties to the listening point does not guarantee a complete auditory experience because the listener uses both ears to perceive the position of the virtual sound. In addition, using both the Ando's conversion and the 3D-VBAP, they all need to constantly select a series of loudspeaker triplets when the virtual source is moved on a given trajectory. The 3D-VBAP technique indicates that the shape of the spherical triangle, corresponding to the loudspeaker triplet, is not too long and narrow. Moreover, Ando's conversion allows you to select the loudspeaker triplet with the smallest spherical triangle of all candidate loudspeaker triplets. Unfortunately, using Andos conversion, the listener's ears can perceive the inaccurate position of the virtual source whenever the virtual sound source trajectory moves from one loudspeaker triplet to another. As shown in Fig. 1(b), each time the loudspeaker triplet changes, the listener's ears will perceive that the position of the virtual source is not correct, even if the least-square errors of the reproduced sound field within head region is small.

In this paper, an important goal is to find the factors that affect the perceptual localization distortion of the virtual source generated by the loudspeaker triplet. First, the framework of perceptual localization estimation was introduced in this paper. Then, the perceptual localization errors of virtual sources were calculated by using PKU HRTFs. After analyzing the perceptual localization errors of virtual sources reproduced by loudspeaker triplets, it was found that the main influence factor, i.e., the convergence angle of the loudspeaker triplet, could constrain the perceptual localization distortion. Experiments show that the perceptual localization is more accurate while selecting loudspeaker triplet with a small convergence angle.

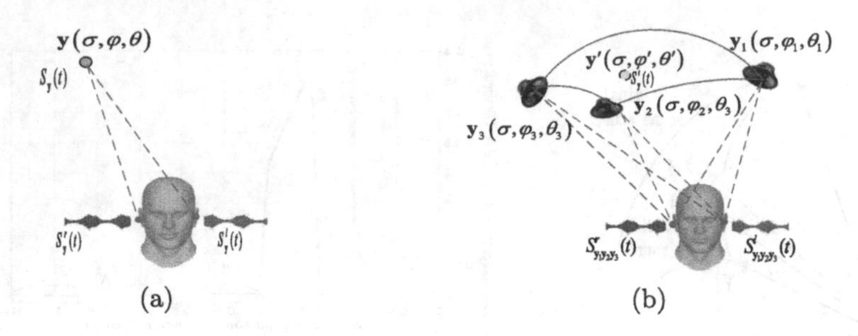

Fig. 2. Binaural signal with different spatial orientation of sound source. (a) Signal of the sound source object at ears; (b) Virtual sound source at ears.

2 Perceptual Localization of Virtual Source

2.1 Framework of Perceptual Localization

Assume that a sound source $\mathbf{y}$ is located at $\mathbf{y}(\sigma, \varphi, \theta)$, where σ represents the distance from the source to the listening point (the center of the listener's head), φ and θ are the azimuthal and elevation angles of the sound source $\mathbf{y}$ respectively; σ is the distance between the center point o of the human head and the sound source $\mathbf{y}$, and the signal of source is $\mathrm{S}_{\mathbf{y}}(\mathrm{t})$. After propagating, left ear will receive $S^l_{\mathbf{y}}(t)$ and right ear will receive $S^r_{\mathbf{y}}(t)$ (shown in Fig. 2(a)). The signal of the source $\mathrm{S}_{\mathbf{y}}(\mathrm{t})$ can be allocated to three loudspeakers (named as loudspeaker triplet $\mathbf{y_1 y_2 y_3}$) $\mathbf{y_1}(\sigma, \varphi_1, \theta_1)$, $\mathbf{y_2}(\sigma, \varphi_2, \theta_2)$ and $\mathbf{y_3}(\sigma, \varphi_3, \theta_3)$. A virtual sound source $\mathbf{y}'(\sigma, \varphi', \theta')$, generated by using this loudspeaker triplet $\mathbf{y_1 y_2 y_3}$, will be posited on the spherical triangle formed by this loudspeaker triplet. That is, the signal $\mathrm{S}_{\mathbf{y}'}(\mathrm{t})$ of virtual source $\mathbf{y}'(\sigma, \varphi', \theta')$ will be represented as three signals of the loudspeaker triplet $\mathbf{y_1 y_2 y_3}$. Moreover, after propagating of the loudspeaker triplet $\mathbf{y_1 y_2 y_3}$, left ear will receive $S^l_{\mathbf{y_1 y_2 y_3}}(t)$ and right ear will receive $S^r_{\mathbf{y_1 y_2 y_3}}(t)$ (shown in Fig. 2(b)). After Fourier transform [16], signals of left and right ears propagated by the loudspeaker triplet $\mathbf{y_1 y_2 y_3}$ satisfy

$$\begin{cases} S^l_{\mathbf{y_1 y_2 y_3}}(f) = S^l_{\mathbf{y_1}}(f) + S^l_{\mathbf{y_2}}(f) + S^l_{\mathbf{y_3}}(f) \\ S^r_{\mathbf{y_1 y_2 y_3}}(f) = S^r_{\mathbf{y_1}}(f) + S^r_{\mathbf{y_2}}(f) + S^r_{\mathbf{y_3}}(f) \end{cases} \tag{1}$$

Since the virtual sound source $\mathbf{y}'$ is synthesized by the loudspeaker triplet, we can also think that the binaural signal $S^l_{\mathbf{y_1 y_2 y_3}}(f)$ and $S^r_{\mathbf{y_1 y_2 y_3}}(f)$ generated by the loudspeaker triplet $\mathbf{y_1 y_2 y_3}$ are consistent with the virtual sound source $\mathbf{y}'$, that is,

$$\begin{cases} S^l_{\mathbf{y}'}(f) = S^l_{\mathbf{y_1 y_2 y_3}}(f) \\ S^r_{\mathbf{y}'}(f) = S^r_{\mathbf{y_1 y_2 y_3}}(f) \end{cases} \tag{2}$$

The head-related transfer function (HRTF) [15] indicates that the binaural sound signal can be regarded as the sound signal of the original sound source formed by a series of reflection, refraction and scattering through the listener's head, shoulder and auricle in the process of transmitting the acoustic signal of a sound source to the ears of the listener in the spatial direction. When the listener is in a free sound field, the HRTF is defined as:

$$\begin{cases} H_L = H_L\left(\sigma,\varphi,\theta,f,\alpha\right) = \frac{\mathrm{P}_L(\sigma,\varphi,\theta,f,\alpha)}{\mathrm{P}_o(\sigma,f)} \\ H_R = H_R\left(\sigma,\varphi,\theta,f,\alpha\right) = \frac{\mathrm{P}_R(\sigma,\varphi,\theta,f,\alpha)}{\mathrm{P}_o(\sigma,f)} \end{cases} \tag{3}$$

Where $\mathrm{P}_L(\cdot)$ and $\mathrm{P}_R(\cdot)$ are the sound pressures of the sound source at the ears; $\mathrm{P}_\mathbf{o}(\cdot)$ is the sound pressure of the sound source at the center point o when the listener is absent; α is the equivalent size of the head.

When the acoustic signal $S_\mathbf{y}\left(f\right)$ of the source $\mathbf{y}$ propagates through the air, the acoustic signal $S_\mathbf{y}^l(f)$ and $S_\mathbf{y}^r(f)$ at the ears are:

$$\begin{cases} S_\mathbf{y}^l(f) = S_\mathbf{y}(f) \cdot H_\mathbf{y}^l\left(\sigma,\varphi,\theta,f,\alpha\right) \\ S_\mathbf{y}^r(f) = S_\mathbf{y}(f) \cdot H_\mathbf{y}^r\left(\sigma,\varphi,\theta,f,\alpha\right) \end{cases} \tag{4}$$

By Ando's conversion method, three loudspeakers of the loudspeaker triplet will obtain three weight coefficients w_1, w_2 and w_3. the acoustic signals $S_{\mathbf{y}_1\mathbf{y}_2\mathbf{y}_3}^l\left(f\right)$ and $S_{\mathbf{y}_1\mathbf{y}_2\mathbf{y}_3}^r\left(f\right)$ at ears, propagated by the loudspeaker triplet $\mathbf{y}_1\mathbf{y}_2\mathbf{y}_3$, can be represented as:

$$\begin{cases} S_{\mathbf{y}_1\mathbf{y}_2\mathbf{y}_3}^l(f) = S_\mathbf{y}(f) \cdot \sum\limits_{j=1}^{3} w_j \cdot H_{\mathbf{y}_j}^l\left(\sigma_j,\varphi_j,\theta_j,f,\alpha\right) \\ S_{\mathbf{y}_1\mathbf{y}_2\mathbf{y}_3}^r(f) = S_\mathbf{y}(f) \cdot \sum\limits_{j=1}^{3} w_j \cdot H_{\mathbf{y}_j}^r\left(\sigma_j,\varphi_j,\theta_j,f,\alpha\right) \end{cases} \tag{5}$$

If the position of the source $\mathbf{y}$ is equal to that of the virtual source $\mathbf{y}'$,

$$\begin{cases} H_\mathbf{y}^l\left(\sigma,\varphi,\theta,f,\alpha\right) = \sum\limits_{j=1}^{3} w_j \cdot H_{\mathbf{y}_j}^l\left(\sigma_j,\varphi_j,\theta_j,f,\alpha\right) = H_{\mathbf{y}'}^l\left(\sigma',\varphi',\theta',f,\alpha\right) \\ H_\mathbf{y}^r\left(\sigma,\varphi,\theta,f,\alpha\right) = \sum\limits_{j=1}^{3} w_j \cdot H_{\mathbf{y}_j}^r\left(\sigma_j,\varphi_j,\theta_j,f,\alpha\right) = H_{\mathbf{y}'}^r\left(\sigma',\varphi',\theta',f,\alpha\right) \end{cases} \tag{6}$$

That is, the perceptual localization of virtual source $(\sigma',\varphi',\theta')$ is equal to (σ,φ,θ). When we got $S_{\mathbf{y}_1\mathbf{y}_2\mathbf{y}_3}^l(f)$ and $S_{\mathbf{y}_1\mathbf{y}_2\mathbf{y}_3}^r(f)$ at ears, we need to find the closest $H_{\mathbf{y}'}^l\left(\sigma',\varphi',\theta',f,\alpha\right)$ and $H_{\mathbf{y}'}^r\left(\sigma',\varphi',\theta',f,\alpha\right)$ in a given HRTF set, such as PKU HRTF (HRTFs acquired by Peking University). And we think that the perceptual localization of virtual source is equal to $(\sigma',\varphi',\theta')$ (shown in Fig. 3). Moreover, the perceptual localization error $\varepsilon\left(\delta_\varphi,\delta_\theta\right)$ between the virtual source and the original source is

$$\varepsilon\left(\delta_\varphi,\delta_\theta\right) = \left(\left|\varphi-\varphi'\right|,\left|\theta-\theta'\right|\right) \tag{7}$$

2.2 Estimation of Perceptual Localization

Through the Fourier transform, the signals of sound source $\mathbf{y}$ at ears should be represented as $\mathrm{S}_\mathbf{y}^l(f)$ and $\mathrm{S}_\mathbf{y}^r(f)$. Since the position (σ,φ,θ) of the source $\mathbf{y}$ is

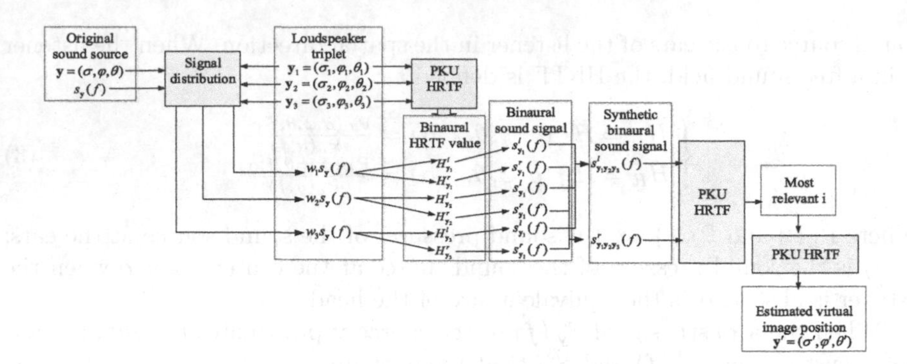

Fig. 3. Framework of perceptual localization estimation of the virtual source.

given, the index number i of the corresponding HRTFs can be found in a certain HRTF set, such as HRTF set of Peking University (PKU HRTF). According to Eq. (4), $H_{\mathbf{y}}^{li}$ and $H_{\mathbf{y}}^{ri}$ can be selected to synthesise the signal of source $S_{\mathbf{y}}(f)$. That is,

$$\begin{cases} S_{\mathbf{y}}(f) = S_{\mathbf{y}}^{l}(f) \cdot H_{\mathbf{y}}^{li}(\sigma, \varphi, \theta, f, \alpha)^{-1} \\ S_{\mathbf{y}}(f) = S_{\mathbf{y}}^{r}(f) \cdot H_{\mathbf{y}}^{ri}(\sigma, \varphi, \theta, f, \alpha)^{-1} \end{cases} \tag{8}$$

When the position of the sound source $\mathbf{y}$ is unknown, i.e., the index number i of the corresponding HRTFs at ears is unknown, the only way is to scan all of HRTFs in the given HRTF set untill $S_{\mathbf{y}}^{l}(f) \cdot H_{\mathbf{y}}^{li}(\sigma, \varphi, \theta, f, \alpha)^{-1}$ is equal to $S_{\mathbf{y}}^{r}(f) \cdot H_{\mathbf{y}}^{ri}(\sigma, \varphi, \theta, f, \alpha)^{-1}$, i.e.,

$$\frac{S_{\mathbf{y}}^{l}(f)}{S_{\mathbf{y}}^{r}(f)} = \frac{H_{\mathbf{y}}^{li}(\sigma, \varphi, \theta, f, \alpha)}{H_{\mathbf{y}}^{ri}(\sigma, \varphi, \theta, f, \alpha)} \tag{9}$$

It indicates that the position $(\sigma_i, \varphi_i, \theta_i)$ is considered to be the position of the source $\mathbf{y}$.

Most of the time, $S_{\mathbf{y}}^{l}(f) \cdot H_{\mathbf{y}}^{li}(\sigma, \varphi, \theta, f, \alpha)^{-1}$ is not accurately equal to $S_{\mathbf{y}}^{r}(f) \cdot H_{\mathbf{y}}^{ri}(\sigma, \varphi, \theta, f, \alpha)^{-1}$ in practical application. So we also calculate the correlation between $S_{\mathbf{y}}^{l}(f) \cdot H_{\mathbf{y}}^{li}(\sigma, \varphi, \theta, f, \alpha)^{-1}$ and $S_{\mathbf{y}}^{r}(f) \cdot H_{\mathbf{y}}^{ri}(\sigma, \varphi, \theta, f, \alpha)^{-1}$ (or calculate the correlation between $S_{\mathbf{y}}^{l}(f) \cdot H_{\mathbf{y}}^{li}(\sigma, \varphi, \theta, f, \alpha)^{-1}$ and $S_{\mathbf{y}}^{r}(f) \cdot H_{\mathbf{y}}^{ri}(\sigma, \varphi, \theta, f, \alpha)^{-1}$). And the index number i is selected when the correlation is the highest. That is, the position of the source corresponding to the index number i is deemed as the perceptual position of the virtual source.

Considering that the sound source $\mathbf{y}$ with the given position $(\sigma, \varphi, \theta)$ can be synthesized by a loudspeaker triplet $\mathbf{y}_1\mathbf{y}_2\mathbf{y}_3$, the position of the virtual sound source $\mathbf{y}'$ generated by the loudspeaker triplet $\mathbf{y}_1\mathbf{y}_2\mathbf{y}_3$ can be estimated by searching the index number i in the given HRTF set, shown in Fig. 3.

3 Perceptual Localization Distortion Analysis

3.1 Setup of Perceptual Distortion Test

In order to analyze the perceptual localization distortion of the virtual source caused by loudspeaker triplets, it needs to describe the position of the loudspeaker triplet and the position of the original source. Furthermore, we need to record the signals or HRTFs at the right and left ears. Fortunately, some researchers have recorded the HRTFs at left and right ears when the sound source has been located. And, in this paper, HRTFs at the right and left ears recorded by Peking University, i.e., PKU HRTFs, have been used to calculate the perceptual distortion of the virtual source localization. Considering that the distances between the center of head and every loudspeaker (or sound source) are more than one meter, 720 sources with 130 cm from the center of the sound source are selected in PKU HRTF set. The azimuthal angle and elevation angle of the loudspeaker sources are selected as follows: (1) Seventy two azimuthal angles φ of the sources are selected to be uniformly distributed from 0° to 359°, and the azimuthal angle between the adjacent source is 5°; and (2) Ten elevation angles θ of sources are selected to be evenly distributed from 40° to 130°, and the elevation angle between the adjacent loudspeakers (or sources) is 10°, which causes the perception distortion of elevation angles to be too large.

Therefore, between a given sound source $\mathbf{y}(\sigma, \varphi, \theta)$ and the virtual source $\mathbf{y}'(\sigma', \varphi', \theta')$ synthesized by a loudspeaker triplet, the perceptual error $\varepsilon(\delta_\varphi)$ of azimuthal angle will be chosen to analyse the perceptual localization factors of the candidate loudspeaker triplets. From Eq. (7), the perceptual error of azimuthal angles $\varepsilon(\delta_\varphi)$ is

$$\varepsilon(\delta_\varphi) = |\varphi - \varphi'| \tag{10}$$

3.2 Result of Perceptual Distortion Test

Li introduced two factors of the loudspeaker triplet [17], i.e., the convergence angle and the deviation angle (as shown in Fig. 4(a) and (b)), which can affect the least-squares errors of the reproduced sound field within a given region, such as the region within head. Li indicated that (1) the smaller the convergence angle is, the smaller the distortion of the sound field within head, reproduced by the loudspeaker triplet, is; (2) the bigger the deviation angle is, the smaller the distortion of the reproduced sound field within head is; and (3) if the loudspeaker triplet is an equilateral loudspeaker triplet, the distortion of the reproduced sound field within a given region is the biggest one among all loudspeaker triplets with the same convergence angles.

Therefore, all equilateral loudspeaker triplets were selected from all loudspeaker triplets consisting of 720 sound sources in the PKU HRTF set. And it was found that the convergence angles were concentrated at 36°, 55° and 86°.

Figure 5(a) indicates that (1) the smaller the perceptual error of azimuthal angle $\varepsilon(\delta_\varphi)$ is, the smaller the convergence angle of the loudspeaker triplet is; and (2) the change in the different perceptual errors of azimuthal angle $\varepsilon(\delta_\varphi)$

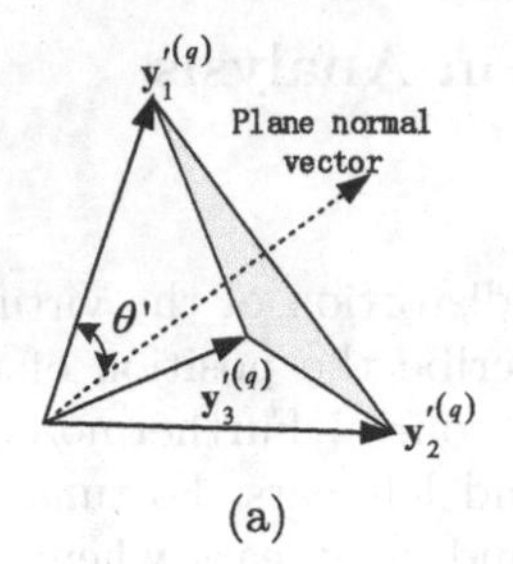

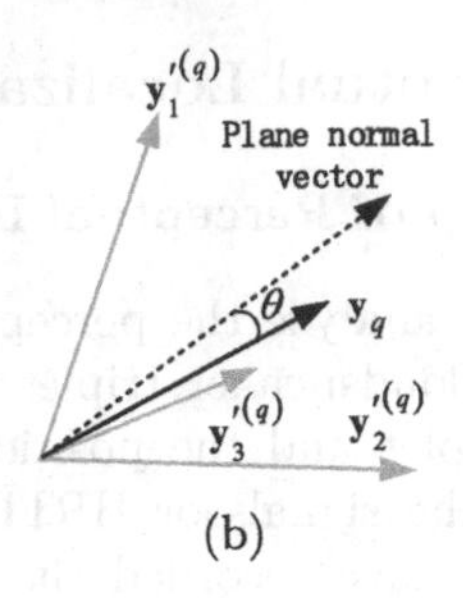

Fig. 4. Two factors of loudspeaker triplet can restrain distortion of the reproduced sound field with a given region. (a) Convergence angle θ' of loudspeaker triplet is the angle between the plane normal vector and the loudspeaker vector; (b) Deviation angle θ of the virtual source is the angle between the plane normal vector and the source vector.

is small when the convergence angles of the different loudspeaker triplets are the same. That is to say, there is only one factor, i.e., the convergence angle of the loudspeaker triplet, which can significantly affect the perceptual localization distortion of the virtual source.

Moreover, three moving trajectories of the virtual source are synthesized by a series of loudspeaker triplets, which are selected from all equilateral loudspeaker triplets with convergence angles of 36°, 55° and 86°. As shown in Fig. 5(b), in the process of synthesizing the moving virtual sound source by a series of loudspeaker triplets, we only consider the trajectory of the virtual source with different azimuthal angles and the same elevation angles. It indicates from the Fig. 5(b) that the smaller the convergence angels of the series of loudspeaker triplets are, the smaller the perceptual errors of azimuthal angle are.

Through the analysis of the factors of the loudspeaker triplet, it is found that the key factor, affecting the perceptual localization distortion of the virtual sound source, is the convergence angle of the loudspeaker triplet. Moreover, the convergence angle of the loudspeaker triplet can also constrain the reproduced sound field distortion within a given region.

4 Experiments

4.1 Experiments Setup

Simulation Experiment Setup. Free-field source conditions were assumed, and the sound field resulted from the loudspeaker was a spherical wave. We let the center of the head be located at the origin. The distance from each loud speaker to the origin was 200 cm, i.e., $\sigma = 200$. The distance from each ear to the center of the head was 8.5 cm, i.e., $\gamma = 8.5$. The loudspeaker positions of a 22.2 multichannel sound system without two LFE channels are used as an example.

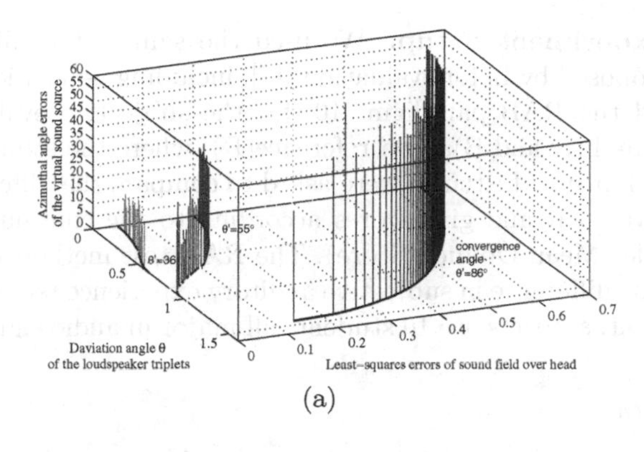

(a)

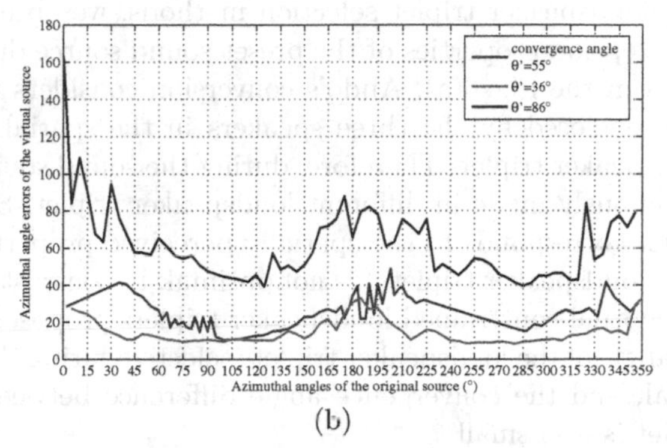

(b)

Fig. 5. Perceptual error of azimuthal angle caused by different equilateral loudspeaker triplets. (a) Perceptual errors of azimuthal angles generated by different convergence angles and deviation angles of the loudspeaker triplets; (b) Loudspeaker triplet senses the azimuthal error of the motion source.

For sound source object audio, we use vocal music with a musical background. The sound quality is not degraded. The audio file has a length of 10 s and the audio is divided into 468 frames.

We have set up four sound source objects in advance, in which the first sound source is fixed, and the other three sound source spatial positions form a motion track. The spatial locations of the four sound sources are described in the Table 1.

Table 1. Description of the simulation experiment environment.

Track object	Position	Azimuthal angle	Elevation angle	Trajectory motion
I	Fixed	30°	30°	Still
II	Moving	0° → 360°	90°	Rotate a circle
III	Moving	0° → 360°	60°	Rotate a circle
IV	Moving	0° → 360°	90° → 60°	Spiral rise

Subjective Experiment Setup. We used the same set of different object audio files as proposed by Li for evaluation [17], including percussion and natural sound. We used the RAB paradigm [10] for the subjective evaluation, which includes two stimuli(A and B)and a reference(R), where the stimulus A or B is equal to the reference R. Listeners were asked to compare the difference between A and B relative to R and give scores according to the continuous five-grade impairment scale (Mean Opinion Score). The RAB test method is divided into five grades for the difference in subjective auditory experience (shown in Table 2). In this experiment, subjects are 16 students all major in audio signal processing.

4.2 Simulation

For two different loudspeaker triplet selection methods, we observed the variation of spatial perception properties of the preset sound source during the entire motion. As shown in the Fig. 6(a), Ando's conversion considers the area of the spherical triangle enclosed by the three speakers in the spatial position when selecting the loudspeaker triplet. Therefore, during the sound source motion, the selection is continuously made in different loudspeaker triplet. So, the selected loudspeaker triplet corresponds to the spatially perceived property (i.e., convergence angle of the loudspeaker triplets) is not optimal. In contrast, the method of selecting the perceptual constrained loudspeaker triplets proposed in this paper, the convergence angle of the loudspeaker triplets selected during the sound source motion is optimal, and the convergence angle difference between the different loudspeaker triplet is also small.

4.3 Subjective Evaluation

It can be seen from Fig. 6(b) that the method in this paper selects the virtual sound source of the original sound source reconstructed by the loudspeaker triplet has an average MOS of 3.5 points in the subjective evaluation of the sound source localization. However, Ando's conversion selects the virtual sound source reconstructed by the loudspeaker triplet, and the average MOS of the subjective evaluation of the sound source localization is 2.303 points. The average MOS score of the proposed method is 1.197 higher than the average MOS score of the Ando's conversion.

Table 2. RAB subjective evaluation scoring criteria.

Score	Description of the perception of sound direction
4–5	Direction of sound source is clear and consistent with the reference sound
3–4	Direction of sound source is slightly different from the reference sound
2–3	Direction of sound source is significantly different from the reference sound, but can be tolerated
1–2	Direction of sound source is obviously distorted and unbearable
0–1	Direction of sound source is completely distorted and annoying

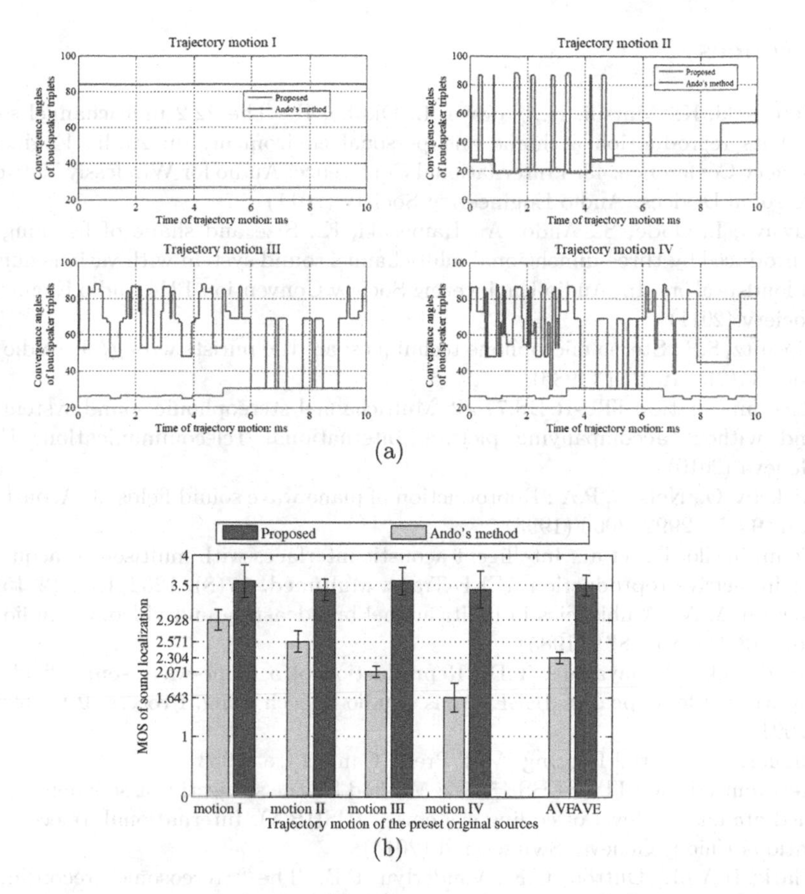

Fig. 6. Experiment results. (a) Simulation: four trajectory motions of the source and the convergence angles of the selected loudspeaker triplets; (b) Subjective evaluation: MOS of perceptual localization of four trajectory motions of the sources.

5 Conclusion

This paper mainly studies the factors of perceptual localization of the virtual source caused by different loudspeaker triplets. After analyzing the perceptual localization distortion caused by different candidate loudspeaker triplets, the loudspeaker triplet with the smallest convergence angle should be selected to generate the position of the virtual source. In addition, whenever the virtual source trajectory moves from one loudspeaker triplet to another, the proposed method indicates that the better perceptual localization of virtual source trajectory should constantly select a series of loudspeaker triplets with smallest convergence angles. Subjective evaluation shows that the perceptual localization of the virtual source used by the proposed method is better than that used by the conversion method, especially for perceptual localization of the moving virtual source.

References

1. Hamasaki, K., Matsui, K., Sawaya, I., Okubo, H.: The 22.2 multichannel sounds and its reproduction at home and personal enviroment. In: Audio Engineering Society Conference: 43rd International Conference: Audio for Wirelessly Networked Personal Devices. Audio Engineering Society (2011)
2. Sawaya, I., Oode, S., Ando, A., Hamasaki, K.: Size and shape of listening area reproduced by three-dimensional multichannel sound system with various numbers of loudspeakers. In: Audio Engineering Society Convention 131. Audio Engineering Society (2011)
3. Lipshitz, S.P.: Stereo microphone techniques: are the purists wrong? J. Audio Eng. Soc. **34**(9), 716–744 (1986)
4. Recommendation ITU-R BS.775-2: Multichannel stereophonic sound system with and without accompanying picture, International Telecommunications Union, Geneva (2010)
5. Kirkeby, O., Nelson, P.A.: Reproduction of plane wave sound fields. J. Acoust. Soc. Am. **94**(5), 2992–3000 (1993)
6. Comminiello, D., et al.: Intelligent acoustic interfaces with multisensor acquisition for immersive reproduction. IEEE Trans. Multimed. **17**(8), 1262–1272 (2015)
7. Gerzon, M.A.: Ambisonics in multichannel broadcasting and video. J. Audio Eng. Soc. **33**(11), 859–871 (1985)
8. Ward, D.B., Abhayapala, T.D.: Reproduction of a plane-wave sound field using an array of loudspeaker. IEEE Trans. Audio Speech Lang. Process. **9**(6), 697–707 (2001)
9. Blauert, J.: Spatial Hearing. MIT Press, Cambridge (1983)
10. Recommendation ITU-R BS.1534-2: Method for the subjective assessment of intermediate quality level of coding systems (MUSHRA), International Telecommunications Union, Geneva, Switzerland (2014)
11. Clark, H.A.M., Dutton, C.F., Vanderlyn, P.B.: The "Stereosonic" recording and production system. IRE Trans. Audio **5**(4), 96–111 (1957)
12. Pulkki, V.: Spatial sound reproduction with directional audio coding. J. Audio Eng. Soc. **55**(6), 503–516 (2007)
13. Ando, A.: Conversion of multichannel sound signal maintaining physical properties of sound in reproduced sound field. IEEE Trans. Audio Speech Lang. Process. **19**(6), 1467–1475 (2011)
14. Recommendation, ITU-R BS. 1284–2: General Methods for the Subjective Assessment of Sound Quality. International Telecommunications Union (2002)
15. Ramos, A., Tommasini, F.: Magnitude modelling of HRTF using principal component analysis applied to complex values. Arch. Acoust. **39**(4), 477–482 (2014)
16. Williams, E.G.: Fourier Acoustics: Sound Radiation and Nearfield Acoustical Holography. Academic Press, London (1999)
17. Li, D., Hu, R., Wang, X., Tu, W.: Loudspeaker triplet selection based on low distortion within head for multichannel conversion of smart 3D home theater. Concurrency Computat Pract Exper. (2018)

TK-Text: Multi-shaped Scene Text Detection via Instance Segmentation

Xiaoge Song[1], Yirui Wu[2], Wenhai Wang[1], and Tong Lu[1](✉)

[1] National Key Lab for Novel Software Technology, Nanjing University, Nanjing, China
sxg514@163.com, lutong@nju.edu.cn

[2] College of Computer and Information, Hohai University, Nanjing, China

Abstract. Benefit from the development of deep neural networks, scene text detectors have progressed rapidly over the past few years and achieved outstanding performance on several standard benchmarks. However, most existing methods adopt quadrilateral bounding boxes to represent texts, which are usually inadequate to deal with multi-shaped texts such as the curved ones. To keep consist detection performance on both quadrilateral and curved texts, we present a novel representation, i.e., text kernel, for multi-shaped texts. On the basis of text kernel, we propose a simple yet effective scene text detection method, named as TK-Text. The proposed method consists of three steps, namely text-context-aware network, segmentation map generation and text kernel based post-clustering. During text-context-aware network, we construct a segmentation-based network to extract feature map from natural scene images, which are further enhanced with text context information extracted from an attention scheme TKAB. In segmentation map generation, text kernels and rough boundaries of text instances are segmented based on the enhanced feature map. Finally, rough text instances are gradually refined to generate accurate text instances by performing clustering based on text kernel. Experiments on public benchmarks including SCUT-CTW1500, ICDAR 2015 and ICDAR 2017 MLT demonstrate that the proposed method achieves competitive detection performance comparing with the existing methods.

Keywords: Multi-shaped scene text detection · Instance segmentation · Text-context-aware network · Text kernel

1 Introduction

Recently, deep-learning based scene text detectors have achieved significant progress on standard benchmarks. Former, most methods are designed on the basis of assumption that text instances have quadrilateral shapes, which fails to handle texts with arbitrary shapes. For instance, EAST and some other methods [9,11,17] predict rectangular bounding boxes for scene texts. Yao and several

Y. M. Ro et al. (Eds.): MMM 2020, LNCS 11962, pp. 201–213, 2020.
https://doi.org/10.1007/978-3-030-37734-2_17

Fig. 1. Scene text detection results achieved by the proposed TK-Text. For text of arbitrary orientions and shapes in **first row**, TK-Text first predicts text kernel segmentation (in red color) and rought text segmentation (in white color) as shown in **second row**, and then draws bounding box for text instances as shown in **third row**. (Color figure online)

typical approaches [14,16] group text pixels into text instance of linear shape, which can not be applied to texts of irregular shapes.

With the development of research on curved text detecting problem, more curved text detector [5,12,15,18] have been proposed recently. However, CTD [15] and several curved text detectors extract curved texts by regressing polygonal bounding boxes with 14 vertices, which are inadequate to give smooth text boundaries for texts with extremely irregular shapes. Moreover, performance of most existing methods for curved texts are highly affected by the complex background. Therefore, text related context information on how to accurately locate text boundary still required to be modelled and involved for higher performance.

To address all these issues, we introduce a text detection method named as TK-Text, which not only keeps consistent performance on multi-shaped scene texts with text kernel, but also properly models text-context information on the basis of accurately located text kernel with an attention scheme, named as Text Kernel Attention Block (TKAB). Text kernel are defined as a non-overlap region inside the center of a text, which could help represent quadrilateral and curved text instances as a cluster of text pixels around its shape. To clearly show the effect of text kernel, we show a brief detection process of TK-Text in Fig. 1, where text kernel and rough text segmentation are generated by the Text-Context-Aware network and bounding boxes representing text instances are achieved after post-processing. Moreover, the proposed TAKB models text context information by describing both channel and spatial interdependencies between text and text kernel features, which help enhance distinguish ability of TK-Text.

We propose text kernel based on three considerations. Acting as the central region of text instances, text kernel remains unchanged on border and background variations, which fits for curved text with complex boundaries. Since they are generally far from each other, text kernels can be easily separated to help accurately represent and locate text instances. Last but not least, text kernel provide unique task-specific contextual information, which helps the proposed network to generate more discriminative feature map for higher performance.

The proposed TK-Text has achieved state-of-the-art performance (Precision 0.805, Recall 0.782 and F-measure 0.793) on SCUT-CTW1500, which indicates the consistent and effective detection performance on multi-shaped texts. To summarize, the contributions of this paper are included as below:

- We propose a novel instance segmentation based method TK-Text for multi-shaped scene text detection, which has achieved state-of-the-art performance on SCUT-CTW1500 comparing with existing methods.
- A novel representation for text, i.e., text kernel has carefully designed to process multi-shaped texts, which remain consistent on border and background variations and can be easily distinguished from complex background.
- The proposed TKAB has been constructed with a dual combination form between channel and spatial attention block, which successfully involves text context information into the TK-Text to reduce false positives that occur at the border of text.

2 Related Work

Current deep learning methods for text detection can be categorized into two types, i.e., Regression based Methods and Segmentation based Methods.

2.1 Regression Based Methods

Mainly inspired by the innovations of end-to-end trainable DNN models on generic object detection, some state-of-the-art scene text detection methods seek to adapt the mechanism of bounding box regression in order to meet the unique attributes of scene text. [9,11,17] successfully adopt the pipelines of object detection into text detection and achieve better performance on public benchmarks than traditional functions. [17] regresses text sides or vertexes on text center, based on shrunk text line segmentation map.

Since in natural scene images there are both quadrangle text lines and curved ones, [15] releases a curve text dataset called SCUT-CTW1500 which contains scene curved texts with polygon labels, and proposes a method called CTD which predicts bounding boxes for curved text by regressing the relative positions for vertices of a 14-sided polygon. Another method SLPR [18] slides a line along horizontal box, then regresses points of intersection of sliding lines and text polygon. TextSnake [5] also concentrates on multi-shaped text lines, it predicts text/non-text and local geometries to reconstruct text instances.

2.2 Segmentation Based Methods

Inspired by FCN [4], the key of segmentation based text detectors is to identify all text instances on a saliency map, which indicates whether a pixel is text or

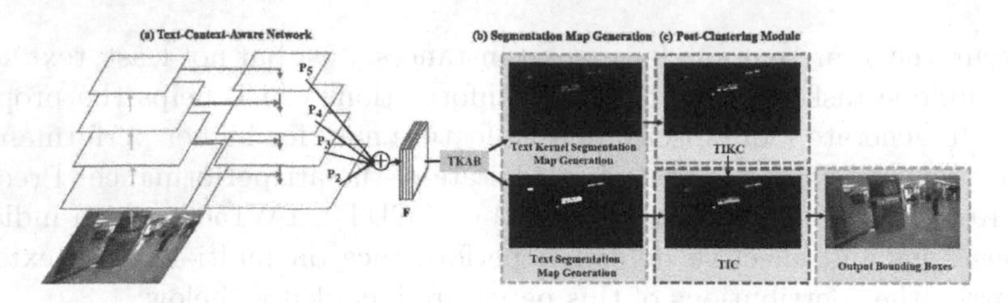

Fig. 2. Workflow of the proposed TK-Text network.

background. [14] first predicts segmentation map of text regions and centroid of each character, then generate text instances based on assumption that text lines are linearly arranged characters. To better distinguish text instances, [1] proposes the 8 direction links between pixels and uses them to group and distinguish text instances. [6] creatively adopts corner detection via position-sensitive segmentation map, groups corners to determine the position and shape of a text bounding box.

Different from existing segmentation methods on object, our method present the concept text kernel to capture general characteristics of multi-shaped texts and use it to extract text instances for both quadrilateral and curve texts through shape-independent post-clustering modules. Also we propose a text context aware unit based on text kernel to enhance the network representational power and segmentation performance.

3 Proposed Method

The whole pipeline of TK-Text is shown in Fig. 2, which is composed of three steps: (a) text-context-aware network, (b) segmentation map generation and (c) text kernel based post clustering. During step (a), a text-context-aware network is conducted to extract feature map, which consists of FCN network and TKAB unit for feature enhancement. During step (b) Text segmentation and Text Kernel segmentation map are generated from enhanced feature map, which is further applied to produce text kernels and rough boundaries of text instances. In step (c), a text kernel based post-clustering module is proposed, which contains two clustering module, i.e., Text Instance Kernel Clustering (TIKC) and Text Instance Clustering (TIC). TIKC generates results of text instance kernels, while TIC utilizes text kernels as cluster centers to assemble text pixels into clusters, which can be further regarded as individual instances, i.e., text lines.

3.1 Architecture of Text-Context-Aware Network

In this subsection, we first describe architecture of the proposed Text-Context-Aware Network, and then give details of the proposed TKAB module.

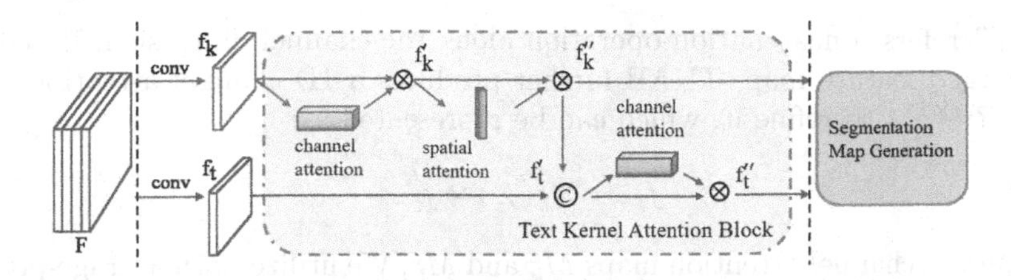

Fig. 3. Overview of TKAB: the scheme first refines text kernel features f_k by sequential channel attention and spatial attention. Then it concatenates the refined features and f_t, which is further enhanced by another channel attention operation.

Network Architecture. The architecture of our network is shown in Fig. 1(a). First we gradually merge features from different layers of backbone network through a standard FPN structure, following the concept of [3]. The backbone can be the widely-used networks proposed for image classification, e.g. ResNet [2]. Then we fuse the intermediate outputs of FPN (i.e. P_2, P_3, P_4, P_5) by resize-concatenation operation "$\oplus$" into F, whose size is 1/4 of the input images. In our experiments, resize operation is implemented as bilinear interpolation layer. After merging, we apply two 3×3 convolution layers to reduce channels of F from 1024 to 256 and produce f_k, f_t in Fig. 3, respectively. Consequently, f_k, f_t are sent to TKAB unit and two 1×1 convolution-sigmoid layers for text and text kernel segmentation. Finally, we interpolate the segmentation maps to original size of input images by additional upsampling layers, obtaining high resolution segmentation results.

Text Kernel Attention Block. Lack of context information may cause misclassification. Inspired by CBAM [13], we introduce a text-context-aware module TKAB to solve this problem, which exploits their cross channel relationship through attention scheme. In this way we involves context information to make text segmentation more robust.

We describe the computation process of TKAB as depicted in Fig. 3. Given the feature maps $f_t, f_k \in R^{c \times H \times W}$ as inputs, Text Kernel Attention Block (TKAB) sequentially computes a 1D channel attention map $M_k^c \in R^{c \times 1 \times 1}$, and a 2D spatial attention map $M_k^s \in R^{1 \times H \times W}$ to refine the text kernel features by exploiting the inter-channel relationship of features. The attention process can be summarized as:

$$\begin{aligned} f_k^{'} &= M_k^c(f_k) \otimes f_k \\ f_k^{''} &= M_k^s(f_k^{'}) \otimes f_k^{'} \end{aligned} \tag{1}$$

where "$\otimes$" refers to element-wise multiplication. Next it concatenates the refined text kernel features $f_k^{''}$ with the text features f_t, and applies a 3×3 convolution layer to merge features. The feature fusion process can be summarized as:

$$f_t^{'} = conv(f_t || f_k^{''}) \tag{2}$$

The "||" refers concatenation operation along the channel dimension. Based on the merged feature map, TKAB further produces a 1D channel attention Map $M_t^c \in R^{2c \times 1 \times 1}$ to refine it, which can be represented as:

$$f_t^{''} = M_t^c(f_t^{'}) \otimes f_t^{'} \tag{3}$$

To generate channel attention maps M_k^c and M_t^c, We utilize both average-pooled features and max-pooled features to aggregate spatial information, and use a shared Multi-Layer Perceptron (MLP) network with one hidden activation layer. The hidden activation layer for M_k^c and M_t^c are set to $R^{c/r \times 1 \times 1}$ and $R^{2c/r \times 1 \times 1}$, respectively, where "r" refers to the reduction ratio. To obtain a spatial attention map, TKAB applies average-pooling and max-pooling operations along the channel axis, then feeds the concatenated feature maps of them into a 3×3 convolution layer. After enhancing and merging features by TKAB, we take $f_t^{''}, f_k^{''}$ as the final refined features for subsequent text and text kernel segmentation, respectively.

3.2 Segmentation Map Generation

Based on the enhanced features $f_k^{''}$ and $f_t^{''}$ produced by TKAB, the text context aware network further generates text and text kernel segmentation map, respectively. The loss function can be written as a linear weighted sum of losses of two segmentation sub-tasks:

$$L = \lambda L_t + (1 - \lambda) L_k \tag{4}$$

where L_t and L_k refer to the loss for text and text kernel segmentation, respectively, and λ is a weight to make a balance between two tasks.

Text Segmentation Map Generation. This branch generates score map indicating whether a pixel is text or background. Ground truths as shown in Fig. 4(a) and (b) are generated according to [9]. We label all pixels inside text bounding boxes as positive, otherwise negative. For text segmentation training, we adopt dice coefficient loss introduced in [8]. It is common that text regions are usually small in natural scene images and dice coefficient loss can help reduce the bias to non-text regions. L_{text} can be calculated as:

$$L_{text} = 1 - 2\sum_{x,y}(P_{x,y} * G_{x,y}) / (\sum_{x,y} P_{x,y}^2 + \sum_{x,y} G_{x,y}^2) \tag{5}$$

where P and G refer to the prediction and ground truth respectively. Moreover, in natural scenes there are plenty of patterns that similar to texts. To better distinguish them, we adopt Online Hard Example Mining (OHEM) [1,10] which automatically selects hard samples based on positive samples to train. When there are S positive pixels, $r \times S$ pixels of largest loss are selected as hard samples, and r is a hyper-parameter fixed to 3 in our experiments.

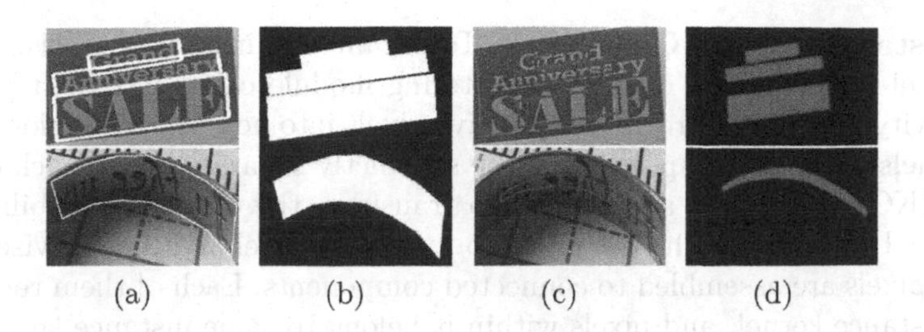

Fig. 4. Ground truth and label generation: (a) original image with corresponding bounding boxes for text region, (b) white masks are the corresponding ground truth of text region, (c) original image with bounding boxes for text kernel, (d) red masks are the ground truth of text kernel segmentation. (Color figure online)

Text Kernel Segmentation Map Generation. This branch aims to segment text kernels. Different from the "shrunk text lines" mentioned in [17] which is applied on quadrangular texts, our text kernels are defined as consistent representatives of multi-shaped scene text instances, which can well locate the central regions of both quadrangle and curved texts therefore guide the following clustering processes. The generation of text kernel ground truths and loss function are given in this section.

To obtain the ground truths in Fig. 4(c) and (d), we first shrink the original text annotation boxes to its center by $\triangle_{off}$ pixels with Vatti clipping algorithm. $\triangle_{off}$ refers to the margin between original bounding box and text kernel. We calculate it based on a hyper-parameter $\hat{r}$, which is the scale ratio between area of text kernel and area of whole text. The formulation of $\triangle_{off}$ is:

$$\triangle_{off} = (1 - \hat{r}^2) \times S/L \tag{6}$$

where S and L represent the area of bounding box and its perimeter, respectively. Next, we label pixels inside the shrunk bounding boxes as positive, otherwise negative. We use dice coefficient loss to train text kernel segmentation and L_{kernel} can be calculated as:

$$L_{kernel} = 1 - 2\sum_{x,y}(P_{x,y} * G_{x,y})/(\sum_{x,y} P_{x,y}^2 + \sum_{x,y} G_{x,y}^2) \tag{7}$$

where P represents the prediction map and G is the ground truth.

3.3 Text Kernel Based Post-clustering

In order to detect and distinguish text lines, we propose a fast post-clustering processing method which is composed of two clustering module TIKC and TIC. Since text segmentation map cannot provide enough information to separate adjacent text instances on their own, while text kernel segmentation map is lack of sufficient information to point out the whole text instances, the combination of TIKC and TIC can bridge the advantages of both sides. TK-Text takes text kernels as instance representatives and use them to group text pixels and conduct the generation of whole text instances.

Text Instance Kernel Clustering. To obtain text instance kernels, we feed text kernel segmentation map to a clustering module called TIKC. It uses the connectivity information to gather positive pixels into non-overlap regions. Since text kernels do not overlap, they can be succinctly separated from each other.

In TIKC, we first set a threshold to transform the output probability map into a 0/1 binary map, where 1 refers to a positive pixel and 0 otherwise. Next, positive pixels are assembled to connected components. Each of them represents a text instance kernel, and pixels within it belong to same instance kernel.

Text Instance Clustering. Assuming that we obtain N text pixels by text segmentation, and K text instance kernels $\mu_1, \mu_2, \mu_3, ..., \mu_K$ predicted by TIKC, then the instance segmentation task can be transformed to divide N text pixels into K instance clusters. Regarding the i_{th} text pixel as x_i, TK-Text assigns text pixels into text instance by minimizing the cost function J as below:

$$J = \sum_{i=1}^{N}\sum_{t=1}^{K} T_{it} \cdot dist(x_i, \mu_t),\ where$$
$$dist(x_i, \mu_t) = \min_{y \in \mu_t} ||x_i - y||^2\ and\ T_{it} = \begin{cases} 1, & \text{if } x_i \text{ is assigned to } \mu_t \\ 0, & \text{otherwise} \end{cases} \tag{8}$$

where x is text pixel, and μ is a text instance kernel, y is the text kernel pixel with smallest $L2$ distance between x among all other kernel pixels.

After Text Instance Clustering step, we achieve results of connected components, which can be regarded as text instances. Based on requirements of different datasets, we utilize minimal area rectangles to generate quadrilateral bounding boxes, and Ramer-Douglas-Peucker algorithm for polygonal ones. In fact, we adopt nearly the same method to generate bounding boxes as PixelLink [1]. To remove false detections, we also implement several extra post-filtering methods proposed in [1]. A predicted box is selected only if it has proper side length, area, and an average confidence $\geq \epsilon$. ϵ is the selected threshold on confidence. We keep the selected boxes as the final results.

4 Experiment

In this section, we firstly introduce dataset. Then, we conduct experiments on quantity of public datasets are performed to prove the efficiency of TK-Text. Finally, we describe implementation details for readers' convenience.

4.1 Dataset

To show the effective and consistent performance of TK-Text on both curved and quadrilateral texts, we conduct experiments on three typical public benchmarks namely SCUT-CTW1500, ICDAR2015 and ICDAR 2017 MLT, where SCUT-CTW1500 is designed for arbitrarily curve text detection contains 1000 training

Fig. 5. Results on public benchmarks produced by TK-Text. The proposed method draws the bounding boxes with red lines. The detection examples of ICDAR 2015, ICDAR 2017 MLT and SCUT-CTW1500 are listed in the first, second and third row, respectively. (Color figure online)

Table 1. The single-scale results on SCUT-CTW1500.

Method	Precision (%)	Recall (%)	F-measure (%)
CTD [15]	74.3	65.2	69.5
CTD + TLOC [15]	77.4	69.8	73.4
SLPR [18]	80.1	70.1	74.8
TextSnake [5]	67.9	**85.3**	75.6
TK-Text	**80.5**	78.2	**79.3**

images and 500 test images, ICDAR 2015 is a commonly used dataset for incidental text detection and ICDAR 2017 MLT is a large scale multi-lingual text dataset proposed on ICDAR2017 Competition.

4.2 Results and Analysis

Several results on testing samples obtained by TK-Text are shown in Fig. 5, where we can notice TK-Text not only properly detects multi-shaped text instances, but also own the ability to clearly distinguish adjacent texts from natural scenes. All these sampling results prove that TK-Text can accurately detect both curved and quadrilateral texts from benefits of text kernel and TKAB.

We perform experiments on SCUT-CTW1500, ICDAR2015 and ICDAR2017 MLT datasets, where the former one and the latter two datasets are used to prove the effectiveness on detecting curve and oriented texts, respectively. Moreover, we conduct ablation experiment on ICDAR2015 to prove the usage on accurately detecting of different modules.

Detecting Curve Text. For SCUT-CTW1500 dataset, we adopt the same evaluation method proposed by [15] to perform single-scale comparison. We report the statics of experiments on SCUT-CTW1500 in Table 1, where F-measure achieved by TK-Text, i.e., 79.3, demonstrates the solid superiority of

Table 2. Comparison results on ICDAR 2015 Dataset.

Method	Precision (%)	Recall (%)	F-measure (%)
MCLAB FCN [16]	70.8	43.0	53.6
CTPN [11]	74.2	51.5	60.9
Yao et al. [14]	72.3	58.7	64.8
SegLink [9]	73.1	76,8	75.0
EAST+PVANET2s RBOX [17]	83.6	73.5	78.2
PixelLink [1]	85.5	82.0	83.7
Lyu et al. [6]	**94.1**	70.7	80.7
TK-Text	86.1	**83.0**	**84.5**

Table 3. Comparison results on ICDAR 2017 MLT Dataset.

Method	Precision (%)	Recall (%)	F-measure (%)
YY AI OCR Group [7]	64.8	44.3	52.6
SARI-FDU-RRPN-v0 [7]	67.1	55.4	60.7
SARI-FDU-RRPN-v1 [7]	71.2	55.5	62.4
TK-Text	**76.8**	**55.9**	**64.7**

the proposed method for detecting curved texts. In fact, text kernel based post-clustering module can greatly refine the rough text instances with accurate text boundaries. With the hyperparameters obtained by grid search on the training set, our method achieved a more balanced trade-off between precision and recall, when comparing with TextSnake [5] which clearly trades recall with precision. Results on SCUT-CTW1500 proves the effectiveness of TK-Text in detecting scene texts of irregular shapes.

Detecting Oriented Text. Comparisons with other methods on ICDAR datasets are shown in Tables 2 and 3, where we can notice that TK-Text achieves comparable F-measure results of 84.5% and 64.7% on ICDAR 2015 and ICDAR 2017 MLT, respectively. It's noted that Lyu [6] achieves 94.1% in precision, which is much higher than 86.1% achieved by TK-Text. The reason of higher precision lies in the fact that Lyu [6] pre-trains their model with a quite large dataset, i.e., 800000 synthetic images and carefully finetunes on ICDAR 2015 to pursue best precision result. Meanwhile, TK-Text achieves balance performance between precision and recall with less training data. The competitive results on the ICDAR datasets indicate the proposed method can obtain consistent performance on quadrilateral texts.

Ablation Experiment. Results of several contrast control experiments on ICDAR 2015 are reported in Table 4, which is designed to show the specific effect of text kernel, TKAB and post processing. Specifically, we directly locate text instances on text segmentation map without text kernel, TKAB unit and

Table 4. Ablation experiment with different settings on ICDAR 2015 Dataset.

Configuration	Precision (%)	Recall (%)	F-measure (%)
Without text kernel	68.0	63.0	65.4
Without post processing	74.1	**86.4**	79.8
Without TKAB	85.9	81.7	83.7
TK-Text	**86.1**	83.0	**84.5**

post processing module to perform three group of ablation experiment, respectively. We can observe a significant decline in both precision and recall achieved by "Without text kernel", which proves text kernel could help improve both precision and recall. Meanwhile, we can find that disable post processing module could result in a sharp decline in precision, which proves that post filtering can effectively reduce false detections. Last but not least, TKAB makes the predicted bounding boxes more accurate, thus improving performance with 0.8 on f-measure.

4.3 Implementation Details

We adopt a data augmentation method to help build the proposed TK-Text, where we rotate images by a random degree in the range of [−10, 10], resize them with a random ratio in the range of [0.5, 1.0, 2.0, 3.0] and uniformly sample a 640 × 640 patch from each image to generate more training samples.

Our method uses ResNet-101 [2] pretrained on ImageNet dataset as backbone, and all networks are trained by SGD. On ICDAR2017 MLT, we train our models for 300 epochs with initial learning rate $1e^{-3}$, which is divided by 10 at 100 and 200 epoch. On ICDAR2015 and SCUT-CTW1500, our model is first pretrained on ICDAR2017 MLT then fine-tuned for 400 epochs, the batch size and learning rate settings are same with [12]. In experiments, reduction ratio of TKAB, $\hat{r}$ of text kernel, and the confidence threshold ϵ is set to 16, 0.4 and 0.8, respectively. All hyper-parameters are tuned by grid search on training set.

5 Conclusion and Future Work

In this paper, we propose a concise method implementing easy instance segmentation to detect multi-shaped text instances in natural scenes. The design of text kernel and TKAB makes TK-Text robust to shapes, which better distinguish text instances. In the future we intend to extend the proposed scene text detection framework to an efficient end-to-end text recognition system.

Acknowledgment. This work is supported by the Natural Science Foundation of China under Grant 61672273 and Grant 61832008, and Scientific Foundation of State Grid Corporation of China (Research on Ice-wind Disaster Feature Recognition and Prediction by Few-shot Machine Learning in Transmission Lines), and National Key

R&D Program of China under Grant 2018YFC0407901, the Natural Science Foundation of China under Grant 61702160, the Science Foundation of Jiangsu under Grant BK20170892.

References

1. Deng, D., Liu, H., Li, X., Cai, D.: PixelLink: detecting scene text via instance segmentation. In: Thirty-Second AAAI Conference on Artificial Intelligence (2018)
2. He, K., Zhang, X., Ren, S., Sun, J.: Deep residual learning for image recognition. In: Proceedings of the IEEE Conference on Computer Vision and Pattern Recognition, pp. 770–778 (2016)
3. Lin, T.Y., Dollár, P., Girshick, R., He, K., Hariharan, B., Belongie, S.: Feature pyramid networks for object detection. In: Proceedings of the IEEE Conference on Computer Vision and Pattern Recognition, pp. 2117–2125 (2017)
4. Long, J., Shelhamer, E., Darrell, T.: Fully convolutional networks for semantic segmentation. In: Proceedings of the IEEE Conference on Computer Vision and Pattern Recognition, pp. 3431–3440 (2015)
5. Long, S., Ruan, J., Zhang, W., He, X., Wu, W., Yao, C.: TextSnake: a flexible representation for detecting text of arbitrary shapes. In: Proceedings of the European Conference on Computer Vision (ECCV), pp. 20–36 (2018)
6. Lyu, P., Yao, C., Wu, W., Yan, S., Bai, X.: Multi-oriented scene text detection via corner localization and region segmentation. In: Proceedings of the IEEE Conference on Computer Vision and Pattern Recognition, pp. 7553–7563 (2018)
7. Nayef, N., et al.: ICDAR 2017 robust reading challenge on multi-lingual scene text detection and script identification - RRC-MLT. https://rrc.cvc.uab.es/?ch=8&com=evaluation&task=1
8. Ronneberger, O., Fischer, P., Brox, T.: U-Net: convolutional networks for biomedical image segmentation. In: Navab, N., Hornegger, J., Wells, W.M., Frangi, A.F. (eds.) MICCAI 2015. LNCS, vol. 9351, pp. 234–241. Springer, Cham (2015). https://doi.org/10.1007/978-3-319-24574-4_28
9. Shi, B., Bai, X., Belongie, S.: Detecting oriented text in natural images by linking segments. In: Proceedings of the IEEE Conference on Computer Vision and Pattern Recognition, pp. 2550–2558 (2017)
10. Shrivastava, A., Gupta, A., Girshick, R.: Training region-based object detectors with online hard example mining. In: Proceedings of the IEEE Conference on Computer Vision and Pattern Recognition, pp. 761–769 (2016)
11. Tian, Z., Huang, W., He, T., He, P., Qiao, Y.: Detecting text in natural image with connectionist text proposal network. In: Leibe, B., Matas, J., Sebe, N., Welling, M. (eds.) ECCV 2016. LNCS, vol. 9912, pp. 56–72. Springer, Cham (2016). https://doi.org/10.1007/978-3-319-46484-8_4
12. Wang, W., et al.: Shape robust text detection with progressive scale expansion network. In: The IEEE Conference on Computer Vision and Pattern Recognition (CVPR), June 2019
13. Woo, S., Park, J., Lee, J.-Y., Kweon, I.S.: CBAM: convolutional block attention module. In: Ferrari, V., Hebert, M., Sminchisescu, C., Weiss, Y. (eds.) ECCV 2018. LNCS, vol. 11211, pp. 3–19. Springer, Cham (2018). https://doi.org/10.1007/978-3-030-01234-2_1
14. Yao, C., Bai, X., Sang, N., Zhou, X., Zhou, S., Cao, Z.: Scene text detection via holistic, multi-channel prediction. arXiv preprint arXiv:1606.09002 (2016)

15. Yuliang, L., Lianwen, J., Shuaitao, Z., Sheng, Z.: Detecting curve text in the wild: new dataset and new solution. arXiv preprint arXiv:1712.02170 (2017)
16. Zhang, Z., Zhang, C., Shen, W., Yao, C., Liu, W., Bai, X.: Multi-oriented text detection with fully convolutional networks. In: Proceedings of the IEEE Conference on Computer Vision and Pattern Recognition, pp. 4159–4167 (2016)
17. Zhou, X., et al.: East: an efficient and accurate scene text detector. In: Proceedings of the IEEE conference on Computer Vision and Pattern Recognition, pp. 5551–5560 (2017)
18. Zhu, Y., Du, J.: Sliding line point regression for shape robust scene text detection. In: 2018 24th International Conference on Pattern Recognition (ICPR), pp. 3735–3740. IEEE (2018)

More-Natural Mimetic Words Generation for Fine-Grained Gait Description

Hirotaka Kato[1(✉)], Takatsugu Hirayama[1], Ichiro Ide[1], Keisuke Doman[2], Yasutomo Kawanishi[1], Daisuke Deguchi[1], and Hiroshi Murase[1]

[1] Nagoya University, Aichi, Japan
katoh@murase.is.i.nagoya-u.ac.jp
[2] Chukyo University, Aichi, Japan

Abstract. A mimetic word is used to verbally express the manner of a phenomenon intuitively. The Japanese language is known to have a greater number of mimetic words in its vocabulary than most other languages. Especially, since human gaits are one of the most commonly represented behavior by mimetic words in the language, we consider that it should be suitable for labels of fine-grained gait recognition. In addition, Japanese mimetic words have a more decomposable structure than these in other languages such as English. So it is said that they have sound-symbolism and their phonemes are strongly related to the impressions of various phenomena. Thanks to this, native Japanese speakers can express their impressions on them briefly and intuitively using various mimetic words. Our previous work proposed a framework to convert the body-parts movements to an arbitrary mimetic word by a regression model. The framework introduced a "phonetic space" based on sound-symbolism, and it enabled fine-grained gait description using the generated mimetic words consisting of an arbitrary combination of phonemes. However, this method did not consider the "naturalness" of the description. Thus, in this paper, we propose an improved mimetic word generation module considering its naturalness, and update the description framework. Here, we define the co-occurrence frequency of phonemes composing a mimetic word as the naturalness. To investigate the co-occurrence frequency, we collected many mimetic words through a subjective experiment. As a result of evaluation experiments, we confirmed that the proposed module could describe gaits with more natural mimetic words while maintaining the description accuracy.

1 Introduction

A mimetic word is used to verbally express the manner of a phenomenon intuitively. The Japanese language is known to have a greater number of mimetic words than most other languages. Researchers have focused on Japanese mimetic words representing the texture of an object to understand the mechanism of cross-modal perception and applied it to information systems [1,2,10]. Human motion, especially gait, is a visually dynamical state most commonly represented

Y. M. Ro et al. (Eds.): MMM 2020, LNCS 11962, pp. 214–225, 2020.
https://doi.org/10.1007/978-3-030-37734-2_18

by mimetic words, but it has not attracted attention from researchers working on the application of mimetic words to information systems. In English, when we wish to properly express the aspect of gaits, we can use lexical verbs such as *stroll*, *stagger*, and so on. Meanwhile, in Japanese, when we wish to describe the slight difference of gaits, we can use mimetic words adverbially. In addition, Japanese mimetic words have a more decomposable structure than these in other languages. So native Japanese speakers can express them briefly using various mimetic words and even modify them impromptu, in order to express their impressions intuitively.

Japanese mimetic words have an interesting property: sound-symbolism, which indicates that there is an association between linguistic sounds and sensory experiences [5]. The phonemes of a mimetic word should be strongly related to the visual sensation when observing a gait so that the mimetic words can describe the difference in the appearances of gaits at a fine resolution [3]. In the Japanese language, there are more than fifty gait-related mimetic words according to a Japanese mimetic word dictionary [7]. For example, *noro-noro* describes "slowly walk without having a vigorous intention to move forward," and *yoro-yoro* describes "walk with an unstable balance." Their difference of only one sound, i.e. /n/ or /y/, can represent a slight difference in gaits. As another example, *suta-suta* describes "walk with light steps without observing around," and *seka-seka* describes "trot as being forced to hurry." As we can see from these examples, the phoneme /s/ seems to express an impression of fast, smooth, and stable motion. Such associations are individual-invariant and linguistic invariant similar to the famous Bouba/kiki-effect [8].

We have focused on gaits and proposed a computational method to convert the kinetic features to mimetic words inspired by this cross-modal perception [4]. We constructed a phonetic space simulating the sound-symbolism and associated it with a kinetic feature space of gaits by a regression model. It allows us to describe the difference of gait impressions as difference in phonemes, computationally. Thanks to this ability, the proposed framework can assign not only existing mimetic words but also a novel one generated from an arbitrary combination of phonemes to gaits. However, although it can generate a mimetic word which is closer to one's intuitive impression than ordinary mimetic words, it has a risk of generating useless mimetic words because an extremely uncommon combination of phonemes will sound strange. To avoid this problem, in this paper, we propose an improved word generation module considering its "naturalness". More specifically, we introduce a "naturalness penalty" into the most suitable mimetic word generation module.

The previous study had one more problem that no public dataset was available at that time. So we newly constructed a public dataset. The most notable point of the dataset is that it includes various mimetic words described in a free description form. In this paper, to define what characteristics of words are natural, we analyze these annotations and define the co-occurrence frequency of phonemes composing the mimetic words as the naturalness.

The rest of the paper is composed as follows: Related work is introduced in Sect. 2. Section 3 introduces the dataset. Section 4 introduces our proposed framework briefly and describes the new description module. Section 5 reports results of experiments. Finally, the paper is concluded in Sect. 6.

2 Related Work

Most previous researches focusing on human gaits work on authentication or soft biometrics. For example, Sakata et al. proposed an age estimation method from gaits [9]. There are few studies on the fine-grained description which is independent from individuals. As a study of describing dynamic states, Takano et al. proposed a sentence generation method from RGB-D videos [13]. They introduced a "motion primitive" representation which intermediates motions and sentences. Though their approach is similar to ours in that translating motions to primitive representations, their proposed representation consists of just latent variables which are not intuitively interpretable by people, and the correctness of the representation itself can not be evaluated directly. Meanwhile, in our method, the primitive representations are Japanese mimetic words, and the correctness can be evaluated directly by any native Japanese speaker.

With regard to researches of mimetic words, there are some previous works on mimetic words associated with auditory, visual, and tactile modalities in the field of Computer Science. Sundaram et al. proposed a "meaning space" having the semantic word-based similarity metric that can be used to cluster acoustic features extracted from audio clips tagged with English onomatopoeias (mimetic words of sound) [11]. They also constructed a latent perceptual space using audio clips categorized by high-level semantic labels and the mid-level perceptually motivated onomatopoeia labels [12]. Fukusato et al. proposed a method to estimate an onomatopoeia imitating a collision sound, e.g. "Bang", from the physical characteristics of objects [2]. Shimoda et al. demonstrated that Web images searched with different mimetic words can be classified with a deep convolutional neural network [10]. Doizaki et al. proposed a mimetic word quantification system [1] which is based on sound-symbolism and prior subjective evaluations using 26 opposing pairs of tactile adjectives such as "hard – soft". These works target mimetic words imitating sounds or representing visually static states. Meanwhile, as mentioned in Sect. 1, in this paper, we focus on human gaits as visually dynamic states, especially human gaits, and attempt to accurately describe human gaits using mimetic words.

3 Dataset

We newly constructed a public dataset[1]. It includes videos recording human gaits and various mimetic word labels annotated manually.

In this section, we introduce the procedure of the video recording session and the mimetic words labeling.

[1] http://www.murase.is.i.nagoya-u.ac.jp/~katoh/hoyo.html.

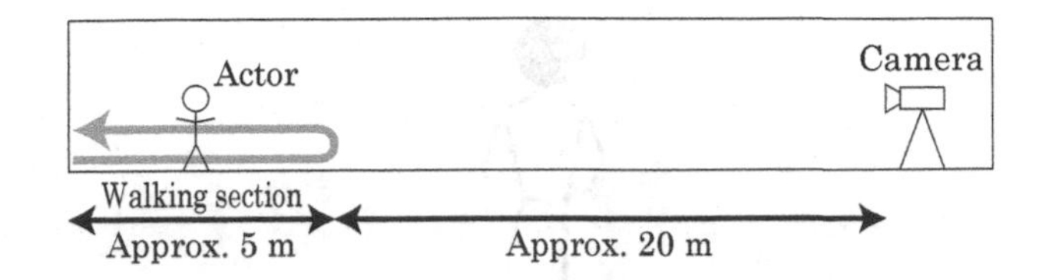

Fig. 1. Video recording environment.

Table 1. Selected mimetic words and their meanings [4,7].

Mimetic word	Meaning
suta-suta	Walk with light steps without observing around
noro-noro	Slowly walk without having a vigorous intention to move forward
yoro-yoro	Walk with an unstable balance
dossi-dossi	Walk with one's weight by stepping on the ground forcefully
seka-seka	Trot as being forced to hurry
teku-teku	Walk by firmly stepping on the ground for a long distance
tobo-tobo	Walk with dropping one's shoulder for a long distance
noshi-noshi	Walk with heavy steps forcefully
yota-yota	Walk with weak steps as with an elderly or a patient
bura-bura	Walk without having any intention

3.1 Video Recording

In this work, we use a kinetic feature following our previous work [4] as an input of the proposed framework. To collect kinetic coordinates, we detect body-parts (automatically detect and manually correct) from an image sequence captured from an ordinary camera, instead of using a depth sensor or a motion capture technique, because the mimetic words labeling procedure requires raw videos.

Figure 1 shows the environment of the video recording. The video recording was made over a single actor at a time. The walking section was approximately five meters long.

We asked ten amateur actors to walk with a gait representing a mimetic word back and forth the walking section. Here, the actors were native Japanese University students in their twenties but without professional acting skills. Table 1 shows a list of mimetic words instructed to the actors and their meanings, for reference. The ten mimetic words are commonly used ones, which were chosen from 56 mimetic words used to describe gaits listed in a Japanese mimetic word dictionary [7]. We asked the actors to walk with ordinary gaits as well. Finally, we recorded 292 gait videos (146 from the front of the actors and the paired 146 from their back).

The videos were taken at a rate of 60 fps, 527×708 pixels resolution, and 8-bit color. We used a USB 3.0 camera Flea3 produced by Point Gray Research,

Fig. 2. Example of fourteen body parts.

Inc. The sensor size was 2/3 in., and the focal length of the lens was 35 mm. The camera was set approximately twenty meters away from the termination of the walking section. It aims to suppress the scale variation of body appearance due to walking along the optical axis of the camera.

3.2 Body-Parts Detection

Li et al. proposed an algorithm for fine-grained classification of walking disorders arising from neuro-degenerative diseases such as Parkinson and Hemiplegia, by referring to relative body-parts movement [6]. In line with this work, we used kinetic features based on the relative movement of body parts in our previous research. To calculate them, we applied Convolutional Pose Machines (CPM) [14] to each frame of the dataset sequences mentioned above. Here, CPM is an articulated pose estimation method based on a deep learning model, which can detect fourteen parts of a human body, and yield their pixel coordinates.

However, the estimated body-parts coordinates are sometimes incorrect. In this paper, we use manually corrected data of the CPM detected coordination. For online applications, we will need a more accurate body-parts detector or a more convenient motion capturing device to obtain correct kinetic coordinates. Note that the dataset mentioned above includes the corrected body-part coordination data, and does not include the raw videos for the sake of the actors' privacies. Figures 2 shows an example of the fourteen body-parts.

3.3 Mimetic Words Labeling

In our previous work [4], the annotation was conducted in the form of choosing among ten types of candidates. Our framework has an ability of generating a variety of mimetic words, not only choosing one of the trained mimetic words. In order to make full use of the ability, the framework needs to learn various mimetic words, but the diversity of candidates was not enough in the previous work. To overcome this problem, in this work, we annotated more data, and also the annotators were allowed to give arbitrary mimetic words in a free description form.

Thirty annotators who are native Japanese University students in their twenties watched 146 videos showing the gaits from the front and annotated each

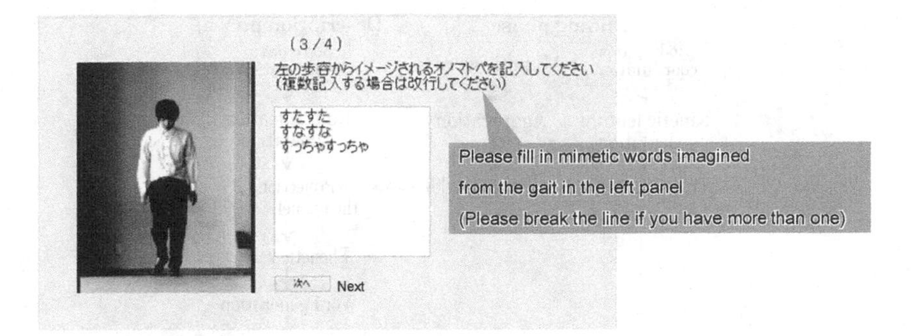

Fig. 3. Annotation tool.

1st consonant		φ	/k/	/s/	/t/	/n/	/h/	/m/
	avg.	0.0175	0.0468	0.1721	0.2882	0.0957	0.1066	0.0019
	s.d.	0.0207	0.0433	0.1580	0.1323	0.0846	0.0989	0.0063
		/y/	/r/	/w/	/g/	/z/	/d/	/b/
	avg.	0.0663	0.0102	0.0010	0.0298	0.0267	0.0707	0.0312
	s.d.	0.0742	0.0271	0.0046	0.0408	0.0359	0.1039	0.0263
1st vowel		/a/	/i/	/u/	/e/	/o/		
	avg.	0.1165	0.0218	0.3661	0.1286	0.3670		
	s.d.	0.0657	0.0245	0.1283	0.0767	0.1433		
2nd consonant		φ	/k/	/s/	/t/	/n/	/h/	/m/
	avg.	0.1549	0.1617	0.1252	0.2092	0.0059	0.0003	0.0059
	s.d.	0.1172	0.1057	0.0036	0.1264	0.0122	0.0020	0.0119
		/y/	/r/	/w/	/g/	/z/	/d/	/b/
	avg.	0.0016	0.2857	0.0058	0.0002	0.0008	0.0042	0.0371
	s.d.	0.0058	0.2440	0.0141	0.0019	0.0042	0.0123	0.0489
2nd vowel		/a/	/i/	/u/	/e/	/o/	/n/	
	avg.	0.3902	0.1020	0.1331	0.0287	0.2154	0.1305	
	s.d.	0.1362	0.0746	0.0790	0.0308	0.1315	0.1136	

Fig. 4. Statistics of the freely described mimetic words.

video with three mimetic words they imagined. Fifteen annotators were assigned to each video, and annotated using the tool shown in Fig. 3. Here, the mimetic words were restricted to the pattern of *ABCD-ABCD*, which is the most common pattern of Japanese mimetic words. Note that A and C are consonants, and B and D are vowels.

Finally, 6,322 mimetic words were collected except for 248 invalid words, e.g. typing error or not in the *ABCD-ABCD* pattern. Statistics of the results are shown in Fig. 4. The upper row shows the mean occurrence frequency of each phoneme, and the lower row shows its standard deviation.

4 Gaits Description by Mimetic Words

The procedure of the proposed method based on our previous work [4] is shown in Fig. 5. In our method, we map the kinetic features extracted from videos

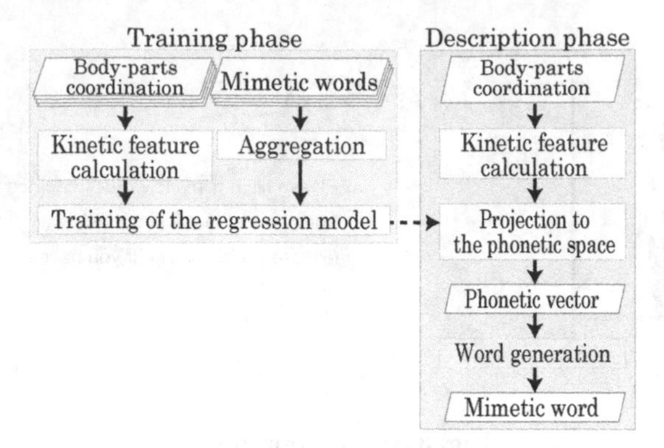

Fig. 5. Procedure of the proposed method.

to the phonetic space by regression. It consists of the training phase and the description phase. The main contribution of this paper is the proposal of the improved word generation module. Firstly, we explain the general framework concisely in Sect. 4.1. Secondly, the updated module is explained in Sect. 4.2.

4.1 General Framework of Describing Gaits

Takano et al. mentioned above showed the effectiveness of body-parts movement as a feature in describing gaits [13]. In addition, Li et al. proposed an algorithm for fine-grained classification of walking disorders arising from neurodegenerative diseases such as Parkinson and Hemiplegia, by referring to relative body-parts movement [6]. In line with these works, our framework [4] uses kinetic features based on the relative movement of body parts. Specifically, a sequence of arbitrary pairs of body-parts is used as an input.

Let the fourteen sequences of pixel coordinates be $\boldsymbol{P}(p,t) \in \mathbb{R}^2$. Here, $p \in \{0,\dots,13\}$ indicates the index of each body part, and $t \in \{1,\dots,T\}$ indicates the index of each video frame where the length of the input video is T [frames]. We calculate the Euclidean distance $D_{p_1,p_2}(t)$ between arbitrary pairs of parts p_1 and p_2. Then, we calculate the human height $H(t)$, namely, the difference in y-coordinates between head and foot, and their average in sequence $\bar{H}$. Finally, we divide all of $D_{p_1,p_2}(t)$ by $\bar{H}$, and obtain a sequence of the normalized body-parts distance $L_{p_1,p_2}(t)$. Note that the number of combinations of p_1 and p_2 under the condition of $p_1 < p_2$ is ${}_{14}\mathrm{C}_2 = 91$.

In order to handle mimetic words corresponding to gaits in a regression model, we express them in the form of "phonetic vector". As we mentioned in Sect. 3, in our dataset, multiple mimetic words can be annotated to each gait sequence. So we use the frequency vector of appearance of each phoneme composing the mimetic words corresponding to the gait as the phonetic vector $\mathbf{v}$. The vector is composed of 41 dimensions because the annotated mimetic words are restricted to the pattern of *ABCD-ABCD*, where *A* and *C* consist of fifteen consonants, B consists of five vowels, and D consists of six vowels [2]. Let the frequency vector of phonemes A, B, C, and D be $\mathbf{v}_A$, $\mathbf{v}_B$, $\mathbf{v}_C$, and $\mathbf{v}_D$ respectively, the phonetic vector $\mathbf{v}$ is represented as $(\mathbf{v}_A, \mathbf{v}_B, \mathbf{v}_C, \mathbf{v}_D)$. Note that $\mathbf{v}_A$, $\mathbf{v}_B$, $\mathbf{v}_C$, and $\mathbf{v}_D$ are normalized so that the summation of each element becomes 1.

Finally, a regression model learns the relation of the kinetic feature $L_{p_1,p_2}(t)$ and phonetic vector $\mathbf{v}$. Let the space constructed by the phonetic vector be named "phonetic space", the procedures can be regarded as estimating the mapping of the kinetic feature space to the phonetic space. In the description phase, the regression model estimates the phonetic vector $\hat{\mathbf{v}}$ from the kinetic feature $L_{p_1,p_2}(t)$.

4.2 Naturalness-Penalized Word Generation Module

This module generates an appropriate mimetic word from the estimated phonetic vector $\hat{\mathbf{v}}$ under consideration of "naturalness". Here, we define the co-occurrence frequency of phonemes composing a mimetic word as the naturalness.

Firstly, $\hat{\mathbf{v}}$ is split into the four frequency vectors for each phoneme; $\hat{\mathbf{v}_A}$, $\hat{\mathbf{v}_B}$, $\hat{\mathbf{v}_C}$, and $\hat{\mathbf{v}_D}$. This module chooses a mimetic word, i.e. series of phonemes, minimizing the following criteria.

$$\mathcal{L} = \mathcal{L}_d + \alpha \mathcal{L}_c \tag{1}$$

$$\mathcal{L}_d = ||\hat{\mathbf{v}_A} - Q(o_A)|| + ||\hat{\mathbf{v}_B} - Q(o_B)|| + ||\hat{\mathbf{v}_C} - Q(o_C)|| + ||\hat{\mathbf{v}_D} - Q(o_D)|| \tag{2}$$

$$\begin{aligned}\mathcal{L}_c = & w_{AB} C_{AB}(o_A, o_B) + w_{BC} C_{BC}(o_B, o_C) + w_{CD} C_{CD}(o_C, o_D) \\ & + w_{AC} C_{AC}(o_A, o_C) + w_{BD} C_{BD}(o_B, o_D) + w_{AD} C_{AD}(o_A, o_D)\end{aligned} \tag{3}$$

Here, each of o_A, o_B, o_C, and o_D is the candidate phoneme for each phoneme A, B, C, and D, respectively, and $Q(\cdot)$ is a function that converts a phoneme into a one-hot vector. $\mathcal{L}_d$ calculates the distance of $\hat{v}$ and mimetic words consisting of an arbitrary combination of phonemes. $\mathcal{L}_c$ is the naturalness penalty term. Note that $\mathcal{L}$ becomes an ordinary Nearest Neighbor method if the hyper parameter $\alpha = 0$, which corresponds to the previous method [4]. $C(\cdot)$ is the naturalness penalty between two phonemes.

For example, $C_{AB}(o_A, o_B)$ indicates a naturalness penalty of the first vowel o_A and the first consonant o_B. Finally, a combination of o_A, o_B, o_C, and o_D which minimizes the criterion $\mathcal{L}$ is obtained, and a mimetic word is output as the concatenation of the four phonemes.

The value of $C(\cdot)$ is calculated from the freely described mimetic words of the dataset introduced in Sect. 3.3. Firstly, all of annotated mimetic words are decomposed into a series of phonemes. Secondly, we aggregate these into histograms of each positional pair of phonemes, e.g. the first vowel and the first consonant. Thus, we obtain six ($= {}_4\mathrm{C}_2$) co-occurrence histograms $C'(\cdot)$. Finally, the naturalness penalty $C(\cdot) = 1 - C'(\cdot)/N_{\text{words}}$ is calculated per each positional pair. Here, N_{words} is the number of collected mimetic words (actually 6,322).

[2] In Japanese language, a special phoneme /n/ sometimes appears except in the first phoneme (it is called syllabic nasal). Although, strictly speaking, it is not a vowel, in this paper, we handle it as a vowel for convenience.

5 Experiments

We performed experiments for evaluating the correctness and the naturalness of the generated mimetic words. In Sect. 5.1, we report the result of a preliminary experiment to decide the weights of naturalness penalty w mentioned in Sect. 4.2. In Sects. 5.2 and 5.3, we report experiments evaluating the correctness and the naturalness of the generated mimetic words, respectively. Here, we define a subjective metric on how well a generated mimetic word expresses the corresponding gait as the correctness.

5.1 Parameter Tuning

As we mentioned in Sect. 4.2, the proposed naturalness penalty criteria is composed of six terms. In this section, we report the result of a preliminary experiment to decide the weights of the penalty terms.

Firstly, we sorted all the 5,700 mimetic words generated from arbitrary combinations of phonemes according to the $\mathcal{L}_c$ criteria with equal weights. Secondly, we extracted ten words from the list of sorted mimetic words at an equal interval. Concretely, the following ten words were extracted: *yura-yura, guri-guri, zuze-zuze, sako-sako, done-done, maba-maba, roya-roya, pubu-pubu, hazo-hazo*, and *hape-hape*, in descending order. Thirdly, we conducted a pairwise comparison experiment for reranking the ten words into actual order of naturalness. We asked four evaluators to choose the more natural one from the pair of extracted words. The number of questions was ${}_{10}\mathrm{C}_2 = 45$. Then, we sorted the words in descending order of the selection rate. Finally, we grid-searched a combination of optimal weights. Each weight had a value of 0 to 9 with an increment of 1, and we calculated the naturalness ranking of the ten words under each condition. We searched the weights in which the calculated naturalness ranking had the highest correlation to the experimentally obtained actual naturalness ranking under Spearman's rank correlation criteria.

As a result, the following combination achieved the highest correlation 0.8389: $w_{AB} = 0$, $w_{BC} = 0$, $w_{CD} = 1$, $w_{AC} = 9$, $w_{BD} = 0$, $w_{AD} = 1$. Note that w_{AC} corresponds to the co-occurrence of the first consonant and the second consonant, w_{CD} corresponds to that of the second consonant and the second vowel, and w_{AD} corresponds to that of the first consonant and the second vowel. This result shows the importance of co-occurrence of two consonants. Incidentally, the most frequently appeared pair of consonants is the pair of the first consonant /t/ and the second consonant /k/. The words including this pair account for 797 words of all the collected 6,322 mimetic words through the annotation mentioned in Sect. 3.3. This pair often appears in popular mimetic words (e.g. "*toko-toko*" or "*teku-teku*"), and such a familiar combination of two consonants may take an important part in making us feel the mimetic word natural.

In the following experiments, we use this combination of weights. In other words, the naturalness penalty term becomes as follows:

$$\mathcal{L}_c = C_{CD}(o_C, o_D) + 9C_{AC}(o_A, o_C) + C_{AD}(o_A, o_D) \tag{4}$$

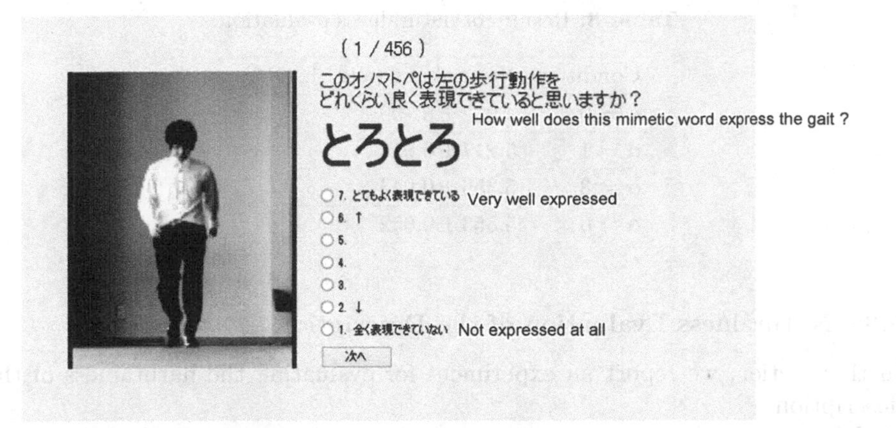

Fig. 6. User interface for correctness evaluation.

Table 2. Results of correctness evaluation.

Condition	Correctness (avg. ± s.d.)
$\alpha = 0$	4.434 ± 0.109
$\alpha = 1$	4.452 ± 0.088
$\alpha = 3$	4.275 ± 0.053
$\alpha = 6$	4.192 ± 0.067

5.2 Correctness Evaluation of the Description

In this section, we report an experiment for evaluating the correctness of the description.

We presented a pair of a gait video and a generated mimetic word to evaluators, and asked them how well the generated mimetic word described the gait from seven levels of Likert scale. Here, we call this metric as "correctness". The presented gaits were the gait videos in the dataset introduced in Sect. 3, and the mimetic words were generated from phonetic vectors based on the freely described mimetic words for those videos. The evaluators were five native Japanese University students. Figure 6 shows the interface used for this evaluation. In this experiment, four methods were compared with hyperparameters $\alpha = 0, 1, 3$, and 6. As mentioned in Sect. 4.2, α is a parameter which decides the weight of the penalty term $\mathcal{L}_c$ to the distance $\mathcal{L}_d$, and when $\alpha = 0$, it becomes equivalent to the ordinary Nearest Neighbor method. The result is shown in Table 2. We can see that as α increases, the naturalness constraint becomes stronger. The correctness and naturalness are in the relation of a trade-off. The result shows that the condition $\alpha = 1$ can keep the correctness compared to the condition $\alpha = 0$. Note that the correctness evaluated under a random condition is 4.014. In the random condition, we presented a pair of a gait video and a random mimetic word to evaluators. Comparing these results, it was confirmed that the proposed method achieved higher correctness than the random description.

Table 3. Results of naturalness evaluation.

Condition	Naturalness (avg. ± s.d.)
$\alpha = 0$	4.962 ± 0.109
$\alpha = 1$	5.217 ± 0.077
$\alpha = 3$	5.356 ± 0.043
$\alpha = 6$	5.553 ± 0.052

5.3 Naturalness Evaluation of the Description

In this section, we report an experiment for evaluating the naturalness of the description.

We presented a generated mimetic word to evaluators, and asked them how natural the generated mimetic word is from seven levels of Likert scale. The evaluators were four native Japanese University students. As the same with the experiment in Sect. 5.2, four methods with $\alpha = 0, 1, 3$, and 6 were compared. The presented mimetic words were the same as in the previous experiment. The result is shown in Table 3. We can see that as α increases, the naturalness becomes higher.

Considering together with the evaluation result of correctness in Sect. 5.2, it turned out that the condition $\alpha = 1$ generates more natural mimetic words than the condition $\alpha = 0$ while maintaining the correctness.

6 Conclusions

In this paper, we proposed an improved mimetic word generation module considering naturalness, and updated our previously proposed description framework [4]. We defined the co-occurrence frequency of phonemes composing a mimetic word as the naturalness. We constructed a new dataset, and used the freely described mimetic words in the dataset to calculate the frequency. We formulated the naturalness penalty in six terms, each term corresponding to the co-occurrence of the positional pair of two phonemes. Through a preliminary experiment, we obtained the optimal weights of naturalness penalty terms, and revealed that the following three kinds of co-occurrences are important: the first consonant and the second consonant, the second consonant and the second vowel, the first consonant and the second vowel. To confirm the effectiveness of the proposed mimetic word generation module, we conducted two subjective experiments. Evaluators assessed the correctness and the naturalness in Likert scale. As a result, we confirmed that the proposed module could describe gaits with more natural mimetic words while maintaining the correctness.

Future works include exploring how the impression of human appearance (e.g. body shape or facial expression) biases a mimetic word we imagine.

Acknowledgements. Parts of this work were supported by MEXT, Grant-in-Aid for Scientific Research and the Kayamori Foundation of Information Science Advancement.

References

1. Doizaki, R., Watanabe, J., Sakamoto, M.: Automatic estimation of multidimensional ratings from a single sound-symbolic word and word-based visualization of tactile perceptual space. IEEE Trans. Haptics **10**(2), 173–182 (2017)
2. Fukusato, T., Morishima, S.: Automatic depiction of onomatopoeia in animation considering physical phenomena. In: Proceedings of the 7th ACM International Conference on Motion in Games, pp. 161–169 (2014)
3. Hamano, S.: The Sound-Symbolic System of Japanese. CSLI Publications, Stanford (1998)
4. Kato, H., et al.: Toward describing human gaits by onomatopoeias. In: Proceedings of the 2017 IEEE International Conference on Computer Vision, pp. 1573–1580 (2017)
5. Köhler, W.: Gestalt Psychology: An Introduction to New Concepts in Modern Psychology. WW Norton & Company, New York (1970)
6. Li, Q., et al.: Classification of gait anomalies from Kinect. Vis. Comput. **34**(2), 229–241 (2018)
7. Ono, M.: Jpn. Onomatopoeia Dict. (In Jpn.). Shogakukan Press, Tokyo (2007)
8. Ramachandran, V.S., Hubbard, E.M.: Synaesthesia–a window into perception, thought and language. J. Conscious. Stud. **8**(12), 3–34 (2001)
9. Sakata, A., Makihara, Y., Takemura, N., Muramatsu, D., Yagi, Y.: Gait-based age estimation using a DenseNet. In: Carneiro, G., You, S. (eds.) ACCV 2018. LNCS, vol. 11367, pp. 55–63. Springer, Cham (2019). https://doi.org/10.1007/978-3-030-21074-8_5
10. Shimoda, W., Yanai, K.: A visual analysis on recognizability and discriminability of onomatopoeia words with DCNN features. In: Proceedings of the 2015 IEEE International Conference on Multimedia and Expo, pp. 1–6 (2015)
11. Sundaram, S., Narayanan, S.: Analysis of audio clustering using word descriptions. In: Proceedings of the 2007 IEEE International Conference on Acoustics, Speech and Signal Processing, vol. 2, pp. 769–772 (2007)
12. Sundaram, S., Narayanan, S.: Classification of sound clips by two schemes: using onomatopoeia and semantic labels. In: Proceedings of the 2008 IEEE International Conference on Multimedia and Expo, pp. 1341–1344 (2008)
13. Takano, W., Yamada, Y., Nakamura, Y.: Linking human motions and objects to language for synthesizing action sentences. Auton. Robot. **43**(4), 913–925 (2019)
14. Wei, S.E., Ramakrishna, V., Kanade, T., Sheikh, Y.: Convolutional pose machines. In: Proceedings of the IEEE Conference on Computer Vision and Pattern Recognition 2016, pp. 4724–4732 (2016)

Lite Hourglass Network for Multi-person Pose Estimation

Ying Zhao[1,2](✉), Zhiwei Luo[2], Changqin Quan[2], Dianchao Liu[1], and Gang Wang[1]

[1] Ricoh Software Research Center (Beijing) Co., Ltd., Beijing, China
{ying.zhao,dianchao.liu,gang.wang}@srcb.ricoh.com
[2] Graduate School of System Informatics, Kobe University, Kobe, Japan
{luo,quanchqin}@gold.kobe-u.ac.jp

Abstract. Recent multi-person pose estimation networks rely on sequential downsampling and upsampling procedures to capture multi-scale features and stacking basic modules to reassess local and global contexts. However, the network parameters become huge and difficult to be trained under limited computational resource. Motived by this observation, we design a lite version of Hourglass module that uses hybrid convolution blocks to reduce the number of parameters while maintaining performance. The hybrid convolution block builds multi-context paths with dilated convolutions with different rates which not only reduces the number of parameters but also enlarges the receptive field. Moreover, due to the limitation of heatmap representation, the networks need extra and non-differentiable post-processing to convert heatmaps to keypoint coordinates. Therefore, we propose a simple and efficient operation based on integral loss to fill this gap specifically for bottom-up pose estimation methods. We demonstrate that the proposed approach achieves better performance than the baseline methods on the challenge benchmark MSCOCO dataset for multi-person pose estimation.

Keywords: Multi-person pose estimation · Human keypoint detection · Deep learning

1 Introduction

Multi-person pose estimation targets to locate and recognize the body keypoints (such as nose, shoulders, wrists, etc.) from multiple person in a given RGB image. It is an essential yet challenging task in computer vision applications and benefits many applications, such as human-computer interaction, human action recognition and sports video analytics. In spite of extensive prior arts, it still remains challenging to get accurate keypoint detection from variant articulation of body limbs, self-occlusion and significant overlap between neighbor persons. Moreover, it is also demanding to allocate the detected keypoints to multiple scales and unknown number of persons. The two major approaches in multi-person pose estimation are structured in top-down and bottom-up. On one hand, the

Y. M. Ro et al. (Eds.): MMM 2020, LNCS 11962, pp. 226–238, 2020.
https://doi.org/10.1007/978-3-030-37734-2_19

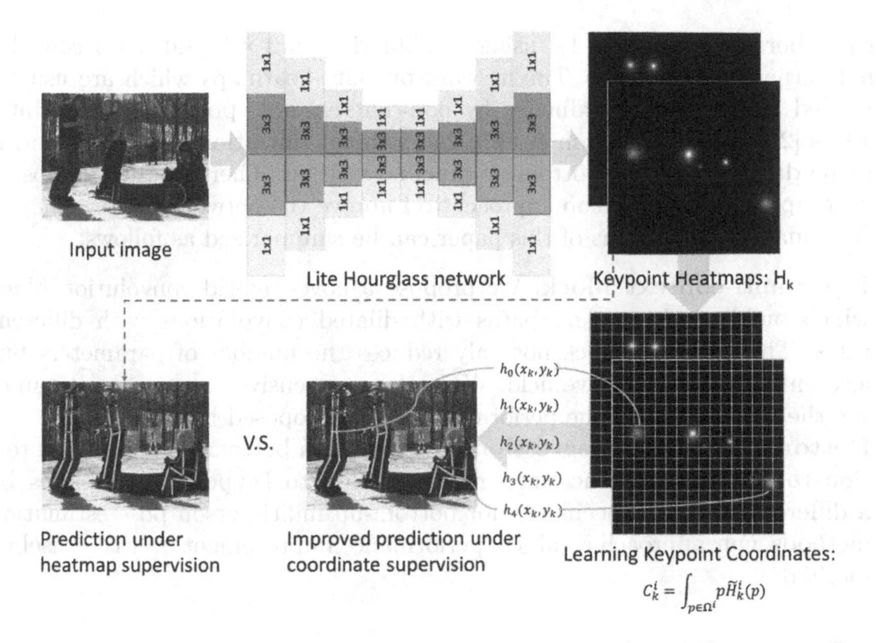

Fig. 1. Overview of proposed lite Hourglass network with bottom-up integral regression.

top-down methods [2–4,6,15,25,27] firstly detect persons and then repeatedly estimate pose for each of them. On the other hand, the bottom-up methods [1,8,9,14,16] detect body keypoints without advance knowledge of person locations and then group them into person instances.

To capture and consolidate information across all scales of the image, the pipeline of repeated downsampling and upsampling are broadly used, such as the classical architecture of the Hourglass network [14,15]. The Hourglass network pools down the feature maps to a very low resolution, and then upsamples and combines features across multiple resolutions. The most significant attribute of the network is the symmetric topology that consists of a series of convolution, pooling and upsampling layers. This architecture provides the benefit of capturing both global and local features for the pixel-wise prediction tasks. However, with the using of stacking multiple Hourglass modules, the network parameters become huge and difficult to be trained under limited computational resource. The top-down pipeline method SHG [15] uses the bottleneck [5] in each layer of the Hourglass module and achieves good performance. However, due to the needs of simultaneously detecting and grouping keypoints, the bottom-up pipeline method PoseAE [14] uses standard 3×3 convolutional kernels in each layer of the Hourglass module. Motivated by this observations, we propose a lite version of Hourglass module which is able to use much less parameters while maintaining the performance. As shown in Fig. 1, our module uses hybrid convolution kernels in each scale rather than uniformly using 3×3 kernels. It reduces the number of parameters by using combination of 1×1 and 3×3 convolutional kernels in each scale. The network outputs heatmaps which are usually converted to keypoint coordinates by non-differentiable post-processing. Integral loss [23] proposed by Sun et al. reduces the quantization error. However, it can't be directly used for bottom-up pipeline method. Therefore, we propose a bottom-up integral regression approach to improve the network performance.

The main contributions of this paper can be summarized as follows:

- **Lite multi-context block.** We propose a novel hybrid convolution block which builds multi-context paths with dilated convolutions with different rates. The proposed block not only reduces the number of parameters but also enlarges the receptive field. We perform extensive experiments to analyse the properties and the performance of the proposed block.
- **Bottom-up integral regression.** We propose a bottom-up integral regression to transform the heatmap representation to keypoint coordinates by a differentiable way specifically for bottom-up multi-person pose estimation methods. Our approach results in performance improvement over the baseline methods.

2 Related Works

Since DeepPose [24], the pose estimation solutions thrive in the presence of deep neural network. The pose estimation network branched out into bottom-up and top-down structures. In the bottom-up branch, the approaches firstly detect body keypoints (or joints) and then group them into person instances. Deepcut [20] proposes a partitioning and labeling formulation of a set of body-part hypotheses generated with CNN-based part detectors. Deepercut [8] and Iqbal et al. [9] also formulate the problem as part grouping and labeling via a linear programming. Following PoseMachine [25], OpenPose [1] uses a part affinity field learn to associate body parts and group them to person instances with greedy bottom-up parsing steps. AE [14] proposes associative embedding to simultaneously generate and group detections. Chu et al. [2] use geometrical transform kernels and a bi-direction tree structured model to capture and pass relationships between joints. PersonLab [16] proposes a part-induced geometric embedding descriptor to associate semantic person pixels with their corresponding person instance. MultiPoseNet [10] receives keypoint and person detections, and produces accurate poses by assigning keypoints to person instances. On the contrary, top-down methods [2–4,6,15,25,27] detect people first and then apply a single person pose estimation to each person detection result.

From the architecture point of view, recent pose estimation networks have universally adopted the architecture consisting of successive bottom-up (from high resolutions to low resolutions) and top-down (from low resolutions to high resolutions) processing. This high-low-high architecture captures and consolidates features across all scales of image with a sequence of downsampling and upsampling. The typical case is the Hourglass Network proposed by Newell et al. [15] which produces keypoint heatmaps by pooling down features to a very low resolution, then unsampling and combining features across multi-resolution. Methods of [14,18,19] are also based on the Hourglass module proposed by [15]. In addition, Xia et al. [26] detect keypoints of the human pose by using a fully convolution network (FCN) [12] which also processes spatial information at multiple scales for dense prediction. Compare to FCN [12], the Hourglass has more symmetric distribution of capacity between bottom-up and top-down processing. Unlike the classical high-low-high structures, the recent pose estimation network names HRNet [22] maintains high-resolution representations through the whole network and gradually connects to lower resolutions in parallel.

3 Method

3.1 Network Overview

As shown in Fig. 1, the main pipeline of the Hourglass module is the repeated process of bottom-up encoding and top-down decoding. It firstly downsamples the feature maps several times to reach the lowest resolution and then upsamples the feature maps to restore the original scale. Meanwhile, it builds a residual connection between the feature maps from shallow and deep layers having same scale and merges them together. By doing this, it captures and consolidates the information across all scales of the input image. For each scale, the computation consists of a main path for the fully multi-scale feature extraction and an identity path for current scale feature strengthen. As points verified by methods [14,15], stacking multiple Hourglass modules with intermediate supervision gradually produces a more accurate final prediction due to the repeated bottom-up and top-down inference. However, the network parameters become huge and difficult to be trained under limited computational resource. Motived by this observation, we design a lite version of Hourglass module that uses hybrid convolution blocks to reduce the number of parameters while maintaining performance.

To detect keypoints from multiple instances, our network is constructed based on the bottom-up pipeline which stacks multiple lite Hourglass modules with two head networks: one head network predicts confidence and precise locations of keypoints, and the other head network predicts associations between keypoints. The network first decreases the input resolution with convolutions and poolings to reduce computational burden. Moreover, the feature maps from previous stack are merged and passed to next stack repeatedly. This processing makes the network process features at both local and global contexts and gradually strengthen the capacity of accurate prediction. With intermediate supervision, each Hourglass module outputs a set of heatmaps indicating keypoints positions and tagmaps for grouping the keypoints into instances. Since the body keypoints only occupy a small area in images, the heatmap matrix is very sparse. Therefore, we propose a bottom-up integral regression approach to reduce the noise of background areas and improve the network performance.

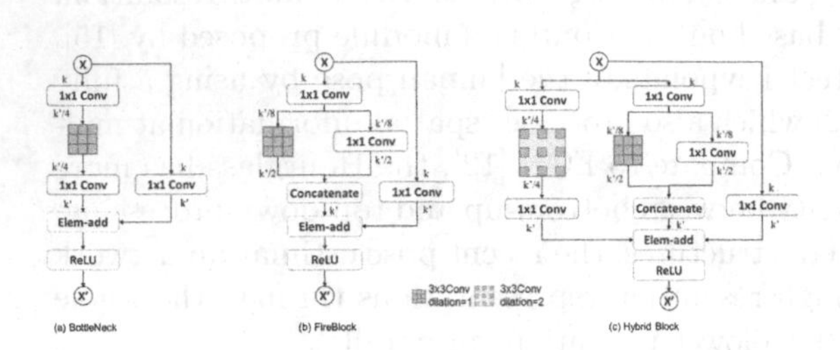

Fig. 2. Illustration of lite blocks for compacting Hourglass module. (a) is the BottleNeck of ResNet [5]. (b) is the FireBlock of SqueezeNet [7]. (c) is our proposed hybrid block.

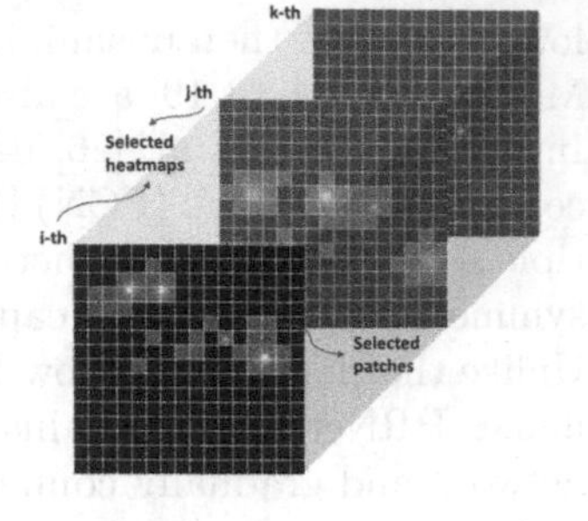

Fig. 3. Illustration of bottom-up integral regression.

3.2 Lite Multi-context Block

The standard convolution layer with 3×3 kernels has more flexible ability of expression while higher computational cost than the one with 1×1 kernels. With the increasing number of the 3×3 convolution layers, the amount of parameters increases to a large extent and at the risk of being redundant, especially for the case of stacking four or more Hourglass modules. To reduce the amount of parameters, the 1×1 convolution kernels are integrated with 3×3 kernels in a block to harmonize the feature map dimensions. Generally, each block consists of head, core and tail parts. The core part is a 3×3 convolution layer that responses for heavy feature extraction. The block uses a head 1×1 convolution layer to reduce the input dimension and a tail 1×1 convolution layer to harmonize the number of output channels. The typical examples of this kind of block are the BottleNeck from ResNet [5] and the FireBlock from SqueezeNet [7], as shown in Fig. 2a and b.

The BottleNeck from ResNet [5] is a quite effective structure and broadly used in many computer vision tasks. It consists of a sequence of 1×1, 3×3, and 1×1 convolution layers, where the 1×1 layers are responsible for reducing and then restoring the amount of feature channels, leaving the 3x3 layer a bottleneck with smaller input/output dimensions. The shortcut connection with 1×1 convolutions is used to harmonize dimensions. To compact network complexity, SqueezeNet [7] proposes a FireBlock and uses it to replace 3×3 convolution layers. The FireBlock utilizes 1×1 convolution kernels to squeeze the amount of input channels that fed to the following 3×3 convolution kernels and expands the number of output channels by the other 1×1 convolution kernels. The output of the fire module is a concatenation of 1×1 and 3×3 convolution results. Figure 3a and b shows the detail structures of the BottleNeck and FireBlock and input/output dimensions of each layer.

Inspired by the insight of ResNet [5] and SqueezeNet [7], we propose a HybridBlock that integrates ResBlock and FireBlock by using 3×3 convolution kernels with different dilation rates and sharing a projection path based on 1×1 convolution kernels. The basic intention of our hybrid convolution block is to generate more expressive feature maps with less parameters. As shown in Fig. 3c, the proposed HybridBlock is a multi-branch convolution block which integrates the BottleNeck and FireBlock with different squeezing and expansion factors. The numbers beside each layer indicated the input and output dimensions. To be specific, its inner structure can be components: the squeezing convolution layer with 1×1 kernels to decrease the number of channels in the feature map, the expanding convolution layers with 1×1 and 3×3 kernels, and the shortcut connection with 1×1 convolution kernels to match the output dimensions. Take FireBlock branch as an example, the input channels are firstly squeezed into 1/8 of the amount of output k by 1×1 convolution kernels. Then, it expands the feature maps by concatenating two sets of k'/2 channels from 1×1 and 3×3 kernels. Similar with the BottleNeck, to aggregate feature and avoid gradient vanishing, the shortcut connection is set through 1×1 convolution kernels in the HybridBlock. Eventually, the feature maps of all the branches are concatenated and merged into the output feature maps.

By using the HybridBlock, we reduce the computational cost and make it possible to use higher resolution feature maps in the limited computation budget. Retaining high resolution provides more spatial information and is important for spatially detailed image understanding, especially for keypoint detection from smaller objects. However, it also reduces the receptive field that corresponds to context cues for prediction. According to [13], for a unit in a certain layer in the network, its receptive field is defined as the region in the input that the unit affected by. As for this point, we use the dilated convolution [28] to enlarge the receptive field of the higher resolution layers.

3.3 Bottom-Up Integral Regression

For each keypoint, there is one ground-truth positive location and all other locations are negative. Instead of equally penalizing negative locations, the common approaches [4,14,17] reduce the penalty given to negative locations within a radius of the positive location. Therefore, by using a 2D Gaussian, the ground-truth locations are converted to a ground-truth heatmap in which each pixel represents the probability of the location being the keypoint. Thus, the amount of penalty is reduced with the reduction of distance from the keypoint location. The groundtruth heatmap representation can be formed as:

$$H_k(i,j) = exp(-\frac{(i-i_k)^2 + (j-j_k)^2}{2\sigma^2}) \quad (1)$$

where (i_k, j_k) is the groundtruth coordinate of the k-th keypoint and H_k is the generated heatmap by using the Gaussian kernel with the standard deviation σ.

Since the body keypoints only occupy a small area in images, the heatmap matrix is very sparse. Moreover, the integral loss [23] is designed for top-down pipeline method which assumes only one person exists in the cropped region of input image. Therefore, we propose a bottom-up integral regression approach to reduce the noise of background areas and quantization error of converting heatmaps to coordinates specifically for bottom-up pipeline method. Our network is trained by minimizing the bottom-up integral loss which is defined as follows:

$$L_k^{det} = \frac{1}{G} \sum_k \sum_g (L_C^{g,k} + L_H^{g,k}) \tag{2}$$

where L_k^{det} is the bottom-up integral loss integrates local grid loss to global heatmap loss. For each grid, the loss consists of a coordinate loss L_C^g and a heatmap loss L_H^g. The L_C^g enables the network learns keypoint locations in a differentiable way without quantization errors and L_H^g forces the network to focus on relevant areas. As shown in Fig. 3, we select top-m grids and top-n heatmaps for final loss calculation.

The coordinate loss L_C^g is calculated in a local region between the predicted heatmap and groundtruth heatmap which are equally divided into grids. The softmax function is applied to each heatmap grid along the spatial axis to generate the coordinate C_k^g for the k-th keypoint of multi-person in a differentiable manner. The definition of the L_C^g is as follows:

$$L_C^{g,k} = ||C_{g,k} - C_{g,k}^*|| \tag{3}$$

$$C_{g,k} = (\sum_i^w \sum_j^h i\hat{H}_{g,k}(i,j), \sum_i^w \sum_j^h j\hat{H}_{g,k}(i,j)) \tag{4}$$

where K is the number of keypoints, $C_{g,k}$ is the groundtruth coordinates for the $g-th$ grid of $k-th$ heatmap, (w,h) indicates the size of a grid patch, $\hat{H}_{g,k}$ is the predicted heatmap with softmax applied, the groundtruth heatmaps are processed in the same way. For the predicted detection heatmap of each grid, the Mean Square Error (MSE) loss is computed by

$$L_H^{g,k} = \frac{1}{M} \sum_i (p_i - g_i)^2 \tag{5}$$

Where, M is the number of pixels in the heatmap grid, p_i and q_i are pixel values at position i in the heatmap grid and ground-truth map grid respectively.

Given a set of keypoints extracted from local peaks of the heatmaps, we have to group them into person instances. Following PoseAE [14], we calculate the loss for grouping keypoints based on "pulling" together those from the same instance and "pushing" away the others from different instances. Therefore, in addition to producing the detection heatmaps, the network correspondingly outputs tagmaps for keypoint-wise relation embedding and instance retrieving. In each tagmap, pixels having similar values indicate the locations belong to the same instance. The loss for grouping keypoints into instances is calculated by

$$\begin{aligned} L_{emb} = \frac{1}{NK} \sum_n \sum_i (h_i - \overline{h}_n)])^2 + \\ \frac{1}{N(N-1)} \sum_n \sum_{m \neq n} exp(-\frac{1}{2\delta^2}(\overline{h}_n - \overline{h}_m)^2) \end{aligned} \tag{6}$$

Where, N is the number of instances, K is the number of visible keypoints, h_i is pixel values at position i in the tagmap, $\overline{h}_n$ and $\overline{h}_m$ are the reference tag embeddings for different instances.

Finally, the fully training loss L enforces the keypoints detection close to the ground-truth and encourages pairs of indexes to have similar values if the corresponding detections belong to the same instance or different values otherwise.

$$L = \lambda_d L_{det} + \lambda_e L_{emb} \tag{7}$$

Where λ_d and λ_e are the weights for the detection and embedding loss respectively.

4 Experiments

4.1 Evaluation on Benchmark Dataset

Our network is trained and validated on the MSCOCO Keypoint2017 [11] dataset which consists of over 150K public available labeled person instances from 56,599 training and 2346 validation images. Its testing set contains 40,670 images and the online evaluation are divided into a long-term opened test-dev (20,880 images) and a competition-oriented test-challenge (19,790 images). The annotation for each people is a sequence of 17 keypoints with the order of nose, eyes, ears, shoulders, elbows, wrists, hips, knees and ankles. Therefore, we can retrieve the type of each keypoint from the predefined dictionary (e.g., the second keypoint is the left eye). The Object Keypoint Similarity (OKS) is a standard metrics for keypoint detection evaluation. Generally, the OKS metric measures the similarity between ground truth keypoints and predicted keypoints based on distance rather than the bounding box overlap. The OKS officially defined in MSCOCO website mimics the evaluation of average precision (AP) and average recall (AR) used for object detection.

Table 1. Dilation setting on COCO held-out500 with training resolution of 512 × 512.

Blocks	AP	AP^{50}	AP^{75}	AP^{M}	AP^{L}	AR	AR^{50}	AR^{75}	AR^{M}	AR^{L}
OurBlock-f1r1	0.590	0.829	0.645	**0.522**	**0.699**	**0.635**	**0.850**	0.677	0.555	0.749
OurBlock-f2r1	0.590	**0.835**	**0.656**	0.521	0.695	0.633	**0.850**	**0.684**	**0.556**	0.744
OurBlock-f2r2	0.584	0.825	0.645	0.513	0.696	0.629	0.841	0.675	0.548	0.745
OurBlock-f1r2	**0.591**	0.834	0.650	**0.522**	0.695	**0.635**	**0.850**	0.681	**0.556**	**0.747**

Table 2. Performances of lite blocks on COCO test-dev with training resolution of 512 × 512.

Blocks	# Parameters	GFLOPs	AP	AP^{50}	AP^{75}	AP^{M}	AP^{L}	AR	AR^{50}	AR^{75}	AR^{M}	AR^{L}
FireBlock [7]	**25,799,568**	**112.16**	0.562	0.821	0.609	0.51	0.636	0.62	0.852	0.666	0.555	0.708
Bottleneck [5]	30,447,248	116.54	0.579	0.831	0.63	0.527	0.651	0.635	0.863	0.683	0.572	0.721
OurBlock	41,789,328	127.52	**0.623**	**0.848**	**0.682**	**0.578**	**0.689**	**0.672**	**0.877**	**0.782**	**0.615**	**0.751**
3 × 3Conv	*138,933,904*	*222.57*	0.633	0.857	0.689	0.580	0.704	0.688	0.884	0.742	0.620	0.781

4.2 Implementation

Our network is implemented under the PyTorch framework and trained on two GTX 1080 Ti GPUs. To make fair comparison, the baseline method PoseAE [14] with lite blocks and our block both use four stacks Hourglass modules and are both trained from scratch. The initialization is the default setting of PyTorch. The trainings are carried on the data with resolution of 512×512, which leads to an output resolution of 128×128. To reduce overfitting, we adopt standard data augmentation techniques including random horizontal flipping, scaling, cropping and adjusting the brightness, saturation and contrast of an image. The learning rate is initialized with 2e−4 and dropped to 1e−5 after 150k epochs and the training terminated after the plateau of precision growth appearing. We use Adam to optimize the full training loss that minimizes the differences between the predicted and the ground truth locations and groupings. The grouping term is weighted by a factor of 1e-3 relative to the keypoint detection term. During each round of iterations, 1000 training steps and 10 evaluation steps are alternatively carried on. The samples of each batch are randomly shuffled from the training dataset.

4.3 Performance

We evaluate our networks from two aspects: computational cost under the number of parameters and GFLOPs and performance under OKS metrics. We study each major change in our network to understand its contribution to achieve the performance.Table 1 shows the results with different dilation settings. By using dilation rates of 1 and 2 for paths of fireblock and bottleneck respectively, our hybrid block achieves best performance on a held-out set containing 500 images. The primary challenge metric AP and AR are averaged over multiple OKS values with 0.05 interval. Small objects (segment area $<32^2$) do not contain keypoint annotations. The AP^M is for the medium objects having areas between of 32^2 and 96^2 and the AP^L is for large objects having area larger than 96^2. Table 2 shows our results compared with the baselines under the input size 512×512. The original structure of PoseAE [14] uses the standard 3×3 convolutional filters in most layers and results in huge number of parameters and GFLOPs. By replacing the 3×3 convolution with the conventional lite blocks of BottleNeck or FireBlock, the number of parameters is greatly reduced but the performance is also drastically degraded. On the contrast, our network not only reduces the computational cost but also maintains the performance compare to using standard 3×3 convolutional layers.

Table 3. Comparison on COCO test-dev dataset with training resolution of 512×512.

Methods	AP	AP^{50}	AP^{75}	AP^M	AP^L	AR	AR^{50}	AR^{75}	AR^M	AR^L
CMU-Pose [1]	0.618	0.849	0.675	0.571	0.682	0.665	0.872	0.718	0.606	0.746
RMPE [3]	0.618	0.837	0.689	**0.586**	0.673	0.676	0.875	0.746	0.630	0.740
Mask-RCNN(ResNet50) [4]	0.629	**0.871**	0.689	0.576	0.713	**0.697**	**0.913**	**0.751**	**0.639**	0.776
PoseAE [14]	0.633	0.857	0.689	0.580	0.704	0.688	0.884	0.742	0.620	0.781
OurBlock+OurLoss	0.621	0.851	0.683	0.58	0.685	0.677	0.886	0.732	0.622	0.751
PoseAE+OurLoss	**0.642**	0.863	**0.706**	**0.586**	**0.719**	0.696	0.892	**0.751**	0.630	**0.785**

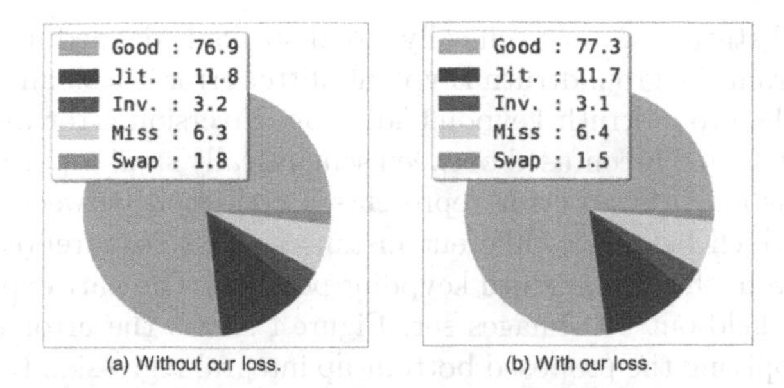

Fig. 4. Error distributions change after applying the proposed bottom-up integral loss to PoseAE [14] network.

Fig. 5. Visualization of pose errors correction comparison.

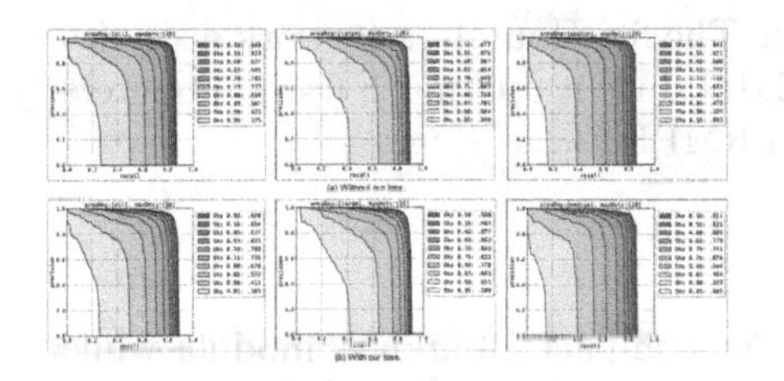

Fig. 6. Illustration the performance improvement according to the size of targets.

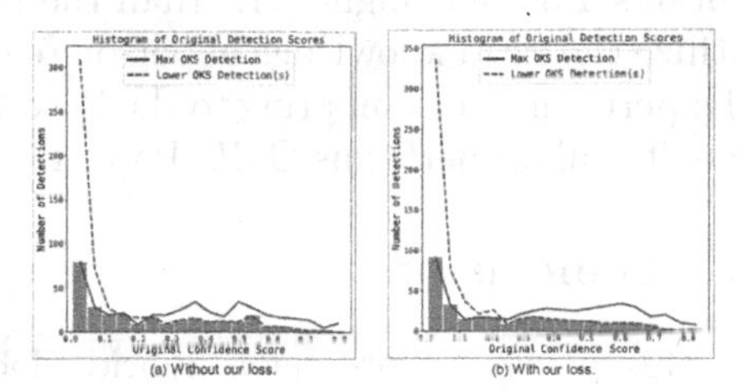

Fig. 7. Confidence score and OKS comparison.

We also study the error distributions in our network to understand its contribution to achieve the performance. Ronchi et al. [21] categorize the error distributions include the frequency of pose errors of jitter, inversion, swap, and miss according to the keypoint type, number of visible keypoints, and overlap in the input image. There may also be keypoints that do not have any error and are called good status. More specifically, good status is defined as a very small displacement from the groundtruth keypoint. Jitter error is a small displacement error around the groundtruth keypoint location. Inversion error occurs when a pose estimation model is confused between semantically similar parts that belong to the same instance. Swap error represents a confusion between the same or similar parts which belong to different instances. Miss error represents a large displacement from the groundtruth keypoint position. The part experiments are carried on the held-out 500 images set. Figure 4 shows the error distributions change after applying the proposed bottom-up integral regression to the PoseAE [14] network. Our method not only corrects the small displacement error of jitter but also the large displacement errors of inversion and swap. To give an intuitive sense of the improvement, Fig. 5 visualizes the comparison results of pose errors correction. Figure 6 illustrates the performance improvement according to the size of targets. The precision-recall curves showing the performance of PoseAE [14] without and with our loss by progressively increasing the OKS evaluation threshold with 0.05 increment. For both large and medium size targets, the proposed loss improves the network performance. Figure 7 represents the changes of heatmap confidence scores which should be OKS monotonic increasing and reflect as much as possible the probability of being a True Positive. It shows the enlarged amount of overlap between the histogram of detection scores with the highest with a given groundtruth (solid line) and all other detections with a lower OKS (dash line). It indicates that the improved heatmap prediction makes less error and its confidence score is a better OKS predictor.

Finally, we compare our method with state-of-the-art of methods on COCO test-dev set and the results are shown in Table 3. Except Mask-RCNN [4], all methods follow the bottom-up detection pipeline which detects keypoints firstly and groups them into instances. As shown in Fig. 3, the PoseAE [14] achieves better performance with the help of our proposed bottom-up integral loss. It obtains 1.3 point higher AP than the top-down method Mask-RCNN [4] which utilize the extra knowledge of person region. The lite Hourglass network degrades the performance comparing to the PoseAE [14] since it uses much less parameters but it still outperforms CMU-Pose [1] and RMPE [3].

5 Conclusion

In this paper, we present a hybrid block for compact Hourglass module while maintaining the network performance. Unlike standard Hourglass module, we use the hybrid convolution block instead of uniformly using 3×3 convolutional kernels in all layers. The hybrid block builds multi-context paths with dilated convolutions with different rates which not only reduces the number of parameters but also enlarges the receptive field. We also introduce a novel bottom-up integral regression operation to reduce the quantization error of converting heatmaps to keypoint coordinates specifically for bottom-up pipeline multi-person pose estimation methods. To meet the end of real-time application, further improvement will be expected by integrating the architecture with more lightweight kernels while achieving a better performance.

References

1. Cao, Z., Simon, T., Wei, S., Sheikh, Y.: Realtime multi-person 2D pose estimation using part affinity fields. In: CVPR, pp. 1302–1310. IEEE Computer Society (2017)
2. Chu, X., Ouyang, W., Li, H., Wang, X.: Structured feature learning for pose estimation. In: CVPR, pp. 4715–4723. IEEE Computer Society (2016)
3. Fang, H., Xie, S., Tai, Y., Lu, C.: RMPE: regional multi-person pose estimation. In: ICCV, pp. 2353–2362. IEEE Computer Society (2017)
4. He, K., Gkioxari, G., Dollár, P., Girshick, R.B.: Mask R-CNN. In: ICCV, pp. 2980–2988. IEEE Computer Society (2017)
5. He, K., Zhang, X., Ren, S., Sun, J.: Deep residual learning for image recognition. In: CVPR, pp. 770–778. IEEE Computer Society (2016)
6. Huang, S., Gong, M., Tao, D.: A coarse-fine network for keypoint localization. In: ICCV, pp. 3047–3056. IEEE Computer Society (2017)
7. Iandola, F.N., Moskewicz, M.W., Ashraf, K., Han, S., Dally, W.J., Keutzer, K.: SqueezeNet: Alexnet-level accuracy with 50x fewer parameters and <1 mb model size. CoRR abs/1602.07360 (2016)
8. Insafutdinov, E., Pishchulin, L., Andres, B., Andriluka, M., Schiele, B.: DeeperCut: a deeper, stronger, and faster multi-person pose estimation model. In: Leibe, B., Matas, J., Sebe, N., Welling, M. (eds.) ECCV 2016. LNCS, vol. 9910, pp. 34–50. Springer, Cham (2016). https://doi.org/10.1007/978-3-319-46466-4_3
9. Iqbal, U., Gall, J.: Multi-person pose estimation with local joint-to-person associations. In: Hua, G., Jégou, H. (eds.) ECCV 2016. LNCS, vol. 9914, pp. 627–642. Springer, Cham (2016). https://doi.org/10.1007/978-3-319-48881-3_44
10. Kocabas, M., Karagoz, S., Akbas, E.: MultiPoseNet: fast multi-person pose estimation using pose residual network. In: Ferrari, V., Hebert, M., Sminchisescu, C., Weiss, Y. (eds.) ECCV 2018. LNCS, vol. 11215, pp. 437–453. Springer, Cham (2018). https://doi.org/10.1007/978-3-030-01252-6_26
11. Lin, T.-Y., et al.: Microsoft COCO: common objects in context. In: Fleet, D., Pajdla, T., Schiele, B., Tuytelaars, T. (eds.) ECCV 2014. LNCS, vol. 8693, pp. 740–755. Springer, Cham (2014). https://doi.org/10.1007/978-3-319-10602-1_48
12. Long, J., Shelhamer, E., Darrell, T.: Fully convolutional networks for semantic segmentation. CoRR abs/1411.4038 (2014)
13. Luo, W., Li, Y., Urtasun, R., Zemel, R.S.: Understanding the effective receptive field in deep convolutional neural networks. In: NIPS, pp. 4898–4906 (2016)
14. Newell, A., Huang, Z., Deng, J.: Associative embedding: end-to-end learning for joint detection and grouping. In: NIPS, pp. 2274–2284 (2017)
15. Newell, A., Yang, K., Deng, J.: Stacked hourglass networks for human pose estimation. In: Leibe, B., Matas, J., Sebe, N., Welling, M. (eds.) ECCV 2016. LNCS, vol. 9912, pp. 483–499. Springer, Cham (2016). https://doi.org/10.1007/978-3-319-46484-8_29
16. Papandreou, G., Zhu, T., Chen, L.-C., Gidaris, S., Tompson, J., Murphy, K.: PersonLab: person pose estimation and instance segmentation with a bottom-up, part-based, geometric embedding model. In: Ferrari, V., Hebert, M., Sminchisescu, C., Weiss, Y. (eds.) Computer Vision – ECCV 2018. LNCS, vol. 11218, pp. 282–299. Springer, Cham (2018). https://doi.org/10.1007/978-3-030-01264-9_17
17. Papandreou, G., et al.: Towards accurate multi-person pose estimation in the wild. In: CVPR, pp. 3711–3719. IEEE Computer Society (2017)
18. Pavlakos, G., Zhou, X., Chan, A., Derpanis, K.G., Daniilidis, K.: 6-DOF object pose from semantic keypoints. In: ICRA, pp. 2011–2018. IEEE (2017)

19. Pavlakos, G., Zhou, X., Derpanis, K.G., Daniilidis, K.: Coarse-to-fine volumetric prediction for single-image 3D human pose. In: CVPR, pp. 1263–1272. IEEE Computer Society (2017)
20. Pishchulin, L., et al.: DeepCut: joint subset partition and labeling for multi person pose estimation. In: CVPR, pp. 4929–4937. IEEE Computer Society (2016)
21. Ronchi, M.R., Perona, P.: Benchmarking and error diagnosis in multi-instance pose estimation. In: ICCV, pp. 369–378. IEEE Computer Society (2017)
22. Sun, K., Xiao, B., Liu, D., Wang, J.: Deep high-resolution representation learning for human pose estimation. CoRR abs/1902.09212 (2019)
23. Sun, X., Xiao, B., Wei, F., Liang, S., Wei, Y.: Integral human pose regression. In: Ferrari, V., Hebert, M., Sminchisescu, C., Weiss, Y. (eds.) ECCV 2018. LNCS, vol. 11210, pp. 536–553. Springer, Cham (2018). https://doi.org/10.1007/978-3-030-01231-1_33
24. Toshev, A., Szegedy, C.: DeepPose: human pose estimation via deep neural networks. In: CVPR, pp. 1653–1660. IEEE Computer Society (2014)
25. Wei, S., Ramakrishna, V., Kanade, T., Sheikh, Y.: Convolutional pose machines. In: CVPR, pp. 4724–4732. IEEE Computer Society (2016)
26. Xia, F., Wang, P., Chen, X., Yuille, A.L.: Joint multi-person pose estimation and semantic part segmentation. In: CVPR, pp. 6080–6089. IEEE Computer Society (2017)
27. Yang, W., Li, S., Ouyang, W., Li, H., Wang, X.: Learning feature pyramids for human pose estimation. In: ICCV, pp. 1290–1299. IEEE Computer Society (2017)
28. Yu, F., Koltun, V.: Multi-scale context aggregation by dilated convolutions. In: ICLR (2016)

Special Session Papers SS1: AI-Powered 3D Vision

Single View Depth Estimation via Dense Convolution Network with Self-supervision

Yunhan Sun[1], Jinlong Shi[1](✉), Suqin Bai[1], Qiang Qian[1], and Zhengxing Sun[2](✉)

[1] School of Computer, Jiangsu University of Science and Technology, Zhenjiang, China
jlshifudan@gmail.com

[2] State Key Lab for Novel Software Technology, Nanjing University, Nanjing, China
szx@nju.edu.cn

Abstract. Depth estimation from single image by deep learning is a hot topic of research nowadays. Existing methods mainly focus on learning neural network supervised by ground truth. This paper proposes a method for single view depth estimation based on convolution neural network with self-supervision. Firstly, a modified dense encoder-decoder architecture is employed to predict the disparity maps of image which can then be converted into depth and only one single image is fed to predict depth at test time. Secondly, the stereo pairs without ground truth are used as samples to generate supervision signals by synthesizing the predicted results during network training, which is referenced to network training in self-supervision manner. Finally, a novel loss function is defined which considers not only the similarity between the stereo and synthesized images, but also the inconsistency between the predicted disparities, which can decrease the influence of illumination of images. Experimental comparisons against the state-of-the-art both supervised and unsupervised methods on two public datasets prove that the proposed method performs very well for single view depth estimation.

Keywords: Single view depth estimation · Dense convolution network · Self-supervision

1 Introduction

Since the emergence of 3D understanding, depth estimation technologies have become the focus of academia and industry for many years. In particular, depth estimation from single view has become more and more important in lots of practical applications recently. As we know, human can reconstruct world view from one eye in different scenes according to the past experience, to replicate this learning ability of human, some researchers introduced deep neural network into the field of monocular depth estimation. According to training strategy,

Y. M. Ro et al. (Eds.): MMM 2020, LNCS 11962, pp. 241–253, 2020.
https://doi.org/10.1007/978-3-030-37734-2_20

existing researches of monocular depth estimation based on deep neural network roughly fall into three categories, namely *single-view supervision methods*, *multi-view supervision methods* and *stereo supervision methods*. More concretely, with regard to the three kinds of methods, one, two or more observations are required for training, in supervised or unsupervised manner depending on whether the training samples require ground-truth data or not, and the learned neural network predicts a depth map or 3D shape from one single 2D image at testing time. *Single-view supervision methods* perform training by minimizing the difference between the predicted depth from monocular image with the corresponding ground truth [1,4,5,12], which usually adopt multi-scale CNN architecture or coarse-to-fine prediction strategy. This kind of methods must be trained in supervised manner, however, it is difficult to obtain dense and accurate ground-truth using laser or structured-light sensor in reality. *Multi-view supervision methods* usually predict 3D shapes of small objects according to multi-view observations based on unprojection or silhouettes theory in multi-view geometry [13,28,34], and the predicted 3D shapes can be converted into depth data. However, multi-view observations are usually not available in reality, especially for large scenes. Therefore, large scale synthetic dataset using graphical rendering are usually adopted for training. *Stereo supervision methods* train a deep neural network by taking stereo image sequences as input, synthesized images are generated according to the output (such as disparities [9,33], or depth map [6,14]), and inconsistency between input images and synthesized images [6,9,33] is minimized during training. There are some advantages for *stereo supervision methods*: convenient to capture stereo image sequences using portable stereo rigs for training; suitable for depth prediction of large scenes; and feasible to use training data without depth ground truth. But it is still an open problem to effectively and accurately learn depth via deep neural network using stereo supervision, and the depth prediction performance is far from practical application. In order to improve the prediction performance, researchers proposed some optimization strategies, such as improving the encoder-decoder architecture in end-to-end learning system, enriching specific details of the network structure, building deeper network, optimizing parameters of the network and designing better loss function. However, the illumination influence of training samples collected under different sun light is also an important aspect, which is not addressed so far to the best of our knowledge.

Accordingly, we propose a method of depth estimation from single view via convolution neural network with self-supervision, by introducing dense convolution framework into depth prediction network and training with the stereo image pairs without ground truth, based on [9,10], as shown in Fig. 1. Concretely, our main contributions are threefold: Firstly, a modified dense encoder-decoder architecture is employed to predict the disparity maps of image which can then be converted into depth and only one single image is fed to predict depth at test time. Secondly, the stereo pairs without ground truth is used as samples to generate supervision signals by synthesizing the predicted results during network training, which is referenced to network training in self-supervision manner. Finally, a novel loss function is defined which considers not only the similarity between the stereo and synthesized images, but also the inconsistency between the predicted disparities, which can decrease the influence of illumination of images. Experimental comparisons on two public datasets demonstrate that the proposed method outperforms existing both supervised and unsupervised methods, especially does better at dealing with details of image.

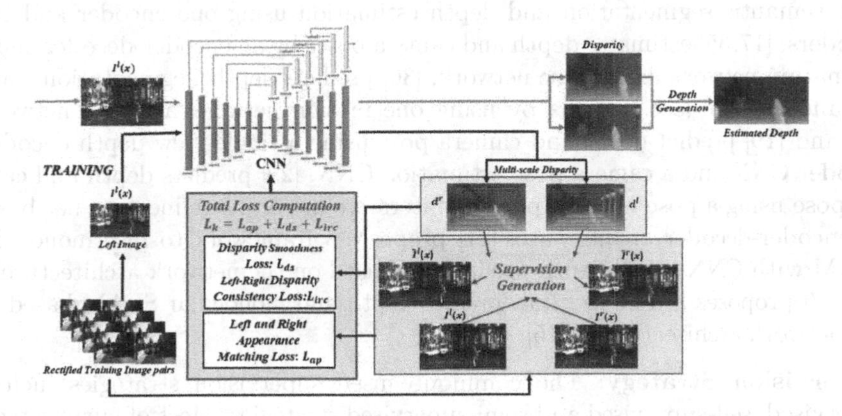

Fig. 1. Illustration of the proposed method. During training, the modified dense encoder-decoder (CNN) takes the left/right image of stereo pairs as input, generates multi-scale left-right and right-left disparity maps, synthesizes them to generate supervisions and performs training using a compound loss function. During testing, the CNN predicts depth by taking only one image as input.

2 Related Work

For current methods, a typical depth estimation model consists of three components: network architecture, supervision strategy and loss function.

Network Architecture: Some methods predict depth by using one network module. [6,9,20,22] adopt one encoder-decoder CNN for depth estimation. [15] introduces a depth prediction network based on ResNet-50. [33] uses one network which generates several branches of feature maps followed by a softmax layer, and the output of the softmax layer is interpreted as a probabilistic disparity map. [2] estimates depth using a variant of "hourglass" network. A number of methods predict depth using two network modules. In [5], a coarse-scale network first predicts the depth at a global level which is then refined by a fine-scale network. In [1], a local network is used to extract features from a image patch around each location, and a scene network with pre-trained VGG-19 layers is used to compute a single scene feature vector. [14] uses two encoder-decoder CNNs based on deep residual network which is similar with that method in [15]. [24] uses two encoder-decoder CNNs based on [9]. [16] predicts depth using two modules, a CNN module is used to estimate depth, and followed by a post processing refining module based on CRF. [18] use three neural network modules, namely a unary part CNN, a pairwise part fully-connected layer and a CRF structured loss layer.

Many methods simultaneously deal with multi prediction tasks such as depth prediction, semantic segmentation, and camera poses. [31] performs depth estimation and semantic prediction using three modules based on [5]. [12] performs depth estimation and semantic prediction using three modules. [4] predicts depths, normals and semantic labels by extending the work of [5]. [23] performs joint semantic segmentation and depth estimation using one encoder and two decoders. [17,35] estimates depth and camera poses by an encoder-decoder depth estimation network and a pose network. [30] predicts depth, segmentation, camera and rigid object motions by using one motion network and one network. [36] and [19] predict depth and camera pose using a single-view depth encoder-decoder CNN and a camera pose estimation CNN. [29] predicts depth and camera pose using a pose bootstrap net, an iterative net and a refinement net based on encoder-decoder architecture. [21] proposes a framework to fuse monocular SLAM with CNN-based depth predictions based on the network architecture of [4]. [27] proposes a framework to predict depth and monocular SLAM based on the network architecture of [15].

Supervision Strategy: The commonly used supervision strategies include supervised, self-supervised and semi-supervised strategies. Most of current techniques belong to supervised methods which require ground-truth depth during training [1,2,4,5,12,15,16,18,20,21,25–27,29,31]. Self-supervised methods [6,9,17,19,22,24,30,35,36] train neural networks by using stereo pairs or monocular image sequence, and usually adopt view synthesis as supervision. Semi-supervised methods take the combination of ground-truth data and view synthesis as supervision signals, for example, [14] adopts sparse ground-truth depth and image view synthesis as supervision signals, [23] relies on view synthesis and ground-truth semantic maps as supervision signals.

Loss Function: Existing methods use different loss functions, for example, L2 loss [21], L2 loss with scale-invariant error in log space [4,5], L2 loss for depth and semantic label estimation in log space [31], CRF loss [18], Euclidean loss [16], relative quadratic distance loss [12], Log RMSE loss [20], combination of an L1 and SSIM term [9,17,19,22–24,35], reverse Huber loss [15,27], ranking loss [2,14], KL-divergence loss [1], L1 loss [30,33,36], combination of L1 loss and L2 loss [29], standard Horn and Schunck optic flow loss [6].

3 Method

In this paper, we predict the depth from one single image by using a new encoder-decoder CNN, as shown in Fig. 1, where we learn the CNN by taking rectified stereo image sequence (left image $I^l(\mathbf{x})$ and right image $I^r(\mathbf{x})$ in Fig. 1) as the training data, and the CNN outputs multi-scale disparity maps which will be converted into depth by the following method: suppose d_s denote the predicted disparity, and we compute the corresponding depth d_p by using $d_p = bf/d_s$, where b is the baseline distance between the left and right cameras, and f is the camera focal length. At test time, by only inputting one single image, the CNN predicts its disparity maps which are then converted into depth information. It consists of three main components: CNN network architecture, supervision generation and loss computation.

3.1 Network Architecture

We propose a dense encoder-decoder CNN with skip connections and multi-scale predictions by introducing the idea of dense convolution network.

Encoder. Our CNN is shown as Fig. 2, where 7 blocks are contained in the encoder. The first block of the encoder is a convolution layer used for pre-processing, denoted by C, where the kernel size is 3, stride is set to 1, and zero-padding is adopted. Other blocks of the encoder are called dense block, and denoted by B_i, $i \in \{1, 2, .., 6\}$. Each dense block includes m BN-ReLU-Conv sub blocks, and each BN-ReLU-Conv sub block includes a batch normalization (BN) [11] layer, followed by a rectified linear unit (ReLU) [8] and a 3×3 convolution (Conv) layer. To increase the information flow between BN-ReLU-Conv sub blocks, a dense connectivity structure is adopted, where we directly connect any BN-ReLU-Conv sub block to all subsequent BN-ReLU-Conv blocks. Thus, each BN-ReLU-Conv sub block can access all the preceding feature-maps in B_i, and can have the collective knowledge of all the preceding feature-maps. Let BRC_j denote the *j-th* BN-ReLU-Conv sub block which receives the feature-maps of all preceding BN-ReLU-Conv sub blocks, $BRC_0, ..., BRC_{j-1}$, as input:

$$BRC_j = H([BRC_0, ...BRC_{j-1}]) \tag{1}$$

where $[BRC_0, ...BRC_{j-1}]$ denotes the concatenation of the feature-maps generated in layers $0, ..., j-1$. $H()$ is defined as a composite function of batch normalization (BN), rectified linear unit (ReLU) and convolution.

BRC_{m-1} is followed by a BN layer, a 1×1 convolution layer, a ReLU and a 2×2 average pooling layer. By using 2×2 average pooling, the size of output from B_k can be reduced by half, which changes the size of output feature-maps. Thus, the size of feature-maps from B_1, B_2,..., B_6 is reduced gradually.

We suppose $H()$ produces r feature-maps, BRC_j in B_i has $r_0 + r \times (j-1)$ input feature-maps, where r_0 is the number of channel of BRC_0.

Decoder. As shown in Fig. 2, the decoder includes 6 deconvolution blocks denoted by U_i ($i \in \{1, 2, ..., 6\}$) which can double the size of input feature-maps. The output of dense block B_i is concatenated to the output of deconvolution blocks U_i, and the concatenation of B_i and U_i will be input into the next deconvolution blocks U_{i+1}. The decoder produces four disparity maps on four different scales, which are represented by D_k, $k \in \{1, 2, 3, 4\}$, and the downscaling factor of D_k relative to the input image is 2^{4-k}. D_k includes two feature maps which represent the left-to-right disparity and right-to-left disparity map, respectively.

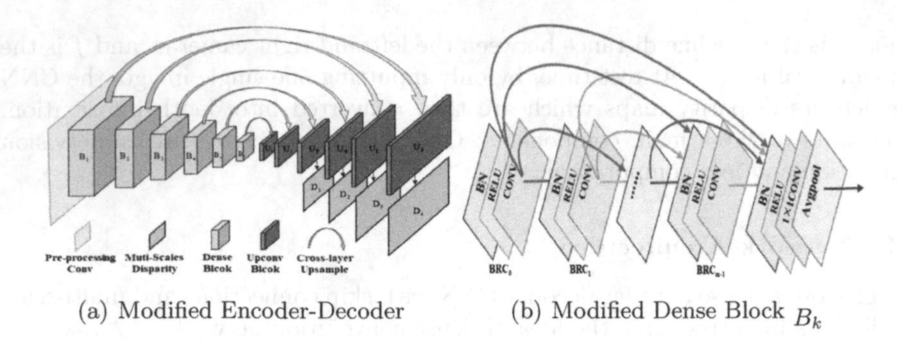

(a) Modified Encoder-Decoder (b) Modified Dense Block B_k

Fig. 2. The Modified Convolution Neural Network architecture

3.2 Supervision Generation

At training time, our aim is to train the CNN to predict the disparity maps between $I^l(\mathbf{x})$and $I^r(\mathbf{x})$. Firstly, the CNN takes the left image sequence $(I^l(\mathbf{x}))$ as input; Secondly, the CNN generates multi-scale disparity maps, where two disparity maps(left-to-right disparity d^l, and right-to-left disparity d^r) are included at each scale; Thirdly, the left image $I^l(\mathbf{x})$ is warped according to the disparity map d^r to generate a synthesized image $\tilde{I}^r(\mathbf{x}) = I^l(d^r + \mathbf{x})$, similarly, a synthesized image $\tilde{I}^l(\mathbf{x}) = I^r(d^l + \mathbf{x})$ is generated according to $I^r(\mathbf{x})$ and d^l; Finally, the synthesized images are considered as supervision signals and compared with the input rectified stereo image pairs to measure the appearance similarity, and we check the consistency between d^r and d^l at the same time.

3.3 Loss Function

We define a loss function at the four output scales D_k. The total loss is defined as $L = \sum_{k=1}^{4} L_k$, where L_k is defined as follows:

$$L_k = \alpha_{ap}(L^l_{ap} + L^r_{ap}) + \alpha_{ds}(L^l_{ds} + L^r_{ds}) + \alpha_{lr}(L^l_{lrc} + L^r_{lrc}) \tag{2}$$

L_k includes three parts: appearance matching loss $L^l_{ap} + L^r_{ap}$, disparity smoothness loss $L^l_{ds} + L^r_{ds}$, and left-right disparity consistency loss $L^l_{lr} + L^r_{lr}$, where α_{ap}, α_{ds} and α_{lr} are the weights of the three parts. We use the same L^l_{ds},L^r_{ds},L^l_{lrc}, and L^r_{lrc} terms as those in [9] except L^l_{ap} and L^r_{ap}.

L^l_{ap} and L^r_{ap} denote the left appearance matching loss and right appearance matching loss, respectively. We take L^l_{ap} as an example to explain this term. We here not only consider the similarity between the input rectified stereo images and the synthesized images, but also consider the gradient inconsistency between the input rectified stereo images and the synthesized images. Because the images are rectified, we here only consider the gradient in x direction. By doing so, the influence of illumination for the training images can be decreased and robustness can be increased. We define L^l_{ap} via three parts as shown in Eq. (3). Here, we use the structural similarity (SSIM) index [32] to measure the appearance similarity between the input image $I^l_{ij}(\mathbf{x})$ and the synthesized image $\tilde{I}^l_{ij}(\mathbf{x})$ using the predicted disparity, where $1 \leq i \leq N, 1 \leq j \leq M$, and N and M are the height and width of the input images, respectively. The first part is used to measure the difference between $I^l_{ij}(\mathbf{x})$ and $\tilde{I}^l_{ij}(\mathbf{x})$ according to SSIM. The second part is used to measure the similarity between the derivative images of $I^l_{ij}(\mathbf{x})$ and $\tilde{I}^l_{ij}(\mathbf{x})$ in x direction according to SSIM. The third part is used to measure the similarity between $I^l_{ij}(\mathbf{x})$ and $\tilde{I}^l_{ij}(\mathbf{x})$ according to $L1$ regularization formation. Parameters α and β are used to control the weights for the three parts.

$$L^l_{ap} = \frac{1}{NM}\sum_{i,j}\alpha\frac{1 - SSIM(I^l_{ij}(\mathbf{x}), \tilde{I}^l_{ij}(\mathbf{x}))}{2} + \beta\frac{1 - SSIM(\partial_x I^l_{ij}(\mathbf{x}), \partial_x \tilde{I}^l_{ij}(\mathbf{x}))}{2} + (1 - \alpha - \beta)||I^l_{ij}(\mathbf{x}) - \tilde{I}^l_{ij}(\mathbf{x})|| \tag{3}$$

Table 1. Results on the disparity images of KITTI 2015 stereo 200 training set [7]. K denotes the KITTI split [7] and CS denotes the Cityscapes dataset [3]. Our proposed method performs the best on both KITTI split and Cityscapes + KITTI split.

Method	Dataset	Abs Rel	Sq Rel	RMSE	RMSE log	D1-all	$\delta < 1.25$	$\delta < 1.25^2$	$\delta < 1.25^3$
		Lower is better					Higher is better		
Godard with Deep3D [33]	K	0.412	16.37	13.693	0.512	66.85	0.690	0.833	0.891
Godard with Deep3Ds [33]	K	0.151	1.312	6.344	0.239	59.64	0.781	0.931	0.976
Godard No LR [9]	K	0.123	1.417	6.315	0.220	30.318	0.841	0.937	0.973
Godard [9]	K	0.124	1.388	6.125	0.217	30.272	0.841	0.936	0.975
Godard [9]	CS	0.699	10.060	14.445	0.542	94.757	0.053	0.326	0.862
Godard [9]	CS+K	0.104	1.070	5.417	0.188	25.523	0.875	0.956	0.983
Godard pp [9]	CS+K	0.100	0.934	5.141	0.178	25.077	0.878	0.961	0.986
Godard resnet pp [9]	CS+K	0.097	0.896	5.093	0.176	23.811	0.879	0.962	0.986
Ours+Godard pp	K	0.106	0.991	5.369	0.189	26.507	0.860	0.952	0.983
Ours	K	0.099	0.965	5.333	0.184	24.308	0.875	0.957	0.985
Ours pp	K	0.096	0.860	5.080	0.176	23.890	0.879	0.961	0.986
Ours+Godard pp	CS	0.294	3.470	9.292	0.305	81.176	0.560	0.879	0.968
Ours	CS	0.304	3.821	9.526	0.318	81.257	0.562	0.872	0.963
Ours pp	CS	0.290	3.212	8.953	0.301	80.948	0.566	0.884	0.971
Ours+Godard pp	CS+K	0.093	0.864	4.964	0.170	22.085	0.888	0.964	0.986
Ours	CS+K	0.091	0.879	4.929	0.171	20.560	0.893	0.964	0.986
Ours pp	CS+K	**0.090**	**0.868**	**4.927**	**0.169**	**20.142**	**0.897**	**0.974**	**0.986**

4 Expriments and Evaluations

4.1 Implementation Details

We here compare our method with the unsupervised methods presented in [9,33], and the supervised methods proposed in [5,18]. All our models were trained for

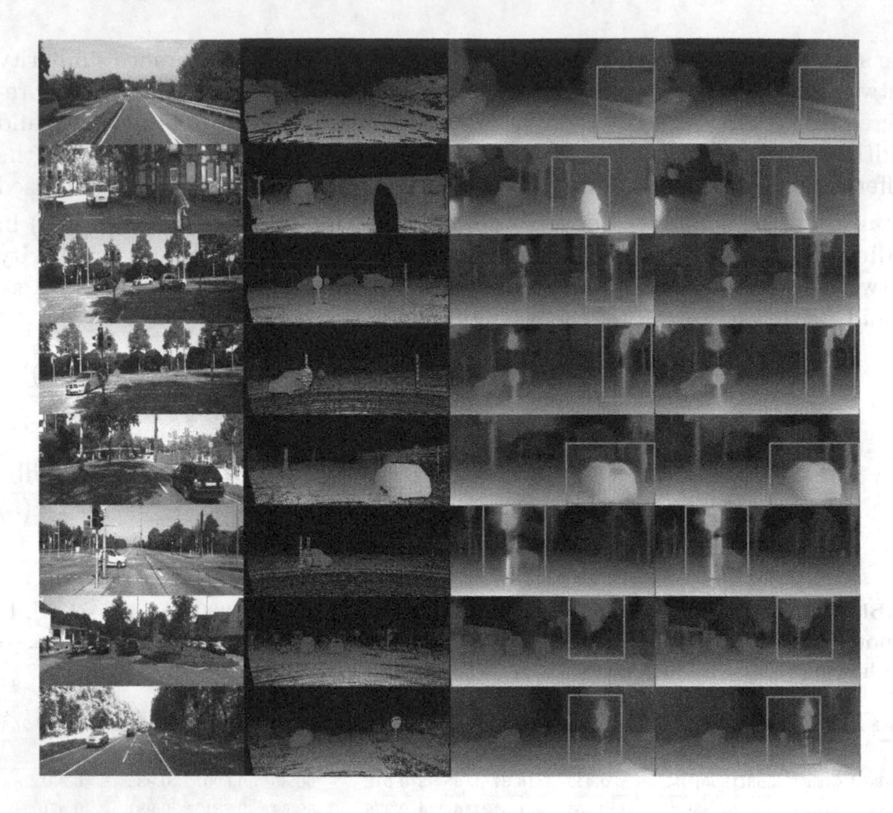

Fig. 3. Experimental results, the second column shows the ground truth which is interpolated for illustration, the third column shows the results of Godard et al. [9], and the fourth column shows our results.

50 epochs, with 512×256 image resolution and a batch size of 8, r in $H()$ is set to 16, 32, 64, 64, 96 and 128 in dense block $B_1, B2, ..., B6$ respectively. For the loss function, we set α_{ap}, α_{ds}, α_{lr}, α and β to 1, 1, 1, 0.45 and 0.45, respectively. Our network is implemented using TensorFlow 1.10 on four Nvidia GTX 1080Ti GPUs. KITTI 2015 [7] dataset and Cityscape [3] dataset are used as the training data. For KITTI dataset, KITTI split and Eigen split are used for the evaluation and comparison with state-of-the-art methods. For Cityscapes dataset, we make use of leftImg8bit_trainvaltest.zip, rightImg8bit_trainvaltest.zip, leftImg8bit_trainextra.zip and rightImg8bit_trainextra.zip downloaded from the Cityscapes website.

4.2 KITTI Split

For KITTI split, we use 29000 images of 33 scenes in KITTI dataset for training, and 200 images which cover 28 scenes are used for test, and the corresponding 200 official disparity images from KITTI stereo 2015 are used for evaluation. The

Fig. 4. Local enlarged images which illustrate the predicted detailed information (the green rectangles), the four columns are input images, ground-truth, the results of Godard et al. [9] and ours, respectively. (Color figure online)

results are evaluated according to the metrics used in [5] and D1-all disparity error metric from [7].

As Table 1 shows, we compare our proposed method with different variants of Godard's method [9] and Deep3D [33]. Here, we compare to a variant of [9] that adopts the original Deep3D [33] image formation model and a modified one with an added smoothness constraint, namely Deep3Ds in Table 1. For training, K means the KITTI split and CS is Cityscapes dataset.

To further improve the results, we first train our model using Cityscape dataset, and then fine-tune the model by KITTI split, namely CS+K in Table 1. To compare the performance, we also perform the method [9] with Cityscape+ KITTI dataset. In addition, we perform some experiments with our proposed dense encoder-decoder convolutional network and the loss function used in [9] on KITTI, Cityscape, and KITTI+Cityscape split, namely Ours+Godard in Table 1. From Table 1, we can see that our proposed method is better than other state-of-the-art methods, and our proposed dense encoder-decoder convolutional network and loss function significantly improve the experimental performance. pp denotes post processing, and we here adopt the same post processing strategy as that in [9].

Figure 3 shows qualitative results on the KITTI Split, where the ground truth data (the second column) are downloaded from KITTI website and interpolated for illustration, and the results of Godard et al. (the third column) are downloaded from the author's website. Figure 4 shows the comparison results of local enlarged images. From Fig. 4 and these regions within rectangular box in Fig. 3, we can see that our method does better at dealing with the details in the image. Even for these regions that are missing from the ground truth, our methods can predict very good results.

4.3 Eigen Split

To compare with the existing methods, we also perform some experiments on Eigen split [5]. For evaluation, we use the 697 test images which are used by [5]

Table 2. Results on KITTI 2015 [7] using the Eigen split et al. [5]. E denotes the Eigen split [7] and CS denotes the Cityscapes dataset [3].

Method	Supervised	Dataset	Abs Rel	Sq Rel	RMSE	RMSE log	$\delta < 1.25$	$\delta < 1.25^2$	$\delta < 1.25^3$
			Lower is better				Higher is better		
Train set mean	No	E	0.361	4.826	8.102	0.377	0.638	0.804	0.894
Eigen et al. [5] *Coarse*^{o}	Yes	E	0.214	1.605	6.563	0.292	0.673	0.884	0.957
Eigen et al. [5] *Fine*^{o}	Yes	E	0.203	1.548	6.307	0.282	0.702	0.890	0.958
Liu et al. [18] DCNF-FCSP	Yes	E	0.201	1.584	6.471	0.273	0.68	0.898	0.967
Godard et al. [9]	No	E	0.148	1.344	5.927	0.247	0.803	0.922	0.964
Godard et al. [9] pp	No	CS+E	0.118	0.923	5.015	0.210	0.854	0.947	0.976
Godard et al. [9] resnet pp	No	CS+E	0.114	0.898	4.935	0.206	0.861	0.949	0.976
SfMlearner [36]	No	E	0.208	1.768	7.527	0.294	0.676	0.885	0.954
SfMlearner [36]	No	CS+E	0.198	1.836	6.565	0.275	0.718	0.901	0.960
GeoNet [35]	No	E	0.155	1.296	5.857	0.233	0.793	0.931	0.973
GeoNet [35]	No	CS+E	0.153	1.328	5.737	0.232	0.802	0.934	0.972
Vid2Depth [19]	No	E	0.163	1.240	6.220	0.250	0.762	0.916	0.968
Vid2Depth [19]	No	CS+E	0.159	1.231	5.912	0.243	0.784	0.923	0.970
UnDeepVO [17]	No	E	0.183	1.73	6.57	0.268	–	–	–
Ours pp	No	E	0.132	1.171	5.269	0.231	0.834	0.938	0.970
Ours pp	No	CS+E	**0.102**	**0.976**	**4.677**	**0.203**	**0.884**	**0.953**	**0.976**

and covers 29 scenes. For the remaining 32 scenes, 22600 image pairs are used for training. In Table 2, E means the Eigen split. The results of [18] are generated on a mix of the left and right images instead of just the left input images, the results of [5] are calculated relative to the velodyne LIDAR instead of the camera. In addition, we also compared some recent SFM based methods [17,19,35,36] on Eigen split, but at input resolution of 416×128. Table 2 shows that our algorithm outperforms all other existing methods, including those supervised methods. We also show the results that are first trained on Cityscapes and then trained on Eigen split, from Table 2, we can see that our method is the best one.

5 Conclusion

As it is easier to acquire rectified stereo image pairs by using calibrated stereo rigs, this paper proposes an method of depth estimation from single image based on deep neural network by using the rectified stereo pairs as training samples. A modified dense encoder-decoder architecture is employed to predict the disparity maps of image which can then be converted into depth and the stereo pairs without ground truth is used as samples to generate supervision signals by synthesizing the predicted results during network training. In addition, a novel loss function is defined which considers not only the similarity between the stereo and synthesized images, but also the inconsistency between the predicted disparities. From the experimental evaluations we can see that the proposed method outperforms the state-of-the-art methods.

Acknowledgments. This work is supported by National Key Research and Development Program of China (No. 2018YFC0309100, No. 2018YFC0309104), National

High Technology Research and Development Program of China (No. 2007AA01Z334), National Natural Science Foundation of China (Nos. 61321491 and 61272219), the China Postdoctoral Science Foundation (Grant No. 2017M621700) and Innovation Fund of State Key Laboratory for Novel Software Technology (Nos. ZZKT2018A09).

References

1. Chakrabarti, A., Shao, J., Shakhnarovich, G.: Depth from a single image by harmonizing overcomplete local network predictions. In: Advances in Neural Information Processing Systems, pp. 2658–2666 (2016)
2. Chen, W., Fu, Z., Yang, D., Deng, J.: Single-image depth perception in the wild. In: Advances in Neural Information Processing Systems, pp. 730–738 (2016)
3. Cordts, M., et al.: The cityscapes dataset for semantic urban scene understanding. In: Proceedings of the IEEE Conference on Computer Vision and Pattern Recognition, pp. 3213–3223 (2016)
4. Eigen, D., Fergus, R.: Predicting depth, surface normals and semantic labels with a common multi-scale convolutional architecture. In: Proceedings of the IEEE International Conference on Computer Vision, pp. 2650–2658 (2015)
5. Eigen, D., Puhrsch, C., Fergus, R.: Depth map prediction from a single image using a multi-scale deep network. In: Advances in Neural Information Processing Systems, pp. 2366–2374 (2014)
6. Garg, R., Vijay Kumar, B.G., Carneiro, G., Reid, I.: Unsupervised CNN for single view depth estimation: geometry to the rescue. In: Leibe, B., Matas, J., Sebe, N., Welling, M. (eds.) ECCV 2016. LNCS, vol. 9912, pp. 740–756. Springer, Cham (2016). https://doi.org/10.1007/978-3-319-46484-8_45
7. Geiger, A., Lenz, P., Urtasun, R.: Are we ready for autonomous driving? The Kitti vision benchmark suite. In: 2012 IEEE Conference on Computer Vision and Pattern Recognition (CVPR), pp. 3354–3361. IEEE (2012)
8. Glorot, X., Bordes, A., Bengio, Y.: Deep sparse rectifier neural networks. In: Proceedings of the Fourteenth International Conference on Artificial Intelligence and Statistics, pp. 315–323 (2011)
9. Godard, C., Mac Aodha, O., Brostow, G.J.: Unsupervised monocular depth estimation with left-right consistency. In: CVPR, p. 7 (2017)
10. Huang, G., Liu, Z., Weinberger, K.Q., van der Maaten, L.: Densely connected convolutional networks. In: Proceedings of the IEEE Conference on Computer Vision and Pattern Recognition, p. 3 (2017)
11. Ioffe, S., Szegedy, C.: Batch normalization: accelerating deep network training by reducing internal covariate shift. In: International Conference on Machine Learning, pp. 448–456 (2015)
12. Jafari, O.H., Groth, O., Kirillov, A., Yang, M.Y., Rother, C.: Analyzing modular CNN architectures for joint depth prediction and semantic segmentation. In: 2017 IEEE International Conference on Robotics and Automation (ICRA), pp. 4620–4627. IEEE (2017)
13. Kar, A., Häne, C., Malik, J.: Learning a multi-view stereo machine. In: Advances in Neural Information Processing Systems, pp. 364–375 (2017)
14. Kuznietsov, Y., Stückler, J., Leibe, B.: Semi-supervised deep learning for monocular depth map prediction. In: Proceedings of the IEEE Conference on Computer Vision and Pattern Recognition, pp. 6647–6655 (2017)

15. Laina, I., Rupprecht, C., Belagiannis, V., Tombari, F., Navab, N.: Deeper depth prediction with fully convolutional residual networks. In: 2016 Fourth International Conference on 3D Vision (3DV), pp. 239–248. IEEE (2016)
16. Li, B., Shen, C., Dai, Y., van den Hengel, A., He, M.: Depth and surface normal estimation from monocular images using regression on deep features and hierarchical CRFs. In: Proceedings of the IEEE Conference on Computer Vision and Pattern Recognition, pp. 1119–1127 (2015)
17. Li, R., Wang, S., Long, Z., Gu, D.: UnDeepVO: monocular visual odometry through unsupervised deep learning. In: 2018 IEEE International Conference on Robotics and Automation (ICRA), pp. 7286–7291. IEEE (2018)
18. Liu, F., Shen, C., Lin, G., Reid, I.: Learning depth from single monocular images using deep convolutional neural fields. IEEE Trans. Pattern Anal. Mach. Intell. **38**(10), 2024–2039 (2016)
19. Mahjourian, R., Wicke, M., Angelova, A.: Unsupervised learning of depth and ego-motion from monocular video using 3D geometric constraints. In: Proceedings of the IEEE Conference on Computer Vision and Pattern Recognition, pp. 5667–5675 (2018)
20. Mancini, M., Costante, G., Valigi, P., Ciarfuglia, T.A.: Fast robust monocular depth estimation for obstacle detection with fully convolutional networks. In: 2016 IEEE/RSJ International Conference on Intelligent Robots and Systems (IROS), pp. 4296–4303. IEEE (2016)
21. Mukasa, T., Xu, J., Stenger, B.: 3D scene mesh from CNN depth predictions and sparse monocular slam. In: Proceedings of the IEEE Conference on Computer Vision and Pattern Recognition, pp. 921–928 (2017)
22. Pillai, S., Ambrus, R., Gaidon, A.: SuperDepth: self-supervised, super-resolved monocular depth estimation. arXiv preprint arXiv:1810.01849 (2018)
23. Ramirez, P.Z., Poggi, M., Tosi, F., Mattoccia, S., Di Stefano, L.: Geometry meets semantics for semi-supervised monocular depth estimation. arXiv preprint arXiv:1810.04093 (2018)
24. Repala, V.K., Dubey, S.R.: Dual CNN models for unsupervised monocular depth estimation. arXiv preprint arXiv:1804.06324 (2018)
25. Saxena, A., Chung, S.H., Ng, A.Y.: Learning depth from single monocular images. In: Advances in Neural Information Processing Systems, pp. 1161–1168 (2006)
26. Saxena, A., Sun, M., Ng, A.Y.: Make3D: learning 3D scene structure from a single still image. IEEE Trans. Pattern Anal. Mach. Intell. **31**(5), 824–840 (2009)
27. Tateno, K., Tombari, F., Laina, I., Navab, N.: CNN-SLAM: real-time dense monocular slam with learned depth prediction. arXiv preprint arXiv:1704.03489 (2017)
28. Tulsiani, S., Zhou, T., Efros, A.A., Malik, J.: Multi-view supervision for single-view reconstruction via differentiable ray consistency. In: CVPR, p. 3 (2017)
29. Ummenhofer, B., et al.: DeMoN: depth and motion network for learning monocular stereo. In: IEEE Conference on Computer Vision and Pattern Recognition (CVPR), vol. 5 (2017)
30. Vijayanarasimhan, S., Ricco, S., Schmid, C., Sukthankar, R., Fragkiadaki, K.: SfM-Net: learning of structure and motion from video. arXiv preprint arXiv:1704.07804 (2017)
31. Wang, P., Shen, X., Lin, Z., Cohen, S., Price, B., Yuille, A.L.: Towards unified depth and semantic prediction from a single image. In: Proceedings of the IEEE Conference on Computer Vision and Pattern Recognition, pp. 2800–2809 (2015)
32. Wang, Z., Bovik, A.C., Sheikh, H.R., Simoncelli, E.P.: Image quality assessment: from error visibility to structural similarity. IEEE Trans. Image Process. **13**(4), 600–612 (2004)

33. Xie, J., Girshick, R., Farhadi, A.: Deep3D: fully automatic 2D-to-3D video conversion with deep convolutional neural networks. In: Leibe, B., Matas, J., Sebe, N., Welling, M. (eds.) ECCV 2016. LNCS, vol. 9908, pp. 842–857. Springer, Cham (2016). https://doi.org/10.1007/978-3-319-46493-0_51
34. Yan, X., Yang, J., Yumer, E., Guo, Y., Lee, H.: Perspective transformer nets: learning single-view 3D object reconstruction without 3D supervision. In: Advances in Neural Information Processing Systems, pp. 1696–1704 (2016)
35. Yin, Z., Shi, J.: GeoNet: unsupervised learning of dense depth, optical flow and camera pose. In: Proceedings of the IEEE Conference on Computer Vision and Pattern Recognition, pp. 1983–1992 (2018)
36. Zhou, T., Brown, M., Snavely, N., Lowe, D.G.: Unsupervised learning of depth and ego-motion from video. In: Proceedings of the IEEE Conference on Computer Vision and Pattern Recognition, pp. 1851–1858 (2017)

Multi-data UAV Images for Large Scale Reconstruction of Buildings

Menghan Zhang[1], Yunbo Rao[1(✉)], Jiansu Pu[1], Xun Luo[2], and Qifei Wang[3]

[1] University of Electronic Science and Technology of China, Chengdu, Sichuan, China
raoyb@uestc.edu.cn

[2] Tianjin University of Technology, Tianjin, China

[3] University of California, Berkeley, CA, USA

Abstract. In this paper, a new energy function is proposed that can aggregate the mesh model generated by the point cloud extracted from the UAV and supplement it with contextual semantics to accurately segment the building, which maximizes the consistency of the extracted buildings to restore detail. The semantic information is also used to improve the consistency of the labels between the semantic segments of the extracted input model to ensure the validity of the separation results. A new method of reconstructing polygon and arc models using unstructured models is proposed to improve large scale reconstruction. It can robustly discover the set of adjacency relations and repairs appropriately the non-watertight model due to point cloud loss. The experimental results show that the proposed large scale reconstruction algorithm is suitable for the modeling of complex urban buildings.

Keywords: Unstructured point clouds · Unmanned aerial vehicle · Energy function · Large scale reconstruaction

1 Introduction

Over the last decade, increasing attention has been attracted in the modeling and reconstruction of large-scale urban buildings. Now, digital 3D models of urban scenes are important for a variety of applications, such as urban planning, public security, transportation, measurement, military, and other fields. However, the digitization of urban scenes with complex architectural structures especially the modeling of curved buildings still remains a challenge [1].

In recent years, various reconstruction methods that can be implemented and can be automatically modeled have been developed. Most of the existing methods were designed based on processing light detection (LiDAR) point cloud data, and achieved good results. Most LiDAR datas use the energy function method to segment the point cloud and generate a mesh model using conventional algorithms and they have proven to be mature methods, such as [2,3]. But there are still some confusions that make these methods impossible to use on a large scale. The most important thing is that extracting LiDAR point clouds

Y. M. Ro et al. (Eds.): MMM 2020, LNCS 11962, pp. 254–266, 2020.
https://doi.org/10.1007/978-3-030-37734-2_21

requires expensive equipment and some occlusions can make the airborne radar data incomplete and lead to reconstruction holes or dents. Simultaneously, in order to reduce the cost of use, there are also aome methods of modeling urban scene images taken in space using satellite images, such as [4,5]. These types of methods collect information from satellite images and then calculate 3D models from multiple satellite images at the same location. However, due to the occlusion of the cloud layer and the long distance of the imaging, these methods do not achieve a good effect on the detail display during the reconstruction.

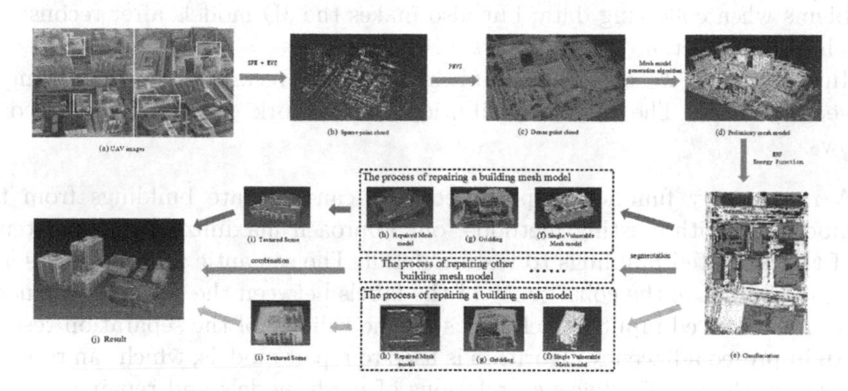

Fig. 1. Our overview of the urban building reconstruction method. From a series of images captured by a camera mounted on the drone (a), a spare point cloud (b) is generated by using SFM and MVS. A dense point cloud (c) is generated after the patch-based MVS algorithm (PMVS). Then, the mesh reconstruction is performed on some scenes first, and then the object is segmented according to the defined energy, and the whole scene is decomposed into buildings and other objects (d). Extract individual buildings separately for optimal modeling (e). For each individual building, use the patching algorithm to repair the mesh model in (g) through the point cloud and the mesh model in (g) to generate a vulnerability-free model (h). The entire scene can be textured (i) for various applications. Finally, put together all the reconstructed models together (j).

As a result, many of the lines of sight have turned to other methods of reconstruction, that is, extracting point cloud data from images acquired by drones and automatically reconstructing. On the data collection, Miiani et al. [6] studied how the formation affects the reconstruction accuracy of the Unmanned Aerial Vehicle (UAV) group in the three-dimensional environment, and can effectively use the side information of the camera in the field of view to overcome the shortcomings of the algorithm. Li et al. [7] proposed a method for reconstructing a building quality model from a drone image, which uses Markov random field optimization to extract the roof of each building and refine it using a contour refinement algorithm. Malihi et al. [8] used the high-density point clouds generated by drone images to perform large-scale reconstruction of buildings. In terms of the lack of point clouds, Arikan et al. [9] proposed an automatic method that simultaneously detects the planar primitives and global laws of local fitting and using these rules can adjust the plane as a reward and effectively correct the local fitting error.

With the rapid development of drone technology, high-quality images of urban architectural areas can be captured at low cost by drones flying at low altitudes (less than 1000 m) equipped with high-resolution cameras. Using these readily available aerial imageries, we propose a new reconstruction method that divides the reconstruction and repairs the 3D scene by extracting the point cloud into the photo collection, which not only overcomes the expensive equipment problems when collecting data, but also makes the 3D models after reconstruction have more detail.

In this paper, we consider the problems of the reconstruction modeling of curved buildings. The main contribution of our work can be summarized as follows:

- A new energy function is proposed that can separate buildings from the model. As with existing methods, our approach maximizes the consistency of the extracted buildings to restore detail. The semantic information is also used to improve the consistency of the labels between the semantic segments of the extracted input model to ensure the validity of the separation results.
- An improved adjacency algorithm is used to repair models, which can robustly discover the set of adjacency relations of mesh models and repair appropriately the non-watertight model due to point cloud loss.

2 The Proposed Algorithm

Our method takes a series of UAV images of the scene as input, and output is the 3D polygon mesh model of the scene. An overview of our approach is shown in Fig. 1. The images were captured by cameras mounted on the drone. In the pre-processing step, we extract a point cloud from these images using structure from motion (SFM) and multi-view system (MVS). Then using these point clouds to generate a mesh model. In this section, we reconstruction large scale of complex buildings including two components. (1) Split mesh model. (2) An improved adjacency algorithm is constructed to repair model.

2.1 Building Segmentation

Inspired by the analysis of [10–12], we use the energy function to classify the model, distinguish it by the energy contained in each category, and finally use some context common sense to adjust the final model. The energy function we use is primarily referenced in [10], we transformed the label classification and use its first partial function as the intrinsic energy of the patch. Since the [10] does not do much processing on the energy relationship between the patches, our energy function chooses to increase the sensitivity of patches to multiple labels and the interaction energy between the patches for more detailed processing.

The cluster relies on an MRF in order to distinguish and extract between four classes of urban objects: roof, ground, façade, clutters. As a part of the input grid is denser, each triangular surface is classified by MRF, which will lead to larger calculation time. Before this step, we subdivide the input grid into hyperplanes: a set of connected triangular faces similar to the concept of super pixels used for image analysis. By clustering and regional growth, triangular faces of similar shape operator matrix are obtained, and hyperplanes are obtained. More specifically, we estimated the shape operator matrices of each triangular face near a local spherical grid with radius R, and compared these matrices by Fresenius norm. Then we use the following equation to describe each hyperplane:

$$E(X) = \sum_{i \in f} D(X_i) + \sum_{i \in f} E(X_i) + \sum_{i,j \in f} E(X_i, X_j) \tag{1}$$

where $D(X_i)$, $E(X_i)$ and $E(X_i, X_j)$)denote the energy of each hyperplane, the incremental energy of each hyperplane and the energy relationship between the adjacent hyperplane and the hyperplane.

In our work, the first part of the proposed energy function is to describe the inherent energy of each patch and is described as following:

$$D(X_i) = \begin{cases} 1 - a_p * a_h * (1 - a_e)) & if\ X_i = ground \\ 1 - a_p * (1 - a_h)) & if\ X_i = facade \\ 1 - a_p * a_h * a_e & if\ X_i = roof \\ 1 - (1 - a_p) * a_h & if\ X_i = clutters \end{cases} \tag{2}$$

The closer $D(X_i)$ get to one, the closer the region is to the assumed classification. And a_p, a_h and a_e denote the planarity of the hyperplane containing, the deviation of the unit normal and the relative height (z coordinate) of the triangle facet centroid.

In order to further describe the energy of each part, we introduce the incremental energy of each hyperplane. There are five geometric attributes are described for each triangle facet of the input mesh in Table 1.

Table 1. Five geometric attributes to describe each triangle facet of the input mesh

Parameter	Parameter description
F_e	Elevation above ground
F_d	Direction of the hyperplane
F_f	Hyperplane flatness, this attribute reaches its maximum at 45°
F_s	Compactness of patches, measured by the area divided by the square of the perimeter of the hyperplane. In the mesh model, most of the patches on the building have large F_s values

To improve the sensitivity of the patch to multiple labels and to make the classification more accurate, we adjust our formula by improving the second part

Table 2. Discrimination of the degree of adaptation of each feature to classification. The symbols "+", "−" and "/" indicate the sensitivity value tends to be large, small, and arbitrary in the respectively corresponding class.

Classification	F_e	F_d	F_f	F_s
Roofs	+	+	−	+
Facades	/	−	−	+
Grounds	−	+	−	+
Clutters	−	/	+	−

of the classification formula in [11]. Since our classification categories are quite different from the classification categories, we adjust and increase the sensitivity of our classifications to labels and features in Table 2.

Before computing the unary energy of MRF the features are normalized to [0, 1] by truncated normalization to balance their contributions as in Eq. (3):

$$x = \begin{cases} 0 & if\ F < F_{min} \\ 1 & if\ F > F_{max} \\ \frac{F - F_{min}}{F_{min} - F_{max}} & otherwise \end{cases} \tag{3}$$

The content in Table 2 is to describe the degree of adaptation of each feature to classification. And we will use the degree of adaptation in Eq. (4) to describe a portion of the energy $\sum E(X_i)$. To simplify the description, we define the following operator $x \bigotimes y$ with regard to a normalized feature x and each label y as:

$$x \bigotimes y = \begin{cases} 1 - x\ if\ \text{"} + \text{"} \\ x\quad if\ \text{"} - \text{"} \\ 0\quad if\ \text{"}/\text{"} \end{cases} \tag{4}$$

For each patch, there are five attributes. We use Table 2 to specify the degree of adaptation of each category to each attribute, and finally to calculate the minimum energy of each patch in each category. The second part of the proposed energy function is defined as:

$$\sum_{i \in f} E(X_i) = \sum_{i \in f} (\frac{1}{n} \sum_{x \in X} x \bigotimes y) \tag{5}$$

At last, we use the last energy function, which describes the energy relationship between the adjacent hyperplane. And the function is given in equation (9):

$$\sum_{i,j \in f} E(X_i, X_j) = w_{ij} 1[x_i, x_j] \tag{6}$$

where w_{ij} is the weights for the distance between two adjacent hyperplane centers, which contains two weight values, one is the Euclidean distance between the center points of the two patches, and the other is the angular difference between the two patch normal vectors. And $1[x_i, x_j]$ is the binary function (which is 0 if $x_i == x_j$ and 1 otherwise).

After all, we use a knowledge-based semantic approach to find the misclassified patches and re-label the classification results before processing the next steps. There are three specific descriptions as follows:

If a connected component contains a hyperplane labeled facade, it must also contain a hyperplane labeled roof, which are directly connected to each other. If a connected component contains tree, the total number of connections labeled as tree must be greater than the number of adjacent hyperplanes. In a connected component, the total 2D area of the hyperplanes that are labeled "roof" connections must be greater than the threshold δ (e.g., $10\,\mathrm{m}^2$). Here, the value of δ is conservatively defined, it's value can be changed according to the actual situation.

2.2 Repair Non-watertight Areas

After segmenting the triangular mesh model, we can get the triangular mesh model of buildings. However, due to the limitations of the generation method, the resulting triangular mesh model cannot be directly utilized by other applications. It contains some limitations, such as holes, self-intersecting triangles, gaps. Some fixes must be made before applying these models to the actual scene. Therefore, some algorithms are presented to repair the gaps and overlaps in the extracted model.

Extracted the mesh model of roofs and facades of the building are point cloud data. Due to the blurring of images, it leads to the occlusion of trees or other objects or the absence of triangular facets in extracted data. And the extracted mesh models are non-watertight. In our work, inspired by [9], we analyze a graph topology algorithm to repair the non-watertight model to achieve watertight. The work in [9] aimed at repairing a topological shape with a regular shape. However, it does not consider a model with rounding properties. It only topographs the various patches of the obtained model to straighten the multiple deformations. Our method is aimed at repairing all topological shapes. Obviously, we can't make the initial model polygonization and the model data we have imported has been triangular facets, that is, the edge of the model has been relatively smooth. Therefore, when model repair is carried out, the initialization is no longer required, and the boundary is extracted, and the boundaries of triangular facets can be directly used. We abandon the polygonalization and directly perform polygon soup snapping of triangular faces. For the boundary problem will occur after the model, in our work, we use the quadric surface fitting method to simulate the patch, which the patch is aggregated to achieve the smoothness of the partial area.

Algorithm 1. Non-watertight model repair

Input: The mesh of model with peripheral point
Parameter: τ = degree, r = radius, p, q = point in V, l = line in L, f = mesh face in F
Output: repaired mesh model
1: **while** p,q in V **do**
2:    **if** $\|p, q\|$ < min(r(p),r(q)) **then**
3:       p=q
4:    **end if**
5: **end while**
6: **while** l_i,l_j in L **do**
7:    **if** cross(l_i,l_j)==0 and orien(l_i,l_j) < τ and $\|l_i, l_j\|$ < min(r(l_i),r(l_j)) **then**
8:       l_i=l_j
9:    **end if**
10: **end while**
11: **while** l in L and f in F **do**
12:    **if** cross(l,f)==0 and orien(l,f) < τ and $\|l, f\|$ < min(r(l),r(f)) **then**
13:       let l in f
14:    **end if**
15: **end while**
16: **return** repaired mesh model

where cross(.) represents no intersection between two objects and orien(.) represents the degree of the normal vector between two objects.

Before repair, we mainly consider the following situations to carry out the limitation of the repair: (1) In order to achieve local stability, self-intersection, flanging, and collapse should be avoided; (2) An extended set of matching candidates allows more free connections, thus achieving a balance with (1); (3) The problem of local pruning repair is mainly treated by the balance of (1) and (2); (4) The global trim can prevent the degradation of the face by considering the global problem that affects the matching of more than two faces.

After the pre-conditions are completed, the Algorithm 1 is summarized for non-watertight model repair in the front.

The gap will be repaired after the triangle surface of the first step is fitted, but this obviously causes the model to be partially stiff and cannot be perfectly reconstructed for some local smooth areas. In our work, we use the quadratic surface method. The fitting method fits the triangular patches that complete the clustering to achieve the smoothness of the local area.

The Algorithm 2 is summarized for how to smooth watertight model is as follows:

Algorithm 2. Smooth watertight model

Input: repaired mesh model
Parameter: f_i = mesh face in F(mesh face group), C_i = clustering faces group, τ = degree(a constant)
Output: smooth mesh model

1: **while** f_i in F **do**
2: let $f_i \in C_i$
3: **end while**
4: **while** f_i in F, C_j in C **do**
5: **if** orien(f_i,C_j) $< \tau$ **then**
6: let $f_i \in C_j$
7: **end if**
8: **end while**
9: **while** C_i in C **do**
10: quadric surface fitting C
11: **end while**
12: **return** smoothed and repaired mesh model

After triangular patch boundary fitting and patch cluster fitting, our model can achieve more successful repair results both locally and in all. Our results will be shown in the experimental section.

3 Experiments and Analysis

In our experiment, the data set consists of 1328 images taken with the Dajiang UAV's own FC550 model camera (9 million pixels) and 15 mm focal length in two 20-minute normal flights, with horizontal and vertical resolution. These two flights are in different areas and the height is about 70 m. The areas scanned by drones include many unique buildings that have not been built to date for more than a decade, with complex architectural features, peculiar new buildings and high-rise facilities of various buildings. Our approach benefits from statistical analysis that is an imperfect point cloud that compensates for the low quality of the data. It can be seen from the figure that although there are missing areas on the roof of the building, our method successfully detects and reconstructs all the buildings in these areas, and obtains a crack-free model. We get firstly a colored 3D point cloud based on SFM and MVS's images. Due to both SFM and MVS are based on local image features, the point cloud obtained by calculation usually has serious problems such as noise, occlusion ,and uneven density. Then our method is implemented to reconstruct the polygon model from the point cloud.

Figure 2 shows the results of the architectural segmentation in Chengdu. Figure 2(a) shows the real scene in the suburbs of Chengdu, and Fig. 2(b) shows the results of the energy splitting of the buildings in Chengdu after the common algorithm reconstruction. Since our reconstruction is only for buildings, we only identify the roof of the building in the same color as the façade, and we will

Fig. 2. Segmentation of the suburb of Chengdu area. The upper row is initial scene; the lower row is building segmentation result.

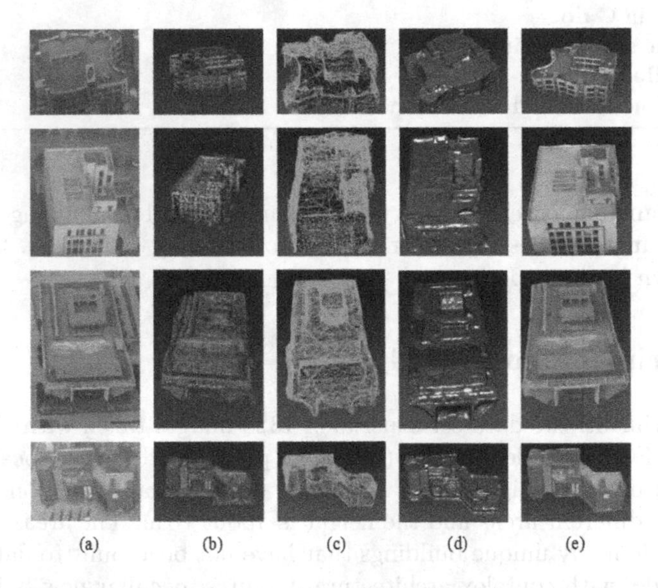

Fig. 3. Four different building repair and reconstruction. (a) Initial photos; (b) building segmentation result; (c) Model repair using algorithms; (d) repaired model; (e) textured polygonal models.

discard them for the properties of other unrelated buildings. It can be seen that the results after our segmentation are quite satisfactory. First of all, the energy splitting function is sensitive to the height attribute. When the high-rise building is divided, the extraction of building attributes is good. Secondly, if the exterior wall of the building is more vertical and unobstructed, the segmentation effect is also good. However, if there is a relatively large forest near the building, the reconstructed forest is similar to a low-rise building cluster. In this case, the effect of the segmentation is not well reflected.

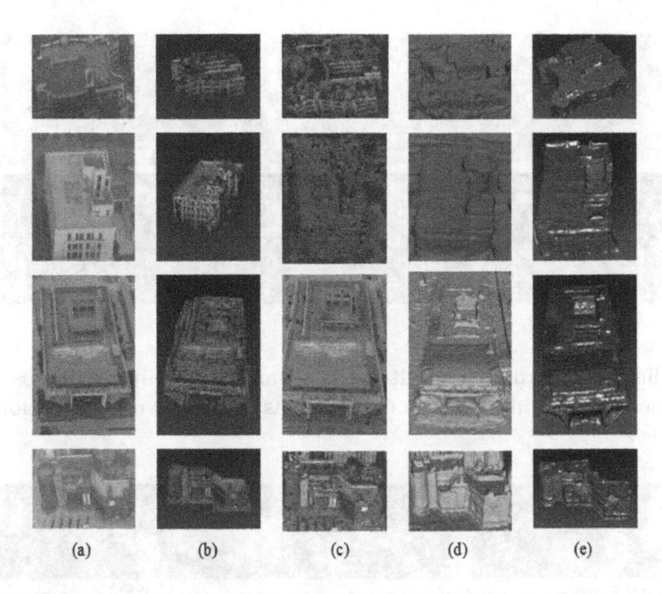

Fig. 4. Comparisons against other methods. (a) Initial photos; (b) building segmentation result; (c) Ball Pivoting arithmetic; (d) Poisson Reconstruction; (e) our method.

Figure 3 provides a more detailed description of the reconstruction and repair process for four different buildings. Figure 3(a) shows the actual scene of the building so that we can make some comparisons later. Figure 3(b) shows that after we have split the building, we take the initial reconstruction result of the building for repair. In Fig. 3(c), we can see that we extract the grid lines of each area and refine them, then add the patches to the building frame composed of these lines in Fig. 3(d) and smooth them. Finally, we paste the texture in Fig. 3(e) as the final result. It can be seen clearly that the results of the repair of a single building are quite satisfactory. In some real scenes, the smoothed area can be displayed smoothly, and some small holes can be filled, compared with the initial one. It is better to use other methods for building modeling.

In the past few years, dozens of buildings have been developed in this area. Figure 4 compares our algorithm with two other competing methods: Screened Poisson Surface Reconstruction (Poisson Reconstruction, in Fig. 4(d)) and Ball Pivoting arithmetic (in Fig. 4(c)). However, the Ball Pivoting algorithm failed to completely reconstruct the model with noise and occlusion. The two main failure modes stem from the fact that it is not suitable for the processing of missing point clouds, resulting in a large number of holes that cannot be modeled in places where there is a little cloud missing. For Poisson Reconstruction, it is obvious that the equation used for Poisson Reconstruction can make it fill all the holes, but this filling is not standardized, it can be clearly seen that when filling the defective point cloud. If it is recessed downward, the results cannot completely fill the defective part of the model, and it cannot complete the surface defect well. Figure 4(e) shows that our method has a relatively large improvement

Fig. 5. Building reconstruction results in large areas. The upper photos are original areas, and the following are corresponding areas after the reconstruction process is completed.

Fig. 6. Point cloud overlaid on the reconstructed models. The coverage of four different buildings is on display.

for the processing of defective point clouds and the modeling of the surface of buildings(our reconstruction here refers to the repair of a single building after the split, the time of the process of generating the mesh model before is not included in this part).

In order to show our method can run in multiple buildings, we selected a part of the conjoined building in a community for reconstruction work, as shown in Fig. 5. We found that we were able to complete the reconstruction and restoration of the residential buildings. But for models with incomplete image groups, the repair is difficult, and it can't be repaired well, Such as Fig. 5(b). However, in Fig. 5(a) and (c), we can see that the interval between each building is relatively large, and the surface of the building is relatively standardized. Several buildings do not have much correlation with each other, so in this case, the repair results for the building will be better.

In Table 3, we quantitatively compare the building shown in Fig. 6 with the above method. It can be seen from the table that the selected Poisson Reconstruction method has higher precision, but the final surface is more fluctuating. Our approach has similar accuracy to the Ball Pivoting algorithm, but its performance is more convincing. Our approach is to strike a balance between accuracy and automatic rebuild.

Simultaneously, in Fig. 6, we superimpose the point cloud extracted by the drone on the repair model to visually observe the accuracy of the reconstructed model after the repair. It can be seen that the point cloud basically covers the model, and no point cloud will appear in a farther place.

Table 3. Statistical comparison of running time (RT, in minute) and mean distance error (DE, in meters, defined as the average distance of the points to the model) of our method with Ball Pivoting and Poisson Reconstruction methods on the buildings shown in Fig. 4.

City scene	Evaluation	Ball pivoting	Poisson	Ours
Figure 6(a)	RT (minutes)	4.56 min	7.26 min	**5.38** min
	DE (meters)	0.095 m	0.078 m	**0.088** m
Figure 6(b)	RT (minutes)	12.57 min	20.16 min	**17.12** min
	DE (meters)	0.111 m	0.103 m	**0.105** m
Figure 6(c)	RT (minutes)	3.47 min	6.29 min	**5.28** min
	DE (meters)	0.084 m	0.073 m	**0.077** m
Figure 6(d)	RT (minutes)	5.48 min	8.07 min	**7.59** min
	DE (meters)	0.090 m	0.099 m	**0.097** m

Experiments have shown that in addition to the single building, our reconstruction framework performs well in large scenes (Fig. 5). We record the running time of these scenarios, as shown in Table 4. The time to divide and rebuild the buildings in these two scenarios takes only a few tens of seconds. After the building is split, the multi-threading technique can be used to repair the reconstruction of each building at the same time, and a large amount of time can be saved if conditions permit. Therefore, our approach is more suitable for dealing with large-scale urban environments.

Table 4. Running times (in seconds) of the two core steps (building segmentation and building reconstruction) for the two large scenes shown in Fig. 5.

City scene	Building segmentation (second)	Building repaired (minute)
Figure 5(a)	64.63 s	31.12 min
Figure 5(b)	65.82 s	37.19 min
Figure 5(c)	75.69 s	42.54 min

4 Conclusions

This paper proposes a framework for a automatic reconstruction of large-scale urban scenes based on drone images. We propose an efficient segmentation algorithm that uses the Markov energy field for statistical analysis to segment the data and extract the mesh building model. The geometrical topology method of model reconstruction is used to fill the surface vulnerabilities of buildings. Experiments in various scenarios show that the reconstructed polygon model is more compact and regular than the existing methods.

Acknowledgements. This work was supported by the Science and Technology Service Industry Project of Sichuan under 2019GFW126, Key R&D project of Sichuan under 2019ZDYF2790.

References

1. Berger, M., et al.: A survey of surface reconstruction from point clouds. Comput. Graph. Forum **36**, 301–329 (2016)
2. Yi, C., et al.: Urban building reconstruction from raw LiDAR point data. Comput.-Aided Des. **93**, S0010448517301331 (2017)
3. Hao, W., Wang, Y., Liang, W.: Slice-based building facade reconstruction from 3D point clouds. Int. J. Remote Sens. **39**, 1–20 (2018)
4. Facciolo, G., De Franchis, C., Meinhardt-Llopis, E.: Automatic 3D reconstruction from multi-date satellite images. In: Computer Vision and Pattern Recognition Workshops (2017)
5. Duan, L., Lafarge, F.: Towards large-scale city reconstruction from satellites. In: Leibe, B., Matas, J., Sebe, N., Welling, M. (eds.) ECCV 2016. LNCS, vol. 9909, pp. 89–104. Springer, Cham (2016). https://doi.org/10.1007/978-3-319-46454-1_6
6. Milani, S., Memo, A.: Impact of drone swarm formations in 3D scene reconstruction. In: IEEE International Conference on Image Processing (2016)
7. Li, M., Nan, L., Smith, N., Wonka, P.: Reconstructing building mass models from UAV images. Comput. Graph. **54**, 84–93 (2016)
8. Malihi, S., Valadan Zoej, M., Hahn, M.: Large-scale accurate reconstruction of buildings employing point clouds generated from UAV imagery, vol. 10, pp. 1148–1156 (2018)
9. Arikan, M., Schwärzler, M., Flöry, S., Wimmer, M., Maierhofer, S.: O-snap: optimization-based snapping for modeling architecture. ACM Trans. Graph. (TOG) **32**, 1–15 (2013)
10. Verdie, Y., Lafarge, F., Alliez, P.: LOD generation for urban scenes. ACM Trans. Graph. **34**, 1–14 (2015)
11. Zhu, Q., Li, Y., Hu, H., Wu, B.: Robust point cloud classification based on multi-level semantic relationships for urban scenes. Isprs J. Photogramm. Remote. Sens. **129**, 86–102 (2017)
12. Blaha, M., et al.: Semantically informed multiview surface refinement. In: IEEE International Conference on Computer Vision (2017)

Deformed Phase Prediction Using SVM for Structured Light Depth Generation

Sen Xiang[1,3](✉), Qiong Liu[2,4], Huiping Deng[1,3], Jin Wu[1,3], and Li Yu[2,4]

[1] School of Information Science and Engineering, Wuhan University of Science and Technology, Wuhan 430081, China
xiangsen@wust.edu.cn

[2] School of Electronic Information and Communication, Huazhong University of Science and Technology, Wuhan 430074, China

[3] Engineering Research Center of Metallurgical Automotive and Measurement Technology, Ministry of Education, Wuhan 430081, China

[4] Wuhan National Laboratory for Opto-electronics, Wuhan 430074, China

Abstract. In phase-based structured light, absolute phase unwrapping, which is a cumbersome step, is often considered necessary before calculating depth. In this paper, we notice that depth is only related to the deformed phase but not the absolute unwrapped phase. Furthermore, the deformed phase is highly related to the changes of the wrapped reference and captured phases. Based on these findings, we propose a classification-based scheme that can directly report deformed phase. To be specific, we cast the problem of inferring fringe order difference as a multi class classification task, where phase samples within half a period are fed to the classifier and the fringe oder difference is the class. Besides, we use a radial basis function support vector machine as the classifier. In such a manner, for every pixel, the deformed phase can be obtained directly without knowing the absolute unwrapped phase. Moreover, the proposed method only needs phase from a single frequency and is pixel-independent, so it is free from troubles such as poor real-time performance in temporal unwrapping or error accumulation in spatial unwrapping. Experiments on 3dsmax data and real-captured data prove that the proposed method can produce high quality depth maps.

Keywords: Structured light · SVM · Phase-shifting · Profilometry

1 Introduction

The recent years have witnessed the booming development of three-dimensional (3D) research and applications [13,17–19], where depth is the key element. Among various depth generation approaches, structured light (SL) [11] is an important technique due to its high accuracy and low cost. A typical SL system has a coupled projector and camera pair as shown in Fig. 1. A pre-designed pattern I_{prj} is projected to a reference plane H_{ref} with known depth and also the measured object with unknown depth, and correspondingly the camera records

Y. M. Ro et al. (Eds.): MMM 2020, LNCS 11962, pp. 267–278, 2020.
https://doi.org/10.1007/978-3-030-37734-2_22

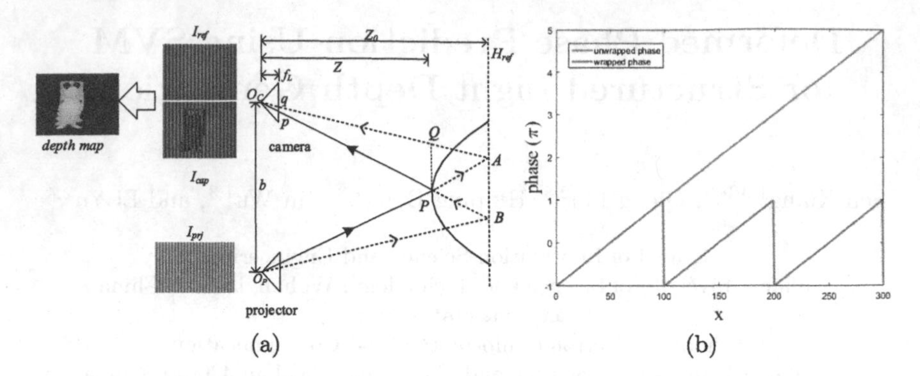

Fig. 1. A typical SL system. (a) Layout of a SL system. f_L: focal length of the camera. b: baseline between the projector and the camera. Z_0: depth of the reference plane H_{ref}. Z: depth of the measured objects. (b) Phase wrapping problem.

a reference pattern I_{ref} and a captured pattern I_{cap}. By checking the pattern deformation, depth values can be obtained [20].

Based on this principle, phase-based approaches embed phases in sinusoidal patterns. After extracting the captured phase and the reference phase, their difference called deformed phase can be directed converted to scene depth. Unfortunately, phase values calculated from the patterns are not continuous but wrapped to the range of $(-\pi, \pi]$ as shown in Fig. 1(b). So, prior to calculating depth, it is necessary to recover the absolute true phase, for both the reference one and the captured one, and this process is known as phase unwrapping (PU).

As shown in Fig. 1(b), PU is in fact an ill-posed problem since only the wrapped phase is available. Classic PU includes spatial phase unwrapping and temporal phase unwrapping [14]. Spatial phase unwrapping is based on the smooth assumption of phase, and is conducted along a specific path. Therefore, phase errors accumulate in the unwrapping. Meanwhile, temporal phase unwrapping uses multiple wrapped phases with specified periods and directly calculate the absolute phase values. Nevertheless, it needs multiple phase maps and is thus in low efficiency. In addition, recently, convolution neural network is being applied in depth generation filed, dealing with tasks such as stereo matching [5], and even recently phase unwrapping [15].

We notice that in conventional phase-based SL, recovering the absolute phase with PU is the most complex part. However, depth is only related to the deformed phase, but not the absolute phase. This innovates us to develop a method that can skip the cumbersome absolute PU and directly predict the deformed phase. We find that tracing the changes in the wrapped phase can predict the deformed phase. More specifically, we try to predict the fringe order difference by inspecting the wrapped phases, and this can be cast to a multi-class classification task. In implementation, a radial basis function support vector machine (RBF-SVM) is applied as the classifier, where the wrapped phases and the fringe order difference are the input feature vector and the output class, respectively. Compared with conventional methods, the proposed method has the following advantages. Most importantly, it avoids the cumbersome absolute phase unwrapping. Moreover, compared with spatial unwrapping, it processes every pixel independently and thus no error accumulation happens. Compared with temporal phase unwrapping, it needs only a single-frequency phase map, and thus enjoys good real-time performance.

2 Related Work

2.1 Phase-Based Depth Measuring

Based on the basic principle of SL as shown in Fig. 1(a), phase-based SL embeds spatial coordinates (x, y) into the phase $\varphi(x, y)$ with sinusoidal fringes. For example, three step phase shifting [9] projects three patterns

$$\begin{cases} I_1(x,y) = A + B\cos\left(\varphi(x,y) - \frac{2\pi}{3}\right) \\ I_2(x,y) = A + B\cos\left(\varphi(x,y)\right) \\ I_3(x,y) = A + B\cos\left(\varphi(x,y) + \frac{2\pi}{3}\right) \end{cases} \tag{1}$$

where the embedded phase $\varphi(x, y)$ linearly increases with the pixel position x. With these patterns, fringe analysis techniques can report the phase as

$$\varphi(x,y) = \arctan\left(\sqrt{3}\frac{I_1 - I_3}{2I_2 - I_1 - I_3}\right) \tag{2}$$

This process is conducted on both the reference patterns and the captured patterns as shown in Fig. 1(a), and correspondingly two phase maps φ^{ref} and φ^{cap} are obtained.

After that, the phase difference between φ^{ref} and φ^{cap}, also named as deformed phase $\Delta\varphi$, is converted to the depth by following Eqs. 3 and 4.

$$\Delta\varphi = \varphi^{cap} - \varphi^{ref} \tag{3}$$

$$Z = \frac{bf_L Z_0}{f_L b + \frac{Z_0}{2\pi f}\Delta\varphi} \tag{4}$$

where f is the fringe frequency in the reference pattern, and other notations are given in Fig. 1(a).

2.2 Phase Unwrapping

In Eq. 2, phase is derived with 'arctan' and thus the obtained phase is wrapped to the range of $(-\pi, \pi]$ as shown in Fig. 1(b). The real unwrapped phase φ and the wrapped phase φ_w are formulated as

$$\begin{cases} \varphi^{ref} = \varphi_w^{ref} + m^{ref}2\pi \\ \varphi^{cap} = \varphi_w^{cap} + m^{cap}2\pi \end{cases} \tag{5}$$

where the fringe order m^{ref} and m^{cap} are integers. Phase unwrapping recovers φ from φ_w, but this is in fact an ill-posed problem since only φ_w is available. Mainstream phase unwrapping methods can be divided into spatial, temporal and learning-based approaches.

Spatial Phase Unwrapping is based on the assumption that phase is smoothly varied, so in case φ_w has abrupts from π to $-\pi$, an additional 2π is compensated to remove the sharp transition and make the phase smooth. Depending on phase difference between neighboring pixels, this method is conducted along a specific unwrapping path, which brings a crucial drawback that phase errors accumulate to the successive pixels. To improve the robustness, the idea of 'quality guidance' is introduced [21], i.e. pixels with higher quality are unwrapped before those with lower quality, where the quality is measured with metrics such as phase derivative variance [3] and the maximum phase gradient [22]. Nevertheless, since neighboring pixels are dependent, the problem of error propagation still exists.

Temporal Phase Unwrapping is based on number theory. It needs multiple wrapped phase maps, which are obtained with patterns with varying periods, and directly computes the unwrapped phase [10,23]. Temporal phase unwrapping is pixel-independent and thus free from error propagation, but it requires a large number of varying-frequency patterns, reducing its efficiency. To overcome this problem, researchers proposed multi-frequency composite patterns [1,2,16], but the robustness or accuracy is weakened.

Learning-Based Phase Unwrapping is also attracting attentions in stereo and SL field in recent years. Fanello [6,7] cast the algorithm of solving the correspondence problem for Kinect-like patterns as a classification-regression task. As to phase unwrapping, Sawaf [12] use a trained kernel to predict phase discontinuities. Dardikman [4] used a ResNet in phase unwrapping. However, learning-based phase unwrapping is just starting and still needs further research.

In general, the existing phase unwrapping focuses on recovering the absolute true phase for both the reference and captured data, which is cubersome. We propose a method which directly infers deformed phase and depth without absolute phase unwrapping. The details are presented in Sect. 3.

3 Proposed Scheme

3.1 Motivation

In the pipeline of conventional phase-based SL, recovering the absolute phase is necessary. However, Eq. 4 indicates that depth is only directly related to the deformed phase $\Delta\varphi$ but not the absolute phase. By combining Eqs. 3 and 5, the deformed phase $\Delta\varphi$ can be rewritten as

$$\Delta\varphi = \Delta\varphi_w + \Delta m 2\pi \tag{6}$$

where

$$\begin{cases} \Delta\varphi_w = \varphi_w^{cap} - \varphi_w^{ref} \\ \Delta m = m^{cap} - m^{ref} \end{cases} \tag{7}$$

Here, $\Delta\varphi_w$ can be computed with known φ_w^{cap} and φ_w^{ref}. So, if the fringe order difference Δm can be directly inferred without knowing m^{ref} and m^{cap}, absolute phase unwrapping is no longer necessary. However, this is not easy since m^{cap} and m^{ref} are unknowns, and we propose a learning-based approach to solve the problem.

We find that the fringe order difference Δm has the following properties.

- Δm varies only when the fringe order, m_{cap} or m_{ref}, changes, which are always companied with sharp transitions in φ_w^{ref} and φ_w^{cap}. Therefore, tracing the changes in φ_w^{ref} and φ_w^{cap} indicates the value of Δm.
- Equation 6 indicates that $\Delta m 2\pi$ fills the gap between $\Delta\varphi$ and $\Delta\varphi_w$, e.g. a correct Δm make them equal to each other.
- SL systems are applied for indoor use with limited depth range, Δm values are integers near zero. Therefore, it is reasonable to predict Δm with a multi-class classifier.

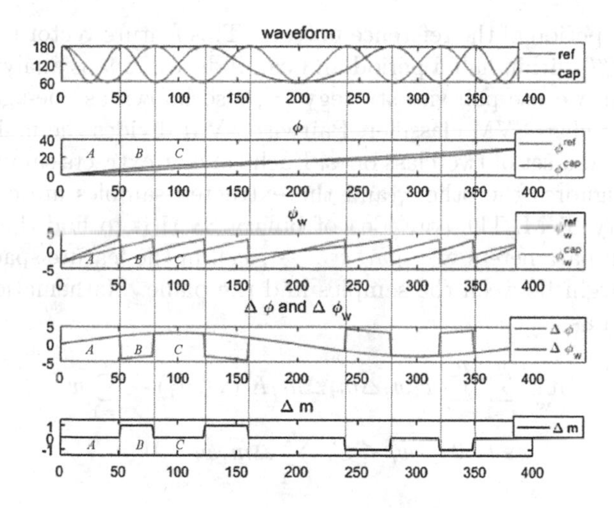

Fig. 2. Relationship between wrapped phase and Δm. First row: waveform of the reference and the captured patterns. Second row: absolute true phase. Third row: wrapped phase. Fourth row: wrapped and unwrapped deformed phase. Last row: fringe order difference Δm. All phase values are in radian.

Without loss of generality, we present an example in Fig. 2, where the relationship between wrapped phases and Δm is illustrated. As shown in the figure, the whole range is horizontally divided to several intervals by the transitions of φ_w^{cap} and φ_w^{ref}, and we will study the intervals A, B and C as examples. In interval A, both φ_w^{cap} and φ_w^{ref} increases smoothly, and thus $\Delta\varphi_w$ coincide well with $\Delta\varphi$. So no compensation is needed between them and $\Delta m = 0$. In transition A to B, φ_w^{cap} jumps from π to $-\pi$, while φ_w^{ref} keeps growing. Therefore, in interval B, $\Delta m = 1$ and an additional 2π compensates the difference between $\Delta\varphi_w$ and

$\Delta\varphi$. In transition B to C, φ_w^{ref} jumps from π to $-\pi$, while φ_w^{cap} increases. In this case, an additional -1 should be added to Δm, which makes Δm=0 in interval C. The successive intervals can be analyzed similarly. In such a manner, we can infer Δm based on the wrapped phases without absolute phase unwrapping.

3.2 RBF-SVM Classification for Δm

In practice, the case is more complicated than Fig. 2, and to reveal the complex relationship, a learning-based method is utilized. Considering that Δm must be integers near zero, we cast the task of predicting Δm to a multi-class classification task where a radial basis function kernel support vector machine (RBF-SVM) is the classifier. The input feature consists of samples in φ_w^{ref} and φ_w^{cap}, and the output class is the fringe order difference Δm. Specifically, for every pixel p, the feature vector $\mathbf{v}(p)$ consists of 18 elements as shown below

$$\mathbf{v}(p) = \left[\varphi_w^{ref}(p-j), \varphi_w^{cap}(p-j)\right], \qquad j = 0, 1, \tfrac{T}{40}, \tfrac{T}{20}, \tfrac{T}{10}, \tfrac{T}{5}, \tfrac{3T}{10}, \tfrac{2T}{5}, \tfrac{T}{2}. \tag{8}$$

where T is the period of the reference pattern. This feature vector traces changes of φ_w^{ref} and φ_w^{cap} within half a period and can indicate Δm as analyzed in Fig. 2.

In addition, we use pairwise strategy [8], also known as one-against-one, to train the multi-class SVM classifier. Pairwise SVM divides the multi-class classification task to a set of two-class ones. Each time, it extracts samples from two classes while ignores the others, and the extracted samples are classified with a classic binary SVM. The core idea of binary SVM is to find the hyperplane, described with parameters $\mathbf{w} = [w_1, w_2, \cdots, w_k]$, in the feature space that maximizes the margin between the samples and the plane. Mathematically, a SVM can be written as

$$\begin{aligned} \min_{\mathbf{w}} \sum_{i=1}^{n} \sum_{j=1}^{n} w_i w_j \Delta m_i \Delta m_j K(\mathbf{v}_i, \mathbf{v}_j) - \sum_{i=1}^{n} w_i \\ s.t.\ \ 0 \le w_i \le C,\ \sum_{i=1}^{n} \Delta m_i w_i = 0 \end{aligned} \tag{9}$$

Here n is the number of samples, and K is a radial basis function (RBF) kernel

$$K(\mathbf{v}_i, \mathbf{v}_j) = \exp\left(-\gamma |\mathbf{v}_i - \mathbf{v}_j|^2\right) \tag{10}$$

that maps samples to higher feature dimension and are thus linearly separable. Note that, the labels of Δm, which are originally integers near zero, are temporally converted to $+1/-1$ when training the SVM binary classifier shown in Eqs. 9 and 10. For samples from N classes, pairwise mutli-class SVM will produce $\frac{N(N-1)}{2}$ binary classifiers. In a classification task, for an specified input sample, every binary SVM will report an output class, which can be regarded as a vote, and the class with the highest vote is the final output.

Once Δm is obtained, the deformed phase and depth can be further calculated by following Eqs. 4, 6 and 7.

4 Results

We have verified the proposed method with both simulated data and real captured data. Before that, we train the multi-class SVM model with synthetic data by following the pipeline of three-step phase shifting [9]. The patterns are in the resolution of 1200×1200 and the period is 80. The deformed phase $\Delta\varphi$ is defined with the absolute value of 'peaks' function in Matlab as shown in Fig. 3, and $-\Delta\varphi$ and its spatially-shifted version are also added to the training data. In addition, the patterns are corrupted with noise (mean value: 0, variance: 33.33). With the synthetic data, 20000 samples are randomly chosen as the training data. After that, a RBF-SVM model is trained with pairwise strategy as the classifier.

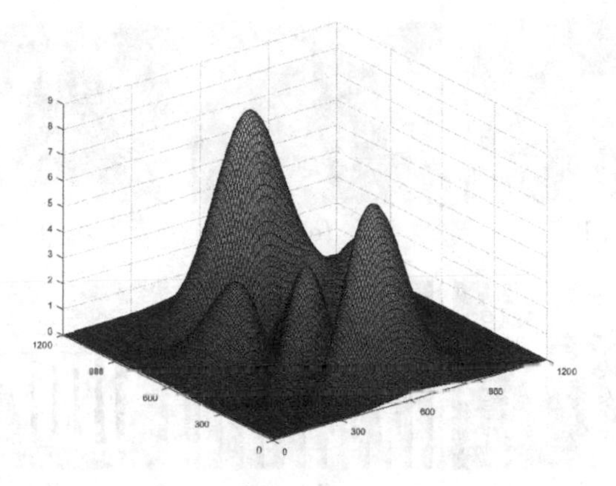

Fig. 3. $\Delta\varphi$, in radian, used in generating the training data.

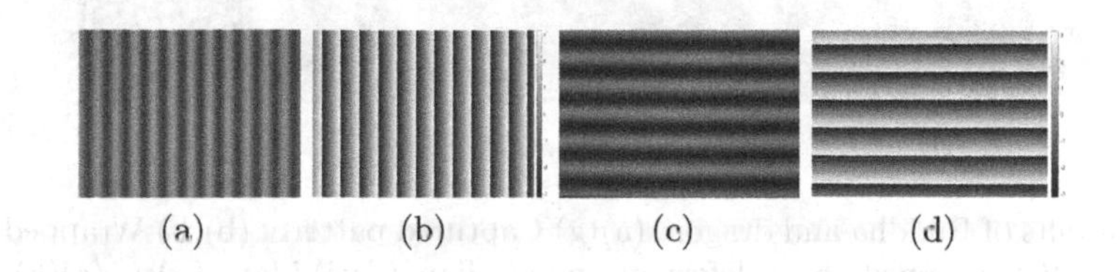

Fig. 4. Reference patterns and phase maps. (a) The second reference pattern in 3dsmax simulation. (b) The wrapped phase of (a). (c) The second reference pattern in real-captured data. (d) The wrapped phase of (c).

4.1 Simulation Results

We construct a SL system with 3dsmax, where the reference pattern and phase maps are shown in Figs. 4(a) and (b), respectively. Important parameters of the

SL systems are as follows. Projector resolution = 800×1280, camera resolution = 960×1280, baseline $b = 80$ mm, focal length $f_L = 35.572$ mm, reference plane $Z_0 = 800$ mm. Two 3D models 'Buddha' and 'dragon', which have many tiny components and foreground-background transitions, are used as the measured objects.

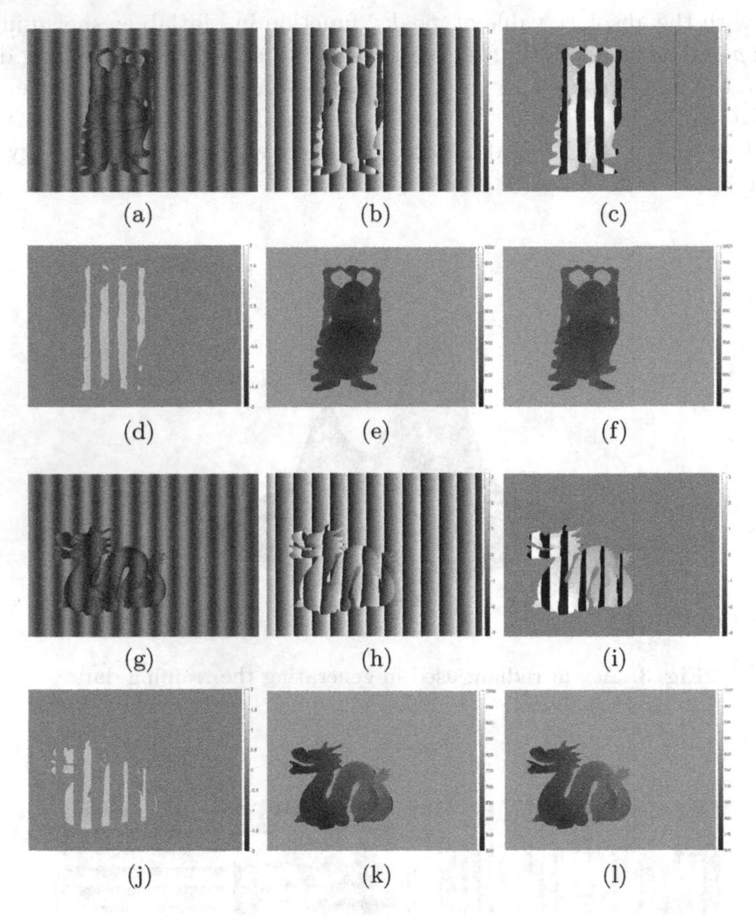

Fig. 5. Results of Buddha and dragon. (a)(g) Captured pattern. (b)(h) Wrapped phase in radian. (c)(i) Wrapped phase deformation in radian. (d)(j) Map of Δm. (e)(k) Resultant depth in millimeters. (f)(l) Ground truth depth in millimeters.

The results are shown in Fig. 5. Based on the captured patterns, the wrapped phases φ_w^{cap} are calculated and shown in Figs. 5(b) and (h). After that, by differencing φ_w^{cap} and φ_w^{ref}, wrapped deformed phase $\Delta\varphi_w$ are obtained and shown in Figs. 5(c) and (i). It is obvious that many pixels have incorrect phases (black regions) since the calculated phase values are wrapped. After that, maps of Δm that obtained with the proposed method are shown in Figs. 5(d) and (j), which exactly compensates the incorrect phases of $\Delta\varphi_w$. The output depth maps are shown in Figs. 5(e) and (k), which are in quite good shapes and very close to the ground truth.

In addition, with the ground truth depth provided by 3dsmax, we evaluate the objective quality with mean absolute difference (MAD) and its relative version in Table 1. The metrics shown that the depth maps are in good quality, with relative error less than 0.7% for Buddha and 0.53% for dragon.

Table 1. Objective quality of the depth values

	Buddha	Dragon
MAD (mm)	4.5587	3.4904
Relative MAD (%)	0.70	0.53

4.2 Results on Real Captured Data

We also conduct experiments with a real SL system and the parameters are as the following. Projector resolution 1920×1080, camera resolution = 2592×1800, baseline $b = 150$ mm, focal length $f_L = 16$ mm(6507pixels), reference plane Z_0=1950 mm. The projector and camera pair is vertically settled for convenience and the fringes are modulated in columns correspondingly. The reference pattern and phase map are shown in Figs. 4(c) and (d), respectively. We test the proposed method with two scene, boy and cones, and the results are shown in Fig. 6.

Like the simulation results, in Figs. 6(d) and (j), the original deformed phase maps are incorrect. With our proposed method, the predicted Δm Figs. 6(e) and (k) can compensate the phase and yield correct depth maps shown in Figs. 6(f) and (l). Note that the pixels in black are occluded or highly-slanted regions, where the pattern information is not enough to provide phase or depth. As to qualitative assessment, since no ground-truth depth is available, we measure the scenes 10 times and take the average as the basis. MAD and relative MAD with respect to this basis are shown in Table 2. It can be observed that the measurement is with high precision with the average relative error being 0.1024% and 0.1017% for boy and cones, respectively.

Last but not least, we compare the performance of the proposed method with spatial phase unwrapping since both of them use only a pair of captured phase map and reference phase map. In the results shown in Fig. 7, scanline phase unwrapping yields incorrect depth values along the unwrapping path. In contrast, the proposed method classifies Δm independently for every pixel, so no error propagation occurs.

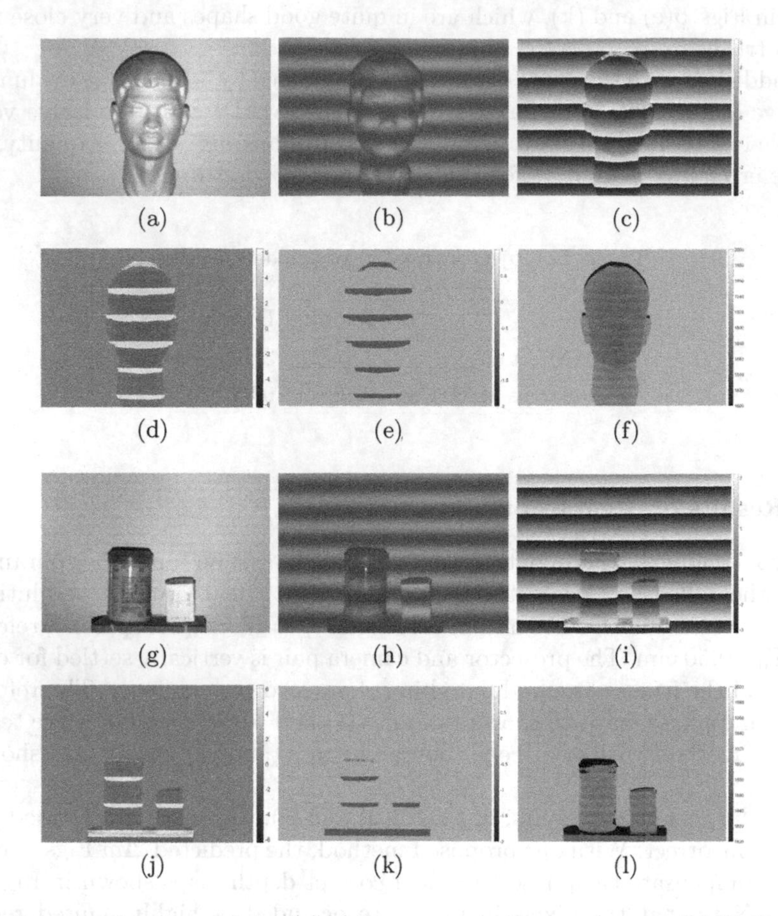

Fig. 6. Results of captured-data. (a)(g) Scene maps of boy and cones. (b)(h) Captured pattern I_2. (c)(i) Wrapped phase in radian. (d)(j) Wrapped deformed phase without unwrapping in radian. (e)(k) Maps of Δm. (f)(l) Resultant depth maps in millimeters.

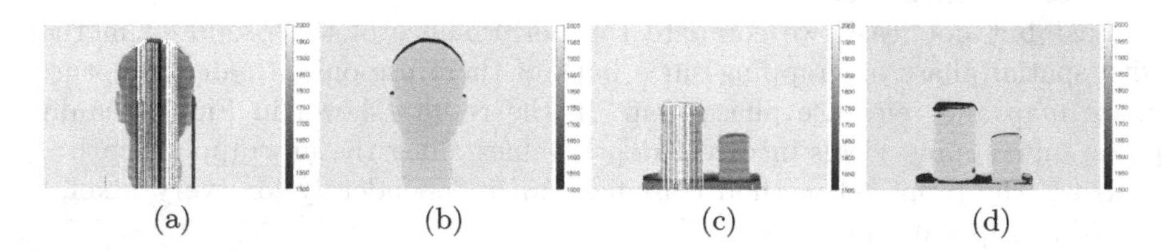

Fig. 7. Performance comparison between scanline phase unwrapping and the proposed scheme. (a)(c) Results with scanline phase unwrapping. (b)(d) Results of the proposed method.

Table 2. Objective quality of the depth values

No	Boy		Cones	
	MAD(mm)	relative MAD (%)	MAD(mm)	relative MAD (%)
1	1.9455	0.1032	1.9300	0.1015
2	1.9316	0.1024	1.9223	0.1011
3	1.9269	0.1022	1.9234	0.1012
4	1.9246	0.1021	1.9275	0.1014
5	1.9269	0.1022	1.9413	0.1021
6	1.9259	0.1021	1.9329	0.1017
7	1.9397	0.1029	1.9457	0.1024
8	1.9312	0.1024	1.9348	0.1018
9	1.9308	0.1024	1.9320	0.1016
10	1.9308	0.1025	1.9400	0.1021
Average	1.9314	0.1024	1.9330	0.1017

5 Conclusion

In this paper, we propose a novel depth measuring scheme without recovering the absolute true phase in structured light systems. We find that depth is only related to deformed phase, and thus absolute phase unwrapping is not always needed if the fringe order difference between the reference and the captured phases can be inferred. Furthermore, we convert the problem of estimating the fringe order difference Δm to a multi-class classification task, where the classifier is a RBF-SVM and the features are wrapped phases in half a period. With the estimated fringe order difference, deformed phase can be directly obtained and further converted to depth even though the absolute true phases are unknown. Compared with conventional methods, the proposed scheme only needs a single captured phase map and also avoids phase error propagation. Experiments show that this novel scheme is effective in generating depth maps for both simulated and captured data where the relative MAD is as low as 0.1%, and thus can be used in various applications.

Fundings. National Natural Science Foundation of China (61702384); Natural Science Foundation of Hubei Province (2017CFB348); Research Foundation for Young Scholars of WUST (2017xz008).

References

1. Chao, Z., Qian, C., Guohua, G., Shijie, F., Fangxiaoyu, F.: High-speed three-dimensional profilometry for multiple objects with complex shapes. Opt. Express **20**(17), 19493–19510 (2012)
2. Cheng, T., Du, Q., Jiang, Y., Zhu, X.: Absolute phase retrieval via color phase-coding. Optik **140**, 1056–1062 (2017)

3. Dai, Z., Zha, X.: An accurate phase unwrapping algorithm based on reliability sorting and residue mask. IEEE Geosci. Remote Sens. Lett. **9**(2), 219–223 (2012)
4. Dardikman, G., Shaked, N.T.: Phase unwrapping using residual neural networks. In: Imaging and Application Optical, p. CW3B.5 (2018)
5. Fanello, S., et al.: UltraStereo: efficient learning-based matching for active stereo systems. In: IEEE CVPR, pp. 6535–6544 (2017)
6. Fanello, S.R., et al.: HyperDepth: learning depth from structured light without matching. In: 2016 IEEE Conference on Computer Vision and Pattern Recognition (CVPR), pp. 5441–5450 (2016)
7. Fanello, S.R., et al.: UltraStereo: efficient learning-based matching for active stereo systems. In: 2017 IEEE Conference on Computer Vision and Pattern Recognition (CVPR), pp. 6535–6544 (2017)
8. Hsu, C.W.C., Lin, C.J.: A comparison of methods for multi-class support vector machines (2015)
9. Huang, P.S., Zhang, S.: Fast three-step phase-shifting algorithm. Appl. Opt. **45**(21), 5086–5091 (2006)
10. Lei, Z., Wang, C., Zhou, C.: Multi-frequency inverse-phase fringe projection profilometry for nonlinear phase error compensation. Opt. Lasers Eng. **66**, 249–257 (2015)
11. Salvi, J., Fernandez, S., Pribanic, T., Llado, X.: A state of the art in structured light patterns for surface profilometry. Pattern Recogn. **43**(8), 2666–2680 (2010)
12. Sawaf, F., Groves, R.M.: Phase discontinuity predictions using a machine-learning trained kernel. Appl. Opt. **53**(24), 5439 (2014)
13. Smolic, A.: 3D video and free viewpoint video-from capture to display. Elsevier Science Inc. (2011)
14. Song, Z.: Absolute phase retrieval methods for digital fringe projection profilometry: a review. Opt. Lasers Eng. **107**, 28–37 (2018)
15. Spoorthi, G.E., Gorthi, S., Gorthi, R.K.S.S.: PhaseNet: a deep convolutional neural network for two-dimensional phase unwrapping. IEEE Signal Process. Lett. **26**, 54–58 (2019)
16. Xiang, S., Deng, H., Yu, L., Wu, J., Yang, Y., Liu, Q., Yuan, Z.: Hybrid profilometry using a single monochromatic multi-frequency pattern. Opt. Express **25**(22), 27195–27209 (2017)
17. Xiang, S., Yu, L., Chen, C.W.: No-reference depth assessment based on edge misalignment errors for t + d images. IEEE Trans. Image Process. **25**, 1479–1494 (2016)
18. Yang, Y., Li, B., Li, P., Liu, Q.: A two-stage clustering based 3D visual saliency model for dynamic scenarios. IEEE Trans. Multimedia **21**(4), 809–820 (2018)
19. Yang, Y., Liu, Q., He, X.X., Liu, Z.: Cross-view multi-lateral filter for compressed multi-view depth video. IEEE Trans. Image Process. **28**, 302–315 (2019)
20. Zhang, S.: High-speed 3D shape measurement with structured light methods: a review. Opt. Lasers Eng. **106**, 119–131 (2018)
21. Zhao, M., Huang, L., Zhang, Q., Su, X., Asundi, A., Kemao, Q.: Quality-guided phase unwrapping technique: comparison of quality maps and guiding strategies. Appl. Opt. **50**(33), 6214–6224 (2011)
22. Zhong, H., Tang, J., Zhang, S., Chen, M.: An improved quality-guided phase-unwrapping algorithm based on priority queue. IEEE Geosci. Remote Sens. Lett. **8**(2), 364–368 (2011)
23. Zuo, C., Huang, L., Zhang, M., Chen, Q., Asundi, A.: Temporal phase unwrapping algorithms for fringe projection profilometry: a comparative review. Opt. Lasers Eng. **85**, 84–103 (2016)

Extraction of Multi-class Multi-instance Geometric Primitives from Point Clouds Using Energy Minimization

Liang Wang[1](✉), Biying Yan[1], Fuqing Duan[2], and Ke Lu[3]

[1] Faculty of Information Technology, Beijing University of Technology, Beijing 100124, China
wangliang@bjut.edu.cn
[2] School of Artificial Intelligence, Beijing Normal University, Beijing 100875, China
[3] School of Engineering Sciences, University of Chinese Academy of Sciences, Beijing 100049, China

Abstract. Point clouds play a vital role in self-driving vehicle, interactive media and other applications. However, how to efficiently and robustly extract multiple geometric primitives from point clouds is still a challenge. In this paper, a novel algorithm for extracting multiple instances of multiple classes of geometric primitives is proposed. First, a new sampling strategy is applied to generate model hypotheses. Next, an energy function is formulated from the view of point labelling. Then, an improved optimization technique is used to minimize the energy. After that, refine hypotheses and parameters. Iterate this process until the energy does not decrease. Finally, multi-class multi-instance of geometric primitives are correctly and robustly extracted. Different to existing methods, the type and number of models can be automatically determined. Experimental results validate the proposed algorithm.

Keywords: Point cloud · Geometric primitives extraction · Multi-class multi-instance · Energy minimization

1 Introduction

The rise of artificial intelligence makes unmanned driving, 3D television-based immersive interactive media and other 3D point cloud-based intelligent applications progress rapidly. Geometric primitives contained in 3D point clouds can further improve these applications by providing not only meaningful and concise abstraction of 3D data [1] but also the possibility of high-level interaction for users. However, how to efficiently and robustly extract multiple geometric primitives from point clouds is still a challenge. The core of the problem is to robustly detect each geometric primitive and accurately fit their parameters from the

Supported by NSFC under Grant No. 61772050 and the Joint Research Fund in Astronomy (U1531242) under cooperative agreement between NSFC and CAS.

Y. M. Ro et al. (Eds.): MMM 2020, LNCS 11962, pp. 279–290, 2020.
https://doi.org/10.1007/978-3-030-37734-2_23

mixture of lots of 3D points supporting an unknown number of instances of an unknown number of classes of geometric primitives and outliers. Although some methods have been proposed, they mainly focus on the problems of one-instance of one-class or multi-instance of one-class. However, point clouds in real scenario generally contain multi-instance of multi-class of geometric primitives.

The existing methods of geometric primitives extraction from 3D point clouds can be classified into three categories: the model-based, the cluster-based and the graph-based methods. The model-based methods mainly rely on the RANdom SAmple Consensus (RANSAC) technique [2]. It can extract single model from data even the outlier rate, the ratio of outliers with respect to the total data, is more than 50%. Sequential-RANSAC [3,4] can sequentially extract multiple instances of one type of geometric primitives. However, accumulated errors inevitably lead to bad results in later stage. MultiRANSAC [5] can simultaneously extract multiple instances of one specific class of model. However, the number of instances has to be known a priori. Most RANSAC-based methods adopt the greedy search without considering the relationship of data, which leads to a huge computational cost. The cluster-based methods are the extension of 2D clustering method [6]. As a typical representative, J-linkage [7,8] performs multi-model fitting by merging models and their inliers with small Jaccard distances, and then re-estimating new models with merged point sets. It can automatically determine the number of model instances. However, the threshold that distinguishes inliers and outliers should be manually specified in advance. In addition, it is prone to get trapped into local optimum. The graph-based methods utilize the graph to describe point cloud [9]. The PEARL algorithm [11] applies the graph-based energy minimization framework [10], which is proposed to slove the graph maximum-flow/minimum-cut problem, to 2D geometric model fitting. Then, this framework is extended to extract planes [12] and spheres [13] from 3D point clouds. This type of methods usually performs better than the above two types of methods. However, most of three types of methods can only extract multiple instances of one specific class of model. In fact, point clouds are more complex, and generally contain multiple instances of multiple classes of geometric primitives in real applications. Although multi-X [14] can first determine the number of 2D models using the Median-Shift algorithm and then label each point using the graph-based energy minimization algorithm, the number of generated hypotheses of models is generally twice of the number of points. Huge computation consumption restricts its 3D application.

In this paper, a novel energy minimization based algorithm is proposed, which can accurately and robustly extract multi-class multi-instance geometric primitives from point clouds. Inspired by the NAPSAC [15], an improved sampling strategy is first adopted to generate model hypotheses. Then, the energy function is constructed from the view of point labeling. Finally, multiple instances of multiple classes of geometric primitives are extracted with the energy minimization framework. Not only the number of instances, but also the corresponding class can be automatically determined. Different to existing methods, it takes less time and depends less on the initial hypothesis. More importantly, it can automatically revise the model hypothesis and accurately fit geometric model.

The main contributions of this paper can be summarized as follows:

1. A novel algorithm for automatically and accurately extracting multi-class multi-instance geometric primitives from point clouds is proposed.
2. A novel sampling strategy is proposed to improve the sampling accuracy and then reduce the number of sampling in the stage of hypothesis generation.
3. Time consumption is significantly reduced by establishing the neighborhood to formulate smooth term of energy function with a new KD-tree based strategy.

The rest of this paper is organized as follows. Section 2 elaborates the proposed algorithm. Extensive experiments with synthetic and real data are reported in Sect. 3. Section 4 concludes this paper.

2 The Proposed Algorithm

Given a point cloud consisting of n points, $\mathcal{P} = \{p_1, p_2, \cdots, p_n\}$, the aim is to extract all geometric primitives contained in this point cloud, $\mathcal{H}_0 = \mathcal{H}_I^P \cup \mathcal{H}_J^C \cup \mathcal{H}_K^S$, where $\mathcal{H}_I^P$, $\mathcal{H}_J^C$ and $\mathcal{H}_K^S$ represents the set of extracted planes, that of extracted cylinders and that of extracted spheres respectively, I, J and K denotes the number of instance of each class of geometric primitives. Here, only three types of geometric primitives, plane, cylinder and sphere are taken into accounts. It is straightforward to extend other types of geometric primitives. An algorithm based on the energy minimization is proposed to solve this problem via labelling each point in the point cloud. The set of initial labels corresponding to $\mathcal{H}_0$ is $\mathcal{L}_0 = \{l_1, l_2, \cdots, l_M\}$, where $M = I + J + K$. With the proposed algorithm, each point in the point cloud can be firstly assigned a label. Secondly, parameters of geometric primitives can be updated with the newly labelled inliers. After that, the model hypothesis and correspondent labels are updated. This process is iterated until the value of energy function does not decrease or termination condition is satisfied. Finally, $\tilde{M}$ geometric primitives, $\mathcal{H} = \{H_1, H_2, \cdots, H_{\tilde{M}}\}$, and their correspondent labels, $\mathcal{L} = \{l_1, l_2, \cdots, l_{\tilde{M}}\}$, are obtained as the output, where l_i is the label of the ith geometric primitive model H_i, $\tilde{M} = \tilde{I} + \tilde{J} + \tilde{K}$. Here, the model H_i is one instance of multiple classes of geometric primitives, it is a plane when $i \leq \tilde{I}$, a cylinder while $\tilde{I} < i \leq \tilde{I} + \tilde{J}$ and a sphere while $\tilde{I} + \tilde{J} < i \leq \tilde{I} + \tilde{J} + \tilde{K}$. In the following, the proposed algorithm is elaborated step by step.

2.1 Hypothesis Generation

Assumed that three types of geometric primitives, plane, cylinder and sphere, are contained in point clouds, the model of geometric primitive can be represented as $\mathbf{C} = \{\mathbf{X}, \boldsymbol{\Psi}, \boldsymbol{\theta}, \varphi\}$, where $\mathbf{X}$ is the minimal support set for one sampling of a certain class of geometric primitives, $\boldsymbol{\Psi}$ is the model generation function, $\boldsymbol{\theta}$ is model parameter corresponding to $\boldsymbol{\Psi}$ and φ is the function of distance from one point to a model $\boldsymbol{\theta}$. The cardinality of set $\mathbf{X}$, $card(\mathbf{X})$, varies with the class of geometric primitives. We have $card(\mathbf{X}^P) = 3$ for planes, $card(\mathbf{X}^C) = 2$ for cylinders and $card(\mathbf{X}^S) = 4$ for spheres. The model generation function, $\boldsymbol{\Psi}$, and correspondent model parameter $\boldsymbol{\theta}$ can be determined as follows.

For a plane, one sample consisting of $card(\mathbf{X}^P) = 3$ points, $\mathbf{X}^P = \{\mathbf{p}_1, \mathbf{p}_2, \mathbf{p}_3\}$, is got first. Then, the normal vector of the plane, $\mathbf{n} = (\mathbf{p}_1 - \mathbf{p}_2) \times (\mathbf{p}_1 - \mathbf{p}_3)$, is computed, which corresponds to unit normal vector $\mathbf{n}_u = (a, b, c)$. Taking one arbitrary point of sampling point set $\mathbf{X}^P = \{\mathbf{p}_1, \mathbf{p}_2, \mathbf{p}_3\}$ into the plane model generation function, $\boldsymbol{\Psi}^P : ax+by+cz+d = 0$, to compute d, the model parameter $\boldsymbol{\theta}^P = (a, b, c, d)$ can be obtained. In addition, the distance function of one point $\mathbf{p}$ to a plane model $\boldsymbol{\theta}_i^P$, φ, can be computed by

$$\varphi(\mathbf{p}, \boldsymbol{\theta}_i^P) = \|\mathbf{p}\cdot[a_i^P, b_i^P, c_i^P]' + d_k^P\| \tag{1}$$

where $(a_i^P, b_i^P, c_i^P, d_i^P)$ are parameters of the ith plane.

For a cylinder, one sample consisting of $card(\mathbf{X}^C) = 2$ points, $\mathbf{X}^C = \{\mathbf{p}_1, \mathbf{p}_2\}$, and their correspondent unit normal vectors $\{\mathbf{n}_1, \mathbf{n}_2\}$, are got first. Then, the directional vector can be computed by $\mathbf{n} = \mathbf{n}_1 \times \mathbf{n}_2$. Project the line determined by point $\mathbf{p}_2$ and its unit normal vector $\mathbf{n}_2$, $\mathbf{p}_2 + t\cdot\mathbf{n}_2 = \mathbf{0}$, onto the plane passing through point $\mathbf{p}_1$ with normal vector $\mathbf{n}$. The intersection point of the projected line and the line $\mathbf{p}_1 + t\cdot\mathbf{n}_1 = \mathbf{0}$ on the plane passing through point $\mathbf{p}_1$ with normal vector $\mathbf{n}$, $\mathbf{p}_0$, is one point on the axis of the cylinder. The radius of the cylinder can be computed by $r = \|\mathbf{p}_0 - \mathbf{p}_1\|$. So the model parameters of the cylinder, $\boldsymbol{\theta}^C = (\mathbf{p}_0, \mathbf{n}, r)$, are obtained. In addition, the distance function of one point $\mathbf{p}$ to a cylinder model $\boldsymbol{\theta}_j^C$, φ, can be computed by

$$\varphi(\mathbf{p}, \boldsymbol{\theta}_j^C) = \|\frac{\|(\mathbf{p} - \mathbf{p}_{0j}^C)\times\mathbf{n}_j^C\|}{\|\mathbf{n}_j^C\|} - r_j^C\| \tag{2}$$

where $(\mathbf{p}_{0j}^C, \mathbf{n}_j^C, r_j^C)$ are parameters of the jth cylinder.

For a sphere, one sample, $\mathbf{X}^S = \{\mathbf{p}_1, \mathbf{p}_2, \mathbf{p}_3, \mathbf{p}_4\}$, contains $card(\mathbf{X}^S) = 4$ points. The model function $(x-a)^2 + (y-b)^2 + (z-c)^2 = r^2$ can be computed with the least-squares algorithm, where (a, b, c) is the sphere center and r is the sphere radius. So parameters of the sphere $\boldsymbol{\theta}^P = (a, b, c, r)$ are obtained. In addition, the function of distance from one point $\mathbf{p}$ to a sphere model $\boldsymbol{\theta}_k^S$, φ, can be computed by

$$\varphi(\mathbf{p}, \boldsymbol{\theta}_k^S) = \|\|\mathbf{p} - [a_k^S, b_k^S, c_k^S]'\| - r_k^S\| \tag{3}$$

where (a_k^S, b_k^S, c_k^S) and r_k^S is the center and radius of the kth sphere respectively.

Sampling Strategy. Points in point cloud are distributed unevenly. In addition, it is inevitable that points are contaminated by noise in real applications. All of these make it hard to effectively generate good model hypothesis. It is worth noting that the probability that points in the neighborhood of one sampling point belong to the same model is high. For example, if four points are sampled in a certain neighborhood, the probability that four points of this sample are simultaneously on the surface of a sphere is higher than the case that four points are randomly selected in the whole volume of point cloud. So inspired by the NAPSAC algorithm [15], we adopt the following sampling strategy. At first, one point is randomly selected in the point cloud. Then, the other three points are randomly selected in the neighborhood of the first selected point. Finally, these four points are used to fit the sphere model. In this case, the obtained model hypothesis takes not only the neighborhood a prior but also the model a prior into account. So this strategy improves the sampling accuracy and efficiency.

Generating Hypothesis. Using the proposed sampling strategy, I_0 hypotheses of plane model $\mathcal{H}_{I_0}^{C}$, J_0 hypotheses of cylinder model $\mathcal{H}_{J_0}^{C}$ and K_0 hypotheses of sphere model $\mathcal{H}_{K_0}^{S}$ are obtained with the above setting. The generated initial model hypotheses and correspondent labels are $\mathcal{H}_0 = \mathcal{H}_{I_0}^{P} \cup \mathcal{H}_{J_0}^{C} \cup \mathcal{H}_{K_0}^{S}$ and $\mathcal{L}_0 = \{l_1, l_2, \cdots, l_M\}$ respectively.

2.2 Formulation and Optimization of Energy Function

Following the graph-based energy minimization framework, the energy function can be defined as follows.

$$E(\mathcal{L}_0) = \sum_{\mathbf{p}\in\mathcal{P}} \varphi_{\mathbf{p}}(\boldsymbol{\theta}_{l(\mathbf{p})}, \mathbf{p}) + \lambda \sum_{(\mathbf{p},\mathbf{q})\in\mathcal{N}} \omega_{\mathbf{pq}} \delta(l_{\mathbf{p}} \neq l_{\mathbf{q}}) + f(\mathcal{L}_0) \tag{4}$$

where the first term is the data term measuring the residual error that the distance between points to the geometrical model corresponding to assigned label, the second term is the smooth term measuring the cost that neighbor points are labelled different labels, the third term is label term measuring the number of labels to prevent over-fitting or under-fitting.

Data Term. The first term of Eq. (4),

$$E_{Data} = \sum_{\mathbf{p}\in\mathcal{P}} \varphi_{\mathbf{p}}(\boldsymbol{\theta}_{l(\mathbf{p})}, \mathbf{p}) \tag{5}$$

is the data term. Take the model parameters $\boldsymbol{\theta}_{l(\mathbf{p})}$ and point coordinate $\mathbf{p}$ into this equation, the function of distance from one point to a model $\boldsymbol{\theta}$, $\varphi_{\mathbf{p}}(\boldsymbol{\theta}_{l(\mathbf{p})}, \mathbf{p})$ can be computed. The shorter the distance $\varphi_{\mathbf{p}}$ is, the more the possibility that point $\mathbf{p}$ is labelled to label $l(\mathbf{p})$ correspondent to model $H(l(\mathbf{p}))$ is. Otherwise, the longer the distance is, the less the possibility. The distance function can be chosen from Eqs. (1), (2) and (3) according to the specific type of geometric primitives which the hypothetic model belongs to.

Smooth Term. The smooth term of energy function takes the pairwise energy

$$E_{Smooth} = \lambda \sum_{(\mathbf{p},\mathbf{q})\in\mathcal{N}} \omega_{\mathbf{pq}} \delta(l_{\mathbf{p}} \neq l_{\mathbf{q}}) \tag{6}$$

where $\mathcal{N}$ denotes a certain neighborhood. Different from the original PEARL algorithm, here a KD-tree based strategy is introduced to determine the neighborhood of one point in the point cloud. In addition,

$$\omega_{\mathbf{pq}} = exp^{\frac{-\|\mathbf{p}-\mathbf{q}\|^2}{\tau^2}} \tag{7}$$

is a penalty function of discontinuity for each pair of neighboring points $(\mathbf{p}, \mathbf{q})$, where τ is a constant coefficient which generally varies from 3 to 5 for different point clouds in real applications. $\delta(\cdot)$ equals to 1 if the specified condition in the bracket holds, otherwise 0. λ is a weight coefficient of smooth term, which takes the value from 0.5 to 2.5 in real applications.

Label Term. The third term in Eq. (4) denotes the label energy,

$$f(\mathcal{L}_0) = h{\cdot}card(\mathcal{L}_0) + \eta \tag{8}$$

where $card(\mathcal{L}_0)$ is the cardinality of label set, which equals to the number of labels, h is the weight coefficient of the label term, which usually takes value from 10 to 20, and η generally takes 10 times of the outlier rate. This term measures the number of labels to avoid over-fitting that few points with noise are fitted to mistaken models.

Once the energy function is defined, the improved energy minimization algorithm [13] can be applied to solve the following energy minimization problem

$$\min_{\mathcal{L}_0} E(\mathcal{L}_0) = \min_{\mathcal{L}_0} \sum_{\mathbf{p}\in\mathcal{P}} \varphi_{\mathbf{p}}(\boldsymbol{\theta}_{l(\mathbf{p})}, \mathbf{p}) + \lambda \sum_{(\mathbf{p},\mathbf{q})\in\mathcal{N}} \omega_{\mathbf{pq}}\delta(l_{\mathbf{p}}{\neq}l_{\mathbf{q}}) + f(\mathcal{L}_0) \tag{9}$$

Then, each point of point cloud is optimally assigned a label of $\mathcal{L}_0$ or outlier.

2.3 Parameter Refinement

Once the energy is minimized, each point in the point cloud is labelled as an outlier or an inlier of a specific instance of a type of geometric primitives. Generally, some wrong hypotheses would have few support set, which means that the label l_i correspondent to the wrong hypothesis will be assigned to few points or even none. In addition, some similar hypotheses are correspondent to one hypothesis. So some wrong hypotheses should be removed, and some similar hypotheses could be merged. After the hypotheses removing and merging, parameters of the current hypotheses should be refined using the least-squares estimation. Finally, refined hypotheses $\tilde{\mathcal{H}}_0$ and correspondent label set $\tilde{\mathcal{L}}_0$ are obtained.

2.4 Iterative Optimization

After refining the hypotheses and labels, current outliers are taken as input to generate new initial hypotheses. The union of the refined hypotheses $\tilde{\mathcal{H}}_0$ and the new initial hypotheses is taken as initial values of energy function to perform energy minimization. With this operation, new labels can be generated and added into the label set, which can overcome the deficiency of the original graph-based energy minimization algorithm that the number of initially generated hypotheses is too small to omit some instances of geometric primitives due to the limited sampling number. Iteratively operate the above process until the energy does not decrease. Finally, parameters and support set of multiple instances of multiple classes of geometric primitives are obtained.

The proposed algorithm can be summarized as follows.

1. Generate initial hypotheses of multiple instances of multiple classes, $\mathcal{H}_0 = \mathcal{H}_I^P \cup \mathcal{H}_J^C \cup \mathcal{H}_K^S$, and correspondent initial label set, $\mathcal{L}_0 = \{l_1, l_2, \cdots, l_M\}$, of geometric primitives by sampling.
2. Take the initial hypotheses and labels into energy minimization problem Eq.(9), then compute the current optimized labelling results by minimizing the energy function.
3. Refine the hypotheses and their correspondent labels and parameters.
4. If the energy does not decrease, terminate the operation, otherwise jump to step 2 and iterates the operation.

3 Experiments

Lots of experiments with synthetic and real data are performed. All of them consistently validate the proposed algorithm. Some of them are reported here.

3.1 Experiment with Synthetic Data

In this experiment, a point cloud simulating measurements of a 3D laser scanner is synthesized, which contains two planes, one cylinder and one sphere. In addition, outliers accounting for 50% of all 3D points are added. The proposed algorithm is applied to extract geometric primitives. To make a comparison, the Sequential-RANSAC and J-Linkage are also applied. To evaluate algorithms, the correction rate of extracted inliers is taken as a measure.

Table 1. The accuracy of inliers extracted by different algorithms with 50% outliers.

Method	Plane 1	Plane 2	Cylinder	Sphere
The proposed	99.55%	99.55%	93.08%	89.77%
Sequential-RANSAC	100%	100%	58.16%	100%
J-Linkage	100%	100%	–	–

Table 1 gives the correction rates of three algorithms. Table 2 shows the ground truth and estimation of fitted parameters. Figure 1 demonstrates the results of geometric primitives extraction. Figure 1(a) gives the result of the proposed algorithm, from which we can see that the proposed algorithm can correctly and simultaneously extracted all instances of all classes of geometric primitives. Figure 1(b) shows the result of the Sequential-RANSAC, which needs

Table 2. Parameters of extracted geometric primitives with 50% outliers.

Method	Plane 1	Plane 2	Cylinder	Sphere
Ground truth	$(0, -1, 0, 10)$	$(0, -1, 0, -20)$	$(0, 0, -5)$	$(-10, -10, 0)$
			$(0, 0, 1)$ 5	5
The proposed	$(0, -1, 0, 10)$	$(0, -1, 0, -20)$	$(0.12, 0.01, -5.08)$	$(-10, -10, 0)$
			$(-0.01, 0.00, 1.00)$ 4.98	5
Sequential-RA	$(0, -1, 0, 10)$	$(0, -1, 0, -20)$	$(-0.02, 0.00, -10.72)$	$(-10, -10, 0)$
-NSAC			$(-0.02, 0.00, 5.00)$ 5.02	5
J-Linkage	$(0, -1, 0, 10)$	$(0, -1, 0, -20)$	–	–

manual intervention to specify the type and number of geometric primitives in advance and has poor robustness. Figure 1(c) presents the result of the J-Linkage, which can only correctly and simultaneously extracted multiple planes. Although the J-Linkage has a high correctness rate, it is quite time consuming and heavily depends on the threshold of inliers. From these results, it can be seen that the proposed algorithm is superior in accuracy and robustness.

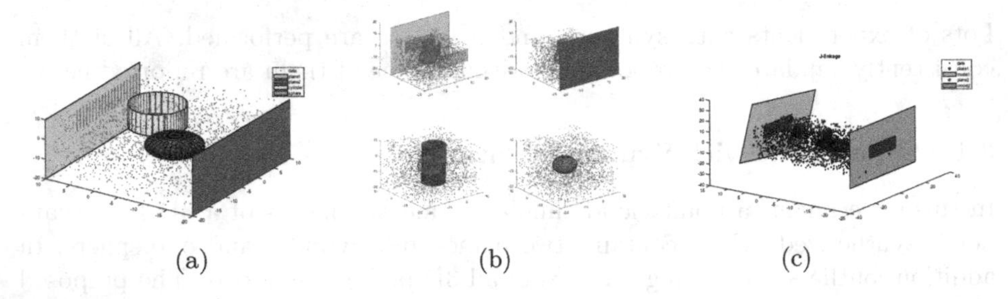

Fig. 1. Results of experiments with synthetic point cloud. (a) The proposed algorithm. (b) Sequential-RANSAC. (c) J-Linkage.

To validate the proposed KD-tree based strategy of establishing the neighborhood relationship, some typical execution runtime of establishing the neighborhood relationship are recorded during the operation of experiments with synthetic data (see Table 3). To make a comparison, the correspondent execution runtime of the start-of-the-art method, the PEARL, are also given in Table 3. It can be seen that the proposed strategy significantly reduces the runtime.

Table 3. Comparison of the runtime of the neighborhood establishing module.

Number of points	PEARL (s)	The proposed (s)
386	0.40	0.04
10160	5.96	0.09
10849	6.16	0.10

3.2 Experiment with Real Point Cloud

In this experiment, 307200 points are captured with a Microsoft Kinect sensor in indoor environment of our lab. There remain 13197 points after voxel filtering (see Fig. 2). The proposed algorithm, the Sequential-RANSAC algorithm and the J-Linkage algorithm are applied to extract geometric primitives from the point cloud after filtering. Figures 3, 4 and 5 gives the results of three algorithms respectively. Parameters of extract geometric primitives are shown in Table 4. To quantitatively evaluate three algorithms, some geometrical measures are used to make a comparison (see Table 5).

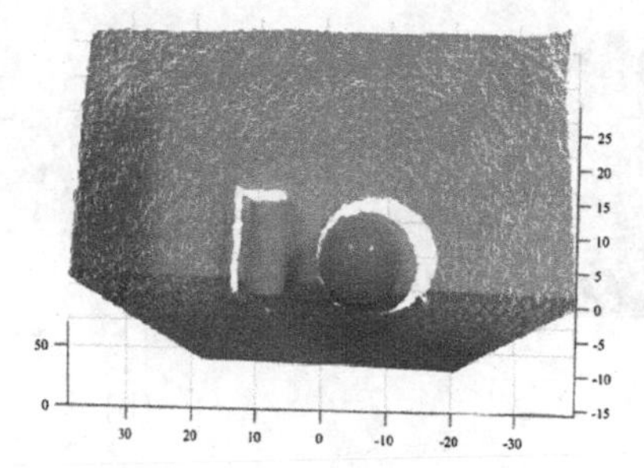

Fig. 2. The original point cloud with texture of indoor environment of our lab.

Table 4. Parameters of geometric primitives extracted from real point cloud.

	The proposed	Sequential-RANSAC	J-Linkage
Plane 1	(−0.06, 0.99, 0.12, 18.37)	(−0.05, 0.99, −0.13, 18.79)	(−0.05, 0.99, −0.13, 18.78)
Inliers	4340	4393	4581
Plane 2	(0.01, −0.12, 0.99, −65.25)	(0.01, 0.10, 1.00, −65.30)	(0.01, −0.12, 0.06, −64.96)
Inliers	7727	6781	3034
Cylinder	(9.02, −10.41, 62.83)	–	–
	(0.14, 0.08, 0.99) 3.62	–	–
Inliers	396	–	–
Sphere	(−6.80, −4.10, 58.16) 7.39	(−7.32, −3.89, 59.56) 8.48	–
Inliers	711	639	–

Results of the proposed algorithm are shown in Fig. 3, where Fig. 3(a) gives the results of multiple geometric primitives extraction and Fig. 3(b) the inliers of each extracted instance. It can be seen that the proposed algorithm can correctly and simultaneously extract all instances of all classes of geometric primitives and their correspondent inliers. Figure 4 gives the results of the Sequential-RANSAC step by step. The Sequential-RANSAC needs manual intervention to specify the type and number of geometric primitives in advance. It is also poor in robustness. For example, it fails to extract the cylinder due to too few points on the cylinder surface. Figure 5 gives results of the J-Linkage. It can only extract two planes.

Table 5. Comparison of some measurements in real point cloud.

	Ground truth	The proposed	Sequential-RANSAC	J-Linkage
Angle between two walls	90°	89.85°	86.47°	85.99°
Radius of cylinder	11.19 cm	10.84 cm	–	–
Radius of sphere	22.39 cm	22.16 cm	25.43 cm	–

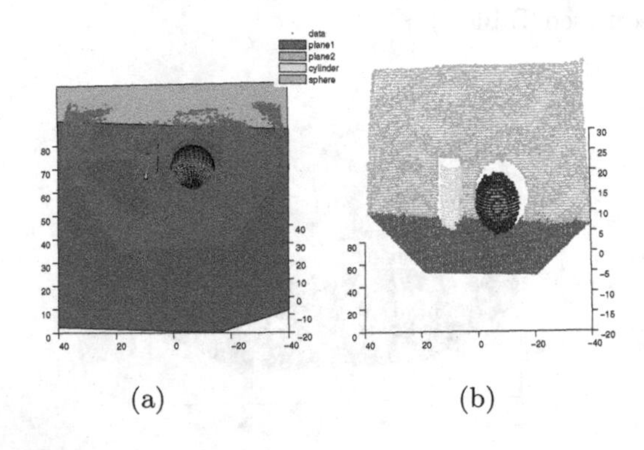

(a) (b)

Fig. 3. Experimental results of the proposed algorithm with real data.

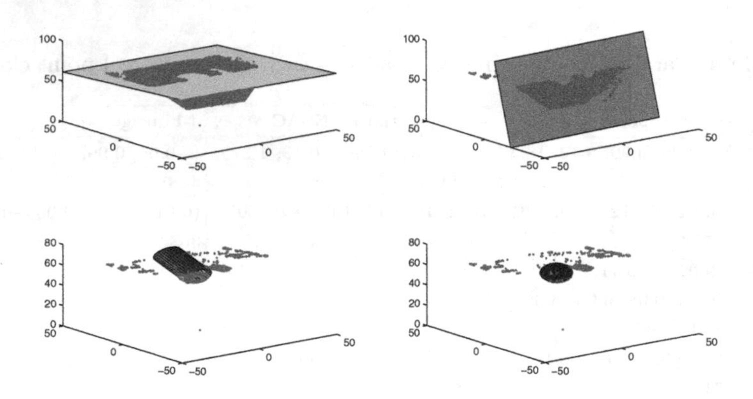

Fig. 4. Experimental results of the Sequential-RANSAC with real data.

Although the J-Linkage can extract multiple instance of geometric primitives, it is quite time consuming and poor in robustness. For example, the inliers number of plane 2 is incomplete (see Fig. 5 and Table. 4). From Table. 4, we can see that the error of the angle between two planes is only 0.15° for the proposed algorithm, which is dramatically superior to the other two algorithms. The advantage of the proposed algorithm can also be seen from the radius of the extracted cylinder and the radius of the extracted sphere.

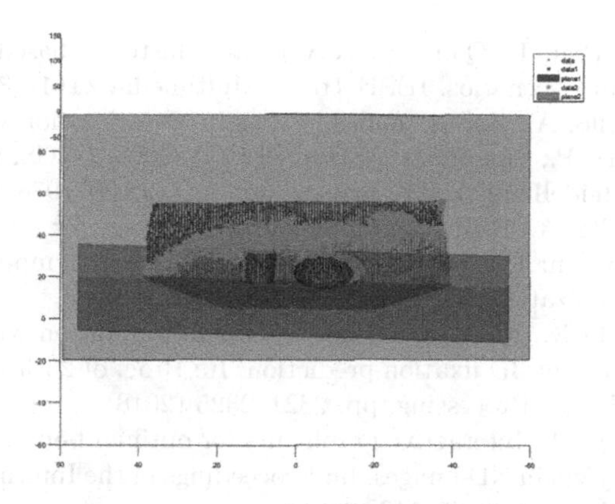

Fig. 5. Experimental results of the J-Linkage with real data.

4 Conclusion

In this paper, a novel energy minimization based algorithm for multi-class multi-instance geometric primitives extraction is proposed. By analyzing the distribution of points in point cloud, a new sampling strategy is first applied to generate model hypotheses, which can improve the sampling accuracy and then reduce the number of sampling. Next, the energy function is constructed from the view of point labeling. Then, the graph-based energy minimization technique is used to optimally assign labels to points. During the process, a KD-tree based strategy is proposed to establish the neighborhood to significantly reduce runtime. After that, refine the hypotheses and parameters. Iterate this process until the energy does not decrease. Finally, models of multi-class multi-instance geometric primitives are correctly and robustly extracted. In comparison with existing methods, it can automatically determine the type and number of model while ensuring small running time. Experimental results validate the proposed algorithm.

References

1. Rao, Y., Fan, B., et al.: Extreme feature regions detection and accurate quality assessment for point-cloud 3D reconstruction. IEEE Access **7**, 37757–37769 (2019)
2. Fischler, M., Bolles, R.: Random sample consensus: a paradigm for model fitting with applications to image analysis and automated cartography. Commun. ACM **24**(6), 381–395 (1981)
3. Vincent, E., Laganire, R.: Detecting planar homographies in an image. In: Proceedings of the 2nd International Symposium on Image and Signal Processing and Analysis, pp. 182–187 (2001)
4. Kanazawa, Y., Kawakami, H.: Detection of planar regions with uncalibrated stereo using distributions of feature points. In: Proceedings of the British Machine Vision Conference, pp. 247–256 (2004)
5. Zuliani, M., Kenney, C., Manjunath, B.: The multiransac algorithm and its application to detect planar homographies. In: Proceedings of IEEE International Conference on Image Processing, Genova, Italy (2005)

6. You, Y., Bei, L., Pian, L., Qiong, L.: A two-stage clustering based 3D visual saliency model for dynamic scenarios. IEEE Trans. Multimedia **21**(4), 809–820 (2019)
7. Toldo, R., Fusiello, A.: Robust multiple structures estimation with J-Linkage. In: Forsyth, D., Torr, P., Zisserman, A. (eds.) ECCV 2008. LNCS, vol. 5302, pp. 537–547. Springer, Heidelberg (2008). https://doi.org/10.1007/978-3-540-88682-2_41
8. Toldo, R., Fusiello, A.: Real-time incremental J-Linkage for robust multiple structures estimation. In: Proceedings of the International Symposium on 3D Data Processing, Visualization and Transmission (2010)
9. Li B., Liu Q., Shi X., Yang Y.: Graph-based saliency fusion with superpixel-level belief propagation for 3D fixation prediction. In: Proc. of 25th IEEE International Conference on Image Processing, pp. 2321–2325 (2018)
10. Boykov, Y., Jolly, M.: Interactive graph cuts for optimal boundary and region segmentation of objects in ND images. In: Proceedings of the International Conference on Computer Vision, pp. 105–112 (2001)
11. Isack, H., Boykov, Y.: Energy-based geometric multi-model fitting. Int. J. Comput. Vis. **97**(2), 123–147 (2012)
12. Wang, L., Shen, C., Duan, F., Guo, P.: Energy-based multi-plane detection from 3D point clouds. In: Hirose, A., Ozawa, S., Doya, K., Ikeda, K., Lee, M., Liu, D. (eds.) ICONIP 2016. LNCS, vol. 9948, pp. 715–722. Springer, Cham (2016). https://doi.org/10.1007/978-3-319-46672-9_80
13. Wang, L., Shen, C., Duan, F., Lu, K.: Energy-based automatic recognition of multiple spheres in three-dimensional point cloud. Pattern Recogn. Lett. **83**(3), 287–293 (2016)
14. Barath, D., Matas, J.: Multi-class model fitting by energy minimization and mode-seeking. In: Ferrari, V., Hebert, M., Sminchisescu, C., Weiss, Y. (eds.) ECCV 2018. LNCS, vol. 11220, pp. 229–245. Springer, Cham (2018). https://doi.org/10.1007/978-3-030-01270-0_14
15. Myatt, D., Torr, P., Nasuto, S., et al.: NAPSAC: high noise, high dimensional robust estimation. In: Proceedings of British Machine Vision Conference, pp. 458–467 (2002)

Similarity Graph Convolutional Construction Network for Interactive Action Recognition

Xiangyu Sun, Qiong Liu(✉), and You Yang

School of Electronic Information and Communications,
Huazhong University of Science and Technology, Wuhan, China
q.liu@hust.edu.cn

Abstract. Interaction action recognition is a challenging problem in the research of computer vision. Skeleton-based action recognition shows great performance in recent years, but the non-Euclidean distance structure of the skeleton brings a huge challenge to the design of deep learning neural network. When meeting interaction action recognition, research in the previous study is based on a fixed skeleton graph, capturing only information about local body movements in a single action and do not deal with the relationship between two or more people. In this article, we present a similarity graph convolutional network that contains two-person interaction information. This model can represent the relationship between two people. Simultaneously, for different body parts (such as head and hand), the relationship can be handled. The model has two construction modes, a skeleton graph and a similarity graph, and the features from the two composition modes is better fused by the hypergraph. Similarity graph is obtained from a two-step construction. First, an encoder is designed, which is aimed to map different characteristics of one joint to a same vector space. Second, we calculate the similarity between different joints to construct the similarity graph. Follow the steps above, similarity graph can indicate the relationship between two people in details. We perform experiments on the NTU RGB+D dataset and verify the effectiveness of our model. The result shows that our approach outperforms the state-of-the-art methods and similarity graph can solve the relationship modeling problem in interactive action recognition.

Keywords: Interactive action recognition · Skeleton-based · Similarity graph convolutional network

1 Introduction

Interactive action recognition has been a popular research in computer vision with applications in human computer interaction, virtual reality, video surveillance and so on. It plays a fundamental and important role, with the purpose of processing interactive actions between different persons from videos. In recent

Y. M. Ro et al. (Eds.): MMM 2020, LNCS 11962, pp. 291–303, 2020.
https://doi.org/10.1007/978-3-030-37734-2_24

years, skeleton-based action recognition is attracting increasing interests. Skeleton is robust to variations of viewpoints, body scales and motion speeds. As a high level representation of human body, skeleton-based action recognition has attracted more and more attention and provides valuable research ideas.

For interactive action recognition, deep learning is widely used and various networks have been exploited, such as graph networks [3,13,21,23]. The type of skeleton data is non euclidean distance [1], while RGB and depth image are euclidean distance and graph network is applied well to process this kind of data. With the advantage in non-euclidean data, more skeleton-based action recognition model is designed by graph neural network. To deal with interactive action recognition, there are methods including interactive recognition [15] and group activity recognition [6,20]. As mentioned above, a person or a subject is regraded as a whole feature and the final recognition result is group activity. The mentioned research do not analysis the interaction between body parts, so how to design construction of graph network to process the interaction between persons is still a challenging work, especially with skeleton data structure. There are still many problems in the construction of the graph worth researching.

To process the skeleton data with the graph convolution network, in [21], a novel model of dynamic skeletons called Spatial-Temporal Graph Convolutional Networks (ST-GCN), which moves beyond the limitations of previous methods by automatically learning both the spatial and temporal patterns from data, is proposed. In [16], a novel Attention Enhanced Graph Convolutional LSTM Network(AGC-LSTM), which can capture discriminative features in spatial configuration and temporal dynamics and explore the co-occurrence relationship between spatial and temporal domains, is proposed. However, the above two articles are aimed at processing the relation between spatial and temporal domain. The graph applied in training model only includes skeleton connection information in one person, without interaction information between different person. In [6], group of activity is recognized with whole action for each person. However, without scene and subject information, skeleton data can not recognize in the same way, and actions like point finger to each other between two persons are not recognized in such research. They can not describe the unconnected parts of the body well, so actions like point finger, giving objects and punch, can not get a great performance. For example, when classify neck pain or clapping, it can not describe the subtle contact between two hands and neck. The researches mentioned above have not processed the relationship between parts of body. However, in recent years, similarity graph has a potent to overcome the relationship between different subjects. Similarity graph modeling can describe the relationship between different joints by mapping different characteristics of one joint to a same vector space and further expressing the relationship between two people in details. For the interactive problem in action recognition, this kind of method to construct a graph have not been tried.

Motivated by this, we propose similarity graph convolution architecture to define the relation of different joints in mutual action to further improve the graph construction of skeleton data for stronger expressive power. The connection in graph is redesigned to express the relation from multi-person. After getting the relation from mutual action, the input and the similarity graph go through a spatio-temporal graph convolutional network to increase the performance for mutual action. Thus making a contribution to interactive action recognition.

In this work, our contributions can be described as follows:

We propose a novel graph convolutional model for skeleton-based interactive action recognition, which attempts to process interaction information between mutual action. With the construction graph of each joint, the method can distinguish the relationship between the details in the body part, rather than the relationship between whole persons.

2 Related Work

Interactive Action Recognition. Interactive action recognition can rely on the help of scenes and objects. For recognizing human and object interactions, in [5], they hypothesis that the appearance of a person is a powerful cue for localizing the objects they are interacting with. However, the interaction between people and objects cannot be transferred to the interaction recognition between people. And in [15], they propose a novel hierarchical long short-term concurrent memory (H-LSTCM) to model the long-term inter-related dynamics among a group of persons for recognizing the human interactions. In [6], relational representations of each person are created based on their connections in the graph. Both of them are aimed at the group of activity, ignoring the details between parts of body. For the action like pointing to each other and punching, the direct relationship between the two hands is also very important. These examples have emphasized the importance of modeling the joints within parts of human bodies. Similarity graph can solve this problem well by representing the relationship between joints.

Neural Networks on Graphs. In recent years, graph-based models have attracted a lot of attention due to the effective representation for the graph structure data. The principle of constructing graph convolutional networks on graph generally follows two streams: the spectral perspective [2,7] and the spatial perspective [9,11,12]. With the applying on graph to process action recognition based on skeleton, more and more people consider in structure of the graph. For example, Kipf et al. [7] introduce Spectral GCNs for semi-supervised classification on graph-structured data. In [3], a generalized graph convolutional neural networks (GGCN) is represented for skeleton-based action recognition, which is aimed to capture the relationship between single body part via spectral graph theory. And [23] proposes to develop convolutions over graph edges that correspond to bones in human skeleton. With the development of graph network, using the graph to construct the relationship is suitable for non-euclidean distance structure of skeleton, but they do not process the association between different people, just the connection between body parts in single person. Similarity graph differentiates from previous approaches in that it can describe interaction

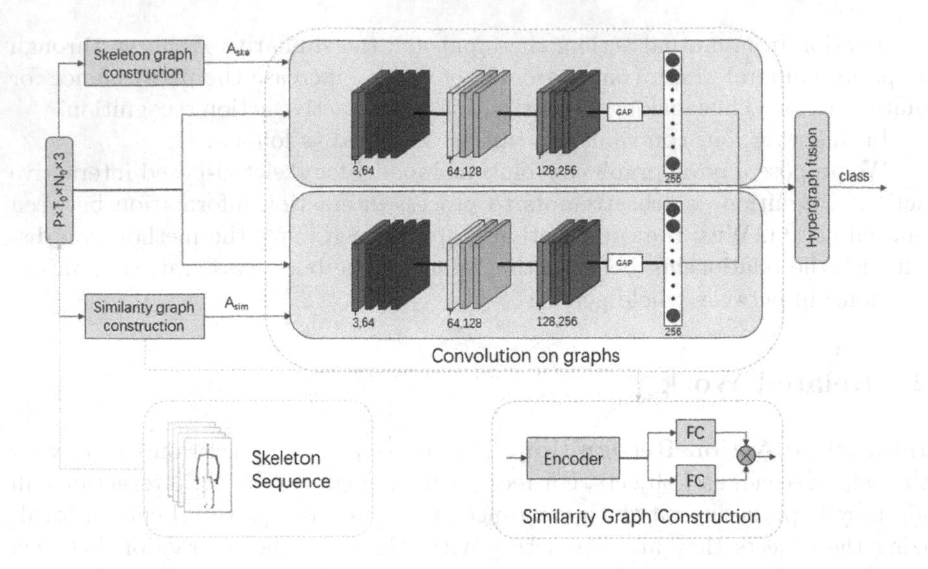

Fig. 1. The framework of the proposed recognition method.

between both of body part in single person and different persons by constructing similarity graph in training network, and the model is potent to learn better action representations.

3 Similarity Graph Convolutional Networks

3.1 The Architecture of Proposed Model

To solve the problem in interactive action recognition, the framework is divided into two streams, corresponding to skeleton graph and similarity graph. The input is a skeleton-based action sequence organized as $P \times T_0 \times N_0 \times 3$ tensor, where P is the number of actors in each sequence, T_0 is the number of frames, N_0 is the number of joints in each frame, and 3 means the dimension of x, y, z coordinates. In order to construct the similarity graph, we firstly use an encoder and two full connected layer (FC). Encoder is a method to represent different joints in the form of vectors and it is illustrated in Sect. 3.3. The affinity between different joints is measured in the feature space, which is used to construct the similarity graph. We then use skeleton method in [21] to construct the skeleton graph. A_{ske} and A_{sim}, which will be used in convolutions on graphs, represent skeleton and similarity construction graph respectively. In convolution on graphs, the two numbers under the layers are input channels and output channels. The input and output channels are same in other layers. Each layer with different input and output channels uses a temporal stride 2 to reduce the sequence length. GAP is a global average pooling operation, and the output layer is 256. Finally, the multi-person graph network and skeleton graph network will be trained, then apply the fusion of hypergraph to get the classification score for classes. We have composed these methods into the framework shown in Fig. 1.

3.2 Construction of Skeleton Graph

Notations. We consider a graph as $\mathcal{G}(\mathcal{V}, \mathcal{E}, \mathcal{A})$ composed of a vertex set $\mathcal{V}$ of cardinality $|\mathcal{V}| =$ n, an edge set $\mathcal{E}$ connecting vertices, and a weighted adjacency matrix $\mathcal{A}$, where $a_{i,j}$ is the weight assigned to the edge (i, j) connecting vertices i and j. In the skeleton graph, $a_(i, j) = 1$ if the $i - th$ and the $j - th$ joints are connected and 0 otherwise. However in similarity graph, we assume non-negative weights, *i.e.*, $a_{i,j} \geq 0$, and the adjacency matrix can be calculated automatically in our model. In similarity graph, each joint is treated as a vertex in graph, and each edge is used to measure the relationship between them.

Skeleton Graph. ST-GCN [21] consists of a series of blocks. Each block is composed of a spatial convolution followed by a temporal convolution. The key component of the ST-GCN is the spatial graph convolution kernel, which is constructed by the connection of joints. The spatial graph convolution is

$$f_{out} = \sum_{p} M_p \circ A_p f_{in} W_p \tag{1}$$

where $f_{in} \in R^{n \times d_{in}}$ is the input features of all joints in one frame, $f_{out} \in R^{n \times d_{out}}$ is the output features obtained from spatial graph convolution, $A_p = D_p^{-1/2} A D_p^{-1/2}$ is the normalized adjacent matrix for each partition group, $\circ$ denotes the Hadamard product, $M_p \in R^{n \times n}$ and $W_p \in R^{n \times d_{out}}$ are trainable weights for each partition group to capture edge weights and feature importance, respectively.

3.3 Construction of Similarity Graph

Different Characteristics Problem Oriented Encoder Design. To map different characteristics in one same joint to same vector space, we design an encoder. The obtained vector brings convenience for calculating similarity graph. As illustrated in Fig. 2. For a given joint X_t^j of type j at time t, it can be identified by its spatial and temporal information. Spatial information is defined as its position $\mathbf{p}_{t,j} = (x_{t,j}, y_{t,j}, z_{t,j})^T$ in the 3D coordinate system, and velocity $\mathbf{v}_{t,j} = \mathbf{p}_{t,j} - \mathbf{p}_{t-1,j}$. Both temporal information and the type of the joint are represented by a one hot vector as $f_t \in R^T, j_j \in R^J$, respectively. Because the four pieces of raw representations are not in the same domain, so in our model, the four pieces of information are encoded to a high dimensional space and aggregated by concatenation.

As example, we encode the position using two fully connected(FC) layers as

$$\tilde{\mathbf{p}_{t,j}} = \sigma(W_1(\sigma(W_2 p_{t,j}))) \tag{2}$$

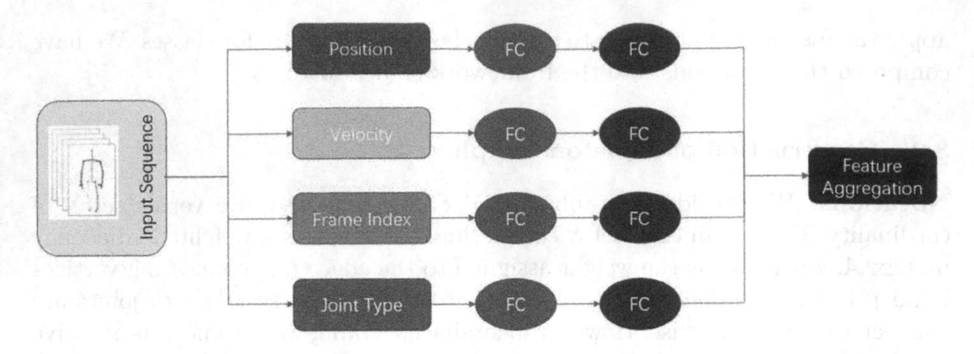

Fig. 2. Encoder. Representing skeleton sequence frames from four different aspects, then go through two full connected layers (FC) to get the feature Aggregation.

where W_1 and W_2 are two matrices, due to the huge amount of calculation, the biases are omitted to simplify the network, σ denotes the ReLU activation function.

Similarly, for the given joint X_t^j, using respective FC layers, we obtain the embedding for velocity, frame index and joint type respectively as $\tilde{v_{t,j}}, \tilde{f_t}, \tilde{j_j}$.

We describe a joint from different aspects. Then aggregate them together through concatenation to fully represent one joint as $[\tilde{\mathbf{p}_{t,j}}, \tilde{\mathbf{v}_{t,j}}, \tilde{\mathbf{f}}_t, \tilde{\mathbf{j}}_j] \in R^d$, where d is the dimension of the joint representation in our experiment.

Similarity Graph for Joints. To describe the interaction information between person in mutual action, e.g. point to each other, we construct a similarity graph. At the same time, it can describe the relationship of the unconnected parts of the body to a certain extent. For example, when classify neck pain, it can describe the contact between hands and neck, with clapping, it can describe the contact between two hands.

To model the graph with similarity, we define an adaptive method to get the all-connected graph. For different actions, the correlations between two joints are different. Thus, we build adaptive graph where the edges between different nodes depend on the content instead of human prior. We propose use spatial and temporal information going through full-connected layer to construct the graph.

The human defined graph connections are pre-defined based on only skeleton connections. This indicates the skeleton connection has already provided useful information. However, with two persons, they do not have any connections with the skeleton, so we propose to use spatial and temporal information to get the interaction between two persons.

Given a skeleton sequence with T frames, J joints and P persons, in each frame, we build a graph of $N = J \times P$ nodes. We denote the input as $Z = (z_1, ..., z_N)^T \in R^{N \times d}$. Similar to [18,19], the edge weight from the i_{th} to the j_{th} joint is represented by their similarity/affinity in the transformed space as

$$F(z_i, z_j) = \phi_1(z_i)^T \phi_2(z_j) \tag{3}$$

where ϕ_1 and ϕ_2 denote two transformation functions with each constructed by an FC layer,i.e.,$\phi_1(z_i) = W_3 z_i + b_3$ and $\phi_2(z_j) = W_4 z_j + b_4$.

By computing the affinities of all the joint pairs, we can obtain the adjacency matrix at every frame, with an average operation on temporal domain, we can obtain the adjacency matrix. Normalization using $SoftMax$ is performed on each row so that the sum of all the edge values connected to one node is 1. We denote the normalized adjacency matrix by A_{sim} for similarity graph, e.g. there are two person in the action, and the size of adjacency matrix is $2N \times 2N$ (In NTU dataset, we repeat the single action twice, so the format of single action is the same as mutual action). Then the graph is used as input to spatial-temporal convolution layer.

3.4 Convolutions on Graphs

We adopt a similarity graph convolution stream and a skeleton graph convolution stream. Different from the skeleton graph convolution, the similarity graph convolution network is adaptive. The weight of the edge in similarity graph is changed with the change of the skeleton object. The intra-body connections of joints within a single frame are represented by an adjacency matrix A_{sim} representing self-connections. In the single frame case, the convolution can be calculated in the following formula

$$f_{out} = A_{sim} f_{in} W \tag{4}$$

where A_{sim} represents one of the adjacency graph we have introduced with $2J \times 2J$ dimensions, and f_{in} is the input of skeleton frame with $2J \times d$ dimensions, and W is the weight matrix of the layer with dimension $d \times d$ in our case. Thus the output of one graph convolutional layer is still in $2J \times d$ dimensions.

Compared to the skeleton graph convolution in Equal.1, because of the adaptive updating, similarity graph do not have a mask matrix.

To combine multiple graph in graph convolutional networks, we simply extend Equal.1 as

$$f_{out} = \sum_i A_i f_{in} W_i \tag{5}$$

where A_i indicates different types of graphs, and the weights for different graphs W_i are not shared.

However, we find that the combination of two graphs (A_{sim}, A_{ske}) actually hurts the performance. The reason is that our similarity graph A_{sim} contains learnable parameters and requires back propagation for updating, while the skeleton graph A_{ske} do not require learning. Thus we train two branches of graph convolutional networks respectively, and only fuse the features we extracted from two graph convolutional networks in the end.

In order to better integrate the extracted features from the two networks, we adopt a hypergraph method [4]. Due to its high-order correlation, hypergraph can calculate the internal relations of different sequence frames during the propagation process, and construct two hypergraph by calculating the relationship between the vertices, thereby better blending the two types of features obtained by the two compositions.

4 Experiments

4.1 Dataset

The NTU RGB+D Dataset [14] is captured from 40 human subjects by 3 Microsoft Kinect v2 cameras. NTU Dataset is a large-scale dataset for RGB+D human action recognition with more than 56 thousand video samples and 4 million frames, collected from 40 distinct subjects. The dataset contains 60 different action classes including daily, mutual, and health-related actions. Each body skeleton is recorded with 25 joints. The benchmark evaluations include Cross-Subject (CS) and Cross-View (CV). In the CS evaluation, 40320 samples from 20 subjects were used for training, and the other samples for testing. In the CV evaluation, samples captured from camera 2 and 3 were used for training, while samples from camera 1 were employed for testing. In our experiment, only Cross-Subject is used.

4.2 Implementation Details

Data Processing. The skeleton data is extracted from original data. Sequence level translation based on the first frame is performed to be invariant to the initial position. If one frame contains two human skeletons, we rebuild the frame to two frames by making each frame contain one human skeleton in skeleton graph model. On the contrary, in similar graph model, we do not rebuild which contains two human skeletons. For frame which contains one human skeleton, in order to get similar graph with two persons, we repeat one frame contains one human skeleton to two same skeletons.

Network Setting. For the encoder, the neuron number is set to 64 for each FC layer. The weights of FC layers are not shared for the four types of input. Then the outputs of FC layer are concatenated to 256 dimension. Then the similar graph is calculated and used as graph in the spatio-temporal graph convolutional kernel. The graph convolution network is composed of 9 layers of spatial temporal graph convolution operators. The first three layers have 64 channels for output. The follow three layers have 128 channels for output. And the last three layers have 256 channels for output. These layers have 9 temporal kernel size.

Optimization Setting. All experiments are conducted on the Pytorch platform. We use the SGD optimizer with the initial learning rate of 0.01. The learning rate is divided by 10 when the epochs is 10 and 50. We use a weight decay of 0.001. The batch size is set to 16.

4.3 Model Analysis

In this subsection, we evaluate the improvement in NTU dataset. Our method can get the improvement classification of mutual action. At the same time, the new graph construction method do not influence the performance on single action, and it works well in single action which is recognized by the relationship between different parts of body, so we analysis confusion matrix of mutual action and part of single action.

	punch/ slap	kicking	pushing	pat on back	point finger	hugging	giving object	touch pocket	shaking hands	walking towards	walking apart
punch/slap	90.32	1.61	3.23	0.00	0.00	0.00	0.00	0.00	0.00	0.00	0.00
kicking	0.00	96.77	1.61	0.00	0.00	0.00	0.00	0.00	0.00	0.00	0.00
pushing	0.00	0.00	100.00	0.00	0.00	0.00	0.00	0.00	0.00	0.00	0.00
pat on back	6.45	0.00	0.00	91.94	0.00	0.00	0.00	1.61	0.00	0.00	0.00
point finger	11.29	0.00	0.00	0.00	88.71	0.00	0.00	0.00	0.00	0.00	0.00
hugging	0.00	0.00	0.00	0.00	0.00	100.00	0.00	0.00	0.00	0.00	0.00
giving object	0.00	0.00	0.00	0.00	0.00	0.00	98.39	0.00	1.61	0.00	0.00
touch pocket	1.61	0.00	0.00	0.00	0.00	0.00	0.00	98.39	0.00	0.00	0.00
shaking hands	0.00	0.00	0.00	0.00	0.00	0.00	1.61	3.23	95.16	0.00	0.00
walking towards	0.00	0.00	0.00	0.00	0.00	0.00	0.00	0.00	0.00	100.00	0.00
walking apart	0.00	0.00	0.00	0.00	0.00	0.00	0.00	0.00	0.00	0.00	100.00

Fig. 3. Confusion matrix of mutual action

The Performance on Mutual Action. Interaction between different persons is mainly dealt with in our model. This subsection evaluates the performance on single action and mutual action, respectively. It shows that with the improvement on mutual action, the method has great robustness on single action too.

Table 1. Experimental results on single and mutual actions in NTU dataset

Method	Result with skeleton graph [21] (%)	Our model (%)
Single action	78.72	82.94
Mutual action	89.28	96.33
All actions	80.66	85.69

In Table 1, original result is training only with skeleton graph, while the fusion results are used both skeleton graph and similarity graph. It is obvious that hypergraph can better fuse features and has the gains of 5.03% on all actions in NTU dataset. With the comparisons to skeleton graph, the fusion of similarity graph and skeleton graph has gains of 4.22% on single action and 7.05% on mutual action. Our proposed model not only has a improvement to interactive action, but also work well on single action.

Confusion Matrix of Mutual Action. In NTU dataset, there are 11 mutual actions. In Fig. 3, the performance of mutual actions is shown and most of the actions are higher than 95% except punch(slap), pat on back and point finger. Even pushing, hugging, walking towards and walking apart can be recognized accurately.

Table 2. Part of classification result with great influence. Single: a single action in NTU dataset. Mutual: a mutual action in NTU dataset.

Action	Result with skeleton graph [21] (%)	our model (%)
clapping(single)	71.86	77.46
tear up paper(single)	84.19	90.45
cheer up(single)	89.96	97.76
neck pain(single)	73.86	81.00
punch/slap(mutual)	85.20	90.32
point finger(mutual)	82.86	88.71
hugging(mutual)	92.09	100.00

Part of the Performance in Confusion Matrix. Table 2 is mainly for part of recognition performance in confusion matrix. It is obvious that whether it is single action like tear up paper, neck pain or mutual action like hugging, point finger, both of them in Table 2 have improved. For single action like neck pain, the similarity graph in our model can establish head-to-hand connection. Our model can adaptively train and obtain the weight of edge in similarity graph to represent the importance of interaction of body parts in action recognition. Mutual action, like pointing finger, is the same. With the weight of the edge increases, the hands interaction of two people can be expressed. Regardless of the interaction between the body parts or the interaction between the two persons, similar graph can get better performance.

4.4 Comparison with State-of-the-Art Method

In this part, we test on NTU dataset, which is a persuasive deep learning dataset, on the model. Then the result is compared to other state-of-the-art methods. We present the comparison with the state-of-the-art methods in Table 3. With the construction of skeleton graph and similarity graph, our performances significantly outperform the LSTM-based methods [22] by about 6.3% for cross-subject evaluation. Our model belongs to the CNN-based methods. Compared with LSTM-CNN for action recognition, our result are about 2.8% better on the NTU dataset. Compared with [23], which is aimed at constructing the graph edge convolutional neural network, the result of our model outperform by 1.0%.

Specifically, compared with the state-of-the-art and CNN-Based method ST-GCN [21], which construction graph only includes skeleton graph, our model leads to 4.2% gain in CS, which demonstrates the superiority of our method.

Table 3. Comparisons on the NTU RGB+D dataset(%)

Methods	Cross subject
Part-aware LSTM [14]	62.9
ST-LSTM + Trust Gate [10]	69.2
VA-LSTM [22]	79.4
LSTM-CNN [8]	82.9
ST-GCN [21]	81.5
SR-TSL [17]	84.8
SLHM [23]	84.7
Our model	85.7

5 Conclusion

Aiming to fully represent interaction information among different persons, we propose a similarity graph convolutional network for interactive action recognition. In our model, we focus designing the part of similarity graph. The similarity graph includes two parts. First is encoder, which maps different characteristics in one same joint to same vector space. Second is constructing the similarity graph for joint, which represent the relationship in interactive action recognition. Experiment result shows that the proposed similarity graph can get gains of 4.2% than only skeleton graph method on the challenging NTU dataset. The proposed model can get better performance in interactive action recognition and provide great help for future applications.

Acknowledgement. This work was partially supported by the National Natural Science Foundation of China (Grant No. 91848107, 61971203, and 61571204) and National Key Research and Development Program of China (Grant No. 2017YFC0806202).

References

1. Bronstein, M.M., Bruna, J., Lecun, Y., Szlam, A., Vandergheynst, P.: Geometric deep learning: going beyond euclidean data. IEEE Sig. Process. Mag. **34**(4), 18–42 (2017)
2. Defferrard, M., Bresson, X., Vandergheynst, P.: Convolutional neural networks on graphs with fast localized spectral filtering. In: Advances in Neural Information Processing Systems, pp. 3844–3852 (2016)
3. Gao, X., Hu, W., Tang, J., Pan, P., Liu, J., Guo, Z.: Generalized graph convolutional networks for skeleton-based action recognition. arXiv preprint arXiv:1811.12013 (2018)

4. Gao, Y., Wang, M., Tao, D., Ji, R., Dai, Q.: 3-D object retrieval and recognition with hypergraph analysis. IEEE Trans. Image Process. **21**(9), 4290–4303 (2012)
5. Gkioxari, G., Girshick, R., Dollár, P., He, K.: Detecting and recognizing human-object interactions. In: Proceedings of the IEEE Conference on Computer Vision and Pattern Recognition, pp. 8359–8367 (2018)
6. Ibrahim, M.S., Mori, G.: Hierarchical relational networks for group activity recognition and retrieval. In: Ferrari, V., Hebert, M., Sminchisescu, C., Weiss, Y. (eds.) ECCV 2018. LNCS, vol. 11207, pp. 742–758. Springer, Cham (2018). https://doi.org/10.1007/978-3-030-01219-9_44
7. Kipf, T.N., Welling, M.: Semi-supervised classification with graph convolutional networks. arXiv preprint arXiv:1609.02907 (2016)
8. Li, C., Wang, P., Wang, S., Hou, Y., Li, W.: Skeleton-based action recognition using LSTM and CNN. In: 2017 IEEE International Conference on Multimedia & Expo Workshops (ICMEW), pp. 585–590. IEEE (2017)
9. Li, Y., Tarlow, D., Brockschmidt, M., Zemel, R.: Gated graph sequence neural networks. arXiv preprint arXiv:1511.05493 (2015)
10. Liu, J., Shahroudy, A., Xu, D., Wang, G.: Spatio-temporal LSTM with trust gates for 3D human action recognition. In: Leibe, B., Matas, J., Sebe, N., Welling, M. (eds.) ECCV 2016. LNCS, vol. 9907, pp. 816–833. Springer, Cham (2016). https://doi.org/10.1007/978-3-319-46487-9_50
11. Monti, F., Boscaini, D., Masci, J., Rodola, E., Svoboda, J., Bronstein, M.M.: Geometric deep learning on graphs and manifolds using mixture model CNNs. In: Proceedings of the IEEE Conference on Computer Vision and Pattern Recognition, pp. 5115–5124 (2017)
12. Niepert, M., Ahmed, M., Kutzkov, K.: Learning convolutional neural networks for graphs. In: International conference on machine learning. pp. 2014–2023 (2016)
13. Seo, Y., Defferrard, M., Vandergheynst, P., Bresson, X.: Structured sequence modeling with graph convolutional recurrent networks. In: Cheng, L., Leung, A.C.S., Ozawa, S. (eds.) ICONIP 2018. LNCS, vol. 11301, pp. 362–373. Springer, Cham (2018). https://doi.org/10.1007/978-3-030-04167-0_33
14. Shahroudy, A., Liu, J., Ng, T.T., Wang, G.: NTU RGB+D: A large scale dataset for 3D human activity analysis. In: Proceedings of the IEEE Conference on Computer Vision and Pattern Recognition, pp. 1010–1019 (2016)
15. Shu, X., Tang, J., Qi, G.J., Liu, W., Yang, J.: Hierarchical long short-term concurrent memory for human interaction recognition (2018)
16. Si, C., Chen, W., Wang, W., Wang, L., Tan, T.: An attention enhanced graph convolutional LSTM network for skeleton-based action recognition. arXiv preprint arXiv:1902.09130 (2019)
17. Si, C., Jing, Y., Wang, W., Wang, L., Tan, T.: Skeleton-Based action recognition with spatial reasoning and temporal stack learning. In: Ferrari, V., Hebert, M., Sminchisescu, C., Weiss, Y. (eds.) ECCV 2018. LNCS, vol. 11205, pp. 106–121. Springer, Cham (2018). https://doi.org/10.1007/978-3-030-01246-5_7
18. Wang, X., Girshick, R., Gupta, A., He, K.: Non-local neural networks. In: Proceedings of the IEEE Conference on Computer Vision and Pattern Recognition, pp. 7794–7803 (2018)
19. Wang, X., Gupta, A.: Videos as space-time region graphs. In: Ferrari, V., Hebert, M., Sminchisescu, C., Weiss, Y. (eds.) ECCV 2018. LNCS, vol. 11209, pp. 413–431. Springer, Cham (2018). https://doi.org/10.1007/978-3-030-01228-1_25
20. Wu, J., Wang, L., Wang, L., Guo, J., Wu, G.: Learning actor relation graphs for group activity recognition (2019)

21. Yan, S., Xiong, Y., Lin, D.: Spatial temporal graph convolutional networks for skeleton-based action recognition. In: Thirty-Second AAAI Conference on Artificial Intelligence (2018)
22. Zhang, P., Lan, C., Xing, J., Zeng, W., Xue, J., Zheng, N.: View adaptive recurrent neural networks for high performance human action recognition from skeleton data. In: Proceedings of the IEEE International Conference on Computer Vision, pp. 2117–2126 (2017)
23. Zhang, X., Xu, C., Tian, X., Tao, D.: Graph edge convolutional neural networks for skeleton based action recognition. arXiv preprint arXiv:1805.06184 (2018)

Content-Aware Cubemap Projection for Panoramic Image via Deep Q-Learning

Zihao Chen[1,3], Xu Wang[1(✉)], Yu Zhou[1], Longhao Zou[2,3], and Jianmin Jiang[1]

[1] College of Computer Science and Software Engineering, Shenzhen University, Shenzhen 510680, China
zihaocheniml@gmail.com, {wangxu,yu.zhou,jianmin.jiang}@szu.edu.cn

[2] Institute of Future Networks, Southern University of Science and Technology, Shenzhen, China
Zoulh@sustech.edu.cn

[3] Peng Cheng Laboratory, PCL Research Center of Networks and Communications, Shenzhen, China

Abstract. Cubemap projection (CMP) becomes a potential panoramic data format for its efficiency. However, default CMP coordinate system with fixed viewpoint may cause distortion, especially around the boundaries of each projection plane. To promote quality of panoramic images in CMP, we propose a content-awared CMP optimization method via deep Q-learning. The key of this method is to predict an angle for rotating the image in Equirectangular projection (ERP), which attempts to keep foreground objects away from the edge of each projection plane after the image is re-projected with CMP. Firstly, the panoramic image in ERP is preprocessed for obtaining a foreground pixel map. Secondly, we feed the foreground map into the proposed deep convolutional network (ConvNet) to obtain the predicted rotation angle. The model parameters are training through the deep Q-learning scheme. Experimental results show our method keep more foreground pixels in center of each projection plane than the baseline.

Keywords: Panoramic images · Deep Q-learning · Content-aware projection

1 Introduction

Recently, panoramic image applications become popular for providing immersive experiences. Unlike the limited field of view (FoV) of traditional planar images, it can provide an omni-directional view, which allows users to view freely in the virtual world. For the storage of panoramic images, many projection schemes have been studied, such as Equirectangular projection (ERP), Cubemap projection (CMP) [1] and other Polyhedron projections [2], to obtain coordinate mapping from sphere to plane.

However, all projection methods will introduce distortion, and the degree of distortion depends on the projection methods. For example, ERP is an equidistant projection that preserves distance between parallels of latitude, but it makes

Y. M. Ro et al. (Eds.): MMM 2020, LNCS 11962, pp. 304–315, 2020.
https://doi.org/10.1007/978-3-030-37734-2_25

serious distortions at the south and north poles. CMP projects panoramas from sphere onto six projection planes of a cube, and each projection plane spans 90° field of view (FOV), which is more in line with human visual experience. Distortion mainly exists at the edge of the projection plane. Nevertheless, default CMP coordinate system may lead to discontinuous distribution of a single object, and the object information across boundary of each projection plane will be distorted. As shown in Fig. 1(a), a "computer" and some equipments are on the "table". Unfortunately, they fall within one of faces and bottom face so that they are incomplete. After rotating a little angle in azimuth, in Fig. 1(b), the "computer" is shown in the forth face completely and equipments are neatly placed on the "table" in the second face which is shown in Fig. 1(a).

Inspired by [3], we propose an content-aware CMP method by minimizing projection distortion. Fist, our proposed approach preprocesses the panoramic image in ERP and extracts the foreground pixel map for feature extraction. Then, we model the optimal angle prediction problem as system control problem in continuous action space. Final, a deep Q-learning scheme is applied to determine the optimal rotation angle.

The rest of this paper is organized as follows. Sect. 2 overviews the related works. Sect. 3 describes the overall algorithm in detail, including the preprocessing method for panoramic image in ERP and deep reinforcement learning algorithm. Experimental results are provided in Sect. 4. Finally, conclusions are given in Sect. 5.

2 Related Work

2.1 Content-Aware Projection

Content-aware projection aims to optimize different projection methods by considering the content in the scene. As for the Panini projection [4], Kim *et al.* [5] attempt to preserve the salient contents such as linear structures and salient regions. As for CMP, Xiong *et al.* [3] proposes to automatically predict snap angle for rendering panoramas into CMP. Their research confirms that content-aware projection can help generate panoramic images with higher image quality in specific projection. Besides, Tehrani *et al.* [6] propose a interactive methods that user can actively sketch the contours of region of interest. We propose a content-aware optimization method for CMP. Unlike [3], we extract foreground object completely to help the model choose the best rotation angle and reducing distortion of foreground object.

2.2 Reinforcement Learning in Continuous Action Space

There are many reinforcement learning algorithms applied in continuous action space. The most representative methods are Deep Deterministic Policy Gradient (DDPG) [7] and Normalized Advantage Functions (NAF) [8]. DDPG is an algorithm based on Actor-Critic framework and an extension of Deterministic

(a) Before

(b) After

Fig. 1. Example of horizontal rotation for CMP method. (a) Shows that computer and some equipments are segmented across the faces for the default CMP setting; (b) is obtained by rotating (a) with a little angle, where all things on the table are complete such as "computer".

Policy Gradient (DPG) [9]. Therefore, DDPG needs to train Actor network used to output the determined action value and Critic network used to estimate the current state and action of Actor respectively. NAF enable Deep Q-Network (DQN) [10] in continuous action spaces, so only Q network needs to be trained. Both of them use off-policy learning method. Random strategy is used to generate empirical samples and put them into replay-buffer. Samples are randomly sampled during training to improve their network parameters. At the same time, using replay-buffer, the correlation between training samples can be minimized. In our method, we use the deep Q-learning algorithm with NAF to train our model, so that the model can find the best rotation angle in the continuous action space.

3 Proposed Approach

In this paper, we concentrate on the optimization of content-aware CMP projection, which maps the sphere to a cube with six unfolded faces. Each face captures a 90° FOV. The goal of proposed approach is to reduce the distortion of foreground object and improve visualization quality of panoramic image in CMP format, by minimizing the total amount of foreground pixels that fall in the boundary area of four faces (front, right, back, and left).

As shown in Fig. 2, the optimization projection angle prediction is implemented for multiple iterations. The initial input of the model is a source

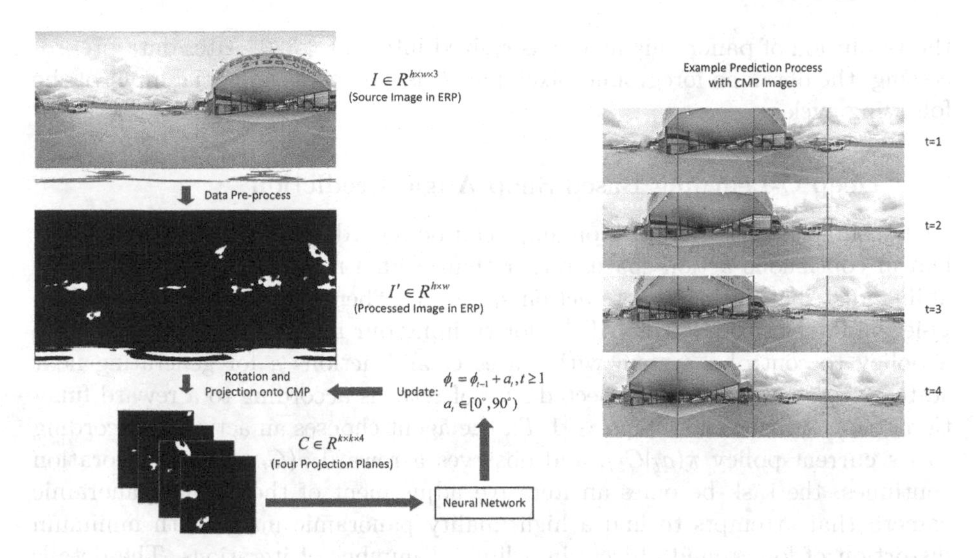

Fig. 2. The iterative process of our propose method for refining the best rotate angle (left), and a series of CMP images (right) produced by multiple predictions in limited number of iterations

panoramic image in ERP format denoted as $I \in \mathbf{R}^{h\times w\times 3}$, where h and w are height and width of the source panoramic image. Then the data pre-processing stage is implemented for obtaining the foreground pixel map $I' \in \mathbf{R}^{h\times w}$ from I. For time step t, I' is rotated with angle ϕ_t and projected into panorama in CMP denoted as $C_t \in \mathbf{R}^{k\times k\times n}$, where $k \times k$ is the spatial resolution and n is the input dimension of the model. Note that we only consider the front/right/back/right faces because users focus on the area near the equator and pay less attention to the north and south poles [11], thus n is set to 4. Detailed descriptions of sub-modules are provided as follows.

3.1 Data Preprocessing

The main purpose of this part is to generate a foreground pixel map from source panoramic image in ERP format, which can be proceeded in all exploration rather than recompute it for each iteration [3]. However, there are little published works on semantic segmentation for panoramic images. Currently, ConvNet based method such as Pixel-Objectness algorithm [12] can identify most of the foreground objects accurately. Su *et al.* [13,14] also used this method to get accurate label data from source panoramic images for training their model, which do not require any annotated data for training.

Inspired by [15,16], we apply the Pixel-Objectness algorithm repeatedly to multiple perspective projections of source panoramic image in ERP, where the parameters of convolution kernels are keep as the same in [12]. To make balance between the foreground segmentation accuracy and computational complexity, the resolution of panoramic images is resized into 640×320. After data preprocessing, the obtained foreground pixel map I' is treated as an initial input of the following cycle.

3.2 Deep Q-Learning Based Snap Angle Prediction

The optimal selection of rotation angle can be regarded as system control problem in continuous action space, rather than a final result determined by probability distribution in discrete action space [3]. Therefore, we employ the deep Q-learning algorithm with NAF [8] for training our model. The goal is to learn a policy to control a system with states C and actions a for generating next states C', to minimize the expected sum of returns according to a reward function $r(C')$. At each time step $t \in [1, T]$, the agent chooses an action a_t according to its current policy $\pi(a_t|C_t)$, and observes a reward $r(C_{t+1})$. As exploration continues, the task becomes an iterative adjustment of the virtual panoramic camera that attempts to find a high quality panoramic image with minimum distortion of foreground objects in a limited number of iterations. The details of the deep Q-learning with NAF based snap angle prediction are provided as follows.

Action. Recall that each projection plane in CMP spans 90° FOV. When the *action* (relative rotation angle prediction) a_t at time step t exceeds $90°$, the effective rotation angle is $a_t\%90°$. Hence we define $a_t \in [0°, 90°)$. In this continuous action space, the angle prediction will be limited to this range. In most cases, top face of cube mainly contains ceiling or sky and bottom face mainly contains floor, camera bracket, or even publicity map for covering up image distortion in pole, in where foreground object are minimal or there are irrelevant informations. We do not need to optimize quality of two faces mentioned above in case it interferes with our experiment. Rotations in azimuth may make many disruption caused by Cubemap edges [3], thus we only rotate in azimuth for the panorama in ERP, to promote quality of front/right/back/left faces in CMP.

Network. Let $C_t = f(I', \phi_{t-1})$ denote the panorama in CMP after rotation by ϕ_{t-1} and projection from I' at time step $t-1$. We set $\phi_0 = 0$ initially. To obtain the relative rotation angle prediction a_t at the time step t, we propose a ConvNet based prediction module. As shown in Fig. 3, the proposed network structure consists of one convolution layer, a ResNet block [17] that contains two convolution layers, and one fully connected layer. Each layer followed by a batch normalization and a ReLU layer. The output is fed into a fully connected layer for non-linear mapping from the features into *action* a_t, which is defined as

$$a_t = \mu(C_t|\theta^{\mu}), \tag{1}$$

where μ is the policy with learnable parameters θ^{μ} obtained from the proposed network. During the inference stage, the rotation angle is calculated as $\phi_t = \phi_{t-1} + a_t$.

During the training stage, a batch of experience are sampled randomly from replay-buffer, including C_t and a'_t generated by the random strategy. To apply

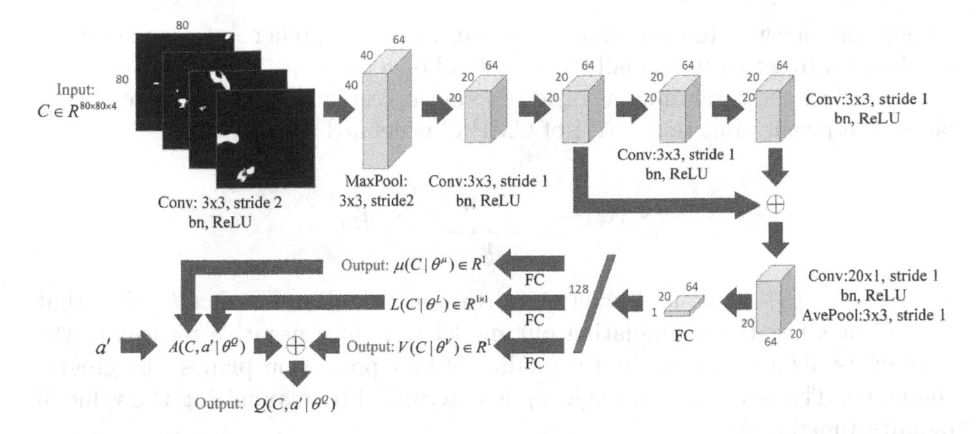

Fig. 3. Network architecture. Note that "FC" denotes a fully connected layer, "Conv" denotes a convolution layer, "bn" denotes batch normalization and "ReLU" denotes a rectified linear unit.

NAF to train our model, the proposed network contains three branches, including relative angle prediction $\mu(C_t|\theta^{\mu})$, a state function term $V(C_t|\theta^V)$ and an advantage term $A(C_t, a'_t)$ separately [8] for calculating Q-function in Q-learning [18]. The Q-function $Q(C_t, a'_t|\theta^Q)$ is defined as

$$Q(C_t, a'_t|\theta^Q) = A(C_t, a'_t) + V(C_t|\theta^V), \tag{2}$$

where θ^Q is the learnable parameters of Q-function. $A(C_t, a'_t)$ [8] is defined as the function of past action value a'_t, current predicted action value $\mu(C_t|\theta^{\mu})$ and $L(C_t|\theta^L)$ that depends on current state C_t.

$$A(C_t, a'_t) = -\frac{1}{2}[(a'_t - \mu(C_t|\theta^{\mu}))\, L(C_t|\theta^L)]^2, \tag{3}$$

To summarize, when training, our model makes use of three fully connected layers to produce $\mu(C_t|\theta^{\mu})$ as a relative rotation angle prediction, $L(C_t|\theta^L)$ for calculating $A(C_t, a'_t)$, and $V(C_t|\theta^V)$ for calculating $Q(C_t, a'_t)$. Note that θ^V and θ^L are also the learnable parameters obtained from the propose network. We only need $\mu(C_t|\theta^{\mu})$ during the inference phases.

Reward. To accurately distinguish whether the foreground pixel falls on the edge of four projection planes, we count the pixels near cube boundaries if its distance is less than β of the cube length. We penalize the foreground pixels that fall on the top/bottom/left/right edges with weights of p_1, p_2, p_3 and p_4, respectively. Xiong *et al.* [3] considered that it is common to place objects near the bottom boundary, so they set p_2 to 0. However, there are two reasons against this consideration. On the one hand, although some objects near bottom boundary owing to standing on the ground, some important objects such as a standing man or books on the table should carry weight. On the other hand, a little horizontal rotation may better preserve a foreground object in a single projection plane rather than allow it to cross to the bottom. After comprehensive consideration, we decided to set p_2 to a small value instead of zero.

To reflect the total amount of foreground pixels located in the edge of four faces, the penalty function $\Psi(C)$ of CMP C is defined as

$$\Psi(C) = -\sum_{k=1}^{4}\sum_{i=1}^{4} p_i \times m_k^i, \tag{4}$$

where m_k^i is the foreground pixel proportion in boundary i of face k. Note that Ψ is always negative, stimulating our model to reduce negative returns to the best of its ability, and the better quality of four projection planes, the greater the value. The best rotation angle $\hat{\phi}_T$ is determined by maximizing the value of penalty function Ψ:

$$\hat{\phi}_T = \underset{t=[0,\ldots,T]}{\operatorname{argmin}} \Psi(C_t) = \underset{t=[0,\ldots,T]}{\operatorname{argmin}} \Psi(f(I', \phi_t)). \tag{5}$$

The target panorama in CMP is generated by rotating the initial input I' by $\hat{\phi}_T$ in limited budget T.

Let $\hat{\phi}_{t-1}$ denote the best angle $\hat{\phi}$ until time step $t-1$, the reward r_t for time step t is updated as [3]

$$r_t = \max\left(\Psi(f(I', \phi_t)) - \Psi(f(I', \hat{\phi}_{t-1})), 0\right). \tag{6}$$

Training. Following the settings of NAF [8], we add a replay-buffer to recover the samples generated by the random strategy when training, and sample them randomly from buffer to update the network parameters. The Ornstein-Uhlenbeck process [19] is employed as random noise, which has a good correlation in time series and can make agent explore the environment with momentum attributes. In this way, the Eq. (1) is modified as

$$a_t = \mu(C_t|\theta^{\mu}) + \mathcal{N}_t, \tag{7}$$

where $\mathcal{N}$ is a random process and it is dependent on time step t in the training cycle.

We set a Q network and a copy of Q, called target network Q', both of them have same network structure in Sect. 3.2. The soft target updating scheme in [7,8] is employed

$$\theta^{Q'} \leftarrow \tau\theta^{Q} + (1-\tau)\theta^{Q'}, \tag{8}$$

where $\tau \ll 1$. In this way, the parameters of Q' change little, and it is used to calculate gradient of Q in the training process, which is more stable and easy to converge. Of course, because they change little, the learning process will slow down. We optimize Q, parameterized by θ^{Q}, by minimizing the following loss function:

$$L(\theta^{Q}) = E\left[\left(y_t - Q(C_t, a_t|\theta^{Q})\right)^2\right], \tag{9}$$

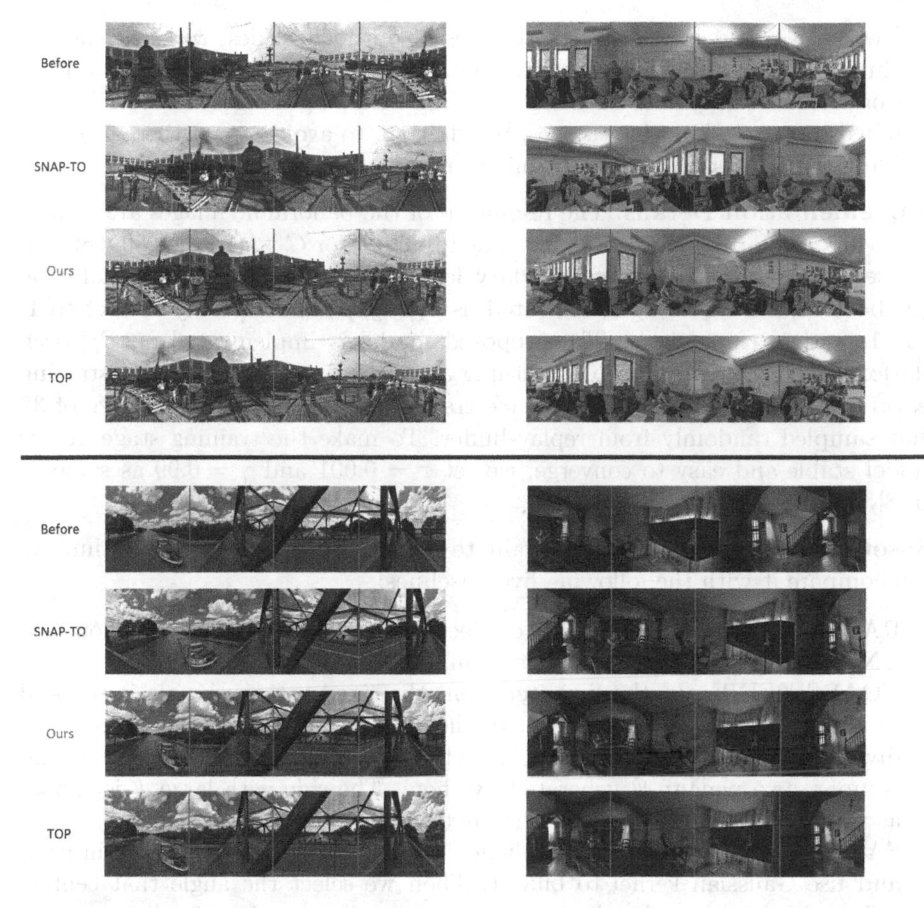

Fig. 4. Example of panoramas in CMP produced by SNAP-TO, our method and TOP. In the first row of each example there are source panoramas in CMP without rotation. In other rows there are panoramas in CMP generated by SNAP-TO, our method, and TOP, respectively.

where y_t is dependent on θ^Q. We define it as:

$$y_t = r_t + \gamma V' \left(C_t | \theta^{Q'} \right), \tag{10}$$

where γ is a discount factor and $V' \left(C_t | \theta^{Q'} \right)$ is the value function produced by Q'.

4 Experimental Results

4.1 Settings

Dataset. We evaluate the proposed approach on the public available SUN360 dataset, which contains indoor and outdoor panoramic images, covering 43 categories of indoor scenes and 28 categories of outdoor scenes, with the highest resolution of 9104×4552. 584 panoramic images are used for training and other 503 panoramic images are used for test. Both training images and test images included indoor and outdoor scenes. In addition, to avoid over fitting, there are no identical categories between training images and test images.

Implementation Details. The resolution of the panoramic images are resized into 640×320 for further processing. The input tensor C is with size $80 \times 80 \times 4$. We set $\beta = 6.25\%$ for fixing boundary length. For the weights of penalty on top/bottom/left/right edges, indicated as p_1, p_2, p_3 and p_4, they are set to 1, 0.1, 1, and 1, respectively. The proposed model is implemented on PyTorch platform, and train with deep Q-learning algorithm with NAF [8]. The starting learning rate is 0.001 for all layers. We train the model with a batch size of 32 that sampled randomly from replay-buffer. To make the training stage of our model stable and easy to converge, we set $\tau = 0.001$ and $\gamma = 0.99$ as same as in [8].

Baselines. Given a budget T, to evaluate the effectiveness of our algorithm, we will compare it with the following five baselines:

- RANDOM : T rotation angles are selected randomly without repetition.
- UNIFORM : T rotation angles are sampled uniformly.
- COARSE2FINE : In the first iteration, the fixed rotation angle is $0°$, and in the second iteration, it is $45°$. In the subsequent exploration process, we divide the optional angle range, search the center angle in each side, and compare two penalty Ψ generated by them. The side with large Ψ is choose as the optional angle range for the next exploration.
- SALIENCY : We compute the saliency map [20] of panoramic image in ERP and use Gaussian kernel to blur it. Then we select the angle that centers a 30×30 cube face that has maximal accumulative value of saliency. Since rotation never change the region, it only needs to be executed once to get the final angle.
- SNAP − TO : Follow the setting in [3], the model are trained trough REINFORCE [21] and output T angles from 20 candidates, which are sampled uniformly in $[0, 90]$.

For fair comparison, all the methods are set with initial rotation angle $0°$, besides SALIENCY directly calculating target rotation angle and Random method randomly choosing T rotation angles. Since SNAP-TO method does not use preprocessed panoramic images I' in the training process, and directly uses source panoramic images in ERP I for training. Thus, SNAP-TO method needs to extract the foreground objects on four projection planes in each iteration.

4.2 Prediction in Limited Budget

This experiment is to observe the efficiency of all methods in prediction efficiency under different iterations. We set the budget $T = 8$, and the final result in each iteration is the sum of penalty until each time step t in all test images.

The average results of panoramic images in test dataset are summarized in Table 1. It is observed that our proposed algorithm achieves the minimum sum of penalty values for most iterations, like $T = 2, 3, 4, 7, 8$. At the 5th and 6th time steps, our method ranks second. Besides, the TOP represents minimum sum of penalty values after exhaustively exploring all rotation angles in $[0°, 90°)$, which help us understand the difficulty of predicting rotation angle because most of images can not avoid the situation that the foreground pixels fall on the boundary of all projection planes at any rotation angle. UNIFORM and COARSE2FINE can find better rotation angles than RANDOM in most cases, mainly because they are designed according to manually rules. Compared with the initial panorama in CMP C_0, SALIENCY method can obtain smaller penalty value, but it can not show any better effect in the later iterations. It is worth mentioning that the training process of SNAP-TO method needs to re-recognize the foreground pixels in each iteration. Because of the serious distortion of the edge of all projection planes, the traditional convolution algorithm may not be able to accurately segment the foreground pixels, which will lead to the misjudgement of the foreground pixel distribution, and make the training process error. Therefore, SNAP-TO cannot obtain a better rotation angle in multiple iterations.

Figure 4 shows that our prediction results at the 8th time step. Regardless of the number of objects in the image, if the accuracy of semantics segmentation in the data preprocessing part is high, our method can predict the best rotation angle to keep the object in the image and reduce distortion of object.

Table 1. Total amount of penalty for all methods under different iterations

Iteration	RANDOM	UNIFORM	COARSE2FINE	SALIENCY	SNAP-TO	OURS	TOP
1	−66.10	−65.29	−65.29	−64.70	−65.29	−65.29	−38.35
2	−55.68	−56.48	−51.77		−53.43	**−51.29**	
3	−51.62	−49.90	−47.92		−48.98	**−47.23**	
4	−48.53	−47.10	−46.19		−46.47	**−45.56**	
5	−47.10	−45.21	**−44.15**		−45.32	−44.46	
6	−46.05	−43.76	**−43.08**		−44.72	−43.11	
7	−44.66	−42.70	−42.35		−43.87	**−42.09**	
8	−43.82	−41.86	−42.04		−43.30	**−41.62**	

5 Conclusion

We propose a content-aware CMP optimization method via deep Q-learning with NAF. Our method can extract the foreground pixel map from panoramic images in ERP and automatically predict the angle for reducing distortion of foreground objects. In order to maintain the continuity of action space, we make use of deep Q-learning with NAF to train a model that outputs a certain angle instead of choosing an angle from discrete candidates based on probability distribution. We demonstrate the advantage of our method in efficient prediction in limited budget and in different variances of images and performance on preserving integrity of objects.

Acknowledgements. This work was supported in part by the National Natural Science Foundation of China (Grant 31670553, Grant 61871270 and Grant 61672443), in part by the Guangdong Natural Science Foundation of China under Grant 2016A030310058, in part by the Natural Science Foundation of SZU (Grant 827000144) and in part by the National Engineering Laboratory for Big Data System Computing Technology of China.

References

1. Ng, K.-T., Chan, S.-C., Shum, H.-Y.: Data compression and transmission aspects of panoramic videos. IEEE Trans. Circuits Syst. Video Technol. **15**(1), 82–95 (2005)
2. Grünheit, C., Smolic, A., Wiegand, T.: Efficient representation and interactive streaming of high-resolution panoramic views. In: Proceedings of the 2002 International Conference on Image Processing (ICIP), pp. 209–212 (2002)
3. Xiong, B., Grauman, K.: Snap angle prediction for 360° panoramas. In: Ferrari, V., Hebert, M., Sminchisescu, C., Weiss, Y. (eds.) ECCV 2018. LNCS, vol. 11209, pp. 3–20. Springer, Cham (2018). https://doi.org/10.1007/978-3-030-01228-1_1
4. Abudahab, K., et al.: Panini: pangenome neighbour identification for bacterial populations. Microbial Genomics **5**(4) (2019)
5. Kim, Y.W., Lee, C.-R., Cho, D.-Y., Kwon, Y.H., Choi, H.-J., Yoon, K.-J.: Automatic content-aware projection for 360° videos. In: 2017 IEEE International Conference on Computer Vision (ICCV), pp. 4753–4761 (2017)
6. Tehrani, M.A., Majumder, A., Gopi, M.: Correcting perceived perspective distortions using object specific planar transformations. In: 2016 IEEE International Conference on Computational Photography (ICCP), pp. 1–10, May 2016
7. Lillicrap, T.P., et al.: Continuous control with deep reinforcement learning. In: Bengio, Y., LeCun, Y. (eds.) 4th International Conference on Learning Representations (ICLR) (2016)
8. Gu, S., Lillicrap, T., Sutskever, I., Levine, S.: Continuous deep q-learning with model-based acceleration. In: International Conference on Machine Learning (ICML), pp. 2829–2838 (2016)
9. Silver, D., Lever, G., Heess, N., Degris, T., Wierstra, D., Riedmiller, M.A.: Deterministic policy gradient algorithms. In: Proceedings of the 31th International Conference on Machine Learning (ICML), vol. 32, pp. 387–395 (2014)
10. Mnih, V., et al.: Human-level control through deep reinforcement learning. Nature **518**(7540), 529 (2015)
11. Xu, M., Song, Y., Wang, J., Qiao, M., Huo, L., Wang, Z.: Predicting head movement in panoramic video: a deep reinforcement learning approach. IEEE Trans. Pattern Anal. Mach. Intell. (2018)
12. Jain, S.D., Xiong, B., Grauman, K.: Pixel objectness: learning to segment generic objects automatically in images and videos. IEEE Trans. Pattern Anal. Mach. Intell. (PAMI) (2018)
13. Su, Y.-C., Grauman, K.: Learning spherical convolution for fast features from 360° imagery. In: Advances in Neural Information Processing Systems, pp. 529–539 (2017)

14. Su, Y.-C., Grauman, K.: Kernel transformer networks for compact spherical convolution. In: Proceedings of the IEEE Conference on Computer Vision and Pattern Recognition (CVPR), pp. 9442–9451 (2019)
15. Su, Y.-C., Jayaraman, D., Grauman, K.: Pano2Vid: automatic cinematography for watching 360° videos. In: Lai, S.-H., Lepetit, V., Nishino, K., Sato, Y. (eds.) ACCV 2016. LNCS, vol. 10114, pp. 154–171. Springer, Cham (2017). https://doi.org/10.1007/978-3-319-54190-7_10
16. Su, Y.-C., Grauman, K.: Making 360° video watchable in 2D: learning videography for click free viewing. In: 2017 IEEE Conference on Computer Vision and Pattern Recognition (CVPR), pp. 1368–1376. IEEE (2017)
17. He, K., Zhang, X., Ren, S., Sun, J.: Deep residual learning for image recognition. In: Proceedings of the IEEE Conference on Computer Vision and Pattern Recognition, pp. 770–778 (2016)
18. Watkins, C.J., Dayan, P.: Q-learning. Mach. Learn. **8**(3–4), 279–292 (1992)
19. Uhlenbeck, G.E., Ornstein, L.S.: On the theory of the Brownian motion. Phys. Rev. **36**(5), 823 (1930)
20. Liu, T., et al.: Learning to detect a salient object. IEEE Trans. Pattern Anal. Mach. Intell. (PAMI) **33**(2), 353–367 (2010)
21. Williams, R.J.: Simple statistical gradient-following algorithms for connectionist reinforcement learning. Mach. Learn. **8**(3–4), 229–256 (1992)

Robust RGB-D Data Registration Based on Correntropy and Bi-directional Distance

Teng Wan[1,2], Shaoyi Du[1,2(✉)], Wenting Cui[1], Qixing Xie[1], Yuying Liu[1], and Zuoyong Li[2]

[1] Institute of Artificial Intelligence and Robotics, Xi'an Jiaotong University, Xi'an 710049, Shaanxi Province, People's Republic of China
dushaoyi@gmail.com

[2] Fujian Provincial Key Laboratory of Information Processing and Intelligent Control, Minjiang University, Fuzhou 350121, People's Republic of China

Abstract. The iterative closest point (ICP) algorithm is most widely used for rigid registration of point sets. In this paper, a robust ICP registration method data is proposed to register RGB-D data. Firstly, the color information is introduced to build more precise correspondence between two point sets. Secondly, to enhance the robustness of the algorithm to noise and outliers, the maximum correntropy criterion (MCC) is introduced to the registration framework. Thirdly, to reduce the possibility of the algorithm falling into local minimum and deal with ill-pose issue, the bidirectional distance measurement is added to the proposed algorithm. Finally, the experimental results of point sets registration and scene reconstruction demonstrate that the proposed algorithm can obtain more precise and robust results than other ICP algorithms.

Keywords: RGB-D data · Point set registration · Correntropy · Bi-directional distance

1 Introduction

Rigid point sets registration is a key technology in pattern recognition and computer vision, which is extensively used in scene reconstruction [1], simultaneous localization and mapping (SLAM) [2], medical image analysis [3] and other fields. In many registration algorithms, the iterative closest point (ICP) algorithm is widely used in rigid registration because of its fast speed and high accuracy [4]. After decades of development, abundant variant ICP algorithms are proposed. These methods are mainly improved in terms of speed, robustness and accuracy of ICP algorithm.

To improve the robustness, the trimmed ICP algorithm is proposed by Chetverikov et al. [5], which is based on the least trimmed squares approach. Ridene et al. [6] enhance the robustness of the ICP algorithm by setting dynamic threshold and using random sample consensus (RANSAC) method. Du et al. [7] presented probability ICP algorithm to deal with noise and a Gaussian model was added to traditional rigid registration. The correntropy based ICP algorithm is proposed, which could effectively suppress the impact of noises and outliers to realize precise registration [8, 9].

Y. M. Ro et al. (Eds.): MMM 2020, LNCS 11962, pp. 316–326, 2020.
https://doi.org/10.1007/978-3-030-37734-2_26

In addition, to speed up convergence, Fitzgibbon [10] uses Levenberg-Marquardt algorithm to improve accuracy and speed via general-purpose non-linear optimization. Benjemaa et al. [11] proposed a three-dimensional sampled surfaces registration method which uses a multi-z-buffer technique to accelerate the search of the nearest neighbors and has an accurate and robust performance in highly curved objects.

Meanwhile, with the popularity of RGB-D sensor, we can easily obtain color and other information of objects or scenes which can further improve the accuracy of registration. Furthermore, the registration method of RGB-D data is proposed. Men et al. [12] proposed 4D ICP algorithm which uses the color information and the original coordinate space to resolve ambiguity in registration, but the registration accuracy will be impacted by noises and outliers in RGB-D data. Danelljan et al. [13] proposed a probabilistic framework for color-based point set registration, which uses expectation maximization (EM) algorithm for estimating the parameters and transformations. However, it uses Gaussian mixture model (GMM) based model and takes much more time to register point sets.

To register RGB-D point cloud with noises and outliers precisely, the correntropy and the color information are introduced. Moreover, as the bidirectional distance metric can enhance the robustness of, it is applied to set up the registration model. To solve this problem, we propose a robust ICP algorithm, which could obtain accurate results in the experiments even if the point sets contain noises and outliers.

The structure of the paper is organized as follows. Section 2 introduce the standard ICP algorithm will be reviewed briefly. In Sect. 3, we describes color analysis and maximum correntropy criterion and presents bidirectional registration based on correntropy and color-assisted. In Sect. 4, experimental results are given to show the robustness of proposed algorithm. Finally, the conclusion is given in Sect. 5.

2 The ICP Algorithm

The registration of m-dimensional (m-D) point sets is a significant problem in computer vision. One of the most commonly used registration method is ICP algorithm. Suppose there are two point sets in $\mathbb{R}^m$, a data point set $X \triangleq \{\vec{x}_i\}_{i=1}^{N_x} (N_x \in \mathbb{N})$ and a target point set $Y \triangleq \{\vec{y}_j\}_{j=1}^{N_y} (N_y \in \mathbb{N})$. The registration is to build the correspondence and compute the rigid transformation between these two point sets, which can be expressed by least squares (LS) criterion:

$$\begin{aligned} \min_{\mathrm{R}, \vec{t}, c(i) \in \{1,2,\cdots,N_y\}} & \sum_{i=1}^{N_x} \|(\mathbf{R}\vec{x}_i + \vec{t}) - \vec{y}_{c(i)}\|_2^2 \\ s.t. \quad & \mathbf{R}^{\mathrm{T}}\mathbf{R} = \mathrm{I}_m, \det(\mathbf{R}) = 1 \end{aligned} \tag{1}$$

where $\mathbf{R} \in \mathbb{R}^{m \times m}$ is a rotation matrix and $\vec{t} \in \mathbb{R}^m$ is a translation vector. The objective function can be solved by two steps:

Firstly, search the new correspondences between data point set X and target point set Y:

$$c_k(i) = \underset{c(i)\in\{1,2,\cdots,N_y\}}{\arg\min} \|(\mathbf{R}_{k-1}\vec{x}_i + \vec{t}_{k-1}) - \vec{y}_{c(i)}\|_2^2,\ i = 1,2,\cdots,N_x \tag{2}$$

Secondly, compute the rigid transformation $(\mathbf{R}_k, \vec{t}_k)$ of two point sets:

$$(\mathbf{R}_k, \vec{t}_k) = \underset{\mathbf{R}^{\mathrm{T}}\mathbf{R}=\mathbf{I}_m, \det(\mathbf{R})=1, \vec{t}}{\arg\min} \sum_{i=1}^{N_x} \|\mathbf{R}\vec{x}_i + \vec{t} - \vec{y}_{c_k(i)}\|_2^2 \tag{3}$$

Repeats the above two steps until two point sets are aligned. However, the ICP is easy to fall into local minimum when the point sets contain noises and outliers.

3 Our Algorithm

In this section, a bidirectional registration method based on correntropy and color-assisted is proposed to realize precise registration even if there are noises and outliers in point sets.

3.1 Problem Statement

In this paper, we mainly focus on three problems of registration. Firstly, ICP algorithm cannot establish correct correspondence between two point sets when the structure of point sets is simple and symmetry, such as a wall. Secondly, the precision of ICP algorithm is influenced by noises and outliers easily. Unfortunately, the noises and outliers are randomly distributed in real scene (see Fig. 1). Thirdly, ICP algorithm is easy to fall into local extremum, which will lead to the failure of the registration finally. Therefore, to overcome those problems, an innovative ICP algorithm is proposed.

Fig. 1. The point set data is collected by RGB-D camera. (Color figure online)

Firstly, to build precise correspondence between the data and target point sets, the color information is introduced into the criteria for selecting corresponding points. It means that the corresponding point pairs are the closest in both the color space and the Euclidean space. This constraint guarantees the accuracy of the correspondence between point sets. Among them, to reduce the impact of illumination, the color of points will be translated from the RGB (red, green, blue) color space to HSV (hue, saturation, value) color space, and the saturation and value will be ignored. Only the hue information is applied in our algorithm, where the hues of the data point set and the target point set are denoted as h_i^x and h_j^y respectively. Therefore, after the hue information is added to the traditional ICP algorithm, the objective function is as shown below:

$$\begin{aligned} &\min_{\mathbf{R},\vec{t},c(i)\in\{1,2,\cdots,N_y\}} \sum_{i=1}^{N_x} \left(\|(\mathbf{R}\vec{x}_i+\vec{t}) - \vec{y}_{c(i)}\|_2^2 + w(h_i^x - h_{c(i)}^y)^2 \right) \\ &s.t. \quad \mathbf{R}^{\mathrm{T}}\mathbf{R} = \mathbf{I}_m, \det(\mathbf{R}) = 1 \end{aligned} \tag{4}$$

where w is the weight of hue values.

Secondly, as mentioned above, noises and outliers in data affects the registration accuracy of the ICP algorithm, so the noises and outliers should be eliminated. Fortunately, the maximum correntropy criterion (MCC) 8 is robust to noises and outliers, which can be expressed as follows:

$$g(\vec{x},\vec{y}) = \sum_{i=1}^{N_x} \exp\left(-\|\vec{x}-\vec{y}\|_2^2\right)/(2\sigma^2) \tag{5}$$

where σ is a variance. Therefore, the new objective function of ICP with color-assisted and maximum correntropy criterion can be expressed as:

$$\begin{aligned} &\max_{\mathbf{R},\vec{t},j\in\{1,2,\ldots,N_y\}} \sum_{i=1}^{N_x} e^{-(\|\mathbf{R}\vec{x}_i+\vec{t}-\vec{y}_{c_k(i)}\|_2^2 + w(h_i^x - h_{c_k(i)}^y)^2)/(2\sigma^2)} \\ &s.t. \quad \mathbf{R}^T\mathbf{R} = \mathbf{I}_m, \det(\mathbf{R}) = 1 \end{aligned} \tag{6}$$

Thirdly, to deal with the ill-pose problem and prevent ICP algorithm from falling into local extremum, the bidirectional distance measure is introduce into our algorithm. Usually, in traditional ICP algorithm, the correspondence between point sets is unidirectional search from data point sets to target point sets. In bidirectional distance measure, both data and target point sets will find correspondence from each other. The advantage of the bidirectional distance measure is that the reverse search from point set Y to point set X can help the algorithm jump out of the local extremum when it falls into local extrema when the point set X searches and registers with point set Y. Therefore, the bidirectional distance algorithm can be used to deal with the ill-posed problem and obtains the stable registration results. Finally, the new objective function is as follow:

$$\begin{aligned} \max_{\substack{\mathbf{R},\vec{t} \\ c(i)\in\{1,2,\cdots,N_y\} \\ d(j)\in\{1,2,\cdots,N_x\}}} \quad & \exp(-(\sum_{i=1}^{N_x}(\|(\mathbf{R}\vec{x}_i+\vec{t})-\vec{y}_{c(i)}\|_2^2+w(h_i^x-h_{c(i)}^y)^2) \\ & +\sum_{j=1}^{N_y}(\|(\mathbf{R}\vec{x}_{d(j)}+\vec{t})-\vec{y}_j\|_2^2+w(h_{d(j)}^x-h_j^y)^2)))/2\sigma^2) \\ s.t. \quad & \mathbf{R}^T\mathbf{R}=\mathrm{I}_m, \det(\mathbf{R})=1 \end{aligned} \tag{7}$$

where h^x and h^y are the hue values of X and Y point sets, $c(\bullet)$ and $d(\bullet)$ are the correspondence index of the point sets. Moreover, we represents the balance between the coordinate values and hue values, which is set to 30.

3.2 A New ICP Algorithm

To solve the objective function of the new ICP algorithm, we propose a new algorithm that is similar to the traditional ICP algorithm and is introduced as follows.

In the first step, the color information of points is used to establish accuracy correspondences between two point sets. In traditional ICP algorithm, the correspondence between two points is established by minimum Euclidean distance. However, if the surface is smooth, such as a surface or hemisphere, the correspondence established by the nearest Euclidean distance in this case may be wrong. To solve this problem, the color information is introduced to find correct correspondence. When we establish the correspondences, the closest distance simultaneously satisfies the closest distance in the Euclidean space and the closest color in the color space.

Moreover, if the color proportion of points is too small and less than a threshold, we can regard those points as noises. Those noises and outliers will cause the algorithm to establish some wrong correspondences and resulting in a decrease in registration accuracy or a registration failure. Similarly, if the proportion is more than a threshold, those points will be regarded as the background points with high possibility. The existence of such background points also cause the algorithm to fall into local extremum. Therefore, both noises and background points should be eliminated before registration. Usually, we divide the color of the points into 8 classes. After that we select the available points according to the number of points in each color. Usually we select the points with the percentage from a to b of the total number of point sets for registration, where a and b are set to be 5% and 30% here.

As with the traditional ICP algorithm, we need to calculate the bidirectional correspondences with hue-assist at the $(k-1)^{th}$ rigid transformation $(\mathbf{R}_{k-1}, \vec{t}_{k-1})$, which could be expressed as follows:

$$c_k(i) = \mathop{\arg\min}_{c(i)\in\{1,2,\cdots N_y\}} \left(\|(\mathbf{R}_{k-1}\vec{x}_i+\vec{t}_{k-1})-\vec{y}_{c(i)}\|_2^2+w(h_i^x-h_{c(i)}^y)^2\right) \tag{8}$$

$$d_k(j) = \mathop{\arg\min}_{d(j)\in\{1,2,\cdots N_x\}} \left(\|(\mathbf{R}_{k-1}\vec{x}_{d(j)}+\vec{t}_{k-1})-\vec{y}_j\|_2^2+w(h_{d(j)}^x-h_j^y)^2\right) \tag{9}$$

In the second step, we compute the rigid transformation with bidirectional distance measurement at the kth step according to the correspondences of $(k-1)^{th}$ step:

$$\begin{aligned}(\mathbf{R}_k,\vec{t}_k) = \underset{\mathbf{R}^T\mathbf{R}=\mathbf{I}_n,\det(\mathbf{R})=1,\vec{t}}{\arg\max} \ & \exp(-(\sum_{i=1}^{N_x}(||(\mathbf{R}\vec{x}_i+\vec{t})-\vec{y}_{c_k(i)}||_2^2+w(h_i^x-h_{c_k(i)}^y)^2) \\ & +\sum_{j=1}^{N_y}(||(\mathbf{R}\vec{x}_{d_k(j)}+\vec{t})-\vec{y}_j||_2^2+w(h_{d_k(j)}^x-h_j^y)^2)))/2\sigma^2)\end{aligned} \tag{10}$$

Then, we repeat the above two steps until k reaches the maximum number of iterations or the registration error is small enough to realize the precise matching. In addition, this algorithm can be proved to be a local convergent algorithm. We take the derivative of (10) and set it to be 0, so we can get:

$$\vec{t} = \frac{\sum_{i=1}^{N_x}(\vec{y}_{c_k(i)}-\mathbf{R}\vec{x}_i)+\sum_{j=1}^{N_y}(\vec{y}_j-\mathbf{R}\vec{x}_{d_k(j)})}{N_x+N_y} \tag{11}$$

Substituting $\vec{t}$ in Eq. (10) and we can get:

$$\begin{aligned}\mathbf{R}_k = \underset{\mathbf{R}^T\mathbf{R}=\mathbf{I}_n,\det(\mathbf{R})=1}{\arg\max} \ & \exp(-(\sum_{i=1}^{N_x}(||(\mathbf{R}\vec{x}_i+\frac{\sum_{i=1}^{N_x}(\vec{y}_{c_k(i)}-\mathbf{R}\vec{x}_i)+\sum_{j=1}^{N_y}(\vec{y}_j-\mathbf{R}\vec{x}_{d_k(j)})}{N_x+N_y})-\vec{y}_{c_k(i)}||_2^2+w(h_i^x-h_{c_k(i)}^y)^2) \\ & +\sum_{j=1}^{N_y}(||(\mathbf{R}\vec{x}_{d_k(j)}+\frac{\sum_{i=1}^{N_x}(\vec{y}_{c_k(i)}-\mathbf{R}\vec{x}_i)+\sum_{j=1}^{N_y}(\vec{y}_j-\mathbf{R}\vec{x}_{d_k(j)})}{N_x+N_y})-\vec{y}_j||_2^2+w(h_{d_k(j)}^x-h_j^y)^2))/2\sigma^2)\end{aligned} \tag{12}$$

Let

$$\vec{p}_i = \frac{(N_x+N_y)\vec{x}_i-\sum_{i=1}^{N_x}\vec{x}_i-\sum_{j=1}^{N_y}\vec{x}_{d_k(j)}}{N_x+N_y},\ \vec{q}_i = \frac{(N_x+N_y)\vec{y}_j-\sum_{i=1}^{N_x}\vec{y}_{c_k(i)}-\sum_{j=1}^{N_y}\vec{y}_j}{N_x+N_y} \tag{13}$$

$$\vec{p}_j = \frac{(N_x+N_y)\vec{x}_{d_k(j)}-\sum_{i=1}^{N_x}\vec{x}_i-\sum_{j-1}^{N_y}\vec{x}_{d_k(j)}}{N_x+N_y},\ \vec{q}_j = \frac{(N_x+N_y)\vec{y}_j-\sum_{i=1}^{N_x}\vec{y}_{c_k(i)}-\sum_{j=1}^{N_y}\vec{y}_j}{N_x+N_y} \tag{14}$$

$$l_i = w(h_i^x-h_{c_k(i)}^y)^2,\ l_j = w(h_{d_k(j)}^x-h_j^y)^2 \tag{15}$$

Equation (12) can be rewritten as:

$$\mathbf{R}_k = \underset{\mathbf{R}^T\mathbf{R}=\mathbf{I}_n,\det(\mathbf{R})=1}{\arg\max} \ \exp(-(\sum_{i=1}^{N_x}(||\mathbf{R}\vec{p}_i-\vec{q}_i||_2^2+l_i^2)+\sum_{j=1}^{N_y}(||\mathbf{R}\vec{p}_j-\vec{q}_j||_2^2+l_j^2)/2\sigma^2) \tag{16}$$

Solving by Lagrangian multiplier method, we can get:

$$\mathbf{L}'\mathbf{R} = -\frac{1}{\sigma^2}F(\mathbf{R})(\sum_{i=1}^{N_x}(\vec{p}_i\vec{p}_i^T) + \sum_{j=1}^{N_y}(\vec{p}_j\vec{q}_j^T)) \tag{17}$$

Then, singular value decomposition (SVD) algorithm is used to solve this problem. Therefore, we can get:

$$\mathbf{L}'\mathbf{R} = \mathbf{U}\Lambda\mathbf{V}^T \tag{18}$$

and the rotation matrix can be calculated via the following equation:

$$\mathbf{R}_k = \mathbf{U}\mathbf{D}^{-1}\mathbf{V}^T \tag{19}$$

where U and V are orthogonal matrices, and the translation vector $\vec{t}$ can be expressed in the following:

$$\vec{t}_k = \frac{\sum_{i=1}^{N_x}(\vec{y}_{c(i)} - \mathbf{R}_k\vec{x}_i) + \sum_{j=1}^{N_y}(\vec{y}_j - \mathbf{R}_k\vec{x}_{d(j)})}{N_x + N_y} \tag{20}$$

4 Experimental Results

In this section, we verify the robustness of the proposed algorithm with simulation and real scene experiments. Firstly, we test our method with RGB-D scenes dataset v2 [14] and RGB-D SLAM Dataset and Benchmark [15] respectively. Secondly, for real data experiment, we test the proposed algorithm with real RGB-D data collected by a RGB-D camera. In addition, we compare our algorithm with the traditional ICP [4], the hue-assist ICP (HICP) [14] and correntropy based ICP (CICP) algorithms [9].

4.1 Simulation Experiment

In simulation experiment, for creating data and target point sets, we rotate a point set along the xyz axes randomly via the rigid transformation. Then, random color noises are added to the point sets (see Fig. 2).

Fig. 2. The position of two point sets before registration.

To conveniently judge whether the registration result is accurate, we use rigid transformation $(\mathbf{R}, \vec{t})$ obtained by each algorithm to calculate registration error $\varepsilon_{\mathbf{R}} = \|\mathbf{R} - \mathbf{R}_G\|_2$ and $\varepsilon_{\vec{t}} = \|\vec{t} - \vec{t}_G\|_2$. After that, we can get the simulation experimental results (see Fig. 3). In addition, we experimented with five indoor scene and the results are shown in Table 1.

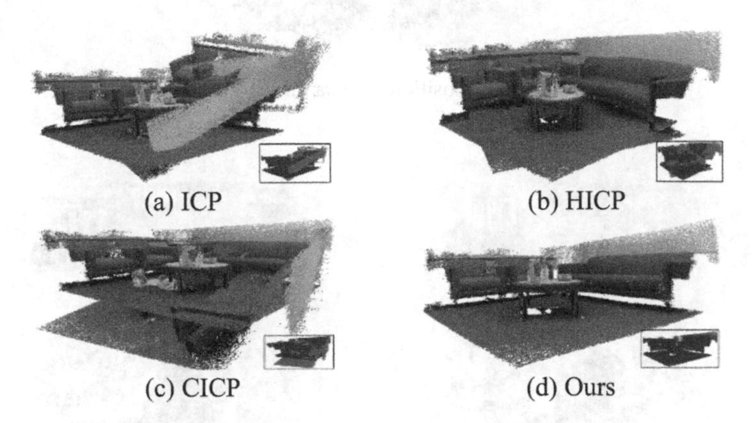

Fig. 3. The registration results of simulation experiments.

Table 1. Simulation experimental results.

Dataset	Error	Algorithms			
		ICP	HICP	CICP	Ours
Room1	ε_R	4.69	0.25	3.28	5.13e−29
	$\varepsilon_{\vec{t}}$	2.51	0.09	3.20	3.86e−29
Room2	ε_R	7.64	7.93	8.00	3.64e−31
	$\varepsilon_{\vec{t}}$	1.60	1.73	1.60	8.41e−32
Desk1	ε_R	3.68	3.83	1.66	1.13e−29
	$\varepsilon_{\vec{t}}$	5.02	4.98	1.57	6.04e-30
Desk2	ε_R	7.49	7.82	5.51	4.82e−30
	$\varepsilon_{\vec{t}}$	3.45	3.26	3.43	1.68e−30
Desk3	ε_R	7.29	4.62	4.98	4.69e−30
	$\varepsilon_{\vec{t}}$	3.26	2.35	2.07	5.10e−30

As shown in Fig. 3 and Table 1, compared with other three registration algorithms, our algorithm could register two point sets precisely.

4.2 Real Scene Experiment

We test our algorithm with real scene data which collected by a RGB-D camera. The original position of data and target point sets are shown in Fig. 4. The experimental results of the ICP, HICP, CICP and the proposed algorithm are shown in Fig. 5.

Fig. 4. The initial position of data and target point sets.

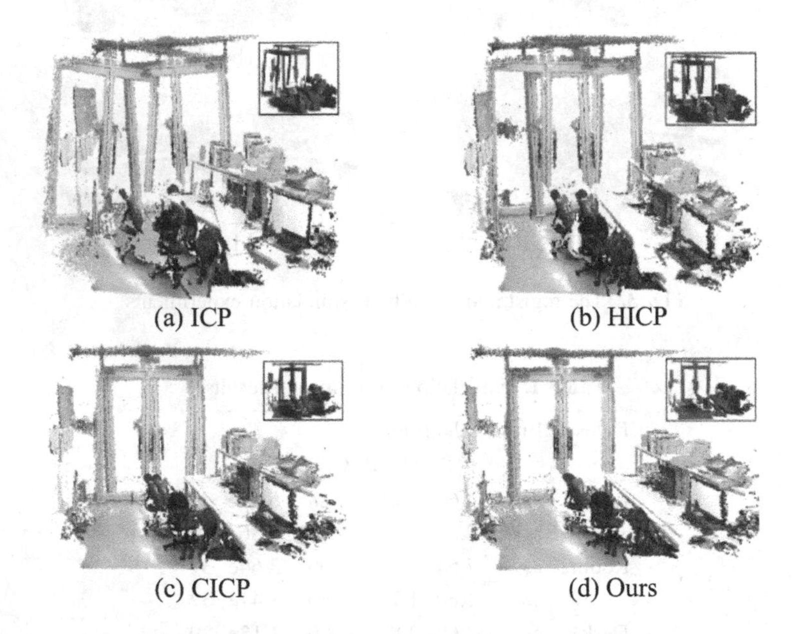

(a) ICP (b) HICP

(c) CICP (d) Ours

Fig. 5. The registration results with real scene data.

As shown in Fig. 5, our algorithm obtains the best registration result than the other contrast algorithms. As mentioned above, the precision of ICP and HICP algorithm are easily affected by noises and outliers. However, real scene data contain lots of the noises and outliers. Therefore, the ICP and HICP algorithm does not properly register the point set of real scene. In contrast, the CICP algorithm has better resistance to noises and outliers, but cannot establish accurate correspondence between data and target point set. Thus, the CICP algorithm fails to register.

Moreover, our algorithm is used for local indoor scene reconstruction. We collect 30 frames of indoor scene, and then the RGB-D data is registered frame by frame. The reconstruct result and some details are shown in Fig. 6.

Fig. 6. Indoor scene reconstruction.

5 Conclusion

In this paper, we propose a robust registration algorithm based on correntropy and color-assisted bidirectional distance measurement for RGB-D data. The experimental results show that our algorithm can obtains precise registration results with good robustness. The contributions of our work are: (1) As the data includes noises and outliers, the color information and correntropy are used to solve this problem, and the registration accuracy is further improved. (2) We use bidirectional distance measurement to avoid the ill-posed problem and get much more robust results. In the future, we will apply our method for large-scale scene reconstruction.

Acknowledgment. This work was supported by the National Natural Science Foundation of China under Grant Nos. 61971343, 61573274 and 61627811, Fujian Provincial Key Laboratory of Information Processing and Intelligent Control (Minjiang University) under Grant No. MJUKF-IPIC201802.

References

1. Henry, P., Krainin, M., Herbst, E., Ren, X., Fox, D.: RGB-D mapping: using depth cameras for dense 3D modeling of indoor environments. Int. J. Robot. Res. **31**(5), 647–663 (2013)
2. Mur-Artal, R., Montiel, J.M.M., Tardós, J.D.: ORB-SLAM: a versatile and accurate monocular SLAM system. IEEE Trans. Rob. **31**(5), 1147–1163 (2015)
3. Bernard, F., et al.: Shape-aware surface reconstruction from sparse 3D point-clouds. Med. Image Anal. **38**, 77–89 (2017)
4. P.J. Besl, N.D. Mckay: A method for registration of 3-D shapes. IEEE Trans. Pattern Anal. Mach. Intell., **14**(2), 239–256 (1992)
5. Chetverikov, D., Stepanov, D., Krsek, P.: Robust Euclidean alignment of 3D point sets: the trimmed iterative closest point algorithm. Image Vis. Comput. **23**(3), 299–309 (2005)

6. Ridene, T., Goulette, F.: Registration of fixed-and-mobile-based terrestrial Laser data sets with DSM. In: IEEE International Symposium on Computational Intelligence in Robotics and Automation, pp. 375–380 (2016)
7. Du, S., Liu, J., Zhang, C., Zhu, J., Li, K.: Probability iterative closest point algorithm for m-D point set registration with noise. Neurocomputing **157**, 187–198 (2015)
8. Wu, Z., Chen, H., Du, S., Fu, M., Zhou, N., Zheng, N.: Correntropy based scale ICP algorithm for robust point set registration. Pattern Recogn. **93**, 14–24 (2019)
9. Du, S., Xu, G., Zhang, S., Zhang, X., Gao, Y., Chen, B.: Robust rigid registration algorithm based on pointwise correspondence and correntropy. Pattern Recogn. Lett. (2018). https://doi.org/10.1016/j.patrec.2018.06.028
10. Fitzgibbon, A.W.: Robust registration of 2D and 3D point sets. Image Vis. Comput. **21**(13), 1145–1153 (2001)
11. Benjemaa, R., Schmitt, F.: Fast global registration of 3D sampled surfaces using a multi-z-buffer technique. In: International Conference on Recent Advances in 3-D Digital Imaging and Modeling Proceedings, pp. 113–123 (1997)
12. Men, H., Gebre, B., Pochiraju, K.: Color point cloud registration with 4D ICP algorithm. In: IEEE International Conference on Robotics and Automation, pp. 1511–1516 (2011)
13. Danelljan, M., Meneghetti, G., Khan, F.S., Felsberg, M.: A probabilistic framework for color-based point set registration. In: Computer Vision and Pattern Recognition, pp. 1818–1826 (2016)
14. Lai, K., Bo, L., Ren, X., Fox, D.: A large-scale hierarchical multi-view RGB-D object dataset. In: IEEE International Conference on Robotics and Automation, pp. 1817–1824 (2011)
15. Sturm, J., Engelhard, N., Endres, F., Burgard, W., Cremers, D.: A benchmark for the evaluation of RGB-D SLAM systems. In: IEEE International Conference on Intelligent Robots and Systems, pp. 573–580 (2012)

InSphereNet: A Concise Representation and Classification Method for 3D Object

Hui Cao, Haikuan Du, Siyu Zhang, and Shen Cai(✉)

School of Computer Science and Technology, Donghua University, Shanghai, China
ch123ui@163.com, Hanson_du@163.com, akirazure@163.com, hammer_cai@163.com

Abstract. In this paper, we present an InSphereNet method for the problem of 3D object classification. Unlike previous methods that use points, voxels, or multi-view images as inputs of deep neural network (DNN), the proposed method constructs a class of more representative features named infilling spheres from signed distance field (SDF). Because of the admirable spatial representation of infilling spheres, we can not only utilize very fewer number of spheres to accomplish classification task, but also design a lightweight InSphereNet with less layers and parameters than previous methods. Experiments on ModelNet40 show that the proposed method leads to superior performance than PointNet in accuracy. In particular, if there are only a few dozen sphere inputs or about 100000 DNN parameters, the accuracy of our method remains at a very high level.

Keywords: 3D object classification · Signed distance field · Deep learning · Infilling sphere

1 Introduction

After intensive research in recent years, convolutional neural networks (CNN) is widely used in many areas, such as computer vision, multimedia, and so on. Despite the great success in detection, recognition, segmentation, and classification tasks for 2D images, the use of deep learning on 3D data remains a big challenge because of the sparsity of most 3D data. To the task of 3D object classification, the commonly available datasets are ModelNet [21] and ShapeNet [22] in which each object has a complete CAD model. Thus the previous works can transform 3D models into multi-view images, voxels, or point clouds which are then fed into convolutional neural networks. For example, 2D CNN based MVCNN [17] recognizes 3D shapes from a collection of their rendered views on 2D images which lack of explicit 3D geometric information. VoxNet [6] represents a 3D shape with a volumetric occupancy grid and trains a 3D CNN to perform classification on voxels. However, volumetric CNNs typically have low resolutions (e.g. 32 × 32 × 32) due to computationally expensive 3D convolutions and therefore have difficulty processing fine object models. PointNet [9]

Y. M. Ro et al. (Eds.): MMM 2020, LNCS 11962, pp. 327–339, 2020.
https://doi.org/10.1007/978-3-030-37734-2_27

is the first method to apply deep learning directly on points. Though achieving record-breaking results, it is unable to extract local features and its inputs should contain enough points to cover the surface of the object.

In addition, signed distance field (SDF) becomes another popular choice for 3D shape representation. As the SDF value of a spatial point stands for the distance between this point and its nearest object surface, the point whose SDF value is equal to zero lies on the surface. Every point on the exterior of the surface is considered positive distance and any point inside the mesh stores a negative distance. Some fusion methods [3,7] use a truncated SDF (TSDF) to reconstruct a single 3D model from noisy depth maps. Voxel-based SDF representations have been extensively used for 3D shape learning [4,16,24] and 3D shape completion [8], but their use of discrete voxels is expensive in memory. Although SDF is capable to express the shape of any 3D object, it has not been used for 3D object classification to the best of our knowledge. The main reason why SDF is difficult to be applied to 3D object classification is that it is a dense field with 3D position and SDF value. It suffers from the same problems as voxels.

In this paper, we propose infilling spheres extracted from the SDF to represent a complete 3D object. For each voxel, we can construct a sphere with its 3D coordinates as the sphere's center and its SDF value as the sphere's radius. A number of spheres (e.g. 64–1024) are selected to represent the object which we name infilling spheres. Intuitively, space infilling spheres are more informative and representative than isolated surface points for 3D objects because a surface point is just equivalent to a sphere with a radius of zero at the specific locations (surface) while a sphere can be anywhere with any size. Figure 1 shows an airplane model represented by four different primitives which are point clouds, voxels, interior infilling spheres and exterior infilling spheres separately. The proposed infilling spheres representation is more concise and effective than other representation methods, especially with a few of primitives.

Specifically, we first normalize 3D objects into a unit size and voxelize them with a high resolution of $512 \times 512 \times 512$. Then we compute the SDF value of each voxel with which we can construct a sphere by using its position as the sphere's center and its SDF value as the sphere's radius. Subsequently, only a number of infilling spheres are constructed according to three criteria we will introduce later. After that, the infilling spheres with four-dimensional vectors are fed into a lightweight PointNet network architecture. Experiments on ModelNet40 verify the representation power of the proposed method. If there are only a few dozen sphere inputs or about 100000 DNN parameters, the accuracy of our method remains at a very high level.

The contributions of our work can be summarized as follows:

- We propose a novel 3D shape representation using infilling spheres which is geometrically intuitive and meaningful.
- The number of infilling spheres can sharply decreases without obvious decrease of classification accuracy.
- The network architecture can be lightweight without obvious decrease of classification accuracy.

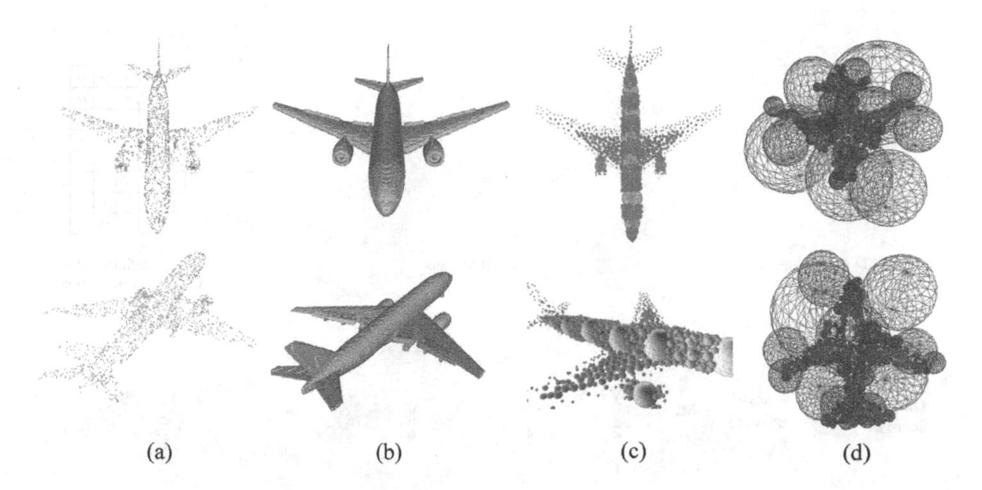

Fig. 1. Four different primitive representations of an airplane model. (a) 2048 surface points; (b) voxels with the resolution 512^3; (c) 1024 interior infilling spheres; (d) 1024 exterior infilling spheres

2 Related Works

Traditionally, hand-crafted features for point clouds can be divided into two categories: *intrinsic* and *extrinsic*. Intrinsic descriptors [12,15,18] treat the 3D shape as a manifold, while extrinsic descriptors [5,13,14] are usually extracted from coordinates of the shape in 3D space.

In the deep learning era, approaches to 3D object classification keep evolving at a fast pace. Volumetric CNNs have been adopted by pioneers on this specific task. [21] proposes to convert depth maps to volumetric representations, and then utilize a convolutional deep belief network to recognize object categories. VoxNet [6] represents point clouds with a volumetric occupancy grid and trains a 3D CNN to accomplish classification on voxels. However, volumetric CNNs typically have low resolutions due to sparsity of points and computationally expensive 3D convolutions and therefore have difficulty processing very large point clouds.

Another family of methods [10,17] classify multi-view 2D images captured from the circular observation of 3D shapes with state-of-the-art 2D CNNs and achieve record-breaking results. However, they are not geometrically intuitive and cannot easily be extended to other 3D tasks such as part segmentation.

To circumvent these issues, PointNet [9] directly consumes point clouds with a simple yet efficient network. It is also robust to inputs perturbation and corruptions. Nonetheless, it only considers global features and ignores local neighborhood information, making it not suitable to fine-grained pattern and complex scenes. Instead of working on individual points, PointNet++ [11] introduces a hierarchical neural network that applies PointNet recursively on several group points in different levels. Consequently, features from multiple scales could be

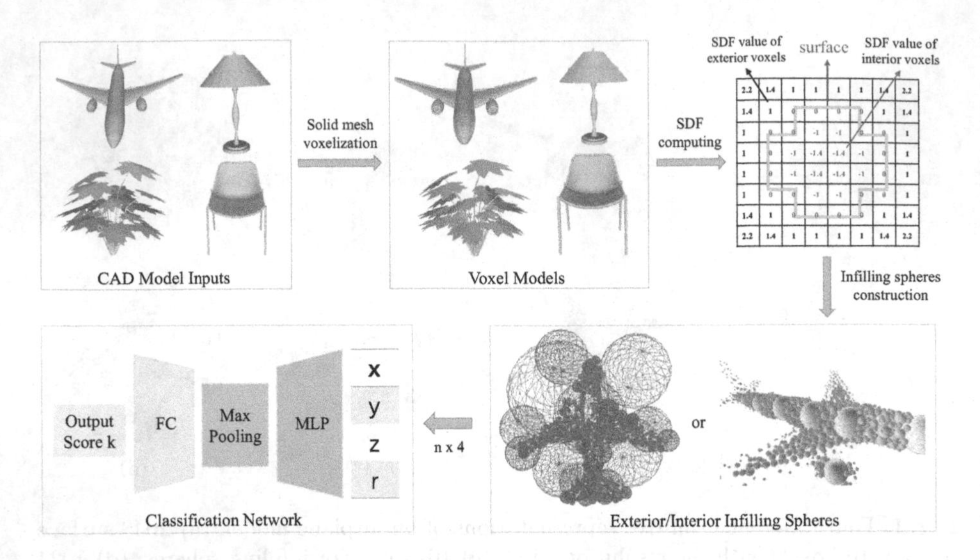

Fig. 2. The flow chart of InSphereNet

extracted hierarchically. One implicit drawback of this family of methods is that they need a sufficient number of points to cover the whole surface. CNNs are very efficient for processing data representation which have a grid structure. But point clouds usually do not have grids thus makes it hard to learn local information. A simple method to overcome this problem is constructing neural networks on graphs [2,19,23]. DGCNN [20] exploits local geometric structures by constructing a local neighborhood graph and applying graph convolutions on the connecting edges between points. This approach fails to take directions and other information into account, which is also essential to 3D object recognition.

Different from above 3D representation methods, the methodology we adopted in this paper is to explore another more concise way, which can express geometric models from coarse to fine. After performing a series of construction operations on the SDF of an object, the proposed infilling spheres can work well for classification task, even if the number of spheres is small or a lightweight network is adopted.

3 Our Approach

This section describes the proposed approach in detail. Firstly, we voxelize the 3D model with a high resolution of $512 \times 512 \times 512$. Secondly, the SDF value of each voxel within an external sphere is computed. Thirdly, a number of voxels with larger SDF values are selected according to three criteria. Finally, positions and radii of selected infilling spheres are fed into the classification network. The detailed workflow is illustrated in Fig. 2.

Fig. 3. Five example objects with the resolution 32^3 in the top row and 512^3 in the bottom row

3.1 Mesh Voxelization

Mesh voxelization is the process of converting a 3D triangular mesh into a 3D voxel grid. As we only use voxel models to compute SDF, resolution is no more a limitation to mesh voxelization, thus high quality shape representation with voxel model is available. In our work, we adopt solid mesh voxelization method in PyMesh [1] with the resolution of 512^3. Figure 3 shows five example objects with the resolution of 32^3 and 512^3 separately. It can be seen that the voxel models with the resolution of 32^3 lose fine details and still have a large number of voxels.

3.2 SDF Computing

After mesh voxelization, we calculate the SDF of each voxel whether it is inside or outside the object. Here we add a sphere with a radius of a half of voxelization resolution (256 in our setting) as an external boundary of the object. As a result, the SDF value of a voxel outside the sphere will be empty. The SDF value of a voxel inside the object is negative while is positive if the corresponding voxel is outside the object but inside the external sphere.

3.3 Infilling Sphere Construction

Instead of using point cloud to represent a 3D model, our key idea is to fill the inside or outside of the 3D model with an appropriate number of infilling spheres. Here a sphere is defined by a voxel with the voxel coordinate as its center and the SDF value as its radius. Thus it is suitable to represent the spatial occupation of an object. However, the problem is how to construct a number of infilling spheres rather than using all spheres (voxels) to represent an object.

First, constructing infilling spheres should follow the principle of from big to small, from coarse to fine. By doing this, no matter how many spheres are used

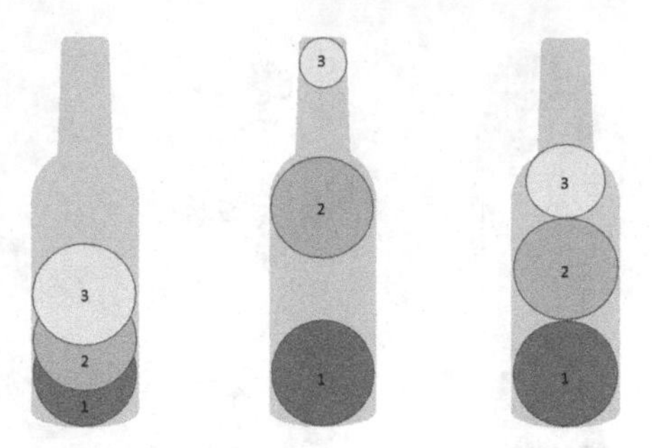

Fig. 4. The relationship of three largest spheres inside a bottle from left to right is: intersecting, separate, tangential.

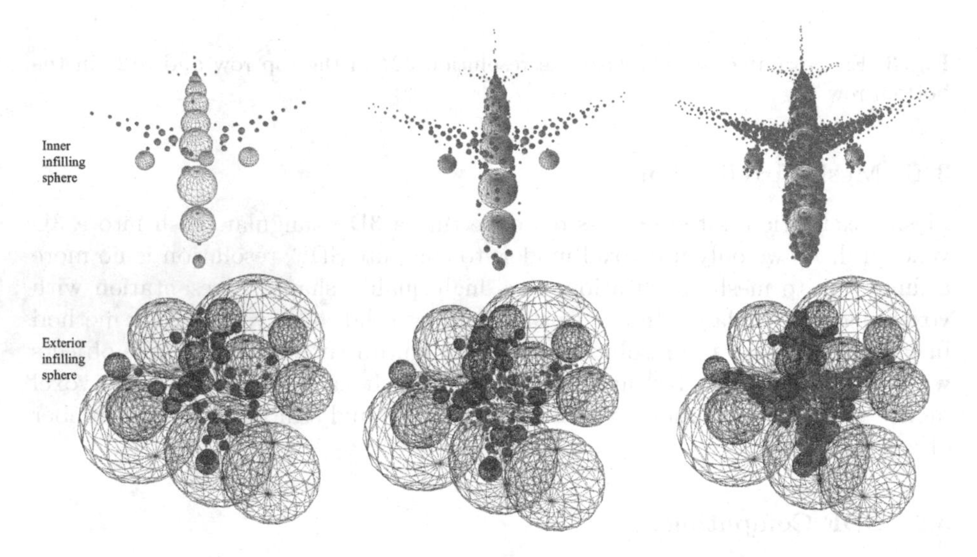

Fig. 5. Infilling spheres construction of an airplane model with different resolutions. The first and the second row draw inner and exterior infilling spheres respectively. The sphere resolutions n from left to right are 64, 256, 1024 respectively.

for object representation, larger spheres occupying the main part of a object as its basic trunk can be firstly constructed followed by filling the resting fine part with smaller spheres.

Moreover, the adjacent relationship of infilling spheres should be considered. Take a bottle scenario as an example shown in Fig. 4. If given three infilling spheres to represent this bottle, the relationship of three largest infilling spheres could be classified as intersecting, tangential, and separate. Obviously, the separate form should be adopted as the preferred occupation representation of the object because it is easier to occupy main space of the object at a given number n of infilling spheres.

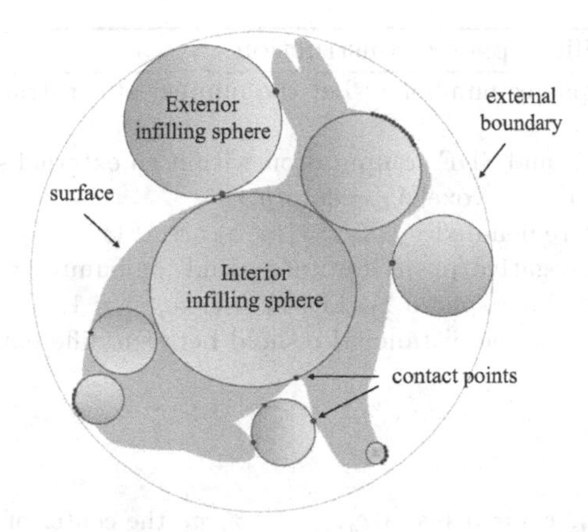

Fig. 6. Spheres with different numbers of contact points drawn in dark blue for interior case and red for exterior case (Color figure online)

Specifically, the ideal separate distance between two infilling spheres is affected by several factors, such as object volume, object shape, the number of infilling spheres, rendering the complicated constructing strategy. Here we finally adopt a simply hierarchical way which set the separate distance $d = 10, 5, 0$ successively. As a result, any object can be represented hierarchically under a given infilling sphere resolution. Figure 5 shows the constructions of inner and exterior infilling spheres of an airplane model with different resolutions.

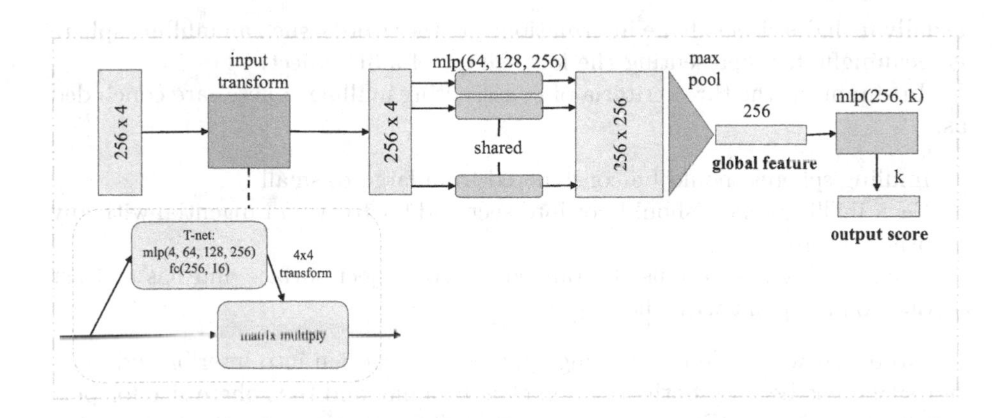

Fig. 7. Lightweight network architecture for 256 infilling spheres

Another thing should be considered is that the selection of infilling spheres should also be related to the number of points contacting on the surface of the object. Figure 6 shows an example of a planar case. The sphere with more contacting points drawn in dark blue for interior case and red for exterior case

Algorithm 1. Infilling spheres construction

0. Given infilling spheres number n; Let the number of constructed infilling spheres $m = 0$.
1. Mesh voxelization and SDF computation within an external sphere.
2. Initialize status of each voxel $V_i = empty$.
3. Obtain each sphere denoted by $X_i := \{(x, s) : SDF(x) = s\}$.
4. Sort all X_i with negative/positive values s and the number of contacting points.
5. Construct first infilling sphere Y_1. Let $V_1 = true$, $m = 1$.
6. Set $d = 10$.   % the distance threshold between different spheres
7. for i = 2,3,4,...

```
repeat
   for j = 1-m
   repeat
      if distance(x_i, x_j) = d + s_j + s_i        % x_j the center of one infilling sphere.
      then
         construct a new infilling sphere Y_{m+1}, V_i = true, and m = m + 1
      else
         if distance(x_i, x_j) < s_j + s_i         % point x_i is inside or near Y_j then
            V_i = false
         end if
      end if
   until maximum number of existing infilling spheres reached
until maximum number of voxels or n reached
```

8. Set $d = 5$ and repeat Step 7 for voxel satisfying $V_i = empty$ until n reached.
9. Set $d = 0$ and repeat Step 7 for voxel satisfying $V_i = empty$ until n reached.

usually includes richer shape information. In other words, such an infilling sphere is meaningful for representing the local shape of a 3D object.

In summary, the three criteria of constructing infilling spheres are concluded as:

- Infilling spheres should be constructed from large to small.
- Each infilling sphere should not intersect and try to avoid tangential with any other sphere.
- Each infilling sphere must be tangent to the object surface and has at least one contact point with the object.

Note that we divide the infilling spheres construction into interior and exterior situations because both the geometric meaning and the sphere size for positive and negative SDF space are somewhat different. However, their processing flow is the same. The pseudo-code of interior/exterior infilling spheres construction is provided in Algorithm 1 for a clear understanding.

3.4 Neural Network Architecture

When the infilling spheres are constructed, we can directly input these 4D primitives (coordinates of the sphere center plus the radius) into PointNet with a little adjustment to accomplish object classification. However, since a few number of spheres are necessary for complete representation of a 3D object, we empirically propose a lightweight network architecture, leading to faster training and inference. The lightweight network architecture with the proposed infilling spheres as inputs are named **InSphereNet**. As demonstrated in experiments, InSphereNet can perform as well as PointNet even with only 12% parameters and 17% FLOPS. Figure 7 shows the designed lightweight network architecture for 256 infilling spheres. It is worth noting that there are only about 100000 parameters in this classification network.

4 Experiment

The experiments are divided into four parts. First, we show infilling spheres can be directly applied to classical classification network PointNet and achieve better performance with 1024 primitives. Second, to validate the robustness of the infilling spheres, we reduce the number of spheres to 512 and 256 separately. Although the number of input spheres decrease by 50% and 75%, the classification accuracy decrease slightly and become much better than PointNet with point clouds as input. Third, since the classification accuracy do not decrease significantly with less infilling sphere inputs, we reduce the dimension of global features and the number of fully connected layer, and the accuracy is still higher than 88%. Fourth, we visualize critical spheres which have the greatest impact on the classification task.

4.1 Preliminary Classification Evaluation on ModelNet40

PointNet learns global point cloud feature from 1024 uniformly sampled points of each 3D object in ModelNet40. To compare the representative ability of our spheres with point clouds, spheres with the same input data size are fed into the PointNet classification network. Table 1 shows that three configurations of 1024 infilling spheres all achieve higher classification accuracy than 1024 points on PointNet.

Table 1. Overall classification accuracy on ModelNet40

Method	Input	Acc (%)
MVCNN 12x	Images	89.5
3D Shapenets	Voxels	84.7
VoxNet	Voxels	85.9
PointNet	Points	89.2
PointNet++	Points with normal	91.9
Ours (1024 interior)	Infilling spheres	90.2
Ours (1024 exterior)	Infilling spheres	90.6
Ours (512 interior and 512 exterior)	Infilling spheres	90.3

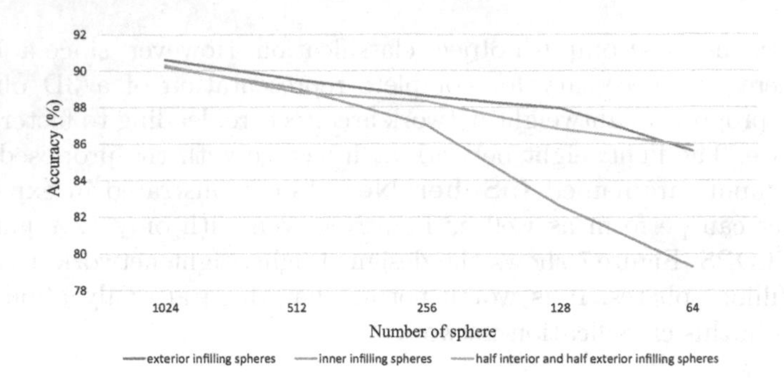

Fig. 8. Accuracy of InSphereNet vs. number of infilling spheres

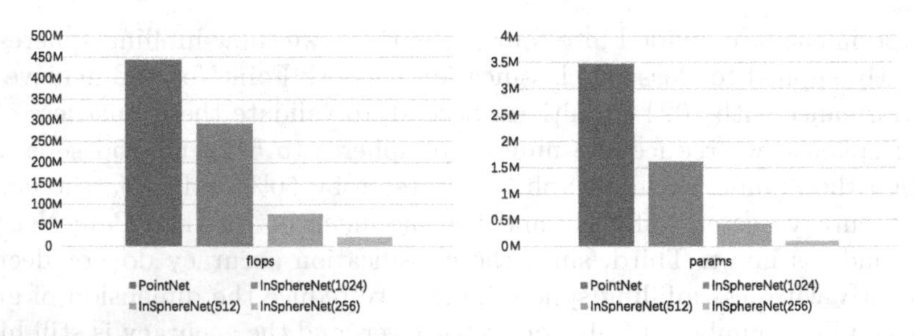

Fig. 9. Comparison of different network architectures in terms of flops and number of parameters

4.2 Less Infilling Spheres Test

In this experiment, we show the infilling spheres for 3D classification task are more robust than point clouds in terms of the reduced network inputs. To point clouds, PointNet reports if there are 50% points missing, the accuracy drops by 2.4%. However, when we reduce the number of infilling sphere inputs by 50%, the accuracy only drop by 1.1% for external infilling sphere and 1.2% for inner infilling sphere separately. And the accuracy of 512 external infilling spheres is still higher than 1024 points. Figure 8 depicts the overall classification accuracy with different numbers of infilling spheres for three configurations.

4.3 Lightweight Neural Network Test

From the above experiments, we found 512 external spheres still achieve higher classification accuracy than 1024 points. Therefore, we try modifying the network architecture settings to further test the effects of infilling spheres. As shown in Fig. 7, when the input size of external spheres is reduced from 1024 to 256, the dimension of SDF features extracted by the MLP layers is reduced accordingly from 1024 to 256. Since the feature dimension extracted by MLP decreases, we also reduce the fully connected layers, which largely reduced network parameters and computational costs. Figure 9 shows the comparison of four different network

Table 2. Classification accuracy with different network setting

Input size	Network setting	Acc (%)
1024	mlp(4, 64, 128, 1024), fc(1024, 512, 256, k)	90.6
512	mlp(4, 64, 128, 512), fc(512, 256, k)	88.8
256	mlp(4, 64, 128, 256), fc(256, k)	88.1

architectures in terms of flops and number of parameters. Table 2 shows the classification accuracy for different network setting with different input data size. For 256 exterior spheres, the accuracy is even higher than 88%, which validates the representation power of infilling spheres.

4.4 Critical Spheres Visualization

In this section, the critical infilling spheres with global feature are visualized. The original 1024 inputs are rendered in the first row of Fig. 10 while the critical spheres are shown in its second row. The number of critical spheres from left to right is only 251, 201, 267 and 234 respectively. It can be also seen that most of larger spheres are critical, which further proves the validity of our representation method for 3D objects.

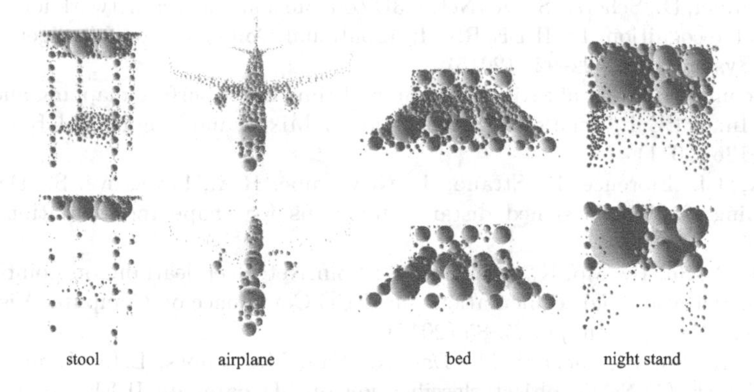

Fig. 10. Visualization of critical infilling spheres

5 Conclusion and Future Work

In this paper, we present how to construct infilling spheres to accomplish 3D object classification. Compared to previous works directly utilizing point clouds on surface as inputs of DNN, the proposed method can represent 3D shape from coarse to fine as the number of infilling spheres increases. Experiment results show that InSphereNet has better performance than PointNet, especially with less number of inputting features. Even if the layers and parameters of DNN decreases sharply, the results are still satisfactory. All of this proves that infilling spheres are more representative and meaningful than point clouds.

One existing drawback of the proposed method is that the infilling spheres are still unstructured. In future work, we will try to extract local information of each infilling sphere by using graph convolution, just like PointNet++ and DGCNN do.

Acknowledgements. The authors would like to thank NSFC 61703092 for supporting this research.

References

1. https://github.com/PyMesh/PyMesh/
2. Bruna, J., Zaremba, W., Szlam, A., LeCun, Y.: Spectral networks and locally connected networks on graphs. CoRR abs/1312.6203 (2013)
3. Curless, B., Levoy, M.: A volumetric method for building complex models from range images. In: SIGGRAPH (1996)
4. Dai, A., Qi, C.R., Nießner, M.: Shape completion using 3D-encoder-predictor CNNs and shape synthesis. In: IEEE Conference on Computer Vision and Pattern Recognition, pp. 6545–6554 (2016)
5. Ling, H., Jacobs, D.W.: Shape classification using the inner-distance. IEEE Trans. Pattern Anal. Mach. Intell. **29**, 286–299 (2007)
6. Maturana, D., Scherer, S.: VoxNet: a 3D convolutional neural network for real-time object recognition. In: IEEE/RSJ International Conference on Intelligent Robots and Systems, pp. 922–928 (2015)
7. Newcombe, R.A., et al.: KinectFusion: real-time dense surface mapping and tracking. In: IEEE International Symposium on Mixed and Augmented Reality, pp. 127–136 (2011)
8. Park, J.J., Florence, P., Straub, J., Newcombe, R.A., Lovegrove, S.: DeepSDF: learning continuous signed distance functions for shape representation. ArXiv (2019)
9. Qi, C.R., Su, H., Mo, K., Guibas, L.J.: PointNet: deep learning on point sets for 3d classification and segmentation. In: IEEE Conference on Computer Vision and Pattern Recognition, pp. 77–85 (2017)
10. Qi, C.R., Su, H., Nießner, M., Dai, A., Yan, M., Guibas, L.J.: Volumetric and multi-view CNNs for object classification on 3D data. In: IEEE Conference on Computer Vision and Pattern Recognition, pp. 5648–5656 (2016)
11. Qi, C.R., Yi, L., Su, H., Guibas, L.J.: PointNet++: deep hierarchical feature learning on point sets in a metric space. In: NIPS (2017)
12. Rustamov, R.M.: Laplace-Beltrami eigenfunctions for deformation invariant shape representation. In: Symposium on Geometry Processing (2007)
13. Rusu, R.B., Blodow, N., Beetz, M.: Fast point feature histograms (FPFH) for 3D registration. In: IEEE International Conference on Robotics and Automation, pp. 3212–3217 (2009)
14. Rusu, R.B., Blodow, N., Marton, Z.C., Beetz, M.: Aligning point cloud views using persistent feature histograms. In: IEEE/RSJ International Conference on Intelligent Robots and Systems, pp. 3384–3391 (2008)

15. Shah, S.A.A., Bennamoun, M., Boussaïd, F., El-Sallam, A.A.: 3D-div: a novel local surface descriptor for feature matching and pairwise range image registration. In: IEEE International Conference on Image Processing, pp. 2934–2938 (2013)
16. Stutz, D., Geiger, A.: Learning 3D shape completion from laser scan data with weak supervision. In: IEEE Conference on Computer Vision and Pattern Recognition, pp. 1955–1964 (2018)
17. Su, H., Maji, S., Kalogerakis, E., Learned-Miller, E.G.: Multi-view convolutional neural networks for 3D shape recognition. In: IEEE International Conference on Computer Vision, pp. 945–953 (2015)
18. Sun, J., Ovsjanikov, M., Guibas, L.J.: A concise and provably informative multi-scale signature based on heat diffusion. Comput. Graph. Forum **28**, 1383–1392 (2009)
19. Wang, R., Yan, J., Yang, X.: Learning combinatorial embedding networks for deep graph matching. In: International Conference on Computer Vision (2019)
20. Wang, Y., Sun, Y., Liu, Z., Sarma, S.E., Bronstein, M.M., Solomon, J.M.: Dynamic graph CNN for learning on point clouds. ArXiv abs/1801.07829 (2018)
21. Wu, Z., et al.: 3D ShapeNets: a deep representation for volumetric shapes. In: IEEE Conference on Computer Vision and Pattern Recognition, pp. 1912–1920 (2015)
22. Yi, L., et al.: A scalable active framework for region annotation in 3D shape collections. ACM Trans. Graph. **35**, 210:1–210:12 (2016)
23. Yu, T., Yan, J., Zhao, J., Li, B.: Joint cuts and matching of partitions in one graph. In: Proceedings of the IEEE Conference on Computer Vision and Pattern Recognition, pp. 705–713 (2018)
24. Zeng, A., Song, S., Nießner, M., Fisher, M., Xiao, J., Funkhouser, T.A.: 3DMatch: learning local geometric descriptors from RGB-D reconstructions. In: IEEE Conference on Computer Vision and Pattern Recognition, pp. 199–208 (2016)

3-D Oral Shape Retrieval Using Registration Algorithm

Wenting Cui[1], Shaoyi Du[1](✉), Teng Wan[1], Yan Liu[2], Yuying Liu[1], Yang Yang[3], Qingnan Mou[4,5], Mengqi Han[4,5], and Yu-cheng Guo[1,4,5]

[1] Institute of Artificial Intelligence and Robotics, Xi'an Jiaotong University, Xi'an 710049, Shaanxi Province, People's Republic of China
dushaoyi@gmail.com

[2] School of Software Engineering, Xi'an Jiaotong University, Xi'an 710049, Shaanxi Province, People's Republic of China

[3] The School of Electronic and Information Engineering, Xi'an Jiaotong University, Xi'an 710049, Shaanxi Province, People's Republic of China

[4] Department of Orthodontics, Stomatological Hospital of Xi'an Jiaotong University, 98 XiWu Road, Xi'an 710004, Shaanxi Province, People's Republic of China

[5] Key Laboratory of Shaanxi Province for Craniofacial Precision Medicine Research, College of Stomatology, Xi'an Jiaotong University, 98 XiWu Road, Xi'an 710004, Shaanxi Province, People's Republic of China

Abstract. In this paper, we present a novel 3-D oral shape retrieval using correntropy-based registration algorithm. Fast matching as the traditional registration method can achieve, its registration accuracy is disturbed by noise and outliers. Since the 3-D oral model contains a large amount of noise and outliers, it may lead to a decrease in registration accuracy, which affects the accuracy of retrieval rate. Therefore, we introduce the correntropy into the rigid registration algorithm to solve this problem. Although the noise and outliers are suppressed by the correntropy-based algorithm, these noises and outliers still participate in the registration. For better retrieval, we choose the matched point cloud data and use mean squared error results to judge the individual differences of the shape. Finally, the accurate retrieval of the oral shape is realized. Experimental results demonstrate our 3-D shape retrieval algorithm can be successfully searched under different models, which can help forensics use the characteristics of biological individuals to accurately search and identify, and improve recognition efficiency.

Keywords: Point set registration · Iterative closest point (ICP) algorithm · Correntropy · Retrieval

1 Introduction

The development of computer information, graphics and other technologies seems as rapid as can be, and meanwhile, 3-D shape retrieval is a research hotspot in computer vision. For example, it can be used for biometrics identification [1], medical image analysis [2], e-commerce [3], and virtual reality [4, 5], etc. Biological individual

Y. M. Ro et al. (Eds.): MMM 2020, LNCS 11962, pp. 340–349, 2020.
https://doi.org/10.1007/978-3-030-37734-2_28

identification, especially forensic science, is a research topic with important application value [6]. Forensic doctors often use dental information as an important basis for judging an individual, and use the teeth and their surrounding information as a biometric model to perform accurate biometric identification. At present, there are many methods for 3-D shape retrieval, such as retrieval using feature information [7], retrieval based on deep learning [8], and text-based retrieval [9], etc. However, these methods do not handle oral data very well. Due to the relatively small number of oral datasets, deep learning methods cannot be used for retrieval. Moreover, the oral plaster model contains a large number of plaster tumors and bubbles, which causes the dataset to contain a large amount of noise and outliers and makes it difficult to extract features.

In this paper, in order to get a better retrieval result, we use the rigid registration algorithm to solve this retrieval problem. The most classic and widely used algorithm in rigid registration is the iterative closest point (ICP) algorithm [10]. Different from the previous algorithms, it achieves fast registration between two sets of points, while saving the steps of the pre-processing and feature extraction. However, the registration accuracy of the algorithm will decrease when the image has noise and outliers. In order to solve these problems, many scholars have improved shortcomings of the traditional ICP algorithm in recent years. For the registration problem of noise and outliers in data sets, Du et al. [11] introduced bidirectional distance into the ICP registration algorithm, which achieved robust and fast registration. Chetverikov et al. [12] put forward a trimmed ICP registration algorithm to achieve fast registration by a given overlapping rate. Phillip et al. [13] improved the trimmed ICP registration algorithm, which could compute the overlapping rate and correspondence simultaneously.

However, some algorithms above are too slow and others have no good solution to deal with noise and outliers. Therefore, the retrieval problem of the oral model is not well handled. To tackle this problem, this paper demonstrates a novel 3-D oral shape retrieval using correntropy registration algorithm for biological individual identification. Firstly, the oral data is sparsely preprocessed for acceleration, and then the correntropy is introduced into the traditional ICP algorithm for the oral data matching. After that, we choose the matched data to judge their individual differences, and finally demonstrate the accurate individual identification of oral data. In short, the proposed algorithm can help forensic doctors to search and identify quickly and accurately by using the characteristics of biological individuals, and improve the efficiency of recognition.

This paper is organized as follows. In the second section, the traditional ICP algorithm is briefly discussed. In the third section, we introduce the correntropy into the algorithm model and apply it to the retrieval of the tooth model. In the fourth section, experiments verify the precision and speed of our algorithm in the retrieval of the tooth model. Finally, the conclusion is given in the last section.

2 Rigid Registration Method

In this section, we introduce the rigid registration algorithm for retrieval. Given two point sets in $\mathbb{R}^n$, the model point set $P = \{\vec{p}_i\}_{i=1}^{N_p} (N_p \in \mathbb{N})$ and the target point set

$Q = \{\vec{q}_j\}_{j=1}^{N_q} (N_q \in \mathbb{N})$. The traditional ICP algorithm aims to find an optimal rigid transformation, with which the model point set is in the best alignment with the objective point set. For the registration of these point sets, the formula expressed by the least squares (LS) criterion as follows:

$$\begin{aligned} \min_{\mathbf{R}, \vec{t}, j \in \{1,2,\cdots,N_q\}} & (\sum_{i=1}^{N_p} ||(\mathbf{R}\vec{p}_i + \vec{t}) - \vec{q}_j||_2^2) \\ s.t.\ & \mathbf{R}^T\mathbf{R} = \mathbf{I}_n, \det(\mathbf{R}) = 1 \end{aligned} \tag{1}$$

where $\mathbf{R}$ is a $n \times n$ dimension rotation matrix in $\mathbb{R}^n$, and $\vec{t}$ is a translation vector in $\mathbb{R}^n$. There are two unknowns in Eq. (1) above that need to be solved:

(1) According to the $(k-1)$th step,the correspondence between two point sets is established:

$$c_k(i) = \arg \min_{j \in \{1,2,\cdots,N_q\}} (||(\mathbf{R}_{k-1}\vec{p}_i + \vec{t}_{k-1}) - \vec{q}_j||_2^2),\ i = 1, 2, \cdots, N_p \tag{2}$$

(2) In order to find the optimal spatial transformation between two point sets, it can be computed according to the known correspondence:

$$(\mathbf{R}^*, \vec{t}^*) = \arg\min_{\mathbf{R}^T\mathbf{R}=\mathbf{I}_n, \det(\mathbf{R})=1, \vec{t}} (\sum_{i=1}^{N_p} ||\mathbf{R}(\mathbf{R}_{k-1}\vec{p}_i + \vec{t}_{k-1}) + \vec{t} - \vec{q}_{c_k(i)}||_2^2) \tag{3}$$

Next, we update the transformation $\mathbf{R}^*$ and $\vec{t}^*$ of the kth step according to the obtained $\mathbf{R}_k$ and $\vec{t}_k$.

$$\mathbf{R}_k = \mathbf{R}^*\mathbf{R}_{k-1},\ \vec{t}_k = \mathbf{R}^*\vec{t}_{k-1} + \vec{t}^* \tag{4}$$

Fast and accurate as the traditional ICP algorithm is, it has a reduced accuracy when there is a lot of noise and outlier interference.

3 3-D Oral Shape Retrieval Using the Correntropy Registration Algorithm

In this section, we introduce the correntropy into the algorithm model and apply it to the retrieval of the tooth model.

3.1 Problem Statement

The oral plaster model contains a large number of plaster tumors and bubbles, which make the data set contain a lot of noise and outliers. This phenomenon causes the registration accuracy of the traditional rigid registration algorithm to be less than the retrieval requirement. It is because the traditional rigid registration algorithm uses a 2-Norm distance between two point sets as a measure. Under this measure, when corresponding points between two point sets have short distance, the error of the corresponding points is close to zero. However, if the distance of corresponding points between two point sets is large, the error of the corresponding points will increase rapidly. Therefore, if the data sets contain a large amount of noise and outliers, the accuracy of the registration result will be affected. For solving these problems above, the correntropy is introduced into the traditional rigid algorithm, and the precise registration is achieved when the data set contains a large amount of noise and outliers. Then, the correntropy form is as follows:

$$W(x,y) = \exp\left(-\frac{(x-y)^2}{2\sigma^2}\right) \tag{5}$$

where σ is a free variable. The closer the values of x and y are, the larger the value of the equation. If x and y contain a large amount of noise and outliers, the values of noise and outliers will decrease in the Eq. (5).

In this way, the correntropy is effective in restraining noise and outliers, which can improve the accuracy of the registration algorithm. According to the above conclusion, the new objective function based on the correntropy between the correspondence is shown as follows:

$$\begin{aligned} &\max_{\mathbf{R},\vec{t},c(i)\in\{1,2,\cdots,N_q\}} \sum_{i=1}^{N_x} \exp\left(-\frac{\|(\mathbf{R}\vec{p}_i+\vec{t})-\vec{q}_{c(i)}\|_2^2}{2\sigma^2}\right) \\ &s.t. \quad \mathbf{R}^T\mathbf{R} = \mathbf{I}_n, \quad \det(\mathbf{R}) = 1 \end{aligned} \tag{6}$$

where $\mathbf{R}$ is a $n \times n$ dimension rotation matrix in $\mathbb{R}^n$, $\vec{t}$ is a translation vector in $\mathbb{R}^n$, and σ is a free variable.

3.2 3-D Oral Shape Retrieval Using the Correntropy-Based Registration Algorithm

In this section, we introduce the correntropy into the registration algorithm to improve the accuracy of the algorithm, which is applied to the retrieval of 3-D oral shape.

It can be seen from the comparison of Eqs. (1) and (6) that the point set registration algorithm based on correntropy is similar to the traditional rigid registration algorithm, but the solution process is slightly different. And each iteration includes the following two steps:

(1) According to the $(k-1)$th step, we can establish a correspondence between two point sets:

$$c_k(i) = \underset{j\in\{1,2,\cdots,N_q\}}{\arg\min} \|(\mathbf{R}_{k-1}\vec{p}_i + \vec{t}_{k-1}) - \vec{q}_j\|_2^2, \; i = 1, \cdots, N_p \tag{7}$$

(2) In order to find the optimal rigid transformation between two point sets, it can be computed according to the known correspondence:

$$(\mathbf{R}^*, \vec{t}^*) = \underset{\mathbf{R}^{\mathrm{T}}\mathbf{R} = \mathbf{I}_n,\ \det(\mathbf{R}) = 1, \vec{t}}{\arg\max} \sum_{i=1}^{N_p} \exp\left(-\frac{\|\mathbf{R}(\mathbf{R}_{k-1}\vec{p}_i + \vec{t}_{k-1}) + \vec{t} - \vec{q}_{c_k(i)}\|_2^2}{2\sigma^2}\right) \tag{8}$$

Next, we update the transformation $\mathbf{R}^*$ and $\vec{t}^*$ of the kth step according to the obtained $\mathbf{R}_k$ and $\vec{t}_k$.

$$\mathbf{R}_k = \mathbf{R}^*\mathbf{R}_{k-1},\ \vec{t}_k = \mathbf{R}^*\vec{t}_{k-1} + \vec{t}^* \tag{9}$$

There are many solutions to Eq. (7), such as the Delaunay triangulation [14], k-d tree [15] and so on. However, the solution of Eq. (8) is relatively difficult, and this problem can be solved by singular value decomposition (SVD) [16]. The following is a derivation of a rigid body transformation based on SVD method and we can get:

$$J = \mathbf{U}\boldsymbol{\Lambda}\mathbf{V}^T \tag{10}$$

where $\mathbf{U}$ and $\mathbf{V}$ are $n \times n$ orthogonal matrices respectively, and $\boldsymbol{\Lambda}$ is a $n \times n$ diagonal matrix. Accordingly, the rotation matrix is calculated as follows:

$$\mathbf{R}^* = \mathbf{VDU}^T \tag{11}$$

where $\mathbf{D}$ is a $n \times n$ diagonal matrix:

$$\mathbf{D} = \begin{cases} \mathbf{I}_n & \det(\mathbf{U})\det(\mathbf{V}) = 1 \\ diag(1, 1, \ldots, 1, -1) & \det(\mathbf{U})\det(\mathbf{V}) = -1 \end{cases} \tag{12}$$

According to Eq. (9), we can get $\mathbf{R}_k$.

After that, the translation vector is calculated as follows:

$$\vec{t}^* = \sum_{i=1}^{N_p}\left(\vec{q}_{c_k(i)} - \mathbf{R}^*\vec{p}_i^{\,'}\right)W_k(i) / \sum_{i=1}^{N_p} W_k(i) \tag{13}$$

then, according to Eq. (9), we can get $\vec{t}_k$.

In addition, the deep learning method has a large demand for sample size, but there are fewer oral data sets. Therefore, the above registration method can be used for retrieval, which can well handle noise and outliers interference. On this basis, we describe in detail how to use the correntropy-based registration algorithm to retrieve the tooth model. As shown in Fig. 1, these two types of models are the most commonly used dental models in the clinic, which include 3-D oral plaster models and 3-D oral scanning models.

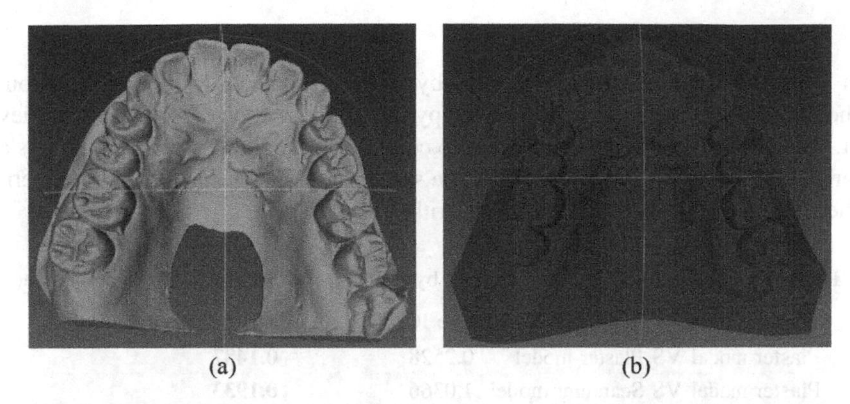

Fig. 1. Tooth models. (a) 3-D oral plaster model. (b) 3-D oral scanning model.

First, the oral plaster model and the oral scanning model are transformed into 3-D point cloud models by using the MeshLab. Second, point cloud data is matched by the correntropy-based registration algorithm. Although these oral model noise and outliers are suppressed by the proposed algorithm, these noise and outliers still participate in the registration. And we use mean squared error to measure the similarity between the two models, but the point pairs generated by these noise and outliers through our registration method will affect the accuracy of retrieval. In order to improve the retrieval accuracy, we only extract the top 50% of matching point pairs after registration as effective points, and it denoted as $\{\vec{u}_s, \vec{v}_{c(s)}\}_{s=1}^{N_s}$, where N_s is the number of effective points, $\vec{v}_{c(s)}$ is the corresponding point of $\vec{u}_s$. Then, we calculate the mean squared error of these pairs, and the formula is as follows:

$$e = \sum_{s=1}^{N_s} ||\mathbf{R}\vec{p}_s + \vec{t} - \vec{q}_{c(s)}||_2^2 / N_s \tag{14}$$

If two oral models are from the same person, the mean squared error between them should be small. In this way, the tooth model of the same person can be searched from the data set, thereby implementing the identification of the individual.

4 Experimental Results

First, registration results for oral plaster models and oral scanning models are given in the first part. Then, in the second part, we test and verify the retrieval accuracy of the oral model. Furthermore, the data set of using for retrieval is obtained from the Stomatological Hospital (College of Stomatology) of Xi'an Jiaotong University, which includes 3-D oral plaster models and 3-D oral scanning model. And we down-sample these data to improve the speed of retrieval.

4.1 Registration of Real Data

This section gives the matching results by different methods from same person to further study the accuracy of the correntropy-based registration algorithm for retrieval. First, we use two registration algorithms to compare errors in the same oral models and different oral models respectively. It can be seen from Table 1 that experimental errors of the correntropy-based registration algorithm is small.

Table 1. The mean squared error results by different methods from the same person.

	The ICP algorithm	The proposed algorithm
Plaster model VS Plaster model	0.2528	**0.1487**
Plaster model VS Scanning model	1.0366	**0.1933**

Second, in order to directly show the effect of the algorithm, we give the registration results of different models from the same person, including an oral plaster model and an oral scanning model. as shown in Fig. 2, the registration result of the proposed algorithm is better than the traditional ICP algorithm. Therefore, this method is effective not just for retrieving the same type of tooth model, but for retrieving different types of tooth models.

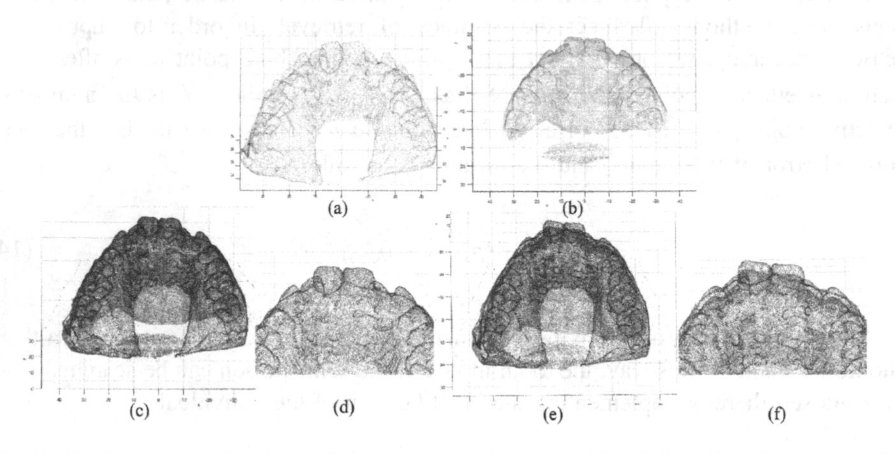

Fig. 2. Registration results of two different types oral models. (a) and (b) 3-D oral plaster model and oral scanning model from the same person respectively. (c) the results of ICP algorithm. (d) a partial enlargement results. (e) the results of the correntropy-based registration algorithm (f) the partial enlargement result.

4.2 Comparison of Retrieval Accuracy

This section further verifies the retrieval accuracy of the oral model. Considering the problem of model diversification, we use the correntropy-based registration algorithm for shape retrieval, and then calculate the error according to Eq. (14). And the Figs. 3 and 4 represent mean squared error results of our algorithm in the two types of oral models respectively.

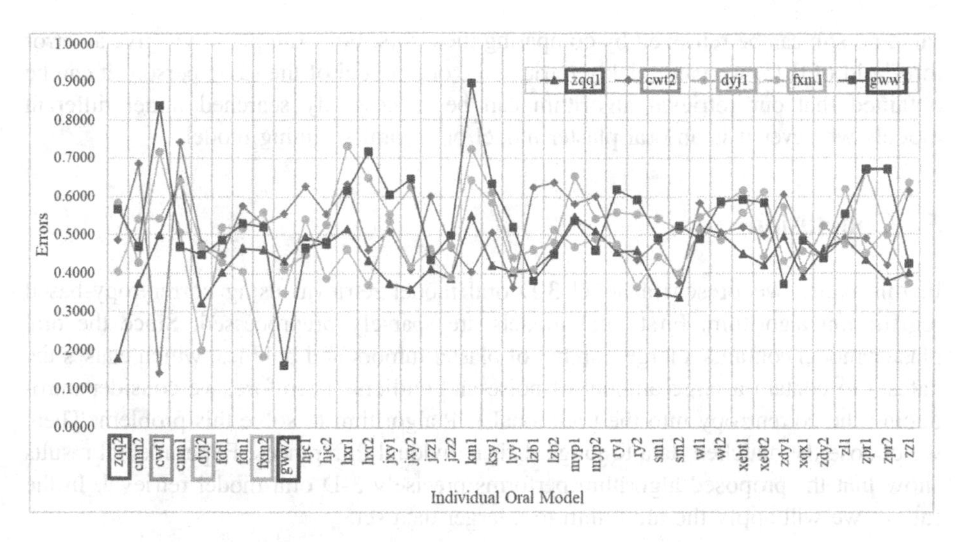

Fig. 3. Retrieval results under the same oral model.

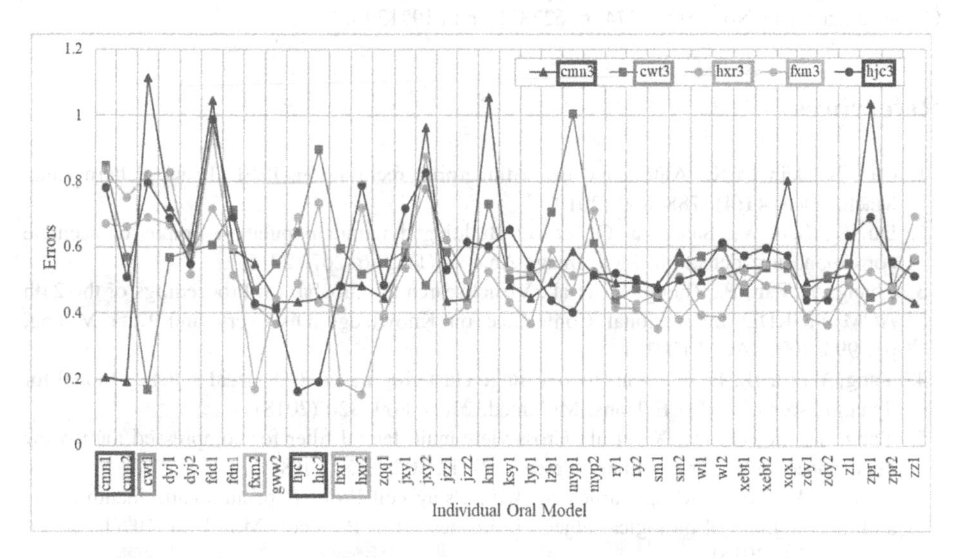

Fig. 4. Retrieval results under different oral models.

When these search results indicate that the model is from the same person, the mean squared error between two point sets is the smallest. Among them, the abscissa represents the individual of the search library, and the ordinate represents the mean squared error between the two individual models. It can be obtained from Figs. 3 and 4, five 3-D oral plaster models are randomly selected as the objects to be retrieved, and the most similar model from the retrieval object is searched from the oral model library. When the same person is matched, the error is very small. On the contrary, the matching error between different people is relatively large. Then, the oral model of the same person can be retrieved by comparing the errors. For example, if we give an error threshold of 0.25, we can quickly retrieve the oral model of the same person. It can be obtained that our retrieval algorithm can be successfully searched under different models whatever it is an oral plaster model or an oral scanning model.

5 Conclusion

In this paper, we present a novel 3-D oral model retrieval using correntropy-based registration algorithm. First, oral models are sparsely preprocessed. Since the oral plaster model contains a large number of plaster tumors and bubbles, which causes the dataset to contain a large amount of noise and outliers. Therefore, we consider introducing the correntropy into the traditional ICP algorithm to solve this problem. Then, we choose the matched data to judge their individual differences. Experimental results show that the proposed algorithm performs precisely 3-D oral model retrieval. In the future, we will apply the algorithm to a larger data set.

Acknowledgment. This work was supported by the National Natural Science Foundation of China under Grant Nos. 61573274, 61627811 and 61971343.

References

1. Cao, K., Jain, A.K.: Automated latent fingerprint recognition. IEEE Trans. Pattern Anal. Mach. Intell. **41**(4), 788–800 (2019)
2. Du, S., Guo, Y., Sanroma, G., et al.: Building dynamic population graph for accurate correspondence detection. Med. Image Anal. **26**(1), 256–267 (2015)
3. Zhang, Y., Pan, P., Zheng, Y., et al.: Visual search at Alibaba. In: Proceedings of the 24th ACM SIGKDD International Conference on Knowledge Discovery and Data Mining, pp. 993–1001. ACM (2018)
4. Yang, Y., Li, B., Li, P., et al.: A two-stage clustering based 3-D visual saliency model for dynamic scenarios. IEEE Trans. Multimed. **21**(4), 809–820 (2018)
5. Yang, Y., Liu, Q., He, X., et al.: Cross-view multi-lateral filter for compressed multi-view depth video. IEEE Trans. Image Process. **28**(1), 302–315 (2018)
6. Bray, M.A., Vokes, M.S., Carpenter, A.E.: Using cell Profiler for automatic identification and measurement of biological objects in images. Curr. Protocols Mol. Biol. **109**(1), 14.17. 1–14.17. 13 (2015)
7. Ke, Q., Deng, J., Baker, S., et al.: Image retrieval using discriminative visual features. U.S. Patent 9,229,956, 5 January 2016
8. Zhao, F., Huang, Y., Wang, L., et al.: Deep semantic ranking based hashing for multi-label image retrieval. In: Proceedings of the IEEE Conference on Computer Vision and Pattern Recognition, pp. 1556–1564 (2015)
9. Li, A., Sun, J., Yue-Hei Ng, J., et al.: Generating holistic 3D scene abstractions for text-based image retrieval. In: Proceedings of the IEEE Conference on Computer Vision and Pattern Recognition, pp. 193–201 (2017)
10. Besl, P.J., Mckay, H.D.: A method for registration of 3-D shapes. IEEE Trans. Pattern Anal. Mach. Intell. (PAMI) **14**(2), 239–256 (1992)

11. Du, S., Zhang, C., Wu, Z., et al.: Robust isotropic scaling ICP algorithm with bidirectional distance and bounded rotation angle. Neurocomputing **215**, 160–168 (2016)
12. Chetverikov, D., Stepanov, D., Krsek, P.: Robust Euclidean alignment of 3-D point sets: the trimmed iterative closest point algorithm. Image Vis. Comput. **23**(3), 299–309 (2005)
13. Phillips, J.M., Liu, R., Tomasi, C.: Outlier robust ICP for minimizing fractional RMSD. In: Proceedings of IEEE International Conference on 3-D Digital Imaging and Modeling (3DIM), pp. 427–434 (2007)
14. Boissonnat, J.D., Dyer, R., Ghosh, A.: Delaunay triangulation of manifolds. Found. Comput. Math. **18**(2), 399–431 (2018)
15. Chen, Y., Zhou, L., Tang, Y., et al.: Fast neighbor search by using revised k-d tree. Inf. Sci. **472**, 145–162 (2019)
16. Arun, K.S., Huang, T.S., Blostein, S.D.: Least-squares fitting of two 3D point sets. IEEE Trans. Pattern Anal. Mach. Intell. (PAMI) **9**(5), 698–700 (1987)

Face Super-Resolution by Learning Multi-view Texture Compensation

Yu Wang, Tao Lu[(✉)], Ruobo Xu, and Yanduo Zhang

Hubei Key Laboratory of Intelligent Robot,
School of Computer Science and Engineering, Wuhan Institute of Technology,
Wuhan 430205, China
lutxyl@gmail.com

Abstract. Single face image super-resolution (SR) methods using deep neural network yields decent performance. Due to the posture of face images, multi-view face super-resolution task is more challenging than single input. Multi-view face images contain complement information from different view. However, it is hard to integrate texture information from multi-view low-resolution (LR) face images. In this paper, we propose a novel face SR using multi-view texture compensation to combine multiple face images to yield a HR image as output. We use texture attention mechanism to transfer high-accurate texture compensation information to fixed view for better visual performance. Experimental results conform that the proposed neural network outperforms other state-of-the-art face SR algorithms.

Keywords: Multi-view face image · Texture compensation · Face super-resolution

1 Introduction

Face super-resolution (SR), which is known as a specific SR algorithm, can reconstruct a high-resolution (HR) images from one or multiple low-resolution (LR) input images. Due to the superb ability of reconstructing image details, face SR is widely used in video surveillance, face recognition, entertainment, etc. In general, face SR methods include three typical methods: Interpolation-based [1], reconstruction-based [2] and learning-based [3] methods. Because learning-based face SR approaches utilize additional priors from training samples to achieve reconstruction task. Thus learning-based face SR becomes more and more popular in recent decades.

Intuitively, the existing learning-based face SR algorithms can be divided into two kinds: single-input face SR (SFSR) and multi-input face SR (MFSR) algorithms. There are plenty of decent SFSR algorithms using sparse coding [4], locality-constrained representation [5], low-rank representation [6]. Dong et al. [7] firstly introduced convolutional neural network (CNN) into SR algorithm in an end-to-end manner. Yu et al. [8] proposed a transformative autoencoder network

Y. M. Ro et al. (Eds.): MMM 2020, LNCS 11962, pp. 350–360, 2020.
https://doi.org/10.1007/978-3-030-37734-2_29

to super-resolve very low-resolution unaligned and noisy face images. Yang et al. [9] proposed a Generative Adversarial Networks (GAN) to restore reasonable visual output HR face images. Recently, Lu et al. [10] proposed a parallel region-based deep residual networks, which utilizes region-based face hallucination to learn further accurate prior information. Although SFSR gives an end-to-end solution for supervised learning. In fact, in real world applications, multi-view images are more common than single images. And SFSR has limitations on dealing with multi-view images.

On the other hand, MFSR methods take additional two or more images as inputs, which uses additional texture information to aid the SR process. Generally, traditional multi-frame reconstruction based SR methods can be directly used for super-resolving facial images. However, the performance of reconstruction based SR relies on sub-pixel registration between LR images. It is very challenging to get high-accuracy sub-pixel level registration over LR images. Thus, using multi-frame images limits its reconstruction performance directly. Jia et al. [11] proposed a general face SR approach using tensor to model expression and posture changes. Ma et al. [12] used a multi-view face SR method to generate frontal facial images from non-frontal ones. Evgeniya et al. [13] proposed a multi-frame deep face SR to solve the registration and SR problems in one network with an end-to-end manner. The performance of these methods relies on the performance of registration sub-network.

In fact, the existing face SR methods mainly focuses on generating a HR face images, which provides key perceptual information for the vision system using single LR fixed posture image. However, in most cases, it is not sufficient to use only the LR frontal image texture information. Therefore, it is an attractive idea to recover an HR face image from multi-view reference images. Inspired by the method of multi-frame face image super-resolution [13] and parallax attention model [14], we extend single input face SR into multi-view approach using texture compensation model which avoids registration. Particularly, multi-view texture compensation (MTC) can adaptively transfer face texture information from a fixed view to another view images. After a face image pair (frontal/fixed-view image and another multi-view image) is given, a residual pooling module (RPM) is first used to generate a texture compensation feature. Then, these features are sent to a texture-attention module (TAM) to fuse the compensation textures by calculating an attention map. Finally, the feature maps of the target view images are updated by feature fusion to yield HR results.

The main contributions of this paper are: (1) We first use the texture information of the multi-view images to solve the face SR problem, and the proposed a method which does not rely on registration between pairs of face images; (2) We introduce a texture-attention module to learn the texture commentation of face images pairs, which can effectively improve the face SR performance; (3) We extend SFSR into its multi-view version named as MFSR which outperforms other state-of-the-art face SR methods.

2 Face Super-Resolution by Learning Multi-view Texture Compensation (MTC)

The proposed MTC has the ability of reconstructing any fixed view face images. For easy understanding, we use side-view images to form the front-view images as output. In this paper, we only verify the front face image SR task. It is worth noting that MTC can generate any fixed-view image. The architecture of MTC is shown in Fig. 1.

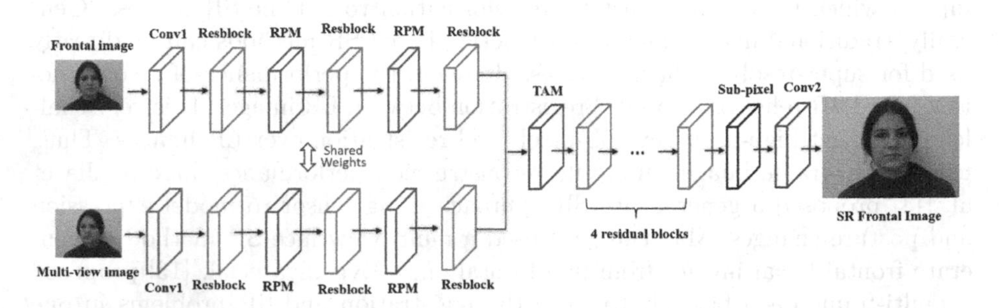

Fig. 1. The overall network structure of MTC. The specific details of RPM and TAM structure are shown in Figs. 2 and 3, respectively.

2.1 Residual Pooling Module (RPM)

Feature representations with rich texture information are important for enhancing SR performance. Therefore, we have to learn the characteristics of the texture information, and obtain its discriminant features. In order to achieve this goal, we propose to use RPM [15] for extracting deep features from face images. As shown in Fig. 2, RPM is constructed by alternately cascading the residual pooling module and the residual block. Features of the face images are first sent to RPM to generate multi-scale facial features, and then the obtained features are sent to the residual block for feature fusion. This process is repeated twice to generate the final face features. In RPM, we first combine three dilated convolutions (dilation rates of 1, 4, 8) with the 1×1 convolution into a RPM group, and then cascade four RPM groups in a residual manner. This RPM groups not only extracts the multi-scale features of the face, but also utilizes the diversity of convolutions to aggregate the convolutions of different dilated rates.

2.2 Texture-Attention Module (TAM)

Inspired by the self-attention mechanism [16,17], we propose TAM to obtain the global correspondence between the frontal images and the multi-view images. TAM can effectively integrate texture information of face images pairs.

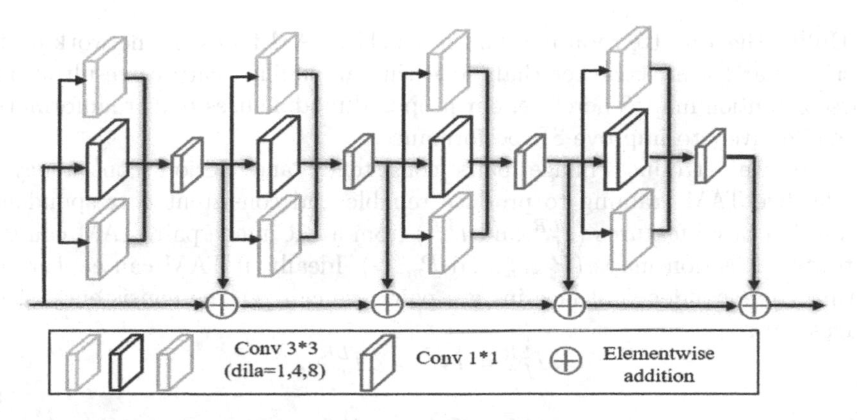

Fig. 2. Residual Pooling Module (RPM). RPM combines three dilated convolutions (dilation rates of 1, 4, 8) with the 1×1 convolution as a RPM group, and then cascades four RPM groups in residual feature spaces.

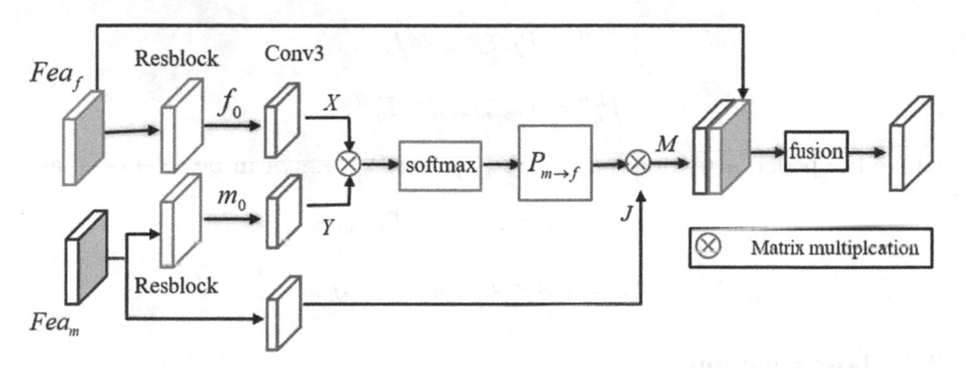

Fig. 3. Texture-attention Module (TAM). The main work of TAM is to integrate the texture features of the generated face images, the details are in Sect. 2.2.

The architecture of TAM is illustrated in Fig. 3. We will first feed the frontal images feature map $Fea_f \in \mathbb{R}^{H \times W \times C}$ and multi-view images feature map $Fea_m \in \mathbb{R}^{H \times W \times C}$ to two residual blocks to generate f_0 and m_0, respectively. And then feed f_0 to the 1×1 convolution layer to generate the feature map $X \in \mathbb{R}^{H \times W \times C}$. At the same time, feeding m_0 to another 1×1 convolution layer produces a feature map $Y \in \mathbb{R}^{H \times W \times C}$, and then reshaping Y to $\mathbb{R}^{H \times C \times W}$. Then, X and Y are subjected to batch matrix multiplication, and then passed through the softmax layer to generate an attention-map $P_{m \to f} \in \mathbb{R}^{H \times W \times W}$. Second, Fea_m is sent to a 1×1 convolution layer to produce $J \in \mathbb{R}^{H \times W \times C}$, which is further multiplied to produce a feature $M \in \mathbb{R}^{H \times W \times C}$. Finally, M and Fea_f are fed to the 1×1 convolutional layer for feature fusion.

Unlike the self-attention mechanism [16,17], TAM focus the network on the most similar features, rather than collecting all similar features resulting in a sparse attention map. Therefore, our proposed module uses texture information more effectively to improve SR performance.

Here, we introduce image pairs consistency and period consistency to standardize TAM training to produce reliable and consistent correspondence. Extracting facial features (I_f^{LR} and I_m^{LR}) from a LR image pair, TAM can generate two attention maps ($P_{f\to m}$ and $P_{m\to f}$). Ideally, if TAM can capture the feature correspondence of face images pairs, we can get the consistency of the images pairs:

$$\begin{aligned} I_f^{LR} &= P_{m\to f} \otimes I_m^{LR}, \\ I_m^{LR} &= P_{f\to m} \otimes I_f^{LR}, \end{aligned} \tag{1}$$

where $\otimes$ represents batch matrix multiplication. Based on Eq. (1), we can further derive the period consistency:

$$\begin{aligned} I_f^{LR} &= P_{f\to m\to f} \otimes I_f^{LR}, \\ I_m^{LR} &= P_{m\to f\to m} \otimes I_m^{LR}, \end{aligned} \tag{2}$$

where the period attention maps $P_{f\to m\to f}$ and $P_{m\to f\to m}$ can be calculated as:

$$\begin{aligned} P_{f\to m\to f} &= P_{m\to f} \otimes P_{f\to m}, \\ P_{m\to f\to m} &= P_{f\to m} \otimes P_{m\to f}. \end{aligned} \tag{3}$$

2.3 Loss Function

We have designed four loss functions for this network structure. Besides an reconstruction loss, we also introduced three kinds of losses, named as: photometric loss, guide loss, and period loss. They help the network to access the most of the correspondence between face images pairs. The overall loss function is formulated as:

$$L_{overall} = L_{rec} + k(L_{pho} + L_{gui} + L_{per}), \tag{4}$$

where k is empirically set to 0.005. Next, we will introduce four kinds of losses respectively.

Reconstruction Loss. The fusion network uses the mean square error (MSE) as loss function to calculate the difference between the merged reconstructed frontal images and the original HR frontal images. The reconstruction loss is:

$$L_{rec} = \| I_f^{SR} - I_f^{HR} \|_2^2, \tag{5}$$

where I_f^{SR} and I_f^{HR} represents the SR version and ground-truth of the frontal images, respectively.

Photometric Loss. Since collecting face images with multi-view images in vary illumination is challenging, we use an unsupervised way to train TAM. Following [18], we introduce a loss of photometric using the mean absolute error (MAE) loss. The photometric loss is:

$$\begin{aligned} L_{pho} &= \sum \| I_f^{LR} - (P_{m\to f} \otimes I_m^{LR})\|_1 \\ &+ \sum \| I_m^{LR} - (P_{f\to m} \otimes I_f^{LR})\|_1, \end{aligned} \tag{6}$$

where I_f^{LR} and I_m^{LR} represent feature maps from a LR face images pair.

Guide Loss. In order to produce accurate and consistent attention in the textureless area, guide loss is defined on the attention maps $P_{f\to m}$ and $P_{m\to f}$. The guide loss is:

$$\begin{aligned} L_{gui} = \sum_P \sum_{x,y,z} (&\|P(x,y,z) - P(x+1,y,z)\|_1 \\ + &\|P(x,y,z) - P(x,y+1,z+1)\|_1), \end{aligned} \tag{7}$$

where $P \in \{P_{f\to m}, P_{m\to f}\}$, $P(x,y,z)$ represents the contribution of position (x,y) in the multi-view images to position (x,z) in the frontal images. The first and second terms in Eq. (7) are used to achieve vertical and horizontal attention consistency, respectively.

Period Loss. In addition to the photometric loss and the guide loss, we further introduce a period loss to achieve period consistency. Since $P_{f\to m\to f}$ and $P_{m\to f\to m}$ can be regarded as identity matrices, we design a period loss as:

$$L_{per} = \sum \|P_{f\to m\to f} - F\|_1 + \sum \|P_{m\to f\to m} - F\|_1, \tag{8}$$

where F is a stack of H identity matrices.

3 Experimental Results

In this section, we first introduce the database and implementation details, and then conduct experiments to test the proposed network.

3.1 Database

In this paper, we use the FEI [23] database to verify the proposed method. There are 200 person in the FEI dataset. Each person has 14 face images. We select two images for each person, one for the frontal image and the other for side-view image. We use 360 images as the training dataset, 40 images as the testing dataset, and the HR image size is 256 × 192 pixels. The LR images is obtained by down-sampling with bicubic interpolation, and the down-sampling factor is 4, so that the LR image size is 64 × 48 pixels. For testing, we select 20 frontal images from the FEI dataset for objective assessment. For verification, we select another face image of 20 person from the FEI dataset as a multi-view image.

3.2 Implementation Details

In the training phase, we first perform a 4× downsampling of the HR images using bicubic interpolation to generate LR images, and then crop the 32 × 24 pixels images patches in steps of 4 pixels from the generated LR images. At the same time, their corresponding patches in the HR images are also cropped and the data is enhanced by random horizontal and vertical flipping. The generated patches are feed into the network as input, the initial learning rate is set to 2×10^{-4}, and reduced to half after every 30 epochs. We use the Adam [20] method to optimize all models, among them $\beta_1 = 0.9$, $\beta_2 = 0.999$. Since more training epochs do not improve the experimental results, we stop training after 470 epochs. Then the proposed method is evaluated by three criteria: Peak Signal to Noise Ratio (PSNR), Structural Similarity (SSIM) [21] and Visual Information Fidelity (VIF) [22] to test SR performance. The boundaries are cropped to achieve a fair comparison.

3.3 Quantitative Evaluation

In this section, we present ablation experiments to demonstrate the effectiveness of the proposed method, including the role of multi-view images and the role of TAM.

Table 1. Comparison of PSNR, SSIM, VIF and Params. results of different models on the FEI datasets.

Model	PSNR	SSIM	VIF	Params.
MTC with SFSR	37.67	0.9612	0.6594	1.55M
MTC without TAM	37.74	0.9612	0.6610	1.56M
MTC	38.17	0.9634	0.6709	1.66M

3.3.1 The Role of Multi-view Images

In order to verify the validity of the multi-view images, we conduct a comparative experiment of different configurations. We remove the TAM from the network and retrained the network using single image. Table 1 shows the PSNR and SSIM for the reconstruction results in different configurations.

The performance of single input model drops 0.50 dB (38.17 dB to 37.67 dB) in PSNR compared to the original network. If there is no texture information introduced by the multi-view images, we can achieve the equivalent reconstruction effect of the existing SFSR technology, and the proposed network should outperform existing SR methods with the assistance of multi-view images. This indicates that the multi-view images can be used to improve the performance of the original network.

3.3.2 The Role of TAM

TAM is introduced to integrate texture information from face images pairs. In order to prove its validity, we remove the TAM and directly merged the generated frontal images features. It can be observed from Table 1 that the PSNR/SSIM/VIF values are decreased from 38.17 dB/0.9634/0.6709 to 37.74 dB/0. 9612/0.6610 if TAM is removed. Because the texture features in the frontal images do not coincide with the texture features in the multi-view images, which prevents the ordinary network from effectively combining these corresponding texture features.

Table 2. Comparison of PSNR, SSIM and VIF results of different algorithms on the FEI datasets.

Algorithm	Bicubic	SelfEx [19]	SRCNN [7]	EDGAN [9]	TDAE [8]	PRDRN [10]	Ours
PSNR/dB	33.30	36.53	36.71	37.89	34.34	37.14	38.17
SSIM	0.9318	0.9546	0.9495	0.9558	0.9320	0.9570	0.9634
VIF	0.5293	0.6369	0.5963	0.6349	0.5527	0.6454	0.6709

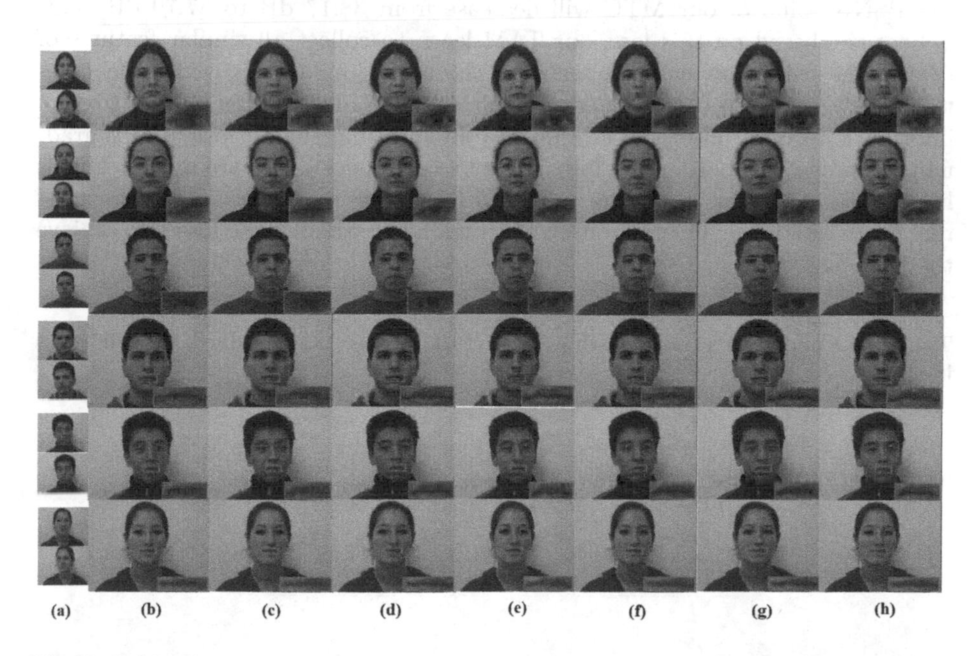

Fig. 4. Subjective comparison of our method with other algorithms on FEI datasets. (a) LR inputs (Top: frontal image; Bottom: side-view image), (b) SelfEx, (c) SRCNN, (d) EDGAN, (e) TDAE, (f) PRDRN, (g) The proposed method, (h) Original HR image.

3.3.3 Performance Comparison with Some State-of-the-art Face SR

As far as we know, the MFSR is a new topic in the field of computers, and there is no relevant open source code. So we will compare with several state-of-the-art algorithms, including SelfEx [19], SRCNN [7], EDGAN [9], TDAE [8], and PRDRN [10] methods. For fair comparison, we retrain and test the comparison algorithm using the same training database.

Quantitative results are shown in Table 2. It can be observed that the proposed method achieves the best performance on the FEI dataset. In particular, MTC is at least 0.28 dB higher than these SFSR algorithms. Because of TAM can get more reliable texture information. The qualitative results are shown in Fig. 4. It should be noted that algorithm (b) to algorithm (f) are only input frontal image for testing. From the magnified area we can observe that some details of EDGAN and TDAE using GAN network have sharper edges. But in terms of PSNR/SSIM/VIF, these algorithms are lower than the proposed method.

3.3.4 Effect of Losses

To test the effectiveness of the loss, we retrain the MTC with different losses. As can be seen from Table 3, if the MTC is trained only by reconstruction loss, the PSNR value of our MTC will decrease from 38.17 dB to 37.79 dB. This is because, based on this loss, our TAM learn to collect all similar features of face image pairs, but can not focus on the most similar face texture features to provide accurate correspondence, and can not make better use of texture information from multi-view face images. In addition, the performance is gradually improved if photometric loss, guide loss and period loss are added. This is because, these losses encourage our TAM to generate reliable and more consistent correspondence. Overall, our MTC is trained with all these losses to achieve the best performance.

Table 3. Comparative results achieved on FEI by our MTC trained with different losses.

Model	L_{rec}	L_{pho}	L_{gui}	L_{per}	PSNR	SSIM
MTC	√				37.79	0.9614
MTC	√	√			37.80	0.9616
MTC	√	√	√		37.84	0.9618
MTC	√	√	√	√	38.17	0.9634

4 Conclusion

In this paper, we propose a face SR network based on multi-view images, which utilizes the texture features of the multi-view images to restore a more reasonable texture for rendering better visual performance. The experimental results show that the proposed network effectively utilizes the texture features of the multi-view images to improve the reconstruction performance of fixed view image. Comparing with single input SR, the proposed method enhances the performance by utilizing multi-view texture compensation. In the future work, we will pay more attention to how to use multiple face multi-views images for image reconstruction.

Acknowledgment. This work was supported by the National Natural Science Foundation of China (61502354), the Hubei Technology Innovation Project (2019AAA045), the Natural Science Foundation of Hubei Province of China (2015CFB451), the Central Committee Guides Local Special Projects for Science and Technology Development (2018ZYYD059), the Scientific Research Foundation of Wuhan Institute of Technology (K201713).

References

1. Zhang, L., Wu, X.: An edge-guided image interpolation algorithm via directional filtering and data fusion. TIP **15**, 2226–2238 (2016)
2. Tsai, R.Y.: Multiple frame image restoration and registration. In: CVIP, pp. 1715–1989 (1989)
3. Zeng, K., Lu, T., Liang, X., Liu, K., Chen, H., Zhang, Y.: Face super-resolution via bilayer contextual representation. In: SPIC, pp. 147–157 (2019)
4. Yang, J., Wright, J., Huang, T.S., Ma, Y.: Image super-resolution via sparse representation. IEEE Trans. Image Process. **19**, 2861–2873 (2010)
5. Lu, T., et al.: Face hallucination using manifold-regularized group locality-constrained representation. In: ICIP, pp. 2511–2515 (2018)
6. Lu, T., Guan, Y., Chen, D., Xiong, Z., He, W.: Low-rank constrained collaborative representation for robust face recognition. In: MMSP, pp. 1–7 (2017)
7. Dong, C., Loy, C.C., He, K., Tang, X.: Learning a deep convolutional network for image super-resolution. In: Fleet, D., Pajdla, T., Schiele, B., Tuytelaars, T. (eds.) ECCV 2014. LNCS, vol. 8692, pp. 184–199. Springer, Cham (2014). https://doi.org/10.1007/978-3-319-10593-2_13
8. Yu, X., Porikli, F.: Hallucinating very low-resolution unaligned and noisy face images by transformative discriminative autoencoders. In: CVPR, pp. 3760–3768 (2017)
9. Yang, X., et al.: Enhanced discriminative generative adversarial network for face super-resolution. In: Hong, R., Cheng, W.-H., Yamasaki, T., Wang, M., Ngo, C.-W. (eds.) PCM 2018. LNCS, vol. 11165, pp. 441–452. Springer, Cham (2018). https://doi.org/10.1007/978-3-030-00767-6_41
10. Lu, T., Hao, X., Zhang, Y., Liu, K., Xiong, Z.: Parallel region-based deep residual networks for face hallucination. IEEE Access **7**, 81266–81278 (2019)
11. Jia, K., Gong, S.: Generalized face super-resolution. TIP **17**, 873–886 (2008)
12. Ma, X., Huang, H., Wang, S., Qi, C.: A simple approach to multiview face hallucination. SPL **17**, 579–582 (2010)
13. Ustinova, E., Lempitsky, V.: Deep multi-frame face super-resolution. arXiv preprint arXiv:1709.03196 (2017)
14. Wang, L., et al.: Learning parallax attention for stereo image super-resolution. In: CVPR, pp. 12250–12259 (2019)

15. Qiao, Z., Cui, Z., Niu, X., Geng, S., Yu, Q.: Image segmentation with pyramid dilated convolution based on ResNet and U-net. In: Liu, D., Xie, S., Li, Y., Zhao, D., El-Alfy, E.S. (eds.) ICONIP. LNCS, vol. 10635, pp. 364–372. Springer, Cham (2017). https://doi.org/10.1007/978-3-319-70096-0_38
16. Zhang, H., Goodfellow, I., Metaxas, D., Odena, A.: Self-attention generative adversarial networks. arXiv preprint arXiv:1805.08318 (2018)
17. Fu, J., et al.: Dual attention network for scene segmentation. In: CVPR, pp. 3146–3154 (2019)
18. Godard, C., Mac Aodha, O., Brostow, G. J.: Unsupervised monocular depth estimation with left-right consistency. In: CVPR, pp. 270–279 (2017)
19. Huang, J.B., Singh, A., Ahuja, N.: Single image super-resolution from transformed self-exemplars. In: CVPR, pp. 5197–5206 (2015)
20. Kingma, D.P. Ba, J.: Adam: a method for stochastic optimization. arXiv preprint arXiv:1412.6980 (2014)
21. Wang, Z., Bovik, A.C., Sheikh, H.R., Simoncelli, E.P.: Image quality assessment: from error visibility to structural similarity. IEEE Trans. Image Process. **13**(4), 600–612 (2004)
22. Sheikh, H.R., Bovik, A.C.: Image information and visual quality. In: IEEE International Conference on Acoustics, Speech, and Signal Processing, pp. iii–709 (2004)
23. Thomaz, C.E., Giraldi, G.A.: A new ranking method for principal components analysis and its application to face image analysis. IVC **28**, 902–913 (2010)

Light Field Salient Object Detection via Hybrid Priors

Junlin Zhang[1,2] and Xu Wang[1,2](✉)

[1] College of Computer Science and Software Engineering, Shenzhen University, Shenzhen 510680, China
wangxu@szu.edu.cn

[2] Guangdong Laboratory of Artificial Intelligence and Digital Economy (SZ), Shenzhen University, Shenzhen 510680, China

Abstract. In this paper, we propose a salient object detection model on light field via hybrid priors. The proposed model extracts four feature maps, including region contrast, background prior, depth prior and surface orientation prior maps. After that, the priors fusion stage is implemented to obtain and optimize the final salient object map. To verify the validity of the proposed model, comprehensive performance evaluation and comparative analysis are conducted on the public datasets LFSD and HFUT-Lytro. Experimental results show that the proposed method is superior to the existing light field saliency object detection model on the public two datasets.

Keywords: Light field · Salient object detection · Priors fusion

1 Introduction

With the rapid development of photography technology, light field imaging [1] has become popular for its potential in 3D application. By using consumer level light field cameras, such as Lytro, Raytrix, the total amount of light intensity and the direction of each incident light can be captured simultaneously during capturing. Thus the information of a light field can be expressed as a 4D function of the light, including their position and orientation [2]. This information can be transformed into various 2D images by rendering and refocusing techniques, like focus slices, all-focus and depth maps [3]. For example, a light field image can produce a set of focus slices that are focused at different depths [2]. The background area can be identified by picking a focus slice focus on the background, and then it can be used to separate the focus areas. An all-focus image contains a series of images captured at different focal planes, providing the sharpest pixels, and can be reconstructed by blurring focus stack images which have invariant depth [4] or rendering algorithm dependent on depth [5]. In addition, the depth of each ray recorded in the sensor can be estimated by measuring the pixels in the focus stack [3].

Y. M. Ro et al. (Eds.): MMM 2020, LNCS 11962, pp. 361–372, 2020.
https://doi.org/10.1007/978-3-030-37734-2_30

Li *et al.* [6] pioneered using light field data to solve challenging problems in saliency object detection. They proposed a new saliency detection method that takes advantage of the foreground and background cues generated by the focus stack. In addition, they collected the first light field dataset by using the Lytro camera. It is proved that the light field can improve the accuracy of saliency object detection in complex scenes. However, it is still in the initial stages of exploration and has some limitations, *e.g.*, when calculating focus and objects to select prospective saliency candidates, it inevitably ignores the explicit use of depth data associated with salient objects. In addition, the type and scale of scenarios included in existing datasets are still limited. Zhang *et al.* [7] explicitly combined depth contrast to fill the defect of color contrast, and utilize focus-based background priors to improve the performance of saliency object detection. Although these methods have proven effective performance by utilizing light field data, the accuracy of saliency detection in real scenes still remains a challenge, due to the inherent or external factors such as illumination, viewpoint changes, occlusion, etc. Thus, it is necessary to develop a more efficient light field saliency object detection model.

In this paper, we propose a novel light field salient objection detection model via hybrid priors, which extract depth prior and orientation prior from depth maps to boost the prediction accuracy. After priors fusion and optimization, the proposed model output the final saliency map. Experimental results demonstrate that our proposed method can achieve a significant improvement on the public datasets.

2 Related Works

2.1 Light Field Data

Light field imaging system records both the intensity and direction information of light [8,9]. Unlike conventional imaging systems, it not only captures the intensity projection but also captures the direction of the incident light that is projected onto the sensor. The light field camera inserts a microlens array in front of the detector, and the microlens array disperses the light collected behind the main lens again. The sensor records the light in different directions, and the pixels on the corresponding sensor after each microlen corresponding to the image pixels at different viewing angles of the same position of the object. From a macro perspective, the light field image is essentially the same as a normal photo. However, from the microscopic point of view, the light field image is composed of different microlens sub-images behind the microlens array. The microlens array records the light structure and records the depth information of the object.

The current widely used LFSD [6] dataset is the earliest light field dataset for saliency detection, but the data set is not challenging enough. A typical scene in a dataset contains only a single centered and unobstructed salient object with a clean background. In the actual scene, there may have problems such as multiple significant objects, brightness changes of an object, etc. The HFUT-Lytro [10] dataset is more massive and more challenging, and the dataset appears to contain multiple salient objects, salient objects may be away from the camera, the light source may be different, and the salient area may be partially occluded.

2.2 Light Field Salient Object Detection

At present, the light field saliency object detection is still in its infancy. In 2014, Li *et al.* [6] proposed the first light field salient object detection model, which shows that the light field can significantly improve the accuracy of saliency detection. The focus prior was employed to extract background information and calculate the contrast saliency between the background and foreground areas. Zhang *et al.* [7] later used the depth information and color information to generate region contrast saliency maps, combined Li's model [6] to extract background and non-background regions for background possibilities calculating. Exiting models did not well exploit the cues such as the depth and direction priors [11–13], which may limit the performance of models on salient object detection task.

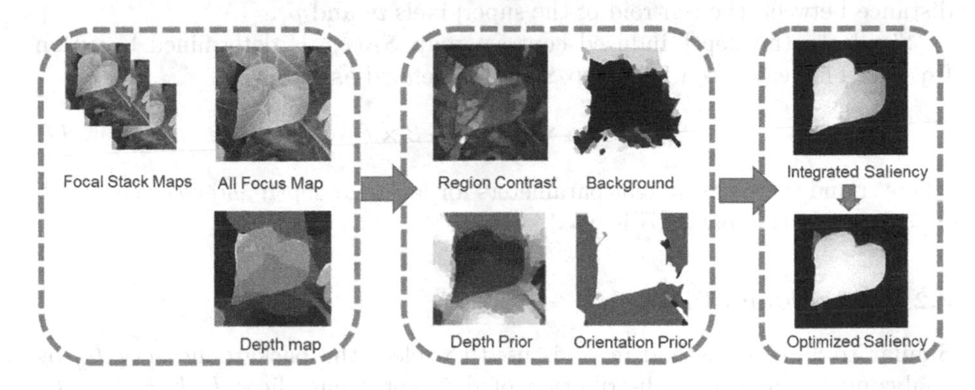

Fig. 1. Framework of proposed salient detection model on light field data.

3 Proposed Salient Object Detection Model

Given a light field sample, consisting of a pair of all-focus image (color image I_c and depth map I_d) and focal stack maps, the task is to obtain a saliency map with regard to the all-focus image. In this paper, we explore multiple saliency cues deriving from the light field data to detect the salient object in the all-focus image.

The framework of proposed hybrid priors based salient object detection model for light field data is shown in Fig. 1. The proposed model first exploits the saliency related cues from light field data, including region contrast map from the all-focus map, the background prior map from the focus stack maps, the depth prior map and the surface orientation prior map from the depth map. Final, the intergraded saliency map is obtained trough the fusion and optimization modules. Detailed descriptions are provided as follows.

3.1 Region Contrast

As same in [7], a simple linear iterative clustering algorithm (SLIC) [14] is employed to segment the all-focus image into a set of compact super-pixel blocks (defined as $\mathbf{P}$). For any superpixel $p_i \in \mathbf{P}$, the region contrast $S_C(p_i)$ for the all-focus image image is defined as follows:

$$S_C(p_i) = \sum_{j=1}^{N} \left\| U_C^f(p_i)) - U_C^f(p_j) \right\| \exp(-\frac{\left\| U_p^*(p_i) - U_p^*(p_j) \right\|^2}{2\sigma_\omega^2}), \quad (1)$$

where N is the total number of superpixels in $\mathbf{P}$. $U_C^f(p_i)$ is the average feature values of the superpixels p_i of all-focus color image. The second term in Eq. (1) is the spatial weighting factor that controls the equidistance between superpixels, where the closer regions with similar texture information make greater contribution to the contrast saliency. $\left\| U_p^*(p_i) - U_p^*(p_j) \right\|$ defines the distance between the centers of the superpixels p_i and p_j, and σ_ω is the standard deviation of the distance between the centroid of the superpixels p_i and p_j.

Similarly, the depth-induced contrast map $S_D(p_i)$ is determined based on Eq. (1). The region contrast map $S_R(p_i)$ is defined as:

$$S_R(p_i) = \alpha \times S_C(p_i) + \beta \times S_D(p_i) \quad (2)$$

where α and β are two weight parameters for leverage depth and color cues with $\beta = 1 - \alpha$. In this paper, α is fixed as 0.3.

3.2 Background Prior

Similar to [6], the method in [7] is used to select the background slice I_{bg} by analyzing the focusness distribution of different focus slices $I_k, k = 1, ..., K$. More specifically, the background likelihood score B_k of each slice is measured by using a one-dimensional U-shaped filter. The slice with the highest likelihood score B_k is selected as the background slice I_{bg}:

$$I_b =_{k=1,..,K}^{argmax} B_k(I_k, u), \quad (3)$$

where

$$B_k(I_k, u) = \rho \cdot \left[\sum_{x=1}^{w} u(x, w) + \sum_{y=1}^{h} u(y, h) \right]. \quad (4)$$

$u(x, w) = \frac{1}{\sqrt{1+(\frac{x}{\eta})^2}} + \frac{1}{\sqrt{1+(\frac{(w-x)}{\eta})^2}}$ is the one-dimensional bandpass filtering function of the x-axis, and $\eta = 28$ controlling the bandwidth.

To improve the saliency contrast, the background probability ω_b of the background slice I_{bg} is measured as:

$$\omega_b(p_i) = 1 - \exp(-\frac{U_b(p_i)^2}{2\sigma_b^2} \left\| C - U_p^*(p_i)^2 \right\|), \quad (5)$$

where $\sigma_{bg} = 1$ and $\omega_b(p_i)$ is the average value of the superpixels p_i on the background slice I_b. $\|C - U_p^*(p_i)^2\|$ measures the spatial information of the super-pixels associated with the image center C. $U_p^*(p_i)$ defines the normalized average coordinates of the super-pixel p_i. Therefore, the regions belongs to the background have a higher background probability Pb_{bg}. This background prior measure method effectively eliminates most of the boundary regions, but it still retains a large portion of the image as saliency, as shown in Fig. 2-(3).

3.3 Depth Prior

A depth prior observed in both visual perception and cognitive psychology is that people always take attention on the closest object. In addition, Lang *et al.* [15] pointed out that the relationship between depth and saliency is nonlinear. They therefore use a Gaussian Mixture Model (GMM) to learn depth priors to characterize the saliency and depth at different depth of field (DOF).

Considering that when the scenes may have different DOFs, the saliency objects may appear in completely different positions, so the absolute depth value in each image need to be rescaled into the range [0, 1] to eliminate the influence of DOFs. It increases the saliency score of closer objects and decreases the score of distant objects.

The method for calculating the depth prior map is as follows:

$$S_F(p_i) = \sqrt{1 - d(p_i)}, \tag{6}$$

where $d(p_i)$ is the average depth value of the superpixel p_i. Using Eq. (6), the object further away from the background is more likely to be considered as a salient object, as shown in Fig. 2-(4). However, when the object is placed on a support plane like the ground, the closer part of the plane will be highlighted, as shown in the second example of Fig. 2.

3.4 Orientation Prior

The surface orientation prior is considered to be an important saliency related cue, and the relative direction between each two superpixels is widely employed for region contrast evaluation. Therefore, we use a global-context orientation prior [12]. This prior is based on an observation that the photographers like to select a viewpoint parallel to the interested object for observation and shooting. In other words, the direction perpendicular to the main axis received most concerned, thus the saliency of the severely inclined plane can be reduced. We use the z-axis to represent the main axis and use it to calculate the orientation prior:

$$S_O(p_i) = \langle z, n(p_i) \rangle, \tag{7}$$

where $n(p_i)$ represents the unit surface normal of the superpixel p_i, and $< \cdot, \cdot >$ denotes the inner product. The orientation prior reduces the saliency score of the plane close to the salient object. As shown in Fig. 5, the orientation prior and the depth prior are complementary to each other for the first example.

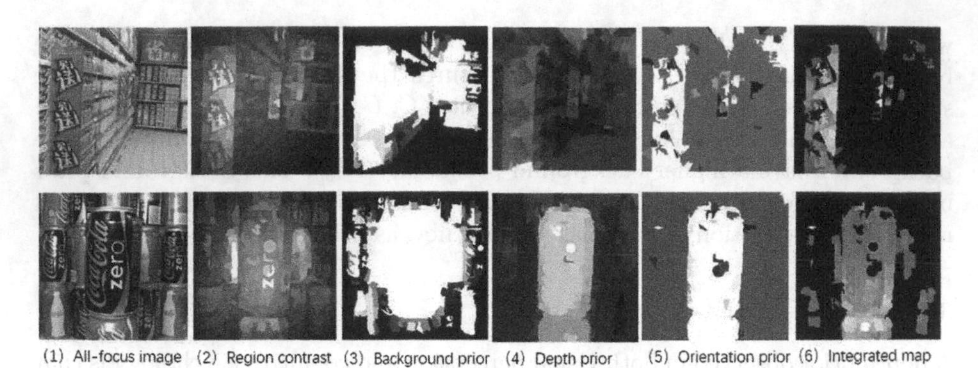

Fig. 2. Examples of priors maps.

3.5 Priors Fusion

Once we have a region contrast map, as well as a background, depth, and orientation prior maps, we integrate the regional contrast with the previous background prior, and then multiply the depth and orientation prior maps to generate a saliency map S_L:

$$S_L(p_i) = \sum_{j=1}^{N} S_R(p_i) \cdot \omega_b(p_j) \cdot S_F(p_i) \cdot S_O(p_i) \tag{8}$$

3.6 Saliency Optimization

In order to obtain a clearer salient object map, the saliency optimization algorithm in [16] is employed, where the salient object region is assigned with value 1 and the background region is set to 0. The final saliency values $S_(p_i)$ of superpixel p_i in image is calculated by minimizing the following cost function:

$$J = \sum_{i=1}^{N} \omega_b(p_i) \cdot S(p_i)^2 + \sum_{i=1}^{N} S_L(p_i) \cdot (S(p_i) - 1)^2 + \sum_{i,j} \omega_{ij} \cdot (S(p_i) - S(p_j))^2. \tag{9}$$

The first item in the cost function is the background part, which suggests that the superpixel with a high background probability $\omega_b(p_i)$ corresponds to a smaller value (close to 0). The second term is the foreground part, which suggests that a superpixel with a higher foreground probability $S_L(p_i)$, corresponds to a larger value (close to 1). The third term is the smoothing part. It is recommended to maintain the saliency value. For each adjacent superpixel pair p_i, p_j, the weight ω_{ij} is defined as

$$\omega_{ij} = exp(-\frac{\left\| U_p^*(p_i) - U_p^*(p_j)) \right\|^2}{2\sigma_\omega^2}) + \mu \tag{10}$$

This weight is larger in the smooth region and smaller in the boundary region, and is mainly used to eliminate noise in the background and foreground boundaries. The parameter μ is a small constant used to regularize the optimization of cluttered image regions. All three terms use the mean square error, and the final saliency map is optimized by least-square.

Table 1. Summarized results of different methods on LFSD and HFUT-Lytro datasets.

Dataset	Metric	DILF	LFS	Proposed
HFUT-Lytro	AUC	0.974	0.510	**0.977**
	F-measure	0.616	0.480	**0.623**
	MAE	0.150	0.223	**0.134**
LFSD	AUC	0.937	0.958	**0.959**
	F-measure	0.766	0.678	**0.813**
	MAE	0.150	0.213	**0.130**

4 Experiment Results

4.1 Experimental Setup

In this section, the evaluation protocols, including datasets and evaluation metric, are described as follows.

Datasets. To evaluate the performance of this paper proposed approach, we conduct experiments using two public available datasets: the LFSD [6] dataset and the HFUT-Lytro [7] dataset. Each scene in these datasets is composed of five types of image data, including raw light field data, focus slices, all-focus map derived from the focus stack, a depth map, and the corresponding 2D binary ground truth map.

- **LFSD dataset:** This dataset contains 100 light field images of different scenes. It contains 60 indoor and 40 outdoor scenes. But most scenes contain only one salient object with a high contrast and a limited depth range.
- **HFUT-Lytro dataset:** This dataset contains 255 light field images. Most scenes contain multiple objects appearing in various locations, and the background is cluttered and occluded, making the dataset more challenging for saliency detection.

Evaluation Metric. Three widely used metrics, F-measure, mean absolute error (MAE) and area under ROC curve (AUC) are used to measure the overall perdition accuracy. F-measure is the weighted harmonic average of precision and recall. MAE measures the average per-pixel difference between the binary ground truth and the saliency map.

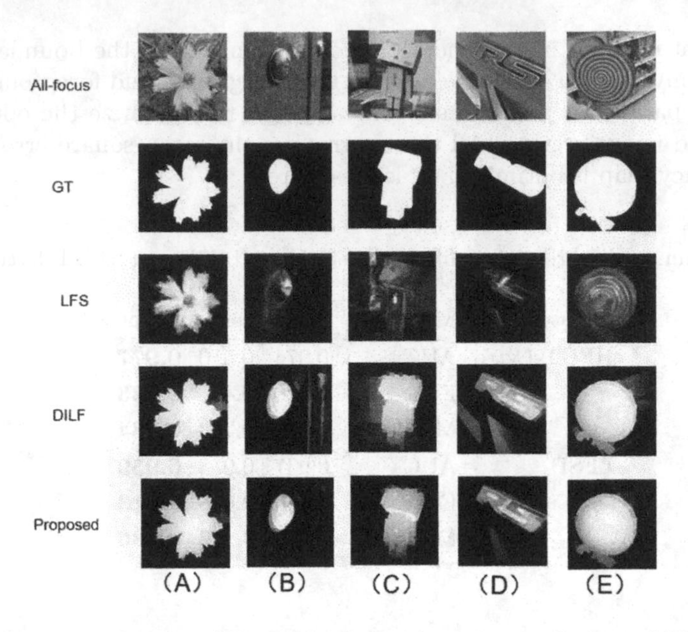

Fig. 3. Comparison of various light field saliency detection methods on LFSD dataset.

4.2 Comparison with Different Methods

The proposed method is compared with two state-of-the-art methods, LFS [6] and DILF [12] on both LFSD [6] and HFUT-Lytro [7] datasets. The results in Table 1 show that our proposed method is superior to the DILF and LFS methods on both LFSD and HFUT-Lytro datasets. More specifically, the proposed method outperforms all other methods in terms of F-measure, MAE and AUC. On average, our proposed method in this paper improves the performance of F-measure by 1.8% and 2.8% compared with the DILF method, and increased by 15.4% and 11.5% compared with the LFS method. In terms of MAE, compared with the DILF algorithm , the average prediction error of our proposed method was reduced by 1.6% and 2.1%, and it is 8.8% and 8.3% lower than the average error of the LFS algorithm.

For an intuitive comparison, we present several representative saliency maps generated by the proposed method and other advanced methods on the LFSD and HFUT-Lytro datasets, respectively. Obviously, most of the saliency detection methods can process images with relatively simple backgrounds and uniform objects, as shown in Fig. 3(A). However, our proposed method can handle many challenging cases. For example, although the contrast between the object and the background in Fig. 3(C) is very high, due to the background noise, some methods cannot accurately highlight the salient region, and some of the backgrounds are also displayed on the salient map. But our proposed method can effectively solve this problem. Even when the salient areas are dispersed by background illumination and shading, the proposed method performs better than other methods,

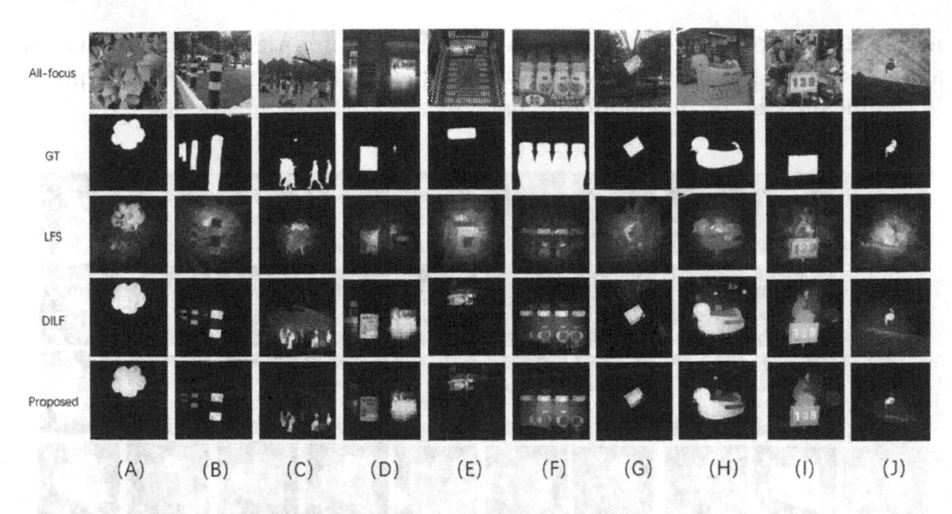

Fig. 4. Comparison of various light field saliency detection methods on HFUT-Lytro dataset.

as shown in Fig. 4(E). In addition, in the case of background clutter which is easily distracting attention or has a similar background, our proposed method can make the salient part more coherent and provide better and cleaner predictions, as shown in Figs. 3(D), and 4(I). In addition, when the background prior is invalid to some extent, the method of this paper still performs well. For example, there are multiple objects in the same scene (Fig. 4(G)), and the significant objects are at the distant depth level (In Fig. 4(F)), or the salient object is very small (Fig. 4(J)).

Table 2. Influence of numbers of superpixels on the performance for dataset LFSD.

Number	300	500	800	1000
AUC	0.960	0.963	**0.966**	0.959
F-measure	**0.802**	0.800	0.793	0.783
MAE	**0.129**	0.134	0.139	0.144
Time(s)	**0.754**	1.014	1.278	1.458

4.3 Ablation Study

To validate the contribution of each important modules in our framework, we conduct ablation studies to demonstrate their effectiveness. Detailed experimental results are provided as follows: **Superpixel Generation** The number of superpixel has a certain impact on the performance of the model. As shown in Table 2, the setting with 300 superpixels can achieve the best performance on saliency detection. Segmentation into 300 superpixels is superior to 500, 800 and 1000 superpixels according to MAE and F-measure. Although the number of superpixels of various divisions is not much different in AUC, the 300 superpixels is significantly better in computational cost than other numbers.

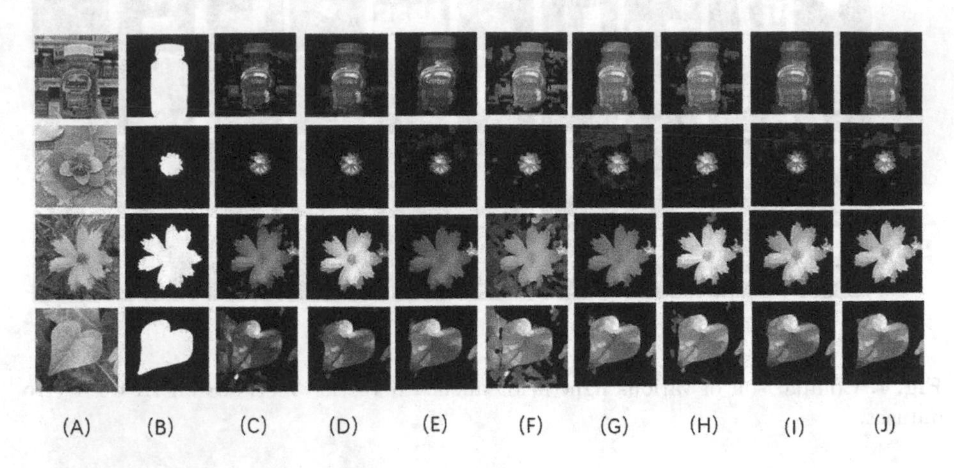

Fig. 5. Saliency map derived from combinations of different priors. (A) All-focus image; (B) GT; (C) RC; (D) RC+BP; (E) RC+DP; (F) RC+OP; (G) RC+DP+OP; (H) RC+BP+OP; (I) RC+BP+DP; (J) RC+BP+DP+OP.

Evalution of Different Priors. Table 3 shows the F-measure, ROC, and MAE results for different combinations. The performance of all metrics has been consistently improved, which further validates the effectiveness of the proposed method. When linearly combining various priors finds that the algorithm combination of this paper is superior to other prior combinations. In addition, from the data in the table we can know that adding background prior can significantly improve the performance of other priors. The orientation prior can improve the predictive performance of the depth prior. The main reason is that in most cases, the depth information helps to pop out the salient object, regardless of whether the object has a boundary with the background, and the orientation prior can eliminate background interference, especially the effects of heavily slanted planes, making the saliency map's boundary cleaner and the salient objects more prominent.

Figure 5 visually compares the performance of different light field characteristics. It can be observed that each prior has a unique advantage for the saliency detection, and the results obtained by a single used prior are not ideal, especially the orientation prior. The use of region contrast and background prior combinations has been able to roughly show salient objects. Furthermore, focusness on different depths depths are beneficial for effective foreground and background separation. However, when contrast of depth is low or the highlighted object is placed in the background, like the example(B), it may be inferior. The examples of Fig. 5(C) and (D) show that background prior and orientation prior help to eliminate background interference and enhance salient foreground objects.

Table 3. Results in terms of MAE, F-measure and AUC of different priors combinations for saliency detection on LFSD.

Model	MAE	F-measure	AUC
RC	0.232	0.559	0.853
RC+DP	0.188	0.652	0.925
RC+OP	0.267	0.593	0.891
RC+BP	0.199	0.642	0.865
RC+DP+OP	0.178	0.695	0.923
RC+BP+OP	0.212	0.673	0.900
RC+BP+DP	0.177	0.678	0.925
RC+BP+DP+OP	**0.168**	**0.717**	**0.937**

5 Conclusion

In this paper, we propose a hybrid priors based salient object detection model for light field data. More specifically, the depth prior and orientation prior are employed to boost the prediction accuracy. Experimental comparison shows that the proposed method is superior to other methods in the publicly available light field datasets by effectively exploring the complementarity of multiple clues and producing better performance.

Acknowledgements. This work was supported in part by the National Natural Science Foundation of China (Grant 31670553, Grant 61871270 and Grant 61672443), in part by the Guangdong Natural Science Foundation of China under Grant 2016A030310058, in part by the Natural Science Foundation of SZU (Grant 827000144) and in part by the National Engineering Laboratory for Big Data System Computing Technology of China.

References

1. Gaochang, W., et al.: Light field image processing: an overview. IEEE J. Sel. Top. Signal Process. **11**(7), 926–954 (2017)
2. Adelson, E., Wang, J.: Single lens stereo with a plenoptic camera. IEEE Trans. Pattern Anal. Mach. Intell. **14**(2), 99–106 (1992)
3. Tao, M.W., Hadap, S., Malik, J., Ramamoorthi, R.: Depth from combining defocus and correspondence using light-field cameras. In: IEEE International Conference on Computer Vision, pp. 673–680 (2013)
4. Kuthirummal, S., Nagahara, H., Zhou, C., Nayar, S.K.: Flexible depth of field photography. IEEE Trans. Pattern Anal. Mach. Intell. **33**(1), 58–71 (2011)
5. Rumin, Z., Yu, R., Dijun, L., Youguang, Z.: All-focused light field image rendering. In: Li, S., Liu, C., Wang, Y. (eds.) CCPR 2014. CCIS, vol. 484, pp. 32–43. Springer, Heidelberg (2014). https://doi.org/10.1007/978-3-662-45643-9_4
6. Li, N., Ye, J., Ji, Y., Ling, H., Yu, J.: Saliency detection on light field. In: IEEE Conference on Computer Vision and Pattern Recognition, pp. 2806–2813 (2014)

7. Zhang, J., Wang, M., Gao, J., Wang, Y., Zhang, X., Wu, X.: Saliency detection with a deeper investigation of light field. In: International Joint Conferences on Artificial Intelligence, pp. 2212–2218 (2015)
8. Gershun, A.: The light field. J. Math. Phys. **18**(1–4), 51–151 (1939)
9. Landy, M., Movshon, J.A.: The plenoptic function and the elements of early vision. In: MITP (1991)
10. Zhang, J., Wang, M., Lin, L., Yang, X., Gao, J., Rui, Y.: Saliency detection on light field: a multi-cue approach. ACM Trans. Multimed. Comput. Commun. Appl. **13**(3), 32 (2017)
11. Zhang, Y., Jiang, G., Yu, M., Chen, K.: Stereoscopic visual attention model for 3D video. In: International Conference on Multimedia Modeling, pp. 314–324 (2010)
12. Ren, J., Gong, X., Yu, L., Zhou, W., Yang, M.Y.: Exploiting global priors for RGB-D saliency detection. In: IEEE Conference on Computer Vision and Pattern Recognition Workshops, pp. 25–32 (2015)
13. Zhang, Q., Wang, X., Wang, S., Li, S., Kwong, S., Jiang, J.: Learning to explore intrinsic saliency for stereoscopic video. In: The IEEE Conference on Computer Vision and Pattern Recognition, pp. 9749–9758 (2019)
14. Achanta, R., Shaji, A., Smith, K., Lucchi, A., Fua, P., Süsstrunk, S.: SLIC superpixels compared to state-of-the-art superpixel methods. IEEE Trans. Pattern Anal. Mach. Intell. **34**(11), 2274–2282 (2012)
15. Lang, C., Nguyen, T.V., Katti, H., Yadati, K., Kankanhalli, M., Yan, S.: Depth matters: influence of depth cues on visual saliency. In: Fitzgibbon, A., Lazebnik, S., Perona, P., Sato, Y., Schmid, C. (eds.) ECCV 2012. LNCS, pp. 101–115. Springer, Heidelberg (2012). https://doi.org/10.1007/978-3-642-33709-3_8
16. Zhu, W., Liang, S., Wei, Y., Sun, J.: Saliency optimization from robust background detection. In: IEEE Conference on Computer Vision and Pattern Recognition, pp. 2814–2821 (2014)

SS2: Multimedia Analytics: Perspectives, Tools and Applications

Multimedia Analytics Challenges and Opportunities for Creating Interactive Radio Content

Werner Bailer[1(✉)], Maarten Wijnants[2], Hendrik Lievens[2], and Sandy Claes[3]

[1] JOANNEUM RESEARCH, Graz, Austria
werner.bailer@joanneum.at

[2] Hasselt University – tUL – EDM, Diepenbeek, Belgium
{maarten.wijnants,hendrik.lievens}@uhasselt.be

[3] VRT, Brussels, Belgium
sandy.claes@vrt.be

Abstract. The emergence of audio streaming services and evolved listening habits notwithstanding, broadcast radio is still a popular medium that plays an important role in contemporary users' media consumption mix. While radio's strength has traditionally lain in the shared live experience that it enables, radio shows are nowadays much more than just a linear broadcast feed: they are about user engagement and interaction over a amalgam of communication channels. Producing interactive radio programs in a cost-effective way thus requires understanding and indexing a large set of multimedia content, not just audio data (but also e.g., text, user-generated content, web resources). This position paper discusses a number of open challenges and opportunities with respect to the application of multimedia analytics in interactive radio production that need to be addressed in order to facilitate content creation at scale. Our work aims to support the future evolution of (interactive) radio, this way helping the radio medium to stay relevant in an ever-changing media ecosystem.

Keywords: Radio production · Interactivity · Automatic content annotation · Content structuring · Summarization · Context · Adaptation · Personalization · User-generated content

1 Introduction

The media landscape is undergoing significant changes, caused by the increasingly diverse and personalized ways in which media is consumed (in terms of time, place, context and content). These changes also impact radio, a medium that has maintained its popularity over a century, despite fierce competition. The proportion of Europeans who listen to the radio at least once a week is stable at 75%, the number of daily consumers is at 50% [1]. While the primary strength of broadcast radio is still the fact that it offers a shared live experience to listeners, radio shows are nowadays much more than merely a linear

Y. M. Ro et al. (Eds.): MMM 2020, LNCS 11962, pp. 375–387, 2020.
https://doi.org/10.1007/978-3-030-37734-2_31

broadcast feed. Indeed, radio increasingly revolves around user engagement and interaction over a multitude of channels, including direct communication (phone, email, instant messaging), social media and visual radio. Many of the devices used to access these channels have screens and provide rich interaction capabilities. For example, 52% of UK adults have downloaded a radio app and 8% of UK adults regularly use radio catch-up services [34]. Radio is thus a medium embedded in a context of social media, interaction and personalization. As such, radio is no longer only about audio and music, but increasingly also about the text, image and video content that is exchanged as part of the listener interactions in contemporary radio consumption practices. This observation has direct implications for radio production workflows, where creating appealing supplemental material and interactive content has become a necessity.

This position paper contributes a number of open challenges and opportunities with respect to the application of multimedia analytics in radio production. We hereby focus specifically on the authoring of interactive instead of purely linear radio content. The identified open challenges are grounded on empiric evidence harvested via desk research, the authors' personal experience in the radio research domain and, perhaps most importantly, the insights from discussions at the Workshop on Interactive Radio Experiences (IRE) at ACM TVX 2019 [9]. The IRE workshop was attended by both practitioners (e.g., radio producers) from broadcasters and researchers from broadcasters' R&D labs, which resulted in a wealth of "insider information" about (interactive) radio production and its practical pitfalls. Identified open challenges are first described on a high level in the remainder of this section (see Sects. 1.1 and 1.2), before diving deeper into the specific challenges and opportunities in terms of *content enrichment*, *context derivation and adaptation* and *production user interfaces* (in Sects. 2, 3 and 4, respectively). A secondary contribution of our work is that it helps uncovering research gaps in the audio domain that typically have already been solved for other media like video and text.

1.1 Challenges for Content Production

The creation of interactive radio experiences is still in an early stage, but very interesting content has already been realized. For example, the BBC has created interactive audio content for smart speakers such as "The Inspection Chamber"[1] or "The Unfortunates"[2]. Listeners can influence the continuation of the story with their interactions, resulting in a myriad of possible paths through the narrative. Similar opportunities have also been explored outside the broadcasting domain. For example, the Financial Times produced interactive audio city guides for Google Assistant[3]. Another dimension of interactivity with audio content is introduced by object-based audio [36], which captures the scene as a set of audio objects and associated metadata, which can then be dynamically composed to a customized stream for individual listeners as needed.

[1] https://www.bbc.co.uk/taster/pilots/inspection-chamber.
[2] https://www.bbc.co.uk/taster/pilots/unfortunates.
[3] https://www.ft.com/hiddenberlin.

However, at both public and commercial broadcasters, radio content production faces budget limitations. While creating rich and bespoke interactive content, built around a hand-crafted story, is likely to provide the most engaging experience, this approach is not economically viable at scale. In addition, there is considerable risk how new forms of content will be received by the audience. The alternative is thus to build on existing content, which has an installed consumer base, and to augment that content with supplemental material and by providing interaction capabilities. An approach as described by Baume, which uses existing radio shows to create enriched and interactive podcasts [6], is thus a more realistic deployment example for the near future. Despite the more incremental nature of interactive content that is produced in this way, the required additional information, links, structure, etc. is currently typically still added manually. Richer time-based metadata is required to streamline and automate this process.

Interactive radio content is consumable on many platforms, including digital radio receivers, smart phones, tablets, smart speakers and TVs. The presentation (e.g., display size) and interaction capabilities (e.g., touch screen, voice interaction) are different for each of them. Interaction options will hence need to be presented in different ways, and must support different means to respond to it. Production tools must be able to simulate this range of options, support authors in defining interaction alternatives for different platforms, and enable them to understand how interaction options will be used and which issues may arise.

Listener co-creation processes grounded on user-generated content (UGC) are one particularly cost-effective way to enrich radio shows and to stimulate interaction. An example case for using UGC in event-related radio content is described in [14]. As UGC-driven co-creation commonly leads to extensive pools of content, the production team needs algorithmic support to (semi-)automatically select contributions that are of good quality in both technical and content aspects.

Finally, fine-grained audience measurements become a necessity in interactive radio experiences, as content creators must become aware how interactive data that supplements the radio signal is used and consumed, and how listeners interact with the radio program. Also, as the range of possible consumption contexts is wide, content should be able to adapt to user context (semi-)automatically at least to some degree. This adaptivity requirement again adds complexity to the radio production process.

1.2 A Case for Multimedia Analytics

Many of the discussed production challenges have in common that a solution can be enabled by fine-grained metadata about professional content and UGC as well as detailed audience measurements. The extraction of semantically meaningful information about the content requires state of the art natural language processing and computer vision tools, which in turn yields large amounts of data that need automation for structuring and organization. However, what sets traditional media apart from the pervasive amounts of content on the web is the curation and creation of a narrative by human creators. Thus the final creative choices and decisions need to stay in the hands of the radio creators, supported by intelligent tools. The requirements for handling large amounts of heterogeneous multimedia data in order to enable creators to efficiently produce richer content makes this a multimedia analytics problem. Despite this, very few papers dealing with multimedia analytics actually address radio content (beyond mentioning the word radio in the introduction); see, for example, [26] and [10].

2 Content Enrichment

The first area related to multimedia analytics for the authoring of interactive radio content concerns enrichment. With this, we refer to the use of technologies that help the production team in performing tasks like structuring content, temporally segmenting content, storing metadata, referencing supplemental material and linkage to associated user-generated content. Content enrichment can be implemented either on existing, non-interactive radio content (i.e., as an afterthought) or could be upfront factored into the radio production processes. A good example of the former approach is given by Cowlishaw et al., who exploit manually entered metadata (e.g., synopses of radio programs) to facilitate the transformation from non-interactive to interactive radio content [15].

Content Segmentation. Studies for both TV and radio content have shown that users tend to consume program segments rather than entire programs when accessing content on demand. For example, the authors of [37] report that 48% of the respondents in their study found it important to easily locate a part (or section) of a radio program. This means that content needs to be structured into semantically meaningful temporal units. Unfortunately, basic segmentation of audio content typically means segmenting into speech, music and other acoustic elements. By drilling down the resulting disassembled elements (i.e., further analyzing them using topic detection algorithms or by leveraging available EPG data), topical units can be identified and interaction options can be added. Speech is particularly relevant, as interaction opportunities can be added based on the spoken content. For music, interaction may mean adding/linking background information related to the music being played.

Speech to Text (ASR). Automatic speech recognition (ASR) is a base technology for other natural language processing tasks, such as named entity recognition, topic detection and clustering. However, the intended purpose of the resulting transcript determines its quality requirements. For further processing, it is important that the semantically relevant terms are correctly captured, while a grammatically completely correct transcription is not needed. If on the other hand the transcript shall also be presented to the user, its quality requirements are significantly higher. The interactive podcast player introduced in [6] visualizes the transcript, and 25% of the users stated it as their preferred feature. Transcript requirements may also depend on the user context, e.g., a full transcript is likely to be useful for users with hearing impairments or who want to exploit the radio content to improve their proficiency in a foreign language.

Topic Detection/Clustering. In cases where detailed structural information is not available from the production process, the topic structure of the content must be recreated. Topic detection and clustering based on the ASR transcript can be applied, and the result can be improved by exploiting external information (e.g., a list of potential topics). Such external information may be helpful even if it is just global, and not associated with the media timeline. If a chapter structure is not only used as a navigation aid for consuming the program but also for consuming content segments independently (i.e., outside the context of the program), then editors need to take care that such segments are self contained. Automated natural language processing tools can support this step by indicating when the main topic of the segment is introduced, or when named entities related to the topic are first mentioned in the entire broadcast [12].

Summarization. Summarization aims at creating shorter or condensed versions of content (while maximally retaining the core "message" of the content) in order to facilitate faster content consumption or to yield quick content overviews for browsing purposes. In the radio production context, *dynamic* (or *elastic*) summaries are mostly of interest, in order to enable consumers to access a version of the content that fits both their interest and time constraints. A large body of work on text and video summarization exists, while most work on audio summarization is geared towards music [5] or audio events [44]. Work on summarising spoken content [42] does not aim to create the summary as an audio segment, but only as a text. Hardly any work addresses the problem of generating re-edited audio content, which means posing the problem as one to be jointly solved on audio and text modalities [43]. In addition, scalable summarization technologies, as proposed for video content [27], would be needed to allow consumers to flexibly adjust the desired content length.

Qualitative and Affective Content Attributes. Audio signals that are of high technical fidelity (i.e., according to objective metrics like sampling rate or encoding bitrate) are not necessarily positively assessed by listeners from a qualitative point of view. This observation makes the case for enriching radio content with subjective attributes that can have either a positive or negative valence. Examples of interesting qualitative content attributes in the context of speech clips are intonation variation from the speaker (or lack thereof) and the presence of disturbing background noise. Detailed analysis of the audio signal (i.e., inspecting the waveform over time to estimate intonation variation) and machine learning models (as proposed in [21] for user-generated video) could support radio producers by automatically flagging content that exhibits undesirable qualitative attributes. The annotation and exploitation of content attributes however does not need to be limited to quality-related aspects. Again considering the case study of speech clips, other potential approaches to uncover interesting content attributes include sentiment analysis, gender classification of the speaker [25,28], speaking mode classification (e.g., yelling versus whispering), and auditory emotion derivation (e.g., sad versus happy). Such non-qualitative subjective attributes could be meaningfully applied in the context of, for example, offensive content identification and to match radio content to the mood of the listener (see also Sect. 3).

Hyperlinking External Content. A survey [38] found that the most popular radio content genres among Generation C listeners are music, arts & culture, events, and local information. All these genres can benefit from linking the radio content to other information on the web, on social media or with other multimedia content. Especially for younger consumer demographics, the notion of hyperlinks in any content is very natural, and tying in links to related content may avoid that they use other services in parallel to retrieve related information.

One obvious target for linking are sources that were used during the creation of the radio content, such as original articles or interviews that are cited. Ideally, these materials are still available from the production process, otherwise they have to be discovered again (e.g., via web search). The study in [6], dealing with information/documentary programs, found that consumers particularly liked visualizations such as diagrams. Such diagrams can be treated like other external content, i.e. as a graphic file or image. However, if a data-driven approach to journalism is used, the data analysis and presentation can also be supported by automatic tools [32]. In such a case visualizations of the data can be created on the fly, and can also be adapted to the user context (e.g., screen real estate, desired level of detail, highlighting local data relevant to the consumer).

Hyperlinking of video content is a well studied problem, among others through a series of benchmarks in the MediaEval and TRECVID evaluation campaigns [18]. The aim is to find cross-links in video collections to enable the user to view contextually relevant segments. This approach could of course also be applied across collections and information sources, including the web. Although some approaches strongly rely on audio content (e.g., [23]), there is little work specifically on hyperlinking of audio content [24].

A final potential application of hyperlinking concerns the discovery of social media content relevant to the radio program at hand. Again, this problem has been studied in more detail for linking video, e.g. with social media content related to events [31].

Annotating and Filtering User-Generated Content. Wardle and Williams provide a classification of different types of UGC in a broadcasting context, ranging from audio comments to networked journalism, but focus mostly on the use of UGC in relation to news coverage [40]. The contribution of non-news UGC in the context of a radio-supported charity event running for 14 weeks is discussed in [14]. Around 68% of the 24,615 received messages contained multimedia content. This poses challenges of selecting content based on content value, technical quality and diversity. A workflow for content selection is described in [3], using automatic quality analysis and similarity matching tools. With the recent advances in object detection and semantic scene segmentation, there is potential to create more fine-grained and directly usable semantic metadata.

A basic way of presenting related UGC in the radio production workflow has been implemented in [7] as part of the radio coverage of live events such as music festivals. Here, the content is provided as a ranked list, from which the editor can choose elements for inclusion in the radio show. In this example, the rank is learned from past editorial decisions, and the use of online random forests enables adaptation to changing trends [4]. While applying UGC in radio contexts is not widely explored yet, examples of leveraging UGC in video or TV contexts are rather plentiful (e.g., [21,41]).

3 Context Derivation and Adaptation

Context adaptation involves technologies that can help in better aligning content to the consumption context, either by simplifying the production of multiple, specialized content versions, or by (semi-)automatic content transformation during delivery. Creating new instantiations of existing content or adapting content to the listener's context hinges on tools that are capable of extracting content metadata, information about the user and contextual data in general, and consumption behavior (e.g., audience measurements).

Technical Capabilities of Target Device. An important piece of the contextual puzzle is given by the listener's playback device and its technical capabilities. As a simple example, it makes little sense to deliver pre-rendered surround sound to a listener who is using a pair of stereo headphones in conjunction with a smartphone. Another principal aspect of the consumption device are its display capabilities. If such capabilities are absent, visual supplemental information need not be delivered to the listener (to avoid wasting network bandwidth on information that the user will not be able to consume anyway). On the other hand, if a display is present, its form factor and hardware characteristics are also of interest. Indeed, the physical size and technical capabilities of the display influence the type of visual content that can be meaningfully consumed on it (e.g., still images, long pieces of text like transcripts, geographic maps, charts [6], video). The object-based media paradigm holds the promise to dynamically tune radio content to device capabilities, yet this paradigm is currently still hampered by the challenge that its production processes differ radically from traditional radio production [20].

Environmental Context. Another invaluable source of contextual information is given by the environment in which the user resides while listening to radio content. Listeners are likely to consume radio differently in solitary versus group settings. When listening together with others, users might be more willing to *go with the flow*, whereas in solitary settings these same users might be more eager to actively engage in content selection. Whether similar behaviors also hold for the witnessed level of interaction with radio content remains to be determined; it might very well be the case that group settings spur radio interactions that would not occur in solitary consumption contexts. Another crucial type of environmental context is the activity the consumer is currently involved in (e.g., working at a desk versus doing a physical workout), and whether or not she is willing or even able to interact. In situations where the user does not have her hands free to perform interaction (e.g., while cooking [16]), smart speaker technology could be helpful [39]. However, smart speakers involve a different way of interacting with radio content as opposed to a typical radio player, which must be taken into account during radio production. The mood of the listener is also likely to affect listener behaviour and is hence valuable contextual information that is best taken into account when delivering radio content [11]. Finally, whether the listener is consuming the radio content live or in an on-demand fashion is also an important type of environmental context. Catching up on radio items has been found to resemble the experience of consuming a podcast, which is a more intimate way of listening compared to live radio [30]. This observation implies that simply hosting (segmented) broadcast content online for on-demand consumption is unlikely to yield optimal listening experiences. Stated differently, live and on-demand radio content demand different, specialized radio production approaches.

Wearable technology, and sensors in general, bring a whole new dimension in gathering analytics about listeners and their consumption environment. A simple example would be to automatically adapt a musical playlist to the current heart rate of a runner. As another example, a seamless handover from IP to DAB+ could automatically be triggered when a user enters her car [17]. However, inferring contextual information that is as intricate as exemplified in the previous paragraph is no small feat and will likely require intelligent reasoning on the fusion of different contextual sources. Also, even if environmental context can be precisely and comprehensively derived, properly adapting radio content to it is far from a solved problem.

Personalization. An important form of context-driven content adaptation is personalization. In effect, personalization and recommendation engines take contextual information as input to deliver relevant pieces of content to the user. Content adaptation through personalization can take many forms in a radio consumption context. A straightforward personalization example is to exploit the listener's preferences and profile information to curate a tailored stream of radio items (e.g., a personalized playlist of relevant recent news items as they have been discussed on radio [33,35]). A more advanced approach would be to replace specific songs in the radio broadcast (using hybrid radio technologies [2]) in accordance with the musical taste of the listener. Personalization can also take place on different levels of individualization. In the most extreme case, personalization is intended to serve a single listener. However, personalization could also cater to groups of like-minded listeners, or even to the radio community as a whole. A real-world example of community-driven personalization is given by the concept of listener curation of the radio playlist, by letting listener voting determine the songs that will be played [29].

Interaction can play an important role in personalized radio experiences. As an example, listeners could provide feedback about the quality and relevance of the recommendations they receive [15]. In certain personalization schemes, interaction is even indispensible, as is exemplified by the use case of listener curation of the radio playlist (see previous paragraph).

A common challenge with personalization and recommendation is the filter bubble effect. By exclusively catering to the taste and preferences of the listener, the risk arises that the listener gets "locked in" in his or her personal interest sphere or, more worrying, that the listener's view on the world becomes too one-sided. This is of particular interest in the context of public service radio, given that fostering diversity and pluralism is one of the six core values of public service media [19]. Personalization and recommendation are furthermore known to have an adverse effect on serendipity, which is still claimed to be one of broadcast radio's strong suits [15]. Finally, by design, radio is intended to deliver a shared, uniting experience to entire communities; clearly, personalization undermines this objective. Finding the sweet spot between serving the community as a whole and catering to the increasing personalization desires from listeners is an important open challenge in radio research.

Adjusting Content Duration. Consumers often have a limited time slot to fill when they turn to the catch-up consumption of radio content (e.g., while commuting). A specialized form of radio personalization therefore revolves around content duration adaptation [33]. The goal of such adaptation approaches is to tell a story that is as complete and as compelling as possible, within a certain time limit. Given that it is practically infeasible to prepare different versions of the story for each possible time budget, coming up with algorithmic solutions that on-the-fly populate the available time slot in an optimal fashion is an important area of future research (cf. the Squeezebox prototype described in [20]).

Deriving Context from Listener Input. A method for users to interact with radio stations that became popular recently is through chatbots that serve as a first line of support [14]. The resulting conversations can lead to novel ways of profiling and analyzing listeners. Consider a listener that queries a chatbot about the currently playing song. After responding with the requested song title and artist information, the chatbot automatically follows up with the question whether the requesting listener actually likes the song. Based on the listener's response to this question (if any), his or her profile information can be refined (specifically with respect to musical preferences), this way allowing the broadcaster to gather deeper knowledge about its listeners. Another important form of listener input in the context of radio interaction is UGC (see Sect. 2). Automatically scanning and analysing such UGC can also provide clues about the user's current context (e.g., location, activity, mood).

4 Production User Interfaces

Radio production user interfaces need to be updated to integrate the rich information provided by automatic tools and present it in a way that enables efficient production processes.

Live Versus Nearly Live Consumption Data. When radio is consumed through a website or application, radio producers are already enabled to monitor listeners' experiences, using off-the-shelf tools as Adobe Analytics[4] or tailored solutions as Voizzup[5]. The latter experimented with offering listener consumption data in real-time to the radio production team, yet learned that radio hosts felt it affected the production of their show. For instance, learning that a subset of listeners is disconnecting during a particular interview does not encourage a radio host to continue that interview, although it still might be relevant. As a result, the tool is developed to disclose consumption data only right after the end of the radio show. Whether this approach of nearly live data delivery also applies to other types of data, such as contextual information (see Sect. 3), is still an open question.

Visualization and Transparency. In a live production environment, data has to be interpreted fast. Text messages (e.g., contributed by listeners through chat or SMS), for instance, provide a rich source of stories that could be told on radio. Nowadays, such stories commonly have to be spotted and distilled manually by radio producers. When text messages contain photos, it becomes easier for the radio producer to interpret and assess the potential story in a fast way [13]. Because of such practical considerations, in present-day radio production, visually augmented listener messages have a higher probability of being included in the radio broadcast. This in turn indicates the potential of enriching data with automatic visual annotations (e.g., a map of geo-tagged text or photos submitted by listeners). Furthermore, as novel types of data (such as those mentioned in previous sections) are being tracked and cause automatic content adaptations, there is a need to present those decisions in an easy and fast-to-understand format to radio producers. Overall, intelligent and transparent data visualization in radio production interfaces should allow radio producers to stay in control to ensure serendipity (as mentioned in Sect. 3) and storytelling quality.

Efficient Overview. Radio producers are currently confronted with a multitude of tools, software, interfaces, and so on during the live production process. As a result, they are often distracted from their core content production tasks (e.g., when searching for the right tool to contact a listener) [8]. In future, a smart production system might automatically reconfigure its user interface by visualizing only the data, content and context that is relevant in the current phase of the radio production process or given the current radio production task at hand [22]. Conversely, currently irrelevant information or tools could be hidden, but remain accessible to the production team when needed. Automatic interface reconfiguration decisions could be inspired by, for example, the pre-produced script of the radio show.

---

[4] https://www.adobe.com/analytics/adobe-analytics.html.
[5] http://www.voizzup.com/.

5 Conclusion

In this position paper, we have analyzed challenges for producing interactive radio content, which fits the need of contemporary *any where, any time, any device* media consumption habits. On the one hand, the production team needs to stay in control to create high quality radio experiences. On the other hand, automation support is needed to handle the large amounts of heterogeneous multimedia content that is involved in interactive radio production. We argue that, to some extent, interactive radio production is in fact a multimedia analytics problem. We have analyzed three major aspects in interactive radio production (i.e., content enrichment, context derivation and adaptation, and the integration in production user interfaces) and have uncovered important challenges and opportunities concerning the use of multimedia analytics for each of them. In this process, we have also identified important research gaps in the analysis and processing of radio content. Equivalent research has commonly already been conducted for media types other than radio (mostly video); it is worthwhile to investigate whether these findings from other media domains are translatable to interactive radio contexts.

Acknowledgments. This work has received funding from the European Union's Horizon 2020 research and innovation programme, under grant agreement n° 761802 MARCONI ("Multimedia and Augmented Radio Creation: Online, iNteractive, Individual"). The authors thank all presenters and participants of the Workshop on Interactive Radio Experiences at ACM TVX 2019.

References

1. Media use in the European Union. Technical report, Standard Eurobarometer 88 - Wave EB88.3, November 2017
2. D2.1: HRADIO User Scenarios. Technical report, H2020 HRADIO Project Deliverable (2018)
3. Bailer, W., et al.: Content and metadata workflow for user generated content in live production. In: Proceedings of European Conference on Visual Media Production, London, UK (2016)
4. Bailer, W., Winter, M., Wechtitsch, S.: Learning selection of user generated event videos. In: Proceedings of 15th International Workshop on Content-Based Multimedia Indexing (2017)
5. Bartsch, M.A., Wakefield, G.H.: Audio thumbnailing of popular music usingchroma-based representations. IEEE Trans. Multimed. **7**(1), 96–104 (2005)
6. Baume, C.: "Even more or less": a data-rich interactive podcast player. In: Proceedings of Workshop on Interactive Radio Experiences at ACM TVX (2019)
7. Bauwens, R.: Interactive content contribution. In: Proceedings of Workshop on Interactive Content Consumption at ACM TVX (2016)
8. Bauwens, R., Claes, S.: MARCONI: towards an integrated, intelligent radio production platform. In: Proceedings of IBC2019 Conference (2019, to appear)
9. Bauwens, R., Lievens, H., Wijnants, M., Pike, C., Jennes, I., Bailer, W.: Interactive radio experiences. In: Proceedings of the 2019 ACM International Conference on Interactive Experiences for TV and Online Video (TVX) (2019)

10. Bois, R., Gravier, G., Jamet, E., Morin, E., Robert, M., Sébillot, P.: Linking multimedia content for efficient news browsing. In: ACM International Conference on Multimedia Retrieval (2017)
11. Buurman, A.: Audio draait om mood management (2016). https://beautifullives.com/news/audio-draait-om-mood-management/
12. Chen, Y., Liu, L.: Development and research of topic detection and tracking. In: Proceedings of IEEE International Conference on Software Engineering and Service Science (2016)
13. Claes, S., Bauwens, R., Matton, M.: Augmenting the radio experience by enhancing interactions between radio editors and listeners. In: Proceedings of ACM International Conference on Interactive Experiences for TV and Online Video (TVX) (2018)
14. Claes, S., Jansen, S.: 360 radio experience: connecting live listening with user interaction and visual radio. In: Proceedings of Workshop on Interactive Radio Experiences at ACM TVX (2019)
15. Cowlishaw, T., Burlington, T., Man, D., Fiala, J., Barrington, R., Wright, G.: Personalising the public: personalising linear radio at a public service broadcaster. In: Proceedings of the IBC2018 Conference (2018)
16. Cox, J., Jones, R., Northwood, C., Tutcher, J., Robinson, B.: Object-based production: a personalised interactive cooking application. In: Adjunct Proceedings of ACM International Conference on Interactive Experiences for TV and Online Video (TVX) (2017)
17. Erk, A., Sattler, F.: DAB over IP. In: Proceedings of Workshop on Interactive Radio Experiences at ACM TVX (2019)
18. Eskevich, M., et al.: Multimedia information seeking through search and hyperlinking. In: Proceedings of the 3rd ACM International Conference on Multimedia Retrieval (2013)
19. European Broadcasting Union (EBU): Empowering Society - A Declaration of the Core Values of Public Service Media (2012). https://www.ebu.ch/files/live/sites/ebu/files/Publications/EBU-Empowering-Society_EN.pdf
20. Evans, M., et al.: Creating object-based experiences in the real world. SMPTE Mot. Imaging J. **126**(6) (2017)
21. Evans, M., Kerlin, L., Larner, O., Campbell, R.: Feels like being there: viewers describe the quality of experience of festival video using their own words. In: Extended Abstracts of the ACM Conference on Human Factors in Computing Systems (CHI) (2018)
22. Gajos, K., Weld, D.S.: SUPPLE: automatically generating user interfaces. In: Proceedings of the 9th International Conference on Intelligent User Interfaces, IUI 2004, pp. 93–100. ACM (2004)
23. Galuščáková, P., Pecina, P.: Audio information for hyperlinking of TV content. In: Proceedings of 3rd Workshop on Speech, Language & Audio in Multimedia (2015)
24. Gehani, S.: Audio hyperlinking. US Patent App. 13/368,129 (2013)
25. Gemmeke, J.F., et al.: Audio set: an ontology and human-labeled dataset for audio events. In: Proceedings of the International Conference on Acoustics, Speech, and Signal Processing (IEEE ICASSP) (2017)
26. Gravier, G., et al.: Shaping-up multimedia analytics: needs and expectations of media professionals. In: Tian, Q., Sebe, N., Qi, G.-J., Huet, B., Hong, R., Liu, X. (eds.) MMM 2016. LNCS, vol. 9517, pp. 303–314. Springer, Cham (2016). https://doi.org/10.1007/978-3-319-27674-8_27
27. Herranz, L., Martinez, J.M.: A framework for scalable summarization of video. IEEE Trans. Circ. Syst. Video Technol. **20**(9), 1265–1270 (2010)

28. Hershey, S., et al.: CNN architectures for large-scale audio classification. In: Proceedings of the International Conference on Acoustics, Speech, and Signal Processing (IEEE ICASSP) (2017)
29. Jackson, W.: Listener driven radio gains popularity (2018). https://www.radioworld.com/news-and-business/listener-driven-radio-gains-popularity
30. Krotoski, A.: Touchies and feelies: everything i know about human interfaces. ACM CHI Opening Keynote (2019)
31. Liu, X., Huet, B.: Linking socially contributed media with events. Multimed. Syst. **22**(4), 433–442 (2016)
32. Montagnuolo, M., Messina, A.: Rai active news: integrating knowledge in newsrooms. In: Proceedings of the IBC2015 Conference (2015)
33. Casagranda, P., Russo, F., Teraoni Prioletti, R.: Personalising linear radio: model and user evaluation. In: Proceedings of IBC2018 Conference (2018)
34. RAJAR/IpsosMori: MIDAS Audio Survey Autumn 2018. Technical report (2018)
35. Sappelli, M., Chu, D.M., Cambel, B., Nortier, J., Graus, D.: SMART radio: personalized news radio. In: Proceedings of 17th Dutch-Belgian Information Retrieval workshop (DIR) (2018)
36. Silzle, A., Weitnauer, M., et al.: ORPHEUS audio project: piloting an end-to-end object-based audio broadcasting chain. In: Proceedings of IBC2017 Conference (2017)
37. Skov, M., Lykke, M.: Unlocking radio broadcasts: user needs in sound retrieval. In: Proceedings of the 4th Information Interaction in Context Symposium (2012)
38. Starkey, G., Gazi, A., Dimitrakopoulou, D., Cordeiro, P.: "Generation C" and audio media: a cross-cultural analysis of differences in media consumption in four European countries. Particip. J. Audience Recept. Stud. **11**(2), 239–257 (2014)
39. VRT Innovation: "Alexa, what's the news?" VRT is experimenting with voice-controlled radio and news (2018). https://innovatie.vrt.be/en/en/article/vrt-is-experimenting-with-voice-controlled-radio-and-news
40. Wardle, C., Williams, A.: Beyond user-generated content: a production study examining the ways in which UGC is used at the BBC. Media Cult. Soc. **32**(5), 781–799 (2010)
41. Wijnants, M., Rovelo, G., Quax, P., Lamotte, W.: Wandercouch. Multimed. Toolsand Appl. **76**(4), 5721–5753 (2017)
42. Zechner, K.: Automatic summarization of open-domain multiparty dialogues indiverse genres. Comput. Linguist. **28**(4), 447–485 (2002)
43. Zlatintsi, A., Iosif, E., Marago, P., Potamianos, A.: Audio salient event detection and summarization using audio and text modalities. In: Proceedings of the 23rd European Signal Processing Conference (EUSIPCO) (2015)
44. Zlatintsi, A., Maragos, P., Potamianos, A., Evangelopoulos, G.: A saliency-based approach to audio event detection and summarization. In: Proceedings of the 20th European Signal Processing Conference (EUSIPCO) (2012)

Interactive Search and Exploration in Discussion Forums Using Multimodal Embeddings

Iva Gornishka, Stevan Rudinac(✉), and Marcel Worring

University of Amsterdam, Amsterdam, The Netherlands
iva.gornishka@gmail.com, {s.rudinac,m.worring}@uva.nl

Abstract. In this paper we present a novel interactive multimodal learning system, which facilitates search and exploration in large networks of social multimedia users. It allows the analyst to identify and select users of interest, and to find similar users in an interactive learning setting. Our approach is based on novel multimodal representations of users, words and concepts, which we simultaneously learn by deploying a general-purpose neural embedding model. The usefulness of the approach is evaluated using artificial actors, which simulate user behavior in a relevance feedback scenario. Multiple experiments were conducted in order to evaluate the quality of our multimodal representations and compare different embedding strategies. We demonstrate the capabilities of the proposed approach on a multimedia collection originating from the violent online extremism forum Stormfront, which is particularly interesting due to the high semantic level of the discussions it features.

Keywords: Multimedia analytics · Search · Exploration · Interactive learning · Multimodal embeddings · Online discussion forums

1 Introduction

In recent years much of our communication is happening on social multimedia platforms, which allow users to connect with others and to exchange ideas and content about topics of their interest. Such fora commonly host lengthy discussions and fierce debates about social issues, and they have become a widely adopted place for cooperation, activism, promotion of different ideologies, and organization of offline events and activities all over the world. Still, as pointed out in [4], even basic descriptive or explanatory research is often missing when it comes to e.g. determining the role of Internet in promoting the ideologies and processes with a potentially cataclysmic societal impact, such as violent extremism and radicalization. One of the main factors hindering domain experts from social sciences fields and law enforcement agencies is a lack of multimedia analytics tools facilitating insight gain into the role of users and groups in dynamic online communities. Tools should be developed that not only model users' interactions with the platform and each other, but go beyond to incorporating analysis of the heterogeneous digital content they consume.

Y. M. Ro et al. (Eds.): MMM 2020, LNCS 11962, pp. 388–399, 2020.
https://doi.org/10.1007/978-3-030-37734-2_32

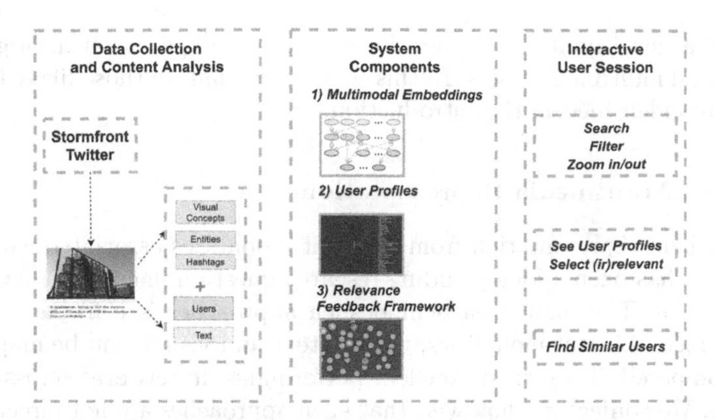

Fig. 1. High-level overview of *ISOLDE*'s full preprocessing pipeline, system components and interactive user sessions

In this paper we design *ISOLDE*, a novel analytics system which aids domain experts in analyzing large collections of social multimedia users. Its main purpose is to enable easy, on the fly categorization of the users into analytic categories and the discovery of new users of interest, in order to assist annotating large datasets for frequently changing communities. In addition, the proposed system needs to facilitate search and exploration in the large and heterogeneous multimedia collections that online discussion forums create. Lastly, the system should fulfill basic requirements for multimedia analytics systems—as outlined by [24], some of the most important being *interactivity*, *scalability*, *relevance* and *comprehensibility*. Based on these technical prerequisites and the common information needs of the domain experts, we develop a prototype of such a system, which contains the following main novel contributions:

- Compact multimodal user and content representations, which can serve as the basis for visualization, interactive learning, categorization and profiling.
- Investigation into the effect multimodal embeddings have on different aspects of system performance. Namely, while the effects of text embeddings, such as word2vec, glove and fasttext, on standard evaluation metrics is relatively well studied, this is not the case for multimodal embeddings.
- Analysis of a number of use cases to identify in which situations traditional vector-space models and multimodal embeddings yield optimal performance.

2 Related Work

Over the last decades a number of excellent multimedia representation approaches and analytics systems have been proposed to aid domain experts in their research. While some of them were specifically developed to support network analysis tasks, others, although not directly applicable, are characterized by plenty of useful features and could serve as a good starting point for developing a novel analytics system for search and exploration in large collections of social multimedia users. In this section we analyze those likely to satisfy requirements identified in the Introduction.

2.1 Social Multimedia Representation

Deriving a joint representation from different modalities associated with a multimedia item has been a long-standing research question in cross-media retrieval [3,14,19,22,23]. The main idea behind such approaches is learning a common space to which different modalities, usually text and visual, can be mapped and directly compared. They yield excellent performance in retrieval across different modalities. We conjecture, however, that such approaches are not directly applicable for modeling the complex relations within social multimedia networks. It requires going beyond text and visual content, which are usually well-aligned, to include user interactions with the online platform and each other.

Inspired by the success of word embedding techniques, such as word2vec [11], glove [13] and fasttext [2], graph and general purpose embeddings for multimodal data started to emerge [7,21]. These approaches were proven effective in a variety of tasks, such as query-by-example retrieval and recommendation. Although they have not been designed or tested on multimedia content, due to their demonstrated potential for modeling heterogeneous data collections, we consider them a solid base for building multimodal user representations.

2.2 Multimedia Analytics

Multimedia analytics systems, such as Multimedia Pivot Tables [20], ICLIC [5], and Blackthorn [24] facilitate search and exploration in large collections of multimedia data as well as interactive multimodal learning. Blackthorn, for example, compresses semantic information from the visual and text domain and learns user preferences on the fly from the interactions with the system in a relevance feedback framework [24]. Serving as the epicenter of research on interactive multimedia retrieval, the initiatives such as Video Browser Showdown produced a number of excellent analytics systems [9]. For example, vitrivr system owes its good performance in interactive multimedia retrieval to an indexing structure for efficient kNN search [15]. Similarly, SIRET tool facilitates interactive video retrieval using several querying strategies, i.e. query by keywords, query by color-sketch and query by example image [8]. Following a different approach, Vibro system relies on a hierarchical graph structure for interactive exploration of large video collections [1]. Yet, none of these systems were designed with the analysis of social graphs in mind.

Finally, while PICTuReVis [6] facilitates interactive learning for revealing relations between users based on their patterns of multimedia consumption, it is not designed for search and exploration of large social multimedia networks, but rather forensic analysis of artifacts from e.g. confiscated electronic devices, featuring a limited number of users.

3 Approach Overview

In this work, we propose *ISOLDE* – a novel multimodal analytics system which allows domain experts to explore large collections of social multimedia users, to identify users of interest and find more similar ones in an interactive framework. Our goal goes beyond modeling social networks shaped by user interactions with the online platform and each other, to discovering "topical communities" based on similarities in multimedia content the users consume. In this section we provide a high-level overview of *ISOLDE*, its main components and their importance for the user's interactive sessions.

ISOLDE's full pipeline is conceptually depicted in Fig. 1 and it consists of three main phases: data preprocessing, preparation of the individual system components and the interactive user sessions.

3.1 Data Preprocessing

The first step is collecting social multimedia data and analyzing the content in order to provide additional context from the text, visual, or any other available modality. Afterwards, the annotated data is indexed in order to provide search and filtering functionality. Section 4 discusses in details our approach to data collection and analysis, however, *ISOLDE*'s framework is general and can easily be adapted to any social multimedia platform or content analysis approach.

3.2 System Components

The following phase in *ISOLDE*'s pipeline is setting up all individual components of the system. First, we need user representations which will be later used to visualize the users and to classify them. While any standard technique can be used to represent the users, our proposed approach is based on a novel general-purpose neural embedding model which allows us to learn representations not only for users, but also for the multimodal content [21].

Next, user and community summaries (profiles) are required to reduce the amount of content that needs to be processed by the interacting user and to support insightful analysis of the different social networks and their members. Our approach to creating such summaries is inspired by standard summarization techniques and relies on identifying diverse and representative items from all modalities. This process is enabled by our multimodal content representations.

Lastly, an interactive learning component enables the discovery of new users of interest based on previously provided examples.

3.3 Interactive User Sessions

Finally, all components of the system are combined into a single interactive user interface. From the point of view of the interacting user (i.e. actor), analytic sessions consist of the following steps:

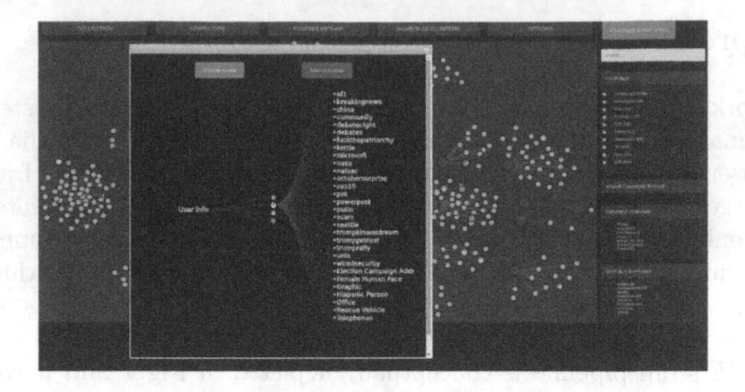

Fig. 2. A screenshot of *ISOLDE*'s interface with the detected topical communities in the background and automatically generated user profile in the foreground.

Step 1: Collection Overview, Search and Exploration. The actor is initially presented with an aggregated overview of all users in the collection, grouped by their topical similarities. They can start interacting with the collection, easily navigating by zooming in and out, filtering the items and searching by text queries. Automatically created sub-community profiles enable quick understanding of the space and the overall structure of the collection.

Step 2: User Interactions and Profiling. Once potential users of interest are identified, the actor can inspect their automatically generated multimodal user profiles, and mark them as relevant or irrelevant (Fig. 2).

Step 3: Identifying Similar Users. When the actor has marked a number of users as relevant, she can look for more similar users. At this moment, an interactive classifier is trained in real time and used to score each item (i.e. users) in the collections. All user nodes are colored in order to reflect the scores, and the top-N users considered most relevant by the system are highlighted in the interface. Although it is preferable that the actor explicitly indicates the relevance of the top-N highlighted results, they are not obliged to do so and can simply continue with another action.

Throughout the whole session, the interacting user can seamlessly switch between the aforementioned actions and continue iterative refinement of their preferences until satisfied with the outcome.

4 Data Collection and Analysis

4.1 Datasets

We demonstrate the potential of the proposed system using a dataset related to the violent online extremism domain and originally collected for the EU VOX-Pol Project[1]. The collection consists of around 2 million posts from the white

[1] http://www.voxpol.eu/.

nationalist, white supremacist, antisemitic neo-Nazi Internet forum Stormfront. After disregarding all posts of suspended users and users with less than 3 posts, the final dataset contains posts from 40 high-level categories, generated by 29.279 users in the period 2001–2015. For the purpose of this research, we distinguish between two different subsets of categories – the *General chapters* (such as *Politics & Continuing Crises* and *Dating Advice*), containing discussions on various topics, and the *National Chapters* (such as *Stormfront Italia* and *Stormfront Britain*), which are commonly frequented by users interested in the specific geographic area and topics related to it.

4.2 Content Analysis

When analysing social multimedia data, domain experts usually start by annotating the content – they commonly label the individual posts and images with concepts that describe them. This process is often done manually, which makes it labor intensive and time consuming. In order to mimic this process, we automatically extract concepts from the textual and visual domain as follows.

Entity Linking: In the preprocessing step, we extract entities (i.e. topics, people, organizations and locations) mentioned in the Stormfront posts using the Semanticizer [12], which links text to English Wikipedia articles. The process resulted in 65.240 unique entities, which are usually much easier to interpret than alternatives such as latent topics.

Visual Concepts: For each image in the collection we extract 346 TRECVID semantic concepts as described in [18]. A large number of TRECVID concepts are related to intelligence and security applications, and have been shown more useful for categorizing extremism content than the semantic concept detectors trained on general-purpose image collections such as ImageNet [16]. After obtaining confidence scores per image for all of the concepts, we only select the top 5 highest-ranking concepts to represent it.

5 User Representation

5.1 Unimodal Representation and Early Multimodal Fusion

As a baseline approach to representing a user based on all modalities (text, visual concepts, and entities) we use a representation based on time and again proven TFIDF weighting [17]. In order to represent a user in the textual modality, we treat all the posts generated by the user as a single document.

In a similar fashion, using the standard definition of TFIDF, we separately create user representations in all other modalities by simply treating all visual concepts and entities extracted from the user posts as terms. Here too we aggregate all posts from a particular user into a single document.

In this manner, we produce user representations having the dimensionality of the corresponding vocabulary – that is number of words or distinct concepts.

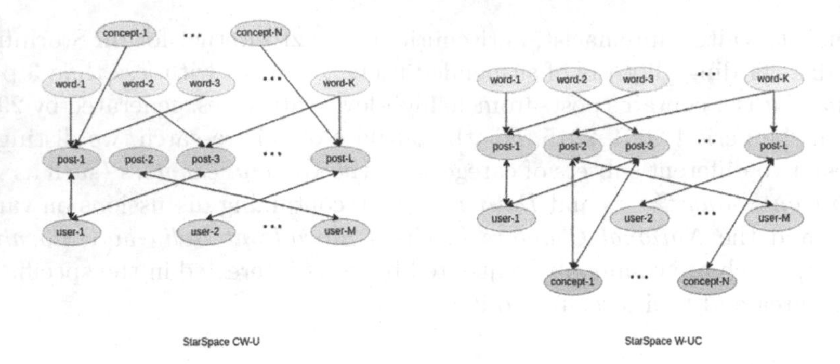

Fig. 3. Different setups for creating user and content representation using a general purpose neural embedding.

Such high-dimensionality vectors are not suitable for interactive systems like *ISOLDE* since they increase the computational time needed for classification, and hence the amount of time that the user waits for a response from the system. Therefore, we reduce the dimensionality of the obtained unimodal user representations using PCA [10].

Preliminary experiments showed that in our evaluation setup early fusion clearly outperforms late fusion approaches independent of the deployed fusion technique. Thus, in all future experiments with TFIDF representations based on multiple modalities, we assume the representations have been normalized and concatenated in advance.

However, separately modeling the individual modalities does not only yield sparse representations in some of them, but it also fails to capture important dependencies between them. When analyzing social multimedia data, analysts are often interested in the co-occurrence of specific topics and the relations between the different modalities within the same posts – phenomena which are not capture by simple unimodal representations which essentially aggregate all of the content produced by the user.

5.2 Multimodal Neural Embeddings

In order to overcome some of the problems posed by unimodal user representations, we propose learning multimodal user and content representations using StarSpace [21] - a general-purpose neural embedding model which was recently shown to be effective for a variety of tasks. While most of these tasks can be adapted in order to learn user representations, we chose to deploy a multilabel text classification task, which allows us to simultaneously learn embeddings not only for users, but also for words, entities and visual concepts. We expect such embeddings to be general enough for solving a wide range of tasks.

While there are multiple possible approaches to training the user and content embeddings through a multilabel text classification task, in the scope of this research we have chosen to compare two different setups, conceptually depicted on Fig. 3. In both setups we generate training examples per post and assign the corresponding user as a positive label. However, the setups differ in two ways - first, in the way we generate the input documents for every example (post), and second, in whether or not we add additional labels next to the user label.

StarSpace **CW-U** trains the model with two separate examples per post - one containing the bag of concepts associated with the post (**C**), and one containing the bag of words (**W**). For both examples, the user (**U**) is a single assigned label.

In StarSpace **W-UC** setup, examples consist again of the bag of words (**W**), however every post is labeled not only with the user (**U**), but also with each of the associated concepts (**C**). In this way, we put more importance on the concepts – such a setup implicitly minimizes the distance between users and the concepts that they commonly use, by simultaneously minimizing the distance between user and a post, and each of the concepts and the post.

6 Evaluation Framework

The usefulness of the system has been evaluated using a protocol inspired by Analytic Quality [25] – a framework which has been adapted for the evaluation of a number of analytics systems in the past years [24,26]. The main idea behind this framework is to automatically simulate user interactions with the system in order to evaluate its performance without the bias of human judgments.

The experiments start by creating multiple artificial actors, each one of them assigned a different task inspired by the intended use of the system. For the purpose of evaluating *ISOLDE*, we assign the different actors a specific subset of the users in the corresponding dataset – a subset which a real-life user could be potentially interested to identify by using the system. Then, the artificial actor's task is to discover as many as possible of the users in their assigned subset by interacting with the system.

According to the protocol, each artificial actor starts by presenting the system with a number of positive seed examples from their own subset. Next, we simulate multiple interaction rounds with the system. At every iteration, the system ranks all users based on the previously shown examples and top N are presented to the actor, where N is a parameter of the system controlling the number of examples highlighted in the interface. At this step, the artificial actor truthfully marks the presented users as relevant or irrelevant, following the assumption that a real-life interacting actor would do so themselves, striving to maximize their own information gain. For all experiments we use the same setup – linear SVM with SGD training as the interactive classifier, $N = 15$ items are presented to the actor and we set representation dimensionality to 128.

In order to fairly evaluate the performance of the system, it is important that the criteria used to form the actor's target subsets do not take into account data used in the user representation (i.e. text, or concepts extracted from the text and the visual content). Thus, we only rely on metadata such as forum structure or information about replies in order to create the target subsets. More details about this process are provided in the following section, together with the analysis of the corresponding experiments.

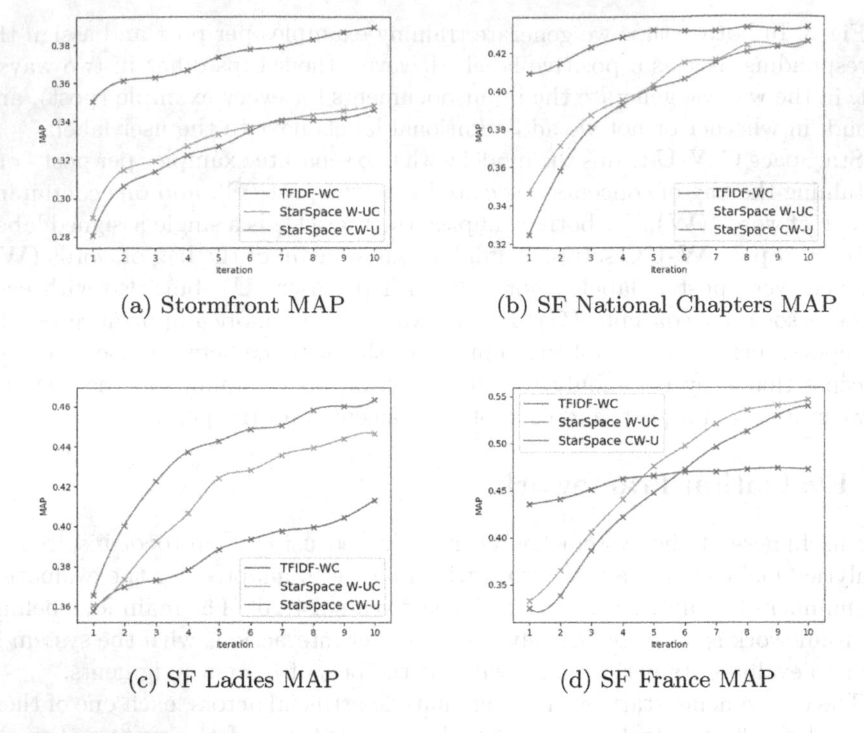

(a) Stormfront MAP

(b) SF National Chapters MAP

(c) SF Ladies MAP

(d) SF France MAP

Fig. 4. Performance of different user representations on Stormfront dataset.

7 Experimental Results

7.1 Baseline Experiments

In our first set of experiments, we compare the performance of the different user representations by conducting the experiments with 40 artificial actors corresponding to each of the Stormfront categories. In these experiments, each actor initially presents the system with the 15 users which produced the highest number of posts within the corresponding category or subcollection.

Figure 4a shows that the multimodal user representation based on TFIDF weighting outperforms multimodal embeddings on Stormfront dataset. A possible explanation lies in a clear difference between the topics discussed in various sub-forums. Most sub-forums further feature narrowly focused discussions, which better suits TFIDF representation than the embeddings optimized for capturing a broader context.

7.2 National Chapters

Our dataset contains 14 categories related to specific countries or geographic regions. These categories present a great opportunity for comparing our user representations due to the specifics of their content – discussions cover a broad range of topics, predominantly related to history and politics, with often mentions of entities (events, people, etc) specific to the region; the discourse is mostly led in English, besides few chapters where the native language prevails. Thus, we next compare the performance of the different user representations in experiments with only the 14 artificial actors corresponding to the National Chapters.

As it can be seen on Fig. 4b, the differences in performance between the TFIDF-based representations and the multimodal embeddings is now noticeably smaller than in the experiments with all chapters. Furthermore, improvement in terms of MAP over time is considerably higher for the multimodal embeddings. It is then possible that retrieving more irrelevant results at the earlier iteration, which are truthfully labeled as such and presented as negative examples at the next round, makes it possible for the classifier based on StarSpace embeddings to learn to better distinguish between the classes.

7.3 Individual Chapters

Finally, the performance varies greatly even between the separate national categories, therefore, we next look into two individual categories – *Stormfront en Français*, which is characterized by the common use of the national language unlike most other national chapters, and *For Stormfront Ladies Only*, which has previously been analyzed in [16] due to the interest of social scientists in the role and portrayal of women in right-wing extremist networks.

The significantly higher results for StarSpace experiments in the experiments with the *For Stormfront Ladies Only* category (cf. Fig. 4c) finally prove the major advantage of the proposed approach over TFIDF representations – that is, its ability to capture context and semantic meaning rather than encoding specific terms. *For Stormfront Ladies Only* is a category which contains a vast majority of topics, including the political and ethnic discussions typical for Stormfront, but presented from the point of view of women and in relation to topics such as family, relationships and culture. This means that the specific terms and language used in the category, as well as visual concepts and entities, are overall general and similar to many other categories. This does not give TFIDF the chance 'hold on' to specific terms, and highlights StarSpace's ability to capture more abstract concepts within the content.

Stormfront en Français is one of the national chapters characterized by predominant use of the national language and a high number of extracted region-specific entities and visual concepts – a setup which is ideal for TFIDF. However, its performance is considerably lower than that of StarSpace (cf. Fig. 4d). While French was hardly ever used within the same post with other languages and semantic similarities between corresponding words have not been captured by StarSpace, entities and visual concepts are more language-independent. Now they become invaluable for StarSpace, since this is the only signal which can be used to expand the topics and find more semantically similar user. Their importance can also be seen in the consistently higher scores for StarSpace W-UC, which so far performed similarly to or worse than StarSpace CW-U. Treating concepts as labels in the training setup (as in StarSpace W-UC) implicitly minimizes the distance between users and concepts, giving them more weight. Thus, using similar concepts becomes more important than using similar words when judging the similarity between users. This allows StarSpace W-UC to diversify the most relevant users at each iteration, helping the classifier to refine the ranking and achieve higher overall results.

8 Conclusion

In this work, we proposed *ISOLDE* – a novel analytics system which facilitates gaining deeper insight into the role of a user or a group in an online community. *ISOLDE* enables search and exploration in large heterogeneous collections, on the fly categorization of social multimedia users and the discovery of new users of interest, in order to assist annotating large datasets for frequently changing communities. As the core component of this system, we proposed a new approach to simultaneously learn multimodal representations of social multimedia users and content using the neural embedding model StarSpace. We showed these representations to be useful not only for categorizing users, but also for automatically generating user and community profiles by selecting diverse and representative content from all modalities. We conducted various experiments in order to automatically evaluate the performance of the system, and to identify the strengths and weaknesses of the proposed user representations. In these experiments, we showcased StarSpace's ability to diversify the results retrieved by the system, ensuring the constant improvement of the model and the high overall long-term information gain for the user. We also saw that this trait of the StarSpace embeddings makes them invaluable for tasks where context is more important than the specific terms which are usually captured by the traditional representations.

Acknowledgments. This project has received funding from the European Union's Seventh Framework Programme for research, technological development and demonstration under grant agreement no. 312827 (NoE VOX-Pol).

References

1. Barthel, K.U., Hezel, N., Mackowiak, R.: Navigating a graph of scenes for exploring large video collections. In: Tian, Q., Sebe, N., Qi, G.-J., Huet, B., Hong, R., Liu, X. (eds.) MMM 2016. LNCS, vol. 9517, pp. 418–423. Springer, Cham (2016). https://doi.org/10.1007/978-3-319-27674-8_43
2. Bojanowski, P., Grave, E., Joulin, A., Mikolov, T.: Enriching word vectors with subword information. TACL **5**, 135–146 (2017)
3. Chen, J.J., Ngo, C.W., Feng, F.L., Chua, T.S.: Deep understanding of cooking procedure for cross-modal recipe retrieval. In: ACM MM 2018, pp. 1020–1028 (2018)
4. Conway, M.: Determining the role of the internet in violent extremism and terrorism. In: Violent Extremism Online: New Perspectives on Terrorism and the Internet, p. 123 (2016)
5. van der Corput, P., van Wijk, J.J.: ICLIC: interactive categorization of large image collections. In: IEEE PacificVis 2016, pp. 152–159 (2016)
6. van der Corput, P., van Wijk, J.J.: Comparing personal image collections with picturevis. In: Computer Graphics Forum, vol. 36, no. 3, pp. 295–304 (2017)

7. Grover, A., Leskovec, J.: Node2vec: scalable feature learning for networks. In: ACM KDD 2016, pp. 855–864 (2016)
8. Lokoč, J., Kovalčík, G., Souček, T.: Revisiting SIRET video retrieval tool. In: Schoeffmann, K., et al. (eds.) MMM 2018. LNCS, vol. 10705, pp. 419–424. Springer, Cham (2018). https://doi.org/10.1007/978-3-319-73600-6_44
9. Lokoč, J., Bailer, W., Schoeffmann, K., Muenzer, B., Awad, G.: On influential trends in interactive video retrieval: video browser showdown 2015–2017. IEEE TMM **20**(12), 3361–3376 (2018)
10. Martin, N., Maes, H.: Multivariate Analysis. Academic Press, Cambridge (1979)
11. Mikolov, T., Sutskever, I., Chen, K., Corrado, G.S., Dean, J.: Distributed representations of words and phrases and their compositionality. In: NIPS 2013, pp. 3111–3119 (2013)
12. Odijk, D., Meij, E., de Rijke, M.: Feeding the second screen: semantic linking based on subtitles. In: OAIR 2013, pp. 9–16 (2013)
13. Pennington, J., Socher, R., Manning, C.: Glove: global vectors for word representation. In: EMNLP 2014, pp. 1532–1543 (2014)
14. Qi, M., Wang, Y., Li, A.: Online cross-modal scene retrieval by binary representation and semantic graph. In: ACM MM 2017, pp. 744–752 (2017)
15. Rossetto, L., Amiri Parian, M., Gasser, R., Giangreco, I., Heller, S., Schuldt, H.: Deep learning-based concept detection in vitrivr. In: Kompatsiaris, I., Huet, B., Mezaris, V., Gurrin, C., Cheng, W.-H., Vrochidis, S. (eds.) MMM 2019. LNCS, vol. 11296, pp. 616–621. Springer, Cham (2019). https://doi.org/10.1007/978-3-030-05716-9_55
16. Rudinac, S., Gornishka, I., Worring, M.: Multimodal classification of violent online political extremism content with graph convolutional networks. In: Thematic Workshops of ACM MM 2017, pp. 245–252 (2017)
17. Salton, G., Buckley, C.: Term-weighting approaches in automatic text retrieval. Inf. Process. Manag. **24**(5), 513–523 (1988)
18. Snoek, C.G.M., et al.: Mediamill at TRECVID 2013: searching concepts, objects, instances and events in video. In: TRECVID Workshop (2013)
19. Wang, B., Yang, Y., Xu, X., Hanjalic, A., Shen, H.T.: Adversarial cross-modal retrieval. In: ACM MM 2017, pp. 154–162 (2017)
20. Worring, M., Koelma, D., Zahálka, J.: Multimedia pivot tables for multimedia analytics on image collections. In: IEEE TMM 2016, vol. 18, no. 11, pp. 2217–2227, November 2016
21. Wu, L.Y., Fisch, A., Chopra, S., Adams, K., Bordes, A., Weston, J.: Starspace: embed all the things! In: AAAI 2018, pp. 5569–5577 (2018)
22. Wu, Y., Wang, S., Huang, Q.: Learning semantic structure-preserved embeddings for cross-modal retrieval. In: ACM MM 2018, pp. 825–833 (2018)
23. Yang, Y., Luo, Y., Chen, W., Shen, F., Shao, J., Shen, H.T.: Zero-shot hashing via transferring supervised knowledge. In: ACM MM 2016, pp. 1286–1295 (2016)
24. Zahálka, J., Rudinac, S., Jónsson, B.T., Koelma, D.C., Worring, M.: Blackthorn: large-scale interactive multimodal learning. IEEE TMM **20**(3), 687–698 (2018)
25. Zahálka, J., Rudinac, S., Worring, M.: Analytic quality: evaluation of performance and insight in multimedia collection analysis. In: ACM MM 2015, pp. 231–240 (2015)
26. Zahálka, J., Rudinac, S., Worring, M.: Interactive multimodal learning for venue recommendation. IEEE TMM **17**(12), 2235–2244 (2015)

An Inverse Mapping with Manifold Alignment for Zero-Shot Learning

Xixun Wu[1(✉)], Binheng Song[1(✉)], Zhixiang Wang[1(✉)], and Chun Yuan[1,2(✉)]

[1] Computer Science and Technology, Graduate School at Shenzhen, Tsinghua University, Shenzhen, China
{wuxx17,wangzhix17}@mails.tsinghua.edu.cn,
{songbinheng,yuanc}@sz.tsinghua.edu.cn
[2] Peng Cheng Laboratory, Shenzhen, China

Abstract. Zero-shot learning aims to recognize objects from unseen classes, where samples are not available at the training stage, by transferring knowledge from seen classes, where labeled samples are provided. It bridges seen and unseen classes via a shared semantic space such as class attribute space or class prototype space. While previous approaches have tried to learning a mapping function from the visual space to the semantic space with different objective functions, we take a different approach and try to map from the semantic space to the visual space. The inverse mapping predicts the visual feature prototype of each unseen class via the semantic vector for image classification. We also propose a heuristic algorithm to select a high density set from data of each seen class. The visual feature prototypes from the high density sets are more discriminative, which is benefit to the classification. Our approach is evaluated for zero-shot recognition on four benchmark data sets and significantly outperforms the state-of-the-art methods on AWA, SUN, APY.

Keywords: Zero-shot learning · High density set · Image classification

1 Introduction

The significant performance improvement of visual object recognition in recent years can largely be attributed to deep neural networks (DNN), which need a huge number of labeled training images [1]. However, it is laboriously difficult and costly to collect and label training samples for some categories in life, or even impossible. For example, samples for penguins which live in Antarctica are hard to obtain and samples for dragons even do not exist. These restrictions are fatal to the visual object recognition task.

Zero-shot learning (ZSL) [2] has proven to be an effective way to address the above difficulty. In zero-shot learning task, we refer to the image categories in the training set as seen classes and those in the test set as unseen classes. There are two basic spaces: visual space which consists of visual features of images extracted by CNN and semantic space which consists of semantic vectors such

Y. M. Ro et al. (Eds.): MMM 2020, LNCS 11962, pp. 400–411, 2020.
https://doi.org/10.1007/978-3-030-37734-2_33

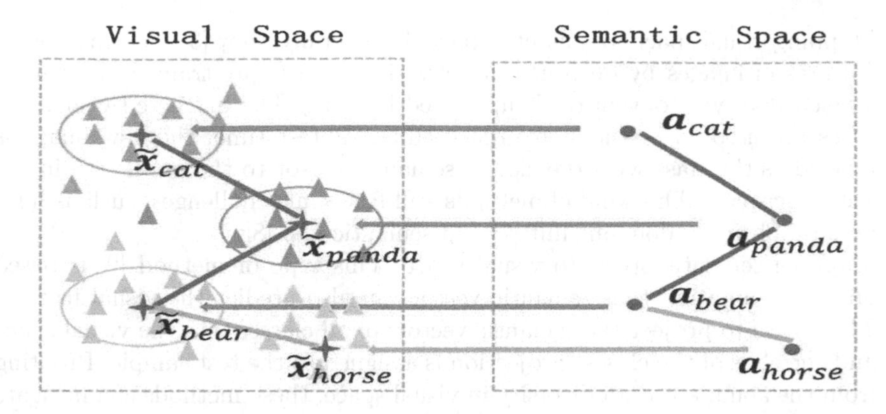

Fig. 1. Illustration of inverse mapping from semantic space to visual space with manifold alignment. We extract visual features $\widetilde{\mathbf{x}}_l$ (four-pointed star) from visual space and extract semantic vector $\mathbf{a}_l$ (red dot) from semantic space. l means the class l. Our approach is to learn a function $f(\mathbf{a}_l) = \widetilde{\mathbf{x}}_l$ (blue arrows) where $\mathbf{a}_l$ denotes the semantic vector and $\widetilde{\mathbf{x}}_l$ denotes the visual feature prototype of the samples in high density set (circles). Then, giving an unseen semantic vector of unseen classes, we project it into the visual space to predict the visual feature prototype (light green arrow). For a novel class image given at test time, the class with the closest visual feature prototype to the visual feature is assigned. (Color figure online)

as class attribute [24,25], word vector representation of class name [10,26], textual description [27,28] and so on. Given a labeled training set from seen classes, zero-shot learning attempts to classify test samples from unseen classes through exploiting a shared semantic space that embeds all classes and enables transferring the knowledge from seen classes to unseen classes. While each sample (e.g., image) is encoded by a feature vector in the visual space, each class corresponds to a unique semantic vector in the semantic space. This paradigm is inspired by the way human beings are able to identify a new object by just reading a description of it, leveraging similarities between the description of the new object and previously learned concepts. As show in Fig. 1, we try to train a classifier on samples from seen classes (cat, panda and bear) to recognize samples from unseen classes (horse) through transferring the shared class attributes among all classes, such as furry, four-legged and mammal.

According to whether unlabeled test samples from unseen classes are available for training or not, existing zero-shot learning methods can be grouped into two categories: inductive zero-shot learning and transductive zero-shot learning [7]. Transductive zero-shot learning assumes that unlabeled samples from unseen classes are also available for training, while inductive zero-shot learning can only access labeled samples from seen classes. Intuitively, inductive zero-shot learning is more practical and challenging, and it also attracts more attention in existing studies. Our work belongs to inductive zero-shot learning. Previous works on inductive zero-shot learning can be divided into the following three categories:

- Mapping visual space to semantic space. In generally, they [3–5] extract visual features of images by deep neural network, which is pre-trained on massive labeled data via conventional supervised learning. The extracted visual features are used to predict semantic vectors. At test time, the new image is labeled as the class with the closest semantic vector to the prediction in the semantic space. This kind of methods still face some challenges, such as hubness problem [6], domain shift [7] and semantic gap [8].
- Mapping semantic space to visual space. This type of method [9] is based on the assumption that semantic vector can also predict the visual feature. They learn to project the semantic vectors of all classes into the visual space and the class of the closest projection is assigned to the test sample. Profiting from the abundant data diversity in visual space, these methods can mitigate the hubness problem at some extent. Nevertheless, this kind of method is usually hard to training since a fixed semantic vector corresponds to multiple visual features.
- Mapping visual features and semantic vector to a common intermediate space. These methods learn to fit a appropriate compatibility function between visual features and semantic vectors to project both of them into a common intermediate space [10–12]. However, the learned comparability function often produces bias results without training samples from unseen classes.

Recently, generative models [13] applied to zero-shot learning are proved to have great potential, such as GAN (Generative Adversarial Networks) and VAE (Variational Auto-Encoder). The generative models are used to generate data for unseen classes to augment original data and the augmented new data set is utilized to train a conventional multi-classifier. Despite their strong performance, these generative models are more difficult to train. Our approach significantly boosts the accuracy of zero-shot learning in the regime of discriminative models, which attains the simplicity of model design. Also, our work is well complementary to the generative models based approaches.

The approach we propose is to learn a map function from semantic space into visual space. A fact can be found in visual space is that the visual features of images from the same class cluster around the visual center, we called visual feature prototype. The visual feature prototype characterizes all visual feature vectors from the corresponding class, shown as Fig. 1. Based on the discovery, we try to learn a function to predict the visual feature prototype through semantic vector of the corresponding class. More importantly, the hubness problem can be avoided due to a large margin between two different visual feature prototypes in visual space. The test sample can be labeled to class of the closest visual feature prototype. However, not all samples can be discriminated easily. To further increase the separability of visual feature prototypes, which is important to recognize test samples, we propose a heuristic algorithm to select a high density set of samples from all samples of each class. The high density set consists of a fixed proportion of the samples closest to the visual feature prototype. We also combine manifold alignment with our approach to cope with the domain shift problem that the projections of unseen class semantic vectors are likely to be misplaced due to the bias of the training seen classes. The manifold alignment is to keep consistency of relations between seen classes and unseen classes in both visual space and semantic space. We validate the effectiveness of our proposed approach on four benchmark datasets for ZSL and the results demonstrate the advantage of our model over current state-of-the-art competitors. For example, on AwA2 dataset, our approach improves the recognition accuracy on unseen classes by 5% in conventional ZSL setting and even by 11.6% in the generalized ZSL setting.

The rest of the paper is organized as follows. We describe our proposed approach in Sect. 2. We demonstrate the superior performance of our method in Sect. 3 and give a conclusion in Sect. 4.

2 The Proposed Method

2.1 Problem Setting

We start by introducing some notations and the problem definition. Let $L_s = \{l_1, ..., l_{N_s}\}$ denote a set of seen classes (N_s denotes number of seen classes) and $L_u = \{l_{N_s+1}, ..., l_{N_s+N_u}\}$ denote a set of unseen classes (N_u denotes number of unseen classes), L_s and L_u are disjoint, i.e. $L_s \cap L_u = \emptyset$. For each class l in $L = L_s \cup L_u$, we have a class semantic vector $\mathbf{a}_l$, that describes the class. We are given a set of labelled training data $D_s = \{(\mathbf{x}_i^s, l_i^s, \mathbf{a}_{l_i^s}^s) : i = 1, ..., T_s\}$, where $\mathbf{x}_i^s \in R^d$ is the d-dimensional visual feature vector of the i-th image in the training set, $l_i^s \in L_s$ is the label of $\mathbf{x}_i^s$, $\mathbf{a}_{l_i^s}^s$ is the semantic vector of $\mathbf{x}_i^s$, and T_s denotes the total number of labelled images. Let $D_u = \{(\mathbf{x}_i^u, l_i^u, \mathbf{a}_{l_i^u}^u) : i = 1, ..., T_u\}$ denote a set of unlabelled test data, where $\mathbf{x}_i^u \in R^d$ is the d-dimensional visual feature vector of the i-th image in the test set, $l_i^u \in L_u$ is the unseen label of $\mathbf{x}_i^u$, $\mathbf{a}_{l_i^u}^u$ is the class semantic vector of $\mathbf{x}_i^u$, and T_u denotes the total number of unlabelled images.

In traditional zero-shot learning setting, the goal is to construct a model $f : R^d \rightarrow L_u$, that can classify the data from the unseen classes L_u. In generalized zero shot setting, we aim to construct a more generic model $f_g : R^d \rightarrow L_s \cup L_u$, that can classify the data from both the seen and unseen classes correctly. The latter setting is much more difficult than the former for two reasons. Firstly, there are more classes in the second setting which leads to more confusion. Secondly, the seen and unseen classes may come from different probability distributions, which could degrade the performance on either the seen or the unseen classes.

2.2 Approach

The key of our method is to establish an inverse mapping from semantic vector to visual feature prototype of corresponding classes with the manifold alignment. Our proposed approach consists of three parts: inverse mapping, high density set, manifold alignment.

Inverse Mapping. Most of previous works are devoted to finding the function $h(\mathbf{x}) = \mathbf{a}$ which projects visual feature $\mathbf{x}$ into semantic vector $\mathbf{a}$, then they predict the class label by various similarity measures implied by the semantic vectors. For example, given a test instance $\mathbf{x}$, the prediction is given by

$$\arg\max_{l} S(h(\mathbf{x}), \mathbf{a}_l) \tag{1}$$

where S is a similarity function. The challenge faced in learning such a mapping are well documented in [6], that is the hubness problem. Mapping the visual features to the semantic space will shrink the variance of the visual features and thus aggravate the hubness problem. To alleviate the problem, we propose a inverse mapping h^{-1} from semantic space to visual space. The visual space with greater variance than the semantic space makes the projected data points less likely to become hubs. For simplicity, we define $f = h^{-1}$. For each class l, we predict a visual feature prototype $\widetilde{\mathbf{x}}_l$ by:

$$f(\mathbf{a}_l) = \widetilde{\mathbf{x}}_l \tag{2}$$

Then, given a instance $\mathbf{x}$, the prediction is given by:

$$\arg\max_{l} S(\mathbf{x}, \widetilde{\mathbf{x}}_l) \tag{3}$$

However, the inverse mapping is hard to train since a semantic vector corresponds to multiple visual features in seen classes. To solve the problem, we create the visual feature prototype (denoted by $\widetilde{\mathbf{x}}_l^s$) for each seen class to replace all visual feature vectors. Then we learn a projection function from semantic vectors to the visual feature prototypes of classes instead of all visual features vectors. In this paper, the visual feature prototype of a class is the average visual feature vector of data belonging to the class.

$$\widetilde{\mathbf{x}}_l^s = \frac{1}{\mathrm{n}_l} \sum \mathbf{x}_i^s, \mathbf{x}_i^s \in D_l^s \tag{4}$$

where n_l denotes the number of feature vectors, D_l^s denotes the training data from class l. We would like to learn the projection $\widetilde{\mathbf{x}}_l^s = f(\mathbf{a}^s)$ to enforce the semantic vectors to be predictive of their visual prototypes. We get the following loss function:

$$L_p = ||\widetilde{\mathbf{x}}_l^s - f(\mathbf{a}_l)||^2 \tag{5}$$

We choose a linear function $f : \widetilde{\mathbf{x}}_l^s = \mathbf{w}\mathbf{a}_l$, where $\mathbf{w}$ is the parameters. We apply a square loss to the learnable parameters $\mathbf{w}$ and add the following implicit regularization term to the minimization formulation:

$$L_p = ||\widetilde{\mathbf{x}}_l^s - f(\mathbf{a}_l)||^2 + \lambda||\mathbf{w}||^2 \tag{6}$$

where λ is regularization parameter. The first term enforces semantic vector to predict visual feature prototype and the second term is to relieve over-fitting.

High Density Set. In our work, we discover fuzzy samples which are far from visual feature prototype or as far as two different visual feature prototypes. The fuzzy samples result in small margin between the two visual feature prototypes, which increases the difficulty of classification. To get more discriminative visual feature prototype, we select a high density set defined in [14] from data of each class. The high density set consists of a fixed proportion of the samples closest to the visual feature prototype and excludes the fuzzy samples.

Algorithm 1. Find High Density Set

Input:
Train data from class l: $D_l^s = \{(\mathbf{x}_i^s, l_i^s, \mathbf{a}_{l_i^{(s)}}^s) : l_i^s = l; i \in \{1, ..., T_s\}\}$; Ratio of samples $k = 0.9$; Distance function: $d_{\mathbf{x}_1,\mathbf{x}_2} = dist(\mathbf{x}_1, \mathbf{x}_2)$;
Output: High density set I_l^s; Visual feature prototypes $\widetilde{\mathbf{x}}_l^s$
$I_l^s \leftarrow D_l^s$;
$\widetilde{\mathbf{x}}_l^s \leftarrow \frac{1}{|I_l^s|}\sum \mathbf{x}_i^s, \mathbf{x}_i^s \in I_l^s$;
$K \leftarrow |I_l^s| \times k$;
$newI_l^s \leftarrow$ top K closest $\mathbf{x}_i^s$ sorted by $d_{\mathbf{x}_1,\mathbf{x}_2}(\mathbf{x}_i^s, \widetilde{\mathbf{x}}_l^s), \mathbf{x}_i^s \in I_l^s$
while $I_l^s \neq newI_l^s$ **do**
  $\widetilde{\mathbf{x}}_l^s \leftarrow \frac{1}{|newI_l^s|}\sum \mathbf{x}_i^s, \mathbf{x}_i^s \in newI_l^s$;
  $newI_l^s \leftarrow$ top K closest $\mathbf{x}_i^s$ sorted by $d_{x_1,x_2}(\mathbf{x}_i^s, \widetilde{\mathbf{x}}_l^s), \mathbf{x}_i^s \in I_l^s$;
end
return I_l^s;$\widetilde{\mathbf{x}}_l^s$;

We propose a heuristic algorithm to find the high density set for each classes (details in Algorithm 1). For each class l, we sort the visual feature vectors by the distance from the initial visual feature prototype $\widetilde{\mathbf{x}}_l^s$ in Eq. 4. The distance which is calculated by distance function $dist(\mathbf{x_1}, \mathbf{x_2})$ can be cosine distance, Euclidean distance or others. We adopt the cosine distance in this paper. Then we select the top k percent visual feature vectors as new high density set $newI_l^s$ and update the visual feature prototype as the average visual feature vector of $newI_l^s$. The algorithm would not stop until the high density set keeps unchange to get the final visual feature prototype.

The algorithm can converge within a few epochs and the final visual feature prototype is computed on the high density set chosen by our algorithm. There are two methods we use for computing a better visual feature prototype: taking the average of all visual features as the Eq. 4 and taking the weighted average of all visual features as the formulation:

$$\widetilde{\mathbf{x}}_l^s = \frac{1}{Z}\sum \frac{\mathbf{x}_i^s}{dist(\widetilde{\mathbf{x}}_l^s, \mathbf{x}_i^s)}, \mathbf{x}_i^s \in D_l^s \qquad (7)$$

where Z is the normalization term: $Z = \sum \frac{1}{dist(\widetilde{\mathbf{x}}_l^s, \mathbf{x}_i^s)}$. We choose the former through controlled experiment in this paper.

Manifold Alignment. In our work, the semantic vector is projected to the visual feature prototype. There is visual-semantic gap existing in the learned inverse mapping function because we lack the data on the unseen classes, that is, the visual feature prototype predicted through semantic vector of unseen class may be far from its real place. We tackle with it by manifold alignment which preserves the relations between seen classes and unseen classes in visual and semantic space.

For the i-th training data $\mathbf{x}_i^s$, we proposed the penalty as follow:

$$L_m = \frac{1}{N_u} \sum_{t=1}^{N_u} |dist(\mathbf{a}_i^s, \mathbf{a}_t^u) - dist(\widetilde{\mathbf{x}}_l^s, f(\mathbf{a}_k^u))|^2 \quad (8)$$

where $\widetilde{\mathbf{x}}_l^s$ is the visual feature prototype for the class l from which $\mathbf{x}_i^s$ is. The penalty ensures that the relations (similarity in this paper) between semantic vectors of both seen classes and unseen classes as same as the relations between their visual feature prototypes. With the manifold alignment penalty, hence the complete learning objective is given by:

$$L = L_p + \beta L_m \quad (9)$$

where L_p is the square loss described in Eq. 6, L_m is the penalty described in Eq. 8 and β is the weighting factor. To optimize the objective function stably, we train it on a new train set. Although we have only N_s samples for training, we sample the new train set from these samples, which is based on the distribution of the train data. For example, the new train set contains the same number of $\widetilde{\mathbf{x}}_l^s$ as the number of feature vectors from class l in the train data. Otherwise, the l2 regularization in Eq. 6 play a key role in avoiding over-fitting due to a small sample size. Once we learn the inverse mapping function $f(.)$, the visual feature prototype of unseen class can be predicted when the semantic vector is provided. Then a nearest neighbor classifier is applied to visual features of test samples. A coming new test image is taken as input by a pre-trained network to extract visual feature. The test image is classified to the class of the closest visual feature prototype to its visual feature.

3 Experiment

3.1 Dataset and Setup

Dateset. Following the setting in [15], we select five widely-used benchmark datasets for evaluation, e.g., AWA1, AWA2, CUB, SUN and APY. AWA1 contains 30,745 images of 50 classes of animals. We use 40 classes (13 for validation) for training while the remaining 10 classes are used for testing. Each class is associated with a 85-dimension continuous attribute vector. AWA2 is an extension of AWA1. CUB (Caltech-UCSD Birds-200-2011) contains 11,788 images of 200 bird species. We split these bird species into 150 seen classes (50 for validation) with 50 disjoint unseen classes and annotate each of them with a 312-dimension continuous attribute vector. SUN consists of 14,340 images of scenes in 717 categories where 645 classes (65 for validation) are selected for training and the remaining 72 classes are used for testing. A 102-dimension continuous attribute vector is utilized to describe the semantic information of each class. APY (Attribute Pascal and Yahoo) contains 32 classes with 64-dimension attribute vectors. Among them, we utilize 20 Pascal classes (5 for validation) for training and 12 Yahoo classes for testing. We follow the proposed split in all datasets introduced by [15], where the test data is disjoint with the data which is used for the pre-training feature module.

ZSL Setting. There are two kinds of ZSL settings we used in our experiments: the conventional ZSL setting and the generalized ZSL setting. In the convention ZSL, test samples are restricted to the unseen classes, while in the generalized ZSL, they may come from seen classes or unseen classes. For evaluation in the convention ZSL, we use the multi-way classification accuracy (averaged over classes) as the evaluation metric and in the generalized ZSL, three metrics are defined as: (1) **tr** - the accuracy of classifying the samples from the seen classes to all the classes (both seen and unseen); (2) **ts** - the accuracy of classifying the samples from the unseen classes to all the classes; (3) **H** - the harmonic mean of **tr** and **ts**. We choose the harmonic mean as our evaluation criteria instead of arithmetic mean because in arithmetic mean if the seen class accuracy is much higher, it effects the overall results significantly. However, our aim is high accuracy on both seen and unseen classes.

Implementation Details. We adopt the 2048-dimension top pooling units of ResNet101 [1] as the initial encodings in the visual feature space for all images, it is noted that the ResNet101 is pre-trained on ImageNet 1K. The attribute vectors defined by human for all classes (we assume that the attribute vectors of unseen classes are known) is used as semantic vectors. In order to retain useful samples, we do not select a high density set in the classes that own a small number of samples. In the process to select the high density set, we set k = 0.9 that means we get an objective set containing 90% samples from a class. The scalar λ and β in the loss function are determined by cross validation on each benchmark. We implement our model with TensorFlow and train it using Adam optimizer with a learning rate 0.001 and the batch size was set to 256. Several epochs is needed in our experiments to converge and we compute the average accuracy in 5 repeated experiments as the final result. To ensure simplicity, its version without manifold alignment and with manifold alignment is denoted as ours1 and ours2 respectively in the following experiments.

Compared Methods. In this paper, We selected 13 existing ZSL methods to prove the effectiveness of our model, including DAP [16], IAP [16], CONSE [5], CMT [17], SSE [18], LATEM [19], ALE [20], DEVISE [10], SJE [11], ESZSL [21], SYNC [22], SAE [4] and GFZSL [23]. Under each ZSL setting, we compare our model with the recent and representative ZSL models that have achieved the state-of-the-art results under the same setting.

Table 1. Zero-shot learning results on AWA1, AWA2, CUB, SUN and APY with ResNet101 features. The results report top-1 accuracy in %.

Methods	AWA1	AWA2	CUB	SUN	APY
DAP	44.1	46.1	40.0	39.9	33.8
IAP	35.9	35.9	24.0	19.4	36.6
CONSE	45.6	44.5	34.3	38.8	26.9
CMT	39.5	37.9	34.6	39.9	28.0
SSE	60.1	61.0	43.9	51.5	34.0
LATEM	55.1	55.8	49.3	55.3	35.2
ALE	59.9	62.5	54.9	58.1	39.7
DEVISE	54.2	59.7	52.0	56.5	39.8
SJE	65.6	61.9	53.9	53.7	32.9
ESZSL	58.2	58.6	53.9	54.5	38.3
SYNC	54.0	46.6	**55.6**	56.3	23.9
SAE	53.0	54.1	33.3	40.3	8.3
GFZSL	68.3	63.8	49.3	60.6	38.4
ours1	68.1	67.5	50.6	60.1	41.8
ours2	**68.8**	**68.2**	51.4	**61.0**	**42.9**

3.2 Evaluation on Conventional Zero-Shot Learning

In conventional zero-shot learning setting, we have the comparative results of all methods in the unseen classes from five benchmarks reported in Table 1. Our experiments have the same setting in [15] and the results of baselines are also from [15].

As shown in Table 1, we can see that for AWA1 and AWA2, ours2 outperforms the state-of-the-art method by 0.5% and 4.9% and obviously outperforms all of other methods since most of them suffer a lot from the hubness problem and visual-semantic gap. For APY, we also have achieved 3.1% improvement compared with state-of-the-art competitors, which suggests that the semantic vector can be predictive for the visual feature prototype of class which owns only several samples. However, existing models require a large amount of data to train and they are easy to underfit when there are not enough data. Then for SUN, we have also achieved the slightly better performance than the state-of-the-art method by 0.4%. The high density set we used to get a more discriminative visual feature prototype is useful for the training on SUN, which actually makes the training of the inverse projection more stable. For CUB, we do not achieve a higher accuracy since there are fine-grained data where the difference among classes is too vague to be distinguished. The dimension of semantic vector of CUB is high, it need exponentially growing number of training samples to cover the whole attribute vector space, but the samples we have are not enough.

Otherwise, comparing ours1 with ours2, we can find that the manifold alignment can bring about 1% improvement, which prove the manifold alignment is useful for avoiding over-fitting.

Table 2. Generalized Zero-Shot Learning measuring *ts*=Top-1 accuracy on unseen classes, *tr*=Top-1 accuracy on seen classes, H = harmonic mean. We measure top-1 accuracy in %.

	AWA1			AWA2			CUB			SUN			APY		
Method	ts	tr	H	ts	tr	H	ts	tr	H	ts	tr	H	ts	tr	H
DAP	0.0	**88.7**	0.0	0.0	84.7	0.0	1.7	67.9	3.3	4.2	25.1	7.2	4.8	78.3	9.0
IAP	2.1	78.2	4.1	0.9	87.6	1.8	0.2	72.8	0.4	1.0	37.8	1.8	5.7	65.6	10.4
CONSE	0.4	88.6	0.8	0.5	**90.6**	1.0	1.6	**72.2**	3.1	6.8	**39.9**	11.6	0.0	**91.2**	0.0
CMT	0.9	87.6	1.8	0.5	90.0	1.0	7.2	49.8	12.6	8.1	21.8	11.8	1.4	85.2	2.8
SSE	7.0	80.5	12.9	8.1	82.5	14.8	8.5	46.9	14.4	2.1	36.4	4.0	0.2	78.9	0.4
LATEM	7.3	71.7	13.3	11.5	77.3	20.0	15.2	57.3	24.0	14.7	28.8	19.5	0.1	73.0	0.2
ALE	16.8	76.1	27.5	14.0	81.8	23.9	23.7	62.8	**34.4**	**21.8**	33.1	**26.3**	4.6	73.7	8.7
DEVISE	13.4	68.7	22.4	17.1	74.7	27.8	**23.8**	53.0	32.8	16.9	27.4	20.9	4.9	76.9	9.2
SJE	11.3	74.6	19.6	8.0	73.9	14.4	23.5	59.2	33.6	14.7	30.5	19.8	3.7	55.7	6.9
ESZSL	6.6	75.6	12.1	5.9	77.8	11.0	12.6	63.8	21.0	11.0	27.9	15.8	2.4	70.1	4.6
SYNC	8.9	87.3	16.2	10.0	90.5	18.0	11.5	70.9	19.8	7.9	43.3	13.4	7.4	66.3	13.3
SAE	1.8	77.1	3.5	1.1	82.2	2.2	7.8	54.0	13.6	8.8	18.0	11.8	0.4	80.9	0.9
GFZSL	1.8	80.3	3.5	2.9	80.1	4.8	0.0	45.7	0.0	0.0	39.6	0.0	0.0	83.3	0.0
ours	**26.5**	75.8	**39.3**	**28.7**	75.4	**41.6**	20.9	55.2	30.3	19.2	33.7	24.5	**12.7**	62.9	**21.1**

3.3 Evaluation on Generalized Zero-Shot Learning

In real situation, the images that image systems have access to can not be classified to seen classes or unseen classes in advance. Hence, we train the same model as the conventional zero-shot learning on the same data and evaluated performance on both seen classes and unseen classes by the Top-1 accuracy denoted by **tr** and **ts** respectively.

As shown in Table 2, the **ts** are significantly lower than **tr** for every dataset in generalized zero-shot learning due to lacking data of unseen classes in training. It is unfair to compare **ts** or **tr** separately with all of methods, therefor we evaluate the comprehensive performance by **H** (the harmonic mean) which balance the accuracy on both seen and unseen classes. For AWA1, AWA2 and APY, compared with state-of-art methods, our method outperforms them by 11.5%, 13.8%, 7.8% on **H** and 9.7%, 11.6%, 5.3% on **ts**. It is obvious that our method outperforms the state-of-the-art method in **ts** and **H**, which suggests that our approach has excellent ability to transfer knowledge from seen classes to unseen classes. Meanwhile, it keeps its ability to classify the images from seen classes. In addition, most of competitors in Table 2 produce obvious bias towards seen classes, i.e., the recognition accuracy on unseen class are much less than that on seen classes, while ours2 produces much more balance results. This makes ours gain the best harmonic mean scores on the three benchmarks with big margin from other competitors. For CUB and SUN, our method has got a slightly worse performance than the state-of-the-art although it still outperforms most of methods. We attribute it to that they are fine grained datasets with high-dimension semantic vector, which results in that samples from different classes can not be dispersed with large enough margin.

4 Conclusion

In this paper we propose a novel method for zero-shot learning by inverse mapping from the semantic space to the visual space to avoid the hubness problem. In addition, we combine the high density set and manifold alignment with the inverse mapping to improve the discrimination of the visual feature prototype and mitigated the visual-semantic gap. We demonstrate through extensive experiments that our approach outperforms existing ZSL models and achieves state-of-the-art performance on three benchmark datasets.

Acknowledgment. This work is supported by NSFC project Grant No. U18331 01, Shenzhen Science and Technologies project under Grant No. JCYJ201604281 82137473 and the Joint Research Center of Tencent and Tsinghua.

References

1. He, K., Zhang, X., Ren, S., Sun, J.: Deep residual learning for image recognition. In: Proceedings of the IEEE Conference on Computer Vision and Pattern Recognition, pp. 770–778 (2016)
2. Larochelle, H., Erhan, D., Bengio, Y.: Zero-data learning of new tasks. In: AAAI, vol. 1, p. 3 (2008)
3. Guo, Y., Ding, G., Han, J., Tang, S.: Zero-shot learning with attribute selection. In: AAAI, pp. 6870–6877. AAAI Press (2018)
4. Kodirov, E., Xiang, T., Gong, S.: Semantic autoencoder for zero-shot learning. In: 2017 IEEE Conference on Computer Vision and Pattern Recognition, CVPR 2017, Honolulu, HI, USA, 21–26 July 2017, pp. 4447–4456 (2017)
5. Norouzi, M., et al.: Zero-shot learning by convex combination of semantic embeddings. CoRR, vol. abs/1312.5650 (2013)
6. Shigeto, Y., Suzuki, I., Hara, K., Shimbo, M., Matsumoto, Y.: Ridge regression, hubness, and zero-shot learning. In: Appice, A., Rodrigues, P.P., Santos Costa, V., Soares, C., Gama, J., Jorge, A. (eds.) ECML PKDD 2015. LNCS (LNAI), vol. 9284, pp. 135–151. Springer, Cham (2015). https://doi.org/10.1007/978-3-319-23528-8_9
7. Fu, Y., Hospedales, T.M., Xiang, T., Gong, S.: Transductive multi-view zero-shot learning. IEEE Trans. Pattern Anal. Mach. Intell. **37**(11), 2332–2345 (2015)
8. Li, Y., Wang, D., Hu, H., Lin, Y., Zhuang, Y.: Zero-shot recognition using dual visual-semantic mapping paths. In: IEEE Conference on Computer Vision and Pattern Recognition (CVPR), pp. 5207–5215 (2017)
9. Changpinyo, S., Chao, W.-L., Sha, F.: Predicting visual exemplars of unseen classes for zero-shot learning. In: IEEE International Conference on Computer Vision, ICCV 2017, Venice, Italy, 22–29 October 2017, pp. 3496–3505 (2017)
10. Frome, A., et al.: DeVISE: a deep visual-semantic embedding model. In: International Conference on Neural Information Processing Systems, pp. 2121–2129 (2013)
11. Akata, Z., Reed, S.E., Walter, D., Lee, H., Schiele, B.: Evaluation of output embeddings for fine-grained image classification. In: CVPR, pp. 2927–2936. IEEE Computer Society (2015)
12. Xian, Y., Akata, Z., Sharma, G., Nguyen, Q., Hein, M., Schiele, B.: Latent embeddings for zero-shot classification. In: Proceedings of the IEEE Conference on Computer Vision and Pattern Recognition, pp. 69–77 (2016)

13. Bucher, M., Herbin, S., Jurie, F.: Generating visual representations for zero-shot classification, pp. 2666–2673 (2017)
14. Jiang, H., Kim, B., Guan, M., Gupta, M.: To trust or not to trust a classifier. In: Advances in Neural Information Processing Systems, pp. 5542–5553 (2018)
15. Xian, Y., Schiele, B., Akata, Z.: Zero-shot learning - the good, the bad and the ugly. In: CVPR, pp. 3077–3086. IEEE Computer Society (2017)
16. Lampert, C.H., Nickisch, H., Harmeling, S.: Attribute-based classification for zero-shot visual object categorization. IEEE Trans. Pattern Anal. Mach. Intell. **36**(3), 453–465 (2014)
17. Socher, R., Ganjoo, M., Manning, C.D., Ng, A.Y.: Zero-shot learning through cross-modal transfer. In: NIPS, pp. 935–943 (2013)
18. Zhang, Z., Saligrama, V.: Zero-shot recognition via structured prediction. In: Leibe, B., Matas, J., Sebe, N., Welling, M. (eds.) ECCV 2016. LNCS, vol. 9911, pp. 533–548. Springer, Cham (2016). https://doi.org/10.1007/978-3-319-46478-7_33
19. Xian, Y., Akata, Z., Sharma, G., Nguyen, Q.N., Hein, M., Schiele, B.: Latent embeddings for zero-shot classification. CoRR, vol. abs/1603.08895 (2016)
20. Akata, Z., Perronnin, F., Harchaoui, Z., Schmid, C.: Label embedding for image classication. IEEE Trans. Pattern Anal. Mach. Intell. **38**(7), 1425–1438 (2016)
21. Romera-Paredes, B., Torr, P.: An embarrassingly simple approach to zero-shot learning. In: International Conference on Machine Learning, pp. 2152–2161 (2015)
22. Morgado, P., Vasconcelos, N.: Semantically consistent regularization for zero-shot recognition. In: 2017 IEEE Conference on Computer Vision and Pattern Recognition, CVPR 2017, Honolulu, HI, USA, 21–26 July 2017, pp. 2037–2046 (2017)
23. Verma, V.K., Rai, P.: A simple exponential family framework for zero shot learning. In: Ceci, M., Hollmén, J., Todorovski, L., Vens, C., Džeroski, S. (eds.) ECML PKDD 2017. LNCS (LNAI), vol. 10535, pp. 792–808. Springer, Cham (2017). https://doi.org/10.1007/978-3-319-71246-8_48
24. Lampert, C.H., Nickisch, H., Harmeling, S.: Learning to detect unseen object classes by between-class attribute transfer (2009)
25. Farhadi, A., Endres, I., Hoiem, D., Forsyth, D.: Describing objects by their attributes. In: 2009 IEEE Conference on Computer Vision and Pattern Recognition, CVPR 2009, pp. 1778–1785. IEEE (2009)
26. Socher, R., Ganjoo, M., Sridhar, H., Bastani, O., Manning, C.D., Ng, A.Y.: Zero-shot learning through cross-modal transfer. In: International Conference on Neural Information Processing Systems (2013)
27. Elhoseiny, M.: Write a classifier: zero shot learning using purely textual descriptions. In: IEEE International Conference on Computer Vision (2014)
28. Lei Ba, J., Swersky, K., Fidler, S., Salakhutdinov, R.: Predicting deep zero-shot convolutional neural networks using textual descriptions (2015)

Baseline Analysis of a Conventional and Virtual Reality Lifelog Retrieval System

Aaron Duane(✉) and Cathal Gurrin

Insight Centre for Data Analytics, Dublin City University, Dublin, Ireland
{aaron.duane,cathal.gurrin}@insight-centre.org

Abstract. Continuous media capture via a wearable devices is currently one of the most popular methods to establish a comprehensive record of the entirety of an individual's life experience, referred to in the research community as a lifelog. These vast multimodal corpora include visual and other sensor data and are enriched by content analysis, to generate as extensive a record of an individual's life experience. However, interfacing with such datasets remains an active area of research, and despite the advent of new technology and a plethora of competing mediums for processing digital information, there has been little focus on newly emerging platforms such as virtual reality. In this work, we suggest that the increase in immersion and spatial dimensions provided by virtual reality could provide significant benefits to users when compared to more conventional access methodologies. Hence, we motivate virtual reality as a viable method of exploring multimedia archives (specifically lifelogs) by performing a baseline comparative analysis using a novel application prototype built for the HTC Vive and a conventional prototype built for a standard personal computer.

Keywords: Lifelog · Virtual reality · Information retrieval

1 Introduction

A natural by-product of progress in computing technology has resulted in the progression from desktop-based computing to mobile computing and (more recently) pervasive and immersive computing. Every individual with a smartphone or other wearable sensors can generate large and continuous archives of multimodal data, while at the same time, new access methodologies are becoming popular, such as augmented and virtual reality. In this position paper, we explore how feasible it is to employ new access methodologies (virtual reality) to provide a novel access mechanism for personal multimodal data and we hypothesise that a well designed virtual reality interactive retrieval system can be as effective as a conventional retrieval system. We do this by developing prototype retrieval systems for archives of continuous multimodal data gathered by individuals, otherwise known as lifelogs [12], which are passively captured, automatic

Y. M. Ro et al. (Eds.): MMM 2020, LNCS 11962, pp. 412–423, 2020.
https://doi.org/10.1007/978-3-030-37734-2_34

and continuous collections of data pertaining to a person's life or life experience. Lifelogs can vary in their comprehensiveness from highly selective [1,14] to indiscriminate total capture [8,18].

Total capture lifelogging typically produces vast image corpora which are often further enriched by a new generation of multimodal content analysis such as visual concept detection [2,4] and event segmentation [13]. Hence such archives pose significant retrieval challenges for the community. Developing applications which enable lifelog retrieval remains an active area of research and there has been notable work designing such systems on a myriad of access mechanisms such as personal computers, tablets and even smartphones [17,20]. However, to date, there has been very little research into developing such applications for less conventional platforms such as virtual reality, which has seen a notable resurgence in recent history. It is our objective in this work to motivate others in the community to consider novel access mechanisms operating over challenging datasets by providing an initial evaluation of how successful a novel virtual realty access mechanism can be used to support interactive access to lifelog archives.

2 Motivation

Though virtual reality has yet to fully mature as a platform, and is not yet as ubiquitous as other access mechanisms, there is evidence to suggest it may effectively support lifelog retrieval. For example, some researchers believe the most valuable aspect of virtual reality is its highly immersive quality and the degree to which it projects stimuli onto the sensory receptors of users in a way that is "extensive, matching, surrounding, vivid, interactive and plot informing" [19]. There has also been well-established research indicating that actively using more of the human sensory capability and motor skills has been known to increase understanding and learning [3] and more recent research has suggested that immersion can greatly improve user recall [15]. For many, the underlying belief motivating most virtual reality research is that it will lead to more natural and effective human-computer interfaces and there have already been promising results in several key application domains [16].

When we consider the varied and multifaceted nature of lifelog datasets, containing text, images, audio, video and metadata, the concept of an immersive virtual world to store and explore this wealth of digital information seems quite enticing. This would be especially true when hardware advancements enable the convergence of virtual and augmented reality so that lifelog information could be exposed to us contextually within our environment at any time. While it is tempting to immediately try and create some early version of these advanced interface concepts and start mapping lifelog data to multiple spatial dimensions to try and create an entirely novel method of digesting information, we must first establish a baseline for interacting with lifelog data inside a virtual environment. In this paper we describe such an analysis, intended to show that a virtual reality-specific interface has strong potential to effectively support lifelog retrieval. This analysis consisted of two prototype lifelog retrieval systems, one designed for virtual reality, specifically the HTC Vive, and one designed for a standard personal computer. The primary goal was to determine a baseline design for a virtual reality application which incorporated conventions found in state-of-the-art lifelog retrieval applications and evaluate its effectiveness in comparison to a conventional alternative which contained the same features and targeted the same dataset. The research described in this paper is part of a larger body of work [6,7] aimed at motivating virtual reality as a viable candidate for the development of lifelog interaction systems.

3 Methodology

3.1 Dataset

The primary data chosen for this analysis was the NTCIR-13 test collection [10] first released for the lifelog workshop at NTCIR-13 in 2016. This dataset consisted of 90 days of continuous images captured via a wearable camera from the perspective of two lifeloggers, where each image was anonymised via face blurring to alleviate data privacy concerns. In total the datatset consisted of 114,547 images which were enriched via computer vision techniques, using feature extraction to provide content analysis and event segmentation. This resulted in each image in the dataset being semantically grouped and automatically labelled with a set of words describing the image's content, referred to as visual concepts, but which we refer to as *lifelog concepts* (e.g. desk, chair, phone, etc.). The dataset also included a selection of biometric, multimedia and activity data, but this data belonged primarily to only one of the two lifeloggers.

The NTCIR-13 test collection was chosen because it was one of the few lifelogging datasets focused on total capture to be publicly released by the research community. This is likely due to privacy concerns, the expense necessary to analyse a sufficiently large corpus of images, and the relatively niche research area lifelogging exists within. A different version of this test collection targeting different data was also made available for NTCIR-12 [9] but the content analysis in this collection was not as accurate and was also less comprehensive. To avoid unnecessary complexity navigating between lifeloggers and their corresponding data, we elected to target only one of the two available lifeloggers, who constituted two thirds of the NTCIR-13 datatset, or 60 of the total 90 days. Furthermore, as the biometric, multimedia and activity data was not as comprehensive or consistent, a decision was made to initially target only the images, events, concepts and timestamps. This did not preclude the possibility of introducing the remaining data at a later stage but time constraints and project scope restricted the possibility of including it for this analysis.

3.2 Evaluation

Our baseline analysis was conducted primarily in the form of a user study consisting of 16 participants of varying technical background. Each participant was asked to perform a total of 16 known-item search tasks, where half were performed on the virtual reality prototype and half were performed on the conventional prototype. In this context, a known-item search task refers to a scenario where the participant is provided with a specific description of an item, for example an image, and are then asked to retrieve it using the designated lifelog system. This style of task was chosen as it is the most commonly used method to evaluate lifelog retrieval [11] and does not necessitate the user being the owner of the lifelog dataset. Further details regarding our precise experiment configuration and the topics used for our known-item search tasks used are outlined in a parallel work [5] which is outside the scope of this paper to describe.

The users were evaluated on the speed of retrieval, the number of incorrect submissions and the number of times they failed to retrieve a correct item within the allotted time (180 s). Furthermore, each user was asked to fill out a user feedback questionnaire after each experiment and also participated in an informal interview regarding their experience. The decision to record this type of feedback was chosen because, while it would have been preferable to recruit several hundred participants of varying experience to produce more robust quantitative data for this analysis, time constraints and project costs made this unfeasible. As a result, an emphasis on qualitative data became a primary focus, utilising open-ended questions to garner user feedback, which could then better inform the quantitative results.

4 System Overview

In this section we will provide an overview of both prototype systems in the context of their two main interactive elements; the user interface and the data visualisation. The design and approaches outlined in this section were the result of a series of iterative user studies [6,7] which are outside the scope of this paper to be fully described in this overview.

4.1 User Interface

There were two primary components to the user interface on both retrieval prototypes; one for concept selection and one for temporal selection. This can be seen clearly in Fig. 1 where we can see a user has generated a query with four concepts. The concepts are arranged alphabetically and filtered by letter whereas, to select a time, the user can choose from the seven days of the week or the twenty-four hours in the day. These two components are identical between the conventional and virtual reality prototypes, the only difference being how each is interacted with. On the personal computer, the interface occupies the entire screen and the user can select interface elements with their mouse. However, within virtual reality, this interface floats in front of the user within the virtual environment. Its position can be adjusted at any time and the user interacts with the interface via a beam emanating from each controller (see Fig. 2).

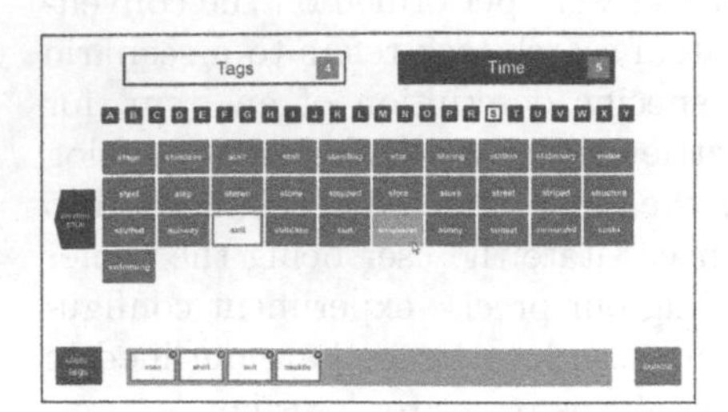

Fig. 1. Interface interaction on conventional lifelog retrieval system

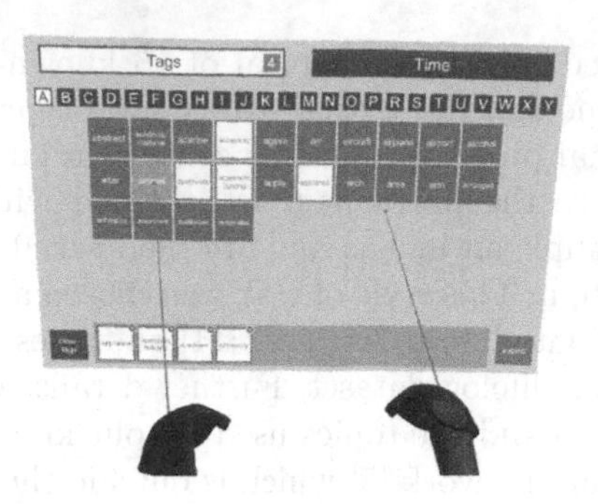

Fig. 2. Interface interaction on virtual reality lifelog retrieval system

4.2 Data Visualisation

The major differences in transitioning from virtual reality to a more conventional medium is in the visualisation and presentation of the lifelog data itself. In a virtual environment the data must be arranged with careful consideration regarding the user's position, as they occupy the same space as the data being explored. This means navigating data from the traditional perspective of top to bottom is poorly suited as it forces the user to crane their neck and can even lead to vertigo when data is presented too far below them. This was addressed in our virtual reality prototype by having the user scroll through data horizontally rather than vertically. However, as we move back to traditional media, we must revise this methodology in favour of common practice, which also has implications regarding the specific arrangement of the data as it is being navigated. In Fig. 3 we can observe a set of results which have been returned after the user submits a query, where each horizontal line of images represents a summary of an event, and each event is ranked from top to bottom based on the user's query. In contrast, within virtual reality (see Fig. 4) we can see these summaries are aligned in a 3×3 grid and are instead ranked from left to right. To explore all the images within an event summary, the necessary interactions are very similar to how each system interacts with its respective user interface. On the conventional prototype, the user simply hovers their mouse over a relevant event and selects it, whereas on the virtual reality prototype, the user simply points their controller at a relevant event, guided by a beam. and selects it.

5 Experiment Results

5.1 Technical Background

It was clear before recruiting the participants that many of them would have significant experience using computers and comparatively less experience using virtual reality, and this is reflected in the nature of the questions that were asked.

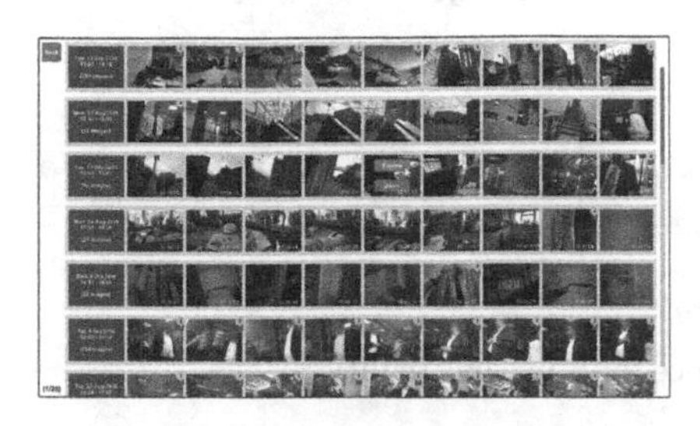

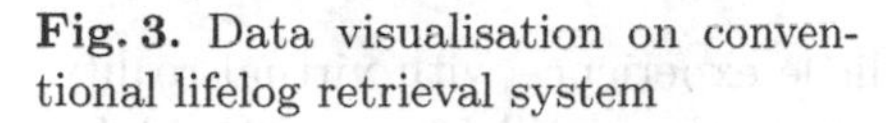

Fig. 3. Data visualisation on conventional lifelog retrieval system

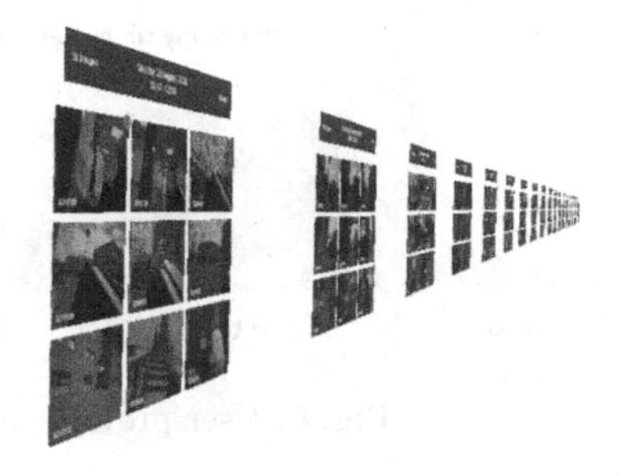

Fig. 4. Data visualisation on virtual reality lifelog retrieval system

In Fig. 5 we can observe that the participants were asked how often they use a computer in their average week and almost all of the participants stated they used computers for over 30 h on average, with the majority of them stating it was over 40 h. In contrast, with respect to virtual reality, participants were not asked about their average time, but rather the total number of times they had used a virtual reality platform in their entire lifetime. In Fig. 6 we can observe that almost every user had some previous experience with virtual reality but it was very limited. Only four users stated they had used a virtual reality platform more than ten times in their life, and only one user stated they actually owned a virtual reality headset.

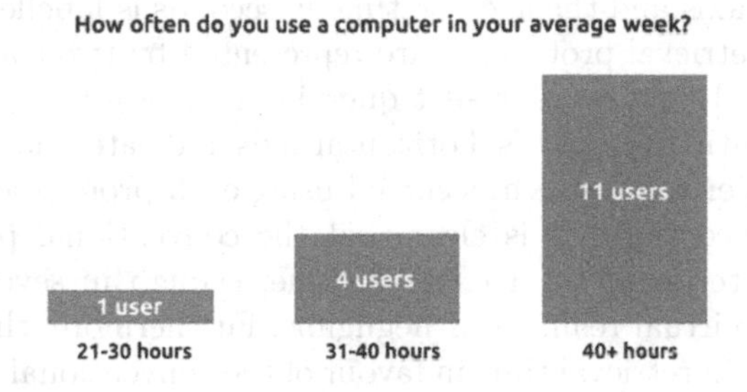

Fig. 5. User weekly exposure to computers

It is clear from these results that the majority of volunteers recruited for this study used computers very regularly throughout their week. Though it may have been valuable to perform a more thorough analysis of their technical abilities, the primary goal was to establish their baseline experience performing general computer tasks and familiarity with digital user interfaces. The stark contrast in experience using computers over virtual reality was expected and likely contributed to both positive and negative outcomes during the study. For example, the fact that every user had at least some technical experience meant that transitioning onto a virtual reality platform wasn't completely unfamiliar. However,

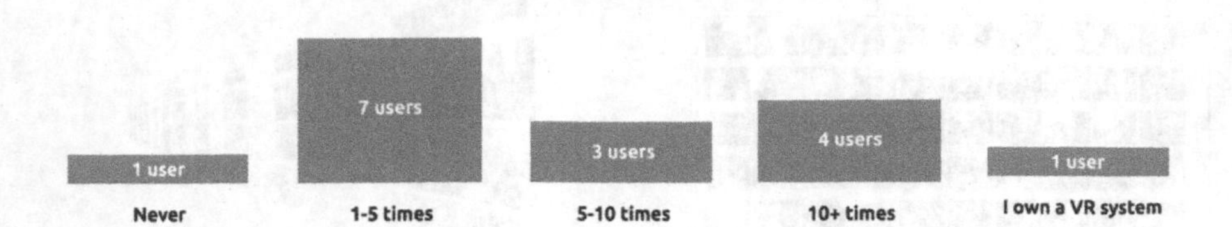

Fig. 6. User previous experience with virtual reality

the fact that so many of the users had so little experience with virtual reality, and so much experience with computers, means there will be an unavoidable bias when trying to use each system effectively. However, since this bias is in favour of the conventional platform, we can assume that as people become more familiar with virtual reality platforms, the potential effectiveness of our baseline prototype can only improve.

5.2 User Performance

After all the users had participated in the experiment, each known-item search task, which were referred to as topics, had been searched for a total of 16 times, 8 times on each of the 2 retrieval prototypes. We have visualised these results in Fig. 7 where we can observe a bar chart displaying the average seconds taken querying and browsing per topic for each prototype. The 16 topics are labelled on the horizontal axis and the average time in seconds is labelled on the vertical axis. The lifelog retrieval prototypes are represented by two coloured bars, each shaded in dark and light to represent querying and browsing respectively. The red squares beneath the chart's horizontal axis indicate the total number of retrieval failures per topic which occurred using each prototype.

With a few exceptions, it is clear that the conventional prototype proved most effective in terms of total retrieval time, though in several instances its effectiveness over virtual reality was negligible. Furthermore, though we can see a notable contrast in retrieval time in favour of the conventional prototype across a number of topics, such as T4 and T6, the largest contrast across all the topics was in favour of virtual reality on T11. This topic also resulted in the largest contrast of failed retrievals, with the virtual reality system failing only once and the conventional system failing a total of five times. It is difficult to speculate on the reason for this outlier, but one explanation is that the topic required users to retrieve an image where the lifelogger entered a home where the house number is clearly visible, and the virtual reality system afforded a better visualisation of the data to detect this relatively small detail in the images.

A small selection of topics proved exceedingly difficult for users irrespective of what prototype they were using. This is clearly evident on T1, T3 and T5 which resulted in the highest average retrieval times and the most retrieval failures, which were comparable on both prototypes. With respect to the ratio of querying

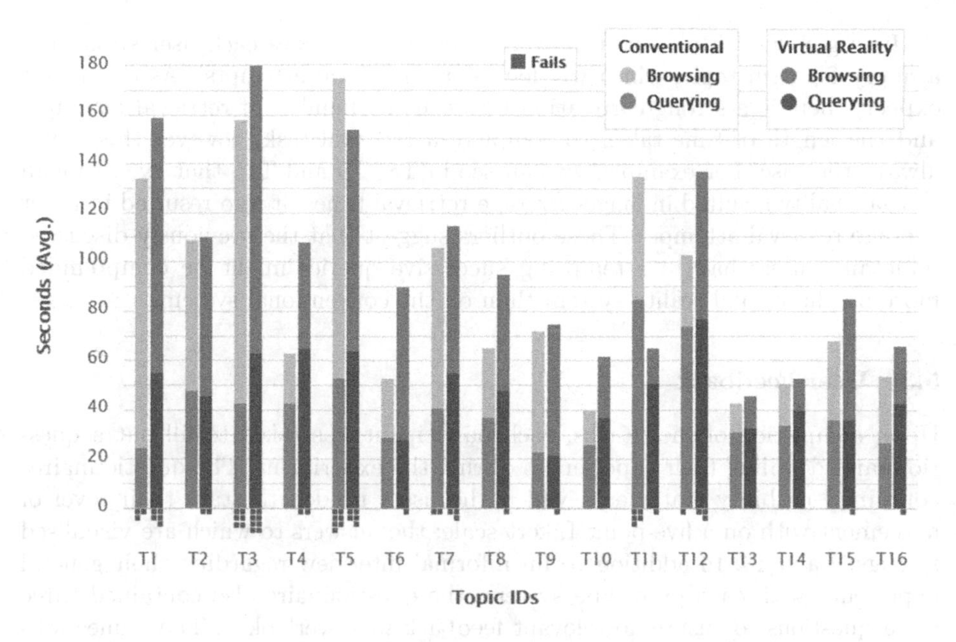

Fig. 7. Average seconds taken querying and browsing per topic for each prototype (with total failures below axis)

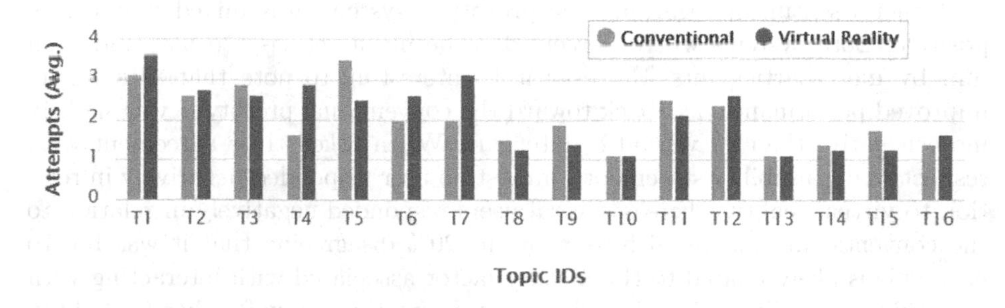

Fig. 8. Average retrieval attempts per topic for each prototype

time versus browsing time, evidence suggests that on average more difficult topics resulted in longer browsing times and easier topics resulted in shorter browsing times. This is most notable in topics T1, T3 and T5 which many users found difficult and resulted in comparably long browsing times, and in topics T13, T14 and T16 which many users found easy and resulted in comparably short browsing times. The source of this trend likely relates to behaviour which was observed during testing, where users were reluctant to adjust their query after they had committed to a specific set of lifelog concepts. Only after browsing a significant number of results did they concede their query was not retrieving what they intended and considered other options.

In Fig. 8 we can observe the average number of times each user submitted a query for each topic, which we defined as 'retrieval attempts'. As one might expect, there is a strong correlation between the number of retrieval attempts and the length of time taken to complete a retrieval task, however this is not always the case. For example, we can see in T8, T9 and T15 that even though virtual reality resulted in longer average retrieval times, it also resulted in fewer average retrieval attempts. These outliers suggest that the previously discussed reluctance users had to attempting successive queries might be compounded more on the virtual reality system than on the conventional system.

5.3 User Feedback

Upon completion of their tasks, each participant was asked to fill out a questionnaire detailing their experiences during the experiment. The questionnaires contained usability statements which the users needed to state their level of agreement with on a five-point Likert scale; the answers to which are visualised in Figs. 9 and 10. In addition to an informal interview regarding their general experience with each prototype system, the questionnaire also contained three open questions to ensure no relevant feedback was overlooked. These questions asked users what they liked about the system, what they disliked about the system, and what they suggest might improve the system.

General sentiment regarding the prototype systems was mixed but mostly positive. Both systems where perceived to be intuitive, easy to use, and even fun, by most participants. However it is interesting to note that, despite its improved performance, feedback toward the conventional prototype was slightly more negative than its virtual counterpart. When asked their agreement with respect to our usability statements, almost no user responded negatively in relation to virtual reality, whereas several users responded negatively in relation to the conventional system, with as many as 20% disagreeing that it was fun to use. This is likely related to the novelty factor associated with interacting with something unfamiliar (virtual reality) versus something very familiar (a desktop computer).

Positive feedback regarding the conventional prototype centred around its familiar user interface and style of interaction. The majority of users required very little instruction prior to interacting with the system and began discovering features naturally without being prompted. There was notably mixed feedback regarding the exploration of lifelog data on the conventional system, as some users felt it utilised its visual space very efficiently whereas others felt it was too cluttered and inhibited retrieval. Related sentiment was also evident during testing, where some users seemed to initially respond well to interacting with the data on the conventional system, but then determined that the presentation of the data was causing them to overlook important information. For example, despite their awareness that highly ranked data is presented at the top of the list, the users' instinct to immediately use the scroll wheel to move down the page often resulted in them scrolling past relevant results.

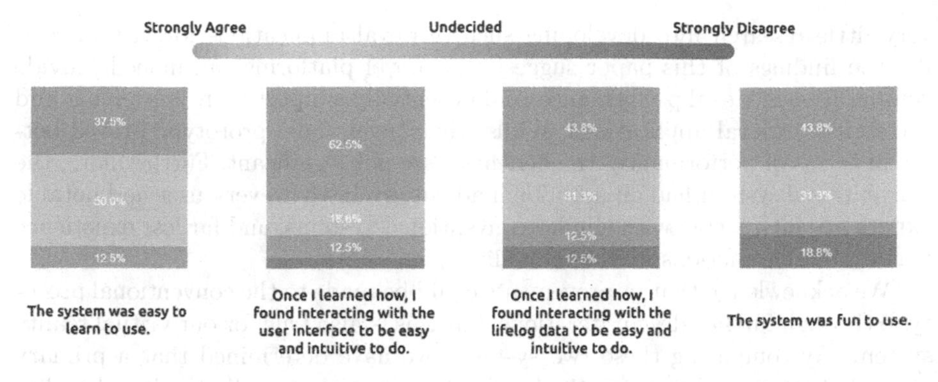

Fig. 9. User feedback for conventional retrieval prototype

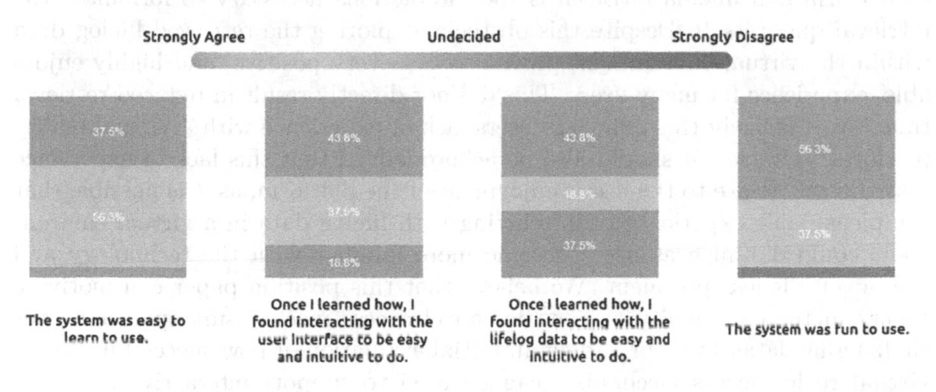

Fig. 10. User feedback for virtual reality retrieval prototype

Positive feedback regarding the virtual reality prototype centred around the immersive experience and the novelty of exploring a virtual environment. Compared to the conventional system, it took noticeably more time for users to become comfortable with their surroundings and it required far more prompting and instruction to discover all of the virtual reality system's features. However, despite the steeper learning curve, many users stated they adapted quickly once they grew accustomed to the environment. Interestingly, despite their increased familiarity with the platform alongside its slightly improved performance, only six out of the sixteen participants stated they preferred the conventional prototype overall, with the remaining ten stating they preferred virtual reality.

5.4 Conclusion

In this paper we have presented a baseline analysis intended to show that a virtual reality-specific interface can effectively support interactive retrieval from a large personal multimodal data archive. This was achieved by presenting two prototype retrieval systems, one designed for the novel virtual reality platform and one designed for a conventional computing platform. Since there has been very little research into developing such retrieval applications for virtual reality, the findings of this paper suggest that novel platforms can indeed provide comparative retrieval performance, and potentially support more convenient and attractive retrieval applications. Whilst the conventional prototype proved better in terms of performance, the benefits were not significant. Furthermore, the conventional system had an additional advantage in that every user had notable experience interacting with similar conventional systems, and far less experience performing interactions in virtual reality.

We acknowledge that improvements could be made to the conventional prototype through further design iterations, but this is also true for our virtual reality system. By comparing these two systems, we have determined that a primary obstacle for users when transitioning from conventional media to virtual reality to perform multimedia retrieval is the interactions necessary to formulate the retrieval query itself. Despite this obstacle, exploring the retrieved lifelog data within the virtual environment proved to be a very positive, and highly enjoyable, experience for many users. This did not directly result in reduced retrieval time but it is likely this relates to users lack of experience with a virtual reality platform. However, it should also be acknowledged that this lack of experience may directly relate to the user's enjoyment of the platform, as it is possible that the pleasurable experience of interacting with lifelog data in a virtual environment could diminish as users become more familiar with the technology and the novelty is less prevalent. We believe that this position paper can motivate others in the community to consider novel access mechanisms operating over challenging datasets by providing an initial evaluation of how successful a novel virtual realty access mechanism can be used to support interactive access to lifelog archives.

References

1. Barrett, M.A., Humblet, O., Hiatt, R.A., Adler, N.E.: Big data and disease prevention: from quantified self to quantified communities. Big Data **1**(3), 168–175 (2013)
2. Byrne, D., Doherty, A.R., Snoek, C.G., Jones, G.J., Smeaton, A.F.: Everyday concept detection in visual lifelogs: validation, relationships and trends. Multimedia Tools Appl. **49**(1), 119–144 (2010)
3. Dale, E.: Audio-Visual Methods in Teaching, 3rd edn. Dryden Press, New York (1969)
4. Doherty, A.R., Moulin, C.J.A., Smeaton, A.F.: Automatically assisting human memory: a SenseCam browser. Memory **19**(7), 785–795 (2011)
5. Duane, A.: Visual Access to Lifelog Data in a Virtual Environment. Ph.D. thesis, Insight Centre for Data Analytics, Dublin City University, Ireland (2019)
6. Duane, A., Gurrin, C.: Lifelog exploration prototype in virtual reality. In: Schoeffmann, K., et al. (eds.) MMM 2018. LNCS, vol. 10705, pp. 377–380. Springer, Cham (2018). https://doi.org/10.1007/978-3-319-73600-6_36
7. Duane, A., Huerst, W.: Virtual reality lifelog explorer. In: Proceedings of the 2018 ACM Workshop on the Lifelog Search Challenge (2018)

8. Gemmell, J., Bell, G., Lueder, R.: MyLifeBits: a personal database for everything. CACM **49**(1), 88 (2006)
9. Gurrin, C., Joho, H., Hopfgartner, F., Zhou, L., Albatal, R.: Overview of NTCIR-12 lifelog task. In: Proceedings of the 12th NTCIR Conference on Evaluation of Information Access Technologies, pp. 354–360 (2016)
10. Gurrin, C., et al.: Overview of NTCIR-13 lifelog-2 Task. In: Proceedings of the 13th NTCIR Conference on Evaluation of Information Access Technologies, pp. 6–11 (2017)
11. Gurrin, C., et al.: Comparing approaches to interactive lifelog search at the lifelog search challenge (LSC2018). ITE Trans. Media Technol. Appl. **7**(2), 46–59 (2019)
12. Gurrin, C., Smeaton, A.F., Doherty, A.R.: LifeLogging: personal big data. Found. Trends Inf. Retrieval **8**(1), 1–125 (2014)
13. Hodges, S., et al.: SenseCam: a retrospective memory aid. In: Dourish, P., Friday, A. (eds.) UbiComp 2006. LNCS, vol. 4206, pp. 177–193. Springer, Heidelberg (2006). https://doi.org/10.1007/11853565_11
14. Hoy, M.B.: Personal activity trackers and the quantified self. Med. Ref. Serv. Q. **35**(1), 94–100 (2016)
15. Krokos, E., Plaisant, C., Varshney, A.: Virtual memory palaces: immersion aids recall. Virtual Reality **23**(1), 1–15 (2018)
16. Mine, M.R., Brooks, J., Sequin, C.: Moving objects in space: exploiting proprioception in virtual-environment interaction. In: 24th Annual Conference on Computer Graphics and Interactive Techniques, pp. 19–26 (1997)
17. Qiu, Z., Gurrin, C., Smeaton, A.F.: Evaluating access mechanisms for multimodal representations of lifelogs. In: Tian, Q., Sebe, N., Qi, G.-J., Huet, B., Hong, R., Liu, X. (eds.) MMM 2016. LNCS, vol. 9516, pp. 574–585. Springer, Cham (2016). https://doi.org/10.1007/978-3-319-27671-7_48
18. Sellen, A., Whittaker, S.: Beyond total capture. Commun. ACM **53**(5), 70 (2010)
19. Slater, M., Wilbur, S.: A framework for immersive virtual environments (FIVE): speculations on the role of presence in virtual environments. Presence Teleoperators Virtual Environ. **6**(6), 603–616 (1997)
20. Yang, Y., Lee, H., Gurrin, C.: Visualizing lifelog data for different interaction platforms. In: CHI 2013 Extended Abstracts on Human Factors in Computing Systems on - CHI EA 2013, p. 1785 (2013)

An Extensible Framework for Interactive Real-Time Visualizations of Large-Scale Heterogeneous Multimedia Information from Online Sources

Aikaterini Katmada(✉), George Kalpakis, Theodora Tsikrika, Stelios Andreadis, Stefanos Vrochidis, and Ioannis Kompatsiaris

Information Technologies Institute, CERTH, Thessaloniki, Greece
{akatmada, kalpakis, theodora.tsikrika, andreadisst, stefanos, ikom}@iti.gr

Abstract. This work presents the user-centered design and development of a generic and extensible visualization framework that can be re-used in various scenarios in order to communicate large–scale heterogeneous multimedia information obtained from social media and Web sources, through user-friendly interactive visualizations in real-time. Using the particular framework as a basis, two Web-based dashboards demonstrating the visual analytics components of our framework have been developed. Additionally, three indicative use case scenarios where these dashboards can be employed are described. Finally, preliminary user feedback and improvements are discussed, and directions for further development are proposed on the basis of the findings.

Keywords: Information visualization · Visual analytics · Multimedia · Social media · Human Computer Interaction · Usability evaluation

1 Introduction

Over the last few decades, advances in Information and Communications Technologies (ICT), as well as the emergence of social media platforms, have revolutionized our ability to create, store, retrieve, and exchange information. Consequently, they have also contributed to an explosion in the volume and complexity of data to which we are exposed, leading to confusion and decision paralysis. Such *information overload* is nowadays a frequent occurrence and refers specifically to the danger of getting lost in data which may be processed or presented in a way that is inappropriate or irrelevant to the current task [1]. Indeed, from everyday navigation information to business decision-making, there is a growing need for presenting the available information in an effective and efficient manner.

Information visualization—a sub discipline within Human Computer Interaction (HCI)—is focused on the graphical mechanisms designed to show the structure of information [2]. *Visual analytics*, on the other hand, constitute an outgrowth of the information visualization field [3], researching the creation of interactive visual representations that enable users to analyze data, often using automatic analysis methods.

Y. M. Ro et al. (Eds.): MMM 2020, LNCS 11962, pp. 424–435, 2020.
https://doi.org/10.1007/978-3-030-37734-2_35

It is argued that in order to sustain growth of the field, we have to examine the ways in which visual analytics techniques and systems elicit user insight, especially through empirical studies [4], and to address various technical challenges, such as *user acceptability*, *data quality*, *scalability*, and *system evaluation* [5].

Towards this direction, this work aims at making a unique contribution by: (a) providing a concise overview of the theoretical framework regarding information visualization and visual analytics for large-scale datasets; and (b) presenting the user-centered design and development of a generic visualization framework that can be re-used in various scenarios. More specifically, our goal is to provide a set of interactive Web-based visualizations where large-scale heterogeneous multimedia information from social media and Web sources is communicated through user-friendly interfaces in real-time. Our framework supports big data analytics, employing different types of visual representations which can be tailored to each specific use case. Here, we present three indicative examples of application in three different domains: (i) social media monitoring on any given topic, (ii) SME internationalization, and (iii) monitoring of violent extremist online content.

The rest of the paper is organized as follows: Sect. 2 discusses the theoretical background and describes relevant applications and studies. Section 3 presents the use case scenarios and user requirements of our work. Section 4 discusses the methodology and architecture of our framework. Section 5 evaluates our work and Sect. 6 discusses the conclusions and future work.

2 Background and Related Work

2.1 Theoretical Background

Information visualization addresses the study of the graphical display of data for the purposes of sense-making and communication. It employs various methods focused on augmenting the perception of abstract data, i.e. data with no inherent spatial layout or physical qualities [6]. Relationships that are not quantitative in nature (e.g., connections between people) are also often visualized. Information visualization is useful to both data consumers and data analysts, as effective representations render complex data more accessible and they enable problems in the data to become apparent [7].

Visual analytics can be considered a research field emerging from information visualization, integrating theories and methodologies from various fields, such as cognitive science, statistical analysis, and data science [3]. It could be argued that it differs in the sense that traditional information visualization does not necessarily use data analysis algorithms to automatically extract information from raw data, or deal with an analysis task [1]. Thus, visual analytics combines analysis techniques (e.g., classification and clustering) with interactive information visualization, in order to facilitate understanding and decision-making on the basis of large and complex datasets [1].

Principles of Information Visualization. While information visualization can help users make sense of complex data, it is also recognized that it bears the danger of distortion. Misleading visualizations are often the result of ignoring fundamental principles of statistics, human perception and design [8]. It is also argued that although perception and cognition theories play a major role in information visualization, the research emphasis has been placed, so far, on developing new visualization techniques [9]. Thus, a concise overview of perception and design principles was conducted before the design of the framework. Accordingly, a number of issues for consideration, e.g. the design process, were also identified in the research literature.

A general process of data visualization is presented in the book *Information visualization: perception for design* [7]. It is based on four stages, including the collection and storage of data; preprocessing and transformation on data; the graphics engine and algorithms that produce an image; and the human information analyst that explores the data. On the receiving end of the proposed visualization is the end user; it was, therefore, useful to understand the way visual information is perceived by the human brain. *Pre-attentive processing* refers to the processing of raw visual information that is subconsciously accumulated from the environment and makes sense of a few image attributes [7], such as color, form, movement, and spatial positioning. The concept of *pre-attentive visual properties* is based on Gestalt psychology [8]; more specifically, the *Gestalt principles* describe how the human mind perceives visual elements as a united form, rather than separate objects. Analysis of the Gestalt principles is outside the scope of this paper; it should be mentioned, however, that they are often used by designers in order to organize content for clarity.

Furthermore, we reviewed guidelines aiming to develop a shared language for visual representations, such as Tufte's guidelines [10]. These comprise the following:

- *Graphical Excellence*. It refers to complex ideas being communicated with clarity, precision, and efficiency.
- *Visual Integrity*. The representation should not distort the underlying data or create a false impression. Explanations and labelling could be used to prevent ambiguity.
- *Maximizing the Data-Ink Ratio*. Priority should be given to the data and not on superfluous visual elements that may distract the viewer.
- *Aesthetic Elegance*. The complexity of the data is evoked clearly by the simplicity of the design.

Organization of Visualizations in Dashboards. A common way to organize a large amount of information is to use *dashboards*. In general, dashboards are single-screen Web pages, providing overviews of indicators relevant to a particular objective. One of their main benefits is that they facilitate the quick identification of data correlations and outliers. Additionally, well-designed dashboards: (a) provide a *central location* where users can access a *broad overview* of the data when needed; (b) let users *"drill-down"* to further visualizations or raw data; and (c) render the *analysis* of data more user-friendly. Building on Tufte's guidelines for data visual representations, we conclude that graphical dashboards should not (a) over-burden users with data that requires further calculations, (b) contain superfluous graphics that may distract users, or (c) include irrelevant elements, consuming much needed space.

2.2 Related Visual Analytics Work

Applications of visual analytics can be encountered in the pertinent bibliography grouped according to the domain (sector). Some key sectors include the following:

- *Journalism*. Due to the increasing quantity of information from both online and traditional sources, professionals are looking for systems that streamline information from various sources, cluster relevant items, and analyze social media metrics. Relevant case studies can be found in [11–13].
- *Digital Forensics and Security*. Visual analytics for security are a research topic of great potential, applicable to areas ranging from network security to terrorism prevention. For instance, the VisAware visualization framework displays a visual representation of network intrusions [14]. Romero-Gomez et al. [15] present an open-source visualization system for network threat analysis.
- *Healthcare*. Visual analytics can provide significant benefits in the domains of personal, clinical, and public health information. As demonstrated in various studies, e.g. [16, 17], visual analytics could facilitate clinicians, educators, patients, etc.
- *Disaster and Emergency Management*. In scenarios such as natural or human-induced catastrophes, visual analytics can help evaluate the progress of an ongoing emergency and identify the countermeasures that must be taken. For example, [18] describes a map-based analytics app leveraging Twitter for crisis management.
- *Business*. Visual analytics are used in financial applications and related research areas, e.g. financial forecasting and stock market monitoring. They can help both non-expert users and financial analysts to gain insights, interpret the risk and correlation aspects of financial data, and take informed financial decisions [19, 20].

3 Use Cases

This section begins by describing three use case scenarios in different domains (i.e., social media monitoring, SME internationalization, and extremist online content monitoring), where our visual analytics framework could support the end user needs for content analysis by providing a set of interactive visualizations, and then lists the high-level user requirements that drove the implementation of our framework.

3.1 Use Case I: International Media Monitoring

Over the past few years, media companies have integrated social media into their workflows and utilized social media accounts in order to engage directly with audiences. News organizations also use social media as part of their wider newsgathering and audience engagement strategies. Monitoring and analyzing large amounts of heterogeneous data streams from social media for any given topic of public interest is of paramount importance for many stakeholders from the news and mass media domain. Therefore, the target users of this scenario would be editors and managers trying to understand what drives the audience interest, reporters interested in uncovering stories that rivals might have missed, and social media experts in their effort to identify trends. In this case, our framework could provide them with dashboards and visualizations helping them identify trends and influential users, such as: maps visualizing aggregated social media activity per location, charts displaying the most popular entities encountered (e.g. hashtags), visuals clustering the posts collected based on their textual similarities and showcasing the topics discussed, etc.

3.2 Use Case II: SME Internationalization

The abundance of information posted on social media by millions of users with different nationalities, cultures, religions, traits and traditions poses a great opportunity for informed business decision making, based on the analysis and extraction of information that can affect their strategy and policy. In this particular scenario, small or medium-sized companies (SMEs) aiming to expand to foreign markets are particularly interested in analyzing information regarding market opportunities and indicators, the potential consumption, and competition. Additionally, market researchers are also focused on finding information about people's likes, interests and habits in geographical areas of interest where a business plans to expand, so as to identify the best opportunities in the market. Thus, in this scenario, our framework could provide the interested stakeholders with dashboards displaying the aggregated user activity within timeframes of interest for a specific market or product, maps visualizing the aggregated activity per location, charts delivering the most trending hashtags encountered within the collected social media posts, etc.

3.3 Use Case III: Violent Extremist Online Content Monitoring

Violent extremist content, including material associated with terrorist groups, has proliferated on Web and social media platforms over recent years. Some terrorist groups, in particular, have launched well-organized social media campaigns to recruit followers and to glorify acts of terrorism and violent extremism. Given that there is increasing concern and research on the part of scholars and policymakers that easy availability of violent extremist content online may have violent radicalizing effects, there is a need to monitor such content in order to both produce strategic insights into violent extremism and terrorism, and also acquire information that could be useful in potential criminal investigations linked to such malicious content. Thus, the target users of the particular scenario would be security analysts, law enforcement investigators, and scholars in the field that would aim to detect and analyze terrorist and violent extremist online content. Here, our framework could provide them with dashboards displaying the aggregated user activity within timeframes of interest, social network analysis graphs grouping users together in communities based on their activity over time and uncovering the most influential actors in them, maps delivering the most active locations at different levels of granularity, etc.

3.4 User Requirements

In order to design and develop our visualizations framework, we extracted several user requirements pertinent to the UI and visualizations design based on the three use case scenarios listed. To this end, we consulted end users dealing with large-scale multimedia data with the goal to design and develop visualizations and UIs that would cover their needs across different domains. The end users created lists of user requirements which were then grouped based on relevance. The high-level user requirements are included in Table 1.

Table 1. High-level user requirements

User Requirement	Description
R1 – User-friendly interface	The visualization UI is easy to use and understand
R2 – Intuitive and interactive visualizations	Important information is visualized in a user-friendly and efficient manner, while users can control aspects of the way the information is visually represented
R3 – Visualization of user activity over time	The visualization includes charts displaying the online activity of social media users over time
R4 – Visualization of connections between users	A visual representation of the most influential social media users and their connections with other users
R5 – Visualization of the most frequent entities encountered	A visualization showing the most frequent entities encountered within the collected posts
R6 – Visualization of geotagged results on a map	An interactive map displaying user activity per location (e.g. country, city)

Additionally, important non-functional requirements ("quality" attributes) were also identified. These were based either on conditions stemming from the aforementioned user requirements or from the design principles described in Sect. 2 and included: (a) good performance (loading and response time), (b) cross-browser compatibility, and (c) reliability and scalability. Additional aspects, such as visual consistency, range of charts, and customization options were also taken into account, so that we could provide a sufficient number of visualizations and interactivity options to the end users.

4 Description of the Visualization Framework

This section first describes the methodology followed for the development of our framework, and then presents its architecture. Next, it discusses the dashboards developed in the context of our activities for demonstrating its capabilities.

4.1 Methodology

The development of the visualization framework followed a user-centered, iterative process, consisting of the following steps: (a) review of related studies and principles; (b) requirements gathering and analysis; (c) definition of the data to be represented and the interactions required from the visualizations; (d) design and development; and (e) evaluation with end users and improvement.

The design of our framework took into consideration both the functional and non-functional high-level requirements extracted, such as *visual consistency* and *standardization* of the visual analytics elements, *good performance,* and *cross-browser compatibility*. Based on these requirements, we selected the appropriate visualization elements incorporated in the UI (e.g., graphs for social networks, bar charts for displaying the posting activity on social media, etc.). Additionally, the interactions required from the visualizations were defined after taking into consideration an established visual analytics model [21], which dictates that the visual analytics should be designed to provide *"Overview first, zoom after, details on demand"*.

4.2 Framework Architecture

The visualization framework follows a decoupled architecture (Fig. 1) based on two layers interacting with each other for delivering the desired output, namely: (i) the *visual analytics elements* and (ii) the *visualization UI.* In order to retrieve the required data, the *visual analytics elements* communicate with a data delivery API which fetches data (gathered from web and social media sources) from a repository where such information is stored. Next, the visual analytics elements apply various visualization techniques in order to deliver the visual representations to the end users. Each visual analytics element represents a different interactive chart. The current version supports various types of charts and graphs, such as line charts, bar charts, maps, tree-maps, pie charts, graphs, and bubble charts. Our architecture supports the easy integration of additional element types, based on the end user requirements.

All *visualizations* of our framework are implemented with the open-source ECharts library (https://echarts.apache.org/) as standalone components that can be easily integrated into different UIs. For demonstration purposes, we created two Web-based dashboards: (i) a "collection-based" dashboard providing visual analytics on large collections of multimedia data gathered from the Web and social media, and (ii) a "profile-based" dashboard presenting information about the activity of a specific social media account. Again, the framework architecture allows the easy integration of custom dashboards including different combinations of visualizations that can be tailored to the specific needs of the end users and reused in many use case scenarios.

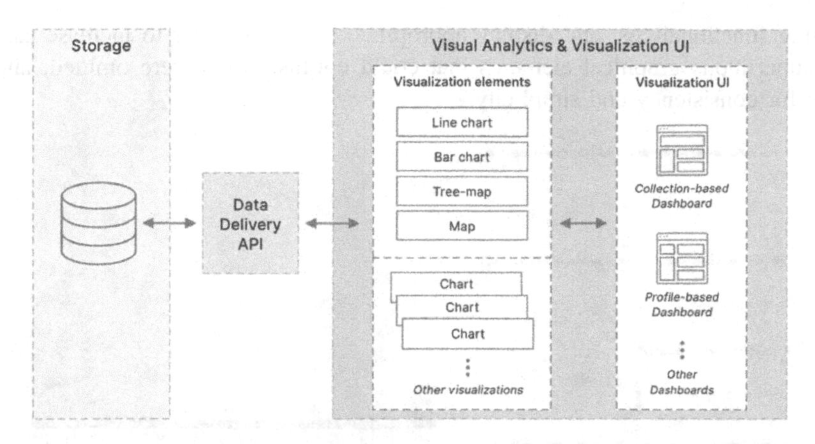

Fig. 1. High-level framework architecture

4.3 Visualization Elements and User Interface

The visual analytics developed as part of the particular framework are demonstrated through two open-source dashboards. The content visualized in our work is gathered from Twitter; however, our visualizations can support collections of data from multiple social media platforms and the Web at the same time.

The collection-based dashboard (Fig. 2(a)) showcases visualizations about collections of data gathered from social media platforms, including the social media posts and the accounts who published this content. The visualizations consist of: (i) charts displaying the aggregated or average user activity within timeframes of interest (minutes/hours/days/weekdays), (ii) a pie chart depicting the posting activity per platform (e.g. Android app, iOS app, etc.) and a bar chart with the respective activity per platforms per weekday, (iii) a chart with the most active users of the particular collection, (iv) a map visualizing the aggregated or average activity per location (country/city), (v) a tree-map presenting the most discussed topics of interest within the collected posts, (vi) a bubble chart delivering the most frequent entities (hashtags) encountered within the collected social media posts, and (vii) a social network graph displaying the most influential social media users and their communities.

The profile-based dashboard (Fig. 2(b)) focuses on delivering analytics related to a specific social media account. It consists of the following visualizations: (i) cards with general information about the particular user, e.g. username/handler, number of followers, etc., (ii) charts showcasing patterns of activity on social media, i.e. aggregated or average activity per minute, hour or weekday, (iii) a pie chart depicting the posting activity per platform and (iv) a bar chart with the respective activity per platform per weekday and (v) a bubble chart with the most common entities encountered within the particular user's social media posts.

The dashboard UI was designed based on the design principles of Sect. 2.1, and the end user requirements. Specifically, the most significant information is instantly available the moment the user accesses the dashboard. More detailed information, such as specific statistics or alternative representations of the data, is available with minimum number of clicks. All visualizations are responsive, support zooming and brushing functionalities, and display appropriate labels, in order to increase ease-of-use. Superfluous graphical elements that could confuse users were omitted, and we aimed for consistency and simplicity.

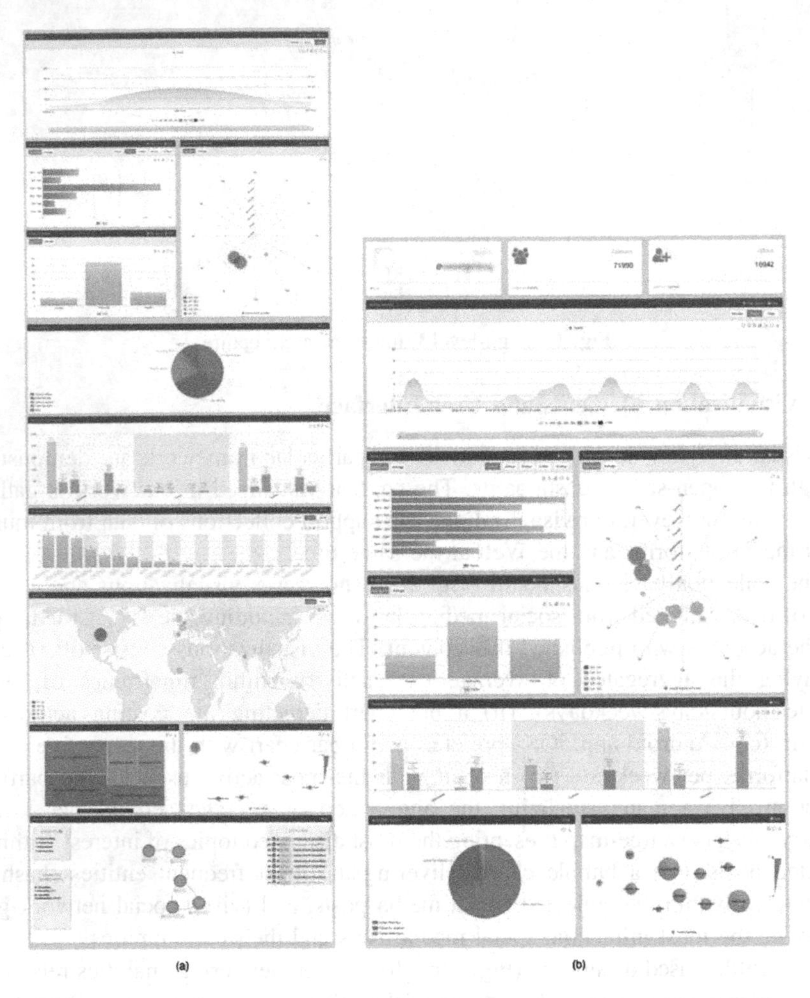

Fig. 2. (a) Dashboard 1 (collection-based), (b) Dashboard 2 (profile-based)

5 Evaluation and Discussion

Our visualization framework was initially evaluated as to its usability and perceived usefulness, following the *think-aloud protocol*, which involved participants commenting as they were performing a set of specific tasks relevant to the third use case (Sect. 3.3), on the two dashboards presented on Sect. 4.3. The participants, who were law enforcement agents, also responded to a short survey including 14 questions[1]

[1] The questions of our survey are not included due to space limitations.

(based on a five-point Likert scale where 1 corresponds to "Strongly disagree" and 5 to "Strongly agree") focused on: (i) the analysis process, (ii) the visualizations UI, and (iii) the interactions.

A total number of seven end users with experience on large datasets and social media content participated in our survey. We used the mean (M) and the standard deviation (SD) value for evaluating their responses. The goal of our survey was to elicit qualitative insights that would drive further improvement; for this type of evaluation, seven end users might not constitute a representative sample for statistical exploration, but they are sufficient for uncovering a substantial number of usability issues in testing sessions [22].

Indeed, the evaluation provided by the end users brought back helpful qualitative feedback. Overall, the participants considered the visualizations user-friendly and were able to understand the information presented without extra instructions. In regard to the analysis process, they appreciated the inclusion of various different charts and the filtering options, while, at the same time, they pointed out usability "pain points". For example, most users agreed that the selection of the particular visualizations were appropriate, whereas two users were neutral and one disagreed (M = 3.71, SD = 1.11). Additionally, most of the participants found the visualizations useful for analysis (M = 3.71, SD = 0.75); however, they did not seem confident as to whether the visualizations could help them uncover outliers in the data (M = 3.28, SD = 2.11).

Questions regarding the visualizations UI yielded neutral to positive results. For instance, four users found the visualizations easy to understand, whereas three users were neutral (M = 3.85, SD = 0.89). The majority also agreed that only a few steps are required in order to access the visualizations; one user encountered difficulties nonetheless (M = 3.85, SD = 0.88). Concerning the UI design, most users agreed that the visualizations included are color consistent, whereas two users were neutral (M = 4.14, SD = 0.89); five users also agreed that the visualizations include explanatory labels, whereas two users were neutral (M = 3.85, SD = 0.69). Furthermore, five users agreed and two users strongly agreed that filters, options and instructions are always near the respective visualization, and that the amount of text is appropriate (M = 4.28, SD = 0.48).

Regarding the available interactivity options, most users agreed that they can apply filters and manipulate complex visualizations in order to view an alternative representation. One user was neutral, and one user was negative (M = 3.71, SD = 0.95). However, even though we received positive comments regarding the existing filtering and zooming/brushing functionalities, the participants also expressed the need for more advanced customization options, e.g. filtering data by inserting a specific date. Additionally, to increase user-friendliness, they also suggested the incorporation of extra information regarding complex visualizations, such as the graph depicting user communities, or specific menu options that could be overlooked. For example, even though raw data can be easily accessed for all charts, only two users agreed that they can drill down to the actual data; three users were neutral, whereas two users disagreed (M = 3, SD = 0.81). Taking their feedback into account, we decided to update the visualization components of the framework with additional features, such as more advanced filtering options, links to the actual content, and informative tooltips.

6 Conclusions and Future Work

This work provided a concise overview of the theoretical background of information visualization and visual analytics and presented (a) a visualization framework that provides real-time interactive visualizations, and (b) two Web-based dashboards demonstrating the visualizations of our framework. The particular work makes a unique contribution by examining theoretical and practical principles, as well as describing the creation of a generic visualization framework that can be re-used in various contexts. Additionally, the paper describes three indicative use cases, and presents the feedback received from end users engaged with the two dashboards during usability evaluation sessions. The visualizations were well-received by end users; it should be mentioned, however, that the particular study had its limitations which deterred us from performing further statistical analyses. These included the small number of participants, as well as the fact that end users did not use the dashboards for an extended period of time. However, this preliminary feedback was invaluable as it illustrated how to improve the current version of the framework by adding more features and configuration options to the visualizations and paved the path for more extensive testing in other scenarios and contexts. Some suggestions for future development include the addition of more advanced configuration and filtering options, the incorporation of informative tooltips on complex visualizations, and the addition of on-boarding which would provide useful tips to newcomers.

Acknowledgements. This work was supported by the TENSOR (H2020-700024) and the V4Design (H2020-779962) projects, both funded by the European Commission.

References

1. Keim, D., Andrienko, G., Fekete, J.-D., Görg, C., Kohlhammer, J., Melançon, G.: Visual analytics: definition, process, and challenges. In: Kerren, A., Stasko, J.T., Fekete, J.-D., North, C. (eds.) Information Visualization. LNCS, vol. 4950, pp. 154–175. Springer, Heidelberg (2008). https://doi.org/10.1007/978-3-540-70956-5_7
2. Averbuch, M., et al.: As you like it: tailorable information visualization. Database Visualization Research Group. Tufts University (2004)
3. Wong, P.C., Thomas, J.: Visual analytics. IEEE Comput. Graph. Appl. **5**, 20–21 (2004)
4. Kang, Y.A., Gorg, C., Stasko, J.: Evaluating visual analytics systems for investigative analysis: deriving design principles from a case study. In: IEEE Symposium on Visual Analytics Science and Technology, pp. 139–146. IEEE (2009)
5. Keim, D.A., Mansmann, F., Schneidewind, J., Thomas, J., Ziegler, H.: Visual analytics: scope and challenges. In: Simoff, S.J., Böhlen, M.H., Mazeika, A. (eds.) Visual Data Mining. LNCS, vol. 4404, pp. 76–90. Springer, Heidelberg (2008). https://doi.org/10.1007/978-3-540-71080-6_6
6. Moere, A.V.: Beyond the tyranny of the pixel: exploring the physicality of information visualization. In: 12th International Conference on Information Visualization. IEEE (2008)
7. Ware, C.: Information Visualization: Perception for Design. Elsevier, Amsterdam (2012)
8. Behrens, C.: The Form of Facts and Figures: Design Patterns for Interactive Information Visualization (2008)

9. Jun, E., Steven, L., Salvendy, G.: A visual information processing model to characterize interactive visualization environments. Int. J. Hum.-Comput. Interact. **27**(4), 348–363 (2011)
10. Globus, Al.: Principles of information display for visualization practitioners. Rev. Econ. Bus. Stud. REBS **2**, 161 (1994)
11. Diakopoulos, N., Naaman, M., Kivran-Swaine, F.: Diamonds in the rough: social media visual analytics for journalistic inquiry. In: IEEE Symposium on Visual Analytics Science and Technology. IEEE (2010)
12. Marcus, A., et al.: Twitinfo: aggregating and visualizing microblogs for event exploration. In: Proceedings of the SIGCHI Conference on Human Factors in Computing Systems. ACM (2011)
13. Becker, H., Naaman, M., Gravano, L.: Beyond trending topics: real-world event identification on Twitter. In: Fifth International AAAI Conference on Weblogs and Social Media (2011)
14. Livnat, Y., et al.: Visual correlation for situational awareness. In: IEEE Symposium on Information Visualization. IEEE (2005)
15. Romero-Gomez, R., Yacin N., Antonakakis, M.: Towards designing effective visualizations for DNS-based network threat analysis. In: IEEE Symposium on Visualization for Cyber Security (VizSec), pp. 1–8. IEEE (2017)
16. Vaitsis, C., Nilsson, G., Zary, N.: Visual analytics in healthcare education: exploring novel ways to analyze and represent big data in undergraduate medical education. PeerJ **2**, e683 (2014)
17. Simpao, A.F., Ahumada, L.M., Rehman, M.A.: Big data and visual analytics in anaesthesia and health care. Br. J. Anaesth. **115**(3), 350–356 (2015)
18. MacEachren, A.M., et al.: Geo-twitter analytics: applications in crisis management. In: 25th International Cartographic Conference (2011)
19. Rudolph, S., Savikhin, A., Ebert, D.S.: FinVis: applied visual analytics for personal financial planning. In: IEEE Symposium on Visual Analytics Science and Technology. IEEE (2009)
20. Ko, S., et al.: A survey on visual analysis approaches for financial data. In: Computer Graphics Forum, vol. 35, no. 3, pp. 599–617 (2016)
21. Shneiderman, B: The eyes have it: a task by data type taxonomy for information visualizations. The craft of information visualization, pp. 364–371 (2003)
22. Nielsen, J.: Why You Only Need to Test with 5 Users. Nielsen Norman Group (2000). https://www.nngroup.com/articles/why-you-only-need-to-test-with-5-users/, Accessed 17 Oct 2019

SS3: MDRE: Multimedia Datasets for Repeatable Experimentation

GLENDA: Gynecologic Laparoscopy Endometriosis Dataset

Andreas Leibetseder[1(✉)], Sabrina Kletz[1], Klaus Schoeffmann[1], Simon Keckstein[2], and Jörg Keckstein[3]

[1] Institute of Information Technology, Klagenfurt University, Klagenfurt, 9020 Klagenfurt, Austria
{aleibets,sabrina,ks}@itec.aau.at

[2] University Hospital, Ludwig-Maximilians-University Munich, 80799 Munich, Germany
simon.keckstein@med.uni-muenchen.de

[3] Ulm University, 89081 Ulm, Germany
joerg@keckstein.at

Abstract. Gynecologic laparoscopy as a type of minimally invasive surgery (MIS) is performed via a live feed of a patient's abdomen surveying the insertion and handling of various instruments for conducting treatment. Adopting this kind of surgical intervention not only facilitates a great variety of treatments, the possibility of recording said video streams is as well essential for numerous post-surgical activities, such as treatment planning, case documentation and education. Nonetheless, the process of manually analyzing surgical recordings, as it is carried out in current practice, usually proves tediously time-consuming. In order to improve upon this situation, more sophisticated computer vision as well as machine learning approaches are actively developed. Since most of such approaches heavily rely on sample data, which especially in the medical field is only sparsely available, with this work we publish the Gynecologic Laparoscopy ENdometriosis DAtaset (GLENDA) – an image dataset containing region-based annotations of a common medical condition named endometriosis, i.e. the dislocation of uterine-like tissue. The dataset is the first of its kind and it has been created in collaboration with leading medical experts in the field.

Keywords: Lesion detection · Endometriosis localization · Medical dataset · Region-based annotations · Gynecologic laparoscopy

1 Introduction

Minimally invasive surgery (MIS) considerably reduces trauma inflicted upon patients during medical interventions, since, as opposed to traditional open surgery, treatments are applied less intrusively. As a typical form of MIS, *endoscopy* is performed by inserting a small camera, the *endoscope*, as well as a variety of instruments into the human body via natural or artificially created orifices.

Y. M. Ro et al. (Eds.): MMM 2020, LNCS 11962, pp. 439–450, 2020.
https://doi.org/10.1007/978-3-030-37734-2_36

In the case of *gynecologic laparoscopy* such incisions are created into the abdomen in order to treat conditions related to the female reproductive system. The accordingly obtained video feed of an individual's inner anatomy is projected onto external monitors providing physicians with adequate visuals for performing surgery.

With the prospect of conducting surgeries in such a manner comes the possibility of recording entire procedures, an opportunity that is in fact pursued by most modern medical facilities. Apart from representing valuable evidence for lawful investigations, these kind of recordings more importantly are consulted by medical practitioners for further treatment planning, case revisitations or even educational purposes. Seemingly a convenient improvement, several downsides, however, considerably diminish the usefulness of archived surgery footage: recording the typically hours-long surgeries filmed in high-definition on a daily basis requires elaborate long-term storage solutions. Furthermore, in order to remain useful, video archives of such magnitudes must easily be searchable even by potentially non tech-savvy staff. The consequentially arising need for more sophisticated systems capable of aiding physicians post- as well as even intra-surgery creates great opportunities and challenges for various scientific communities, not least the ones concerned with multimedia [7].

Although machine learning has successfully been applied in the field of medical imaging [5], specifically for the task of disease classification and diagnosis, much needed published datasets for feeding corresponding algorithms are only sparsely available. This not only is due to the increased sensitiveness of such data but as well a consequence of the broad spectrum of different imaging technologies[1] utilized for a great variety of purposes. When merely regarding endoscopy in general the number of publically available datasets is reduced even more drastically, leaving only a few for the sub-discipline of laparoscopy: Cholec80 [11], LapChole [9], GI dataset [12], SurgicalActions160 [8] and LapGyn4 [4] to name some recent ones.

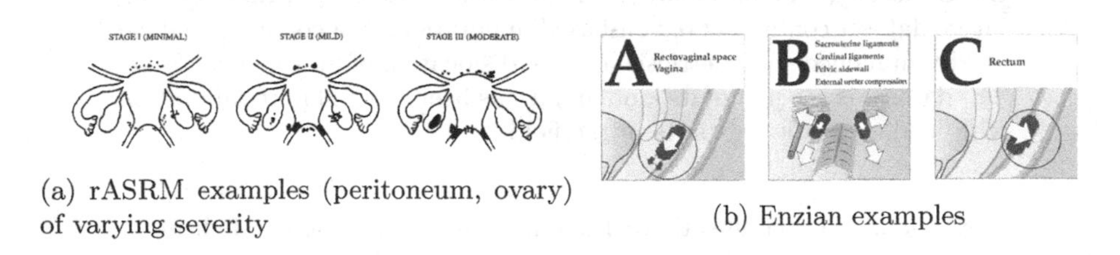

(a) rASRM examples (peritoneum, ovary) of varying severity

(b) Enzian examples

Fig. 1. Example endometriosis locations for rASRM (a) and Enzian (b).

As cholecystectomy, i.e. the removal of the gallbladder, is the most frequently conducted laparoscopic surgery [10], released datasets commonly are

[1] e.g. X-ray, computed tomography (CT) scans, magnetic resonance imaging (MRI), ultrasound, ...

created from this procedure. Keeping that in mind, with this work we specifically target a different kind of procedure, which typically as well is treated laparoscopically: the diagnosis, inspection and surgical removal of *endometriosis* – a benign but painful anomaly among women in child bearing age involving the growth of uterine-like tissue in locations outside of the uterus. The condition can be found in various positions and severities, often in multiple instances per patient requiring a physician to determine its extent. This most frequently is accomplished by calculating its magnitude via utilizing the combination of two popular classification systems, the revised American Society for Reproductive Medicine (rASRM) score [2] and the European [1] Enzian classification [3], which describe the anomaly's potential anatomical location and severity on a three-level scale. Figure 1 shows a few examples of these locations as described by both of these systems. Our contribution, the Gynecologic Laparoscopy ENdometriosis DAtaset[2] (GLENDA) dataset comprises a subset of these locations and has been created with leading medical experts in the field of endometriosis treatment. The dataset and with it our contribution can be characterized as follows:

Source. 300+ video segments and frames selected from a pool of 400+ individual full surgery videos.

Images. 25K+ Images, consisting of 12K+ positive, i.e. pathological images associated with endometriosis, and 13K+ negative examples, i.e. non-pathological images without visible endometriosis.

Annotations. 500+ hand-drawn region-based class-specific endometriosis annotations on 300+ images/keyframes.

Classes. Five pathological categories, of which four are based on the location of the condition (peritoneum, ovary, uterus, DIE – deep infiltrating endometriosis) and one indicating no visible endometriosis (no pathology).

Purposes. Binary as well as multi-label (endometriosis) classification, detection and localization tasks with the option of tracking pathology over video segments, thus, augmenting the overall annotated sample count.

The remainder of this paper discusses details about the dataset, starting with its creation in Sect. 2, its structure in Sect. 3 and, finally, discussing its limitations in Sect. 4 before drawing conclusions in Sect. 5.

2 Dataset Creation

Overall, there are very numerous potential locations for endometriosis[3] and the condition's size determines its severity level on a scale from one to three. Hence, for creating a complete dataset in terms of a sufficient amount of examples for every possible combination of location and severity extent requires the collection of samples for well over 50 different category types or classes. This, in fact, can be considered an overly challenging task due to the following reasons:

[2] http://www.itec.aau.at/ftp/datasets/GLENDA.

[3] e.g. peritoneum, ovary, tube, ligaments, vagina, rectum, bladder, ureter, ...

Expert Knowledge. Endometriosis can not reliably be recognized by laymen or even untrained medical practitioners, which stresses the need for employing specific experts in the field and at the same time severely reduces the amount of capable annotators for such a dataset.

Time. GLENDA has been created with fully active surgeons restricting all annotation and research effort to non-working hours, which considerably slows down the data collection process.

Rarity. Several lesion locations are diagnosed much more rarely than others, hence, including them prolongs data accumulation even further.

Completeness. Finding representative examples of a class for each of the three potential severity levels even for a reduced set of categories poses an additional challenge outweighing the time and effort for spent annotating, at least for the dataset's current first version.

Therefore, for our initial GLENDA version we constrain annotations to a subset of four endometriosis locations (see Sect. 3 for details) consisting of region-based annotations of single video frames, which either are associated with specific video positions (frame annotations) or sequences over time (keyframe annotations in video segments). Although for video segments only keyframes are annotated, they have been created keeping in mind that all of the endometriosis regions identified on them are visible throughout the sequences, i.e. camera motion is kept at a minimal level. This offers the possibility of augmenting the number of annotations by applying annotation tracking mechanisms to these segments (e.g. point/kernel/silhoutte tracking).

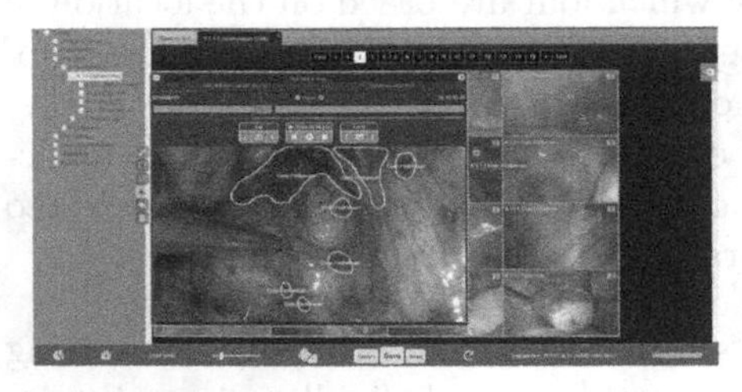

(a) Creating annotations using closed free-hand drawings, polygons and rectangles.

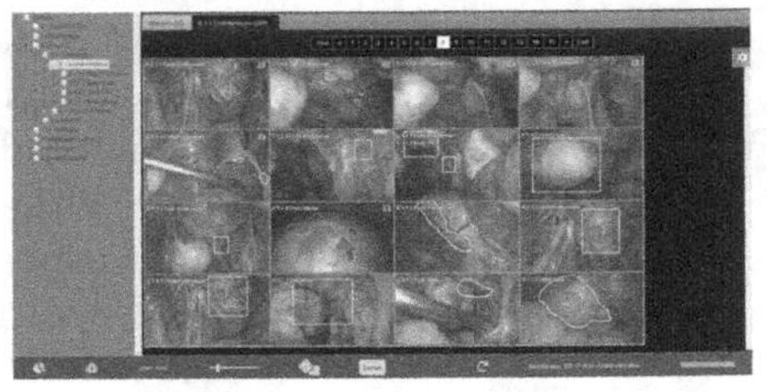

(b) Different endometriosis annotations in a summary view.

Fig. 2. Dataset creation and exploration using the Endoscopic Concept Annotation Tool (ECAT).

The entire dataset has been created using the Endoscopic Concept Annotation Tool [6] (ECAT), shown in Fig. 2. ECAT is a web-technologies-based tool that allows for importing large video databases and creating concept annotations for video sequences as well as frames. It in particular enables users to annotate frames by creating rectangles as well as closed polygons and free-hand drawings, meaning that every annotation always needs to enclose a region. Further, a single annotation on a frame that potentially can contain many different annotations, is required to be associated with one of GLENDA's four endometriosis categories.

For video sequences, a keyframe must be chosen first before being able to draw an annotation region.

As the system can be utilized via a standard web browser, it has been made remotely accessible to all involved medical experts for increasing the convenience when creating annotations. Finally, all data for the current GLENDA version has been collected over the course of four months time.

3 The GLENDA Dataset

GLENDA is a multi-faceted endometriosis dataset that has been extracted from over 400 gynecologic laparoscopy videos, many of which show endometriosis cases of varied severities. It is summarized in Table 1 and composed of following elements:

Categories. Five categories/classes describe a distinct endometriosis locations:
- pathology: peritoneum, ovary, uterus, deep infiltrating endometriosis (DIE)
- no pathology: (no visible endometriosis)

Annotations. Region-based as well as temporal annotations in the form of:
- Annotated frames: single video frames annotated with hand-drawn sketches (regions), which indicate one or more out of four endometriosis categories.
- Annotated sequences: sets of consecutive video frames associated with one or several categories over certain periods of time with annotated keyframes (pathology) or no additional region-based annotations (no pathology).

As a consequence of choosing above structure, the dataset allows for a multitude of utilization purposes. Splitting up the dataset into pathology and no pathology images allows for attempting binary classification, disregarding all endometriosis sub-classes. Furthermore, when including individual class annotations multi-class endometriosis prediction can be approached, as already mentioned in above Sect. 2 potentially by augmenting the amount of annotations via tracking them throughout their corresponding video segments. Aside from possible disadvantages outlined in Sect. 4, additionally collecting video segments has the advantage of enabling the inclusion of temporal information in proposed methodologies for analysis. Finally, the multitude of region-based annotations can be leveraged for localization tasks as well as representing a basis for learning further annotations.

Following sections more thoroughly describe GLENDA's class categories as well as structure on a file basis, while pointing out the dataset's limitations.

3.1 Categories

Peritoneum. The peritoneum is a serous membrane lining the abdominal cavity (parietal) as well as its contained upper organs (visceral). Endometrial tissue

Table 1. GLENDA summary: number of annotations (annot.) per category (cat.), number of annotated frames per category, maximum (max.) annotations per frame, max. categories (cat.) per frame, number of sequences (seq.) and amount of frames.

Category[a]		annot.	annot. frames	max. annot. per frame	seq.	Frames
Pathology	Peritoneum	402	203	9	73	6470
	ovary	51	48	2	15	2478
	uterus	14	8	3	5	475
	DIE	53	43	3	18	2821
no pathology		0	0	0	27	13 438
Total		**520**	**302**	**9 (max. cat.: 3)**	**138**	**25 682**

[a]Note: A sequence/keyframe/frame is attributed to a specific category if it is the dominant one in all of its corresponding annotations in terms of annotation count/area covered.

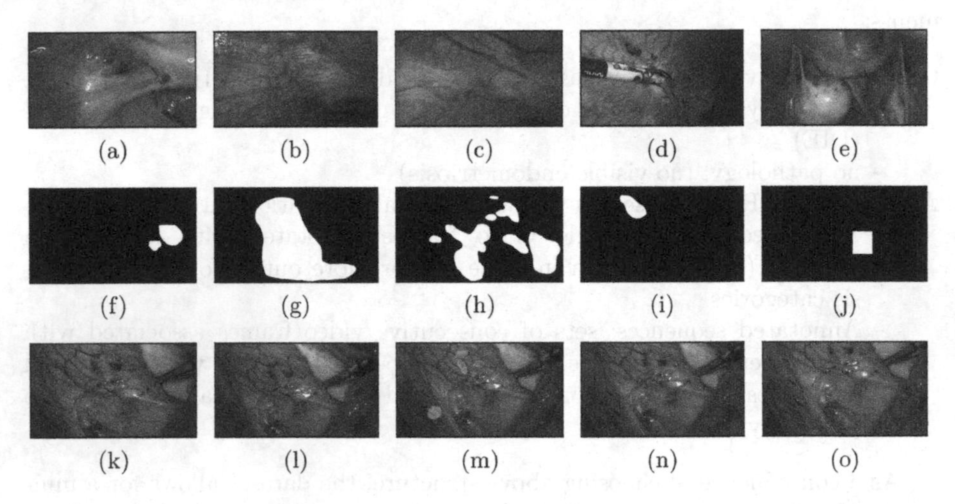

Fig. 3. Peritoneum: differing example images (3a–e) with corresponding annotations (3f–j) and video sequence example including keyframe annotations (3k–o). (Color figure online)

annotated in GLENDA is associated with the pelvic cavity, which is enclosed by the parietal peritoneum. Figure 3 shows various peritoneum dataset examples together with their annotations[4] (binary images) and selected frames of a video sequence with its annotated keyframe (green overlay). Since the peritoneum covers a very large area and as well surrounds organs that are part of other GLENDA classes, corresponding images are often very different to one another and can contain non-relevant other areas that may even contain

[4] Note that due to the possibility of annotating several categories per image, e.g. GLENDA includes region-based annotations of up to three classes per image, for simplicity only frames with exactly one associated class have been chosen as examples.

additional endometrial tissue. Another implication of the membrane's proportionally large size is its consequently very frequent visibility in many of the dataset's images, be it pathologoical or non pathological. Visually the peritoneum occurs in a mixture of red, yellow and white colors.

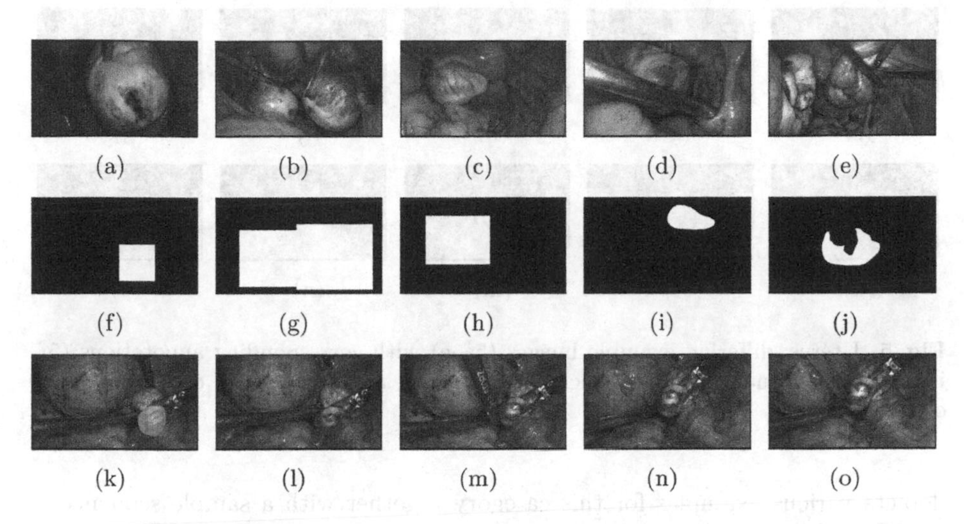

Fig. 4. Ovary: differing example images (4a–e) with corresponding annotations (4f–j) and video sequence example including keyframe annotations (4k–o). (Color figure online)

Ovary. Apart from carrying several important functions like producing hormones, the main purpose of the two ovaries is to produce mature ova. Together with the peritoneum class, the ovaries are the most common locations for endometriosis (see Fig. 4 for dataset examples), which is the reason why both of them (together with the fallopian tubes) are the only lesion locations described by the rASRM score [2], specifically as well for diagnosing *adhesions*, i.e. endometrial tissue connecting other tissue – a class that, however, is not yet included in GLENDA. Visually ovaries are easily distinguishable from other organs even for laymen, since their oval-shaped outer capsule in non pathological state is colored in a shade of white contrasting them from the typical red-yellowish color spectrum of other anatomical structures.

Uterus. The uterus is intended for bringing up a fetus from a fertilized ovum. Uteri can show different types of endometrial dislocation: endometrial tissue growing into the muscle wall of the uterus and thickening it is called *adenomyosis* (adenomyosis may alter the shape and consistency of the uterus), while there is no special term for the case that the tissue is found on the uterine surface, which is covered by the visceral peritoneum. Similar to the previous classes, Fig. 5

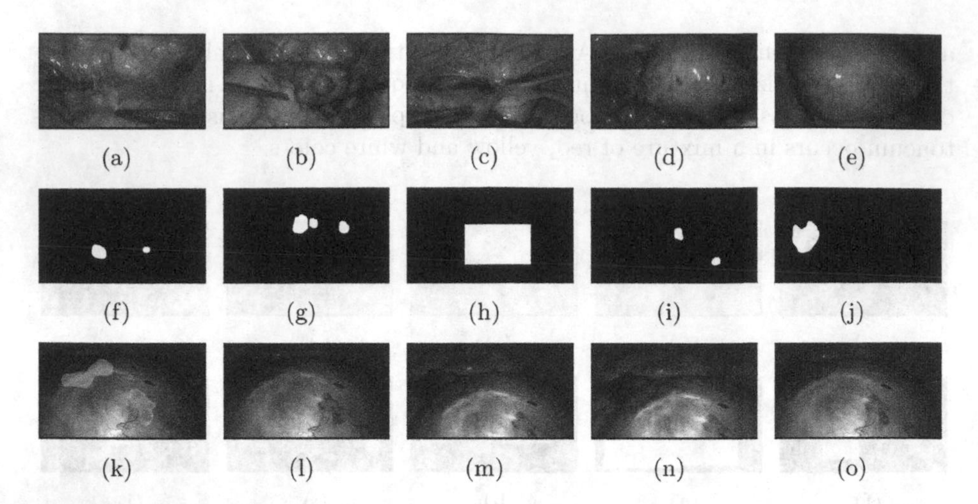

Fig. 5. Uterus: differing example images (5a–e) with corresponding annotations (5f–j) and video sequence example including keyframe annotations (5k–o). (Color figure online)

depicts various examples for this category together with a sample sequence of an affected uterus. A non pathological uterus is pear-shaped, visually appears in shades of red and is located in-between the two ovaries and in connection to them via the fallopian tubes.

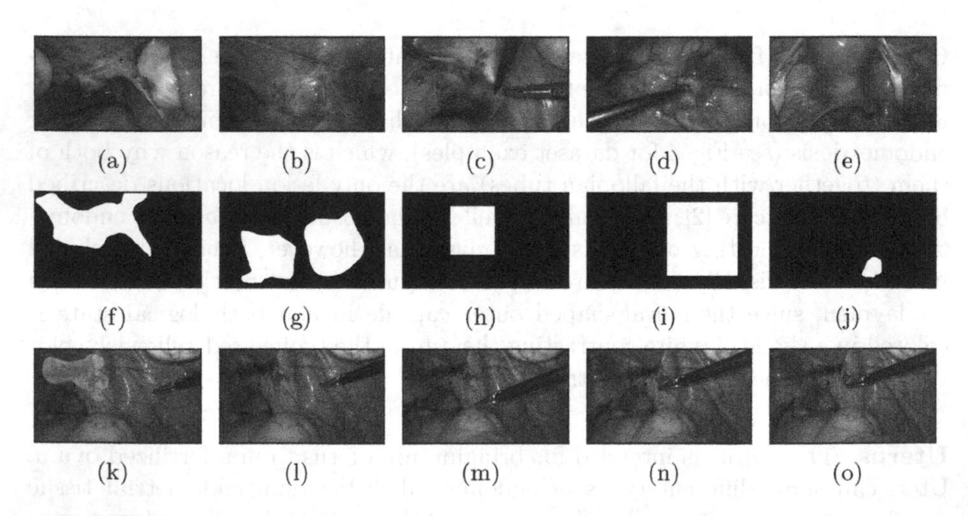

Fig. 6. Deep Infiltrating Endometriosis (DIE): differing example images (6a–e) with corresponding annotations (6f–j) and video sequence example including keyframe annotations (6k–o). (Color figure online)

DIE. Non-shallow endometriosis that is found on specific locations such as the rectum, the rectovaginal space or uterine ligaments is described as Deep Infiltrating Endometriosis (DIE) and is usually rated using the Enzian classification system [3] in addition to the rASRM score [2]. Figure 6 shows several examples of this class including lesions in the pelvic wall and uterine ligaments. Since all of the previously described anatomical structures can be affected by DIE rendering example pictures very similar to the other classes, it is a challenging task to classify DIE correctly. Additionally, as this type of endometriosis describes a large variety of lesion locations, no distinct visual appearance can be attributed to this type of class, other than highlighting that typically the color spectrum in recorded laparoscopic videos lacks green tones.

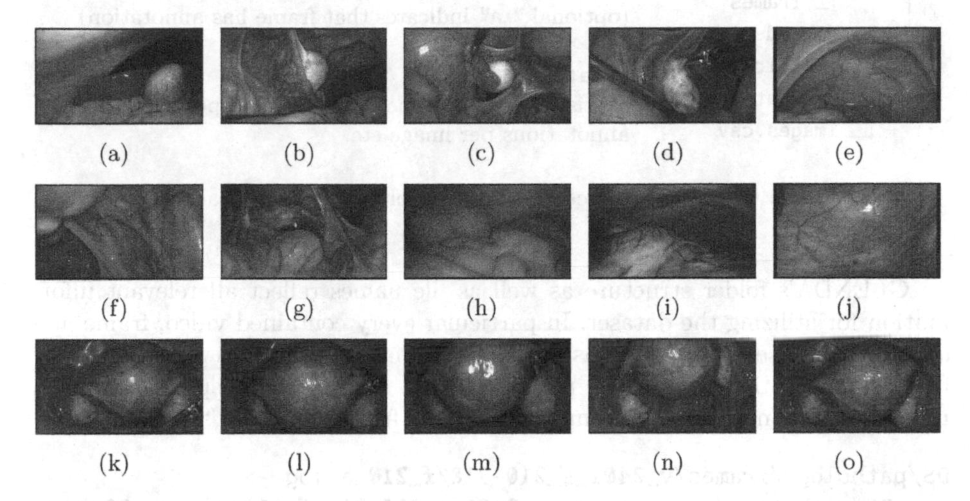

Fig. 7. No Pathology: differing example images (7a–j) and video sequence example (7k–o).

No Pathology. Video sequences containing no visible pathology in relation to endometriosis are included in the dataset, providing counter examples to above categories. Since this class does not contain any region-based annotations, in addition to a sequence showing a non-pathological uterus, Fig. 7 particularly includes examples of several anatomical structures from above pathological classes (e.g. peritoneum and ovaries). Again it is not possible to make any assumptions about the color and shape of objects within this class, since it includes images covering most areas of the pelvic region.

3.2 Structure

Although originally extracted from videos, GLENDA is an image-based dataset, hence, contains a structured collection of images. Besides images of video frames, all annotations have been extracted separately and are also provided as images, albeit in binary format (as depicted in Figs. 3, 4, 5 and 6, but with the restriction of one annotation per image). The dataset archive addionally includes a Readme file as well as some dataset statistics in comma separated value (CSV) tables. Its directory structure is listed and explained in Fig. 8.

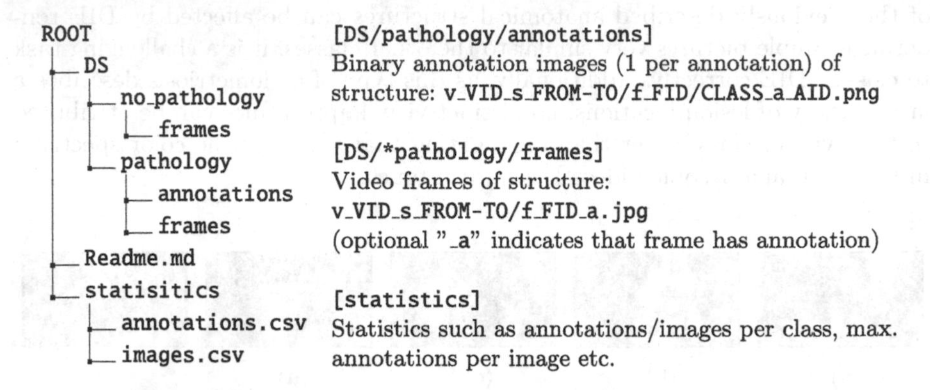

Fig. 8. GLENDA's directory structure (placeholders capitalized).

GLENDA's folder structure as well as file names reflect all relevant information for utilizing the dataset. In particular every contained video, frame and annotation possesses a unique ascending ID number and frames can be mapped to their annotations by partial path matching, which can be sped up by first removing all non-annotated frames, i.e. finding frames with an "_a" suffix:

```
DS/pathology/frames/v_2401_s_210-318/f_210_a.jpg ->
    DS/pathology/annotations/v_2401_s_210-318/f_210/die_a_629.png
    DS/pathology/annotations/v_2401_s_210-318/f_210/die_a_630.png
    DS/pathology/annotations/v_2401_s_210-318/f_210/die_a_631.png
    ...
```

Region-based annotations, which, as mentioned above, are in binary format (black background, white annotation) need to appropriately be transformed into the required format, e.g. rectanglar bounding boxes, polygons etc. For conducting binary classification region-based annotations are disregarded, hence, images can simply be retrieved from their corresponding folders (`DS/pathology/frames` and `DS/no_pathology/frames`).

4 Limitations

When thoroughly examining GLENDA in its current version, several shortcomings can be identified. Although the total amount of images is approximately balanced between examples for pathology and no pathology (12K+ vs. 13K+), single pathology classes are uneven: e.g. peritoneum contains more annotations than all three other classes combined. Especially the sample count of the uterus category with a total of merely 8 annotated images with 14 annotations is rather low. Therefore, researchers may either choose to omit this class altogether or attempt to augment it via tracking the annotations over the class' 5 included video segments. Although this will yield a bigger sample count of 475 images, it is of course less diverse than creating new annotations.

Paying even more attention to data diversity, when using the full 25K+ image corpus with the goal of machine learning based classification, it is important to carefully consider data preparation: sequential video frames within small periods of time (e.g. a few seconds) are very similar to each other, which can have a grave detrimental impact on the training process. Thus, training, validation and test splits should be constructed from distinct video sequences rather than from the entire image pool, specifically for non pathological samples, which exclusively are comprised of merely 27 sequences. Although more effortful, this approach has the advantage that the data across the splits is always truly different, preventing the classifier from validating/testing on exactly what it has been trained on, yielding a perfect classification score. In order to increase the amount of dissimilar sequences, it may also be feasible to uniformly sample from the existing sequences with a large enough interval or apply a shot detection technique for finding boundaries between dissimilar content.

Finally, not least due to the varied sample count for pathological classes, in order to ensure an optimal training split that is balanced similarly to the dataset, it should be proportional to the amount of examples per class and not the total number of images, i.e. every split should contain a certain percentage of examples from each class.

5 Conclusion

With the aim of inspiring research in gynecologic laparoscopy, we introduce the first Gynecologic Laparoscy ENdometriosis DAtaset (GLENDA), created in collaboration with medical experts in the domain of endometriosis treatment. GLENDA contains over 25K images, about half of which are pathological, i.e. showing endometriosis, and the other half non-pathological, i.e. containing no visible endometriosis. We thoroughly describe the data collection process, the dataset's properties and structure, while also discussing its limitations. We plan on continuously extending GLENDA, including the addition of other relevant categories and ultimately lesion severities. Furthermore, we are in the process of collecting specific "endometriosis suspicion" class annotations in all categories for capturing a common situation among endometriosis experts: at times it proves difficult even for specialists to classify the anomaly without further inspection, which may be due to several reasons, such as visible video artifacts or DIE regions with a small surface area. Although doubling the amount of classes, having such difficult examples may greatly improve the quality of endometriosis classifiers.

Acknowledgements. This work was funded by the FWF Austrian Science Fund under grant P 32010-N38.

References

1. Andrews, W., et al.: Revised american fertility society classification of endometriosis: 1985. Fertil. Steril. **43**(3), 351–352 (1985)
2. Canis, M., et al.: Revised american society for reproductive medicine classification of endometriosis: 1996. Fertil. Steril. **67**(5), 817–821 (1997). https://doi.org/10.1016/S0015-0282(97)81391-X
3. Keckstein, J.: Endometriosis in the intestinal tract – important facts for diagnosis and therapy. Coloproctology **39**(2), 121–133 (2017). https://doi.org/10.1007/s00053-017-0144-5
4. Leibetseder, A., Petscharnig, S., Primus, M.J., Kletz, S., Münzer, B., Schoeffmann, K., Keckstein, J.: LapGyn4: a dataset for 4 automatic content analysis problems in the domain of laparoscopic gynecology. In: Proceedings of the 9th ACM Multimedia Systems Conference, pp. 357–362. ACM (2018)
5. Litjens, G., et al.: A survey on deep learning in medical image analysis. Med. Image Anal. **42**, 60–88 (2017)
6. Münzer, B., Leibetseder, A., Kletz, S., Schoeffmann, K.: ECAT - endoscopic concept annotation tool. In: Kompatsiaris, I., Huet, B., Mezaris, V., Gurrin, C., Cheng, W.-H., Vrochidis, S. (eds.) MMM 2019. LNCS, vol. 11296, pp. 571–576. Springer, Cham (2019). https://doi.org/10.1007/978-3-030-05716-9_48
7. Münzer, B., Schoeffmann, K., Böszörmenyi, L.: Content-based processing and analysis of endoscopic images and videos: a survey. Multimed. Tools Appl. (2017). https://doi.org/10.1007/s11042-016-4219-z
8. Schoeffmann, K., Husslein, H., Kletz, S., Petscharnig, S., Muenzer, B., Beecks, C.: Video retrieval in laparoscopic video recordings with dynamic content descriptors. Multimed. Tools Appl. **77**(13), 16813–16832 (2018). https://doi.org/10.1007/s11042-017-5252-2
9. Stauder, R., Ostler, D., Kranzfelder, M., Koller, S., Feußner, H., Navab, N.: The TUM LapChole dataset for the M2CAI 2016 workflow challenge. arXiv preprint arXiv:1610.09278 (2016)
10. Tsui, C., Klein, R., Garabrant, M.: Minimally invasive surgery: national trends in adoption and future directions for hospital strategy. Surg. Endosc. **27**(7), 2253–2257 (2013)
11. Twinanda, A.P., Shehata, S., Mutter, D., Marescaux, J., de Mathelin, M., Padoy, N.: EndoNet: a deep architecture for recognition tasks on laparoscopic videos. IEEE Trans. Med. Imag. **36**(1), 86–97 (2017). https://doi.org/10.1109/TMI.2016.2593957
12. Ye, M., Giannarou, S., Meining, A., Yang, G.Z.: Online tracking and retargeting with applications to optical biopsy in gastrointestinal endoscopic examinations. Med. Image Anal. **30**, 144–157 (2016)

Kvasir-SEG: A Segmented Polyp Dataset

Debesh Jha[1,2(✉)], Pia H. Smedsrud[1,3,4], Michael A. Riegler[1,7], Pål Halvorsen[1,6], Thomas de Lange[4,5], Dag Johansen[2], and Håvard D. Johansen[2]

[1] SimulaMet, Oslo, Norway
debesh@simula.no
[2] UIT The Arctic University of Norway, Tromsø, Norway
[3] Augere Medical AS, Oslo, Norway
[4] University of Oslo, Oslo, Norway
[5] Oslo University Hospital, Oslo, Norway
[6] Oslo Metropolitan University, Oslo, Norway
[7] Kristiania University College, Oslo, Norway

Abstract. Pixel-wise image segmentation is a highly demanding task in medical-image analysis. In practice, it is difficult to find annotated medical images with corresponding segmentation masks. In this paper, we present Kvasir-SEG: an open-access dataset of gastrointestinal polyp images and corresponding segmentation masks, manually annotated by a medical doctor and then verified by an experienced gastroenterologist. Moreover, we also generated the bounding boxes of the polyp regions with the help of segmentation masks. We demonstrate the use of our dataset with a traditional segmentation approach and a modern deep-learning based Convolutional Neural Network (CNN) approach. The dataset will be of value for researchers to reproduce results and compare methods. By adding segmentation masks to the Kvasir dataset, which only provide frame-wise annotations, we enable multimedia and computer vision researchers to contribute in the field of polyp segmentation and automatic analysis of colonoscopy images.

Keywords: Medical images · Polyp segmentation · Semantic segmentation · Kvasir-SEG dataset · Fuzzy C-mean clustering · ResUNet

1 Introduction

Colorectal cancer is the second most common cancer type among women and third most common among men [25]. Polyps are precursors to colorectal cancer and therefore important to detect and remove at an early stage. Polyps are found in nearly half of the individuals at age 50 that undergo a colonoscopy screening, and their frequency increase with age [21]. Polyps are abnormal tissue growth from the mucous membrane, which is lining the inside of the GI tract, and can sometimes be cancerous. Colonoscopy is the gold standard for detection and

Y. M. Ro et al. (Eds.): MMM 2020, LNCS 11962, pp. 451–462, 2020.
https://doi.org/10.1007/978-3-030-37734-2_37

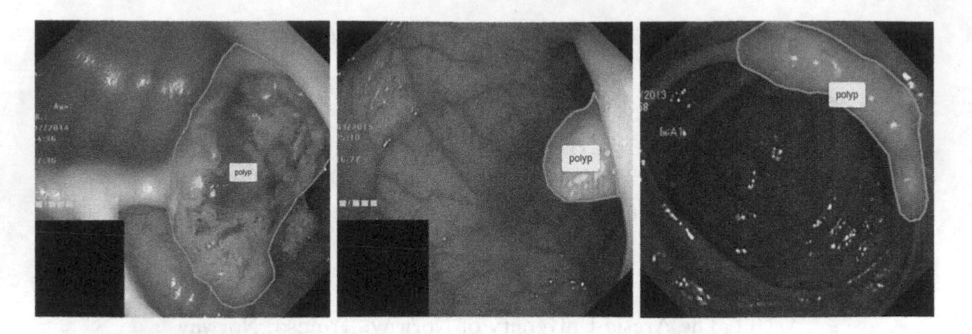

Fig. 1. Example frames from the Kvasir dataset where we additionally have marked the polyp tissue with green outlines. (Color figure online)

assessment of these polyps with subsequent biopsy and removal of the polyps. Early disease detection has a huge impact on survival from colorectal cancer [11]. In addition, several studies show that polyps are often overlooked during colonoscopies, with polyp miss rates of 14 to 30% depending on type and size of the polyps [26]. Increasing the detection of polyps has been shown to decrease risk of colorectal cancer [12]. Thus, automatic detection of more polyps at an early stage can play a crucial role in prevention and survival from colorectal cancer. This is the main motivation behind the development of a polyp segmentation dataset.

Image segmentation is the technique of dividing images into meaningful Regions of Interests (ROIs) that are simple to analyze and interpret. Further research in medical image segmentation can assist processes such as monitoring pathology, improving the diagnostic ability by increasing accuracy, precision, and reducing manual intervention [15]. In particular, for Computer Assisted Interventions (CAIs), pixel-wise semantic segmentation methods have a huge potential to become part of fast, accurate and cost-effective systems.

The goal of image segmentation is to assign a label to each pixel of the image so the pixels with the same label share specific characteristics, e.g., the pixels covered by the outline in the Fig. 1 show a polyp. Manual segmentation by physicians is still the gold standard for most of the medical imaging modalities, for example, Magnetic Resonance Imaging for evaluating hippocampal atrophy in Alzheimer's Disease [5] and tumor segmentation of glioma [27]. However, manual image segmentation is tedious, time-consuming, and subject to physician's bias and inter-observer variation. Therefore, there is a need for an automated and efficient image segmentation technique. Methods for automated and efficient image segmentation are difficult to develop as state-of-the art machine learning methods often require large number of annotated and labelled quality data, which is difficult to obtain in this field. Annotating medical data such as polyp images manually requires a lot of time and effort. It also requires medical experts, gastroenterologists in our case, which can be expensive and inaccessible. Also, there are problems related to the collection of medical images, with concern to privacy and security for patients and hospitals. Riegler et al. [19] have raised several open questions about the medical world that need to be addressed, where they emphasized the need for test datasets, including annotations and ground truth that meet current medical standards. Although there are a few available datasets, open-access datasets for comparable evaluations are missing in this field. We therefore provide the Kvasir-SEG dataset and propose a baseline model for evaluation.

The main contribution of this paper are as follows:

1. We extend the Kvasir dataset [16] with polyp images along with their corresponding segmentation masks and bounding boxes. The ROIs are the pixels depicting polyp tissue. These are represented by a white foreground in the segmentation masks. The ROIs are generated from manual annotations verified by an experienced gastroenterologist. The bounding boxes are the set of coordinates that encloses the polyp regions. The Kvasir-SEG dataset is made publicly available and open access.
2. In this article, we include a first attempt to use the Kvasir-SEG dataset for pixel-wise semantic segmentation based analysis. For the experiment, we have used Fuzzy C-mean clustering (FCM) [6] and Deep Residual U-Net (ResUNet) [28] architecture. We achieved promising results with our proposed methods when evaluated on the same dataset. We evaluated the proposed method using Dice Coefficients and mean Intersection over Union (IoU). These metrics were selected for fair comparison, and we encourage the use of these and similar metrics in future work on the dataset. The promising results demonstrated in this paper serves as baseline and motivation for further research and evaluation done on the same dataset.
3. Multiple datasets are prerequisites for comparing computer vision based algorithms, and this dataset is useful both as a training dataset or as a validation dataset. This dataset can assist the development of state-of-the-art solutions on images captured by colonoscopes. Further research in this field has the potential to help reduce the polyp miss rate and thus improve examination quality.

This paper is organized as follows: Sect. 2 discusses related datasets. We discuss the Kvasir-SEG dataset in Sect. 3. In Sect. 4, we define the suggested metrics for the segmentation of polyps. Section 5 describes the baseline experiments, results and discussion. We conclude our work and give future directions in Sect. 6.

2 Related Work

There are only few available polyp datasets that consist of ground truth and corresponding segmentation mask. These are CVC-ColonDB [24], ASU-Mayo Clinic Colonoscopy Video © Database [3], ETIS-Larib Polyp DB [23], and CVC-Clinic DB [2].

CVC-ColonDB [24] is the second largest database available and consists of annotated video sequences from colonoscopy videos. From 15 short colonoscopy sequences, 1200 image frames are extracted. Out of these images, only 300 frames are annotated. These annotated frames were specifically chosen to maximize the the visual differences between them. Use of the CVC-ColonDB requires registration.

The ASU-Mayo Clinic Colonoscopy Video © Database [3] is the first and largest available dataset captured using standard colonoscopes. The training dataset consists of 18,781 frames extracted from 20 short videos. Of these, there are 10 videos of polyps (positive) and 10 videos without polyps (negative). Ground truth and its corresponding segmentation masks are provided with the more than 3,500 frames showing polyps. For testing, 18 videos without ground truth are included. The images in the dataset are very similar to each other, which raise the problem of overfitting [16]. The ASU-Mayo Clinic Colonoscopy database is copyrighted, and is only available through direct contact with the administrators at Arizona State University.

The ETIS-Larib Polyp DB [23] consists of 196 frames of polyps extracted from colonoscopy videos and their corresponding masks. This database is available through registration.

The CVC-Clinic DB [2] consists of 612 image frames extracted from 29 different colonoscopy sequences and their corresponding ground truth as segmentation masks. The use of this database is public and open access.

The CVC-Clinic DB, ETIS-Larib and ASU-Mayo Clinic Colonoscopy Video DB were used at Medical Image Computing and Computer Assisted Intervention (MICCAI) 2015 Automatic Polyp Detection in Colonoscopy Videos Sub-Challenge. More details about the dataset and competition can be found in the paper by Bernal et al. [4].

The literature review shows that there are few available datasets. However, an open-access dataset for comparable evaluation is missing in this field. Therefore, it was a logical next step to extend the Kvasir dataset with segmentation masks. The presented data and baseline work can be a important source for addressing the problem of standard datasets for evaluation, and help develop robust and efficient systems.

3 The Kvasir-SEG Dataset

The Kvasir-SEG dataset is based on the previous Kvasir [16] dataset, which is the first multi-class dataset for gastrointestinal (GI) tract disease detection and classification.

3.1 The Original Kvasir Dataset

The original Kvasir dataset [16] comprises 8,000 GI tract images from 8 classes where each class consists of 1000 images. We replaced the 13 images from the polyp class with new images to improve the quality of the dataset. These images were collected and verified by experienced gastroenterologists from Vestre Viken Health Trust in Norway. The classes include anatomical landmarks, pathological

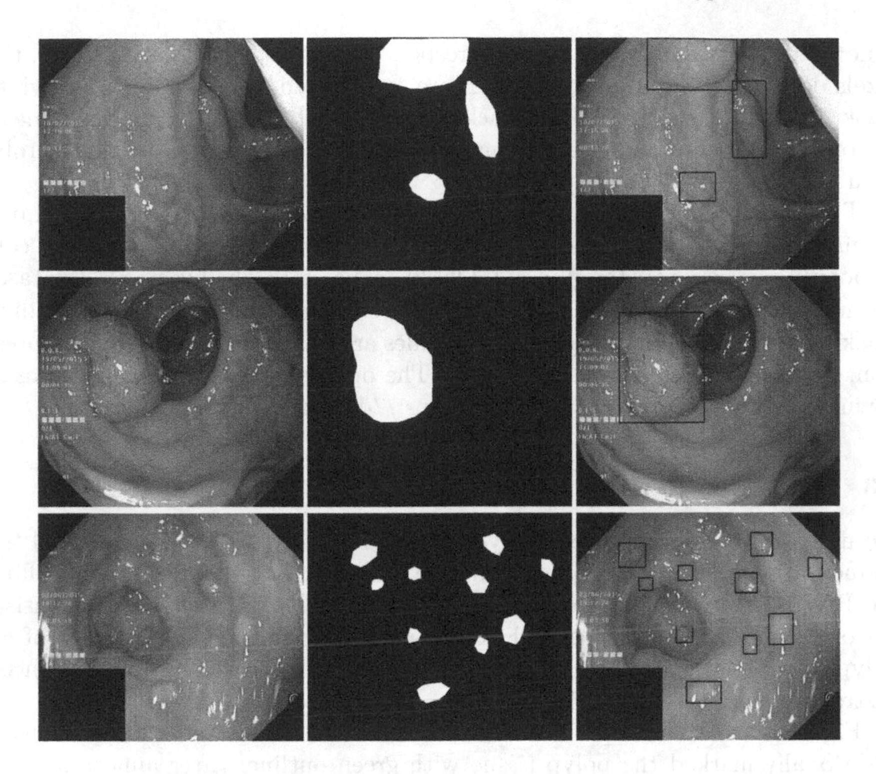

Fig. 2. Examples of polyp images and their corresponding masks from Kvasir-SEG. The third image is generated from the original image using the bounding box information from the JSON file.

findings and endoscopic procedures. A more detailed explanation about each image classes, the data collection procedure and the dataset details can be found in [16].

The Kvasir dataset was used for the Multimedia for Medicine Challenge (the Medico Task) in 2017 [20] and 2018 [17] at the MediaEval Benchmarking Initiative for Multimedia Evaluation[1] to develop and compare methods to reach clinical level performance on multiclass classification of endoscopic findings in the large bowel. However, the dataset was limited to frame classification only, due to only a frame-wise annotations. Thus, Pozdeev et al. [18] trained their model on the CVC-ClinicDB, and tried to predict the segmentation masks for the Kvasir dataset, but could not report the experimental scores because of missing ground truth.

3.2 The Kvasir-SEG Dataset Details

To address the high incidence of colorectal cancer, we selected the polyp class of the Kvasir dataset for the initial investigation. The Kvasir-SEG dataset contains

[1] http://www.multimediaeval.org.

annotated polyp images and their corresponding masks. As shown in Fig. 2, the pixels depicting polyp tissue, the ROI, are represented by the foreground (white mask), while the background (in black) does not contain positive pixels. Some of the original images contain the image of the endoscope position marking probe from the ScopeGuide (Olympus).

The Kvasir-SEG dataset is made up of two folders: one for images and one for masks. Each folder contains 1000 images. The bounding boxes for the corresponding images are stored in a JSON file. Therefore, the kvasir-SEG dataset has image folder, masks folder and JSON file. The image and its corresponding mask have the same filename. The image files are encoded using JPEG compression, and online browsing is facilitated. The open-access dataset can be easily downloaded for research purposes at: https://datasets.simula.no/kvasir-seg/.

3.3 Mask Extraction

We uploaded the entire Kvasir polyp class to Labelbox [22] and created all the segmentations using this application. The Labelbox is a tool used for labelling the ROI in image frames, i.e., the polyp regions for our case. A team consisting of an engineer and a medical doctor manually outlined the margins of all polyps in all 1000 images. The annotations were then reviewed by an experienced gastroenterologist.

Figure 1 shows example frames from the kvasir dataset where we have additionally marked the polyp tissue with green outline. After annotation, we exported the files to generate masks for each annotation. The exported JSON file contained all the information about the image and the coordinate points for generating the mask. To create a mask, we used ROI coordinates to draw contours on an empty black image and fill the contours with white color. The generated masks are a 1-bit color depth images with white foreground and black background. Figure 2 shows example images, their corresponding segmentation masks and bounding boxes from the Kvasir-SEG dataset.

4 Suggested Metrics

Different metrics for evaluating and comparing the performance of the architectures exist. For medical image segmentation tasks, the perhaps most commonly used metrics are Dice coefficient and IoU. These are used in particular for several medical related Kaggle competitions [10]. In this medical image segmentation approach, each pixel of the image either belongs to a polyp or non-polyp region. We calculate the Dice coefficient and mean IoU based on this principle.
Dice coefficient: Dice coefficient is a standard metric for comparing the pixel-wise results between predicted segmentation and ground truth. It is defined as:

$$\text{Dice coefficient}(A, B) = \frac{2 \times |A \cap B|}{|A| + |B|} = \frac{2 \times TP}{2 \times TP + FP + FN} \tag{1}$$

where A signifies the predicted set of pixels and B is the ground truth of the object to be found in the image. Here, TP represents true positive, FP represents false positive, and FN represents the false negative.

Intersection over Union: The Intersection over Union (IoU) is another standard metric to evaluate a segmentation method. The IoU calculates the similarity between predicted (A) and its corresponding ground truth (B) as shown in the equation below:

$$IoU(A, B) = \frac{A \cap B}{A \cup B} = \frac{TP(t)}{TP(t) + FP(t) + FN(t)} \tag{2}$$

In Eq. 2, t is the threshold. At each threshold value t, a precision value is calculated based on the above equation and parameters, which is done by calculating the predicted object to all the ground truth objects. There are other parameters such as recall, specificity, precision, and accuracy which are mostly used for frame-wise image classification tasks. The detailed explanation about these parameters can be found in the Kvasir dataset paper [16].

5 Evaluation

The Kvasir-SEG dataset is intended for research and development of new and improved methods for segmentation, localization, and classification of polyps. To show that the dataset is useful for these purposes, we conducted several experiments, which we will described next.

5.1 Baseline Models

As our baseline, we have conducted initial investigations using two different methods. The first method is based on the efficient FCM [6] unsupervised clustering algorithm. The second method is based on the deep-learning ResUNet [28] architecture, utilizing the advantage of the residual block.

When using basic CNN architectures to predict outcomes in computer-vision tasks, millions of labelled training data are often needed to counteract overfitting and ensuring the model's ability to generalize when tested on new data [9]. Because large datasets of medical images are hard to come by, using CNNs for medical-image segmentation systems remains challenging. Image augmentation techniques [7] and encoder-decoder architecture such as ResUNet [28] are popular methods to use CNNs with smaller training sets.

5.2 Implementation Details

Before applying the FCM algorithm, several pre-processing steps were applied to the dataset. First, we converted the image to grayscale and applied median blur to reduce noise. Then, we applied the Median-based Otsu method [14], which gave us the ROI. Next, we converted image pixels between 0 and 1 and subtracted

Table 1. Quantitative performance of ResUNet model on Kvasir-SEG dataset.

ResUNet	Loss	Dice coefficient	Mean IoU
Train	0.059389	0.940609	0.920957
Validation	0.196520	0.803479	0.792339
Test	0.212236	0.787763	0.777771

the image with its blurred version. We then used a threshold value and created an image with edges in it. Afterwards, we performed the dilation operation, which increases the foreground (white) region of the image. We subtracted edges from the image and clipped the image pixels value between 0 and 1. After that, we reshaped the image into 1D, which is the input to the FCM. Finally, the output of the FCM was reshaped into a 2D binary mask.

For our experiment with the ResUNet model, we used image augmentation techniques like flipping, random crop, scaling, rotation, brightness, cutout, and random erasing to increase the size of our training dataset. After all preprocessing was completed, we resized our images to 320 × 320 pixels. We used 80% of the dataset for training, and 10% for validation. The remaining of 10% was used for testing. We used five convolutional blocks both in the encoder and the decoder of the ResUNet model. The batch size was set to 8, and we trained the model for 150 epochs. The proposed model converged at 91 epochs. We used a Nadam optimizer with the learning rate of 0.0001, $\beta 1$ of 0.9 and $\beta 2$ of 0.999. We chose Dice coefficient as the loss function and Relu as non-linearity. We used a threshold value t of 0.5 to convert the predicted masks pixels to foreground or background.

For our deep-learning implementations, we used the Keras framework [8] and Tensorflow [1] as a backend. We performed our experiment on a single Volta 100 GPU on a powerful Nvidia DGX-2 [6] AI system capable of 2 PFLOPS tensor performance. The system is part of Simula Research Laboratories heterogeneous cluster and has dual Intel(R) Xeon(R) Platinum 8168 CPU@2.70 GHz, 1.5 TB of DDR4-2667 MHz DRAM, 32 TB of NVMe scratch space, and 16 of NVIDIAs latest Volta 100 GPGPUs [7] interconnected using Nvidia's NVlink fully non-blocking crossbars switch capable of 2.4 TB/s of bisectional bandwidth. The system was running Ubuntu 18.04.3 LTS OS and had the latest Cuda 10.1.243 installed.

5.3 Results and Discussions

The FCM clustering algorithm achieved a Dice coefficient of 0.239002 and a mean IoU of 0.314187. The ResUNet model achieved a Dice coefficient of 0.787763 and mean IoU of 0.777771 (see Table 1) using the test dataset. We have included the training, validation and testing scores for the ResUNet model in Table 1. Examples of qualitative result comparisons for the FCM algorithm and ResUNet model on the Kvasir-SEG dataset is shown in the Fig. 3.

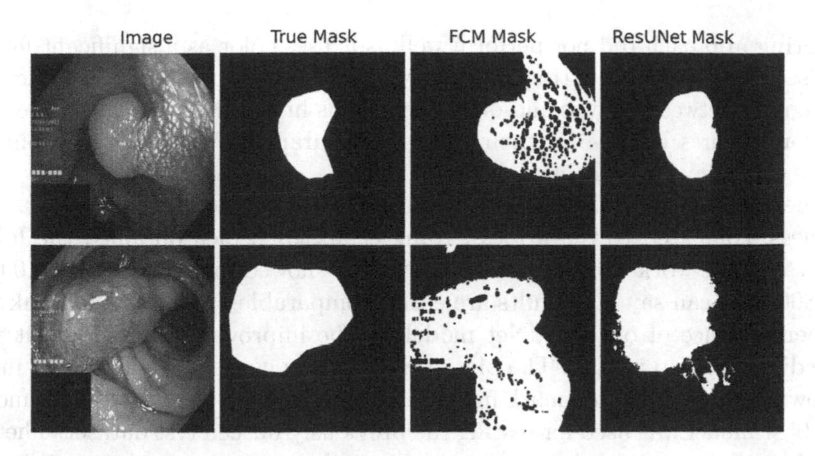

Fig. 3. Qualitative comparison provided by both methods: Coloumn one shows the original image, column two shows the ground truth of the corresponding image. Column three shows the result of FCM clustering and column four shows the results of ResUNet. (Color figure online)

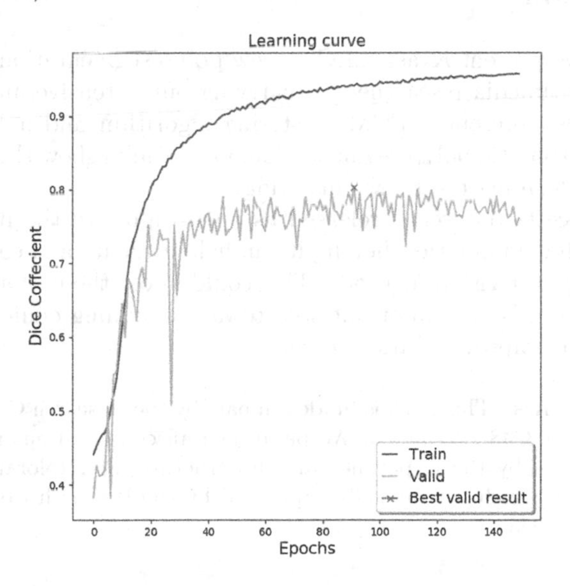

Fig. 4. The learning curve of the proposed ResUNet model on Kvasir-SEG dataset showing Dice coefficient versus number of epochs. (Color figure online)

Considering the quantitative and qualitative results (see Table 1 and Fig. 3), the study shows a superior performance of the ResUNet model over the FCM algorithm in segmenting the polyp pixels. It should be noted that the FCM algorithm uses no data augmentation because it does not have any learning mechanism or learning parameters, whereas the ResUNet utilizes the advantage of the data augmentation techniques. Another important reason why FCM clustering approach did not perform well as it uses color as a significant feature for discriminating normal tissue and polyp. However, in practice, it is difficult to distinguish between polyps and other conditions inside the GI tract on the basis of color features because of their similar appearances. We achieved promising results with the ResUNet model.

There are no directly comparable papers with regards to our results. Nevertheless, compared to the work of Kang et al. [13] which obtained the IoU of 0.6607 and the work of Pozdeev et al. [18] that showed dice ranging from 0.6200 to 0.8600, we can say our results are either comparable or better. We think that the performance of our ResUNet model can be improved by providing it with more diverse polyp images. The plot of the learning curve of the ResUNet model is shown in Fig. 4. The red mark in the learning curve "x" denote the best model. This best model was used for testing the previously unseen test dataset. The presented results are good; however, we believe that more research is required to achieve performance applicable to the clinic.

6 Conclusion

In this paper, we present Kvasir-SEG: a new polyp segmentation dataset developed to aid multimedia researchers in carrying out extensive and reproducible research. We also present a FCM clustering algorithm and a ResUNet-based approach for automatic polyp segmentation. Our results show that the ResUNet model is outperforming the FCM clustering.

The Kvasir-SEG dataset is released as open-source to the multimedia and medical research communities, hoping it can help evaluate and compare existing and future computer vision methods. This could boost the performance of computer vision methods, an important step towards building clinically acceptable CAI methods for improved patient care.

Acknowledgements. This work is funded in part by the Research Council of Norway projects number 263248 (Privaton). We performed all computations in this paper on equipment provided by the Experimental Infrastructure for Exploration of Exascale Computing (eX^3), which is financially supported by the Research Council of Norway under contract 270053.

References

1. Abadi, M., et al.: Tensorflow: a system for large-scale machine learning. In: Proceeding of the ACM Symposium on Operating Systems Design and Implementation (SOSP), pp. 265–283 (2016)
2. Bernal, J., Sánchez, F.J., Fernández-Esparrach, G., Gil, D., Rodríguez, C., Vilariño, F.: WM-DOVA maps for accurate polyp highlighting in colonoscopy: validation vs. saliency maps from physicians. Comput. Med. Imag. Graph. **43**, 99–111 (2015)
3. Bernal, J., Sánchez, J., Vilarino, F.: Towards automatic polyp detection with a polyp appearance model. Pattern Recogn. **45**(9), 3166–3182 (2012)

4. Bernal, J., et al.: Comparative validation of polyp detection methods in video colonoscopy: results from the MICCAI 2015 endoscopic vision challenge. IEEE Trans. Med. Imag. **36**(6), 1231–1249 (2017)
5. Boccardi, M., et al.: Survey of protocols for the manual segmentation of the hippocampus: preparatory steps towards a joint EADC-ADNI harmonized protocol. J. Alzheimer's Dis. **26**(s3), 61–75 (2011)
6. Cai, W., Chen, S., Zhang, D.: Fast and robust fuzzy c-means clustering algorithms incorporating local information for image segmentation. Pattern Recogn. **40**(3), 825–838 (2007)
7. Chollet, F.: Building powerful image classification models using very little data. Keras Blog (2016)
8. Chollet, F.: Keras: The Python Deep Learning Library. Astrophysics Source Code Library (2018)
9. Dravid, A.: Employing deep networks for image processing on small research datasets. Microsc. Today **27**(1), 18–23 (2019)
10. Goldbloom, A., Hamner, B., et al.: Kaggle: your home for data science. Competition, Kaggle Inc. (2019). https://www.kaggle.com. Accessed 12 July 2019
11. Haggar, F.A., Boushey, R.P.: Colorectal cancer epidemiology: incidence, mortality, survival, and risk factors. Clin. Colon Rectal Surg. **22**(04), 191–197 (2009)
12. Kaminski, M.F., et al.: Increased rate of adenoma detection associates with reduced risk of colorectal cancer and death. Gastroenterology **153**(1), 98–105 (2017)
13. Kang, J., Gwak, J.: Ensemble of instance segmentation models for polyp segmentation in colonoscopy images. IEEE Access **7**, 26440–26447 (2019)
14. Otsu, N.: A threshold selection method from gray-level histograms. IEEE Trans. Syst. Man Cybern. **9**(1), 62–66 (1979)
15. Pham, D.L., Xu, C., Prince, J.L.: Current methods in medical image segmentation. Ann. Rev. Biomed. Eng. **2**(1), 315–337 (2000)
16. Pogorelov, K., et al.: Kvasir: a multi-class image dataset for computer aided gastrointestinal disease detection. In: Proceedings of Multimedia Systems Conference (MMSYS), pp. 164–169. ACM (2017)
17. Pogorelov, K., et al.: Medico multimedia task at MediaEval 2018. In: CEUR Workshop Proceedings - Multimedia Benchmark Workshop (MediaEval) (2018)
18. Pozdeev, A.A., Obukhova, N.A., Motyko, A.A.: Automatic analysis of endoscopic images for polyps detection and segmentation. In: IEEE Conference of Russian Young Researchers in Electrical and Electronic Engineering (EIConRus), pp. 1216–1220. IEEE (2019)
19. Riegler, M., et al.: Multimedia and medicine: teammates for better disease detection and survival. In: Proceedings of ACM Multimedia (ACM MM), pp. 968–977. ACM (2016)
20. Riegler, M., et al.: Multimedia for medicine: the medico task at Mediaeval 2017. In: CEUR Workshop Proceedings - Multimedia Benchmark Workshop (MediaEval) (2017)
21. Rundle, A.G., Lebwohl, B., Vogel, R., Levine, S., Neugut, A.I.: Colonoscopic screening in average-risk individuals ages 40 to 49 vs 50 to 59 years. Gastroenterology **134**(5), 1311–1315 (2008)
22. Sharma, M., Rasmuson, D., Rieger, B., Kjelkerud, D., et al.: Labelbox: the best way to create and manage training data. Software, LabelBox Inc. (2019). https://www.labelbox.com/. Accessed 21 May 2019
23. Silva, J., Histace, A., Romain, O., Dray, X., Granado, B.: Toward embedded detection of polyps in wce images for early diagnosis of colorectal cancer. Int. J. Comput. Assist. Radiol. Surg. **9**(2), 283–293 (2014)

24. Tajbakhsh, N., Gurudu, S.R., Liang, J.: Automated polyp detection in colonoscopy videos using shape and context information. IEEE Trans. Med. Imag. **35**(2), 630–644 (2015)
25. Torre, L.A., Bray, F., Siegel, R.L., Ferlay, J., Lortet-Tieulent, J., Jemal, A.: Global cancer statistics, 2012. CA: Cancer J. Clin. **65**(2), 87–108 (2015)
26. Van Rijn, J.C., Reitsma, J.B., Stoker, J., Bossuyt, P.M., Van Deventer, S.J., Dekker, E.: Polyp miss rate determined by tandem colonoscopy: a systematic review. Am. J. Gastroenterol. **101**(2), 343 (2006)
27. Visser, M., et al.: Inter-rater agreement in glioma segmentations on longitudinal MRI. NeuroImage: Clin. **22**, 101727 (2019)
28. Zhang, Z., Liu, Q., Wang, Y.: Road extraction by deep residual U-net. IEEE Geosci. Rem. Sens. Lett. **15**(5), 749–753 (2018)

Rethinking the Test Collection Methodology for Personal Self-tracking Data

Frank Hopfgartner[1(✉)], Cathal Gurrin[2], and Hideo Joho[3]

[1] University of Sheffield, Sheffield, UK
f.hopfgartner@sheffield.ac.uk
[2] Dublin City University, Dublin, Ireland
[3] University of Tsukuba, Tsukuba, Japan

Abstract. While vast volumes of personal data are being gathered daily by individuals, the MMM community has not really been tackling the challenge of developing novel retrieval algorithms for this data, due to the challenges of getting access to the data in the first place. While initial efforts have taken place on a small scale, it is our conjecture that a new evaluation paradigm is required in order to make progress in analysing, modeling and retrieving from personal data archives. In this position paper, we propose a new model of Evaluation-as-a-Service that re-imagines the test collection methodology for personal multimedia data in order to address the many challenges of releasing test collections of personal multimedia data.

Keywords: Lifelogging · Evaluation · Self-tracking

1 Introduction

The Information Retrieval community has a long and rich tradition of creating and using reusable test collections which, if carefully curated, can support valid comparative evaluation of multiple systems and techniques. Within the past two decades, we have seen the emergence of various workshops and conferences that support community driven benchmarking activities. TREC [38], TRECVid [3], ImageCLEF [23], MediaEval [26], etc., all have played a part in supporting the community to generate test collections and coordinate such international comparative benchmarking efforts. In most cases, these activities have focused on the release of test collections that support the retrieval of online content, such as web pages, online or professional videos, blogs, and other crawlable content. In effect these can be considered to be DtA (Data-to-Algorithm) evaluation efforts where the test collection is centrally gathered and organised before being sent to participants to be used to evaluate their algorithms.

However, most of these DtA evaluation efforts have ignored user-generated content such as self-tracking or lifelogging data. This is due to many reasons,

Y. M. Ro et al. (Eds.): MMM 2020, LNCS 11962, pp. 463–474, 2020.
https://doi.org/10.1007/978-3-030-37734-2_38

such as the difficulty of gathering personal user data, privacy concerns or data governance/legal issues. It is our conjecture that the community is consequently failing to address the very real need of managing modern personal data, such as personal photo archives, email archives, or even health-data archives. As a consequence, the data created by individuals every day is not being well served by the current generation of test collections and benchmarking activities. While there have been some initial efforts, such as the lifelogging challenge at NTCIR [16], or the lifelogging tasks at ImageCLEF [7] and MediaEval, even these can be considered to be pseudo-personal data challenges, since the test collections involved (lifelogs) are typically small in nature (from a few individuals). Furthermore, due to the constraints of DtA evaluation, the datasets have, by necessity, been filtered to remove content such as identifiable entities or content that the data gatherers were unwilling to make public. Clearly, if the community is to assist the real problem of individuals managing their own personal data collections, then an alternative approach is required that facilitates researchers to evaluate algorithms while reducing the risks inherent in releasing personal data test collections. Addressing this need, the contribution of this position paper is to propose an alternative approach, based on replacing the DtA evaluation effort with an AtD (Algorithm-to-Data) effort. This contribution is framed by considering the challenges of releasing a rich personal data archive for conventional DtA evaluation. The paper is structured as follows: In Sect. 2, we provide an overview of related work to set this position paper into perspective. Section 3 discusses steps necessary to enable collaborative research on personal data. The paper concludes with a discussion on future work in Sect. 4.

2 Background

While many forms of personal data exist, passively captured data, such as self-tracking data [8] or lifelog data [9], are likely to pose the biggest research challenges due to their diverse nature, volume and difficulty of managing. Self-tracking is concerned with individual-driven quantisation of some aspect of human life experience by passively (or actively) capturing data in order to achieve some form of self enhancement or betterment, whereas lifelogging is more focused on the indiscriminate passive capture of a wide range of personal data, from audio or visual data, right up to the total capture proposed in the MyLifeBits project [10].

Focusing on self-tracking data, this section provides a literature survey on the use of such data for research purposes. We first provide an introduction to self-tracking data in Sect. 2.1. Section 2.2 then describes ongoing efforts of archiving personal data. An overview of prior efforts on the creation of test collections for research is given in Sect. 2.3.

2.1 Self-tracking Data

Self-tracking applications are usually developed to "help people collect personally relevant information for the purpose of self-reflection and gaining self-knowledge" [27]. In clinical psychology, the act of collecting personal data is also referred to as self-monitoring [25]. Inspired by the work of Gurrin et al. in [13], we list different categories of self-tracking data which can be applied at the time of writing:

- Passive visual capture. Utilising wearable devices such as the Narrative Clip[1], the Microsoft SenseCam [20], or a first-generation Augmented Reality glasses, will allow for the continuous and passive capture of life activities as a sequence of digital images. Studies suggest that passive visual capture can be employed to help patients to cope with various memory difficulties, such as offsetting the effects of early stage dementia [32].
- Passive audio capture. Audio capture could allow for the identification of events or identification people who were speaking. Audio can easily be captured by smartphones. Audio recordings such as the ICSI Meeting Corpus [24] have played an essential role in the field of speech research.
- Personal biometrics. Sensing devices are becoming more common and widely used by self-trackers as it allow them to monitor their sleep duration, distance traveled, caloric output, and other biometrics data. The popularity of wearable devices such as Fitbit or Garmin suggest that capturing biometrics is a very common activity.
- Mobile device context. This refers to using the phone to continuously and passively capture the user's context (e.g., location, movement, or acceleration). Combined with smart watches, mobile devices are able to capture a detailed trace of life activity and can be used e.g., to adapt information services [29].
- Communication activities. This refers to the phone or PC passively logging messages, emails, phone calls, or other means of communications. Tracking such activities help us to better understand the impact of technology on our communication behaviour (e.g., [2]).
- Data creation/access activities. Logging data consumed and created on a computer, for example, words typed, web pages visited, videos watched and so on. Collated analysis of such data can provide valuable insights on users' interests (e.g., [39]).
- Environmental context and media. Other sources such as external sensor data or surveillance cameras could also be employed for self-tracking.
- Manual logging. This refers to the manual or direct logging of activity that is initiated by the user, for example, video recording, personal logs and diaries.

2.2 Personal Data Archiving

As evident by the emergence of self-tracking communities such as The Quantified Self movement[2] or parkrun [36], more and more people now own personal data as described above. As Hopfgartner and Davidson [21] point out though, although self-tracking has become very popular, efforts to archive such data is very limited

[1] http://getnarrative.com.
[2] https://quantifiedself.com.

in scale. They argue that this is mainly due to several challenges that need to be resolved first, including the creation of data, its active use, appraisal & selection, data transfer, storage & preservation, and access & re-use.

First organised efforts by the public sector to address these challenges can be observed in Japan where, in July 2019, the Information Technology Federation of Japan certified two companies as "information banks" to allow them to collect and use personal data for business purposes. This certification is based on the Japanese government's guidelines compiled in June 2018 for information banking services to utilize personal information while protecting privacy for individuals[3]. This is an important movement for personal data since, just like a monetary bank, if a user prefers, they can delegate the collection and management of their personal data to a third-party institution, rather than managing by themselves. Although this could facilitate the use of personal data for business purposes, it could impact the development of community-based approaches to personal data.

Another development is the implementation of trading market platforms for personal data. For example, the company EverySense[4] has introduced a platform to connect a business entity in need for relevant data to develop or enhance their services and products, with another party or individuals who agree to use sensors to collect and sell such data. This type of platform aims to trade various sensor data including personally collected data, in several domains such as healthcare, construction, car manufacturing, sports, or agriculture. This could include blood pressure, step counter, car navigation, smartphone, wearable devices, temperature, noise level, and so forth. Such a platform has a significant implication for the future of personal data since it could directly relate to the monetary benefit at a scale much bigger than what we have now.

Concluding from these developments, we argue that there are opportunities emerging that can result in the creation of centrally managed personal archives. An interesting research challenge of today is to explore how these archives can be used for further research. Following the argumentation of Chang et al. [6], we argue that this can be of particular importance in the field of computational social science where behavioural data is analysed to gain insights on society. Similar thoughts are presented by Sellen and Whittaker [33] who outline the usage domains of personal lifelog and sensor data. In the next section, we point to a number of initial efforts in the space.

2.3 Personal Data Test Collections

For decades, the information retrieval research community has been at the forefront of exploring methods to enable reproducible and comparable research. As evidence, we point to success stories such as the creation of shared test collections and the development of widely accepted evaluation metrics. Please refer to Harman [17] for an historic overview of this development.

[3] https://www.nippon.com/en/news/yjj2019070800965/aeon-unit-sumitomo-mitsui-trust-bank-certified-as-1st-ever-info-banks.html.

[4] https://every-sense.com/eng/.

In the context of the creation of test collections consisting of personal sensor/lifelog data, the first thoroughly annotated dataset was developed for the Lifelog task of the Japanese-based evaluation conference NTCIR-12 [14]. This dataset consists of 79 days of data from three lifeloggers, totalling around 88k filtered and anonymised images with substantial metadata (locations, activities). This first dataset was followed by another richer dataset for the NTCIR-13 competition [16], this time grouping visual, activity, biometric (e.g., heart rate, galvanic skin response, calorie burn, steps, etc.), location and metadata information. This new dataset consists of 90 days of data from two lifeloggers, totalling around 114k filtered and anonymised images. Subsequently, following the trend in society for richer personal data, a third related collection was released for NTCIR-14 [16], which consisted of 81k filtered and anonymised images from two users, spanning over 43 days, with rich personal activities and biometric data, which was focused on quantising the health, activities and diet of the two individuals.

While such datasets may have addressed the challenges of supporting initial efforts at comparative benchmarking for retrieval and analytics tasks, as outlined in the relevant overview papers from the NTICR competitions [14–16], they are still limited by the focus on a small number of (two or three) individuals and the datasets are anonymised in order to meet ethical, legal and privacy-by-design [5] principles. In fact, anonymisation of such datasets requires that the organisers of benchmarking efforts ignore the significant use-cases of data retrieval that require named individuals, which would be an important aspect of any lifelog retrieval system. While they serve their purpose, to fully address the challenges of personal data analytics and retrieval, larger archives of raw data are required.

We note some efforts at gathering limited or focused datasets from larger numbers of individuals. In most cases, these datasets have gathered egocentric video or lifelog image data. The Nagoya-COI [18] dataset is a collection of multimodal data recorded by one long-term and 18 short-term subjects, containing accelerometer, sound and video information captured by a smartphone and a video-camera. Heruzzo et al. [19] propose the LAP dataset, where they address the problem of analyzing socializing, eating and sedentary lifestyle patterns by recognizing the lifelogger's activities. In total, they gathered 45k images from four different people in consecutive days and labeled them for diet-related activities. Lidon et al. [28] created a dataset with 10 day lifelogs from 5 different subjects producing a total of 7.1k images. A larger dataset named EgoSum+gaze [40] was generated by five subjects with 21 videos, each lasting between 15 and 90 min, adding up to about 15 hours of data. Miyanishi et al. [30] propose a daily living question-answering dataset which contains 20 continuous activities in six different places, each performed ten times, by eight subjects. Aghaei et al. [1] released the EgoSocialStyle dataset of 130k images from eight users, for the purpose of characterising the social patterns of a person relying exclusively on visual data. UT EE [37] gathered and crowd source annotated 27 videos from nine users, covering 14 hours in order to detecting the wearer's engagement with the surrounding environment. An event segmentation dataset was published by

Gupta and Gurrin [12], consisting of 14k images from ten participants. Each participant segmented their day into a set of activities, which was then labeled as the ground truth data for subsequent evaluation.

Where larger numbers of users are involved, in some cases the data released was limited to a feature vector, as opposed to the raw data, or the data was not released at all. For example, the R3 dataset [31] covers 57 users, over a period of 1,723 days (1.5M images) and was used for event segmentation. However, due to privacy concerns, only the extracted visual features were ever publicly released. In the KidsCam dataset [35], 169 children captured 1.5M egocentric images with the purpose of detecting the presence of food and non-alcoholic beverages marketing and availability. The dataset was manually annotated with an custom vocabulary, but it was never released for community use, due to the sensitive nature of the data. It is the authors conjecture that few of these datasets are of sufficient volume or completeness to fully support the research community. While the NTCIR datasets are among the richest and largest, they are limited to a small number of individual data gatherers. At the same time, the KidsCam dataset was extensive in numbers, but limited in media (image and location) and could not be released. Additionally, all of these datasets are traditional centrally-hosted DtA collections where willing volunteers gather data and release datasets, which pose major challenges for researchers to release for community use, as outlined in the following section.

3 Enabling Collaborative Research on Personal Data

Above efforts illustrate that there is a clear desire in the research community to perform further research on self-tracking data. However, as has been shown, there are several shortcomings that hinder us in exploring open research challenges further. We argue that while it would be preferable to release datasets to the community in a conventional DtA manner, that are rich, non-anonymised and sourced from a large number of people, there are a number of reasons, for this not happening. In this section, we first elaborate further on the challenges for releasing personal test collections in a conventional manner (Sect. 3.1). In Sect. 3.2, we then argue to employ Evaluation-as-a-Service as an option to address these issues and challenges. Finally, in Sect. 3.3, we describe what an evaluation campaign on self-tracking data employing the Evaluation-as-a-Service paradigm would look like.

3.1 The Challenges of Releasing Personal Datasets in a Conventional DtA Manner

Prior efforts at releasing test collections of personal data faced a number of challenges, that ultimately reduced the number of such collections available. In particular, we can identify the following challenges from past work:

- Willing Volunteers. It has always proven difficult to recruit willing volunteers to gather data in a free-living, long-term environment.

- Legal Constraints. Recent data legislation (in Europe and elsewhere) means that the risks for challenge organisers are significantly higher once any form of personal data is released. While efforts at pseudo-anonymisation have been performed, it is likely that any effort to balance anonymisation and usefulness of data will mean that individuals could potentially be identified in the data.
- Maintaining Control of Test Collections. Legal and ethical expectations require that data owners (creators) maintain control of their data, so that it can be deleted after its lifetime, or upon request from a subject in the collection. Once a test collection is released to the public, even with comprehensive data agreements in place, the control of the data is effectively lost by the organisers and owners.
- Data Pre-processing. Data anonymisation efforts, e.g., as presented in [4], can go a long way toward the solving of legal and ethical constraints, however these occur at the expense of test collection usefulness, such efforts are actually very costly in terms of human effort. Cross-checking and ensuring effective anonymisation is still a human process, even if the anonymisation (e.g., blurring) algorithms are automatic. Legal requirements insist that state-of-the-art tools and reasonable effort are required to ensure appropriate levels of annonymisation.
- Ethical Data Release. To release a personal data from an academic or industrial source would usually require the prior-approval of an institutional ethics committee, which may not always be possible, due to the sensitive nature of the personal data.

Of course, there are benefits to the implementation of centrally controlled DtA test collections and evaluation campaigns, such as the ability of organisers to pre-process, filter and manually ensure accuracy and coverage of the data. It is also easier to control the process of creating appropriate research tasks and sourcing carefully curated information needs. Nevertheless, we argue that above barriers have often been to hard to overcome and therefore hampered further efforts to create and release public test collections. In the next section, we discuss how a methodology referred to as Evaluation-as-a-Service can help us to move one step forward.

3.2 Data Banks as Evaluation Platforms

Looking at above challenges, it is clear that the public release of self-tracking data for research is far more problematic than the release of test collections that do not reveal any personal information. We therefore have to explore options on how to allow further research on self-tracking data while at the same time guaranteeing and respecting users' privacy.

Considering recent developments on the establishment of data banks as a central facility to archive personal data, we argue that these archives could be used to gather data from large numbers of people, hence solving the challenge of finding users willing to share their data as outlined above. The potential of gaining access to this data depends on several factors. Most importantly, users have to be willing for their data can be used for research purposes. This is in particular important to address ethical issues as highlighted above. As outlined in Sect. 2, first services have entered the market now that allow users to sell their data. It is yet to be seen whether such services will be accepted by society and whether self-tracking data from a sufficient number of people could be employed for research purposes.

Addressing the challenge of maintaining control of data in the context of shared evaluation campaigns, Hopfgartner et al. [22] outline a new evaluation paradigm referred to as Evaluation-as-a-Service (EaaS). The basic idea of EaaS is to employ the so-called "Algorithms-to-Data paradigm" (AtD) rather than the established "Data-to-Algorithm" (DtA) approach, that we have considered thus far in this paper. The AtD paradigm would also facilitate comparative evaluation of systems and approaches using the same test collections, but in a less problematic manner. The difference between these two paradigms is as follows: The DtA paradigm is based on the approach of allowing researchers to download test collections and then run their experiments on their own IT infrastructure. Almost all evaluation campaigns that have been organised in the past few decades follow this approach. The AtD paradigm is approaching this from a different perspective. Rather than allowing full download of a test collection, participants are required to deploy their algorithms on a central IT infrastructure. So instead of having to give up control over the spreading of the collection, evaluation campaigns following the EaaS methodology can lock up their data on a central server where it can only be accessed for the purpose outlined in the evaluation protocol. As the authors clarify in [22], the benefits of this approach is manifold and for a detailed discussion, we refer to their paper. In the context of this paper, we consider the ability to maintain control over the data and to protect users' privacy the main benefits of employing this approach. So instead of having to perform all the privacy-preserving steps outlined by Gurrin et al. [13], EaaS allows us to run algorithms on complete and unmodified datasets. In addition, since access to the full data is restricted to the algorithms, there is no need for tedious data cleaning. Careful configuration of the evaluation service can guarantee that no data is released without the consent of the data owner. It is also feasible then, to gather real-world information needs from the central IT infrastructure, as would be done by a real-world search engine evaluating ranking algorithm variations.

Summarising, in order to address the challenges that hinder the release of test collections containing personal data, we argue for the application of the EaaS paradigm where data banks play a key role in guaranteeing control over the data to protect users privacy. In the next section, we describe how a data challenge that employs this methodology could look like.

3.3 Toward a New Personal Data Challenge

By applying the AtD evaluation, we are able to facilitate the same comparative benchmarking efforts that the research community is accustomed to, while at the same time reducing the burden of creating and sharing a suitable dataset.

Assuming that users are willing to keep their data with data banks, the challenge is now how to use these data banks as the backbone of a privacy-preserving EaaS infrastructure.

The first challenge is to employ an entity to serve as data bank. This has to be an entity that is able to attract large numbers of self-trackers, and at the same time gained their trust to handle their data with care.

Next, this data bank needs to run an EaaS platform. With the open source TIRA platform [11], a AtD solution already exists that allows researchers to upload software and data collections to the cloud, where the software can then be executed remotely. Technically, this is done by asking participants to deploy binaries within virtual machines, which are then executed on the platform. Apart from allowing these binaries to operate on a protected data collection, the platform also provides a web front-end to display evaluation results. A similar idea is presented by [34] who propose to rely on the cloud for training privacy-preserving activity recognition models using personal sensor data.

Having both data and infrastructure in place, a more demanding challenge becomes the need for the creation of realistic information needs with relevance judgements if an IR-like task is to be introduced. At prior evaluation campaigns that dealt with personal data (e.g., the NTCIR Lifelog task), the task of identifying information needs was given to the creator of the personal data. The main argument for this was that it is the user who is most familiar with their own data and therefore is most suitable to identify suitable known-item search tasks. Potentially, however, this is a very time consuming task as the creator needs to reflect on their behaviour and go over the dataset to identify suitable tasks, often generating complete relevance judgements in the process, or in some cases, pooled judgements. If a new data challenge uses data shared by users of data banks, the burden of formulating information needs should be kept to a very minimum and real-world user interactions with their archives, could be used as the basis of the queries and relevance judgments. Additionally, an automated analysis of the data collection might help to identify additional challenges and tasks for the research community to tackle.

4 Conclusion and Future Work

In this position paper, we discussed the challenge of enabling research on personal self-tracking data. After providing a detailed overview of prior research on the creation and use of self-tracking data for research, we identify issues that emerge when creating test collections of self-tracking data as commonly used by shared evaluation campaigns. This includes in particular the challenge of finding self-trackers willing to share their data, legal constraints that require expensive data preparation and cleaning before a potential release to the public, as well as ethical considerations. In order to address these challenges, we then argue to employ Evaluation-as-a-Service as a novel evaluation paradigm to enable collaborative research on personal self-tracking data. Evaluation-as-a-Service relies on the idea of a central data infrastructure that guarantees full protection of the data, while at the same time allowing algorithms to operate on this protected data. We further highlight the importance of data banks in this scenario. Finally, we briefly outline technical aspects that would allow setting up a shared evaluation campaign on self-tracking data.

As future work, we intend to explore this idea further by setting up an evaluation campaign on self-tracking data that fully implements the Evaluation-as-a-Service methodology.

References

1. Aghaei, M., Dimiccoli, M., Ferrer, C.C., Radeva, P.: Towards social pattern characterization in egocentric photo-streams. Comput. Vis. Image Underst. **171**, 104–117 (2018)
2. Alsuhaibani, A., Cox, A., Hopfgartner, F.: Investigating the role of social media during the transition of international students to the UK. In: iConference 2019 Poster Proceedings, IDEALS (2019)
3. Awad, G., et al.: TRECVID 2018: benchmarking video activity detection, video captioning and matching, video storytelling linking and video search. In: TRECVid 2018: Proceedings of the TREC Video Retrieval Evaluation Conference. NIST, Gaithersburg (2018)
4. Bailer, W.: Face swapping for solving collateral privacy issues in multimedia analytics. In: MMM 2019, pp. 169–177 (2019)
5. Cavoukian, A.: Privacy by design: the 7 foundational principles. Implementation and mapping of fair information practices. Information and Privacy Commissioner of Ontario, Canada (2010)
6. Chang, R.M., Kauffman, R.J., Kwon, Y.: Understanding the paradigm shift to computational social science in the presence of big data. Decis. Support Syst. **63**, 67–80 (2014)
7. Dang-Nguyen, D.T., Piras, L., Riegler, M., Zhou, L., Lux, M., Gurrin, C.: Overview of ImageCLEFlifelog 2018: daily living understanding and lifelog moment retrieval. In: CLEF2018 Working Notes, Avignon, France (2018)
8. Dix, A., Ellis, G.: The Alan Walks Wales Dataset: Quantified Self and Open Data, pp. 56–66. Open data as open educational resources: case studies of emerging practice, The Open University (2015)
9. Dodge, M., Kitchin, R.: 'Outlines of a world coming into existence': pervasive computing and the ethics of forgetting. Environ. Plann. B Plann. Design **34**(3), 431–445 (2007). https://doi.org/10.1068/b32041t
10. Gemmell, J., Bell, G., Lueder, R., Drucker, S., Wong, C.: Mylifebits: fulfilling the memex vision. In: Proceedings of the Tenth ACM International Conference on Multimedia, MULTIMEDIA 2002, pp. 235–238. ACM, New York (2002)
11. Gollub, T., Stein, B., Burrows, S.: Ousting ivory tower research: towards a web framework for providing experiments as a service. In: The 35th International ACM SIGIR Conference on Research and Development in Information Retrieval, SIGIR 2012, Portland, OR, USA, 12–16 August 2012, pp. 1125–1126 (2012)
12. Gupta, R., Gurrin, C.: Approaches for event segmentation of visual lifelog data. In: Schoeffmann, K., et al. (eds.) MMM 2018. LNCS, vol. 10704, pp. 581–593. Springer, Cham (2018). https://doi.org/10.1007/978-3-319-73603-7_47
13. Gurrin, C., Albatal, R., Joho, H., Ishii, K.: A privacy by design approach to lifelogging. In: Digital Enlightenment Yearbook 2014, pp. 49–73. IOS Press (2014)

14. Gurrin, C., Joho, H., Hopfgartner, F., Zhou, L., Albatal, R.: Overview of NTCIR-12 lifelog task. In: Kando, N., Kishida, K., Kato, M.P., Yamamoto, S. (eds.) Proceedings of the 12th NTCIR Conference on Evaluation of Information Access Technologies, pp. 354–360 (2016)
15. Gurrin, C., et al.: Overview of NTCIR-13 lifelog-2 task. In: Proceedings of the 13th NTCIR Conference on Evaluation of Information Access Technologies (2017)
16. Gurrin, C., et al.: Overview of the NTCIR-14 lifelog-3 task. In: Online Proceedings of the Fourteenth NTCIR Conference (NTCIR-14), NII (2019)
17. Harman, D.: Information retrieval: the early years. Found. Trends Inf. Retrieval **13**(5), 425–577 (2019)
18. Hayashi, T., Nishida, M., Kitaoka, N., Toda, T., Takeda, K.: Daily activity recognition with large-scaled real-life recording datasets based on deep neural network using multi-modal signals. IEICE Trans. Fundam. Electron. Commun. Comput. Sci. **E101.A**, 199–210 (2018)
19. Herruzo, P., Portell, L., Soto, A., Remeseiro, B.: Analyzing first-person stories based on socializing, eating and sedentary patterns. In: Battiato, S., Farinella, G.M., Leo, M., Gallo, G. (eds.) ICIAP 2017. LNCS, vol. 10590, pp. 109–119. Springer, Cham (2017). https://doi.org/10.1007/978-3-319-70742-6_10
20. Hodges, S., et al.: SenseCam: a retrospective memory aid. In: Dourish, P., Friday, A. (eds.) UbiComp 2006. LNCS, vol. 4206, pp. 177–193. Springer, Heidelberg (2006). https://doi.org/10.1007/11853565_11
21. Hopfgartner, F., Davidson, J.: Digital preservation and curation of self-tracking data: a position paper. In: Proceedings of the 1st Workshop on Knowledge Discovery and User Modelling for Smart Cities Co-located with 24th ACM SIGKDD Conference on Knowledge Discovery and Data Mining, UMCit at KDD 2018, London, United Kingdom, 20 August 2018, pp. 1–5 (2018)
22. Hopfgartner, F.: Evaluation-as-a-service for the computational sciences: overview and outlook. J. Data Inf. Quality **10**(4), 15:1–15:32 (2018)
23. Ionescu, B., et al.: ImageCLEF 2019: multimedia retrieval in lifelogging, medical, nature, and security applications. In: Azzopardi, L., Stein, B., Fuhr, N., Mayr, P., Hauff, C., Hiemstra, D. (eds.) ECIR 2019. LNCS, vol. 11438, pp. 301–308. Springer, Cham (2019). https://doi.org/10.1007/978-3-030-15719-7_40
24. Janin, A., et al.: The ICSI meeting corpus. In: ICASSP 2003, April 2003
25. Korotitisch, W.J., Nelson-Gray, R.O.: An overview of self-monitoring research in assessment and treatment. Psychol. Assess. **11**, 415–425 (1999)
26. Larson, M. (eds.): Working Notes Proceedings of the MediaEval 2018 Workshop, Sophia Antipolis, France, 29–31 October 2018, CEUR Workshop Proceedings, vol. 2283 (2018). CEUR-WS.org
27. Li, I., Dey, A.K., Forlizzi, J.: A stage-based model of personal informatics systems. In: Proceedings of the 28th International Conference on Human Factors in Computing Systems, CHI 2010, Atlanta, Georgia, USA, 10–15 April 2010, pp. 557–566 (2010)
28. Lidon, A., Bolaños, M., Dimiccoli, M., Radeva, P., Garolera, M., Giró, X.: Semantic summarization of egocentric photo stream events. In: LTA@MM (2017)
29. Lorenz, F., et al.: Countering contextual bias in TV watching behavior: introducing social trend as external contextual factor in TV recommenders. In: Proceedings of the 2017 ACM International Conference on Interactive Experiences for TV and Online Video, Hilversum, The Netherlands, 14–16 June 2017, pp. 21–30 (2017)
30. Miyanishi, T., Hirayama, J., Kanemura, A., Kawanabe, M.: Answering mixed type questions about daily living episodes. In: Proceedings of the 27th International Joint Conference on Artificial Intelligence, IJCAI 2018, pp. 4265–4271 (2018)

31. Garcia del Molino, A., Lim, J.H., Tan, A.H.: Predicting visual context for unsupervised event segmentation in continuous photo-streams. In: ACM Multimedia Conference (ACMMM 2018), MM 2018, pp. 10–17. ACM, New York (2018)
32. Piasek, P.: Case Studies in Therapeutic SenseCam Use Aimed at Identity Maintenance in Early Stage Dementia. Ph.D. thesis, Dublin City University (2015)
33. Sellen, A.J., Whittaker, S.: Beyond total capture: a constructive critique of lifelogging. Commun. ACM **53**(5), 70–77 (2010)
34. Servia-Rodriguez, S., Wang, L., Zhao, J., Mortier, R., Haddadi, H.: Privacy-preserving personal model training. In: ACM/IEEE International Conference on Internet of Things Design and Implementation, pp. 153–164 (2018)
35. Smeaton, A.F., et al.: Semantic indexing of wearable camera images: Kids'Cam concepts. In: Proceedings of the 2016 ACM Workshop on Vision and Language Integration Meets Multimedia Fusion (2016)
36. Stevinson, C., Wiltshire, G., Hickson, M.: Facilitating participation in health-enhancing physical activity: a qualitative study of parkrun. Int. J. Behav. Med. **22**(2), 170–177 (2015)
37. Su, Y.C., Grauman, K.: Detecting engagement in egocentric video. In: Proceedings of the European Conference on Computer Vision (ECCV) (2016)
38. Voorhees, E.M., Harman, D.K.: TREC: Experiment and Evaluation in Information Retrieval. The MIT Press, Cambridge (Digital Libraries and Electronic Publishing) (2005)
39. Walsh, D., Clough, P., Hall, M.M., Hopfgartner, F., Foster, J., Kontonatsios, G.: Analysis of transaction logs from National Museums Liverpool. In: Doucet, A., Isaac, A., Golub, K., Aalberg, T., Jatowt, A. (eds.) TPDL 2019. LNCS, vol. 11799, pp. 84–98. Springer, Cham (2019). https://doi.org/10.1007/978-3-030-30760-8_7
40. Xu, J., Mukherjee, L., Li, Y., Warner, J., Rehg, J.M., Singh, V.: Gaze-enabled egocentric video summarization via constrained submodular maximization. In: Proceedings of CVPR (2015)

Experiences and Insights from the Collection of a Novel Multimedia EEG Dataset

Graham Healy(✉), Zhengwei Wang, Tomas Ward, Alan Smeaton, and Cathal Gurrin

Insight Centre for Data Analytics, Dublin City University, Glasnevin, Dublin, Ireland
{graham.healy,zhengwei.wang,tomas.ward,alan.smeaton,cathal.gurrin}@dcu.ie

Abstract. There is a growing interest in utilising novel signal sources such as EEG (Electroencephalography) in multimedia research. When using such signals, subtle limitations are often not readily apparent without significant domain expertise. Multimedia research outputs incorporating EEG signals can fail to be replicated when only minor modifications have been made to an experiment or seemingly unimportant (or unstated) details are changed. This can lead to overoptimistic or overpessimistic viewpoints on the potential real-world utility of these signals in multimedia research activities. This paper describes an EEG/MM dataset and presents a summary of distilled experiences and knowledge gained during the preparation (and utilisiation) of the dataset that supported a collaborative neural-image labelling benchmarking task. The goal of this task was to collaboratively identify machine learning approaches that would support the use of EEG signals in areas such as image labelling and multimedia modeling or retrieval. The contributions of this paper can be listed thus; a template experimental paradigm is proposed (along with datasets and a baseline system) upon which researchers can explore multimedia image labelling using a brain-computer interface, learnings regarding commonly encountered issues (and useful signals) when conducting research that utilises EEG in multimedia contexts are provided, and finally insights are shared on how an EEG dataset was used to support a collaborative neural-image labelling benchmarking task and the valuable experiences gained.

Keywords: Brain-computer interface · Electroencephalography · RSVP

1 Introduction

EEG (Electroencephalography) has recently become an accessible method to support the building and operation of BCI (Brain-Computer Interface) applications. While the initial use of such techniques began in clinical/rehabilitative settings for the purposes of augmenting communication and control, a recent

Y. M. Ro et al. (Eds.): MMM 2020, LNCS 11962, pp. 475–486, 2020.
https://doi.org/10.1007/978-3-030-37734-2_39

trend has been to use such signals and methods in novel domains, such as image annotation, which relies on the identification of target brain events to trigger semi-automated image labeling [5,11,14,18]. This trend is particularly relevant to multimedia and HII (Human-Information Interaction) communities because in recent years EEG has demonstrated its potential for several applications including annotation of multimedia content, identifying when a user's attention is drawn to something in the real world, or as a source of wearable sensor data to be indexed for later retrieval or analysis.

EEG signals when used in a multimedia application can often be naively expected to carry meaningful information that will directly measure a particular mental state or concept. Many multimedia researchers embark on a course of research intending to use EEG signals without a clear understanding of which phenomena in the signal should be useful. In such circumstances, it is often quickly realised that the signals offer little utility. Conversely, a naively applied off-the-shelf machine-learning strategy to an arbitrary selection of features from EEG might not readily reveal if the source of the useful information is of neural origin or from non-neural artefacts imparted onto the EEG (e.g. eye movements), therefore it can be erroneously assumed that since EEG was used the only explanation is that the useful signals are directly of a neural origin.

EEG data is rife with sources of variability including those related to the task, the environment and the participants themselves. Moreover, EEG is typically contaminated by non-neural sources of activity emerging from the body such as eye movements (EOG - Electrooculography), facial movement (EMG - Electromyography) and ECG (Electrocardiography). These signals are typically orders of magnitude larger than EEG phenomena, and can be difficult to disentangle from the EEG. Hence, we decided that the community needed to have access to multimedia datasets containing EEG signals and a better understanding of the methodologies for extracting semantic value from such data. Therefore, an EEG/multimedia modelling comparative benchmarking task was proposed and run at NTCIR-13.

NTCIR (NII Testbeds and Community for Information access Research) is a repeating participation conference (with an 18-month cycle) that brings together researchers to develop evaluation methodologies and performance measures for IA (Information Access) technologies across single and multiple-media data. This brings together an active research community in which findings based on comparable experimental results are shared and exchanged in an open, collaborative manner. One topical focus of this is mining knowledge from a large amount of human generated data. NAILS (Neurally Augmented Image Labelling Strategies) was an affiliated task at NTCIR-13 (the 13th NTCIR conference) to support the collaborative evaluation of best-practice strategies for RSVP-EEG image search applications, where researchers benchmarked their machine-learning strategies.

This paper extends previous work with the NAILS task by sharing experiences gained in collecting the novel dataset, and importantly, offering not only a template experimental protocol but also an understanding of common pitfalls and issues. We describe the experimental protocol used to capture the dataset for this task, and compliment this with an understanding of the motivation behind its construction to allow others to extend upon this approach integrating it as relevant with their application domain.

2 Motivation to Use EEG

When coupled with a suitable visual presentation paradigm, EEG can enable the detection of attention-related events that are understood to be indicative of user interest – or more specifically the allocation of their attention to one particular stimulus as opposed to some other. One characteristic pattern of activity, commonly known as the P300 signal [19], has been a focus of investigation as it can be used as an index of attentional resource allocation to a stimulus such as an attention-captivating image (due to its infrequency) when presented on a screen. This finding has enabled BCI systems to leverage the ability of a user to be able to guide their attention in such a manner so as to be able to provide relevance judgements/ratings on visual stimuli. For example, a user can actively 'look out' for a particular type of image so that when relevant images appear in a high-speed visual presentation sequence known as RSVP (Rapid Serial Visual Presentation) [25], they will subsequently elicit a P300 response that can be detected using signal processing and machine-learning methods. Ultimately this allows the image to be 'neurally' labelled by the participant.

While systems like these have been explored in a proof-of-concept manner in BCI research using a multitude of image-search tasks, the datasets used usually remain unshared between studies, making it difficult to meaningfully compare the machine-learning and feature-processing strategies used, to find those that offer the best generalisability both across tasks and participants. This is what NTCIR-13 NAILS sought to address, by developing and releasing a dataset and setting achievable research challenges for participants. While the NAILS task showed some classification approaches from participating groups were better than others, it also provided clear evidence, that even with a pristine cleaned dataset (removing potential non-neural sources of useful information), that applications relying on such signals would still need to ultimately rely on noisy labels for the time being i.e. a balanced accuracy of 0.8839 might not be good enough yet to support the type of image target detection applications it is targeting.

While this might appear as a roadblock for applications using EEG signals in this way, it's important to realise the developments that have been made in this space over the past number of years, where through refined experimental protocols, better sensing equipment [10,15,16] and improved signal processing/machine-learning [12], the accuracy of such neural-labelling systems are improving. Moreover, applications replying upon the RSVP-EEG paradigm are being realised where the objective of the system might be to extract other information such as the believability of images generated by GANs [27], memorability of media [23], or to use the signals across users on the same dataset collectively to overcome issues with noise [8]. It is the opinion of the authors that sharing datasets, as well as experience and knowledge in how to conduct EEG data gathering and use of the data from a RSVP-EEG BCI, could enable other researchers to leverage a RSVP-EEG BCI as a component to drive other applications within the multimedia modelling space although the intended application may not be specifically for image labelling.

Fig. 1. Examples of four target images used in the NAILS experiment.

3 NAILS Data Set and Collection

Before discussing experiences in executing the NAILS task at NTCIR-13, we provide a concise description of the dataset [6,7].

3.1 Experimental Task Description

The NAILS dataset[1] collection contained EEG responses to 97,200 images from 10 experimental participants. Data collection was carried out with approval from Dublin City University's Research Ethics Committee (DCUREC/2016/099). Each participant completed 6 different search tasks for a particular type of target, where each search task was divided into 9 (approximately 35 second) blocks

[1] To gain access to the NAILS dataset and related benchmark implementations please contact graham.healy@dcu.ie.

which were completed in a self-paced manner so as to alleviate strain on participants. In each search task, a participant searched for a known type of target (e.g. an airplane), and was instructed to covertly count occurrences of target images in the RSVP sequence so as to maintain their attention on the task. Figure 1 shows examples of the target search images used. In each RSVP block, images were presented successively at a rate of 6 Hz with target (search-relevant) images randomly interspersed among standard (non-search relevant) images with a percentage of 5% across all blocks. In each block, 180 images (9 targets/171 standards) were presented in rapid succession on screen. Per participant, there were 486/9234 target/standard examples available.

3.2 Image Dataset

Image tasks were constructed using freely available datasets [21,22,28]. These were selected as a good choice given that they are commonly used datasets with well-researched characteristics that are representative of the visual content typically encountered in multimedia-IR tasks whilst remaining similar to content used in previous RSVP-BCI studies.

3.3 EEG Data Filtering

As contaminant eye-movement related activity on the EEG can often contain useful information, epochs (from -1000ms to 2000ms) containing such activity were excluded as they might encourage developed strategies to utilise these non-neural sources of discriminative information. In the NTCIR-13 NAILS task, epochs were filtered to exclude those with a peak-to-peak amplitude greater than 70 on EOG (Electrooculogram) and frontal EEG channels to remove trials that contained such contaminant eye-movement activity. A commonly employed strategy in EEG signal processing is ICA (Independent Component Analysis), and in the NAILS dataset this was used alongside a wavelet based analysis to confirm that the remaining epochs did not contain non-neural sources of discriminative information. For further details please refer to [7]. For the NAILS task, this dataset was split into a training/testing set, where 15/285 target/standard trials from each search task (for each participant) were selected to act as a withheld test set in the evaluation.

3.4 Collaborative Evaluation Task Description

Nine competing teams took part in the collaborative evaluation using the supplied training data (remaining epochs from blocks not used to extract test set data) and they were asked to build machine-learning models that maximised the BA (Balanced Accuracy) score on the withheld testing set (withheld by the NAILS organisers). That means for an evaluation run, a team needed to submit binary predictions for the 18,000 examples given in the test set (900/17100 targets/standards respectively). There were more than 2500/47000 target/standard training examples available across all participants for model training.

3.5 Provided Features/Pre-processing

Three types of preprocessed data were made available to participating organisations: time-series features (time), wavelet magnitude features (w-mean) and wavelet magnitude ratio (w-ratio) features. It was at the discretion of each participating team which combination of these features to use.

3.6 Dataset Validation

In order to validate that the captured data contained useful information for classification prior to sharing the dataset, we applied a basic machine learning analysis using a RBF (Radial Basis Function) kernel SVM (Support Vector Machine) [17]. Each model was trained on a participant-by-participant basis where hyper-parameters (C and gamma) were learned using a randomised grid-search approach. Each model was then applied to the unseen test set data where accuracy measures were calculated (presented in Tables 1 and 2). A range (and combination) of feature sources (used in baseline approaches) were presented so as to support a better interpretation of the results of participating teams. Importantly, a functioning pipeline was shared with participants (developed in python using mne [3] and sklearn [17]) demonstrating how this result was achieved. In Fig. 2, we show a characteristic P3b response acquired from one experimental participant. These measures verified that the chosen tasks were eliciting the expected characteristic (oddball) P300 response i.e. it was possible for a participant to do the search tasks as intended.

Table 1. Balanced accuracy scores for each participating team's best performing method broken down by experimental participant.

Dataset	*Team-1*	*Team-2*	*Baseline*
101	.8219	.7670	.7503
102	.8781	.8512	.8211
103	.8646	.8275	.7664
104	.8877	.8743	.8322
105	.9304	.8921	.8257
106	.8781	.8705	.8026
107	.9170	.8719	.8295
108	.8804	.8658	.8041
109	.8763	.8523	.7930
110	.9041	.8556	.8246
Average	.8839	.8528	.8049

4 Experiences from Gathering Usable EEG Data

Given the challenges of gathering usable EEG data for valid experimental use, we now provide on overview of experiences gained from gathering the NTCIR dataset, as well as other related activities over the recent years.

Table 2. Balanced accuracy scores for each participating team's best performing method broken down by experimental task.

Task ID	*Team-1*	*Team-2*	*Baseline*
WIND1	.8905	.8609	.8237
WIND2	.8846	.8356	.7746
INSTR	.8114	.7895	.7616
BIRD	.8616	.8191	.7805
UAV1	.9216	.9053	.8381
UAV2	.9335	.9065	.8512
Average	.8839	.8528	.8049

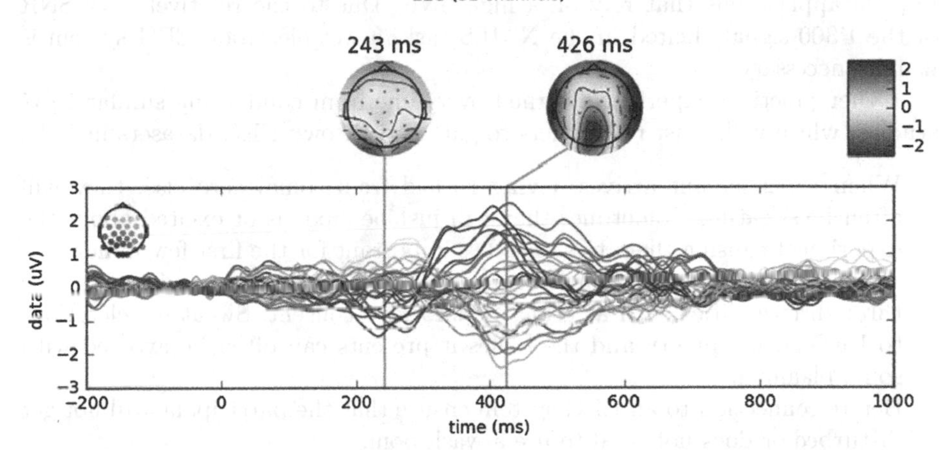

Fig. 2. Butterfly plot (ERP averages) of target epochs across all blocks minus average standard epochs across all blocks. Plots are generated using CAR (common average reference). Characteristic P3b activity can be seen at posterior scalp sites approximately between 300 ms and 600 ms following target detection (peaking at 426 ms). The colors on time-series plots indicate electrode location on scalp (upper left). (Color figure online)

4.1 Data Gathering

While EEG data clearly has a lot of potential to assist the multimedia modeling, analysis and retrieval communities, recording clean EEG data is a laborious activity requiring a coordinator to strike a balance between multiple factors such as experiment length, a participant's motivation to maintain attention during the task and task complexity. There is little point in recording data if the participant is no longer engaged in a task that requires their active engagement for the data to be meaningful (as is the case with the endogenous P300 [1]).

Furthermore, if aiming for high quality signals, it requires the careful connection of an EEG cap ensuring the impedance on each electrode is kept low.

This typically involves using an instrument to mechanically abrade the top layer of (dead) skin and using a conductive paste or liquid to enable conduction of electrical signals generated by the brain to the electrodes [13]. This is a messy business requiring participants after an experiment to wash their hair (necessitating some basic washing facilities on site). Moreover, care must be taken not to use too much conductive gel as electrodes can bridge together when this gel creeps along the scalp. This becomes particularly cumbersome when using more than 32 electrodes in an experiment as the electrodes will be closer together. For those new to recording EEG, this can often be daunting as there's a valid fear that they may injure a participant, which leads to over-cautious scalp preparation behaviour that in fact counter-productively results in more discomfort than necessary [2]. While many dry electrode EEG systems (not requiring a conductive gel) are available, their SNR (Signal-to-Noise Ratio) issues can often impede applications that rely on a high SNR. Due to the relatively low SNR of the P300 signal elicited in the NAILS task, a wet electrode EEG system is usually necessary.

Other practical experience learned over time from conducting similar EEG studies, which will assist researchers to gather their own EEG datasets include:

- When a participant arrives having rushed from somewhere else, they will often be sweating. Sometimes they will just be anxious or excited about the experiment causing them to sweat. It's important for the first few minutes to allow a participant to get their bearings, and this is often a good time to run through formalities such as ethics or informed consent. Sweat is deleterious to EEG signal quality and the issues it presents can often be avoided with some planning.
- Before connection to an EEG system ensure that the participant will not get disturbed or does not need to use a washroom.
- Allow a participant a practise session to get comfortable with the general requirements of the task.
- Do some pilot tests before committing to executing a large study (and have a pipeline to analyse and inspect the data from the start). It's easy to overlook what seems like a minor detail that can have deleterious effects that are only realised during data analysis when it's too late to fix a timing synchronisation or trigger problem [26].
- Check impedance of the electrodes during the experiment.
- Pay careful attention to the instructions you use to ask a participant to complete a task as they can have undesired consequences i.e. asking a participant to minimise eye blinks can often result in the subject in a RSVP experiment withholding eye blinks until they see a target image in a stream resulting in confounding eye blinks consistently occurring directly after a target image.
- Instruct the participant to try and avoid physical movements during the experimental blocks (and similarly make it apparent if the participant needs to adjust themselves physically that between experimental blocks is a good time to do so). Avoid swivel and recliner chairs as they can encourage movement during the experiment.

- Choose a quiet location to do the experiment where the participant will not be interrupted with distractions e.g. overhearing a hallway conversation distracting them from the task.
- Use small experimental blocks; in long experimental blocks it's unlikely a participant will be able to consistently sustain their attention throughout.
- EEG experiments are often long and boring, and it is often vitally important that the participant remains engaged in the task. Conversing with the participant during electrode setup and between experimental blocks will make them feel less objectified as a data point and more likely to want to do the task correctly.
- Ensure the participant is comfortable. The distraction of hunger/thirst or an uncomfortable chair (requiring regular readjustment) is not only likely to affect a participant's performance but will also likely add to giving your experiment a bad reputation when recruiting future participants.

4.2 Experiences from Running NTCIR-13 NAILS

Only two of the nine teams successfully submitted an overview paper along with valid predictions to the NAILS task. Teams were contacted prior to the due date of submission of results (i.e., predictions on the test set), and the most common reason for not continuing participation was due to not achieving any significant improvements over the baseline approach. All participants in the task were provided with an implementation for the baseline approach so as to ease their participation. A table of results related to the competition are presented in Table 1. These results have been subsequently interpreted in an overview paper [7]. Elements of the NAILS task that happened at NTCIR-13, particularly the use of EEG in an informational retrieval context, will be married with a previous core task [4] as part of NTCIR-15.

Invariance of Ranking of Participant Accuracies. Although not explicitly stated in the overview paper [7], each team's winning approach (and the baseline) showed high correlation in their respective balanced accuracy scores when analysing on a per-participant basis i.e. balanced accuracy scores for individual experimental participants data tended to be similarly ranked regardless of approach. Using a Spearman's rho correlation test we find the balanced accuracy scores for Team 1's and Team 2's best approaches significantly correlate ($r_s = .86$, $p = .0015$, $N = 10$). This is similarly the case when performing the same correlation test against the baseline approaches for both Team 1 ($r_s = .89$, $p = .0005$, $N = 10$) and Team 2 ($r_s = .82$, $p = .0038$, $N = 10$). This is an important observation as it indicates some participant's EEG data was difficult to classify regardless of the explored approaches taken. When conducting a future study like this, we may actively seek to screen participants in order to collect a more directed dataset that focuses on participants who have difficult-to-classify EEG data. Similarly, we intend to explore whether it's possible to identify such experimental participants via a proxy measure like reaction time [20].

Invariance of Ranking of Task Accuracies. Performing a similar Spearman's rho correlation analysis on the balanced accuracy scores of the tasks (where scores are averaged across participants for a task) we find the scores of Team 1's and Team 2's best approaches significantly correlate ($r_s = 1$, $p = .0000$, $N = 6$). This is similarly the case when performing a similar correlation test against the baseline approaches for both Team 1 (r_s=.94, $p = .0048$, $N = 6$) and Team 2 ($r_s = .94$, $p = .0048$, $N = 6$). These results indicate that balanced accuracy scores for experimental task's data tended to be similarly ranked regardless of approach.

ARL17 [24] and QUT [9] both made successful submissions whose respective balanced accuracies on the test set are shown in Tables 1 and 2. Both team's best results achieved balanced accuracy scores on the test set greater than any of the naive baseline approaches. This indicates that both participating team's approaches used a suitably developed strategy i.e. they outperformed a classical off-the-shelf machine-learning strategy like a SVM. In Tables 1 and 2 we present a breakdown across participants and tasks (respectively) of the balanced accuracies achieved by each team's best performing method. Notably, independent subject nor task (or a combination thereof) models were not used as runs as it was found that these models performed sub-optimally to those trained on the data both per task and per participant. This is particularly important, as it shows there may be a need for much larger datasets to accomplish such feats.

5 Conclusions

There is a growing interest in utilising novel signal sources such as EEG (Electroencephalography) in multimedia research. While these signals can provide a useful source of evidence in multimodal media analytics, significant domain expertise is required to gather EEG datasets and make use of the resulting data. This paper presents a summary of distilled experiences and knowledge gained during the preparation (and utilisiation) of an EEG dataset that supported a collaborative neural-image labelling benchmarking task. This paper also highlights the nature of the novel EEG dataset and provides details on how it was made and how it can be accessed.

Acknowledgments. This work is funded as part of the Insight Centre for Data Analytics (which is supported by Science Foundation Ireland under Grant Number SFI/12/RC/2289) and Dublin City University's Research Committee.

References

1. Bennington, J.Y., Polich, J.: Comparison of p300 from passive and active tasks for auditory and visual stimuli. Int. J. Psychophysiol. **34**(2), 171–177 (1999)
2. Furyk, J.S., O'Kane, C.J., Aitken, P.J., Banks, C.J., Kault, D.A.: Fast versus slow bandaid removal: a randomised trial. Med. J. Aust. **191**(11–12), 682–683 (2009)
3. Gramfort, A., et al.: MEG and EEG data analysis with MNE-python. Front. Neurosci. **7**, 267 (2013)

4. Gurrin, C., Joho, H., Hopfgartner, F., Zhou, L., Albatal, R.: NTCIR Lifelog: the first test collection for lifelog research. In: Proceedings of the 39th International ACM SIGIR Conference on Research and Development in Information Retrieval, pp. 705–708. ACM (2016)
5. Healy, G., Smeaton, A.F.: Eye fixation related potentials in a target search task. In: 2011 Annual International Conference of the IEEE Engineering in Medicine and Biology Society, pp. 4203–4206, August 2011
6. Healy, G., Wang, Z., Gurrin, C., Ward, T.E., Smeaton, A.F.: An EEG image-search dataset: a first-of-its-kind in IR/IIR. NAILS: neurally augmented image labelling strategies. In: Proceedings of CHIR Workshop on Challenges in Bringing Neuroscience to Research in Human-Information Interaction, Oslo, Norway, 11 March 2017
7. Healy, G., Ward, T.E., Gurrin, C., Smeaton, A.F.: Overview of NTCIR-13 NAILS task (2017)
8. Healy, G.F., Gurrin, C., Smeaton, A.F.: Informed perspectives on human annotation using neural signals. In: Tian, Q., Sebe, N., Qi, G.-J., Huet, B., Hong, R., Liu, X. (eds.) MMM 2016. LNCS, vol. 9517, pp. 315–327. Springer, Cham (2016). https://doi.org/10.1007/978-3-319-27674-8_28
9. Hutson, H., Geva, S., Cimiano, P.: Ensemble methods for the NTCIR-13 NAILS task. In: Proceedings of the 13th NTCIR Conference on Evaluation of Information Access Technologies, NTCIR-13, Tokyo, Japan, 5–8 December 2017 (2017)
10. Kam, J.W., et al.: Systematic comparison between a wireless EEG system with dry electrodes and a wired EEG system with wet electrodes. NeuroImage **184**, 119–129 (2019)
11. Koelstra, S., et al.: Deap: a database for emotion analysis using physiological signals **3**(1), 18–31 (2012). eemcs-eprint-21368
12. Lawhern, V.J., Solon, A.J., Waytowich, N.R., Gordon, S.M., Hung, C.P., Lance, B.J.: Eegnet: a compact convolutional neural network for EEG-based brain-computer interfaces. J. Neural Eng. **15**(5), 056013 (2018)
13. Luck, S.J.: An Introduction to the Event-related Potential Technique. MIT Press (2014)
14. Marathe, A.R., et al.: The effect of target and non-target similarity on neural classification performance: a boost from confidence. Front. Neurosci. **9**, 270 (2015)
15. Mathewson, K.E., Harrison, T.J., Kizuk, S.A.: High and dry? Comparing active dry eeg electrodes to active and passive wet electrodes. Psychophysiology **54**(1), 74–82 (2017)
16. Mullen, T.R., et al.: Real-time neuroimaging and cognitive monitoring using wearable dry EEG. IEEE Trans. Biomed. Eng. **62**(11), 2553–2567 (2015)
17. Pedregosa, F., et al.: Scikit-learn: machine learning in Python. J. Mach. Learn. Res. **12**, 2825–2830 (2011)
18. Pohlmeyer, E.A., et al.: Closing the loop in cortically-coupled computer vision: a brain-computer interface for searching image databases. J. Neural Eng. **8**(3), 036025 (2011)
19. Polich, J.: Updating P300: an integrative theory of P3a and P3b. Clin. Neurophysiol. **118**(10), 2128–2148 (2007)
20. Ramchurn, A., de Fockert, J.W., Mason, L., Darling, S., Bunce, D.: Intraindividual reaction time variability affects p300 amplitude rather than latency. Front. Hum. Neurosci. **8**, 557 (2014)
21. Razakarivony, S., Jurie, F.: Vehicle detection in aerial imagery : a small target detection benchmark. J. Vis. Commun. Image Representation **34**, 187–203 (2016)

22. Russakovsky, O., et al.: ImageNet large scale visual recognition challenge. Int. J. Comput. Vis. (IJCV) **115**(3), 211–252 (2015)
23. Smeaton, A.F., et al.: Dublin's participation in the predicting media memorability task at mediaeval 2018 (2018)
24. Solon, A.J., Gordon, S.M., Lance, B.J., Lawhern, V.J.: Deep Learning Approaches for P300 classification in image triage: applications to the NAILS task. In: Proceedings of the 13th NTCIR Conference on Evaluation of Information Access Technologies, NTCIR-13, Tokyo, Japan, 5–8 December 2017 (2017)
25. Thorpe, S., Fize, D., Marlot, C.: Speed of processing in the human visual system. Nature **381**, 520 (1996)
26. Wang, Z., Healy, G., Smeaton, A.F., Ward, T.E.: An investigation of triggering approaches for the rapid serial visual presentation paradigm in brain computer interfacing. In: 2016 27th Irish Signals and Systems Conference (ISSC), pp. 1–6. IEEE (2016)
27. Wang, Z., Healy, G., Smeaton, A.F., Ward, T.E.: Use of neural signals to evaluate the quality of generative adversarial network performance in facial image generation. Cognitive Computation, August 2019
28. Zhou, B., Khosla, A., Lapedriza, A., Torralba, A., Oliva, A.: Places: an image database for deep scene understanding. CoRR, abs/1610.02055 (2016)

SS4: MMAC: Multi-modal Affective Computing of Large-Scale Multimedia Data

Relation Modeling with Graph Convolutional Networks for Facial Action Unit Detection

Zhilei Liu[1], Jiahui Dong[1], Cuicui Zhang[2](✉), Longbiao Wang[1], and Jianwu Dang[1,3]

[1] College of Intelligence and Computing, Tianjin University, Tianjin, China
{zhileiliu,2118216008,longbiao_wang}@tju.edu.cn
[2] School of Marine Science and Technology, Tianjin University, Tianjin, China
cuicui.zhang@tju.edu.cn
[3] School of Information Science, JAIST, Nomi, Japan
jdang@jaist.ac.jp

Abstract. Most existing AU detection works considering AU relationships are relying on probabilistic graphical models with manually extracted features. This paper proposes an end-to-end deep learning framework for facial AU detection with graph convolutional network (GCN) for AU relation modeling, which has not been explored before. In particular, AU related regions are extracted firstly, latent representations full of AU information are learned through an auto-encoder. Moreover, each latent representation vector is feed into GCN as a node, the connection mode of GCN is determined based on the relationships of AUs. Finally, the assembled features updated through GCN are concatenated for AU detection. Extensive experiments on BP4D and DISFA benchmarks demonstrate that our framework significantly outperforms the state-of-the-art methods for facial AU detection. The proposed framework is also validated through a series of ablation studies.

Keywords: AU detection · Graph convolutional network · Multi-label prediction

1 Introduction

In recent years, research on Facial Action Unit (AU), as a comprehensive description of facial movements, has attracted more and more attention in the field of human-computer interaction and affective computing. Facial AU detection is beneficial to facial expression recognition and analysis. According to statistical calculation and facial anatomy information, strong relationships are exist among different AUs under different facial expressions, e.g., happiness might be the combination of AU12 (Lip Corner Puller) and AU13 (Cheek Puffer).

Most of existing AU detection methods focus on AU relationship modeling implicitly. For example, probabilistic graphic models including Bayesian

Y. M. Ro et al. (Eds.): MMM 2020, LNCS 11962, pp. 489–501, 2020.
https://doi.org/10.1007/978-3-030-37734-2_40

Networks [22], Dynamic Bayesian Networks [27] and Restrict Boltzmann Machine [23] have demonstrated their effectiveness of relation modeling for AU detection. However, these generative models are always integrated with manually extracted feature, i.e. LBP, SIFT, HoG, which limits its extension ability with state-of-the-art deep discriminative models.

With the recent development of deep graph networks, relation modeling with graph based deep graph models has attracted more and more attention. In this paper, we use the graph convolutional network (GCN) [9] for AU relation modeling to strengthen the facial AU detection. In particular, reference to EAC-Net [11], AU related regions are extracted at first, these AU regions are feed into some specific AU auto-encoder for deep representation extraction in the next. Moreover, each latent representation is pull into GCN as a node, the connection mode of GCN is determined by the relationship of AUs. Finally, the assembled features are concatenated for AU detection. These auto-encoders are trained firstly, then the whole framework is trained together.

The contributions of this paper are twofold. (1) We propose a deep learning framework for AU detection with graph convolutional network for AU relation modeling. (2) Results of extensive experiments conducted on two benchmark datasets demonstrate that our proposed framework significantly outperforms the state-of-the-art.

2 Related Work

Our proposed framework is closely related to facial AU detection and graph convolutional network.

Facial AU Detection: Based on previous research [20,23,27], AUs are in contact, which make itself a problem different from standard expression recognition. To capture such correlations, a generative dynamic Bayesian networks (DBN) [27] was proposed to model the AU relationships and their temporal evolution. Rather than learning, pairwise AU relations can be explicitly inferred using statistics in annotations, and then injected such relations into a multi-task learning framework to select important patches for each AU. In addition, a restricted Boltzmann machine (RBM) [23] was developed to directly capture the dependencies between image features and AU relationships. Following this direction, image features and AU outputs were fused in a continuous latent space using a conditional latent variable model. Song et al. [20] studied the sparsity and co-occurrence of AUs. Although improvements can be observed considering the relationships among AUs, these approaches rely on manually extracted features such as SIFT, LBP, or Gabor, rather than deep features.

With the recent rise of deep learning, CNN have been widely adopted to extract AU features. Zhao et al. [26] proposed a deep region and multi-label learning (DRML) network to divide the face images into 8 × 8 blocks and used individual convolutional kernels to convolve each block. Although this approach treats each face as a group of individual parts, it divides blocks uniformly and does not consider the FACS knowledge, thereby leading to poor performance. Wei Li et al. [11] proposed Enhancing and Cropping Net (EAC-Net), which intends to give significant attention to individual AU centers; however, this approach does not consider AU relationship modeling, and the lack of RoI-level supervised information can only give coarse guidance. All these researches demonstrate the effectiveness of deep learning on feature extraction for AU detection task. However, they all do not consider the AU relation modeling.

Graph Convolutional Network: There have been a lot of works for graph convolution, whose principle of constructing GCNs mainly follows two streams: spatial perspective [1,4,19] and spectral perspective [2,3,7,8,18]. Spatial perspective methods directly perform the convolution filters on the graph vertices and their neighbors. Atwood et al. [1] proposed the diffusion-convolutional neural networks (DCNNs). Transition matrices are used to define the neighborhood for nodes in DCNN. Niepert et al. [19] extracts and normalizes a neighborhood of exactly k nodes for each node. And then the normalized neighborhood serves as the receptive field for the convolutional operation. Different with the spatial perspective methods, spectral perspective methods utilize the eigenvalues and eigenvectors of graph Laplace matrices. Bruna et al. [2] proposed the spectral network. The convolution operation is defined in the Fourier domain by computing the eigendecomposition of the graph Laplacian.

Recently, Li et al. [10] proposed the AU semantic relationship embedded representation learning (SRERL) framework to combine facial AU detection and Gated Graph Neural Network (GGNN) [12] and achieved good results. But the commonly used Graph Convolutional Network (GCN) for classification task with relation modeling is adopted for AU relation modeling in our proposed method, while the Gated Graph Neural Network (GGNN) adopted in [13] is inspired by GRU and mainly used for the task of Visual Question Answering and Semantic Segmentation. In addition, our method has only about 2.3 million parameters, but SRERL [13] has more than 138 million parameters.

In this paper, we apply the spectral perspective of GCNs [9] for AU relation modeling. Our GCN is bulit by stacking multiple layers of graph convolutions with AU relation graph. The outputs of the GCNs are updated features for each AU region node by modeling their relationships, which can be used to perform classification.

3 Proposed Method

3.1 Overview

The propose AU-GCN framework for AU detection by considering AU relation modeling through GCN is shown in Fig. 1, in which, four modules are included: AU local region division, AU local region representation, AU relation graph, Convolutions on graph. Given the face image with facial landmark key points, AU related local regions are extracted at first by taking EAC-Net [11] as a reference. After that, deep representations of each AU region are represented

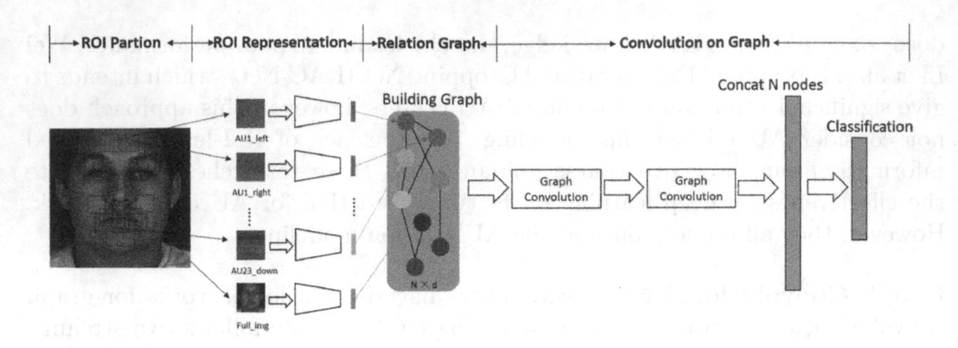

Fig. 1. The proposed AU-GCN framework for AU detection.

by the latent vectors of an auto-encoder supervised through the reconstruction loss and the AU classification loss. In the next, each latent vector is pull into GCN as a node, and AU relationships are modeled through the edges of GCN. Multiple layers of graph convolution operations will be applied on the input data and generating higher-level feature maps on the graph. It will then be classified by the modified multi-label cross entropy loss and Dice loss to the AU correct classification. We will now go over the components in the AU-GCN model as following.

3.2 AU ROI Partition Rule

The most recent deep learning based image classification methods make use of CNN for feature extraction, and the basic assumption for a standard CNN is the shared convolutional kernels for an entire image. For an image with the relatively fixed structure, such as a human face, a standard CNN may fail to capture those subtle appearance changes. In order to focus more on AU specific regions, the AU local region partition rules are defined at first by taking FACS [5] and EAC-Net [11] as reference.

The first step is to use the facial landmark information to get the AUs centers. The landmark points provide rich information about the face, which help us to locate specific AU related facial areas. Then, taking this AU related landmark as the center to extract the n × n size region as AU local region. Figure 2(a) shows the AU region partition of the face, in which, the face image is partitioned into 19 basic ROIs using AU related landmarks, AU12, AU14 and AU15 share a ROI, AU23, AU24, AU25 and AU26 share a ROI. These 12 ROIs are shared by different benchmark datasets, i.e. BP4D [24] and DISFA [16] datasets, in which, 6 AU ROIs for BP4D dataset, and addition one for DISFA dataset. Due to the fact that previous ROIs are all the facial local feature, the facial global feature is ignored, another special ROI representing the whole face image in introduced. All these AU related ROIs will be resized into n × n for further representation learning and relation modeling. Finally, BP4D dataset has 19 ROIs, DISFA dataset has 14 ROIs.

3.3 AU Deep Representation Extraction

Figure 2(b) shows the architecture of network for AU deep representation extraction. This purpose of this step is to get d_0-dim deep representations full of AU information for further AU relation modeling and AU detection.

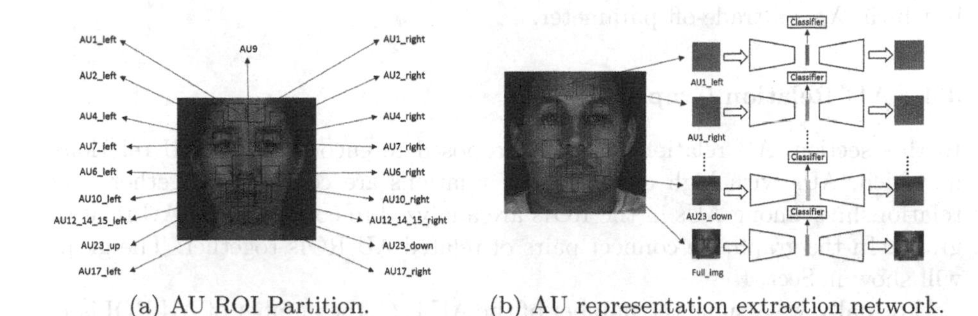

(a) AU ROI Partition. (b) AU representation extraction network.

Fig. 2. AU ROI partition and AU deep representation extraction network.

The AU specific ROIs obtained in the previous step are feed into AU specific auto-encoders (AEs) [15] to reconstruct each AU ROI. To get latent vectors full of AU information, two kinds of losses are introduced here to constrain the extracted deep representations. The first loss is the pixel-wise L1-reconstruction loss L_R:

$$L_R(I^{GT}, I^R)) = \frac{1}{n^2}\sum_{i=1}^{n}\sum_{j=1}^{n}|I_{ij}^{GT} - I_{ij}^{R}| \tag{1}$$

where n is the size of each AU ROI, I^{GT} denotes the ground truth AU ROI image, I^R denotes the reconstructed AU ROI image.

To make sure that the extracted AU deep representation contains as more AU information as possible, the second loss $L_{ROI\_softmax}$ for ROI-level multi-label AU detection is introduced as following:

$$\begin{aligned} &L_{ROI\_softmax}(Y_r^{ROI}, \hat{Y}_r^{ROI}) = \\ &\quad -\frac{1}{C}\sum_{c=1}^{C}\left[Y_{rc}^{ROI} log\hat{Y}_{rc}^{ROI} + (1 - Y_{rc}^{ROI})log(1 - \hat{Y}_{rc}^{ROI})\right] \end{aligned} \tag{2}$$

where C is the number of the classes, R is the number of the ROIs obtained in the previous step, i.e., 19 ROIs and 14 ROIs are defined in BP4D dataset and DISFA dataset respectively according to the provided AU labels, the ground truth of AU label is $Y^{ROI} \in \{0,1\}^{R\times C}$, $Y_{i,j}^{ROI}$ indicates the (i, j) -th element of Y, where $Y_{i,j}^{ROI} = 0$ denotes AU j is inactive in AU ROI i, and $Y_{i,j}^{ROI} = 1$ denotes AU j is active in AU ROI i. In addition, the ground truth Y^{ROI} must satisfy the constraint of AU region partition rule: $Y_{i,j}^{ROI} = 0$ if AU j does not belong to the i-th AU ROI. In particular, when an AU ROI consists of multiple AUs, just like the ROI containing AU12, AU14 and AU15 in BP4D, the $Y_{i,j}^{ROI}$ also follows the above rules. The ROI-level label also helps to improve AU detection performance through the space constraint and supervised information of the ROIs. Finally, the overall loss function for AU deep representation extraction is shown below:

$$L_{ROI} = L_{ROI\_softmax} + \lambda_1 L_R \tag{3}$$

in which, λ_1 is a trade-off parameter.

3.4 AU Relation Graph

In this section, AU relation graph is proposed to encoder those AU relations, in which, AUs with high confidence of relations are connected together. The relationships among AUs in the ROIs are analyzed to construct the AU relation graph. In the graph, we connect pairs of related AU ROIs together. The graph will show in Sect. 4.

Formally, we assume the number of the AU is C, the number of AU ROI is R. Given all labels in the training-set, the conditional probability that AU j equals 1 when AU i equals 1 is calculated. Relation matrix M of C × C dimension is obtained, and then in order to transform M into symmetric matrix M^{sym}, the following function is introduced as:

$$M_{ij}^{sym} = M_{ij} + M_{ji} \tag{4}$$

where M^{ij} denotes the (i, j)-th element of the matrix M. Then, a threshold h is set to convert M_{ij}^{sym} into a 0–1 matrix M^{bool} as following:

$$M_{ij}^{bool} = \begin{cases} 1 \; if \; M_{ij}^{sym} \geq threshold \\ 0 \; if \; M_{ij}^{sym} < threshold \end{cases} \tag{5}$$

In the next, graph G with R AU ROI nodes is built according M^{bool}, in which, R is the number of AU ROIs. Firstly, the node in G is connected to itself. Secondly, each node is connected with its symmetrical node, i.e.: AU1_left ROI and AU1_right ROI, AU23_up and AU23_down. Thirdly, if $M_{ij}^{bool} = 1$, it shows that AU i is strongly related to AU j, so these nodes belonging to AU i are connected to those nodes belonging to AU j. Finally, the last node representing the whole facial image is connected to all nodes, which lets the global feature help the local features learn more AU information. By building the AU relation graph G, we can obtain richer AU relation information and enlarge the ability of classifiers in subsequent inference process.

3.5 Convolutions on Graph G

To perform reasoning on the graph, we apply the Graph Convolutional Networks (GCNs) proposed in [9]. Different from standard convolutions which operates on a local regular grid, the graph convolutions allow us to compute the response of a node based on its neighbors defined by the graph relations. Thus performing graph convolutions is equal to performing message passing inside the graphs. The outputs of the GCNs are updated features of each ROI node. Inspired by the above, we design a GCN-based multi-label encoder for AU detection. We can represent one layer of graph convolution as:

$$Z_{i+1} = G \times Z_i \times W_i \tag{6}$$

where G represents the adjacency graph we have introduced above with R $\times$ R dimension. Z_i denotes the input features in the i-th graph convolution operation, in particular, Z_0 denotes the latent vectors with $R \times d_0$, and W_i is the weight matrix of the layer. W_0 with dimension $d_0 \times d_1$, W_1 with dimension $d_1 \times d_2$. Thus, the output of two graph convolution layers Z_2 is in $R \times d_2$ dimension. After each layer of graph convolutions, we apply two functions including the Dropout and then ReLU before the updated feature Z_2 is forwarded to the next layer.

3.6 Facial AU Detection:

As illustrated in Fig. 1, the updated feature Z_2 after graph convolutions is flatten. Then, the flatten feature is forwarded to a fully connected network (FCN) for AU detection. Finally, we get the detection results $\hat{Y}$ with C-dim.

Facial AU detection can be regarded as a multi-label binary classification problem with the following weighted multi-label softmax loss $L_{softmax}$:

$$L_{softmax}(Y, \hat{Y}) = -\frac{1}{C}\sum_{i=1}^{C} w_i \left[Y_i log\hat{Y}_i + (1 - Y_i)log(1 - \hat{Y}_i)\right] \tag{7}$$

where Y_i denotes the ground-truth probability of occurrence for the i-th AU, which is 1 if occurrence and 0 otherwise, and $\hat{Y}_i$ denotes the corresponding predicted occurrence probability for the i-th AU. The trade-off weight w_i is introduced to alleviate the data imbalance problem. For most facial AU detection benchmarks, the occurrence rates of AUs are imbalanced [13,14]. Since AUs are not mutually independent, imbalanced training data has a bad influence on this multi-label learning task. Particularly, we set $w_i = \frac{(1/r_i)C}{\sum_{i=1}^{C}(1/r_i)}$, where r_i is the occurrence rate of the i-th AU in the training set.

In some cases, some AUs appear rarely in training samples, for which the softmax loss often makes the network prediction strongly biased towards absence. To overcome this limitation, a weighted multi-label Dice coefficient loss L_{dice} [17] is further introduced as following:

$$L_{dice}(Y, \hat{Y}) = \frac{1}{C}\sum_{i=1}^{C} w_i (1 - \frac{2Y_i\hat{Y}_i + \epsilon}{Y_i^2 + \hat{Y}_i^2 + \epsilon}) \tag{8}$$

where ϵ is the smooth term. Dice coefficient is also known as F1-score: $F1 = 2pr/(p + r)$, the most popular metric for facial AU detection, where p and r denote precision and recall respectively. With the help of the weighted Dice coefficient loss, we also take into account the consistency between the learning process and the evaluation metric. Finally, the AU detection loss is defined as:

$$L_{au} = L_{softmax} + \lambda_2 L_{dice} \tag{9}$$

where λ_2 is a trade-off parameter.

4 Experiments

4.1 Setting

Dataset: The effectiveness of our proposed AU-GCN is evaluated on two benchmark datasets: BP4D [24] and DISFA [16]. For BP4D and DISFA, a 3-fold partition is adopted to ensure subjects were mutually exclusive in train/val/test sets by following previous related work [11,26]. The frames with intensities equal or greater than 2 are considered as positive, while others are treated as negative. BP4D contains 2D and 3D videos of 41 young adults during various emotion inductions while interacting with an experimenter. We used 328 videos (41 participants $\times$ 8 videos each) with 10 AUs coded, resulting in ~140,000 valid face images. For each AU, we sampled 100 positive frames and 200 negative frames for each video. DISFA [16] contains 27 subjects watching video clips, and provides 8 AU annotations with intensities. There were ~130,000 valid face images. We used the frames with AU intensities with 2 or higher as positive samples, and the rest as negative ones. To be consistent with the 8-video setting of BP4D, we sampled 800 positive frames and 1600 negative frames for each video.

Metrics: The AU detection performance was evaluated on two commonly used frame-based metrics: F1-score and area under curve (AUC). F1-score is the harmonic mean of precision and recall, and widely used in AU detection. AUC quantifies the relation between true and false positives. For each method, we computed average metrics over all AUs (denoted as Avg.).

Implementation: For each face image, we perform similarity transformation to obtain a $200 \times 200 \times 3$ color face. This transformation is shape-preserving and brings no change to the expression. In order to enhance the diversity of training data, the face images are flipped for data augmentation. Our AU-GCN is trained using PyTorch with stochastic gradient descent (SGD), a mini-batch size of 256, a momentum of 0.9 and a weight decay of 0.0005. We decay the learning rate by 0.1 after every 10 epochs. The structure parameters of AU-GCN are chosen as $d_0 = 150$, $d_1 = 30$, $d_2 = 12$, n is 25, C is 12 for BP4D and 8 for DISFA, R is 19 for BP4D and 14 for DISFA. The graph connection matrix M^{bool} on BP4D and DISFA are shown in Table 1. The hyperparameters λ_1, λ_2 are obtained by cross validation. In our experiments, set $\lambda_1 = 3$ and $\lambda_2 = 4$. AU-GCN is firstly trained with AE optimized with 12 epochs. Next, we read the parameters before getting the R latent vectors and train with all the modules optimized with 40 epochs.

4.2 Comparison with State-of-the-Art Methods

We compare our method AU-GCN against state-of-the-art single-image based AU detection works under the same 3-fold cross validation setting. These methods include both traditional methods, LSVM [6], JPML [25], and deep learning

Table 1. Graph connection matrix M^{bool} on BP4D and DISFA

(a) BP4D

AU	1	2	4	6	7	10	12	14	15	17	23	24
1	1	1	0	0	0	1	0	0	0	0	0	0
2	1	1	0	0	0	1	1	0	0	0	0	0
4	0	0	1	0	1	0	0	0	0	0	0	0
6	0	0	0	1	1	1	1	1	1	1	0	0
7	0	0	1	1	1	1	1	1	1	1	1	0
10	1	1	0	1	1	1	1	1	1	1	1	0
12	0	1	0	1	1	1	1	1	1	1	1	0
14	0	0	0	1	1	1	1	1	1	1	1	1
15	0	0	0	1	1	1	1	1	1	1	0	0
17	0	0	0	1	1	1	1	1	1	1	1	1
23	0	0	0	0	1	1	1	1	0	1	1	0
24	0	0	0	0	0	0	0	1	0	1	0	1

(b) DISFA

AU	1	2	4	6	9	12	25	26
1	1	1	0	0	0	0	0	0
2	1	1	0	0	0	0	0	0
4	0	0	1	0	1	0	0	0
6	0	0	0	1	0	1	1	0
9	0	0	1	0	1	0	0	0
12	0	0	0	1	0	1	1	0
25	0	0	0	1	0	1	1	1
26	0	0	0	0	0	0	1	1

Table 2. F1-score and AUC for 12 AUs on BP4D

AU	F1-score						AUC				
	LSVM	JPML	LCN	DRML	EAC-Net	AU-GCN	LSVM	JPML	LCN	DRML	AU-GCN
1	23.2	32.6	45.0	36.4	39.0	**46.8**	20.7	40.7	51.9	55.7	**58.3**
2	22.8	25.6	41.2	**41.8**	35.2	38.5	17.7	42.1	50.9	54.5	**71.2**
4	23.1	37.4	42.3	43.0	48.6	**60.1**	22.9	46.2	53.6	58.8	**85.6**
6	27.2	42.3	58.6	55.0	76.1	**80.1**	20.3	40.0	53.2	56.6	**89.7**
7	47.1	50.5	52.8	67.0	72.9	**79.5**	44.8	50.0	63.7	61.0	**83.5**
10	77.2	72.2	54.0	66.3	81.9	**84.8**	73.4	75.2	62.4	53.6	**86.7**
12	63.7	74.1	54.7	65.8	86.2	**88.0**	55.3	60.5	61.6	60.8	**93.5**
14	64.3	65.7	59.9	54.1	58.8	**67.3**	46.8	53.6	58.8	57.0	**78.0**
15	18.4	38.1	36.1	33.2	37.5	**52.0**	18.3	50.1	49.9	56.2	**86.6**
17	33.0	40.0	46.6	48.0	59.1	**63.2**	36.4	42.5	48.4	50.0	**81.2**
23	19.4	30.4	33.2	31.7	35.9	**40.9**	19.2	51.9	50.3	53.9	**80.3**
24	20.7	42.3	35.3	30.0	35.8	**52.8**	11.7	53.2	47.7	53.9	**91.4**
Avg	35.3	45.9	46.6	48.3	55.9	**62.8**	32.2	50.5	54.4	56.0	**87.3**

methods, LCN [21], DRML [26] and EAC-Net [11]. Note that EAC-Net [11] is not compared AUC due to its metrics of accuracy instead of AUC.

Table 2 reports the F1-score and AUC results of different methods on BP4D. It can be seen that our AU-GCN outperforms all these previous works on the challenging BP4D dataset. AU-GCN is superior to all the conventional methods, which demonstrates the strength of deep learning based methods. Compared to the state-of-the-art methods, AU-GCN brings significant relative increments of 6.9% and 31.3% respectively for average F1-score and AUC, which verifies the effectiveness of AU relation modeling with GCN. In addition, our method obtains high accuracy without sacrificing F1-score, which is attributed to the integration of the softmax loss and the Dice coefficient loss.

Table 3. F1-score and AUC for 8 AUs on DISFA

AU	F1-score						AUC				
	LSVM	APL	LCN	DRML	EAC-Net	AU-GCN	LSVM	APL	LCN	DRML	AU-GCN
1	10.8	11.4	12.8	17.3	**41.5**	32.3	21.6	32.7	44.1	**53.3**	47.1
2	10.0	12.0	12.0	17.7	**26.4**	19.5	15.8	27.8	52.4	53.2	**61.1**
4	21.8	30.1	29.7	37.4	**66.4**	55.7	17.2	37.9	47.7	60.0	**72.5**
6	15.7	12.4	23.1	29.0	50.7	**57.9**	8.7	13.6	39.7	54.9	**77.9**
9	11.5	10.1	12.4	10.7	**80.5**	61.4	15.0	**64.4**	40.2	51.5	62.3
12	70.4	65.9	26.4	37.7	**89.3**	62.7	93.8	**94.2**	54.7	54.6	91.6
25	12.0	21.4	46.2	38.5	88.9	**90.9**	3.4	50.4	48.6	48.6	**95.8**
26	22.1	26.9	30.0	20.1	15.6	**60.0**	20.1	47.1	47.0	45.3	**88.4**
Avg	21.8	23.8	24.0	26.7	48.5	**55.0**	27.5	46.0	46.8	52.3	**74.6**

Experimental results on DISFA dataset are shown in Table 3, from which it can be observed that our AU-GCN outperforms all the state-of-the-art works with even more significant improvements. Specifically, AU-GCN increases the average F1-score and AUC relatively by 6.5% and 22.3% over the state-of-the-art methods, respectively. Due to the serious data imbalance issue in DISFA, performances of different AUs fluctuate severely in most of the previous methods. For instance, the accuracy of AU 12 is far higher than that of other AUs for LSVM and APL. Although both AU-GCN and EAC-Net use the AU local features, the GCN better expresses the AU relation information.

4.3 Ablation Study

To investigate the effectiveness of each component in our framework, Table 4 present the average F1-score and AUC for different variants of AU-GCN on BP4D benchmark, where "w/o" is the abbreviation of "without". Each variant is composed by different components of our framework. AU-Net is the framework without GCN relation modeling (GCN), Dice loss (D) and global facial information (F).

Table 4. F1-score on BP4D for ablation study

Methods	GCN	D	F	F1-score	AUC
AU-Net	×	×	×	54.0	81.3
AU-Net+D	×	✓	×	56.4	83.7
AU-GCN w/o F, D	✓	×	×	59.1	83.9
AU-GCN w/o F	✓	✓	×	61.5	85.8
AU-GCN w/o D	✓	×	✓	61.9	86.8
AU-GCN	✓	✓	✓	**62.8**	**87.3**

Contribution of the GCN: By integrating the graph convolutional network (GCN), AU-GCN w/o F, D achieves higher F1-score and AUC results than AU-Net. In particular, the AU-Net is to concatenate R node features and put the concatenated features into FCN instead of GCN. This result illuminates that GCN can capture the strong relationship between AUs, and strength the relation learning for AU detection.

Integrating of Whole Facial Information: By adding the resized whole facial image as a node to GCN and connecting this node with all the other nodes, AU-GCN w/o D achieves better F1-score and AUC results compared to AU-GCN w/o F, D. Since the previous features are all local AU features, benefiting from the whole facial image to add global feature for GCN, our method obtains more significant performance, which demonstrates that global facial information is helpful for local AU detection.

Integrating of Dice Loss: After integrating the weighted softmax loss with the Dice loss, AU-GCN w/o F attains higher average F1-score and AUC than AU-GCN w/o F, D. The softmax loss focus more on the classification accuracy, rather than the balance between precision and recall, the Dice loss which optimizes the network from the perspective of F1-score, so this loss can make F1-score and AUC achieve good results.

5 Conclusion

In this paper, to makes full use of AU local features and their relationship, we have presented a facial AU detection methods by integrating graph convolution network for explicit AU relation modeling. To the best of our knowledge, this is the first study that combines facial AU detection and GCN with one end-to-end framework. Extensive experiments on two benchmark AU datasets demonstrate that the proposed network outperformed state-of-the-art methods for AU detection, the effectiveness of the proposed modules in the framework are also validated through a series of ablation study.

Acknowledgements. This work is supported by the National Natural Science Foundation of China under Grants of 41806116 and 61503277. We gratefully acknowledge the support of NVIDIA Corporation with the donation of the Titan V GPU used for this research.

References

1. Atwood, J., Towsley, D.: Diffusion-convolutional neural networks. In: Advances in Neural Information Processing Systems, pp. 1993–2001 (2016)
2. Bruna, J., Zaremba, W., Szlam, A., LeCun, Y.: Spectral networks and locally connected networks on graphs. arXiv preprint arXiv:1312.6203 (2013)

3. Defferrard, M., Bresson, X., Vandergheynst, P.: Convolutional neural networks on graphs with fast localized spectral filtering. In: Advances in Neural Information Processing Systems, pp. 3844–3852 (2016)
4. Duvenaud, D.K., et al.: Convolutional networks on graphs for learning molecular fingerprints. In: Advances in Neural Information Processing Systems, pp. 2224–2232 (2015)
5. Ekman, R.: What the Face Reveals: Basic and Applied Studies of Spontaneous Expression Using the Facial Action Coding System (FACS). Oxford University Press, Oxford (1997)
6. Fan, R.E., Chang, K.W., Hsieh, C.J., Wang, X.R., Lin, C.J.: Liblinear: a library for large linear classification. J. Mach. Learn. Res. **9**(Aug), 1871–1874 (2008)
7. Hammond, D.K., Vandergheynst, P., Gribonval, R.: Wavelets on graphs via spectral graph theory. Appl. Comput. Harmonic Anal. **30**(2), 129–150 (2011)
8. Henaff, M., Bruna, J., LeCun, Y.: Deep convolutional networks on graph-structured data. arXiv preprint arXiv:1506.05163 (2015)
9. Kipf, T.N., Welling, M.: Semi-supervised classification with graph convolutional networks. arXiv preprint arXiv:1609.02907 (2016)
10. Li, G., Zhu, X., Zeng, Y., Wang, Q., Lin, L.: Semantic relationships guided representation learning for facial action unit recognition. arXiv preprint arXiv:1904.09939 (2019)
11. Li, W., Abtahi, F., Zhu, Z., Yin, L.: EAC-Net: a region-based deep enhancing and cropping approach for facial action unit detection. In: 2017 12th IEEE International Conference on Automatic Face & Gesture Recognition (FG 2017), pp. 103–110. IEEE (2017)
12. Li, Y., Tarlow, D., Brockschmidt, M., Zemel, R.: Gated graph sequence neural networks. arXiv preprint arXiv:1511.05493 (2015)
13. Liu, Z., Song, G., Cai, J., Cham, T.J., Zhang, J.: Conditional adversarial synthesis of 3D facial action units. arXiv preprint arXiv:1802.07421 (2018)
14. Martinez, B., Valstar, M.F., Jiang, B., Pantic, M.: Automatic analysis of facial actions: a survey. IEEE Trans. Affect. Comput. **10**, 325–347 (2017)
15. Masci, J., Meier, U., Cireşan, D., Schmidhuber, J.: Stacked convolutional auto-encoders for hierarchical feature extraction. In: Honkela, T., Duch, W., Girolami, M., Kaski, S. (eds.) ICANN 2011. LNCS, vol. 6791, pp. 52–59. Springer, Heidelberg (2011). https://doi.org/10.1007/978-3-642-21735-7_7
16. Mavadati, S.M., Mahoor, M.H., Bartlett, K., Trinh, P., Cohn, J.F.: DISFA: a spontaneous facial action intensity database. IEEE Trans. Affect. Comput. **4**(2), 151–160 (2013)
17. Milletari, F., Navab, N., Ahmadi, S.A.: V-Net: fully convolutional neural networks for volumetric medical image segmentation. In: 2016 Fourth International Conference on 3D Vision (3DV), pp. 565–571. IEEE (2016)
18. Ng, Y.C., Colombo, N., Silva, R.: Bayesian semi-supervised learning with graph gaussian processes. In: Advances in Neural Information Processing Systems, pp. 1683–1694 (2018)
19. Niepert, M., Ahmed, M., Kutzkov, K.: Learning convolutional neural networks for graphs. In: International Conference on Machine Learning, pp. 2014–2023 (2016)
20. Song, Y., McDuff, D., Vasisht, D., Kapoor, A.: Exploiting sparsity and co-occurrence structure for action unit recognition. In: 2015 11th IEEE International Conference and Workshops on Automatic Face and Gesture Recognition (FG). vol. 1, pp. 1–8. IEEE (2015)

21. Taigman, Y., Yang, M., Ranzato, M., Wolf, L.: DeepFace: closing the gap to human-level performance in face verification. In: Proceedings of the IEEE Conference on Computer Vision and Pattern Recognition, pp. 1701–1708 (2014)
22. Wang, S., Hao, L., Ji, Q.: Facial action unit recognition and intensity estimation enhanced through label dependencies. IEEE Trans. Image Process. **28**(3), 1428–1442 (2019). https://doi.org/10.1109/TIP.2018.2878339
23. Wang, Z., Li, Y., Wang, S., Qiang, J.: Capturing global semantic relationships for facial action unit recognition. In: IEEE International Conference on Computer Vision (2014)
24. Zhang, X., et al.: A high-resolution spontaneous 3D dynamic facial expression database. In: 2013 10th IEEE International Conference and Workshops on Automatic Face and Gesture Recognition (FG), pp. 1–6. IEEE (2013)
25. Zhao, K., Chu, W.S., De la Torre, F., Cohn, J.F., Zhang, H.: Joint patch and multi-label learning for facial action unit and holistic expression recognition. IEEE Trans. Image Process. **25**(8), 3931–3946 (2016)
26. Zhao, K., Chu, W.S., Zhang, H.: Deep region and multi-label learning for facial action unit detection. In: Proceedings of the IEEE Conference on Computer Vision and Pattern Recognition, pp. 3391–3399 (2016)
27. Zou, M., Conzen, S.D.: A new dynamic Bayesian network (DBN) approach for identifying gene regulatory networks from time course microarray data. Bioinformatics **21**(1), 71–79 (2005)

Enhanced Gaze Following via Object Detection and Human Pose Estimation

Jian Guan[1], Liming Yin[2], Jianguo Sun[1], Shuhan Qi[2], Xuan Wang[2(✉)], and Qing Liao[2,3]

[1] College of Computer Science and Technology, Harbin Engineering University, Harbin 150001, China
[2] Department of Computer Science and Technology, Harbin Institute of Technology (Shenzhen), Shenzhen 518055, China
wangxuan@cs.hitsz.edu.cn
[3] Peng Cheng Laboratory, Shenzhen 518000, China

Abstract. The aim of gaze following is to estimate the gaze direction, which is useful for the understanding of human behaviour in various applications. However, it is still an open problem that has not been fully studied. In this paper, we present a novel framework for gaze following problem, where both the front/side face case and the back face case are taken into account. For the front/side face case, head pose estimation is applied to estimate the gaze, and then object detection is used to further refine the gaze direction by selecting the object that intersects with the gaze in a certain range. For the back face case, a deep neural network with the human pose information is proposed for gaze estimation. Experiments are carried out to demonstrate the superiority of the proposed method, as compared with the state-of-the-art method.

Keywords: Gaze following · Objection detection · Human pose estimation · Deep neural network

1 Introduction

Human gaze is an important clue to the understanding of human behaviour. By following the gaze, we may probably know where a person is looking, how he is interacting with object or other person, and even infer what he is thinking about. Therefore, it is of great value for emotion recognition, cognitive process research, and human-machine interaction [3,14].

There are many works focus on eye tracking or gaze estimation, however, these are different from gaze following, as either eye tracking or gaze estimation usually requires specialized hardware (e.g., head-mounted camera, infra-red light source) to capture users' face or eye region [3]. Although these methods are useful for human-machine interaction and psychology experiment, the specialized hardware and the tedious calibration procedure often limit the application of such methods [13].

Y. M. Ro et al. (Eds.): MMM 2020, LNCS 11962, pp. 502–513, 2020.
https://doi.org/10.1007/978-3-030-37734-2_41

Recently, appearance-based deep learning methods have been studied for gaze estimation, which only need one camera [4,16]. To obtain the gaze point, the relative position of the camera and the user is applied, it often requires the user to face the camera. This restriction leads to the difficulty of processing the surveillance video, where people are far away from the camera without looking at the camera. For example, the method proposed in [5] is only applicable for the situation that people are looking at each other. The method in [1] achieved gaze following by finding the regions in which multiple lines of gaze intersect. This method is applicable for the scene with multi-people, where each one has an ego-centric camera. In [7] and [6], these works proposed a system to infer the region attracting the attention of a group of people (social saliency prediction), which require a set of images taken from the viewpoint of each people in the image. [8] improved the models of free-viewing saliency prediction via gaze following, however, it relies on people that face the camera.

Gaze following aims to estimate the gaze direction, and localize the gaze point. This can be beneficial for many applications, e.g., the recognition of abnormal case, and finding the most noticeable product in a shopping mall. However, it is still a challenging problem. Because of the differences of human appearances and poses in the scene, it often requires the analysis of the complex background [10]. To the best of our knowledge, the method in [10] is the first to apply a single third-person view of the scene to infer gaze, where the authors stimulate the procedure of human gaze following. Their results show that when people infer where another person is looking, they often first look at the person's head and eyes to estimate their view field, and subsequently seek salient objects in their perspective to predict where they are looking. However, this method also has the limitation as the methods mentioned above that people need to face the camera.

Motivated by [10], a novel gaze following framework is proposed in this paper, which can solve the gaze following problem without additional equipment or any limitation on person, i.e., face the camera. In this framework, the gaze following problem is divided into two cases by employing a face detection method, the front/side face case and the back face case. For the front/side case, the human face is front or side to the camera; and for the back face case, the human face is back to the camera. In the first case, the gaze can be estimated by head pose, moreover, we use an object detection module to refine the result of gaze estimation. For the second case, we propose a deep neural network (DNN) framework that incorporates the human pose information to estimate gaze. Therefore, our proposed method not only can be used for gaze following in front/side face situation as the method in [10], but also can be applied in back face situation.

The remainder of the paper is organized as follows: Sect. 2 presents the proposed gaze following method in detail. Section 3 shows the experiment results. Section 4 gives the conclusion and the potential future work.

2 Proposed Method

Here we briefly introduce our proposed gaze following framework. First, object detection is performed to locate object and human. Then, face detection is conducted to detect the image is front/side face case or the back face case. For front/side face case, gaze direction is achieved via head pose estimation and then refined by object location process. For back face case, human keypoint detection is applied to locate the back face, and the gaze is estimated by using DNN that incorporates the information of full image, e.g., head image and human keypoints. The proposed framework is given in Fig. 1. Note that, this framework can be extended to process the case of multi-person gaze following.

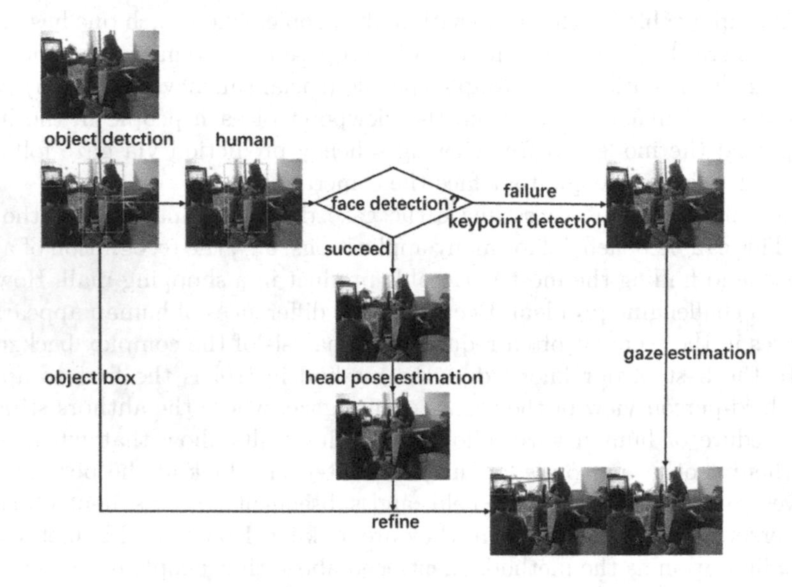

Fig. 1. The proposed gaze following framework.

2.1 Gaze Following via Head Pose Estimation and Object Detection

In this section, we give the proposed gaze following method for front/side face situation, where the gaze direction is estimated by head pose estimation, and further refined by an object detection operation. As the appearance of front/side face has adequate information for head pose estimation, the state-of-the-art method can already provide enough estimation accuracy. Therefore, we apply a state-of-the-art method hopenet [12] for head pose estimation. Here, we suppose that although the gaze direction is different from head pose sometimes, they should be approximately equal in most cases.

Then, object detection is conducted to refine the gaze direction by employing a Faster R-CNN method [11]. Specifically, among the objects that are intersected with gaze, the nearest one is assumed as being looking at. The distance between the center of the object and the center of face is calculated. After the object being looking at is selected, its center is set to be as the point of attention, and is used to refine the gaze direction. The result is illustrated in Fig. 2.

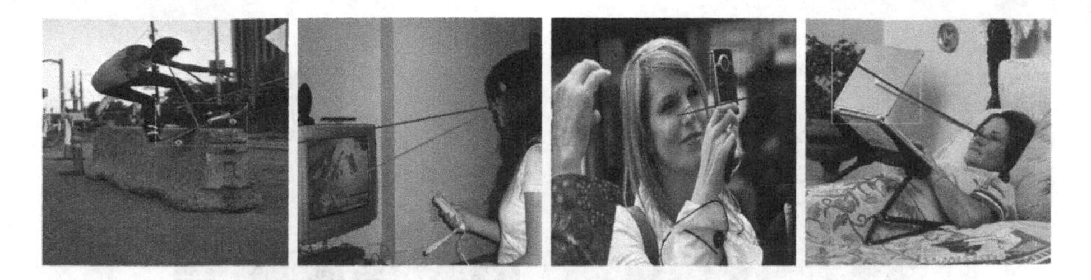

Fig. 2. Illustration of the proposed method for front/side face. Blue line is the estimation of head pose. Red line is the estimation of the gaze refined by the object detection. Object is in green box. (Color figure online)

However, there exist two problems in gaze following: (1) the size of the object is too small, which may lead to the object box cannot intersect with the gaze direction; (2) the size of the object is too big, which may lead to the center of the object deviates from the gaze direction, as demonstrated in Fig. 3. Therefore, we proposed two principles to address these problems. First, search the object in a certain range $[\theta_{down}, \theta_{up}]$, where $\theta_{down} = \theta_g - \theta_s$ and $\theta_{up} = \theta_g + \theta_s$. Here, θ_g is the gaze direction, and θ_s is the parameter that controls the search range. Second, we set a threshold for gaze direction refinement, if $|\theta_g - \theta_r| > \theta_t$, the gaze direction doesn't need to be corrected. θ_r is the new refined gaze direction, and θ_t is the threshold that rejects the refinement.

Here, the angles of the four vertexes of the object box are computed to determine whether or not the object is intersected with the gaze (the object is within the range of eye sight). And the vertex angle θ is defined as $\theta = atan2(x, y)$, where (x, y) are the vertex coordinates of the object box, and the center of human head is the origin of the coordinate. As $atan2$ is discontinuous when the object box crosses the second and third quadrant, there are two cases need to be handled to estimate the gaze that interacts with the object, which are illustrated in Fig. 4.

(a) when the object box doesn't cross the second and the third quadrant, the object that intersects with gaze should satisfy following condition

$$[\theta_B, \theta_A] \cap [\theta_{down}, \theta_{up}] \neq \varnothing \tag{1}$$

where $[\theta_B, \theta_A]$ stands for the angle range of the object box, θ_A and θ_B are the largest and the least angle among four vertexes, respectively.

(b) when the object box crosses the second and the third quadrant, the satisfied condition is

$$[\theta_B, \pi] \cap [\theta_{down}, \theta_{up}] \neq \varnothing \vee [-\pi, \theta_A] \cap [\theta_{down}, \theta_{up}] \neq \varnothing \tag{2}$$

where θ_A and θ_B denote the second largest and the second least angle among four vertexes, respectively. Hence, the angle range of the object box is spit into two parts $[\theta_B, \pi]$ and $[-\pi, \theta_A]$.

Fig. 3. Two groups of images (a) and (b), both include the original image (left up), object detection (right up), head pose estimation (left down), gaze direction refined by object box (right down). Here, (a) shows the situation that the object is too small to intersect with the initially estimated gaze direction, so that refinement is needed to find the object within a certain range; (b) shows the situation that the center of the large object is far from the true gaze direction, where refinement of the object center is unnecessary. Green box denotes object box, blue line denotes head pose and red line stands for the gaze direction refined by object centre. (Color figure online)

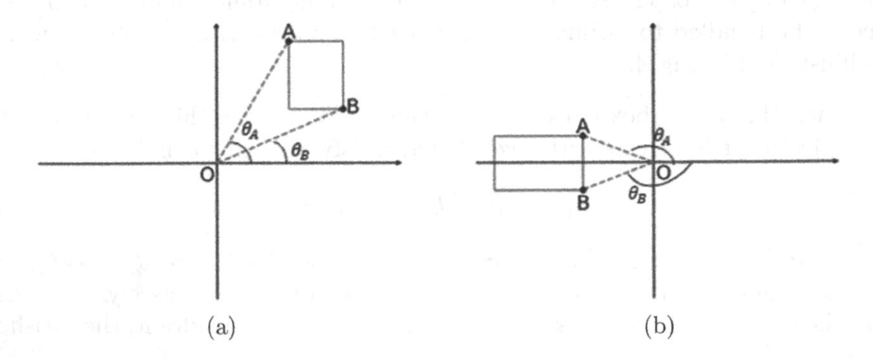

Fig. 4. Two cases are given to explain the conditions that the object box intersects with gaze depending on the object box crosses the second and the third quadrant or not. The center of human head is the coordinate origin, and blue box denotes the object box. In (a), object box does not cross the second and the third quadrant. In (b), object box crosses the second and the third quadrant. (Color figure online)

2.2 Gaze Following via Human Pose Estimation

In [10], the authors use the appearance and location of head to learn the gaze direction. It cannot be applied for the situation when human face cannot be seen, in other words, the case of back face. Because there is inadequate information for the network to infer the gaze direction.

In our work, we improve the gaze following via human pose estimation, which can achieve the gaze following for back face case. This is because human pose has certain relation with head pose and gaze direction, therefore, we assume that with the human pose information, the deep convolution neural network can predict gaze direction more robustly and accurately. In addition, the human pose also has the relation with the object that is interacted with. Recent work on human object interaction [2] has proven this point. This method uses human image to localize the object that is interacted with. Another benefit of using human pose estimation is that the keypoint location of head top and neck can be applied to localize the head position and determine its size. Hence, we employ the human pose estimation in our proposed gaze following framework for back face case. Figure 5 shows how human pose estimation effects on gaze following for back face case. It can be seen, by using the human pose information, we can obtain the human keypoint location, which can be used as the input of in our proposed gaze following network, as detailed next.

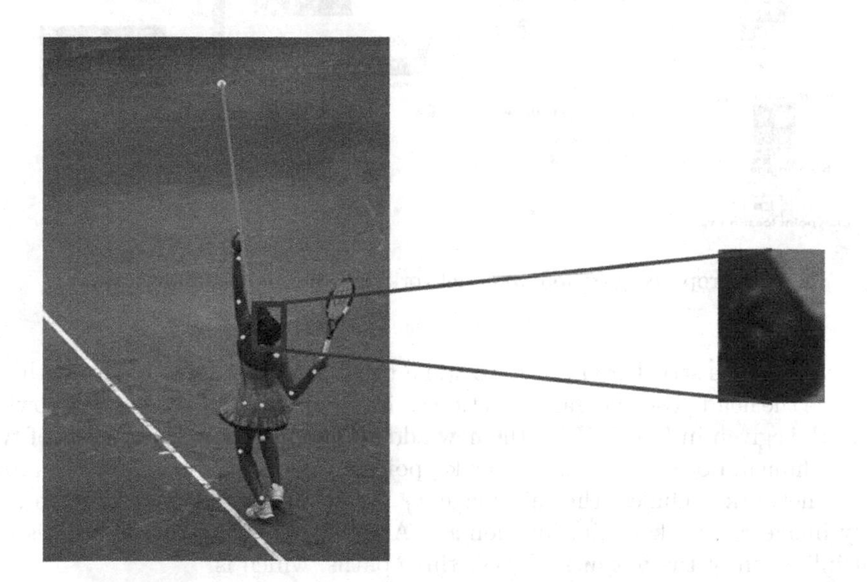

Fig. 5. Illustration of human pose estimation effects on gaze following for back face case. Although few information is provided by head appearance, with human pose information, we can obtain human keypoint locations (green dots). (Color figure online)

Here, the position of head center h_c and size h_s can be calculated as follows

$$h_c = \frac{p_h + p_n}{2} \tag{3}$$

$$h_s = \|p_h - p_n\| \tag{4}$$

where p_h is the location of the keypoint of head top, and p_n is the location of the keypoint of neck.

In [10], the main structure of the gaze following network contains two paths: saliency path and head pose path. The saliency path aims to find the saliency object; and the head pose path is used to estimate the head pose. Then, the saliency object in the head pose direction can be found by a multiplication operation on these two paths. This saliency object is assumed to be the object being looking at, and its direction is the gaze direction to be estimated. However, this structure cannot achieve a promised estimation result for back face case, which is the case as shown in Fig. 5 without the human keypoints, only black pixels can be seen.

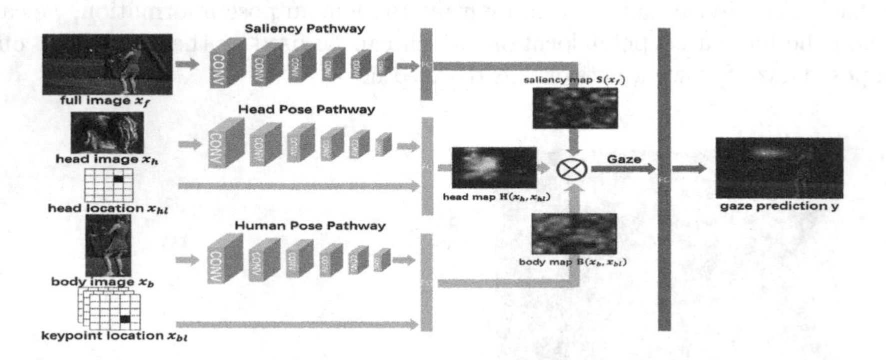

Fig. 6. Proposed gaze following network with human pose estimation.

Based on the structure in [10], we add a third path (i.e. human pose path) to improve the head pose and gaze direction estimation, the proposed gaze following network is given in Fig. 6. Here, the new added human pose path consists of two inputs: human body image x_b and the keypoint location x_{bl}. Therefore, the input of our network includes: the full image x_f, head image x_h, head location x_{hl}, body image x_b and keypoint location x_{bl}. And the output of the network is the multiplication of the outputs of these three paths, which is

$$Y = F(S(x_f) \otimes H(x_h, x_{hl}) \otimes P(x_b, x_{bl})) \tag{5}$$

where $F(\cdot)$ denotes the fully connection operation, $S(\cdot)$, $H(\cdot)$, and $P(\cdot)$ denote the output of these three paths, respectively. $Y \in R^{M \times M}$ is the predicted gaze location.

A spatially smooth cross-entropy [9] is used as the loss of our gaze following network, which is

$$L(Y,Y^*) = \sum_{i=1}^{M}\sum_{j=1}^{M} w_{ij} E_{ij}(Y,Y^*) \tag{6}$$

where $i \times j$ is the size of the grid cell, w_{ij} is the weight, Y and Y^* are the predicted gaze location and the ground truth respectively. $E_{ij}(Y,Y^*)$ is the smooth cross-entropy, which can be calculated as follows

$$E_{ij}(Y,Y^*) = -\sum_{k=0}^{M-1}\sum_{l=0}^{M-1} \overline{S}_{ij}(Y^*) \log \overline{S}_{ij}(Y) \tag{7}$$

where $\overline{S}_{ij}(\cdot)$ denotes the spatially smooth operation as follows

$$\overline{S}_{ij}(Y) = \sum_{m=-i}^{i}\sum_{n=-j}^{j} Y[k+m][l+n] \tag{8}$$

3 Experiments and Results

3.1 Experimental Setup

Experiments are conducted on the Gazefollow dataset [10]. Several baseline methods are evaluated on the test dataset, which are the same as that in [10], Random, Center, and Fixed bias. In order to demonstrate the gaze following performance of our method, especially for back face case, the test set is split into front/side face case and back face case by face detection, where S^3FD [15] is employed for face detection in all experiments.

To evaluate the gaze following performance, the same performance metrics as in [10] are employed, which are the angle error between prediction and the ground truth (Ang.), the distance between prediction and the ground truth (Dist.), and area under ROC curve (AUC). Here, Ang. and Dist. are computed as follows

$$\text{Ang.} = \frac{1}{N}\sum_{n=1}^{N} |\theta_n - \theta_n^*| \tag{9}$$

where n indicates the nth test sample, and N is the total number of test samples. θ_n denotes the predicted direction, and θ_n^* is the ground truth.

$$\text{Dist.} = \frac{1}{N}\sum_{n=1}^{N} \sqrt{\left(\frac{x_n - x_n^*}{width}\right)^2 + \left(\frac{y_n - y_n^*}{height}\right)^2} \tag{10}$$

where (x_n, y_n) represents the predicted location, and (x_n^*, y_n^*) is the ground truth. *width* and *height* are the width and height of the image respectively.

3.2 Experimental Results

First, experiment is conducted on training set to show the convergence of the proposed method, as compared with the method in [10] (Recasens). The result is given in Fig. 7. In the training stage, we can see that with the human pose information, the loss decreases sharply when compared with Recasens' no pose network, and both networks converge after 250K iterations.

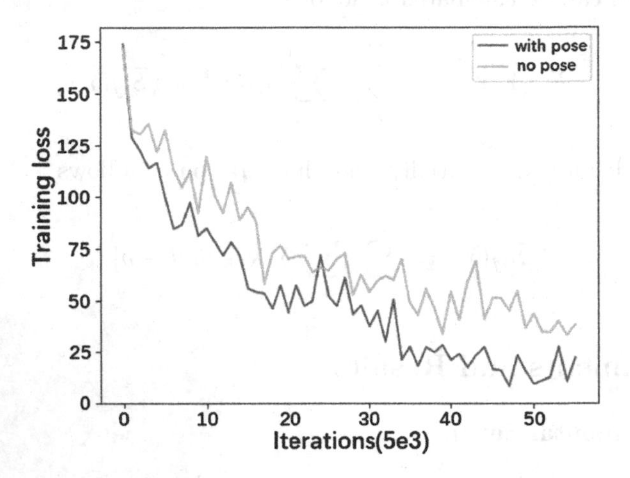

Fig. 7. Training loss with pose and no pose network on Gazefollow dataset, where the network with pose information has lower training loss.

Then, in order to show the capability of our proposed method for gaze following in both front/side face and back face cases, we carry out experiments in the case of front/side and back face respectively. In the case of front/side face, experiments are conducted to evaluate the performance of our proposed method, as compared with baseline methods. As can be seen from Table 1(a), Recasens gives a significant improvement when compared with other methods, which shows the superiority of this deep learning method. However, by applying object detection to refine gaze direction, our proposed method can achieve the least angle error, with 2.5° improvement over Recasens in the case of front/side face. Regarding the back face case, with the human pose information, our proposed method can achieve the best gaze following performance as shown in Table 1(b). However, both gaze following results in Table 1 are still far away from the human level performance, which is only 11° angle error [10]. Hence, more efforts are needed in gaze following problem.

In addition, to show the validity of using human pose information, we conduct another experiment for gaze following, as compared with Recasens' model. The result is given in Fig. 8. We find that with human pose information, in

Table 1. Performance comparison of gaze following in front/side face case and back face case. (a) Gaze following in the case of front/side face. (b) Gaze following in the case of back face.

Method	Ang.
Random	69.75°
Center	48.52°
Fixed	42.22°
Recasens	22.88°
Ours	**20.37°**

(a) front or side face

Method	AUC	Dist.	Ang.
Random	0.501	0.474	69.75°
Center	0.505	0.299	48.52°
Fixed	0.507	0.264	42.22°
Recasens	0.864	0.219	26.88°
Ours	**0.865**	**0.210**	**25.80°**

(b) back face

Fig. 8. Illustration of gaze following performance by using the proposed gaze following network, as compared with Recasens'. Red line stands for Recasens', blue line denotes ours with human pose network, and green line is the ground truth. (Color figure online)

the case of back face, our model can predict the gaze direction around hands, whereas Recasens' model can only estimate the gaze direction around human head, as illustrated in Fig. 8. This is reasonable, as people are often looking at the object that they are interacting with. In other words, when people are holding something in hands or pointing at something, our model can achieve better prediction.

Fig. 9. Failure caused by lacking of depth information: blue line is the result of our method, and green line is the ground truth. (Color figure online)

However, in both front/side face and back face case, the proposed model and other models that we compared are all misled by object in different depth positions as shown in Fig. 9. This is because the object is in a different depth position, and the gaze is often considered as the object being looking at, thus misleading our model. Therefore, without depth information, this problem can be very hard to resolve, which is an interesting direction for our future work.

4 Conclusions

In this paper, we presented a novel gaze following framework, which could be used for both front/side face and back face cases. Experiments showed the proposed framework can achieve better performance for the gaze following in both front/side face case and back face case. Especially for the back face case, which is rarely considered by other methods, with human pose information, the proposed model can estimate gaze more accurately. However, the result is still far from the human level, more efforts are needed for gaze following problem. Future work will focus on exploiting depth information to solve this problem.

Acknowledgement. This work is partly supported by the Fundamental Research Funds for the Central Universities (No. 3072019CFJ0602).

References

1. Fathi, A., Hodgins, J.K., Rehg, J.M.: Social interactions: a first-person perspective. In: Proceedings of IEEE Conference on Computer Vision and Pattern Recognition (CVPR), pp. 1226–1233 (2012)
2. Gkioxari, G., Girshick, R.B., Dollár, P., He, K.: Detecting and recognizing human-object interactions. CoRR abs/1704.07333 (2017). http://arxiv.org/abs/1704.07333
3. Hansen, D.W., Ji, Q.: In the eye of the beholder: a survey of models for eyes and gaze. IEEE Trans. Pattern Anal. Mach. Intell. **32**(3), 478–500 (2010)
4. Krafka, K., et al.: Eye tracking for everyone. In: Proceedings of IEEE Conference on Computer Vision and Pattern Recognition (CVPR), pp. 2176–2184 (2016)
5. Marin-Jimenez, M.J., Zisserman, A., Eichner, M., Ferrari, V.: Detecting people looking at each other in videos. Int. J. Comput. Vis. **106**(3), 282–296 (2014)
6. Park, H.S., Jain, E., Sheikh, Y.: Predicting primary gaze behavior using social saliency fields. In: Proceedings of IEEE International Conference on Computer Vision, pp. 3503–3510 (2013)
7. Park, H.S., Shi, J.: Social saliency prediction. In: Proceedings of IEEE Conference on Computer Vision and Pattern Recognition (CVPR), pp. 4777–4785 (2015)
8. Parks, D., Borji, A., Itti, L.: Augmented saliency model using automatic 3D head pose detection and learned gaze following in natural scenes. Vis. Res. **116**, 113–126 (2015)
9. Recasens, A., Vondrick, C., Khosla, A., Torralba, A.: Following gaze in video. In: Proceedings of IEEE International Conference on Computer Vision (ICCV), pp. 1444–1452 (2017)

10. Recasens, A., Khosla, A., Vondrick, C., Torralba, A.: Where are they looking? In: Proceedings of Advances in Neural Information Processing Systems, pp. 199–207 (2015)
11. Ren, S., He, K., Girshick, R., Sun, J.: Faster R-CNN: towards real-time object detection with region proposal networks. IEEE Trans. Pattern Anal. Mach. Intell. **39**(6), 1137–1149 (2017)
12. Ruiz, N., Chong, E., Rehg, J.M.: Fine-grained head pose estimation without keypoints. CoRR abs/1710.00925 (2017). http://arxiv.org/abs/1710.00925
13. Santini, T., Fuhl, W., Kasneci, E.: CalibMe: fast and unsupervised eye tracker calibration for gaze-based pervasive human-computer interaction. In: Proceedings of the CHI Conference on Human Factors in Computing Systems, pp. 2594–2605. ACM (2017)
14. Shepherd, S.V.: Following gaze: gaze-following behavior as a window into social cognition. Front. Integr. Neurosci. **4**, 1–13 (2010)
15. Zhang, S., Zhu, X., Lei, Z., Shi, H., Wang, X., Li, S.Z.: S^3FD: single shot scale-invariant face detector. In: Proceedings of IEEE International Conference on Computer Vision (ICCV), pp. 192–201 (2017)
16. Zhang, X., Sugano, Y., Fritz, M., Bulling, A.: Appearance-based gaze estimation in the wild. In: Proceedings of IEEE Conference on Computer Vision and Pattern Recognition (CVPR), pp. 4511–4520 (2015)

Region Based Adversarial Synthesis of Facial Action Units

Zhilei Liu(✉), Diyi Liu, and Yunpeng Wu

College of Intelligence and Computing, Tianjin University, Tianjin, China
{zhileiliu,liudiyi,wuyupeng}@tju.edu.cn

Abstract. Facial expression synthesis or editing has recently received increasing attention in the field of affective computing and facial expression modeling. However, most existing facial expression synthesis works are limited in paired training data, low resolution, identity information damaging, and so on. To address those limitations, this paper introduces a novel Action Unit (AU) level facial expression synthesis method called Local Attentive Conditional Generative Adversarial Network (LAC-GAN) based on face action units annotations. Given desired AU labels, LAC-GAN utilizes local AU regional rules to control the status of each AU and attentive mechanism to combine several of them into the whole photo-realistic facial expressions or arbitrary facial expressions. In addition, unpaired training data is utilized in our proposed method to train the manipulation module with the corresponding AU labels, which learns a mapping between a facial expression manifold. Extensive qualitative and quantitative evaluations are conducted on commonly used BP4D dataset to verify the effectiveness of our proposed AU synthesis method.

Keywords: Facial action unit · Facial expression synthesis/editing · Conditional generative adversarial network

1 Introduction

Recently, identity preserving facial expression generation or synthesis from a single facial image has attracted continuously increasing attention in the field of affective computing and computer vision [3,18,27]. Ekman and Friesen [4] developed the Facial Action Coding System (FACS) for defining facial expressions with some basic facial action units (AUs), each of which represents a basic facial muscle movement or expression change. However, with the challenges of time-consuming AU annotation and imbalanced databases, FACS based facial expression analysis with large-scaled data dependent deep learning methods is not widely conducted. To address those issues, facial expression synthesis combined and coordinated by a certain association of AUs has recently received increased attention in the method of facial editing and transformation [18,27]. The generated facial expressions corresponding to desired AU labels can be applied to create a facial expression dataset with multiple diverse AU labels.

Y. M. Ro et al. (Eds.): MMM 2020, LNCS 11962, pp. 514–526, 2020.
https://doi.org/10.1007/978-3-030-37734-2_42

Most recent existing studies working on facial expression synthesis based on distinct AU states pay more attention on the global face and some of them train with the paired data. Zhou et al. [27] proposed a conditional difference adversarial autoencoder (CDAAE) to transfer AUs from absence to presence on the global face. This method divides the database into two groups according to absence or presence of AU labels and trains with paired images of the same subject, which increases the complexity of training and the difficulties of preprocess. Moreover, CDAAE employs the low resolution images, which can lose facial details vital for AU synthesis. GANimation proposed by Pumarola et al. [18], transfers AUs on the whole face which can produce a co-generated phenomenon between different AUs. It is difficult for the method to synthesize a single AU respectively without keeping the other AU untouched. Liu et al. [13] uses 3D Morphable Model (3DMM) to achieve AU synthesis, where the transformation from a image to 3D model damages the texture details of the original images.

In this paper, aiming at building a model for facial action unit synthesis with more local texture details, we propose a facial action unit synthesis framework named LAC-GAN by integrating local AU regions with conditional generative adversarial network. With personal identity information well preserved, our proposed LAC-GAN manipulates AUs between different states, which learns a mapping between a facial manifold related to AU manipulation same as CAAE proposed by Zhang et al. [26]. Specifically, our AU manipulation model is trained on unpaired samples and the corresponding AU labels without grouping the database by different states of labels. In addition, the key point of our method is to make the manipulation module focus only on the synthesis of local AU region without touching the rest identity information and the other AUs. For this purpose, AU region of interest(ROI) localization mechanism without co-generated phenomenon between different AUs is applied to synthesize a single AU respectively and correctly. Finally, to evaluate the performance of proposed method, quantitative analyses on our synthesized facial images are conducted with state-of-the-art facial action unit detectors.

In summary, the contributions of our work are as follows: (1) The proposed AU manipulation module learns a mapping between the facial expression manifold with unpaired samples and corresponding AU labels. (2) Specific AU related local attention is considered to manipulate AU features locally. (3) The proposed AU synthesis framework LAC-GAN enables facial expression synthesis given any desired AU combination of AU combinations. To demonstrate the effectiveness of our proposed framework, both qualitative and quantitative evaluations are performed.

2 Related Work

Our proposed framework is closely related to existing studies on GAN based image generation and facial expression synthesis.

2.1 Conditional Generative Adversarial Network

Generative Adversarial Network (GAN) [5] and Deep Convoluntional GAN (DCGAN) [19] are powerful class of generative models based on game theory. The typical GAN optimization consists in simultaneously training a generator network to produce realistic fake samples and a discriminator network to distinguish between real and fake data. This idea is embedded by the so-called adversarial loss.

An active area of research is designing CGAN [15] models extended by GAN that incorporate conditions and constraints into the generation process. Prior studies have explored combining several conditions on transformation task, such as class information [16], particularly, interesting for which are those methods exploring image based conditioning as in image super-resolution [10], image inpainting [17], image-to-image translation [8] and face age progression or regression [23,26]. Facial expression editing mostly focus on using the methods of CGAN, similar to the above transferring work.Based on face age progression method [26], we proposed a conditional model to learn the face manifold conditioned on AUs.

2.2 Facial Expression Synthesis

In recent years, the study on facial expression editing/synthesis has been actively investigated in computer vision. Recently, Yeh et al. [24] proposed to edit the facial expression by image warping with appearance flow. Although the model can generate high-resolution images, paired samples as well as the labeled query image are required. GANimation [18] proposed a method of virtual avatar animation on the whole facial images while training a cycle conditional generative adversarial network to achieve the transformation of expression. Recently, Zhou et al. [27] proposed a conditional difference adversarial autoencoder (CDAAE) for facial expression synthesis that considers AU labels. However, the resolution of its generated facial image is only 32×32, and the generated facial images with AU labels are not well quantitatively evaluated. By integrating with the 3D Morphable Model (3DMM), Liu et al. [13] proposed an 3D AU synthesis framework to transfer AUs in the range of intensities, however, some texture details are lost for certain AUs because of the limitations of 3D face model. In addition, while generating a single AU, all these above mentioned methods can damage the other AU without keeping the identity information untouched.

It is a certain reference for AU synthesis that most works on AU detection make full use of landmark-based geometry to improve the performance. Li et al. [12] proposed a deep learning based approach named EAC-Net for facial action unit detection by enhancing and cropping the AU regions of interest(ROI) with roughly extracted facial landmark information. Therefore, in this paper, imitating EAC-Net, our proposed framework separates the facial image into multiple local AU regions which are integrated in modern deep learning model. In addition, attention-GAN [1] proposed adopts attention mechanism to focus on generating objects of interests without touching the background region.

Similar to them, we proposed AU ROI localization module to maintain the other information except the concerned AU.

3 LAC-GAN for Facial Action Unit Synthesis

In this section, the overall framework of our proposed LAC-GAN for AU synthesis as shown in Fig. 1 is presented at first. The details of the AU manipulation module with conditional AU region generator (CARG) for single AU synthesis as shown in Fig. 2 are introduced in the next.

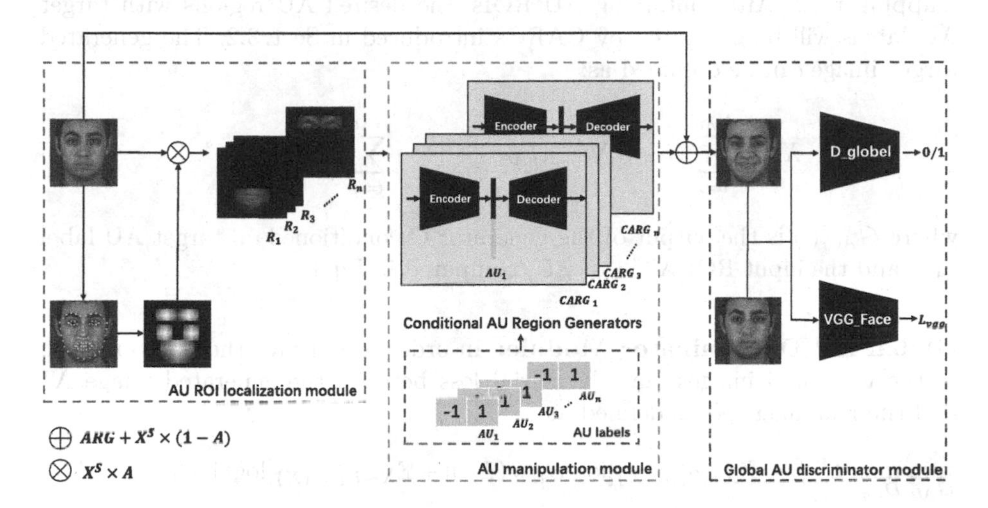

Fig. 1. The overall framework of LAC-GAN

3.1 The Overall Framework of LAC-GAN

AS shown in Fig. 1, our proposed LAC-GAN consists of three modules: AU ROI localization module with fixed local attention, AU manipulation module, and global AU discriminator module. In the AU ROI localization module, AU specific ROIs are defined as local regions of the original facial image $X^s \in \mathbb{R}^{H \times W \times 3}$. Given the input image X^s and the target one-hot AU label vector $l_{AU_i} \in \{-1, +1\}^{N_{AU} \times 2}$, the AU manipulation module focuses on transforming the AU ROI from the source state to the target state. The resulting image is therefore a combination of all the changed AU regions with the rest regions of original facial image. Finally, the global AU discriminator aims to distinguish the real images and the generated images.

AU ROI Localization Module: AUs appear in specific facial regions that are not limited to facial landmark points. Instead of directly using facial landmarks, AU center rules are adopted by us to localize AU specific ROIs. Similar to EAC-net, AU local attention map containing several AUs are designed here for the purpose of generating AU ROIs. In addition, we capture the AU local attention map by applying the Manhattan distance to the AU center. The local AU ROI is defined as:

$$X^{AU_i} = A_{AU_i} \times X^s, \tag{1}$$

where X^{AU_i} is the pixel-level weight of the AU_i with the local attention map $A_{AU_i} \in \{0, ..., 1\}^{H \times W}$.

In order to preserve the original facial information outside of the AU ROIs, an local AU attention localization is considered in this module. Concretely, the whole face is divided into multiple AU regions based on the local AU attention mapping rules. After obtaining AU ROIs, the desired AU regions with target AU labels will be generated by CARGs introduced in Sect. 3.2. The generated target image can be obtained as:

$$X^t = \sum_{i=1}^{N_{AU}} G_{AU_i}(X^{AU_i}, l_{AU_i}) + (1 - \sum_{i=1}^{N_{AU}} A_{AU_i}) \times X^s, \tag{2}$$

where $G_{AU_i}(\cdot)$ is the output of the generator G conditioned on target AU label l_{AU_i} and the input ROI X^{AU_i} of AU_i computed in Eq. 1.

Global AU Discriminator Module: In order to improve the photo-realism of the generated images, an adversarial loss between the generated image X^t and the real image X^r is defined as:

$$\min_{G_{AU}} \max_{D_{img}} L_{adv}^{img} = \mathbb{E}_{X \sim P_{data}(X)}[\log D_{img}(X^r)] + \mathbb{E}_{X \sim P_{data}(X)}[\log(1 - D_{img}(X^t))], \tag{3}$$

where X^t is synthetic output obtained by Eq. 2.

To preserve more identity information between X^t and X^r, a pre-trained VGG-face model is leveraged to enforce the similarity in the feature space with following loss:

$$\min_{G_{AU}} L_{id} = \sum_l \alpha_l L_1(\phi_l(X^t), \phi_l(X^r)), \tag{4}$$

where $\phi_l(\cdot)$ is the feature map of the l_{th} layer of the VGG-face network, and α_l is the corresponding weight. Similar to [22], the activations at the *conv*1_2, *conv*2_2, *conv*3_2, *conv*4_2 and *conv*5_2 layer of the VGG-face model are used.

3.2 AU Manipulation Module:

As shown in Fig. 2, the proposed AU manipulation module contains multiple local conditional AU regional generators (CARGs) for single facial action unit synthesis. Base on the face manifold assumption demonstrated experimentally in CAAE, the inputs of our proposed CARG are the source ROI of X^{AU_i} and the target label l_{AU_i}. On the other hand, additional local critic discriminator is used to evaluate the quality of the generated regional image.

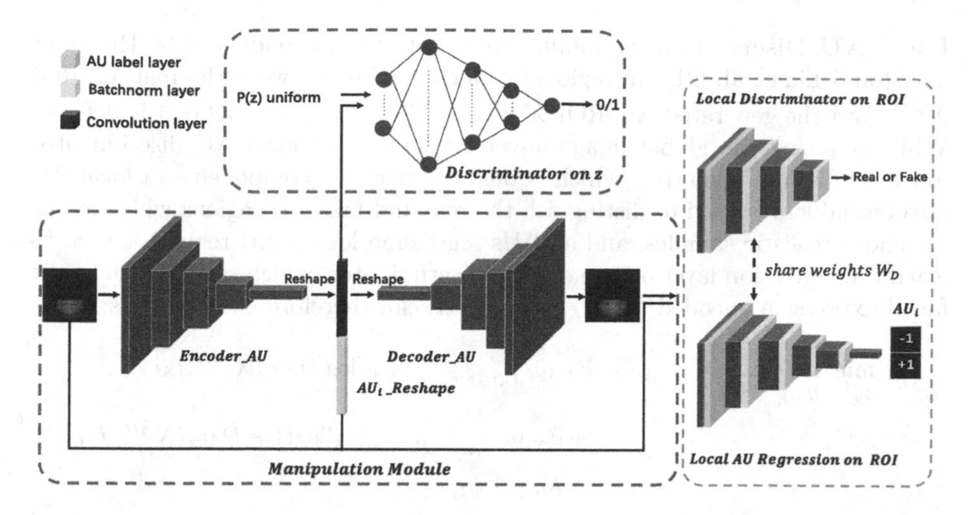

Fig. 2. Proposed conditional AU regional generator of AU manipulation module

Local Conditional AU Regional Generators: Given the specific AU ROI X^{AU_i} of the source image and the desired AU label, the generator network $G_{AU_i} = (G_{en}^{AU_i}, G_{de}^{AU_i})$ with encoder-decoder structure is proposed. At first, the encoder $G_{en}^{AU_i}$ maps the input X^{AU_i} into a latent feature vector z_{AU_i}, N_z is the dimension of the latent feature vector z_{AU_i}. By concatenating the obtained z_{AU_i} and the desired AU labels l_{AU_i} together, the decoder $G_{de}^{AU_i}$ is designed to generate the target AU ROI $X^{\hat{AU}_i} = G_{de}^{AU_i}(G_{en}^{AU_i}(X^{AU_i}), l_{AU_i})$ with original identity information and target AU information. A pixel-wise image reconstruction loss is defined as:

$$\min_{G_{en}^{AU_i}, G_{de}^{AU_i}} L_{pixel}^i = \mathbb{E}_{X^{AU_i} \sim P_{data}(X^{AU_i})}[\|G_{de}^{AU_i}(G_{en}^{AU_i}(X^{AU_i}), l_{AU_i}) - X^{AU_i}\|_1], \tag{5}$$

in which, l_1-norm is adopted to capture low-level structure information. In preliminary experiments, we also tried replacing l_1-norm with the other perceptual loss, although we did not observe significant improved performance.

Discriminator D_z on Latent Feature: The fact is demonstrably authenticated that face images lie on a manifold [6,11]. For the purpose of maintaining the AU regions generated by the face manifold [26], we employ the uniform distribution to z_{AU_i} through the discriminator $D_z^{AU_i}$, which imposes z_{AU_i} on the uniform distribution without "holes". The adversarial training process is of D_z is defined as:

$$\begin{aligned} \min_{G_{en}^{AU_i}} \max_{D_z^{AU_i}} L_{adv\_z}^i = & \mathbb{E}_{z \sim P(z)}[\log D_z^{AU_i}(z)] \\ & + \mathbb{E}_{X^{AU_i} \sim P_{data}(X^{AU_i})}[\log(1 - D_z^{AU_i}(G_{en}^{AU_i}(X^{AU_i}))]. \end{aligned} \tag{6}$$

Local AU Discriminator: Similar to recent studies conducted by Huang et al. [7] and Liu et al. [21], an regional adversarial loss between the real AU ROI X^{AU_i} and the generated AU ROI $X^{\hat{AU}_i} = G_{de}^{AU_i}(G_{en}^{AU_i}(X^{AU_i}), l_{AU_i})$ is defined. While reducing the global image adversarial loss, the local AU discriminator must also reduce the error, which is defined with two components: a local AU adversarial loss is used to distinguish the real and fake AU regions which learns to render realistic samples; and an AUs regression loss of AU regions is used to learn the regression layer on top of local discriminator, which satisfies the target facial expression encoded by l_{AU_i}. Those loss can therefore be defined as:

$$\begin{aligned}\min_{G_{en}^{AU_i}, G_{de}^{AU_i}, R_{AU_i}} \max_{D_{AU_i}} L_{adv\_AU}^i = & \mathbb{E}_{X^{AU_i}, l_{AU_i} \sim P_{data}(X,l)}[\log D_{AU_i}(X^{AU_i}, l_{AU_i})] \\ & + \mathbb{E}_{X^{AU_i}, l_{AU_i} \sim P_{data}(X,l)}[\log(1 - D_{AU_i}(X^{\hat{AU}_i}, l_{AU_i}))] \\ & + \lambda_{AU} L_{label}^i,\end{aligned} \tag{7}$$

where $\lambda_{AU} L_{label}$ is a trade-off parameter of the AU regression loss which keeps the facial region with a specific AU state generated by manipulating the corresponding expression code. This loss is completed as follow:

$$\min_{R_{AU_i}} L_{label}^i = \mathbb{E}_{X^{AU_i}, l_{AU_i} \sim P_{data}(X,l)}[\|R_{AU_i}(X^{\hat{AU}_i}, l_{AU_i}) - l_{AU_i}\|_2^2] \tag{8}$$

Overall Objective Function: To generate the target face with desired AU label vector, following loss function L_{CARG} is defined by linearly combining all previous partial losses:

$$\min_{G_{en}^{AU_i}, G_{de}^{AU_i}, R_{AU_i}} \max_{D_{AU_i}, D_z^{AU_i}} L_{CARG}^i = L_{pixel}^i + \lambda_1 L_{adv\_z}^i + \lambda_2 L_{adv\_AU}^i. \tag{9}$$

The final training loss function of LAC-GAN is a weighted sum of all these losses defined above:

$$\min_{G_{AU}, R_{AU}} \max_{D_{AU}, D_z^{AU}} L_{LAC-GAN} = \sum_{i=1}^{N_{AU}} \beta_i L_{CARG}^i + \lambda_3 L_{id} + \lambda_4 L_{tv}. \tag{10}$$

where $\lambda_j (j = 1, 2, 3, 4)$ is a trade-off parameter, $\beta_i (j = 1, ..., N_{AU})$ is the corresponding weight of $CARG_i$ loss.The total variation regularization L_{tv} [14] is adopt on the reconstructed image to reduce spike artifacts.

4 Experimental Evaluation

4.1 Experimental Dataset and Implementation Details

Dataset: Our LAC-GAN is evaluated on widely used database for facial AU detection, named BP4D [25]. BP4D contains 41 participants with 23 female and 18 male, each of which is involved in 8 sessions captured both 2D and

3D videos for each participant. Each video frame is manually coded with an intensity for each of the 12 AUs, namely AU1, AU2, AU4, AU6, AU7, AU10, AU12, AU14, AU15, AU17, AU23, and AU24, with AU labels of occurrence or absence according to the FACS. In this work, all annotated video frames with successful face registration (100,767 frames) of 31 subjects are selected as the training set, and all annotated video frames (39,233 frames) for the remaining 10 subjects are used as the testing set. The data partition rule is the same as the AU detection model JAA-Net [20] with two folds for training and the remaining one for testing.

Implementation Details: For each facial image, similarity transformations including rotation, uniform scaling, translation, and normalization are performed to obtain a $200 \times 200 \times 3$ color facial image. The kernel size of the multiple convolution and de-convolution layers in our proposed framework is set to be 5×5. The encoder consists of 5 convolutional layers and a reshaped fully connection layer, while the decoder consists of the other reshaped layer and 5 de-convolutional layers. The dimensions of z and AU labels are set to be 60. Discriminator D_z employs four fully connection layers. The batch normalization is adopted on local AU discriminator to make the framework more stable. Simultaneously local AU Regression shares the weight of 4 convolution layers with local AU discriminator.

All models are trained using Tensorflow using the Adam optimizer [9], with learning rate of 0.0002, $\alpha_1 = 0.5, \alpha_2 = 0.9, \alpha_3 = 0.75, \alpha_4 = \alpha_5 = 1$. The weight coefficients for the loss terms in Eqs. 9 and 10 are set to $\lambda_1 = 0.01, \lambda_2 = 0.1, \lambda_3 = 1, \lambda_4 = 0.001, \lambda_{AU} = 10$. During training, we set $\beta_i = 1$, where i is corresponded with original AU labels.

4.2 Qualitative Analysis of AU Synthesis Performance

Synthetic Results of Single AU: We firstly evaluate our model's ability to activate the status of AUs by transforming the neutral face to the absence or the presence of specific AU while preserving the person's identity. Figure 3 shows a subset of 12 AUs individually manipulated at different status during the testing session.

For AU1 (inner brow raiser), AU2 (outer brow raiser), and AU4 (inner brow lowerer) located in the brow region, the changes of synthesis face between absence and presence of AU can be obviously perceived. For AU6 (cheek Raiser) located in the cheek region, the movement of cheek muscle can be observed. For AU10 (Upper Lip Raiser), AU12 (Lip Corner Puller), AU14 (Dimpler), and AU15 (Lip Corner Depressor) located in the mouth region, obvious movements of AU muscles can be observed in the synthetic images. For the other AUs corresponding to the movements in the mouth and chin regions, AU23 (Lip Tightener) can be observed like pouting and AU24 (Lip Pressor) seem like closing mouse obviously. However, Subtle variation of AU7 (Lid Tightener) and AU17 (Chin Raiser) which accounts for minor wrinkling in the synthetic faces.

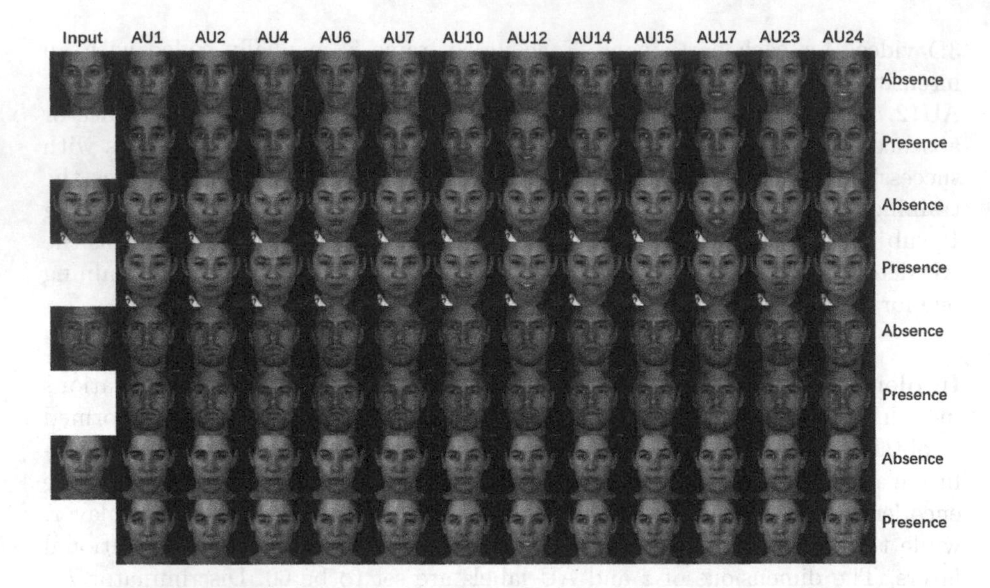

Fig. 3. Synthetic results of single AU.

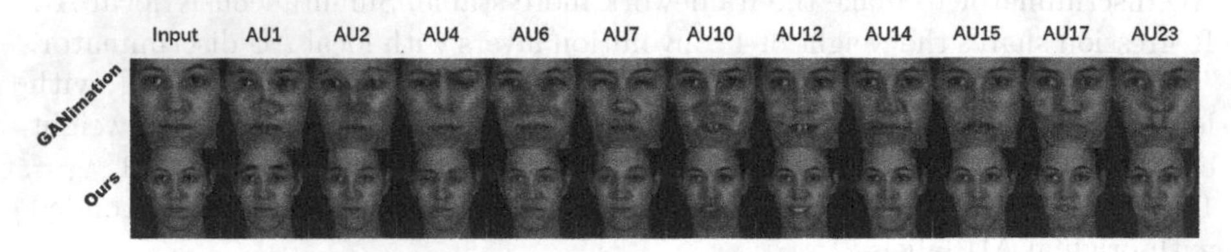

Fig. 4. Qualitative comparison with GANimation [18].

Qualitative Comparison with GANimation: We compare our approach again the baseline GANimation [18]. For a fair comparison, we adopt the same dataset and experimental details with training GANimation. Figure 4 shows our method performs better than GANimation on synthetic of single AUs, with keeping identity information and the other AUs untouched. Owing to the dataset BP4D with poor diversity and unbalanced labels distribution, the generated results we trained is not as well as in their paper. However, ours model can be trained to generate the better results with the same dataset.

Synthetic Results of AU Combinations: Our LAC-GAN can synthesize spontaneous facial expression incorporated by multiple AUs, such as happy and angry. Figure 5 shows the generated happy (AU2, AU6, AU7 and AU12) and angry (AU4 and AU23), which are substantially similar to the ground-truth expressions. The slight difference is probably caused by the different intensity of the presence of AUs.

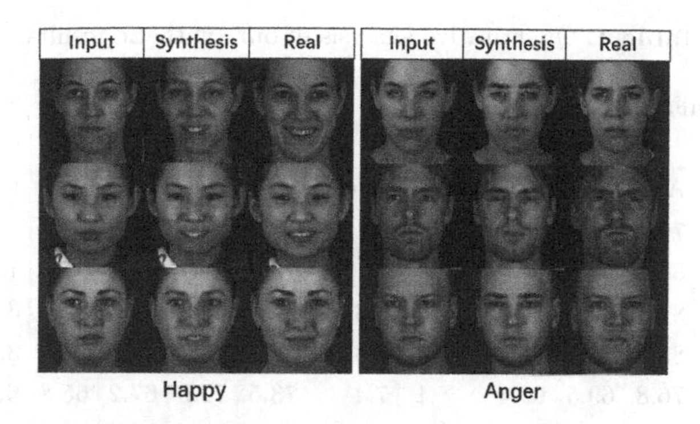

Fig. 5. Synthetic results of common AU combinations.

4.3 Quantitative Analysis of the Synthetic Results

To assess whether the synthetic images are capable of being accurately detected by the AU detection methods, we evaluate our synthetic images with state-of-the-art AU detection models. We firstly generated the augmentation dataset by our synthesis model of which the person's subject and corresponding AUs labels distribution is same as the ground-truth test dataset. Afterwards, the real images and synthesis images are estimated by two AU detectors respectively which are OpenFace AU classifier [2] and JAA-Net [20]. These two models are demonstrated state-of-the-art results in the task of AU detection. F1 score and accuracy are adopted as metrics. In the following section, all the results are simplified without %.

Table 1 shows the quantitative analysis results of synthesis images augmentation. 'Gaps' is regarded as the different value between the detection results of 'Real' dataset and 'Synthesis' dataset. '–' means there are no results of AU24 with OpenFace classifier. Specifically, the results of synthesis images approaches to the real images, between which the gaps is approximately 6%∼7% with average metrics which means our synthesis images are highly homologous with the real images on AU detection level. While JAA-Net used as the detector, the gaps between Real and Synthesis is less than while OpenFace is used as the detector, on account of the local AU attention localization JAA-Net adopts similar with our model. AU1, AU4, AU12, AU14, AU23 generated by our model is demonstrably close to the ground truth images with both detectors, especially for AU1 and AU14. However, the performance of generated face on AU17 is poor, which accounts the occurrence of AU17 is lower than the other AUs in the dataset. Substantially, the images generated by our model is effective to be detected by the state-of-the-art AU detection models.

Table 1. Quantitative analysis of our synthetic results.

AU	OpenFace						JAA-Net					
	Real		Synthesis		Gaps		Real		Synthesis		Gaps	
	F1	Acc	F1	Acc	F1	Acc	F1	Acc	F1	Acc	F1	Acc
AU1	64.1	76.1	75.8	88.7	−11.7	−12.6	46.2	69.7	59.5	76.5	−13.3	−6.8
AU2	44.3	66.2	33.0	51.3	11.3	14.9	48.7	78.4	33.7	67.1	15	11.3
AU4	71.9	87.4	67.7	77.6	4.2	9.8	56.4	84.7	52.6	78.7	3.8	6
AU6	84.3	83.5	73.1	75.2	11.2	8.3	80.4	80.2	72.3	75.9	8.1	4.3
AU7	77.6	76.8	69.5	69.4	8.1	7.4	73.5	72.9	67.2	65.8	6.3	7.1
AU10	88.2	85.0	76.8	72.3	11.4	12.7	84.9	80.4	74.3	68.5	10.6	11.9
AU12	73.6	68.7	72.8	78.0	0.8	−9.3	88.4	85.7	83.6	80.1	4.8	5.6
AU14	91.0	89.2	85.1	84.8	5.9	4.4	59.4	60.2	63.7	65.1	−4.3	−4.9
AU15	44.3	85.7	35.7	76.7	6.8	9	45.6	84.7	34.1	76.4	11.5	8.3
AU17	69.6	78.8	40.4	51.2	29.3	27.6	61.1	73.3	35.8	54.7	25.3	18.6
AU23	53.6	80.3	47.5	74.9	6.1	5.4	36.2	81.0	31.7	74.9	4.5	6.1
AU24	–	–	–	–	–	–	37.4	83.9	30.6	76.2	6.8	−7.7
Avg	69.3	79.8	61.7	72.7	7.6	7.1	59.9	77.9	53.3	71.7	6.6	6.3

5 Conclusion

In this paper, we presents LAC-GAN for facial action units synthesis, which is incorporated into the photo-realistic facial expressions, without destroying the other facial information except the AU. The generator can manipulate the AU in different status, such as transferring from absence to presence. The local discriminator and AU classifier in CARGs guarantees the consistency between the desired faces and the corresponding target AU. The AU regional localization is proposed to combine all the AU regions to an integral face with keep the background untouched. We further conducted extensive experimental quantitative analysis to evaluate our synthesis model. Our future work will explore how to apply LAC-GAN to other larger and more unconstrained facial expression dataset with intensity-level generation.

Acknowledgements. This work is supported by the National Natural Science Foundation of China under Grants of 41806116 and 61503277. We gratefully acknowledge the support of NVIDIA Corporation with the donation of the Titan V GPU used for this research.

References

1. Chen, X., Xu, C., Yang, X.: Attention-GAN for object transfiguration in wild images. arXiv preprint arXiv:1803.06798 (2018)
2. Cmusatyalab: Openface: facial action units recognition with deep neural networks. http://cmusatyalab.github.io/openface/
3. Ding, H., Sricharan, K., Chellappa, R.: ExprGAN: facial expression editing with controllable expression intensity. arXiv preprint arXiv:1709.03842 (2017)
4. Ekman, P., Rosenberg, E.L.: What the Face Reveals: Basic and Applied Studies of Spontaneous Expression using the Facial Action Coding System (FACS). Oxford University Press, USA (1997)
5. Goodfellow, I.J., Pouget-Abadie, J.: Generative adversarial nets. In: Advances in Neural Information Processing Systems, pp. 2672–2680 (2014)
6. He, X., Yan, S., Hu, Y.: Face recognition using laplacianfaces. IEEE TPAMI **27**(3), 328–340 (2005)
7. Huang, R., Zhang, S., Li, T., He, R.: Beyond face rotation: global and local perception GAN for photorealistic and identity preserving frontal view synthesis. In: ICCV (2017)
8. Isola, P., Zhu, J.Y., Zhou, T.: Image-to-image translation with conditional adversarial networks. In: CVPR 2017 (2017)
9. Kingma, D., Ba, J.: Adam: a method for stochastic optimization. In: ICLR (2014)
10. Ledig, C., Theis, L., Huszar, F.: Photo-realistic single image super- resolution using a generative adversarial network. In: CVPR 2017 (2017)
11. Lee, K.C., Ho, J., Yang, M.H.: Video-based face recognition using probabilistic appearance manifolds. In: CVPR, vol. 1(1) (2003)
12. Li, W., Abtahi, F., Zhu, Z.: EAC-net: a region-based deep enhancing and cropping approach for facial action unit detection. In: IEEE Conference on Computer Vision and Pattern Recognition Workshop, pp. 103–110 (2017)
13. Liu, Z., Song, G.: Conditional adversarial synthesis of 3D facial action units. arXiv preprint arXiv:1802.07421 (2018)
14. Mahendran, A., Vedaldi, A.: Understanding deep image representations by inverting them. In: CVPR, pp. 5188–5196 (2015)
15. Mirza, M., Osindero, S.: Conditional generative adversarial nets. arXiv preprint arXiv:1411.1784 (2014)
16. Odena, A., Olah, C., Shlens, J.: Conditional image synthesis with auxiliary classifier GANs. In: ICML 2017 (2017)
17. Pathak, D., Krahenbuhl, P., Donahue, J.: Context encoders: feature learning by inpainting. In: CVPR 2016 (2016)
18. Pumarola, A., Agudo, A., Martinez, A.M., Sanfeliu, A., Moreno-Noguer, F.: GANimation: anatomically-aware facial animation from a single image. In: Ferrari, V., Hebert, M., Sminchisescu, C., Weiss, Y. (eds.) ECCV 2018. LNCS, vol. 11214, pp. 835–851. Springer, Cham (2018). https://doi.org/10.1007/978-3-030-01249-6_50
19. Radford, A., Metz, L.: Unsupervised representation learning with deep convolutional generative adversarial networks. In: ICLR 2016 (2016)
20. Shao, Z., Liu, Z., Cai, J., Ma, L.: Deep adaptive attention for joint facial action unit detection and face alignment. In: Ferrari, V., Hebert, M., Sminchisescu, C., Weiss, Y. (eds.) ECCV 2018. LNCS, vol. 11217, pp. 725–740. Springer, Cham (2018). https://doi.org/10.1007/978-3-030-01261-8_43
21. Tran, L., Yin, X., Liu, X.: Disentangled representation learning GAN for poseinvariant face recognition. In: CVPR, vol. 4(7) (2017)

22. Wang, M., Deng, W.: Deep face recognition: a survey. BMVC **1**(6) (2015)
23. Wang, Z., Tang, X.: Face aging with identity-preserved conditional generative adversarial networks. In: CVPR 2018 (2018)
24. Yeh, R., Liu, Z., Goldman, D.B.: Semantic facial expression editing using autoencoded flow. arXiv preprint arXiv:1611.09961 (2016)
25. Zhang, X., Yin, L., Cohn, J.F.: Bp4d-spontaneous: a high-resolution spontaneous 3D dynamic facial expression database. Image Vis. Comput. **32**(10), 692–706 (2014)
26. Zhang, Z., Song, Y.: Age progression/regression by conditional adversarial autoencoder. In: CVPR 2017 (2017)
27. Zhou, Y., Shi, B.E.: Photorealistic facial expression synthesis by the conditional difference adversarial autoencoder. In: ACII 2017 (2017)

Facial Expression Restoration Based on Improved Graph Convolutional Networks

Zhilei Liu[1], Le Li[1], Yunpeng Wu[1], and Cuicui Zhang[2](✉)

[1] College of Intelligence and Computing, Tianjin University, Tianjin, China
{zhileiliu,le_li,wuyunpeng}@tju.edu.cn
[2] School of Marine Science and Technology, Tianjin University, Tianjin, China
cuicui.zhang@tju.edu.cn

Abstract. Facial expression analysis in the wild is challenging when the facial image is with low resolution or partial occlusion. Considering the correlations among different facial local regions under different facial expressions, this paper proposes a novel facial expression restoration method based on generative adversarial network by integrating an improved graph convolutional network (IGCN) and region relation modeling block (RRMB). Unlike conventional graph convolutional networks taking vectors as input features, IGCN can use tensors of face patches as inputs. It is better to retain the structure information of face patches. The proposed RRMB is designed to address facial generative tasks including inpainting and super-resolution with facial action units detection, which aims to restore facial expression as the ground-truth. Extensive experiments conducted on BP4D and DISFA benchmarks demonstrate the effectiveness of our proposed method through quantitative and qualitative evaluations.

Keywords: Facial expression restoration · Generative adversarial network · Graph convolutional network · Facial action units

1 Introduction

Facial restoration aims to recover the valuable missing information of faces caused by low resolution, occlusion, large pose, etc, which has gained increasing attention in the field of face recognition, especially with the emergence of convolution neural networks (CNN) [11,21] and generative adversarial networks (GAN) [6]. Many sub tasks of facial restoration have achieved great breakthroughs, consisting of face completion [15,27], face super-resolution or hallucination [1,12], and face frontal view synthesis [8]. Most of these previous works just conduct these face restoration tasks independently, and what's more, only facial identity restoration is considered, without taking facial expression information restoration into consideration. Recently, some studies [22] try to jointly deal with these ill situations with the help of deep learning and GAN. And three kinds of ill facial images is shown in Fig. 1 including both low resolution and

Y. M. Ro et al. (Eds.): MMM 2020, LNCS 11962, pp. 527–539, 2020.
https://doi.org/10.1007/978-3-030-37734-2_43

Fig. 1. Example images showing face images with low resolution, partial occlusion and both in the wild.

occlusion faces, which give us the necessity to address both low resolution and occlusion jointly. While face super-resolution, the model takes more relations on intra-patches into account, but the relations on inter-patch during face inpainting. Concerning that graph can have intra-patch and inter-patch relationships with edges, we attempt to jointly address low resolution and partial occlusion.

Facial expression restoration is beneficial to the study of facial emotion analysis, which is easily affected by challenging environment, i.e. low resolution, occlusion, etc. In the field of facial expression analysis, facial action units (AUs) refer to a unique set of basic facial muscle actions at certain location defined by Facial Action Coding System (FACS) [3], which is one of the most comprehensive and objective systems for describing facial expressions. Considering facial structure and patterns of facial expression are relatively fixed, it should be beneficial for facial expression restoration if taking their relations of different AUs into consideration under occlusion and low resolution situations. However, in literature it is rare to see such facial expression restoration study by exploring the relations of different facial regions under different facial expressions.

In this paper, we propose a novel facial expression restoration framework by exploiting the correlations of different facial AUs. Our idea appears that firstly restoring the whole face and then detecting AUs to verify whether the facial expression appears or not, which can be called facial expression restoration. In order to learn the features of facial occluded patches from other unoccluded patches, we propose an improved graph convolutional network (IGCN), of which the structure is shown in Fig. 3. In addition, IGCN also can help to improve the resolution of unoccluded face patches from other visible face patches, by exploring the correlations of different facial components. In the next, with the help of the proposed IGCN, a Region Relation Modeling Block (RRMB) is built to capture the facial features with different scales for face restoration. Given more finer facial division, more accurate relations of different face patches can be built with the help of our proposed framework. With more accurate adjacency matrix in the proposed IGCN, our proposed model can well restore the feature map in deep networks with visible patches' features. We can also use IGCN to build AU detector by exploring these correlations among AUs to help generator to restore more accurate facial expressions. Last but not least, a discriminator is designed to help generator to generate realistic faces, and additional perceptual loss is helpful to improve the quality of the generated faces to some extent.

The contributions of this paper are threefold. First, a novel end-to-end facial expression restoration framework is proposed by jointly addressing face inpainting and face super-resolution. Second, an IGCN is proposed for facial patch relation modeling, and a RRMB is built with the aid of the proposed IGCN. Third, we exploit facial action units detector in generative model to improve the facial expression restoration capability of the generator.

2 Related Works

Our proposed framework is closely related to existing image restoration methods, facial action units detection methods, and graph convolutional network related studies, since we aim to study facial expression restoration by modeling AU relations with the aid of GCN based methods.

2.1 Image Restoration

Recently, image restoration has attracted more attentions due to the existence of generative adversarial network(GAN) [6], which generates an image from a random vector and uses a discriminator to distinguish the real image from generated image. In order to improve the generated images' quality, many works use perceptual loss to supervise model learning [2]. Also, conditional GAN is proposed to limit the generated images' distribution [17]. Image restoration consists of image super-resolution or hallucination [1,12], image completion [15,27], face frontal view synthesis [8], image denoise [18], image derain [25], image dehaze [4], image deblurring [13] and shadow removal [24]. Many topics lack the true datasets. For image super-resolution, it usually uses bicubic interpolation to synthesis low-resolution image as [12]. For image completion, it usually uses a binary mask to synthesis masked image as [27] and etc. We follow this setting for ill image synthesis in this paper. Also, [22] tries to jointly deal with face hallucination and deblurring. The situation of both problems co-occurring is common in the wild environment, which is depicted in Fig. 1. Here, we try to jointly deal with face inpainting and super-resolution for facial expression restoration concerning on relations on inter and intra patches. Considering that face image has structure information, [1] achieves amazing success with the aids of face parsing and facial landmarks information, which motivate us to restore face with facial action units information.

2.2 Action Units Detection

Automatic facial AUs detection plays an important role in describing facial actions. To recognize facial action units under complex environment, many works have been devoted to explore various features and classifier. [26] jointly detects facial action units and landmarks, which want to recognize AUs with the help of landmarks. [9] uses convolutional networks to capture deep representations to recognize AUs via deep learning model. [23] designs AUs-related region, Zhao

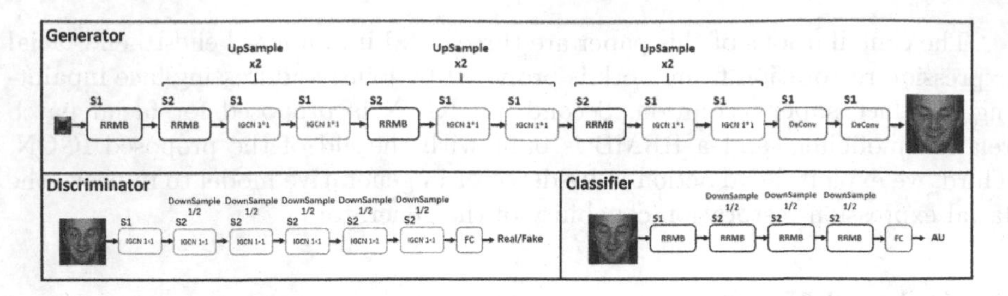

Fig. 2. Framework of the proposed facial expression restoration network. During training, generator generates restored facial expression images with the supervision of pre-trained AU classifier and the adversarial loss from discriminator. During testing, only the generator is adopted to restore the ill facial images.

et al. [29] exploits patches centered at facial landmarks, Li et al. [14] exploits hand-crafted heatmaps centered at facial landmarks based on Manhattan distance and [30] proposes deep region layer to help detect AUs. These defined regions help attention these regions while model learning. [19] also uses AUs co-existence relations to help recognize AUs. These methods achieve good performances for AUs detection, which motivate us to exploit the relations among AUs-related face patches. With the relations, improved graph convolutional network well fuses the features of different face patches to detect AUs, which is the supervisory information to help restore facial expression.

2.3 Graph Convolutional Networks

Recently, there has been a rich line of research on graph neural networks [5]. [10] proposes graph convolutional networks (GCN), which is inspired by the first order graph Laplacian methods. GCN mainly achieves promising performance on graph node classification task. Adjacency matrix is defined by the links between nodes of the graph. The transformation on nodes is linear transformation without learning trainable filters. Using the relations among nodes, graph convolutional networks can embed the features of relational nodes and itself. We improve conventional graph convolutional network with the tensor-inputs and standard convolutional layer instead of linear transformation in conventional graph convolutional network.

3 Facial Expression Restoration Based on IGCN

In this section, the proposed model is introduced in Sect. 3.1 at first. Then, the details of improved graph convolutional networks (IGCN) are explained in Sect. 3.2 and the region relation modeling block (RRMB) is explained in Sect. 3.3.

3.1 Proposed Model

The structure of our proposed method is shown in Fig. 2, which consists of a generator to restore the whole face image, a discriminator to justify whether the generated face is real or fake, a classifier to recognize the facial action units (AUs) to supervise the generated face image. To make full use of unoccluded face patches, we jointly deal with face completion and super-resolution problem. For face completion, it models the relations between unoccluded face patches and occluded patches. For face super-resolution, it models the relations among different unoccluded face patches. This aims to ensure the global harmony of generated face images.

The losses of our proposed model consist of three parts: the loss for generator learning, the loss for discriminator learning, the loss for AUs classifier learning. For generator, to help learn the generator network, we use pixel loss L_{pix}, which is defined as

$$L_{pix} = \sum \mathbb{E}_{I_{gt},I_{out}} \left[\|I_{gt} - I_{out}\|_2 \right], \tag{1}$$

where I_{out} is the generated facial expression image by generator, I_{gt} is the ground-truth facial image. Besides, we use the pre-trained 19-layer VGG to compute perceptual loss L_{per} to gain more facial details [21]. The perceptual loss L_{per} is defined as

$$L_{per} = \sum \mathbb{E}_{I_{gt},I_{out}} \left[\left\| f_{I_{gt}}^{2,2} - f_{I_{out}}^{2,2} \right\|_2 + \left\| f_{I_{gt}}^{5,4} - f_{I_{out}}^{5,4} \right\|_2 \right], \tag{2}$$

where $f_{I_{gt}}^{i,j}$ is the ground-truth's feature map obtained by the j-th convolution layer before the i-th max-pooling layer in VGG-19, and $f_{I_{out}}^{i,j}$ is the generated face's. Adversarial loss is used to improve the quality and reality of generated face image after restoration, the loss of discriminator L_{adv} is defined as

$$L_{adv} = \sum \mathbb{E}_{I_{out} \sim p(I_{out})} \left[\log D_I \left(I_{out} \right) \right] + \mathbb{E}_{I_{gt} \sim p(I_{gt})} \left[\log \left(1 - D_I \left(I_{gt} \right) \right) \right], \tag{3}$$

where D_I is the discriminator to discriminate the ground-truth face from the generated face. In order to retain the facial expression, AUs are one way to convey the facial action, such as six basic facial expressions. AU classifier is used to help generator learn the facial action units' distributions. The loss of AU classifier is defined as

$$L_{cls} = \sum \mathbb{E}_{I_{out} \sim p(I_{out})} \left[\|C_I(I_{gt}) - C_I(I_{out})\|_2 \right], \tag{4}$$

where C_I is the AU classifier to recognize facial action units. $C_I(I_{gt})$ are ground-truth's logits of the last fully connection (FC) layer before activation of AU classifier, $C_I(I_{out})$ are generated face's logits of the last FC layer before activation of AU classifier. The overall loss of the proposed facial expression restoration framework is

$$L_{\mathrm{G}} = L_{pix} + \lambda_1 L_{adv} + \lambda_2 L_{cls} + \lambda_3 L_{per}, \tag{5}$$

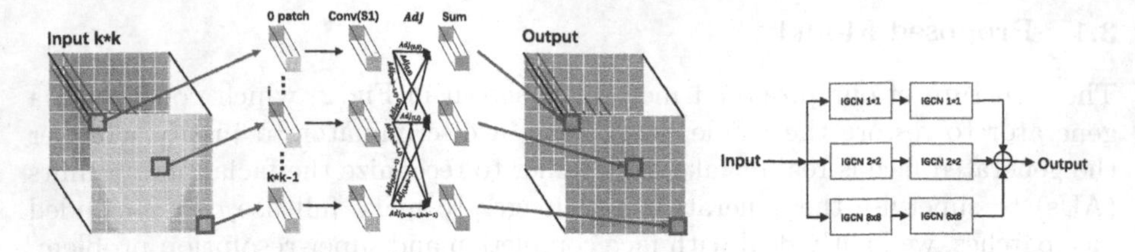

Fig. 3. Structure of the IGCN $8*8$ with stride 1 in the left. $Adj_{(i,j)}$ represents the link between i-th patch and j-th patch, *Adj* represents adjacency matrix. The right is the structure of RRMB, which consists of IGCN $1*1$, $2*2$, $8*8$. $1*1$ represents splitting only 1 patch for the inputs, $2*2$ represents splitting 4 patches for the inputs, and $8*8$ represents splitting 64 patches for the inputs.

where λ_1, λ_2, and λ_3 are trade-off parameters. General GAN loss for learning discriminator and cross-entropy loss for learning classifier. This max-min game will help to generate realistic face image. Note that for each AU, we should calculate the cross-entropy loss for AU classifier, because it is a multi-label task. The activation function used in this paper is sigmoid function.

3.2 Improved Graph Convolutional Networks

The features of the nodes are vectors in conventional graph convolutional network [10], which is called as non-euclidean data. For face image, every patch of face image is associated with other patches and is euclidean data. In order to use the face patches as nodes directly via modeling the relations among different facial patches, an improved graph convolutional network is proposed, of which the whole structure is shown in Fig. 3. Due to the ability of graph convolutional network, We can use unoccluded regions to complete the occluded regions via pre-defined relations, such as using unoccluded left eyes to restore occluded right eyes, also can using unoccluded region to enhance the quality of other unoccluded regions.

Firstly, we split the feature F of face image into $k*k$ face patches with certain order position ID. For each face patch, we use convolutional layer to transform its representation. Here, it should be noted that conventional graph convolutional networks use vectors as features, and use linear transformation layer to capture representations. Different from conventional GCNs, our proposed IGCN uses 4-D tensor of face patches as input features, and uses convolution layer to capture representations. The weights of all convolutional layers for each patch are shared under one layer of IGCN. According to symmetrical adjacency matrix, we get every face patch feature after sum operation. Lastly, we convert $k*k$ face patch features into a feature map according the origin position ID. Note that we also can use deconvolutional layer in IGCN. Adjacency matrix is predefined via facial structure. IGCN can be defined as:

$$F_{upd} = A : Relu\left(W * F + b\right), \tag{6}$$

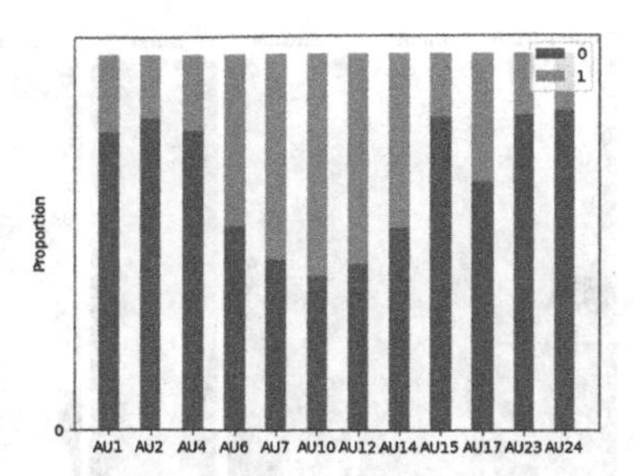

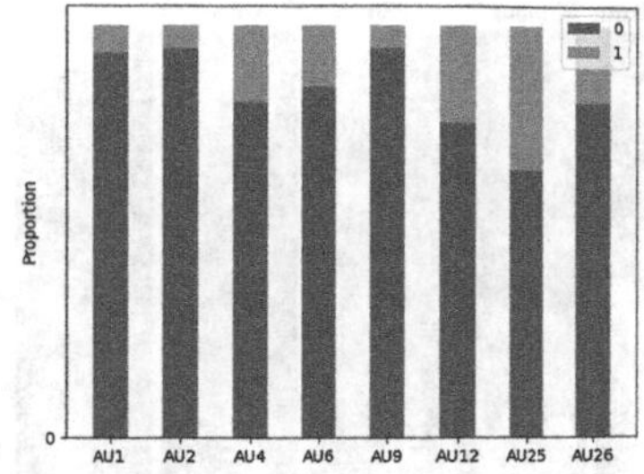

Fig. 4. Sample distributions of BP4D dataset (left) and DISFA dataset (right). 1 represents AU appearance, 0 represents AU disappearance.

where F is the stacked patches features, A is the normalized adjacency matrix and : represents tensor product. The adjacency matrixis defined by the correlations of facial structure, such as the symmetry of left face and right face and AUs correlation. Supposing that two patches have relation, then the link between the two patches are supposed to be 1, the opposite is 0. Here we define the relation by cosine similarity between two patches and the co-existence and exclusive relation between two patches consisting of two AUs according landmarks.

3.3 Region Relation Modeling Block

Region Relation Modeling Block (RRMB) is designed to model the relations of different face patches. This multi-scale structure design is popular in image feature representation learning area. In order to capture different scales' features, we use three scales, such as splitting $1 * 1$ patch, $2 * 2$ patches, $8 * 8$ patches. While splitting $1 * 1$ patch in IGCN $1 * 1$, which is same with standard convolutional layer. This scale is to capture global image-level features. The second scale is splitting $2 * 2$ patches, IGCN $2 * 2$ is to ensure stable features during flipped situation. This scale setting is exploited to capture object-level features. The third scale is splitting $8 * 8$ patches, IGCN $8 * 8$ is to construct associations between relational spatial patches, such as eyes and mouth. This scale setting is exploited to capture patch-level features. All these scales features are summed pixel-wisely to get the final output features.

4 Experiments

4.1 Datasets and Settings

Datasets: Our proposed facial expression restoration network is evaluated on two wildely used datastes for facial expression analysis: BP4D [28] and DISFA [16]. The settings of two datasets are similar with [20]. For **BP4D**, we split the dataset to training/testing sets according to subject. There are 28 subjects in training set and 13 subjects in testing set. Each set contains 12 AUs with AU labels of occurrence or absence. Total of 100760 frames are used for

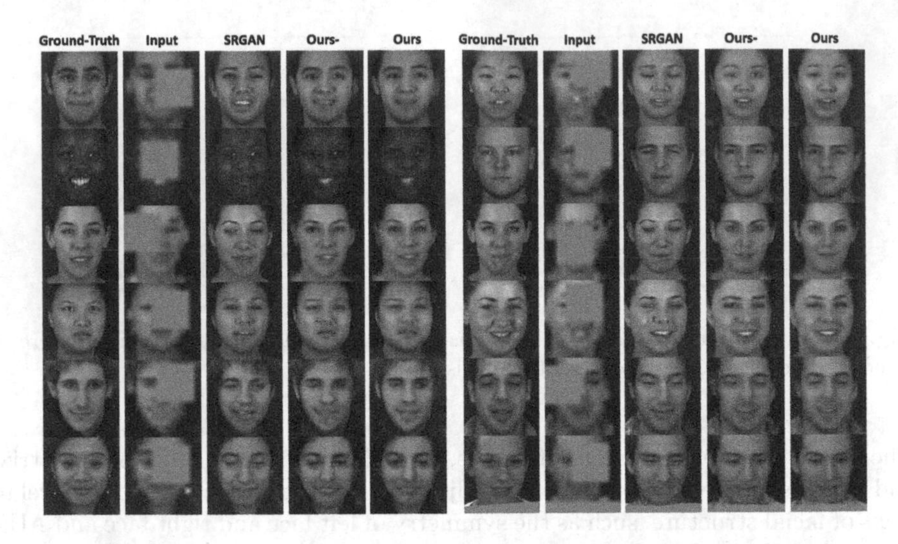

Fig. 5. Facial expression restoration results on test datasets, top four rows show the comparison on BP4D and others on DISFA. Zoom in for better view on details.

training and 45809 frames are used for testing. For **DISFA**, the processing of the dataset is same as BP4D, there are 18 subjects in training set and 9 subjects in testing set. Each set contains 8 AUs with AU labels of occurrence or absence. Total of 87209 frames are adopted as training set and 43605 frames are used for testing. Note that the color and background of face image are large of differences in DISFA dataset, which is difficult for model to learn well results. The sample distributions of two datasets are shown in Fig. 4, which illustrates the extreme unbalance situation of labels.

Preprocessing: For each face image, we perform similarity transformation including rotation, uniform scaling, and translation to obtain a $128 * 128 * 3$ face. This transformation is shape-preserving and brings no change to the expression. The input ill face images are produced by resizing high resolution face image to $16 * 16$ via bicubic interpolation method and added a random binary mask, of which size is one fourth of the input size.

Implementation Details: We firstly pre-train the AUs classifier, then jointly learn the generator and discriminator, about learning one time of discriminator every three times of generator. For AUs classifier learning, we get the good metrics, which are little lower than the state of the arts. The settings of trade-off parameters are $\lambda_1 = 0.001$, $\lambda_2 = 0.001$, $\lambda_3 = 0.5$. We use Adam for optimization. The learning rate is 0.0001, the batch size is 8, and the kernel size is 3.

Table 1. F1-score and accuracy for 12 AUs on BP4D. Ours is the total loss to learn the proposed model, ours- lacks the loss of AUs classifier.

BP4D	F1-score				Accuracy			
	SRGAN	Ours-	Ours	Ground-truth	SRGAN	Ours-	Ours	Ground-truth
1	0.097	0.349	0.412	0.412	0.700	0.690	0.674	0.720
2	0.065	0.214	0.267	0.331	0.754	0.770	0.749	0.725
4	0.168	0.284	0.298	0.276	0.692	0.798	0.803	0.785
6	0.545	0.575	0.672	0.730	0.503	0.705	0.731	0.732
7	0.560	0.619	0.594	0.646	0.500	0.662	0.650	0.646
10	0.680	0.768	0.905	0.825	0.565	0.748	0.775	0.777
12	0.616	0.882	0.861	0.874	0.528	0.840	0.837	0.845
14	0.569	0.676	0.594	0.634	0.494	0.606	0.587	0.595
15	0.177	0.258	0.299	0.307	0.712	0.713	0.792	0.784
17	0.446	0.748	0.723	0.548	0.464	0.597	0.626	0.595
23	0.204	0.433	0.454	0.333	0.652	0.755	0.744	0.684
24	0.142	0.080	0.086	0.411	0.753	0.763	0.832	0.794
Avg	0.356	0.491	0.514	0.525	0.610	0.721	0.733	0.724

Table 2. F1-score and accuracy for 8 AUs on DISFA. Ours is the total loss to learn the proposed model, ours- lacks the loss of AUs classifier.

DISFA	F1-score				Accuracy			
	SRGAN	Ours-	Ours	Ground-truth	SRGAN	Ours-	Ours	Ground-truth
1	0.107	0.217	0.214	0.210	0.901	0.863	0.866	0.908
2	0.010	0.159	0.185	0.198	0.958	0.806	0.836	0.949
4	0.091	0.202	0.217	0.286	0.739	0.739	0.716	0.735
6	0.392	0.336	0.348	0.362	0.870	0.797	0.804	0.855
9	0.039	0.185	0.365	0.270	0.903	0.945	0.939	0.885
12	0.576	0.548	0.558	0.628	0.763	0.741	0.752	0.844
25	0.509	0.654	0.765	0.746	0.608	0.809	0.811	0.772
26	0.270	0.506	0.504	0.524	0.685	0.725	0.723	0.755
Avg	0.249	0.351	0.395	0.404	0.803	0.803	0.806	0.838

4.2 Visual Results

We aim to jointly address face inpainting and super-resolution problem for facial expression restoration. General face inpainting methods are not proper to deal with this case, because the numbers of downsample and upsample layers are same. Here we aim to verify our proposed method's effectiveness in two dataset with SRGAN [12], which is notable on image super-resolution area and when we use IGCN $1 * 1$, the proposed model is similar with residual block [7], which is the main component for SRGAN. Comparison with SRGAN and proposed model without AUs detection is shown in Fig. 5. In order to observe the difference between different methods, we emphasize the difference of the eye area and mouth area. Obviously, in the results of first row, SRGAN method generates tooth but our proposed method generates closed mouth, which is similar with

Table 3. SSIM and PSNR on BP4D and DISFA.

	SSIM			PSNR		
	SRGAN	Ours-	Ours	SRGAN	Ours-	Ours
BP4D	0.625	0.738	0.748	23.324	25.297	25.418
DISFA	0.598	0.624	0.655	20.855	21.621	21.826

ground-truth corresponding to AU 25, and in the results of third row, SRGAN generates closed eyes but our proposed method generates opened eyes corresponding to AU 43. For quality and reality, the results of SRGAN have virtual streak and blur, such as the first row. It is worth noting that the shown results are from 13 subjects of BP4D dataset and 9 subjects of DISFA dataset for testing respectively. It is observed that our proposed method outperforms SRGAN in the aspects of reality and quality. And also, our proposed method can well retain the facial action or expression after restoration.

4.3 Quantity Results

In order to investigate the effectiveness of AU classifier in our framework for facial expression restoration, Tables 1 and 2 present the AU detection results on our restored facial expression images compared with corresponding ground truth images in terms of F1-score and accuracy, where "*Ours-*" is the proposed framework without AU classifier. Note that AU classifier is trained on training dataset but the quantity results are compared in results of different model on test dataset.

The results shown in Table 1 demonstrates that our proposed method outperforms SRGAN in BP4D dataset, even "*Ours-*" brings significant increments of 13.6% and 11.1% respectively for average f1-score and accuracy than SRGAN. It is also observed that learning framework with AU classifier gain a few increments of 2.3% and 1.2% for average f1-score and accuracy. The large gaps between our proposed method and SRGAN are associated with the distribution of BP4D. Due to the unbalanced distribution of status for each AU as is shown in Fig. 4, our proposed facial expression restoration method is inclined to learn the '0' status for each AU. For accuracy, ours result is similar with ground-truth, even better than ground-truth. And the AU classifier is strong to make the logits of generated face image incline to the distribution of the AUs, which results in the our proposed model getting little higher accuracy than ground-truth.

Similar results in DISFA dataset are shown in Table 2, from which it can be observed that our proposed method with or without AUs classifier outperforms SRGAN. Specifically, our proposed method increase 14.6% and 0.3% for average f1-score and accuracy than SRGAN. For accuracy, our proposed method has a few improvements, it is also associated with AUs occur distribution in the dataset. For most face images, AUs do not occur in DISFA dataset as shown in Fig. 4, so AU classifier always recognizes '0' status. On the other hand, lower f1-score also tell us that model learns the nature situation easier than activate situation for each AU.

When it comes to image restoration task, many works often compare the structural similarity (SSIM) and Peak Signal to Noise Ratio (PSNR). The results can be observed in Table 3. Our proposed method outperforms 0.123 and 0.057 for SSIM, 2.094 and 0.971 for PSNR respectively in BP4D and DISFA dataset, which demonstrate the effectiveness of our proposed method on facial expression restoration. Note that there are few improvements in DISFA datasets due to its extreme unbalance distribution.

5 Conclusion

In this paper, we have proposed a novel facial expression restoration method by integrating a region relation modeling block with the aid of an improved graph convolution network to model the relations among different facial regions. The proposed method is beneficial to facial expression analysis under challenging environments, i.e. low resolution and occlusion. Extensive qualitative and quantitative evaluations conducted on BP4D and DISFA have demonstrated the effectiveness of our method for facial expression restoration. The proposed framework is also promising to be applied for other face restoration tasks and other multi-task problems, i.e. face recognition, facial attribute analysis, etc.

Acknowledgements. This work is supported by the National Natural Science Foundation of China under Grants of 41806116 and 61503277. We gratefully acknowledge the support of NVIDIA Corporation with the donation of the Titan V GPU used for this research.

References

1. Chen, Y., Tai, Y., Liu, X., Shen, C., Yang, J.: FSRNet: end-to-end learning face super-resolution with facial priors. In: Proceedings of the IEEE Conference on Computer Vision and Pattern Recognition, pp. 2492–2501 (2018)
2. Cheon, M., Kim, J.-H., Choi, J.-H., Lee, J.-S.: Generative adversarial network-based image super-resolution using perceptual content losses. In: Leal-Taixé, L., Roth, S. (eds.) ECCV 2018. LNCS, vol. 11133, pp. 51–62. Springer, Cham (2019). https://doi.org/10.1007/978-3-030-11021-5_4
3. Ekman, R.: What the Face Reveals: Basic and Applied Studies of Spontaneous Expression Using the Facial Action Coding System (FACS). Oxford University Press, Oxford (1997)
4. Engin, D., Genç, A., Kemal Ekenel, H.: Cycle-Dehaze: enhanced cyclegan for single image dehazing. In: Proceedings of the IEEE Conference on Computer Vision and Pattern Recognition Workshops, pp. 825–833 (2018)
5. Gilmer, J., Schoenholz, S.S., Riley, P.F., Vinyals, O., Dahl, G.E.: Neural message passing for quantum chemistry. In: Proceedings of the 34th International Conference on Machine Learning, vol. 70, pp. 1263–1272. JMLR. org (2017)
6. Goodfellow, I., et al.: Generative adversarial nets. In: Advances in Neural Information Processing Systems, pp. 2672–2680 (2014)

7. He, K., Zhang, X., Ren, S., Sun, J.: Deep residual learning for image recognition. In: Proceedings of the IEEE Conference on Computer Vision and Pattern Recognition, pp. 770–778 (2016)
8. Huang, R., Zhang, S., Li, T., He, R.: Beyond face rotation: Global and local perception GAN for photorealistic and identity preserving frontal view synthesis. In: Proceedings of the IEEE International Conference on Computer Vision, pp. 2439–2448 (2017)
9. Khorrami, P., Paine, T., Huang, T.: Do deep neural networks learn facial action units when doing expression recognition? In: Proceedings of the IEEE International Conference on Computer Vision Workshops, pp. 19–27 (2015)
10. Kipf, T.N., Welling, M.: Semi-supervised classification with graph convolutional networks. arXiv preprint arXiv:1609.02907 (2016)
11. Krizhevsky, A., Sutskever, I., Hinton, G.E.: ImageNet classification with deep convolutional neural networks. In: Advances in Neural Information Processing Systems, pp. 1097–1105 (2012)
12. Ledig, C., et al.: Photo-realistic single image super-resolution using a generative adversarial network. In: Proceedings of the IEEE Conference on Computer Vision and Pattern Recognition, pp. 4681–4690 (2017)
13. Li, L., Pan, J., Lai, W.S., Gao, C., Sang, N., Yang, M.H.: Learning a discriminative prior for blind image deblurring. In: Proceedings of the IEEE Conference on Computer Vision and Pattern Recognition, pp. 6616–6625 (2018)
14. Li, W., Abtahi, F., Zhu, Z., Yin, L.: EAC-Net: a region-based deep enhancing and cropping approach for facial action unit detection. In: 2017 12th IEEE International Conference on Automatic Face & Gesture Recognition (FG 2017), pp. 103–110. IEEE (2017)
15. Li, Y., Liu, S., Yang, J., Yang, M.H.: Generative face completion. In: Proceedings of the IEEE Conference on Computer Vision and Pattern Recognition, pp. 3911–3919 (2017)
16. Mavadati, S.M., Mahoor, M.H., Bartlett, K., Trinh, P., Cohn, J.F.: DISFA: a spontaneous facial action intensity database. IEEE Trans. Affect. Comput. **4**(2), 151–160 (2013)
17. Mirza, M., Osindero, S.: Conditional generative adversarial nets. arXiv preprint arXiv:1411.1784 (2014)
18. Muhammad, N., Bibi, N., Jahangir, A., Mahmood, Z.: Image denoising with norm weighted fusion estimators. Pattern Anal. Appl. **21**(4), 1013–1022 (2018)
19. Peng, G., Wang, S.: Weakly supervised facial action unit recognition through adversarial training. In: Proceedings of the IEEE Conference on Computer Vision and Pattern Recognition, pp. 2188–2196 (2018)
20. Shao, Z., Liu, Z., Cai, J., Ma, L.: Deep adaptive attention for joint facial action unit detection and face alignment. In: Ferrari, V., Hebert, M., Sminchisescu, C., Weiss, Y. (eds.) ECCV 2018. LNCS, vol. 11217, pp. 725–740. Springer, Cham (2018). https://doi.org/10.1007/978-3-030-01261-8_43
21. Simonyan, K., Zisserman, A.: Very deep convolutional networks for large-scale image recognition. arXiv preprint arXiv:1409.1556 (2014)
22. Song, Y., et al.: Joint face Hallucination and deblurring via structure generation and detail enhancement. Int. J. Comput. Vis. **127**, 1–16 (2018)
23. Taheri, S., Qiu, Q., Chellappa, R.: Structure-preserving sparse decomposition for facial expression analysis. IEEE Trans. Image Process. **23**(8), 3590–3603 (2014)
24. Wang, J., Li, X., Yang, J.: Stacked conditional generative adversarial networks for jointly learning shadow detection and shadow removal. In: Proceedings of the IEEE Conference on Computer Vision and Pattern Recognition, pp. 1788–1797 (2018)

25. Wang, Y.T., Zhao, X.L., Jiang, T.X., Deng, L.J., Chang, Y., Huang, T.Z.: Rain streak removal for single image via kernel guided CNN. arXiv preprint arXiv:1808.08545 (2018)
26. Wu, Y., Ji, Q.: Constrained joint cascade regression framework for simultaneous facial action unit recognition and facial landmark detection. In: Proceedings of the IEEE Conference on Computer Vision and Pattern Recognition, pp. 3400–3408 (2016)
27. Yeh, R.A., Chen, C., Yian Lim, T., Schwing, A.G., Hasegawa-Johnson, M., Do, M.N.: Semantic image inpainting with deep generative models. In: Proceedings of the IEEE Conference on Computer Vision and Pattern Recognition, pp. 5485–5493 (2017)
28. Zhang, X., et al.: A high-resolution spontaneous 3D dynamic facial expression database. In: 2013 10th IEEE International Conference and Workshops on Automatic Face and Gesture Recognition (FG), pp. 1–6. IEEE (2013)
29. Zhao, K., Chu, W.S., De la Torre, F., Cohn, J.F., Zhang, H.: Joint patch and multi-label learning for facial action unit detection. In: Proceedings of the IEEE Conference on Computer Vision and Pattern Recognition, pp. 2207–2216 (2015)
30. Zhao, K., Chu, W.S., Zhang, H.: Deep region and multi-label learning for facial action unit detection. In: Proceedings of the IEEE Conference on Computer Vision and Pattern Recognition, pp. 3391–3399 (2016)

Global Affective Video Content Regression Based on Complementary Audio-Visual Features

Xiaona Guo[1], Wei Zhong[1(✉)], Long Ye[1], Li Fang[1], Yan Heng[2], and Qin Zhang[1]

[1] Key Laboratory of Media Audio and Video, Ministry of Education, Communication University of China, Beijing 100024, China
{guoxiaona, wzhong, yelong, lifang8902, zhangqin}@cuc.edu.cn

[2] Shanghai Radio Equipment Research Institute, Shanghai 201109, China
hengyan822@126.com

Abstract. In this paper, we propose a new framework for global affective video content regression with five complementary audio-visual features. For the audio modality, we select the global audio feature eGeMAPS and two deep features SoundNet and VGGish. As for the visual modality, the key frames of original images and those of optical flow images are both used to extract VGG-19 features with finetuned models, in order to represent the original visual cues in conjunction with motion information. In the experiments, we perform the evaluations of selected audio and visual features on the dataset of Emotional Impact of Movies Task 2016 (EIMT16), and compare our results with those of competitive teams in EIMT16 and state-of-the-art method. The experimental results show that the fusion of five features can achieve better regression results in both arousal and valence dimensions, indicating the selected five features are complementary with each other in the audio-visual modalities. Furthermore, the proposed approach can achieve better regression results than the state-of-the-art method in both evaluation metrics of MSE and PCC in the arousal dimension and comparable MSE results in the valence dimension. Although our approach obtains slightly lower PCC result than the state-of-the-art method in the valence dimension, the fused feature vectors used in our framework have much lower dimensions with a total of 1752, only five thousandths of feature dimensions in the state-of-the-art method, largely bringing down the memory requirements and computational burden.

Keywords: Affective video content regression · eGeMAPS · SoundNet · VGG · Optical flow

---

This work is supported by the National Natural Science Foundation of China under Grant Nos. 61801440 and 61631016, and the Fundamental Research Funds for the Central Universities under Grant Nos. 2018XNG1824 and YLSZ180226.

Y. M. Ro et al. (Eds.): MMM 2020, LNCS 11962, pp. 540–550, 2020.
https://doi.org/10.1007/978-3-030-37734-2_44

1 Introduction

Affective content is an important component of video content analysis and it can be considered as an objective characteristic of the video. Affective video content analysis aims to automatically recognize the type and intensity of the emotion expected to arise when people watch a given video clip. With the rapid developments of multimedia technologies, the modeling and analysis of affective video contents has attracted more and more attentions.

The research works on affective video content analysis can be mainly categorized into two subgroups: continuous affective video content analysis and global affective video content analysis [1]. In this work, we focus on the global affective video content analysis which assigns an affective score to the entire video clip. It should be noticed that, a large number of reliable annotated training and test data is highly required for affective content modeling and analysis, while the scientific labeling of emotion is extremely difficult due to the subjectivity and complexity of human emotions. To the best of our knowledge, LIRIS-ACCEDE [2] is the largest dataset with scientific annotations for global affective video content analysis. It contains 9800 short video clips with each ranging from 8 to 12 s. For the global affective video content analysis, MediaEval organized competitions including Affective Impact of Movies Task in 2015 (AIMT15) [3] and Emotional Impact of Movies Task in 2016 (EIMT16) [4]. The dataset used in these two competitions are both the extensions of LIRIS-ACCEDE. The AIMT15 extended 1100 video clips with discrete annotations which leads to the classification task, while the EIMT16 extended 1200 video clips with continuous annotations and thus leading to the regression task.

For the regression task of EIMT16, there are five teams participated in [5–9]. Among them, RUC [5] achieved the best results. This method used the baseline features provided by the competition organizers, audio features (IS09, IS10, IS13, MFCC), image features (VGG-16, VGG-19) and motion features (iDT, C3D), and then the support vector regression (SVR) and Random Forest were trained for each kind of features. Finally, they applied late fusion to fuse different features by training a second-layer SVR with the input of the best predictions for each kind of features using the local validation set, and then the best subset of feature types was found with Sequential Backward Selection algorithm. Liu [6] proposed an algorithm named Arousal-Valence Discriminant Preserving Embedding to extract features, and then the neural network and SVR were used as regressor respectively for two of the four run submissions. THU [7] used baseline features, eGeMAPS, VGG-19 and SVR on this task, early fusion and late fusion were also used respectively for their submissions. But they finetuned VGG-19 with the input images being static frames extracted from video clips at the rate of 2 Hz, which leads to large proportion of redundant information of input data and huge computational burden of training process. AUTH-SGP [9] extracted iDT, CNN feature, DenseSIFT, HSH, MFCC as multimodal features besides the baseline features, and then SVR was used for regression. Furthermore, Yi and Wang [10] also proposed their framework on this task and got the state-of-the-art results. In their work, they utilized motion keypoint trajectory (MKT) and temporal segment networks (TSN) to depict the visual modality of elicited emotions, and emoBase10 to describe the audio modality.

And then SVR was used to learn the affective models for regression. However, the proposed features are extremely high dimensional which leads to the problem of large memory requirement and heavy computational burden.

In this paper, a new framework is proposed for global affective video content regression with five complementary audio-visual features. For the audio modality, we choose the global audio feature eGeMAPS and two deep features SoundNet and VGGish. And for the visual modality, in order to represent the original visual cues and motion information together, the key frames of original images and those of optical flow images are both utilized to extract VGG-19 features with finetuned models. With the three audio features and two visual features obtained, we concatenate the selected five features together and then employ the Passive Aggressive algorithm and LarsCV for regression model learning and prediction. In the experiments, we perform the evaluations of selected audio and visual features on the dataset of EIMT16, and compare our results with those of competitive teams in EIMT16 and state-of-the-art method. The experimental results show that the fusion of five features can achieve better regression results in both arousal and valence dimensions, indicating that the selected five features are complementary with each other in the audio-visual modalities. Furthermore, the proposed approach can achieve better regression results than the state-of-the-art method in both evaluation metrics of MSE and PCC in the arousal dimension and comparable MSE results in the valence dimension. Although our approach obtains slightly lower PCC result than the state-of-the-art method in the valence dimension, the fused feature vectors used in our framework have much lower dimensions with a total of 1752, only five thousandths of feature dimensions in the state-of-the-art method, bringing down the memory requirements and computational burden largely.

The remainder of the paper is organized as follows. Section 2 introduces the proposed framework including the audio and visual features and model learning. Then the experimental results and discussions are given in Sect. 3. Finally, some conclusions are drawn in Sect. 4.

2 The Proposed Framework

In this section, we elaborate the proposed framework for affective video content regression, and its main components are shown in Fig. 1. For the audio modality, we select the global audio feature eGeMAPS and two deep features SoundNet and VGGish. Among them, eGeMAPS is a basic standard acoustic parameter set, SoundNet can generate rich natural sound representations by training with two-million unlabeled videos, while VGGish is trained with two million human-labeled video sound-tracks. As for the visual modality, the key frames of original images and those of optical flow images are both used to extract VGG-19 features with finetuned models. Finally, we choose the Passive Aggressive algorithm and LarsCV for model learning and prediction.

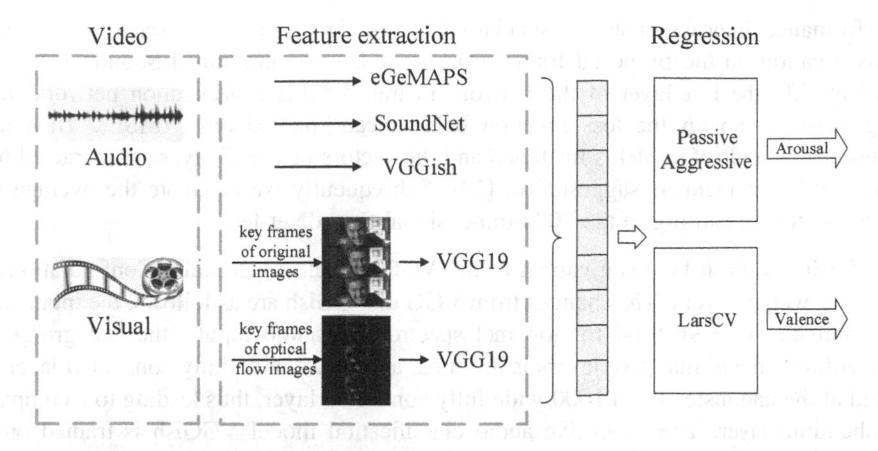

Fig. 1. The proposed framework for affective video content regression.

2.1 Audio Features

For the audio modality as shown in Fig. 1, we utilize three complementary features to depict audio cues. Among them, eGeMAPS is a standard acoustic parameter set, while SoundNet and VGGish features are extracted from the finetuned models with high-level semantics.

eGeMAPS. The extended Geneva Minimalistic Acoustic Parameter Set (eGeMAPS) [11] is a basic standard acoustic parameter set for automatic voice analysis. In contrast to a large brute-force parameter set, eGeMAPS is a minimalistic set of voice parameters with 88-dimensions, which is an extension of the 62-dimensional GeMAPS. GeMAPS contains a compact set of 18 low-level descriptors (LLDs), the arithmetic mean and coefficient of variation are applied as functionals to all 18 LLDs, yielding 36 parameters. In addition, 8 functionals applied to loudness and pitch give additional 16 parameters. Also, the arithmetic mean of Alpha Ratio and Hammarberg Index, the spectral slopes from 0–500 Hz and 500–1500 Hz over all unvoiced segments, and 6 temporal features are included. As an extension of 62-dimensional GeMAPS, the cepstral parameters including MFCC 1–4, spectral flux and Formant 2–3 bandwidth are added as additional 7 LLDs, and the arithmetic mean and coefficient of variation are applied to 7 additional LLDs to all segments, and thus 14 extra descriptors are added. The arithmetic mean of spectral flux in unvoiced regions only, the arithmetic mean and coefficient of variation of spectral flux and MFCC 1–4 voiced regions only are included, resulting in another 11 descriptors. Finally, the equivalent sound level is also included, presenting eGeMAPS as a minimalistic set of voice parameters with compact 88-dimensional vectors.

SoundNet. SoundNet [12] is a one-dimensional deep convolutional network which can generate rich natural sound representations. It learns directly on raw audio waveforms using two-million unlabeled videos and is trained by transferring discriminative visual knowledge from well-established visual models into the sound modality. It has been shown that SoundNet representation can yield significant performance improvements on standard benchmarks for acoustic scene and object classification. In the proposed framework, we utilize the pretrained SoundNet model and modify the last layer of the network to transfer this classification network into regression one with the loss function being mean squared error (MSE). Then the modified SoundNet model is finetuned and the vectors of conv7 layer are extracted for each audio segment as suggested in [12]. Subsequently we calculate the average of these vectors, resulting in the 1024-dimensional SoundNet feature.

VGGish. VGGish [13] is a variant of the VGG model, in particular Configuration A with 11 weight layers. The changes from VGG to VGGish are as follows: the input size is changed to be 96×64 for log mel spectrogram audio inputs, the last group of convolutional and maxpool layers is dropped, and a 128-wide fully connected layer is used at the end instead of a 1000-wide fully connected layer, thus leading to a compact embedding layer. The VGG-like audio classification model VGGish is trained on a large YouTube dataset [14], which includes over 2 million human-labeled 10-second YouTube video soundtracks. In the proposed framework, by using the pretrained VGGish model provided by [13], we extract 128-dimensional embeddings of each audio segment for one audio, and treat the average of these embeddings as the 128-dimensional VGGish feature.

2.2 Visual Features

For the visual modality as shown in Fig. 1, in order to utilize the original images and motion information together, we train two modified VGG-19 models with the input being the key frames of original images and optical flow images, respectively. And then the visual features can be extracted from the two modified VGG-19 models complementarily.

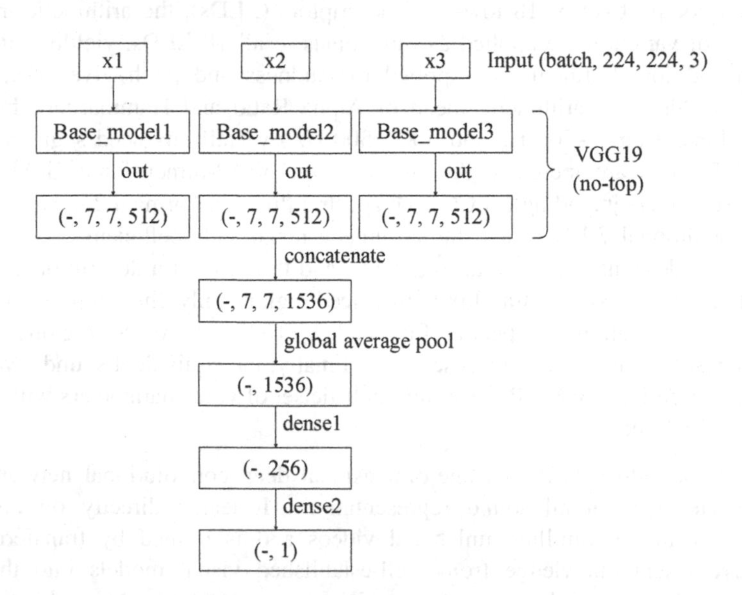

Fig. 2. The modified VGG-19 network for affective video content regression.

VGG-19 [15] is one of the most frequently used networks in image localization and classification, and it secured the first and the second places in the localization and classification tracks of ImageNet challenge 2014, respectively. It has been shown that VGG-19 can generalize well to other datasets and achieve state-of-the-art results on VOC-2007, VOC-2012, Caltech-101 and Caltech-256 for image classification, action classification and other recognition tasks. In the pro-posed framework, the modified VGG19 network with three key frames is shown in Fig. 2. Here in order to avoid the large proportion of redundant information of input data and huge computational burden of training process, we choose three key frames as the inputs of the modified VGG-19 model. It can be seen from Fig. 2 that, for each input of key frame, a VGG-19 no-top network is employed as one base model, and thus the inputs of three key frames result in three outputs with each shape being (batch size, 7, 7, 512). In this paper, we set the batch size to be 8, while the smaller or bigger batch size can also be chosen. Then the three out-puts of VGG-19 no-top models are concatenated and pooled through the added global average pool layer. Subsequently, we utilize the "dense1" layer with 256 filters to extract the deep visual features. By adding the "dense2" layer with one filter and setting the loss function to be MSE between this filter and actual label, we finetune the modified VGG-19 model on the dataset of LIRIS-ACCEDE.

For the modified VGG-19 model shown in Fig. 2, there are two types of inputs we used to train the network. One is the key frames of original images and the other is the key frames of optical flow images. Here the three key frames of original images can be obtained directly by k-means algorithm, which aims to seek a reasonable division by grouping the similar samples into the same cluster and classifying dissimilar objects into different clusters. While for the key frames of optical flow images, we need to calculate the optical flow images first, which are used to describe the motion information of the videos. In the experiments, we employ the Farneback algorithm to get the velocity in the directions of x and y, and then transfer them to HSV values and further convert to RGB values to form the optical flow images. Subsequently, the three key frames can also be extracted from the optical flow images by k-means algorithm. With two types of inputs being the key frames of original images and optical flow images respectively, we finetune two modified VGG-19 models and extract the vectors of "dense1" layer as visual features, resulting in two 256-dimensional deep visual features per video.

2.3 Regression Models

In this paper, we choose the Passive Aggressive algorithm as a regressor for the arousal dimension and LarsCV for the valence dimension.

Passive Aggressive Algorithm. Passive Aggressive (PA) algorithm [16] is a family of margin based online learning algorithms for various prediction tasks. The update taken by PA is aggressive in the sense that even a small loss forces an update of the hypothesis. The performance of PA has been proofed to be superior to many other alternative methods, we choose it as a regressor for the arousal dimension.

LarsCV. Least-angle regression (Lars) [17] is a regression algorithm for high-dimensional data, it is numerically efficient in contexts where the number of features is significantly greater than the number of samples at each step. It finds the feature most correlated with the target. When there are multiple features having equal correlation, it proceeds in a direction equiangular between the features instead of continuing along the same feature. LarsCV is cross-validated Lars to automatically select the best hyper-parameters, we choose it as a regressor for the valence dimension.

3 Experiments

In the experiments, we first evaluate the performance of single features in the audio and visual modalities respectively. And then the evaluation of feature fusion is given and the comparisons with the competition results of EIMT16 and state-of-the-art method are also made. Here all experiments are performed on the global emotion prediction task of EIMT16, and it is the largest dataset for global affective video content regression to the best of our knowledge. This dataset is an extension of LIRIS-ACCEDE, which includes 11000 short video clips from movies. The video clips are ranging from 8 to 12 s and split into a development set of 9800 samples and a test set of 1200 samples. All training experiments are operated using a server with 8 T M40 with 24 GB GPU memory for each.

3.1 Evaluation of Single Features

In this subsection, we evaluate the performance of single features in the audio and visual modalities respectively and the performance is evaluated in terms of MSE and Pearson correlation coefficient (PCC).

For the audio modality, we extract the mp3 and wav formatted audio files from the video clips for feature extraction by using FFMPEG. For the audio feature of eGe-MAPS, the wav audio files are used to extract 88-dimensional feature vectors by employing openSMILE toolkit with the configuration file 'eGMAPSv01a.conf'. Then for the deep feature of SoundNet, the mp3 audio files are used to finetune the pretrained model provided by [12] employing the Torch toolbox with learning rate being 0.0001. Here we extract the output of conv7 layer (1024 dimension) from the finetuned SoundNet model for each audio segment as suggested in [12], and the average of these vectors is calculated as the final SoundNet feature of each audio. As for the VGGish feature, we use Tensorflow toolbox to extract the 128-dimensional embedding from the pretrained model provided by [13] for each audio segment, and then the average of these embeddings is calculated as the VGGish feature for each audio.

Now we can give the evaluation of single features in audio modality as shown in Table 1, where MFCC, IS13, EmoLarge and EmoBase10 are four baseline audio features given in [10] and their regression results are obtained by SVR. It can be seen from Table 1 that, the three features selected in the proposed framework can achieve better regression results in terms of MSE in both arousal and valence dimensions.

Table 1. Evaluation of single features in audio modality

Single features	Arousal		Valence	
	MSE	PCC	MSE	PCC
MFCC	1.818	–	0.504	–
IS13	1.513	–	0.236	–
EmoLarge	1.497	–	0.276	–
EmoBase10	1.400	–	0.228	–
eGeMAPS	**0.732**	0.268	**0.226**	0.221
SoundNet	**0.603**	0.087	**0.224**	0.226
VGGish	**1.000**	0.219	**0.211**	0.315

For the visual modality, we extract the jpeg formatted image files from the video clips for feature extraction by using FFMPEG. And then the optical flow images are calculated from original images using OpenCV and the *k*-means clustering is implemented to extract three key frames from both original images and optical flow images for each video by employing sklearn. To finetune the VGG-19 network, we use the Keras toolbox with TensorFlow as backend. With the inputs being three key frames of original images and optical flow images respectively, we finetune two VGG-19 models with learning rate being 0.001 and the maximum numbers of iterations to be 12250 with batch size of 8. Finally, the vectors from 'dense1' layer are extracted as the visual features, resulting in two 256-dimensional deep visual features.

Table 2. Evaluation of single features in visual modality

Single features	Arousal		Valence	
	MSE	PCC	MSE	PCC
HSH	3.160	–	1.340	–
DSIFT	1.401	–	0.353	–
MKT	1.390	–	0.318	–
TSN	1.254	–	0.215	–
OVGG[a]	**0.776**	0.178	**0.214**	0.391
OFVGG[b]	**0.707**	0.189	**0.232**	0.121

a. OVGG: feature extracted from VGG19 finetuned with key frames of original images.
b. OFVGG: feature extracted from VGG19 finetuned with key frames of optical flow images.

Next we can give the evaluation of single features in visual modality as shown in Table 2, where Hue-Saturation Histogram (HSH), Dense Scale Invariant Feature Transform (DSIFT), MKT and TSN are four baseline visual features given in [10] and their regression results are also obtained by SVR. It can be seen from Table 2 that, the two features selected in the proposed framework can achieve better regression results in terms of MSE in the arousal dimension and comparable results in the valence dimension.

3.2 Comparisons with the State-of-the-Art Results

With the three audio features and two visual features obtained, we concatenate the selected five features together and then employ the PA algorithm in the arousal dimension and LarsCV in the valence dimension for regression model learning and prediction. In order to validate the proposed framework for affective video content regression task, the comparisons are also made among the regression results of the proposed approach and those of competitive teams participated in EIMT16 [5–9] and state-of-the-art method [10], as shown in Table 3.

Table 3. Comparisons with the state-of-the-art results

EIMT16 results	Arousal		Valence		Feature dimension
	MSE	PCC	MSE	PCC	
AUTH-SGP [9]	–	0.265	–	0.110	>35481
BUL [8]	1.431	0.271	0.231	0.146	–
THU-HCSI [7]	1.467	0.344	0.214	0.296	**745**
HKBU [6]	**1.182**	0.212	0.236	**0.379**	**44**
RUC [5]	1.479	**0.467**	**0.201**	**0.419**	>24740
MML [10]	**1.173**	**0.446**	**0.198**	**0.399**	365102
Our approach	**0.543**	**0.459**	**0.209**	0.326	**1752**

It can be seen from Table 3 that, the fusion of five features can achieve better regression results in both arousal and valence dimensions than single features shown in Tables 1 and 2, indicating that the selected five features are complementary with each other in the audio-visual modalities. Furthermore, the proposed approach can achieve better regression results than the state-of-the-art method [10] in both evaluation metrics of MSE and PCC in the arousal dimension and comparable MSE results in the valence dimension. It should be noticed that, although our approach obtains slightly lower PCC result than the methods [5] and [10] in the valence dimension, the fused feature vectors employed in the proposed framework have much lower dimensions with a total of 1752, only about one fourteenth of feature dimensions used in [5] (1752 versus 24740) and five thousandths of feature dimensions used in [10] (1752 versus 365102). It will bring down the memory requirements and computational burden largely.

4 Conclusion

This paper proposes a new framework for global affective video content regression by utilizing five complementary audio-visual features. In the proposed framework, we select the traditional global feature GeMAPS and two deep features SoundNet and VGGish as audio features. As for the visual modality, the key frames of original images and those of optical flow images are both utilized to extract VGG-19 features with finetuned models, in order to represent the original visual cues and motion information together. In the experiments, we perform the evaluations of selected audio and visual features on the dataset of EIMT16, and compare our results with those of competitive teams in EIMT16 and state-of-the-art method. The experimental results show that the fusion of five features can achieve better regression results in both arousal and valence dimensions, indicating the complementariness of the selected five features in the audio-visual modalities. Furthermore, the proposed approach can achieve better regression results than the state-of-the-art method in both evaluation metrics of MSE and PCC in the arousal dimension and comparable MSE results in the valence dimension. Although our approach obtains slightly lower PCC result than the state-of-the-art method in the valence dimension, the fused feature vectors used in our framework have much lower dimensions with a total of 1752, only five thousandths of feature dimensions in the state-of-the-art method, bringing down the memory requirements and computational burden largely.

References

1. Baveye, Y., Chamaret, C., Dellandréa, E., Chen, L.M.: Affective video content analysis: a multidisciplinary insight. IEEE Trans. Affect. Comput. **9**(4), 396–409 (2018)
2. Baveye, Y., Dellandréa, E., Chamaret, C., Chen, L.M.: LIRIS-ACCEDE: a video database for affective content analysis. IEEE Trans. Affect. Comput. **6**(1), 43–55 (2015)
3. Sjöberg, M., Baveye, Y., Wang, H.L., Quang, V.L., Ionescu, B., et al.: The MediaEval 2015 affective impact of movies task. In: MediaEval (2015)
4. Dellandréa, E., Chen, L.M., Baveye, Y., Sjöberg, M.V., Chamaret, C.: The MediaEval 2016 emotional impact of movies task. In: MediaEval (2016)
5. Chen, S.Z., Jin, Q.: RUC at MediaEval 2016 emotional impact of movies task: fusion of multimodal features. In: MediaEval (2016)
6. Liu, Y., Gu, Z.L., Zhang, Y., Liu, Y.: Mining emotional features of movies. In: MediaEval (2016)
7. Ma, Y., Ye, Z.P., Xu, M.X.: THU-HCSI at MediaEval 2016: emotional impact of movies task. In: MediaEval (2016)
8. Jan, A., Gaus, Y.F.B.A., Meng, H.Y., Zhang, F.: BUL in MediaEval 2016 emotional impact of movies task. In: MediaEval (2016)
9. Timoleon, A.T., Hadjileontiadis, L.J.: AUTH-SGP in MediaEval 2016 emotional impact of movies task. In: MediaEval (2016)
10. Yi, Y., Wang, H.L.: Multi-modal learning for affective content analysis in movies. Multimedia Tools Appl. **78**(10), 13331–13350 (2019)
11. Eyben, F., Scherer, K.R., Schuller, B.W., Sundberg, J., Andre, E., et al.: The geneva minimalistic acoustic parameter set (GeMAPS) for voice research and affective computing. IEEE Trans. Affect. Comput. **7**(2), 190–202 (2016)
12. Aytar, Y., Vondrick, C., Torralba, A.: SoundNet: learning sound representations from unlabeled video. In: Advances in Neural Information Processing Systems, pp. 892–900. Barcelona, Spain (2016)
13. Gemmeke, J.F., Ellis, D.P.W., Freedman, D., Jansen, A., Lawrence, W., et al.: Audio set: an ontology and human-labeled dataset for audio events. In: IEEE International Conference on Acoustics, Speech and Signal Processing, pp. 776–780. New Orleans, USA (2017)
14. Hershey, S., Chaudhuri, S., Ellis, D.P.W., Gemmeke, J.F., Jansen, A., et al.: CNN architectures for large-scale audio classification. In: IEEE International Conference on Acoustics, Speech and Signal Processing, pp. 131–135. New Orleans, USA (2017)

15. Simonyan, K., Zisserman, A.: Very deep convolutional networks for large-scale image recognition. In: International Conference on Learning Representations. San Diego, USA (2015)
16. Crammer, K., Dekel, O., Keshet, J., Shalev-Shwartz, S., Singer, Y.: Online passive-aggressive algorithms. J. Mach. Learn. Res. **7**(3), 551–585 (2006)
17. Efron, B., Hastie, T., Johnstone, I., Tibshirani, R., Ishwaran, H., et al.: Least angle regression. Ann. Stat. **32**(2), 407–499 (2004)

SS5: MULTIMED: Multimedia and Multimodal Analytics in the Medical Domain and Pervasive Environments

Studying Public Medical Images from the Open Access Literature and Social Networks for Model Training and Knowledge Extraction

Henning Müller[1,2(✉)], Vincent Andrearczyk[1], Oscar Jimenez del Toro[1], Anjani Dhrangadhariya[1], Roger Schaer[1], and Manfredo Atzori[1]

[1] University of Applied Sciences Western Switzerland (HES-SO), Sierre, Switzerland
henning.mueller@hevs.ch
[2] University of Geneva, Geneva, Switzerland

Abstract. Medical imaging research has long suffered problems getting access to large collections of images due to privacy constraints and to high costs that annotating images by physicians causes. With public scientific challenges and funding agencies fostering data sharing, repositories, particularly on cancer research in the US, are becoming available. Still, data and annotations are most often available on narrow domains and specific tasks. The medical literature (particularly articles contained in MedLine) has been used for research for many years as it contains a large amount of medical knowledge. Most analyses have focused on text, for example creating semi-automated systematic reviews, aggregating content on specific genes and their functions, or allowing for information retrieval to access specific content. The amount of research on images from the medical literature has been more limited, as MedLine abstracts are available publicly but no images are included. With PubMed Central, all the biomedical open access literature has become accessible for analysis, with images and text in structured format. This makes the use of such data easier than extracting it from PDF. This article reviews existing work on analyzing images from the biomedical literature and develops ideas on how such images can become useful and usable for a variety of tasks, including finding visual evidence for rare or unusual cases. These resources offer possibilities to train machine learning tools, increasing the diversity of available data and thus possibly the robustness of the classifiers. Examples with histopathology data available on Twitter already show promising possibilities. This article adds links to other sources that are accessible, for example via the ImageCLEF challenges.

Keywords: Medical imaging · Biomedical literature · Machine learning · Training

Y. M. Ro et al. (Eds.): MMM 2020, LNCS 11962, pp. 553–564, 2020.
https://doi.org/10.1007/978-3-030-37734-2_45

1 Introduction

Machine learning, in particular deep learning, relies on large annotated datasets to reach sometimes impressive results, as for example in the ImageNet competition [9]. Whereas web images are easily available and annotations can be obtained via crowdsourcing without a need for expensive specialists, the medical domain suffers more difficulties in creating large-scale image resources that are publicly available. All medical data acquisitions require ethics approval and privacy constraints can sometimes limit the distribution and sharing of such data even when it is considered of high importance [39]. As a consequence, small and non publicly available datasets limit the use of state-of-the-art machine learning algorithms that require large amounts of data, as well as the reproducibility of many reported results in the literature. Many funding organizations in the US and Europe have started pushing for data sharing and for making resources available over 15 years ago. The outcomes are now visible with large scale repositories such as the TCIA[1] (The Cancer Imaging Archive) and TCGA[2] (The Cancer Genome Atlas) being increasingly used by research projects. These repositories take some of the legal responsibilities from the medical institutions that acquired that data, easing data sharing for them. Scientific challenges have also contributed to making medical data available for concrete tasks with strong baselines. ImageCLEF [11,20] has had medical challenges each year since 2004 and, together with other challenges such as VISCERAL [18], BraTS [28] or Camelyon [4], has strongly gained in popularity. Even though scientific challenges have strongly advanced many domains, there is a risk of bias (depending on the exact setup and performance measures used) and results need to be evaluated with care [25]. Other resources for access to images and videos include [32,34].

The biomedical literature stores a very large amount of available medical knowledge. Medical knowledge is estimated to have a half-life of about 5–10 years [13], meaning that knowledge needs to be checked regularly and it may be important to use recent data to assure veracity when training systems. Similarly for images, the acquisition devices change continuously. Ways to harmonize images across the imaging devices also need to be developed [1].

While a large amount of work has been dedicated to the automatic analysis of text in biomedical literature [37,40], work on extracting and practically using images present in the literature is still limited. A major difficulty that explains this limited amount of work is the unstructured nature of the data, with images not being easily extracted from the literature and associated with meaningful information or labels. The biomedical literature also contains an extreme variability of information, making it necessary to filter out the unwanted data [20].

The PubMed Central (PMC) repository[3] has allowed this type of analysis in recent years, since an exponentially increasing number of images has become available with the free text and limited structured data (such as attached MeSH

[1] https://www.cancerimagingarchive.net/.
[2] https://www.genome.gov/Funded-Programs-Projects/Cancer-Genome-Atlas.
[3] http://www.ncbi.nlm.nih.gov/pmc/.

terms, keywords, place where a figure is referenced, etc.) (see Fig. 1). With more than 2 million articles in total, an average of 3.5 figures per article including 1.5 compound figures of 4 subfigures each, it sums up to approximately seven million figures, including 3 million compound figures with 12 million subfigures for a total of >16 million figures available in 2018 if separated correctly. With an expected increase of nearly 3 million figures in 2019 and more in the following years, it promises in the near future very large amounts of training data in various applications, modalities and particularly rare cases that are strongly oversampled in the literature compared to clinical archives [12]. Difficulties related to this type of data, that will be developed in more details in Sect. 3, include the heterogeneity and non-guaranteed quality of the images, the presence of compound images and the automation of ground truth labels extraction from the text. This article has as objective the systematic analysis of work towards using publicly available sources of medical images, such as PMC. It reviews much of the existing work in the field of making such resources usable for machine learning. The main contribution of this text is the systematic collection of available articles in the field including resources of annotated data sets that can be used for model training. Thus, this article makes the available resources (articles, data sets, source code) accessible for researchers, resources that are currently scattered and not easy to find. It solves the problem of where to start when filtering the medical literature for relevant images for a specific problem. The example problem chosen here is that of histopathology image analysis.

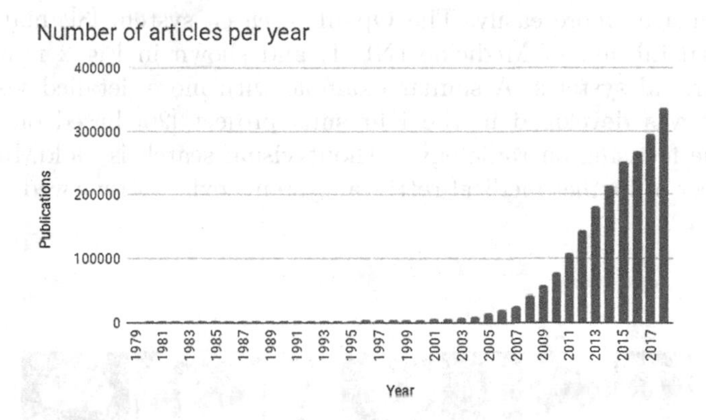

Fig. 1. The growth in the number of published open access articles in the biomedical literature has been exponential in the past 30 years.

2 Methods

For gathering the articles cited in this text, two approaches were chosen as a more qualitative methodology. As a first approach, the work of the ImageCLEF benchmark [20] that has extensively worked on images from the biomedical open-access literature was analyzed over the past 12 years, a period in which most image resources have come from the literature or other public sources. Several steps were analyzed in this context to extract information from images in the literature, to filter our relevant clinical images and to retrieve visual content or answer questions based on this visual content. In a second step, the literature search tool Google scholar was used to add articles working on related fields and for specific tasks. Search terms include "medical image classification" and "medical literature" and "publicly available resources" and "machine learning". Articles found were chosen based on being complementary to the already cited articles, journal papers were favored over conference papers and dynamically growing data sets (such as PMC) were favored over fixed data sets. The found resources are sorted into several categories based on the steps required for the data extraction and data enrichment.

3 Analyzing Images from the Biomedical Literature

3.1 Retrieval of Medical Images

One of the first ways to exploit images from the biomedical literature was image retrieval systems, that indexed images and allowed to search by keywords and visual examples or for visually similar regions of interest. This made the visual content accessible and allowed to reuse single images with specific patterns or groups of images more easily. The OpenI research system [8], maintained by the National Library of Medicine (NLM) and shown in Fig. 2 is an example of such retrieval systems. A similar example with more detailed visual search capabilities was developed in the Khresmoi project [26] based on [30], while another one focusing on radiology without visual search is GoldMiner [19]. A large number of further medical retrieval systems exist as reviewed in [31].

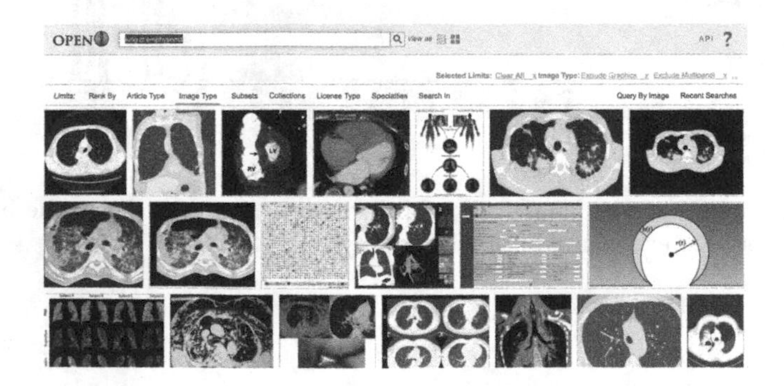

Fig. 2. Screenshot of the OpenI image retrieval system [8].

3.2 Extracting Content from Medical Images

When the objectives go beyond finding specific images and require filtering the entire PMC, then it is necessary to extract metadata from the images, which is described in the following sections.

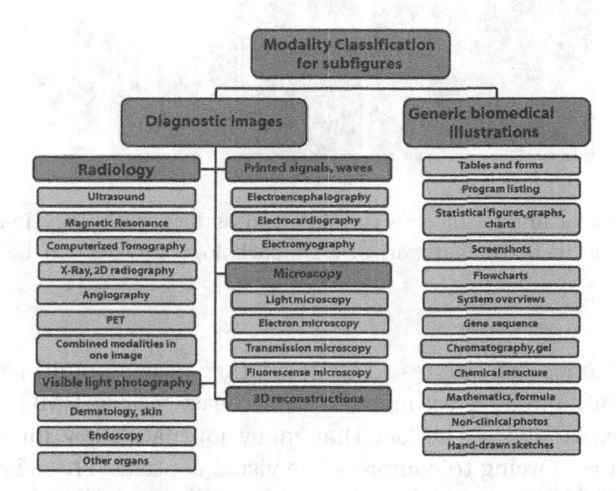

Fig. 3. A hierarchy of images types in the biomedical literature, taken from [29].

Image Types. The first basic information to use for filtering an image collection is the image type, for example, the imaging modality that produced the image but also whether a flow chart or other general graph is shown. Image search engines such as GoldMiner [19], for instance, allow to filter a search by image modality and it was shown that filtering by modality can improve retrieval quality [21]. Specifically for the biomedical literature in PMC, a hierarchy of image types was developed in [29]. This hierarchical structure is also shown in Fig. 3. Several challenges on identifying the image types were run in ImageCLEF [15]. The currently best results for the really challenging and very unbalanced data set of over 30 classes reached over 90% [2].

In order to underline the diversity in the image types, we show in Fig. 4 a set of images that were initially classified as histopathology images but in manual control found to be different types. These examples illustrate the visual similarity of some image types and, in one case, a hand-drawn histopathology image which clearly looks like histopathology but is a different type in the hierarchy. Besides the figure type that was also described in the IRMA (Image Retrieval in Medical Applications) hierarchy [22] (that focuses only on medical modalities) there is also an interest to identify the anatomical region of the images, its orientation and the biological system that is imaged (the heart vs. the lung for a chest X-ray, for example). These meta-data allow for good filtering and search. Pathology is the most frequently requested functionality for search [27] but it also very difficult to obtain from the image data alone, as often more information on a case is required.

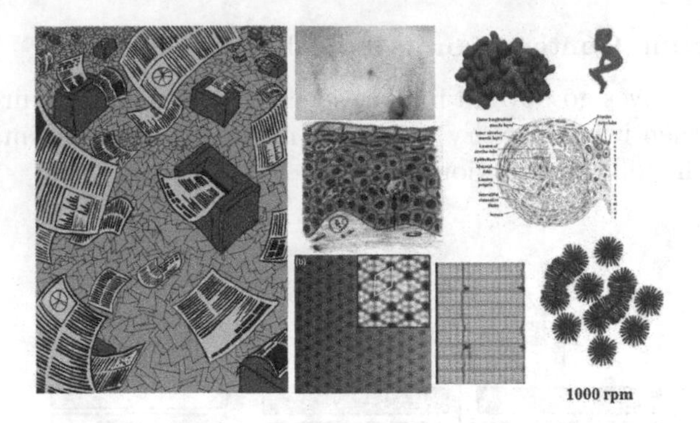

Fig. 4. Examples of images incorrectly classified as histopathology images and manually identified as incorrect categories. Histopathology images can be seen in Fig. 5.

Dealing with Compound Figures. The percentage of compound figures (consisting of several subfigures) is estimated to be at least 40% in PMC [15]. This high ratio can be explained by the fact that many journals allow for a very limited number of figures, forcing to compress the visual content. These images are only available in a single image block limiting their utility in computer analysis or for further analysis. Making the individual subfigures accessible requires detecting the compound figures among the millions of figures and splitting them into subfigures as explained in [3,6]. Several challenges arise, as the subfigures are often related and sometimes it is even hard to identify whether a figure is a single figure or contains independent subparts. An example of journal compound figures with several subfigures that are automatically separated is shown in Fig. 5, in this case focusing on histopathology images.

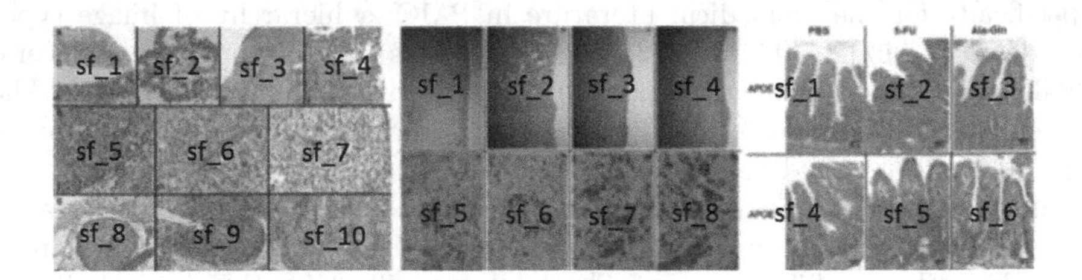

Fig. 5. Examples of compound figures and the automatically detected separation lines.

As with the image types described before, the variety of images and ways in which images are put into compound figures is enormous. Again, several challenges in ImageCLEF tackled this problem with often very good results for both detecting the subfigures and separating them [16]. After subfigures are cut they can again be classified into image types and then be used for specific tasks.

Focusing on Regions of Interest. In medical images, the actual region of interest is often small. In journal articles, the raw data are usually not made available and replaced by cropped images that are already in the optimal level/window setting for viewing. These images show a subset of the original image and for tomographic images most frequently only the best slices, for example where a tumor is largest. This reduction of information, intrinsic to the purpose of reporting images in scientific articles, presents inconveniences. Information is lost with the compression and transfer to jpeg format (256 grey levels instead of 4000 in DICOM) and with the omission of slides in tomographic series. Yet, the content is also more focused and often shows only the environment around the region of interest. This can possibly allow weakly annotated approaches if a sufficiently large amount of data is available. Another particularity of images from the literature is the presence of arrows to highlight regions that are further discussed in the caption or the full text [5]. These arrows can relatively easily be detected and allow to further focus the search on small regions of interest [5].

3.3 Combining Text and Images for Data Analysis

Much of the description in the preceding sections has focused on image analysis approaches to enrich the information of images from the medical literature by filtering specific image types, cutting compound figures and detecting the region of interest. In the case of the biomedical literature, there is also text information available, notably the figure caption and the full text surrounding the reference to a figure. In PMC, most articles have manually attached MeSH (Medical Subject Headings) terms. Text has been used in most retrieval applications [10] but has also obtained very good results in modality classification [2,17], as it is complementary to visual information. In the case of compound figure detection, a caption with several subparts can also be indicative for the presence of subfigures. The text can then be split to correspond to each of the subfigures [3].

For images detected as histopathology to be useful for training clinical decision support systems, further steps are required [12]. Much of the cancer research is on animals so, when learning human tissue classification, it is important to filter out animal tissue samples even from the same organ. The species is most often present in the manually attached MeSH terms (for humans even the group of children, or older adults is usually given) and these can be used as a good indicator for filtering out those of mice and rats. The specific organ is often mentioned in the MeSH terms or in the article title but is only rarely mentioned in the figure caption. This again allows filtering out tissue of organs that are not relevant for a given task.

Image Heterogeneity in the Case of Histopathology. Histopathology has several specificities that increase the possible image heterogeneity. Different types of stainings can highlight various molecular aspects in the images in differing colors. The most frequent one, the H&E (Hematoxylin and Eosin) staining, is low in cost and accounts for approximately 90% of the histopathology images in the literature based on a small sample that we evaluated. Within H&E staining, color heterogeneity can strongly affect the performance of the machine learning algorithms [7], so heterogeneity needs to be added in the training data. In pathology images, color variations can be due to tissue preparation and are related to the complex set of preparation phases related to staining procedures, section thickness and scanner differences [23]. Color heterogeneity can be approached with many methods, such as color normalization [7,24,38] and color augmentation [36] directly in the learning phase. Particularly, color augmentation has recently led to excellent results in challenges [7]. Interpretability methods can evaluate the impact of color shifts and texture transformations [14]. Besides this, detecting the scale of figures [33] is another challenge. With structures being analyzed at differing scales on a microscope, it is important to know the image scale when comparing images or when using them for machine learning. Sometimes, this information can be found in the image caption but it may not actually be reliable, as the editors can modify the image size and resolution.

3.4 An Example of Using Twitter Histopathology Images

Images and information posted by pathologists on social media (in this case Twitter) were used in [35] to create a dataset and train machine learning algorithms to identify stains and discriminate between different tissues in histopathology images. The results obtained by Schaumberg et al. [35] show that such data can actually be used. However, they also highlight the limitations of the approach. Despite having a large number of manually curated images, good performance was only obtained for tasks that can be defined as very simple for a human. For instance, the authors reported Area Under Receiver Operating Characteristic (AUROC) over 0.9 for tasks such as: differentiating between human H&E stained microscopy images from all other types of images or distinguishing H&E from immunohistochemistry (IHC) stained microscopy images, a very simple task. AUROC reduces to 0.803 when distinguishing among breast, dermatological, gastrointestinal, genitourinary and gynecological pathology tissue types. Finally, the performance for more relevant tasks noticeably drops. Distinguishing between low-grade and malignant tumors on the mentioned tissues obtains an average AUROC of 0.703, while the three-class classification of nontumoral diseases, low-grade tumors, and malignant tumors drops to an average AUROC of 0.683. Both results should be considered in the light of the considered number of classes (respectively 2 and 3), which leads to chance level accuracies of respectively 50% and 33.3% in case of a balanced distribution.

4 Conclusions

The objective of this article is to gather and review research that aims at leveraging the usefulness of medical images publicly available on the Internet via a variety of sources. The most frequently used resource is the biomedical literature, although some communities shared images on social networks such as Twitter and there is potentially useful content in public teaching files and possibly other resources. With an exponentially increasing amount of images, it is important to develop automatic pipelines that adapt to the changing images and regularly add such up-to-date content to learn from it and really optimize generalization performance of classifiers with limited manual work. Many of the examples shown in this paper focused on basic classification and filtering tasks to augment the value of the extracted images. This allowed, in internal experiments, to find around 100,000 histopathology images among the five million images in PMC (a number that is increasing very quickly). This number gets further reduced when removing non-human tissue and also when focusing on specific organs such as prostate or breast tissue.

Still, such teaching files, social networks or literature can provide important complements to clinical archives if the information contained in the images can be accurately extracted. Moreover, these resources focus on rare cases or abnormal situations and can complement clinical archives where the most common conditions are usually oversampled and rare or unusual cases are not often seen.

This paper focused on a scenario using histopathology images and it shows the steps of how to make images from the biomedical literature usable for machine learning tasks. A quantitative evaluation is clearly required to show the usefulness of these images to machine learning. A very similar approach can be employed in radiology or dermatology, simply filtering for a different set of images and different subclasses. Each time, resources can be created that have few problems in terms of privacy constraints and ethics because the data have already been made available in the biomedical literature with a clear license. The work required can be important in a first step to create a fully automated pipeline but it is still much less than extracting images from clinical archives. Quickly increasing data sources offer the possibility to have within a few years a much larger resource available and being able to reuse such an automatic pipeline to retrain existing systems.

Using images from the literature is complementary to using images from clinical archives for training, as clinical archives focus on local specificities whereas images in the literature allow for better generalization. Images from the literature contain mainly unusual or rare cases whereas images in clinical archives contain many normal or frequent cases. Thus, the two sources can be used together. Finally, the literature also allows groups without connections to a medical center to work on medical data. The next steps in this work are to show that training with such heterogeneous images is possible for a well-defined task such as grading of prostate cancer histopathology images. Other useful targets would be to create an automated pipeline for all the steps required to enrich images from the literature and then run this at several moments over time to estimate data increase. If several research groups can collaborate, a possible critical mass can be reached and combinations of automatic labels could reach a high quality. It would be even more useful if information on image type, compound figures etc. could be distributed directly with PMC, so all research using the data can profit from it. In the case of uncertain labels, a confidence score could be added.

Acknowledgment. This work was partially funded by the EU H2020 ExaMode project (grant agreement 825292).

References

1. Andrearczyk, V., Depeursinge, A., Müller, H.: Neural network training for cross-protocol radiomic feature standardization in computed tomography. J. Med. Imaging **6**(2), 024008 (2019)
2. Andrearczyk, V., Müller, H.: Deep multimodal classification of image types in biomedical journal figures. In: Bellot, P., et al. (eds.) CLEF 2018. LNCS, vol. 11018, pp. 3–14. Springer, Cham (2018). https://doi.org/10.1007/978-3-319-98932-7_1
3. Apostolova, E., You, D., Xue, Z., Antani, S., Demner-Fushman, D., Thoma, G.R.: Image retrieval from scientific publications: text and image content processing to separate multi-panel figures. J. Am. Soc. Inf. Sci. **64**, 893–908 (2013)
4. Bejnordi, B.E., et al.: Diagnostic assessment of deep learning algorithms for detection of lymph node metastases in women with breast cancer. J. Am. Med. Assoc. **318**(22), 2199–2210 (2017)
5. Cheng, B., Stanley, R.J., De, S., Antani, S., Thoma, G.R.: Automatic detection of arrow annotation overlays in biomedical images. Int. J. Healthcare Inf. Syst. Inform. **6**(4), 23–41 (2011)
6. Chhatkuli, A., Markonis, D., Foncubierta-Rodríguez, A., Meriaudeau, F., Müller, H.: Separating compound figures in journal articles to allow for subfigure classification. In: SPIE Medical Imaging (2013)
7. Cruz-Roa, A., et al.: Accurate and reproducible invasive breast cancer detection in whole-slide images: a deep learning approach for quantifying tumor extent. Sci. Rep. **7**, 46450 (2017)
8. Demner-Fushman, D., Antani, S., Simpson, M.S., Thoma, G.R.: Design and development of a multimodal biomedical information retrieval system. J. Comput. Sci. Eng. **6**(2), 168–177 (2012)
9. Deng, J., Dong, W., Socher, R., Li, L.J., Li, K., Fei-Fei, L.: ImageNet: a large-scale hierarchical image database. In: IEEE Conference on Computer Vision and Pattern Recognition, CVPR 2009, pp. 248–255 (2009)
10. Depeursinge, A., Müller, H.: Sensors, medical images and signal processing: comprehensive multi-modal diagnosis aid frameworks. In: IMIA Yearbook of Medical Informatics, vol. 5, no. 1, pp. 43–46 (2010)
11. Deselaers, T., Deserno, T.M., Müller, H.: Automatic medical image annotation in ImageCLEF 2007: overview, results, and discussion. Pattern Recogn. Lett. **29**(15), 1988–1995 (2008)
12. Dhrangadhariya, A.K., Jimenez-del Toro, O., Andrearczyk, V., Atzori, M., Müller, H.: Exploiting the PubMed central repository to mine out a large multimodal dataset of rare cancer studies. In: SPIE International Society for Optics and Photonics (2020)
13. Emanuel, E.: A half-life of 5 years. Can. Med. Assoc. J. **112**(5), 572 (1975)
14. Graziani, M., Andrearczyk, V., Müller, H.: Regression concept vectors for bidirectional explanations in histopathology. In: Stoyanov, D., et al. (eds.) MLCN/DLF/IMIMIC -2018. LNCS, vol. 11038, pp. 124–132. Springer, Cham (2018). https://doi.org/10.1007/978-3-030-02628-8_14
15. García Seco de Herrera, A., Kalpathy-Cramer, J., Demner Fushman, D., Antani, S., Müller, H.: Overview of the ImageCLEF 2013 medical tasks. In: Working Notes of CLEF 2013 (Cross Language Evaluation Forum), September 2013

16. García Seco de Herrera, A., Müller, H., Bromuri, S.: Overview of the ImageCLEF 2015 medical classification task. In: Working Notes of CLEF 2015 (Cross Language Evaluation Forum), September 2015
17. García Seco de Herrera, A., Schaer, R., Bromuri, S., Müller, H.: Overview of the ImageCLEF 2016 medical task. In: Working Notes of CLEF 2016 (Cross Language Evaluation Forum), September 2016
18. Jimenez-del-Toro, O., et al.: Cloud-based evaluation of anatomical structure segmentation and landmark detection algorithms: VISCERAL Anatomy benchmarks. IEEE Trans. Med. Imaging **35**(11), 2459–2475 (2016)
19. Kahn Jr., C.E., Thao, C.: GoldMiner: a radiology image search engine. Am. J. Roentgenol. **188**, 1475–1478 (2008)
20. Kalpathy-Cramer, J., García Seco de Herrera, A., Demner-Fushman, D., Antani, S., Bedrick, S., Müller, H.: Evaluating performance of biomedical image retrieval systems: overview of the medical image retrieval task at ImageCLEF 2004–2014. Comput. Med. Imaging Graph. **39**, 55–61 (2015)
21. Kalpathy-Cramera, J., Hersh, W.: Automatic image modality based classification and annotation to improve medical image retrieval. Stud. Health Technol. Inform. **129**, 1334–1338 (2007)
22. Lehmann, T.M., Schubert, H., Keysers, D., Kohnen, M., Wein, B.B.: The IRMA code for unique classification of medical images. In: Huang, H.K., Ratib, O.M. (eds.) Medical Imaging 2003: PACS and Integrated Medical Information Systems: Design and Evaluation. SPIEProc, vol. 5033, pp. 440–451. San Diego, California, USA (2003)
23. Leo, P., Lee, G., Shih, N.N.C., Elliott, R., Feldman, M.D., Madabhushi, A.: Evaluating stability of histomorphometric features across scanner and staining variations: prostate cancer diagnosis from whole slide images. J. Med. Imaging **3**(4), 047502 (2016)
24. Li, X., Plataniotis, K.N.: A complete color normalization approach to histopathology images using color cues computed from saturation-weighted statistics. IEEE Trans. Biomed. Eng. **62**(7), 1862–1873 (2015)
25. Maier-Hein, L., et al.: Why rankings of biomedical image analysis competitions should be interpreted with care. Nat. Commun. **9**(1), 5217 (2018)
26. Markonis, D., et al.: Khresmoi for radiologists - visual search in radiology archives and the open-access medical literature. Health Manage. **13**(3), 23–24 (2013)
27. Markonis, D., et al.: A survey on visual information search behavior and requirements of radiologists. Methods Inf. Med. **51**(6), 539–548 (2012)
28. Menze, B.H., et al.: The multimodal brain tumor image segmentation benchmark (BRATS). IEEE Trans. Med. Imaging **34**(10), 1993–2024 (2015)
29. Müller, H., Kalpathy-Cramer, J., Demner-Fushman, D., Antani, S.: Creating a classification of image types in the medical literature for visual categorization. In: SPIE Medical Imaging (2012)
30. Müller, H., Rosset, A., Vallée, J.P., Geissbuhler, A.: Integrating content-based visual access methods into a medical case database. In: Proceedings of the Medical Informatics Europe Conference, MIE 2003, St. Malo, France, vol. 95, pp. 480–485, May 2003
31. Müller, H., Unay, D.: Retrieval from and understanding of large-scale multi-modal medical datasets: a review. IEEE Trans. Multimedia **19**(9), 2093–2104 (2017)
32. Münzer, B., Schoeffmann, K., Böszörmenyi, L.: Content-based processing and analysis of endoscopic images and videos: a survey. Multimedia Tools Appl. **77**(1), 1323–1362 (2018)

33. Otálora, S., Atzori, M., Andrearczyk, V., Müller, H.: Image magnification regression using densenet for exploiting histopathology open access content. In: Stoyanov, D., et al. (eds.) OMIA/COMPAY -2018. LNCS, vol. 11039, pp. 148–155. Springer, Cham (2018). https://doi.org/10.1007/978-3-030-00949-6_18
34. Pogorelov, K., et al..: KVASIR: a multi-class image dataset for computer aided gastrointestinal disease detection. In: Proceedings of the 8th ACM on Multimedia Systems Conference, pp. 164–169. ACM (2017)
35. Schaumberg, A.J., et al.: Large-scale annotation of histopathology images from social media. bioRxiv 396663 (2018)
36. Tellez, D., et al.: Quantifying the effects of data augmentation and stain color normalization in convolutional neural networks for computational pathology. arXiv preprint arXiv:1902.06543 (2019)
37. Tsatsaronis, G., et al.: An overview of the BIOASQ large-scale biomedical semantic indexing and question answering competition. BMC Bioinform. **16**(1), 138 (2015)
38. Valavanis, L., Stathopoulos, S.: IPL at ImageCLEF 2017 concept detection task. In: CLEF2017 Working Notes. CEUR Workshop Proceedings, Dublin, Ireland, 11–14 September 2017. CEUR-WS.org. http://ceur-ws.org
39. Vannier, M.W., Summers, R.M.: Sharing images. Radiology **228**, 23–25 (2003)
40. Westergaard, D., Stærfeldt, H.H., Tønsberg, C., Jensen, L.J., Brunak, S.: A comprehensive and quantitative comparison of text-mining in 15 million full-text articles versus their corresponding abstracts. PLoS Comput. Biol. **14**(2), e1005962 (2018)

AttenNet: Deep Attention Based Retinal Disease Classification in OCT Images

Jun Wu[1(✉)], Yao Zhang[1], Jie Wang[2], Jianchun Zhao[3], Dayong Ding[3], Ningjiang Chen[4], Lingling Wang[4], Xuan Chen[5(✉)], Chunhui Jiang[6], Xuan Zou[7], Xing Liu[8], Hui Xiao[8], Yuan Tian[4], Zongjiang Shang[1], Kaiwei Wang[1], Xirong Li[2], Gang Yang[2], and Jianping Fan[9]

[1] School of Electronics and Information, Northwestern Polytechnical University, Xi'an, China
junwu@nwpu.edu.cn
[2] Key Lab of DEKE, Renmin University of China, Beijing, China
[3] Vistel AI Lab, Visionary Intelligence Ltd., Beijing, China
[4] Carl Zeiss (Shanghai) Co., Ltd., ZEISS Group, Shanghai, China
[5] The Second People's Hospital of Ji'nan, Ji'nan, China
lhgcx@163.com
[6] Eye and ENT Hospital of Fudan University, Shanghai, China
[7] Peking Union Medical College Hospital, Beijing, China
[8] The State Key Laboratory of Ophthalmology; Zhongshan Ophthalmic Center, Sun Yat-sen University, Guangzhou, China
[9] University of North Carolina-Charlotte (UNCC), Charlotte, NC, USA

Abstract. An optical coherence tomography (OCT) image is becoming the standard imaging modality in diagnosing retinal diseases and the assessment of their progression. However, the manual evaluation of the volumetric scan is time consuming, expensive and the signs of the early disease are easy to miss. In this paper, we mainly present an attention-based deep learning method for the retinal disease classification in OCT images, which can assist the large-scale screening or the diagnosis recommendation for an ophthalmologist. First, according to the unique characteristic of a retinal OCT image, we design a customized pre-processing method to improve image quality. Second, in order to guide the network optimization more effectively, a specially designed attention model, which pays more attention to critical regions containing pathological anomalies, is integrated into a typical deep learning network. We evaluate our proposed method on two data sets, and the results consistently show that it outperforms the state-of-the-art methods. We report an overall four-class accuracy of 97.4%, a two-class sensitivity of 100.0%, and a two-class specificity of 100.0% on a public data set shared by Zhang et al. with 1,000 testing B-scans in four disease classes. Compared to their work, our method improves the numbers by 0.8%, 2.2%, and 2.6% respectively.

Keywords: Optical Coherence Tomography (OCT) · Retinal disease classification · Deep learning · Attention model

---

The original version of this chapter was revised: a missing funding number in the acknowledgement section was added. The correction to this chapter is available at https://doi.org/10.1007/978-3-030-37734-2_75

Y. M. Ro et al. (Eds.): MMM 2020, LNCS 11962, pp. 565–576, 2020.
https://doi.org/10.1007/978-3-030-37734-2_46

1 Introduction

Optical Coherence Tomography (OCT) has become an emerging biomedical imaging technology in ophthalmological diagnosis. Different from color fundus photographs, the OCT imaging offers a non-invasive real-time, high-resolution 3D volumetric scan for the highly-scattering human retinal tissues, where a cross-sectional tomograph (B-scan) is widely used [6,9]. Retinal diseases such as Age-related Macular Degeneration (AMD), Diabetic Retinopathy (DR) and Glaucoma have become the most essential ophthalmological problems to be solved. Early diagnosis and timely treatment can greatly reduce the possibility of vision loss or even blindness. For efficient screening in a large population, the automatic diagnosis of retinal diseases based on OCT images is very crucial and necessary.

To tackle this issue, some existing works are using traditional image processing and machine learning technologies. To classify normal, and three types of macular pathologies as the Macular Edema (ME), macular hole and AMD, Liu et al. [15] proposed a Support Vector Machine (SVM) based method based on multi-scale spatial texture and geometric shape features using Local Binary Pattern (LBP) descriptors. A Histogram of the Gradient (HoG) based SVM method was proposed by Srinivasan et al. [20] to classify normal, AMD, and Diabetic Macular Edema (DME) [3]. Naz et al. [16] proposed an SVM-based method using coherent tensors to identify the DME. Venhuizen et al. [23] proposed a random forest based method to classify the AMD patients.

Except for these, in recent years deep learning is also popular in retinal disease classification in OCT images. After the denoising and clipping were applied as the pre-processing steps, Awais et al. [1] used a VGG16 network to extract image features, and then the K-Nearest Neighbour (KNN) and random forest were utilized to classify retinal lesions. Lee et al. [14] proposed an AMD classification algorithm based on a modified VGG16 network, where the random descent gradient (SGD) was applied. Gulshan et al. [8] applied a deep convolutional neural network (CNN) for automated detection of DR and DME. Ravenscroft et al. [18] applied a CNN to extract low-level primitive filter kernels, and then a histogram-based descriptor was formed as the discriminative image features that were fed into a traditional neural network to classify different stages of the AMD.

Further, Karri et al. [12] utilized the GoogleNet to classify the ME, dry AMD, and normal images. After the image pre-processing and de-noising, transfer learning was applied. Similarly, Kermany et al. [13] applied the transfer learning to create an Inception-V3 model [21] to classify Normal, DME, Choroidal Neovascularization (CNV) and Drusen, reporting an overall accuracy of 96.6%. In [5], a unified method combining the segmentation and classification was proposed by De Fauw et al. First, OCT images were segmented using a 3D U-net [2]. Then, they were fed into the DenseNet [11] for training. Finally, the classification results were obtained based on the trained model. In [17], a OCT-NET model was proposed to classify retinal diseases from 3D SD-OCT volumes.

Most of the existing OCT retinal disease classification methods do not consider the attention mechanism and directly feed the OCT images, which is prone to be affected by background noises. Generally, speckle noise reduces the OCT quality where an attention model is required to emphasize the main signal. The attention mechanism for general image classification has been widely researched, i.e. residual attention model [24], while its very-deep structure is not tailored for OCT images. For fundus images, there are some works for attention models [4,22], which are related but using a different modality.

Another drawback of the existing methods is a disease-specific design with special domain knowledge, which is difficult to generalize for other diseases. By contrast, Fang et al. [7] proposed a lesion-aware CNN to generate a soft attention map, resulting in local lesion-related regions for further classification networks. However, it is tightly coupled with the lesion classification network, which cannot be easily integrated with other existing retinal disease classification models.

Therefore, a lesion-free decoupled attention model for general retinal disease classification is in demand. Different from a color fundus photograph, a B-Scan is a gray image with a simple dark background, and possible pathological changes occur only in the main signal region. Previous studies find that noisy backgrounds still hurt model optimization [19]. To tackle this issue, we need to highlight specific informative areas and reduce background interferences effectively.

As a result, in this paper we propose a simple but effective design for extracting a lesion-free attention map, amplifying the retinal signals of the low-intensity pixels and restraining the background noises. Its advantages are: (1) As an independent and decoupled module, it is easy to integrate with any existing retinal disease models. (2) This simple feed-forward structure has a few parameters and it has less demand for the training data. (3) It can achieve bigger perception fields to obtain a global retinal structure, as the pair of down-sampling and up-sampling is applied. Finally, this lesion-free attention-based deep learning framework (AttenNet) is applied to classify the retinal diseases in OCT images.

2 Our Proposed Method: AttenNet

As illustrated in Fig. 1, the main ideas of our proposed *AttenNet* are as follows. First, a pre-processing step is applied for an input OCT B-scan. The main signal area for retinal structures is detected and preserved. Then, an attention model is designed to capture the most informative and critical region. Next, based on the obtained attention map, a deep learning model for retinal disease classification is trained. Finally, test images are classified based on the pre-trained model.

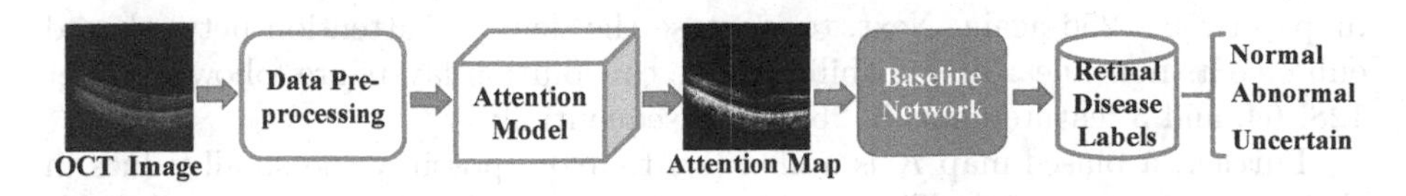

Fig. 1. Workflow of our proposed AttenNet for retinal disease classification in OCT.

2.1 Data Preprocessing

As the image regions above the upper retinal boundary and below the lower retinal boundary are the backgrounds that are irrelevant w.r.t. the task, we introduce a pre-processing module to roughly identify these two boundaries. To that end, the precise edge detection is unnecessary. We therefore use the computationally efficient Sobel operator. Our experiments show that this simple operator is sufficient. Also, the morphology method such as open and close operations is an effective way to remove the isolated noisy pixels from the background.

Background Removal: First, the OTSU binarization is applied to a gray B-scan, and then it is further de-noised by a filter composed of morphological open and close operations. Next, a retinal contour is obtained by the Sobel operator, resulting in a binary edge map. Then, four coordinates of a bounding box are determined based on active pixel ranges, where all the background pixels are eliminated to remove possible noises to avoid local maxima in optimization, as in Fig. 2. Finally, the refined B-scans are fed into the deep learning pipeline.

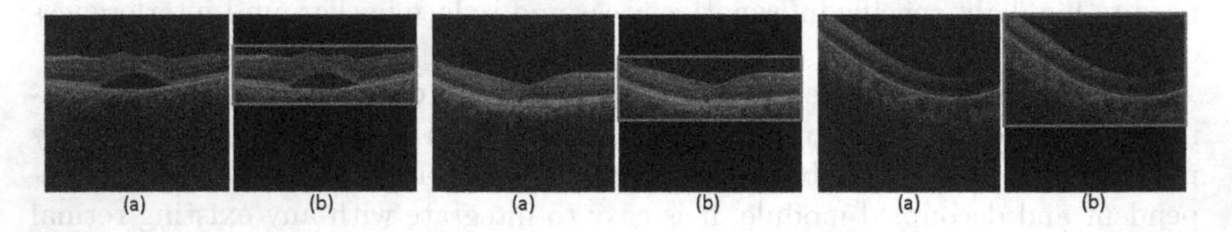

Fig. 2. B-scan examples of the pre-processing step: (a) original, (b) pre-processed.

Data Augmentation: Also, traditional data augmentation is applied for the training data to avoid over-fitting, such as the random mirroring, clipping, and rotation, where their operating probabilities are all 50%. The edge clipping is between 10–20 pixels, and the rotation angle is within 0–360°.

2.2 The Designed Attention Model

As in Fig. 3, we propose an attention model to capture critical signal regions. Given 256×256 B-scans, a convolution operation is first carried out, and 64 corresponding feature maps in 256×256 are created. And, a down-sampling is further applied to reduce them into 128 smaller feature maps in 128×128. Then, an up-sampling by the de-convolution operation is employed to restore 64 feature maps in 256×256 again. Next, to increase the depth of attention network and enhance its non-linear fitting ability, three convolution layers are followed to get 128, 64, and 3 feature maps in 256×256 sequentially.

Further, a biased map K is added ($\oplus$) to avoid possibly too small values in the current feature maps. The biased map K is a constant image where all pixels are 1 in our evaluation, which is a residual structure as

$$y = (1 + \text{mask}) * x = x + (\text{mask} * x) = x + \text{residual}. \quad (1)$$

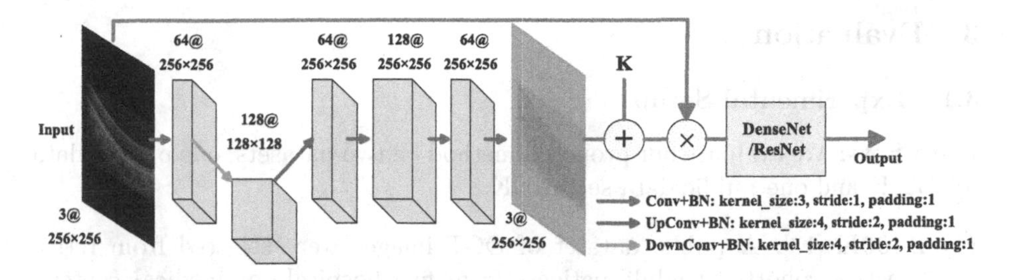

Fig. 3. Flowchart of the AttenNet network structure for attention model.

It tries to amplify the signals of the low-intensity pixels from the up-sampling output images, resulting in keeping target details for further model learning.

In addition, a batch normalization layer is applied after each convolutional operation to force the neurons back to the normal distribution. Finally, an element-wise multiplication ($\otimes$) is executed and the corresponding results are fed into the next input in the pipeline, such as a DenseNet or ResNet.

As shown in Fig. 4(d), the designed attention module has succeeded to highlight the pixels of the critical signal region, which is referred to as an activation map enhancing the retinal signals. In addition, it can also increase the model perception field in a global view to improve classification performance.

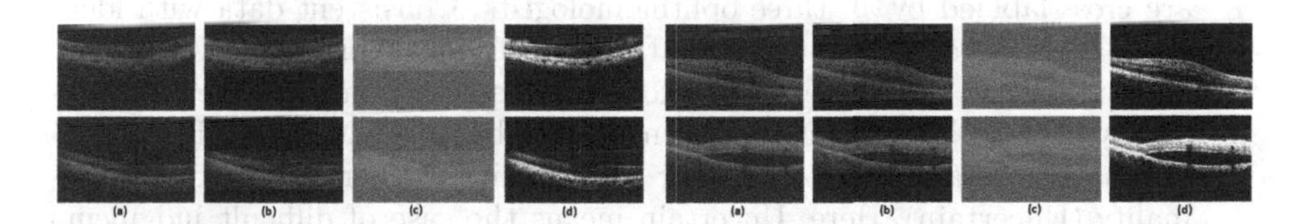

Fig. 4. Image examples for the attention model. (a) original, (b) pre-processed, (c) feature map before adding K, and (d) feature map after element-wise multiplication.

2.3 Basic Deep Learning Network

Followed by our attention model, a typical deep learning network for the image classification task can be applied, such as DensetNet [11], ResNet [10], or InceptionV3 [21]. We will evaluate different models such as DenseNet169, ResNet34, ResNet50, and InceptionV3 in Sect. 3. For the network optimization, a cross entropy loss function will applied for single-label classification tasks, and a binary cross entropy (BCE) loss is for multi-label classification tasks. For an abbreviation, we use *Atten(DP)* to denote the *DP*-based attention model, where *DP* is a typical deep learning network such as ResNet, DenseNet, Inception, and so on.

3 Evaluation

3.1 Experimental Setup

Data Sets: We evaluate our proposed method on two datasets, one private data set B28K and one public data set Z109K.

(1) **Z109K** [13]**:** A public dataset of OCT images were selected from retrospective cohorts of adult patients from five hospitals or medical centers. Validated OCT Images are labeled as (disease)-(randomized patient ID)-(image number by this patient). They are centered on the macular are split into a training set (108,309 images) and a testing set (1,000) of independent patients. They have four classes: CNV, DME, Drusen, and Normal.
(2) **B28K:** This private data set is collected from a local hospital with randomly-selected 2,564 OCT scans from 2017 to 2018 calendar years, including 599 32-line cube scans and 1,965 high-resolution 5-line scans. A total of 28,624 B-scan is obtained as 369 B-scans were eliminated due to the lack of any consensus among annotators. The OCT images are taken centered on macular or non-macular areas. Many kinds of lesions and severe pathological changes occur. The 28,624 B-scan images are split into the training (20,000), validation (3,500) and test sets (5,124) of independent patients. Each B-scan slice in the training set is graded by one of three ophthalmologists with at least 5-year experience. B-scan slices in the test set are cross-labeled by all three ophthalmologists. Consistent data with identical labels are collected as the final test set. Eight involved classes include: Normal, retinal deformation (R-deform), fovea abnormality (Fovea), abnormality over ELM (O-ELM), abnormality in/below ELM (I/B-ELM), Subretinal abnormality (Sub-R), other abnormality (Other), uncertain abnormality (Uncertain). Here, Uncertain means the case of difficult judgments for the extremely low-quality images. Further, to make the classification task easier, another simplified version with three categories are also considered as Normal (15,344), Abnormal (11,130) and Uncertain (2,150).

Parameter Settings: Experiments are conducted under Ubuntu 16.04 with an NVIDIA 1080Ti GPU. The original images in 1536×1024 are resized to 256×256. The deep learning models are trained by stochastic gradient descent with a batch size of 16 and a learning rate of 1.0×10^{-3}.

3.2 Evaluation Metrics

As eight classes in the B28K test set are not balanced, *sensitivity* (sens.), *specificity* (spec.), and F1 are applied as the metrics. Considering a binary classification for pixels, define TP as true positive, FP as false positive, TN as true negative, FN as false negative. Sensitivity = Recall = TP/(TP + FN), Specificity = TN/(TN + FP), Precision = TP/(TP + FP), and Accuracy = (TP + TN)/(TP + TN + FP + FN). Generally, F1 represents the harmonic mean of two trade-off metrics. Especially, F1(PR) represents the harmonic mean of Precision and Recall, and F1(SS) represents the harmonic mean of Sensitivity and Specificity, which is affected by imbalanced data. Precisely, their definitions are as follows:

$$F1(PR) = \frac{2 * \text{Precision} * \text{Recall}}{\text{Precision} + \text{Recall}}, \tag{2}$$

$$F1(SS) = \frac{2 * \text{Sensitivity} * \text{Specificity}}{\text{Sensitivity} + \text{Specificity}}. \tag{3}$$

However, the balance of our dataset B28K is acceptable (1.87:1 for the positive-negative ratio) for binary classification, normal (3339) vs abnormal (1785).

Since four classes in the public Z109K test set is accurately balanced, except for the above metrics, *accuracy* is also considered as an extra metric.

3.3 Results

(1) Results on the B28K Dataset. We compare our proposed method to the original ResNet50 [10], ResNet34 [10], Densenet169 [11], and InceptionV3 [21] with different settings to solve a single-label classification task with three categories (see details in Sect. 3.1) on the B28K dataset, as in Table 1. In addition, the parameter settings of the learning rate and batch size have already been clarified in Sect. 3.1.

(a) Three-label OCT Disease Classification. From Table 1, we can conclude that our attention-based method achieves the best sensitivity (90.14% for T4* using *Atten(ResNet50)* model), the best specificity (95.30% for I4 using *Atten(Inception)*), and the best harmonic mean F1(PR) for T4*, *Atten(ResNet50)*, which all outperform their original networks (I4 vs. I1, T4* vs. T1, R2 vs. R1, and D2 vs. D1). For example, comparing our method (T4*) to ResNet50 (T1), the sensitivity and specificity have been increased by 2.92% and 3.53% respectively. Further, to prove the effectiveness of every single module, the pre-processing step can compare different settings (I2 vs. I1, T2 vs. T1, and T4* vs. T3), and the attention module can compare *Atten(ResNet50)* (T3) to ResNet50 (T1).

In addition, considering the residual attention model [10] as our main baseline model. Based on our private dataset with 28,624 B-scan images for disease classification, our method is better than the residual attention model [10]. We optimize the parameters for residual attention-56 model as in Table 2, and residual attention-92 model as in Table 3. Compared to the residual attention-56 model, our method (T4*) increase sensitivity by 10.08% (from 80.06%–90.14%), and F1 by 7.23% (from 83.74% to 90.97%). Compared to the residual attention-92 model, our method (T4*) increase sensitivity by 5.5% (from 84.59%–90.14%), and F1 by 9.3% (from 81.67% to 90.97%).

For Tables 2 and 3, it should be noted: a binary cross entropy (BCE) loss is applied for this multi-label classification task. Sensitivity and Specificity are

Table 1. Comparisons of different methods on the B28K dataset to classify three labels: Normal, Abnormal, and Uncertain. A cross entropy loss function is applied during model training. Some abbreviations are Prep: pre-processing, Atten: attention.

No.	Models	Prep	Atten	Sens.(%)	Spec.(%)	F1(PR)(%)
B1	Residual attention-56 [24]	×	×	80.06	94.04	83.74
B2	Residual attention-92 [24]	×	×	84.59	87.93	81.67
I1	InceptionV3 [21]	×	×	87.17	89.40	88.27
I2	InceptionV3+Prep	✓	×	88.07	89.97	89.01
I3	InceptionV3+Atten	×	✓	84.59	93.86	86.29
I4	Atten(InceptionV3)	✓	✓	86.05	**95.30**	88.33
T1	ResNet50 [10]	×	×	87.22	88.29	87.75
T2	ResNet50+Prep	✓	×	88.18	90.42	89.29
T3	ResNet50+Atten	×	✓	88.23	91.85	90.00
T4*	**Atten(ResNet50)**	✓	✓	**90.14**	91.82	**90.97**
R1	ResNet34 [10]	×	×	88.57	89.43	89.00
R2*	Atten(ResNet34)	✓	✓	88.18	92.45	90.26
D1	Densenet169 [11]	×	×	87.34	89.91	88.61
D2	Atten(Densenet169)	✓	✓	88.18	92.00	90.05

Table 2. Comparisons of different settings of the Residual Attention-56 Network [24] on the B28K dataset to classify three labels.

No.	B-Size	L-rate	Sens.(%)	Spec.(%)	F1(PR)(%)	F1(SS)(%)
1	6	0.0001	66.33	**95.93**	76.26	78.43
2	60	0.0001	42.75	86.25	50.75	57.16
3	60	0.001	73.78	95.39	80.90	83.20
4*	**60**	**0.01**	80.06	94.04	**83.74**	**86.49**
5	60	0.1	**81.62**	86.67	79.03	84.07
6	60	0.5	75.80	90.93	78.64	82.68
7	60	1	77.42	92.69	81.03	84.37

Table 3. Comparisons of different settings of the Residual Attention-92 Network [24] on the B28K dataset to classify three labels.

No.	B-Size	L-rate	Sens.(%)	Spec.(%)	F1(PR)(%)	F1(SS)(%)
1	6	0.0001	70.36	**95.72**	78.89	81.10
2	40	0.0001	47.34	95.00	60.42	63.19
3	40	0.001	78.38	91.76	80.89	84.54
4*	**40**	**0.01**	**84.59**	87.93	**81.67**	**86.23**
5	40	0.1	80.62	83.14	76.00	81.86
6	40	0.5	74.34	92.57	78.99	82.46

Table 4. Comparisons of different methods on the B28K dataset to classify eight labels. A binary cross entropy (BCE) loss is applied for this multi-label classification task. Sensitivity and Specificity are calculated based on a two-class evaluation as Anti-Normal (including six Abnormal sub-classes and Uncertain) vs. Normal.

No.	Models	Prep	Atten	Sens.(%)	Spec.(%)	F1(PR)(%)
E1	ResNet50 [10]	×	×	89.75	87.33	88.52
E2*	Atten(ResNet50)	✓	✓	89.36	**92.51**	90.91
E3	ResNet34 [10]	×	×	87.34	88.41	87.87
E4*	Atten(ResNet34)	✓	✓	90.14	90.36	90.25
E5	DenseNet169 [11]	×	×	90.25	90.39	90.32
E6*	**Atten(DenseNet169)**	✓	✓	**92.38**	91.52	**91.95**

calculated based on a two-class evaluation as Anti-Normal (including six Abnormal sub-classes and Uncertain) vs. Normal. B-size means the Batch Size, L-rate means the learning rate.

(b) Eight-label OCT Disease Classification. To solve a multi-label classification task with eight classes (see Sect. 3.1) on the B28K dataset, as in Tables 4 and 5, the ResNet50 [10], ResNet34 [10], and DenseNet169 [11] are all evaluated. The conclusions can be made that the attention model using the DenseNet169 achieves the best sensitivity of 92.38%, and the attention model using the ResNet50 achieves the best specificity of 92.51%. Further, the effectiveness of our attention-based method can be proved by comparing different settings as E2* vs. E1, E4* vs. E3, and E6* vs. E5.

Table 5. Comparisons of different methods on the B28K dataset to classify eight labels. The detailed results of Table 4. Some abbreviations are R50: ResNet50, R34: ResNet34, D169: DenseNet169, and Atten: Attention.

Models	Metrics (%)	Normal	Abnormal (including six sub-classes)						Uncertain
			R-deform	Fovea	O-ELM	I/B-ELM	Sub-R	Other	
R50	Sens	87.33	82.98	88.19	91.57	80.99	77.39	88.56	86.96
	Spec	89.75	95.71	88.07	91.26	92.46	95.48	80.74	93.81
Atten (R50)	Sens	92.51	95.74	93.70	93.17	86.95	89.57	94.44	85.22
	Spec	89.36	91.73	80.35	90.67	91.67	91.40	78.17	96.55
R34	Sens	88.41	85.82	85.04	88.27	86.95	91.74	88.56	76.52
	Spec	87.34	92.90	89.71	90.72	87.94	92.91	74.18	96.42
Atten (R34)	Sens	90.36	91.49	76.38	93.17	84.79	90.00	93.79	94.78
	Spec	90.14	91.01	89.45	88.18	90.03	93.05	78.21	94.59
D169	Sens	90.39	93.62	92.91	93.74	87.58	93.91	93.14	82.17
	Spec	90.25	90.35	82.25	90.44	91.95	91.62	76.88	97.22
Atten (D169)	Sens	91.52	90.07	92.13	93.39	88.59	90.43	91.50	74.78
	Spec	92.38	92.96	85.67	89.90	91.53	93.60	80.82	98.06

As the final judgment threshold is optimized in the validation dataset based on the maximum harmonic mean of Sensitivity and Specificity. The validation set is divided from the original training set, which is annotated by only one ophthalmologist. While the test set is independently labeled by three different ophthalmologists. For our attention model based on different baseline networks, there exist certain distribution deviations between the verification set and the test set, which leads to the performance drop, resulting in the inconsistency of selecting the optimal threshold in these two datasets. For example, the specificity of Atten (R50) is lower than that of other models. In addition, the Atten(R50) method has low specificity, but its sensitivities are higher.

(2) Results on the Public Z109K Dataset. Further, the evaluations are carried out on the Z109K dataset. As the B-scans in the Z109K have relatively high image quality, we do not apply the data pre-processing step here, which is fair to the same setting as in [13]. For the model optimization, we randomly select 1948 images from the training set as a validation set.

For the disease classification of CNV, DME, Drusen, and Normal, our attention model is better than Kermany et al. [13] on their public dataset, which integrates transfer learning into deep learning network, as in Table 6.

Compared to the existing methods [10,13], our proposed method achieves the best accuracy of 97.50% (Z2*), the best sensitivity of 100.00% (Z2* and Z6*), and the best specificity of 100.0% (Z5 and Z6*). More precisely, compared to [13], the best setting of our proposed method (Z6*), *Atten(ResNet34)* with the batch size as 32, can achieve the state-of-the-art performance, where the

Table 6. Comparisons of the different methods on the public Z109K dataset [13] for identifying four classes: CNV, DME, Drusen, and Normal. As a four-class classification task, Accuracy is computed based on four class confusion matrix. Sensitivity, Specificity, and F1 are calculated based on a two-class evaluation as Normal vs. Rest (CNV, DME, Drusen). Some abbreviations are Atten: attention, Acc.: accuracy. Note: Accuracy is computed based on the four-class confusion matrix and other metrics such as Sensitivity, Specificity and F1 are calculated based on a two-class evaluation.

No.	Models	Atten	Batch	4-class	Two-class Metrics		
			Size	Acc.(%)	Sens.(%)	Spec.(%)	F1(%)
Z0	Kermany et al. [13]	×	-	96.60	97.80	97.40	97.60
Z1	ResNet50 [10]	×	16	95.90	99.20	<u>99.86</u>	99.53
Z2*	**Atten(ResNet50)**	✓	16	**97.50**	**100.0**	98.00	98.99
Z3	ResNet34 [10]	×	16	95.70	99.73	99.60	99.66
Z4	Atten(ResNet34)	✓	16	97.00	99.60	99.60	99.60
Z5	ResNet34 [10]	×	32	95.70	<u>99.86</u>	**100.0**	<u>99.93</u>
Z6*	**Atten(ResNet34)**	✓	32	<u>97.40</u>	**100.0**	**100.0**	**100.0**
Z7	ResNet50 [10]	×	20	96.30	99.73	**100.0**	99.86
Z8	Atten(ResNet50)	✓	20	96.70	100.0	99.6	99.80

accuracy has increased by 0.8%, sensitivity by 2.2%, and specificity by 2.6%. In addition, for *ResNet50*, increasing the batch size from 16 to 20 seems helpful (Z7 vs. Z1). While for *Atten(ResNet50)*, this improvement is not consistent as the specificity increases 1.6% but the accuracy decreases 0.8% (Z8 vs. Z2).

4 Conclusions

In this paper, we mainly propose a novel and effective deep attention learning method for the retinal disease classification in OCT images. First, a pre-processing method is introduced to deal with OCT data in low image quality that include out-of-center, noisy background, and so on. Next, motivated by the human attention mechanism, an attention deep learning model is specially designed to learn an active B-scan image mask that can more emphasize critical regions. Finally, a typical deep learning network is followed in the pipeline to execute the task of the retinal disease classification. Experiment results on two data sets show that both the pre-processing step and the proposed attention model are effective, and they can improve the overall classification performance. For the public Z109K data set with four classes, our proposed method can achieve the state-of-the-art performance where the accuracy has increased by 0.8%, sensitivity by 2.2%, and specificity by 2.6%. For our private B28K data set with eight classes that is a relatively difficult task, the pre-trained deep attention framework achieves a sensitivity of 92.38% and a specificity of 91.52%, which outperforms other state-of-the-art methods.

Acknowledgement. This work is supported by the CSC State Scholarship Fund (201806295014), NSFC (No. 61672523), CAMS Initiative for Innovative Medicine (2018-I2M-AI-001), Beijing NSF (No.4192029, No.7184236), National Key Research & Development Plan (No.2017YFC0108200), and NSF of Guangdong Province (No.2017A030313649).

References

1. Awais, M., et al.: Classification of SD-OCT images using a deep learning approach. In: IEEE ICSIPA, pp. 489–492 (2017)
2. Çiçek, Ö., Abdulkadir, A., Lienkamp, S.S., Brox, T., Ronneberger, O.: 3D U-Net: learning dense volumetric segmentation from sparse annotation. In: Ourselin, S., Joskowicz, L., Sabuncu, M.R., Unal, G., Wells, W. (eds.) MICCAI 2016. LNCS, vol. 9901, pp. 424–432. Springer, Cham (2016). https://doi.org/10.1007/978-3-319-46723-8_49
3. Ciulla, T.A., et al.: Diabetic retinopathy and diabetic macular edema: pathophysiology, screening, and novel therapies. Diabetes Care **26**(9), 2653–2664 (2003)
4. Dai, B., Bu, W., Wang, K., Wu, X.: Fundus lesion detection based on visual attention model. In: Che, W., et al. (eds.) ICYCSEE 2016. CCIS, vol. 623, pp. 384–394. Springer, Singapore (2016). https://doi.org/10.1007/978-981-10-2053-7_34
5. De Fauw, J., et al.: Clinically applicable deep learning for diagnosis and referral in retinal disease. Nat. Med. **24**(9), 1342–1350 (2018)

6. Drexler, W., et al.: State-of-the-art retinal optical coherence tomography. Progress Retinal Eye Res. **27**(1), 45–88 (2008)
7. Fang, L., et al.: Attention to lesion: lesion-aware convolutional neural network for retinal optical coherence tomography image classification. IEEE Trans. Med. Imaging **38**(8), 1959–1970 (2019)
8. Gulshan, V., et al.: Development and validation of a deep learning algorithm for detection of diabetic retinopathy in retinal fundus photographs. JAMA **316**(22), 2402–2410 (2016)
9. Hassan, T., et al.: Review of OCT and fundus images for detection of macular edema. In: IEEE IST, pp. 1–4 (2015)
10. He, K., et al.: Deep residual learning for image recognition. In: IEEE CVPR, pp. 770–778 (2016)
11. Huang, G., et al.: Densely connected convolutional networks. In: IEEE CVPR, pp. 4700–4708 (2017)
12. Karri, S.P.K., et al.: Transfer learning based classification of optical coherence tomography images with diabetic macular edema and dry age-related macular degeneration. Biomed. Optics Express **8**(2), 579–592 (2017)
13. Kermany, D.S., et al.: Identifying medical diagnoses and treatable diseases by image-based deep learning. Cell **172**(5), 1122–1131 (2018)
14. Lee, C.S., et al.: Deep learning is effective for classifying normal versus age-related macular degeneration oct images. Ophthalmol. Retina **1**(4), 322–327 (2017)
15. Liu, Y.Y., et al.: Automated macular pathology diagnosis in retinal oct images using multi-scale spatial pyramid and local binary patterns in texture and shape encoding. Med. Image Anal. **15**(5), 748–759 (2011)
16. Naz, S., et al.: A practical approach to OCT based classification of diabetic macular edema. In: IEEE ICSigSys, pp. 217–220 (2017)
17. Perdomo Charry, O., et al.: Classification of diabetes-related retinal diseases using a deep learning approach in optical coherence tomography. Comput. Methods Programs Biomed. **178**, 181–189 (2019)
18. Ravenscroft, D., et al.: Learning feature extractors for AMD classification in OCT using convolutional neural networks. In: IEEE EUSIPCO, pp. 51–55 (2017)
19. Reif, R., et al.: Motion artifact and background noise suppression on optical microangiography frames using a Naive Bayes mask. Appl. Opt. **53**, 4164–4171 (2014)
20. Srinivasan, P.P., et al.: Fully automated detection of diabetic macular edema and dry age-related macular degeneration from optical coherence tomography images. Biomed. Opt. Express **5**(10), 3568–3577 (2014)
21. Szegedy, C., et al.: Rethinking the inception architecture for computer vision. In: IEEE CVPR, pp. 2818–2826 (2016)
22. Varadarajan, A.V., et al.: Deep learning for predicting refractive error from retinal fundus images. Invest. Ophthalmol. Vis. Sci. (IOVS) **59**, 2861–2868 (2018)
23. Venhuizen, F.G., et al.: Automated age-related macular degeneration classification in OCT using unsupervised feature learning. In: Medical Imaging, vol. 9414 (2015)
24. Wang, F., et al.: Residual attention network for image classification. In: IEEE CVPR, pp. 3156–3164 (2017)

NOVA: A Tool for Explanatory Multimodal Behavior Analysis and Its Application to Psychotherapy

Tobias Baur[1(✉)], Sina Clausen[2], Alexander Heimerl[1], Florian Lingenfelser[1], Wolfgang Lutz[2], and Elisabeth André[1]

[1] Lab for Human-Centered Multimedia, Augsburg University, Augsburg, Germany
{baur,heimerl,lingenfelser,andre}@hcm-lab.de

[2] Klinische Psychologie und Psychotherapie, Trier University, Trier, Germany
{clausen,lutz}@uni-trier.de

Abstract. In this paper, we explore the benefits of our next-generation annotation and analysis tool NOVA in the domain of psychotherapy. The NOVA tool has been developed, tested and applied in behaviour studies for several years and psychotherapy sessions offer a great way to expand areas of application into a challenging yet promising field. In such scenarios, interactions with patients are often rated by questionnaires and the therapist's subjective rating, yet a qualitative analysis of the patient's non-verbal behaviours can only be performed in a limited way as this is very expensive and time-consuming. A main aspect of NOVA is the possibility of applying semi-supervised active learning where Machine Learning techniques are already used during the annotation process by giving the possibility to pre-label data automatically. Furthermore, NOVA provides therapists with a confidence value of the automatically predicted annotations. This way, also non-ML experts get to understand whether they can trust their ML models for the problem at hand.

Keywords: Annotation tools · Psychotherapy · Cooperative Machine Learning · Explainable AI

1 Introduction

In psychotherapy emotions appear to have a central role for the activation of change processes and therapeutic success [25,32]. Most mental disorders are characterised by disturbed affect (e.g. depression) and dysfunctional emotion regulation (e.g. substance abuse disorders) [17,22]. Many therapeutic approaches (e.g. emotion-focused therapy, schema therapy, dialectical-behavioural therapy) emphasise the need of changing emotional coping styles during the therapy process [32]. Multiple studies have shown that psychotherapy is generally effective

This work has received funding from the BMBF under FKZ 01IS17074, FMLA, the DFG under project number 392401413, DEEP and LU 660/10-1, LU660/8-1.

Y. M. Ro et al. (Eds.): MMM 2020, LNCS 11962, pp. 577–588, 2020.
https://doi.org/10.1007/978-3-030-37734-2_47

[8]. Yet, there is often high variability in outcomes [9]. Patient-focused psychotherapy research deals with the question how, when and why psychotherapy works in order to improve therapeutic success for the individual patient [20]. This field of research makes use of frequently repeated measures, mainly questionnaires, to examine session processes and outcomes (routine outcome monitoring, feedback) [18,21]. It includes for example the assessment of current symptoms and common factors (e.g. therapeutic relationship, problem solving, problem actuation) to predict symptom change (e.g. sudden gains and losses) and provide empirically supported feedback to therapists [19,21]. In this context, additional or alternative data sources would be highly valuable because humans, especially patients with depressive symptoms, tend to have a distorted recall of emotions and mood [3]. Further, the reported subjective feeling captures one component of emotions. Complementary information about the more objective (bodily) expression is of major importance to better understand interpersonal processes and communication (e.g. [15]).

Thus, the analysis of emotions by means of nonverbal signals in recorded psychotherapy sessions bears great potential for advancing both, the psychotherapy process as well as outcome research. In order to analyse recorded therapy sessions for identifying relevant behaviour patterns with this degree of refinement, in classical approaches a huge bottleneck is given by the necessity of manual labelling effort. That means, segments in the observed material need to be labelled using sets of discrete classes or continuous scores, e. g. a certain type of gesture, a social situation, or the emotional state of a person. Especially in the field of practical psychotherapy, where thousands of hours of data are generated, manually annotating would be an overambitious task. A solution to this problem is exploitation of computational power to accomplish some of the annotation work automatically. However, to ensure the quality of the predicted annotations this still requires human supervision to identify and correct errors. To keep human effort as low as possible, it is useful to understand why a model makes wrong assumptions. Therefore, it is not only important to provide tools that ease the use of semi-automated labelling, but also to increase the transparency of the decision process. By visualising the predictions, therapists get an idea about the strengths and weaknesses of the underlying classification model and can immediately decide which parts of a prediction are worth keeping. Ideally, the system even guides the users' attention towards parts where manual revision is necessary. Once an annotation has been revised, the model can be retrained by end-users of the system themselves to improve its performance for the next cycle. This procedure can be repeated until a desired performance is reached.

Once the model achieves a satisfying performance it may be used to predict new, unlabelled sessions in a fully automated manner. This automated analysis of emotional expression during the session can provide vital additional information that helps to understand the emotional activation of the patient and the emotional interaction with the therapist (e.g. affective co-regulation, synchrony). In this paper, we first introduce a next-generation annotation tool called NOVA, which implements a cooperative machine learning workflow. In particular, NOVA offers semi-automated annotations and provides visual feedback to inspect and correct machine-generated labels. We further report on a pilot study that describes first experiences with NOVA in the practical application in the area of psychotherapy.

2 Related Work

2.1 Annotation Tools

In the past, several annotation tools with focus on analysing social signals in various contexts have been developed. The general user interface of NOVA has been inspired by existing annotation tools. Prominent examples include ELAN [33], ANVIL [16], and EXMARALDA [28]. These tools offer layer-based tiers to insert time-anchored labelled segments, that we call *discrete* annotations. *Continuous* annotations, on the other hand, allow an observer to track the content of an audiovisual stimulus over time based on a continuous scale. One of the first tools that allow annotators to trace emotional content in real-time on two dimensions (activation and evaluation) was FEELTRACE [6]. Its descendant GTRACE (general trace) [7] allows the user to define their own dimensions and scales. More recent tools to accomplish continuous descriptions are CARMA (continuous affect rating and media annotation) [10] and DARMA (dual axis rating and media annotation) [11].

Unfortunately, almost all of the tools offer none or only little automation. In former studies, labelling of several hours of interaction turned out to be an extremely time consuming task, so methods to automate the coding process were highly desirable. In the targeted scenario, bearing the potential of several thousands of hours of recorded sessions, automation of the labelling process becomes imperative.

2.2 Active and Cooperative Machine Learning

A common approach to reduce human labelling effort is the selection of instances for manual annotation based on active learning techniques. The basic idea is to forward only instances with low prediction certainty or high expected error reduction to human annotators [29]. Estimation of most informative instances is an art of its own. A whole range of options to choose from exist, such as calculation of 'meaningful' confidence measures, detecting novelty (e. g. by training auto-encoders and seeing for the deviation of input and output when new data runs through the auto-encoder), estimating the degree of model change the data instance would cause (e.g. seeing whether knowing the label of a data point would make a change to the model at all), or trying to track 'scarce' instances, e.g. trying to find those data instances that are rare in terms of the expected label. Further, more sophisticated approaches aggregate the results of machine learning and crowd-sourcing processes to increase the efficiency of the labelling process. Kamar et al. [14] make use of learned probabilistic models to fuse results from computational agents and human annotators. They show how to allocate tasks to coders in order to optimise crowdsourcing processes based on expected utility. Relatively little attention has been paid, however, to the question of how to make these techniques available to human annotators. There is a high demand for annotation tools that integrate cooperative machine learning in order to reduce human effort.

Most studies in this area focus on the gain obtained by the application of specific active learning techniques. However, little emphasis is given to the question of how to assist users in the application of these techniques for the creation of their own corpora. While the benefits of integrating active learning with annotation tasks has been demonstrated in a variety of experiments, annotation tools that provide users with access to active learning techniques are rare.

3 NOVA Tool

The NOVA tool aims to enhance the standard annotation process with the latest developments from contemporary research fields such as Cooperative Machine Learning by giving annotators easy access to automated model training and prediction functionalities, as well as sophisticated explanation algorithms via its user interface.

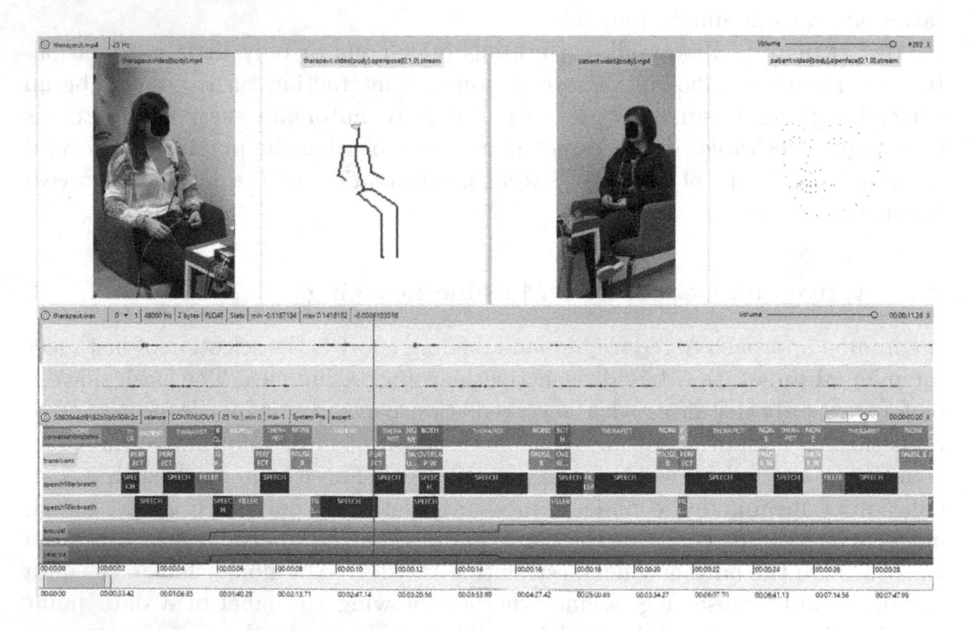

Fig. 1. NOVA allows to visualise various media and signal types and supports different annotation schemes. This figure illustrates an instance of a clinical therapy session with a therapist and a patient. From top downwards: full-body videos along with skeleton and face tracking, and audio streams of two persons during an interaction. In the lower part, several discrete and continuous annotation tiers are displayed.

The NOVA user interface has been designed with a special focus on the annotation of long and continuous recordings involving multiple modalities and subjects. A screenshot of a loaded clinical therapy session is shown in Fig. 1. On the top, several media tracks are visualised and ready for playback. Note that the number of tracks that can be displayed at the same time is not limited and various types of signals (video, audio, facial features, skeleton, depth images, etc.) are supported. In the lower part, we see multiple annotation tracks describing the visualised content with multiple types of annotations (Discrete, Free and Continuous).

To support a collaborative annotation process, NOVA maintains a database back-end, which allows users to load and save annotations from and to a MongoDB[1] database running on a central server. This gives annotators the possibility to immediately commit changes and follow the annotation progress of others. Beside human annotators, a database may also be visited by one or more "machine users". Just like a human operator, they can create and access annotations. Hence, the database also functions as a mediator between human and machine. NOVA provides instruments to create and populate a database from scratch. At any time new annotators, schemes and additional sessions can be added. NOVA provides several functions to process the annotations created by multiple human or machine annotators. For instance, statistical measures such as Cronbach's α, Pearson's correlation coefficient, Spearman's correlation coefficient or Cohen's κ can be applied to identify inter-rater agreement. Thus, the foundations have been laid to fine-tune the number of annotators based on inter-rater agreement in order to further reduce work load by allocating human resources to instances that are difficult to label (see [34]).

Tasks related to machine learning (ML) are handed over and executed by our open-source Social Signal Interpretation (SSI) framework [31]. Since SSI is primarily designed to build online recognition systems, a trained model can be directly used to detect social cues in real-time. A typical ML pipeline starts by prepossessing data to input data for the learning algorithm, a step known as *feature extraction*. An XML template structure is used to define extraction chains from individual SSI components. A dialogue helps users to extract features by selecting an input stream and a number of sessions. The result of the operation is stored as a new signal in the database. This way, feature streams can be reviewed in NOVA and accessed by all users. Based on the extracted features, a classifier, which may also be added using XML templates, can be trained. Alternatively, NOVA supports Deep and Transfer Learning by providing Python interfaces to Tensorflow and Keras. This way convolutional networks may be trained, respectively retrained, based on annotations saved in NOVA's annotation database on raw video data.

[1] https://www.mongodb.com/.

4 Cooperative Machine Learning

In this paper, we subsume learning approaches that efficiently combine human intelligence with the machine's ability of rapid computation under the term *Cooperative Machine Learning* (CML). In Fig. 2, we illustrate our approach to CML, which creates a loop between a machine learned model and human annotators: an initial model is trained (1) and used to predict unseen data (2). An active learning module then decides which parts of the prediction are subject to manual revision by human annotators (3 + 4). Afterwards, the initial model is retrained using the revised data (5). Now the procedure is repeated until all data is annotated. By actively incorporating the user into the loop it becomes possible to interactively guide and improve the automatic predictions while simultaneously obtaining an intuition for the functionality of the classifier.

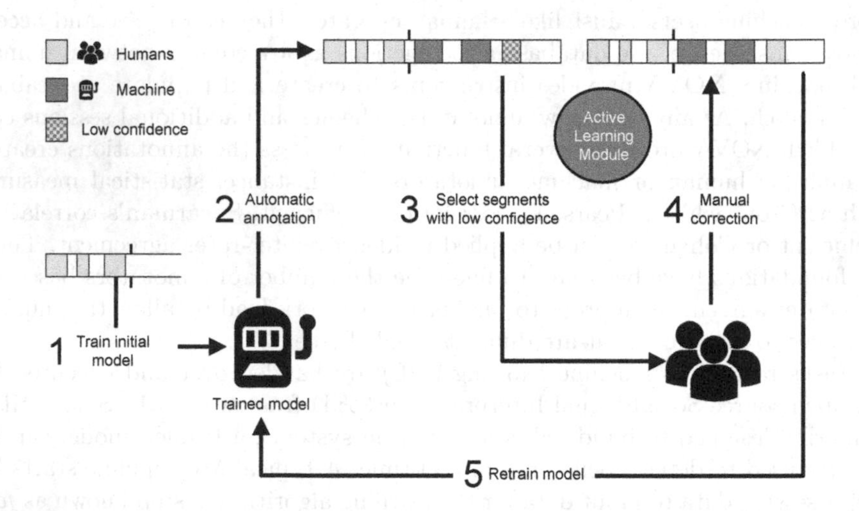

Fig. 2. The scheme depicts the general idea behind Cooperative Machine Learning (CML): (1) An initial model is trained on partially labelled data. (2) The initial model is used to automatically predict unseen data. (3) Labels with a low confidence are selected and (4) manually revised. (5) The initial model is retrained with the revised data.

However, the approach does not only bear the potential to considerably cut down manual efforts, but also to come up with a better understanding of the capabilities of the classification system. For instance, the system may quickly learn to label some simple behaviours, which already facilitates the work load for human annotators at an early stage. Then, over time, it could learn to cope with more complex social signals as well, until at some point it is able to finish the task in a completely automatic manner.

To automatically finish an annotation, the user either selects a previously trained model or temporarily builds one using the labels on the current tier.

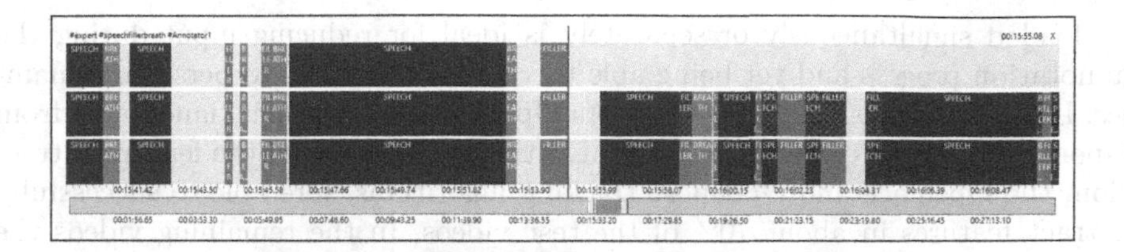

Fig. 3. The upper tier shows a partly finished annotation. ML is now used to predict the remaining part of the tier (middle), where segments with a low confidence are highlighted with a red pattern. The lower tier shows the final annotation after manual revision. (Color figure online)

An example before and after the completion is shown in Fig. 3. Note that labels with a low confidence are highlighted with a pattern. This way, the annotator can immediately see how well the prediction worked. To evaluate the efficiency of the integrated CML strategy, in our earlier work [30] we performed a simulation study on an audio-related labelling task. Following this approach we were able to reduce the initial annotation labour of 9.4 h to 5.9 h, which is a reduction of 37.23%.

5 Pilot Study in Psychotherapy Research

The application of NOVA for the analysis of psychotherapy sessions could lead to multiple advantages for understanding nonverbal signals and communication in psychotherapy. Yet, the transfer to naturalistic conditions sometimes involves obstacles. Therefore, we conducted a pilot study in order to evaluate the applicability of NOVA for this setting.

5.1 Study Setup

The pilot study comprises therapy videos from a protocol-based treatment for test anxiety [26]. The protocol includes cognitive-behavioural therapy components and imagery rescripting which is a experiential and emotionally activating technique. The sample includes therapy videos from 12 patient-therapist dyads with 6 sessions each with a duration of 50–60 min. The patients were students with high scores on test anxiety (partly with depressive symptoms). The therapists were three graduates of a masters' programme of psychology who were awaiting the beginning of their clinical training and two PhD-students in clinical psychology who each had prior experience of one year as a clinician.

The starting module involved the installation and database set up at the outpatient clinic as well as an introduction for the main features of NOVA. Since the therapy videos are very confidential material, all annotations need to be conducted within the clinic. First, the recorded therapy videos were converted to suit the requirements of NOVA (i.a. single video streams for each role). The data structure of sessions with different roles (therapist and patient) which can be loaded simultaneously or separately is ideal for reducing input during the annotation process and yet being able to visually observe interpersonal dynamics. In the following, body features from OpenPose [5] and facial landmarks from OpenFace [2] were extracted. Concerning the performance of the feature extraction, the Openface and Openpose tracking algorithms were able to successfully extract features in about 70% of the test videos. In the remaining videos the feature extraction partly failed due to known challenges, such as problematic head and body orientations (facing/sitting non-frontal to the camera) or characteristics of the person in the video (beard, hat etc.).

For the manual annotations two advanced master students awaiting the beginning of their clinical training were trained in NOVA and the circumplex-model of emotions (valence, arousal) in a 3h-training session. A training video was annotated and discussed in order to achieve a common understanding. A difficulty in this context evolved through cases with incongruent signals on the verbal and non-verbal canal or suppressed emotions. It was decided to annotate by means of the global impression and to give the nonverbal signals a higher weight in unclear situations. This is in line with findings of a higher importance of nonverbal signals in unclear communicative situations (nonverbal dominance, e.g. [13]). Further, NOVA was introduced to six additional students in the master programme of psychology in the context of a seminar. They rated each about 6 h of recorded sessions and also gave qualitative feedback. Since the rating is still in progress, this paper presents qualitative feedback of the experiences with applying NOVA so far.

5.2 Results

The qualitative feedback from the eight raters (two with >20 h of rating experience with NOVA and six with about 6 h) included the following aspects. Every rater gave positive feedback concerning the use of NOVA being "intuitive" and ergonomic in main functions (e.g. start/ stop, Live-Mode, the possibility to correct and overwrite incorrect annotations, adaptation of the pace of the annotation stream). Critical feedback was mainly concerned with the general task of continuously annotating arousal and valence in recorded sessions of psychotherapy. Raters reported that, despite psychological knowledge and training, the external rating of emotions with valence and arousal is still prone to subjective interpretations. This was reflected in low inter rater agreement in some segments, especially for persons with low congruence of verbal and nonverbal signals or low expressiveness. Here, NOVA was helpful in identifying the corresponding parts of the interaction. Thus, a good training and the creation of merged annotations from multiple ratings seems important to achieve more objective training data. The rating is challenging because the context often creates ambiguity. For example laughter implies positive valence yet the arousal can be different. In general, laughter often marks joy and therefore a higher arousal. Yet, in a context of heightened tension and personal distress it can be a sign of relief and thus a lower arousal. The context-dependent ambiguity possibly leads to lower quality of the training data and basis for the machine learning process. Further, manual continuous annotation for longer videos was described to be "very tiring", thus the required annotated video time should be as short as possible. Some raters said that it is especially difficult to rate the same video twice (once for each valence- and arousal dimension). A simultaneous 2-dimensional rating (e.g. by means of a joystick) might help to reduce to rating time, yet might lead to other problems, like a drop in annotation accuracy due to multi-tasking on the side of the annotators. Additional aspects of qualitative feedback for functions in NOVA apart from the direct rating process involved the following positive points: The possibility to conduct all relevant steps of nonverbal behaviour analysis within one tool (annotation, model training, model evaluation) leads to high usability. Multiple annotators can be assigned to databases and annotations with different rights, this is very practical. NOVA offers a high level of adaptability and flexibility concerning the concrete steps (e.g. which annotations to merge, which models to train and apply). The study participants pointed out that the rating effort to build a first model appears quite high, especially for continuous variables in naturalistic settings where strong emotional changes do not occur very often. Thus, for the future the use of pre-trained models under similar conditions would seem helpful. This is likely feasible as NOVA also allows for multi-database training. In summary, the experiences with NOVA so far indicate that it encompasses many important functions for the analysis of emotions in psychotherapy sessions.

5.3 Perspectives for NOVA in Psychotherapy Research and Practice

Multiple topics of major importance in psychotherapy research can presumably profit from a successful application of NOVA, both in process and outcome research. In process research an automated emotion recognition can add knowledge about beneficial therapeutic processes (e.g. successfully targeting emotions, characteristics of sessions prior to sudden gains or early positive change of symptoms, associations with the therapeutic relationship) [1,27]. Further, data concerning the emotions could be linked to problematic developments (e.g. alliance ruptures, sudden losses, dropout) [23]. After having achieved knowledge about the associations between emotional activation and co-regulation patterns with developments in therapy it can be included into the routine feedback systems (e.g. [21]). Feedback could include for example the following "Your patient had almost no phases of positive valence in the last session, you may consider to improve resource activation and supporting needs of the patient". For outcome research emotional activation could potentially be employed as an outcome measure. One could expect for example for depressed patients an increase in emotional variability and positive emotions in the course of therapy [4]. Emotional activation in the beginning compared to the end of therapy could act as a measure of change. Further, patients would possibly reveal atypical patterns of emotional co-regulation (i.e. synchrony) which could change towards more typical patterns during the course of therapy and thus act as another indicator of change [12,24].

For psychotherapists in clinical practice NOVA could be a helpful tool to achieve more objective insight to in-session processes. For example, the therapist could use it to reveal discrepancies between self-perception of the patient and external perception and discuss it with the patient. A potential scenario would be, that a patient is convinced that his grief is clearly observable for others and, in contrast, there is no sign of negative valence during the sessions. The therapist could also use it for self-reflection. For example if he has very low arousal and negative valence with one patient compared to others he could use it as an indicator to make use of supervision.

6 Conclusion

In this paper we presented an initial application of the NOVA annotation and analysis tool in the context of patient-focused psychotherapy. NOVA offers a collaborative workflow for multiple types of annotation tasks. Additionally it provides interfaces to machine-learning techniques that allow even non-experts to make use of these technologies in order to speed up the annotation labour.

The qualitative feedback for working with NOVA was consistently very positive. The experiences with feature extraction, annotation and machine learning in NOVA under real-life conditions give reason for optimism concerning the further application of NOVA in psychotherapy research and practice.

With little effort, models can be retrained and fine-tuned to specific scenarios and types of patients without the need of programming-skills. Yet, more technically interested users can also extend NOVA's ML tools by adding new templates. This way NOVA is not limited to current state of the art methods such as Deep Neural Networks but is also extendable in the future. Additionally, we are working on extending NOVA to provide capabilities for the latest explainable AI techniques on pre-trained as well as self-trained models. This way, users should get an even better understanding when they can trust their ML model and what might cause issues, respectively when more training examples are required.

NOVA is open-source software and available on Github: https://github.com/hcmlab/nova.

References

1. Atzil-Slonim, D., et al.: Emotional congruence between clients and therapists and its effect on treatment outcome. J. Couns. Psychol. **65**(1), 51–64 (2018)
2. Baltrušaitis, T., Robinson, P., Morency, L.P.: OpenFace: an open source facial behavior analysis toolkit. In: 2016 IEEE Winter Conference on Applications of Computer Vision (WACV), pp. 1–10, March 2016. https://doi.org/10.1109/WACV.2016.7477553
3. Ben-Zeev, D., Young, M.A., Madsen, J.W.: Retrospective recall of affect in clinically depressed individuals and controls. Cogn. Emot. **23**(5), 1021–1040 (2009)
4. Bylsma, L.M., Morris, B.H., Rottenberg, J.: A meta-analysis of emotional reactivity in major depressive disorder. Clin. Psychol. Rev. **28**(4), 676–691 (2008)

5. Cao, Z., Hidalgo, G., Simon, T., Wei, S.E., Sheikh, Y.: OpenPose: realtime multi-person 2D pose estimation using part affinity fields. arXiv preprint arXiv: 1812.08008 (2018)
6. Cowie, R., Douglas-Cowie, E., Savvidou, S., McMahon, E., Sawey, M., Schröder, M.: 'FEELTRACE': an instrument for recording perceived emotion in real time. In: ISCA Tutorial and Research Workshop (ITRW) on Speech and Emotion (2000)
7. Cowie, R., McKeown, G., Douglas-Cowie, E.: Tracing emotion: an overview. IJSE **3**(1), 1–17 (2012)
8. Cuijpers, P., van Straten, A., Andersson, G., van Oppen, P.: Psychotherapy for depression in adults: a meta-analysis of comparative outcome studies. J. Consult. Clin. Psychol. **76**(6), 909–922 (2008)
9. Delgadillo, J., Moreea, O., Lutz, W.: Different people respond differently to therapy: a demonstration using patient profiling and risk stratification. Behav. Res. Ther. **79**, 15–22 (2016)
10. Girard, J.M.: CARMA: software for continuous affect rating and media annotation. J. Open. Res. Softw. **2**(1), e5 (2014)
11. Girard, J.M., Wright, A.G.C.: DARMA: dual axis rating and media annotation (2016)
12. Hofmann, S.G.: Interpersonal emotion regulation model of mood and anxiety disorders. Cogn. Ther. Res. **38**(5), 483–492 (2014)
13. Jacob, H., Kreifelts, B., Brück, C., Nizielski, S., Schütz, A., Wildgruber, D.: Nonverbal signals speak up: association between perceptual nonverbal dominance and emotional intelligence. Cogn. Emot. **27**(5), 783–799 (2013)
14. Kamar, E., Hacker, S., Horvitz, E.: Combining human and machine intelligence in large-scale crowdsourcing. In: van der Hoek, W., Padgham, L., Conitzer, V., Winikoff, M. (eds.) International Conference on Autonomous Agents and Multiagent Systems, AAMAS 2012, Valencia, Spain, 4–8 June 2012, vol. 3 , pp. 467–474. IFAAMAS (2012)
15. Kennedy-Moore, E., Watson, J.C.: How and when does emotional expression help? Rev. Gen. Psychol. **5**(3), 187–212 (2001)
16. Kipp, M.: ANVIL: the video annotation research tool. In: Handbook of Corpus Phonology. Oxford University Press (2013)
17. Lukas, C.A., Ebert, D.D., Fuentes, H.T., Caspar, F., Berking, M.: Deficits in general emotion regulation skills-evidence of a transdiagnostic factor. J. Clin. Psychol. **74**(6), 1017–1033 (2018)
18. Lutz, W., et al.: Chancen von e-mental-health und eprozessdiagnostik in der ambulanten psychotherapie: Der trierer therapie navigator. Verhaltenstherapie 1–10 (2019)
19. Lutz, W., et al.: The ups and downs of psychotherapy: sudden gains and sudden losses identified with session reports. Psychother. Res. **23**(1), 14–24 (2013)
20. Lutz, W., de Jong, K., Rubel, J.: Patient-focused and feedback research in psychotherapy: where are we and where do we want to go? Psychother. Res. **25**(6), 625–632 (2015)
21. Lutz, W., Rubel, J.A., Schwartz, B., Schilling, V., Deisenhofer, A.K.: Towards integrating personalized feedback research into clinical practice: development of the Trier Treatment Navigator (TTN). Behav. Res. Ther. **120**, 103438 (2019)
22. Marwood, L., Wise, T., Perkins, A.M., Cleare, A.J.: Meta-analyses of the neural mechanisms and predictors of response to psychotherapy in depression and anxiety. Neurosci. Biobehav. Rev. **95**, 61–72 (2018)

23. Paulick, J., et al.: Nonverbal synchrony: a new approach to better understand psychotherapeutic processes and drop-out. J. Psychother. Integr. **28**(3), 367–384 (2018)
24. Paulick, J., et al.: Diagnostic features of nonverbal synchrony in psychotherapy: comparing depression and anxiety. Cogn. Ther. Res. **42**(5), 539–551 (2018)
25. Peluso, P.R., Freund, R.R.: Therapist and client emotional expression and psychotherapy outcomes: a meta-analysis. Psychotherapy **55**(4), 461–472 (2018). (Chicago, Ill.)
26. Prinz, J.N., Bar-Kalifa, E., Rafaeli, E., Sened, H., Lutz, W.: Imagery-based treatment for test anxiety: a multiple-baseline open trial. J. Affect. Disord. **244**, 187–195 (2019)
27. Rubel, J.A., Rosenbaum, D., Lutz, W.: Patients' in-session experiences and symptom change: session-to-session effects on a within- and between-patient level. Behav. Res. Ther. **90**, 58–66 (2017)
28. Schmidt, T.: Transcribing and annotating spoken language with EXMARaLDA. In: 2004 Proceedings of the International Conference on Language Resources and Evaluation: Workshop on XML Based Richly Annotated Corpora, Lisbon, pp. 879–896. ELRA (2004). eN
29. Settles, B.: Active Learning. Synthesis Lectures on Artificial Intelligence and Machine Learning. Morgan & Claypool Publishers, San Rafael (2012)
30. Wagner, J., Baur, T., Zhang, Y., Valstar, M.F., Schuller, B., André, E.: Applying cooperative machine learning to speed up the annotation of social signals in large multi-modal corpora. arXiv preprint arXiv:1802.02565 (2018)
31. Wagner, J., Lingenfelser, F., Baur, T., Damian, I., Kistler, F., André, E.: The social signal interpretation (SSI) framework: multimodal signal processing and recognition in real-time. In: Proceedings of the 21st ACM International Conference on Multimedia, pp. 831–834. ACM (2013)
32. Whelton, W.J.: Emotional processes in psychotherapy: evidence across therapeutic modalities. Clin. Psychol. Psychother. **11**(1), 58–71 (2004)
33. Wittenburg, P., Brugman, H., Russel, A., Klassmann, A., Sloetjes, H.: ELAN: a professional framework for multimodality research. In: Calzolari, N., et al. (eds.) Proceedings of the Fifth International Conference on Language Resources and Evaluation, LREC 2006, Genoa, Italy, 22–28 May 2006, pp. 1556–1559. European Language Resources Association (ELRA) (2006)
34. Zhang, Y., Michi, A., Wagner, J., André, E., Schuller, B., Weninger, F.: A generic human-machine annotation framework based on dynamic cooperative learning. IEEE Trans. Cybern. 1–10 (2019)

Instrument Recognition in Laparoscopy for Technical Skill Assessment

Sabrina Kletz[1(✉)], Klaus Schoeffmann[1], Andreas Leibetseder[1], Jenny Benois-Pineau[2], and Heinrich Husslein[3]

[1] Klagenfurt University, Klagenfurt, Austria
{sabrina,ks,aleibets}@itec.aau.at
[2] University of Bordeaux, Bordeaux, France
jenny.benois@labri.fr
[3] Medical University of Vienna, Vienna, Austria
heinrich.husslein@meduniwien.ac.at

Abstract. Laparoscopic skill training and evaluation as well as identifying technical errors in surgical procedures have become important aspects in Surgical Quality Assessment (SQA). Typically performed in a manual, time-consuming and effortful post-surgical process, evaluating technical skills for a large part involves assessing proper instrument handling as the main cause for these type of errors. Therefore, when attempting to improve upon this situation using computer vision approaches, the automatic identification of instruments in laparoscopy videos is the very first step toward a semi-automatic assessment procedure. Within this work we summarize existing methodologies for instrument recognition, while proposing a state-of-the-art instance segmentation approach. As a first experiment in the domain of gynecology, our approach is able to segment instruments well but a much higher precision will be required, since this early step is critical before attempting any kind of skill recognition.

Keywords: Surgical instrument detection · Multi-instance segmentation · Multiclass classification · Skill assessment · Gynecology · Laparoscopy

1 Introduction and Motivation

Laparoscopy is a minimally invasive surgical procedure where a laparoscope with additional surgical instruments is inserted into the human body. It has become common that surgeons record their procedures for retrospective analysis and post-operative *Surgical Quality Assessment (SQA)*, where the surgical actions are closely investigated and the surgeon's skill level is assessed. This includes all kinds of surgical errors that lead to complications or unnecessarily prolong the surgery such as in the case when a surgeon tries to grasp tissue with a grasper instrument in a wrong orientation and slips off. Researchers in the medical community have shown that SQA with error ratings via recorded videos significantly

Y. M. Ro et al. (Eds.): MMM 2020, LNCS 11962, pp. 589–600, 2020.
https://doi.org/10.1007/978-3-030-37734-2_48

improve surgical quality over time [3]. This is also the reason why even standardized error rating schemes like the *Generic Error Rating Tool (GERT)* [2], have been developed over the years.

GERT defines specific surgical activities that are typical in laparoscopic procedures and medical experts have proposed to carry out continuous error analyses for these activities in order to improve their quality [7,24,25]. However, this error-rating process is currently performed manually, which means assessors interact with a conventional video player, watch the recorded procedure from the beginning to the end and make notes of errors and their timestamps. One can imagine that rating errors in this way is extremely effortful and time-consuming as well as error-prone. Both, manual notes of timestamps can be erroneous and technical errors can be easily overlooked if instrument handling is not carefully observed. Since most technical errors are caused by mishandling of instruments, automatic instrument recognition is highly relevant for improving the skill assessment process using computer vision approaches.

However, the automatic detection of laparoscopic instruments in videos is not a trivial task and is accompanied by many research challenges in vision-based object recognition like large variations in appearance of instruments due to viewpoint changes, scale, occlusion, orientation, illumination and camera motion. Also extreme conditions like specular reflections, blurriness, smoke, blood and strong motion have a big impact on the automatic instrument recognition task. In this paper, we propose a multiclass multiple-instance segmentation approach with convolutional neural networks (CNNs) addressing the task of instrument recognition as instance segmentation task using images of gynecological surgeries. Since instrument recognition in laparoscopy is a broad research field and many attempts have been made in the domain of *cholecystectomy* and *robotic-assisted laparoscopy*, we summarize existing approaches toward instrument recognition in laparoscopy.

2 Instrument Recognition Approaches

The task of instrument recognition comprises methods that can recognize a specific instrument type while merely processing an image or a sequence of video frames. However, instrument types differ strongly in appearance depending on the surgical procedure and also more than one instrument can be visible at any point. In recent years, different approaches have been proposed ranging from multi-label classification identifying the presence of specific instrument types over only classifying the visible amount of instruments to the pixel-wise classification of instrument parts and up to region-based detection and classification. In the following, we summarize methodologies proposed in the literature to address the task of instrument recognition grouped by their approaches.

2.1 Image Classification

The most basic approach to recognize instruments is to classify entire images, which has been attempted by extracting hand-crafted features as well as by utilizing CNNs. Many of such approaches are validated on data from cholecystectomy procedures and one dataset has been made publicly available that includes instrument annotations *(Cholec80)* [27]. This dataset contains 80 different laparoscopic cholecystectomy videos with annotations for the presence or absence of seven instruments. A subset of this dataset forms the *mcai16-tool* dataset [27] utilized for the M2CAI 2016 tool presence detection challenge [17], which yielded the insight that CNNs overall are better full-image classifiers than other approaches. Recently, a four-part dataset (*LapGyn4*) [13] has been introduced which includes an individual instrument count dataset. This subset consists of over 20k frames equally categorized into images showing zero to three instruments, which partially was taken from the domain of cholecystectomy but as well from laparoscopic gynecology videos.

In early work addressing the image-based instrument classification task, authors in [21] use an individually collected dataset consisting of 14 chunks of a specific cholecystectomy phase comprising 160k images. Aiming at classifying different types of instruments (i.e. two types of graspers, suction and irrigation probe, scissors, clipper, monopolar spatula), they utilize SVMs, bag-of-features constructed from ORB features and report a *mean average precision (mAP)* of 56%. Another approach is to disregard instrument types altogether as investigated by authors in [13], where they classify images in the LapGyn4 dataset according to the amount of visible instruments, yielding an AP of 84% when using GoogLeNet. Finally, authors in [27] attempting to classify seven surgical tools (i.e. grasper, bipolar forceps, instrument with a hook, clipper, scissors, suction and irrigation probe and specimen bag) develop *(Endo) ToolNet* as a component of their bigger surgical phase recognition architecture *EndoNet* and their evaluations on the mcai16-tool dataset results in a mAP of 52.5%.

2.2 Pixel-Wise Classification

In recent years, many attempts have been made to address the task of robotic instrument recognition by segmenting instruments and separate them from their background. This is probably due to the fact that in the field of robotic laparoscopy there are existing benchmark datasets, one is released as part of the EndoVis challenge 2015 [5] and one of the challenge 2017 [4]. The first dataset *(EV15)* consists of 4,5k training images and 4,5k test images showing ex-vivo video recordings of phantom tissue. This dataset provides two types of segmentation masks: a binary mask as well as a mask that segments the manipulator (i.e., operating part) and shaft. The dataset used in the EndoVis 2017 *(EV17)* consists of approx. 2k training and 1,2k test examples of in-vivo video recordings and supports three different segmentation tasks: binary segmentation, parts (e.g., shaft, wrist, claspers and ultrasound probes) and type segmentation (e.g., needle driver, forceps, scissors, sealer, grasper and others).

Authors in [9] address the task of binary instrument segmentation by using a *fully convolutional network (FCN)* model, pre-trained on the PASCAL-context 59-class dataset and fine-tuned on robotic instrument images. They achieve a mean *Jaccard similarity coefficient (i.e., Intersection over Union (IoU))* of 70.9%

and mean *Dice similarity coefficient (DSC)* of 78.8% calculated for the test images included in EV15 dataset. In [8], authors propose *(FCN) ToolNet* and have shown that a FCN-based architecture with a combined loss at different scales improves the IoU and DSC by approx. 3%. A similar approach is used by [19] where a residual network architecture *(ResNet)* is transformed into a FCN architecture. The usage of residual blocks outperforms (FCN) ToolNet with 11.3% compared on the balanced accuracy. Furthermore, they evaluate their approach for multiclass segmentation where image pixels are classified either as background, shaft or manipulator and report an IoU of 77.7% based on the EV15 dataset. Authors in [26] compare different encoder-decoder architectures such as *U-Net*, *TernausNet* and *LinkNet*. They have shown that a TernausNet outperforms remaining architectures in all three tasks with a resulting DSC of 83.8% for binary, 75.97% part-based and 45.86% type-based segmentation. However, authors in [10] modify the U-Net architecture and propose *U-NetPlus* by modifying the decoder part. They have shown that this modification together with data augmentation outperform U-Net, TernausNet and LinkNet on the EV17 dataset with an increase of 6.4% for the binary, 0.29% for the part-based segmentation and 0.21% for segmenting instrument types.

2.3 Region-Based Classification

As a final category, region-based instrument classification can be considered the latest topic of interest in the field, involving tool detection, classification as well as localization. Recent approaches with such goals again mostly utilize the above mentioned Cholec80 [27] dataset or subsets of it, enhancing it with spatial instrument information [12]. The authors of [12] focus on instrument localization as well as tracking for the purpose of surgical skill assessment and enhance the M2CAI 2016 tool presence challenge dataset with spatial tool bounds, publishing it under the name *m2cai16-tool-locations*. Their approach is based on *Faster R-CNN* using a pre-trained VGG model on ImageNet data as backbone network and they achieve a mean AP with 50% IoU (AP_{50}) of 63.1% for spacial detection, and mAP 81.8% for presence detection. In [28], the authors address the lack of spatially annotated example data by applying weakly-supervised approach and propose an FCN architecture consisting of a modified ResNet that is as well pre-trained on ImageNet data. They further train their network on a Cholec80 sub-set of 5 videos annotated with image-level instrument bounding boxes and achieve a mAP of 87.2% for binary tool presence classification. A similar approach is taken by [18], where the authors improve upon the FCN architecture by long short-term memories and achieves a mAP of 92.9% for tool presence detection and an AP_{50} of 38.2% for tool detection and localization.

3 Multiclass Multiple-Instance Segmentation with CNNs

Methods for instance segmentation can be broadly classified into two different categories: bottom-up and top-down segmentation approaches. Previously described methods, considering pixel-wise classifications like works relying on FCNs [9,19] or decoder-encoder architectures [10,26] can be assigned to bottom-up approaches because an additional approach is necessary to group per-pixel predictions in order to assign them to a single instance. In contrast, top-down approaches utilize region proposal in order to classify pixels only within these regions. Recently, Mask R-CNN [11] has been proposed as a convolutional neural network to learn to segment multiple-instances in images. Authors in [11] have shown that this network architecture outperforms state-of-the-art instance segmentation methods such as SGN [16] or DIN [1] on the Cityscapes dataset [6] and has also reached a better score in the COCO segmentation task [15] in comparison to FCIS [14]. Mask R-CNN splits up the task of instance segmentation into different sub-tasks and extends Faster R-CNN [23] for predicting a segmentation mask. For a given image, a Mask R-CNN model predicts the class, bounding box and the binary mask for multiple-instances. To train a model the following multi-task loss is minimized: $\mathcal{L} = \mathcal{L}_{rpn} + \mathcal{L}_{cls} + \mathcal{L}_{box} + \mathcal{L}_{mask}$, where $\mathcal{L}_{cls}, \mathcal{L}_{box}$ is defined by Faster R-CNN and $\mathcal{L}_{rpn}$ additionally comprises $\mathcal{L}_{rpn} = \mathcal{L}_{cls} + \mathcal{L}_{box}$. The loss $\mathcal{L}_{rpn}$ trains the underlying region proposal network (RPN) based on the binary cross-entropy loss calculated between a set of region proposals and a positive region. The mask loss $\mathcal{L}_{mask}$ is the average binary cross-entropy loss between the predicted mask and the mask of the target class. Since masks are predicted for each class, only the error for the mask of the target label contributes to the loss.

3.1 Dataset

Surgical instruments in laparoscopy are long thin tools and vary in appearance, but essentially they consist of a shaft and a tissue manipulator as considered in the EndoVis challenges [4,5]. However, most of these instruments differ from each other mainly by their manipulators. These manipulators can be either flexible like instruments with jaws (e.g., graspers and scissors) or rigid with a blunt tip (e.g., suction and irrigator probes or instruments with a hook). However, this is only a coarse classification and it is important to highlight that instrument types within these groups vary strongly depending on their purpose. For example, a grasper may have two movable jaw members or only one of them is capable of being moved. An instrument with a hook as tip, are mostly rigid manipulators but the tip can vary in form like a J, I or spatula [21,27]. On the other side, probes for suction and irrigation do not have a tissue manipulating part per se, but they have a blunt tip and are additionally used to interact with tissue. Also, there are many other types of instruments which cannot be assigned to one of these groups like trocars or morcellators.

Gynecological Surgery. Together with a medical expert, we identified eleven different types of instruments in gynecologic myomectomy and hysterectomy which are highly relevant for automatic skill assessment and error detection, namely: (1) bipolar forceps, (2) graspers, (3) instruments with a hook, (4) suction and irrigation probes, (5) knot-pushers, (6) morcellators, (7) needles, (8)

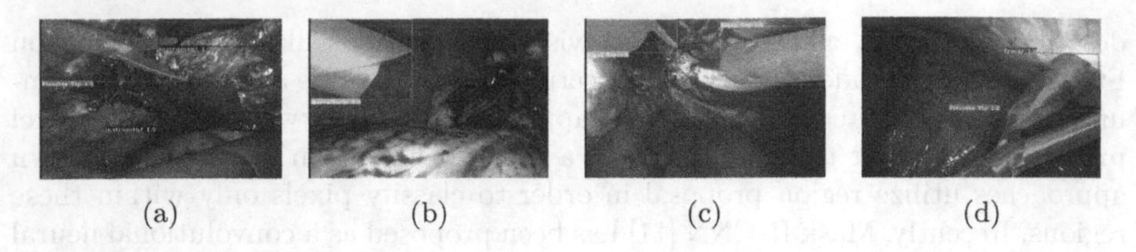

Fig. 1. Instruments with segmented areas: (a) Instrument with flexible tip (left, orange) and "unknown" instruments (bottom and top, navy), (b) Morcellator (left sky blue) (c) Instruments with rigid tips (top, green) (d) Trocar (right, aqua). (Color figure online)

needle-holders, (9) scissors, (10) sealer and divider instruments, and (11) trocars. However, instruments like forceps, grasper, scissors, needle-holder as well as sealer and divider are very similar looking but have a flexible tip in common. In contrast, instruments with a hook or suction and irrigation probes have a rigid tip. Instruments like morcellators, needles and trocars have a different structure, and cannot be coarsely categorized into shaft and manipulator. For example, a morcellator is a tubed-shaped blade used together with a grasper to catch the tissue. A trocar is used to prepare the initial access to the abdomen, therefore, the cannula with a sharp tip is mainly seen. In contrast, a needle is a very thin tool with a point, curved or straight body and a swaged end comprising the thread to perform suturing.

Table 1. Details of the dataset distributed over three splits.

Category	Total instances	Train	Val	Test
Flexible	279	199	38	42
Morcellator	42	29	6	7
Needle	55	39	8	8
Rigid	114	76	18	20
Trocar	42	29	7	6
Unknown	56	41	8	7
Total Images	**344**	**243**	**50**	**51**

Classification. Studies in [10,26] have demonstrated that performance decreases when the segmentation task gets harder like for example segmenting five different robotic instrument types plus one additional type "other". Since our previous study [22] confirms this because many types are very similar, we further group the eleven instruments by their manipulators into (1) *flexible* and (2) *rigid* instruments accompanied with (3) *morcellators*, (4) *needles*, and (5) *trocars*. Resulting dataset is detailed in Table 1, describing the number of collected samples per category, distributed over three splits. Figure 1 demonstrates some examples included in the dataset. Similarly to the category "other" in [4], the last type "*unknown*" in Table 1 represents instruments that are not identifiable due to occlusion caused by other instruments or tissue or due to distorted appearance.

3.2 Implementation Details

Our experiments are conducted using PyTorch [20] which also provides a publicly available implementation of the Mask R-CNN architecture. For a training setup, we follow the strategy proposed in [11] and use a ResNet-50 architecture as backbone network together with a feature pyramid network (FPN). To be able to compare the performance in train and test mode, we process 2k proposals obtained from the RPN. However, we reduce detection rate and utilize only the top 10 scores, since no more than four instruments are visible in one image. Since data augmentation is beneficial for training the instrument segmentation task [10,22], we additionally utilize data augmentation techniques in training such as mirroring, blurring and contrasting. To be more precise, we use Gaussian blur with $\sigma \in [0, 3.0]$ sharpening in the range of $[0.75, 1.5]$, as well as mirroring along the x-axis and y-axis, where 25% of the total input sequence is transformed using mirroring and blurring or mirroring and contrasting. We use stochastic gradient descent (SGD) with momentum $\mu = 0.9$ and weight decay $\lambda = 0.001$ as proposed in [11,23] and additionally schedule the learning rate automatically. In training, we decay the learning rate step-wise with an initial learning rate α_0 and drop it by a fraction of γ after N epochs. Since learning rate α is reduced during training it is important to mention that the computation of stochastic gradient descent with momentum in PyTorch [20] differs from some other frameworks. The difference is that when the learning rate is decreased also the step size decreases immediately because of α influences not only the step size but also the momentum μ.

4 Experimental Results

As a baseline, we fine-tune a Mask R-CNN model for our seven instrument classes using a pre-trained model on the COCO dataset [15] (available in the PyTorch Model Zoo [20]). We use an initial learning rate $\alpha_0 = 0.001$ with a step decay of $\gamma = 0.50, N = 20$ and train one batch with 2 images, where each image has a size of 540×360. We initialize the model with a pre-trained model on COCO data and fine-tune this model for our data. The training is conducted for 6.1k iterations resulting in 50 epochs with 122 batches per epoch, comprising 243 training samples. Since the loss value is obtained per batch, in the following we report the averaged loss overall batches for one epoch. The average precision (AP) of the model after each epoch is measured based on the COCO metric [15] using segmentation masks. This metric represents the average precision for all categories considering ten IoU thresholds (i.e., Jaccard similarity coefficients) in the range of 50% to 95% ($AP_{50:95}$). Since the maximum number of possible instruments is less than 10 instruments per image, we calculate the average precision for a maximum number of 10 detections per image.

Detection Performance. Figure 2 shows the loss values on the training data (blue dashed-dotted line) and the validation data (orange dashed-dotted line) over 50 epochs. As can be seen, the training loss decreases and achieves a minimum value of 0.108 at the 50th epoch. The validation loss decreases rapidly in the first few epochs and has a minimum value of 0.316 at the 20th epoch. Afterward, the validation loss fluctuates slightly but stays nearly steady through training for remaining epochs and has a value of 0.348 at the last epoch. In addition, the figure shows the average precision for predicted categories based on their segmentation masks ($AP_{50:95}$) for both, training data (green line) and validation data (red line). The $AP_{50:95}$ at epoch 20 is 68.9% for the training data and 41.8% for the validation data, respectively. The maximum average precision of 48.4% is achieved at the 48th epoch, where the $AP_{50:95}$ is 77.9% for the training data. Further training of two more epochs increases the $AP_{50:95}$ only for training data to 78,4% but decrease it for validation data to 47,0%. Since selecting the best model based on the validation loss at epoch 20 seems too early, because the $AP_{50:95}$ on the validation data is further increasing until epoch 48, we additionally took a closer look at the prediction results of trained models at different epochs.

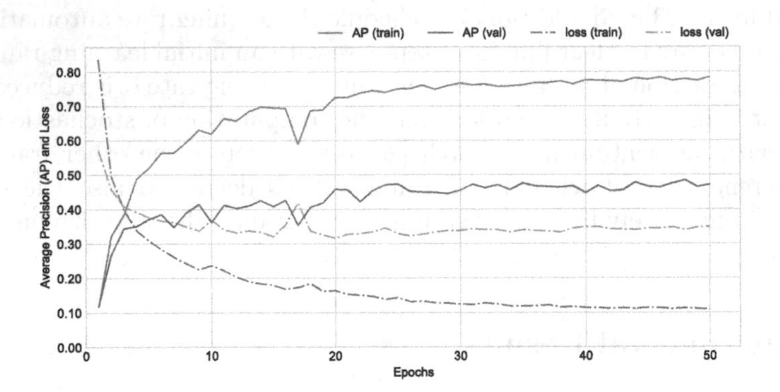

Fig. 2. Average Precision and loss during training a model for 50 epochs. (Color figure online)

Figure 3, shows a sample image selected from the validation data and predicted results for this image at three different epochs. The first image 3a represents the ground-truth and shows two instruments with a rigid tip (green areas) and a third instrument (blue area) which is not clearly visible and categorized as "unknown". It becomes clear, that predicted positions and shapes are already representative after the 20th epoch, however, further training improves the classification performance. In the 40th epoch, both instruments with the rigid tips are correctly classified with a score of 1.0 and only the third instrument is misclassified and has a score of 0.99. The image in the last epoch shows that further

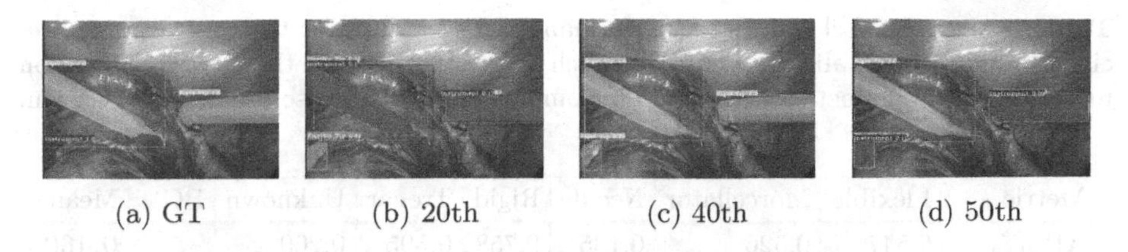

(a) GT (b) 20th (c) 40th (d) 50th

Fig. 3. Segmentation results at different epochs: (a) ground-truth sample showing two instruments with rigid tips (green areas) and one unknown instrument (blue area); (b)–(c) predicted instrument categories. (Color figure online)

training the model induces the classifier again to categorize instruments into the category "unknown" but come with the burden that the third instrument is still misclassified as a rigid instrument with a score of 0.91 but with a second proposal that classifies the instrument as "unknown" with a score of 0.08.

Classification Performance. Additionally, Table 2 details the classification performance of the model on the test data at the selected epoch 48, evaluated for each category in comparison to pixel-wise classification performance. Although the average precision (AP) for classifying and segmenting instruments in the test data is slightly lower with 40.6% compared to 48.4% in the validation data, it represents a good baseline for further comparisons. When regarding each category in detail one can observe that classification results are similar for each instrument except for needles and "unknown" instruments. This can be attributed to the small area that is covered by needles which is difficult to segment precisely. This is underlined by the average precision (AP_{50}) of 45.5% solely considering an IoU threshold of 50% compared to 3.2% (AP_{75}) for an IoU threshold of 75%. Also, instruments categorized as "unknown" are somehow difficult to distinguish from instruments with flexible or rigid tips since this category includes parts of instruments which can be assigned to another type of instruments.

Pixel-Wise Classification Performance. Furthermore, we report the precision obtained by pixel-wise classification using a score threshold of 0.7. This metric reflects how many pixels for an entire image are correct classified compared to the ground-truth segmentation mask. In Table 2, precision, sensitivity, IoU as well as DSC for each class, including background is reported. The IoU shows that instruments with a rigid tip are predicted most precisely with 80.6%, however, sensitivity shows that this class is also more often predicted in comparison to other instruments. Since a rigid and flexible instrument only differs at the manipulator (i.e., tip) and have a shaft in common, instruments that do not show clearly a flexible tip are misclassified as rigid instrument. This misclassification is also reflected by the class "unknown" which is a class that represents rather a subset of these both classes. Therefore, it seems that the class "unknown" is redundant and not independently from classes like flexible and rigid instruments.

Table 2. Details of classification performance on test data for the best average precision, obtained on validation data at epoch 48, evaluated with the COCO evaluation metric for multiple-instance detection in comparison to pixel-wise prediction precision.

Metric	Flexible	Morcellator	Needle	Rigid	Trocar	Unknown	BG	Mean
$AP_{50:95}$	0.547	0.526	0.135	0.758	0.595	0.200	–	**0.460**
AP_{50}	0.786	0.913	0.455	0.945	0.784	0.308	–	**0.698**
AP_{75}	0.606	0.558	0.032	0.891	0.663	0.238	–	**0.498**
Precision	0.915	0.772	0.681	0.882	0.938	0.293	0.985	**0.781**
Sensitivity	0.844	0.853	0.645	0.903	0.863	0.225	0.990	**0.761**
IoU	0.782	0.681	0.495	0.806	0.816	0.146	0.976	**0.672**
DSC	0.878	0.811	0.662	0.892	0.899	0.255	0.988	**0.769**

5 Conclusion

With the aim to semi-automatically assess skills and detect errors in handling instruments in gynecology, we summarize existing instrument recognition approaches in a much broader field of laparoscopy. In comparison to other works, we propose a top-down segmentation approach for instrument recognition in gynecological surgeries using a state-of-the-art multiclass multiple-instance segmentation method based on CNNs. Although it is not directly comparable to other approaches in this field since underlying datasets differ as well as the recognition task is different, we have shown that using Mask R-CNN with a limited labeled dataset achieves an average precision ($AP_{50:95}$) of 46% as well as an AP_{50} of 69.8%, measured by the COCO metric. Furthermore, it yields a pixel-wise precision of 67.2% measured by IoU and 76.9% by DSC. In literature, the best results reported for a multiclass segmentation approach [10] concerning robotic instruments is a DSC of 46.07% using an encoder-decoder architecture as bottom-up segmentation approach on a much larger dataset. Our approach in comparison to an existing top-down approach [12] targeting multiclass and multiple instrument detections yields an AP_{50} of 63.1% using data from cholecystectomies.

For the task of automatic skill assessment and error detection in laparoscopy, it would require more accurate instrument recognition results in order to avoid poor rating quality. In a previous study [22], we found that classifying eleven instrument types plus a category "unknown" requires stronger data augmentation including geometric transformations in order to achieve a similar $AP_{50:95}$ of 42.9% and AP_{50} of 61.3%. However, when we consider this task as a binary segmentation problem, the detection performance increases to 54.3% $AP_{50:95}$ accompanied by an AP_{50} of 81.4%. For future work, we will rethink our introduced instrument categorization because we found that they are not independent enough and share at least visible characteristics such as an instrument shaft. However, most of the instrument types are distinguishable by their tips and a more fine-grained classification approach in which this diversity will be considered could yield more accurate classification results. Furthermore, not clearly visible instruments but labeled as "unknown" instruments share at least some features with known instruments and considering these correlations could contribute to avoiding misclassifications. Since we have limited labeled data, approaches like domain-adaption seem promising where trained models in the field of cholecystectomy and robotic-assisted laparoscopy are used and transferred to our domain of gynecological laparoscopy.

Acknowledgments. This work was funded by the FWF Austrian Science Fund under grant P 32010-N38.

References

1. Arnab, A., Torr, P.H.: Pixelwise instance segmentation with a dynamically instantiated network. In: Proceedings of 30th IEEE Conference on Computer Vision and Pattern Recognition, vol. 2017-Jan, pp. 879–888 (2017)
2. Bonrath, E.M., Zevin, B., Dedy, N.J., Grantcharov, T.P.: Error rating tool to identify and analyse technical errors and events in laparoscopic surgery. Br. J. Surg. **100**(8), 1080–1088 (2013)
3. Bonrath, E.M., Dedy, N.J., Gordon, L.E., Grantcharov, T.P.: Comprehensive surgical coaching enhances surgical skill in the operating room. Ann. Surg. **262**(2), 205–212 (2015)
4. MICCAI EndoVis Sub Challange: Robotic Instrument Segmentation (2017). endovissub2017-roboticinstrumentsegmentation.grand-challenge.org
5. MICCAI EndoVis Sub-Challange: Instrument Segmentation and Tracking (2015). endovissub-instrument.grand-challenge.org
6. Cordts, M., et al.: The cityscapes dataset for semantic urban scene understanding. In: Proceedings of the IEEE International Conference on Computer Vision, pp. 3213–3223 (2016)
7. De Vries, E.N., Ramrattan, M.A., Smorenburg, S.M., Gouma, D.J., Boermeester, M.A.: The incidence and nature of in-hospital adverse events: a systematic review. Qual. Saf. Health Care **17**(3), 216–223 (2008)
8. Garcia-Peraza-Herrera, L.C., et al.: ToolNet: holistically-nested real-time segmentation of robotic surgical tools. In: Proceedings of the IEEE/RSJ International Conference on Intelligent Robots and Systems, pp. 5717–5722. IEEE, September 2017
9. García-Peraza-Herrera, L.C., et al.: Real-time segmentation of non-rigid surgical tools based on deep learning and tracking. In: Peters, T., et al. (eds.) CARE 2016. LNCS, vol. 10170, pp. 84–95. Springer, Cham (2017). https://doi.org/10.1007/978-3-319-54057-3_8
10. Hasan, S.M.K., Linte, C.A.: U-NetPlus: a modified encoder-decoder U-net architecture for semantic and instance segmentation of surgical instrument. CoRR, pp. 1–7 (2019)
11. He, K., Gkioxari, G., Dollar, P., Girshick, R.: Mask R-CNN. In: Proceedings of the IEEE International Conference on Computer Vision, pp. 2980–2988 (2017)
12. Jin, A., et al.: Tool detection and operative skill assessment in surgical videos using region-based convolutional neural networks. In: Proceedings of the IEEE Winter Conference on Applications of Computer Vision, pp. 691–699. IEEE, March 2018

13. Leibetseder, A., et al.: LapGyn4: a dataset for 4 automatic content analysis problems in the domain of laparoscopic gynecology. In: Proceedings of the ACM Multimedia Systems Conference, pp. 357–362. ACM Press, New York (2018)
14. Li, Y., Qi, H., Dai, J., Ji, X., Wei, Y.: Fully convolutional instance-aware semantic segmentation. In: Proceedings of the IEEE International Conference on Computer Vision, pp. 2359–2367 (2017)
15. Lin, T.-Y., et al.: Microsoft COCO: common objects in context. In: Fleet, D., Pajdla, T., Schiele, B., Tuytelaars, T. (eds.) ECCV 2014. LNCS, vol. 8693, pp. 740–755. Springer, Cham (2014). https://doi.org/10.1007/978-3-319-10602-1_48
16. Liu, S., Jia, J., Fidler, S., Urtasun, R.: SGN: sequential grouping networks for instance segmentation. In: Proceedings of the IEEE International Conference on Computer Vision, vol. 2017-Oct, pp. 3516–3524 (2017)
17. M2CAI Challenge: Tool Presence Detection. Workshop and Challenges on Modeling and Monitoring of Computer Assisted Interventions (2016). camma.u-strasbg.fr/m2cai2016/index.php/tool-presence-detection-challenge-results
18. Nwoye, C.I., Mutter, D., Marescaux, J., Padoy, N.: Weakly supervised convolutional LSTM approach for tool tracking in laparoscopic videos. Int. J. Comput. Assist. Radiol. Surg. **14**, 1–9 (2019)
19. Pakhomov, D., Premachandran, V., Allan, M., Azizian, M., Navab, N.: Deep residual learning for instrument segmentation in robotic surgery. CoRR, pp. 1–9 (2017)
20. Paszke, A., Gross, S., Chintala, S., Chanan, G., Yang, E.: Automatic differentiation in PyTorch. In: NIPS Autodiff Workshop, pp. 1–4 (2017)
21. Primus, M.J., Schoeffmann, K., Böszörmenyi, L.: Instrument classification in laparoscopic videos. In: Proceedings of the International Workshop on Content-Based Multimedia Indexing, pp. 1–6. IEEE, June 2015
22. Kletz, S., Schoeffmann, K., Benois-Pineau, J., Husslein, H.: Identifying surgical instruments in laparoscopy using deep learning instance segmentation. In: Proceedings of the International Conference on Content-Based Multimedia Indexing, pp. 1–6. IEEE (2019)
23. Ren, S., He, K., Girshick, R., Sun, J.: Faster R-CNN: towards real-time object detection with region proposal networks. IEEE Trans. Pattern Anal. Mach. Intell. **39**(6), 1137–1149 (2017)
24. Rosenthal, R., Hoffmann, H., Dwan, K., Clavien, P.A., Bucher, H.C.: Reporting of adverse events in surgical trials: critical appraisal of current practice. World J. Surg. **39**(1), 80–87 (2014)
25. Rothschild, J.M., et al.: The critical care safety study: the incidence and nature of adverse events and serious medical errors in intensive care. Crit. Care Med. **33**(8), 1694–1700 (2005)
26. Shvets, A., Rakhlin, A., Kalinin, A.A., Iglovikov, V.: Automatic instrument segmentation in robot-assisted surgery using deep learning. In: Proceedings of the IEEE International Conference on Machine Learning and Applications, pp. 624–628, March 2018
27. Twinanda, A.P., Shehata, S., Mutter, D., Marescaux, J., De Mathelin, M., Padoy, N.: EndoNet: a deep architecture for recognition tasks on laparoscopic videos. IEEE Trans. Med. Imaging **36**(1), 86–97 (2016)
28. Vardazaryan, A., Mutter, D., Marescaux, J., Padoy, N.: Weakly-supervised learning for tool localization in laparoscopic videos. In: Stoyanov, D., et al. (eds.) LABELS/CVII/STENT -2018. LNCS, vol. 11043, pp. 169–179. Springer, Cham (2018). https://doi.org/10.1007/978-3-030-01364-6_19

Real-Time Recognition of Daily Actions Based on 3D Joint Movements and Fisher Encoding

Panagiotis Giannakeris(✉), Georgios Meditskos, Konstantinos Avgerinakis, Stefanos Vrochidis, and Ioannis Kompatsiaris

Centre for Research and Technology Hellas, Information Technologies Institute, Thessaloniki, Greece
{giannakeris,gmeditsk,koafgeri,stefanos,ikom}@iti.gr

Abstract. Recognition of daily actions is an essential part of Ambient Assisted Living (AAL) applications and still not fully solved. In this work, we propose a novel framework for the recognition of actions of daily living from depth-videos. The framework is based on low-level human pose movement descriptors extracted from 3D joint trajectories as well as differential values that encode speed and acceleration information. The joints are detected using a depth sensor. The low-level descriptors are then aggregated into discriminative high-level action representations by modeling prototype pose movements with Gaussian Mixtures and then using a Fisher encoding schema. The resulting Fisher vectors are suitable to train Linear SVM classifiers so as to recognize actions in pre-segmented video clips, alleviating the need for additional parameter search with non-linear kernels or neural network tuning. Experimental evaluation on two well-known RGB-D action datasets reveal that the proposed framework achieves close to state-of-the-art performance whilst maintaining high processing speeds.

Keywords: Action recognition · 3D human joints · Gaussian Mixture modeling · Fisher encoding

1 Introduction

Action recognition in general is an important task in computer vision with a very wide range of possible applications. Recently, many of those are part of ambient assisted living environments where users are monitored by static cameras placed inside their homes. Many of the patients do not feel comfortable wearing any sensory equipment or wearable cameras that may generally feel bulky and invasive.

For those reasons, depth cameras that can capture 3D positions of human skeleton joints are very well suited to this task. Not only the joint locations can be captured at real time speeds, but also the amount of processing time required is small compared to techniques that involve processing RGB video

Y. M. Ro et al. (Eds.): MMM 2020, LNCS 11962, pp. 601–613, 2020.
https://doi.org/10.1007/978-3-030-37734-2_49

frames. Many of the recent works in action recognition follow closely the deep learning trend [10–12,19,20,27] in order to achieve competitive results, however they do not give much attention to efficiency. Deep learning techniques usually require lots of training data and careful parameter tuning to avoid overfitting. Additionally, expensive GPUs are needed during training or inference in order to run at acceptable speeds.

In this paper, inspired by [31], we use the Moving Pose descriptor at the basis of our approach for representing actions and extend its applicability by incorporating an aggregation scheme that transforms multiple pose descriptors of an action clip into a compact meaningful encoding using prototypical pose features. The Moving Pose was originally proposed as a descriptor that captured for each frame 3D pose configurations along with differential properties, like the speed and acceleration of human parts. It was paired with a modified kNN classifier which characterized each sequence based on the action label that the majority of the individual frame descriptors had been assigned to.

While the low-level frame descriptors are powerful and are calculated very fast, the application of the modified kNN that is proposed inserts model parameters that need to be optimized (i.e. the number of neighbors and a confidence threshold for classification). Another drawback is that the kNN classifier can be generally slower in some cases of high data dimensionality. Our contribution lies mainly on the creation of compact representations by a sophisticated descriptor aggregation scheme that are suitable for Linear Support Vector Machine classification. The aggregation scheme involves building of a vocabulary of pose prototypes using Gaussian Mixture modeling during training and encoding a sequence of an arbitrary number of frame descriptors into meaningful high-level action representations using Fisher encoding.

Our proposed scheme alleviates the need to search the training data for discriminative neighbors during inference. It also achieves comparable performance even without carefully tuning the weighting parameters that control the relative importance of the pose derivatives like in the original method. Additionally, it results in higher classification accuracy when paired with a Linear Support Vector Machine and improves the overall processing speed which is now faster by 100%. In this work we perform our experiments on public RGB-D datasets that use the Microsoft Kinect V1 sensor to acquire skeletons, but the method can be generally applied to every sensor of this type.

The rest of this paper is structured as follows: In Sect. 2 we present the state-of-the-art related work, while in Sect. 3 we describe in detail our proposed methodology. In Sect. 4 our experimental work and evaluation results are reported and in Sect. 5 conclusions are drawn and future work is discussed.

2 Related Work

Previous works on third person action recognition can be categorized based on the type of data that they process, whether it is RGB or depth videos. For the first category, most of the pre-CNN era works dealt with motion analysis using optical flow and dense trajectories [1,8,9,25,26], extracting legacy low-level descriptors like Histograms of Oriented Gradients (HOG), Histograms of Optical Flow (HOF) and Motion Boundary Histograms (MBH), to represent the visual and motion features around keypoints tracked in time. More advanced techniques quickly began to take advantage of the temporal structure of visual patterns [7,16]. Shortly after the CNN breakthrough, the direction was steered naturally towards deep learning approaches. Some of them combined various modes of video frames, mainly an RGB channel and an optical flow channel, constructing multi-stream CNNs [6,23,29], in order to extract deep CNN visual and motion features and represent actions based on multimodal fusion. In later works, information from human pose was more effectively captured using pose-based CNN features [2]. Other techniques that leverage temporal information rely on RNNs. More specifically, the modern technique of deep visual attention was combined with RNNs in [4]. Very recently, modifications on legacy techniques were presented, like in [22] where optical flow derivation features (OFF) were plugged in a legacy CNN-based action recognition framework, or in [5] where the two-stream CNN approach was modernized by injecting residual connections.

More related to this work are techniques that fall into the second category, i.e. the ones that use information from depth videos and more specifically try to represent actions from 3D human skeleton joint positions. Earlier works focused on extracting features from human joints to characterize their movement [28,30,31]. In addition, the features were designed to be invariant to noise, translation and viewpoint temporal misalignment. In [28] LOP features of joints were combined into actionlets that represented particular conjunctions of the joints. A data mining approach was used in order to find the most significant combinations and make an ensemble out of them to represent the actions. In [30] view invariant joint features, named HOJ3D, were extracted and used to discover prototypical poses and Hidden Markov Models were used to describe their temporal evolution in order to represent actions. Temporal joint displacement features were combined with spatial features to form a simple spatiotemporal fusion scheme in [32] by calculating pairwise distances of joint positions. A more elaborate technique was proposed in [24] that represented human actions as curves in a Lie group in order to model 3D geometric relationships between human joints. The processing of those curves involved mapping them from the Lie group to Lie algebra and then using Dynamic Time Warping and Linear SVM for classification.

Later works gravitate towards deep learning methods and specifically Long Short Term Memory networks (LSTM). A spatio-temporal LSTM was proposed in [14] which aimed to model the temporal dynamics and spatial dependencies. [17] extends upon the Lie group representation of [24] with the inclusion of CNNs and LSTMs in the framework. The transformed vectors sequenced from the Lie group were fed into stacked units of a 1-D CNN across the temporal domain and then a separate LSTM layer was trained to learn temporal dependencies and classify the action segments. A non deep learning method has been recently proposed in [15] which deployed a similar encoding scheme with ours.

Its purpose is to encode multiple spatial and temporal features of different joint subgroups. Features were aggregated using VLAD encoding and then optimal feature combinations were found based on metric learning.

3 Methodology

The extraction of human skeleton movement patterns constitute the basis of our approach so as to characterize pre-segmented action sequences. Action videos can be seen as sequential frames of body pose configurations. Therefore, spatial relationships between joints that form body poses in still frames are very informative towards understating the action that is taking place. This holds true for certain actions more than it does for others. For example, "walking" instances can be easily separated from "lying down" instances based on the relative positions of the head or torso joints. However, the movement and transitions of joint configurations is also critical in order to understand actions that cannot be characterized by static pose information only. For example, a still pose taken from a "walking" instance is not enough to uniquely define it and separate it from a "standing up" instance, because movement information is not present. Therefore, we focus on extracting low-level frame descriptors based not only on joint positions but also on joint displacement features inside short temporal windows centered around the current frame. Another important aspect is the expected variance of natural skeletal dimensions between different subjects. Directly computing displacement vectors in 3D space will result in inconsistent results due to lack of invariance to the subjects' natural body shapes. For this reason temporal features that encode velocity and acceleration quantities between adjacent frames are selected instead. The speed and direction of joint movement are informative features that can separate actions that are built by similar static poses but involve different direction of movement and the changes in speed and direction of joint movement can separate actions that involve periodic movements of joints like "walking" or "hand waving". Accordingly, we adopt the Moving Pose descriptor [31] which assumes that the pose, $P(t)$, is a continuous and differentiable function of the joint positions over time; thus, its second-order Taylor approximation in a short temporal window around the current time-step t_0 can be expressed as:

$$P(t) \approx P(t_0) + \delta P(t_0)(t - t_0) + \frac{1}{2}\delta^2 P(t_0)(t - t_0)^2 \tag{1}$$

where $\delta P(t)$ and $\delta^2 P(t)$ are the first and second order derivatives of the pose function and are effectively encoding information about the temporal changes in pose configuration regarding the center frame inside a short temporal window. This approximation can be used in order to describe every action frame with respect to the current static pose and the joint kinematics between adjacent frames, thus, incorporating the temporal dynamics of the movement.

3.1 Low-Level Pose Descriptors

We assume that for every video frame the 3D joint positions of the skeleton are available as 3D vectors $j_i = [x_i, y_i, z_i]^T$, where $i = \{1, 2, \ldots n\}$ is the total number of joints that the sensor can capture. At any given moment the static pose is given by concatenating all the joint vectors $P = [j_1, j_2, \ldots j_n]$. The derivatives are approximated numerically by using a temporal window of 5 frames centered at the current frame, as such:

$$\delta P(t_0) \approx P(t_1) - P(t_{-1}) \tag{2}$$

$$\delta^2 P(t_0) \approx P(t_2) + P(t_{-2}) - 2P(t_0) \tag{3}$$

The final low-level moving pose descriptor is the concatenation of the static pose vector and the first and second order derivatives. The derivative vectors are rescaled to unit norm. The original descriptor was proposed to insert two weighting parameters for the two derivatives that would effectively control their relative importance. However, we reject the insertion of the parameters in order to avoid optimizing them via cross-validation for specific datasets.

In order to compensate for skeleton variations across different subjects and to deal with noise in the data, the static poses are first normalized before the final low-level descriptor is formed. The average length of each limp of the skeleton is calculated first. Then, all the train and test skeleton limps are normalized to have the same average length for each limp type whilst maintaining the angles between joints (the direction vectors) that form each static pose. Normalizing the skeletons guarantees that the same types of limps will have the same length across not only different subjects but also different instances of the same subject. Each joint's position is also expressed using relative distance from the hip center, by subtracting the coordinates of the root joint. The last step ensures that the descriptor is invariant to camera parameters.

3.2 High-Level Action Representations

Each action clip may have arbitrary duration and as such, an arbitrary number of moving pose descriptors are going to be extracted. What follows is our proposed framework for moving pose descriptor aggregation and encoding into high level meaningful action representations.

We initiate the process by reducing the descriptor dimensionality using Principal Component Analysis. We choose as many principal components in order to guarantee that at least 98% of the original variance of the training set is maintained to the lower-dimensional space. Next, we intent to create a statistical model that can generate a number of prototypical descriptors from the training set. Those will represent the most discriminative static poses and pose transitions from the full training set of low-level descriptors across all subjects and action sequences. We do that using mixtures of Gaussians (GMM) which is a probabilistic model that assumes all the data points are generated from a mixture of a finite number of Gaussian distributions with unknown parameters. The

EM algorithm is applied in order to fit the mixture of Gaussians to the training set. This way, a moving pose vocabulary based on the most discriminative low-level descriptors is constructed. Any set of low-level action descriptors extracted from a sequence can then be expressed by the gradients of the log-likelihood of each descriptor under the GMM, with respect to the GMM parameters. This process is known as Fisher Encoding [18] and the final representation is called a Fisher vector (FV).

Let $\{\mu_j, \Sigma_j, \pi_j; j \in R^L\}$ be the set of parameters for L Gaussian models, with μ_j, Σ_j and π_j standing respectively for the mean, the covariance and the prior probability weights of the jth Gaussian. Assuming that the D-dimensional early descriptor is represented as $\overline{M}_i \in R^D; i = \{1, \ldots, N\}$, with N denoting the total number of descriptors, Fisher encoding is then built upon the first and second order statistics:

$$\begin{aligned} f_{1j} &= \frac{1}{N\sqrt{\pi_j}} \sum_{i=1}^{N} q_{ij} \sigma_j^{-1} (\overline{x}_i - \overline{\mu}_j) \\ f_{2j} &= \frac{1}{N\sqrt{2\pi_j}} \sum_{i=1}^{N} q_{ij} [\frac{(\overline{x}_i - \overline{\mu}_j)^2}{\sigma_j^2} - 1] \end{aligned} \tag{4}$$

where q_{ij} is the Gaussian soft assignment of descriptor M_i to the jth Gaussian and is given by:

$$q_{ij} = \frac{exp[-\frac{1}{2}(M_i - \mu_j)^T \Sigma_j^{-1} (M_i - \mu_j)]}{\sum_{t=1}^{L} exp[-\frac{1}{2}(M_i - \mu_t)^T \Sigma_j^{-1} (M_i - \mu_t)]} \tag{5}$$

Distances that are calculated by Eq. 4 are next concatenated to form the final $2LD$-dimensional Fisher vector, $F_X = [f_{11}, f_{21}, \cdots, f_{1L}, f_{2L}]$, that characterizes each action clip. The final Fisher vector is calculated for every action clip sequence in the train and test set. One of the benefits of Fisher encoding is that it leads to representations that can now be classified using cost-less linear SVM classifier with high accuracy.

4 Experimental Work

In order to evaluate our proposed framework we experiment on two well-known RGB-D datasets for action recognition. Namely, they are the UT-Kinect dataset [30] and the MSR-Action3D dataset [13]. The UT-Kinect dataset contains 10 action classes performed twice by 10 subjects. This dataset poses significant intra-class, viewpoint variations and occlusions because the actors are interacting with objects during the action clips. The MSR-Action3D contains 20 classes and 10 subjects, each performing a single action 2 or 3 times. Both datasets provide 20 skeletal joint locations for each action frame. In the case of UT-Kinect not all action frames contain skeletal joint positions which makes the calculation of the pose derivatives tricky since the pose function may not be considered continuous in this case. Still, the method performs well even in this case as we will see.

We followed a common evaluation method among relevant works for the UT-Kinect dataset, which is the leave-one-subject-out-cross-validation (LOOCV). For the MSR-Action3D dataset there are two popular evaluation protocols. The first approach is the 5-fold split where half the subjects are used for training and the other half is kept for testing. The second approach is the average result among all possible half-splits keeping a different set out for testing in each iteration (cross-validation). It is considered the most stable approach since the results are being averaged across many splits. We followed the second evaluation protocol for the MSR-Action3D.

The modified-kNN classifier that the moving pose authors originally proposed [31] was not evaluated on the UT-Kinect and also on the MSR-Action3D under the second and most reliable protocol, thus, we perform the above experiments ourselves in order to compare it with our approach. The modified-kNN classifier that was proposed works by accumulating votes at every time step using at most k neighbors, but with the modification that a single vote of a training sample is weighted by a "goodness" probability assigning method. A training sample's goodness is derived by treating it as an unknown instance and finding what percentage of its k-neighbors belong to its class. The authors propose this method as a measure to weaken the votes of irrelevant samples or outliers in the training set.

Table 1. Experiments with Moving Pose and modified-kNN.

K neighbors	UT-Kinect accuracy (%)	MSR-Action3D accuracy (%)
5	90.47	92.18
7	**90.47**	**92.51**
10	90.44	91.63
15	87.94	91.47

Table 2. Experiments with Moving Pose and Fisher encoding.

GMM gaussians	UT-Kinect accuracy (%)	MSR-Action3D accuracy (%)
4	**94**	–
8	91.47	–
12	90.47	–
16	–	90.87
24	–	**92.38**
32	–	91.27

For the modified-kNN we experimented with 4 different values for the K number of neighbors, as Table 1 shows. Optimal performance is obtained when setting $K = 7$ for both datasets. This method reaches 90.47% and 92.51% mean classification accuracy on the UT-Kinect and MSR-Action3D respectively. Note that we rejected the derivative weighting parameters as we mentioned earlier. This simply means that we set them both to 1 so that they have no effect on the low-level descriptors, thus, no other parameters were needed to be optimized here. During inference time the modified-kNN approach ran on 50–100 fps depending on the action clip.

For our proposed framework, we experimented with the number of Gaussians for the GMM moving pose vocabulary that is created during training time. It is expected that the optimal vocabulary size is different for each dataset and that it should be generally larger for the MSR-Action 3D since it contains a lot more action classes. Table 2 shows our experiments with different GMM vocabulary sizes for each dataset. We manage to achieve 3.53% increase in classification accuracy with as many as 4 Gaussians on our mixture model on the UT-Kinect dataset compared to the best modified-kNN score. A decrease in performance is observed as the vocabulary size gets larger, however the dataset contains a small set of actions and as such, redundancy in the vocabulary may be prominent in these settings. Similarly, the sweet spot for the MSR-Action3D is around 24 Gaussians. We managed to reach the accuracy of the modified-kNN in this case but not surpass it. Our proposed method ran on average on 100–200 fps during inference time, doubling the efficiency when compared with the modified-kNN. All the experiments were performed using an Intel i7-3770K @ 3.50 GHz CPU.

Table 3. Comparison with SoA on UT-Kinect dataset.

Method	Accuracy (%)
Grassmann manifold [21]	88.5
Histogram of 3D joints [30]	90.9
Riemannian manifold [3]	91.5
ST-LSTM + trust gate [14]	97.0
Lie Group [17]	98.5
Moving pose + knn	90.47
Moving pose + Fisher	94.0

Tables 3 and 4 show the comparison of our proposed method with State-of-the-art related works. We can see that our method achieves very good classification accuracy on both datasets when compared to elaborate techniques, like the ones that use manifolds [3,21], as well as the more simple techniques [30]. Moreover in the case of MSR-Action3D we managed to surpass the approach of [15] which deploys a VLAD encoding scheme. Our method is only topped by a maximum of 4.5% in the UT-Kinect and 2.29% in the MSR-Action3D by the powerful deep learning methods.

In Figs. 1 and 2 the confusion matrices are shown for action recognition on the UT-Kinect and MSR-Action3D respectively (Table 5 shows the action names

Table 4. Comparison with SoA on MSR-Action3D dataset.

Method	Accuracy (%)
Grassmann manifold [21]	91.21
Feature learning [15]	90.36
Lie group [17]	94.27
ST-LSTM + trust gate [14]	94.80
Moving pose + knn	92.51
Moving pose + Fisher	92.38

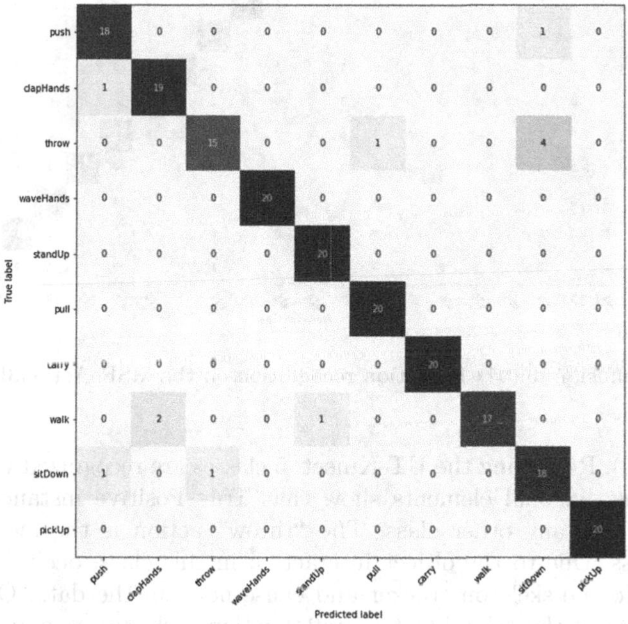

Fig. 1. Confusion matrix for action recognition on the UT-Kinect dataset.

Table 5. Class labels of the MSR-Action3D dataset.

Label	Action name	Label	Action name	Label	Action name
a01	High arm wave	a08	Draw tick	a15	Side-kick
a02	Horizontal arm wave	a09	Draw circle	a16	Jogging
a03	Hammer	a10	Hand clap	a17	Tennis swing
a04	Hand catch	a11	Two-hand wave	a18	Tennis serve
a05	Forward punch	a12	Side-boxing	a19	Golf swing
a06	High throw	a13	Bend	a20	Pick-up and throw
a06	Draw cross	a14	Forward kick		

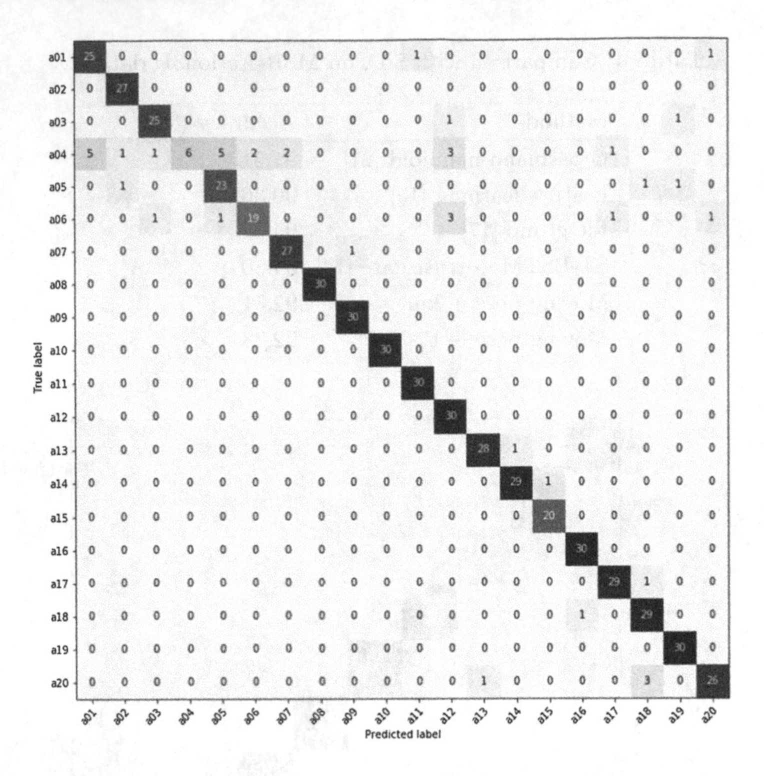

Fig. 2. Confusion matrix for action recognition on the MSR-Action3D dataset.

for each label). Regarding the UT-Kinect, 5 classes are recognized with a perfect score and the diagonal elements show that True Positive instances never fall bellow 15/20 for any other class. The "throw" action is the most frequently confused class. Due to the object interaction in this class, occlusion may pose a challenge to the skeleton tracker and cause noise in the data. On the MSR-Action3D dataset the "Hand Catch" (a04) action is the most confused class due to fast arm movement and human-object interaction. The second most confused class is the "High Throw" with 19/30 instances correctly predicted. Nevertheless, for the rest of the classes the True Positive instances do not fall below 25/30 which shows very good performance of the proposed method in a large scale dataset with a higher number of classes and complex actions.

5 Conclusions

We have presented a descriptor aggregation and encoding scheme to pair with the Moving Pose descriptor for action recognition using skeleton data. Evaluation results indicate that our proposed framework can reach close to State-of-the-art performance without the use of deep learning and surpass the modified-kNN method whilst achieving higher processing speed rates. Our future plans are to explore other aggregation techniques and incorporate features regarding human-object interaction into the framework.

Acknowledgments. This research has been co-financed by the European Regional Development Fund of the European Union and Greek national funds through the Operational Program Competitiveness, Entrepreneurship and Innovation, under the call RESEARCH - CREATE - INNOVATE (T1EDK-00686) and the EC funded project V4Design (H2020-779962).

References

1. Avgerinakis, K., Briassouli, A., Kompatsiaris, Y.: Activity detection using sequential statistical boundary detection (SSBD). Comput. Vis. Image Underst. **144**, 46–61 (2016)
2. Chéron, G., Laptev, I., Schmid, C.: P-CNN: pose-based CNN features for action recognition. In: Proceedings of the IEEE International Conference on Computer Vision, pp. 3218–3226 (2015)
3. Devanne, M., Wannous, H., Berretti, S., Pala, P., Daoudi, M., Del Bimbo, A.: 3-D human action recognition by shape analysis of motion trajectories on riemannian manifold. IEEE Trans. Cybern. **45**(7), 1340–1352 (2014)
4. Du, W., Wang, Y., Qiao, Y.: RPAN: an end-to-end recurrent pose-attention network for action recognition in videos. In: Proceedings of the IEEE International Conference on Computer Vision, pp. 3725–3734 (2017)
5. Feichtenhofer, C., Pinz, A., Wildes, R.: Spatiotemporal residual networks for video action recognition. In: Advances in Neural Information Processing Systems, pp. 3468–3476 (2016)
6. Feichtenhofer, C., Pinz, A., Zisserman, A.: Convolutional two-stream network fusion for video action recognition. In: Proceedings of the IEEE Conference on Computer Vision and Pattern Recognition, pp. 1933–1941 (2016)
7. Gaidon, A., Harchaoui, Z., Schmid, C.: Actom sequence models for efficient action detection. In: CVPR 2011, pp. 3201–3208. IEEE (2011)
8. Jain, M., Jegou, H., Bouthemy, P.: Better exploiting motion for better action recognition. In: Proceedings of the IEEE Conference on Computer Vision and Pattern Recognition, pp. 2555–2562 (2013)
9. Jhuang, H., Gall, J., Zuffi, S., Schmid, C., Black, M.J.: Towards understanding action recognition. In: Proceedings of the IEEE International Conference on Computer Vision, pp. 3192–3199 (2013)
10. Lee, I., Kim, D., Kang, S., Lee, S.: Ensemble deep learning for skeleton-based action recognition using temporal sliding LSTM networks. In: Proceedings of the IEEE International Conference on Computer Vision, pp. 1012–1020 (2017)
11. Li, C., Zhong, Q., Xie, D., Pu, S.: Skeleton-based action recognition with convolutional neural networks. In: 2017 IEEE International Conference on Multimedia and Expo Workshops (ICMEW), pp. 597–600. IEEE (2017)
12. Li, C., Cui, Z., Zheng, W., Xu, C., Yang, J.: Spatio-temporal graph convolution for skeleton based action recognition. In: Thirty-Second AAAI Conference on Artificial Intelligence (2018)
13. Li, W., Zhang, Z., Liu, Z.: Action recognition based on a bag of 3D points. In: 2010 IEEE Computer Society Conference on Computer Vision and Pattern Recognition-Workshops, pp. 9–14. IEEE (2010)

14. Liu, J., Shahroudy, A., Xu, D., Kot, A.C., Wang, G.: Skeleton-based action recognition using spatio-temporal lstm network with trust gates. IEEE Trans. Pattern Anal. Mach. Intell. **40**(12), 3007–3021 (2017)
15. Luvizon, D.C., Tabia, H., Picard, D.: Learning features combination for human action recognition from skeleton sequences. Pattern Recogn. Lett. **99**, 13–20 (2017)
16. Pirsiavash, H., Ramanan, D.: Parsing videos of actions with segmental grammars. In: Proceedings of the IEEE Conference on Computer Vision and Pattern Recognition, pp. 612–619 (2014)
17. Rhif, M., Wannous, H., Farah, I.R.: Action recognition from 3D skeleton sequences using deep networks on lie group features. In: 2018 24th International Conference on Pattern Recognition (ICPR), pp. 3427–3432. IEEE (2018)
18. Sánchez, J., Perronnin, F., Mensink, T., Verbeek, J.: Image classification with the fisher vector: theory and practice. Int. J. Comput. Vis. **105**(3), 222–245 (2013)
19. Si, C., Chen, W., Wang, W., Wang, L., Tan, T.: An attention enhanced graph convolutional lstm network for skeleton-based action recognition. In: Proceedings of the IEEE Conference on Computer Vision and Pattern Recognition, pp. 1227–1236 (2019)
20. Si, C., Jing, Y., Wang, W., Wang, L., Tan, T.: Skeleton-based action recognition with spatial reasoning and temporal stack learning. In: Proceedings of the European Conference on Computer Vision (ECCV), pp. 103–118 (2018)
21. Slama, R., Wannous, H., Daoudi, M., Srivastava, A.: Accurate 3D action recognition using learning on the grassmann manifold. Pattern Recogn. **48**(2), 556–567 (2015)
22. Sun, S., Kuang, Z., Sheng, L., Ouyang, W., Zhang, W.: Optical flow guided feature: a fast and robust motion representation for video action recognition. In: Proceedings of the IEEE Conference on Computer Vision and Pattern Recognition, pp. 1390–1399 (2018)
23. Tran, A., Cheong, L.F.: Two-stream flow-guided convolutional attention networks for action recognition. In: Proceedings of the IEEE International Conference on Computer Vision, pp. 3110–3119 (2017)
24. Vemulapalli, R., Arrate, F., Chellappa, R.: Human action recognition by representing 3D skeletons as points in a lie group. In: Proceedings of the IEEE Conference on Computer Vision and Pattern Recognition, pp. 588–595 (2014)
25. Wang, H., Kläser, A., Schmid, C., Liu, C.L.: Dense trajectories and motion boundary descriptors for action recognition. Int. J. Comput. Vis. **103**(1), 60–79 (2013)
26. Wang, H., Schmid, C.: Action recognition with improved trajectories. In: Proceedings of the IEEE international Conference on Computer Vision, pp. 3551–3558 (2013)
27. Wang, H., Wang, L.: Modeling temporal dynamics and spatial configurations of actions using two-stream recurrent neural networks. In: Proceedings of the IEEE Conference on Computer Vision and Pattern Recognition, pp. 499–508 (2017)
28. Wang, J., Liu, Z., Wu, Y., Yuan, J.: Mining actionlet ensemble for action recognition with depth cameras. In: 2012 IEEE Conference on Computer Vision and Pattern Recognition, pp. 1290–1297. IEEE (2012)
29. Wang, L., Xiong, Y., Wang, Z., Qiao, Y.: Towards good practices for very deep two-stream convnets. arXiv preprint arXiv:1507.02159 (2015)
30. Xia, L., Chen, C.C., Aggarwal, J.K.: View invariant human action recognition using histograms of 3d joints. In: 2012 IEEE Computer Society Conference on Computer Vision and Pattern Recognition Workshops, pp. 20–27. IEEE (2012)

31. Zanfir, M., Leordeanu, M., Sminchisescu, C.: The moving pose: an efficient 3D kinematics descriptor for low-latency action recognition and detection. In: Proceedings of the IEEE International Conference on Computer Vision, pp. 2752–2759 (2013)
32. Zhu, Y., Chen, W., Guo, G.: Fusing spatiotemporal features and joints for 3D action recognition. In: Proceedings of the IEEE Conference on Computer Vision and Pattern Recognition Workshops, pp. 486–491 (2013)

Model-Based and Class-Based Fusion of Multisensor Data

Athina Tsanousa(✉), Angelos Chatzimichail, Georgios Meditskos, Stefanos Vrochidis, and Ioannis Kompatsiaris

Information Technologies Institute, Center for Research and Technology Hellas, 6th km Charilaou-Thermi, 57001 Thessaloniki, Greece
{atsan,angechat,gmeditsk,stefanos,ikom}@iti.gr
https://mklab.iti.gr/

Abstract. In the recent years, the advancement of technology, the constantly aging population and the developments in medicine have resulted in the creation of numerous ambient assisted living systems. Most of these systems consist of a variety of sensors that provide information about the health condition of patients, their activities and also create alerts in case of harmful events. Successfully combining and utilizing all the multimodal information is an important research topic. The current paper compares model-based and class-based fusion, in order to recognize activities by combining data from multiple sensors or sensors of different body placements. More specifically, we tested the performance of three fusion methods; weighted accuracy, averaging and a recently introduced detection rate based fusion method. Weighted accuracy and the detection rate based fusion achieved the best performance in most of the experiments.

Keywords: Activity recognition · Wearable sensors · Fusion

1 Introduction

Population of elderly people is constantly rising and will continue to increase significantly according to expectations. Although this creates many problems in the health care, including higher costs and larger number of people with difficulties in self-serving, the advancement in technology is able to provide solutions [6]. Systems that employ artificial intelligence applications, have the ability to recognize the daily activities of a subject, provide information about heart rates, blood pressure or temperature and detect the occurrence of a harmful event, such as fall.

Assisted living systems utilize a variety of sensors, devices and technologies. Inertial sensors are usually included in such systems, however they can also be used separately to provide information about the activities performed by a person. Nowadays, such sensors can be easily found in mobile and wearable devices. Most commonly used sensors are accelerometers, gyroscopes and magnetometers.

Y. M. Ro et al. (Eds.): MMM 2020, LNCS 11962, pp. 614–625, 2020.
https://doi.org/10.1007/978-3-030-37734-2_50

Accelerometers, which are the most popular, are quite effective in recognizing activities with repetitive body movement [5] while gyroscopes are capable of recognizing the orientation of an object [16]. Accelerometers and gyroscopes can be used separately and produce adequate results, while magnetometers are known to perform poorly when used individually [18]. Inertial sensors in general, are very prone to environmental noise, thus combining them tends to increase the accuracy of the recognition rate. Combination of sensors is algorithmically achieved through combination of the features extracted from each sensor, referred to as early fusion, or combination of the classification results of each individual sensor, also known as late fusion. It is easily understood that late fusion can also be applied to an individual sensor, combining the results of different classification algorithms and improve its performance.

In human activity recognition problems, fusion can also be applied to combine the results of the same sensor placed on different body parts, since there is claim that the placement of accelerometer affects its performance [7]. Although it is not considered mistaken to ignore the location of the sensor when analyzing its recordings, there are studies that investigate the affect the body placement has on the recognition of activities. In [7], the authors propose a late fusion methodology that combines accelerometers placed on ankle, wrist and chest. Authors in [18] investigate how five different body locations of a smartphone affect the performance of its built-in sensors in recognizing particular activities. Performance of individual sensors and their combination by concatenating feature vectors is also studied. [4] and [8] combine accelerometers of different body placements by applying early fusion.

In the current study, late fusion is employed to combine three inertial sensors, namely accelerometer, gyroscope and magnetometer, by body placement. Furthermore, the fusion of different placements of the same sensor is investigated. For the late fusion, two weighting schemes are incorporated and compared with a baseline late fusion method. The first one is a model-based method, the weighted accuracy [6], which reflects the total performance of a classifier. The second scheme is a class-based method, recently proposed by the current authors in [21], that utilizes the detection rate of a class, so as to emphasize the ability of a classifier in detecting certain classes and not its overall performance. In the latter, we suggested using fusion weights that are equal to the supplement of the class detection rate. We incorporated the suggested weights in a typical late fusion function and in a framework with posterior adapted class probabilities. The suggested method was compared with known late fusion methods, like averaging and stacking and with a novel framework suggested in [7]. Finally, we compare the model and class based fusion schemes with a simple form of late fusion, the averaging of class probability vectors produced by different models.

In summary the contribution of this paper lies in the following:

- The application of a new fusion method to more data
- The comparison of the performance of three fusion methods

The rest of the paper is organized as follows: Sect. 2 includes a brief mention of related work. Section 3 explains the theory used and Sect. 4 presents the results of the application. Section 5 concludes the paper.

2 Related Work

Although fusion has recently started gaining popularity, there is already a wide variety of available research work. As already stated, fusion can be applied to combine different sensors, even quite heterogeneous ones, sensors placed on different locations or improve the performance of an individual sensor by combining results of several algorithms. A methodology for recognizing activities from wearable sensors is proposed in [22]. The methodology is based on the late fusion of classification results obtained from Neural Networks (NN) and Hidden Markov Models (HMM) using two sensors placed on different body locations of the participants. In [20] a wireless sensor network is developed to observe the status of persons in need of assistance. Accelerometer data are combined with images from three different cameras to detect falls and improve the system's ability to create true alerts. In [10] data from a wearable inertial sensor and two cameras are combined in order to detect events. For the fusion step a probabilistic scheme is proposed by the authors. Many studies use audio visual sensors to recognize activities, although this process is usually more time consuming and the equipment needed requires bigger budgets. As already mentioned, input from wearable sensors is often combined with video images, especially in platforms that provide support at home for people with disabilities. In [17] the authors implement three types of fusion, early, intermediate and late, to analyze input from wearable cameras and recognize activities. HMM algorithm is incorporated in the process to classify the data. Different forms of fusion allow for the combination of multiple modalities in different levels. In [19] accelerometer and video data are combined in different stages of the classification process. The authors combine the different inputs before the feature extraction step, after feature extraction by concatenating the different vectors and at results' level by combining the algorithm outputs.

In [18] the authors explored the individual performance of each one of the three smartphone sensors, accelerometer, gyroscope and magnetometer, the combination of two of them, and the affect of the location of the sensor in the recognition process. For the combination of sensors or placements, the authors use the simplest form of early fusion, the concatenation. The current paper, on the contrary, uses late fusion to combine three sensors rather than two. In [11], the authors use built-in sensors of smart devices, separately and combined, and apply several well known classifiers to recognize activities. With the assistance of GPS and light sensors the activities can be further categorized to indoor or outdoor. Accelerometer, gyroscope and magnetometer data are combined with light and pressure data, and after being interpolated and filtered, features are extracted and combined with GPS information in order to enter a classification algorithm. The authors don't apply any fusion techniques, they focus however on the preprocessing of the data so as to eliminate noise and heterogeneity. Accelerometers and gyroscopes are most often combined in fusion schemes, probably due to their satisfactory performance in the daily activities recognition. Early and late fusion is applied in [13] to combine accelerometer and gyroscope features. The authors use concatenation for early fusion, a weighted scheme for late fusion and a descriptor-based framework for the activity recognition. Authors in [2] fuse accelerometer and gyroscopes to recognize activities and detect falls and focus on the importance of the window size for signal segmentation.

Weights are quite often utilized in fusion schemes, especially in late fusion ones. Out of bag errors acquired from the random forest algorithm are used in order to combine classifier results of different modalities in [15]. The classification problem is not relevant to the activity recognition, the methodology though could be easily implemented on multisensor data. In [6] the authors make use of a multisensor platform and apply several fusion weights combined with different fusion functions in order to recognize activities. The authors also propose a genetic algorithm to calculate weights. The weighted accuracy included in the latter, is also utilized in the current paper.

3 Methodology

The current human activity recognition framework comprises of the following steps:

1. Sliding window segments
2. Feature extraction
3. Classification algorithm
4. Model-based or class-based fusion

Sliding windows of 2 s without overlap were taken in order to extract features, similar to [7]. Time domain features, mentioned in Table 1, were extracted from the sliding windows without any further filtering or preprocessing of the data. The initial dataset was then segmented in the required subsets, responding to the sensor and body placement we wanted to analyze. Several multilabel classification algorithms were tested and the four that achieved better results are included here: Support Vector Machines (SVM) [9], Random Forests (RF) [12], C5 trees [14] and k-Nearest Neighbors (kNN) [1]. Each classifier was applied separately to a sensor and the classification results of the algorithms were combined afterwards. For the fusion step, two types of fusion were tested. **Model-based**, which characterizes the overall performance of the classifier and **class-based** which pays attention to the recognition of specific classes. The results were compared with those of the simple late fusion method of averaging class probabilities. To derive both types of weights for the fusion step, the typical steps of a classification framework were applied. An algorithm was trained on the trainset and then applied to the testset in order to predict the types of activities. The fusion schemes applied, combine sensors according to the following two scenarios:

1. Different sensors with the same placement
2. Identical sensors of different placement

Table 1. Extracted features

Features
Maximum
Mean
Median
Minimum
Standard Deviation
Variance

Model-Based Fusion. For the model-based approach the weighted accuracy was used. The accuracy (Eq. 2) of a classifier applied to a sensor, divided by the sum of accuracies, was multiplied by the class probability vectors (Eq. 1) and the products of all three sensors were finally added together to create a final class probability vector [6]. The class with the maximum probability was assigned to each test case. This method gives advantage to the model that has the best performance overall. The formula for weighted accuracy, as described in [6] is given in Eq. 3 and is calculated for each one of the i models:

$$P_{ij} = \{p_{i1}(x_1), \dots, p_{ik}(x_n)\}, i = 1, .., m \tag{1}$$

$$Accuracy = (TP + TN)/(TP + TN + FP + FN) \tag{2}$$

$$WACC = \frac{Accuracy^{(i)}}{\sum_{i=1}^{m} Accuracy^{(i)}} \tag{3}$$

Class-Based Fusion. For the class-based fusion, a novel method proposed by the authors of the current paper in [21] is applied. Class-based methods pay attention to the recognition of each class, which is usually characterized by F1-score [7] or balanced accuracy. This method multiplies the class probabilities with the supplement of the detection rate, which was chosen as weight, to assist the recognition of classes not so easily predicted. This is performed for each sensor separately and the weighted probability vectors of all sensors are afterwards summed together. Again, to assign a class to a test case, we find the class with the maximum fused probability. The detection rate is defined in Eq. 4.

$$DR = TP/(TP + TN + FP + FN) \tag{4}$$

The weights are calculated for each class j by calculating the supplement of the class detection rate (Eq. 5).

$$W_{ij} = 1 - DR_{ij} \tag{5}$$

Both types of weights are then multiplied with the class probabilities of an algorithm (Eq. 6). In the model based fusion, the class probability vectors are multiplied by the same number, the weighted accuracy, while in the class-based weight, each class probability vector is multiplied by a different weight.

$$P_w = W_{ij} P_{ij} \tag{6}$$

Averaging. Each model of those that will be combined, produces k ($j = 1, .., k$) class probability vectors (Eq. 1). To combine the results, a probability vector is calculated for each class, by averaging the respective class probability vectors of the m models combined (Eq. 7).

$$P_j = \frac{\sum_{i=1}^{m} P_{ij}}{m} \tag{7}$$

To evaluate the performance of the individual classifiers and the fusion results, we report two typical evaluation metrics. The accuracy of the model (Eq. 2) and the F1-score (Eq. 8). For multilabel classification, the F1-score is calculated for all classes and then averaged. The F1-score embodies both sensitivity and specificity and especially in multiclass problems, is considered more indicative of the accuracy metric, since it assesses the recognition of each class. In multiclass problems, high accuracy values may arise, while few of the classes may have not been recognized at all, a finding that is also confirmed in the current paper, as it can be seen in the following section.

$$F1\text{-}score = 2 * precision * recall/(precision + recall) \tag{8}$$

4 Application

In order to compare the model-based fusion method of weighted accuracy with the class-based fusion method, proposed by the authors in [21], and with the simple late fusion method of averaging and assess the influence of location on the sensors' performances, we utilize the MHEALTH dataset [3]. The MHEALTH contains recordings of numerous sensors, some of which were placed at different parts of the subject's body. The activities were performed by ten participants. Since a testset needs to be independent from the trainset, the users were separated: nine users constituted the training set and the recordings of one participant constituted the test set. The models were trained using 10-fold cross validation. The subjects performed 13 daily activities, 8 of which are kept as a subset for the current application. The activities were "Standing still", "Sitting and relaxing", "Lying down", "Walking", "Climbing stairs", "Cycling", "Jogging" and "Running". The time domain features that are mentioned in Table 1 are extracted from a sliding window of 2 s without overlap, which in the current datasets responds to 100 recordings, since the sampling frequency is 50 Hz.

Since it has been reported that body placement of a sensor affects its performance [7], we chose to combine (a) results of accelerometers, gyroscopes and magnetometers of the same body location and (b) accelerometers placed on three different locations, as well as gyroscopes placed at two different locations. More specifically, the results reported here for (a) refer to the fusion of

1. The three aforementioned sensors placed on the left ankle
2. The three sensors placed on the right lower arm

and the results reported for (b) refer to the fusion of

1. Accelerometer placed on chest, with that placed on the left ankle and the one of the right lower arm
2. Gyroscope placed on left ankle with the gyroscope of the right lower arm.

The flowchart in Fig. 1 provides a graphic demonstration of the procedure. The flowchart describes the fusion of two sensors as an example, while three sensors are fused in the current application. The same procedure is repeated for the sensors on the right lower arm and for the fusion of identical sensors of different locations.

Table 2 presents the evaluation metrics of the four classifiers applied on each sensor of the left ankle separately and of the three fusion methods, the weighted accuracy, which characterizes the performance of the algorithm, the detection rate based weighted fusion which evaluates the ability of an algorithm to detect each class and averaging. Table 3 contains the respective results for the sensors placed on the right lower arm. In most of the classifiers, fusion schemes exceed the best performing classifier on individual sensor data. In half of the cases the class-based fusion outperforms the model-based one.

Table 2. Accuracy (ACC) and F1-score for the fusion of sensors placed on left ankle, using weighted accuracy (WACC), detection rate based (DR) fusion and averaging

	SVM		RF		C5		KNN	
	ACC	F1	ACC	F1	ACC	F1	ACC	F1
Accelerometer	0.5750	0.5004	0.775	0.7670	0.5667	0.5649	0.7500	0.7489
Gyroscope	0.7000	0.6900	1.0000	1.0000	0.9542	0.9537	0.8583	0.8167
Magnetometer	0.3458	0.2724	0.825	0.8245	0.8208	0.8166	0.7708	0.7706
WACC	0.7542	0.7311	**0.9875**	**0.9874**	**0.9708**	**0.9706**	0.8792	0.8486
DR	**0.7667**	**0.7474**	0.9500	0.9500	0.8958	0.8834	**0.8833**	**0.8535**
Averaging	0.7500	0.7272	0.9583	0.9585	0.9167	0.9112	0.8875	0.8638

SVM has the worst performance among all four classifiers at all cases. In general, although the accuracy and F1-score may indicate good performance, some classes were not recognized at all from certain sensors and classifiers. Three classifiers, namely SVM, RF and C5, applied on the accelerometer placed on the left ankle, failed to recognize one activity, "sitting and relaxing", while SVM was

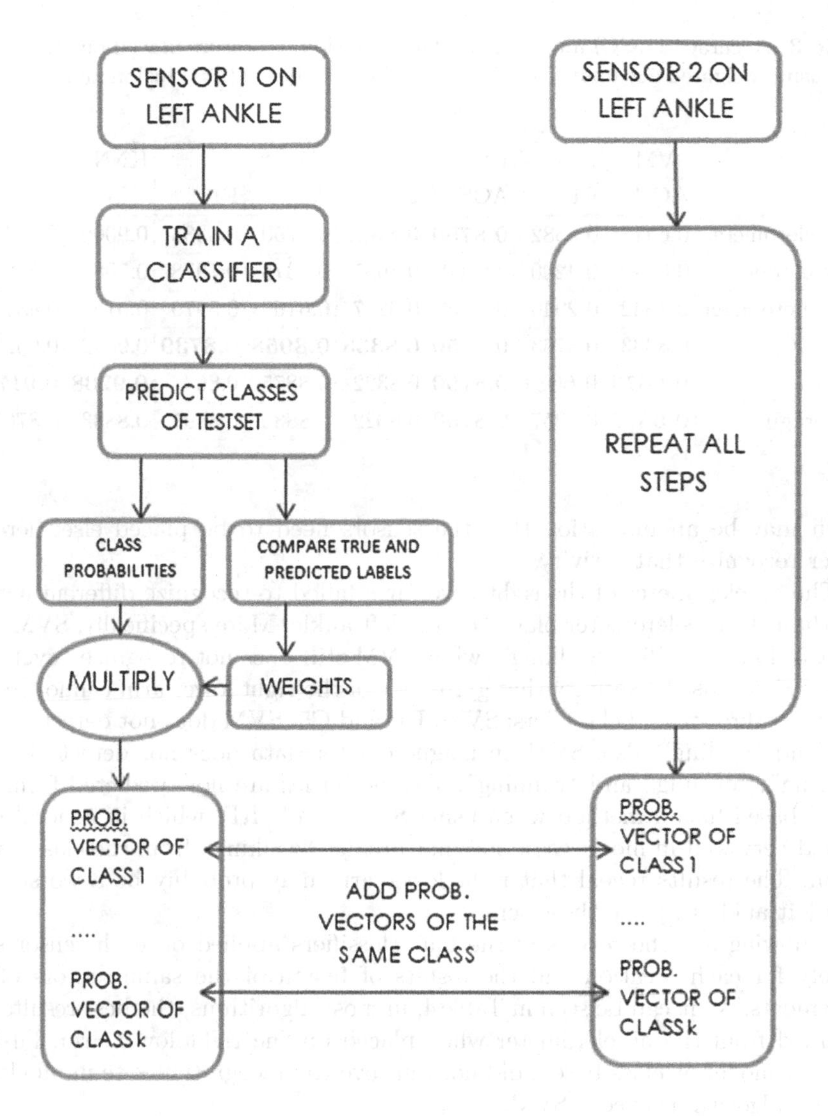

Fig. 1. Example flowchart of the weighted fusion of two sensors.

not able to predict at all two more activities: "climbing stairs" and "cycling". SVM applied on gyroscope of the left ankle, does not again recognize "cycling", while kNN on gyroscope data does not predict "standing still". Three activities were not detected from the worst performing classifier, SVM, on magnetometer of the left ankle, namely "lying down", "running" and "jogging". It is obvious that each sensor provides better recognition of some activities, therefore the fusion of all of them is expected to utilize all information in order to detect all performed activities. SVM, however, failed to detect "cycling" on both fusion methods,

Table 3. Accuracy (ACC) and F1-score for the fusion of sensors placed on right lower arm, using weighted accuracy (WACC), detection rate based (DR) fusion and averaging

	SVM		RF		C5		KNN	
	ACC	F1	ACC	F1	ACC	F1	ACC	F1
Accelerometer	0.6417	0.5582	**0.8750**	**0.8333**	0.8750	0.8333	0.9000	0.8845
Gyroscope	0.5292	0.4200	0.8500	0.8085	0.8375	0.7978	0.7083	0.6823
Magnetometer	0.3542	0.2940	0.6458	0.6257	0.6167	0.5979	0.5167	0.4812
WACC	0.8333	0.5763	**0.8750**	**0.8333**	**0.8958**	**0.8739**	0.9542	0.9529
DR	**0.6875**	**0.6081**	**0.8750**	0.8322	0.8875	0.8637	**0.9208**	**0.9174**
Averaging	**0.6875**	0.6057	**0.8750**	0.8322	0.8833	0.8595	0.8833	0.8765

which may be an indication that the sensors need to be placed elsewhere to better recognize that activity.

The accelerometer of the right lower arm failed to recognize different activities than the accelerometer placed on the left ankle. More specifically, SVM, RF and C5 do not predict "walking", while SVM still does not recognize "cycling". "Lying down" is the activity that gyroscope of the right lower arm cannot recognize with three tested classifiers: SVM, RF and C5. SVM does not detect "walking" and "cycling" also. SVM on magnetometer data does not detect "lying", "jogging", "cycling" and "running". Two activities are not predicted from the model-based fusion method when using SVM, while RF, which in general performed very well in most cases, does not predict "walking" from the class-based fusion. The results reveal that right lower arm may probably be a worst spot than left ankle to place those sensors.

Following are the results of the four classifiers applied on each sensor separately for each location and the results of fusion of the same sensors of all placements. As it can be seen in Table 4, in most algorithms, the best results are obtained from the accelerometer when placed on the right lower arm. Fusion, whether model or class based, did not improve the recognition rate in all classification algorithms except SVM.

Table 5 shows the results for gyroscope. Gyroscope seems to perform better when placed on the left ankle. Here, fusion of gyroscopes of different placements, improves the recognition rate compared to that of individual gyroscopes.

In general, fusion of gyroscopes results in better recognition than the fusion of accelerometers, an indication that these activities are better detected by a gyroscope. However in some cases, there were still activities not detected at all, like "lying", that was not recognized by gyroscopes and three algorithms, kNN, RF and SVM when using class-based fusion.

Table 4. Accuracy (ACC) and F1-score for the fusion of accelerometers of different placements, using weighted accuracy (WACC), detection rate based (DR) fusion and averaging

	SVM		RF		C5		KNN	
	ACC	F1	ACC	F1	ACC	F1	ACC	F1
Accel, chest	0.6458	0.5721	0.7792	0.7255	0.7208	0.6379	0.6208	0.5726
Accel, left ankle	0.5750	0.5004	0.7750	0.7670	0.5667	0.5649	0.7500	0.7489
Accel, right lower arm	0.6417	0.5582	**0.8750**	**0.8333**	**0.8750**	**0.8333**	**0.9000**	**0.8845**
WACC	**0.6833**	0.6202	0.8042	0.7563	0.8375	0.7955	0.8708	0.8565
DR	**0.6833**	**0.6211**	0.7792	0.7210	0.7458	0.6627	0.7667	0.7498
Averaging	0.6750	0.6132	0.7792	0.7210	0.7458	0.6627	0.7667	0.7498

Table 5. Accuracy (ACC) and F1-score for the fusion of gyroscopes of different placements, using weighted accuracy (WACC), detection rate based (DR) fusion and averaging

	SVM		RF		C5		KNN	
	ACC	F1	ACC	F1	ACC	F1	ACC	F1
Gyro, left ankle	**0.7000**	**0.6900**	**1.0000**	**1.0000**	0.9542	0.9537	0.8583	0.8167
Gyro, right lower arm	0.5292	0.4200	0.8500	0.8085	0.8375	0.7978	0.7083	0.6823
WACC	0.6417	0.5626	0.8750	0.8333	**0.9958**	**0.9958**	**0.8708**	**0.8292**
DR	0.6375	0.5621	0.8750	0.8333	0.8708	0.8270	0.8042	0.7669
Averaging	0.6458	0.5606	0.8750	0.8333	**0.9958**	**0.9958**	0.8667	0.8249

5 Conclusion

The fusion of the three sensors improved the recognition rate, whether the sensors were placed on the left ankle or the right lower arm. For half of the classification algorithms, class-based fusion outperformed the others. In almost all cases, model-based fusion and class-based fusion outperform the baseline method of averaging. Furthermore, for the current application, the left ankle placement achieves higher recognition rates than the right lower arm.

Fusion of the same sensors placed on different body placements did not prove so promising for the prediction of the specific activities. The fusion of accelerometers of three placements, did not exceed the individual sensor's performance in most cases, while for gyroscopes, model-based fusion with the weighted accuracy, improved the recognition rate for half of the algorithms applied. Fusion of magnetometers of different placements was not attended due to the poor performance of the sensor.

Overall, for the particular implementation, combining different sensors of the same location proved better than combining same sensor placed on different locations. The class-based fusion scheme suggested in [21] performed equally well with the model-based fusion with the use of weighted accuracy. Both fusion schemes outperform fusion with averaging of class probabilities. The fact that for some tests there were classes not predicted, may have affected the performance of the class-based fusion.

For future work, the authors will investigate fusion frameworks that combine different sensors and different placements, that will eliminate the heterogeneity caused by both factors.

Acknowledgments. This research has been co–financed by the European Regional Development Fund of the European Union and Greek national funds through the Operational Program Competitiveness, Entrepreneurship and Innovation, under the call RESEARCH - CREATE - INNOVATE (T1EDK-00686) and the EC funded project V4Design (H2020-779962).

References

1. Altman, N.S.: An introduction to kernel and nearest-neighbor nonparametric regression. Am. Stat. **46**(3), 175–185 (1992)
2. Banos, O., Galvez, J.M., Damas, M., Pomares, H., Rojas, I.: Window size impact in human activity recognition. Sensors **14**(4), 6474–6499 (2014)
3. Banos, O., et al.: mHealthDroid: a novel framework for agile development of mobile health applications. In: Pecchia, L., Chen, L.L., Nugent, C., Bravo, J. (eds.) IWAAL 2014. LNCS, vol. 8868, pp. 91–98. Springer, Cham (2014). https://doi.org/10.1007/978-3-319-13105-4_14
4. Bao, L., Intille, S.S.: Activity recognition from user-annotated acceleration data. In: Ferscha, A., Mattern, F. (eds.) Pervasive 2004. LNCS, vol. 3001, pp. 1–17. Springer, Heidelberg (2004). https://doi.org/10.1007/978-3-540-24646-6_1
5. Chen, L., Hoey, J., Nugent, C.D., Cook, D.J., Yu, Z.: Sensor-based activity recognition. IEEE Trans. Syst. Man Cybern. Part C (Appl. Rev.) **42**(6), 790–808 (2012)
6. Chernbumroong, S., Cang, S., Yu, H.: Genetic algorithm-based classifiers fusion for multisensor activity recognition of elderly people. IEEE J. Biomed. Health Inform. **19**(1), 282–289 (2014)
7. Chowdhury, A.K., Tjondronegoro, D., Chandran, V., Trost, S.G.: Physical activity recognition using posterior-adapted class-based fusion of multiaccelerometer data. IEEE J. Biomed. Health Inform. **22**(3), 678–685 (2017)
8. Cleland, I., et al.: Optimal placement of accelerometers for the detection of everyday activities. Sensors **13**(7), 9183–9200 (2013)
9. Cortes, C., Vapnik, V.: Support-vector networks. Mach. Learn. **20**(3), 273–297 (1995)
10. Crispim-Junior, C.F., Ma, Q., Fosty, B., Romdhane, R., Bremond, F., Thonnat, M.: Combining multiple sensors for event detection of older people. In: Briassouli, A., Benois-Pineau, J., Hauptmann, A. (eds.) Health Monitoring and Personalized Feedback using Multimedia Data, pp. 179–194. Springer, Cham (2015). https://doi.org/10.1007/978-3-319-17963-6_10
11. Guiry, J., Van de Ven, P., Nelson, J.: Multi-sensor fusion for enhanced contextual awareness of everyday activities with ubiquitous devices. Sensors **14**(3), 5687–5701 (2014)
12. Ho, T.K.: Random decision forests. In: Proceedings of 3rd International Conference on Document Analysis and Recognition, vol. 1, pp. 278–282. IEEE, August 1995
13. Jain, A., Kanhangad, V.: Human activity classification in smartphones using accelerometer and gyroscope sensors. IEEE Sens. J. **18**(3), 1169–1177 (2017)

14. Kuhn, M., Johnson, K.: Applied Predictive Modeling, vol. 26. Springer, New York (2013). https://doi.org/10.1007/978-1-4614-6849-3
15. Liparas, D., HaCohen-Kerner, Y., Moumtzidou, A., Vrochidis, S., Kompatsiaris, I.: News articles classification using random forests and weighted multimodal features. In: Lamas, D., Buitelaar, P. (eds.) IRFC 2014. LNCS, vol. 8849, pp. 63–75. Springer, Cham (2014). https://doi.org/10.1007/978-3-319-12979-2_6
16. Luštrek, M., Kaluža, B.: Fall detection and activity recognition with machine learning. Informatica **33**(2), 205–212 (2009)
17. Pinquier, J., et al.: Strategies for multiple feature fusion with hierarchical HMM: application to activity recognition from wearable audiovisual sensors. In: Proceedings of the 21st International Conference on Pattern Recognition, pp. 3192–3195. IEEE (2012)
18. Shoaib, M., Bosch, S., Incel, O., Scholten, H., Havinga, P.: Fusion of smartphone motion sensors for physical activity recognition. Sensors **14**(6), 10146–10176 (2014)
19. Stein, S., McKenna, S.J.: Combining embedded accelerometers with computer vision for recognizing food preparation activities. In: Proceedings of the 2013 ACM International Joint Conference on Pervasive and Ubiquitous Computing, pp. 729–738. ACM (2013)
20. Tabar, A.M., Keshavarz, A., Aghajan, H.: Smart home care network using sensor fusion and distributed vision-based reasoning. In: Proceedings of the 4th ACM International Workshop on Video Surveillance and Sensor Networks, pp. 145–154. ACM (2006)
21. Tsanousa, A., Meditskos, G., Vrochidis, S., Kompatsiaris, I.: A weighted late fusion framework for recognizing human activity from wearable sensors. In: 10th International Conference on Information, Intelligence, Systems and Applications (IISA). IEEE (2019, Accepted for publication)
22. Zhu, C., Sheng, W.: Human daily activity recognition in robot-assisted living using multi-sensor fusion. In: 2009 IEEE International Conference on Robotics and Automation, pp. 2154–2159. IEEE (2009)

Evaluating the Generalization Performance of Instrument Classification in Cataract Surgery Videos

Natalia Sokolova[1(✉)], Klaus Schoeffmann[1], Mario Taschwer[1], Doris Putzgruber-Adamitsch[2], and Yosuf El-Shabrawi[2]

[1] Klagenfurt University, Klagenfurt, Austria
{natalia,ks,mt}@itec.aau.at
[2] Klinikum Klagenfurt, Klagenfurt, Austria
{doris.putzgruber-adamitsch,yosuf.el-shabrawi}@kabeg.at

Abstract. In the field of ophthalmic surgery, many clinicians nowadays record their microscopic procedures with a video camera and use the recorded footage for later purpose, such as forensics, teaching, or training. However, in order to efficiently use the video material after surgery, the video content needs to be analyzed automatically. Important semantic content to be analyzed and indexed in these short videos are operation instruments, since they provide an indication of the corresponding operation phase and surgical action. Related work has already shown that it is possible to accurately detect instruments in cataract surgery videos. However, their underlying dataset (from the CATARACTS challenge) has very good visual quality, which is not reflecting the typical quality of videos acquired in general hospitals. In this paper, we therefore analyze the generalization performance of deep learning models for instrument recognition in terms of dataset change. More precisely, we trained such models as ResNet-50, Inception v3 and NASNet Mobile using a dataset of high visual quality (CATARACTS) and test it on another dataset with low visual quality (Cataract-101), and vice versa. Our results show that the generalizability is surprisingly low in general, but slightly worse for the model trained on the high-quality dataset.

Keywords: Instrument classification · Cataract surgery videos · Deep learning

1 Introduction

In ophthalmic surgery, interventions are performed on the human eye with tiny instruments under a microscope. Examples are retina laser treatments, refractive surgery, or cataract surgery (lens replacement). These operations are typically very challenging and require special operation techniques and psycho-motor skills that need to be trained intensively. Due to the setup involving the microscope, however, it is impossible for more than 1–2 trainee surgeons to closely follow a surgery. Therefore, many surgeons nowadays record videos of entire surgeries and use them later for educational purposes.

Y. M. Ro et al. (Eds.): MMM 2020, LNCS 11962, pp. 626–636, 2020.
https://doi.org/10.1007/978-3-030-37734-2_51

To use recorded videos efficiently, their content needs to be analyzed and indexed in order to be used with a content-based information retrieval system, which would allow to search for specific moments in these videos. In terms of content analysis of videos of ophthalmic surgeries, researchers have proposed to segment the content into different operation phases [1] and detect surgical actions/tasks and events [2]. One basic step is instrument detection, which aims at detecting the usage of specific surgical instruments in the entire video/surgery. For example, Al Hajj et al. [3] have recently demonstrated instrument detection with high accuracy for 21 different types of instruments, using their dataset released for the CATARACTS challenge [4].

However, the usage of instruments and the quality of videos recorded for ophthalmic surgeries varies greatly between different hospitals. For example, videos in the CATARACTS dataset [4] were recorded with very good lighting conditions, nearly perfect focus, and full-HD resolution. In contrast, videos in the Cataract-101 dataset [5] were recorded with much smaller resolution and – more importantly – suffer from out-of-focus problems of the microscope and bad lighting conditions. Additionally, due to different instrument manufacturers and varying operation techniques, different instruments appear in the two datasets for the same action or purpose.

In this work we evaluate the generalization performance of instrument detection in cataract surgery for different datasets. More precisely, we train an instrument classifier for a dataset with high visual quality (the CATARACTS dataset [4], forth-on called *DS-A*) and test it with a dataset using much lower visual quality (the Cataract-101 dataset [5], forth-on called *DS-B*).

We show that with commonly used convolutional neural network (CNN) architectures – in particular ResNet-50 [6], Inception v3 [7] and NASNet Mobile [8] – it is possible to achieve high accuracy for the dataset the model is trained on. Furthermore, results show that it is possible to correctly detect some instruments in the other dataset, even though their visual appearance differs from instruments used for training.

However, when applying the model to a video dataset recorded in a different hospital (showing actions performed by different surgeons with slightly different instruments, and using video recording with a different visual quality), the performance strongly degrades. This is true for both directions in our evaluation – i.e., when applying a model trained on DS-A to DS-B, or vice versa. Even more interesting, the evaluations show that in average the models trained on DS-B (with lower visual quality) perform better on DS-A (with higher visual quality) than the models trained on DS-A and tested on DS-B. Finally, we found that the NASNet Mobile architecture [8], which is known for its superior performance with general image data, is outperformed by Inception v3 and ResNet in terms of generalization performance for the datasets tested in our work.

2 Related Work

A major part of research work published in the field of cataract surgery analysis is devoted to surgical workflow analysis, and in particular to the problem of automatically segmenting and recognizing surgical phases in video recordings. Early methods apply algorithms using motion features [9] or spatiotemporal polynomials [2], more recent methods are based on conditional random fields or hidden Markov models [10–12].

Due to the fact that usage of surgical tools is closely related to operational phases they are used in, research in this area soon focused on tool recognition. Recent methods apply convolutional neural networks (CNNs) to recognize surgical tools, either on the surgical tray [13] or when they are used for surgical actions [3,4,14,15]. In [14] a CNN is used to process a sequence of consecutive images for instrument classification, achieving an area under ROC curve (AuC) of 0.953. Tool recognition performance can be improved significantly when the temporal dependency between tool usage in cataract surgeries is modeled explicitly. In [15] and [3] a combination of a CNN and a recurrent neural network achieved an AuC of 0.9959 and 0.9961, respectively. From the various approaches submitted to recent editions of the CATARACTS challenge [4], the best-performing one achieved an AuC of 0.9865. Authors used an ensemble of CNNs to make predictions for each fame and then smoothed the predictions using a Markov Random Field.

3 Datasets

In order to evaluate generalizability of instrument detection, we used two publicly available datasets of cataract surgery videos. Both datasets are highly similar in terms of content, but quite different in terms of visual quality, as also described below. According to medical experts, a regular cataract surgery consists of 12 phases (*incision, viscoelastic, capsulorhexis, hydrodissection, phacolysation, irrigation/aspiration, capsule polishing, viscoelastic, IOL insertion, viscoelastic aspiration, sealing of incisions, antibiotic*). Each of them consists of one or more surgical actions performed with certain tools. Some of the instruments are specific for some phase, while others can be used in more than one phase.

3.1 CATARACTS Dataset (DS-A)

The first dataset consists of 25 videos of phacoemulsification cataract surgeries, performed in Brest University Hospital (France) between January 22, 2015 and September 10, 2015. It was used for the CATARACTS challenges [4] as training subset and led to outstanding tool recognition performance of >99% AuC for some instruments [4]. This dataset consists of age-related and traumatic cataract and refractive surgeries and has annotations for 21 different instruments. In each video frame up to three instruments can be visible. Tools are considered to be in use when they are in touch with the eye. The frame resolution of videos is 1920 × 1080 pixels and the frame rate is 30 fps. The visual quality is high in terms of lighting and focus; it contains almost no blurry frames. The dataset was annotated independently by two non-clinical experts. For this paper, we used only video frames where both experts agreed on the tool being used. More details about the CATARACTS dataset can be found in [4].

Figure 3 shows the class distribution of frames in the CATARACTS dataset (the tools are labeled by short identifiers explained in Sect. 3.3). Due to the different length of surgical phases there is an inherent class imbalance. This can result in decreased accuracy for minority classes when training instrument classifiers. In order to aobtain a balanced dataset, we randomly sampled 800 frames for each label/class. For a few instruments (*biomarker*, *needle holder*, *Mendez ring* and *Vannas scissors*) that had less than 800 examples, we applied an oversampling method for balancing the dataset (we did not use any data augmentation in this study). To gain the required frames amount for such classes, we first duplicated the existing frames until the frame number became equal or exceed 800, and then randomly sampled 800 examples from the obtained frames. The resulting dataset, which we call dataset *DS-A* throughout this paper, was randomly split into training, validation, and test subsets with a ratio of 70:15:15.

3.2 Cataract-101 Dataset (DS-B)

The second dataset is based on the Cataract-101 dataset [5] which was collected in 2017 and 2018 at Klinikum Klagenfurt (Austria) and recently released as an open dataset. It consists of 101 age-related cataract surgeries without serious complications and comes with ground truth for phase segmentation only. For evaluation of instrument classification in this study we randomly selected 26 videos and manually annotated them for instrument usage in cooperation with medical experts. In every video frame a maximum of two instruments can be visible.

Each surgical action in the dataset can be associated with a main instrument. If a second instrument is visible at the same time, it is used as a supportive instrument (e.g., to fix the eye). Only video frames where the main instrument is in touch with the eye were selected for this study. Due to the fact that the Cataract-101 dataset does not contain traumatic cataract surgeries, we were only able to annotate 10 types of instruments (see left part of Table 1). Furthermore, not all videos contain all 10 types of instruments. For example, the instrument *cannula* appears only in nine out of the 26 selected videos.

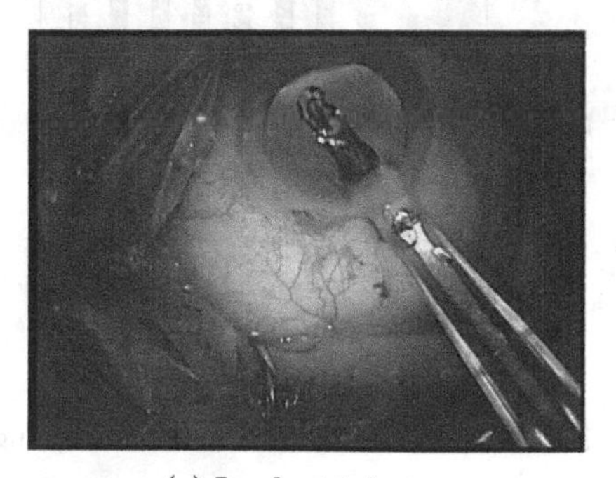

(a) Implant injector

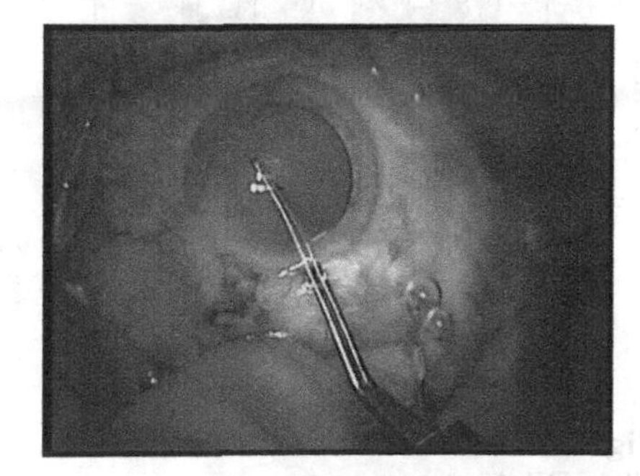

(b) Capsulorhexis forceps

Fig. 1. Example frames from DS-B with good quality.

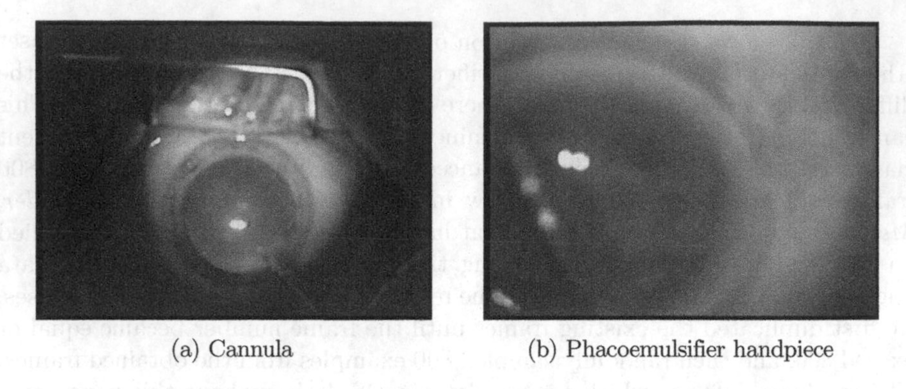

(a) Cannula (b) Phacoemulsifier handpiece

Fig. 2. Example frames from DS-B with bad quality.

Like DS-A, video frames in the selected video dataset display an inherent class imbalance of video frames, see Fig. 4 (instrument identifiers are explained in Sect. 3.3). As for DS-A, we randomly selected 800 video frames for each label/class in order to obtain a balanced dataset, called *DS-B* in this study, and randomly split it into training, validation, and test subsets using a ratio of 70:15:15.

Compared with DS-A, the videos of DS-B have a lower frame resolution of 720 × 540 pixels and a lower frame rate of 25 fps. Moreover, DS-B displays a larger variance in terms of zoom, lighting conditions, and blur level (obviously due to some focus problems and a lower-quality camera system than used for DS-A). Some example video frames of good quality are shown in Fig. 1, while others of low quality are depicted in Fig. 2. It seems obvious that such images pose a challenge for content classification, which is known to work better for higher image quality [16].

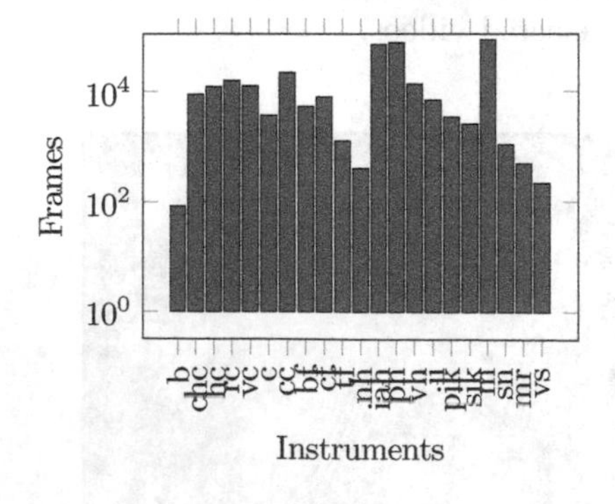

Fig. 3. Class imbalance before sampling DS-A

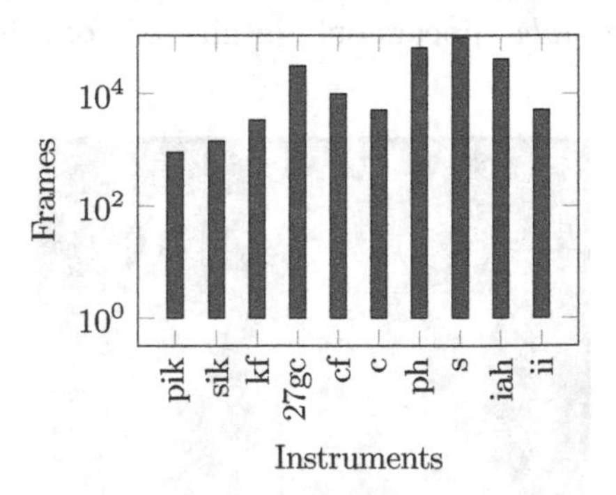

Fig. 4. Class imbalance before sampling DS-B

3.3 Mapping Instruments in Different Datasets

In addition to visual quality, the chosen datasets also differ in terms of used instruments (i.e., models and manufacturers, but also in the number of different instruments). However, in order to evaluate for generalization performance we need a mapping of similar instruments between the two datasets. Most of them can be mapped directly, due to similar names or by usage for the same purpose, as described in the following paragraph and illustrated in Table 1.

Table 1. Mapping instruments from DS-B to DS-A

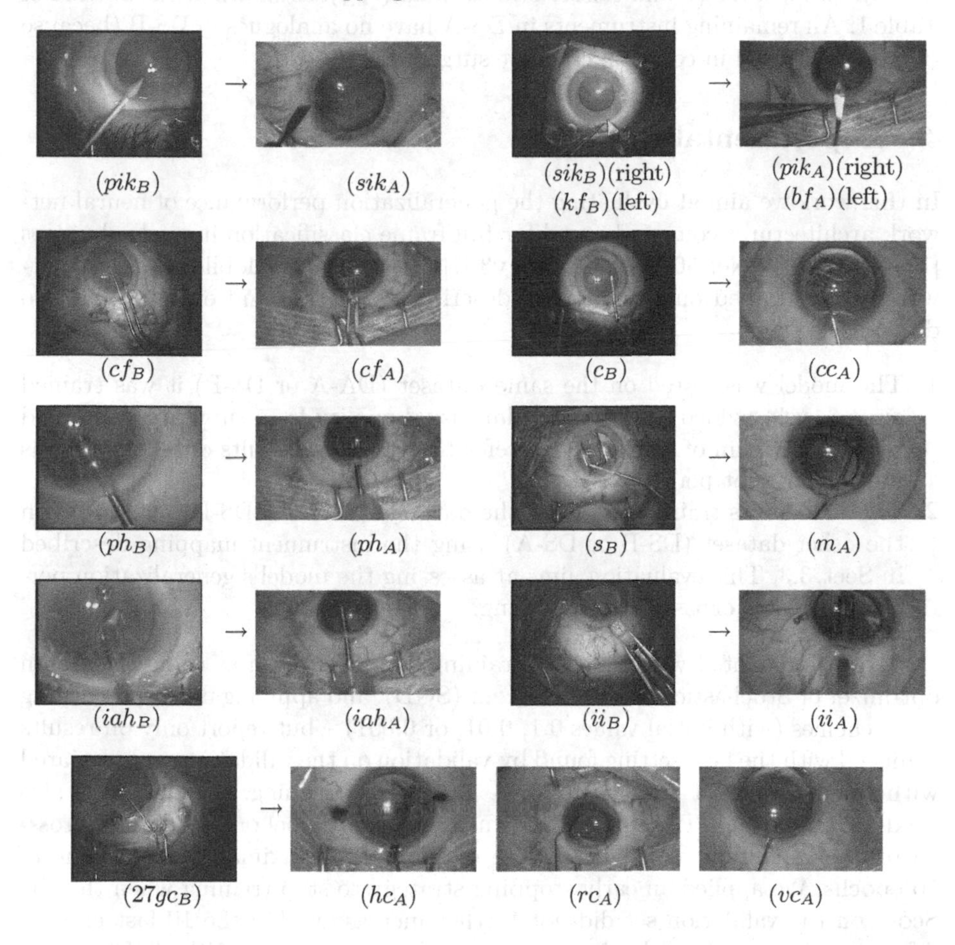

Direct mappings from DS-B (10 instruments) to DS-A (21 instruments) were found for the following instruments: *primary incision knife* (pik_B) → *secondary incision knife* (sik_A), *secondary incision knife* (sik_B) → *primary incision knife* (pik_A), *Katena forceps* (kf_B) → *Bonn forceps* (bf_A), *capsulorhexis forceps* (cf_B) → *capsulorhexis forceps* (cf_A), *cannula* (c_B) → *capsulorhexis cystotome* (cc_A), *phacoemulsifier handpiece* (ph_B) → *phacoemulsifier handpiece* (ph_A), *spatula*

(s_B) → *micromanipulator* (m_A), *irrigation/aspiration handpiece* (iah_B) → *irrigation/aspiration handpiece* (iah_A), *implant injector* (ii_B) → *implant injector* (ii_A). Some of the pairs are visually quite similar, e.g. phacoemulsifier handpieces and implant injectors, while others display a difference in visual appearance, like spatula and incision knives.

Although most of the classes from DS-B are mapped directly, one class has three corresponding classes in DS-A, because surgeons of DS-B use one type of cannula for different tasks, while surgeons of DS-A use different ones. The *27 gauge cannula* ($27gc_B$) therefore relates to *hydrodissection cannula* (hc_A), *Rycroft cannula* (rc_A), and *viscoelastic cannula* (rc_A), as shown at the bottom of Table 1. All remaining instruments in DS-A have no analogues in DS-B (because they are not used in common cataract surgeries).

4 Experimental Results

In this work we aim at evaluating the generalization performance of neural network architectures commonly used for full frame classification in medical videos [17], such as ResNet-50 [6], Inception v3 [7], and NASNet Mobile [8]. These networks were trained on the datasets described in Sect. 3 and evaluated in two different settings:

1. The model was tested on the same dataset (DA-A or DS-B) it was trained on; i.e., using video frames of similar visual quality from surgeries performed by a single team of surgeons. We refer to evaluation results of this setting as **single-dataset** performance.
2. The model was trained on one of the datasets (DS-A or DS-B) but tested on the other dataset (DS-B or DS-A) using the instrument mapping described in Sect. 3.3. This evaluation aims at assessing the model's generalization performance in a **cross-dataset** setting.

We experimented with different training settings – such as using the Adam optimizer or Stochastic Gradient Descent (SGD), and applying different learning rate schemes (with initial values 0.1, 0.01, or 0.001) – but report only on results achieved with the best setting found by validation on the validation set associated with the training set (i.e. when DS-A is used for training, then DS-A is also used for validation). Training is performed with multilabel output, binary cross-entropy as loss function, a batch size of 32, and a maximal training time of 50 epochs. We applied an early stopping strategy to stop training when the F1-Score on the validation set did not further increase within the 10 last epochs. After hyperparameter selection, the networks were trained with SGD and an initial learning rate of 0.01 that was decreased by a factor of 10 after every eight epochs. All networks were trained on an NVIDIA TITAN RTX N graphics card with 24 GB of RAM using the Keras framework with TensorFlow backend.

Results of single-dataset experiments (averaged over all instrument classes) are presented in Table 2 for DS-A and Table 3 for DS-B (IoU means *Intersection-over-Union* and represents partial accuracy). The best results across all networks for each dataset are highlighted in bold face. The results clearly show that the

Table 2. Average single-dataset performance on DS-A.

Architecture	Recall	Precision	Specificity	IoU	F1
ResNet-50	0.8335	0.9473	0.9976	0.8043	0.8798
Inception v3	0.9532	0.9642	0.9979	0.9224	0.9583
NASNet mobile	**0.9580**	**0.9700**	**0.9983**	**0.9320**	**0.9636**

Table 3. Average single-dataset performance on DS-B.

Architecture	Recall	Precision	Specificity	IoU	F1
ResNet-50	0.7998	0.9344	0.9932	0.7679	0.8533
Inception v3	0.9229	0.9510	0.9937	0.8857	0.9365
NASNet mobile	**0.9606**	**0.9654**	**0.9954**	**0.9299**	**0.9628**

mobile-optimized NASNet achieves the best performance for the single-dataset setting, while Inception v3 performs almost equally well, whereas ResNet-50 gives significantly worse results according to F1 measure.

Note that since we use multilabel classification (labels are k-dimensional binary vectors representing k instruments), accuracy is not an appropriate measure due to the high true negative rate for non-detected instruments. Therefore, we rely on the F1-score as our main evaluation criterion, which also correlates with the Intersection-over-Union measure (partial accuracy), according to presented results.

However, for cross-dataset performance the situation changes quite significantly. As shown in Tables 4 and 5, the performance drastically decreases to a maximum F1-score of 0.0844 when tested on DS-A, and to 0.0325 when tested on DS-B. For both datasets, ResNet-50 gave best results in Recall and F1-score, and NasNet Mobile in Specificity.

Table 4. Cross-dataset performance (trained on DS-B, tested on DS-A).

Architecture	Recall	Precision	Specificity	IoU	F1
ResNet-50	**0.2851**	0.1505	0.7542	**0.0465**	**0.0844**
Inception v3	0.0910	**0.1699**	0.9263	0.0452	0.0785
NASNet mobile	0.0862	0.0964	**0.9421**	0.0207	0.0383

Table 5. Cross-dataset performance (trained on DS-A, tested on DS-B).

Architecture	Recall	Precision	Specificity	IoU	F1
ResNet-50	**0.0643**	**0.0418**	0.9370	**0.0178**	**0.0325**
Inception v3	0.0292	0.0329	0.9628	0.0112	0.0210
NASNet mobile	0.0263	0.0405	**0.9747**	0.0117	0.0214

Although cross-dataset performance is surprisingly low for models trained on any of the two datasets, there seems to be a significant difference depending on whether models have been trained on the dataset with high (DS-A) or low (DS-B) visual quality. When trained on DS-A, ResNet-50 achieves only 6.43% recall and 4.18% precision on DS-B, whereas the same neural network trained on DS-B gives 28.51% recall and 15.05% precision on DS-A. We may therefore conclude that training with high-quality images seems to have a greater tendency to overfit than training with low-quality images, although high-quality images are known to be advantageous in single-dataset experiments [16].

Detailed results for individual classes achieved by ResNet-50 models are given in Tables 6 and 7. These results confirm the good single-dataset classification performance of the tested ResNet-50 models by displaying high F1-scores for all classes. However, when the same network trained on DS-A is applied to the test subset of DS-B, only five out of 12 mapped ground truth classes (i.e., 42%) are detected at all – with rather low F1-scores.

Table 6. Detailed performance of ResNet-50 trained on DS-A.

Tool	DS-A (single-dataset)					DS-B (cross-dataset/mapped)				
	Rec	Pre	Spe	IoU	F1	Rec	Pre	Spe	IoU	F1
(sik_A)	0.9496	0.9741	0.9985	0.9262	0.9617	**0.2773**	0.1209	0.7282	0.0919	**0.1684**
(ph_A)	0.7227	0.8776	0.9942	0.6565	0.7926	**0.0420**	0.0617	0.9139	0.0256	**0.0500**
(m_A)	0.6000	0.9474	0.9981	0.5806	0.7347	0.0000	0.0000	1.0000	0.0000	0.0000
(iah_A)	0.4750	0.8382	0.9947	0.4351	0.6064	0.0000	0.0000	1.0000	0.0000	0.0000
(ii_A)	0.7833	0.9495	0.9976	0.7520	0.8584	**0.3500**	0.1284	0.6769	0.1037	**0.1879**
(pik_A)	0.9076	0.9818	0.9990	0.8926	0.9432	**0.0252**	0.4286	0.9955	0.0244	**0.0476**
(bf_A)	0.8673	0.9515	0.9976	0.8305	0.9074	**0.6555**	0.1381	0.4485	0.1287	**0.2281**
(cf_A)	0.8417	0.9806	0.9990	0.8279	0.9058	0.0000	0.0000	1.0000	0.0000	0.0000
(cc_A)	0.7815	0.8857	0.9942	0.7099	0.8304	0.0000	0.0000	1.0000	0.0000	0.0000
(hc_A)	0.6500	0.9512	0.9981	0.6290	0.7723	0.0000	0.0000	1.0000	0.0000	0.0000
(rc_A)	0.5833	0.9333	0.9976	0.5600	0.7179	0.0000	0.0000	1.0000	0.0000	0.0000
(vc_A)	0.5254	0.8378	0.9942	0.4769	0.6458	0.0000	0.0000	1.0000	0.0000	0.0000
(b_A)	1.0000	1.0000	1.0000	1.0000	1.0000	0.0000	0.0000	1.0000	0.0000	0.0000
(c_A)	0.9833	0.9833	0.9990	0.9672	0.9833	0.0000	0.0000	1.0000	0.0000	0.0000
(chc_A)	0.9417	0.9576	0.9976	0.9040	0.9496	0.0000	0.0000	1.0000	0.0000	0.0000
(mr_A)	1.0000	1.0000	1.0000	1.0000	1.0000	0.0000	0.0000	0.9301	0.0000	0.0000
(nh_A)	1.0000	0.9672	0.9981	0.9672	0.9833	0.0000	0.0000	1.0000	0.0000	0.0000
(sn_A)	0.9655	0.9912	0.9995	0.9573	0.9782	0.0000	0.0000	0.9990	0.0000	0.0000
(tf_A)	0.9746	0.9350	0.9961	0.9127	0.9544	0.0000	0.0000	1.0000	0.0000	0.0000
(vh_A)	0.9500	0.9500	0.9971	0.9048	0.9500	0.0000	0.0000	0.9840	0.0000	0.0000
(vs_A)	1.0000	1.0000	1.0000	1.0000	1.0000	0.0000	0.0000	1.0000	0.0000	0.0000

When the same network is trained on DS-B, it is able to detect six out of 10 mapped ground truth classes (60%) in the test subset of DS-A – instruments (ph_B), (s_B), (iah_B), and (ii_B) are not detected due to confusion with

Table 7. Detailed performance of ResNet-50 trained on DS-B.

Tool	DS-B (single-dataset)					DS-A (cross-dataset/mapped)				
	Rec	Pre	Spe	IoU	F1	Rec	Pre	Spe	IoU	F1
(pik_B)	0.9664	1.0000	1.0000	0.9664	0.9829	**0.6471**	0.1264	0.5529	0.1183	**0.2115**
(ph_B)	0.8571	0.9533	0.9943	0.8226	0.9027	0.0000	0.0000	1.0000	0.0000	0.0000
(s_B)	0.6218	0.8222	0.9819	0.5481	0.7081	0.0000	0.0000	1.0000	0.0000	0.0000
(iah_B)	0.5294	0.7875	0.9807	0.4632	0.6332	0.0000	0.0000	1.0000	0.0000	0.0000
(ii_B)	0.8583	0.9196	0.9898	0.7984	0.8879	0.0000	0.0000	1.0000	0.0000	0.0000
(sik_B)	0.9496	1.0000	1.0000	0.9496	0.9741	**0.6218**	0.1375	0.6101	0.1269	**0.2253**
(kf_B)	0.8571	0.9903	0.9989	0.8500	0.9189	**0.1062**	0.0563	0.8319	0.0382	**0.0736**
$(27gc_B)$	0.4500	0.9474	0.9966	0.4390	0.6102	**0.0028**	1.0000	1.0000	0.0028	**0.0056**
(cf_B)	0.9083	0.9397	0.9921	0.8583	0.9237	**0.6583**	0.0866	0.2994	0.0829	**0.1531**
(c_B)	1.0000	0.9836	0.9977	0.9836	0.9917	**0.8151**	0.0978	0.2479	0.0957	**0.1746**

other instruments – with a similar per-class performance as in the cross-dataset experiment of the model trained on DS-A.

We suspect the reason for the problem of missing several classes in cross-dataset experiments to be the rather small size of the dataset (800 images per label) and the fact that no transfer learning has been used in this study (this will be addressed in future work).

5 Conclusions

In this work we have evaluated the generalizability of instrument detection in videos from cataract surgeries for two different datasets with significantly different visual quality. Our evaluation results show that the selected neural network models achieve good performance when trained and tested on separate data from the same dataset. It also shows a significant performance drop when the model is tested with data from the other dataset (i.e., with cross-dataset evaluation). However, interestingly our results further show that the dataset with lower visual quality (DS-B) enables better results in terms of cross-dataset evaluation. In future work we want to perform additional evaluations with larger datasets, transfer learning, and several data augmentation methods.

Acknowledgments. This work was funded by the FWF Austrian Science Fund under grant P 31486-N31.

References

1. Primus, M.J., et al.: Frame-based classification of operation phases in cataract surgery videos. In: Schoeffmann, K., et al. (eds.) MMM 2018. LNCS, vol. 10704, pp. 241–253. Springer, Cham (2018). https://doi.org/10.1007/978-3-319-73603-7_20
2. Quellec, G., Lamard, M., Cochener, B., Cazuguel, G.: Real-time task recognition in cataract surgery videos using adaptive spatiotemporal polynomials. IEEE Trans. Med. Imaging **34**(4), 877–887 (2014)

3. Hajj, H.A., Lamard, M., Conze, P.-H., Cochener, B., Quellec, G.: Monitoring tool usage in surgery videos using boosted convolutional and recurrent neural networks. Med. Image Anal. **47**, 203–218 (2018)
4. Hajj, H.A., et al.: CATARACTS: challenge on automatic tool annotation for cataract surgery. Med. Image Anal. **52**, 24–41 (2019)
5. Schoeffmann, K., Taschwer, M., Sarny, S., Münzer, B., Primus, M.J., Putzgruber, D.: Cataract-101: video dataset of 101 cataract surgeries. In: Proceedings of the 9th ACM Multimedia Systems Conference, pp. 421–425. ACM (2018)
6. He, K., Zhang, X., Ren, S., Sun, J.: Deep residual learning for image recognition. In: Proceedings of the IEEE Conference on Computer Vision and Pattern Recognition, pp. 770–778 (2016)
7. Szegedy, C., Vanhoucke, V., Ioffe, S., Shlens, J., Wojna, Z.: Rethinking the inception architecture for computer vision. CoRR, vol. abs/1512.00567 (2015)
8. Zoph, B., Vasudevan, V., Shlens, J., Le, Q.V.: Learning transferable architectures for scalable image recognition. CoRR, vol. abs/1707.07012 (2017)
9. Charrière, K., Quellec, G., Lamard, M., Coatrieux, G., Cochener, B., Cazuguel, G.: Automated surgical step recognition in normalized cataract surgery videos. In: 2014 36th Annual International Conference of the IEEE Engineering in Medicine and Biology Society, pp. 4647–4650, August 2014
10. Quellec, G., Lamard, M., Cochener, B., Cazuguel, G.: Real-time segmentation and recognition of surgical tasks in cataract surgery videos. IEEE Trans. Med. Imaging **33**(12), 2352–2360 (2014)
11. Charriere, K., et al.: Real-time multilevel sequencing of cataract surgery videos. In: 2016 14th International Workshop on Content-Based Multimedia Indexing (CBMI), pp. 1–6, June 2016
12. Charrière, K., et al.: Real-time analysis of cataract surgery videos using statistical models. Multimed. Tools Appl. **76**(21), 22473–22491 (2017)
13. Al Hajj, H., Lamard, M., Cochener, B., Quellec, G.: Smart data augmentation for surgical tool detection on the surgical tray. In: 2017 39th Annual International Conference of the IEEE Engineering in Medicine and Biology Society (EMBC), pp. 4407–4410, July 2017
14. Al Hajj, H., Lamard, M., Charrière, K., Cochener, B., Quellec, G.: Surgical tool detection in cataract surgery videos through multi-image fusion inside a convolutional neural network. In: 2017 39th Annual International Conference of the IEEE Engineering in Medicine and Biology Society (EMBC), pp. 2002–2005, July 2017
15. Zisimopoulos, O., et al.: DeepPhase: surgical phase recognition in CATARACTS videos. In: Frangi, A.F., Schnabel, J.A., Davatzikos, C., Alberola-López, C., Fichtinger, G. (eds.) MICCAI 2018. LNCS, vol. 11073, pp. 265–272. Springer, Cham (2018). https://doi.org/10.1007/978-3-030-00937-3_31
16. Halevy, A., Norvig, P., Pereira, F.: The unreasonable effectiveness of data. IEEE Intell. Syst. **24**(2), 8–12 (2009)
17. Vardazaryan, A., Mutter, D., Marescaux, J., Padoy, N.: Weakly-supervised learning for tool localization in laparoscopic videos. In: Stoyanov, D., et al. (eds.) LABELS/CVII/STENT-2018. LNCS, vol. 11043, pp. 169–179. Springer, Cham (2018). https://doi.org/10.1007/978-3-030-01364-6_19

SS6: Intelligent Multimedia Security

Compact Position-Aware Attention Network for Image Semantic Segmentation

Yajun Xu[1], Zhendong Mao[2(✉)], Peng Zhang[1], and Bin Wang[3]

[1] Institute of Information Engineering, School of Cyber Security, Chinese Academy of Sciences, Beijing, China
{xuyajun,pengzhang}@iie.ac.cn
[2] University of Science and Technology of China, Hefei, China
maozhendong2008@gmail.com
[3] Xiaomi AI Lab, Beijing, China
wangbin11@xiaomi.com

Abstract. In intelligent multimedia security, automatic image semantic segmentation is a fundamental research, which facilitates to accurately recognizing important targets from multimedia data and performing subsequent security analysis. Most existing semantic segmentation methods have made remarkable progress via modeling interactions between image pixels based on fully convolutional networks (FCN). However, they neglect the fact that semantic features extracted by FCN have poor ability to represent original image details, which always makes it hard to attend true positive relevant information within adjacent regions in spatial position for interactions modeling based methods. To tackle above problem, we take position information into account and adaptively model position relevance between pixels for enhancing local consistent in segmentation results. We propose a novel compact position-aware attention network (CPANet), containing spatial augmented attention module and channel augmented attention module, to simultaneously learn semantic relevance and position relevance between image pixels in a mutually reinforced way. In spatial augmented module, we introduce relative height and width distance to model position relevance based on self-attention mechanism. In channel augmented module, we exploit bilinear pooling to model compact correlation between pixels at any position across any channels. Our proposed CPANet can mutually learn accurate position and semantic of image pixels in a compact manner for improving semantic segmentation performance. Experimental results demonstrate that our approach has achieved the state-of-the-art performance in Cityscapes dataset.

Keywords: Intelligent multimedia security · Semantic segmentation · Self-attention · Semantic relevance · Position relevance

Supported by the National Key Research and Development Program of China (grants No. 2016YFB0800902) and the National Natural Science Foundation of China (grants No. 61502477).

Y. M. Ro et al. (Eds.): MMM 2020, LNCS 11962, pp. 639–650, 2020.
https://doi.org/10.1007/978-3-030-37734-2_52

1 Introduction

Semantic segmentation is an essential and fundamental research, which aims at segmenting the given image into object-category image regions. This study develops a large group of various successful applications such as intelligent multimedia security, where some important objects in multimedia image data can be recognized and subsequent security analysis works can be employed successfully. Fully convolutional networks (FCN) [11] is a typical and effective framework to accomplish semantic segmentation task. The successive convolution and pooling operations in FCN framework promote to extract deep semantic features, while the dependencies between pixels are still limited to simple overlap of convolution calculating kernels. It is necessary to further enrich interactions between pixels and capture comprehensive contextual information for boosting segmentation performance.

Recently, most existing frameworks [6,8,17,20] demonstrate astonishing results via modeling relationship between pixels based on FCN. Among these works, one of the efficient strategy is multi-scale information fusion, which aggregates generated features with multiple scales to encode object context for each pixel location [17]. Some model captures pixel-wise contextual information via combining feature maps with learnable attention maps [20]. Another type of works adopt self-attention mechanism learned from transformer model [14]. For example, Fu et al. [6] explicitly models long-range dependencies between all pixel pairs according to their semantic similarities and refines feature representations with global relationship. Huang et al. [8] designs a lightweight criss-cross module to replace heavy similarities calculation in non-local network [16]. However, these methods neglect the fact that semantic features are lacking in representing original image details. This makes it hard to attend true positive relevant information within spatial adjacent regions for interactions modeling based methods, which leads to producing inaccurate and unmatched label assignments. Therefore it is indispensable to take into consideration of spatial position information in relationship modeling for accurately semantic segmentation results prediction.

To address above problems, we introduce relative distance between pixels in original images. Through embedding position-aware information into the prediction process of attention maps learning, our method can enhance the ability in relationship modeling. Specifically, we propose a novel framework, called as compact position-aware attention network (CPANet), which is illustrated in Fig. 1. It consists of two key modules: spatial augmented attention module and channel augmented attention module. The spatial augmented attention module is designed to attend similar features in semantic and position via integrating relative height and width information based on self-attention modeling. Meanwhile, the channel augmented attention module takes responsibilities for constructing compact relationship across different channels at any position and obtaining relevant features. With flexible distance constraints, we can focus on refining feature maps with their semantic relevance and position relevance, which further facilitates to capturing compact contextual interactions. The contributions of our paper can be summarized as follows:

1. We design novel position-aware attention modules from spatial and channel dimension to enhance compact interactions between image pixels in a mutually reinforced way.
2. We propose a compact position-aware network taking advantage of augmented attention modules for capturing contextual information flexibly.
3. Extensive experimental results on Cityscapes dataset demonstrate the effectiveness of our proposed CPANet compared with the state-of-the-arts.

2 Related Work

Semantic Segmentation. Most existing semantic segmentation methods [1,3,15,19] based on FCN have achieved remarkable progress on different benchmarks. FCN based framework is a typical encoder-decoder structure, which is designed to extract semantic features with successive convolutional layers in encoder stage. Meanwhile decoder stage predicts labeling results using fully convolutional layer and restore resolution with upsampling operations. The common challenge in semantic segmentation task exists in how to accurately predicting image semantic while capturing image details. Recently, state-of-the-art segmentation methods are mainly working on address above problem. Some works mainly focus on designing novel module to replace problematic ones in FCN framework. Wang et al. [15] propose dense learnable upsampling module and remove ambiguous parameter-free upsampling component. Chen et al. [2] exploit dilated convolution to alleviate resolution loss instead of regular max pooling, while U-net directly [13] adds skip-connections to enhance structure prediction ability. Noh et al. [12] apply the proposed de-convolution and un-pooling layer to efficiently restore the resolution of segmentation results. However, this branch of methods just recover and preserve the image details without consideration of diverse feature representation. This leads to the emergency of inconsistent problems in segmentation results.

Another types of works have proven that capturing contextual information can further enrich feature representation and boost segmentation performance. Liu et al. [10] introduce global average pooling to encode global image content while Zhao et al. [19] apply the spatial pyramid pooling to extract multi-scale feature. Chen et al. [2] propose atrous spatial pyramid pooling to enlarge the receptive fields on feature extraction procedure. Chen et al. [3] build multi-scale architectures with search techniques. Peng et al. [1] propose global convolutional network to guide contextual information aggregation. Our network is belonged to this direction and utilize a compact strategy to harvest contextual information by considering semantic and detail content simultaneously.

Attention Mechanism. Attention mechanism is a general and efficient tool and has been widely used in a variety of research topics. Attention based modules haven been adopted to tackle semantic segmentation task in recent years. For example, Chen et al. [4] firstly use attention mechanism to fuse multi-scale feature maps in semantic segmentation task. Squeeze-and-Excitation [9] framework explores channel-wise relationships with attention mechanism to improve

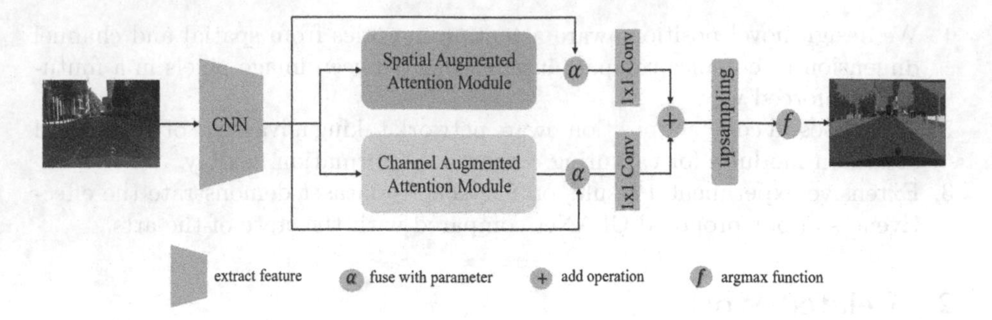

Fig. 1. Compact position-aware attention network for image semantic segmentation

the modeling ability of ConvNets. These works take advantage of powerful representation ability via fusing multi-level features with learned weights separately from spatial and channel dimension. While above methods lack relationships between image pixels and have the limitation to capturing contextual information, which brings inconsistent segmenting objects in labeling assignment results. Non-local module [16] is proposed to collect global context by calculating similarity between pixels. OCNet [17] and CCNet [8] further extend non-local module in different strategies to capture dense contextual information. PSANet [20] aggregates multi-level feature maps with their produced attention maps directly. Our work also takes advantage of self-attention to build semantic segmentation framework but is different to above attention based methods. We focus on addressing existing demerits of semantic features extracted by FCN and novelly introduce relative distance to model spatial location relationships. Our proposed CPANet can model compact relationships between image pixels via integrating semantic relevance and position relevance.

3 Method

In this section, we first describe our proposed compact position-aware attention network containing spatial augmented module and channel augmented module. Then we separately elaborate how these two modules capture contextual interactions between pixels from semantic and position relevance in a compact manner. Finally, we give the details of our complete network architecture for semantic segmentation task.

3.1 Overall

The framework of our network is given in Fig. 1. Given an input image, the goal of our segmentation network is to assign each pixel with certain category label in image. A given image I is fed into convolutional neural network (CNN, which is the former part of FCN), producing feature maps. Then this feature map is passed through two augmented attention modules in parallel, separately

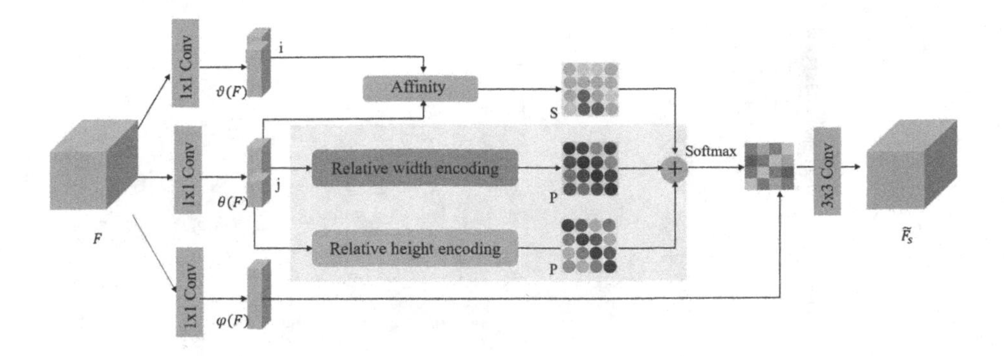

Fig. 2. Spatial augmented module

yielding fused feature maps with learnable parameter weights assignment. These produced feature maps are transformed into semantic score maps with 1×1 fully convolutional layers. Adding operation on these two score maps in final score map. For ensuring efficient gradient propagating, we introduce residual connection through identity mapping operation during two augmented attention pathes. Finally, our network performs up-sampling with original image size on score map and predicts label of each pixel via argmax function along channel dimensionality. The whole framework is named as CPANet, and our key contribution are spatial augmented modules and channel augmented module.

3.2 Spatial Augmented Module

Recently, modern attention based methods propose to capture long-range context via non-local module [16]. However, their approaches are short of modeling spatial position relationship of image pixels, which leads to miss relevant feature in local adjacent regions. The essential problem consists in inherent demerit of semantic features. Since modeling on semantic features alone only attend relevant feature in semantic. The true positive relevant information have been lost in the learning process about similarity calculations.

In order to compensate for the missing spatial location in the process of relationship modeling with semantic features, we introduce position information of original image spaces and novelly design a position-aware self-attention method to model interactions of image pixels. The detail design of spatial augmented module can be shown in Fig. 2. Suppose that given the local feature map $F \in \mathbb{R}^{W \times H \times C}$, where W, H, C represents width, height and the number of channel respectively. The attention operation computes updated feature maps $\tilde{F}_s$ via the weighted sum of the features F (Fig. 3),

$$\tilde{F}_s = \alpha f(\theta(F), \vartheta(F), \phi(F))\varphi(F) + F \tag{1}$$

where $\theta(\cdot), \vartheta(\cdot), \phi(\cdot), \varphi(\cdot)$ are learnable transformations on the input F. α is initialized as zero and gradually learns to assign more weight during network

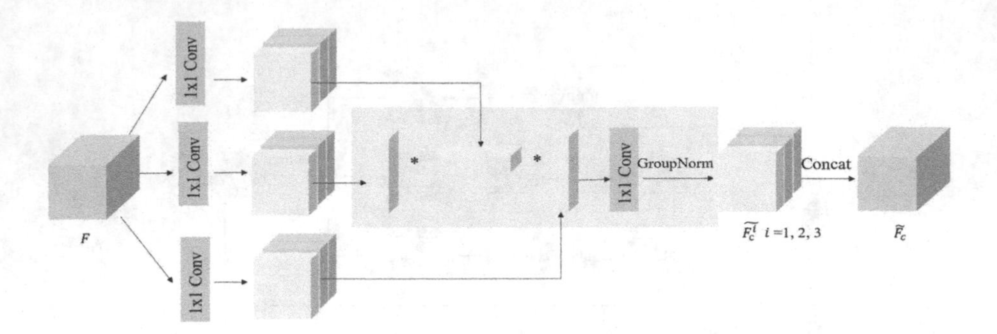

Fig. 3. Channel augmented module

training. The function $f(\cdot,\cdot,\cdot)$ corresponds to our position-aware augmented self-attention, which can be formulated as:

$$f(\theta(F), \vartheta(F), \phi(F)) = Softmax(\theta(F)\vartheta(F)^T + \phi(F)) \tag{2}$$

where $\theta(F)\vartheta(F)^T$ is semantic affinities and $\phi(F)$ is position affinities for all pixel pairs. we apply the softmax operation to generate attention map. The location of each pixel can be described into two dimension axis in original image. Similarly, We model spatial location relationship in position affinity part via encoding relative height and width distance information. Through relative height and width encoding, our module can learn the position affinity from two directions.

In this module, we apply three convolution layers with 1×1 filters as transformations to reduce dimensionality and get three feature maps $\theta(F), \vartheta(F), \varphi(F) \in \mathbb{R}^{W\times H\times C'}$. We flatten above three matrix into $\mathbb{R}^{N\times C'}$, where $N = W \times H$. The semantic affinities can be calculated as $\theta(F)\vartheta(F)^T$, notated as S, which is the inner product of the C dimension feature vector in spatial direction. The entry in S satisfies $S[i,j] = q_i k_j^T$, where q_i is the row vector of matrix $\theta(F)$ and k_j is the column vector of matrix $\vartheta(F)^T$ (They are corresponding to position i in the flattened matrix $\theta(F)$ and position j in the flattened matrix $\vartheta(F)$). As for the position term of $\phi(F)$, it can be extended as

$$\phi(F) = g(\theta(F)W_\phi^h) + g(\theta(F)W_\phi^w) \tag{3}$$

where W_ϕ^h, W_ϕ^w are learned relative height embedding and width embedding. We exploit the skew function $g(\cdot,\cdot)$ referenced to [7], which is a simple and efficient training mode, to inference these relative position affinities with flattened matrix $\theta(F)$. As the same as semantic affinities, we notate relative width affinity as P, where the entry $P[i,j]$ is learned width affinity between position i and position j in matrix $\theta(F)$. The affinity learning in height direction are analogous to the width one. Our spatial augmented module optimize local consistency of segmentation results through capturing position relevance and semantic relevance of per pixel pairs simultaneously.

3.3 Channel Augmented Module

The channel augmented module aims to select and enhance semantic relevant features via typical bilinear pooling method. Inspired to the success [18] in discriminating relevant features in fine-grained objects, we exploit bilinear pooling across channels to attend and extract significant features in a compact manner. Different to spatial augmented module, our channel augmented module improves semantic segmentation performance via modeling pixels interactions in channel dimension.

As shown in Fig. 4, we divide feature map $F \in \mathbb{R}^{W \times H \times C}$ into disjoint groups along channel direction, each group represent $F_i \in \mathbb{R}^{W \times H \times C''}$, where $C'' = C/G$ (G is the number of group). For attending relevant significant features across different channels, each group further flatten into vector $\mathbb{R}^{N''}$, where $N'' = W \times H \times C''$. The channel augmented module can be formulated as:

$$\tilde{F}_c = concat(BN(\tilde{F}_c^i)) + F \tag{4}$$

$$\tilde{F}_c^i = \theta(F^i)\vartheta(F^i)^T\varphi(F^i) \tag{5}$$

where $\theta(F^i), \vartheta(F^i)^T$ is bilinear pooling representation, which models semantic affinities between pixels at any position of any channel, Different from above spatial augmented module, the dot product formulation without Softmax function is an simplified kernel to extract features in bilinear pooling feature space. With matrix associative law, the implementation on trilinear equation can be largely reduced computations via firstly calculating latter two. For reducing the data shifting after division, we apply group normalization on disjoint groups and fuse into feature maps with concat function. Analogue to spatial augmented module, $\theta(\cdot), \vartheta(\cdot), \varphi(\cdot)$ can be applied convolution layers with 1×1.

4 Experiments

We evaluate our approach on the standard benchmark Cityscapes [5]. Our baseline is DANet [6], which applies self-attention mechanism to model long-range interactions between image pixels. Our segmentation performance is evaluated by the metric of mean intersection-over-union(mean IOU). In the following, we first describe the cityscapes dataset and our employed data processing techniques in experiments, then show the implementation details related to our proposed network, finally expound experimental results on cityscapes in the aspects of qualitative and quantitative analysis.

4.1 Cityscapes Datasets

The cityscapes is a well-known semantic segmentation dataset which contains large amount of urban street scene photos from the perspective of cars. Cityscapes dataset covers about 30 classes, of which 19 classes are used for semantic segmentation task. There are 3479 images provided with annotations. We split the whole dataset into training set, validation set and testing set. All images have 2048×1024 resolution. For data augmentation, we adopt random horizontal flipping and random scale on 0.5 to 2. We crop input images into 691×691 size in training stage, which is an important factor to improve segmentation performance apparently. For inference stage, we still use sliding window with fixed size 691×691, moving 3 strides to predict labeling results. The scales are set as 0.5, 0.75, 1, 1.5, 1.75, 2.0 on the final predictions.

4.2 Implementation Details

We conduct our experiments on PyTorch deep learning frameworks. We train our network using min-batch stochastic gradient descent (SGD) with 0.9 momentum. Due to the limited resources of GPU, we set 4 batch sizes with synchronized batch normalization on 4 GPUs. The maximum epoch number is set to 140 epoches, with 0.0004 weight decay. Inspired by the traditional settings, we still use the "poly" learning rate policy, which is multiplied by $(1 - \frac{iter}{maxiters})^{power}$ with 0.9 power and $4e^{-3}$ initial learning rate. We use ResNet101 with dilated convolution as our network backbone to extract initial image features and our initial parameters are pretrained on the ImageNet dataset. For accelerating the convergency of new added layers in network, the initial learning rate is set to 5 times higher than old layers in actual training process.

4.3 Experimental Results

Comparing with State-of-the-Arts. For evaluating the effectiveness of our proposed CPANet, we compare our testing results with the current state-of-the-art methods on the Cityscapes datasets. The results are illustrated in Table 1 and we can see that our method achieves top performance over all previous methods based on ResNet-101 backbone. The compared methods are centering on learning semantic relationship between image pixels, while they lose spatial location relationship in the original images. We employ a typical attention based work [6] as our baseline and optimize it with our proposed spatial augmented module and channel augmented module in a mutually reinforced way. The improved segmentation result on Cityscapes shows that it is important to modeling compact and comprehensive relationships between pixels via taking position and semantic into consideration, especially for dense scene parsing task.

The visualization results of our method are illustrated in Fig. 4. We randomly show some examples of the validation sets in Cityscapes dataset. For every row, we list (a)input images, (b) produced results of DANet [6], which is our baseline, (c) produced results of our proposed CPANet, which is our proposed model, and (d) the ground truth. Some objects can be kept consistency with the constraint of relative distance in adjacent regions. Some indistinguishable objects can be

Table 1. Comparison to state-of-the arts on the testing set of Cityscapes. Our approach achieves top performance over the state-of-the arts.

Method	Mean IoU (%)
GCN [1]	76.9
PSPNet [19]	78.4
DeepLab-v2 [2]	70.4
DUC [15]	77.6
PSANet [20]	78.6
OCNet [17]	80.1
Ours	**80.9**

recognized and assigned accurately. For example, as for the blue bus of red dotted rectangular region in the second row, it can be seen that some regions belonged to object bus is misclassified in the baseline. Our method can take advantage of local consistency and smooth it accurately. In terms of the third row, the vegetation object is hardly found in the baseline compared to the ground truth. While these subtle and tiny regions can be successfully figured out by ours and we can segment more accurate and complete results. The visual analysis in Cityscapes dataset further demonstrates the superiority of our method.

Ablation Study. We apply channel and spatial augmented module on top of the dilated convolutional backbone for modeling compact relationship between image pixels. To verify the effectiveness of spatial augmented module and channel augmented module separately, we conduct extra experiments with each separate module and evaluate segmentation performance in Cityscapes testing sets. We notated that our spatial augmented module as SAM, channel augmented module as CAM, combinations of both as CAM plus SAM (CPANet).

As shown in Table 2, different augmented modules improve segmentation results to different extent. Compared to baseline, employing position relevance in spatial augmented module yields results of 80.14%, which brings approximately 1.09% improvement. For the channel augmented module, we exploit bilinear pooling to extract compact features of any position across any channels, the segmentation results outperform baseline about 0.35% in mean IoU. Combining both, our proposed CPANet gets a larger improvement by 1.83%. The above statistic results show that our designed network can achieve a top performance through integrating spatial augmented and channel augmented modules in a mutually reinforced manner. It means that each module can work, but not remarkable in part.

Table 2. The effect of baseline, our channel augmented module (CAM), our spatial augmented module (SAM) and our CPANet (the combination of CAM and SAM). Submodule and combination are all higher than baseline, while combination are more remarkable than each separated module.

Method	Mean IoU (%)
baseline	79.05
Ours(CAM)	79.40 (↑ 0.35%)
Ours(SAM)	80.14 (↑ 1.09%)
Ours(CAM+SAM)	80.88 (↑ 1.83%)

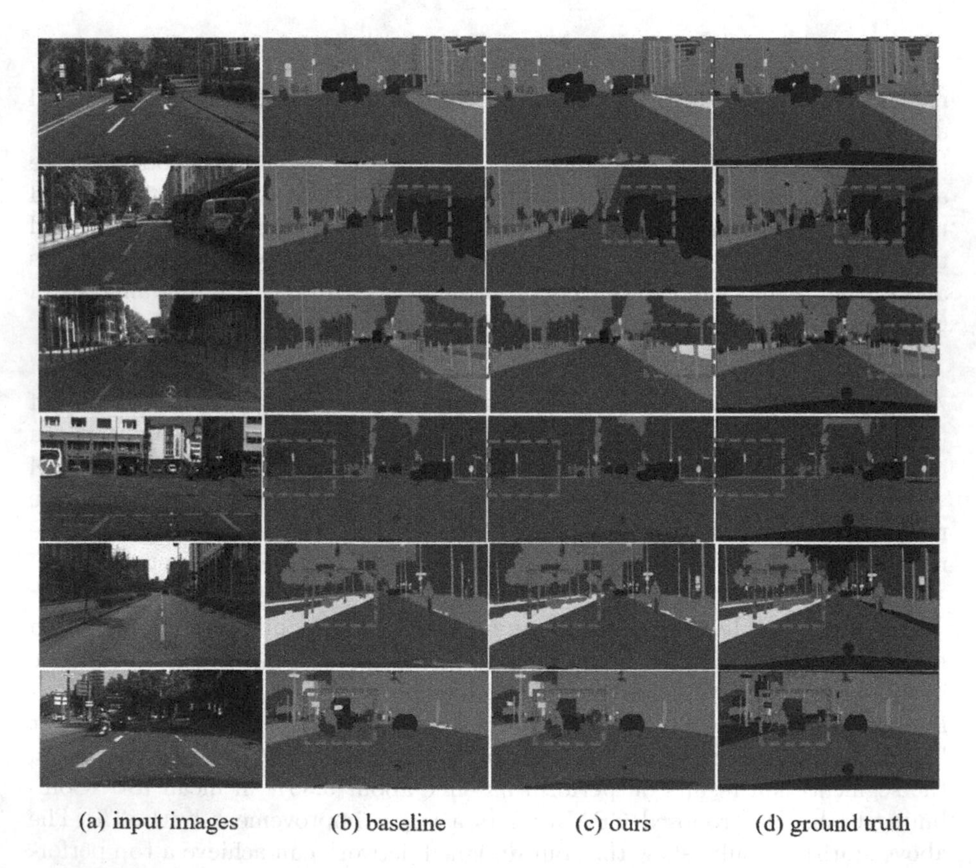

Fig. 4. Examples of semantic segmentation results on Cityscapes validation sets. For every row we list input images (a), produced results of DANet, which is our baseline (b), produced results of our proposed CPANet (c), the ground truth (d). Our Proposed CPANet gets more complete and accurate segmentation results than baseline. (Color figure online)

Table 3. The top10 category IoU on Cityscapes testing set. Deep gray color and light gray color separately represent the scores ranking in the first and second place on each category.

Method	s.walk	build.	t.light	t.sign	veg.	terrain	rider	car	bus	train
baseline	84.72	93.08	73.81	80.79	92.96	66.18	63.24	95.67	85.40	78.13
Ours(CAM)	85.42	93.05	73.46	80.40	92.97	67.05	65.25	95.48	86.23	78.83
Ours(SAM)	85.81	93.50	75.56	82.43	93.10	66.84	68.81	96.01	84.51	80.13
Ours(SAM+CAM)	85.71	94.60	75.60	82.64	93.15	67.47	69.13	96.02	89.85	80.35

Furthermore, we list the top10 category IoU on Cityscapes testing sets in Table 3. These selected categories occupy the majority of whole dataset. From Table 3, we observe that our method no matter separated submodule or combinations all outperforms baseline at reported category. For comparing effectiveness separately, we use deep gray color and light gray color to identify the scores ranking in first and second place at each category. As illustrated in deep gray color regions, we can obtain that combination is superior to individuals in almost categories. As for the light gray colored regions, we can figure out SAM is the majority, and CAM appears minor. This statistics states that our spatial augmented module is more effect in channel augmented module. While integrating both together, which is designed by our CPANet, can take advantage of both modules and significantly improves the segmentation performance.

5 Conclusion

In this paper, we propose a compact position-aware attention network (CPANet) for image semantic segmentation task. Our network mainly consists of two key modules: spatial augmented attention module and channel augmented attention module. With two parallel path, our segmentation network can extract the compact and accurate relevant features in terms of semantic and position simultaneously. Our relation modeling method can capture spatial location relationship and semantic relationship of image pixels with our position-aware augmented attention mechanism. Our experimental results demonstrate the effectiveness of our proposed CPANet.

References

1. Peng, C., Zhang, X., Yu, G., Luo, G., Sun, J.: Large kernel matters - improve semantic segmentation by global convolutional network (2017)
2. Chen, L.C., Papandreou, G., Kokkinos, I., Murphy, K., Yuille, A.L.: DeepLab: semantic image segmentation with deep convolutional nets, atrous convolution, and fully connected CRFs. IEEE Trans. Pattern Anal. Mach. Intell. **40**(4), 834–848 (2018)
3. Chen, L.C., et al.: Searching for efficient multi-scale architectures for dense image prediction (2018)

4. Chen, L.C., Yi, Y., Jiang, W., Wei, X., Yuille, A.L.: Attention to scale: scale-aware semantic image segmentation. In: IEEE Conference on Computer Vision and Pattern Recognition (2016)
5. Cordts, M., et al.: The cityscapes dataset for semantic urban scene understanding (2016)
6. Fu, J., Liu, J., Tian, H., Fang, Z., Lu, H.: Dual attention network for scene segmentation (2018)
7. Huang, C.Z.A., et al.: Music transformer (2018)
8. Huang, Z., Wang, X., Huang, L., Huang, C., Wei, Y., Liu, W.: CCNet: criss-cross attention for semantic segmentation (2018)
9. Jie, H., Li, S., Albanie, S., Gang, S., Wu, E.: Squeeze-and-excitation networks **PP**(99), 1–1 (2017)
10. Liu, W., Rabinovich, A., Berg, A.C.: ParseNet: looking wider to see better. Comput. Sci. (2015)
11. Long, J., Shelhamer, E., Darrell, T.: Fully convolutional networks for semantic segmentation. IEEE Trans. Pattern Anal. Mach. Intell. **39**(4), 640–651 (2014)
12. Noh, H., Hong, S., Han, B.: Learning deconvolution network for semantic segmentation. In: IEEE International Conference on Computer Vision (2015)
13. Ronneberger, O., Fischer, P., Brox, T.: U-net: convolutional networks for biomedical image segmentation. In: International Conference on Medical Image Computing and Computer-assisted Intervention (2015)
14. Vaswani, A., et al.: Attention is all you need (2017)
15. Wang, P., et al.: Understanding convolution for semantic segmentation. In: IEEE Winter Conference on Applications of Computer Vision (2018)
16. Wang, X., Girshick, R., Gupta, A., He, K.: Non-local neural networks (2017)
17. Yuan, Y., Wang, J.: OCNet: object context network for scene parsing (2018)
18. Yue, K., Sun, M., Yuan, Y., Zhou, F., Ding, E., Xu, F.: Compact generalized non-local network. In: Advances in Neural Information Processing System, pp. 6510–6519 (2018)
19. Zhao, H., Shi, J., Qi, X., Wang, X., Jia, J.: Pyramid scene parsing network (2016)
20. Zhao, H., et al.: PSANet: point-wise spatial attention network for scene parsing. In: Proceedings of the European Conference on Computer Vision (ECCV), pp. 267–283 (2018)

Law Is Order: Protecting Multimedia Network Transmission by Game Theory and Mechanism Design

Chuanbin Liu[1,2], Youliang Tian[1(✉)], and Hongtao Xie[1,2]

[1] Guizhou Provincial Key Laboratory of Public Big Data, Guizhou University, Guiyang 550025, China
yltian@gzu.edu.cn
[2] School of Information Science and Technology, University of Science and Technology of China, Hefei 230026, China

Abstract. Nowadays, the computer network plays as the most important medium in the transmitting of multimedia. Correspondingly, the orderliness of network is the protection of multimedia transmission. However, due to the Packet Switching design, the network can only provide best-effort service, in which the multimedia applications compete for its network resource. In the lawless competition, the applications are obliged to be greedy and deceptive driven by their best self-interest. As a result, the transmission of multimedia applications becomes disorderly and inefficiently, and we lose the protection of multimedia network transmission. In this paper, we first investigate the behaviors of multimedia applications with Game Theory, and summarize the disorderly transmission as a Prisoner's Dilemma. The lost of law leads to the disorderly transmission in multimedia network. Then, we investigate the relationship between application's media-attribute and its required transmission service, and resolve this Prisoner's Dilemma with Mechanism Design. Specifically, a novel Media-attribute Switching (MAS) is proposed, where the network allocate the transmission resources according to the application's claimed media-attribute. In MAS, differentiated services are provided to applications with different claimed media-attribute. We design MAS to have the honesty application gets compatible service while the deceptive application gets incompatible service. Therefore, the MAS can provide incentives for multimedia applications to label their data media-attributes honestly and allocate the network resources according to their attributes, thus to protect the multimedia network transmission. The theoretical analysis and experimental comparison both prove our MAS's protection to the multimedia network.

Keywords: Multimedia transmission · Network protection · Game theory · Mechanism design

Y. M. Ro et al. (Eds.): MMM 2020, LNCS 11962, pp. 651–668, 2020.
https://doi.org/10.1007/978-3-030-37734-2_53

1 Introduction

Nowadays, the computer network plays as the most important medium in the transmitting of the multimedia [1,2]. With the rapid increment of multimedia application [3,4], the multimedia transmission is under a sustained growth in the current network. According to Cisco's report [5], the annual global multimedia traffic will reach 4.8 ZB per year by 2022, and the busy hour network traffic is will increase by a factor of 4.8 between 2017 and 2022. The ever-increasing multimedia network transmission raises a tremendous demand of network resources.

Different multimedia applications with different media-attribute demand different types of network resources. For example, realtime-video media (e.g. Skype [6]) is sensitive to latency, but can tolerate a little bit of packet loss. Content media (e.g. BitTorrent [7]) requires "the more the better" amount of bandwidth, but does not care about latency, and can tolerant fluctuation of available bandwidth. Control-signal media (e.g. online gaming and autonomous vehicles) has the highest demands on latency and the most sensitive to packet loss, but only requires a little fragment of bandwidth. According to media-attribute, allocating corresponding network resources to different multimedia applications can guarantee the Quality of Experience (QoE) and utilization of network. On the contrary, a chaotic network will lead to poor QoE of multimedia application. Correspondingly, the orderliness of network is the protection of multimedia transmission [8].

However, the current network is a packet switching network, which treats all the packets equally with a best-effort service. As a result, it cannot provide guaranteed service due to its property of equally sharing network resources. Moreover, fighting for more network resources, the applications can be greedy driven by their best self-interest. They will send packets repeatedly with multiple paths for lowest latency and packet-loss. For example, Skype claims to keep multiple connections open and dynamically chooses the best path in terms of quality. Bittorrent maintains 4 active paths with an additional path periodically chosen at random together with a mechanism that retains the best paths. The greedy behavior of application leads to huge waste of network resources and high latency and packet-loss. To the end, the multimedia applications can only obtain poor QoE.

To overcome this weakness in the best-effort network, researchers have tried for years to introduce differentiated services into the packet-switching networks [9–12], e.g. LLQ and DiffServ. Generally speaking, differentiated services is realized according to the differentiated packet priority [9] or code point [10,13] labeled by applications. However, all of these researches ignore the fact that the allocation of network resources is a competition among applications. An application can deceive network nodes and get additional network resources by labeling its packets with high priority. In the lawless competition, the application will be deceptive to label its packets with highest priority driven by their best self-interest. Therefore, differentiated service never works. As a result, "*differentiated IP service is not widely deployed, even though today's routers fully support LLQ, DiffServ, as well as other similar mechanisms*" [14].

In this paper, we first investigate the behaviors of multimedia applications with Game Theory [15], and summarize the fail of differentiated services as a Prisoner's Dilemma. Specifically, we regard the multimedia applications as game players in the competition of network resources. Although a series of differentiated services have been proposed, they ignore the competition among applications, and has no sanction for these deceiving behavior. Therefore, the applications will label its packets with highest priority for their best self-interest. When all packets are labeled with the highest priority, the differentiated service degenerates to the best-effort service with orderliness transmission, which goes against their initial wishes. To sum up, the lost of law leads to the disorderly transmission in multimedia network.

After finding out the reason for disorderly transmission, we further resolve this Prisoner's Dilemma with Mechanism Design [16]. Specifically, we investigate the relationship between application's media-attribute and its required transmission service. Then, a novel Media-attribute Switching (MAS) is proposed, where the network allocates the transmission resources according to the application's claimed media-attribute, instead of their claimed priority or DSCP. In MAS, differentiated services are provided to applications with different claimed media-attribute. We design MAS to have the honesty application gets compatible service while the deceptive application gets incompatible service. Driven by their best self-interest, the applications have to label their data media-attributes honestly. Therefore, the MAS can provide incentives for multimedia applications with honest and orderly behavior and allocate the network resources according to their media-attributes. In return, the multimedia applications can enjoy guaranteed service and the network can work in an orderly way. Law is order, we finally realize the protection of multimedia network by our novel Media-attribute Switching mechanism.

Our contributions are as follows:

- While all the existing researched on differentiated service ignore the competition behavior of multimedia applications in network, we investigate this behavior with Game Theory for the first time, and figure out the failure of the existing differentiated service network as a Prisoner's Dilemma.
- A novel Media-attribute Switching (MAS) is proposed with Mechanism Design, which can provide incentives for multimedia applications with honest and orderly behavior and allocate the network resources according to their media-attributes.
- In MAS, differentiated services are provided to applications according to their claimed media-attribute, which can guarantee the Quality of Experience and the protection of network.
- Theoretical analysis and experimental comparison both prove the protection of multimedia network with our MAS.

2 Related Work

2.1 Nash Equilibrium

Nash equilibrium [17] is a concept of game theory where the optimal outcome of a game is one where no player has an incentive to deviate from his chosen strategy after considering an opponent's choice.

Let (S, f) be a game with $n <$ players, where S_i is the strategy set for player i, $S = S_1 \times S_2 \times \cdots \times S_n$ is the set of strategy and $f(x) = (f_1(x), \ldots, f_n(x))$ is its payoff function evaluated at $x \in S$. Let x_i be a strategy profile of player i and x_{-i} be a strategy profile of all players except for player i. When each player $i \in \{1, \ldots, n\}$ chooses strategy x_i resulting in strategy profile $x = (x_1, \ldots, x_n)$ then player i obtains payoff $f_i(x)$. Note that the payoff depends on the strategy profile chosen, i.e., on the strategy chosen by player i as well as the strategies chosen by all the other players.

Theorem 1. *A strategy profile $x^* \in S$ is a* ***Nash Equilibrium*** *(NE) if no unilateral deviation in strategy by any single player is profitable for that player, that is*

$$\forall i, x_i \in S_i : f_i(x_i^*, x_{-i}^*) \geq f_i(x_i, x_{-i}^*). \tag{1}$$

2.2 Prisoner's Dilemma in Differentiated Service Network

The current packet switching network treats all the packets equally with a best-effort service. Due to its property of equally sharing network resources, it cannot provide guaranteed service due to multimedia application. To overcome this weakness in the best-effort network, researchers have tried for years to introduce differentiated services into the packet-switching networks. Generally speaking, differentiated services is realized according to the differentiated packet priority [9] or code point [10,13] labeled by applications. For example, the priority queueing (PQ) [9] operates by providing a special queue with high scheduling priority in a network node. Hence those control-signal media applications can choose this queue to achieve lower latency. The DiffServ [10,13] operates by stamping each incoming packet with a label named Differentiated Services Code Point (DSCP). A network node will classify incoming packets according to its DSCP value and provide suitable scheduling priority. With an enormous amount of researches on differentiated services network, the protection of multimedia transmission seems to be solved perfectly. However, all of these researches ignore the fact that the allocation of network resources is a competition among applications. An application can deceive network nodes and get additional network resources by labeling its packets with high priority.

Let's see an analysis of a simplified case. Assuming there are two Scalable Video Coding (SVC) [18,19] applications sending realtime streaming in a differentiated service network with bandwidth of 1.6 Mbps. They have one base-layer stream with bandwidth of 0.5 Mbps and one enhanced-layer stream with bandwidth of 0.5 Mbps, and two strategies (honest and dishonest) to label their packets. With honest strategy, the application only labels the BL packets as highest-priority and the EL packet as best-effort. Meanwhile, with the dishonest strategy, the application labels all of its packets as highest priority. The bandwidth allocation result is list in Table 1.

According to the Eq. 1, the **Nash Equilibrium** of the two application is $(Dishonest, Dishonest)$. This indicates that, the applications are obliged to be deceptive to label all the packets with highest priority driven by their best self-interest. While all packets are labeled with the highest priority, the differentiated service degenerates to the best-effort service with orderliness transmission, which goes against their initial wishes. This is a **Prisoner's Dilemma** [20] in Differentiated Service Network.

Table 1. The bandwidth allocation result of two realtime video-media application in a differentiated service network. This is a Prisoner's Dilemma in Differentiated Service Network.

Bandwidth (Mbps) (APP1, APP2)		APP1	
		Honest	Dishonest
APP	Honest	(0.8, 0.8)	(1, 0.6)
	Dishonest	(0.6, 1)	**(0.8, 0.8)**

2.3 Mechanism Design Theory

Mechanism design theory focuses on how to design such game rules that align those players' self-interests with their overall benefits. It studies how to maximize the overall benefit on condition that players are all rational and only consider their benefits.

We assume that there are N players in a game. Each player i has available to it some private information $\theta_i \in \Theta_i$ which is termed its type. They may not truthfully report its type, hence we assume $\hat{\theta}_i \in \Theta_i$ be the strategy type of player i and $\hat{\theta} = (\hat{\theta}_1, \hat{\theta}_2, ..., \hat{\theta}_N)$. The outcome o is the game result from players' strategy, i.e., $o = f(\hat{\theta})$, where f is the mechanism function from Θ_i to O. Let $u_i(o, \theta_i)$ denotes the utility benefit that player i of type θ_i receives from an outcome o. And we use the sum of all players' utility benefit to express the utility function of mechanism designer $u_0(o, \theta)$, where $u_0(o, \theta) = \sum_{i=1}^{n} u_i(o, \theta_i)$.

When the mechanism f is given, players choose their strategies for their own best benefits. A dominant strategy is optimal for a player no matter what the other players do.

Theorem 2. *A strategy $\hat{\theta}_i \in \Theta_i$ is dominant if, for all $\hat{\theta}'$ and $\hat{\theta}_{-i}$*

$$u_i\left(f\left(\hat{\theta}_i, \hat{\theta}_{-i}\right), \theta_i\right) \geq u_i\left(f\left(\hat{\theta}'_i, \hat{\theta}_{-i}\right), \theta_i\right). \tag{2}$$

There are two principle for the mechanism designer. One is the **principle of honesty** to make all players tell their true types. Which means designing a mechanism f so that truth-telling is a dominant strategy, as $\theta_i = \hat{\theta}_i$ for all i satisfies the definition of a dominant strategy. The other is **principle of optimality** to find a mechanism f with maximized $u_0(o, \theta)$.

3 Method

In this section, we first divide the multimedia applications into three categories according to there media-attribute, and define the corresponding QoE function for each category of application. Then we regard the competition of network resources among applications as a game among gamblers. Accordingly, the designing of multimedia network is mapped to the Mechanism Design of game rules. Finally, a novel Media-attribute Switching (MAS) is proposed, where the network allocate differentiated services according to the application's claimed media-attribute. Law is order, the protection of multimedia network can be realized by the proposed MAS.

3.1 QoE of Multimedia Application

Multimedia applications with different media-attribute demand different types of network resources, and possess different function for quality of experience. According to the media-attribute of the application, we classify the applications into three category as CR, RT, BK, and define their QoE function, respectively.

Critical (CR): CR attribute is suitable for control-signal media and those applications that are very sensitive to latency and packet drop. It can be seen as a highest prior class but with limited bandwidth, e.g. online gaming and autonomous vehicles We assume the CR packet is generated by application at a constant rate of r_{CR}, while the toleration time of CR packet is T_{CR}. Since CR packet is sensitive to delay and packet drop, the quality of experience of CR packet is defined as followed.

$$QoE_{CR} = \begin{cases} 0 & packet-loss \quad or \quad over-delay \\ 100 & else \end{cases} \tag{3}$$

Real-Time (RT): RT attribute is designed for realtime media that need low latency and relatively high bandwidth, e.g. video conference and real-time monitoring. We assume the RT packet is generated by application at a constant rate of r_{RT}, while the toleration time of CR packet is T_{RT}. Let L denote the data amount of all packets that is dropped or cannot be sent within toleration time, A denotes the data amount of the application. The quality of experience of RT packet is defined as followed.

$$QoE_{RT} = 100 * (1 - \frac{L}{A}) \tag{4}$$

Bulk (BK): BK attribute is suitable for those applications that need a large amount of bandwidth, but do not care about latency. These bandwidth-hungry applications can use retransmission to handle packet drop, e.g. FTP. We assume the BK packet is generated by application with a volume of V. As the BK packet only care about speed of transmission, we use the tolerance time T_{BK} and the used time D the describe the quality of experience.

$$QoE_{RT} = 100 * (1 - \frac{D}{T_{BK}}). \quad (5)$$

3.2 Mapping of Network Design to Mechanism Design

We map the network design to mechanism design as below.

Game Player. There are N applications as game players.

Type. In each application, its type is defined as $\theta_i : \left(d^i_{CR}, d^i_{RT}, d^i_{BK}\right)$ where $d^i_{CR}, d^i_{RT}, d^i_{BK}$ represent the amounts of CR, RT, and BK data in the ith application, respectively.

Strategy. Applications may or may not truthfully label their data attributes. The motivation of such a behavior is to obtain more network resources such as higher capacity allocation, lower latency, and/or higher reliability. However, they cannot misrepresent the time when they send their data and the amounts of their data, because the network node can accurately know when data come in and how many bytes of data come in. Therefore, the player strategy is defined as $\hat{\theta}_i : \left\{d^i_{a.b}\right\}$, where $d^i_{a.b}$ is the amount of data in app i with attribute a and labeled to be b, and a and b may be CR, RT, or BK. The network node allocates resources for data scheduling per the attributes that applications label.

Outcome. The outcome o is the result of delivering the data through the network node.

Mechanism. This is what we need to design, namely, the outcome of our scheduling method. We provide the design in the next section.

Utility Function of Applications. This is the quality of experience (QoE) of the application users, according to the outcome of the data delivery mechanism and the application's true media-attributes. We follow the Eqs. 3, 4 and 5 as the QoE function.

Utility Function of Network Designer. We use the sum of utility functions of all applications to express the utility function of the network designer, $u_0(o, \theta) = \sum_{i=1}^{n} u_i(o, \theta_i)$.

3.3 Scheduling Principle of MAS Network

We design the scheduling principle of MAS Network as Fig. 1:

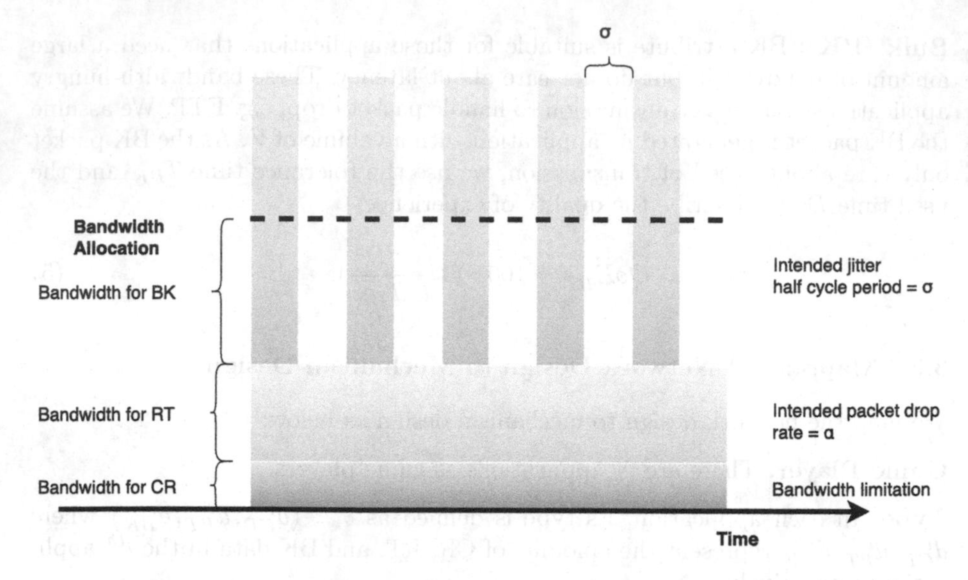

Fig. 1. Scheduling principle for media-attribute switching network.

Assuming the total channel capacity is C. Firstly, we will allocate bandwidth for the applications without BK queue: For the application with CR queue we give their CR queue channel bandwidth with c_{CR}, for applications with RT queue we giving c_{RT} but take off the bandwidth their CR queue has already taken c_{CR} (if there is CR queue). Secondly, the applications which have BK queue will share the bandwidth equally, while their CR queue and RT queue (if there is) will take channel bandwidth from the shared bandwidth as the first step does, and the BK queue will take the channel bandwidth which is left.

For example, if there is three applications on the network, application 1 has only packet in CR queue, application 2 has only packet in RT queue, application 3 has only packet in BK queue, and the application 4 has packet in CR queue RT queue and BK queue. In the step of bandwidth allocation, the application 1 will get bandwidth as c_{CR}, the application 2 will get c_{RT}, then the left bandwidth $C - c_{CR} - c_{RT}$ will be divided equally to application 3 and 4. For application 3, since it only has BK queue, the BK queue will totally take the bandwidth as $(C - c_{CR} - c_{RT})/2$. For application 4, the CR queue will take bandwidth as c_{CR} and RT queue will take bandwidth as $c_{RT} - c_{CR}$ firstly and the BK queue will get the bandwidth as $(C - c_{CR} - c_{RT})/2 - c_{RT}$.

The result of this allocation are: First, the BK queue will always take the left bandwidth, where there may jitter however BK queue does not care. Second, the RT queue will not get higher bandwidth by label part of its packet as CR queue. Third, the BK queue will not get higher bandwidth by label part of its packet as CR or RT or both.

We intentionally introduce jitter for BK data. We set a parameter σ as a half cycle time period. During the first half cycle σ seconds, no BK data are sent out and during the second half cycle σ seconds, the BK data are sent out at a rate $2c_{BK}$ equal to double of the allocated capacity. Therefore, within the entire cycle 2σ seconds, the BK data are sent out at a rate equal to the allocated capacity c_{BK}, but with an intentionally introduced jitter of σ seconds.

We also intentionally introduce packet drop for the RT data and set a parameter α as the data drop rate.

In MAS, differentiated services are provided to applications with different claimed media-attribute. The MAS is designed to guarantee the honesty application gets compatible service while the deceptive application gets incompatible service. Therefore, the MAS can provide incentives for multimedia applications to label their data media-attributes honestly and allocate the network resources according to their attributes, thus to protect the multimedia network transmission.

4 Evaluation

In this section, we conduct theoretical analysis and experimental comparison to prove the protection of multimedia network with our MAS.

4.1 Theoretical Analysis

In the scheduling of MAS, the parameters we already grasped are, (a) total channel bandwidth: C, (b) the number of applications: N, (c) application sending rate of CR, RT: r_{CR},r_{RT}, (d) volume of BK: V, (e) toleration time of CR, RT, BK: T_{CR}, T_{RT}, T_{BK}. Also, the parameters should obey $r_{RT} > r_{CR}$, $T_{RT} > T_{CR}$, $c_{BK} > c_{RT}$.

The parameters of MAS that we need to design are, (a) the channel bandwidth that we allocate for CR and RT: c_{CR}, c_{RT}, (b) the probability of packet drops for RT: α, (c) the intended jitter for BK: σ.

We need to design a mechanism with: The *principle of honesty*, that truth-telling is a dominant strategy. And the *principle of optimality*, to maximize the utility function of mechanism designer. The solving process is attached on the **Supplementary Material** of our paper. Finally, we have the solution of our MAS mechanism design as,

$$\begin{cases} \frac{T_{RT}}{1-2\alpha} \leq \sigma \ll T_{BK} \\ c_{CR} = r_{CR}, c_{RT} = r_{RT} \\ \alpha \to 0 \end{cases} \quad (6)$$

From the simple game-theory analysis, we can see that, for the best self-interest, all applications will honestly label their packets with attributes according to their real needs, so that the global protection of multimedia network is achieved.

Fig. 2. Experimental comparison on the application of Scalable Video Coding.

4.2 Experimental Comparison

In this subsection, we conduct experimental comparison of MAS with the application of Scalable Video Coding. The MAS is realized on a modified JVT simulator [21], while the YUV video is encoded by JSVM9 [22] experiment platform.

We simplify the transmission of multiple applications into transmission of one honest application and one dishonest application. In our experiment, the application with honest strategy will label its I frame with CR attribute while label its P frame and B frame with RT attribute. Meanwhile, the application with dishonest strategy will label its P frame and B frame with CR attribute for higher priority, or BK attribute for larger bandwidth. Figure 2 exhibits the video quality of the two application. As we can see, the quality of the video is quite good for honest application, as it can enjoy guaranteed differentiated service in MAS. On the contrary, the dishonest application cannot get additional network resources by fraudulently labeling its attribute. Moreover, the limited bandwidth for CR attribute and the jitter for BK attribute will cause packet loss or delay, which finally lead to terrible "mosaic" in the video. Drive by their best self-interest, the application will choose honest strategy and tell the true media-attribute to the network. Therefore the lawless competition with greedy and deceptive behavior can get effectively solved by MAS.

Furthermore, we conduct comparison experiment between our MAS and the existing best-effort service network. In this experiment, we set one SVC application sending stream at a stable bit-rate, and limit the network bandwidth to simulate network congestion. We calculate the average SSIM of all frames as the video quality. As shown in Fig. 3, the best-effort network will drop packets randomly regardless of their importance, hence it provides poor service with terrible video quality. Meanwhile, the MAS will drop the RT packet but keep the CR packet when congestion happens, which means the I frame with high importance can get delivered with high priority. Therefore, the SVC application can get better video quality in MAS.

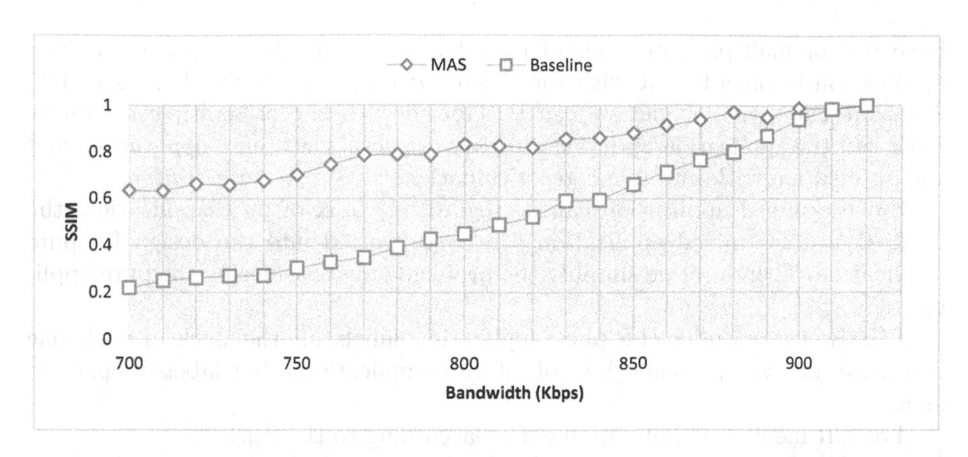

Fig. 3. Experimental comparison between MAS and baseline under network congestion.

The experimental comparison demonstrates that, our MAS can provide incentives for multimedia applications to label their data media-attributes honestly, and allocate the network resources according to their attributes. Therefore, it can protect the multimedia network transmission.

5 Conclusion

In this paper, we study the network transmission protection problem among multimedia application. We consider the multimedia application to be autonomously driven by their best self-interest. The failure of the existing differentiated service network is pointed out in our research for the first time by Game Theory. Then a novel MAS is proposed with Mechanism Design, where the network allocates differentiated services according to the applications claimed media-attribute. Law is order, we finally realize the protection of multimedia network by our MAS mechanism.

Our research highlights the rightness of applying Game Theory and Mechanism Design in the multimedia network. In the future we will focus on experiments of MAS in a real network environment.

6 Supplementary Material

As we mentioned in Sect. 3.1, we need to design MAS with: The *principle of honesty*, that truth-telling is a dominant strategy. And the *principle of optimality*, to maximize the utility function of mechanism designer.

6.1 Requirement from Principle of Honesty

The principle of honesty require the MAS to provide best QoE for applications when they label their packets with true attribute. Notice one application can have one or multiple categories of packets, i.e. the handshake packets of SIP application belongs to CR with the video stream packet of SIP belong to RT. Also one categories of packets can be labeled with one or multiple attribute. Let's call the application with one category of packets as a *pure application*, and the application with multiple categories packets as a *mixed application*.

Since a mixed application can be regard as a mix of pure application, the MAS design for mixed application can be converted into the design for pure application. Therefore, we simplify the problem only considering the pure application.

Firstly, we consider the pure application labels all the packets with one attribute. Let $S_{a,b}$ presents the QoE of pure application a but labels its packets as b.

For CR media-attribute application, according to the Eq. 3,

If a CR application labels as CR, only if the channel bandwidth c_{CR} is bigger than its sending rate r_{CR}, the score will be 100.

$$S_{CR,CR} = 100 \qquad (c_{CR} \geq r_{CR}) \tag{7}$$

If a CR application labels as RT, it will suffer packet loss, so its score will be zero.

$$S_{CR,RT} = 0 \qquad (\alpha > 0) \tag{8}$$

If a CR application labels as BK, it will suffer delay, so its score will be zero.

$$S_{CR,BK} = 0 \qquad (\sigma > T_{CR}) \tag{9}$$

For RT media-attribute application, according to the Eq. 4,

If a RT application labels as RT, it will only suffer the packet loss we intended introduce.

$$S_{RT,RT} = 100 * (1 - \alpha) \qquad (c_{RT} \geq r_{RT}) \tag{10}$$

If a RT application labels as CR, since the channel for CR is rather low and the bit-rate of RT is high, the CR channel could not deliver the RT packets in time then there will be delay. Assuming the packet is generated at the time t_g from RT application and delivered at t_d in channel CR, since the toleration time of RT is T_{RT}, we have

$$t_d \leq t_g + T_{RT} \tag{11}$$

$$t_d * c_{CR} = t_g * r_{RT} \tag{12}$$

The function can be solved with $t_g \leq \frac{T_{RT} * c_{CR}}{r_{RT} - c_{CR}}$. Manning during a period of time $\frac{T_{RT} * c_{CR}}{r_{RT} - c_{CR}} + T_{RT}$, only the packet generated before time $\frac{T_{RT} * c_{CR}}{r_{RT} - c_{CR}}$ can be delivered in time. The score of this situation is be

$$S_{RT,CR} = 100 * \frac{\frac{T_{RT} * c_{CR}}{r_{RT} - c_{CR}} + T_{RT}}{\frac{T_{RT} * c_{CR}}{r_{RT} - c_{CR}}} = 100 * \frac{r_{RT} - c_{CR}}{r_{RT}} \tag{13}$$

If a RT application labels as BK, during the first σ, the bandwidth for BK queue is 0 while at the second σ, the bandwidth is $2 * c_{BK}$. Assume there is a packet sent into the queue in the first σ at the time t, there will be $t * r_{CR}$ packet ahead of it waiting for channel of BK to "open the gate" to transmit. So it will cost the packet $\sigma - t$ to wait for the second σ and $(t * r_{CR})/(c_{BK})$ to transmit the packet ahead of it, so the delay of this packet is $\sigma - t - (t * r_{CR})/(2 * c_{BK})$, and it cannot be bigger than its tolerance time T_{RT}, meaning,

$$\sigma - t - (t * r_{CR})/(2 * c_{BK}) \leq T_{RT} \tag{14}$$

The solution is,

$$t \geq \frac{2c_{BK} * (\sigma - T_{RT})}{2 * c_{BK} - r_{RT}} \qquad (2 * c_{BK} > r_{RT}) \tag{15}$$

Meaning during the jitter cycle 2σ the packet which sent into the queue after the time $\frac{2c_{BK}*(\sigma - T_{RT})}{2*c_{BK} - r_{RT}}$ will be delivered within tolerance. So the score is

$$S_{RT,BK} = 100 * \frac{2\sigma - \frac{2c_{BK}*(\sigma - T_{RT})}{2*c_{BK} - r_{RT}}}{2\sigma} \qquad (2 * c_{BK} > r_{RT}) \tag{16}$$

For BK media-attribute application, according to the Eq. 5,

If a BK application labels as BK, assuming the volume of these data is V, it will cost V/c_{BK} time to deliver into network, also the half jitter cycle σ should be rather small compared with the toleration time T_{BK}. So the score will be

$$S_{BK,BK} = 100 * (1 - \frac{V}{c_{BK}T_{BK}}) \qquad (\sigma \ll T_{BK}) \tag{17}$$

If a BK application labels as CR, it will cost V/c_{CR} time to deliver into network, so the score will be

$$S_{BK,CR} = 100 * (1 - \frac{V}{c_{CR}T_{BK}}) \tag{18}$$

If a BK application labels as RT, since we intended introduce packet drop rate as α, the equivalent bandwidth of RT queue can be considered as $c_{RT} * (1 - \alpha)$, so it will cost $V/(c_{CR}(1 - \alpha))$ time to deliver into network, so the score will be

$$S_{BK,RT} = 100 * (1 - \frac{V}{(1 - \alpha)c_{CR}T_{BK}}) \tag{19}$$

According to the Eq. 2, the principle of honesty requires,

$$\begin{cases} S_{CR,CR} \geq S_{CR,RT} \\ S_{CR,CR} \geq S_{CR,BK} \\ S_{RT,RT} \geq S_{RT,CR} \\ S_{RT,RT} \geq S_{RT,BK} \\ S_{BK,BK} \geq S_{BK,CR} \\ S_{BK,BK} \geq S_{BK,RT} \end{cases} \tag{20}$$

According to the Eqs. 7, 8 and 9 and the principle of our scheduling, we can figure

$$c_{CR} \geq r_{CR}, \sigma > T_{RC}, \alpha > 0 \tag{21}$$

According to the Eq. 10, we have

$$c_{RT} \geq r_{RT} \tag{22}$$

According to $S_{RT,RT} \geq S_{RT,CR}$, we have $1 - \alpha \geq r_{RT} - c_{CR} r_{RT}$, it can be solved as

$$\alpha \leq \frac{c_{CR}}{r_{RT}} \tag{23}$$

According to $S_{RT,RT} \geq S_{RT,BK}$, we have $1 - \alpha \geq \frac{2\sigma - \frac{2c_{BK} * (\sigma - T_{RT})}{2 * c_{BK} - r_{RT}}}{2\sigma}$, it can be solved as

$$\frac{T_{RT}}{1 - 2\alpha(1 - \frac{r_{RT}}{2c_{BK}})} \leq \sigma \tag{24}$$

According to Eq. 17, we have

$$\sigma \ll T_{BK} \tag{25}$$

According to $S_{BK,BK} \geq S_{BK,CR}$ and $S_{BK,BK} \geq S_{BK,RT}$, we have

$$c_{BK} \geq c_{RT}(1 - \alpha), c_{BK} \geq c_{CR} \tag{26}$$

these requirement has already been meet in our principle.

Since $\frac{T_{RT}}{1 - 2\alpha(1 - \frac{r_{RT}}{2c_{BK}})} > T_{RT} > T_{CR}$, finally we have solution

$$c_{CR} \geq r_{CR}, c_{RT} \geq r_{RT} \tag{27}$$

$$0 < \alpha \leq \frac{c_{CR}}{r_{RT}} \tag{28}$$

$$\frac{T_{RT}}{1 - 2\alpha(1 - \frac{r_{RT}}{2c_{BK}})} \leq \sigma \ll T_{BK} \tag{29}$$

Under these conditions, there will be no extra profit for a pure application by labeling all the packets with fraudulent attribute.

Let's go further to discuss the situation a pure application labels the packets dividedly with multiple attributes.

The analysis for CR application is quite easy, since one packet-drop or over-delay will cause the sore of whole function be zero, so CR application will not divided its to RT channel or BK channel.

The analysis for BK application is easy too, as we can figure out, under scheduling principle of MAS, the maximal bandwidth for one application will never be higher than a pure BK application. Since the BK application only care about the allocated channel bandwidth, there is no extra profit for a BK application to tell lies.

The analysis for RT will be just a little difficult. Assume the RT application label part of its packets as CR with the bit-rate of $r_{RT,CR}$, this part of packets will get a score of S'_{CR}. And so it does with $r_{RT,RT}$, S'_{RT}, $r_{RT,BK}$, S'_{BK}. Since the score of RT is defined as the proportion of the delivered packets among the total generated packets, it can be presented as a weighted mean of each part.

$$\bar{S}_{RT} = \frac{r_{RT,CR} * S'_{CR} + r_{RT,RT} * S'_{RT} + r_{RT,BK} * S'_{BK}}{r_{RT,CR} + r_{RT,RT} + r_{RT,BK}} \tag{30}$$

The CR application will not label part of its packet with BK, if

$$S_{RT,RT} \geq S'_{BK} \tag{31}$$

According to Eq. 16, we have

$$S'_{BK} = 100 * \frac{2\sigma - \frac{2c_{BK}*(\sigma - T_{RT})}{2*c_{BK} - r'_{RT}}}{2\sigma} \tag{32}$$

According to Eq. 32, the smaller r'_{BK} is, the bigger S'_{BK} will be. The maximal of S'_{BK} will be acquired as $\frac{\sigma+T_{RT}}{2\sigma}$ when r'_{BK} equals to 0. So we have,

$$1 - \alpha \geq \frac{\sigma + T_{RT}}{2\sigma} \tag{33}$$

And the solution is

$$\sigma \geq \frac{T_{RT}}{1 - 2\alpha} \tag{34}$$

Now that the RT application will not labels part of its packets as BK, its strategy only left labeling part of its packets as CR. So we have,

$$\bar{S}_{RT} = \frac{r_{RT,CR} * 100 + r_{RT,RT} * 100(1 - \alpha)}{r_{RT,CR} + r_{RT,RT}} \tag{35}$$

Notice $c_{RT,CR} + c_{RT,RT} = c_{RT}$ since a rational application will always sent all of its packets out. We have

$$\bar{S}_{RT} = 100 * \frac{\alpha c_{RT,CR}}{c_{RT}} + 100(1 - \alpha) \tag{36}$$

Donate S^e_{RT} as the extra score for RT application when partly labels its packets as CR. We have

$$S^e_{RT} = \bar{S}_{RT} - S_{RT,RT} = 100 * \frac{\alpha r_{RT,CR}}{r_{RT}} \tag{37}$$

Since the channel bandwidth for CR is limited as c_{CR}, we have $r_{RT,CR} \leq c_{CR}$, so the maximal of S^e_{RT} is acquired as $100 * \frac{\alpha c_{CR}}{r_{RT}}$ when $r_{RT,CR} = c_{CR}$. In Eq. 28 there is no lower limit for α and our MAS is required to design α as small as possible, so we have $S^e_{RT} \to 0$. Meaning there will be negligible extra score for

RT application when partly labels its packets as CR. So a RT application will not likely to partly labels its packets as CR.

As we discuss above, when our MAS meet the requirement of Eqs. 27, 28, 29 and 34, a pure application will not label part or entire of its packets with fraudulent attribute. Since $1 - \frac{r_{RT}}{2c_{BK}} < 1$, then $\frac{T_{RT}}{1-2\alpha(1-\frac{r_{RT}}{2c_{BK}})} \leq \frac{T_{RT}}{1-2\alpha}$, so we further optimize σ with $\frac{T_{RT}}{1-2\alpha} \leq \sigma \ll T_{BK}$.

To conclude, MAS meet the principle of honesty in mechanism design when

$$\begin{cases} \frac{T_{RT}}{1-2\alpha} \leq \sigma \ll T_{BK} \\ c_{CR} \geq r_{CR}, c_{RT} \geq r_{RT} \\ 0 < \alpha \leq \frac{c_{CR}}{r_{RT}} \end{cases} \tag{38}$$

6.2 Requirement from Principle of Optimality

The principle of optimality requires us to design mechanism from Θ to O, $f : \Theta \to O$, which can maximize the utility function of the network designer $u_0(o, \theta)$.

$$\arg\max_f \|u_0(o, \theta)\| \tag{39}$$

In our MAS, we use the sum of utility functions of all applications to express the utility function of the network designer, $u_0(o, \theta) = \sum_{i=1}^{n} u_i(o, \theta_i)$. As we analyse before, a mixed application can be regard as a mix of pure application, we can simplify the question as maximize the sum of pure application's utility $u_i(o, \theta_i)$. The mechanism we need to design is

$$\arg\max_f \|n_{CR}S_{CR,CR} + n_{RT}S_{RT,RT} + n_{BK}S_{BK,BK}\| \tag{40}$$

where n_i stands for the account number of application i.

We have already defined the utility function of application as

$S_{CR,CR} = 100 \quad (c_{CR} \geq r_{CR})$

$S_{RT,RT} = 100 * (1 - \alpha) \quad (c_{RT} \geq r_{RT})$

$S_{BK,BK} = 100 * (1 - \frac{V}{c_{BK}T_{BK}})$

To maximize the $u_i(o, \theta_i)$, we need maximize $S_{CR,CR}$, $S_{RT,RT}$, $S_{BK,BK}$, respectively.

$$\arg\max_f \|100 * (1 - \alpha)\| \tag{41}$$

$$\arg\max_f \left\|100 * (1 - \frac{V}{c_{BK}T_{BK}})\right\| \tag{42}$$

So the α should be as small as possible, and the c_{BK} as big as possible.

$$\alpha \to 0 \tag{43}$$

Since BK application take the left channel bandwidth from total channel bandwidth C, we have

$$c_{BK} = \frac{C - n_{CR} * c_{CR} - n_{RT} * c_{RT}}{n_{BK}} \tag{44}$$

So we need to minimize c_{CR} and c_{RT}, the solution will be

$$c_{CR} = r_{CR}, c_{RT} = r_{RT} \tag{45}$$

6.3 Conclusion

Based on the analysts above, Combing the condition on Eqs. 38, 43 and 45, our MAS is designed with below requirement,

$$\begin{cases} \frac{T_{RT}}{1-2\alpha} \leq \sigma \ll T_{BK} \\ c_{CR} = r_{CR}, c_{RT} = r_{RT} \\ \alpha \to 0 \end{cases} \tag{46}$$

Acknowledgment. This work is supported by the Major Scientific and Technological Special Project of Guizhou Province (20183001).

References

1. Schwartz, M.: Network management and control issues in multimedia wireless networks. IEEE Pers. Commun. **2**(3), 8–16 (1995)
2. Sahinoglu, Z., Tekinay, S.: On multimedia networks: self-similar traffic and network performance. IEEE Commun. Mag. **37**(1), 48–52 (1999)
3. Xie, H., Mao, Z., Zhang, Y., Deng, H., Yan, C., Chen, Z.: Double-bit quantization and index hashing for nearest neighbor search. IEEE Trans. Multimed. **21**(5), 1248–1260 (2018)
4. Xie, H., Fang, S., Zha, Z.J., Yang, Y., Li, Y., Zhang, Y.: Convolutional attention networks for scene text recognition. ACM Trans. Multimed. Comput. Commun. Appl. (TOMM) **15**(2), 3 (2019)
5. Cisco Visual: Cisco visual networking index: forecast and trends, 2017–2022. White Paper 1 (2018)
6. Baset, S.A., Schulzrinne, H.: An analysis of the Skype peer-to-peer internet telephony protocol. arXiv preprint cs/0412017 (2004)
7. Cohen, B.: Incentives build robustness in BitTorrent. In: Workshop on Economics of Peer-to-Peer Systems, vol. 6, pp. 68–72 (2003)
8. Park, L.T., Baek, J.W., Hong, J.W.K.: Management of service level agreements for multimedia internet service using a utility model. IEEE Commun. Mag. **39**(5), 100–106 (2001)
9. Semeria, C.: Supporting differentiated service classes: queue scheduling disciplines, pp. 11–14. Juniper Networks (2001)
10. Carpenter, B.E., Nichols, K.: Differentiated services in the Internet. Proc. IEEE **90**(9), 1479–1494 (2002)
11. Yang, X., Liu, J., Li, N.: Congestion control based on priority drop for H.264/SVC. In: Proceedings - 2007 International Conference on Multimedia and Ubiquitous Engineering, MUE 2007, pp. 585–589 (2007). https://doi.org/10.1109/MUE.2007.107
12. Dyahadray, A., Shringarpure, H., Mulay, N., Saraph, G.: Congestion control using scalable video streaming. In: National Conference on Communications 2008 (2008)

13. Semeria, C.: Supporting Differentiated Service Classes: Queue Scheduling Disciplines, pp. 1–27. Juniper Networks (2000). http://users.jyu.fi/~timoh/kurssit/verkot/scheduling.pdf
14. Shetty, N.: Design of network architectures: role of game theory and economics. Ph.D. thesis, UC Berkeley (2010)
15. Osborne, M.J., Rubinstein, A.: A Course in Game Theory. MIT Press, Cambridge (1994)
16. Nisan, N., Ronen, A.: Algorithmic mechanism design. In: Proceedings of the Thirty-First Annual ACM Symposium on Theory of Computing, pp. 129–140. ACM (1999)
17. Maskin, E.: Nash equilibrium and welfare optimality. Rev. Econ. Stud. **66**(1), 23–38 (1999)
18. Li, W.: Overview of fine granularity scalability in MPEG-4 video standard. IEEE Trans. Circuits Syst. Video Technol. **11**(3), 301–317 (2001)
19. Alreshoodi, M., Woods, J., Musa, I.K.: QoE-enabled transport optimisation scheme for real-time SVC video delivery. In: 2014 9th International Symposium on Communication Systems, Networks and Digital Signal Processing, CSNDSP 2014, pp. 865–868 (2014). https://doi.org/10.1109/CSNDSP.2014.6923949
20. Rapoport, A., Chammah, A.M., Orwant, C.J.: Prisoner's Dilemma: A Study in Conflict and Cooperation, vol. 165. University of Michigan Press, Ann Arbor (1965)
21. Guo, H., Wang, Y.: SVC/AVC loss simulator donation, ISO. Technical report, IEC JTC1/SV29/WG11 and ITU-T SG16 Q. 6, Document JVTP069 (2005)
22. Wiegand, T., Sullivan, G., Reichel, J., Schwarz, H., Wien, M.: Joint scalable video model JSVM-9. Joint Video Team, Document JVT-V202 (2007)

Rational Delegation Computing Using Information Theory and Game Theory Approach

Qiuxian Li[1] and Youliang Tian[2(✉)]

[1] School of Big Data Engineering, Kaili University, Kaili 556011, China
[2] The State Key Laboratory of Public Big Data, College of Computer Science and Technology, Guizhou University, Guiyang 550025, China
youliangtian@163.com

Abstract. Delegation computing is a calculation protocol between non-cooperative participants, and its results are influenced by the participant's choice of behavior. The goal of this paper is to solve the problem of high communication overhead in traditional delegation computing schemes. Combining the advantages of information theory and game theory, we propose a rational delegation computing scheme, which guarantees the correctness of the calculation results through the participant utility function. First, by analyzing the participant behavior strategy, we design the game model, which includes the participant set, information set, behavior strategy set and utility function. Second, according to the combination of Nash equilibrium and channel capacity limit in the game model, we construct a rational delegation computing scheme in this paper. Finally, we analyze and prove the scheme. When both the delegation party and computing party choose the honesty strategy, their utility reaches the maximum, that is, the global can reach the Nash equilibrium state, and the calculation efficiency has also been improved.

Keywords: Delegation computation · Game theory · Information theory · Channel capacity · Nash equilibrium

1 Introduction

Delegation computing [8] is an important methods to solve the problem of result reliability in the process of multi-task delegation to an untrusted server in big data and cloud computing environments. Traditional delegation computing mainly refers to the client delegating the computing task of computing complex functions to a server with strong computing power due to its own computing power or resources, and the server returns the result of the calculation and the

Y. Tian—Supported by organization x.

Y. M. Ro et al. (Eds.): MMM 2020, LNCS 11962, pp. 669–680, 2020.
https://doi.org/10.1007/978-3-030-37734-2_54

proof of the correctness of the result. After receiving the feedback from the server, the client verifies the correctness of the returned result by executing its own verification protocol. In this process, the cost of the verification process is much less than the cost of the computation task itself, otherwise the meaning of the delegation service will lose its significance.

There are two types of traditional delegation computing schemes: The first is the construction scheme based on the complexity theory. The main application tools are the interactive proof system [7], the probabilistic verification technique [1], the computational rationality proof technique based on the random oracle [5,6,12], etc. Goldwasser et al. propose an interactive correcting system for language L, which is an interactive process consisting of a common input certifier P and verifier V; As early as 1993, Chaum [4] et al. proposed the "Electronic Wallet" model, and used the group signature to construct a specific agreement, which opened the prelude to the application of cryptography to the study of the delegation calculation. Then Zhang [11] et al. constructed multiple schemes for proxy calculations of polynomial functions and matrix products.

In recent years, rational proof has become a hot topic for many scholars. As early as 2012, Azar [2] proposed a rational proof system based on appropriate scoring rules. The participants in the system are neither honest nor malicious, but rational. Then Azar [3] et al. used the idea of Utility Gaps to construct an super-efficient rational proof system. Rosen [9] et al. solved the rational proof system problem of the prover's computational ability through the study of the rational proof system. Tian [13] et al. analyzed the problem of secure communication from a rational perspective, and proposed a Bayesian rational secret sharing scheme. Subsequently, Chen [10] et al. also studied the rational proof problem of rational proof system when there are multiple provers from the perspective of complexity theory.

This paper introduces rational participants in the delegation calculation, and combines game theory with information theory technology [14] to construct a new rational delegation calculation protocol. In this protocol, only when participants choose the optimal action strategy, the interests of the delegation party and the computing party can reach the optimal value and reach the Nash equilibrium point. At this point, the utility function between the participants is the channel capacity of the both channels.

2 System Model

In the game model, rational participants must choose the optimal action strategy to interact in order to achieve the purpose of their delegation computing. If the rational participants violate the rules of the agreement, they will pay a greater price. In this section, the game model of delegation calculation is given in the framework of game theory. As shown in Fig. 1, this is the rational delegation calculation model diagram.

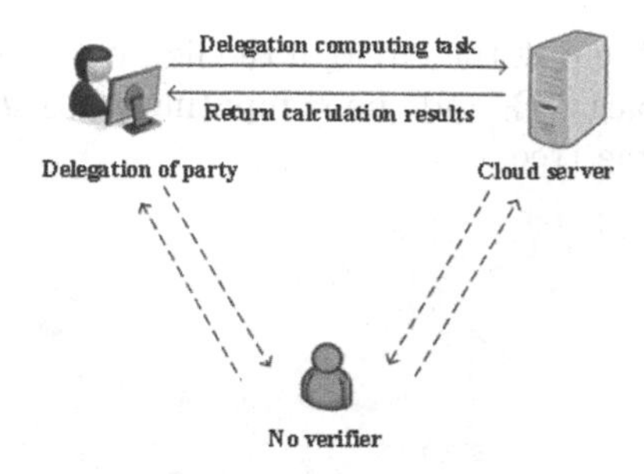

Fig. 1. Rational delegation computing model diagram

The game model of rational delegation calculation is a four-tuple (P, Σ, S, U).

1. Players set: A set of rational delegation and computing parties involved in performing the delegation calculation.
2. Information set: It refers to all the information that the rational participant knows at a particular moment, so that it can make the next decision.
3. Strategy set: A set of all actions that a rational participant may take in a delegated calculation.
4. Utility function: Representing the rewards that rational participants can get after choosing a strategy.

2.1 Players Set

The set of participants is composed of rational delegation party and computing party. This agreement takes into account the situation where one client delegates the computing task to multiple computing party. Therefore, there are mainly two participants in the rational delegation computing model: delegation party and computing party. The set of participants for this rational delegation calculation can be defined as. The delegation party can maximize its own interests under the condition of ensuring the best overall interests. The computing party maximizes its own interests while ensuring the perfect execution of the delegation task.

2.2 Information Set

Information refers to the knowledge of the participants about the game, especially the knowledge about the characteristics and actions of other participants. Information set in game theory refers to all the information that rational participants know at a particular moment, so that they can make the next decision. In the delegation computing game model, after the participant selects the strategy s_i, each participant $i \in P$ will have a local state, which is denoted as $\sum_i (s_i)$, which means that the participant knows all the information at this time. This information will provide a reference for participants $i \in P$ when they make their next action strategy.

As shown in Figs. 2 and 3, the circle in the figure is the selection information set of the delegation party P_0 and the computing party $P = \{1, 2, \cdots, n\}$, and is represented by a game tree.

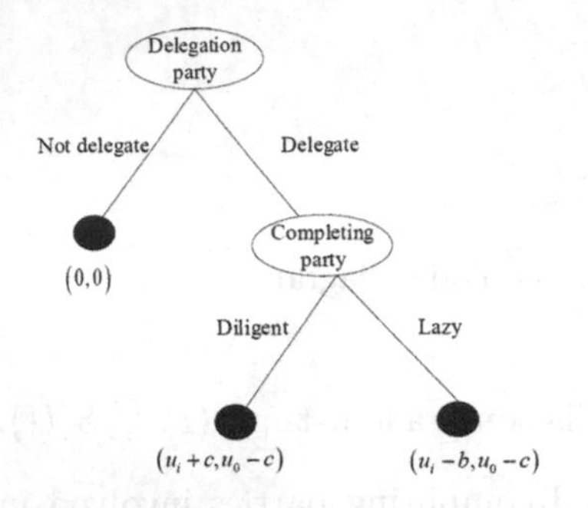

Fig. 2. Computing party game tree

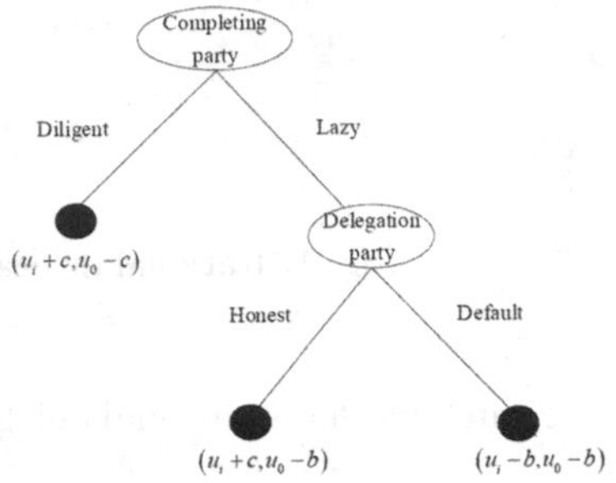

Fig. 3. Delegation party game tree

2.3 Strategy Set

When the participants begin to implement the rational delegation computing protocol, the participants $i \in P$ make the next decision based on their information set and utility. First, the rational delegation party P_0 will choose whether to delegate it to the computing party $P = \{1, 2, \cdots, n\}$ according to its own computing tasks. If the delegation party does not delegate, this agreement will not be executed.

Next, if the delegation party delegates the calculation task to the computing party, it needs to consider the feedback of the two action strategies of the computing party, namely "Diligent" computing delegation task, that is, return the correct answer, or "Lazy" computing delegation task, return the wrong answer. At this point, the strategy set is {Diligent, Lazy}, which can be defined as $S_i = \{s_{i1}, s_{i2}\}$, where $1 \leq i \leq n$ and s_{i1} means the computing party chooses an diligent strategy, and s_{i2} means that the computing party chooses a lazy strategy.

If the delegation party follows the execution of the agreement, the delegation party P_0 will select "Honest" to reward the computing party. However, the delegation party P_0 will choose "Default" and will not send the reward to the computing party. At this point, the strategy set of the delegation party is {Honest, Default}, which can be defined as $S_0 = \{s_{01}, s_{02}\}$, where s_{01} indicates that the delegation party chooses the conservation strategy, s_{02} indicates that the delegation party chooses default strategy.

2.4 Utility Function

According to the analysis of rational delegation party and computing party, the feasible strategy set of standard game $G = \{S_0, S_1, \cdots, S_n; u_0, u_1, \cdots, u_n\}$

between $n+1$ participants in this agreement can be known. For any set of pure strategies $P_0, P_1, \cdots, P_n$, the utility functions between $n+1$ rational participants in the protocol are also different according to different interest targets, and their corresponding channel capacities are also different.

First, from the perspective of the delegation party P_0, he can divide the n computing parties into K groups $T_1, T_2, \cdots, T_K$, so that each computing party is in and only in one group. Moreover, the delegation party P_0 does not distinguish between different computing parties in the same group. For these K groups, the delegation party also assigned weighting factors $a_1, a_2, \cdots, a_K$. Where $a_1 + a_2 + \cdots + a_K = 1$, for each $1 \leq i \leq K, 0 \leq a_i \leq 1$.

Therefore, it can be known that the delegation party P_0's revenue function is:

$$u_0(P_0, P_1, \cdots, P_n) = \sum_{i=1}^{K} a_i I\left(P_0; T_i \left| T_i^C \right.\right) \tag{1}$$

Where T_i^C represents a set of all other computing parties except T_i, and $I\left(X; T_i \left| T_i^C \right.\right)$ represents the mutual information between the rational delegation party and the computing parties T_i combination under condition T_i^C.

Second, for n rational computing parties, suppose they voluntarily divide into M alliances $R_1, R_2, \cdots, R_M$, so that each computing party $P = \{1, 2, \cdots, n\}$ is in and only in one alliance. In this agreement, the computing parties in the same alliance do not consider their own interests, and the interests of the alliance are the most important. The selfish computing parties can form an alliance by themselves. Therefore, for each rational computing party $P_i\,(0 \leq i \leq n)$, if $i \in R_j\,(1 \leq j \leq M)$, then its revenue function can be defined as:

$$u_i(P_0, P_1, \cdots, P_n) = I\left(P_0; R_j \left| R_j^C \right.\right) \tag{2}$$

Where R_j^C denotes a set of all other computing party alliances except R_j. Where $I\left(P_0; R_j \left| R_j^C \right.\right)$ represents the mutual information between the rational delegation party P_0 and the computing party alliance R_j under the condition R_j^C.

3 Rational Delegation Computing Scheme

In this section, rational delegation computing protocol is constructed based on the above rational delegation computing game model and information theory knowledge. In the process of constructing a protocol, the validity and correctness of the protocol are related to the utility function of each participant. In order to obtain the maximum benefit, all rational participants must follow the agreement. Any participants who deviate from the agreement will be severely punished, and the penalty is far greater than the benefit obtained in the protocol. The rational delegation calculation we construct are divided into an initialization phase, a delegation calculation phase, limit of ability and a payment phase.

3.1 Protocol Parameter

The protocol parameters used in this paper are shown in Table 1 below:

Table 1. Scheme parameters

Symbol	Meaning
a	Computational cost of the function F
b	Penalty from the agreement
c	Calculate the bonus of the function F

3.2 Initialization Phase

First, the rational delegation party P_0 chooses whether to delegate the function F according to the amount of computing tasks. If the client chooses not to delegate to the computing party, the protocol is not executed. If the rational delegation party P_0 chooses to delegate the function F to the computing party, the execution of this protocol shall begin. In this protocol, the computation cost of the function F is a.

Then, the delegation party will pre-process the calculating function F that needs to be delegated to prevent the computing party from tampering with the calculating function. The delegate sends the processed function to the computing party $P = \{1, 2, \cdots, n\}$, and the computational power will receive the computing task.

After receiving the computing task, n rational computing parties will voluntarily divide into M alliances $R_1, R_2, \cdots, R_M$, so that each computing party is in and only in one alliance. The computing parties in the same alliance do not consider their own interests, and they all focus on the interests of the alliance. Selfish computing parties can form a single alliance.

3.3 Delegation Calculation Phase

Then, M computing alliances use their own resources, combined with the calculation method of function F to obtain the calculation result of the calculation function. After the computing party completes the calculation task, it forms a collection with all other computing parties and returns the calculation result to P_0. At this stage, the computing parties that require arbitrary probability polynomial time cannot obtain any information about the function F.

3.4 Limit of Ability

This section first considers the case of a delegation computing between a rational delegation party and two rational computing parties, and uses the two-dimensional random variable $P_0 = (P_{01}, P_{02})$ to represent the rational in this scheme according to its experiment.

If the P_1 returns the correct answer, then $P_1 = 1$, and the P_1 returns the wrong answer, then $P_1 = 0$. Similarly, if the P_2 returns the correct answer, then $P_2 = 1$, the P_2 returns the wrong answer, then $P_2 = 0$.

The delegation party and the computing party interact with the computing task and record the interaction results of both parties. Since the participants are all rational, they keep the information of the interaction confidential, but according to their rational behavior, their choice behavior strategy has certain probability as follows:

The probability that P_1 returns the correct calculation result and the wrong result is $0 < P_r(P_1 = 1) = p < 1$ and $0 < P_r(P_0 = 1) = 1 - p < 1$, respectively. And the probability that P_2 returns the correct calculation result and the wrong result is $0 < P_r(q_1 = 1) = q < 1$ and $0 < P_r(q_0 = 1) = 1 - q < 1$, respectively.

The P_0 receives the correct answer from P_1, and the probability that P_2 returns the correct answer is $0 < P_r(P_{01} = 1, P_{02} = 1) = a_{11} < 1$. The P_0 receives the correct answer from P_1, and the probability that P_2 returns the wrong answer is $0 < P_r(P_{01} = 1, P_{02} = 0) = a_{10} < 1$. The P_0 receives the wrong answer from P_1, and the probability that P_2 returns the correct answer is $0 < P_r(P_{01} = 0, P_{02} = 1) = a_{01} < 1$. The P_0 receives the wrong answer from P_1, and the probability that P_2 returns the wrong answer is $0 < P_r(P_{01} = 0, P_{02} = 0) = a_{00} < 1$.

Where $a_{00} + a_{01} + a_{10} + a_{11} = 1$.

Construct a random variable $Z = (P_0 + P_i) \bmod 2$, where $i = 1, 2$, so the joint probability distribution of (P_0, Z) from the probability distribution of P_0 and P_i is:

$$\begin{aligned} & I(P_0, Z) \\ & = \sum_{p_0}\sum_{z} p(p_0, z) \log \frac{p(p_0,z)}{p(p_0)p(z)} \\ & = a_{00} \log \frac{a_{00}}{(1-p)(a_{10}+a_{00})} + a_{01} \log \frac{a_{01}}{(1-p)(a_{11}+a_{00})} \\ & \quad + a_{10} \log \frac{a_{10}}{p(a_{00}+a_{10})} + a_{11} \log \frac{a_{11}}{p(a_{01}+a_{11})} \end{aligned} \tag{3}$$

Since $a_{00} + a_{01} + a_{10} + a_{11} = 1$, $p = a_{10} + a_{11}$, $q = a_{01} + a_{11}$, the above equation can be further transformed into a formula related only to the variables a_{11} and p, where q is a fixed value:

$$\begin{aligned} & I(P_0, Z) \\ & = (1 + a_{11} - p - q) \log \frac{1+a_{11}-p-q}{(1-p)(1+2a_{11}-p-q)} \\ & \quad + (q - a_{11}) \log \left[q - \frac{a_{11}}{(1-p)(p+q-2a_{11})} \right] \\ & \quad + a_{11} \log \frac{a_{11}}{p(1+2a_{11}-p-q)} \\ & \quad + (p - a_{11}) \log \frac{p-a_{11}}{p(p+q-2a_{11})} \end{aligned} \tag{4}$$

Similarly, the mutual information between the random variables P_i and Z is as follows, and p is a fixed value at this time:

$$\begin{aligned} & I(P_i, Z) \\ & = (1 + a_{11} - p - q) \log \frac{1+a_{11}-p-q}{(1-q)(1+2a_{11}-p-q)} \\ & \quad + (p - a_{11}) \log \frac{p-a_{11}}{(1-q)(p+q-2a_{11})} \\ & \quad + a_{11} \log \frac{a_{11}}{q(1+2a_{11}-p-q)} \\ & \quad + (q - a_{11}) \log \frac{q-a_{11}}{q(p+q-2a_{11})} \end{aligned} \tag{5}$$

The above is the mutual information between the rational delegation party P_0 and the rational computing party P_i. And can extend to a one-to-many delegation computing scheme.

3.5 Payment Phase

After completing the calculation task, the computing party returns the calculation result to the P_0. At this point, the utility function of the computing party $P = \{1, 2, \cdots, n\}$ is $u_i (P_0, P_1, \cdots, P_n) = I \left(P_0; R_j \left| R_j^C \right. \right)$. Upon receipt of the returned calculation results, the P_0 shall pay the reward c to the $P = \{1, 2, \cdots, n\}$ according to the agreement. If the delegation party breaches the agreement and fails to pay the reward to the completing party, the delegation party shall be fined b and $b > a, b > c$ according to its utility function.

When the P_0 receives the calculation result returned by the completing party, the transformation of function F is restored according to its pre-processing stage. If the delegation party successfully restores the function, according to the utility of the delegation party in the game model, the utility of the P_0 at this time is $u_0 (P_0, P_1, \cdots, P_n) = \sum_{i=1}^{K} a_i I \left(P_0; T_i \left| T_i^C \right. \right)$. If the delegation party fails to restore the function F successfully, it will refuse to receive the returned result and punish the computing party. The penalty at this time is b, and $b > a$.

Since the penalty in the agreement deviates from the protocol is $b > a$, the penalty is much greater than the value of the calculation function F itself. Therefore, according to the rational behavior of the participants, they will choose the optimal strategy to maximize their own interests. By setting the utility functions of both parties, the behavior strategy is selected according to the judgment of their effectiveness in the agreement, which greatly reduces the risk of participants deviating from the agreement, and can motivate the participants to actively abide by the agreement.

Based on the above analysis, we can get a utility matrix of rational participants. According to the rational computing party's behavior strategy and the rational delegation party's behavior strategy, the corresponding utility function can be obtained, as shown in Table 2.

Table 2. Participant utility matrix

Delegation party	Completing party		
		Diligent	Lazy
	Honest	$u_i + c, u_0 - c$	$u_i - b, u_0 - c$
	Default	$u_i + c, u_0 - b$	$u_i - b, u_0 - b$

4 Scheme Analysis

This section discusses the Nash equilibrium state of the scheme and analyzes the performance of the scheme.

4.1 Nash Equilibrium

Theorem 1. *According to the designed rational delegation computation scheme, when rational participants choose honest strategies, the scheme can reach Nash equilibrium.*

Proof. This paper analyzes and proves the game state from the three stages of rational delegation computing scheme.

Stage 1: In the initialization phase of the scheme, the rational computing party $P = \{1, 2, \cdots, n\}$ will accept the calculation task sent by the delegation party P_0 within its computing power. If both the rational participants abide by the scheme rules, both parties will choose the most favorable behavior strategy.

Stage 2: Then, in the delegation computing stage, the rational computing party $P = \{1, 2, \cdots, n\}$ will use its own resources to complete the computing task F and send the calculated results to the P_0 as the calculation output. At this time, the behavior strategy of rational participants should be considered. If both the P_0 and $P = \{1, 2, \cdots, n\}$ adopt an honest strategy, the delegation party can get the utility of the $u_0 - c$, and the computing party can also get the utility of the $u_i + c$. If the P_0 chooses the honest strategy and returns the reward to $P = \{1, 2, \cdots, n\}$ on time, and the latter chooses the lazy strategy, the delegation party can get the utility of the $u_0 - c$, and the computing party can also get the utility of $u_i - b$. If the P_0 chooses the default strategy and does not return the reward to the computing party, but the computing party chooses the honest strategy, the delegation party can get the utility of $u_0 - b$, and the computing party can get the utility of $u_i + c$. If both the P_0 and $P = \{1, 2, \cdots, n\}$ choose to deviate from the scheme, the delegation party can get the utility of $u_0 - b$, and the computing party can get the utility of $u_i - b$.

Stage 3: Finally, in the payment utility stage, the penalty b is much larger than the calculation cost a and reward c in the game model. That is $u_i + c > u_i - b$ and $u_0 - c > u_0 - b$. Therefore, only when the rational participants choose the honest strategy can the P_0 and $P = \{1, 2, \cdots, n\}$ will obtain the maximum utility, and the global state is also optimized.

According to the analysis of the scheme, we can use the sub-game refining Nash equilibrium to analyze the rational delegation computing. Only when the rational participant chooses the honest strategy, the overall situation can reach the optimal state, the scheme is executed and the Nash equilibrium state is satisfied.

4.2 Capability Limit Experiment

According to the self-interested behavior of the rational delegation party P_0 and the rational computing party P_i, we can consider the mutual information between the delegation party and the computing party at different probabilities. As shown in Fig. 4, we performed a simulation experiment on mutual information $I(P_0, Z)$.

When the P_0 is at different probabilities, the value of its mutual information is also different, but its mutual information has an extreme value.

As shown in Fig. 5, we performed a simulation experiment on mutual information $I(P_i, Z)$. When P_i is at different probabilities, the value of its mutual information is also different, but its mutual information also has an extreme value. Of course, the overall mutual information limit between the rational delegation party P_0 and the rational computing party P_i is shown in Fig. 6.

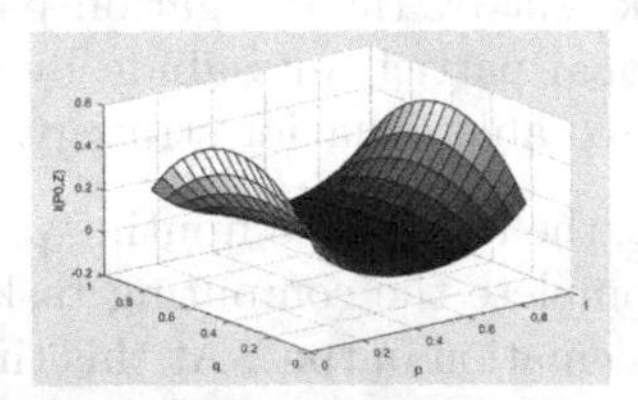

Fig. 4. The mutual information $I(P_0, Z)$ of the rational delegation party P_0

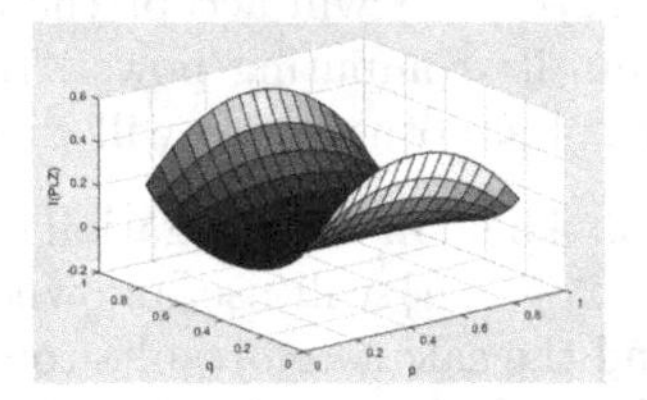

Fig. 5. The mutual information $I(P_i, Z)$ of the rational computing party P_i

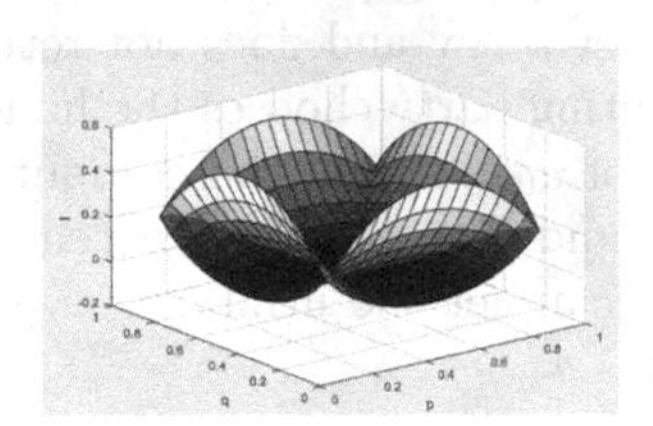

Fig. 6. Mutual information limit

4.3 Simulation Experiment

In this section, we conduct experimental simulation of the rational delegation computing scheme based on information theory. We delegate different numbers of modular exponential function operations to the rational computing side party, and compare the time consumption required for direct calculation and delegate computing. As shown in Fig. 7, it is a comparison diagram of the time consumption required for the direct calculation function and the delegation computing.

It can be seen from the Fig. 7, since the rational computing party does not need to verify the calculation result, the calculation time is much smaller than the time of directly calculating the function, and when the number of delegations increases, the required time gap also increases.

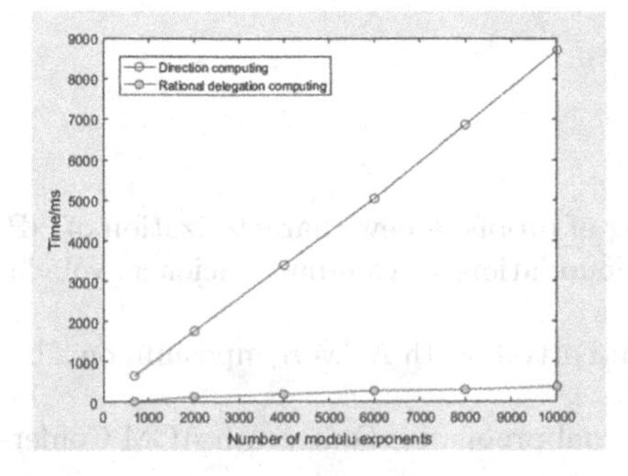

Fig. 7. The results of the multiple modulus exponential delegation scheme

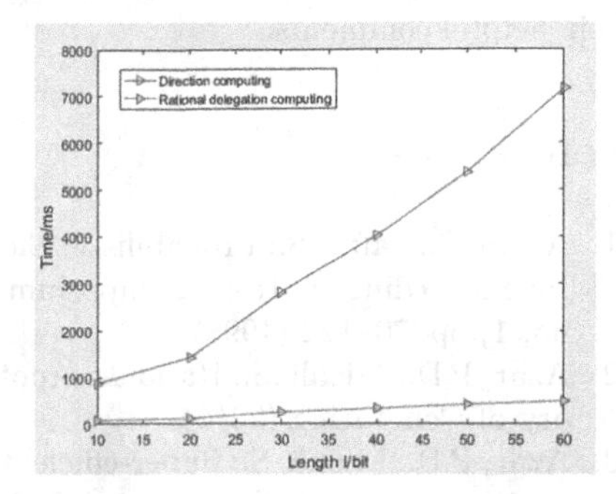

Fig. 8. The delegation computing result of polynomial number $|f|$=1000

Of course, for the delegation computing of special functions, we also simulated the multivariate polynomial delegate calculation. When the number of polynomial terms $|f|$ is fixed at 1000, as the length l of the polynomial input α_i changes, the direct computing function is compared with the time consumption required by the delegation computing, as shown in Fig. 8.

It can be seen from the figure that the delegation computing time consumption of the scheme is smaller than the direct computing time consumption, and as the number of delegation functions increases, the required calculation consumption time will also increase.

5 Conclusion

In this paper, we study the delegation computing problem with game theory and information theory, and analysis the behavioral strategies and utility of each participant in detail under the framework of game theory. Then, we proposed a pair of multiple rational delegation computing schemes based on average mutual information. In this scheme, the delegation party and the computing party select their own behavioral strategies according to their utility, and choose the best behavioral strategies for their own best interests. Finally, the analysis of the scheme proves that Nash equilibrium exists in the game, and the scheme is also effective. The next work for us is that how to consider the Game equilibrium of many-to-many delegation computing based on the existing research.

Acknowledgement. We would like to thank the anonymous reviewers for their valuable suggestions. This work is supported by The National Natural Science Foundation of China (Grant No. 61662009, 61772008); Science and Technology Major Support

Program of Guizhou Province (Grant No. 20183001); Guizhou provincial science and technology plan project (Grant No. [2017]5788); Ministry of Education - China Mobile Research Fund Project (Grant No. MCM20170401); Guizhou University Cultivation Project (Grant No. [2017]5788) Research on Block Data Fusion Analysis Theory and Security Management Model of Data Sharing Application No. U1836205 Research on Key Technologies of Blockchain for Big Data Applications Grant No. [2019]1098 for their helpful comments.

References

1. Arora, S., Safra, S.: Probabilistic checking of proofs: a new characterization of NP. In: Proceedings of IEEE Symposium on Foundations of Computer Science, vol. 45, no. 1, pp. 70–122 (1998)
2. Azar, P.D., Micali, S.: Rational proofs. In: Forty-Fourth ACM Symposium on Theory of Computing (2012)
3. Azar, P.D., Micali, S.: Super-efficient rational proofs. In: Fourteenth ACM Conference on Electronic Commerce (2013)
4. Chung, K.-M., Kalai, Y., Vadhan, S.: Improved delegation of computation using fully homomorphic encryption. In: Rabin, T. (ed.) CRYPTO 2010. LNCS, vol. 6223, pp. 483–501. Springer, Heidelberg (2010). https://doi.org/10.1007/978-3-642-14623-7_26
5. Gennaro, R., Gentry, C., Parno, B.: Non-interactive verifiable computing: outsourcing computation to untrusted workers. In: Rabin, T. (ed.) CRYPTO 2010. LNCS, vol. 6223, pp. 465–482. Springer, Heidelberg (2010). https://doi.org/10.1007/978-3-642-14623-7_25
6. Gennaro, R., Wichs, D.: Fully homomorphic message authenticators. In: Sako, K., Sarkar, P. (eds.) ASIACRYPT 2013. LNCS, vol. 8270, pp. 301–320. Springer, Heidelberg (2013). https://doi.org/10.1007/978-3-642-42045-0_16
7. Goldwasser, S., Micali, S., Rackoff, C.: The knowledge complexity of interactive proof systems (1985)
8. Goldwasser, S., Kalai, Y.T., Rothblum, G.N.: Delegating computation: interactive proofs for muggles. In: ACM Symposium on Theory of Computing (2008)
9. Guo, S., Hubáčk, P., Rosen, A., Vald, M.: Rational arguments: single round delegation with sublinear verification (2014)
10. Chen, J., Mccauley, S., Singh, S.: Rational proofs with multiple provers. In: ACM Conference on Innovations in Theoretical Computer Science (2016)
11. Zhang, L.F., Safavi-Naini, R.: Verifiable delegation of computations with storage-verification trade-off. In: Kutyłowski, M., Vaidya, J. (eds.) ESORICS 2014. LNCS, vol. 8712, pp. 112–129. Springer, Cham (2014). https://doi.org/10.1007/978-3-319-11203-9_7
12. Micali, S.: CS proofs. In: Symposium on Foundations of Computer Science (2002)
13. Tian, Y.L., Peng, C.G., Lin, D.D., Ma, J.F., Qi, J., Ji, W.J.: Bayesian mechanism for rational secret sharing scheme. Sci. China Inf. Sci. **58**(5), 52109–052109 (2015)
14. Yang, Y.X., Niu, X.X.: Covering information-theory with game-theory by the general theory of security-general theory of security(GTS)(11). J. Beijing Univ. Posts Telecommun. (2016)

Multi-hop Interactive Cross-Modal Retrieval

Xuecheng Ning[1], Xiaoshan Yang[2,3,4], and Changsheng Xu[1,2,3,4](✉)

[1] HeFei University of Technology, Hefei, China
nxuecheng@gmail.com
[2] National Lab of Pattern Recognition, Institute of Automation,
Chinese Academy of Sciences, Beijing, China
xiaoshan.yang@nlpr.ia.ac.cn
[3] University of Chinese Academy of Sciences, Beijing, China
csxu@nlpr.ia.ac.cn
[4] Peng Cheng Laboratory, ShenZhen, China

Abstract. Conventional representation learning based cross-modal retrieval approaches always represent the sentence with a global embedding feature, which easily neglects the local correlations between objects in the image and phrases in the sentence. In this paper, we present a novel Multi-hop Interactive Cross-modal Retrieval Model (MICRM), which interactively exploits the local correlations between images and words. We design a multi-hop interactive module to infer the high-order relevance between the image and the sentence. Experimental results on two benchmark datasets, MS-COCO and Flickr30K, demonstrate that our multi-hop interactive model performs significantly better than several competitive cross-modal retrieval methods.

Keywords: Cross-modal retrieval · Deep learning · LSTMs

1 Introduction

Over the last decade, there has been an explosion of multimedia data generated on Internet, including texts, images and videos. Traditional single-modality-based retrieval methods, such as [24,26], only perform similarity search of the same media type, such as text retrieval, image retrieval, and video retrieval. However, the single modality retrieval can hardly satisfy all the requirements of various users. For example, some users may want to find the relevant text descriptions for a landmark photo while others may want to search the relevant videos for phrases, such as "a person is playing the piano". These new demands have inspired research interest in cross-modal retrieval, which aims to take one type of data as the query to retrieve relevant data of another type.

In this work, we mainly focus on the image-text bidirectional retrieval, which is one of the mostly studied and hard problems in cross-media retrieval. It is also concerned by a wide range of applications in multimedia research, such as image

Y. M. Ro et al. (Eds.): MMM 2020, LNCS 11962, pp. 681–693, 2020.
https://doi.org/10.1007/978-3-030-37734-2_55

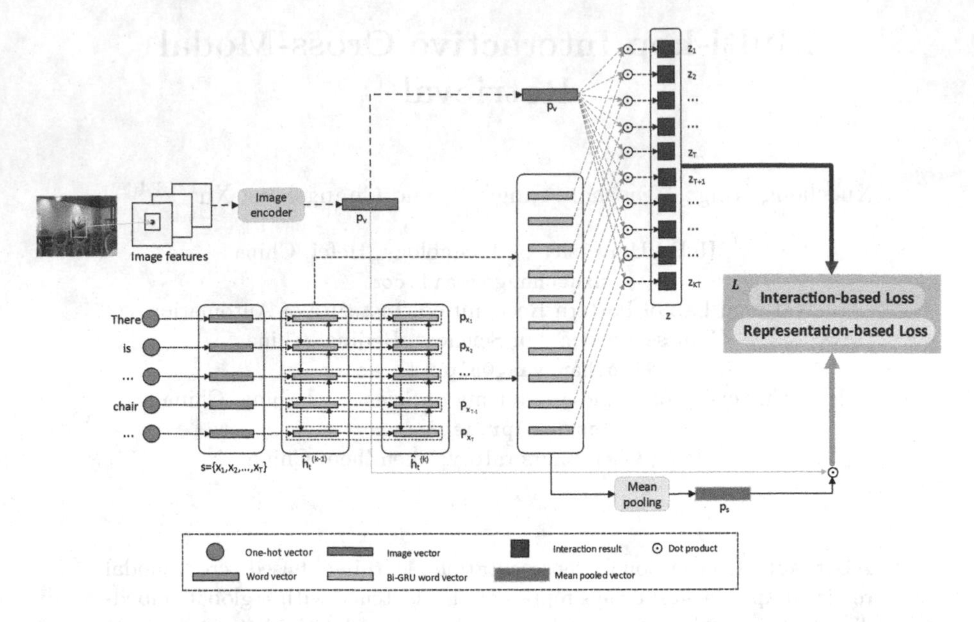

Fig. 1. An illustration of the framework of our model. A stacked bi-directional GRU network is used to generate text representations, and an interactive module implements the multi-hop interactions between image-word representation pairs. Our objective consists of the representation-based loss and the interaction-based loss.

caption generation [19,29], visual question answering [2,18]. Different modalities usually have inconsistent representation and distribution. The major difficulty of cross-media retrieval is to bridge the modality gap. One of the popularly used traditional strategy is to learn linear or non-linear projections to generate a shared feature space, where modality-invariant representations are obtained for handcraft features of different media types. Then the cross-media similarity can be directly measured by using common distance metric such as Euclidean distance. Conventional existing DNN-based cross-media retrieval models typically focus on how to find better ways to project images and sentences as global embedding pairs into the common space, and easily neglect the interactions between the images and single words.

To solve this problem, prior work such as [10], try to infer the latent alignment between segments of sentences and the region of the image that they describe. However, conventional representation-based methods generate text information as single global sentence embedding vectors, which can be redundant and hard to parse. In this paper, We propose to promoting the existing DNN-based cross-media retrieval methods by combining the representation-based and interaction-based methods that we refer to as Multi-hop Interactive Cross-Model Retrieval (MICMR) and that is built around the multi-hop interactions between images and texts.

As illustrated in Fig. 1, the core of the framework is feature representation learning and multi-hop interaction. We use an image encoder to generated the image representations while using a stacked bi-directional GRU [5] network to generate text representations, which is consisted of a series of word embeddings. Then, our interactive module implement the multi-hop interactions between image-word representation pairs. The major contributions of this paper are briefly summarized as follows:

- We propose an Multi-hop Interactive Cross-modal Retrieval model, which combined representation-based and interaction-based methods and focused on image-word interactions for bidirectional image-text retrieval.
- We explore a multi-hop interactive scheme to neglect the redundant information and infer the high-order relevance between images and texts.
- We have conducted experiments on two widely accepted multi-modal datasets: MS-COCO dataset [15] and Flickr30K [30]. Experimental results show that our proposed models obtain highly competitive results.

2 Related Work

In this section, we briefly review existing cross-modal retrieval methods. Since the cross-modal retrieval is considered as an important problem in real applications, various approaches have been proposed to deal with it. There are mainly two kinds of methods: real-valued representation learning [6,27] and binary representation learning [20,28]. The later is also referred as cross-modal hashing [4]. For real-valued representation learning, the learned common representations are real values. The binary representation learning aims to transform different modalities of data into a common Hamming space, in which the similarity of different modalities of data can be efficiently measured.

In this work, we mainly focus on the real-valued representation method. Many different ways have been proposed to learn the common representation subspace [1,25]. The similarity of heterogeneous data can be calculated by using the projected features in the joint subspace. For example, early methods, such as CCA-based methods [3] and graph-based methods [8], learn linear projections to generate a joint representation subspace. With the successful applications in computer vision and natural language processing, DNNs have increasingly been deployed in the cross-modal retrieval task. For example, m-CNN [16] adopts convolutional neural networks to exploit image representation, word composition, and the matching relations between the two modalities. UVS [12] model and its improved version VSE++ [7] learn joint image-sentence embedding space, where the image and the sentence are projected. The embedding space is learned by a constrain of triplet ranking loss with margin α.

There are few works focused on learning image-sentence matching patterns from multi-level interactions. In our work, the multi-level similarities are calculated from pre-trained word2vec embeddings. The interactive similarity between images and sentences are measured at different levels. Previous work, such as [10], try to infer the latent alignment between segments of sentences and the region of the image that they describe. Different from existing works, we present a multi-hop interactive framework to tackle the cross-model retrieval problem. The proposed method introduces an multi-hop interactive mechanism to focus on capturing the most attentive region of the image for each word. By this way, we effectively combine the conventional global features of images and sentences and the interaction-based similarity to improve the performance.

3 Methods

In this section, we describe the proposed multi-hop interactive cross-modal retrieval model (MICRM), in detail. We firstly present the problem formulation of the image-text retrieval task, followed by feature representations of the image and text instances. After that, we introduce the proposed multi-hop interactive retrieval module.

3.1 Problem Formulation

Let $\{(v_i, s_i)\}_{i=1,...,N}$ be a set of image-text pairs, where v_i and s_i are the original features of the image and text instances. Since the image feature v_i and the text feature s_i are from different modalities, they usually have inconsistent distribution and representation which cannot be directly used to measure the similarity. Thus, the main task of cross-media retrieval is to build a common feature subspace, where the pairwise distance between the image feature $p_v = f_v(v; \theta_v)$ and the text feature $p_s = f_s(s; \theta_s)$ can be minimized. The f_v and f_s are the mapping functions while p_v and p_s are the embedding features.

3.2 Image Embedding

Given an image, we use a convolutional neural neural network (CNN) [14] to extract the visual feature v. The CNN was pre-trained on image classification task. We replace the last layer with a fully-connected (FC) projecting layer to map the visual feature into the common space:

$$p_v = (W_v * v) + b_v \tag{1}$$

where the W_v is a learnable parameter vector, b_v is a bias unit, and p_v is the embedded feature vector in the common feature space.

3.3 Sentence Embedding

In this section, we mainly introduce our text representation learning module based on a stacked bi-directional GRU network. By combining the stacked forward and backward GRUs, our text representation can incorporate the hierarchical contextual semantic information of all words in the sentence.

Word Representation. We firstly utilize the off-the-shelf NLP tools to preprocess the input documents and extract tokenized words from the text. Then, we initialize all words of the sentence with 300-dimensional embedding vectors $s = \{x_1, x_2, ..., x_t, ..., x_T\}$, where x_t is the embedded feature of the tth word. This can be implemented by multiplying the one-hot vector of each word with a learnable embedding matrix.

Multi-hop Representation. We use x_t to denote the embedded feature vector for the tth word of a sentence. Then, the GRU architecture is given by:

$$\begin{aligned} r_t &= \sigma(W_{ir}x_t + b_{ir} + W_{hr}h_{(t-1)} + b_{hr}) \\ z_t &= \sigma(W_{iz}x_t + b_{iz} + W_{hz}h_{(t-1)} + b_{hz}) \\ n_t &= tanh(W_{in}x_t + b_{in} + r_t(W_{hn}h_{(t-1)} + b_{hn})) \\ h_t &= (1 - z_t)n_t + z_t h_{(t-1)} \end{aligned} \tag{2}$$

where (r_t, z_t, n_t, h_t) denote the reset date, update gate, candidate and hidden state at time step t. The σ denotes the sigmoid activation function.

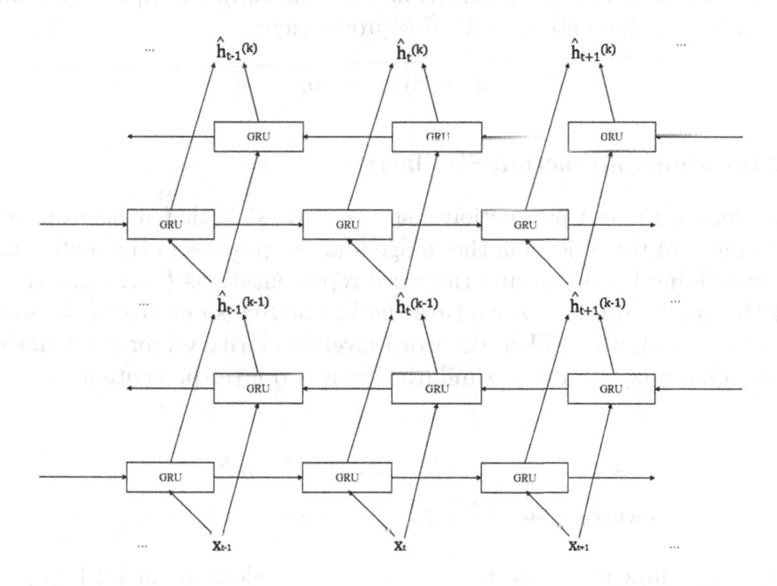

Fig. 2. An example of the stacked bi-directional GRU network.

To further exploit the context semantics of the sentence, we extend the GRU into a bi-directional structure as follows:

$$\hat{h}_t = GRU_{\rightarrow}(x_t, h_{t-1}^{\rightarrow}) + GRU_{\leftarrow}(x_t, h_{t+1}^{\leftarrow}) \tag{3}$$

where $GRU_t^{\rightarrow}$ and $GRU_t^{\leftarrow}$ represent the forward and backward GRU networks which have the same architecture as Eq. (2). The $\hat{h}_t$ is the concatenation hidden

feature of the forward and backward hidden states at the t-th step.
By processing the word sequence from two directions with two separate hidden layers, our sentence representation can capture both the previous and future context information.
Furthermore, we stack multiple layers of bi-directional GRU networks. The output $\hat{h}_t^{k-1}$ from the previous Bi-GRU layer is used as the input of the next layer which produce the output $\hat{h}_t^k$. Figure 2 shows an example of a two-layer stacked bi-directional GRU networks. The final embedded feature p_s of the sentence is obtained by mean-pooling the output of each Bi-GRU layer.

$$p_s = \frac{1}{TK} \sum_{t=1}^{T} \sum_{k=1}^{K} \hat{h}_{x_t^k} \tag{4}$$

3.4 Sentence-Level Similarity

As illustrated in Sects. 3.2 and 3.3, we have obtained the image embedding feature p_v by a fully-connected layer and the sentence embedding feature p_s by a stacked bi-directional GRU network. Then, we can simply compute the similarity of the image and the sentence with dot production:

$$d_1(v, s) = p_v \cdot p_s \tag{5}$$

3.5 Multi-hop Interaction Similarity

The problem of the dot production distance $d_1(v, s)$ is that it neglects the specific semantics of the objects in the image and the phrases in the sentence. With image embedding feature p_v and the word representations $\{p_{x_1}, p_{x_2}, ..., p_{x_T}\}$, we extend the dot production to capture the interactive similarity z_t^k between the image and the t-th word. Then the word-level similarity vector z is transformed into the global image-sentence similarity by a two-layer perception:

$$\begin{aligned} z_t^k &= p_v \cdot \hat{h}_{x_t^k}, \quad t = 1, ..., T, \ k = 1, ..., K \\ d_2(v, s) &= tanh(W_1 * (relu((W_2 * z) + b_2) + b_1) \end{aligned} \tag{6}$$

where the TK-dimensional vector z consists of all elements of $\{z_t^k\}_{t=1,k=1}^{T,K}$. The $d_2(v, s)$ denotes the multi-hop interaction similarity between the image embedding p_v and the sentence embedding p_s. The W_1, W_2, b_1, b_2 are learnable parameters.

3.6 Multi-task Learning

In Sects. 3.4 and 3.5, we have defined two kinds of similarities. Now we will introduce the optimization objectives we used to learn the proposed multi-modal embedding framework. The objective consists of the representation-based loss and the interaction-based loss:

$$L = L_{representation} + L_{interaction} \tag{7}$$

where each item will be illustrated in as follows.

Representation-Based Loss. Based on the global representation similarity $d_1(v, c)$, we adopt a representation-based, triplet ranking loss with a margin α to constrain the similarity of paired or unpaired image and sentence instances:

$$L_{representation} = \max_{\hat{s}}[\alpha - d_1(v, s) + d_1(v, \hat{s})]_+ + \max_{\hat{v}}[\alpha - d_1(v, s) + d_1(\hat{v}, s)]_+ \tag{8}$$

where $d_1(v, s)$ denotes the representation-based similarity score of the positive image-text pair, while $d_1(v, \hat{s})$ and $d_1(\hat{v}, s)$ represent the scores of negative pairs. The + denotes the hard negative instance mining scheme proposed in [14].

Interaction-Based Loss. Based on the multi-hop interaction similarity $d_2(v, s)$, we design an extra interaction-based loss with margin β:

$$L_{interaction} = max(\max_{\hat{s}}(\beta - d_2(v, s) + d_2(v, \hat{s})), \max_{\hat{v}}(\beta - d_2(v, s) + d_2(\hat{v}, s))) \tag{9}$$

where $d_2(v, s)$ denotes the interaction-based similarity score of positive the image-text pair, while $d_2(v, \hat{s})$ and $d_2(\hat{v}, s)$ represent the scores of negative pairs.

4 Experiment

In this section, we evaluate the effectiveness of our MICRM on bidirectional image and sentence retrieval. We begin by a brief description of our experimental settings including datasets, evaluation metric and implementation details. Then we present result analysis and discussions.

Table 1. Details of the two datasets used in our experiments.

Dataset	#Training	#Testing	Image feature dim	Word feature dim	Embedding size
MS-COCO	82783	1000	4096-d	300-d	1024-d
Flickr30K	29000	1000	4096-d	300-d	1024-d

4.1 Datasets

MS-COCO [15] consists of 82783 training images, 40000 validation images, which belong to 80 categories. In this paper, we randomly select 1000 images for the test split. Flickr 30K [30] has a standard 29000 images for training. We use 1000 images for validation and 1000 images for testing according to the "Karpathy" splits which have been extensively used in prior work. Among the above datasets, each image has 5 captions. The statistics of the two datasets are described in Table 1.

Table 2. Experiments on MS-COCO dataset

Model	Image to text				Text to image			
	R@1	R@5	R@10	Med r	R@1	R@5	R@10	Med r
DVSA [10]	38.4	69.9	80.5	-	27.4	60.2	74.8	-
GMM-FVS [13]	39.4	67.9	80.9	-	25.1	59.8	76.6	3
m-CNN [16]	42.8	73.1	84.1	-	32.6	68.6	82.8	-
UVS [12]	43.4	-	85.8	2	31.0	-	79.9	3
Order [23]	46.7	-	88.9	2	37.9	-	85.9	2
VSE++ [7]	43.6	-	84.6	2	33.7	-	81.0	3
Our model	**48.1**	**78.5**	**88.9**	2	**35.4**	**70.9**	**84.0**	2

4.2 Implementation Details

In this subsection, we will illustrate the hyper-parameter setting and training details. The word embedding layer uses pre-trained 300 dimensional vectors. The dimensionality of the image embedding is 4096, extracted by the fc7 layer of VGG19 network [21]. For the model optimization, we use the Adam optimizer with the batch size of 128 and learning rate of 0.0002. Our model is trained end-to-end for 30 epochs and the learning rate is rescaled for every 5 epochs.

4.3 Evaluation Metric

In this paper, we normalize the embedded image and sentence vectors and use dot product as the similarity measurement. We adopt Recall@k at $k = 1, 5, 10$ to measure the items correctly retrieved among the top k results. And the two margins in the representation-based loss and the interaction-based loss are set to $\alpha = 0.2$ and $\beta = 1$. We also present the median rank (Med r) of the ground truth result. We compare our method with several competitive baselines, which have been widely used as benchmark models in the previous work.

- m-CNN model composes different semantic fragments from words and learns the inter-modal relations between images and the composed fragments at different levels. It fully exploits the matching relations between the image and the sentence. Since convolutional neural networks (CNNs) have powerful abilities on learning of image representation and sentence representation, m-CNN model can achieve superior performances than traditional representation based approaches.
- UVS model uses an encoder-decoder pipeline, which allows encoder to learn a joint image-sentence embedding. The decoder uses the structure-content neural language model to generate realistic image captions. Due to the effectiveness of LSTM cells for encoding dependencies across descriptions and learning meaningful distributed sentence representations, UVS model makes significant progress in cross-modal retrieval task.

- Order model is concentrated on the antisymmetric relation of the visual-semantic hierarchy. This model exploits the partial order structure of the visual-semantic hierarchy by learning a mapping which is not distance-preserving but order-preserving between the visual-semantic hierarchy. Thus, the order embeddings also provide a marked improvement.
- VSE++ model, which is based on the UVS model, uses augmented data and fine-tuning scheme to produce a significant improvement in caption retrieval.

Table 3. Experiments on Flickr30K dataset

Model	Image to text				Text to image			
	R@1	R@5	R@10	Med r	R@1	R@5	R@10	Med r
DeViSE [9]	4.5	18.1	29.2	26	6.7	21.9	32.7	25
SDT-RNN [22]	9.6	29.8	41.1	16	8.9	29.8	41.1	16
DeFrag [11]	14.2	37.7	51.3	10	10.2	30.8	44.2	14
m-RNN [17]	18.4	40.2	50.9	10	12.6	31.2	41.5	16
UVS [12]	23.0	50.7	62.9	5	16.8	42.0	56.5	8
VSE++ [7]	31.9	-	68.0	4	23.1	-	60.7	6
Our model	**35.2**	**62.1**	**71.3**	3	**25.2**	**52.2**	**62.9**	5

4.4 Experimental Results

Table 2 summarizes the performance of our model on the MS-COCO dataset. We obtain 4.5% improvement on R@1 for caption retrieval and 1.7% on R@1 for image retrieval compared with the second best model. Table 3 shows the results on the Flickr30K dataset. We obtain 3.3% improvement on R@1 for caption retrieval and 2.1% improvement on R@1 for image retrieval compared with the second best model. The performance improvement shows that our interactive method can contextually exploit the similarity between the multiple objects and semantics for cross-modal retrieval task. And the multi-hop scheme can also remove the redundant information and infer the high-order relevance between images and texts.

Table 4. R@1 results with different number of hop K on MS-COCO and Flickr30K.

Datasets	$K=1$		$K=2$	
	Img2Txt	Txt2Img	Img2Txt	Txt2Img
MS-COCO	46.0	35.0	48.1	35.4
Flickr30K	33.5	24.9	35.2	25.2

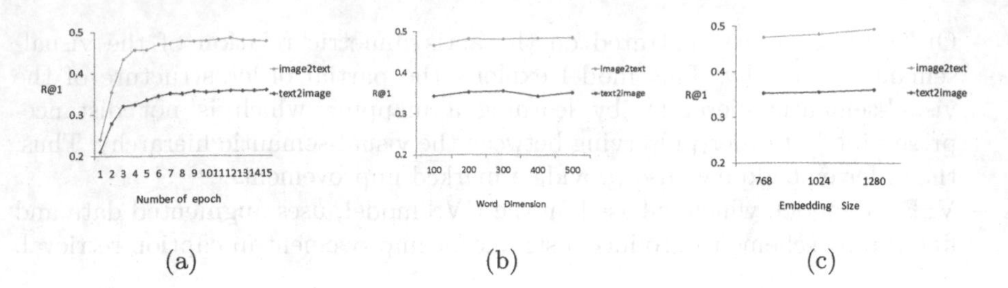

Fig. 3. Model analysis on the MS COCO dataset. Left: validation performance with different training epochs. Middle: impact of the dimension of the word embedding. Right: Impact of the embedding size.

To further explore the effectiveness of the multi-hop interactive module, we examined the performance of the proposed interactive module with different interaction hops. As shown in Table 4, there is a significant improvement from 1 to 2, which shows the effectiveness of our multi-hop interactive module. Figure 4 presents some examples of test images and top-1 retrieved captions based on our MICRM model.

4.5 Model Analysis

Figure 3(a) shows the validation results in first 15 epochs of the training. It is worth noting that in the first 5 epochs, our model already achieves a relatively good performance. After the 6-th epoch, the accuracy does not increase much. This indicates that our model converges very fast. To further evaluate the proposed framework, we also test our model with various word dimensions and embedding sizes.

As shown in Fig. 3(b), it is obvious that retrieval performance is related to the word dimension. When the dimension of the encoded word vector increases from 100 to 500, the retrieval accuracy also increases. Because more text features will

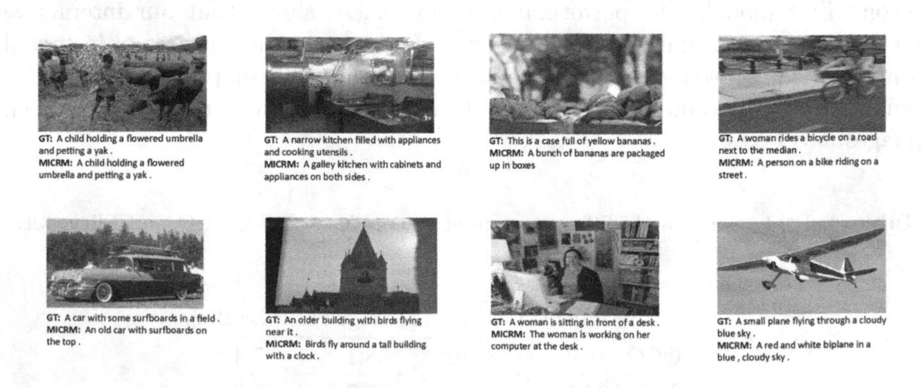

Fig. 4. Examples of test images and top1 captions retrieved by the MICRM model

be captured with larger dimension of word vectors. To keep a balance between the performance and the efficiency, we set the dimension of the word vector as 300 in our experiment.

Figure 3(c) shows that the embedding size has slight impact on the model performance. By increasing the number of embedding size, the retrieval accuracy of our model will be improved. But it will cost much time for the parameter optimization. Thus, we set the embedding size to 1024 in our experiment.

5 Conclusion

In this paper, we proposed MICRM, a novel interaction based and representation embedding model for cross-modal retrieval. The proposed method can effectively capture multi-level semantic correlations between images and sentences by the multi-hop interactive module. We evaluated the proposed method on MS-COCO and Flickr30K datasets. The extensive experiment results showed that our proposed model achieves significant improvement for cross-modal retrieval task, compared with several competitive existing approaches.

Acknowledgments. This work was supported by National Key Research and Development Program of China (No. 2018AAA0100604, 2017YFB1002804), National Natural Science Foundation of China (No. 61872424, 61702511, 61720106006, 61728210, 61751211, 61620106003, 61532009, 61572498, 61572296, 61432019, U1836220, U1705262) and Key Research Program of Frontier Sciences, CAS, Grant NO. QYZD-JSSWJSC039. This work was also supported by Research Program of National Laboratory of Pattern Recognition (No. Z-2018007) and CCF-Tencent Open Fund.

References

1. Aigrain, P., Zhang, H., Petkovic, D.: Content-based representation and retrieval of visual media: a state-of-the-art review. Multimedia Tools Appl. **3**(3), 179–202 (1996)
2. Anderson, P., et al.: Bottom-up and top-down attention for image captioning and visual question answering. In: Proceedings of the IEEE Conference on Computer Vision and Pattern Recognition, pp. 6077–6086 (2018)
3. Andrew, G., Arora, R., Bilmes, J., Livescu, K.: Deep canonical correlation analysis. In: International Conference on Machine Learning, pp. 1247–1255 (2013)
4. Cao, Y., Long, M., Wang, J., Yang, Q., Yu, P.S.: Deep visual-semantic hashing for cross-modal retrieval. In: Proceedings of the 22nd ACM SIGKDD International Conference on Knowledge Discovery and Data Mining, pp. 1445–1454. ACM (2016)
5. Cho, K., et al.: Learning phrase representations using RNN encoder-decoder for statistical machine translation. arXiv preprint arXiv:1406.1078 (2014)
6. Dooly, D.R., Zhang, Q., Goldman, S.A., Amar, R.A.: Multiple-instance learning of real-valued data. J. Mach. Learn. Res. **3**(Dec), 651–678 (2002)
7. Faghri, F., Fleet, D.J., Kiros, J.R., Fidler, S.: VSE++: improving visual-semantic embeddings with hard negatives. arXiv preprint arXiv:1707.05612 (2017)
8. Felzenszwalb, P.F., Huttenlocher, D.P.: Efficient graph-based image segmentation. Int. J. Comput. Vis. **59**(2), 167–181 (2004)

9. Frome, A., Corrado, G.S., Shlens, J., Bengio, S., Dean, J., Mikolov, T., et al.: DeViSE: a deep visual-semantic embedding model. In: Advances in Neural Information Processing Systems, pp. 2121–2129 (2013)
10. Karpathy, A., Fei-Fei, L.: Deep visual-semantic alignments for generating image descriptions. In: Proceedings of the IEEE Conference on Computer Vision and Pattern Recognition, pp. 3128–3137 (2015)
11. Karpathy, A., Joulin, A., Fei-Fei, L.F.: Deep fragment embeddings for bidirectional image sentence mapping. In: Advances in Neural Information Processing Systems, pp. 1889–1897 (2014)
12. Kiros, R., Salakhutdinov, R., Zemel, R.S.: Unifying visual-semantic embeddings with multimodal neural language models. arXiv preprint arXiv:1411.2539 (2014)
13. Klein, B., Lev, G., Sadeh, G., Wolf, L.: Associating neural word embeddings with deep image representations using fisher vectors. In: Proceedings of the IEEE Conference on Computer Vision and Pattern Recognition, pp. 4437–4446 (2015)
14. Krizhevsky, A., Sutskever, I., Hinton, G.E.: ImageNet classification with deep convolutional neural networks. In: Advances in Neural Information Processing Systems, pp. 1097–1105 (2012)
15. Lin, T.-Y., et al.: Microsoft COCO: common objects in context. In: Fleet, D., Pajdla, T., Schiele, B., Tuytelaars, T. (eds.) ECCV 2014. LNCS, vol. 8693, pp. 740–755. Springer, Cham (2014). https://doi.org/10.1007/978-3-319-10602-1_48
16. Ma, L., Lu, Z., Shang, L., Li, H.: Multimodal convolutional neural networks for matching image and sentence. In: Proceedings of the IEEE International Conference on Computer Vision, pp. 2623–2631 (2015)
17. Mao, J., Xu, W., Yang, Y., Wang, J., Yuille, A.L.: Explain images with multimodal recurrent neural networks. arXiv preprint arXiv:1410.1090 (2014)
18. Ray, A., Christie, G., Bansal, M., Batra, D., Parikh, D.: Question relevance in VQA: identifying non-visual and false-premise questions. arXiv preprint arXiv:1606.06622 (2016)
19. Rennie, S.J., Marcheret, E., Mroueh, Y., Ross, J., Goel, V.: Self-critical sequence training for image captioning. In: Proceedings of the IEEE Conference on Computer Vision and Pattern Recognition, pp. 7008–7024 (2017)
20. Shen, F., Zhou, X., Yang, Y., Song, J., Shen, H.T., Tao, D.: A fast optimization method for general binary code learning. IEEE Trans. Image Process. **25**(12), 5610–5621 (2016)
21. Simonyan, K., Zisserman, A.: Very deep convolutional networks for large-scale image recognition. arXiv preprint arXiv:1409.1556 (2014)
22. Socher, R., Karpathy, A., Le, Q.V., Manning, C.D., Ng, A.Y.: Grounded compositional semantics for finding and describing images with sentences. Trans. Assoc. Comput. Linguist. **2**, 207–218 (2014)
23. Vendrov, I., Kiros, R., Fidler, S., Urtasun, R.: Order-embeddings of images and language. arXiv preprint arXiv:1511.06361 (2015)
24. Wan, J., et al.: Deep learning for content-based image retrieval: a comprehensive study. In: Proceedings of the 22nd ACM International Conference on Multimedia, pp. 157–166. ACM (2014)
25. Wang, C., Yang, H., Meinel, C.: A deep semantic framework for multimodal representation learning. Multimedia Tools Appl. **75**(15), 9255–9276 (2016)
26. Wang, D., Nyberg, E.: A long short-term memory model for answer sentence selection in question answering. In: Proceedings of the 53rd Annual Meeting of the Association for Computational Linguistics and the 7th International Joint Conference on Natural Language Processing (Volume 2: Short Papers), pp. 707–712 (2015)

27. Wang, L., Li, Y., Lazebnik, S.: Learning deep structure-preserving image-text embeddings. In: Proceedings of the IEEE Conference on Computer Vision and Pattern Recognition, pp. 5005–5013 (2016)
28. Xu, X., Shen, F., Yang, Y., Shen, H.T., Li, X.: Learning discriminative binary codes for large-scale cross-modal retrieval. IEEE Trans. Image Process. **26**(5), 2494–2507 (2017)
29. You, Q., Jin, H., Wang, Z., Fang, C., Luo, J.: Image captioning with semantic attention. In: Proceedings of the IEEE Conference on Computer Vision and Pattern Recognition, pp. 4651–4659 (2016)
30. Young, P., Lai, A., Hodosh, M., Hockenmaier, J.: From image descriptions to visual denotations: new similarity metrics for semantic inference over event descriptions. Trans. Assoc. Comput. Linguist. **2**, 67–78 (2014)

Demo Papers

Browsing Visual Sentiment Datasets Using Psycholinguistic Groundings

Marc A. Kastner[1(✉)], Ichiro Ide[1], Yasutomo Kawanishi[1], Takatsugu Hirayama[2], Daisuke Deguchi[3], and Hiroshi Murase[1]

[1] Graduate School of Informatics, Nagoya University, Furo-cho, Chikusa-ku, Nagoya 464-8601, Japan
kastnerm@murase.is.i.nagoya-u.ac.jp, {ide,kawanishi,murase}@i.nagoya-u.ac.jp

[2] Institute of Innovation for Future Society, Nagoya University, Furo-cho, Chikusa-ku, Nagoya 464-8601, Japan
takatsugu.hirayama@nagoya-u.jp

[3] Information Strategy Office, Nagoya University, Furo-cho, Chikusa-ku, Nagoya 464-8601, Japan
ddeguchi@nagoya-u.jp

Abstract. Recent multimedia applications commonly use text and imagery from Social Media for tasks related to sentiment research. As such, there are various image datasets for sentiment research for popular classification tasks. However, there has been little research regarding the relationship between the sentiment of images and its annotations from a multi-modal standpoint. In this demonstration, we built a tool to visualize psycholinguistic groundings for a sentiment dataset. For each image, individual psycholinguistic ratings are computed from the image's metadata. A sentiment-psycholinguistic spatial embedding is computed to show a clustering of images across different classes close to human perception. Our interactive browsing tool can visualize the data in various ways, highlighting different psycholinguistic groundings with heatmaps.

Keywords: Visual sentiment · Psycholinguistics · Visualization

1 Introduction

The use of text and imagery from Social Media for tasks related to sentiment and emotion research became ubiquitous in recent research. However, there has been little research regarding the multi-modal implications of images and its annotations related to human perception. In this demonstration, we show a tool to visualize psycholinguistic groundings for a sentiment dataset. Using this, we analyze the relationship between texts and images, trying to get a better understanding of the groundings of human perception. For each image, individual psycholinguistic ratings are computed from the image's textual metadata.

Y. M. Ro et al. (Eds.): MMM 2020, LNCS 11962, pp. 697–702, 2020.
https://doi.org/10.1007/978-3-030-37734-2_56

Combined with sentiment scores available from the used dataset, a sentiment-psycholinguistic spatial embedding is computed. It shows a distribution of sentiment images close to human perception. Based on this, we create an interactive browsing tool, which can visualize the data in various ways. The tool allows to highlight different psycholinguistic ratings in heatmaps separately, as well as understand the structure of different datasets based on their ontology.

In Sect. 2 we briefly overview related research. Section 3 then discusses the idea of combining the sentiment scores of a given dataset with psycholinguistic groundings from the image metadata to compute individual scores for each image. Lastly, Sect. 4 showcases the interactive dataset browser we built to visualize embeddings of the sentiment-psycholinguistic space, which can be filtered across different nouns and adjectives. Various color modes allow for highlighting the different sentiment and psycholinguistic ratings.

2 Related Work

The human perception of natural language is part of the field of Psycholinguistics. In the 1960s, Paivio et al. [6] analyzed the concreteness, imagery, and meaningfulness of nouns. The most recent database for psycholinguistics is published by Scott et al. [7], which provides nine psycholinguistic ratings for 5,500 words. As these values describe human perception, the scores in such databases are typically obtained through psychological experiments. Our previous research on the visual variety of images in datasets [3] shows a connection in how humans perceive semantics of text and images.

There is various research on sentiment and emotion in multimedia applications [4], spanning visualization, datasets [2] and recognition techniques [1]. The connection between psycholinguistics features of text and visual features in sentiment images has not been researched to the best of our knowledge.

3 Approach

In this demonstration, we aim to present a means to analyze psycholinguistic groundings for sentiment image datasets. As a first step, a visual sentiment dataset having a large number of images annotated with adjective-noun pairs is retrieved. Using the textual metadata attached to an individual image, nine psycholinguistic scores are computed for each image. Lastly, a set of spatial embeddings based on each individual images' sentiment-psycholinguistic scores are computed for each noun, adjective and adjective-noun pair, respectively.

3.1 MVSO Dataset

As the baseline for the visualization tool, we use the MVSO dataset [2]. The dataset consists of seven million images, their textual metadata, and sentiment scores, collected through Flickr and crowd-sourcing. Each image is annotated

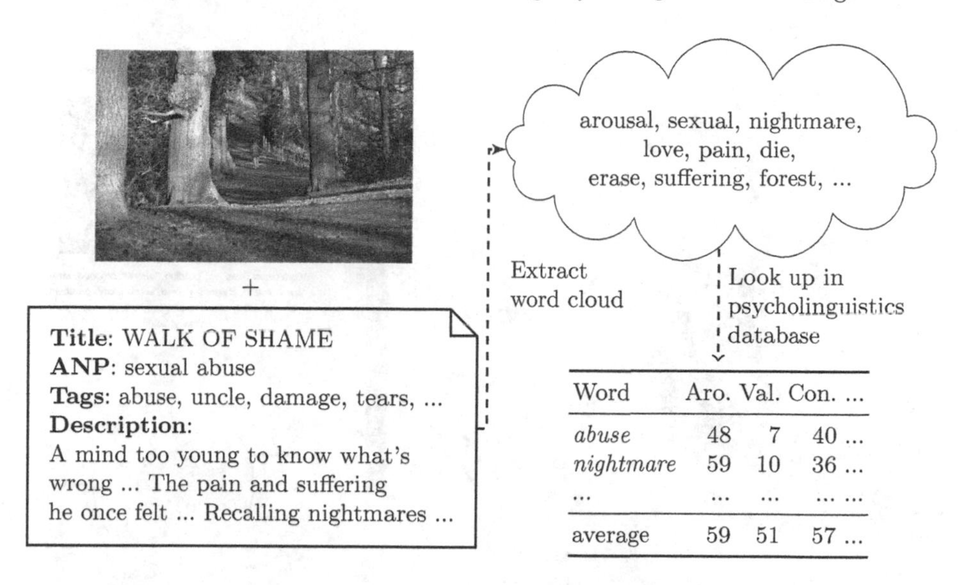

Fig. 1. The process of calculating per-image psycholinguistic scores. For each image, a word cloud is extracted from the textual metadata. Using a psycholinguistics database, an average score describing the image is computed for each psycholinguistic rating (Aro.=*Arousal*, Val.=*Valence*, Con.=*Concreteness*). The example image is courtesy of Flickr user despitestraightlines (http://flickr.com/photos/despitestraightlines/6677983565/).

with a single adjective-noun pair (ANP), e.g. *abandoned_city* or *old_dog*, describing its sentiment. We split the ANP into two labels; *noun* and *adjective*, to create a flat ontology-like structure. Using this, images related to the same noun but for different adjectives, and vice versa, can be filtered. Each ANP comes with 21 sentiment scores (e.g., $joy = 0.6$, $ecstasy = 0.8$), but all images with the same ANP share the same sentiment score. Each image also comes with textual metadata containing a title, a description text, and tags. This metadata is used in the following section to compute an individual psycholinguistic grounding for each image.

3.2 Per-Image Psycholinguistic Scores

To create an embedding with a meaningful spatial distribution per image, individual scores for each image are needed. We compute a psycholinguistic grounding of the textual metadata for each image. Scott et al. [7] provide a psycholinguistics dataset with nine ratings each for 5,500 words. The nine ratings available are: arousal, dominance, valence, imageability, concreteness, familiarity, semantic size, age of acquisition, and gender association. For each image, we extract the title, description, and tags from the MVSO dataset. All these data are provided by the image uploader, which makes them noisy. We generate a word-cloud from all words used in the metadata, stripping grammatical affixes through

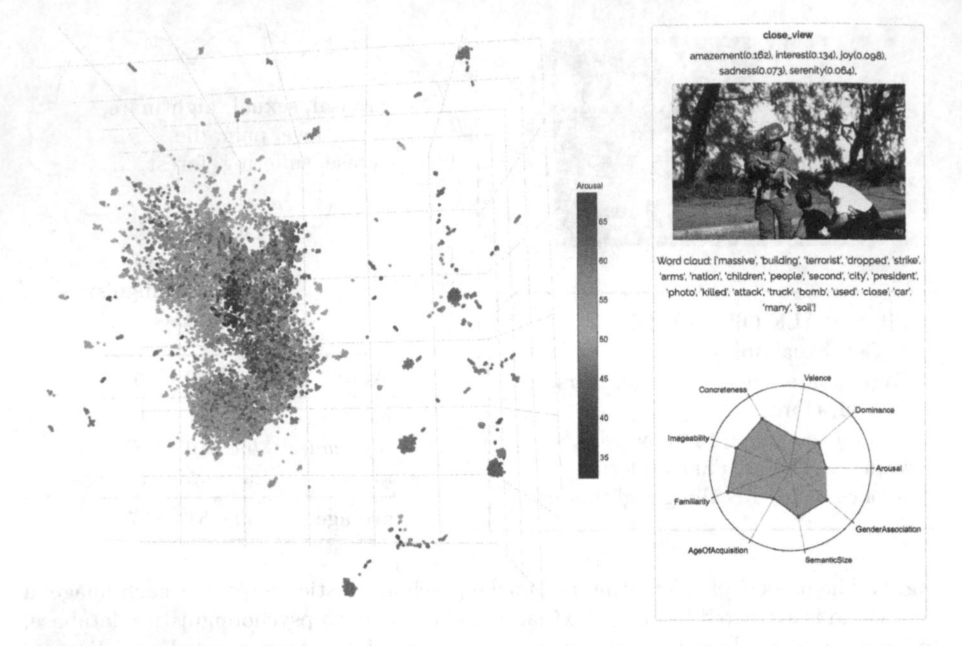

Fig. 2. The user interface of the tool. The upper left shows a three-dimensional embedding of the sentiment-psycholinguistics space. Detailed information for a selected image is shown on the right. The embedding can be filtered by noun, adjective, or ANP. Different color grading options are shown in Fig. 3. (Color figure online)

lemmatization. Furthermore, all words not contained in the psycholinguistics database are filtered out. Lastly, we compute nine psycholinguistic ratings by averaging the corresponding scores for each word in the word-cloud. The process of calculating per-image psycholinguistic scores is shown in Fig. 1. Filtering out images where the number of words available in the psycholinguistics dictionary was not sufficient, this results in approximately 400,000 images with nine individual psycholinguistic ratings each.

For each noun, adjective, and ANP, we compute a spatial embedding using UMAP [5]. Additionally, we compute an embedding including all images, filtering for extreme cases with very high or very low scores for some psycholinguistic ratings. As input, we use a 30-dimensional vector for each image, composed of the 21 sentiment scores of its ANP as well as the nine psycholinguistic ratings calculated through the metadata.

4 Visualization

To visualize the relationship between human sentiment ratings of an image and the psycholinguistic characteristics of words used in the image metadata, we built a dataset browser. Using this tool, it is possible to browse the dataset, filter it

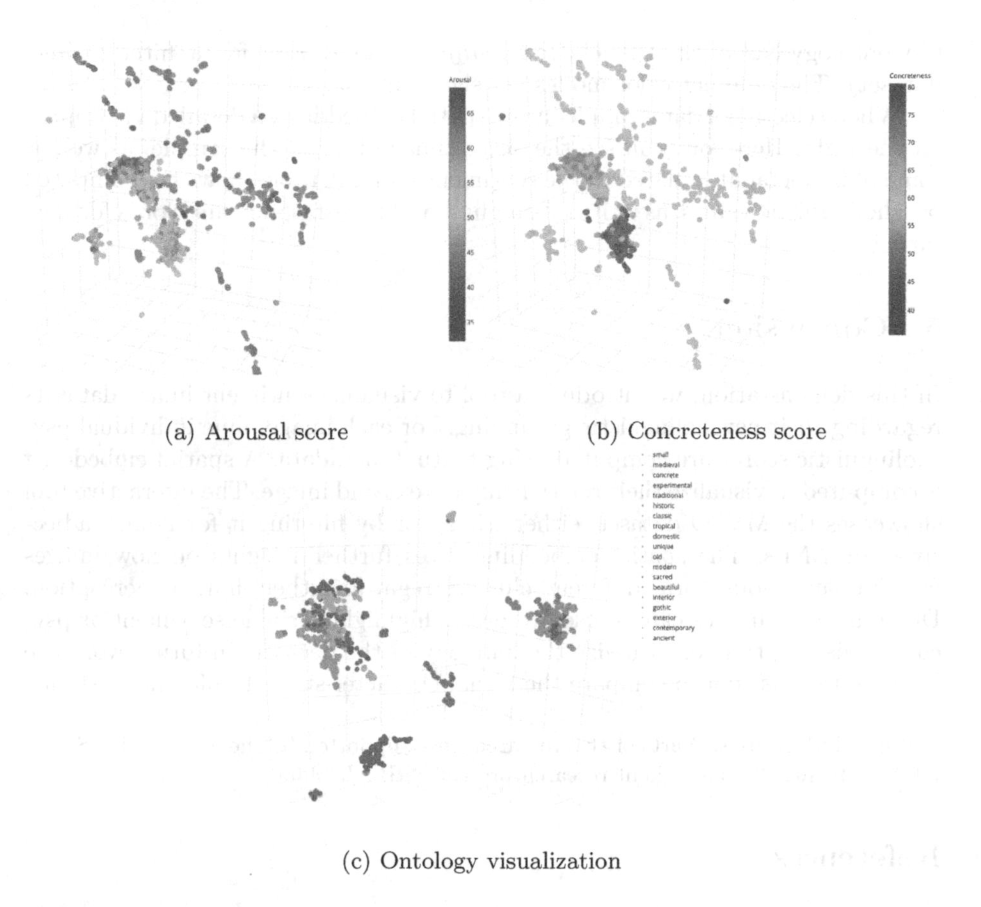

(a) Arousal score (b) Concreteness score

(c) Ontology visualization

Fig. 3. The spatial embedding can be colored in different ways. The psycholinguistic grounding can be shown in a heat map as shown in (a) and (b) highlighting each image's arousal and concreteness scores, respectively. Alternatively, the ontology of adjectives or nouns can be highlighted as shown in (c). (Color figure online)

for different adjective or nouns, and see the scoring for different images. A three-dimensional view shows the sentiment-psycholinguistic spatial embedding of the selected dataset. Different color modes allow for analyzing the dataset regarding its ontology and human perception scores established in Sect. 3. The full user interface of the proposed tool is shown in Fig. 2.

The sentiment-psycholinguistic space is shown with an interactive interface allowing for zooming and panning. Each data-point represents one image from the MVSO dataset plotted on a three-dimensional embedding based on its individual psycholinguistic scores. The user can switch between sampling a selection of images across the whole dataset, or showing all images of a selected noun, adjective, or ANP.

The color displayed in the spatial embedding can be selected to either show scores related to human perception as heatmap-based color gradings, or highlight the ontology-based class labels (e.g., *different adjectives* for a filtered *noun* dataset). The different color modes are shown in Fig. 3.

When selecting a data sample in the spatial embedding, a detailed view opens on the right. Here, one can see the actual image behind the sample, as well as some of its metadata related to the sentiment score. A table shows the computed psycholinguistic values, as well as its highest and lowest significant words for each rating.

5 Conclusion

In this demonstation, we introduce a tool to visualize sentiment image datasets regarding their psycholinguistic grounding. For each image, nine individual psycholinguistic scores are computed using textual metadata. A spatial embedding is computed to visualize their relationship of text and image. The interactive tool showcases the MVSO dataset, either wholly or by filtering it for nouns, adjectives, or ANPs. The spatial embedding gives further insights on how images for the same noun form different clusters regarding their human perception. Different color modes can be used to either highlight a single sentiment or psycholinguistic rating, or visualize the ontology of the dataset. In future work, we plan to use this tool to compare the visual characteristics of different clusters.

Acknowledgments. Parts of this research were supported by the MEXT, JSPS KAKENHI 16H02846, and a joint research project with NII, Japan.

References

1. Jindal, S., Singh, S.: Image sentiment analysis using deep convolutional neural networks with domain specific fine tuning. In: 2015 International Conference on Information Processing (ICIP), pp. 447–451, December 2015. https://doi.org/10.1109/INFOP.2015.7489424
2. Jou, B., Chen, T., Pappas, N., Redi, M., Topkara, M., Chang, S.: Visual affect around the world: A large-scale multilingual visual sentiment ontology. ArXiv e-prints 1508.03868 (2015)
3. Kastner, M.A., Ide, I., Kawanishi, Y., Hirayama, T., Deguchi, D., Murase, H.: Estimating the visual variety of concepts by referring to web popularity. Multimed. Tools Appl. **78**(7), 9463–9488 (2019). https://doi.org/10.1007/s11042-018-6528-x
4. Kim, E., Klinger, R.: A survey on sentiment and emotion analysis for computational literary studies. ArXiv e-prints 1808.03137 (2018)
5. McInnes, L., Healy, J.: UMAP: Uniform Manifold Approximation and Projection for dimension reduction. ArXiv e-prints 1802.03426. February 2018
6. Paivio, A., Yuille, J.C., Madigan, S.A.: Concreteness, imagery, and meaningfulness values for 925 nouns. J. Exp. Psychol. **76**(1), 1–25 (1968)
7. Scott, G.G., Keitel, A., Becirspahic, M., Yao, B., Sereno, S.C.: The Glasgow norms: ratings of 5,500 words on nine scales. Behav. Res. Methods **51**(3), 1258–1270 (2019). https://doi.org/10.3758/s13428-018-1099-3

Framework Design for Multiplayer Motion Sensing Game in Mixture Reality

Chih-Yao Chang[1], Bo-I Chuang[2], Chi-Chun Hsia[2], Wen-Cheng Chen[1], and Min-Chun Hu[3(✉)]

[1] National Cheng Kung University, Tainan, Taiwan
[2] Industrial Technology Research Institute, Zhudong, Taiwan
[3] National Tsing Hua University, Hsinchu, Taiwan
anitahu@cs.nthu.edu.tw

Abstract. Mixed reality (MR) is getting popular, but its application in entertainment is still limited due to the lack of intuitive and various interactions between the user and other players. In this demonstration, we propose an MR multiplayer game framework, which allows the player to interact directly with other players through intuitive body postures/actions. Moreover, a body depth approximation method is designed to decrease the complexity of virtual content rendering without affecting the immersive fidelity while playing the game. Our framework uses deep learning models to achieve motion sensing, and a multiplayer MR interaction game containing a variety of actions is designed to validate the feasibility of the proposed framework.

Keywords: Mixed reality · Motion sensing game · Multiplayer

1 Introduction

With the progress of multimedia technology and the breakthrough of hardware architecture, several MR headsets[1,2,3] have been developed in recent years. These MR systems aim to create immersive experience by visualizing vivid virtual content with the real scene. Moreover, users are enabled to interact with virtual objects through controller or simple gestures, is kind of interaction is still not intuitive enough for multi-user interaction in MR. Multi-user interaction has been introduced in several VR (virtual reality), AR (augmented reality), and MR applications. For example, Pool Nation VR[4] is a VR game in which the user is able to interact with other online players via manipulating all sorts of virtual objects with controllers. Niantic Labs[5] developed a series AR multiplayer

[1] Microsoft Hololens, https://www.microsoft.com/en-us/hololens.
[2] Magic Leap, https://www.magicleap.com/magic-leap-one.
[3] Windows Mixed Reality, https://www.acer.com/ac/zh/TW/content/series/wmr.
[4] Pool Nation VR, https://www.roadtovr.com/pool-nation-vr-review-htc-vive-steam/.
[5] NIANTIC AR Games, https://nianticlabs.com/zh_hant/blog/nrwp-update/.

Y. M. Ro et al. (Eds.): MMM 2020, LNCS 11962, pp. 703–708, 2020.
https://doi.org/10.1007/978-3-030-37734-2_57

interactive games which utilize the camera on smart phone to take a real scene and show the virtual object on the screen. Through internet connection, the player can share images and information with other players. Fact or Fantasy[6] is a multi-user MR game developed by Framestore, which synchronizes the real and virtual spaces of all users. Users can interactive with each other through the shared virtual content displayed by Magic Leap.

However, the existing multi-user applications in VR/AR/MR lack direct interaction between players, i.e. virtual objects are needed to trigger the interaction. In this work, we aim to design an MR multiplayer game framework that allow the players to have more direct interactions. The core concept of the proposed framework is to take the camera on the MR headset of the other user as the motion sensor (as illustrated in Fig. 1) and allow the player to interact with other players directly through intuitive body postures/actions. Game commands are triggered when the captured user takes a specific action, and the corresponding virtual content will be rendered on specific part of the captured user according to his/her pose. We apply lightweight deep learning models to more accurately but immediately estimate the pose and recognize the action.

Unlike the mobile AR system which draws the virtual content on only one flat-panel display, MR systems render a pair of stereo images considering the parallax of two eyes according to depth information. The acquisition of depth information usually requires complex procedures of aligning multiple outside cameras, including tedious calibration process. Instead, we design a simple body depth approximation method based on the proportion between the height of human body and the number of pixels on the image plane to decrease the complexity of virtual content rendering.

Our contributions are summarized as follows: (1) We build a framework for multiplayer motion sensing games based on Hololens. Players can interact directly with other players through their poses. (2) We propose a body depth approximation method for visual effect rendering, which costs less computation and avoids tedious camera calibration process. (3) To verify the feasibility of the proposed framework, we designed a motion sensing game with a variety of actions that are used for triggering attacks or defenses. Video clips of these actions are captured by Hololens and four outside cameras to train the deep learning models for our motion sensing game.

2 The Proposed System

Our game scenario is shown in Fig. 1, in which players can against each other directly through pre-defined body actions. When player 1 makes an action to attack player 2, player 2 can see the corresponding visual effect of that attack on HoloLens and try to make a defensive action. At the mean time, the corresponding visual effect of the defensive action will be displayed on player 1's HoloLens. To ensure that the action of each player can be detected and recognized by the other player, two players have to stand at a distance of 5 m apart. Furthermore,

[6] Fact or Fantasy? https://www.framestore.com/work/fact-or-fantasy.

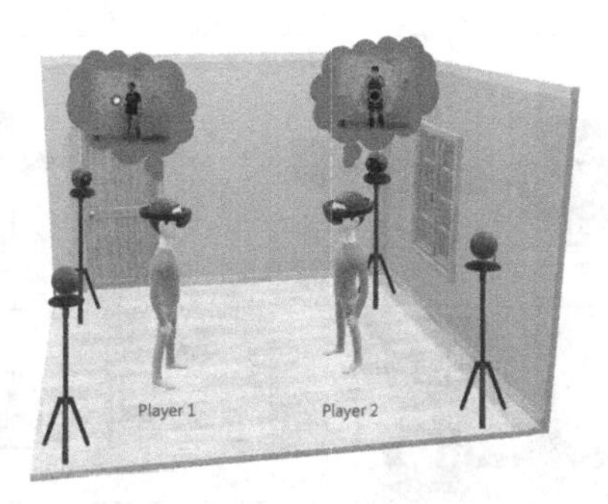

Fig. 1. Scenario of our system.

4 auxiliary outside cameras are placed around the corner of the playground (8 m long and 6 m wide) to recognize the player actions when players are out of the camera view of the others' Hololens.

2.1 System Framework

The framework of the entire system is illustrated in Fig. 2, which consists of three main parts: game server (red box), HoloLens (orange box) and auxiliary server (purple box). The game server utilizes the pre-trained deep learning models to estimate the pose and recognize the action of each captured player, and both the pose and action information are transmitted back to HoloLens via streaming. After receiving the information, HoloLens will render visual effects at specific body joint if a specific action is detected to trigger an attack or defense event. The game server contains a game system to update the game status, including calculating the health point of each player, creating damage, judging the winning/losing, etc. The auxiliary server receives the images from the 4 outside cameras and uses them to detect players, track players and recognize player actions. If the game server fails to detect player in the image sent by HoloLens (i.e. the player is not looking at his/her opponent), the tracking and action recognition results obtained by the auxiliary server will be immediately send to the game server to update the game status.

2.2 Pose Estimation Network and Action Recognition Network

The recent pose estimation and action recognition models have achieved high accuracy while cost much time and computation resources for the inference process. Considering both the accuracy and time performance of the proposed motion sensing game, we evaluate several light-weight pose estimation and action recognition models (cf. Tables. 2 and 3) and finally choose OpenPose [3] with MobileNet backbone as the pose estimation network and TSN (Temporal Segment Network) [8] without the network branch of optical flow as the action recognition network.

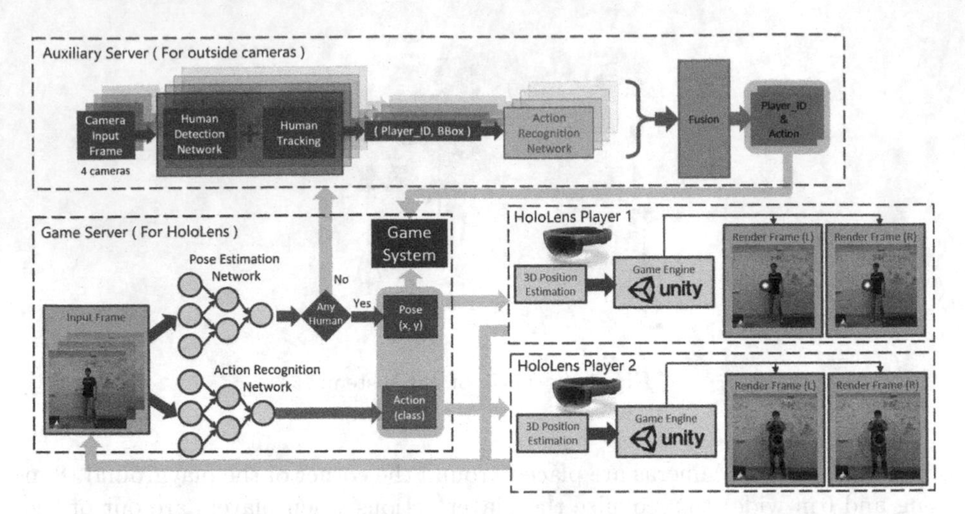

Fig. 2. Our proposed system framework for multiplayer motion sensing game. (Color figure online)

2.3 Player Depth Approximation for 3D Rendering

As mentioned in the introduction section, depth information of the virtual content is required to generate a pair of stereo images for rendering immersive 3D visual effect on Hololens. Instead of using tedious multi-camera alignment process for 3D position estimation, we simply approximate the player depth based on similar triangles. As illustrated in Fig. 3, the ratio between player height in real space (denoted as H_{real}) and the number of pixels on the image plane (denoted as H_{img}) is equals to the ratio of player distance in real space (denoted as Z_{real}) and the focal length (denoted as Z_{img}). The focal length Z_{img} can be obtained by placing an object of a fixed height H'_{real} at a defined distance Z'_{real} and measuring the number of pixels for the object on the image plane (denoted as H'_{img}). That is,

$$Z_{img} = Z'_{real} \times H'_{real}/H'_{img} \tag{1}$$

During playing, we can utilize the number of pixels measured by the pose estimation model, focal length, and the known player height, to estimate the player distance in real space. That is,

$$Z_{real} = Z_{img} \times H_{real}/H_{img}. \tag{2}$$

3 Experiments

To validate the proposed multiplayer motion sensing framework, we collected an action dataset containing videos of 6 kinds of human actions (including 5 action categories for triggering attack/defense game events and one category

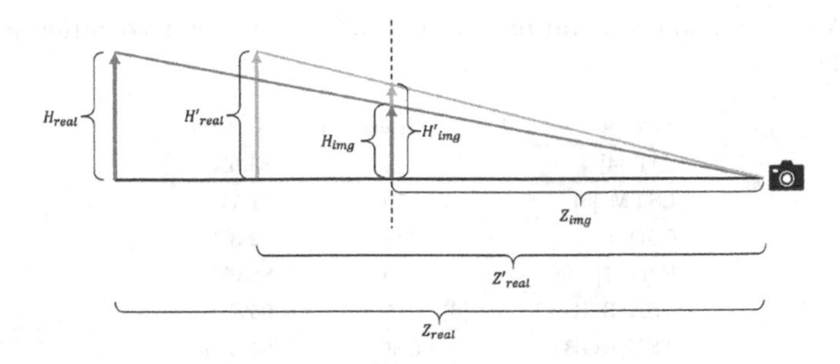

Fig. 3. Illustration of the proposed 3D position estimation method.

for "no action"). The videos were captured in the playground environment (as illustrated in Fig. 1). The videos captured by Hololens were used to train the action recognition models on the game server, and the videos captured by the four outside cameras were used to train the action recognition model on the auxiliary server. Table 1 lists the details of the collected action dataset and the action recognition results. We used leave one participant out cross validation to evaluate the accuracy. The comparisons of using different deep neural network models for pose estimation and action recognition are shown in Tables 2 and 3, respectively.

Table 1. Details of the collected action dataset and the accuracy of action recognition.

	HoloLens videos	Outside camera videos
# of Subjects	12	16
# of Actions	6	6
# of Angles	1	3
# of Repetition(per action per subject)	10 times	15 times
# of Cameras	1	4
# of Segments	≅1000	≅8000
Accuracy of Action Recognition	97.7%	93.3%

Table 2. The performance of different pose estimation methods on COCO dataset.

Model	AP	FPS
Mask RCNN [1]	62.7	5
RMPE(AlphaPose) [2]	68.0	13
OpenPose(CMU) [3]	58.4	9
OpenPose(Mobilenet-Large) [3]	**32.3**	**31**
OpenPose(Mobilenet-Small) [3]	17.3	35

Table 3. Accuracy and computation speed of different action recognition methods on UCF-101 dataset.

Method	Speed (fps)	Accuracy
iDT [4]	2	85.9%
LSTM [5]	150	71.1%
C3D [6]	314	82.3%
P3D [7]	140	88.6%
TSN(RGB+Flow) [8]	15	95%
TSN(RGB)	**680**	**85.7%**

4 Conclusions

We propose an MR multiplayer game framework, which allows the player to interact directly with other players through intuitive body postures/actions. A body depth approximation method is designed to decrease the complexity of virtual content rendering without affecting the immersive fidelity while playing the game. To validate the feasibility of the proposed framework, we designed an MR game that uses 5 kinds of human actions to trigger attack/offense game events. The experimental results show that the proposed framework can achieve real-time and accurate motion-sensing for multiplayer gaming on Hololens.

Acknowledgement. This research was supported by the Ministry of Science and Technology (Contract MOST 108-2218-E-007-055, 108-2221-E-007-106-MY3, and 108-2627-H-155-001), Taiwan.

References

1. He, K., et al.: Mask R-CNN. In: Proceedings of the IEEE International Conference on Computer Vision (2017)
2. Fang, H.-S., et al.: RMPE: regional multi-person pose estimation. In: Proceedings of the IEEE International Conference on Computer Vision (2017)
3. Cao, Z., et al.: Realtime multi-person 2D pose estimation using part affinity fields. In: Proceedings of the IEEE Conference on Computer Vision and Pattern Recognition (2017)
4. Wang, H., Schmid, C.: Action recognition with improved trajectories. In: Proceedings of the IEEE International Conference on Computer Vision (2013)
5. Donahue, J., et al.: Long-term recurrent convolutional networks for visual recognition and description. In: Proceedings of the IEEE Conference on Computer Vision and Pattern Recognition (2015)
6. Tran, D., et al.: Learning spatiotemporal features with 3D convolutional networks. In: Proceedings of the IEEE International Conference on Computer Vision (2015)
7. Qiu, Z., Yao, T., Mei. T.: Learning spatio-temporal representation with pseudo-3D residual networks. In: Proceedings of the IEEE International Conference on Computer Vision (2017)
8. Wang, L., et al.: Temporal segment networks: towards good practices for deep action recognition. In: Leibe, B., Matas, J., Sebe, N., Welling, M. (eds.) ECCV 2016. LNCS, vol. 9912, pp. 20–36. Springer, Cham (2016). https://doi.org/10.1007/978-3-319-46484-8_2

Lyrics-Conditioned Neural Melody Generation

Yi Yu[1(✉)], Florian Harscoët[2], Simon Canales[3], Gurunath Reddy M[4], Suhua Tang[5], and Junjun Jiang[1]

[1] National Institute of Informatics, Tokyo, Japan
yiyu@nii.ac.jp, junjun0595@163.com

[2] Institut Supérieur d'Informatique, de Modélisation et de leurs Applications, Aubiére, France
florian.harscoet@etu.uca.fr

[3] École Polytechnique Fédérale de Lausanne, Lausanne, Switzerland
simon.canales@epfl.ch

[4] Indian Institute of Technology Kharagpur, Kharagpur, India
mgurunathreddy@gmail.com

[5] The University of Electro-Communications, Chofu, Japan
shtang@uec.ac.jp

Abstract. Generating melody from lyrics to compose a song has been a very interesting research topic in the area of artificial intelligence and music, which tries to predict generative music relationship between lyrics and melody. In this demonstration paper, by exploiting a large music dataset with 12,197 pairs of English lyrics and melodies, we develop a lyrics-conditioned AI neural melody generation system that consists of three components: lyrics encoder network, melody generation network, and MIDI sequence tuner. Most importantly, a Long Short-Term Memory (LSTM)-based melody generator conditioned on lyrics, is trained by applying a generative adversarial network (GAN), to generate a pleasing and meaningful melody matching the given lyrics. Our demonstration illustrates the effectiveness of the proposed melody generation system.

Keywords: Lyrics-conditioned melody generation · Long Short-Term Memory · Generative adversarial network

1 Background

Generating melody from lyrics to compose a song by computers has been a very challenging research issue. Through understanding music rules and concepts, creating pleasing sounds could be possible [9]. To learn these kinds of rules and concepts such as mathematical relationships between notes, timing, and melody, the earliest research of various music computational techniques such as Markov

Florian Harscoët, Simon Canales, and Gurunath Reddy M were involved in this work during their internship in National Institute of Informatics (NII), Japan.

Y. M. Ro et al. (Eds.): MMM 2020, LNCS 11962, pp. 709–714, 2020.
https://doi.org/10.1007/978-3-030-37734-2_58

models [7] has emerged for music melody generation since the middle of 1950s. However, due to the limited availability of paired lyrics-melody dataset with alignment information [10], it has difficulty in capturing the sequential alignment relationship between lyrics and melody. With the development of available lyrics-melody dataset and deep learning techniques, more and more AI techniques have been exploited in music generation [5]. But how to accurately model music attributes such as the distribution of MIDI notes remains a challenge.

In this demonstration paper, we develop a lyrics-conditioned neural melody generation system based on exploring the method proposed in [11], which has the capability of automatically composing an AI song matching the lyrics selected by a user. To the best of our knowledge, this is the first lyrics-conditioned neural melody generation system trained on a large dataset with paired English lyrics and melodies. It contains three components: lyrics encoder network, melody generation network, and MIDI sequence tuner. In particular, skip-gram models are trained in lyrics encoder network to extract syllable and word embedding vectors respectively, which are concatenated together as a more meaningful semantic lyrics embedding vector. Then, lyrics-conditioned LSTM-based generator and discriminator networks are trained by applying a generative adversarial network (GAN) to generate a melody matching the given lyrics. Finally, a sheet music with the meaningful alignment between lyrics and generated melody is presented and a synthesizer is applied to integrate the lyrics and generated melody to produce an audio track.

2 Lyrics-Conditioned Neural Melody Generation System

The proposed AI lyrics-to-melody generation system mainly consists of three parts as shown in Fig. 1: lyrics encoder, lyrics-conditioned melody generation with an adversarial training, and MIDI sequence tuner. The lyrics encoder encodes the syllables/words of lyrics into a sequence of hidden vectors, which together with a noise vector is taken as the input of the generator. The goal of the generator is to capture the distribution of real MIDI samples. In particular, by deep learning and generative modeling, sequential alignment relationship between lyrics and melody is automatically learned from the training musical dataset and used to generate new melodies following the estimated distribution.

2.1 Lyrics Encoder

To the best of our knowledge, there is no public lyrics embedding model which can be used for extracting lyrics feature. On the other hand, lyrics embedding model trained on a large lyrics dataset is more meaningful, which can have more capability of capturing semantic information. Therefore, a large dataset is built, and on this basis syllable- and word-level skip-gram models are respectively trained over the entire MIDI song lyrics to obtain a semantic representation of the lyrics [11]. Vector representations explicitly encode many linguistic regularities and patterns which can be regarded as linear translations.

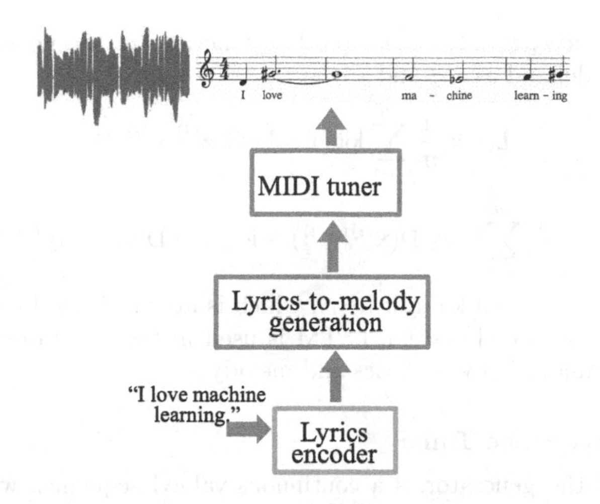

Fig. 1. Overview of lyrics-conditioned neural melody generation system.

A skip-gram model is trained to predict the surrounding tokens (syllables or words) given a token at position t in a sequence of input lyrics [8] with T tokens, as follows:

$$\frac{1}{T}\sum_{t-1}^{T}\sum_{-c\leq i\leq c, i\neq 0}\log p(s_{t+i}|s_t), \tag{1}$$

where s_t is the tth token, $p(s_{t+i}|s_t)$ represents the probability of s_{t+i} conditioned on s_t, and c is the length of the context window around s_t.

In the vanilla skip-gram model, the conditional probability $p(\cdot|\cdot)$ is formulated as a softmax function

$$p(s_O|s_I) = \frac{\exp(v_{s_0}^T v_{s_I})}{\sum_{t=1}^{T}\exp(v_{s_0}^T v_{s_I})}. \tag{2}$$

2.2 Lyrics-to-Melody Generation

The original GAN [6] consists of a generator and a discriminator. The generator $\mathrm{G}(\cdot)$ takes a noise vector $\mathbf{z}$ as an input and generates a MIDI vector $\tilde{\mathbf{x}} = \mathrm{G}(\mathbf{z})$, aiming to pass the test of the discriminator. The discriminator $\mathrm{D}(\cdot)$ discriminates a given MIDI vector $\mathbf{x}$ from the training data and a generated MIDI vector $\tilde{\mathbf{x}}$ from $\mathrm{G}(\cdot)$. The generator and discriminator are jointly trained via a minimax game.

In the conditional GAN, a lyrics condition $\mathbf{y}$ is introduced into both the generator and discriminator. Let $\mathrm{D}(\cdot)$ represents the probability that the discriminator regards a sample as true. With a batch of m pairs of lyrics $\mathbf{y}^{(i)}$ and

MIDI melodies $\mathbf{x}^{(i)}$, $i = 1, \cdots, m$, the loss functions of the generator and discriminator are defined as L_G and L_D in the following:

$$L_G = \frac{1}{m}\sum_{i=1}^{m} \log(1 - \mathrm{D}(\mathrm{G}(\mathbf{z}^{(i)}|\mathbf{y}^{(i)}))) \tag{3}$$

$$L_D = \frac{1}{m}\sum_{i=1}^{m}[-\log\mathrm{D}(\mathbf{x}^{(i)}|\mathbf{y}^{(i)}) - \log(1 - \mathrm{D}(\mathrm{G}(\mathbf{z}^{(i)}|\mathbf{y}^{(i)})))] \tag{4}$$

LSTM [1] is a special kind of RNN, which is able to learn long-term dependencies. In the proposed system, LSTM is used in the generator to model the sequential alignment between lyrics and melody.

2.3 MIDI Sequence Tuner

The output of the generator is a continuous-valued sequence, which needs to be constrained to the most likely standard scale with underlying musical representation of discrete-valued MIDI attributes. Therefore, the fine-tuned music attributes are estimated to see if each generated sequence has a perfect scale consistency of melody containing constraints of music composition.

3 Experiment and Demonstration

Three musical attributes are used to represent a melody sequence: MIDI note number, note duration, and rest (a silent interval between adjacent notes). The sequences of triplets (three musical attributes) are obtained through parsing each MIDI file in the source datasets ("LMD-full" MIDI Dataset [2] and reddit MIDI dataset [3]), resulting in a total number of 12,197 MIDI files.

Two different formats used in our demonstration are described as below:

- Syllable level: A numpy object [[Syllable 1, Syllable 1 attribute], [Syllable 2, Syllable 2 attribute],...]
- Word level: A numpy object [[[Syllable 1 Word 1, Syllable 2 Word 1][Syllable 1 Word 1 attribute, Syllable 2 Word 1 attribute]], [[$\cdots$] for Word 2], $\cdots$]

In each format, three kinds of music attributes are extracted. The continuous attributes contain start of the note, length, frequency and velocity. The discrete attributes contain pitch of the note, duration, and rest. Currently the discrete attributes are utilized to generate melodies in our system. We have successfully parsed 11,678 syllable-level and 11,528 word-level. A full dataset with lyrics-melody pairs and related sources is available in [4].

Figure 2 shows that with the increase of training epochs, the distribution of the MIDI numbers of the generated melodies on the testing set better approaches that of actual MIDI numbers in the ground truth set.

Figure 3 demonstrates the GUI of our lyrics-conditioned AI neural melody generation system. Given lyrics, the system predicts melody, and the alignment between syllables and notes, and on this basis produces music sheet. The lyrics and generated melody are further synthesized for playing, using MIDI number of the piano and mimicking human voice.

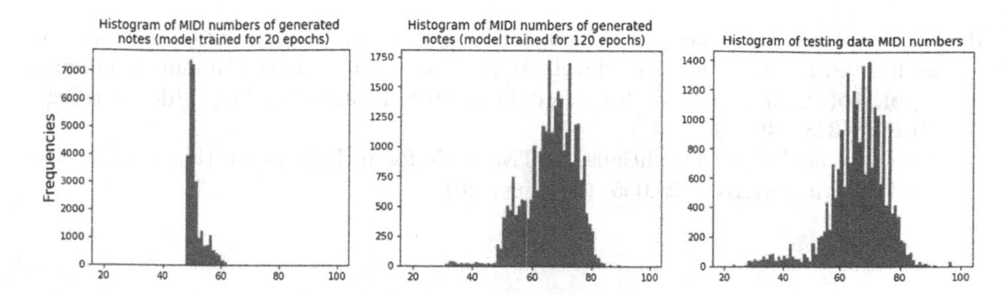

Fig. 2. Histograms of MIDI number for melodies generated using a generator trained for 20 epochs (left), 120 epochs (middle) and directly sampled (DS) from the testing dataset (right). Means are $\mu_{20\text{ epochs}} = 50.69$, $\mu_{120\text{ epochs}} = 65.73$ and $\mu_{\text{DS}} = 65.23$ respectively. Variances are $\sigma^2_{20\text{ epochs}} = 7.46$, $\sigma^2_{120\text{ epochs}} = 72.38$ and $\sigma^2_{\text{DS}} = 98.20$.

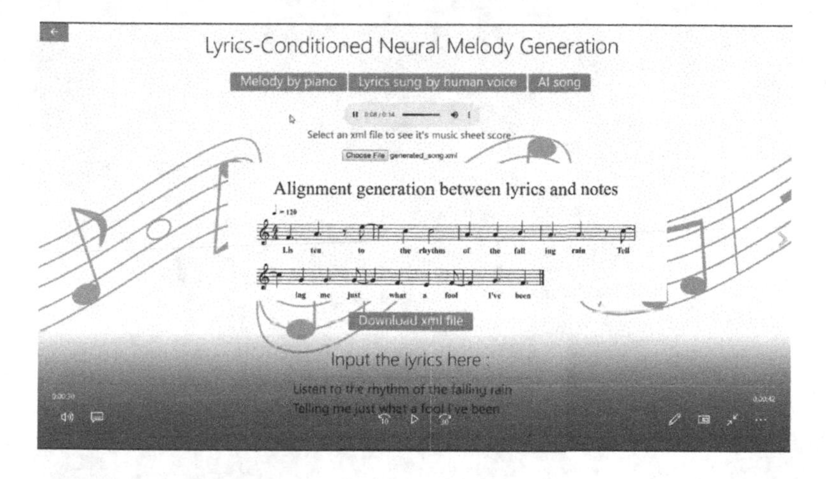

Fig. 3. Screen shot of lyrics-conditioned neural melody generation system.

References

1. https://colah.github.io/posts/2015-08-Understanding-LSTMs/
2. https://colinraffel.com/projects/lmd/
3. https://www.reddit.com/r/datasets/
4. https://github.com/yy1lab/Lyrics-Conditioned-Neural-Melody-Generation
5. Bao, H., et al.: Neural melody composition from lyrics. CoRR abs/1809.04318 (2018). http://arxiv.org/abs/1809.04318
6. Goodfellow, I.J., et al.: Generative Adversarial Networks. arXiv e-prints, June 2014
7. Hiller, L.A., Isaacson, L.M.: Musical composition with a high-speed digital computer. J. Audio Eng. Soc. **6**(3), 154–160 (1958)
8. Mikolov, T., Sutskever, I., Chen, K., Corrado, G.S., Dean, J.: Distributed representations of words and phrases and their compositionality. In: Advances in Neural Information Processing Systems, pp. 3111–3119 (2013)
9. Ponsford, D., Wiggins, G., Mellish, C.: Statistical learning of harmonic movement. J. New Music Res. **28**(2), 150–177 (1999)

10. Yu, Y., Tang, S., Raposo, F., Chen, L.: Deep cross-modal correlation learning for audio and lyrics in music retrieval. ACM Trans. Multimedia Comput. Commun. Appl. **15**(1), 20–20 (2019). https://doi.org/10.1145/3281746. http://doi.acm.org/10.1145/3281746
11. Yu, Y., Canales, S.: Conditional LSTM-GAN for melody generation from lyrics. arXiv e-prints arXiv:1908.05551, August 2019

A Web-Based Visualization Tool for 3D Spatial Coverage Measurement of Aerial Images

Abdullah Alfarrarjeh[1](✉), Zeyu Ma[2], Seon Ho Kim[1], Yeonsoo Park[1], and Cyrus Shahabi[1]

[1] Integrated Media Systems Center, University of Southern California, Los Angeles, USA
{alfarrar,seonkim,yeonsoop,shahabi}@usc.edu
[2] Electronic Engineering Department, Tsinghua University, Beijing, China
mzy16@mails.tsinghua.edu.cn

Abstract. Drones are becoming popular in different domains, from personal to professional usages. Drones are usually equipped with high-resolution cameras in addition to various sensors (e.g., GPS, accelerometers, and gyroscopes). Therefore, aerial images captured by drones are associated with spatial metadata that describe the spatial extent per image, referred to as aerial field-of-view (Aerial FOV). Aerial FOVs can be utilized to represent the visual coverage of a particular region with respect to various viewing directions at fine granular-levels (i.e., small cells composing the region). In this demo paper, we introduce a web tool for interactive visualization of a collection of aerial field-of-views and instant measurement of their spatial coverage over a given 3D space. This tool is useful for several real-world monitoring applications that are based on aerial images to simulate the 3D spatial coverage of the collected visual data in order to analyze their adequacy.

Keywords: Geo-tagged aerial image · 3D spatial coverage · Aerial Field of View · Visualization web tool

1 Introduction

Unmanned aerial vehicles (UAVs) (e.g., drones) are increasingly utilized for collecting massive amounts of aerial images at different geographical regions. Consequently, several monitoring applications that use these images have emerged[1]. Such applications are looking for a more systematic way to collect and manage

[1] The success of smart city applications based on ground images (e.g., street cleanliness classification [1] and material recognition [3]) encouraged utilizing drone images for other applications.

A. Alfarrarjeh, Z. Ma—These authors contributed equally to this work.
Z. Ma—This author contributed to this work during his research visit at USC.

Y. M. Ro et al. (Eds.): MMM 2020, LNCS 11962, pp. 715–721, 2020.
https://doi.org/10.1007/978-3-030-37734-2_59

aerial images. These needs are highlighted by current trends in the use of drones. When we deal with a large amount of geo-tagged visual data, especially including drone imagery data, one of the challenges is how to measure the coverage of visual information regarding a specific region of interest. For example, when we have thousands of geo-tagged images in Los Angeles, how do we intuitively measure how much they visually cover the city? How do we identify unrecorded street blocks in the dataset? One solution is to use traditional computer vision techniques [6,12]; however, they are computationally intensive so not feasible for applications in which instant answers are needed. Alternatively, our previous work [2] proposed spatial coverage measurement models to quantify the visual coverage where these models rely solely on the spatial metadata tagged with ground-level images reducing significant computational cost. Recently, we extended the models to 3D space to enable quantifying the visual coverage of aerial image [4] (described in Subsect. 2.3).

In this paper, we focus on aerial images tagged with spatial metadata (referred to as *Aerial Field-of-View* (Aerial FOV)) which describe its spatial extent in 3D space. An aerial FOV [9] (see Fig. 1) is represented by the eight parameters acquired at the image capturing time, Aerial FOV $\equiv \langle lat, lng, hgt, \theta_y, \theta_p, \theta_r, \alpha, R\rangle$, where lat and lng are the GPS coordinates (i.e., latitude and longitude) of the camera location, hgt is the camera height with respect to the ground, θ_y, θ_p, and θ_r are three rotation angles of the camera pose (θ_y is the yaw angle rotating around the vertical axis, θ_p is the pitch angle rotating around the lateral axis, θ_r is the roll angle rotating around the longitudinal axis), α is the camera visibility angle, and R is the maximum visible distance. Our web-based tool is to visualize these geo-tagged aerial FOVs in a systematic way. To demonstrate the 3D spatial coverage measurement models in a user-friendly way, our tool integrates them on a web interface, enables visualizing the collected aerial FOVs at a specific geographical region, and displays the coverage results of three coverage measurement models. The tool was demonstrated with two real datasets [10,11]. To demonstrate various scenarios of visualization cases, our demo also used synthesized datasets, i.e., augmented aerial FOVs, which simulate images captured at different levels of height or using different camera poses. The source code of the proposed tool is available at https://github.com/mazeyu/3D_Spatial_Coverage_Model_Demo.

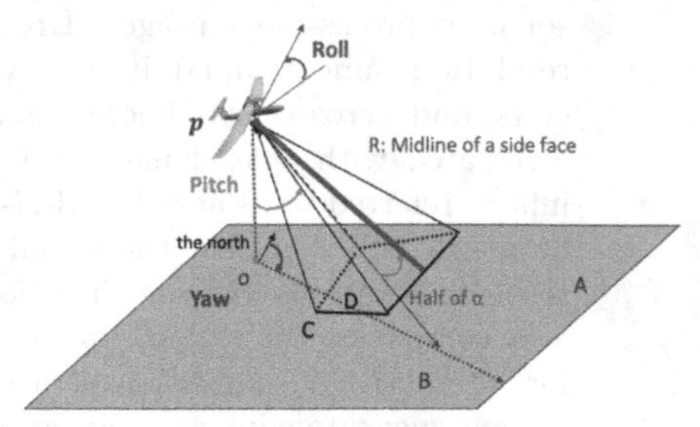

Fig. 1. Aerial Field of View (Aerial FOV)

2 Web Tool Architecture

The proposed tool (see Fig. 2) consists of four main components: data loader, 3D visualization of aerial FOVs, spatial coverage measurement, and interactive querying. Each component supports different features of the web tool as described in what follows.

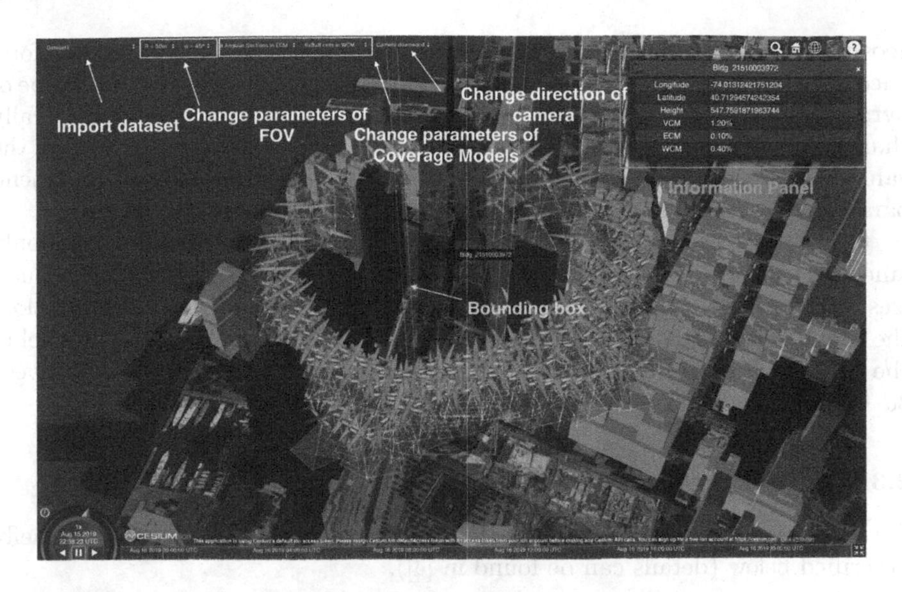

Fig. 2. The GUI of the web tool

2.1 Data Loader

The first step of the spatial coverage visualization is to specify the dataset of interest. For a demonstration purpose, the tool is equipped with multiple datasets, and a user can choose one of them using the first menu bar. In particular, the tool presents two real datasets [10,11] of Aerial FOVs collected by a drone flying over different places of open fields in Switzerland. In the datasets, the heights of the majority of FOVs were in the range of 530 to 600 m, and both pitch and roll angles were almost constant. To simulate various visualization scenarios, the tool also provides additional synthesized datasets based on the real ones with two types of augmentation operations: *height-based*, and *angle-based* augmentations. Through the height-based augmentation, new FOVs were added using the same parameter values of the existing FOVs except the height value was modified to display three cases: low height (i.e., simulating ground images), moderate height (simulating drone images), and very high height (simulating satellite images). Similarly, the angle-based augmentation generates several variants of the existing FOVs[2] by varying the pitch angle (θ_p), the roll angle (θ_r), or both of them simultaneously. Moreover, the FOVs of these datasets did not include values for two fundamental parameters: the maximum visible distance (R), and the viewing angle (α). Therefore, the tool enables setting the values of these parameters using the second and third menu bars.

2.2 3D Visualization of Spatial Metadata of Aerial Images

For visualization, the tool uses the Cesium package (https://cesiumjs.org), which is an open-source JavaScript library for 3D maps and 3D visualization of

[2] In the existing FOVs, yaw angles (θ_y) varies widely.

geospatial data based on geometrical operations provided by WebGL[3]. Therefore, once a dataset is loaded, the tool draws the 3D coverage of each FOV as a shape of pyramid (in blue). Moreover, the visualization of these FOVs can be dynamically changed as a function of the FOV parameters. For example, when changing the value of a parameter (e.g., changing R or α values using the second and third menu bars), the corresponding FOVS are re-rendered and displayed immediately.

Given that the datasets were captured in a rural area which includes only landscape scenes (i.e., no interesting item is visible), the tool "virtually" visualizes buildings in the geographical area of the datasets. For virtual visualization, the tool displays the buildings of New York City using the 3D Building model in the CityGML format available at https://www1.nyc.gov/site/doitt/initiatives/3d-building.page.

2.3 3D Spatial Coverage Measurement

For a 3D spatial coverage measurement, the tool supports three models as briefly described below (details can be found in [4]).

- *Volume Coverage Measurement (VCM) Model* which calculates the overlapping ratio between the volume occupied by the extent of the FOVs and that of a 3D region of interest.
- *Euler-based Directional Coverage Measurement (ECM) Model* which calculates the volume of the overlapping region considering various Euler-angle directional views.
- *Weighted Cell Coverage Measurement (WCM) Model* which partitions the region of interest into fine-granular sub-regions (i.e., cubes) and calculates the coverage of each cube using ECM. After that, the coverage measurements of all cubes are aggregated by weighting the coverage of each cube.

The ECM and WCM models mainly depend on two parameters (the number of sectors which divide Euler-angle viewing direction, and the number of cubes for region division, respectively) that directly affect the calculation of the coverage measurement. Therefore, the tool enables specifying these parameters using the fourth and fifth menu bars. The default values for the ECM and WCM model parameters are set to $8 \times 8 \times 8$. Note that, to support the execution of these models through a web interface conveniently, they were implemented in JavaScript, and integrated into the tool.

2.4 Interactive Querying for 3D Spatial Coverage Measurement

For an interactive querying, the tool enables selecting one of the visible buildings as a geographical region ($\mathcal{Q}_R$) to measure its spatial coverage in the 3D space. When a building is selected, a yellow bounding box is overlayed over it, and this box is considered as a geographical region ($\mathcal{Q}_R$) intended for the coverage

[3] WebGL is an extended version of OpenGL (a standard library in computer graphics) for web content rendered in a web browser.

query. Then, the Cesium package provides the longitude, latitude, and height of the building but not its width and length. Thus, for simplicity, the tool uses default values (100 m) for the width and length when creating the bounding box while using the provided height value of the building. Once an $\mathcal{Q}_R$ is defined, its spatial coverage is computed using the three coverage measurement models (VCM, ECM, and WCM) and the results are displayed on the information panel that is positioned in the upper-right corner of the window.

3 Demonstration Plan

During the demonstration, we highlight the effectiveness of spatial coverage measurement models in several scenarios. Namely, we study the effect of: (1) varying the parameters of the loaded aerial FOVs, (2) varying the parameters of the coverage models, and (3) varying the loaded datasets associated with FOVs for images taken at various heights (see Figs. 3 and 4).

For the scenario of varying the parameters of FOVs, we vary R from a small to a large value (e.g., 50 m to 200 m) to show how the coverage can be affected by such a change when querying for a region of a short or tall building. For the scenario of varying the coverage model's parameters, we demonstrate how the estimated coverage (especially using ECM) changes as the number of angular sections decreases or increases. Additionally, we show the effect of changing the number of cubes on the estimated coverage (especially using WCM). Finally, for the scenario of using datasets augmented with FOVs of various heights, we demonstrate the changes in the estimated coverage of a dataset that includes high-height, moderate-height, or low-height FOVs.

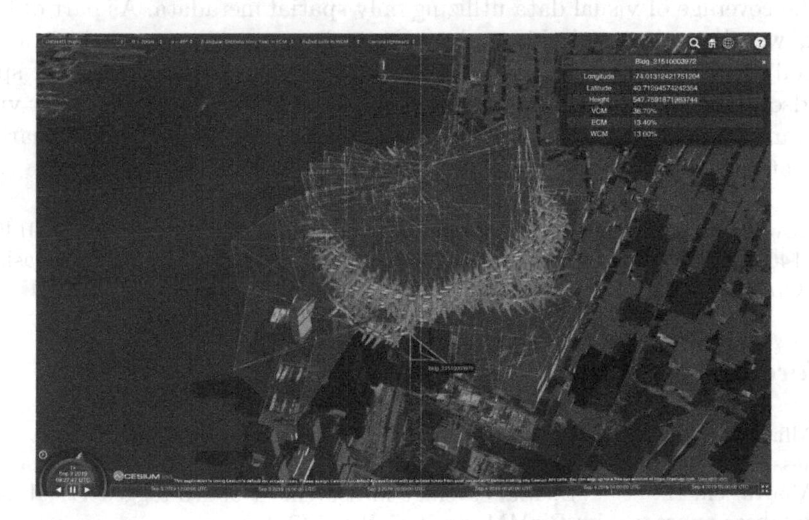

Fig. 3. Spatial coverage measurement of a selected building (marked in yellow) using a dataset of aerial FOVs captured at a high level of height. (Color figure online)

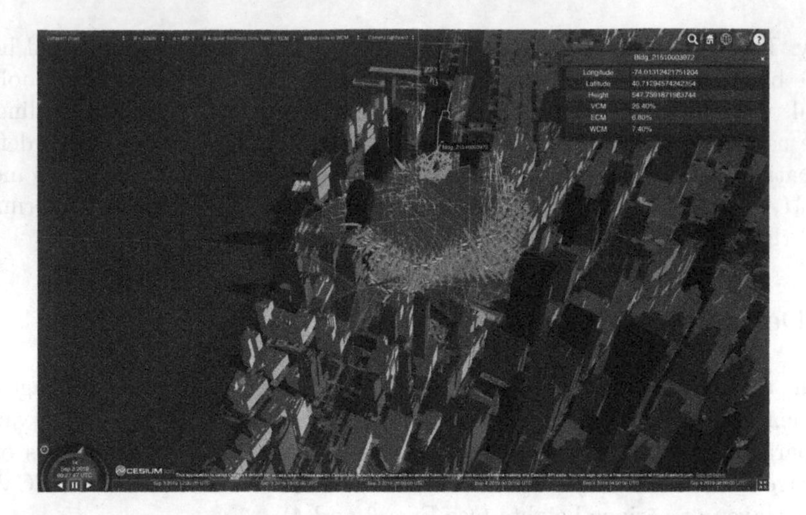

Fig. 4. Spatial coverage measurement of a selected building (marked in yellow) using a dataset of aerial FOVs captured at a low level of height. (Color figure online)

4 Conclusion

This paper introduces a web tool for an interactive visualization of spatial coverage of metadata tagged with aerial images, i.e., aerial FOVs. Our demo showcases 3D spatial coverage measurement using different models for various datasets (both real and synthetic). In addition, the tool is supported with visualization features to show the effectiveness of the spatial coverage calculation by estimating the coverage of visual data utilizing only spatial metadata. As part of future work, we plan to extend this tool to locate holes in 3D space which are not covered by the images in a given dataset to automate the planning of spatial crowdsourcing [5,7] by UAVs. We also plan to integrate this tool into our visionary framework (Translational Visual Data Platform, TVDP [8]) for smart city applications.

Acknowledgment. This work was supported in part by NSF grants IIS-1320149 and CNS-1461963, the USC Integrated Media Systems Center, and unrestricted cash gifts from Oracle and Google.

References

1. Alfarrarjeh, A., et al.: Image classification to determine the level of street cleanliness: a case study. In: BigMM, pp. 1–5. IEEE (2018)
2. Alfarrarjeh, A., et al.: Spatial coverage measurement of geo-tagged visual data: a database approach. In: BigMM, pp. 1–8. IEEE (2018)
3. Alfarrarjeh, A., et al.: Recognizing material of a covered object: a case study with graffiti. In: ICIP, pp. 2491–2495. IEEE (2019)

4. Alfarrarjeh, A., et al.: A Web-Based Visualization Tool for 3D spatial coverage measurement of aerial images. In: Cheng, W.-H., et al. (eds.) MMM 2020. LNCS, vol. 11962, pp. 715–721. Springer, Cham (2020)
5. Alfarrarjeh, A., et al.: Scalable spatial crowdsourcing: a study of distributed algorithms. In: MDM, vol. 1, pp. 134–144. IEEE (2015)
6. Del, B.A., et al.: Visual coverage using autonomous mobile robots for search and rescue applications. In: SSRR, pp. 1–8. IEEE (2013)
7. Kazemi, L., Shahabi, C.: Geocrowd: enabling query answering with spatial crowdsourcing. In: SIGSPATIAL GIS, pp. 189–198. ACM (2012)
8. Kim, S.H., et al.: TVDP: Translational visual data platform for smart cities. In: ICDEW, pp. 45–52. IEEE (2019)
9. Lu, Y., Shahabi, C.: Efficient indexing and querying of geo-tagged aerial videos. In: SIGSPATIAL GIS, pp. 1–10. ACM (2017)
10. Oettershagen, P., et al.: Long-endurance sensing and mapping using a hand-launchable solar-powered UAV. In: Wettergreen, D.S., Barfoot, T.D. (eds.) Field and Service Robotics. STAR, vol. 113, pp. 441–454. Springer, Cham (2016). https://doi.org/10.1007/978-3-319-27702-8_29
11. Oettershagen, P., et al.: Design of small hand-launched solar-powered UAVs: from concept study to a multi-day world endurance record flight. J. Field Robot. **34**(7), 1352–1377 (2017)
12. Papatheodorou, S., et al.: Collaborative visual area coverage. Robot. Auton. Syst. **92**, 126–138 (2017)

An Attention Based Speaker-Independent Audio-Visual Deep Learning Model for Speech Enhancement

Zhongbo Sun[1], Yannan Wang[2], and Li Cao[1(✉)]

[1] Department of Automation, Tsinghua University, Beijing, China
caoli@tsinghua.edu.cn
[2] Media Lab, Tencent, Shenzhen, China

Abstract. Speech enhancement aims to improve speech quality in noisy environments. While most speech enhancement methods use only audio data as input, joining video information can achieve better results. In this paper, we present an attention based speaker-independent audio-visual deep learning model for single channel speech enhancement. We apply both the time-wise attention and spatial attention in the video feature extraction module to focus on more important features. Audio features and video features are then concatenated along the time dimension as the audio-visual features. The proposed video feature extraction module can be spliced to the audio-only model without extensive modifications. The results show that the proposed method can achieve better results than recent audio-visual speech enhancement methods.

Keywords: Speech enhancement · Audio-visual · Attention mechanism · Deep learning

1 Introduction

Speech enhancement aims to separate the speech of the target speaker from background noise and other speakers. The results of speech enhancement have significant effects on the performance of automatic speech recognition [10], speaker recognition [4] and so on. In the past few years, speech enhancement models based on deep learning have made great progress. These models outperform most conventional speech enhancement models [17], such as spectral restoration [13], Wiener filtering [11].

Most single-channel speech enhancement methods use only audio data as input. Inspired by lip reading [1], using visual information to assist speech enhancement has gradually become a hot topic. The movement of the mouth and the changes in the facial muscles help people understand the speech information, especially in noisy environment. Ngiam et al. [12] propose the concept of multimodal deep learning. They demonstrate that better results can be achieved

Supported by Media Lab at Tencent.

Y. M. Ro et al. (Eds.): MMM 2020, LNCS 11962, pp. 722–728, 2020.
https://doi.org/10.1007/978-3-030-37734-2_60

if multimodal features are used. Gabby et al. [6] train a Convolutional Neural Network (CNN) model for denoising the speech signals. Their model uses a sequence of frames cropped into the lip regions of the speaker as visual features and outputs a Mel-spectrogram representing the enhanced speech. Erphat et al. [5] are the first to propose a speaker-independent audio-visual model. They use face embedding for face recognition as visual information, which has been shown to contain more facial features than face landmarks [2].

However,the quality of the extracted video features has a great impact on the performance of the speech enhancement models [3]. Using attention mechanism can focus on important video features and suppress unnecessary features. The idea of the attention mechanism is derived from the perception of human visual systems. The human visual system focuses on several places in the scene, not all of them. Over the years, attention mechanism has been widely used in various fields of deep learning.

In our work, we present an attention based speaker-independent audio-visual deep learning model for single channel speech enhancement. In the audio preprocessing section, we perform short-time Fourier transform (STFT) on each audio segment to obtain time frequency (TF) bins. Each speech-related video is composed of consecutive frames. The pre-trained face recognition model in Dlib [8] is used to extract the face embedding of the target speaker by frame. The attention mechanism is introduced in the video feature extraction module. We sequentially calculate the feature maps along the time dimension and the spatial dimension of the video feature, and then the two attention maps are multiplied with the video features to obtain re-weight features. In this way, not only the spatial information of the video data but also the features of the time series are utilized. Audio features and video features are then concatenated along the time dimension as shared embeddings representing the audio-visual features. Our model outputs a multiplicative complex ideal ratio mask (cRM) [15] of the spectrogram. Our model has been trained and tested on the GRID audio-visual dataset [3]. To the best of our knowledge, our model has achieved state-of-the-art results on the GRID dataset.

2 Model Architecture

The audio-visual feature extraction module consists of a dual tower CNN which takes the audio and video inputs. Shared representation is obtained by concatenating audio and visual features and then processed using bidirectional Long Short-Term Memory (BLSTM) and deep neural network (DNN) layers. The entire model is trained end-to-end. The network is trained to minimize the mean square error loss between the predicted spectrogram and the clean speech spectrogram. Figure 1 shows the model architecture.

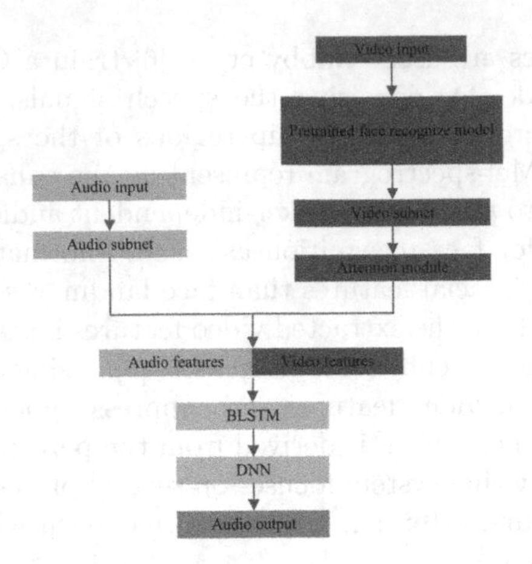

Fig. 1. Model architecture

2.1 Audio Feature Extraction Module

All mono channel audio signals are resampled to 16 kHz. STFT is computed on each 3-s audio segment. Each TF bin contains the real and imaginary parts of a complex number, both of which are used as input.

The state-of-the-art audio-only model on the GRID dataset is proposed by Erphat [5], which we use as audio feature extraction module. The audio module uses dilated convolutional neural networks to extract audio features.

2.2 Video Feature Extraction Module

In the task of audio-visual speech enhancement, using face embeddings has been observed more effective than using raw face area image [5]. Because face embedding retains the necessary information to recognize faces, regardless of the environment in which the face is located. All speech-related videos are resampled to 25 fps. For the target speaker, we use the pre-trained face recognition neural network [9] to extract face embedding of 128-dimensional. Then an input video feature of 75×128 scalars is obtained.

The video feature extraction module has 6 consecutive convolution layers and 1 transposed convolution layer to upsample the output of the visual stream to match the output of the audio feature extraction module, resulting in a video feature of 301×256 scalars. Each neural network layer is followed by Batch Normalization and ReLU.

Both Hu and Sanhyun's attention modules [7,16] are based on image data. However, the video features are a time series. To utilize not only the spatial information of the video data but also the characteristics of the time series, we apply both the time-wise attention and spatial attention in the video feature extraction module.

We first aggregate spatial information of a frame of video features by using average-pooling and max-pooling operations. A vector of spatial information in time-wise is obtained, which is then fed into a DNN with one hidden layer to produce a time-wise attention map. The hidden activation size is set to match the total number of frames of the raw video segment. The final time-wise attention map is normalized by the sigmoid function. Then, we aggregate time-wise information of a frame of video features by using average-pooling and max-pooling operation simultaneously. Average-pooled features and max-pooled features across the time-wise are then concatenated and fed into a convolution layer to produce a spatial attention map. The final spatial attention map is normalized by the sigmoid function. Finally, we obtained the filtered video features by multiplication of the video features and the attention maps in turn. Figure 2 shows the module architecture.

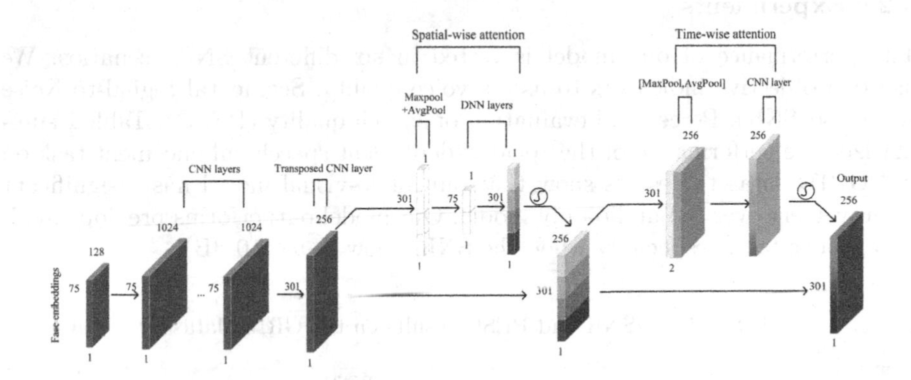

Fig. 2. Attention based video feature extraction subnetwork architecture

2.3 Shared Representation Module

The extracted audio features and video features are concatenated along the time dimension, and then subsequently fed into a BLSTM followed by DNN with one hidden layer. The output of the model is the cRM of the noisy speech spectrogram. The cRM is defined as the ratio of the complex clean and noisy spectrograms. The predicted spectrogram is computed by multiplication of the noisy input spectrogram and the output mask. The enhanced waveform is then obtained by using ISTFT.

3 Experiments

3.1 Datasets

The GRID dataset is used to train the model. GRID audio-visual corpus is a large dataset of audio and video recordings of 33 people (17 male, 16 female).

Each recorded 1000 different sentences. In the experiment of speaker-independent speech enhancement, we use 26 speakers' data as the training set (79%), and 3 speakers' data as the validation set (9%), 4 speakers' data as the test set (12%). Speakers in the training set, the verification set, and the test set do not overlap each other.

The GRID dataset contains only clean speech, so we choose to add noise in different signal-to-noise ratios (SNRs) to artificially create noisy speech. In the test set, we use the open source noise set noisex92 [14] as the noise set to test the generalization ability of the model. The noise added to the test set is completely different from the noise added to the training set and the validation set. The results of the models at the six SNRs of −5 dB, 0 dB, 5 dB, 10 dB, 15 dB, and 20 dB are then tested in turn.

3.2 Experiments

The performance of our model is tested in six different SNR scenarios. We use two objective indicators to assess voice quality: Segmental Signal-to-Noise Ratio (segSNR), Perceptual evaluation of speech quality (PESQ). Table 1 summarizes the performance of the speaker-dependent speech enhancement task on full GRID dataset. Results show that our audio-visual model has a significant improvement over the audio-only model. Our model outperforms previous models on both tasks, especially when the SNR is low (−5 – 10 dB).

Table 1. segSNR and PESQ results on the GRID dataset.

SNR	segSNR						PESQ					
	Model											
	−5 dB	0 dB	5 dB	10 dB	15 dB	20 dB	−5 dB	0 dB	5 dB	10 dB	15 dB	20 dB
Noisy	−7.479	−4.793	0.532	8.827	**18.337**	**25.916**	1.059	1.115	1.366	2.072	2.835	3.618
Audio-only	−3.833	−1.263	3.203	8.979	14.953	19.005	1.090	1.237	1.602	2.287	3.027	3.694
Erphat	−2.755	−0.287	4.358	10.484	16.309	19.400	1.124	1.344	1.771	2.473	3.212	3.825
Ours	**−1.728**	**1.039**	**5.601**	**11.434**	17.241	18.975	**1.152**	**1.435**	**1.919**	**2.595**	**3.296**	**3.840**

Figure 3 shows an example of the output of our model and Erphat's model [5], in SNR of 0 dB. It can be seen that our model is better in the place where the speech energy is concentrated, and the noise is more completely suppressed.

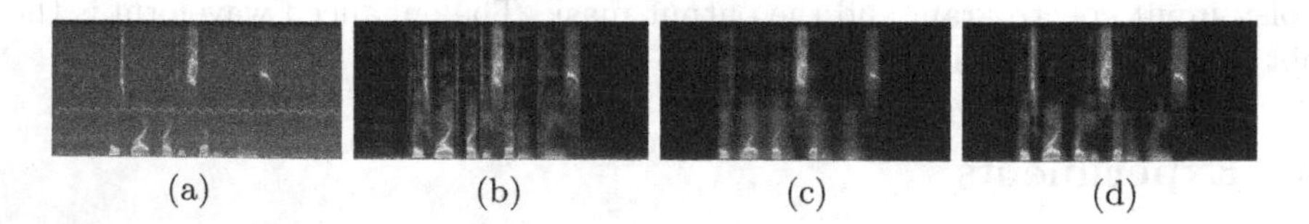

(a) (b) (c) (d)

Fig. 3. (a) The spectrogram of noisy speech (b) The spectrogram of clean speech (c) The spectrogram of the speech signal predicted by the Erphat's audio-visual model [5] (d) The spectrogram of the speech signal predicted by our model

4 Conclusion

In this work, we have proposed an attention based speaker-independent audio-visual deep learning model for single channel speech enhancement. Both the time-wise attention and spatial attention are applied in the video feature extraction module to focus on more important features. Experiments on speaker-independent speech enhancement task show that our model can achieve better results than recent audio-visual methods. We note that our method needs speakers to appear in the video all the time. In future research, we will optimize the model for more realistic scenarios.

References

1. Chung, J.S., Zisserman, A.: Lip reading in the wild. In: Lai, S.-H., Lepetit, V., Nishino, K., Sato, Y. (eds.) ACCV 2016. LNCS, vol. 10112, pp. 87–103. Springer, Cham (2017). https://doi.org/10.1007/978-3-319-54184-6_6
2. Cole, F., et al.: Synthesizing normalized faces from facial identity features. In: Proceedings of the IEEE Conference on Computer Vision and Pattern Recognition (2017)
3. Cooke, M., et al.: An audio-visual corpus for speech perception and automatic speech recognition. J. Acoust. Soc. Am. **120**(5), 2421–2424 (2006)
4. El-Solh, A., Cuhadar, A., Goubran, R.A.: Evaluation of speech enhancement techniques for speaker identification in noisy environments. In: Proceedings of ISMW, pp. 235–239 (2007)
5. Ephrat, A., et al.: Looking to listen at the cocktail party: a speaker-independent audio-visual model for speech separation. ACM Trans. Graph. (TOG) **37**(4), 112 (2018)
6. Gabbay, A., Shamir, A., Peleg, S.: Visual speech enhancement. In: Proceedings of Interspeech 2018, pp. 1170–1174 (2018)
7. Hu, J., Li, S., Sun, G.: Squeeze-and-excitation networks. In: Proceedings of the IEEE Conference on Computer Vision and Pattern Recognition (2018)
8. Kazemi, V., Sullivan, J.: One millisecond face alignment with an ensemble of regression trees. In: The IEEE Conference on Computer Vision and Pattern Recognition (CVPR), June 2014
9. King, D.E.: Dlib-ml: a machine learning toolkit. J. Mach. Learn. Res. **10**, 1755–1758 (2009)
10. Li, J., Deng, L., Haeb-Umbach, R., Gong, Y.: Robust Automatic Speech Recognition: A Bridge to Practical Applications, vol. 1. Academic Press, Amsterdam (2015)
11. Lim, J., Oppenheim, A.: All-pole modeling of degraded speech. IEEE Trans. ASSP **26**(3), 197–210 (1978)
12. Ngiam, J., et al.: Multimodal deep learning. In: Proceedings of the 28th International Conference on Machine Learning, ICML 2011 (2011)
13. Scalart, P., et al.: Speech enhancement based on a priori signal to noise estimation. In: ICASSP 1996, vol. 2, pp. 629–632 (1996)
14. Varga, A., Steeneken, H.J.: Assessment for automatic speech recognition: II. NOISEX-92: a database and an experiment to study the effect of additive noise on speech recognition systems. Speech Commun. **12**(3), 247–251 (1993)

15. Williamson, D.S., Wang, Y., Wang, D.: Complex ratio masking for joint enhancement of magnitude and phase. In: IEEE International Conference on Acoustics, Speech and Signal Processing (ICASSP). IEEE (2016)
16. Woo, S., Park, J., Lee, J.-Y., Kweon, I.S.: CBAM: convolutional block attention module. In: Ferrari, V., Hebert, M., Sminchisescu, C., Weiss, Y. (eds.) ECCV 2018. LNCS, vol. 11211, pp. 3–19. Springer, Cham (2018). https://doi.org/10.1007/978-3-030-01234-2_1
17. Xu, Y., Du, J., Dai, L.R., Lee, C.H.: An experimental study on speech enhancement based on deep neural networks. IEEE Signal Process. Lett. **21**, 65–68 (2014)

DIME: An Online Tool for the Visual Comparison of Cross-modal Retrieval Models

Tony Zhao[1](✉), Jaeyoung Choi[2], and Gerald Friedland[1]

[1] University of California, Berkeley, USA
tonyzhao@berkeley.edu
[2] International Computer Science Institute, Berkeley, USA

Abstract. Cross-modal retrieval relies on accurate models to retrieve relevant results for queries across modalities such as image, text, and video. In this paper, we build upon previous work by tackling the difficulty of evaluating models both quantitatively and qualitatively quickly. We present DIME (Dataset, Index, Model, Embedding), a modality-agnostic tool that handles multimodal datasets, trained models, and data preprocessors to support straightforward model comparison with a web browser graphical user interface. DIME inherently supports building modality-agnostic queryable indexes and extraction of relevant feature embeddings, and thus effectively doubles as an efficient cross-modal tool to explore and search through datasets.

Keywords: Cross-modal retrieval · CBIR · Evaluation

1 Introduction

With the exponentially increasing amount of multimedia content on the Internet of different modalities, cross-modal retrieval becomes increasingly important for indexing and searching through either large multi-modal datasets or between datasets of different modalities. Such cross-modal models allow retrieval across modalities such as text, image, video, etc. [1,2]. Standard evaluation metrics such as mean average precision (mAP) allow quantitative comparison between models, however, visual inspection of retrieval results allows qualitative evaluation of the models which provides much practical insight into the behavior of the models. Demands for interactive search-and-retrieval tools that can accommodate large-scale datasets have been rapidly increasing in the multimedia community and many such tools [3,4,6] have been released in this regard, or to showcase the underlying cross-modal retrieval models.

In this paper, we present DIME (Dataset, Index, Model, Embedding) that builds upon related work in creating systems to index and explore large datasets of images as well as other modalities. For instance, systems such as ImageX [3] share similar functionality such as ranking images by their similarity to a query

Y. M. Ro et al. (Eds.): MMM 2020, LNCS 11962, pp. 729–733, 2020.
https://doi.org/10.1007/978-3-030-37734-2_61

image or classification concept instead of search through filtering. Most general-purpose content-based multimedia retrieval stacks such as Vitrivr [4] support two major workflows. Within these workflows, DIME adds several key features that we found to be very useful in cross-modal retrieval research, which are either lacking or missing in previous works.

First, the *extraction workflow* is used to process different media objects such as images, audio, and video to generate relevant features. DIME adds some minor efficiency improvements and functionality to this workflow such as binarization and bit-packing of embeddings. These improvements allows for memory-efficient extraction of feature vectors and removes the need to repeatedly process datasets while testing models.

Second, the *query workflow* is used when users query a dataset through an interface. This involves extracting the relevant features of the query and dataset look-up before ranking results by their measured similarity. DIME also adds some minor improvements to this workflow by adding metadata and diagnostic information on top of the database look-up.

Finally, DIME improves the flexibility of these systems by supporting a completely new workflow that we found to be highly useful for cross-modal retrieval research. Since feature-based retrieval relies on accurate models, DIME implements the *model workflow*, which is used to compare models against each other both quantitatively with metrics as well as qualitatively with the visual presentation of results that are returned by queries.

On top of these new features, DIME automates the process of building modality-agnostic queryable indexes from corresponding datasets and models as well as presenting information useful for model comparison. Lastly, we implemented a graphical user interface in the web browser to support online and remote functionality (Figs. 1 and 2).

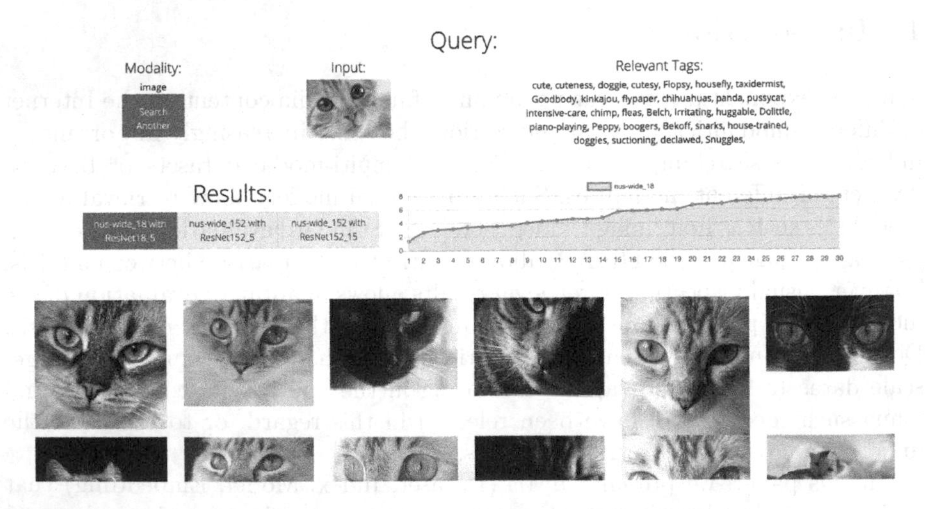

Fig. 1. DIME provides information between models such as a graph of the distribution of similarity (Euclidean distance) among the results for the query (an image in this figure). The relevant tags are the results returned from a dataset lookup of the text-modality index specific to the relevant model.

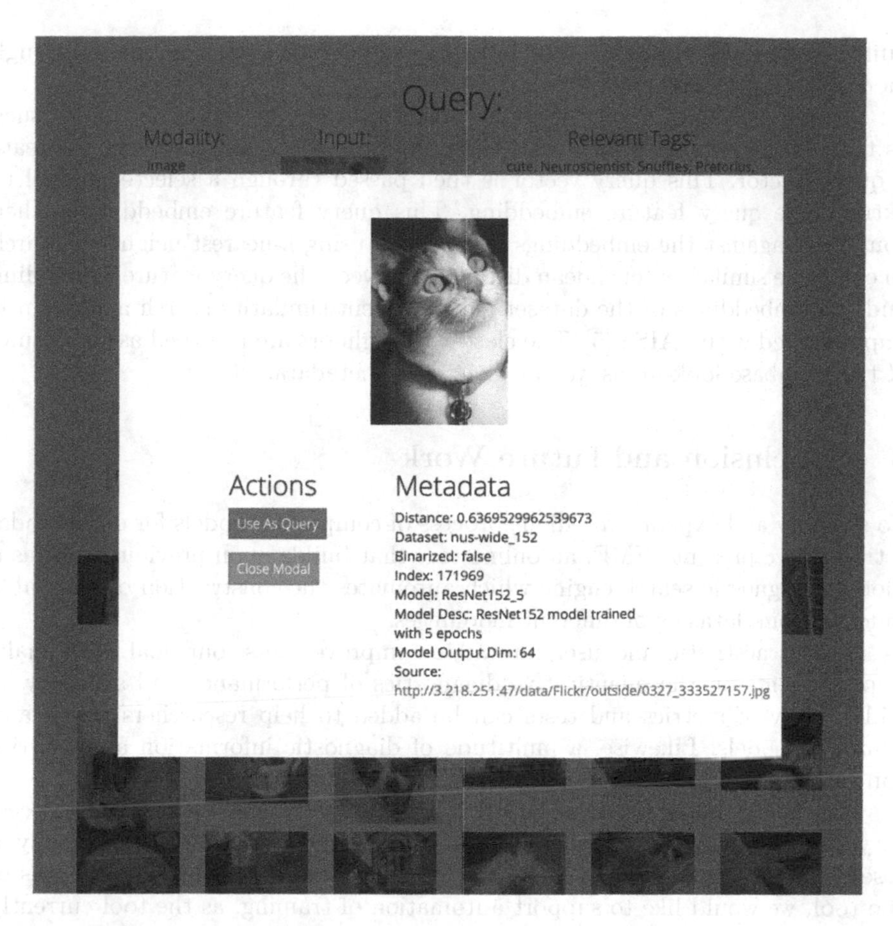

Fig. 2. DIME provides diagnostic metadata as well as other minor functionality such as using results as queries

2 DIME: Dataset, Index, Model, Embedding

DIME is comprised of its titular parts: *dataset*, *index*, *model*, and *embedding*. We define *model* as an object with a callable function. This function has specified input dimensions and output dimensions respectively. A *dataset* is defined as an iterable of vectors. DIME takes a dataset and a model to extract *embeddings* for that dataset from that specific model. Finally, it constructs a queryable *index* from those embeddings to support search and exploration.

DIME receives datasets along with any preprocessors and a specific output dimension. Any pair of model and dataset with matching input and output dimensions respectively, can then be built into an index. Users can specify if these embeddings should be binarized, which will greatly reduce the amount of memory and time needed to build and load indexes. Once the index has finished building, the entire processed dataset can support queries that pass through modality-appropriate processing.

Database lookup is supported by efficient similarity search. A query such as text or image is first vectorized through appropriate preprocessors to create a query vector. This query vector is then passed through a selected model to extract the query feature embedding. This query feature embedding is then compared against the embeddings in an index using k-nearest neighbors search to calculate similarity (euclidean distance) between the query feature embedding and the embeddings of the dataset. This efficient similarity search algorithm is implemented with FAISS [5]. The closest n neighbors are returned as the results of the database look-up as well as diagnostic metadata.

3 Conclusion and Future Work

To simplify and expedite a tedious process of comparing models for cross-modal retrieval, we present DIME, an online tool that builds upon previous work as a modality-agnostic search engine which automates the construction of queryable indexes from datasets of different modalities.

Besides aesthetic and user interaction improvements, our goal is to make improvements on the quantitative diagnostics of performance and accuracy. A wider array of metrics and tests can be added to help researchers assess and compare models. Likewise, a multitude of diagnostic information and metrics can be implemented for datasets as well.

Ultimately the end goal of DIME is to remove tedious but currently necessary steps needed to train and compare cross-modal retrieval models. Ideally, a researcher will only need to focus on designing models. In future iterations of the tool, we would like to support automation of training, as the tool currently only supports usage and comparison of pre-trained models.

Acknowledgments. Parts of this work was performed under the auspices of the U.S. Department of Energy by Lawrence Livermore National Laboratory under Contract DE-AC52-07NA27344 and was supported by the LLNL-LDRD Program under Project No. 17-SI-003. Computation resources used in this work were partially supported by AWS Cloud Credits for Research. Any findings and conclusions are those of the authors, and do not necessarily represent the views of the funders.

References

1. Zhen, L., Peng H., Wang, X., Peng, D.: Deep supervised cross-modal retrieval. In: CVPR (2019)
2. Wang, K., Yin Q., Wang W., Wu S., Wang L.: A comprehensive survey on cross-modal retrieval (2016)
3. Hezel, N., Barthel, K.U., Jung, K.: ImageX - explore and search local/private images. In: Schoeffmann, K., et al. (eds.) MMM 2018. LNCS, vol. 10705, pp. 372–376. Springer, Cham (2018). https://doi.org/10.1007/978-3-319-73600-6_35

4. Gasser R., Rossetto L., Schuldt, H.: Multimodal multimedia retrieval with Vitrivr. In: ICMR (2019)
5. Johnson, J., Douze, M., Jégou, H.: Billion-scale similarity search with GPUs. arXiv preprint arXiv:1702.08734 (2017)
6. Amato, G., Falchi, F., Gennaro, C., Rabitti, F.: YFCC100M-HNfc6: a large-scale deep features benchmark for similarity search. In: Amsaleg, L., Houle, M.E., Schubert, E. (eds.) SISAP 2016. LNCS, vol. 9939, pp. 196–209. Springer, Cham (2016). https://doi.org/10.1007/978-3-319-46759-7_15

Real-Time Demonstration of Personal Audio and 3D Audio Rendering Using Line Array Systems

Jung-Woo Choi(✉)

School of Electrical Engineering,
Korea Advanced Institute of Science and Technology (KAIST),
Daejeon 34141, Republic of Korea
jwoo@kaist.ac.kr

Abstract. Control of sound fields using array loudspeakers has been attempted in many practical areas, such as 3D audio, active noise control, and personal audio. In this work, we demonstrate two real-time sound field control systems involving a line array of loudspeakers. The first one, a personal audio system, aims to reproduce two independent sound zones with different audio programs at the same time. By suppressing acoustic interference between two sound zones, the personal audio system allows users at different locations to enjoy independent sounds. In the second demonstration, active control of spatial audio scene is presented. It has been found that the interaction between the radiation from a sound source and surrounding environment is linked with many perceptual cues of spaciousness. Especially, the perceived stage width and distance are strongly related to the interaural cross-correlation and direct-to-reverberation ratio, which can be easily manipulated by changing the directivity of a loudspeaker array. The smooth transition of spaciousness is demonstrated by changing the shapes of multiple beam patterns radiated from the line array.

Keywords: Sound field control · Personal audio · Spatial audio

1 Introduction of Demonstration Systems

1.1 Personal Audio System

Personal audio [1] is one of the active applications of sound field control. Its objective is to produce two or more independent zones of sound simultaneously, such that a listener in one zone can enjoy individual audio program without being disturbed by the sound played in other zones. One important concept to realize this objective was disclaimed in 2002, with the name of *acoustic contrast* [2]. The acoustic contrast is defined as the acoustic energy ratio of one zone of interest to the others. The zone of interest is denoted as *acoustically bright zone*, and the other zone in which sound is suppressed is called *acoustically dark zone* (Fig. 1). For reproducing two independent audio programs, the sound of

Y. M. Ro et al. (Eds.): MMM 2020, LNCS 11962, pp. 734–738, 2020.
https://doi.org/10.1007/978-3-030-37734-2_62

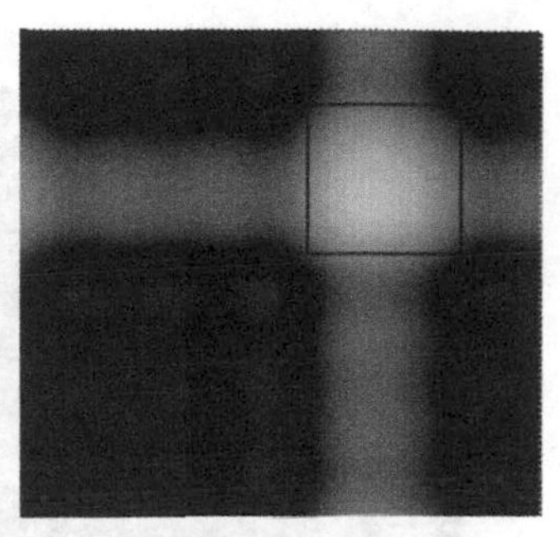

Fig. 1. Concept of personal audio at home. The objective of personal audio is to produce the bright zone (listening zone) and dark zone (quiet zone) simultaneously.

each zone is focused by finding the loudspeaker excitation signals maximizing the acoustic contrast at the corresponding zone, and then two excitation signals for two different zones are superposed, thereby minimizing audio interference between zones. Various strategies to find optimal excitation signals of loudspeakers have been developed. The initial approach, which is now called acoustic contrast control (ACC), solved the maximization problem through the eigenvalue analysis [2]. This energy ratio maximization, however, yields several artifacts such as reduced radiation efficiency, irregular spatial or spectral responses. To circumvent these problems, several alternatives incorporating joint optimization strategies have been proposed [3,4]. Among them, the technique incorporating both the acoustic contrast and energy efficiency (acoustic brightness) [5] is utilized for this demonstration.

Nowadays, there are various personal audio systems developed for different applications. For example, the personal audio system for automotive vehicles can reproduce different audio programs at individual seat locations [6]. Among them, the system demonstrated in this work has to do with its home application. A line array of loudspeakers is chosen as the control system, which can be installed with flat-panel TVs in form of a soundbar (Fig. 2). Using 24 loudspeakers of aperture size of 1.7 m, it is shown that over 30 dB of sound pressure level (SPL) difference, i.e., acoustic contrast, can be produced between the zone of interest defined over 30-degree width and the others (Fig. 3). This performance can be achieved with energy efficiency loss less than −10 dB.

1.2 3D Audio Demonstration

The second part of the demonstration is devoted to the real-time manipulation of spatial audio cues for 3D audio: the auditory source width (ASW) [7–9] and distance [10] of auditory scenery. There have been studies to reveal the relation of these perceptual cues and physical properties of a sound field. The previous studies have shown that the perception of ASW is involved with the inter-aural cross-correlation coefficient (IACC) [7,8], which represents the peak value of

Fig. 2. Linear array system for the demonstration of personal audio. Two audio programs from different video contents are presented in the left and right-half spaces, respectively.

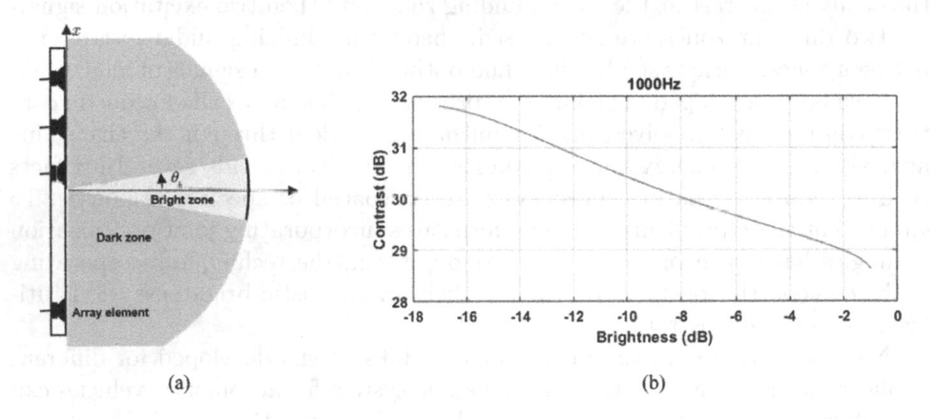

Fig. 3. Generation of an isolated sound zone for personal audio. (a) Configuration of the bright and dark zones for line-array of loudspeakers. (b) Energy ratio between the bright and dark zones (contrast) versus the energy efficiency (brightness) presented in dB scale.

the short-term cross-correlation of two ear signals. In practice, most of the decorrelation of inter-aural signals occurs due to the non-symmetric reflection from the sidewall reflections. The amount of reflections in the listening space can be controlled by changing the directivity of the loudspeaker array. For the synthesis of a directive sound field, the linear array is controlled through the holographic source rendering algorithm [11]. The algorithm approximates the Porter-Bojarski integral [12] for finite set of sound sources by replacing an ideal virtual sound source with a directional multipole source (Fig. 5). The sound generated by this principle is focused at the location of the virtual source, thereby delivering strong direct sound at the location of the virtual source and listener. The extra widening effect can also be provided by producing additional virtual sources near the

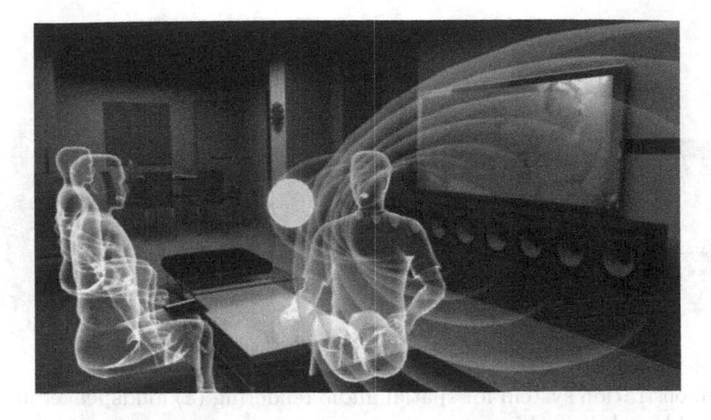

Fig. 4. Concept of holographic reproduction of a virtual sound source.

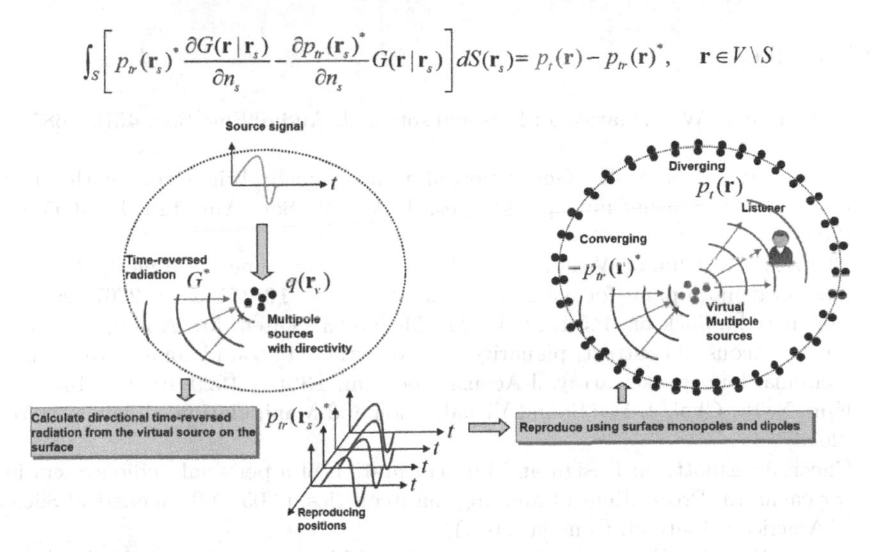

Fig. 5. Approximation of holographic sound source reproduction. The target sound field $p_t(\mathbf{r})$ is reproduced by time-reversing the pressure field and its derivative at the surface of boundary S. Using the directional multipole radiation as the target field, the target area near the listener can be separated from the converging wave front $p^*_{tr}(\mathbf{r})$.

points of reflected image sources. This also enables the control of the direct-to-reverberation ratio, which plays a key role in the distance perception of a sound source.

The demonstration system includes a touchpad interface (Fig. 6) to control the locations of virtual sources, and the changes of virtual source positions are rendered by the real-time control algorithm. The control signals are fed into the line array of loudspeakers that synthesizes desired sound field in space. Participants in this demonstration are allowed to change their positions and can set the best stage width and distance by changing the location of virtual sound sources (Fig. 4).

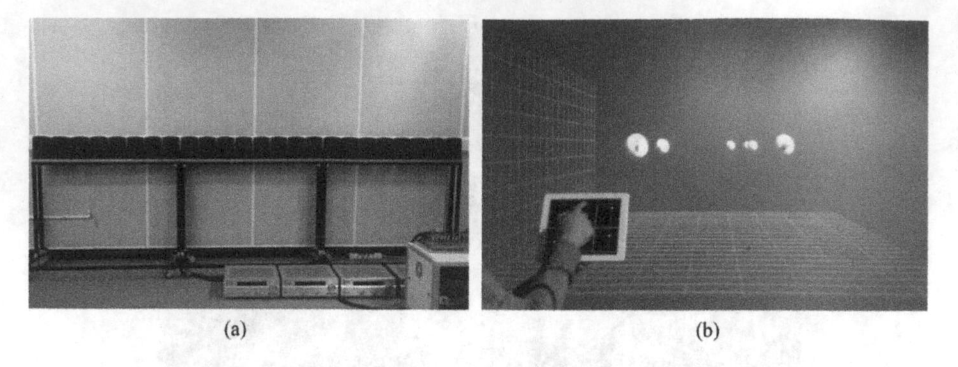

(a) (b)

Fig. 6. Demonstration system for spatial audio rendering (a) loudspeaker array system (b) touchpad-based control interface

References

1. Druyvesteyn, W.F., Garas, J.: Personal sound. J. Audio. Eng. Soc. **45**(9), 685–701 (1997)
2. Choi, J.-W., Kim, Y.-H.: Generation of an acoustically bright zone with an illuminated region using multiple sources. J. Acoust. Soc. Am. **111**(4), 1695–1700 (2002)
3. Chang, J.-H., Choi, J.-W., Kim, Y.-H.: A plane wave generation method by wave number domain point focusing. J. Acoust. Soc. Am. **128**(5), 2758–2767 (2010)
4. Coleman, P., Jackson, P.J.B., Olik, M., Møller, M., Olsen, M., Abildgaard Pedersen, J.: Acoustic contrast, planarity and robustness of sound zone methods using a circular loudspeaker array. J Acoust. Soc. Am. **135**(4), 1929–1940 (2014)
5. Kim, Y.-H., Choi, J.-W.: Sound Visualization and Manipulation. Wiley, New York (2013)
6. Cheer, J., Elliott, S.: Design and implementation of a personal audio system in a car cabin. In: Proceedings of Meetings on Acoustics, p. 055009. Acoustical Society of America, Montreal, Canada (2013)
7. Sayers, B.M.A., Cherry, E.C.: Mechanism of binaural fusion in the hearing of speech. J. Acoust. Soc. Am. **29**(9), 973–987 (1957)
8. Kendall, G.: The decorrelation of audio signals and its impact on spatial imagery. Comp. Music J. **19**(4), 71–87 (1995)
9. Rumsey, F.: Spatial quality evaluation for reproduced sound: terminology, meaning, and a scene-based paradigm. J. Audio Eng. Soc. **50**(9), 651–666 (2002)
10. Kang, D.S., Choi, J.-W., Martens, W.: Distance perception of a virtual sound source synthesized near the listener position. Multimedia Tools Appl. **75**(9), 5161–5182 (2015)
11. Choi, J.W., Kim, Y.-H.: Integral approach for reproduction of virtual sound source surrounded by loudspeaker array. IEEE Trans. Audio Speech Lang. Process. **20**(7), 1976–1989 (2012)
12. Devaney, A.J., Porter, R.P.: Holography and the inverse source problem. Part II: Inhomogeneous media. J. Opt. Soc. Am. A. **2**(11), 2006 (1985)

A CNN-Based Multi-scale Super-Resolution Architecture on FPGA for 4K/8K UHD Applications

Yongwoo Kim[1], Jae-Seok Choi[2], Jaehyup Lee[2], and Munchurl Kim[2](✉)

[1] Artificial Intelligence Research Division, Korea Aerospace Research Institute, Daejeon 34133, Republic of Korea
ywkim85@kari.re.kr

[2] Video and Image Computing Lab, School of Electrical Engineering, Korea Advanced Institute of Science and Technology, KAIST, 291 Daehak-ro, Yuseong-gu, Daejeon 34141, Republic of Korea
{jschoi14, woguq365, mkimee}@kaist.ac.kr

Abstract. In this paper, based on our previous work, we present a multi-scale super-resolution (SR) hardware (HW) architecture using a convolutional neural network (CNN), where the up-scaling factors of 2, 3 and 4 are supported. In our dedicated multi-scale CNN-based SR HW, low-resolution (LR) input frames are processed line-by-line, and the number of convolutional filter parameters is significantly reduced by incorporating depth-wise separable convolutions with residual connections. As for 3× and 4× up-scaling, the number of channels for point-wise convolution layer before a pixel-shuffle layer is set to 9 and 16, respectively. Additionally, we propose an integrated timing generator that supports 3× and 4× up-scaling. For efficient HW implementation, we use a simple and effective quantization method with a minimal peak signal-to-noise ratio (PSNR) degradation. Also, we propose a compression method to efficiently store intermediate feature map data to reduce the number of line memories used in HW. Our CNN-based SR HW implementation on the FPGA can generate 4K ultra high-definition (UHD) frames of higher PSNR at 60 fps, which have higher visual quality compared to conventional CNN-based SR methods that were trained and tested in software. The resources in our CNN-based SR HW can be shared for multi-scale upscaling factors of 2, 3 and 4 so that can be implemented to generate 8K UHD frames from 2K FHD input frames.

Keywords: Super-resolution · Multi-scale · 4 K UHD · Deep learning · CNN · Real-time · Hardware · FPGA

1 Introduction

While many high-end TVs and smartphones support 4K ultra high-definition (UHD) videos, there are still many video streams with qHD (960 × 540) resolution, high-definition (HD) resolution (1280 × 720) and full-high-definition (FHD) resolution (1,920 × 1,080), due to legacy acquisition devices and services. Therefore, a

Y. M. Ro et al. (Eds.): MMM 2020, LNCS 11962, pp. 739–744, 2020.
https://doi.org/10.1007/978-3-030-37734-2_63

delicate up-scaling technique, which can convert low-resolution (LR) contents into high-quality high-resolution (HR) ones, is essential, especially when it comes to up-scaling legacy contents to 4K UHD videos. Recently, deep neural networks (DNNs), especially deep convolutional neural networks (CNNs), have demonstrated superior performance in a variety of computer vision research areas, including image classification, object detection, segmentation, etc.

CNN-based SR methods have been proposed to enhance the visual quality of reconstructed HR images. However, it is known that conventional CNN-based SR methods are difficult to implement in low complexity hardware (HW) for real-time applications. In addition, the conventional CNN-based SR HW is difficult to apply in real-time applications using the method of reading data from an external frame. In this paper, we present a CNN-based multi-scale SR hardware, which can up-scale qHD, HD and FHD to 4K UHD at 60 fps on FPGA.

The remainder of the paper is organized as follows: Sect. 2 describes our multi-scale CNN-based hardware architecture for SR. Section 3 demonstrates our HW implementation on FPGA. Finally, we conclude our work in Sect. 4.

2 CNN-Based Multi-scale SR HW Architecture

Figure 1 illustrates our proposed HW architecture for multi-scale SR to support 2×, 3× and 4×. As shown in Fig. 1, we propose two novel modules to improve upon our previous 2× SR hardware structure [1]. First, as for scale factors of 3 and 4, the number of channels in a point-wise convolution layer before a pixel-shuffle layer is increased to 9 and 16, respectively. From an HW's perspective, using only 16 channels in the last pointwise convolution layer can support all scales. Here, the number of filter parameters used in 2×, 3× and 4× SR is 2,560, 2,640 and 2,752, respectively, which are fewer than that of FSRCNN-s [2]. Secondly, we propose an integrated timing generator module that supports 3× and 4× scale. Timing signals (DE, HSYNC, VSYNC) in the unified timing generator module are required to control the output line buffers.

The processing of our proposed multi-scale SR HW in Fig. 1 is performed as follows: (i) Convolutional filter parameters (weights) in our multi-scale SR HW are loaded from weight buffers. Afterwards, we extract YCbCr values from an RGB input stream. From the YCbCr LR input image, we store its four rows into line buffers, which will be used for nearest neighbor up-sampling to obtain an interpolated image to be used in a residual connection at the end of our network. (ii) A data aligner rearranges the data in both the four line buffers and the input stream, and generates 3 × 3- sized YCbCr LR patches. Here, Y channels of the LR patches are sent to the first 3 × 3 convolution layer. After the first convolution, its feature map data goes through a ReLU activation function. After that, the output is passed to a 1D horizontal residual block. (iii) The intermediate feature maps after the residual block and ReLU are then compressed by the compressor and stored in the line memories. The data stored in the line memories is then read and decompressed at one-delayed line data enable (DE) timing. The decompressed data then goes through 3 × 3 depth-wise and 1 × 1 pointwise convolution. (iv) During the 1 × 1 pointwise convolution, the number of feature map channels is reduced by half from 32 to 16. Next, the operation from the step (iii) is

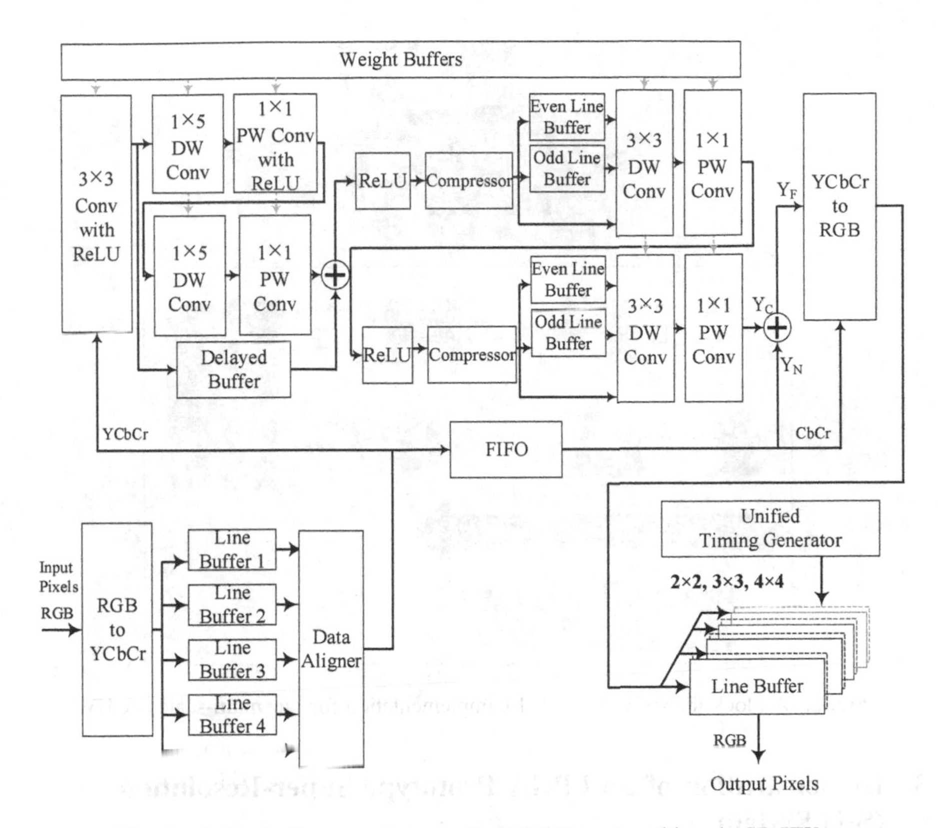

Fig. 1. A block diagram of our unified CNN-based multi-scale SR HW.

repeated for the feature maps of 16 channels. Here, it should be noted that the feature maps at the output (1×1 pointwise) convolution layer are 4 channels for $2\times$ SR, 9 channels for $3\times$ SR, 16 channels for $4\times$ SR, which are then used to construct a 2×2-sized HR patch for $2\times$ SR, a 3×3-sized HR patch for $3\times$ SR, a 4×4-sized HR patch for $4\times$ SR, similarly as in sub-pixel convolution [3]. (v) Finally, the final Y (Y_F) is obtained by adding the multi-scale-sized ($2\times$, $3\times$ and $4\times$) super-resolved Y data (Y_C) to the multi-scale up-sampled data by using nearest-neighbor interpolation (Y_N).

To synchronize the two timings of Y_C and Y_N data, Y_N data is stored in a first-in-first-out (FIFO) block and is read at the same timing as Y_C. Delayed CbCr data from the FIFO is also up-sampled by a factor of 2, 3 and 4 using nearest-neighbor interpolation, which is then transferred to a YCbCr-to-RGB converter to obtain RGB pixels. Four output line buffers (LBs) store the generated multi-scale RGB HR patches which are then delivered to display devices per output clock cycle on output timing. Here, we use eight output line buffers to avoid read/write conflict for multi-scale RGB HR output patches using a double-buffering scheme for stream processing.

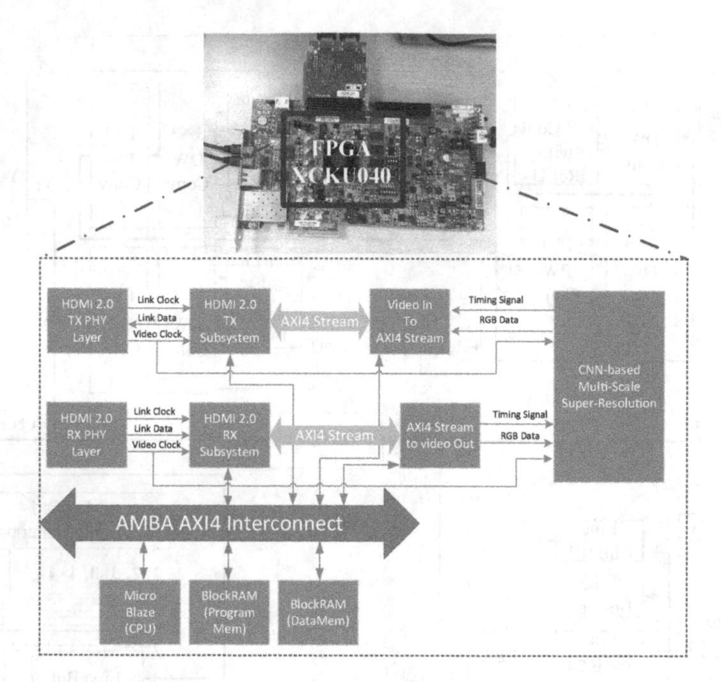

Fig. 2. A block diagram of an FPGA implementation for our multi-scale SR HW.

3 Demonstration of an FPGA Prototype Super-Resolution (SR) System

Figure 2 shows a block diagram of an FPGA implementation for our SR HW. To verify our SR HW, we used a Xilinx Kintex UltraScale FPGA KCU105 evaluation board [4] and a TED's HDMI 2.0 expansion card [5] to support qHD, HD and FHD input and 4K UHD output video interfaces. TED's FMC (FPGA Mezzanine Card) card is designed to be compatible with the HDMI 2.0 specification, with an individual TMDS channel throughput of up to 6 Gbps thus enabling support of 4K resolution at 60 fps.

Our FPGA design is built around the HDMI 2.0 Transmitter Subsystem (HDMI_TX_SS), HDMI 2.0 Receiver Subsystem (HDMI_RX_SS), and Video PHY (VPHY) Controller cores and leverages existing Xilinx IP cores to form the FPGA prototype SR system. All Xilinx IP cores associated with the HDMI 2.0 interface are controlled by the microblaze CPU. The internal clock of this SR system uses two clocks with different input and output clocks. When supporting 2× SR, the frequency relation is 4 times faster than the input frequency. To support 3× and 4×, the output frequency must be 9 and 16 times, respectively, faster than the input frequency, and our SR HW processes four pixels per clock cycle to support 4K UHD video streams of 60 fps. In addition, our SR HW applied the constraints of the 150 MHz target operating frequency to the synthesis phase and the place and route (P&R) phase, which was implemented using Vivado Design Suite 2015.4. Figure 3 shows an FPGA prototype system of our multi-scale SR HW.

Fig. 3. Demonstration of our multi-scale SR FPGA prototype.

4 Conclusion

In this paper, we presented an efficient CNN-based multi-scale SR hardware that can reconstruct 4K UHD at 60 fps. Our multi-scale SR hardware does not use any frame buffer to store intermediate feature maps and uses a small number of filter parameters. Additionally, we used a simple and effective quantization scheme for weight parameters and activations to further reduce computational complexity and memory usage. As a result, our SR HW can reconstruct 4K UHD videos at 60 fps, and capable of handling multi-scale factors of 2, 3 and 4.

Acknowledgement. This work was supported by Institute for Information & communications Technology Promotion (IITP) grant funded by the Korea government (MSIT) (No. 2017-0-00419, Intelligent High Realistic Visual Processing for Smart Broadcasting Media).

References

1. Kim, Y., Choi, J., Kim, M.: A real-time convolutional neural network for super-resolution on FPGA with applications to 4 K UHD 60 fps video services. IEEE Trans. Circuits Syst. Video Technol. **29**(8), 2521–2534 (2019). https://doi.org/10.1109/TCSVT.2018.2864321

2. Dong, C., Loy, C.C., Tang, X.: Accelerating the super-resolution convolutional neural network. In: Leibe, B., Matas, J., Sebe, N., Welling, M. (eds.) Computer Vision – ECCV 2016, ECCV 2016. LNCS, vol. 9906, pp. 391–407. Springer, Cham (2016). https://doi.org/10.1007/978-3-319-46475-6_25
3. Shi, W., et al.: Real-time single image and video super-resolution using an efficient sub-pixel convolutional neural network. In: Proceedings of the IEEE Conference on Computer Vision and Pattern Recognition (CVPR), pp. 1874–1883. IEEE, Las Vegas, June 2016
4. Xilinx. https://www.xilinx.com/products/boards-and-kits/kcu105.html. Accessed 19 Sept 2019
5. TED's TB-FMCH-HDMI4K Hardware User Manual. https://solutions.inrevium.com/products/pdf/TB_FMCH_HDMI4K_HWUserManual_2.04.pdf. Accessed 19 Sept 2019

Effective Utilization of Hybrid Residual Modules in Deep Neural Networks for Super Resolution

Abdul Muqeet and Sung-Ho Bae(✉)

Department of Computer Science and Engineering,
Kyung-Hee University, Yongin, South Korea
{amuqeet,shbae}@khu.ac.kr

Abstract. Recently, Single-Image Super-Resolution (SISR) has attracted a lot of researchers due to its numerous real-life applications in multiple domains. This paper focuses on efficient solutions of SISR with Hybrid Residual Modules (HRM). The proposed HRM allows the deep neural network to reconstruct very high quality super-resolved images with much lower computation compared to the conventional SISR methods. In this paper, we first describe the technical details of our HRM in SISR and introduce interesting applications of the proposed SISR method, such as surveillance camera system, medical imaging, astronomical imaging.

Keywords: Super-resolution · Efficient framework · Image restoration

1 Introduction

For the given single low-resolution (LR) image, SISR aim to reconstruct the high-resolution (HR) image. Presently, several deep learning methods have been proposed to solve the SISR problem. SRCNN [1] come up with three convolutional layers for SISR. Their results surpassed the traditional techniques. EDSR and MDSR [4] utilized the residual blocks [2] to increase the depth of CNN. MSRN [3] exploited the multi-scale spatial features to improve performance. These features are combined through a hierarchical feature fusion (HFF) structure. HRAN [5] proposed the binarized feature fusion (BFF) structure and hybrid residual attention blocks (HRAB) to solve these problems.

Due to the ubiquitous computing applications, SR has become popular in various domains from satellite imaging [6] to medical imaging [7]. However, small hand-held devices require smaller and efficient models and in contrast, medical applications require complex models since critical decisions are required.

In this paper, we present a solution to the above-mentioned problem. We utilize the HRAN network architecture [5] and propose an efficient way such that it could work as both light and complex models.

The remaining paper is organized as follows: In Sect. 2, we discuss the HRAN Architecture. We discuss the real-life applications of SR in Sect. 3. In Sect. 4, we discuss the complexity and accuracy trade-off.

Y. M. Ro et al. (Eds.): MMM 2020, LNCS 11962, pp. 745–750, 2020.
https://doi.org/10.1007/978-3-030-37734-2_64

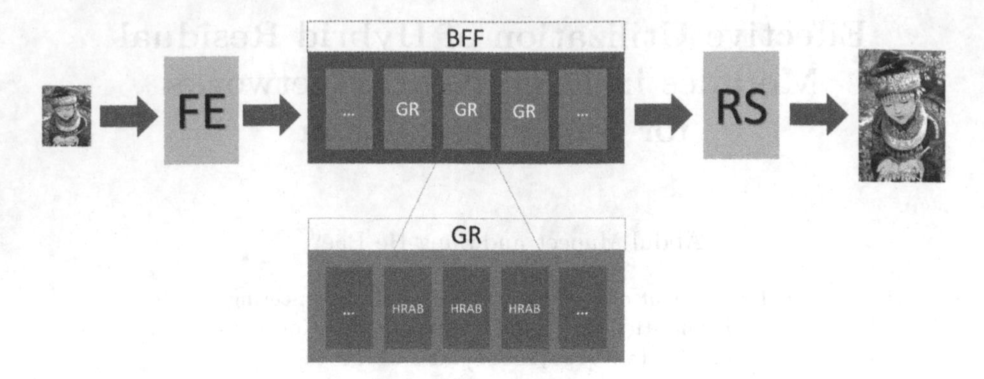

Fig. 1. The HRAN network architecture [5]

2 HRAN Architecture

In this section, we briefly describe the HRAN (Hybrid residual attention network) architecture, it can be seen in Fig. 1. It is decomposed it into feature extraction (FE), BFF, and reconstruction stage (RS). FE and BFF both are responsible for shallow and deep feature extraction respectively. BFF consists of a stack of GR modules, and each GR has a stack of HRAB. The HRAN also contains short (SSC), long (LSC), and global skip connections (GSC), but for the simplicity, we have not shown them in the figure.

3 SR Applications

In this section, we identify the potential applications of SISR and briefly review them. Since, SR can improve the performance of high-level vision algorithms, it has been utilized in various domains as shown in Figure 2. These domains include medical imaging, satellite imaging, microscopic imaging, astronomical imaging, virtual/augmented reality (VR/AR), infrared imaging (IR), E-commerce, broadcasting.

Medical Imaging

There are numerous approaches of SR proposed for medical imaging [8–10]. In [8], authors proposed 3D CNN for brain magnetic resonance (MR) imaging. The authors in [9] improved the previous method and proposed the densely connected 3D CNN. Similarly, for the retinal image analysis, the authors in [10] proposed a generative adversarial network (GAN) based method to solve this problem.

Satellite Imaging

In [11], the authors proposed a neural network for target identification by using remote sensing images. In these problems, to identify the targets, the images

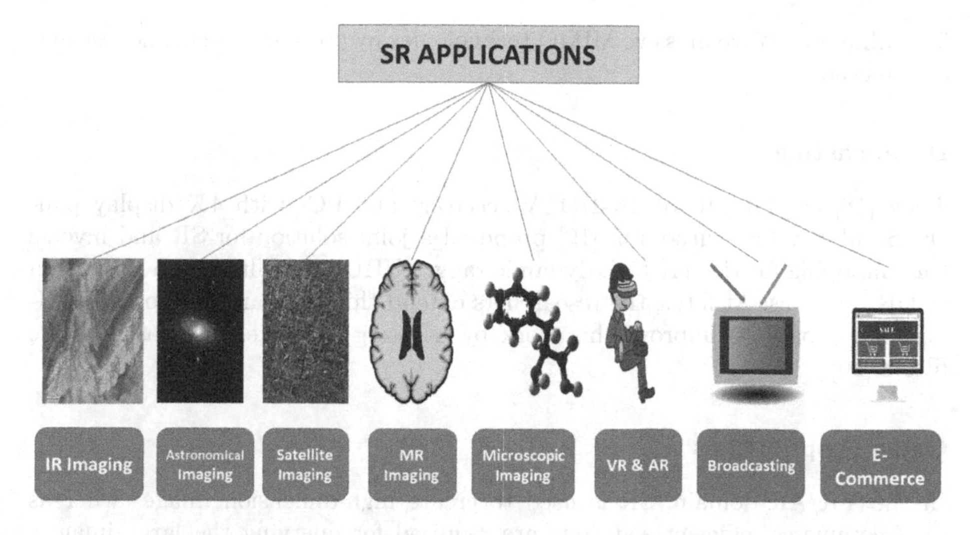

Fig. 2. Applications of Single-Image Super-Resolution (SISR).

were super-resolved beforehand. Similarly, authors in [12] proposed a system for monitoring the tunnel activities using super-resolved images. Furthermore, [13] presented a robust CNN model for video satellite imagery.

Microscopic Imaging

The SR methods have also attracted the biologists. In [14], the author focused on nanoscopic cellular structure and increased the resolution of an image to 50 to 60 nm. Similarly, the authors in [15] worked on vascular imaging. In [16], the authors presented a complete road-map for the microscopy researchers for the potential of SR methods in microscopy.

Astronomical Imaging

SR also has applications in the field of Astronomy. The authors proposed a blind SR approach for the astronomical images in [17]. They have shown through their extensive experiments that faint stars can become more distinct whereas bright stars can have sharper profiles after super-resolving the images. The authors in [21] proposed a SR method by using unregistered aliased images. Likewise, authors [22] proposed a geometric technique for SR. In the optical system, CCD pixel is chosen as detection unit though it generates ill-sampling images. The authors come up with a SR method to avoid the resolution decline cause by ill-sampling.

Infrared Imaging (IR)

In the IR domain, researchers have used SR for infrared surveillance proposed group sparse representations method [24]. Whereas, authors in [23] utilized SISR for Millimeter-Wave massive MIMO technologies by proposing a channel estimation method.

Broadcasting

They [18] employ SR for 4K-HDTV receivers and PCs with 4 K display panels. Similarly, The authors in [19] proposed a joint solution for SR and inverse tone-mapping for the 4 K high dynamic range (UHD) and Ultra High Definition (HDR) systems. At later, the researchers extend this work and proposed GAN-based approach to improve this work by utilizing the pixel-wise task-specific filters [20]

Other Applications

In the VR/AR domain, SR is used to create high-dimension images whereas in E-commerce, efficient solutions are required for querying the large images, thus, images are initially down-sampled on client-side and then super-resolved on server-end to recover the full query image.

4 Complexity and Accuracy Trade-Off

In this section, we utilize the HRAN architecture [5] to propose an efficient SR model. The HRAN mainly consists of GR modules and HRAB blocks. We identify the Microscopic, Astronomical, MR imaging as the critical domains. We will be using over 20 GR modules and 10 HRAB blocks for it. In contrast, for edge applications, we have very low computation power, hence, we can reduce the number of GR modules to 5 and HRAB blocks to 3. Meanwhile, there are many applications, for which, we have to decide on run-time about the trade-off between accuracy and memory computations such as E-commerce. For the E-commerce applications, if we have a lot of traffic on the servers, we may compromise the accuracy by having a low-power model i.e. with GR = 5 and HRAB = 3, otherwise, a model with GR = 0 and HRAB = 10.

For the edge devices and large applications, we will have a single pre-trained models stored on the devices. In contrast, for the applications having mercurial complexity, we will train multiple model with different combinations of GR and HRAB modules in the server. For the testing time, we obtain best model which fit on the given scenario.

5 Conclusion

In this paper, we identified the several potential real-life applications of SR from satellite imaging [6] to medical imaging [7]. We presented an efficient way to handle SR techniques by utilizing the HRAN architecture such that we can have a better trade-off between accuracy and complexity.

Acknowledgement. This research was supported by the MSIT (Ministry of Science and ICT), Korea, under the Grand Information Technology Research Center support program (IITP-2019-2015-0-00742) supervised by the IITP (Insititute of Information & Communications Technology Planning & Evaluation)

References

1. Dong, C., Loy, C.C., He, K., Tang, X.: Image super-resolution using deep convolutional networks. IEEE Trans. Pattern Anal. Mach. Intell. **38**(2), 295–307 (2016)
2. He, K., Zhang, X., Ren, S., Sun, J.: Deep residual learning for image recognition. In: Proceedings of the IEEE Conference on Computer Vision and Pattern Recognition, pp. 770–778 (2016)
3. Li, J., Fang, F., Mei, K., Zhang, G.: Multi-scale residual network for image super-resolution. In: The European Conference on Computer Vision (ECCV), September 2018
4. Lim, B., Son, S., Kim, H., Nah, S., Lee, K.M.: Enhanced deep residual networks for single image super-resolution. In: The IEEE Conference on Computer Vision and Pattern Recognition (CVPR) Workshops, July 2017
5. Muqeet, A., Iqbal, M.T., Bae, S.H.: Hybrid Residual Attention Network for Single Image Super Resolution. arXiv preprint arXiv:1907.05514 2019
6. Thornton, M.W., Atkinson, P.M., Holland, D.A.: Sub-pixel mapping of rural land cover objects from fine spatial resolution satellite sensor imagery using super-resolution pixel-swapping. Int. J. Remote Sens. **27**(3), 473–491 (2006)
7. Greenspan, H.: Super-resolution in medical imaging. Comput. J. **52**(1), 43–63 (2008)
8. Pham, C.H., Ducournau, A., Fablet, R., Rousseau, F.: Brain MRI super-resolution using deep 3D convolutional networks. In: 2017 IEEE 14th International Symposium on Biomedical Imaging (ISBI 2017), pp. 197–200 (2017)
9. Chen, Y., Xie, Y., Zhou, Z., Shi, F., Christodoulou, A.G., Li, D.: Brain MRI super resolution using 3D deep densely connected neural networks. In: 2018 IEEE 15th International Symposium on Biomedical Imaging (ISBI 2018), pp. 739–742 (2018)
10. Mahapatra, D., Bozorgtabar, B., Hewavitharanage, S., Garnavi, R.: Image super resolution using generative adversarial networks and local saliency maps for retinal image analysis. In: International Conference on Medical Image Computing and Computer-Assisted Intervention, pp. 382–390 (2017)
11. Tatem, A.J., Lewis, H.G., Atkinson, P.M., Nixon, M.S.: Super-resolution target identification from remotely sensed images using a Hopfield neural network. IEEE Trans. Geosci. Remote Sens. **39**(4), 781–796 (2001)
12. Dao, M., Kwan, C., Koperski, K., Marchisio, G.: A joint sparsity approach to tunnel activity monitoring using high resolution satellite images. In: 2017 IEEE 8th Annual Ubiquitous Computing, Electronics and Mobile Communication Conference (UEMCON), pp. 322–328 (2017)
13. Luo, Y., Zhou, L., Wang, S., Wang, Z.: A joint sparsity approach to tunnel activity monitoring using high resolution satellite images video satellite imagery super resolution via convolutional neural networks. IEEE Geosci. Remote Sens. Lett. **14**(12), 2398–2402 (2017)
14. Huang, B., Wang, W., Bates, M., Zhuang, X.: Three-dimensional super-resolution imaging by stochastic optical reconstruction microscopy. Science **319**(5864), 810–813 (2008)

15. Errico, C., et al.: Ultrafast ultrasound localization microscopy for deep super-resolution vascular imaging. Nature **527**(7579), 499 (2015)
16. Hell, S.W., et al.: The 2015 super-resolution microscopy roadmap. J. Phys. D: Appl. Phys. **48**(44), 443001 (2015)
17. Li, Z., Peng, Q., Bhanu, B., Zhang, Q., He, H.: Super resolution for astronomical observations. Astrophys. Space Sci. **363**(5), 92 (2018)
18. Goto, T., Fukuoka, T., Nagashima, F., Hirano, S., Sakurai, M. Super-resolution System for 4K-HDTV. In: 22nd IEEE International Conference on Pattern Recognition, pp. 4453–4458 (2014)
19. Kim, S.Y., Oh, J., Kim, M.: Deep SR-ITM: Joint Learning of Super-resolution and Inverse Tone-Mapping for 4K UHD HDR Applications. arXiv preprint arXiv:1904.11176 (2019)
20. Kim, S.Y., Oh, J., Kim, M.: JSI-GAN: GAN-Based Joint Super-Resolution and Inverse Tone-Mapping with Pixel-Wise Task-Specific Filters for UHD HDR Video. arXiv preprint arXiv:1909.04391 (2019)
21. Guo, R., Shi, X., Wang, Z.: Super-resolution from unregistered aliased astronomical images. J. Electron. Imaging **28**(2), 023032 (2019)
22. Zhang, S., Ling, J., Huang, C.: Super-resolution geometry processing technology for Ill-sampled astronomical images. J. Phys.: Conf. Ser. **1229**(1) 012017 (2019)
23. Hu, C., Dai, L., Mir, T., Gao, Z., Fang, J.: Super-resolution channel estimation for mmWave massive MIMO with hybrid precoding. IEEE Trans. Veh. Technol. **67**(9), 8954–8958 (2018)
24. Liu, H.C., Li, S.T., Yin, H.T.: Infrared surveillance image super resolution via group sparse representation. Opt. Commun. **289**, 45–52 (2013)

VBS Papers

diveXplore 4.0: The ITEC Deep Interactive Video Exploration System at VBS2020

Andreas Leibetseder(✉), Bernd Münzer, Jürgen Primus, Sabrina Kletz, and Klaus Schoeffmann

Klagenfurt University, Institute of Information Technology (ITEC), Klagenfurt, Austria
{aleibets,bernd,mprimus,sabrina,ks}@itec.aau.at

Abstract. Having participated in the three most recent iterations of the annual Video Browser Showdown (VBS2017–VBS2019) as well as in both newly established Lifelog Search Challenges (LSC2018–LSC2019), the actively developed *Deep Interactive Video Exploration (diveXplore)* system combines a variety of content-based video analysis and processing strategies for interactively exploring large video archives. The system provides a user with browseable self-organizing feature maps, color filtering, semantic concept search utilizing deep neural networks as well as hand-drawn sketch search. The most recent version improves upon its predecessors by unifying deep concepts for facilitating and speeding up search, while significantly refactoring the user interface for increasing the overall system performance.

Keywords: Video retrieval · Interactive video search · Video analysis

1 System Overview

Developed by the Multimedia Information Systems group of Klagenfurt University's Institute of Information Technology (ITEC), diveXplore (Deep Interactive Video Exploration) is an iteratively evolving interactive video retrieval system originally designed for the annual Video Browser Showdown [5,6,10] (VBS). It is intended for enabling quickly searching large video datasets such as the competition's current V3C1 collection [1] (approx. 1 000 h of video) – the first part of a three-part Vimeo clip compilation labeled V3C [9] (approx. 3 800 h of video). While operating on videos, diveXplore was employed in past VBS iterations (VBS2017 [13], VBS2018 [3,8], VBS2019 [11]) but as well specifically modified to *lifeXplore* for taking part in the most recent two image-based Lifelog Search Challenge runs (LSC2018 [7], LSC2019 [4]) – an interactive competition aimed at determining the best systems and approaches for fast moment retrieval in lifelogging data [2]. Being able to participate in such different competitions providing distinct kinds of data with a mere moderate amount of changes to the

Y. M. Ro et al. (Eds.): MMM 2020, LNCS 11962, pp. 753–759, 2020.
https://doi.org/10.1007/978-3-030-37734-2_65

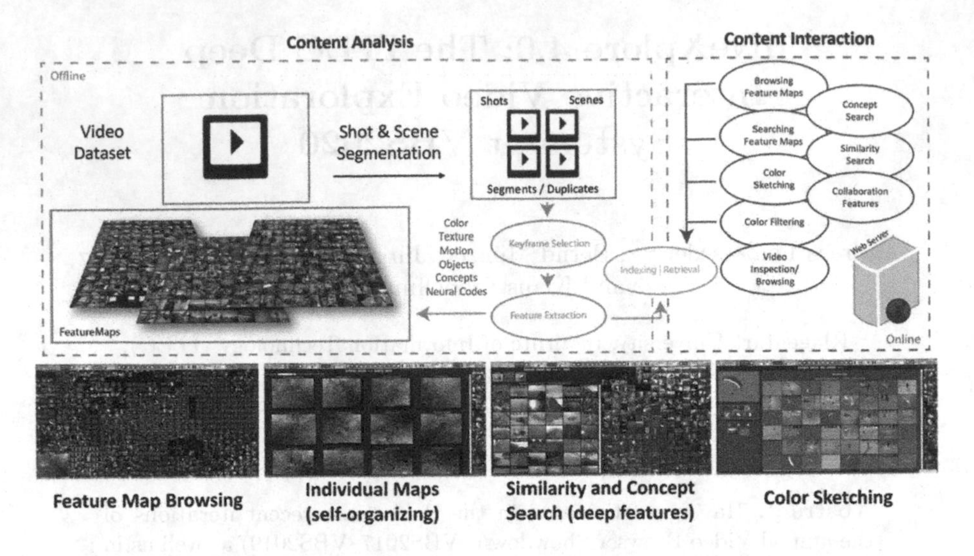

Fig. 1. Architecture and features of the *diveXplore* system

system, shows its versatility for multimedia retrieval in general, which as well becomes apparent when regarding the multitude of browsing and search features offered by diveXplore.

Said feature variety as well as the the core architecture of the current diveXplore version is shown in Fig. 1, highlighting its most prominent search strategies. At the lowest level the system operates on shots, i.e. automatically extracted video chunks optimally representing coherent scenes. Further, at any point in time a pre-processed self-organizing browseable feature map is loaded that arranges all or a subset of these shots as a multi-level wall of keyframes according to certain criteria such as deep features (e.g. `pool5/7x7_s1` of GoogLeNet), colors, faces or visible text (see featuremap examples in Fig. 2). While these maps can be switched via keyword search or choosing from several useful ones pinned to the interface, diveXplore offers many additional tools which accompany and are linked to this core strategy of featuremap exploration: video browsing, inspecting storyboards listing all shots of a video, color filtering, hand-drawn sketch search and concept as well as similarity search based on metadata, deep features or color descriptors.

In diveXplore's 4.0 version, targeted at this year's VBS2020, we combine deep features obtained by different convolutional neural networks (CNNs) improving concept search and introduce a search history for similarity search, while conducting major interface changes and refactorings in order to improve search strategy to featuremap interlinking, system performance and its overall usability. Following sections describe the most significant improvements in detail.

(a) Deep features featuremap. (b) Green color featuremap.

(c) Multiple faces featuremap. (d) Visible text featuremap.

Fig. 2. Example self-organizing featuremaps of diveXplore's extensive map catalogue. (Color figure online)

2 Improved Deep Feature Search

The diveXplore system's deep feature search allows users to retrieve shots according to dataset-specific metadata and deep concepts as well as features using pre-trained CNN models such as Inception-BN, Places-CNN and Sun397.

2.1 Concept Search

The concept search view (see Fig. 3) is accessed via an overlay window on top of the featuremap and provides the user with a textual input for searching shots according to fully or partially matching concepts from a pool of over 22 000 categories (ImageNet + Places-CNN + Sun397), which can be searched via an input field providing autocomplete suggestions to a user.

Whereas in previous system versions, users were able to choose which CNN model to utilize for retrieval, diveXplore 4.0 drops this proven to be rather confusing and time-consuming feature combining all concepts analyzed by the entirety of CNN models. In the pre-processing phase, these concepts formerly were extracted from shot keyframes only, yet for diveXplore 4.0 additionally uniformly sampled shot frames are analyzed. Apart from accumulating much more data, such a strategy is much more advantageous for retrieving result shots, since those can now be ordered according to the majority of detected concepts, weighted by their classification confidence. Finally, a smarter algorithm is applied for metadata filtering improving corresponding search as well.

(a) CNN search for "school bus". (b) Metadata search for "interview".

Fig. 3. Improved concept search.

2.2 Similarity Search

Similarity search allows users to select any shot on any kind of view and find similar shots according to its keyframe's CNN features (last fully-connected layer) or a custom created color histogram-based descriptor (*HistMap* [12]), which has been developed for sketch search. Figure 4 depicts this type of search applied on several keyframes showing various turtles.

Fig. 4. Similarity search of shots showing a turtle with history. (Color figure online)

As a convenience for quickly finding and viewing past similarity searches diveXplore 4.0 provides a newly implemented similarity search history (top row in result area of Fig. 4), including similarity criteria, shot preview as well as an indicator for the currently active search (red border in Fig. 4).

3 Interface Improvements

Among the most integral interface improvements, we place the hover-submit feature, as shown in Fig. 5: mouse-hovering over shots alters the keyframe preview and reveals uniformly sampled shot frames depending on the hover cursor's horizontal hover position (Fig. 5a). Previously, for submitting non keyframes, it has been necessary to open the video browser and jump to corresponding frames before pressing a submit button. Hover-submit improves upon this situation by enabling participants to perform a Ctrl- or Alt-click for more quickly submitting any preview frame (Fig. 5b).

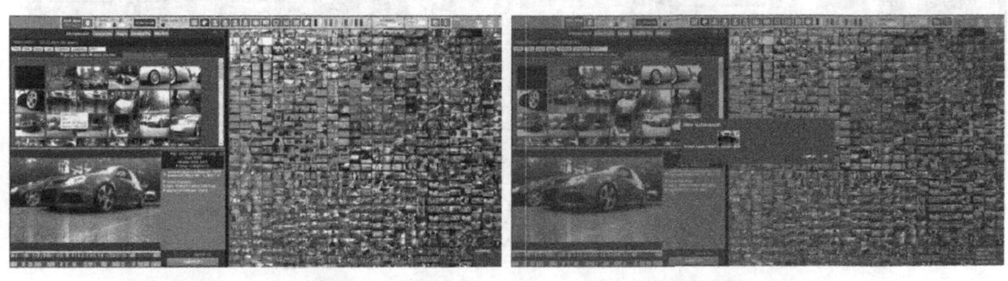

(a) Video shots preview (mouse hovering) allows for previewing non-keyframes.

(b) Ctrl-/Alt-clicking a hover preview image allows for quick-submitting that frame.

Fig. 5. Hover-submit feature (upper left in above figures) for quickly submitting hover preview shots, without the need to search the video (lower left in above figures).

All remaining major and minor improvements are illustrated in Fig. 6. In order to speed up submitting shots for ad-hoc video search (AVS) tasks a single click submit mode can be activated via the top navigation bar, switching left-click shot selection to shot submission without confirmation (Fig. 6a). Another useful new addition is the option to turn on five small permanent preview thumbnails for shots of a certain length, which specifically provides valuable additional information in case shot keyframes displayed in any of the system's views are non-representative, e.g. the preview thumbnail of a faded shot is a mere black image (cf. Fig. 6b). Furthermore, diveXplore 4.0 features some interface modifications that more appropriately interlink the featuremap and all search view overlays: highlighting shots on the featuremap or any other view will synchronize the current shot selection in the featuremap as well as any result shot lists together with the video browser position. The latter, instead of appearing in a separate overlay, can now be toggled and resized as the bottom part of any retrieval view (Fig. 6b–c). Finally, all of these views are resizable and can either be used together (half size, Fig. 6b–d) or without a featuremap (full size, Fig. 6a).

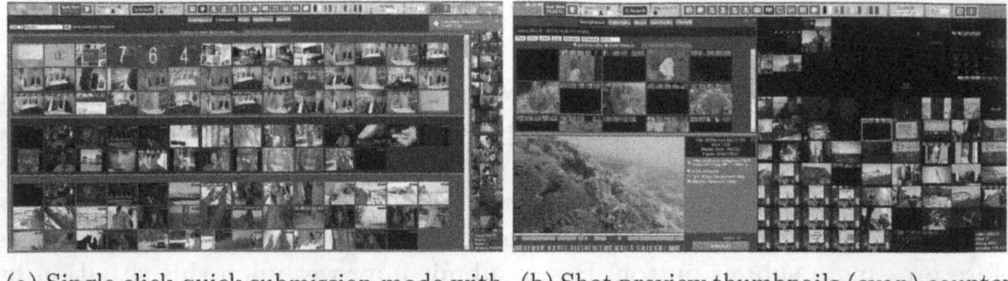

(a) Single click quick submission mode with submission history.

(b) Shot preview thumbnails (cyan) countering non-representative keyframes (black).

(c) Toggleable video player in every retrieval view.

(d) Resizable retrival views, synchronized with feature map and video player.

Fig. 6. Miscellaneous improvements.

4 Conclusions

We introduce our improved diveXplore 4.0 system for participating in VBS2020, which is a web-technologies based interactive video analysis tool offering various browsing and search strategies for exploring large video datasets. Improvements made for this system's version include an enhanced concept, metadata and similarity search as well as major interface refactorings in addition to smaller changes to increase performance and usability. We are confident that many of these improvements in combination with the system's rich set of features are especially beneficial for novice users of the system, thus, expect increasing performance in corresponding tasks.

Acknowledgements. This work was funded by the FWF Austrian Science Fund under grant P 32010-N38.

References

1. Berns, F., Rossetto, L., Schoeffmann, K., Beecks, C., Awad, G.: V3C1 dataset: an evaluation of content characteristics. In: Proceedings of the 2019 on International Conference on Multimedia Retrieval, pp. 334–338. ACM (2019)
2. Gurrin, C., et al.: [Invited papers] Comparing approaches to interactive lifelog search at the lifelog search challenge (LSC2018). ITE Trans. Media Technol. Appl. **7**(2), 46–59 (2019)

3. Leibetseder, A., Kletz, S., Schoeffmann, K.: Sketch-based similarity search for collaborative feature maps. In: Schoeffmann, K., et al. (eds.) MMM 2018. LNCS, vol. 10705, pp. 425–430. Springer, Cham (2018). https://doi.org/10.1007/978-3-319-73600-6_45
4. Leibetseder, A., et al.: lifeXplore at the lifelog search challenge 2019. In: Proceedings of the ACM Workshop on Lifelog Search Challenge, pp. 13–17. ACM (2019)
5. Lokoc, J., Bailer, W., Schoeffmann, K., Muenzer, B., Awad, G.: On influential trends in interactive video retrieval: video browser showdown 2015–2017. IEEE Trans. Multimed. **20**, 3361–3376 (2018)
6. Lokoč, J., et al.: Interactive search or sequential browsing? A detailed analysis of the video browser showdown 2018. ACM Trans. Multimed. Comput. Commun. Appl. **15**(1), 29:1–29:18 (2019)
7. Münzer, B., Leibetseder, A., Kletz, S., Primus, M.J., Schoeffmann, K.: lifeXplore at the lifelog search challenge 2018. In: Proceedings of the 2018 ACM Workshop on the Lifelog Search Challenge, LSC 2018, pp. 3–8, New York, NY, USA. ACM (2018)
8. Primus, M.J., Münzer, B., Leibetseder, A., Schoeffmann, K.: The ITEC collaborative video search system at the video browser showdown 2018. In: Schoeffmann, K., Chalidabhongse, T.H., Ngo, C.W., Aramvith, S., O'Connor, N.E., Ho, Y.-S., Gabbouj, M., Elgammal, A. (eds.) MMM 2018. LNCS, vol. 10705, pp. 438–443. Springer, Cham (2018). https://doi.org/10.1007/978-3-319-73600-6_47
9. Rossetto, L., Schuldt, H., Awad, G., Butt, A.A.: V3C - a research video collection. In: Kompatsiaris, I., Huet, B., Mezaris, V., Gurrin, C., Cheng, W.-H., Vrochidis, S. (eds.) MMM 2019. LNCS, vol. 11295, pp. 349–360. Springer, Cham (2019). https://doi.org/10.1007/978-3-030-05710-7_29
10. Schoeffmann, K.: A user-centric media retrieval competition: the video browser showdown 2012–2014. IEEE MultiMed. **21**(4), 8–13 (2014)
11. Schoeffmann, K., Münzer, B., Leibetseder, A., Primus, J., Kletz, S.: Autopiloting feature maps: the deep interactive video exploration (diveXplore) system at VBS2019. In: Kompatsiaris, I., Huet, B., Mezaris, V., Gurrin, C., Cheng, W.-H., Vrochidis, S. (eds.) MMM 2019. LNCS, vol. 11296, pp. 585–590. Springer, Cham (2019). https://doi.org/10.1007/978-3-030-05716-9_50
12. Schoeffmann, K., Münzer, B., Primus, M.J., Kletz, S., Leibetseder, A.: How experts search different than novices-an evaluation of the divexplore video retrieval system at video browser showdown 2018. In: 2018 IEEE International Conference on Multimedia & Expo Workshops (ICMEW). IEEE (2018)
13. Schoeffmann, K., et al.: Collaborative feature maps for interactive video search. In: Amsaleg, L., Guðmundsson, G., Gurrin, C., Jónsson, B., Satoh, S. (eds.) MMM 2017. LNCS, vol. 10133, pp. 457–462. Springer, Cham (2017). https://doi.org/10.1007/978-3-319-51814-5_41

Combining Boolean and Multimedia Retrieval in vitrivr for Large-Scale Video Search

Loris Sauter[1(✉)], Mahnaz Amiri Parian[1,3], Ralph Gasser[1], Silvan Heller[1], Luca Rossetto[1,2], and Heiko Schuldt[1]

[1] Department of Mathematics and Computer Science, University of Basel, Basel, Switzerland
{loris.sauter,mahnaz.amiriparian,ralph.gasser, silvan.heller,luca.rossetto,heiko.schuldt}@unibas.ch

[2] Department of Informatics, University of Zurich, Zurich, Switzerland
rossetto@ifi.uzh.ch

[3] Numediart Institute, University of Mons, Mons, Belgium

Abstract. This paper presents the most recent additions to the vitrivr multimedia retrieval stack made in preparation for the participation to the 9th Video Browser Showdown (VBS) in 2020. In addition to refining existing functionality and adding support for classical Boolean queries and metadata filters, we also completely replaced our storage engine ADAM$_{pro}$ by a new database called *Cottontail DB*. Furthermore, we have added support for scoring based on the temporal ordering of multiple video segments with respect to a query formulated by the user. Finally, we have also added a new object detection module based on Faster-RCNN and use the generated features for object instance search.

Keywords: Video Browser Showdown · Interactive video retrieval

1 Introduction

In this paper, we present the recent improvements made to vitrivr [18], our multimedia retrieval stack capable of processing several different types of media documents [3]. vitrivr (and its predecessor, the IMOTION system [16]) has participated in the Video Browser Showdown (VBS) [9] for several years [17] and recently also made its debut [13] at the Lifelog Search Challenge (LSC) 2019 [6]. Throughout its development history, vitrivr has gained a large amount of content-based retrieval related functionality. Some of these capabilities however have been discontinued due to the replacement or re-implementation of certain components of the stack. Other capabilities have become impractical in a competitive retrieval context due to changing circumstances, such as the introduction of larger datasets, most recently the V3C [21], the first shard of which already contains 1000 h of video [1]. Our primary focus for this year's participation to the VBS is to consolidate several recent changes made to vitrivr as well as to re-introduce some of these past capabilities, as outlined in Sect. 3.3.

Y. M. Ro et al. (Eds.): MMM 2020, LNCS 11962, pp. 760–765, 2020.
https://doi.org/10.1007/978-3-030-37734-2_66

The remainder of this paper is structured as follows: Sect. 2 provides an overview of the vitrivr stack and its primary components and illustrates its current capabilities. Section 3 then goes into some detail regarding the newly added as well as the re-introduced functionality with which vitrivr will participate to this iteration of the competition. Finally, Sect. 4 concludes this paper.

2 System Overview and Existing Capabilities

vitrivr is a content-based multimedia retrieval stack that is able to retrieve results from mixed media collections [3] containing images, audio, 3D data, and video – of which only the latter is relevant to the VBS competition. vitrivr enables a multitude of query modes, such as Query-by-Sketch (QbS) with both visual and semantic representations, Query-by-Example (QbE) using external example documents from all supported media domains, textual and Boolean queries using structured metadata as well as any combination of the above.

For visual QbS and QbE, vitrivr uses several low-level image features, the combination of which is configurable by the user. The semantic sketch capabilities are realized using a DNN pixel-wise semantic annotator as described in [14]. The textual features encompass OCR and ASR data extracted from the videos as well as automatically generated scene-wise descriptions. The structured metadata contains the data that is part of V3C1 itself along with several object annotations generated by various semantic annotators or obtained from publicly available sources [12].

The vitrivr stack is comprised of three primary components: the persistence layer, a retrieval engine called *Cineast* and a browser-based user interface called *Vitrivr NG*. The persistence layer, for which up and until now we have used our own database system ADAM_{pro} [5], manages all the data required for retrieval, i.e., feature vectors, IDs, attributes, and facilitates query execution. The retrieval engine Cineast generates features from the raw input, such as images, sketches or text, orchestrates the execution of different queries through the persistence layer, fuses results and communicates with the user interface. The user interface Vitrivr NG offers different modes of result presentation and provides all the tools required for query formulation. Furthermore, it employs a secondary late-fusion step that gives the end-user some control over how partial results should be merged.

The entire vitrivr stack and its components are open source[1] and publicly available from GitHub[2].

3 New Functionality in vitrivr

This section provides an overview of improvements compared to the system which won the 2019 iteration of the Video Browser Showdown [19]. One major

[1] https://vitrivr.org/.
[2] https://github.com/vitrivr/.

focus was the introduction of a new storage layer to address performance issues discussed in [20] which will be summarized in Sect. 3.5. Other major additions are based on our winning participation at the Lifelog Search Challenge [13], where metadata and Boolean retrieval was important given the content of the dataset [6].

3.1 Boolean Queries

As discussed in [4], unifying the traditional Boolean retrieval model used in structured data with the world of multimedia retrieval remains an open challenge. To briefly summarize our approach introduced in [13], Boolean feature modules return all matching elements. In the result-fusion step, these results are then used as a filter in contrast to results from similarity modules, where non-matching segments simply do not contribute to the score.

Another design option would have been to do early filtering, only considering elements for similarity queries which match the Boolean filter criteria. Our reasoning to go for late filtering is discussed in [13].

3.2 Metadata Filters

In addition to the Boolean queries discussed in Sect. 3.1, vitrivr offers the possibility to refine results in the user interface. To improve performance and responsiveness, filtering is only done on the client's side, meaning no new queries are executed. The available filters are based on query results and a whitelist of filter keys. This is especially sensible for novices since it hides metadata which is not useful for filtering. This is in line with the focus on usability which has served vitrivr well in competitive settings. Figure 1 shows an example of the metadata filter UI in action.

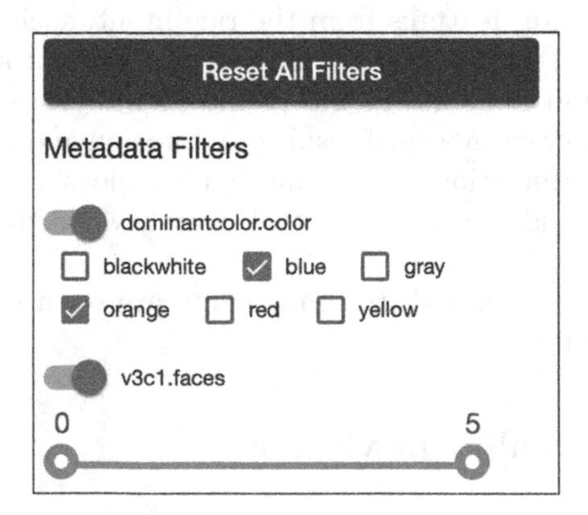

Fig. 1. Metadata filters with both checkboxes and slider values. Results are dynamically updated on changing filters.

3.3 Temporal Scoring

Inspired by the successful application of temporal queries and scoring by other teams [10], we re-introduced this once available feature [15,16] into vitrivr. Temporal queries enable the user to specify multiple queries in a given order, which is then used as a relative temporal reference. For scoring the results, we introduce an expansion to our media description model with the notion of *temporal closeness*. Two segments s_i and s_j are *temporally close*, if $s_j.startTime - s_i.endTime < \varepsilon$, where ε is a configurable threshold. Such temporally close segments s_i and s_j are merged to a single *temporal segment*, if the first segment matches the first query condition and the second segment matches the second query condition. This rule can be applied recursively to other segments as well. The configurable scoring function then assures that temporally close segments occurring in the specified order are boosted.

The user interface reflects the re-introduction of temporal scoring by enabling users to re-order their queries as well as by adding adequate visualization of temporal closeness.

3.4 Object Instance Search

To enhance the feature extraction module of vitrivr, we use the idea proposed in [2] to incorporate the feature embedding extracted by an object detection module in a retrieval task. More specifically, the feature embedding acts as a hard attention module and is used to assign scores to the parts of the feature maps which represent these objects.

To perform the object instance search, two steps are taken: First, the Faster-RCNN [11] framework – pre-trained on the Openimages V4 dataset [8] – is used to extract the regions of interests (ROIs). These ROIs are bounded by boxes and localize objects in the keyframe of the video clip. Second, the ROIs are fed to the feature extraction module as hard attention. The feature extraction is performed by ResNet-50 [7] pre-trained on ImageNet for the classification task. The convolutional features prior to the fully connected layer of ResNet-50 are extracted and used for similarity search. The attended features from ResNet-50 increase the relevance of the search results based on the existing objects in the video clips which eventually enhances the performance of the retrieval task.

3.5 Storage Layer

The vitrivr stack generates and operates on a variety of different types of data ranging from primitive data types to feature vectors. In the past, Cineast has delegated persistent storage as well as lookup to an underlying storage engine called ADAM_{pro}.

In preparation for LSC 2019, we have completely replaced that storage engine by a new system called *Cottontail DB*. This step was necessitated by performance considerations. Even though ADAM_{pro} was designed with scalability and distribution in mind, it always under-performed in a single-node setup and on workloads typically found during competitions such as LSC or VBS. The high query times, especially for similarity based queries, severely limited our choices time-critical settings.

Cottontail is a columnar storage engine. Hence, data can be accessed very efficiently if entire columns are read, e.g., for full scans of a particular attribute. *Cottontail* allows to organize such columns into entities, which in turn can be organized into different schemas. Hence, the data model is very similar to the one found in a classical relational database and ADAM_{pro}.

In addition to Boolean queries and full text search (powered by Apache Lucene), *Cottontail* offers support for k nearest neighbour (kNN) lookup, typically used for feature-based similarity search. In that area, it outperforms the ADAM_{pro} system by at least an order of magnitude without relying on any index structures. However, secondary indexes are supported and the addition of index structures for kNN lookups is planned for future versions.

4 Conclusion

In this paper, we presented the additions made to vitrivr for VBS 2020. We expect the transition to the new storage engine to provide us with better performance and thus with more flexibility as to what types of queries we can use in a competitive setting. Additionally, we see VBS as the final test before *Cottontail* can be published and released as the new, official storage subsystem that powers the vitrivr stack.

Acknowledgements. This work was partly supported by the Hasler Foundation in the context of the project City-Stories (contract no. 17055).

References

1. Berns, F., Rossetto, L., Schoeffmann, K., Beecks, C., Awad, G.: V3C1 dataset: an evaluation of content characteristics. In: Proceedings of the 2019 on International Conference on Multimedia Retrieval, pp. 334–338. ACM (2019)
2. Chen, B.C., Davis, L.S., Lim, S.N.: An analysis of object embeddings for image retrieval. arXiv preprint arXiv:1905.11903 (2019)
3. Gasser, R., Rossetto, L., Schuldt, H.: Towards an all-purpose content-based multimedia information retrieval system. arXiv preprint arXiv:1902.03878 (2019)
4. Giangreco, I.: Database support for large-scale multimedia retrieval. Ph.D. thesis, University of Basel (2018)
5. Giangreco, I., Schuldt, H.: ADAM$_{pro}$: database support for big multimedia retrieval. Datenbank-Spektrum **16**(1), 17–26 (2016)
6. Gurrin, C., et al.: A test collection for interactive lifelog retrieval. In: Kompatsiaris, I., Huet, B., Mezaris, V., Gurrin, C., Cheng, W.-H., Vrochidis, S. (eds.) MMM 2019. LNCS, vol. 11295, pp. 312–324. Springer, Cham (2019). https://doi.org/10.1007/978-3-030-05710-7_26
7. He, K., Zhang, X., Ren, S., Sun, J.: Deep residual learning for image recognition. CoRR abs/1512.03385 (2015). http://arxiv.org/abs/1512.03385

8. Krasin, I., et al.: Openimages: a public dataset for large-scale multi-label and multi-class image classification (2017). Dataset available from https://storage.googleapis.com/openimages/web/index.html
9. Lokoč, J., et al.: Interactive search or sequential browsing? A detailed analysis of the video browser showdown 2018. ACM Trans. Multimed. Comput. Commun. Appl. (TOMM) **15**(1), 29 (2019)
10. Lokoč, J., Kovalčík, G., Souček, T., Moravec, J., Čech, P.: VIRET: a video retrieval tool for interactive known-item search. In: Proceedings of the 2019 on International Conference on Multimedia Retrieval, pp. 177–181. ACM (2019)
11. Ren, S., He, K., Girshick, R.B., Sun, J.: Faster R-CNN: towards real-time object detection with region proposal networks. CoRR abs/1506.01497 (2015). http://arxiv.org/abs/1506.01497
12. Rossetto, L., Berns, F., Schoeffman, K., Awad, G., Beeks, C.: The V3C1 dataset: advancing the state of the art in video retrieval. ACM SIGMultimedia Rec. **11**(2) (2019)
13. Rossetto, L., Gasser, R., Heller, S., Amiri Parian, M., Schuldt, H.: Retrieval of structured and unstructured data with vitrivr. In: Proceedings of the ACM Workshop on Lifelog Search Challenge, pp. 27–31. ACM (2019)
14. Rossetto, L., Gasser, R., Schuldt, H.: Query by semantic sketch. CoRR abs/1909.12526 (2019). https://arxiv.org/abs/1909.12526
15. Rossetto, L., Giangreco, I., Heller, S., Tănase, C., Schuldt, H.: Searching in video collections using sketches and sample images – the Cineast system. In: Tian, Q., Sebe, N., Qi, G.-J., Huet, B., Hong, R., Liu, X. (eds.) MMM 2016. LNCS, vol. 9517, pp. 336–341. Springer, Cham (2016). https://doi.org/10.1007/978-3-319-27674-8_30
16. Rossetto, L., et al.: IMOTION – searching for video sequences using multi-shot sketch queries. In: Tian, Q., Sebe, N., Qi, G.-J., Huet, B., Hong, R., Liu, X. (eds.) MMM 2016. LNCS, vol. 9517, pp. 377–382. Springer, Cham (2016). https://doi.org/10.1007/978-3-319-27674-8_36
17. Rossetto, L., et al.: IMOTION—a content-based video retrieval engine. In: He, X., Luo, S., Tao, D., Xu, C., Yang, J., Hasan, M.A. (eds.) MMM 2015. LNCS, vol. 8936, pp. 255–260. Springer, Cham (2015). https://doi.org/10.1007/978-3-319-14442-9_24
18. Rossetto, L., Giangreco, I., Tanase, C., Schuldt, H.: Vitrivr: a flexible retrieval stack supporting multiple query modes for searching in multimedia collections. In: Proceedings of the 24th ACM International Conference on Multimedia, pp. 1183–1186. ACM (2016)
19. Rossetto, L., Amiri Parian, M., Gasser, R., Giangreco, I., Heller, S., Schuldt, H.: Deep learning-based concept detection in vitrivr. In: Kompatsiaris, I., Huet, B., Mezaris, V., Gurrin, C., Cheng, W.-H., Vrochidis, S. (eds.) MMM 2019. LNCS, vol. 11296, pp. 616–621. Springer, Cham (2019). https://doi.org/10.1007/978-3-030-05716-9_55
20. Rossetto, L., Parian, M.A., Gasser, R., Giangreco, I., Heller, S., Schuldt, H.: Deep learning-based concept detection in vitrivr at the video browser showdown 2019-final notes. arXiv preprint arXiv:1902.10647 (2019)
21. Rossetto, L., Schuldt, H., Awad, G., Butt, A.A.: V3C – a research video collection. In: Kompatsiaris, I., Huet, B., Mezaris, V., Gurrin, C., Cheng, W.-H., Vrochidis, S. (eds.) MMM 2019. LNCS, vol. 11295, pp. 349–360. Springer, Cham (2019). https://doi.org/10.1007/978-3-030-05710-7_29

An Interactive Video Search Platform for Multi-modal Retrieval with Advanced Concepts

Nguyen-Khang Le, Dieu-Hien Nguyen, and Minh-Triet Tran(✉)

University of Science, VNU-HCM, Ho Chi Minh City, Vietnam
tmtriet@fit.hcmus.edu.vn

Abstract. The previous version of our retrieval system has shown some significant results in some retrieval tasks such as Lifelog's moment retrieval tasks. In this paper, we adapt our platform to the Video Browser Showdown's KIS and AVS tasks and present how our system performs in video search tasks. In addition to the smart features in our retrieval system that take advantage of the provided analysis data, we enhance the data with object color detection by employing Mask R-CNN and clustering. In this version of our search system, we try to extract the location information of the entities appearing in the videos and aim to exploit the spatial relationship between these entities. We also focus on designing efficient user interaction and a high-performance way to transfer data in the system to minimize the retrieval time.

Keywords: Retrieval system · User interaction · Concept detection

1 Introduction

Content retrieval is one of the popular topics in research community over the years. Many conferences and challenges about content searching and retrieval have been established over the years as a means of evaluating and encouraging research on efficient retrieval systems. The Video Browser Showdown [6–9] is one of the international search competition that focuses on video content.

The previous version of our system has accomplished promising results in retrieval challenges that work with a Lifelog dataset [1,3,5]. Lifelog datasets share some very similar characteristics with video dataset. Therefore, we expect the system to have adequate performance in video search tasks. In this paper, we describe some modifications to the system so that it can handle the KIS and AVS tasks of Video Browser Showdown.

In comparison with the previous Lifelog retrieval version, this new version of our system has some improvements. For concept retrieval, the system displays the list of concepts in a grid instead of a dropdown in the previous version. Also, the date and location search in the Lifelog version is replaced with the text and transcript search. The search feature for the dominant color of video frames is added. The new system can view videos instead of only images.

Y. M. Ro et al. (Eds.): MMM 2020, LNCS 11962, pp. 766–771, 2020.
https://doi.org/10.1007/978-3-030-37734-2_67

This paper describes the overview of our video retrieval system and goes into details in Sect. 2. Section 2.3 illustrates how the system supports interactive video search. Finally, a conclusion is presented in Sect. 3.

2 Proposed Video Search System

2.1 System Overview

The process of our system is straight forward and intuitive. We first perform our analysis on the given dataset to extract metadata that supports the system's retrieval features. These metadata, along with the provided analysis data, are stored in the system. In the retrieval process, the retrieval application interacts with metadata and search for contents. The process is described in Fig. 1.

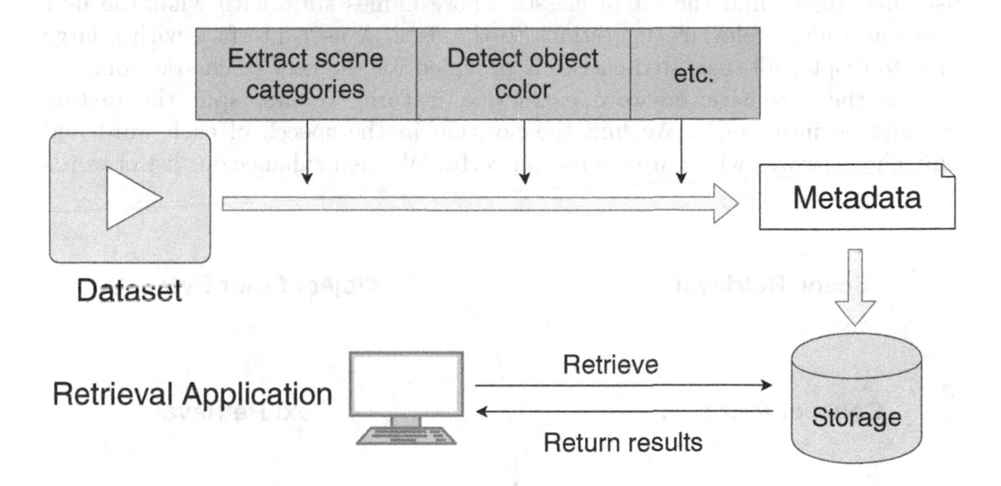

Fig. 1. The retrieval system's process

To support the multi-modality of retrieval, our system consists of many components. Figure 2 illustrates the components in our system, each component support one aspect of retrieval.

2.2 System Components

The Scene Retrieval component extracts scene categories and scene attribute from the keyframes of the video. In the development of this component, we utilize the results in [10]. This component employs ResNet 152 and trains the model on Places365-Standard dataset. With this component, the system can classify the scenes in the keyframes among various scene attributes and approximately 365 scene categories.

The Concept Retrieval component supports the system to retrieve videos where specific concepts appear. We take advantages of the provided analysis data about detected ImageNet classes. This allows the system to cover a large number of classes in ImageNet dataset [2]. We also extract the location information of some of the classes and use it to support the system to search by spatial relationship between appearing classes.

Because the ImageNet dataset contains more than 20,000 classes, when the user of the system tries to retrieve videos with specific concepts appearing, they will struggle to find those classes, or similar classes, in the ImageNet dataset. Therefore, our system supports a high-performance auto-completing feature that helps the user to find the classes' names more efficiently and an automatic feature that extracts keywords from the textual description (in Textual KIS) and finds ImageNet classes automatically based on those keywords. For the auto-completing feature, we construct a prefix tree from the classes' names. We then use this tree to find the set of classes whose names start with what the user types and make relevant suggestions to the user. A user-interface with a large area to display all suggested classes is provided for the user to choose from.

For the automatic keyword extracting feature, we first split the textual description into words. We find the position in the speech of each word and only choose words which are nouns and verbs. We then enhance our list of words

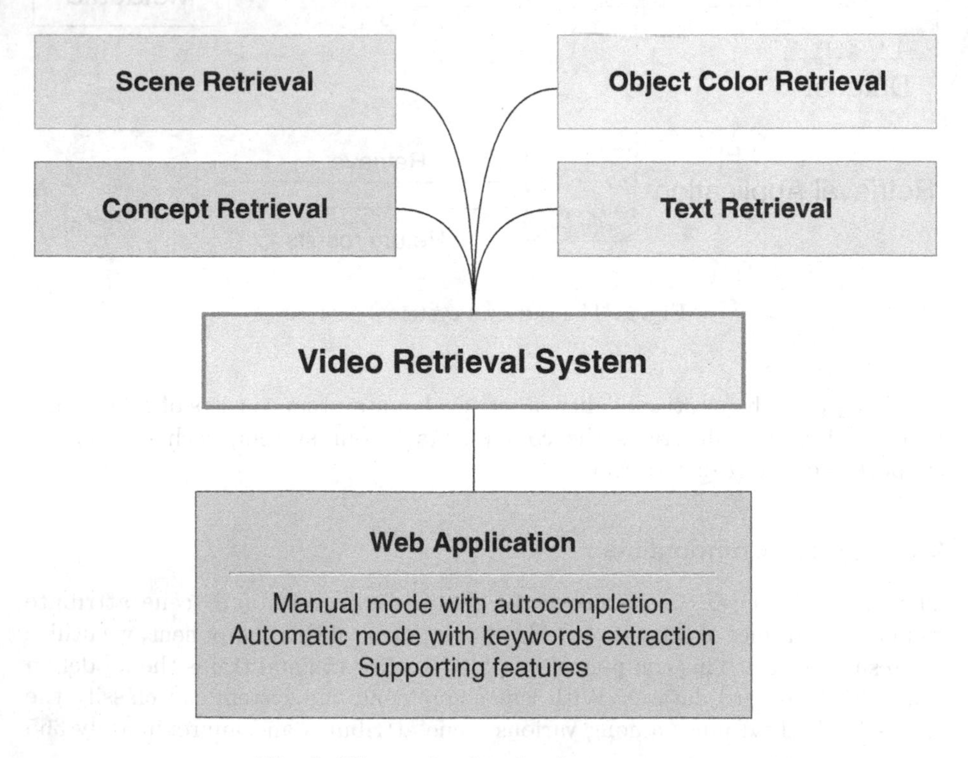

Fig. 2. The retrieval system's components

with their thesaurus. Finally, we check if these keywords are in the ImageNet classes' names and automatically fill them in the input fields.

Object colors play an important role in the retrieval process. By extracting this information, the efficiency of retrieval can be improved. We add a new detector that aims to detect the dominant colors of the object by employing Mask R-CNN [4] and K-means clustering. The details is described in [1].

2.3 System Demonstrations

There are three modes in our system: the default mode with both search panel and result panel displaying, search mode with the expanded search panel, and result mode with expanded result panel. Figures 3 and 4 show a screenshot of our system in default mode and search mode respectively.

As shown in the screenshot (Fig. 4), the user can interact with different aspects of the retrieval such as concepts appearing on the screen, the frame colors, the object colors, or texts that appear in the video or captions. By combining all of these aspects, the user can create complex queries and perform the retrieval efficiently. The user can either manually input the concepts, colors, texts, etc. or simply input the textual description of the task and the system will automatically fill in the input fields.

In Fig. 3, the concept search tab is shown on the left panel. The input field allows the user to input various concepts and retrieve videos which these concepts appear in. When the user types in the input field, the auto-completing feature will suggest relevant concepts which are shown below the input field. The user

Fig. 3. Screenshot of the system in default mode

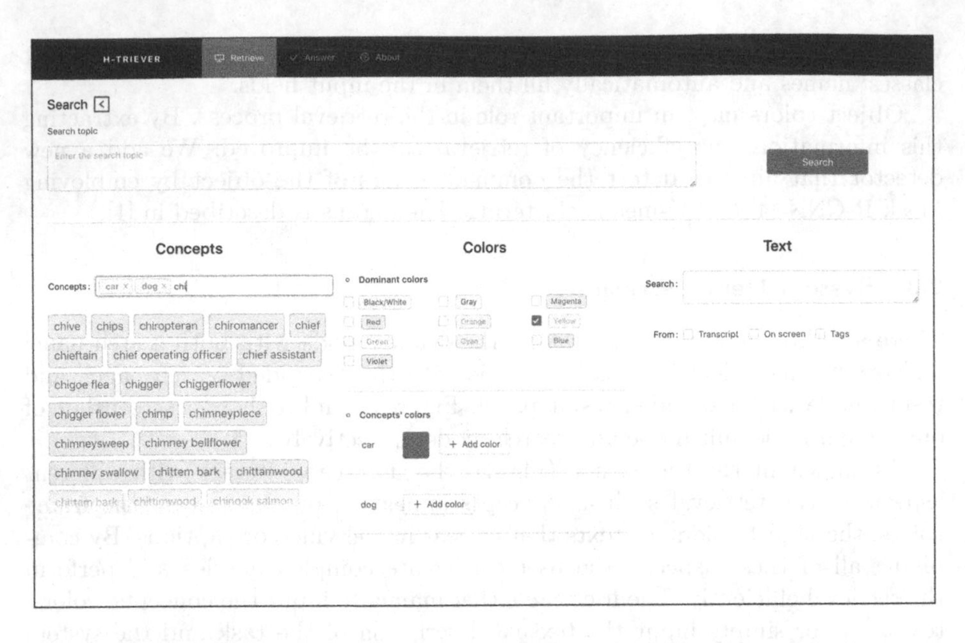

Fig. 4. Screenshot of the system in search mode (Color figure online)

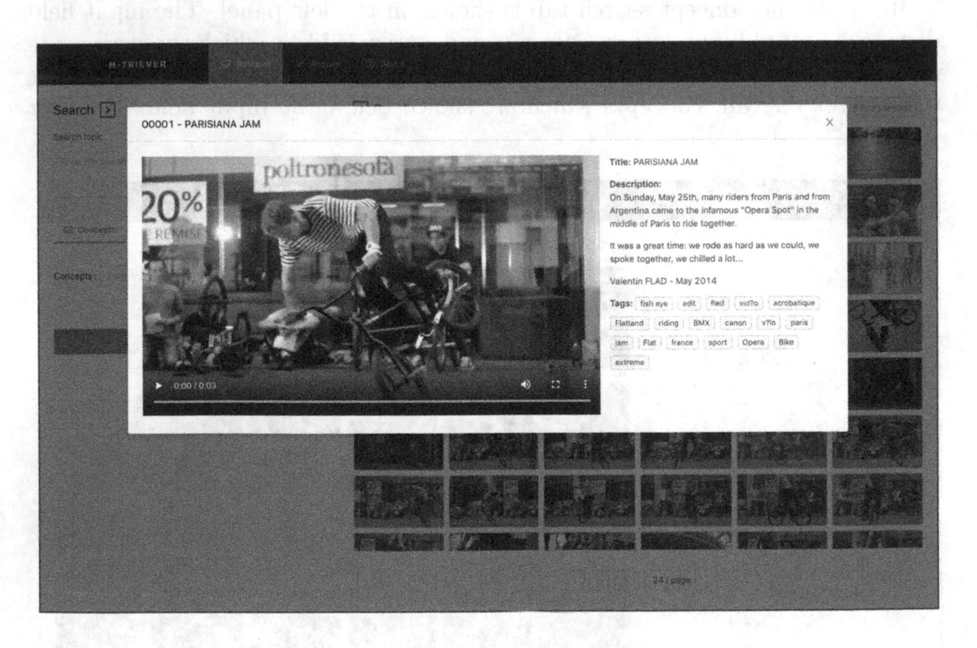

Fig. 5. Screenshot of the system when viewing a result video

can quickly select these concepts and add them to the search criteria. When the user selects one of the concepts, a modal with a rectangle grid will appear and allow the user to optionally select the regions of the screen for that concept entity. As illustrated in Fig. 5, the user of the system can choose to view a video shot and its detail including the video's title, description, and tags.

3 Conclusion

In this version, our system is modified to handle the Video Browser Showdown KIS and AVS tasks. Our video retrieval system has good performance when working with video dataset. The interaction system can support both expert and novice user to perform the video search tasks. The system still has limitations and there are rooms for improvements in the future.

Acknowledgement. Research is supported by Vingroup Innovation Foundation (VINIF) in project code VINIF.2019.DA19. We would like to thank AIOZ Pte Ltd for supporting our research team with computing infrastructure.

References

1. Lifelog moment retrieval with advanced semantic extraction and flexible moment visualization for exploration. In: CEUR Workshop Proceedings, Lugano, Switzerland, 09–12 September 2019, vol. 2380 (2019). CEUR-WS.org http://ceur-ws.org
2. Deng, J., Dong, W., Socher, R., Li, L.J., Li, K., Fei-Fei, L.: ImageNet: a large-scale hierarchical image database. In: CVPR 2009 (2009)
3. Gurrin, C., et al.: Overview of the NTCIR-14 lifelog-3 task. In: Proceedings of the Fourteenth NTCIR Conference (NTCIR-14) (2019)
4. He, K., Gkioxari, G., Dollár, P., Girshick, R.B.: Mask R-CNN. In: IEEE International Conference on Computer Vision, ICCV 2017, Venice, Italy, 22–29 October 2017, pp. 2980–2988 (2017)
5. Le, N.K., Nguyen, D.H., Tran, M.T.: Smart lifelog retrieval system with habit-based concepts and moment visualization. In: LSC 2019 @ ICMR 2019 (2019)
6. Lokoč, J., et al.: Interactive search or sequential browsing? A detailed analysis of the video browser showdown 2018. ACM Trans. Multimed. Comput. Commun. Appl. **15**(1), 29:1–29:18 (2019). https://doi.org/10.1145/3295663
7. Lokoč, J., Bailer, W., Schoeffmann, K., Muenzer, B., Awad, G.: On influential trends in interactive video retrieval: video browser showdown 2015–2017. IEEE Trans. Multimed. **20**(12), 3361–3376 (2018). https://doi.org/10.1109/TMM.2018.2830110
8. Rossetto, L., Schuldt, H., Awad, G., Butt, A.A.: V3C – a research video collection. In: Kompatsiaris, I., Huet, B., Mezaris, V., Gurrin, C., Cheng, W.-H., Vrochidis, S. (eds.) MMM 2019. LNCS, vol. 11295, pp. 349–360. Springer, Cham (2019). https://doi.org/10.1007/978-3-030-05710-7_29
9. Schoeffmann, K.: A user-centric media retrieval competition: the video browser showdown 2012–2014. IEEE Multimed. **21**(4), 8–13 (2014). https://doi.org/10.1109/MMUL.2014.56
10. Zhou, B., Lapedriza, A., Khosla, A., Oliva, A., Torralba, A.: Places: a 10 million image database for scene recognition. IEEE Trans. Pattern Anal. Mach. Intell. **40**, 1452–1464 (2017)

VIREO @ Video Browser Showdown 2020

Phuong Anh Nguyen[1(✉)], Jiaxin Wu[1], Chong-Wah Ngo[1], Danny Francis[2], and Benoit Huet[2]

[1] Computer Science Department, City University of Hong Kong, Hong Kong, China
{panguyen2-c,jiaxin.wu}@my.cityu.edu.hk, cscwngo@cityu.edu.hk
[2] Data Science Department, EURECOM, Biot, France
{danny.francis,benoit.huet}@eurecom.fr

Abstract. In this paper, we present the features implemented in the 4th version of the VIREO Video Search System (VIREO-VSS). In this version, we propose a sketch-based retrieval model, which allows the user to specify a video scene with objects and their basic properties, including color, size, and location. We further utilize the temporal relation between video frames to strengthen this retrieval model. For text-based retrieval module, we supply speech and on-screen text for free-text search and upgrade the concept bank for concept search. The search interface is also re-designed targeting the novice user. With the introduced system, we expect that the VIREO-VSS can be a competitive participant in the Video Browser Showdown (VBS) 2020.

Keywords: Sketch-based retrieval · Query-by-object-sketch · Video retrieval · Video Browser Showdown

1 Introduction

The VIREO-VSS has participated in the Video Browser Showdown [1] for three consecutive years since 2017. The latest version of the VIREO-VSS [2] is composed of three retrieval modules: query-by-text, query-by-sketch, and query-by-example. Given a query, a user firstly makes an input into one of these search modules. Then the retrieved ranked list is represented in a user interface, which allows the user to browse and judge the result. This process is repeated in a loop until the user finds a satisfactory answer.

In VBS 2019, the VIREO-VSS ranked 3th over 6 teams participated despite the system flaws exposed in the benchmark. The system has proved its capability for the new large-scale video dataset V3C1 and its performance in the visual known-item search and the ad-hoc search tasks. The retrieval modality contributions are as follows:

- The simplified query-by-color-sketch model proposed in [3] plays the leading role in solving the visual known-item search task.
- The query-by-concept model [3], together with the nearest neighbor search and quick submission [2], enhance the efficiency of submission in the ad-hoc search task.

Y. M. Ro et al. (Eds.): MMM 2020, LNCS 11962, pp. 772–777, 2020.
https://doi.org/10.1007/978-3-030-37734-2_68

However, the system still can not solve the textual known-item search task efficiently. The reason is that we did not utilize the temporal relation between video segments, which leads to inefficient retrieval result with the correct answer stays pretty low in the rank list. As a consequence, the user needs to browse tediously to find the correct answer. Besides, the user interface is not friendly to the novice user with various functions and configurations.

Facing different shortcomings of the system, we propose the 4th version of the VIREO-VSS with three revisions. First, the color-sketch-based retrieval models from the SIRET [4], VIREO [3]; the object-sketch-based retrieval model from the VISIONE [5]; and the semantic-sketch-based retrieval model from the vitrivr [6] are critical approaches to solve the visual KIS task. Motivated by these approaches, we initiate the idea of utilizing the object color for object-sketch-based retrieval targeting both visual and textual KIS task. As learned from VBS 2019, the temporal information is the deciding factor to solve the textual KIS confirmed by the result of VIRET team [7]. Hence, we utilize the temporal information for both sketch-based and concept-based retrieval model. Second, we supply more data for text-based search including the video speech, the on-screen text, and 1200 additional concepts. Third, the simple and friendly user interface from vitrivr [6] has proved its advantages in the novice session of VBS 2019. Therefore, we update the user interface to make it more compact and user-friendly. The setup details of these revisions are described in the next section.

2 Object-Sketch-Based Retrieval Model

2.1 Feature Extraction

Given a set of video key-frames, we use the Faster-RCNN architecture [8] with Inception ResNetV2 feature extractor [9] pre-trained on Open Images V4. The network can detect up to 600 objects together with the bounding boxes after performing non-maxima suppression. For each key-frame, we keep the objects that have the detection score larger than 0.1 and their bounding boxes. To extract the color attribute, we first define a list of 15 colors, including 12 primary colors from the RGB color wheel and three neutral colors (black, grey, and white). From each bounding box, we map each pixel color to the nearest color in the list; then we calculate the percentage of each color. In the end, from an image O extracted from the video, we have a set of tuples $\{\langle n_i^o, s_i^o, B_i^o, C_i^o \rangle\}_{i=1}^n$ with each tuple representing an object o_i. Each object o_i contains an object name n_i^o, a detection score s_i^o, a bounding box B_i^o, and a 15 dimensions color feature C_i^o.

2.2 Retrieval Model

The user can draw their memo using a canvas where he determines rectangles depicting objects. For each box created by clicking on a clear area of the canvas, the user can add an object with its name and its color by clicking on the rectangle's top and bottom bar. It is noted that the user can leave the object's name and color empty. The user also can drag and resize the box to specify the location and size of the object. An example of the query canvas and the object detection result can be seen in Fig. 1.

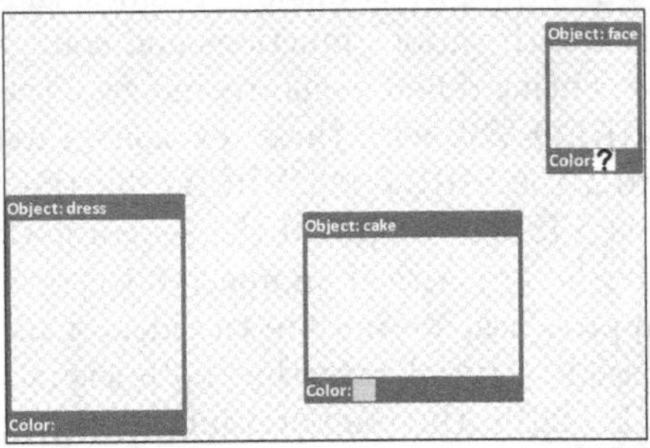

Fig. 1. An example of the object detection result (left) and a possible query to retrieve the image (right). Note that the user can choose a question mark option to specify the color, which represents no specific color. (Color figure online)

Formally, the user's query Q is a set of tuples $\{\langle n_j^q, B_j^q, c_j^q \rangle\}_{j=1}^m$ with each tuple representing an object query q_j. The scoring function to match between a query object q_j to a detected object o_i in the detected is defined as:

$$S(q_j, o_i) = \alpha * match\_obj(n_j^q, n_i^o) + \beta * match\_clr(c_j^q, C_i^o) + \gamma * IoU(B_j^q, B_i^o)$$

with $match\_obj(n_j^q, n_i^o) = s_i^o$ if $n_j^q = n_i^o$, and 0 otherwise; $match\_clr(c_j^q, C_i^o)$ returns the percentage of the color c_j^q from the color feature C_i^o; $IoU(B_j^q, B_i^o)$ return the intersection over union of two bounding boxes; α, β, and γ are the weights of the properties. In this trial, we intuitively select $\alpha = 0.6$, $\beta = 0.3$, and $\gamma = 0.1$.

Then, the similarity of a query Q and a key-frame O in the dataset is defined as:

$$Sim(Q, O) = \underset{\forall q_j \in Q}{\text{avg}} \left(\max_{\forall o_i \in O} S(q_j, o_i) \right)$$

We calculate the similarities from the query to all key-frames in the dataset to get the rank list of key-frames. In addition, we perform $MinMax$ normalization to map these similarities to the range $[0, 1]$ to enable fusing with other search modalities.

2.3 Temporal Query for Object-Sketch-Based Retrieval

We provide two canvases enabling the user to input two object-sketch queries at the timestamp t and t' with $t < t'$. We follow these steps to define the similarity of a video $V = \{O_1, \ldots, O_k\}$ and two query Q_t, $Q_{t'}$:

1. Calculate two sets of similarities $\{Sim(Q_t, O_1), \ldots, Sim(Q_t, O_k)\}$ and $\{Sim(Q_{t'}, O_1), \ldots, Sim(Q_{t'}, O_k)\}$
2. Construct an array $MaxSim(Q_t, V) = [s_1^t, \ldots, s_k^t]$ with $s_1^t = Sim(Q_t, O_1)$ and $s_i^t = max(s_{i-1}^t, Sim(Q_t, O_i))$ for $i > 1$; the order from 1 to k representing the temporal order of the key-frames. This is an increasing array. An element s_i^t of this array represents the maximum similarity of the query Q_t to the video segment starting from the first key-frame to the key-frame i.
3. Construct an array $MaxSim(Q_{t'}, V) = [s_1^{t'}, \ldots, s_k^{t'}]$ with $s_k^{t'} = Sim(Q_{t'}, O_k)$ and $s_i^{t'} = max(s_{i+1}^{t'}, Sim(Q_{t'}, O_i))$ for $i < k$; the order from 1 to k representing the temporal order of the key-frames. This is a decreasing array. An element $s_i^{t'}$ of this array represents the maximum similarity of the query $Q_{t'}$ to the video segment starting from the key-frame i to the last key-frame.
4. Calculate the $Sim((Q_t, Q_{t'}), V) = \max_{i=1}^{k-1}(s_i^t + s_{i+1}^{t'})$

Each step described above has the complexity as $O(k)$ with k is the number of key-frames in a video. To process the whole video dataset, this approach has the complexity as $O(l)$ with l is the total number of key-frames. With this approach, the user needs to remember the order of the key-frames that ensure $t < t'$ rather than the exact interval between two queries.

3 Video Retrieval Tool Description

At first, we integrate the query-by-object-sketch module proposed in Sect. 2 to the VIREO-VSS. Next, we focus on improving the tool at three points:

- *Query-by-text.* For free text search, we add in the video speech shared by vitrivr and the on-screen text detected by Tesseract-OCR. For concept-based search, we update the concept bank with an addition of 600 object detectors trained on Open Images V4 using FasterRCNN and 600 activity detectors trained on Kinetics using I3D [10]. In the latest version of the VIREO-VSS, the query-by-concept module requires the user to initiate the query from scratch with exact concept selection. As our observation in the novice session of VBS 2019, this constraint creates difficulties for the user who has no prior understanding of the concept bank. To overcome this shortcoming, we let the user input free-text and kick off the concept selection step by automatically picking related concepts. This step is done by using Universal Sentence Embedding to match between the free-text query and the concept definitions. Moreover, the temporal query model presented in Sect. 2.3 is employed for concept-based search targeting the textual KIS task.
- *The rank list for AVS task.* From VBS 2018, the scoring function of AVS task favors the diversity than the quantity of submitted video segments. To compromise with this scoring function, we push the video segments that come from different videos up to the top of the rank list. This rank list allows the user to look at the video segments coming from different videos and leads him to submit these video segments, which are in favor of diversity.

- *The user interface.* As we enable free text search for concept-based retrieval, we provide only one text box for text-based search. The user can select the sources of searching by checking in the corresponding checkboxes. The temporal queries using in concept-based and object-sketch-based retrieval module are presented under different tabs (see Fig. 2).

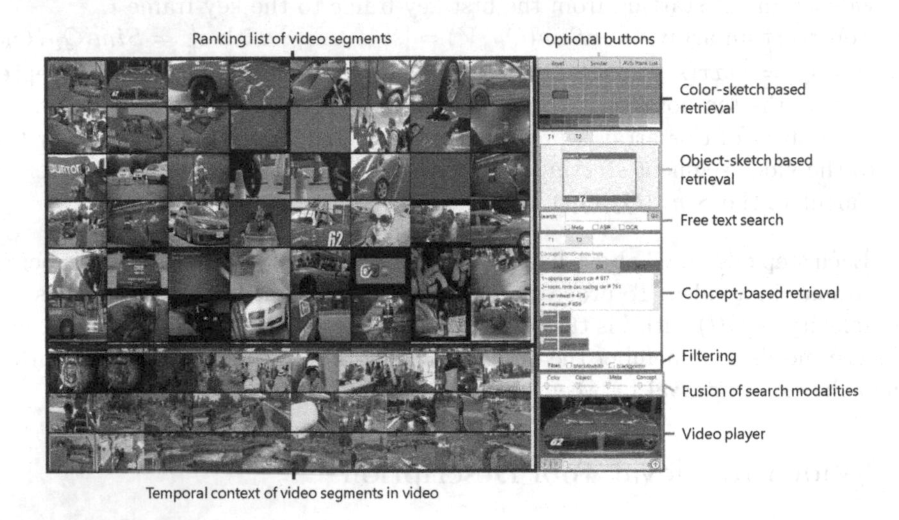

Fig. 2. The user interface of the VIREO-VSS.

We maintain existing modules without further modification, including: the query by color-sketch model, the query-by-example model, and the filtering functions. The detail setup of these models and functions can be found in [2].

4 Conclusion

In this 4th version of the VIREO-VSS, we focus on solving textual KIS task and improving the submission efficiency for AVS task. The proposed query-by-object-sketch model supports both visual and textual KIS task. The temporal query for object-sketch-based retrieval and concept-based retrieval concretely favors the textual KIS task. The modification on the user interface and the rank list of AVS result enhances the submission speed and the diversity of the AVS answer. With these improvements, we expect that the VIREO-VSS can tackle all types of tasks in VBS 2020 efficiently.

Acknowledgments. The work described in this paper was supported by a grant from the Research Grants Council of the Hong Kong SAR, China (Reference No.: CityU 11250716), and a grant from the PROCORE-France/Hong Kong Joint Research Scheme sponsored by the Research Grants Council of Hong Kong and the Consulate General of France in Hong Kong (Reference No.: F-CityU104/17).

References

1. Lokoč, J., et al.: Interactive search or sequential browsing? A detailed analysis of the video browser showdown 2018. ACM Trans. Multimedia Comput. Commun. Appl. **15**(1), 29:1–29:18 (2019)
2. Nguyen, P.A., Ngo, C.-W., Francis, D., Huet, B.: VIREO @ video browser showdown 2019. In: Kompatsiaris, I., Huet, B., Mezaris, V., Gurrin, C., Cheng, W.-H., Vrochidis, S. (eds.) MMM 2019. LNCS, vol. 11296, pp. 609–615. Springer, Cham (2019). https://doi.org/10.1007/978-3-030-05716-9_54
3. Nguyen, P.A., Lu, Y.-J., Zhang, H., Ngo, C.-W.: Enhanced VIREO KIS at VBS 2018. In: Schoeffmann, K., et al. (eds.) MMM 2018. LNCS, vol. 10705, pp. 407–412. Springer, Cham (2018). https://doi.org/10.1007/978-3-319-73600-6_42
4. Lokoč, J., Kovalčík, G., Souček, T.: Revisiting SIRET video retrieval tool. In: Schoeffmann, K., et al. (eds.) MMM 2018. LNCS, vol. 10705, pp. 419–424. Springer, Cham (2018). https://doi.org/10.1007/978-3-319-73600-6_44
5. Amato, G., et al.: VISIONE at VBS2019. In: Kompatsiaris, I., Huet, B., Mezaris, V., Gurrin, C., Cheng, W.-H., Vrochidis, S. (eds.) MMM 2019. LNCS, vol. 11296, pp. 591–596. Springer, Cham (2019). https://doi.org/10.1007/978-3-030-05716-9_51
6. Rossetto, L., Amiri Parian, M., Gasser, R., Giangreco, I., Heller, S., Schuldt, H.: Deep learning-based concept detection in vitrivr. In: Kompatsiaris, I., Huet, B., Mezaris, V., Gurrin, C., Cheng, W.-H., Vrochidis, S. (eds.) MMM 2019. LNCS, vol. 11296, pp. 616–621. Springer, Cham (2019). https://doi.org/10.1007/978-3-030-05716-9_55
7. Lokoč, J., Kovalčík, G., Souček, T., Moravec, J., Bodnár, J., Čech, P.: VIRET tool meets NasNet. In: Kompatsiaris, I., Huet, B., Mezaris, V., Gurrin, C., Cheng, W.-H., Vrochidis, S. (eds.) MMM 2019. LNCS, vol. 11296, pp. 597–601. Springer, Cham (2019). https://doi.org/10.1007/978-3-030-05716-9_52
8. Ren, S., He, K., Girshick, R.B., Sun, J.: Faster R-CNN: towards real-time object detection with region proposal networks. IEEE Trans. Pattern Anal. Mach. Intell. **39**, 1137–1149 (2015)
9. Szegedy, C., Ioffe, S., Vanhoucke, V., Alemi, A.A.: Inception-v4, inception-resnet and the impact of residual connections on learning. In: Proceedings of the Thirty-First AAAI Conference on Artificial Intelligence, AAAI 2017, pp. 4278–4284. AAAI Press, San Francisco (2017)
10. Carreira, J., Zisserman, A.: Quo vadis, action recognition? A new model and the kinetics dataset. In: 2017 IEEE Conference on Computer Vision and Pattern Recognition (CVPR), pp. 4724–4733 (2017)

VERGE in VBS 2020

Stelios Andreadis(✉), Anastasia Moumtzidou, Konstantinos Apostolidis, Konstantinos Gkountakos, Damianos Galanopoulos, Emmanouil Michail, Ilias Gialampoukidis, Stefanos Vrochidis, Vasileios Mezaris, and Ioannis Kompatsiaris

Information Technologies Institute, Centre for Research and Technology Hellas, Thessaloniki, Greece
{andreadisst,moumtzid,kapost,gountakos,dgalanop, michem,heliasgj,stefanos,bmezaris,ikom}@iti.gr

Abstract. This paper demonstrates VERGE, an interactive video retrieval engine for browsing a collection of images or videos and searching for specific content. The engine integrates a multitude of retrieval methodologies that include visual and textual searches and further capabilities such as fusion and reranking. All search options and results appear in a web application that aims at a friendly user experience.

1 Introduction

VERGE is an interactive video retrieval system that provides users with efficient browsing and various search capabilities inside a set of video collections. For more than ten years, VERGE has been participating in numerous video retrieval related conferences and showcases, including TRECVID [1] and Video Browser Showdown (VBS) [2], thus the system is adapted to support the Known Item Search (KIS), Instance Search (INS) and Ad-Hoc Video Search (AVS) tasks. Experience from previous participation drove this year's selection of mature solutions (Sect. 2.1), the improvement of old modalities (Sects. 2.2, 2.6), the integration of new (Sects. 2.3, 2.4, 2.5) and also any advances regarding the user experience.

2 Video Retrieval System

VERGE serves as a video search engine with user-friendly browsing and a variety of modules to retrieve an image or a video from a collection. Furthermore, different search functionalities can be fused to create a combined query or they can be used consecutively to rerank the top results. A detailed description of the implemented indexing and retrieval modules follows in the next subsections, while the general architecture of VERGE can be seen in Fig. 1. It should be noted here that all shot-based algorithms are based on the keyframes that derived from the provided V3C1 segmentation.

Y. M. Ro et al. (Eds.): MMM 2020, LNCS 11962, pp. 778–783, 2020.
https://doi.org/10.1007/978-3-030-37734-2_69

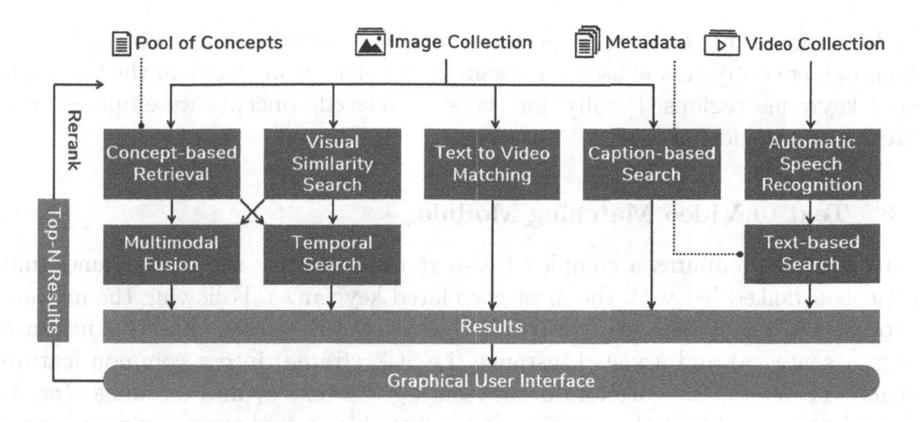

Fig. 1. VERGE system architecture

2.1 Visual Similarity Search

This module performs visual-based retrieval similarity of relevant content using convolutional neural networks (CNNs) upon a deep hashing architecture. A deep hashing approach will be followed in order to represent the visual information into a few bits (12, 24, 32, 48) [3]. Then, the retrieval framework will retrieve the relevant visual content by comparing the hamming distance of the generated binary vectors between the gallery images and the query. The backbone convolutional network will be an architecture similar to AlexNet or VGG16. Eventually, an IVFADC index database vector will be created for fast binary indexing and K-Nearest Neighbors will be computed for the query image [4].

2.2 Concept-Based Retrieval

This module annotates each keyframe with a pool of concepts, which comprises 1000 ImageNet concepts, 345 concepts of the TRECVID SIN task [5], 500 event-related concepts, 80 action-related, 365 scene classification concepts, 580 object labels and 30 style-related concepts. For performing the annotation, each keyframe was split to 9 equally-sized regions by applying a 3×3 grid, and each region, as well as the whole image, were processed separately so as to incorporate coarse localization information to the annotations. To obtain the annotation scores for the 1000 ImageNet concepts, we used an ensemble method, averaging the concept scores from four pre-trained models that employ different DCNN architectures, namely the VGG16, InceptionV3, InceptionResNetV2, as well as a hybrid model that combines the ImageNet and Places365 concept pools [6]. To obtain scores for the 345 TRECVID SIN concepts, we used the deep learning framework of [7]. For the event-related concepts we used the pre-trained model of EventNet [8] while for the action-related concepts we used a model trained on the AVA dataset [9]. Regarding the extraction of the scene-related concepts, we utilized the publicly available VGG16 model fine-tuned on the Places365 dataset. Object detection scores were extracted using models pre-trained on the established MS COCO and Open Images V4 datasets, with 80 and 500 detectable objects, respectively, and the bounding box information for each detected object was used for assigning the detection to one of the 9 considered keyframe regions. Finally, for the style-related concepts we employed the pre-trained models of [10].

2.3 Text to Video Matching Module

This module compares a complex free-text query with a set of keyframes and returns a ranked list with the most correlated keyframes. Following the method proposed in [11], we use an architecture that learns to represent a textual instance (e.g. a sentence) and a visual instance (i.e. a keyframe) into a common feature space. Therefore, the correlation between a given text S_i and an image Im_j is directly comparable in the common space. For this, a dual encoding deep neural network that projects a natural language sentence and a shot keyframe into the common feature space is used. The network performs multi-level encoding in parallel, for both sentence and keyframes. A pre-trained Resnet-152 model is used for the initial keyframe representation, whereas each word sentence is initially encoded as a bag-of-words vector. Then, both the sentence and the keyframe representations go through three different encoders (i.e. mean-pooling, bi-GRU-based sequential model [12], and biGRU-CNN [13]). To train this module, we followed the approach of [14], and in terms of training data we combined two datasets, TGIF [15] and MSR-VTT [16]. The TGIF dataset contains approx. 100k short animated GIFs with one short description per each, while MSR-VTT consists of 10k short video clips, each accompanied by 20 short descriptions.

2.4 Automatic Speech Recognition

Acoustic content from videos is also exploited, by extracting audio channels and applying Automatic Speech Recognition (ASR) on them, in order to produce speech transcriptions for the whole collection. The basis for ASR is the open source framework CMU Sphinx-4 [17], a widely used, portable and flexible ASR system. The main components of the CMU Sphinx-4 Transcriber are (a) a phonetic dictionary, which contains a mapping from words to phones, which are the basic units of speech, (b) an acoustic model, which contains acoustic properties for each unit of speech, and (c) a language model, which provides word-level language structure, by defining which word could follow previously recognized words and significantly restricting the matching process by stripping words that are not probable. Existing open source language and acoustic models are used in the context of VERGE platform. A priori extracted transcriptions and provided metadata are then fed into a text-based search module that uses Apache Lucene and enables the identification of a video by using words from the plot.

2.5 Video Captioning - Caption-Based Search

This module describes each video by a sentence/caption that is constructed from words included in a vocabulary, and thus the user can retrieve videos by simple text search. Video captioning approaches comprise two separate components: (i) a feature extractor that typically extracts the features of a video by sampling among the frames using a fixed number as a step, and (ii) an encoder-decoder that encodes the content and subsequently assigns it to words. To address this, an RNN-based neural network is used similar to [18]. The model is pre-trained on MSR-VTT [16], a widely-known dataset in video captioning domain. Finally, an approach based on [19] using reinforcement learning is implemented.

2.6 Multimodal Fusion and Temporal Search

This module fuses the results of two or more search modules, such as the visual descriptors (Sect. 2.1), the concepts (Sect. 2.2) and the color features mentioned in Sect. 3. Similar shots are retrieved by performing center-to-center comparisons among keyframes by using the selected modules. The query is described with multiple features (e.g. a shot, a color and/or concepts) and one of the features is considered by the user as dominant (i.e the most important one). The system returns the top-N relevant shots by considering solely the dominant feature (e.g. color), and then the other features are used for re-ranking the initial list by using a non-linear graph-based fusion method [20]. In order to perform temporal search, a query using multiple features of two adjacent shots is received, the top-N relevant images for one of the query shots are retrieved and finally this list is re-ranked by considering the features of the adjacent shot.

3 VERGE User Interface and Interaction Modes

The VERGE web application (Fig. 2) aims to provide end users with a friendly and effective way to utilise the developed retrieval algorithms, in a modern environment. Since this year we decided to incorporate a large number of modalities to offer more search options, our main goal is to serve them to the user in a non-complex way.

The VERGE user interface consists of three principal components: (i) a dashboard menu on the left, (ii) a results panel that covers most of the screen, and (iii) a filmstrip on the bottom. The menu contains a countdown timer that shows the remaining time to submit during VBS, a slider that adjusts the size of results, a back button that restores outcomes of previous queries and a switch button that defines whether a retrieval module will bring new matching shots or rerank existing results. Next, the various search modules are visualised as boxes that can be expanded or collapsed for reasons of compactness. In detail, *Concepts* and *Filters* present the entire list of visual concepts and filters respectively (Sect. 2.2), while both provide the option of auto-complete search. The selection of multiple concepts is also supported. *Colors* is a color palette in order to retrieve images of a specific shade. *Text Search* looks for the typed words in the video metadata, in the speech-to-text transcriptions (Sect. 2.4), and/or in the summaries described in Sect. 2.5, and it can also map the words to visual concepts and return most relevant shots (Sect. 2.3). Furthermore, *Combination*

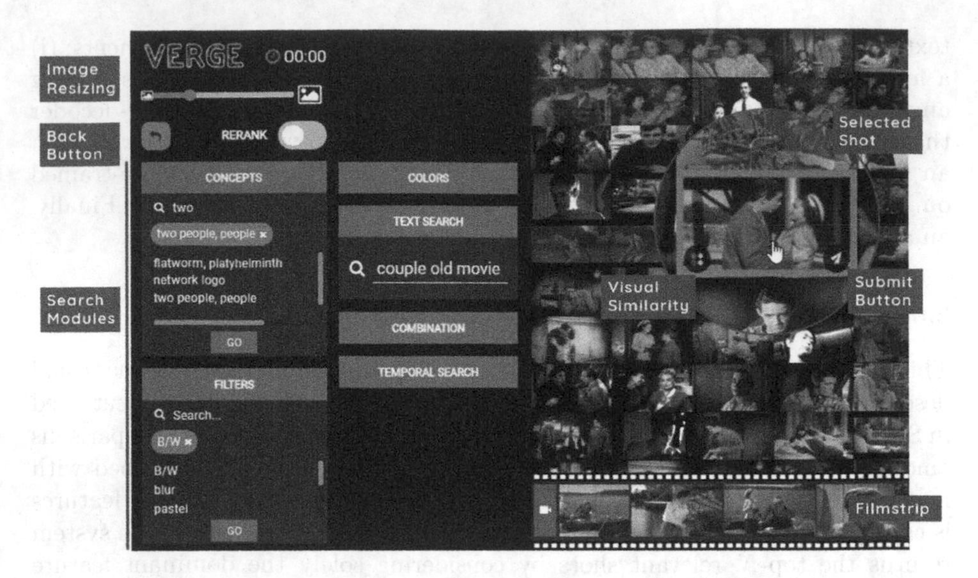

Fig. 2. Screenshot of the VERGE web application

allows the fusion of some of the aforementioned modalities and *Temporal Search* offers the option to describe two consecutive shots (Sect. 2.6). The results of each search module are displayed in the main component, either as single images or groups of images (videos) in a grid view, sorted by highest relevance. Hovering over an image reveals the options to run the *Visual Similarity Search* (Sect. 2.1) or submit it to the contest. Clicking on the image shows the complete video in the bottom filmstrip, in the form of sequential shots.

To illustrate the capabilities of VERGE, a simple scenario is described, where users try to find shots of *a couple hugging in a black-and-white movie.* Search can be initiated by applying the "B/W" filter from the available list of filters and then combining it with the concept "two people". Once a relevant image appears among the results, then visual similarity can be used in order to retrieve more similar shots. An alternative strategy is to look for relevant keywords (e.g., "couple old movie") inside the metadata, the transcripts and the video summaries.

4 Future Work

Since some of the aforementioned retrieval modalities are introduced to VERGE for the first time, we will evaluate their performance during the VBS contest and we will decide accordingly on their further enhancement or modification.

Acknowledgements. This work was supported by the EU's Horizon 2020 research and innovation programme under grant agreements H2020-779962 V4Desi-gn, H2020-786731 CONNEXIONs and H2020-780656 ReTV.

References

1. Awad, G., Butt, A., et al.: TRECVID 2018: benchmarking video activity detection, video captioning and matching, video storytelling linking and video search (2018)
2. Lokoč, J., Kovalčík, G., et al.: Interactive search or sequential browsing? A detailed analysis of the video browser showdown 2018. ACM TOMM **15**(1), 29 (2019)
3. Yang, H.-F., Lin, K., Chen, C.-S.: Supervised learning of semantics-preserving hash via deep convolutional neural networks. IEEE Trans. PAMI **40**(2), 437–451 (2017)
4. Jegou, H., Douze, M., Schmid, C.: Product quantization for nearest neighbor search. IEEE Trans. PAMI **33**(1), 117–128 (2011)
5. Markatopoulou, F., Moumtzidou, A., Galanopoulos, D., et al.: ITI-CERTH participation in TRECVID 2017. In: Proceedings of TRECVID 2017 Workshop, USA (2017)
6. Zhou, B., Lapedriza, A., et al.: Places: a 10 million image database for scene recognition. IEEE Trans. PAMI **40**(6), 1452–1464 (2017)
7. Markatopoulou, F., Mezaris, V., Patras, I.: Implicit and explicit concept relations in deep neural networks for multi-label video/image annotation. IEEE Trans. Circuits Syst. Video Technol. **29**(6), 1631–1644 (2018)
8. Guangnan, Y., Yitong, L., Hongliang, X., et al.: EventNet: a large scale structured concept library for complex event detection in video. In Proceedings of ACM MM (2015)
9. Gu, C., Sun, C., Ross, D.A., et al.: AVA: a video dataset of spatio-temporally localized atomic visual actions. In: Proceedings of the IEEE Conference on CVPR, pp. 6047–6056 (2018)
10. Tan, W.R., Chan, C.S., Aguirre, H.E., Tanaka, K.: Ceci n'est pas une pipe: a deep convolutional network for fine-art paintings classification. In 2016 IEEE ICIP, pp. 3703–3707. IEEE (2016)
11. Dong, J., Li, X., Xu, C., et al.: Dual encoding for zero-example video retrieval. In: Proceedings of the IEEE Conference on CVPR, pp. 9346–9355 (2019)
12. Cho, K., Van M.B., Gulcehre, C., et al.: Learning phrase representations using RNN encoder-decoder for statistical machine translation. arXiv preprint. arXiv:1406.1078 (2014)
13. Kim, Y.: Convolutional neural networks for sentence classification. arXiv preprint. arXiv:1408.5882 (2014)
14. Faghri, F., Fleet, D.J., Kiros, J.R., Fidler, S.: VSE++: improving visual-semantic embeddings with hard negatives (2018)
15. Li, Y., Song, Y., Cao, L., et al.: TGIF: a new dataset and benchmark on animated GIF description. In: The IEEE Conference on CVPR (2016)
16. Xu, J., Mei, T., Yao, T., Rui, Y.: MSR-VTT: a large video description dataset for bridging video and language. In: The IEEE Conference on CVPR (June 2016)
17. Lamere, P., Kwok, P., Gouvea, E., et al.: The CMU SPHINX-4 speech recognition system. In: IEEE ICASSP 2003, vol. 1, pp. 2–5, Hong Kong (2003)
18. Venugopalan, S., Rohrbach, M., Donahue, J., et al.: Sequence to sequence-video to text. In: Proceedings of the IEEE ICCV, pp. 4534–4542 (2015)
19. Phan, S., Henter, G.E., Miyao, Y., Satoh, S.: Consensus-based sequence training for video captioning. arXiv preprint. arXiv:1712.09532 (2017)
20. Gialampoukidis, I., Moumtzidou, A., Liparas, D., et al.: A hybrid graph-based and non-linear late fusion approach for multimedia retrieval. In: 2016 14th International Workshop on CBMI, pp. 1–6 (June 2016)

VIRET at Video Browser Showdown 2020

Jakub Lokoč(✉), Gregor Kovalčík, and Tomáš Souček

SIRET Research Group, Department of Software Engineering,
Faculty of Mathematics and Physics, Charles University, Prague, Czech Republic
lokoc@ksi.mff.cuni.cz, gregor.kovalcik@gmail.com, tomas.soucek1@gmail.com

Abstract. During the last three years, the most successful systems at the Video Browser Showdown employed effective retrieval models where raw video data are automatically preprocessed in advance to extract semantic or low-level features of selected frames or shots. This enables users to express their search intents in the form of keywords, sketch, query example, or their combination. In this paper, we present new extensions to our interactive video retrieval system VIRET that won Video Browser Showdown in 2018 and achieved the second place at Video Browser Showdown 2019 and Lifelog Search Challenge 2019. The new features of the system focus both on updates of retrieval models and interface modifications to help users with query specification by means of informative visualizations.

1 Introduction

State-of-the-art interactive video retrieval systems [1,2,14,16,17,20] try to face difficult video retrieval tasks by a combination of information retrieval [3], deep learning [8], and interactive search [19,21] approaches. Such systems are annually compared at the Video Browser Showdown (VBS) [5,11,12] evaluation campaign, where participating teams compete in one room in the concurrent way, trying to solve a presented video retrieval task within a given time frame. The competition tasks are revealed one by one at the competition, while the video dataset[1] is provided to teams in advance. This paper presents new features of the VIRET tool prototype that regularly participates at interactive video/lifelog search competitions [9,12].

VIRET [14,15] is a frame-based interactive video retrieval framework, relying mostly on a set of three basic image retrieval approaches for searching a set of selected video frames – keyword search based on automatic annotation, color sketching based on position-color signatures, and query by example image relying on deep features. The basic approaches can be further used to construct more complex multi-modal and/or temporal queries, which turned out to be an important VIRET tool feature at VBS 2019. In order to provide information about location of frequent semantic concepts, the sketch canvas supports construction of filters for faces or a displayed text. In addition, several filters are

[1] The V3C1 dataset [18] is currently used at VBS.

Y. M. Ro et al. (Eds.): MMM 2020, LNCS 11962, pp. 784–789, 2020.
https://doi.org/10.1007/978-3-030-37734-2_70

supported as well, either based on content (e.g., black and white filter) or the knowledge of video/shot boundaries (e.g., show only top ranked frames for each video/shot).

The interface is divided into two blocks, one for query formulation and one for top ranked results and context inspection. Extracted small thumbnails are used to display frames. All the entered queries are visible as well as other query settings like a sorting model or filters limiting the number of returned frames for each basic query model. Once a query is provided, users can browse temporal context of each displayed frame, observe video summary or an image map dynamically computed for top ranked frames.

Whereas the presented VIRET features were competitive in expert[2] VBS search sessions, in novice sessions the previous version of the VIRET tool prototype did not perform well. Specifically, while expert VIRET users solved all ten visual KIS tasks and six out of eight textual KIS tasks (the most of all participating teams), the novice VIRET users solved just two out of five evaluated visual KIS tasks (a subset of the expert tasks). According to our analysis, in two unsolved novice tasks the searched frame appeared on the first page, but it was overlooked. In addition, the novice users faced problems with keyword search without the knowledge of the set of supported labels used for automatic annotation. Hence, we focus both on updates of retrieval models and several modifications of the user interface for the next installment of the Video Browser Showdown.

2 New VIRET Features for VBS 2020

This section summarizes considered updates of employed retrieval models and interfaces.

2.1 Retrieval Models

Since the basic retrieval models and their multi-modal temporal combination used by VIRET often turned out to be effective to bring searched frames to the first page, we plan to keep the main querying scheme. However, several updates are considered for VBS 2020.

First, the automatic annotation process employing a retrained NASNet deep classification network [22] is modified to produce different score values for the network output vector (i.e., scores of assigned labels). Instead of softmax which is used for training, the employed feature extraction process currently uses another form of network output normalization of scores that enables more effective retrieval with queries comprising a combination of multiple class labels. In the normalized vectors, all potential zero scores are further replaced with a small constant. We also plan to investigate performance benefits of additional annotation sources (e.g., using object detection networks).

[2] Authors of a tool are considered to be experts as they are expected to use the tool more effectively.

Second, the performance of the vitrivr tool [17] keyword search in ASR annotations[3] was impressive at the previous VBS event. Since the vitrivr team shared the ASR data with other teams, we plan to integrate the data to the VIRET framework. Specifically, we plan to include a video filter based on the presence of a spoken word or phrase.

Third, given a set of collected query logs, we plan to investigate and optimize meta parameters of the retrieval models with respect to the whole set of logged queries. More specifically, we plan to fine-tune the initial setting of filters for the number of top ranked frames for each model and presentation filters. Given a detected effective setting, the corresponding interface controls can be hidden or simplified for novice sessions.

Last but not least, we plan to include free-form text search using a variant of recently introduced W2VV++ model [10], extending the W2VV model [7] and relying on visual features from deep networks leveraging the whole ImageNet hierarchy [6] for training effective representations [13].

2.2 User Interface

Since the VIRET tool focuses on frequent query (re)formulations, informative visualizations are important to aid with querying and help with the semantic gap problem. For VBS 2020, we consider the following updates of the VIRET tool prototype interface.

So far, the keyword search component prompted only supported class labels and their descriptions during query formulation. In the new version, we consider to automatically show also top ranked selected frames for prompted labels (see Fig. 1).

Fig. 1. Top ranked frames for prompted labels.

Without the knowledge of supported labels used for automatic annotation, (especially) novice users may face problems with keyword search initialization. Trying to bridge the gap, the interface was updated to show a few automatically assigned labels with the highest score for a displayed frame, once the mouse cursor hovers over the frame. This feedback helps novice users to observe and gradually learn how the automatic annotation works. Based on this feedback, users can interactively extend the query expression with labels that originally did not come to their mind.

[3] https://cloud.google.com/speech-to-text/.

In order to construct temporal queries using example images, we consider a hierarchical static image map [4] with an organized/sorted representative sample of the whole dataset. Let us emphasize that the primary purpose of the map is to find a suitable query example frame as finding one particular searched frame is a way more difficult task.

The last modification focuses on result presentation displays (used already at the Lifelog Search Challenge 2019). One display shows a classical long list of frames sorted by relevance (using larger thumbnails), where users can navigate using the scroll bar. The second display shows one larger page of the ranked result set, where frames are locally rearranged such that frames from one video are collocated and sorted by frame number (see Fig. 2). The video groups on one page are sorted with respect to the most relevant frame from each group and separated by a green vertical line.

Fig. 2. Top ranked frames grouped by video ID on one page. (Color figure online)

3 Conclusion

This paper presents a new version of the VIRET system, focusing on updates of the utilized retrieval toolkit and interface. The updates aim at more convenient query formulation, new modality (speech), and fine-tuning of the employed ranking and filtering models.

Acknowledgments. This paper has been supported by Czech Science Foundation (GAČR) project 19-22071Y and by Charles University grant SVV-260451. We would also like to thank Přemysl Čech and Vít Škrhák for their help with interface in WPF.

References

1. Amato, G., et al.: VISIONE at VBS2019. In: Kompatsiaris, I., Huet, B., Mezaris, V., Gurrin, C., Cheng, W.-H., Vrochidis, S. (eds.) MMM 2019. LNCS, vol. 11296, pp. 591–596. Springer, Cham (2019). https://doi.org/10.1007/978-3-030-05716-9_51
2. Andreadis, S., et al.: VERGE in VBS 2019. In: Kompatsiaris, I., Huet, B., Mezaris, V., Gurrin, C., Cheng, W.-H., Vrochidis, S. (eds.) MMM 2019. LNCS, vol. 11296, pp. 602–608. Springer, Cham (2019). https://doi.org/10.1007/978-3-030-05716-9_53
3. Baeza-Yates, R.A., Ribeiro-Neto, B.A.: Modern Information Retrieval - The Concepts and Technology Behind Search, 2nd edn. Pearson Education Ltd., Harlow (2011)
4. Barthel, K.U., Hezel, N.: Visually exploring millions of images using image maps and graphs. In: Huet, B., Vrochidis, S., Chang, E. (eds.) Big Data Analytics for Large-Scale Multimedia Search, pp. 251–275. John Wiley and Sons Inc. (2019)
5. Cobârzan, C., et al.: Interactive video search tools: a detailed analysis of the video browser showdown 2015. Multimed. Tools Appl. **76**(4), 5539–5571 (2017). https://doi.org/10.1007/s11042-016-3661-2
6. Deng, J., Dong, W., Socher, R., Li, L., Li, K., Fei-Fei, L.: Imagenet: A large-scale hierarchical image database. In: 2009 IEEE Conference on Computer Vision and Pattern Recognition, pp. 248–255 (June 2009). https://doi.org/10.1109/CVPR.2009.5206848
7. Dong, J., Li, X., Snoek, C.G.M.: Predicting visual features from text for image and video caption retrieval. IEEE Trans. Multimedia **20**(12), 3377–3388 (2018). https://doi.org/10.1109/TMM.2018.2832602
8. Goodfellow, I., Bengio, Y., Courville, A.: Deep Learning. MIT Press, Cambridge (2016). http://www.deeplearningbook.org
9. Gurrin, C., et al.: [invited papers] Comparing approaches to interactive lifelog search at the lifelog search challenge (lsc2018). ITE Trans. Med. Technol. Appl. **7**(2), 46–59 (2019). https://doi.org/10.3169/mta.7.46
10. Li, X., Xu, C., Yang, G., Chen, Z., Dong, J.: W2VV++: fully deep learning for ad-hoc video search. In: Proceedings of the 27th ACM International Conference on Multimedia, MM 2019, Nice, France, 21–25 October 2019, pp. 1786–1794 (2019). https://doi.org/10.1145/3343031.3350906
11. Lokoč, J., Bailer, W., Schoeffmann, K., Münzer, B., Awad, G.: On influential trends in interactive video retrieval: video browser showdown 2015–2017. IEEE Trans. Multimed. **20**(12), 3361–3376 (2018). https://doi.org/10.1109/TMM.2018.2830110
12. Lokoč, J., et al.: Interactive search or sequential browsing? A detailed analysis of the video browser showdown 2018. ACM Trans. Multimed. Comput. Commun. Appl. **15**(1), 29:1–29:18 (2019). https://doi.org/10.1145/3295663
13. Mettes, P., Koelma, D.C., Snoek, C.G.: The imagenet shuffle: Reorganized pre-training for video event detection. In: Proceedings of the 2016 ACM on International Conference on Multimedia Retrieval, pp. 175–182. ICMR '16, ACM, New York, NY, USA (2016). https://doi.org/10.1145/2911996.2912036, http://doi.acm.org/10.1145/2911996.2912036
14. Lokoč, J., Kovalčík, G., Souček, T., Moravec, J., Čech, P.: A framework for effective known-item search in video. In: Proceedings of the 27th ACM International Conference on Multimedia, MM 2019, pp. 1777–1785, ACM, New York (2019). https://doi.org/10.1145/3343031.3351046

15. Lokoč, J., Kovalčík, G., Souček, T., Moravec, J., Čech, P.: Viret: a video retrieval tool for interactive known-item search. In: Proceedings of the 2019 on International Conference on Multimedia Retrieval, ICMR 2019, pp. 177–181. ACM, New York (2019). https://doi.org/10.1145/3323873.3325034
16. Nguyen, P.A., Ngo, C.-W., Francis, D., Huet, B.: VIREO @ video browser showdown 2019. In: Kompatsiaris, I., Huet, B., Mezaris, V., Gurrin, C., Cheng, W.-H., Vrochidis, S. (eds.) MMM 2019. LNCS, vol. 11296, pp. 609–615. Springer, Cham (2019). https://doi.org/10.1007/978-3-030-05716-9_54
17. Rossetto, L., Amiri Parian, M., Gasser, R., Giangreco, I., Heller, S., Schuldt, H.: Deep learning-based concept detection in vitrivr. In: Kompatsiaris, I., Huet, B., Mezaris, V., Gurrin, C., Cheng, W.-H., Vrochidis, S. (eds.) MMM 2019. LNCS, vol. 11296, pp. 616–621. Springer, Cham (2019). https://doi.org/10.1007/978-3-030-05716-9_55
18. Rossetto, L., Schuldt, H., Awad, G., Butt, A.A.: V3C – a research video collection. In: Kompatsiaris, I., Huet, B., Mezaris, V., Gurrin, C., Cheng, W.-H., Vrochidis, S. (eds.) MMM 2019. LNCS, vol. 11295, pp. 349–360. Springer, Cham (2019). https://doi.org/10.1007/978-3-030-05710-7_29
19. Schoeffmann, K., Hudelist, M.A., Huber, J.: Video interaction tools: a survey of recent work. ACM Comput. Surv. **48**(1), 14:1–14:34 (2015). https://doi.org/10.1145/2808796
20. Schoeffmann, K., Münzer, B., Leibetseder, A., Primus, J., Kletz, S.: Autopiloting feature maps: the deep interactive video exploration (diveXplore) system at VBS2019. In: Kompatsiaris, I., Huet, B., Mezaris, V., Gurrin, C., Cheng, W.-H., Vrochidis, S. (eds.) MMM 2019. LNCS, vol. 11296, pp. 585–590. Springer, Cham (2019). https://doi.org/10.1007/978-3-030-05716-9_50
21. Thomee, B., Lew, M.S.: Interactive search in image retrieval: a survey. Int. J. Multimed. Inf. Retrieval **1**(2), 71–86 (2012). https://doi.org/10.1007/s13735-012-0014-4
22. Zoph, B., Vasudevan, V., Shlens, J., Le, Q.V.: Learning transferable architectures for scalable image recognition. CoRR abs/1707.07012 (2017). http://arxiv.org/abs/1707.07012

SOM-Hunter: Video Browsing with Relevance-to-SOM Feedback Loop

Miroslav Kratochvíl(✉), Patrik Veselý, František Mejzlík, and Jakub Lokoč(✉)

SIRET Research Group, Department of Software Engineering,
Faculty of Mathematics and Physics, Charles University, Prague, Czech Republic
{kratochvil,lokoc}@ksi.mff.cuni.cz

Abstract. This paper presents a prototype video retrieval engine focusing on a simple known-item search workflow, where users initialize the search with a query and then use an iterative approach to explore a larger candidate set. Specifically, users gradually observe a sequence of displays and provide feedback to the system. The displays are dynamically created by a self organizing map that employs the scores based on the collected feedback, in order to provide a display matching the user preferences. In addition, users can inspect various other types of specialized displays for exploitation purposes, once promising candidates are found.

Keywords: Interactive video retrieval · Deep features · Relevance feedback · Self-organizing maps

1 Introduction

The astonishing progress in deep learning (e.g. deep features [3], image classification [11,13], and image captioning [12]) starts to significantly aid with multimedia retrieval tasks that originally represented a difficult challenge for search engines. An example of such task is known-item search (KIS), where users search for one particular "known" scene in a given annotation-free multimedia collection [6]. However, even though the known-item search systems can benefit from ranking models based on more effective automatic annotations and various other visual modalities, interactive searching is still required to aid the ranking model in order to target the searched item precisely [7]. For example, the VIRET system [8] provides multi-modal and temporal query formulation interface, and allows the user to iteratively update the query with new terms derived from observation of the candidate result set. Similarly, the vitrivr system [9] incorporates a multitude of state-of-the-art deep learning approaches for automatic extraction of annotations and features for various query modes. Smart browsing of the candidate result set is another successful strategy for known-item search, implemented for example in the Vibro system [1] that considers a hierarchical image map approach for top ranked results combined with a precomputed similarity graph to potentially inspect all relevant dataset objects. At VBS 2016, a

Y. M. Ro et al. (Eds.): MMM 2020, LNCS 11962, pp. 790–795, 2020.
https://doi.org/10.1007/978-3-030-37734-2_71

video browsing system based on a Bayesian framework [4] was tested for known-item search tasks. Each search consisted of iterations, where users select from a provided display one object that corresponds to the mental target. The feedback is used to update probabilities maintained for all dataset images.

In this work, we focus on a simplified combination of three relatively basic techniques: Keyword search query initialization with VIRET-like queries [8] for candidate set selection, a relevance feedback approach considering maintenance of relevance scores, and self-organizing maps (SOMs) [5] for creating comprehensible displays reflecting relevance score distribution in large candidate result sets. With SOMs, the number of objects that can be effectively inspected in a single display can range to several hundreds. In many cases, the organized display of agglomerations of similar images has proven to be convenient for browsing, and therefore was employed by several VBS systems (e.g., diveXplore [10] or Vibro systems [1]).

2 SOM-Hunter

The presented interactive video retrieval system focuses on a search workflow depicted in Fig. 1.

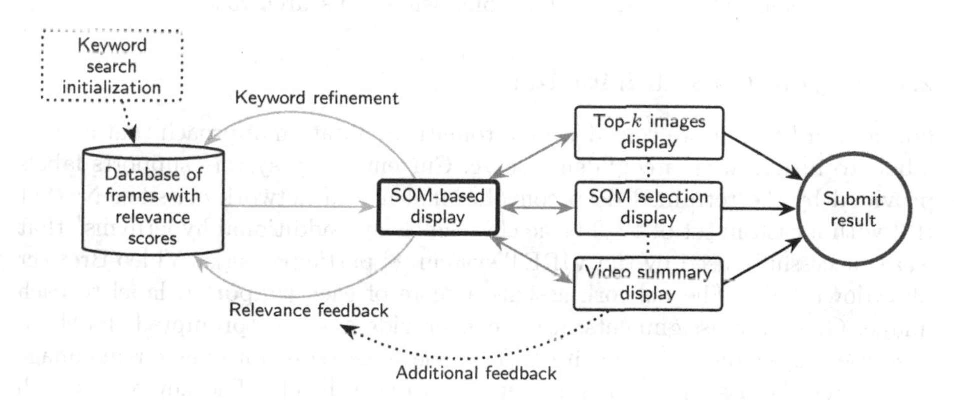

Fig. 1. Overview of a typical SOM-Hunter search workflow. The browsing is optionally initialized with keyword search that reduces the initial dataset. Database of relevance scores of all frames is maintained for the whole browsing process. Relevance-weighted-SOM display is constructed for the user; which he uses for either dataset exploration (green arrows) or exploitation if the user decides the target frame can be reached from a displayed frame (red arrows). (Color figure online)

Users can start either with keyword search initialization returning a pre-ranked fraction of the dataset frames, or the whole dataset with uniformly distributed relevance scores. The first display is computed using a relevance-weighted self-organizing map trained on the deep features. The considered SOM displays are not large (i.e. 12×12 frames), so that the corresponding self organizing map can be computed efficiently, and comprehended by the user in seconds. The workflow continues with several possible search options:

- Based on the SOM display observation, users may provide feedback in form of positive and negative examples, influencing the next SOM display to better match the search intents. Similarly, the keywords relevant for individual frames can be observed and used as a basis for keyword refinement.
- Users may inspect a cluster assigned to several selected SOM nodes in a new window. This action is highly efficient as it exploits information already available from the SOM and provides relevant samples from the neighbourhood of the SOM node.
- Users pick a very promising query example and open a new window with the most similar frames to the query (or, similarly, explore the currently top-ranked frames, which is beneficial after running keyword-search queries).
- Users recognize a frame that could belong to the same video as the searched known item, and open a new window for exploring the video summary accessible from the frame.

As in VIRET, the user can easily inspect temporal context of each displayed frame using the mouse wheel. The searched frame can be marked any time in the set of displayed images, which accomplishes the search task.

2.1 Keyword Search Initialization

For keyword search, we consider an automatic annotation approach that assigns labels to images with a confidence score. Currently, thy system supports labels provided by the retrained deep convolutional neural network classifier NasNet [13] with a custom set of 1243 basic class labels and additional hypernyms[1] that were successfully used by the VIRET system [8] participating at Video Browser Showdown 2019. The network assigns a score of each supported label to each image. Given the assignments, users can provide a set of (prompted) labels to describe the searched known item. The relevance score formula for an image aggregates the assigned scores for provided query labels. The keyword search system is experimentally supplemented with other models that can assign scores to individual video frames based on a free form text query, including the state-of-the-art query representation learning approach W2VV++ by Li et al. [14]. The keyword search system can be easily extended to any additional labels provided by selected state-of-the-art annotation models (e.g. for object detection).

2.2 SOM-Based Display

SOMs (self-organizing maps), introduced by Kohonen [5], are a class of unsupervised learning algorithms, used for finding a low-dimensional manifold in high-dimensional pointcloud data. SOMs have been successfully used to produce

[1] A hypernym represents a set of supported basic labels.

comprehensible visualisations of high-dimensional data for humans. SOM algorithms usually output a 2-D grid where vertices represent clusters of the original data, arranged in the grid in a similarity-respecting manner.

In SOM-Hunter, the SOM-organized displays are produced as such: The SOM grid is first trained in the space of frame deep features; the nodes of the grid are then used as a nearest-neighbor classifier for this space. From each group of frames with same classification, a single example is chosen to represent the group at the corresponding position in the SOM display.

To produce the relevance-weighted SOM, a modified single-update training algorithm is used: The current relevance scores of frames are normalized so that they can be treated as probabilities. The SOM training process then samples the training example frames for each iteration from this score distribution. The approach ensures that the highly scored items are over-represented in the SOM, while diminishing the effect (and number of assigned SOM nodes) of the low-score items.

SOM-Hunter exploits the high malleability of the SOM training process to achieve almost real-time performance. Mainly, a good (although not optimal) SOM that sufficiently describes the whole dataset can be successfully trained on less than 5% of actual frames used as training examples. Possible missed outliers are still accessible in the exploitation-based displays (see Fig. 1), or targeted with relevance feedback.

The effect of using the relevance-weighted-SOM training is illustrated in Fig. 2 on artificial and real data.

2.3 Relevance Score Updates

Users may provide feedback on individual images by assigning either positive feedback, optional negative feedback, or (implicitly) leaving the images unclassified. Compared to binary input models (e.g. PicHunter [2]), ternary feedback allows clear distinction between 'unwanted' and 'untouched' frames, allowing the user to save time by skipping evaluation of subjectively irrelevant frames, without the danger of producing invalid negative feedback.

The management of relevance scores admits various approaches for updating the scores after each iteration. Both the Bayesian approaches [2] and simple distance-based rankings require the model to estimate the 'area of effect' of each user feedback to work well with various exploration/exploitation trade-offs. This area is usually represented as a parameter of a probability distribution around the selected samples. In the current version of SOM-Hunter, we test several simple versions of the update models based on the similarity measure on deep features from retrained NasNet [13] or features used in the W2VV++ model [14]. For example, matching the user choice on SOMs to the statistical properties of the underlying SOM clusters is both efficient as a strategy for guiding the model and intuitive for the user estimation of the update effect.

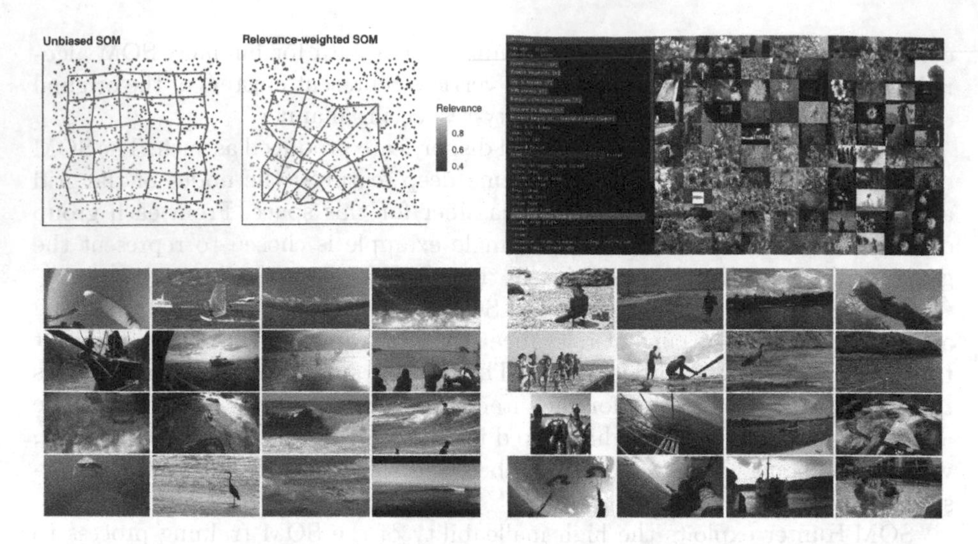

Fig. 2. Effect of relevance scores on SOMs. Top left: Illustration of the difference between unbiased and relevance-weighted trained 6×6 SOMs on artificial data. Bottom row: The effect on SOM display of a real dataset with a small 4×4 SOM; trained without bias (bottom left), and after modifying the relevance scores with positive feedback on frames containing a person (bottom right). Top right: The trained SOM as viewed in SOM-Hunter, focusing on images with flowers.

3 Conclusion

This paper presents an interactive video retrieval system SOM-Hunter for known-item and ad-hoc search tasks that is supposed to extend the list of exploration-based VBS systems. SOM-Hunter focuses on smart, time-efficient browsing of larger candidate result sets, utilizing self-organizing maps combined with provided relevance feedback. The system also supports the standard effective approaches, such as keyword search, temporal context inspection, and a set of additional presentation displays.

Acknowledgments. This paper has been supported by Czech Science Foundation (GAČR) project 19-22071Y and by Charles University grant SVV-260451. M.K. was supported by ELIXIR CZ (MEYS), grant number LM2015047.

We are extremely grateful to Vladimír Vondruš for his helpful advices on using the Magnum engine, and to Tomáš Souček and Gregor Kovalčík for their help with frame selection and feature extraction.

References

1. Barthel, K.U., Hezel, N., Jung, K.: Fusing keyword search and visual exploration for untagged videos. In: Schoeffmann, K., et al. (eds.) MMM 2018. LNCS, vol. 10705, pp. 413–418. Springer, Cham (2018). https://doi.org/10.1007/978-3-319-73600-6_43

2. Cox, I.J., Miller, M.L., Minka, T.P., Papathomas, T.V., Yianilos, P.N.: The Bayesian image retrieval system, pichunter: theory, implementation, and psychophysical experiments. IEEE Trans. Image Process. **9**(1), 20–37 (2000)
3. Donahue, J., et al.: DeCAF: a deep convolutional activation feature for generic visual recognition. In: Proceedings of the 31st International Conference on Machine Learning, ICML 2014, vol. 32, pp. 647–655. JMLR.org (2014)
4. He, J., Shang, X., Zhang, H., Chua, T.S.: Mental visual browsing. In: Tian, Q., Sebe, N., Qi, G.J., Huet, B., Hong, R., Liu, X. (eds.) MMM 2016. LNCS, vol. 9517, pp. 424–428. Springer, Cham (2016). https://doi.org/10.1007/978-3-319-27674-8_44
5. Kohonen, T.: The self-organizing map. Neurocomputing **21**(1–3), 1–6 (1998)
6. Lokoč, J., Bailer, W., Schoeffmann, K., Münzer, B., Awad, G.: On influential trends in interactive video retrieval: video browser showdown 2015–2017. IEEE Trans. Multimedia **20**(12), 3361–3376 (2018). https://doi.org/10.1109/TMM.2018.2830110
7. Lokoč, J., et al.: Interactive search or sequential browsing? A detailed analysis of the video browser showdown 2018. ACM Trans. Multimedia Comput. Commun. Appl. **15**(1), 29:1–29:18 (2019). https://doi.org/10.1145/3295663
8. Lokoč, J., Kovalčík, G., Souček, T., Moravec, J., Čech, P.: A framework for effective known-item search in video. In: Proceedings of the 27th ACM International Conference on Multimedia, MM 2019, pp. 1777–1785. ACM, New York (2019). https://doi.org/10.1145/3343031.3351046
9. Rossetto, L., Amiri Parian, M., Gasser, R., Giangreco, I., Heller, S., Schuldt, H.: Deep learning based concept detection in vitrivr. In: Kompatsiaris, I., Huet, B., Mezaris, V., Gurrin, C., Cheng, W.-H., Vrochidis, S. (eds.) MMM 2019. LNCS, vol. 11296, pp. 616–621. Springer, Cham (2019). https://doi.org/10.1007/978-3-030-05716-9_55
10. Schoeffmann, K., Münzer, B., Leibetseder, A., Primus, J., Kletz, S.: Autopiloting feature maps: the deep interactive video exploration (diveXplore) system at VBS2019. In: Kompatsiaris, I., Huet, B., Mezaris, V., Gurrin, C., Cheng, W.-H., Vrochidis, S. (eds.) MMM 2019. LNCS, vol. 11296, pp. 585–590. Springer, Cham (2019). https://doi.org/10.1007/978-3-030-05716-9_50
11. Szegedy, C., et al.: Going deeper with convolutions. In: IEEE Conference on Computer Vision and Pattern Recognition, CVPR 2015, 7–12 June 2015, Boston, MA, USA, pp. 1–9 (2015)
12. Vinyals, O., Toshev, A., Bengio, S., Erhan, D.: Show and tell: lessons learned from the 2015 MSCOCO image captioning challenge. IEEE Trans. Pattern Anal. Mach. Intell. **39**(4), 652–663 (2017)
13. Zoph, B., Vasudevan, V., Shlens, J., Le, Q.V.: Learning transferable architectures for scalable image recognition. CoRR abs/1707.07012 (2017). http://arxiv.org/abs/1707.07012
14. Li, X., Xu, C., Yang, G., Chen, Z., Dong, J.: W2VV++: fully deep learning for ad-hoc video search. In: Proceedings of the 27th ACM International Conference on Multimedia, MM 2019, 21–25 October 2019, Nice, France, pp. 1786–1794 (2019). https://doi.org/10.1145/3343031.3350906

Exquisitor at the Video Browser Showdown 2020

Björn Þór Jónsson[1(✉)], Omar Shahbaz Khan[1], Dennis C. Koelma[2], Stevan Rudinac[2], Marcel Worring[2], and Jan Zahálka[3]

[1] IT University of Copenhagen, Copenhagen, Denmark
bjorn@itu.dk
[2] University of Amsterdam, Amsterdam, Netherlands
[3] Czech Technical University in Prague, Prague, Czech Republic

Abstract. When browsing large video collections, human-in-the-loop systems are essential. The system should understand the semantic information need of the user and interactively help formulate queries to satisfy that information need based on data-driven methods. Full synergy between the interacting user and the system can only be obtained when the system learns from the user interactions while providing immediate response. Doing so with dynamically changing information needs for large scale multimodal collections is a challenging task. To push the boundary of current methods, we propose to apply the state of the art in interactive multimodal learning to the complex multimodal information needs posed by the Video Browser Showdown (VBS). To that end we adapt the Exquisitor system, a highly scalable interactive learning system. Exquisitor combines semantic features extracted from visual content and text to suggest relevant media items to the user, based on user relevance feedback on previously suggested items. In this paper, we briefly describe the Exquisitor system, and its first incarnation as a VBS entrant.

Keywords: Interactive learning · Video browsing · Scalability

1 Introduction

The Video Browser Showdown (VBS) is a series of annual live competitions, where researchers are asked to study and develop methods to solve search-related tasks for a benchmark video collection. The VBS tasks, which are independent queries of three different flavours, are unknown to the researchers, who must prepare their systems and data representations for any potential task. At competition time, users of all systems are then given a few minutes to solve the tasks. Furthermore, depending on the task, the query may be gradually refined by adding information as time passes, to simulate real users with imperfect memories. While the systems taking part in previous VBS editions employ a variety of advanced search and retrieval techniques, a common observation is that they are highly interactive, requiring users to review and refine results of

Y. M. Ro et al. (Eds.): MMM 2020, LNCS 11962, pp. 796–802, 2020.
https://doi.org/10.1007/978-3-030-37734-2_72

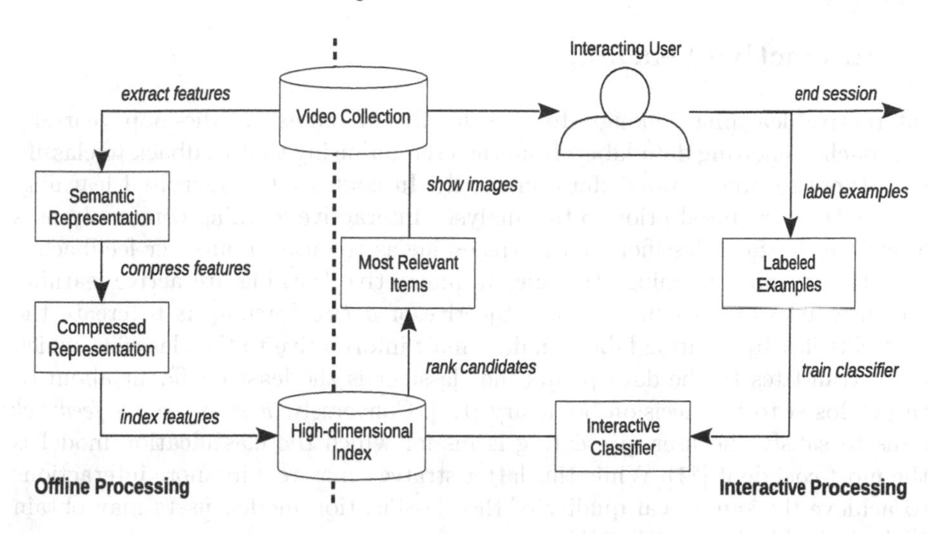

Fig. 1. Exquisitor's interactive learning pipeline. Initially, the video collection is processed to produce a compressed semantic representation, that is stored in a scalable high-dimensional index. In each round of the interactive learning process, the user is shown a set of potentially relevant videos. The user's judgments are then used to train a classifier, which in turn is used to retrieve a new set of videos to show to the user.

queries, resulting in a highly interactive process. Interactive multimodal learning has been proposed as an interactive method capable of satisfying users with uncertain information needs [15]. Given the format of VBS, it is of significant academic interest to apply interactive multimodal learning to VBS.

We have recently developed Exquisitor, a highly scalable interactive multimodal learning approach [5,9]. Figure 1 illustrates the iterative feedback process employed by Exquisitor with video data. When a new task starts, the user is initially presented with a set of randomly selected video scenes from the collection and asked to give (positive or negative) feedback on (some of) the scenes. The feedback is used to build (and subsequently update) a classification model, which in turn is used to provide new suggestions; this iterative process continues as long as the user deems necessary. The Exquisitor system has been used to interactively explore the YFCC100M collection [9], and to compete in the Lifelog Search Challenge (LSC) 2019 [6], where it ranked 6th out of 9 competition entrants. A key feature that distinguishes Exquisitor from previous interactive learning systems is its scalability [5]; while the VBS video collection contains more than 1,000 h of video, video suggestions can be retrieved in a fraction of a second in each interaction round. In this paper, we describe the adaptation of Exquisitor for participation in the Video Browser Showdown.

The remainder of the paper is organized as follows. In Sects. 2 and 3, we briefly give background for interactive learning and the Video Browser Showdown, respectively. In Sect. 4, we then describe Exquisitor and its adaptation to VBS, before concluding in Sect. 5.

2 Interactive Learning

Interactive learning belongs to the family of human-in-the-loop learning approaches, eliciting data labels from the user and using that feedback to classify the otherwise unannotated data on the fly. In contrast to supervised learning, no labels are required prior to the analysis. Interactive learning commonly uses a lightweight, fast classifier that learns online as the user inputs her feedback.

The two main learning strategies in interactive learning are active learning and user relevance feedback. The objective of *active learning* is to create the best classifier by eliciting labels on data most informative to the classifier, which often translates to the data points the classifier is the least confident about or those closest to the decision boundary [1,4]. Conversely, *user relevance feedback* aims to satisfy the user, presenting items for which the classification model is the most confident [11]. While this latter strategy may require more interactions to achieve the same final quality of the classification model, users may obtain their desired insights earlier [15].

The increasing drive towards interactivity, personalized user experience, and higher-level semantic understanding, combined with recent advances in related scientific disciplines [12,15,16], have motivated us to re-visit user relevance feedback with our Exquisitor approach [5,9].

3 The Video Browser Showdown

Involving users in the evaluation of retrieval processes has long been a challenge [7,12,14]. The majority of multimedia and computer vision benchmark competitions are held offline, allowing scientists to devote both significant computational power and time, which has helped solve difficult closed-world problems. Over the last two decades, however, international interactive search benchmarking events have emerged, where systems and their users must solve unknown and complex tasks within a limited time frame. From its inception in 2001, the TRECVID benchmark initiative included an interactive search task [14]. The VideOlympics [13] then started in 2008 and ran for five years, introducing the concept of live interactive video search benchmarking. The Video Browser Showdown (VBS) has been running since 2012 [8], and is now the premier live event, where participants must explore and search a collection of 1,000 hours of video [10]. A recent event series is the Lifelog Search Challenge (LSC), where a collection of lifelog image data must be explored [3]. While VBS and LSC represent only subsets of multimedia analytics applications, participation is important as it allows comparison with related state-of-the-art interactive systems.

The tasks in VBS have three different flavours. Visual Known-Item-Search (KIS) tasks present a randomly selected video clip to competitors, who must then identify the correct clip in the collection and submit it to the VBS server. Textual KIS tasks present a gradually evolving text description, which again has a specific matching scene in the collection. Finally, Ad-hoc Video Search (AVS) tasks ask for scenes matching a description; in this task judges evaluate

Fig. 2. Exquisitor's current user interface. The interface is browser-based and used primarily via mouse-based interaction. When hovering over a video, the user can choose to view the video in full, submit it to the VBS server, label it as a positive/negative example, or mark it as seen (using a 'next' button, the user can also mark all videos as seen and get a full screen of new videos). Positive (green column) and negative (red column) examples are immediately used to update the model. (Color figure online)

the relevance of answers as they are submitted to the VBS server. The VBS competition has an expert session, where the teams use their own systems to solve all types of tasks, and a novice session, where conference participants, who have never seen the system, are asked to solve visual KIS and AVS tasks.

4 Exquisitor

Exquisitor is a user relevance feedback approach capable of handling large scale collections in real time [5,9]. The Exquisitor system used for VBS consists of three parts: (1) a web-based user interface for receiving and judging video suggestions; (2) an interactive learning server, which receives user judgments and produces a new round of suggestions; and (3) a web server which serves videos and video thumbnails. All three components run locally on the laptop of the VBS participants. In the following, we describe the first two parts of the system.

Exquisitor Interface: The current Exquisitor user interface is shown in Fig. 2. In this initial incarnation, it is a pure interactive learning interface: the user is asked to label examples, which are subsequently used to learn the user's preference and suggest further examples. As the process to generate new suggestions is very efficient, however, new suggestions are retrieved each time the user identifies new positive or negative examples.

Exquisitor Server: Exquisitor has been developed to handle large-scale media collections, where each media item is described with feature vector data from both visual and text modalities. The main components of the server are (a) data representation and indexing, and (b) the scoring process, described briefly below.

Each of the (just over) million scenes in the VBS collection is represented by a high-dimensional concept feature vector extracted from a selected keyframe. The high-dimensional feature vectors are compressed using an index-based compression method [16], where each feature vector is represented using the top 6 features of the modality and compressed into only three 64-bit integers. The compressed feature vectors are then indexed using the eCP high-dimensional indexing algorithm [2]. A set of representative vectors is chosen from the collection and each vector is assigned to the closest representative, thus forming clusters in the compressed high-dimensional space. To facilitate retrieval, the cluster representatives are recursively indexed to form an approximate cluster-based index.

Exquisitor uses a Linear SVM classifier learned from user interactions to score items in the compressed feature space. In each interaction round, the Linear SVM model yields a classification hyperplane, which is used to form a farthest neighbor query to the cluster-based index. The goal is to yield $k = 25$ suggestions, which can be presented to the user. The clusters farthest from the SVM hyperplane are selected and their contents scanned to yield the k furthest neighbors.

Solving VBS Tasks: In KIS tasks, the aim of positive and negative examples is to create a model that is good enough to bring the correct answer to the screen. If the user is satisfied that all videos displayed are neither useful as positive/negative examples nor the answer to the task, the user can use the 'next' button to continue browsing the results, similar to the typical 'query and browse' approach of many current VBS entrants. A submitted result is considered as a positive example, regardless of whether it is the correct result or not; once the correct result has been submitted the task is complete. For AVS tasks the process is identical, except that all videos on screen can be submitted at once using a special button, and the process only ends once time has expired.

5 Conclusions

This paper has outlined the adaptation of the Exquisitor system to the Video Browser Showdown, both in terms of the data used to represent the video collection and the interface changes made for video browsing. As a new entrant in the competition, our primary goal is to learn from our participation in the competition, aiming to understand both how well the interactive learning approach suits the different competition tasks, and how we can improve our preliminary interface to be better suited to the competitive environment.

Acknowledgments. This work was supported by a PhD grant from the IT University of Copenhagen and by the European Regional Development Fund (project Robotics for Industry 4.0, CZ.02.1.01/0.0/0.0/15 003/0000470).

References

1. Cohn, D.A., Ghahramani, Z., Jordan, M.I.: Active learning with statistical models. J. Artif. Intell. Res. **4**(1), 129–145 (1996)
2. Guðmundsson, G.T., Jónsson, B.T., Amsaleg, L.: A large-scale performance study of cluster-based high-dimensional indexing. In: Proceedings of International Workshop on Very-large-scale Multimedia Corpus, Mining and Retrieval (VLS-MCM), Firenze, Italy (2010)
3. Gurrin, C., Schoeffmann, K., Joho, H., Dang-Nguyen, D., Riegler, M., Piras, L. (eds.): Proceedings of the 2018 ACM Workshop on The Lifelog Search Challenge, LSC@ICMR 2018, Yokohama, Japan (2018)
4. Huijser, M.W., van Gemert, J.C.: Active decision boundary annotation with deep generative models. In: Proceedings of IEEE ICCV, Venice, Italy, pp. 5296–5305 (2017)
5. Jónsson, B.Þ., et al.: Exquisitor: Interactive learning at large. arXiv:1904.08689 (2019)
6. Khan, O.S., Jónsson, B.Þ., Zahálka, J., Rudinac, S., Worring, M.: Exquisitor at the lifelog search challenge 2019. In: Proceedings of the ACM Workshop on Lifelog Search Challenge, LSC@ICMR, Ottawa, ON, Canada, pp. 7–11 (2019)
7. Larson, M., et al. (eds.): Working Notes Proceedings of the MediaEval 2018 Workshop, CEUR Workshop Proceedings, vol. 2283. CEUR-WS.org, Sophia Antipolis (2018)
8. Lokoč, J., Bailer, W., Schoeffmann, K., Münzer, B., Awad, G.: On influential trends in interactive video retrieval: video browser showdown 2015–2017. IEEE Trans. Multimedia **20**(12), 3361–3376 (2018)
9. Ragnarsdóttir, H., et al.: Exquisitor: breaking the interaction barrier for exploration of 100 million images. In: Proceedings of the ACM Multimedia Conference, Nice, France (2019)
10. Rossetto, L., Schuldt, H., Awad, G., Butt, A.A.: V3C – a research video collection. In: Kompatsiaris, I., Huet, B., Mezaris, V., Gurrin, C., Cheng, W.-H., Vrochidis, S. (eds.) MMM 2019. LNCS, vol. 11295, pp. 349–360. Springer, Cham (2019). https://doi.org/10.1007/978-3-030-05710-7_29
11. Rui, Y., Huang, T.S., Mehrotra, S.: Content-based image retrieval with relevance feedback in MARS. In: Proceedings of ICIP, Santa Barbara, CA, USA, pp. 815–818 (1997)
12. Schoeffmann, K., Bailer, W., Gurrin, C., Awad, G., Lokoč, J.: Interactive video search: where is the user in the age of deep learning? In: Proceedings of ACM Multimedia, Seoul, Republic of Korea, pp. 2101–2103 (2018)
13. Snoek, C.G.M., Worring, M., de Rooij, O., van de Sande, K.E.A., Yan, R., Hauptmann, A.G.: VideOlympics: real-time evaluation of multimedia retrieval systems. IEEE MultiMedia **15**(1), 86–91 (2008)
14. Thornley, C., Johnson, A.C., Smeaton, A.F., Lee, H.: The scholarly impact of TRECVID (2003–2009). J. Am. Soc. Inf. Sci. Technol. (JASIST) **62**(4), 613–627 (2011)

15. Zahálka, J., Worring, M.: Towards interactive, intelligent, and integrated multimedia analytics. In: Proceedings of the IEEE Conference on Visual Analytics Science and Technology (VAST), Paris, France, pp. 3–12 (2014)
16. Zahálka, J., Rudinac, S., Jónsson, B.T., Koelma, D.C., Worring, M.: Blackthorn: large-scale interactive multimodal learning. IEEE Trans. Multimedia **20**(3), 687–698 (2018)

Deep Learning-Based Video Retrieval Using Object Relationships and Associated Audio Classes

Byoungjun Kim(✉), Ji Yea Shim(✉), Minho Park, and Yong Man Ro

School of Electrical Engineering, KAIST, Daejeon, South Korea
{braian98, jiyeashim, roger618, ymro}@kaist.ac.kr

Abstract. This paper introduces a video retrieval tool for the 2020 Video Browser Showdown (VBS). The tool enhances the user's video browsing experience by ensuring full use of video analysis database constructed prior to the Showdown. Deep learning based object detection, scene text detection, scene color detection, audio classification and relation detection with scene graph generation methods have been used to construct the data. The data is composed of visual, textual, and auditory information, broadening the scope to which a user can search beyond visual information. In addition, the tool provides a simple and user-friendly interface for novice users to adapt to the tool in little time.

Keywords: Scene graph · Scene text · Audio classification

1 Introduction

In this section, we introduce the five methodologies utilized in our video retrieval tool, namely, object detection, scene text detection, scene color detection, audio classification and relation detection with scene graph generation. Each methodology serves a role for visual Known-Item Search (KIS), textual KIS, and/or Ad-hoc Video Search (AVS) [1] of VBS 2020 [2]. The implementation of five methodologies are based on deep learning in analyzing the big V3C1 dataset [3, 4]. We would like to highlight the integration of audio classification of our tool, as we have noticed that most systems that participated in the past VBS competitions query visual information [5]. With our tool, we aim to integrate auditory and context relation information to broaden the scope of query-able data.

Object detection detects object classes and their locations in each video clip. Users can query object names, such as "person", "car", to search the video clips with the scenes containing those objects. Users can also query object locations on the 3×3 grid, which can be seen in the tool shown in Fig. 1. This method comes in handy with all three tasks, textual KIS, visual KIS, and AVS, where, in most cases, object location queries would be used in visual KIS tasks [11].

B. Kim and J. Y. Shim—Both authors have equally contributed.

Y. M. Ro et al. (Eds.): MMM 2020, LNCS 11962, pp. 803–808, 2020.
https://doi.org/10.1007/978-3-030-37734-2_73

Scene text detection detects texts in video clips. We use a high functioning scene text detection tool that is able to locate small and noisy texts in images. It is able to locate shop names in street views, or texts on people's t-shirts. Users are able to search texts shown on screen during visual KIS to distinguish target clips from the dataset [8].

Scene color detection detects dominant colors of video clips [17]. This could be used when a clip has specific dominant color. For example, if a video clip portrays mountain climbing, then dominant color would be green. This method is useful for visual KIS tasks.

Audio classification provides a method to distinguish clips with video sound. Predefined classes include rain, thunder, vehicle, speech, and more. An AVS task that asks users to find "all shots with a car in a rainy day" could be tackled easily by querying audio class "rain" and "vehicle" [10]. A textual KIS task that includes keywords such as talking, shouting, or screaming, could be solved with audio query as well. The practicality of audio classification could not be more emphasized as it can be used for all three tasks along with object detection.

Relation detection using scene graph generation [11, 12] can be used to interpret the contextual meaning of shots. Relation detection produces a full sentence that describes object attributes and relationships between objects, such as "A man sitting next to a woman". This method compensates the limitations of object detection, which does not detect actions, such as sitting or running. Users can search in full sentences given in the three tasks with relational detection.

Although we listed the methods that could be used for each task above, users are free to combine five query methods to their taste. The search tool that we provide to not limit the choices of users.

Fig. 1. Screenshot of video retrieval tool UI. The sidebar at the left contains the query methods. Users are expected to select, type, or click query inputs. Small helper texts are provided for novice users. Users can scroll down the sidebar for more query methods and to submit input. (The UI can undergo minor reconstructions until VBS 2020).

Section 2 describes the architecture of the retrieval tool and Sect. 3 provides full description of the five methods.

2 Architecture

The video retrieval tool presented in this paper is a MERN stack application, an abbreviation for MongoDB, ExpressJS, ReactJS, and Node.js.

MongoDB is the database containing the organized result data from the five deep learning based methods. Mongo DB is a NoSQL database where data is stored in JSON style documents. MongoDB allows big data to be easily and rapidly manipulated and delivered. This characteristic benefits our purpose of handling the huge V3C1 dataset.

ExpressJS and Node.js compose the backend server side of the application. The server side and the MongoDB are connected at all times while the application is running. When user submits query inputs via post type, the server side queries MongoDB and receives corresponding video shots sorted in descending order of highest match by indexing technique available in MongoDB.

ReactJS and Node.js compose the frontend client side of the application. The client side receives input from users, and sends it to the server side once the submit button is clicked. The inputs are not refreshed unless users delete or click on the clear button, considering the fact that textual KIS tasks provide additional information to users every time interval. The query results are then displayed in grid on the right side of the UI as shown in Fig. 1. The video is loaded and played once the user clicks on the video from the grid display. Also, descriptive helper texts are provided above and/or below each input fields so that novice users could adapt to the tool rapidly.

The application avoids unnecessary rendering to minimize time consumption and ensures accuracy of search query via indexing method. The synchronization between the database, server, and the client sides complete the video retrieval tool, ready for VBS 2020.

3 System Explanation

3.1 Object Detection

Textual KIS, visual KIS, and AVS are prone to utilize object detection category for the majority of cases. Hence, detection of object occurrences and locations in each video frame is crucial to achieve high performance in VBS challenges. We apply YOLOv3 model [7] pre-trained on the COCO-dataset on video shots to classify objects and create bounding boxes.

First, we extract frames at a rate of 1fps from each video clip and run YOLOv3 on each frame. Then the model returns object class and its bounding box coordinates consisting of the bottom-left x and y coordinates and top-right x and y coordinates. The box coordinates are translated to 3 × 3 sections (top left, top center, top right, center left, center, center left, bottom left, bottom center and bottom right) that overlap. Users can query object locations with the 3 × 3 grid click box query as can be seen in Fig. 1. All the object classes, locations, and numbers of each frame are organized into the document of the video shot containing that frame.

3.2 Scene Text Detection

Video frames frequently contain texts, ranging from subtitles, logos, street signs, shop names, and shirt labels. VBS analysis data provided by VBS lists video shots containing few and much text, which allows users to go through three categories. Scene text detection further locates the texts and detects the letters via CRAFT and Pytesseract. Hence, visual KIS tasks could utilize texts seen on screen.

Two functionalities are undergone in order for scene text detection. Firstly, an optical character recognition (OCR) model called Character Region Awareness for Text detection (CRAFT) [8] locates text letters in images. The model is edited to return polygonal bounding box coordinates around consecutive text letters instead of images with bounding boxes drawn. Then we crop the text sectors from the original frame. Secondly, Pytesseract in python library runs text detection to each cropped text image and the resulting text is associated to the database document of the video shot containing the frame.

3.3 Scene Color Detection

Scene color detection identifies the dominant color of a video clip. For instance, users could query color blue and/or green for an AVS task that asks for all water sports clips, or color green for a visual KIS task that asks for a video clip with a person hiking.

VBS pre-defined ten representative colors and associated each video clip to one color. The analysis data was re-organized to fit the tool's database structure for efficient querying.

3.4 Audio Classification

Every video clips contains audio. Audio query is key category of our video retrieval tool. With audio classification, users are able to query inputs not available in object detection results, such as shout, thunder, crying, laughter, speech, rain, vehicle, music, soundtrack, and much more. For example, users can query shout, male speech, conversation, or yell for an AVS task asking for all scenes of people having an argument. Without audio classification, it would be an extremely challenging task: users can only search object "people", which would yield clips containing people of all actions.

The audio classification model for our video retrieval tool regards "IBM Developer Model Asset Exchange: Audio Classifier" [9], introduced as the state of the art model for audio classification in the paper, "Multi-level Attention Model for Weakly Supervised Audio Classification" [10]. The framework of the model is Keras and Tensorflow and the model is pre-trained on Google Audioset with up to 527 audio classes.

Firstly, we convert .webm video files into.wav format with ffmpeg encoder. Secondly, we run the classifier on each.wav file. Then it returns the corresponding audio classes and probability of the result ranging from 0 to 1. Hence, when users query audio, requested results can be weighted based on probability of the accuracy of audio classes.

3.5 Relation Detection Using Scene Graph Generation

TRECVID analysis introduces ten hardest topics of AVS task [6]. The major feature of the introduced hardest topics is that the keyword(s) that characterizes the sentence is a verb or attributes, such as "Find shots of two men fighting". Relation detection using scene graph generation generates attribute information of an object and relational information between objects in a frame.

Scene graph generation necessitates two processes: object detection and graph generation. Object detection is conducted with faster R-CNN model [14] and Res-101 [15] as backbone [11], and graph generation is conducted with vanilla model and Res-101 as backbone [12, 13] on Visual Genome dataset [16]. The pre-trained models detect objects with faster R-CNN model then run vanilla model to generate scene-graph. Attribute and relational data of objects are extracted and stored in database. Users can query relations, attributes, or objects by selecting the search field on the first row of the sidebar (Fig. 1 shows "Object" select option). Textual KIS, visual KIS, and AVS tasks will hopefully all aid from relation detection data.

4 Conclusion

This paper introduces our tool presented by VBS 2020, and discusses the architecture of video retrieval tool, the five methodologies employed for database construction, and their integration into the user application for retrieval tasks of VBS 2020. The presented system suggests a simple yet well-integrated tool for video retrieval.

References

1. Lokoč, J., Bailer, W., Schoeffmann, K., Muenzer, B., Awad, G.: On influential trends in interactive video retrieval: video browser showdown 2015–2017. IEEE (2018)
2. Lokoč, J., et al.: Interactive search of sequential browsing? A detailed analysis of the video browser showdown 2018. ACM TOMM **15**, 29 (2019)
3. Rossetto, L., Schuldt, H., Awad, G., Butt, Asad A.: V3C – a research video collection. In: Kompatsiaris, I., Huet, B., Mezaris, V., Gurrin, C., Cheng, W.-H., Vrochidis, S. (eds.) MMM 2019. LNCS, vol. 11295, pp. 349–360. Springer, Cham (2019). https://doi.org/10.1007/978-3-030-05710-7_29
4. Berns, F., Rossetto, L., Schoeffmann, K., Beecks, C., Awad, G.: V3C1 dataset: an evaluation of content characteristics. In: ICMR (2019)
5. Schöffmann, K.: A user-centric media retrieval competition: the video browser showdown 2012–2014. IEEE (2014)
6. Awad, G., Butt, A., Curtis, K.: TRECVID 2018: benchmarking video activity detection, video captioning and matching, video storytelling linking and video search. In: TRECVID (2018)
7. PyImageSearch. https://www.pyimagesearch.com/201811/12/yolo-object-detection-with-opencv/. Accessed 12 Nov 2018
8. Baek, Y., Lee, B., Han, D.: Character Region Awareness for Text Detection. arXiv:1904.01941 (2019)

9. Kong, Q., Xu, Y., Wang, W.: Audio set classification with attention model: a probabilistic perspective. arXiv preprint arXiv:1711.00927 (2017)
10. Hershey, S., Chaudhuri, S., Ellis, D.P.W.: Multi-level attention model for weakly supervised audio classification. arXiv preprint arXiv:1803.02353 (2018)
11. Yang, J., Lu, J., Lee, S.: Graph R-CNN for scene graph generation. arXiv preprint arXiv: 1808.00191 (2018)
12. Xu, D., Zhu, Y., Choy, C.B.: Scene graph generation by iterative message passing. arXiv preprint arXiv:1701.02426 (2017)
13. Zhang, J., Shih, K.J., Elgammal, A.: Graphical contrastive losses for scene graph parsing. arXiv preprint arXiv:1903.02728 (2019)
14. Ren, S., He, K., Girshick, R., Sun, J.: Faster R-CNN: towards real-time object detection with region proposal networks. arXiv preprint arXiv:1506.01497 (2016)
15. He, K., Zhang, X., Ren, S., Sun, J.: Deep residual learning for image recognition. In: CVPR (2016)
16. Krishna, R., et al.: Visual genome: connecting language and vision using crowdsourced dense image annotations. Int. J. Comput. Vis. **123**, 32–37 (2017)
17. Shrivastava, N., Tyagi, V.: An efficient technique for retrieval of color images in large databases. Comput. Electr. Eng. **46**, 314–327 (2014)

IVIST: Interactive VIdeo Search Tool in VBS 2020

Sungjune Park(✉), Jaeyub Song(✉), Minho Park, and Yong Man Ro

Image and Video Systems Lab, School of Electrical Engineering, KAIST, Daejeon, South Korea
{sungjune-p, jsong0327, roger618, ymro}@kaist.ac.kr

Abstract. This paper presents a new video retrieval tool, Interactive VIdeo Search Tool (IVIST), which participates in the 2020 Video Browser Showdown (VBS). As a video retrieval tool, IVIST is equipped with proper and high-performing functionalities such as object detection, dominant-color finding, scene-text recognition and text-image retrieval. These functionalities are constructed with various deep neural networks. By adopting these functionalities, IVIST performs well in searching users' desirable videos. Furthermore, due to user-friendly user interface, IVIST is easy to use even for novice users. Although IVIST is developed to participate in VBS, we hope that it will be applied as a practical video retrieval tool in the future, dealing with actual video data on the Internet.

Keywords: Video Browser Showdown (VBS) · Video retrieval tool · Text-image retrieval

1 Introduction

In this paper, we present a new video retrieval tool, Interactive VIdeo Search Tool (IVIST) to participate in the Video Browser Showdown (VBS) [1]. In VBS 2020, there are two main tasks: Known-Item Search (KIS) and Ad-hoc Video Search (AVS). For KIS tasks, users search for one target scene by using information in visualized scene (visual KIS) or specific descriptions without any visualized scene (textual KIS). For AVS tasks, users search for as many target segments as possible from a rough description, without any prior knowledge regarding their specific information [2].

To handle those tasks, IVIST mainly focuses on four functions: object detection, scene-text detection, dominant-color finding, and text-image retrieval. To our knowledge, text-image retrieval function has not been presented in the past VBS contests. In IVIST, we adopt it to mainly deal with textual KIS and AVS tasks. This function can directly take given specific (textual KIS) descriptions or a rough (AVS) description as an input. Moreover, user interface of IVIST is developed to be well-organized and user-friendly, particularly for novice users. It helps users to make queries and acquire results

S. Park and J. Song—have equally contributed.

Y. M. Ro et al. (Eds.): MMM 2020, LNCS 11962, pp. 809–814, 2020.
https://doi.org/10.1007/978-3-030-37734-2_74

Fig. 1. (a) Query results from "A group of boys wearing blue Dodgers and Royals shirts." by using a sentence query (text-image retrieval). (b) Query results from "A man with two boys entering a comic bookstore, they are greeted by the owner. People inside and outside the store cheering." by using object query (person, book). The answers for each query are boxed with red line. (Color figure online)

with good quality. Also, the database used for retrieval is optimized for searching and retrieving results efficiently.

The following sections are described as follows: Sect. 2 introduces an overall architecture of the system. Section 3 explains the main functions of IVIST. Section 4 concludes the paper.

2 Overall Architecture of IVIST

IVIST uses ReactJS for the front-end, Flask for the back-end server, and MongoDB for the database. The front-end is responsible for taking user inputs, delivering a query to the back-end server via a 'post' request, and displaying the results. Users can check results of a query, play the videos associated with the query, and finally select a range of frame they want to find. Users can also choose to search with complex conditions like 'AND'/'OR' options and assign priority to options.

The back-end server receives requests from the front-end and processes the requests properly. For object detection, scene text recognition and dominant color models, results for each frame have already been processed and saved in the database. So, the server looks up frames satisfying the query inside the database and returns the found frames back to the front-end. For text-image retrieval model, it runs in the back-end server and returns the results when users put a sentence input and sends search request by clicking on the search button.

We selected MongoDB as it is advantageous in searching documents inside quickly and supports flexible schema. In the database, information such as scene-texts, objects and colors for each key frame is included. This database can be accessed by back-end server for finding specific frames.

When all these components are integrated and operated together, IVIST performs in a proper way. We ran a simulation on IVIST, based on the queries from the descriptions given in last year's textual KIS. The simulation results are shown in Fig. 1. Figure 1(a) is acquired by making the given description as a sentence query input. Figure 1(b) is acquired by an object query, where objects are inferred from the given description.

3 Main Functions in IVIST

By using the keyframes given in the dataset offered by VBS2020, there are four ways for query formation in IVIST: object, scene-text, dominant-color and sentence query. These are implemented based on the existing pre-trained models and training datasets.

3.1 Object Detection

Object detection can be used in all three tasks. In visual KIS, users can simply search for the objects they saw on the projector. In case of textual KIS and AVS tasks, users can use object detection if certain objects in target scene or shot can be inferred from given descriptions. For instance, one of last year's textual KIS tasks was "A man with two boys entering a comic bookstore, they are greeted by the owner. People inside and outside the store cheering". From this query, users can infer that the scene contains people and books.

The main object detection model used in IVIST is HTC [8]. HTC ranked 1st at COCO [9] 2018 Challenge Object Detection Task. It makes use of Cascade R-CNN [13] and Mask R-CNN [14] by using spatial contexts and cascading on each stage.

While 91 classes of COCO dataset may be sufficient for many tasks, there are still many objects that do not belong in the scope of COCO's classes. To deal with objects that are not within COCO dataset, IVIST also uses the model trained from Open Images Dataset V4 [10] that consists of 500 classes. The model which is submitted by user ZFTurbo [11], uses RetinaNet [12]. Therefore, our main model for object detection is HTC, and RetinaNet is used when user searches for objects that are not in the COCO dataset.

3.2 Scene-Text Detection and Recognition

People sometimes want to find videos that they watched before, which is simulated by visual KIS tasks. In this situation, they can use objects they remember as mentioned in Sect. 3.1. However, if they can remember any texts in the scene, it can be used as strong and powerful method to find the particular scene. To employ this method, we leverage and combine scene-text detector and recognizer together.

The first step is to detect and crop probable scene-text regions as precisely as possible. To perform this process, we adopt PixelLink as a scene-text detector, which detects scene-texts via instance segmentation. It is based on VGG16 as a feature extractor with converting fully connected layers into convolutional layers and trained on the CDAR 2015 dataset [3].

Then, those processed cropped images which contain probable scene-text regions have to be interpreted by a scene-text recognizer. For this purpose, we make use of the model named ASTER [4]. ASTER takes each cropped image from PixelLink as an input and interprets a scene-text. This helpful model is composed of two networks: rectification network and recognition network. In the rectification network, Thin-Plate-Spline [5] is adopted as the transformation to take care of text irregularities. Also, the recognition network is composed of an encoder with convolutional layers and multi-layer bidirectional LSTM [6], and a decoder with attentional sequence-to-sequence LSTM [18, 19]. We use pre-trained ASTER, so that ASTER returns and stores interpreted scene-texts in the database.

3.3 Dominant Color

In visual KIS, color can also be an intuitive and helpful method to find desirable results. For example, say that users want to find a particular scene, such as playing soccer or a cow grazing in a meadow. In this case, users know that one of the dominant colors is green, and can make a query for scenes that are colored by green dominantly. This method might not find one particular scene; however, it can help narrow the range of probable candidates of scenes. For implementation, we used K-Means clustering to determine several dominant colors for each image. Also, we chose output colors that are relatively familiar to people to help them make a color query easily. For example, ‘red’ and ‘green’, which are familiar to many people, are one of the output colors, but ‘cattleya’, which is seldomly used, is not one of our output colors.

3.4 Text-Image Retrieval

In textual KIS and AVS tasks, text-image retrieval functions can be very useful. By making use of the given descriptions, users can generate a proper sentence query or put one of the given descriptions as an input query directly. Therefore, users can search the videos that they want to find, even if they did not watch the videos before.

To make use of text-image retrieval, we deploy SCAN that predicts image-text similarity by dealing with latent alignments in images and sentences [7]. SCAN, which is trained on the MS-COCO dataset, uses a novel stacked cross attention that gives an attention to the image region regarding to words in sentences, and determines where and how much to give an attention to each word afterwards. For acquiring attended features from images and sentences, SCAN adopts Faster R-CNN [15] with ResNet-101 [16] and a sequence of bi-directional GRUs [17, 18].

Due to SCAN, for textual KIS and AVS tasks, users can put the description itself, or a properly modified sentence, as a query to find a video/videos with only a textual description. SCAN then converts an input sentence into embedding features, compares it with every embedding feature of keyframes, and returns images in a high similarity order.

To our knowledge, in the previous VBS challenges, there were no teams that used the sentence itself to compare with image features. Possible reasons are that it is a challenging problem to solve and running the model on site might be time-consuming and make it difficult to solve the problems within the time limit (5–7 min in VBS). However, we adopt and modify SCAN, so that it is performed in time to fit in the tasks of VBS. As a result, it performs and solves the problems successfully.

4 Conclusion

In this paper, we present a new video retrieval tool, IVIST to participate in VBS 2020. We adopt various deep learning models, a flexible user interface, and an efficient database. Through its functionalities and options in the user interface, IVIST helps users make a query with good quality and acquire desirable results. However, to have better performance and more user-friendly user interface, we plan to improve the user interface and develop IVIST’s functionalities to be more efficient.

References

1. Cobârzan, C., Schoeffmann, K., Bailer, W., et al.: Interactive video search tools: a detailed analysis of the video browser showdown 2015. Multimedia Tools Appl. **76**, 5539–5571 (2017)

2. Lokoč, J., et al.: Interactive search or sequential browsing? a detailed analysis of the video browser showdown 2018. ACM Trans. Multimedia Comput. Commun. Appl. **15**(29), 18 (2019)
3. Deng, D., Liu, H., Li, X., Cai, D.: PixelLink.: detecting scene text via instance segmentation. arXiv preprint arXiv:1801.01315 (2018)
4. Shi, B., Yang, M., Wang, X., Lyu, P., Yao, C., Bai, X.: ASTER: an attentional scene text recognizer with flexible rectification. IEEE Trans. Pattern Anal. Mach. Intell. (TPAMI) **41**(9), 2035–2048 (2018)
5. Bookstein, F.L.: Thin-plate splines and the decomposition of deformations. IEEE Trans. Pattern Anal. Mach. Intell. **11**(6), 567–585 (1989)
6. Graves, A., Liwicki, M., Fernandez, S., Bertolami, R., Bunke, H., Schmidhuber, J.: A novel connectionist system for unconstrained handwriting recognition. IEEE Trans. Pattern Anal. Mach. Intell. **31**(5), 855–868 (2009)
7. Lee K.-H., Xi, C., Gang, H., Houdong, H., Xiaodong, H.: Stacked cross attention for image-text matching. arXiv preprint arXiv:1803.08024 (2018)
8. Chen, K., et al.: Hybrid task cascade for instance segmentation. arXiv preprint arXiv:1901.07518 (2019)
9. Lin, T.-Y., et al.: Microsoft COCO: common objects in context. arXiv preprint arXiv:1405.0312 (2014)
10. Kuznetsova, A., et al.: The open images dataset V4: unified image classification, object detection, and visual relationship detection at scale. arXiv preprint arXiv:1811.00982 (2018)
11. ZFTurbo: Keras-RetinaNet-for-Open-Images-Challenge-2018. https://github.com/zfturbo/keras-retinanet-for-open-images-challenge-2018
12. Lin, T.-Y., Goyal, P., Girchick, R., He, K., Dollar, P.: Focal loss for dense object detection. arXiv preprint arXiv:1708.02002 (2018)
13. Cai, Z., Vasconcelos, N.: Cascade R-CNN: delving into high quality object detection. arXiv preprint arXiv:1712.00726 (2017)
14. He, K., Gkioxari, G., Dollár, P., Girshick, R.: Mask R-CNN. arXiv preprint arXiv:1703.06870 (2018)
15. Ren, S., He, K., Girshick, R., Sun, J.: Faster R-CNN: towards real-time object detection with region proposal networks. arXiv preprint arXiv:1506.01497 (2016)
16. He, K., Zhang, X., Ren, S., Sun, J.: Deep residual learning for image recognition. In: CVPR. IEEE Computer Society, pp. 770–778 (2016)
17. Schuster, M., Paliwal, K.K.: Bidirectional recurrent neural networks. IEEE Trans. Signal Process. **45**(11), 2671–2673 (1997)
18. Bahdanau, D., Cho, K., Bengio, Y.: Neural machine translation by jointly learning to align and translate. In: ICLR (2015)
19. Chorowski, J., Bahdanau, D., Serdyuk, D., Cho, K., Bengio, Y.: Attention-based models for speech recognition. arXiv preprint arXiv:1506.07503 (2015)

Correction to: MultiMedia Modeling

Yong Man Ro, Wen-Huang Cheng, Junmo Kim, Wei-Ta Chu,
Peng Cui, Jung-Woo Choi, Min-Chun Hu, and Wesley De Neve

Correction to:
Y. M. Ro et al. (Eds.): *MultiMedia Modeling*, LNCS 11962, https://doi.org/10.1007/978-3-030-37734-2

The original version of this book was revised. Due to a technical error, the first volume editor did not appear in the volumes of the MMM 2020 proceedings. A funding number was missing in the acknowledgement section of the chapter titled "AttenNet: Deep Attention Based Retinal Disease Classification in OCT Images." Both were corrected.

The updated version of the book can be found at
https://doi.org/10.1007/978-3-030-37734-2_46
https://doi.org/10.1007/978-3-030-37734-2

Y. M. Ro et al. (Eds.): MMM 2020, LNCS 11962, p. C1, 2020.
https://doi.org/10.1007/978-3-030-37734-2_75

Author Index

Printed in the United States
By Bookmasters